THE JOSEPH SMITH PAPERS

Ronald K. Esplin
Matthew J. Grow
Matthew C. Godfrey
GENERAL EDITORS

PREVIOUSLY PUBLISHED

THE
JOSEPH SMITH
PAPERS

DOCUMENTS
VOLUME 6: FEBRUARY 1838–AUGUST 1839

Mark Ashurst-McGee
David W. Grua
Elizabeth A. Kuehn
Brenden W. Rensink
Alexander L. Baugh
VOLUME EDITORS

THE CHURCH
HISTORIAN'S
PRESS

www.josephsmithpapers.org

The Joseph Smith Papers Project is endorsed by
the National Historical Publications and Records Commission.

Art direction: Richard Erickson.
Cover design: Scott Eggers. Interior design: Richard Erickson and Scott M. Mooy.
Typography: Carolyn Call.

Library of Congress Cataloging-in-Publication Data

Documents / Dean C. Jessee, Ronald K. Esplin, Richard Lyman Bushman, Matthew J. Grow, general editors.
volumes cm — (The Joseph Smith papers)
Planned publication in 12 volumes.
Includes bibliographical references and index.
ISBN 978-1-60907-577-4 (hardbound: alk. paper; v. 1)
ISBN 978-1-60907-598-9 (hardbound: alk. paper; v. 2)
ISBN 978-1-60907-987-1 (hardbound: alk. paper; v. 3)
ISBN 978-1-62972-174-3 (hardbound: alk. paper; v. 4)
ISBN 978-1-62972-312-9 (hardbound: alk. paper; v. 5)
ISBN 978-1-62972-353-2 (hardbound: alk. paper; v. 6)
1. Church of Jesus Christ of Latter-day Saints—History—19th century—Sources. 2. Mormon Church—
History—Sources. I. Jessee, Dean C., editor. II. Esplin, Ronald K., editor. III. Bushman, Richard L., editor.
IV. Grow, Matthew J., editor. V. Smith, Joseph, Jr., 1805–1844. VI. Series: Smith, Joseph, Jr., 1805–1844.
Joseph Smith papers.

BX8611.D63 2017   289.309'034—dc23   2013017521

Printed in the United States of America on acid-free paper.
10 9 8 7 6 5 4 3 2 1

The Joseph Smith Papers

Contents

Detailed Contents

PART 1: 15 FEBRUARY–28 JUNE 1838

Part 2: 8 July–29 October 1838

Part 3: 4 November 1838–16 April 1839

PART 4: 24 APRIL–12 AUGUST 1839

Illustrations and Maps

TEXTUAL ILLUSTRATIONS

CONTEXTUAL ILLUSTRATIONS

Maps

Other Visuals

Timeline of Joseph Smith's Life

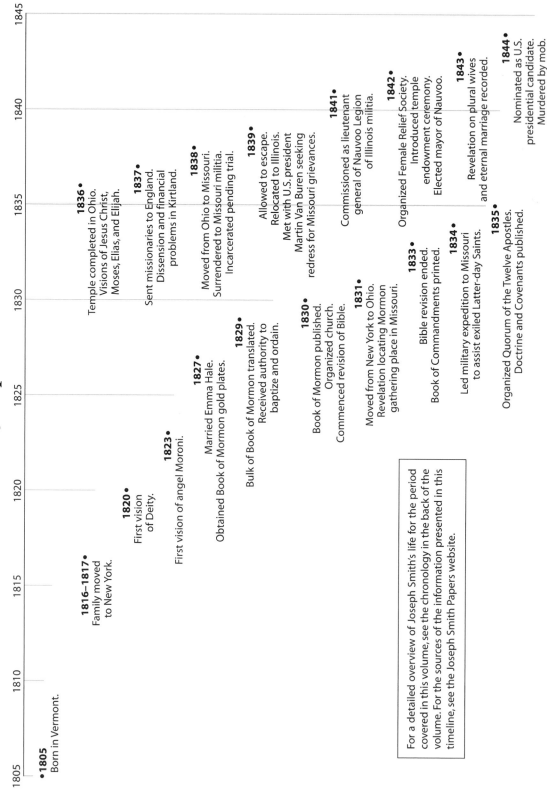

1805
Born in Vermont.

1816–1817
Family moved to New York.

1820
First vision of Deity.

1823
First vision of angel Moroni.

1827
Married Emma Hale.
Obtained Book of Mormon gold plates.

1829
Bulk of Book of Mormon translated.
Received authority to baptize and ordain.

1830
Book of Mormon published.
Organized church.
Commenced revision of Bible.

1831
Moved from New York to Ohio.
Revelation locating Mormon gathering place in Missouri.

1833
Bible revision ended.
Book of Commandments printed.

1834
Led military expedition to Missouri to assist exiled Latter-day Saints.

1835
Organized Quorum of the Twelve Apostles.
Doctrine and Covenants published.

1836
Temple completed in Ohio.
Visions of Jesus Christ, Moses, Elias, and Elijah.

1837
Sent missionaries to England.
Dissension and financial problems in Kirtland.

1838
Moved from Ohio to Missouri.
Surrendered to Missouri militia.
Incarcerated pending trial.

1839
Allowed to escape.
Relocated to Illinois.
Met with U.S. president Martin Van Buren seeking redress for Missouri grievances.

1841
Commissioned as lieutenant general of Nauvoo Legion of Illinois militia.

1842
Organized Female Relief Society.
Introduced temple endowment ceremony.
Elected mayor of Nauvoo.

1843
Revelation on plural wives and eternal marriage recorded.

1844
Nominated as U.S. presidential candidate.
Murdered by mob.

For a detailed overview of Joseph Smith's life for the period covered in this volume, see the chronology in the back of the volume. For the sources of the information presented in this timeline, see the Joseph Smith Papers website.

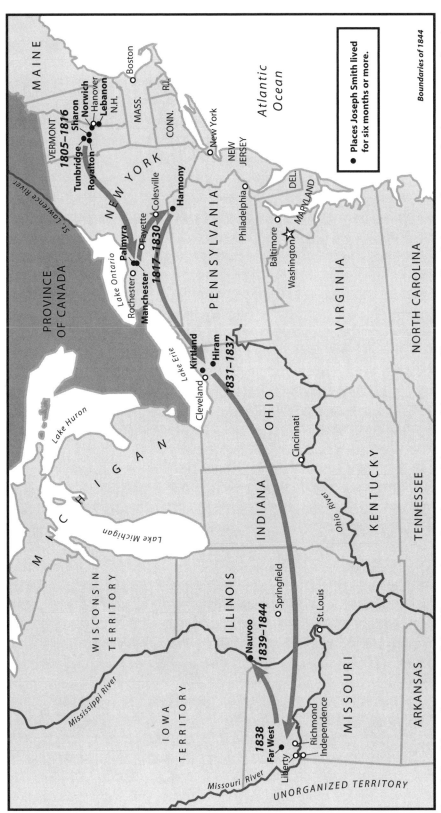

Joseph Smith's residences. Joseph Smith's major places of residence and the general direction of his migrations. Detailed maps relevant to the places mentioned in this volume appear on pages 598–610. (Design by John Hamer.)

About the Joseph Smith Papers Project

Joseph Smith was the founding prophet and first president of The Church of Jesus Christ of Latter-day Saints. The Joseph Smith Papers Project is an effort to gather together all extant Joseph Smith documents and to publish complete and accurate transcripts of those documents with both textual and contextual annotation. All such documents are being published electronically on the project website, josephsmithpapers.org, and a large number of the documents are being published in print. The print and electronic publications constitute an essential resource for scholars and students of the life and work of Joseph Smith, early Mormon history, and nineteenth-century American religion. For the first time, all of Joseph Smith's known surviving papers, which include many of the foundational documents of The Church of Jesus Christ of Latter-day Saints, will be easily accessible in one place.

The Joseph Smith Papers Project is not a "documentary history" project comprising all important documents relating to Joseph Smith. Instead, it is a "papers" project that is publishing, according to accepted documentary editing standards, documents created by Joseph Smith or by staff whose work he directed, including journals, revelations and translations, contemporary reports of discourses, minutes, business and legal records, editorials, and notices. The project also includes papers received and "owned" by Joseph Smith or his office, such as incoming correspondence.

The Joseph Smith Papers Project is a comprehensive edition, meaning it will include all known and available documents meeting the project's criteria as Joseph Smith documents. While selective editions may exclude some documents because they are of less interest or importance, comprehensive editions such as this one make no such exclusions. All Joseph Smith documents, even routine ones such as certificates, will be published.

The print and digital editions of the Joseph Smith Papers are divided into six series. The Documents series is the core of the edition, presenting, with the exception of some documents featured in other series, all of Joseph Smith's papers from July 1828 to June 1844. The other series will publish larger record books and standalone genres. The Journals series presents Joseph Smith's diaries from 1832 to 1844; the Histories series publishes Joseph Smith's many attempts to record his own story and the story of the church; the Revelations and Translations series provides textual studies of Smith's revelatory texts;

the Administrative Records series presents minute books, letterbooks, and records of organizations Smith was associated with, such as the Council of Fifty; and the Legal, Business, and Financial Records series presents the legal cases Smith was involved in as well as the documents related to his business and financial dealings.

Because the Joseph Smith Papers Project meets the requisite scholarly and documentary editing criteria, it has earned an endorsement by the National Historical Publications and Records Commission. To ensure accuracy of the texts, project editors undertake three independent levels of text verification for each manuscript, including a final verification against the original.

The project is staffed by scholars, archivists, and editors employed by the Church History Department of The Church of Jesus Christ of Latter-day Saints in Salt Lake City, Utah, and is funded by the church and by the Larry H. and Gail Miller Family Foundation. Each print volume is submitted to peer review by a national board of scholars prior to publication. The publisher of the project's print and web publications is the Church Historian's Press, an imprint of the Church History Department.

Joseph Smith Documents from February 1838 through August 1839

In March 1839, while writing to the Latter-day Saints from a jail in Missouri, Joseph Smith expressed anguish and frustration over his imprisonment and the expulsion of his people from the land they called Zion. As he reflected on these afflictions, his prose broke into prayer: "O God where art thou and where is the pavilion that covereth thy hiding place how long shall thy hand be stayed and thine eye yea thy pure eye behold from the etearnal heavens the [w]rongs of thy people and of thy servants and thine ear be penetrated with their cyes [cries]."[1] The letter containing this prayer, like many documents produced in the surrounding months, opens to view one of the most difficult periods in the Mormon prophet's personal life and for the Latter-day Saints generally. The sixth volume in the Documents series of *The Joseph Smith Papers* covers the period from February 1838 to August 1839. During these nineteen months, Joseph Smith moved from Kirtland, Ohio, to Far West, Missouri; established new communities in Adam-ondi-Ahman and De Witt, Missouri; and was involved in the armed conflict between the Latter-day Saints and other Missourians. Further, he was arrested and imprisoned based on charges of treason and other crimes; escaped custody and fled to Quincy, Illinois; and helped establish new settlements of Saints at Commerce, Illinois, and at Montrose, Iowa Territory.

The Mormon experience in Missouri illuminates the broader culture of antebellum America. During the early nineteenth century, the United States saw a general increase in the number and intensity of violent conflicts between differing cultural, racial, and political groups. The Latter-day Saints had typically been viewed by other Missourians as outsiders—they came mostly from the North, whereas most Missourians came from the South. Their conflict can be seen in part as a representation of the cultural divide between North and South that was widening in the mid-nineteenth century. This divide would harden into a political struggle over the expansion of slavery into the West, with Missouri the westernmost state at the time, and would eventually culminate in a civil war. The conflict between the Saints and other Missourians

---

1. Letter to the Church and Edward Partridge, 20 Mar. 1839, p. 362 herein.

took place in the far reaches of the state. Western Missouri had weak legal institutions that easily gave way to vigilantism and violence.[2] The experience of the Saints thus highlights the young nation's regional dynamics. The experience also reveals the problems of democracy and the blurry line between the rule of law and the rule of the people when it came to emerging groups on the margins of society. Of course, the difference between the Latter-day Saints and their Missouri neighbors was not only cultural but also religious. The Mormon experience in Missouri therefore also sheds light on the tenuous status of unpopular religious minorities in early America.

During February 1838, Joseph Smith was traveling from Kirtland to Far West, where he planned to relocate his family. Smith had intended to move to Missouri for several years. In July 1831, little more than a year after organizing the Church of Christ, he dictated a revelation designating Missouri as the "land of Zion." The revelation further designated Independence, in Jackson County, as the "centre place" of Zion, at which to build "the City of Zion."[3] Church members soon began migrating to Independence and other parts of the county. The earlier non-Mormon settlers in the area became increasingly suspicious of the growing population of Mormons and forcibly drove them from the county in 1833. Most of the displaced Saints took refuge on the other side of the Missouri River, in Clay County. Meanwhile, Joseph Smith and church members in Kirtland—which by then had been designated as a "stake" of Zion—continued building up the community of Saints living there.[4] While the Kirtland Saints were busy building a temple and developing the community, the growing population of Mormons in Clay County was becoming a concern to non-Mormons. By summer 1836, non-Mormon residents demanded that the Mormons leave Clay County. At the close of 1836, the Missouri legislature created Caldwell County, northeast of Clay County, as a place for the Saints to settle. Thereafter, many Missourians believed the Saints were obligated to confine their settlement to that location.[5]

The Saints moved from Clay County to Caldwell County and established the town of Far West as their central settlement. William W. Phelps and John Whitmer, who were David Whitmer's counselors in the Zion church presidency, used money borrowed from Saints in Kentucky and Tennessee to help buy more land in the vicinity of Far West to begin an aggressive plan of

---

2. See, for example, Gilje, *Rioting in America,* 60–86; and Brown, *Strain of Violence,* 95–133; see also Grimsted, *American Mobbing,* chaps. 3, 7.

3. Revelation, 20 July 1831, in *JSP,* D2:7–8, 12 [D&C 57:1–3, 14].

4. Revelation, 26 Apr. 1832, in *JSP,* D2:236 [D&C 82:13].

5. See LeSueur, "Missouri's Failed Compromise," 113–135.

development. Some church leaders in Missouri strongly believed that Phelps and Whitmer were circumventing the church's council system of decision making and were profiteering from land sales. As a result, in early 1837, apostles Thomas B. Marsh and David W. Patten, the Zion high council, and the Zion bishopric pressured Phelps and John Whitmer into transferring the Far West property to Bishop Edward Partridge.

At this time, the church in Ohio was also embroiled in financial issues and leadership concerns. As the population of Latter-day Saints in Kirtland had continued to grow, JS and other church leaders had conceived expansive plans for the community, including a bank to help provide capital for development. This bank, called the Kirtland Safety Society, was organized in November 1836. Though church leaders were unable to obtain a bank charter from the Ohio legislature—or much in the way of capital—they nevertheless opened their financial institution in January 1837. The safety society struggled to acquire funding and support, with some economic competitors in the area actively opposing the bank. In May a nationwide financial panic caused wide-scale bank failures. The Kirtland banking venture succumbed, as did several other local Mormon enterprises, and unpaid debts brought on a tide of litigation against Joseph Smith and other Ohio Saints. These events contributed to the discontent with Joseph Smith that had been growing since winter 1836–1837. Even some of Smith's closest associates now joined the ranks of the disillusioned.[6]

In the following months, Smith took action to reconfirm his authority as the head of the church. He began by reorganizing the church's leadership in Kirtland and Far West in fall 1837. In September, Smith convened a conference in Kirtland at which the church voted to accept or reject the current leaders. Those who attended voted to sustain the First Presidency, with Joseph Smith as church president; Sidney Rigdon and Frederick G. Williams as counselors; and Oliver Cowdery, Joseph Smith Sr., Hyrum Smith, and John Smith as assistant counselors. The members voted against three apostles and four members of the Kirtland high council, all of whom had been involved in the dissent against Smith's leadership. A week later, the three apostles publicly confessed their errors and were consequently allowed to retain their office.[7]

Following the conference, Joseph Smith conveyed the minutes in a letter to the church in Zion. In the letter, he also stated that Oliver Cowdery and David Whitmer were in transgression and that if they did not humble themselves

6. See, for example, Letter from Parley P. Pratt, 23 May 1837, in *JSP*, D5:386–391; and Warren Parrish, Kirtland, OH, 5 Feb. 1838, Letter to the Editor, *Painesville (OH) Republican,* 15 Feb. 1838, [3]; see also Introduction to Part 6: 20 Apr.–14 Sept. 1837, in *JSP*, D5:363–366.

7. Minutes, 3 Sept. 1837, in *JSP*, D5:422–423; Minute Book 1, 10 Sept. 1837.

they would lose their standing in the church. A revelation that Smith dictated the same day, which may have been enclosed with the letter to the church in Zion, stated that William W. Phelps and John Whitmer had also transgressed against the Lord and would be removed from office if they did not repent.[8]

Later in September, Joseph Smith and other church leaders in Kirtland traveled to Far West to resolve issues and to convene a reorganization conference similar to the one just held in Kirtland. During the Far West conference, held in November, the members of the Zion church presidency were retained after they confessed their faults. Also during the conference, Hyrum Smith was appointed to replace Williams in the First Presidency. Satisfied that leadership problems had been resolved, Joseph Smith and other church leaders visiting from Kirtland returned home.[9] When Smith arrived in Kirtland in December, he found that dissent there had grown dramatically in his absence. As the year was coming to an end and Smith turned thirty-two years old, the Latter-day Saint community that he had been building up for seven years in Kirtland was crumbling around him.

On 12 January 1838, as Joseph Smith faced threats of physical violence and further litigation, he dictated a revelation directing the First Presidency to move to Missouri as soon as possible, with the faithful Saints to follow. Smith and Rigdon fled Kirtland that night and were soon joined by their families. Over the next two months, they traveled the approximately eight hundred miles to Far West. Other Saints left Ohio for Missouri during the spring, summer, and autumn. While Joseph Smith was en route to Far West, his supporters there were working to root out dissent that persisted among local church leadership. In February 1838, senior apostle Thomas B. Marsh and the Zion high council convened a general meeting of the church in which members of the high council accused William W. Phelps and John Whitmer of mismanaging church money. The assembly voted to remove both men, as well as David Whitmer, who had sided with his counselors. In their place, the high council appointed Marsh and David W. Patten as pro tempore presidents. Toward the beginning of the next month, Marsh and Patten presided over a church trial in which former counselors Phelps and Whitmer were excommunicated.

Joseph Smith arrived in Far West in mid-March, determined that the Saints there would pursue their goals without the harassment he had experienced in Ohio and without the persecution the Saints had suffered in Jackson and Clay

---

8. Letter to John Corrill and the Church in Missouri, 4 Sept. 1837, in *JSP*, D5:427–431; Revelation, 4 Sept. 1837, in *JSP*, D5:433.

9. Minutes, 6 Nov. 1837, in *JSP*, D5:466–468; Minutes, 7 Nov. 1837, in *JSP*, D5:469–472; see also "Joseph Smith Documents from October 1835 through January 1838," in *JSP*, D5:xix–xxxvi.

counties. In a conference held in early April 1838, the Saints in Missouri sustained the pro tempore Zion presidency, with Marsh as president and Patten and Brigham Young as assistant presidents, in addition to appointing other new officers. After this further reorganization, Smith and other church leaders turned their attention back to prominent dissenters, excommunicating Oliver Cowdery and David Whitmer in mid-April.

With the church reorganized and the most prominent dissenters cut off, Joseph Smith and the Zion high council focused on developing Far West as the gathering place for the church. In late April, they passed resolutions to construct new church buildings and to reestablish the church press and newspaper. On 26 April, Joseph Smith dictated a revelation directing the Saints to continue gathering to Missouri, to develop Far West, and to begin building a temple in the town on 4 July 1838. This revelation marked a change in the church's plans in Missouri. During the Mormon sojourn in Clay County, no revelations had instructed the Saints to establish a city of gathering or to construct a temple. Similarly, the plan for Far West up until this time had been merely to develop it as a temporary settlement while the Saints waited to return to the "centre place" of Zion at Independence, Jackson County. In contrast, the 26 April revelation commanded them to engage in "building up" Far West as a city of Zion with a temple.

The revelation ended by stating that Joseph Smith would be guided to designate new locations for Mormon settlement. Much of the best land in Caldwell County was already occupied, and hundreds of Saints were expected to gather to Zion from the Kirtland stake and from the various branches of the church in the United States and in British North America. In mid-May 1838, Smith and others left for Daviess County, just north of Caldwell County, to select and survey lands in anticipation of future church growth. It was during this time that Smith identified a bluff rising above the Grand River as Adam-ondi-Ahman, which he had previously taught was the place where Adam blessed his posterity after being driven from the Garden of Eden. Smith spent much of May and June in Daviess County surveying and creating a city plat and supervising the construction of new homes. By the end of June, Adam-ondi-Ahman was sufficiently populated and developed to organize a stake there. During this period, church leaders were also directing Mormon migration to the small town of De Witt, situated at the confluence of the Grand River and the Missouri River in Carroll County.

As the church established settlements in Daviess and Carroll counties, tensions continued to escalate between church members in Far West and prominent excommunicants who remained in Caldwell County. In mid-June, during a brief return to Far West, Smith attended a church meeting in which Rigdon delivered a scathing sermon accusing the dissenters of stealing and other crimes. Around the same time, more than eighty Latter-day Saint men signed a letter directed to Cowdery, the former members of the Zion presidency, and former apostle Lyman Johnson, warning them to leave Caldwell County or suffer "a more fatal calamity."[10] Within a few days, the warned men had either fled the county or reconciled with church leaders. At about this time, several Mormon men organized as a private militia known as the Society of the Daughter of Zion—later called the Danites—to defend the church from any remaining internal and external opposition. The intent of the organization was to support the members of the First Presidency and their policies, as well as to defend the church against any future aggression.

On 4 July 1838, thousands of Saints and others attended a church-sponsored Independence Day celebration in Far West, with Joseph Smith presiding. In an oration during the event, Rigdon venerated America's revolutionary forefathers and the country's heritage of civil and religious liberty. He affirmed the loyalty of the Saints to the United States and claimed the Saints had the same rights as other American citizens. At the conclusion of the oration, Rigdon declared that if the Saints faced further mob violence, they would not only defend but also avenge themselves. The printed version of the discourse circulated broadly throughout northwestern Missouri, and Joseph Smith encouraged church members to obtain their own copies.

Four days later, on 8 July, Joseph Smith dictated five revelations focused on building up the church. One revelation provided directions for reorganizing the Quorum of the Twelve Apostles and for planning a proselytizing mission the apostles were to begin the following spring, sailing "over the great waters" to Britain.[11] Other revelations established a program for gathering and administering donations. Through the remainder of the summer, Joseph Smith was engaged in directing the further settlement of Far West, Adam-ondi-Ahman, and De Witt. By the end of the summer, Far West had over one hundred homes and several mills and shops, with hundreds of farms in the surrounding countryside.

The growing population of Latter-day Saints, especially outside of Caldwell County, eventually led to conflict with other Missourians. Violence between the Mormons and non-Mormons of northwestern Missouri broke out in Gallatin, Daviess County, on an election day in early August 1838. When William Peniston, a candidate for the state legislature, persuaded a crowd of men at the polls to prevent the Saints from voting, one of the men attempted to strike one of

---

10. Sampson Avard et al., Far West, MO, to Oliver Cowdery et al., Far West, MO, ca. 17 June 1838, copy, Mormon War Papers, MSA, also available at josephsmithpapers.org.

11. Revelation, 8 July 1838–A, p. 175 herein [D&C 118:4–5].

the Saints, and a fight between the two groups quickly ensued. When a report of the affray reached Far West, with exaggerated claims that church members had been killed, Joseph Smith accompanied a large body of Danites and other armed men from Caldwell County to Daviess County to investigate and seek assurance from local magistrates that the civil rights of the Saints would be protected. Joined by Mormon men from Daviess County, who were led by Danite officer Lyman Wight, the group visited Adam Black, a justice of the peace living near Adam-ondi-Ahman. The previous year, Black had participated in an effort to pressure the small number of Saints then living in Daviess to leave the county. However, now feeling threatened by the Saints at his house, he promised to uphold their rights in Daviess County.

Soon thereafter, Black, Peniston, and their friends claimed that Black had been attacked, and they filed charges against Smith and Wight. Black and his friends apparently recognized that whereas Jackson and Clay county residents were able to compel the Saints to leave those counties because the Saints were a minority, the small number of non-Mormons in Daviess County could not expel the rapidly increasing population of Saints without help from residents of other counties. The men used the alleged attack as the pretext for soliciting aid from other counties to drive the Saints out. After Wight reportedly resisted arrest and Smith sought a change of venue, Black and his associates claimed that the two Mormon leaders were evading the law. Black and his friends called for volunteers from surrounding counties to meet in Daviess County in early September to take Smith and Wight by force if necessary. The pair attempted to defuse the situation by arranging to appear before a judge, but they were unable to forestall the vigilantism that was already in motion. Men from the northwestern counties soon gathered in Daviess and began terrorizing Saints living in outlying areas of the county. In mid-September, the state militia intervened, disbanding the vigilantes and sending them home. The rule of law was restored in Daviess County.

Some of the vigilantes, however, regrouped and traveled to Carroll County to attack the Saints living at De Witt. In early October 1838, after the Saints refused demands to leave, vigilantes surrounded De Witt and began attacking the Saints. Again, the state militia was sent to keep the peace, but this time the militia was unsuccessful. So many soldiers in the militia sympathized with the vigilantes that their commanding officer removed them from De Witt to prevent them from joining the attack against the Saints. Outnumbered, the Saints at De Witt soon surrendered, and Joseph Smith helped them relocate to Far West. Emboldened, the vigilantes returned to Daviess and rallied their forces with the intent to drive the Saints from that county. The state militia's failure to defend the Saints at De Witt demonstrated to the Saints that they could not rely on the rule of law. When church leaders in Far West learned that the vigilantes were regrouping in Daviess County, the Saints mobilized for self-defense. Rather than waiting to be attacked, they launched preemptive strikes, targeting houses and property in vigilante havens. Soon, vigilantes on both sides were burning buildings and plundering. By the end of October 1838, the Mormon forces had prevailed and most of the other citizens had fled Daviess County.

This conflict, however, led to hostilities along the borders of Caldwell County. In Ray County, bordering Caldwell County to the south, a company of militiamen received orders to patrol the boundary between the counties. The men were directed to prevent Mormon forces in Caldwell County from invading Ray County, citing as precedent the recent Latter-day Saint raids in Daviess County. The Ray County company crossed over into Caldwell County, where the soldiers harassed small communities of Saints living along the border and then captured three Mormon men, at least two of whom were scouts who had been following the company's movements. David W. Patten mobilized a company of Saints from Caldwell County to rescue the three men. The rescue party crossed over the border of Caldwell County and engaged the company of Ray County militia at Crooked River, routing them and liberating the scouts. One Ray County soldier and three Caldwell County soldiers, including Patten, were killed. A few days later, over two hundred vigilantes from Livingston, Daviess, and other counties targeted the small Mormon settlement at Jacob Hawn's mill on the eastern boundary of Caldwell County, where about thirty Mormon families had gathered. The attack was apparently a retaliatory response to the Saints' recent military operations in Daviess County. The vigilantes struck on 30 October, brutally killing ten men and boys—some of whom were unarmed—and fatally wounding seven others.

In the final days of October, Missouri governor Lilburn W. Boggs also took action against the Saints, responding to exaggerated reports of Mormon depredations in Daviess and Ray counties—especially rumors that the Saints had killed most of the company of Ray County militia at Crooked River. Boggs ordered an overwhelming contingent of state militia to restore peace in the northwestern counties by subduing the rumored Mormon insurgency. In a letter to one of his generals, Boggs stated that the Saints were now to be considered enemies of Missouri who should be "exterminated or driven from the state." Boggs explicitly ordered the general and his men to "operate against the Mormons."[12] On 30 October, approximately eighteen hundred troops laid siege to Far West. In early November, Missouri's "Mormon War" concluded

---

12. Lilburn W. Boggs, Jefferson City, MO, to John B. Clark, Fayette, MO, 27 Oct. 1838, copy, Mormon War Papers, MSA.

with the surrender of Far West, the arrest and imprisonment of Joseph Smith and several other Latter-day Saints, confiscation of the Saints' weapons and property, and the Saints' agreement to leave Missouri.

Joseph Smith was held in state custody for almost six months, from 31 October 1838 to 16 April 1839. In a November 1838 preliminary hearing in Richmond, Ray County, the judge found probable cause that Smith and other church members were guilty of treason and other crimes. In December, Smith and a few other Saints were committed to the Clay County jail in Liberty to await a trial in the spring. Through the winter of 1838–1839, Smith and his fellow prisoners wrote several letters to family members and to the church generally, offering words of counsel and support.

Meanwhile, the Latter-day Saints began their forced departure from Missouri. A large-scale evacuation started in February 1839. Approximately eight to ten thousand Saints, including the families of the prisoners, trudged eastward across the state, most seeking refuge in Illinois. Many were poorly provisioned and suffered considerably from cold, hunger, and illness during the journey of nearly two hundred miles. Many found refuge in the town of Quincy, just across the Mississippi River from Missouri.

Joseph Smith and his fellow prisoners continued their correspondence with family and church leaders who had temporarily resettled in Quincy. In March 1839, Smith dictated two general epistles to church members. In the letters, he reflected on the suffering of the Saints and on the deeper significance of persecution. Parts of the epistles were presented in the voice of Deity, providing revelatory counsel and comfort to the prisoners as well as to the Mormon refugees in Illinois. The prisoners also produced several legal documents petitioning for habeas corpus hearings and a change of venue. In addition to pursuing these legal avenues for liberty, the prisoners attempted to escape on two occasions but were unsuccessful. Through this time of great difficulty, Smith was able to stay abreast of the circumstances of the church and provide leadership, even from within the walls of a jail.

In April 1839, after spending much of the winter confined in a cold and dirty dungeon, Joseph Smith and his fellow prisoners were taken to Daviess County for a grand jury investigation. There they were indicted for treason and other alleged crimes but were granted a change of venue to Boone County for their trial. The prisoners escaped during the journey to Boone County, possibly with the complicity of the guards. In late April, Joseph Smith and his companions crossed the Mississippi River into Illinois, where they reunited with their families and with thousands of other Mormon refugees.

Joseph Smith arrived in Illinois determined to find a new place in which to gather his people and rebuild their strength. He soon held church meetings to help organize and regulate the affairs of the church and to identify locations to purchase land for the displaced Saints. By the end of April, the church acquired land approximately fifty miles upriver, at Commerce, Illinois. About this time, some of the apostles were returning to Quincy from a covert trip to Far West. While Smith and his companions were escaping custody and fleeing to Illinois, the apostles were traveling back to Far West to fulfill the commandment in an 8 July 1838 revelation that the apostles were to depart from Far West on 26 April 1839 to begin their mission "over the great waters." The apostles visited the temple lot in the early morning hours of that day to formally commence their mission and then headed back to Illinois, where they stayed a few months before pressing on to the Atlantic.

In early May, the church held a conference at Quincy in which the apostles' actions in Far West were ratified and their mission was reaffirmed. During the conference, the church also appointed a committee to collect libelous reports about the Saints and appointed Rigdon to go to the nation's capital to seek redress for the Saints' tremendous losses of property and goods in Missouri. After this conference, Smith and others began moving from Quincy to Commerce, where they started a new settlement. Over the next few months, Smith and other church officers purchased additional land at Commerce and across the river at Montrose, Iowa Territory.

The riverside land included a swampy floodplain plagued with mosquitoes. A malaria epidemic ravaged the community of Saints from July to November 1839, hampering their efforts to settle the area and resume church affairs—and delaying the apostles' departure for Britain. For months, the Smith home and yard served as a hospital of sorts, with Joseph and his wife Emma nursing those stricken with disease. Joseph also fell ill but soon recovered and continued to minister to the sick. He also met frequently with the apostles to help them prepare for their mission. In June and July, he gave several discourses, instructing the apostles on the importance of unity and harmony, the order of the priesthood, discernment of false spirits, and other doctrines. In August 1839, the final month of this volume, four of the twelve apostles departed for England, and three more followed in September and October 1839.[13]

The church projects that were established by the end of the summer carried on for several years. At a general conference of the church held at Commerce in early October 1839, Joseph Smith proposed—and the membership of the church affirmed—that Commerce was a suitable location for a stake of Zion

---

13. Woodruff, Journal, 8 Aug. 1839; JS History, vol. C-1, 965, 967; John Taylor, Germantown, IL, to Leonora Taylor, Montrose, Iowa Territory, 19 Sept. 1839, John Taylor, Collection, CHL; Allen et al., *Men with a Mission*, 67–72, 77.

and a gathering place for the Saints.[14] Smith soon renamed the settlement Nauvoo, a Hebrew word denoting beauty.[15] Nauvoo became the most successful city-building project Smith undertook in his life. Saints continued to gather to Nauvoo, including those who were baptized in England during the apostles' dramatically successful mission. Yet even while the Saints were successfully building up a new city, the land of Zion still occupied much of their attention. In the months and years following their expulsion from Missouri, they persistently called attention to the injustices they had suffered there and they continued their efforts to obtain federal redress for their losses. The expulsion of Joseph Smith and other church members from Missouri profoundly influenced Latter-day Saint identity throughout the rest of Smith's lifetime and for decades afterward.

Joseph Smith produced documents sporadically between February 1838 and August 1839. There are several gaps in the documentary record, most notably during the conflict in Missouri in late 1838. During the first few months in Far West, Smith kept a journal with the assistance of a scribe, wrote and received several letters, participated in several meetings for which minutes were kept, dictated several revelations, and produced a variety of other documents. As the conflict in neighboring counties escalated, Joseph Smith and his scribes apparently became too preoccupied to continue journal keeping and other documentary efforts. However, while languishing in the Clay County jail during winter 1838–1839, Smith wrote several letters and produced several other documents. In April 1839, when he reunited with the main body of the Saints in Illinois, he reengaged a scribe and resumed the documentary endeavors interrupted by the October 1838 conflict and then by his incarceration and separation from the body of the church. Despite the difficult and fluctuating circumstances of their creation, the letters, minutes, revelations, and other texts produced by Joseph Smith between early 1838 and mid-1839 provide essential documentation of these tumultuous times.

---

14. Minutes, Commerce, IL, 5–7 Oct. 1839, in *Times and Seasons,* Dec. 1839, 1:30.

15. "A Proclamation, to the Saints Scattered Abroad," *Times and Seasons,* 15 Jan. 1841, 2:273–274; Gibbs, *Manual Hebrew and English Lexicon,* 142; Seixas, *Hebrew Grammar,* 111; Zucker, "Joseph Smith as a Student of Hebrew," 48.

Editorial Method

The goal of the Joseph Smith Papers Project is to present verbatim transcripts of Joseph Smith's papers in their entirety, making available the most essential sources of Smith's life and work and preserving the content of aging manuscripts from damage or loss. The papers include documents that were created by Joseph Smith, whether written or dictated by him or created by others under his direction, or that were owned by Smith, that is, received by him and kept in his office (as with incoming correspondence). Under these criteria—authorship and ownership—the project intends to publish, either in letterpress volumes or electronic form, every extant Joseph Smith document to which its editors can obtain access. This sixth volume of the Documents series presents unaltered and unabridged transcripts of letters, discourses, revelations, and other Joseph Smith documents created between February 1838 and August 1839.

Document Selection

For many Joseph Smith documents, multiple versions were created during his lifetime. For example, a revelation originally recorded on loose paper might have been copied into a more permanent bound volume, and that version might then have been revised and published in one or more print editions. Individuals with access to the handwritten or printed versions might have made or obtained copies for personal use, or in some cases for unauthorized publication. For this volume, original documents are featured when they are extant; in cases when the original is not extant (as with most Joseph Smith revelations), the editors selected either the earliest extant version of the text or the version that in their judgment best represents the nonextant original. The source notes and historical introductions preceding the individual documents provide additional information about version selection. Editors compared the featured version against other early versions, and any significant differences are described in annotation.

Rules of Transcription

Because of aging and sometimes damaged texts and imprecise orthography and penmanship, not all handwriting is legible. Hurried writers often rendered words carelessly, and even the best writers and spellers left out letters on occasion or formed them imperfectly and incompletely. Even with rigorous methods, transcription and verification are not an exact science. Judgments about capitalization, for example, are informed not only by looking at the specific case at hand but by understanding the usual characteristics of each particular writer. The same is true for interpreting original spelling and punctuation. If a letter or other character is ambiguous, deference is given to the author's or scribe's usual spelling and punctuation. Where this is ambiguous, modern spelling and punctuation are favored. Even the best transcribers and verifiers will differ from one another in making such judgments. Interested readers may wish to compare the transcripts with images of the original documents at the Joseph Smith Papers website, josephsmithpapers.org, to better understand how our transcription rules have been applied to create these transcripts. Viewing the originals also provides other information that cannot be conveyed by typography.

To ensure accuracy in representing the texts, transcripts were verified three times, each time by a different set of eyes. The first two verifications were done using high-resolution scanned images. The first was a visual collation of the document images with the transcripts, while the second was an independent and double-blind image-to-transcript tandem proofreading. The third and final verification of the transcripts was a visual collation with the original document. At this stage, the verifier employed magnification and ultraviolet light as needed to read badly faded text, recover heavily stricken material, untangle characters written over each other, and recover words canceled by messy "wipe erasures" made when the ink was still wet or removed by knife scraping after the ink had dried. The verified transcripts meet or exceed the transcription and verification requirements of the National Archives and Records Administration's National Historical Publications and Records Commission.

The approach to transcription employed in *The Joseph Smith Papers* is a conservative style of what is known as "expanded transcription." The transcripts render most words letter by letter as accurately as possible, preserving the exact spelling of the originals. This includes incomplete words, variant spellings of personal names, repeated words, and idiosyncratic grammatical constructions. The transcripts also preserve substantive revisions made by the original scribes. Canceled words are typographically rendered with the strikethrough bar, while inserted words are enclosed within angle brackets. Cancellations and insertions are also transcribed letter by letter when an original word was changed to a new word simply by canceling or inserting letters at the beginning or end of the word—such as "sparing~~ly~~" or "attend⟨ed⟩". However, for cases in which an original word was changed to a new word by canceling or inserting letters in the middle of the word, to improve readability the original word is presented stricken in its entirety, followed by the revised word in its entirety. For example, when "falling" was revised to "failing" by canceling the first "l" and inserting an "i", the revision is transcribed as "~~falling~~ ⟨failing⟩" instead of "fal⟨i⟩ling". Insubstantial cancellations and insertions—those used only to correct spelling and punctuation—are silently emended, and only the final spelling and punctuation are reproduced. For example, a manuscript reading "Joseph, Frederick, & and Oliver" will be rendered in the transcript as "Joseph, Frederick, and Oliver". And a manuscript reading "on Thirsday 31th⟨st⟩ arrived at Buffalo" will be rendered "on Thirsday 31st arrived at Buffalo".

The transcription of punctuation differs from the original in a few other respects. Single instances of periods, commas, apostrophes, and dashes are all faithfully rendered without regard to their grammatical correctness, except that periods are not reproduced when they appear immediately before a word, with no space between the period and the word. Also, in some cases of repetitive punctuation, only the final mark or final intention is transcribed while any other characters are silently omitted. Dashes of various lengths are standardized to a consistent pattern. The short vertical strokes commonly used in early American writing for abbreviation punctuation are transcribed as periods, except that abbreviation punctuation is not reproduced when an abbreviation is expanded in square brackets. Pilcrows are silently omitted, represented instead with a paragraph break. Flourishes and other decorative inscriptions are not reproduced or noted. Ellipsis marks appear in the featured text only where they occur in the original manuscript and are standardized to a consistent format; they do not represent an editorial abridgment. Punctuation is never added silently. When the original document sets off a quotation by using quotation marks at the beginning of each line that contains quoted matter, the quotation is formatted as a block quote, without the original quotation marks preserved.

Incorrect dates, place names, and other errors of fact are left to stand. The intrusive *sic,* sometimes used to affirm original misspelling, is never employed, although where words or phrases are especially difficult to understand, editorial clarifications or corrections are inserted in brackets. Correct and complete spellings of personal names are supplied in brackets the first time each incorrect or incomplete name appears in a document, unless the correct name cannot be determined. Place names that may be hard to identify are also clarified or corrected within brackets. When two or more words were inscribed or typeset together without any intervening space and the words were not a compound according to standard contemporary usage or the writer's or printer's consistent practice, the words are transcribed as separate words for readability.

Formatting is standardized. Original paragraphing is retained. All paragraphs are given in a standard format, with indention regularized and with empty lines between paragraphs omitted. Blank space of approximately five or more lines in the original is noted, as are lesser amounts of blank vertical space that appear significant. Extra space between words or sentences is not captured unless it appears the scribe left a blank space as a placeholder to be filled in later. Documents featured herein that are copies of nonextant original documents sometimes contain large blank spaces within a line of text, which seem to indicate where paragraph breaks appeared in the original documents. Where this occurs, the blank space is rendered as a paragraph break. Block quotations of letters, minutes, revelations, and other similar items within the texts are set apart with block indentions, even when such items are not set off in the original. Horizontal rules and other separating devices inscribed or printed in the original are not reproduced. Line ends are neither typographically reproduced nor symbolically represented. Because of the great number of words broken across a line at any point in the word, with or without a hyphen, end-of-line hyphens are not transcribed and there is no effort to note or keep a record of such words and hyphens. This leaves open the possibility that the hyphen of an ambiguously hyphenated compound escaped transcription or that a compound word correctly broken across a line ending without a hyphen is mistakenly transcribed as two words. As many end-of-line hyphens have been editorially introduced in the transcripts, a hyphen appearing at the end of a line may or may not be original to the document.

In transcripts of printed sources, typeface, type size, and spacing have been standardized. Characters set upside down are silently corrected. When the text could not be determined because of broken or worn type or damage to the page, the illegible text is supplied based on another copy of the printed text, if possible. Printers sometimes made changes to the text, such as to correct spelling mistakes or replace damaged type, after printing had already begun, meaning that the first copies to come off the press often differ from later copies in the same print run. No attempt has been made to analyze more than one copy of the printed texts transcribed here, aside from consulting another copy when the one used for transcription is indeterminable or ambiguous.

Within some of the documents, the ink color of the original text changes often, even in the middle of sentences. Such changes in ink color are not noted. In some cases, cancellations and insertions were made in a different color than the original inscription. Because these cancellations and insertions are already marked as revisions—with the horizontal strikethrough bar for cancellations and with a pair of angle brackets for insertions—the color of the ink used for the revision is not noted.

Redactions and other changes made to a document after the original production of the text are not transcribed, nor are labeling and other forms of archival marking. Source notes identify documents that include such redactions or labeling. Most handwritten documents in this volume were inscribed in black or brown ink using a quill pen. Exceptions are identified in source notes.

Transcription Symbols

The effort to render mistakes, canceled material, and later insertions sometimes complicates readability by putting Joseph Smith and his scribes behind the "barbed wire" of symbolic transcription. However, conveying such elements with transcription symbols can aid in understanding the text and the order and ways in which the words were inscribed. Typesetting can never effectively represent all the visual aspects of a document; it cannot fully capture such features as the formation of letters and other characters, spacing between words and between paragraphs, varying lengths of dashes and paragraph indentions, and varying methods of cancellation and the location of insertions. Despite its limitations, a conservative transcription method more faithfully represents the process by which the text was inscribed—especially cancellations and insertions—rather than just the final result.

The following symbols are used to transcribe and expand the text:

/ⁿ	In documents inscribed by more than one person, the slash mark indicates a change in handwriting. A footnote identifies the previous and commencing scribes.
[roman]	Brackets enclose editorial insertions that expand, correct, or clarify the text. This convention may be applied to the abbreviated or incorrect spelling of a personal name, such as Brigham Yo[u]ng, or of a place, such as Westleville [Wesleyville]. Obsolete or ambiguous abbreviations are expanded with br[acket]s. Bracketed editorial insertions also provide reasonable reconstructions of badly miss[p]elled worsd [words]. Missing or illegible words may be supplied within brackets when the supplied word is based on textual or contextual evidence. Bracketed punctuation is added only when necessary to follow complex wording.
[roman?]	A question mark is added to conjectural editorial insertions, such as where an entire word was [accidentally?] omitted and where it is difficult to maintain the sense of a sentence without some editorial insertion.
[*italic*]	Significant descriptions of the writing medium—especially those inhibiting legibility—and of spacing within the text are italicized and enclosed in brackets: [*hole burned in paper*], [*leaf torn*], [*blank*], [*9 lines blank*], [*pages 99–102 blank*].
[*illegible*]	An illegible word is represented by the italicized word [*illegible*] enclosed in brackets.

◊   An illegible letter or other character within a partially legible word is rendered with a diamond. Repeated diamonds represent the approximate number of illegible characters (for example: sto◊◊◊◊s).

[p. x]   Bracketed editorial insertions indicate the end of an originally numbered page, regardless of the location of the page number on the original page. No page indicator is given for the last page of a document if the document was transcribed from a multiple-entry source (such as an article from a newspaper or a letter from a letterbook) and if there is text following the featured document on that same page.

[p. [x]]   Bracketing of the page number itself indicates that the page was not originally numbered and that the number of the page is editorially supplied.

<u>underlined</u>   Underlining is typographically reproduced, with multiple underlining typographically standardized to a single underline. <u>Individually</u> <u>underlined</u> <u>words</u> are distinguished from <u>passages underlined with one continuous line</u>. When underlining includes <u> leading and trailing spaces </u>, it indicates handwritten additions to preprinted forms.

superscript   Superscription is typographically reproduc^{ed}.

~~canceled~~   A single horizontal strikethrough bar is used to indicate any method of cancellation: strikethrough, cross-out, wipe erasure, knife erasure, overwriting, or other methods. ~~Individually~~ ~~canceled~~ ~~words~~ are distinguished from ~~passages eliminated with a single cancellation~~. Characters individual~~ly~~ canceled at the begin~~ning~~ or end of a word are distinguished from ~~words canceled in their entirety~~.

⟨inserted⟩   Insertions in the text—whether interlinear, intralinear, or marginal—are enclosed in angle brackets. Letter⟨s⟩ and other characters individual⟨ly⟩ insert⟨ed⟩ at the beginning or end of a word are distinguished from ⟨words⟩ inserted in ⟨their⟩ entirety.

bold   Joseph Smith's handwriting is rendered in boldface type. Bracketed editorial insertions made within passages of **Smith's own h[and]writing** are also rendered in boldface type.

[roman]   Stylized brackets represent [brackets] used in the original text.

⟦shorthand⟧   Instances of Pitman shorthand—a phonetic system of symbols first published by Isaac Pitman in 1837—are expanded into longhand in the running text and enclosed by ⟦stylized brackets⟧, with precise transliterations and any necessary description or explanation appearing in footnotes.

✉   An envelope symbol signifies the beginning of a mailing address, postmark, or address panel on an original letter.

TEXT   The word TEXT begins textual footnotes describing significant details not comprehended by this scheme of symbolic transcription.

| A line break artificially imposed in an original document is rendered as a vertical line in source notes and textual footnotes.

Annotation Conventions

The Joseph Smith Papers do not present a unified narrative. Annotations—including historical introductions, editorial notes, and footnotes—supply background and context to help readers better understand and use the documents. The aim of the annotation is to serve scholars and students of early Mormon history and American religious history generally, whose familiarity with these fields may vary widely.

The *Papers* cite original sources where possible and practical. Secondary sources of sound scholarship are cited when they distill several primary sources or provide useful general context. Quotations from primary sources preserve original spelling but silently emend cancellations and insertions (unless judged highly significant).

Certain conventions simplify the presentation of the annotation. Joseph Smith is usually referred to by the initials JS. Most sources are referred to by a shortened citation form, with the complete citation given in the Works Cited. Some documents are referred to by editorial titles rather than by their original titles or the titles given in the catalogs of their current repositories. These editorial titles are in some cases similar to informal names by which the documents have come to be known. The editorial titles are listed in the Works Cited along with the complete citations by which the documents can be found in repositories. In cases in which two or more documents of the same genre bear the same date, a letter of the alphabet is appended to the date so that each document has a unique editorial title—for example, Revelation, 8 July 1838–A and Revelation, 8 July 1838–B. The most important sources used in annotation are discussed in the Essay on Sources preceding the Works Cited. Many of the documents featured in the Documents series have been extracted from letterbooks, minute books, or other records that contain multiple individual documents or entries. When more than one text in this volume came from the same record book, bibliographic and other information may be found in "Source Notes for Multiple-Entry Documents" in the back of the volume.

This volume uses a citation style that lists all source citations at the end of the footnote. Because of the complexity of some footnotes and the difficulty readers might have in determining which source citations document particular statements within such footnotes, superscript letters are sometimes used to key specific statements to their corresponding documentation. Though it goes

beyond conventional citation style, this detailed approach may best serve researchers using this volume as a reference work.

Source citations in this volume identify revelations by their original date
and by a citation of the version most relevant to the particular instance of annotation (usually the version published in the Documents series of *The Joseph
Smith Papers*). For revelations that were later canonized by The Church of Jesus
Christ of Latter-day Saints, revelation citations also include a bracketed
"D&C" reference that provides the Doctrine and Covenants section and verse
numbers that have been standard in the church since 1876. Bracketed D&C
references are provided for the benefit of Latter-day Saints, who can easily
access the revelations in their familiar canon of scriptural works, and other
students of early Mormonism who may wish to access the most widely available editions of these revelations. A table titled Corresponding Section
Numbers in Editions of the Doctrine and Covenants is provided following the
Works Cited to help readers refer from the cited version of a canonized revelation to other published versions of the same revelation. For more information
about revelation citations, see the aforementioned table and the introduction
to the Works Cited.

Smith's revelations and revelatory translations published outside of the
Doctrine and Covenants, such as the Book of Mormon, are referenced in
The Joseph Smith Papers to an early published or manuscript version, with references to modern Latter-day Saint publications added in brackets. These books
of Latter-day Saint scripture are described in more detail in the introduction
to the Works Cited. When the Bible is used in annotation, the King James
Version—the version read by Smith and his followers and contemporaries as
well as by English-speaking Latter-day Saints today—is referenced.

In addition to the annotation in the main body of a volume, several sup-
plementary resources in the back of each volume and at josephsmithpapers.org
aid in understanding the text. As many of the places, people, organizations,
and terms mentioned in the documents appear more than once, the reference
material serves to remove duplicate footnotes and to otherwise systematically
reduce the annotation in the main body. To minimize repetition and interrup-
tion, only rarely will annotation within the documents directly refer readers to
the reference material in the back.

Many of the people whose names appear in the documents have been
identified. Many of the first or last names supplied in square brackets in the
transcripts presented in this volume have been inferred from the historical
context of the document, without specific documentation. In most cases, information about people named in the documents appears in the Biographical

Directory rather than in the notes. Some names have silently been left without identification either because resources did not permit research or because no information was found. Complete documentation for reference material in the back and for the timeline included earlier in the volume may be found at josephsmithpapers.org, as may other resources, including a complete calendar of Smith's papers, a glossary of Mormon terminology from Joseph Smith's time, and expanded versions of many of the reference resources.

DOCUMENTS
FEBRUARY 1838–AUGUST 1839

PART 1: 15 FEBRUARY– 28 JUNE 1838

During the period from February to June 1838, JS moved to Far West, Missouri, and helped reorganize church leadership there; some of the principal dissenters in Caldwell County were excommunicated and driven out; and the new settlement of Adam-ondi-Ahman, Daviess County, was surveyed, populated, and organized as a stake of Zion. JS had been planning to move to Far West for some time, and as tensions worsened at the end of 1837, he intended to move as soon as possible. In early January 1838, dissenters, excommunicated church members, and others threatened the lives of JS and his counselors in the First Presidency. In addition, JS and Sidney Rigdon faced litigation that was initiated by excommunicated members and other adversaries.[1] On 12 January, JS dictated a revelation directing him and his counselors in the First Presidency to halt their work in Kirtland "as soon as it is praticable" and move to Missouri; faithful Saints were to follow. That night, JS and Rigdon fled Kirtland on horseback, escaping the threat of violence. JS's wife Emma and their three children soon joined him on his journey to Far West, the central gathering place for Saints in Missouri.[2] Hyrum Smith and other church leaders departed for Missouri during the ensuing weeks and months.[3] Among those remaining in Ohio were William Marks, the newly appointed president of the Kirtland stake of Zion; John Smith and Reynolds Cahoon, who were appointed as assistant presidents to Marks; and Newel K. Whitney, the Kirtland bishop.[4] Marks endeavored to settle the debts of JS and Rigdon and to help the faithful members of the church migrate to Missouri, and Whitney oversaw other temporal operations of the church in Ohio.[5] While these men conducted JS's business and produced documents on his behalf, JS understandably wrote little if at all as he traveled west for two months. JS, Rigdon, and their families encountered several difficulties during

---

1. See Introduction to Part 7: 17 Sept. 1837–21 Jan. 1838, in *JSP*, D5:441–442.

2. Revelation, 12 Jan. 1838–C, in *JSP*, D5:501; Adams, "Grandison Newell's Obsession," 175, 178–180; "History of Luke Johnson," 6, Historian's Office, Histories of the Twelve, 1856–1858, 1861, CHL; JS History, vol. B-1, 780; see also JS, Journal, 29 Dec. 1842, in *JSP*, J2:196.

3. See Hyrum Smith, Commerce, IL, to "the Saints Scattered Abroad," Dec. 1839, in *Times and Seasons,* Dec. 1839, 1:21; and Kirtland Camp, Journal, 17 Mar. 1838.

4. John Smith and Clarissa Lyman Smith, Kirtland, OH, to George A. Smith, Shinnston, VA, 1 Jan. 1838, George Albert Smith, Papers, CHL; Hepzibah Richards, Kirtland, OH, to Willard Richards, Bedford, England, 18–19 Jan. 1838, Willard Richards, Papers, CHL.

5. See, for example, Pay Order to Edward Partridge for William Smith, 21 Feb. 1838, pp. 27–30 herein.

this move in the middle of the winter. Rigdon stopped traveling for several days because of family illness, while JS and his family pushed on toward Far West.[6]

Situated on Shoal Creek, the principal waterway in Caldwell County, Far West was already a sizable town. By summer 1837, Far West had reached a population of approximately fifteen hundred Saints.[7] Because the town was now the center of the Latter-day Saint gathering in Missouri and a revelation had identified that state as the "land of Zion," the church in Far West was usually referred to in contemporary documents as "Zion."[8] However, church members in Missouri were far from living the ideal of social harmony meant to exist in Zion. Internal dissent was a problem there as it was in Kirtland, in part because Oliver Cowdery, Lyman Johnson, and other dissenters had moved from Ohio to Missouri and were holding meetings with the Zion church presidency—David Whitmer, William W. Phelps, and John Whitmer—in which they vented their frustrations toward other church leaders. Additionally, several church authorities in Caldwell County were concerned because members of the Zion presidency had recently sold land in Jackson County, which many church leaders still hoped to reoccupy, and had disregarded the "Word of Wisdom," the church's divinely revealed dietary code.[9] Therefore, in early February 1838, senior apostles Thomas B. Marsh and David W. Patten, the Zion high council, and the Zion bishopric conducted meetings in which the Zion presidency members were removed from office and replaced with a pro tempore presidency consisting of Marsh and Patten. Marsh indicated that the proceedings were carried out according to JS's instructions. On 10 March, Phelps and John Whitmer were excommunicated from the church.[10] Thus, reassertion of the authority of JS and those loyal to him was well underway when JS and his family arrived in Far West on 14 March.[11]

The day after arriving in Far West, JS met with the Zion high council and bishopric. He reviewed the minutes of previous council meetings and apparently approved of the decisions to remove the former Zion presidency and to excommunicate Phelps and Whitmer.[12] The minutes of this meeting, as well as various other council meetings that JS attended, were copied into Minute Book 2, a volume containing minutes of church meetings primarily held in Missouri. Within a few days of arriving, JS composed a motto declaring the church's devotion to the revolutionary legacy of the United States, loyalty to the Constitution, and consent to obey all laws that were "good and wholesome"—while at the same time condemning tyranny, mob violence, and "vexatious lawsuits." The motto signaled JS's determination to vigorously assert the civil rights of the Latter-day Saints, including their right to settle in Missouri and to pursue their goals without being legally or illegally harassed. JS was deeply concerned about his personal liberty, as well as the

---

6. Letter to the Presidency in Kirtland, 29 Mar. 1838, pp. 57–58 herein; JS History, vol. B-1, 780; Van Wagoner, *Sidney Rigdon,* 203–204, 211–212.

7. Letter from William W. Phelps, 7 July 1837, in *JSP,* D5:402.

8. Revelation, 20 July 1831, in *JSP,* D2:12 [D&C 57:14].

9. Minute Book 2, 26 Jan. 1838; see also Minutes, 12 Apr. 1838, p. 88 herein.

10. Letter from Thomas B. Marsh, 15 Feb. 1838, pp. 18–23 herein; Minute Book 2, 10 Mar. 1838.

11. JS, Journal, Mar.–Sept. 1838, p. 16, in *JSP,* J1:237.

12. Minutes, 15 Mar. 1838, pp. 41–43 herein.

Kirtland, Ohio. 1907. In January 1838, amid dissent against Joseph Smith's leadership and threats against his life, he dictated a revelation directing him to leave Kirtland and move to Missouri. Loyal church members were to follow. Smith arrived in Missouri in March, where he continued to face the problems of the church's debt, dissent and disaffection among church members, and persecution against the church. (Church History Library, Salt Lake City. Photograph by George Edward Anderson.)

freedom and safety of the Saints, especially after he faced lawsuits, threats of violence, and the possibility of arrest in Ohio.[13]

Two weeks after JS's arrival, church clerk and recorder George W. Robinson arrived in Far West and was immediately engaged in clerical duties. Within a day or two, he began keeping a "Scriptory Book"—a record of "scripts," or transcripts, of various letters, revelations, and other documents. Toward the end of April, the content recorded in the book began to transition from document transcripts to journal entries of JS's activities. Accordingly, the Scriptory Book is also referred to herein as JS's journal for March to September 1838. This important volume is the source of the church motto and several other documents in part 1.[14] With JS and Robinson both in Far West, the number of JS documents produced in March and April considerably increased. On 29 March, JS wrote to the Kirtland presidency with news of his safe arrival in Far West, the illness delaying Rigdon's family, and recent

13. Motto, ca. 16 or 17 Mar. 1838, pp. 44–45 herein.
14. See JS, Journal, Mar.–Sept. 1838, in *JSP*, J1:236–320.

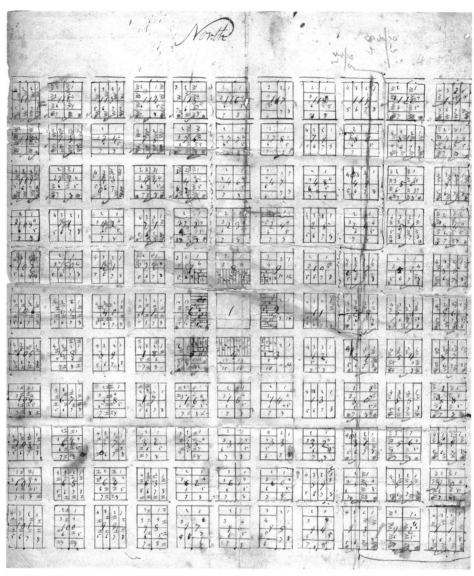

Far West plat. Circa 1838. William W. Phelps and John Whitmer purchased land in 1836 for a new Mormon settlement. A plat for this town, named Far West, was registered with Caldwell County in 1837. Joseph Smith and other church leaders spent much of 1838 developing Far West as the principal Mormon settlement in the county. This copy of the city plat illustrates the vision church leaders had for Far West. (Courtesy L. Tom Perry Special Collections, Harold B. Lee Library, Brigham Young University, Provo, UT.)

adjustments to leadership in the church in Missouri.[15] This and other correspondence between JS and church members in Kirtland, as well as in other places, form an important part
of the corpus of JS documents created during the period covered in part 1. JS's mid-March
letters and other documents may have been produced in the home of George and Lucinda
Pendleton Harris, where JS initially took up residence.[16] Within a few weeks of arriving in Far
West, JS apparently moved into the Samuel Musick tavern on the central block of the town.[17]

JS and Rigdon, who arrived in Far West on 4 April,[18] spent much of that month further
reorganizing church leadership in Missouri and dealing with dissenters. On 6 April, the
Latter-day Saints in Missouri assembled in Far West to commemorate the anniversary of
the church's organization, sustain the pro tempore presidency, and appoint new officers.
Brigham Young was appointed to join Marsh and Patten in the pro tempore presidency.
Partly to fill the vacancies resulting from the excommunication of John Whitmer, who
had served as the church's clerk, record keeper, and historian,[19] John Corrill and Elias
Higbee were appointed as historians, and George W. Robinson was named general church
recorder and clerk, as well as scribe for the First Presidency.[20] Ebenezer Robinson was appointed clerk and recorder for the church in Zion and for the Zion high council.[21] The
reorganization of church officers on 6 April prepared the way for the conference held over
the next two days.[22] The conference meetings were apparently held indoors, perhaps in the
town's schoolhouse, which was the setting of several other meetings held during this period. The Far West schoolhouse was originally in the southwest quarter of town but was
moved to the center of town and used for various civic purposes and church meetings.[23]
The meetings during the April conference were the first of several held in Far West that JS
presided at and Ebenezer Robinson kept minutes for. The minutes of several of these
church meetings are included in part 1.

---

15. Letter to the Presidency in Kirtland, 29 Mar. 1838, pp. 57–61 herein.

16. JS, Journal, Mar.–Sept. 1838, p. 16, in *JSP*, J1:237.

17. Receipt from Samuel Musick, 14 July 1838, pp. 204–206 herein; Kimball, "History," 105–106;
Lucy Mack Smith, History, 1844–1845, bk. 15, [6].

18. JS History, vol. B-1, 786.

19. Minutes, 6 Apr. 1838, p. 67 herein.

20. The minutes of the meeting state that Robinson was officially appointed "general Church Recorder
and Clerk for the first Presidency." When recording his own version of the minutes in JS's Scriptory Book,
Robinson wrote that he was appointed "as general Church Clerk & Recorder to keep a record of the whole
Church also as Scribe for the first Presidency." (Minutes, 6 Apr. 1838, p. 69 herein; Minutes, 6 Apr. 1838,
in JS, Journal, Mar.–Sept. 1838, p. 29, in *JSP*, J1:250.)

21. The minutes of the meeting state that Robinson was officially appointed "Church Clerk and
Recorder for this stake of Zion and Clerk for the high Council." When recording a version of the minutes
in JS's Scriptory Book, George W. Robinson wrote that Ebenezer Robinson was appointed "Clerk &
Recorder for the Church in Mo. also for the High Council," indicating that Ebenezer Robinson was also
appointed as a recorder for the Zion high council. At this time, Ebenezer Robinson began recording
past minutes of the Zion high council in Minute Book 2. (Minutes, 6 Apr. 1838, p. 70 herein; Minutes,
6 Apr. 1838, in JS, Journal, Mar.–Sept. 1838, p. 29, in *JSP*, J1:250; Minute Book 2, title page, 1–93.)

22. Minutes, 7–8 Apr. 1838, pp. 70–74 herein.

23. According to an early history of Caldwell County, "The school-house in Far West was used as a
church, as a town hall and as a court-house, as well as for a school-house." (*History of Caldwell and
Livingston Counties, Missouri*, 121.)

Following the quarterly conference, JS and other church leaders dealt with matters related to prominent dissenters. On 9 April, JS and Rigdon wrote to John Whitmer, requesting the writings he had in his possession as the former church historian.[24] That day, other church leaders sent letters to Oliver Cowdery, Lyman Johnson, and David Whitmer, informing them that councils would be held on 12 and 13 April to consider the men's church membership. JS testified in the trials of Cowdery and Johnson, and all three dissenters were excommunicated.[25]

With the church reorganized and major dissenters removed, JS and the high council turned their attention to developing Far West as the central gathering place for the church. On 21 April, they passed resolutions to improve the schoolhouse in which they were meeting, build one or more storehouses for provisioning poor Saints, and reestablish the church press. They resolved to recommence the *Elders' Journal,* with Marsh as the publisher; to solicit new subscriptions; and to publish minutes of some council meetings in the periodical.[26] Over the next few weeks, a prospectus for the *Elders' Journal* was printed and JS prepared material to include in the periodical.[27] Ultimately, two issues of the recommenced *Elders' Journal* were published; these issues, dated July and August 1838, included minutes of meetings JS participated in and documents written by JS and others during spring and summer 1838.

JS and the Saints also developed the church in Far West by following the direction given in revelations he dictated in spring 1838. In mid-April, he dictated brief revelations for David W. Patten and Brigham Young.[28] A revelation on 26 April stated that Far West was "most holy" and a place in "the land of zion" in which to build up a city. The revelation directed the Saints to continue gathering in Far West, to construct a temple there, and to establish new settlements in the area.[29] Migration to Far West and its vicinity was accelerating because Kirtland was no longer an authorized gathering place; hundreds from Kirtland were expected to arrive in Far West within the next few months.[30] Many more were expected to migrate from the various branches of the church in the United States and British North America. The gathering of the Saints would require settlement beyond the bounds of Far West, and church leaders had been searching for several months to locate other places to settle.[31]

Entries in JS's journal for late April and early May document a brief interlude of relative tranquility in Far West, with JS and Rigdon collaborating on a new church history, studying grammar, and attending meetings. In late May, after Hyrum Smith arrived in Far West,[32] the First Presidency left for Daviess County to select and survey lands for settlement. The

---

24. Letter to John Whitmer, 9 Apr. 1838, pp. 78–79 herein.

25. Minutes, 12 Apr. 1838, pp. 84–94 herein; Minutes, 13 Apr. 1838, pp. 95–104 herein.

26. Minutes, 21 Apr. 1838, pp. 110–111 herein.

27. See Prospectus for *Elders' Journal,* 30 Apr. 1838, pp. 128–133 herein.

28. Revelation, 11 Apr. 1838, pp. 81–82 herein [D&C 114]; Revelation, 17 Apr. 1838, pp. 107–108 herein.

29. Revelation, 26 Apr. 1838, pp. 114–115 herein [D&C 115:6–7].

30. Backman, *Heavens Resound,* 354–355.

31. See Minutes, 10 Nov. 1837, in *JSP,* D5:475; and Minute Book 2, 6–7 Dec. 1837.

32. Hyrum Smith, Commerce, IL, to "the Saints Scattered Abroad," Dec. 1839, in *Times and Seasons,* Dec. 1839, 1:21; JS, Journal, 28 May 1838, in *JSP,* J1:274; O'Driscoll, *Hyrum Smith,* 167–170.

previous year, non-Mormon residents of Daviess County had warned the small number of Latter-day Saints who had settled there to leave or be driven out.[33] However, the Saints in Daviess County had remained, and the First Presidency now planned to expand church settlement there. During this time, JS identified Spring Hill, where church member Lyman Wight had settled, as Adam-ondi-Ahman. Latter-day Saint John Corrill stated that when JS applied the name Adam-ondi-Ahman to Spring Hill, he explained that Adam-ondi-Ahman was "the valley of God, in which Adam blessed his children."[34] According to JS's journal, the location was "the place where Adam shall come to visit his people, or the Ancient of days shall sit as spoken of by Daniel the Prophet."[35] Therefore, the central Mormon settlement in Daviess County took on both primordial and millenarian significance. JS's labors in Daviess County were punctuated by brief visits home. During one of these visits, his wife Emma gave birth to their son Alexander. JS soon returned to Daviess County, and according to his journal, he and others working with him "continued surveying and building houses &c for some time day after day."[36] The selection and surveying of Daviess County land culminated in the completion of a city plat and provided the basis for an orderly and relatively compact settlement coordinated by church officials.[37] While JS was busy with these activities, his involvement in producing documents was greatly diminished.

At this time in Far West, tensions continued to increase between the church and prominent excommunicants who remained in Caldwell County. For example, Oliver Cowdery continued his emerging law practice by encouraging lawsuits among and against the Latter-day Saints for debts they owed.[38] JS and Rigdon came to believe that peace and harmony—which they viewed as essential to establishing Zion in Missouri—were impossible to achieve among the Latter-day Saints as long as dissenters remained in the area. On 17 June, Rigdon railed against the excommunicants in a public sermon. According to Reed Peck, who recounted the sermon after leaving the church several months later, Rigdon accused the dissenters of various crimes and of seeking to undermine the First Presidency. He also called upon the Latter-day Saints to rid the community of their antagonists. Peck also stated that JS spoke afterward and approved of Rigdon's remarks.[39] Around the same time, a letter was signed by eighty-three Latter-day Saint men, warning former Latter-day Saints Oliver Cowdery, David Whitmer, John Whitmer, William W. Phelps, and Lyman E. Johnson that they had three days to leave Caldwell County peacefully.[40] The authorship of

---

33. JS, Journal, 7–9 Aug. 1838, in *JSP*, J1:300; Baugh, "Call to Arms," 106.

34. Corrill, *Brief History*, 28, in *JSP*, H2:163; see also Letter to Stephen Post, 17 Sept. 1838, p. 242 herein.

35. JS, Journal, 18 May–1 June 1838, in *JSP*, J1:271.

36. JS, Journal, 4–5 June 1838, in *JSP*, J1:275.

37. JS, Journal, 4–5 June 1838, in *JSP*, J1:275; see also "Record Book A," in Sherwood, Record Book, CHL; and Walker, "Mormon Land Rights," 30–31.

38. See Minutes, 12 Apr. 1838, p. 85 herein; see also Oliver Cowdery, Far West, MO, to Warren Cowdery and Lyman Cowdery, Kirtland, OH, [10] Mar. 1838, in Cowdery, Letterbook, 92.

39. Reed Peck, Quincy, IL, to "Dear Friends," 18 Sept. 1839, pp. 23–26, Henry E. Huntington Library, San Marino, CA. The journal of JS's uncle John Smith confirms that JS, as well as his brother and counselor Hyrum Smith, attended the church services in Far West on 17 June. (John Smith, Journal, 17 June 1838.)

40. See Oliver Cowdery et al., Far West, MO, ca. 17 June 1838, at josephsmithpapers.org.

the letter is neither stated nor implied, but one of the signatories, Ebenezer Robinson, re-called decades later that according to common belief, the letter "was gotten up in the office of the First Presidency."[41] While Phelps, one of the dissenters named in the letter, reconciled with church leaders and was permitted to remain, the other dissenters fled the county on 19 June.[42] George W. Robinson approvingly noted the flight of the dissenters in the journal he was keeping for JS.[43]

By the end of June, the population in Adam-ondi-Ahman was sufficient for JS to orga-nize a stake, including a presidency, a high council, and a pro tempore bishop. Some of these positions were filled by those who had served in the presidency and bishopric of the Kirtland stake.[44] Around this time, the church also sent a group of Saints to settle in the small town of De Witt in Carroll County, downriver from Adam-ondi-Ahman where the Grand River emptied into the Missouri River. Church leaders purchased land at this strategic site to bene-fit from Grand River commerce.[45] The rapidly growing number of church members in the area further angered Missourians who objected to Latter-day Saint settlement outside of Caldwell County.[46] These tensions eventually led to the trouble that unfolds in the docu-ments included in part 2 of this volume.

———— ✑ ————

Letter from Thomas B. Marsh, 15 February 1838

Source Note

Thomas B. Marsh, Letter, Far West, Caldwell Co., MO, to JS, [Kirtland Township, Geauga Co., OH], 15 Feb. 1838, with Minutes, 5–9 and 10 Feb. 1838. Featured version published in "Minutes of the Proceedings of the Committee of the Whole Church in Zion," Elders' Journal, July 1838, 44–46. For more information on Elders' Journal, see Source Notes for Multiple-Entry Documents, p. 563 herein.

Historical Introduction

In early February 1838, David Whitmer, John Whitmer, and William W. Phelps—who composed the presidency of the church in Zion—were removed from office and replaced by apostles Thomas B. Marsh and David W. Patten as presidents pro tempore. Marsh wrote to JS on 15 February 1838 to inform him of the change and to convey formal statements

---

41. Ebenezer Robinson, "'Saints' Herald,' Again," *Return,* Feb. 1890, 218–219.

42. William W. Phelps, Testimony, Richmond, MO, Nov. 1838, p. [85]; Reed Peck, Testimony, Richmond, MO, Nov. 1838, p. [55], State of Missouri v. JS et al. for Treason and Other Crimes (Mo. 5th Jud. Cir. 1838), in State of Missouri, "Evidence"; Whitmer, Daybook, 19 June 1838; R. Peck to "Dear Friends," 18 Sept. 1839, pp. 25–27; see also Corrill, *Brief History,* 30, in *JSP,* H2:165.

43. JS, Journal, 4 July 1838, in *JSP,* J1:278.

44. Minutes, 28 June 1838, pp. 165–167 herein.

45. Murdock, Journal, 23 June 1838, 95; John Murdock, Affidavit, Adams Co., IL, 10 Jan. 1840, photo-copy, Material relating to Mormon Expulsion from Missouri, 1839–1843, CHL; Sidney Rigdon, Testimony, Nauvoo, IL, 1 July 1843, pp. [2]–[3], Nauvoo, IL, Records, CHL; [Rigdon], *Appeal to the American People,* 36–37; see also Perkins, "Prelude to Expulsion," 264–268.

46. LeSueur, "Missouri's Failed Compromise," 140–144.

exculpating JS from an implied accusation of adultery made by Oliver Cowdery. The letter also included copies of minutes from the meetings in which the former presidency was removed and replaced.

Problems with the presidency had been developing for over a year. While David Whitmer was in Kirtland, Ohio, in summer 1836, counselors William W. Phelps and John Whitmer presided over the Saints in Missouri.[47] In late June, non-Mormon residents in Clay County, Missouri, demanded that the Saints leave the county.[48] Consequently, in July the Missouri Saints met in a "general assembly" and appointed Phelps, John Whitmer, and the Zion bishopric to find a new area to settle. The Saints also appointed Marsh and Elisha Groves to collect donations and obtain loans from the Saints in Missouri and elsewhere to give to Phelps and Whitmer for resettlement efforts.[49] While Marsh and Groves collected donations, Phelps and Whitmer purchased the land for what would become Far West, Missouri. After Marsh and Groves returned from Kentucky and Tennessee, where they borrowed $1,450 from church members,[50] Phelps and Whitmer used the money to buy more land in the vicinity of Far West. However, they did not consult with the bishopric and the high council before selecting and purchasing the land, and they appointed a committee to help build a temple in Far West.[51]

The Missouri Saints followed Phelps and Whitmer to Far West, but the high council and bishopric questioned the control Phelps and Whitmer were asserting. On 3 April 1837, the high council met without Phelps and Whitmer and drew up a list of questions for the two men. The council challenged the authority of the two men to unilaterally select and purchase the land for the new settlement, to sell lots in the city plat for their own profit, to designate the temple site, to appoint a committee to help build the temple, and to take other actions. The council resolved to meet again in two days and invited Phelps and Whitmer to answer the questions. The council also invited the bishopric and resident apostles Thomas B. Marsh and David W. Patten to the meeting.[52]

At the beginning of the council meeting held 5 April 1837, Phelps and Whitmer requested that the bishopric and apostles leave, to which everyone else objected. Phelps insisted that they leave or he would dissolve the high council. Marsh declared that if Phelps took such action, Marsh would prefer formal charges against Phelps in a church court held by the bishop. Phelps relented, and the members of the high council proceeded with their questions. Phelps and Whitmer were unable to answer the questions to the council's satisfaction, which "led the Council & others to strongly rebuke the late improper proceedings of the Presidents." Patten, who was particularly incensed, stated that their actions "had been iniguitous [iniquitous] & fraudulent in the extreme, in the unrighteously appropriating

47. Minute Book 2, 25 July 1836.

48. "Public Meeting," *LDS Messenger and Advocate*, Aug. 1836, 2:353–355; Stokes, "Wilson Letters," 504–509.

49. Minute Book 2, 25 July 1836.

50. Letter to Wilford Woodruff, ca. 18 June 1838, p. 157 herein; see also "T. B. Marsh," [2], Historian's Office, Histories of the Twelve, 1856–1858, 1861, CHL.

51. Minute Book 2, 15 Nov. 1836; 3 and 7 Apr. 1837.

52. Minute Book 2, 3 Apr. 1837.

church funds to their own emolument."[53] Similarly, Marsh wrote in a letter to Wilford Woodruff that the two presidents had purchased the land in Far West "with Church funds, in their own name, for their own agrandisement."[54]

After further discussion over the next few weeks, church officers approved the Far West plat as planned by Phelps and Whitmer and approved of their authority to supervise the construction of a temple and appoint the temple building committee. In response, Phelps and Whitmer agreed to turn over ownership of the Far West plat and surrounding property to Bishop Edward Partridge and to relinquish control of the pricing and sale of this property to a combined council of the presidency, the bishopric, and other officers. Furthermore, the proceeds would be dedicated to the general building up of Zion in Missouri.[55] In spite of these resolutions, the underlying issues persisted.

In the following months, the failure of the Kirtland Safety Society and the general state of depression that followed the nationwide financial panic contributed to significant upheaval in Kirtland. At this time some of JS's closest associates, including former secretary Warren Parrish and several apostles, became disaffected. Discontent and dismay with JS's financial or religious leadership eventually spread to nearly one-third of the church's general leadership and over one-tenth of the membership in Ohio. Declaring JS a fallen prophet, Parrish and others attempted to establish a church of their own, which they called the Church of Christ—the original name of the church JS had founded. They also attempted to take control of the House of the Lord.[56] Further, some dissidents sought to replace JS with David Whitmer as church president.[57] Even Oliver Cowdery, who had been close to JS since the time they had worked together on translating the Book of Mormon, began criticizing JS about financial issues and leadership concerns.

Dissent against JS's leadership was apparently also fueled by the beginnings of plural marriage. JS's introduction of the practice of polygamy—following the model of Old Testament patriarchs—was well attested in Nauvoo in the 1840s. A few individuals who knew JS well recounted later that he had received a revelation about the doctrine of plural marriage as early as 1831, possibly in connection with his work on the revision, or new "translation," of the Bible.[58] Several Latter-day Saints who lived in Kirtland in the 1830s later reported that JS married Fanny Alger, a young Latter-day Saint who worked in the Smith household. These reports, some of which were from members of Alger's family, include statements that a wedding "ceremony" or "sealing" had taken place or that Alger and her parents agreed to the marriage beforehand.[59] Little is known of JS's

---

53. Minute Book 2, 5–7 Apr. 1837.

54. Letter to Wilford Woodruff, ca. 18 June 1838, p. 157 herein.

55. Minute Book 2, 5–7 Apr. 1837, pp. 68–69, 73; Edward Partridge, Bonds, Far West, MO, to William W. Phelps and John Whitmer, 17 May 1837, John Whitmer Family Papers, CHL.

56. Introduction to Part 7: 17 Sept. 1837–21 Jan. 1838, in *JSP*, D5:441–442; Backman, *Heavens Resound*, 323–329; Esplin, "Emergence of Brigham Young," chap. 6.

57. Historian's Office, Brigham Young History Drafts, 14.

58. Bachman, "Ohio Origins of the Revelation on Eternal Marriage," 24–26; Hales, *Joseph Smith's Polygamy*, 1:85–91.

59. See, for example, Andrew Jenson, Research Notes, Andrew Jenson Collection, CHL; Benjamin F. Johnson, [Mesa, Arizona Territory], to George F. Gibbs, Salt Lake City, UT, ca. Apr.–ca. Oct. 1903,

marriage to Alger, which was largely kept confidential and which ended in separation before JS's move to Missouri. Other Kirtland Mormons, including Cowdery, viewed the relationship as immoral. Patten recounted that in summer 1837, Cowdery insinuated that JS was guilty of "committing adultery with a certain girl," an allegation that Cowdery repeated in a letter to one of his brothers in January 1838.[60] On 12 April 1838, Cowdery faced a church trial over a variety of issues. At the trial, JS stated that as Cowdery had been his bosom friend, therefore he entrusted him with many things, and JS then "gave a history respecting the girl buisness."[61] After his separation from Alger and the controversy arising from Cowdery's accusations, JS set aside the practice of plural marriage for several years.

In autumn 1837, JS began to reassert his authority as church president. On 3 September, he convened a conference in Kirtland, during which he was sustained as president and several dissenting church leaders were rejected.[62] This conference was considered a "reorganization of the Church in Kirtland."[63] The following day, JS wrote a letter to the Saints in Missouri, informing them of the "difficulties in Kirtland which are now about being settled." He included a copy of the conference minutes and referred the Missouri Saints to his brother Hyrum Smith and Marsh, who were traveling to Missouri, for further information about the reorganization in Kirtland so they would know "how to proceed to set in order & regulate the affairs of the Church in zion." The letter also warned them of Cowdery, David Whitmer, and others who were or would soon be in Missouri and whose support JS questioned. JS indicated that Cowdery had been in transgression and that if he did not humble himself and magnify his calling, the Saints would "soon be under the necessaty of raising their hands against him." The letter also stated that Whitmer had transgressed and that he had been warned that if he did not "make sattisfaction to the Church," he would lose his standing.[64]

On the same day JS wrote this letter, 4 September, he dictated a revelation declaring that John Whitmer and William W. Phelps must repent of their offenses or they would be removed from office.[65] JS sent the letter, and presumably the revelation, to Missouri with Marsh, who had likely informed JS of the Missouri leadership issues. Together, these documents raised questions about Cowdery and the entire Zion presidency, all of whom were in Missouri by the time JS and other leaders arrived there to hold a reorganization conference similar to the one they had held in Ohio.

Benjamin Franklin Johnson, Papers, CHL; Hancock, "Autobiography of Levi Ward Hancock," 50, 61–65; Young, *Wife No. 19*, 66–67; and Eliza Jane Churchill Webb, Lockport, NY, to Mary Bond, 24 Apr. 1876; Eliza Jane Churchill Webb, Lockport, NY, to Mary Bond, 4 May 1876, Myron F. Bond Folder, Biographical Folder Collection, CCLA; see also Bradley, "Relationship of Joseph Smith and Fanny Alger," 14–58.

　60. Minutes, 12 Apr. 1838, p. 91 herein; Oliver Cowdery, Far West, MO, to Warren Cowdery, 21 Jan. 1838, in Cowdery, Letterbook, 80–83. The timing of the conversation between Cowdery and Patten was clarified in a subsequent remark by Marsh. (Minutes, 12 Apr. 1838, p. 91 herein.)

　61. Minutes, 12 Apr. 1838, p. 91 herein.

　62. Minutes, 3 Sept. 1837, in *JSP*, D5:422.

　63. Minutes, 7 Nov. 1837, in *JSP*, D5:469.

　64. Letter to John Corrill and the Church in Missouri, 4 Sept. 1837, in *JSP*, D5:428, 430.

　65. Revelation, 4 Sept. 1837, in *JSP*, D5:433.

Prominent dissenters. Conflicts over financial management and church authority led to a schism between the Zion high council and the Zion presidency, which consisted of President David Whitmer (top left, photographed circa 1855) and counselors William W. Phelps (top right, circa 1865) and John Whitmer (bottom left, circa 1870). In early February 1838, members of the church in Missouri voted to remove the members of the presidency from office. The high council and the bishopric then met and voted to release William W. Phelps and John Whitmer, as well as Oliver Cowdery (bottom right, circa 1845), as priesthood licensing officers. Thomas B. Marsh and David W. Patten were appointed to serve as a pro tempore presidency. Marsh wrote to Joseph Smith to inform him of these developments. (David Whitmer image courtesy Community of Christ Library-Archives, Independence, MO. Other images: Church History Library, Salt Lake City. Phelps photograph by Charles R. Savage.)

JS arrived in Far West in late October or early November 1837. On 6 November, JS, Sidney Rigdon, Hyrum Smith, and other leaders from Kirtland met with Phelps, John Whitmer, Marsh, and other church leaders living in Missouri to further resolve problems. After those at the council meeting discussed the recent land purchases, the Far West plat, and related issues, "all difficulties were satisfactorily settled except a matter between J. Smith jr. Oliver Cowdery and T. B. Marsh, which was refered to themselves with the agreement that their settlement of the affair should be sufficient for the Council."[66] This unresolved matter was apparently Cowdery's contention that JS was guilty of adultery. The three met to discuss the issue later that evening or sometime before JS returned to Kirtland.

At the 7 November reorganization conference, which was also called a "general assembly," Marsh served as the moderator. JS was sustained as president of the entire church, and Sidney Rigdon was sustained as a counselor in the First Presidency. Marsh and others objected to the other counselor, Frederick G. Williams, who was consequently rejected by the general assembly and replaced by Hyrum Smith. When the names of David and John Whitmer were presented for reappointment to the Zion presidency, Marsh and others objected. However, apostle William E. McLellin "made satisfaction" on behalf of David Whitmer, and John Whitmer offered words of confession, after which the two men were retained in office. When Phelps's name was presented, he also offered a confession and was reappointed to the Zion presidency. In another meeting, held 10 November, the problems with John Whitmer and Phelps were further resolved and the authority of the bishopric to oversee land issues was reaffirmed.

Having addressed the problems in Missouri, JS and his party from Kirtland departed for home.[67] Although the church had been reorganized in Kirtland, JS returned only to face continued efforts by dissidents to undermine his leadership. Marsh's 15 February 1838 letter suggests that rumors of JS committing adultery were circulating in Kirtland or that Marsh understood that to be the case based on a letter he had recently received from JS.

Such rumors and the spirit of dissent were also spreading in Missouri. As tensions involving Cowdery and the Zion presidency resurfaced, it became evident that the dissension required further attention. In a letter JS wrote to Partridge in Missouri on 7 January 1838, JS included a revelation warning the Saints to "be aware of dissensions among them lest the enemy have power over them" and commanding church leaders to warn the members, "for behold the wolf cometh to destroy them!"[68] JS apparently sent a similar letter to Marsh around the same time. Marsh presumably received the letter by 20 January, when he held a meeting at his house to initiate an effort to remove the Zion presidency. Marsh was a member of the Quorum of the Twelve Apostles, which held jurisdiction over only the branches and missionary work outside of Zion and its stakes. However, on 5 February 1838, when

---

66. Minutes, 6 Nov. 1837, in *JSP,* D5:467–468.

67. Minutes, 7 Nov. 1837, in *JSP,* D5:469–472; Minutes, 10 Nov. 1837, in *JSP,* D5:475–476; JS History, vol. B-1, 775–778; Esplin, "Emergence of Brigham Young," chaps. 6–7.

68. Letter and Revelation to Edward Partridge, 7 Jan. 1838, in *JSP,* D5:494.

Marsh held a meeting to remove the Zion presidency, he stated that he was following special instructions from JS, which were apparently included in a letter from JS. John Murdock, who was also at the meeting, stated that he likewise knew about the instructions from JS to Marsh.[69]

In the "social meeting" Marsh hosted on 20 January, he met with fellow apostle Patten and several members of the Zion high council. After considering grievances against the Whitmer brothers, Phelps, and Cowdery, those at the meeting appointed a committee to present their concerns to "the Presidents" and Cowdery, who was serving as the Zion presidency's clerk, and then report back to the larger group. The chief concern, apparently, was that Phelps, John Whitmer, and Cowdery had recently sold land in Jackson County. The committee also challenged the men regarding their adherence to the "Word of Wisdom," the church's dietary code. In general, the men insisted on their individual rights to sell or otherwise control their land and to interpret and observe the dietary revelation as they saw fit. In short, they "would not be controlled by any ecclesiastical power or revelation whatever in their temporal concerns." When the committee reported this response in a council meeting on 26 January, the council members resolved to reject the presidency and to hold "general assembly" meetings to lay the case before church officers in Far West and in some surrounding settlements. The council members planned the general assembly meetings and resolved that Marsh would inform the Zion presidency and Cowdery of the decisions made at the council meeting.[70]

On 30 January, the Zion presidency met with Cowdery and other dissenters, during which the group declared their opposition to JS for "endeavoring to unite ecclesiastical with civil authority and force men under the pretence of incurring the displeasure of heaven to use their earthly substance contrary to their own interest and privilege." Cowdery copied the meeting minutes into a 4 February 1838 letter to his brothers regarding recent events in Far West. He also explained that the high council had decided not to try him and that the Zion presidency had decided not to attend a meeting to be held in Far West the following day.[71] Also on 4 February, Marsh followed through on a request from JS to send Marsh's and George W. Harris's accounts of a meeting with Cowdery in which he discussed Alger.

The general assembly meetings began in Far West on 5 February 1838. Marsh served as the moderator, as he had in the general assembly held on 7 November 1837. He began by rehearsing the recent reorganization meetings in Kirtland and Far West and also some of the problems with the Zion presidency. The members of the committee appointed to visit the presidency also spoke. Bishop Partridge, one of his counselors, and his financial agent argued that the proceedings of the general assembly were hasty and improper, while

---

69. As Marsh noted in his 15 February letter to JS, Marsh had sent a letter to JS on 4 February in response to JS's request for statements from Marsh and George W. Harris regarding what Oliver Cowdery said about Fanny Alger. This 4 February missive to JS may have been a response to the same letter in which JS instructed Marsh to take action against Cowdery and the Missouri presidency.

70. Minute Book 2, 20 and 26 Jan. 1838.

71. Oliver Cowdery, Far West, MO, to Warren Cowdery and Lyman Cowdery, [Kirtland, OH], 4 Feb. 1838, in Cowdery, Letterbook, 83–86.

Partridge's other counselor pleaded for mercy for Phelps and Whitmer. Two members of the high council were sympathetic, but most were against the presidency. Similarly, Marsh, Patten, and high council member Lyman Wight vigorously opposed the presidency. After hearing from the various leaders, the men holding priesthood offices in Far West voted to remove the presidency from office.

Over the next four days, sessions of the general assembly were held in four of the smaller outlying settlements, all with the same result. On 10 February a council meeting was held, probably in Far West, in which Cowdery, Phelps, and John Whitmer were removed from their appointments to license church officers and were replaced by Marsh and Patten. At the same time, Marsh and Patten were appointed presidents pro tempore for the church in Missouri. Five days later, on 15 February, George M. Hinkle wrote a statement regarding a conversation with Cowdery about Alger; Hinkle apparently gave his statement to Marsh that day.

After receiving Hinkle's statement, Marsh wrote to JS. Marsh began with copies of the minutes of the general assembly held 5–9 February and of the council meeting held 10 February.[72] Marsh then explained that the high council had acted in order to avoid a widespread rebellion among the general church membership, which strongly opposed the ongoing actions of the presidency. Marsh was probably writing to report on the fulfillment of JS's earlier instructions. He also wrote to follow through on JS's request for statements regarding Cowdery and his insinuations that JS was guilty of adultery. Marsh included new versions of his and Harris's statements and also included the statement from Hinkle.

Marsh may have written the letter at his home in Far West.[73] He expressed some concern in his letter that the letter he had sent in the mail on 4 February might be intercepted by enemies before it reached JS, so Marsh may have sent his 15 February letter in the hands of a Latter-day Saint he trusted. As Marsh's letter indicates, he was not yet aware that JS had already departed Kirtland and was en route to Far West.[74] Because JS had left already, he would not be able to use the statements collected by Marsh to stop the rumors of adultery in Kirtland, but the statements may have been of some use to him after arriving in Far West. If the letter was sent by a Mormon courier rather than through the mail, JS may have received the letter en route and become apprised of the recent developments in Far West prior to his arrival. In any case, he most likely received the original letter or read a retained copy of it before it was published in the July issue of the *Elders' Journal,* which he was the editor of.

---

72. The letter from Marsh refers to the minutes as if they were part of the letter. In the *Elders' Journal,* the minutes and the letter were printed together as one text.

73. In June 1837, the high council determined to give Marsh "a lot in the Town of Far West." Marsh later recounted that he "immediately procured a lot built a house & moved into it." The minutes for the 20 January meeting designate Far West as the location of the meeting and further specify that the meeting was "held at the house of Thos B. Marsh," affirming that Marsh had moved to Far West by this time. (Minute Book 2, 11 June 1837 and 20 Jan. 1838; "T. B. Marsh," [2], Historian's Office, Histories of the Twelve, 1856–1858, 1861, CHL.)

74. Information regarding JS's departure arrived in a letter to Phelps by 24 February, when it was read in a council meeting. (Minute Book 2, 24 Feb. 1838.)

Document Transcript

MINUTES OF THE PROCEEDINGS OF THE COMMITTEE OF THE WHOLE CHURCH IN ZION.[75]

The following are the minutes of the proceedings of a general assembly of the Church of Jesus Christ, of Latter Day Saints,[76] assembled at the following places, to transact the business of said Church.[77]

1st. At Far West,[78] Feb. 5, 1838; Thomas B. Marsh was chosen Moderator,[79] and John Cleminson Clerk.

The Moderator addressed the throne of grace in prayer,[80] after which he laid before the assembly the object of the meeting, giving a relation of the recent

---

75. The minutes of the 3 September 1837 conference held in Kirtland began with similar language, explaining that they were "minutes of a conference assembled in the house of the Lord, in committee of the whole." Furthermore, when JS sent a copy of the minutes to Missouri, his cover letter referred to the conference as "the comittee, of the whole Church of Kirtland the authorities &.c." The 3 September 1837 and 5 February 1838 meetings may have followed the conventional parliamentary procedure for resolving to form a committee of the whole, in which business ordinarily delegated to a committee was opened to the general body, the regular chairman turned his duties over to a committee chair, and all members could speak as often as they liked. Or the phrase "committee of the whole" may have been used merely to signify the attendance of priesthood holders from all the councils and quorums, as well as other church members. (Minutes, 3 Sept. 1837, in *JSP*, D5:422; Letter to John Corrill and the Church in Missouri, 4 Sept. 1837, in *JSP*, D5:428; Jefferson, *Manual of Parliamentary Practice*, sec. 12.)

76. When JS organized the church on 6 April 1830, it was named the Church of Christ. In 1834, church leaders changed the name of the church to the Church of the Latter Day Saints. After that time, various combinations of the two names were occasionally used. On 26 April 1838, JS dictated a revelation announcing that the church would be called the Church of Jesus Christ of Latter Day Saints. The name of the church used at the beginning of Marsh's letter as published in the July issue of the *Elders' Journal* and as recorded in Minute Book 2 may be a combination of the first two names of the church or may be an emendation made after the new name of the church was revealed. (Revelation, 6 Apr. 1830, in *JSP*, D1:129, 130 [D&C 21:3, 11]; Articles and Covenants, ca. Apr. 1830, in *JSP*, D1:120 [D&C 20:1]; Minutes, 3 May 1834, in *JSP*, D4:44; Revelation, 26 Apr. 1838, p. 114 herein [D&C 115:4]; Minute Book 2, 5–9 Feb. 1838; see also Anderson, "What Changes Have Been Made in the Name of the Church?," 13–14.)

77. Section 3 in part 2 of the 1835 Doctrine and Covenants instructed that an unrighteous decision made by any governing quorum in the church, including a "quorum of three presidents," could be "brought before a general assembly of the several quorums, which constitute the spiritual authorities of the church." (Instruction on Priesthood, between ca. 1 Mar. and ca. 4 May 1835, in *JSP*, D4:314, 315 [D&C 107:29, 32].)

78. This general assembly of church officers may have met in a schoolhouse. Other meetings were held in one or more schoolhouses in Far West in 1837 and 1838. (Minute Book 2, 29 July and 5 Aug. 1837; 24 Feb. and 17 Mar. 1838; JS, Journal, 6 Aug. 1838, in *JSP*, J1:297–298.)

79. Seven members of the high council, including Elias Higbee, were originally designated to conduct the sessions of the general assembly. At a 26 January 1838 meeting, Marsh, who was not a member of the high council, was chosen to replace Higbee in the upcoming series of meetings. During the 5 February session, Marsh stated that he had recently received directions from JS. It is possible that those instructions were relevant to the discipline of the presidency or the regulation of the church, which might explain why Marsh was chosen as Higbee's replacement. (Minute Book 2, 26 Jan. 1838.)

80. See Hebrews 4:16.

organization of the Church here, and in Kirtland.[81] He also read a certain revelation given in Kirtland, Sept. 4, 1837; which made known that John Whitmer and William W. Phelps were in transgression, and that if they repented not, they should be removed out of their places.—[82] Also, read a certain clause contained in the appeal, published in the old Star, under the 183rd page, as follows:— "And to sell our lands would amount to a denial of our faith, as that is the place where Zion of God shall stand according to our faith and belief in the revelations of God."[83]

Elder John Murdock then took the stand, and showed to the congregation why the High Council proceeded thus,[84] was, that the Church might have a voice in the matter; and that he considered it perfectly legal, according to the instructions of President Joseph Smith jr.[85]

Elder G[eorge] M. Hinkle then set forth the way in which the Presidency of Far West had been labored with, that a committee of three, of whom he was one, had labored with them.—[86] He then read a written document containing

---

81. At the reorganization conference held in Kirtland on 3 September 1837, several members of the Kirtland high council and of the Quorum of the Twelve Apostles were removed from their positions. When a reorganization conference was held in Far West on 7 November, Hyrum Smith was appointed to replace Frederick G. Williams in the First Presidency of the church. (Minutes, 3 Sept. 1837, in *JSP*, D5:423; Minutes, 7 Nov. 1837, in *JSP*, D5:469.)

82. Revelation, 4 Sept. 1837, in *JSP*, D5:433.

83. The appeal regarded the lands the Saints owned in Jackson County, from which they had been driven. In 1833, after the Saints were driven out of the county, a revelation indicated that rather than selling their land in Jackson County, the Saints should continue to purchase land there. An 1834 revelation directed the Saints to purchase additional land in Jackson County and to "make proposals for peace unto those who have smitten you." In response to this revelation, church leaders in Missouri apparently wrote an appeal to "the people" of the nation, requesting that the Saints be allowed to possess their lands in peace. ("An Appeal," *The Evening and the Morning Star,* Aug. 1834, 183; Revelation, 16–17 Dec. 1833, in *JSP*, D3:390–391, 394–395 [D&C 101:17–20, 67–75]; Revelation, 22 June 1834, in *JSP*, D4:76, 77 [D&C 105:26–29, 40].)

84. Murdock probably spoke first and on behalf of the high council as a leader in that group. (See 23n104 herein.)

85. Canonized instruction indicated that charges against a president of the high priesthood would be heard by a bishop who was counseled by twelve high priests. However, JS dictated a revelation on 12 January 1838 that instituted a new procedure, whereby "the presidency of said Church may be tried by the voice of the whole body of the Church of Zion, and the voice of a majority of all her stakes." It is possible that this revelation, perhaps with related instructions from JS to Marsh or Murdock, had reached the high council by this time, as had the 7 January letter for Edward Partridge, although Marsh apparently did not yet know that JS had left Kirtland for Far West on the night of 12 January. (Revelation, 11 Nov. 1831–B, in *JSP*, D2:135 [D&C 107:82–84]; Revelation, 12 Jan. 1838–A, in *JSP*, D5:497.)

86. Hinkle, Thomas Grover, and George Morey were appointed to visit the Missouri presidency by Marsh, Patten, and several members of the Missouri high council who met for a "social meeting" in Marsh's home in Far West on 20 January 1838. (Minute Book 2, 20 Jan. 1838.)

a number of accusations against the three presidents.[87] He spake many things against them, setting forth in a plain and energetic manner, the iniquity of Phelps and Whitmer, in using the monies which were loaned for the Church. Also D[avid] Whitmer's wrong, in persisting in the use of tea, coffee, and tobacco.[88]

Bishop [Edward] Partridge then arose, and endeavored to rectify some mistakes of minor importance made by Elder Hinkle. Also, the Bishop spake against the proceedings of the meeting, as being hasty and illegal, for he thought they ought to be had before the common council;[89] and said, that he could not lift his hand against the presidency at present; he then read a letter from President Joseph Smith jr.[90]

A letter was then read by T. B. Marsh from William Smith,[91] who made some comments on the same,[92] and also on the letter read by E. Partridge.

---

87. This document was apparently presented or summarized in a meeting held 26 January 1838. The minutes of that meeting include a transcript or summary of the committee's report. (Minute Book 2, 26 Jan. 1838.)

88. In 1833, JS dictated a revelation proscribing the use of tobacco, wine, "strong drinks," and "hot drinks." "Strong drinks" were understood to be distilled liquors, and "hot drinks" were identified as tea and coffee. In the conference held in Far West on 7 November 1837, the members of the congregation voted that they would not support "Stores and Shops selling spirituous liquors, Tea, Coffee or Tobacco." The committee appointed by the high council to labor with the Missouri presidency reported in the council meeting held 26 January 1838 that "David and John Whitmer said they did use tea and coffee but they did not consider them to come under the head of hot drinks." (Revelation, 27 Feb. 1833, in *JSP*, D3:20–21 [D&C 89:1–3, 5–9]; Minutes, 7 Nov. 1837, in *JSP*, D5:472; Minute Book 2, 26 Jan. 1838.)

89. As the bishop, Partridge oversaw a "common council." In 1835 JS provided instruction on the priesthood, stating that "inasmuch as a president of the high priesthood shall transgress, he shall be had in remembrance before the common council of the church." In May 1837, Sidney Rigdon presided over a high council meeting to try Frederick G. Williams and David Whitmer, both of whom appealed to the 1835 regulation and held that they should be tried in a bishop's court. After much debate on this issue, the council "dispersed in confusion." (Instruction on Priesthood, between ca. 1 Mar. and ca. 4 May 1835, in *JSP*, D4:318–320 [D&C 107:68–84]; Minute Book 1, 29 May 1837.)

90. The 7 January 1838 letter from JS to Partridge included words of a revelation: "And again thus saith the Lord, let my people be aware of dissensions among them lest the enemy have power over them, Awake my shepherds and warn my people! for behold the wolf cometh to destroy them! receive him not." (Letter and Revelation to Edward Partridge, 7 Jan. 1838, in *JSP*, D5:494.)

91. William Smith was a member of the Quorum of the Twelve Apostles, with Marsh serving as president of the quorum. The previous year, apostles Marsh, Patten, and Smith traveled together from Far West to Kirtland, where they participated in the September 1837 reorganization of the church there, and then all returned to Missouri to attend the November 1837 reorganization of the church in Far West. (Letter to Wilford Woodruff, ca. 18 June 1838, p. 155 herein; Minutes, 7 Nov. 1837, in *JSP*, D5:469–472.)

92. Marsh commented on the letter from William Smith, who was still living in Kirtland and would not move to Far West until later in the year. (Letter from Don Carlos Smith, ca. Late May 1838, p. 151 herein; see also Lucy Mack Smith, History, 1844–1845, bk. 15, [3]–[6].)

Elder G. Moery [George Morey], who was one of the committee sent to labor with the Presidency, then spake, setting forth in a very energetic manner, the proceedings of the presidency, as being iniquitous.

Elder [Thomas] Grover also, being one of the committee, spake against the conduct of the presidency and O[liver] Cowdery,[93] on their visit to labor with them.

Elder David W. Patten, then spake with much zeal against this presidency, and in favor of brother Joseph Smith jr.[94] and that the wolf alluded to in his letter, were the dissenters in Kirtland.[95]

Elder Lyman Wight next stated that he considered that all other accusations were of minor importance compared to their selling their lands in Jackson County, that they (Phelps and Whitmer) had set an example which all the members were liable to follow; he said that it was a hellish principle, and that they had flatly denied the faith in so doing. Elder Elias Higbee then sanctioned what had been done by the council, speaking against the presidency.

Elder Murdock again took the stand, and stated that sufficient had been said to substantiate the accusations against them.

Elder Solomon Hancock plead in favor of the presidency, stating that he could not raise his hand against them.

Elder John Corrill then spake against the High Council in regard to their proceedings, and labored hard to show that the meeting was illegal, and that the presidency ought to be had before a proper tribunal, which he considered to be a bishop and twelve high priests;[96] he labored in favor of the presidency, and said that he should not raise his hands against them at present, although he did not uphold the presidents in their iniquity.

Elder Simeon Carter, next arose and spake against the meeting as being hasty. Elder [Elisha] Groves followed brother Carter, in like observations and of like nature. Elder [David W.] Patten again took the stand in vindidcation of the cause of the meeting.

---

93. Two months earlier, Cowdery was appointed clerk of the Missouri high council. (Minute Book 2, 6–7 Dec. 1837.)

94. Patten was second in seniority in the quorum and therefore likely had a close relationship with Marsh, who was the most senior apostle and was leading the charge against the Zion presidency. (Minutes and Discourse, 2 May 1835, in *JSP*, D4:301.)

95. See Letter and Revelation to Edward Partridge, 7 Jan. 1838, in *JSP*, D5:494; John 10:12; and Book of Mormon, 1830 ed., 484 [3 Nephi 14:15].

96. Corrill referred to the same revelation that Partridge had. Corrill had served as a counselor to Partridge for several years but had recently been released as a counselor in the bishopric and appointed as "an agent to the Church and Keeper of the Lord's store House"—an appointment in which he probably worked closely with Partridge. (Minute Book 2, 22 May and 1 Aug. 1837.)

Elder [Isaac] Morley then spake against the presidency, at the same time pleading mercy. Titus Billings said that he could not vote until they had a hearing in the common council.[97]

Elder Marsh said that the meeting was according to the direction of br. Joseph, he, therefore, considered it legal.

Elder Moses Martin then took the stand, and with great energy spake in favor of the legality of the meeting, and against the conduct of the presidency of Zion, alledging that the present corruptions of the church here, were owing to the wickedness and mismanagement of her leaders.

The Moderator then called the vote in favor of the present presidency. The negative was then called, and the vote against David Whitmer, John Whitmer, and William W. Phelps was unanimous, excepting 8 or 10 and [p. 44] this minority only wished them to continue in offioe [office] little longer, or until Joseph Smith jr. came up.

In S. Carter's settlement, the saints assembled, agreeable to appointment,[98] on the 6th inst. when they unanimously rejected the three above named presidents.

Also, on the 7th, the saints assembled at Edmond Durfey's [Durfee's] agreable to appointment, where the above named presidents were unanimously rejected.[99]

Also, on the 8th, at Nahom Curts' [Nahum Curtis's] dwelling house,[100] they were unanimously rejected by the assembly.

Also, at Hauns' mill, on the 9th, the Saints unanimously rejected them.[101]

---

97. Billings, who served as a counselor to Partridge, repeated Partridge's argument and presumably would have participated with Partridge in this "common council." (Minute Book 2, 1 and 5 Aug. 1837; 24 Feb. 1838; Minutes, 7 Nov. 1837, in *JSP*, D5:471; Instruction on Priesthood, between ca. 1 Mar. and ca. 4 May 1835, in *JSP*, D4:320 [D&C 107:82].)

98. On 26 January 1838, the high council decided to send notice of the appointed meeting times to this and other outlying settlements. The council members appointed Murdock, Carter, Marsh, Grover, Hinkle, Morey, and Wight to conduct the meetings. The meeting in "S. Carter's settlement" may have been held in the home of Simeon Carter, who owned 160 acres in the area of the Carter settlement, which was along Goose Creek a few miles southwest of Far West. (Minute Book 2, 26 Jan. 1838; Hamer, *Northeast of Eden,* 26, 56, 64, 82; Caldwell Co., MO, Original Land Entries, 1835–1859, pp. 10–11, microfilm 2,438,695, U.S. and Canada Record Collection, FHL.)

99. Edmond Durfee may have lived on or near land owned by James and Perry Durfee in the Durfee settlement, which was located along Goose Creek between Far West and the Carter settlement. (Berrett, *Sacred Places,* 4:298–299; Hamer, *Northeast of Eden,* 26, 30, 56–57, 84, 93.)

100. Nahum Curtis may have lived on or near land owned by Charles, Jeremiah, or Philip Curtis in the Curtis settlement, which was located along Log Creek about five miles south of Far West. (Berrett, *Sacred Places,* 4:292; Hamer, *Northeast of Eden,* 26, 30, 65, 83–84.)

101. Hawn's Mill was a hamlet named for Jacob Hawn's gristmill along Shoal Creek, about twenty miles downstream from Far West. Hawn had settled the area before the Latter-day Saints moved into the county, and he apparently never joined the church. The meeting may have been hosted by David Evans,

At a meeting of the High Council, the Bishop and his Council, Feb. 10, 1838, it was moved, seconded and carried, that Oliver Cowdery, William W. Phelps and John Whitmer, stand no longer as Chairmen and Clerk, to sign and record liscences.[102]

Also, voted that Thomas B. Marsh and David W. Patten be authorized to attend to said business for the time being.

Also, voted that Thomas B. Marsh and David W. Patten be Presidents, pro tempore, of the church of Latter Day Saints in Missouri, or until Presidents J. Smith Jr. and S[idney] Rigdon arrives in the land of Zion.[103]

J. MURDOCK, Moderator.[104]

T. B. MARSH, Clerk

BELOVED BROTHER JOSEPH:

You will see by the above, that quite a change has taken place among us, of late, and we hope it is for the better; and we rejoice that we have a prospect of having things in a good degree straightened by the time you arrive here. We saw plainly, from the movement of things that the church was about to go to pieces, in consequence of the wickedness of those men, we therefore have done what we have; which thing has given the church general satisfaction, they also appear to be well united, and determined to cleave to the first presidency, that is, the three first.[105]

---

as he was the president of the branch. (Berrett, *Sacred Places,* 4:337; Baugh, "Jacob Hawn and the Hawn's Mill Massacre," 4–5, 9; McBride, Autobiography, 25.)

102. About two months earlier, David Whitmer and William W. Phelps were appointed to sign licenses for priesthood officers—Whitmer as chairman and Phelps as clerk. John Whitmer was appointed to sign licenses as clerk pro tempore in the absence of Phelps. Oliver Cowdery was appointed as "Recording Clerk." Those at the 10 February council meeting may have reviewed the voting results of the church branches participating in the general assembly. (Minute Book 2, 6–7 Dec. 1837.)

103. It appears that Marsh had received word from JS that JS and Rigdon intended to come to Missouri as soon as feasible. Hyrum Smith did not come to Missouri until later, perhaps according to plan.

104. On the rare occasions when the council met without the Zion church presidency, the oldest member of the council served as "moderator." In accordance with that arrangement, Murdock was designated president of the Zion high council in 1836, while the Zion presidency continued to preside over the high council when the presidency members were present. In 1837, in a unique instance of listing a moderator, the high council minutes named Murdock in this role. (Murdock, Journal, 3 Mar. 1836, 81; Murdock, Autobiography, 34, 36; Minute Book 2, 3 Apr. 1837; 10 Feb. and 26 Jan. 1838.)

105. In the September 1837 reorganization meeting held in Kirtland, JS, Rigdon, and Williams were upheld as "the three first presidents of the church," and Oliver Cowdery, Joseph Smith Sr., Hyrum Smith, and John Smith were upheld as "assistant councillors," with the entire group "to be considered the heads of the Church." In the November 1837 reorganization meeting held in Far West, Williams was replaced by Hyrum Smith. Marsh's clarification that the church in Zion upheld the "three first" members of the general church presidency may have consciously avoided expressing support for the assistant counselors. Cowdery, one of the assistant counselors, was considered to be in league with

Had we not taken the above measures, we think that nothing could have prevented a rebellion against the whole high council and bishop; so great was the disaffection against the presidents, that the people began to be jealous, that the whole authorities were inclined to uphold these men in wickedness, and in a little time the church, undoubtedly, would have gone, every man to his own way, like sheep without a shepherd.[106]

We concluded, that as you were coming up soon, it would be well to not appoint regular presidents of this branch; as probably more satisfaction would be had among the people, to have none but the three first.

The High Council are well united together, and with yourself. The Bishop and his council are united with us now, and all misunderstanding removed. We believe that brother Corrill intends to be with you and us; although he was not with us in the meetings.

We hear that the above men intend to call the church together again, for a rehearing; but as they have no authority now, we think that their influence will not be sufficient to bring the people together. We know that such an attempt would be to divide and scatter the flock; and we intend to be faithful to warn the people of this thing.[107] The people seem to wish to have the whole law of God lived up to; and we think that the church will rejoice to come up to the law of consecration, as soon as their leaders shall say the word, or show them how to do it.[108] In a word, we are persuaded that the most part of the people wish to become sanctified by the law of God.[109] Dear Brother, may our God speedily open the way for you and your father's family, with our beloved brother S. Rigdon, to come among us. Your presence is absolutely necessary for the salvation of this church: Do hasten therefore, to our relief, our enemies

---

the recently deposed Zion presidency. (Minutes, 3 Sept. 1837, in *JSP*, D5:422–423; Minutes, 7 Nov. 1837, in *JSP*, D5:469–470.)

106. See Isaiah 53:6.

107. Marsh was apparently alluding to JS's 7 January letter to Edward Partridge, which included words of revelation warning about dissension. (Letter and Revelation to Edward Partridge, 7 Jan. 1838, in *JSP*, D5:494.)

108. The law of consecration was one of the revealed "Laws of the Church of Christ" that JS dictated in 1831 and was the subject of several subsequent revelations. In December, the Zion high council and bishopric held meetings to solve financial problems and work out a plan for the Saints to consecrate part of their assets to the church. The committee sent to talk to the members of the Zion presidency expressed dissatisfaction with them for not teaching the law of consecration. (Revelation, 9 Feb. 1831, in *JSP*, D1:249, 251–252 [D&C 42:30–39]; Minute Book 2, 6–7 and 23 Dec. 1837; Oliver Cowdery, Far West, MO, to Warren Cowdery and Lyman Cowdery, [Kirtland, OH], 4 Feb. 1838, in Cowdery, Letterbook, 84; see also Revelation, 12 Nov. 1831, in *JSP*, D2:140 [D&C 70:7–9].)

109. JS's revelations stated that the Saints would be sanctified by adhering to the laws of God. (Revelation, Feb. 1831–A, in *JSP*, D1:258 [D&C 43:9]; Revelation, 27–28 Dec. 1832, in *JSP*, D2:338 [D&C 88:21, 34–35].)

are bitter against us, and will do all the injury they can to you, to us, and to the church.

In the name of the church, we say hold us by your faith, until you get here. We flatter ourselves that you will have the church in Kirtland, in a situation to leave them as soon as the rivers open.[110] Although these men speak against your proceedings, they are mute when you are present,[111] and the great body is determined to follow you.

Agreable to your request, brother [George W.] Harris and myself wrote, and sent to you our testimony, relative to what Oliver Cowdery said about the girl,[112] and mailed it on the 4th inst. but lest that letter should not reach you through the iniquity of men, I here send you the same, with the addition of brother Hinkle's testimony. They may not be the same words as the other, for we have not a copy of the former letter, however, this is the same in substance, with some addition.

> This may certify, that I heard O. Cowdery say to Joseph Smith Jr., while at George W. Harris' house, in Far West,[113] that he (Joseph) never confessed to him, (Oliver) that he was guilty of the crime alledged to him.[114] And O. Cowdery gave me to understand that Joseph Smith Jr.

---

110. According to an early American steamboat directory, ice on the Ohio River usually broke up in February, rendering the river "open for navigation." In March 1838, the chief engineer of the Baltimore and Ohio Railroad reported that "the navigation of the Ohio River opens always by the 1st of March, and generally by the middle of February." The Missouri River usually opened for navigation between mid-February and early March. (Lloyd, *Lloyd's Steamboat Directory*, 50–51; *Documents Submitted by the Baltimore and Ohio Rail Road Company*, 12; Lass, *Navigating the Missouri*, 89; see also Roberts, *Improvement of the Ohio River*, 14, 25.)

111. The minutes of the November 1837 reorganization meeting contain no mention of dissent against JS. (See Minutes, 7 Nov. 1837, in *JSP*, D5:469–472.)

112. Cowdery had alleged an immoral relationship between JS and Fanny Alger. In the 1840s, JS taught the doctrine of plural marriage to an inner circle of followers, but he never publicized the doctrine. JS's earlier polygamous marriage to Alger was apparently even more secret. In late 1837 and early 1838, JS was apparently attempting to stop the rumors regarding the relationship. (Bushman, *Rough Stone Rolling*, 323–327, 437–446; Leonard, *Nauvoo*, 343–356; see also Compton, *In Sacred Loneliness*, 25–42.)

113. Harris later recounted that this conversation took place "one evening last fall," which would have been during JS's late 1837 visit to Far West. During the evening council meeting held on 6 November, the council resolved that "all difficulties were satisfactorily settled except a matter between J. Smith jr. Oliver Cowdery and T. B. Marsh, which was refered to themselves with the agreement that their settlement of the affair should be sufficient for the Council." JS was apparently staying with Harris during this visit, as JS did again when he returned to Caldwell County in March 1838. Harris owned property along Shoal Creek near Far West. (Minutes, 12 Apr. 1838, p. 90 herein; Minutes, 6 Nov. 1837, in *JSP*, D5:467–468; JS History, vol. B-1, 775–778; JS, Journal, Mar.–Sept. 1838, p. 16, in *JSP*, J1:237; Hamer, *Northeast of Eden*, 49, 85.)

114. Marsh later recounted that Cowdery made this statement "after a considerable winking &c." (Minutes, 12 Apr. 1838, p. 91 herein.)

never acknowledged to him, that he ever confessed to any one, that he was guilty of the above crime.[115]

THOMAS B. MARSH.

This may certify, that I heard Oliver Cowdery say, in my house, that Joseph Smith Jr. never confessed to him, that he was guilty of the crime alledged against him, and Joseph asked if he ever said to him, (Oliver) that he confessed to any one that he, (Joseph) was guilty of the above crime, and Oliver, after some hesitation, answered, no.

GEORGE W. HARRIS.

This may certify, that having heard the report about the crime above referred to, I asked Oliver Cowdery, last fall, when Joseph Smith was in the Far West, if the report was true, for said I, if it is, as he is to be presented before the church, I wish to know of the truth of this matter before hand.[116] And he gave me to understand, either in plain words or implications, that it was false. I bear this testimony for the good of the honest hearted in the east, and else where, and for the good of brother Joseph Smith Jr. Brother Marsh will please copy this in the letter to the east, and keep the original here.

GEORGE M. HINKLE.

Far West, Feb. 15, 1838.

Dear Brother, we lament that such foul and false reports should be circulated in Kirtland concerning yourself. We are persuaded that none but those who wish your overthrow, will believe them, and we presume that the above [p. 45] testimonies will be sufficient to stay the tongue of the slanderer.

Yours, in the bonds of
the New Covenant,[117]

THOMAS B. MARSH.

Joseph Smith Jr.
Far West, Feb. 15, 1838.

———— ∾ ————

115. Patten later recounted that Cowdery said, "Joseph told him, he had confessed to Emma." (Minutes, 12 Apr. 1838, p. 91 herein.)

116. This conversation apparently occurred after JS's arrival in Far West in late October or early November and before the reorganization meeting held on 7 November. (JS History, vol. B-1, 775; Minutes, 7 Nov. 1837, in *JSP*, D5:469–472.)

117. See Philemon 1:13; Jeremiah 31:31; Ezekiel 20:37; and Hebrews 12:24.

Pay Order to Edward Partridge for William Smith, 21 February 1838

Source Note

William Marks, agent, on behalf of JS and Sidney Rigdon, Pay Order, to Edward Partridge for William Smith, [Kirtland Township, Geauga Co., OH], 21 Feb. 1838; one page; handwriting of William Marks; photocopy, JS Collection, CHL. Includes docket.

Single leaf. The photocopied image of the document measures 5–5⅜ × 8 inches (13–14 × 20 cm), which is similar in size to other pay orders produced the same day.[118] The photocopy shows file folds in the original. A two-line docket on the verso of the original bled through and is slightly visible in the photocopy. The docket was made legible through producing a digital mirror image. The docket, which is in unidentified handwriting, reads: "Land order | for $100". The location of the original document is unknown.

Historical Introduction

On 21 February 1838, church financial agent William Marks wrote several "orders" for JS's brother William Smith. These orders functioned like receipts for money given to the church in Ohio, and Smith could redeem them for money or land after moving to Missouri. Marks wrote and signed these and other pay orders on behalf of JS and Sidney Rigdon, members of the First Presidency. The pay orders for William Smith were apparently given in exchange for land he sold to Marks at a reduced rate, which Marks could then sell at market value in order to pay debts JS and Rigdon owed.

In 1836 JS and other church leaders began renegotiating old debts and incurring new ones as they attempted to finance the House of the Lord and expand the economy of the Mormon community in Kirtland Township. Ultimately, they contracted thousands of dollars of debt.[119] In April 1837, JS and Rigdon began engaging Marks as an agent for church business holdings and dealings. In September 1837, Marks was appointed to the high council and appointed as an agent for Kirtland bishop Newel K. Whitney.[120] Marks was appointed to preside over the Saints in Kirtland shortly before JS and Rigdon left for Missouri in January 1838.[121] In these roles, he worked to settle the debts of JS and Rigdon and helped the faithful members of the church prepare to migrate to Missouri. Following directions from JS, Marks sold land in Kirtland Township to raise money to pay creditors.[122] He kept a

---

118. See Orders on Edward Partridge, for William Smith, 21 Feb. 1838, JS Office Papers, CHL.

119. See, for example, Statement of Account from John Howden, 29 Mar. 1838, pp. 61–65 herein; Statement of Account from Perkins & Osborn, ca. 29 Oct. 1838, pp. 252–261 herein; and Statement of Account from Hitchcock & Wilder, between 9 July and 6 Nov. 1838, pp. 285–290 herein.

120. Staker, *Hearken, O Ye People,* 519–522; Minutes, 3 Sept. 1837, in *JSP,* D5:425; Minute Book 1, 9 Sept. 1837; Minutes, 17 Sept. 1837–A, in *JSP,* D5:443.

121. John Smith and Clarissa Lyman Smith, Kirtland, OH, to George A. Smith, Shinnston, VA, 1 Jan. 1838, George Albert Smith, Papers, CHL; Hepzibah Richards, Kirtland, OH, to Willard Richards, Bedford, England, 18–19 Jan. 1838, Willard Richards, Papers, CHL.

122. See, for example, Geauga Co., OH, Deed Record, 1795–1921, vol. 25, pp. 570–571, 5 Feb. 1838; vol. 26, pp. 298–299, 300–301, 15 and 23 Feb. 1838, microfilm 20,241, U.S. and Canada Record Collection, FHL.

register of people who gave money or land, which he used to settle church debts.[123] In return for these goods, Marks wrote pay orders on behalf of JS and Rigdon. Saints could redeem their pay orders after moving to Missouri, where Bishop Edward Partridge would exchange the orders for money or for property the church owned there.[124]

Marks eventually listed twenty donors in his register, which ran from 1 February through 19 April. Many of these orders are still extant.[125] The extant pay orders were issued the day the donations were made or within a day after, as dated in Marks's register.[126] The number of pay orders Marks wrote per donation varied. In some cases, Marks apparently wrote a single order for one donation. For example, Asahel Perry sold his farm on 30 January 1838 for $3,300.[127] Two days later, Marks noted a donation from Perry for $3,200 and wrote him an order for the same amount.[128] In other cases, Marks wrote two or more orders to compensate for one donation. For example, on 1 March, John Isham sold his property for $1,300 and donated $1,100 to the church.[129] The same day, Marks noted the donation in his register and made out four orders totaling $1,100.[130] Breaking the donated amount into smaller quantities may have allowed the donor more financial flexibility. While each pay order names the donor, it then indicates that Partridge should remit the specified amount to "the bearer" in land or money, suggesting that the notes could be transferred in subsequent financial dealings.[131]

---

123. "List of Demands on J Smith & S. Rigdon," 1 Feb.–19 Apr. 1838, JS Collection, CHL.

124. See Corrill, *Brief History,* 27, in *JSP,* H2:161; and Reed Peck, Quincy, IL, to "Dear Friends," 18 Sept. 1839, pp. 14–15, Henry E. Huntington Library, San Marino, CA. The orders that Marks wrote functioned similarly to the certificates Saints received before moving to Jackson County earlier in the 1830s. Saints would present to Partridge a certificate from Bishop Whitney in Kirtland or another authorized officer who vouched for the faithfulness of the individual; the certificate entitled the individual to receive an inheritance of land from the bishop. (See Revelation, 9 Feb. 1831, in *JSP,* D1:251–252, 255 [D&C 42:31–36, 71–72]; Revelation, 20 July 1831, in *JSP,* D2:11 [D&C 57:7]; and Revelation, 4 Dec. 1831–B, in *JSP,* D2:153 [D&C 72:17].)

125. See, for example, Orders on Edward Partridge, Feb.–Apr. 1838, JS Office Papers, CHL.

126. See "List of Demands on J Smith & S. Rigdon," 1 Feb.–19 Apr. 1838; Order on Edward Partridge, for Aaron Johnson, 21 Mar. 1838, JS Collection, CHL; Order on Edward Partridge, for Oliver Granger, 3 Mar. 1838, JS Collection (Supplement), CHL; and Orders on Edward Partridge, for Winslow Farr, 5 Mar. 1838, JS Office Papers, CHL. On 26 April 1838, Marks wrote Granger another pay order, which is also located in the JS Office Papers collection at the Church History Library. One other order, for $200, is extant, but the recipient and date are unknown. (See Order on Edward Partridge, no date, JS Collection, CHL.)

127. Geauga Co., OH, Deed Record, 1795–1921, vol. 25, pp. 463–464, 30 Jan. 1838, microfilm 20,241, U.S. and Canada Record Collection, FHL.

128. "List of Demands on J Smith & S. Rigdon," 1 Feb.–19 Apr. 1838, JS Collection, CHL; Order on Edward Partridge, for Asahel Perry, 1 Feb. 1838, JS Office Papers, CHL. Perry may have decided to keep $100 for traveling expenses.

129. Geauga Co., OH, Deed Record, 1795–1921, vol. 25, pp. 423–424, 1 Mar. 1838, microfilm 20,241, U.S. and Canada Record Collection, FHL.

130. "List of Demands on J Smith & S. Rigdon," 1 Feb.–19 Apr. 1838, JS Collection, CHL; Orders on Edward Partridge, for John Isham, 1 Mar. 1838, JS Office Papers, CHL; Order on Edward Partridge, for John Isham, 1 Mar. 1838, Newel K. Whitney, Papers, BYU.

131. Financial notes were often constructed in this way so they could be transferred to another party. (See, for example, Promissory Note to John Gillet and Smith Tuttle, 12 Aug. 1839, pp. 556–557 herein.)

The donations William Smith made and the pay orders he received differ somewhat from the general pattern. Marks noted a donation of $500 from Smith in an entry dated 14 February 1838. The next day, Smith deeded two pieces of his Kirtland property to Marks. One of these properties, deeded for $1,500, was Smith's land in lot 30, near the House of the Lord.[132] Smith may have deeded this land in an attempt to safeguard his property from creditors, as suggested by the fact that Marks did not sell this property for money to pay JS's and Rigdon's debts. Instead, three years later, when the church's financial troubles in Kirtland had diminished considerably, Marks sold the property back to Smith for $1,800.[133] The other property Smith deeded to Marks on 15 February was his land in lot 31, which he had purchased five months earlier for $1,500.[134] This property apparently coincides with the donation noted in the register the previous day. Instead of selling land to someone else and giving Marks money from the sale, Smith apparently made his donation by selling the property to Marks at the greatly reduced price of $100.[135] Smith's pay orders note that his donations were made "in Lands." If this property were still worth the $1,500 Smith had recently paid for it, his donation in land value would have been closer to $1,400 than to the $500 Marks noted in his register on 14 February. Determining how much to compensate Smith may have taken some time; Marks did not issue pay orders to Smith until almost a week later. There may have been other properties, debts, or considerations involved in the dealings between Smith and Marks, so it is impossible to establish with certainty the details of their agreement.

In any case, on 21 February, Marks made out several pay orders for Smith. It is not certain how many orders Marks wrote or for what total value. Six orders are known to be extant, totaling $625 in value: two notes for $150, three notes for $100, and one note for $25.[136]

Smith deeded his land to Marks in preparation for leaving with the extended Smith family for Missouri. On 15 February, the same day Marks received deeds for Smith's land, Marks's register notes that Wilkins Jenkins Salisbury, the husband of William's sister Katharine, paid Marks $300. On 7 March, Katharine Smith Salisbury sold property in Kirtland for $300 and perhaps gave the proceeds to Marks.[137] Two months later, William and Caroline Rockwell Smith, Wilkins Jenkins and Katharine Salisbury, and other members of the Smith family departed Ohio for Missouri.[138] Upon arriving in Far West, William Smith apparently redeemed some of his pay orders for land or money. Five extant orders have the signatures torn off, indicating they were redeemed. As late as

132. Geauga Co., OH, Deed Record, 1795–1921, vol. 30, pp. 382–383, 15 Feb. 1838, microfilm 20,242, U.S. and Canada Record Collection, FHL.

133. Lake Co., OH, Deeds, 1840–1950, vol. C, p. 536, 10 Feb. 1841, microfilm 974,941, U.S. and Canada Record Collection, FHL.

134. Geauga Co., OH, Deed Record, 1795–1921, vol. 30, p. 384, 4 Sept. 1837, microfilm 20,242, U.S. and Canada Record Collection, FHL.

135. Geauga Co., OH, Deed Record, 1795–1921, vol. 30, p. 383, 15 Feb. 1838, microfilm 20,242, U.S. and Canada Record Collection, FHL.

136. See Orders on Edward Partridge, for William Smith, 21 Feb. 1838, JS Office Papers, CHL.

137. Geauga Co., OH, Deed Record, 1795–1921, vol. 30, pp. 381–382, 7 Mar. 1838, microfilm 20,242, U.S. and Canada Record Collection, FHL.

138. Letter from Don Carlos Smith, ca. Late May 1838, p. 151 herein; Lucy Mack Smith, History, 1844–1845, bk. 15, [3]–[6].

January 1839, when the Saints were preparing for their forced removal from the state, he had not redeemed at least one of the orders. On 7 January 1839, he received $20 from Partridge as a partial payment for one order.[139] The pay order featured here, which represents all of the William Smith orders, as well as the pay orders from this period generally, is complete, with the signatures still intact, indicating it was never canceled and may not have been redeemed.

Document Transcript

Kirtland Febuary 21ˢᵗ 1838

Received of William Smith one hundeed Dollars in Lands to apply on the debts in Kirtland agreeable To the directions of the presidaccy there fore

Mʳ Edward Partridge Sir

Please to pay the bearer One hundred Dollars in money or Lands as shall accommodate and oblige yours

Joseph Smith Jun.

Sidney Rigdon—[140]

By

William Marks there agent

———— ∽ ————

139. William Smith, Receipt, Far West, MO, to JS and Sidney Rigdon, 7 Jan. 1839, JS Collection, CHL.

140. Through various partnerships—such as Rigdon, Smith & Co.ᵃ—JS and Rigdon had contracted much of the debt that church leaders incurred in their attempt to develop the economy of the Mormon community in Kirtland Township.ᵇ Frederick G. Williams, who had served as the second counselor in the First Presidency, had been less involved in business activities. In fact, JS and Rigdon assumed some of the business he previously supervised, as reflected in the transfer of the church printing company from the firm F. G. Williams & Co. to O. Cowdery & Co. and then to JS and Rigdon (and eventually to William Marks).ᶜ In November 1837, Williams was replaced by Hyrum Smith as the third member of the general church presidency.ᵈ Hyrum Smith had not incurred business debts; in fact, he donated land or money to Marks to help JS and Rigdon.ᵉ (a. See, for example, "Mormonism in Ohio," *Yankee Farmer* [Portland, ME], 4 Feb. 1837, 38; and Rigdon, Smith & Co., Store Ledger. b. Statement of Account from Hitchcock & Wilder, between 9 July and 6 Nov. 1838, pp. 285–290 herein. c. "Notice," *LDS Messenger and Advocate,* June 1836, 2:329–330; "Notice," *LDS Messenger and Advocate,* Feb. 1837, 3:458–459; Advertisement, *LDS Messenger and Advocate,* Mar. 1837, 3:480; "Notice," *LDS Messenger and Advocate,* Apr. 1837, 3:496. d. Minutes, 7 Nov. 1837, in *JSP,* D5:469–470. e. "List of Demands on J Smith & S. Rigdon," 1 Feb.–19 Apr. 1838, JS Collection, CHL.)

Letter from Wilford Woodruff and Others, 9 March 1838

Source Note

Wilford Woodruff, James Townsend, and Joseph Ball, Letter, Vinalhaven, Fox Islands, Hancock Co., ME, to Edward Partridge, JS, Sidney Rigdon, Hyrum Smith, and "Saints in Zion," [Far West, Caldwell Co., MO], 9 Mar. 1838. Featured version published in Elders' Journal, *July 1838, 35–36. For more information on* Elders' Journal, *see Source Notes for Multiple-Entry Documents, p. 563 herein.*

Historical Introduction

On 9 March 1838, while proselytizing in Maine, Wilford Woodruff wrote a letter to Bishop Edward Partridge, JS and his counselors in the First Presidency, and the Saints in Missouri generally. As a member of the First Quorum of the Seventy, Woodruff was expected to travel, proselytize, organize branches of the church, and encourage church members to gather to Zion in Missouri.[141] At the time of the letter, Woodruff had been proselytizing in the northeastern United States for almost a year—most recently in the Fox Islands, about halfway along Maine's coast in the middle of Penobscot Bay. In May 1837, within a few weeks after marrying Phebe Carter, he had departed Kirtland on a mission "into the eastern country" with Jonathan H. Hale.[142] Woodruff had a compelling desire to gather the house of Israel from "the islands of the sea," as Isaiah had prophesied and as JS's revelations had commanded.[143] Later in life, Woodruff recounted that after feeling "impressed by the Spirit of God to take a mission to the Fox Islands," he expressed his desire to President Sidney Rigdon and apostle Heber Kimball and they advised him to go.[144] Woodruff preached in many places along the way to Maine, including Farmington, Connecticut, where he shared with his parents and family members the Mormon message of a restored gospel. While in Farmington, he was met by his wife, who traveled with him to Scarborough, Maine, to share the gospel with her parents and other family members. Then Woodruff left Phebe with her family and pressed on with Hale to the Fox Islands.

Woodruff and Hale were very successful proselytizing in the Fox Islands during August and September 1837, and in early October they organized a branch of the church there. The men then returned to Scarborough, where Hale determined to return home to Kirtland while Wilford and Phebe Woodruff traveled to the Fox Islands so Wilford could

---

141. See Woodruff, Journal, 3 Jan. 1837; and Instruction on Priesthood, between ca. 1 Mar. and ca. 4 May 1835, in *JSP,* D4:314 [D&C 107:25].

142. Woodruff, Journal, 30–31 May 1837.

143. See Isaiah 11:11; and Revelation, 3 Nov. 1831, in *JSP,* D2:117 [D&C 133:8]. Woodruff frequently expressed his interest in proselytizing upon the "Islands of the sea." (See Letter from Wilford Woodruff and Jonathan H. Hale, 18 Sept. 1837, in *JSP,* D5:451; and Woodruff, Journal, 20 Aug. 1837; 3–5 Sept. 1837; 1 Oct. 1837; 15–16 Nov. 1837; 31 Dec. 1837; 26 Apr. 1838.)

144. Woodruff, "Autobiography of Wilford Woodruff," 11; "History of Wilford Woodruff," 23–24, Historian's Office, Histories of the Twelve, 1856–1858, 1861, CHL.

continue his labors there.[145] In January 1838, he received a new mission companion: Joseph Ball, an elder from Boston.[146] In February, Woodruff returned to the mainland to preach in Bangor, Maine, and other towns along the way, accompanied by another Mormon elder named James Townsend, while Ball continued preaching on the islands.[147]

The church elders and new converts kept in contact with the gathered Saints through the church newspapers. The *Elders' Journal,* the church's new periodical, had been designed for this purpose.[148] Woodruff collected several subscriptions for the *Elders' Journal* in the Fox Islands and mailed them to Don Carlos Smith, who was in Kirtland and completed the editorial work for the paper.[149]

Woodruff also corresponded occasionally with church members in Kirtland and heard news as he traveled.[150] While staying with a Latter-day Saint on the way to Bangor, Woodruff "heard that Kirtland was in difficulty," a continuation of the dissent that Woodruff had witnessed before leaving on his mission.[151] He learned of further trouble when he and Townsend returned from the mainland to the Fox Islands on 8 March and Phebe gave Wilford letters that had arrived during his absence. One of these letters, from an "Elder Robbins" in Kirtland, informed Woodruff that dissenters in Kirtland had caused great turmoil in the church, that the printing office had been "burned to the ground with all its contents," that JS and Rigdon had fled Kirtland for Far West, and that "the faithful are to follow them for Kirtland will be scorged."[152]

The following day, Woodruff discussed this troubling news with Ball and Townsend. The three missionaries decided to write a letter to Bishop Edward Partridge, the First Presidency, and the Saints in Missouri. Woodruff probably wrote the letter while at the home of Latter-day Saint Malatiah Luce on North Fox Island, where Woodruff was living at the time.[153]

---

145. Woodruff, Journal, 31 May 1837–13 Jan. 1838; Letter from Wilford Woodruff and Jonathan H. Hale, 18 Sept. 1837, in *JSP,* D5:451–457; see also Thompson, "Wilford Woodruff's Missions to the Fox Islands," 97–117.

146. Woodruff was preaching on South Fox Island when Ball arrived on North Fox Island. By the time Woodruff returned to North Fox Island to meet his new mission companion, Ball had already baptized six people. (Woodruff, Journal, 13 Jan. 1838.)

147. Woodruff, Journal, 13 Feb.–8 Mar. 1838.

148. "Prospectus," *LDS Messenger and Advocate,* Sept. 1837, 3:571–572; see also *Elders' Journal,* Oct. and Nov. 1837. When Woodruff received the first issue of the *Elders' Journal,* he wrote in his journal that it "warmed my Soul." When he and Ball received the second issue, Woodruff noted, "It did our souls good." (Woodruff, Journal, 13 Dec. 1837 and 17 Jan. 1838.)

149. See Woodruff, Journal, 20 Nov. and 31 Dec. 1837.

150. See, for example, Letter from Wilford Woodruff and Jonathan H. Hale, 18 Sept. 1837, in *JSP,* D5:451–457; and Woodruff, Journal, 14 Feb. 1838.

151. Woodruff, Journal, 19 Feb. and 28 May 1837; 14 Feb. 1838.

152. Woodruff, Journal, 8 Mar. 1838. "Elder Robbins" is likely Lewis Robbins, a fellow member of the First Quorum of the Seventy. Lewis Robbins was the only known Robbins in Kirtland during this time, as identified by Milton V. Backman in his extensive survey of local records. Robbins lived with Don Carlos Smith, to whom Woodruff had been writing and sending subscriptions for the *Elders' Journal.* (Minutes and Blessings, 28 Feb.–1 Mar. 1835, in *JSP,* D4:258; Robbins, Autobiographical Sketch, 3–4; Backman, *Profile,* 59.)

153. Woodruff, Journal, 8–15 Mar. 1838. Woodruff had stayed with Luce before. Luce owned several pieces of property on North Fox Island. He may have been living along the stream between Fresh Pond

Woodruff began his letter with a general address to "friends in the new and ever-lasting covenant" and then reported on proselytizing in the Fox Islands. In the middle of the letter, Woodruff explicitly addressed the members of the First Presidency and asked them to recommence the *Elders' Journal* in Missouri. Woodruff expressed the missionaries' dire need for church literature to help combat false information about the church that was being circulated in the region. Woodruff concluded by expressing loyalty to JS and the church and by admonishing the Saints in Missouri not to make the mistakes being made by church members in Ohio. The letter was apparently composed by Woodruff, who wrote in the first-person singular voice, but Ball and Townsend signed the letter with him, indicating their agreement with the letter's content. The original letter is apparently not extant, but the letter states that it was written on one page.

Woodruff noted in his journal that on the following Wednesday he walked to the post office, presumably to mail this and other letters he had recently written.[154] Woodruff's letter made its way safely across half the continent, likely arriving in Far West sometime in early or mid-April.[155] Whenever Woodruff's letter was received, it was probably read by or to JS. Sometime on or after 30 April 1838, Thomas B. Marsh wrote a reply to Woodruff on JS's behalf, remarking that Woodruff's letter arrived "some days, since."[156] Woodruff's request for a church newspaper was fulfilled when JS and Marsh began publishing the *Elders' Journal* in Far West in summer 1838. As the editor of the *Elders' Journal*, JS may have reviewed Woodruff's letter again when it was prepared for publication in the July issue.

---

and North Harbor. (Woodruff, Journal, 26 and 29 Aug. 1837; Hancock Co., ME, Deeds, 1791–1861, vol. 67, p. 101, 12 Apr. 1838, microfilm 10,980; Waldo Co., ME, Record of Deeds, 1828–1896, vol. 47, p. 445, 7 Sept. 1838, microfilm 12,373, U.S. and Canada Record Collection, FHL; see also Wells, *Provisional Report upon the Water-Power of Maine*, 227; Woodruff, Journal, 13 Aug. 1838; and Chace et al., *Map of Waldo County, Maine* [Portland, ME: J. Chace Jr., 1859].)

154. Woodruff, Journal, 10–14 Mar. 1838. Notes in Woodruff's journal indicate that the post office, located in John Kent's store, was in the hamlet of North Haven on the south side of North Fox Island. However, the post office was possibly on the southeast side of the island, where an 1859 map of Waldo County shows two Kent domiciles at Kent's Cove. In September 1837, Woodruff "walked to the Post Office. Took a sail boat to cross to South fox Island." In February 1838, he "walked to Mr Kents crossed the thoroughfare," the channel between North Fox Island and South Fox Island. On 5 April, Woodruff walked "to Mr John Kents store & Post Office" to receive mail. (Woodruff, Journal, 4 Sept. 1837; 13 Feb. and 5 Apr. 1838; Chace et al., *Map of Waldo County, Maine* [Portland, ME: J. Chace Jr., 1859].)

155. In the summer, a letter from Marsh reached Woodruff in less than four weeks, suggesting that the 9 March letter from Woodruff traveled at about the same speed. Marsh's 14 July letter was postmarked 15 July 1838 in Far West and was directed to Woodruff in Vinalhaven, Maine. Woodruff, who had been absent from the Fox Islands for several weeks, returned to Vinalhaven on 7 August and noted that he received Marsh's 14 July letter from a local member on 9 August. (Thomas B. Marsh, Far West, MO, to Wilford Woodruff, Vinalhaven, ME, 14 July 1838, Wilford Woodruff, Journals and Papers, CHL; Woodruff, Journal, 7 and 9 Aug. 1838.)

156. Letter to Wilford Woodruff, ca. 18 June 1838, p. 154 herein. Marsh's letter bears an 18 June 1838 postmark.

Document Transcript

Vinalhaven, Fox Islands, Me.

March 9th, 1838.

BISHOP EDWARD PARTRIDGE, AND PRESIDENTS JOSEPH SMITH JR., SIDNEY RIGDON, HYRUM SMITH, and THE SAINTS IN ZION, GREETING:

Dear friends in the new and everlasting covenant;[157]

I, Willford [Wilford] Woodruff, sit down to inform you, that I have just heard, correctly, of the deplorable state of things in Kirtland, and I have this day held a council with Elders J[oseph] Ball and J[ames] Townsend, who are now with me upon these Islands,[158] and we resolved to address a few lines to you concerning our feelings, and set before you a brief account of things with us, and the course we intend to pursue. I have labored principally alone upon these Islands, since Elder [Jonathan H.] Hale left last fall,[159] and the work of the Lord has prospered in my hands, or in other words, the Lord has worked with me during the winter. Elder Joseph Ball has been with me for a number of weeks past upon the Islands.[160] There is rising of 40 members in the church on these Islands, and they are strong in the faith.[161] I returned last evening from a mission in company with Elder James Townsend. we have been visiting the most notable cities and vilages in the eastern country, and delivering unto them the word of God.[162]

We preached in their City Halls, Chapels, School houses, dwellings &c., in such places as Camden, Belfast, Northport, Frankfort, Hampden and the City of Bangor.[163] Doors were open in all of these places, and many others I

---

157. See Revelation, 16 Apr. 1830, in *JSP,* D1:138 [D&C 22:1].

158. Woodruff, Ball, and Townsend may have met in the home of fellow Latter-day Saint Malatiah Luce. (See Woodruff, Journal, 8–15 Mar. 1838.)

159. Hale, Woodruff's principal mission companion, returned to Kirtland in October 1837. (Woodruff, Journal, 31 May 1837; 19 Aug. 1837; 1 and 9 Oct. 1837.)

160. Ball joined Woodruff on North Fox Island on 13 January 1838. (Woodruff, Journal, 13 Jan. 1838.)

161. In September 1837, Woodruff wrote, "Although we have not baptized but few on these Islands, yet there is hundreds believing and many are almost ready to enter into the kingdom." By the time Woodruff left in late April 1838, he had organized two branches of the church, one on each island, and each branch had about fifty members. (Letter from Wilford Woodruff and Jonathan H. Hale, 18 Sept. 1837, in *JSP,* D5:456; Woodruff, Journal, 28 Apr. 1838; Wilford Woodruff, Scarborough, ME, to Asahel Woodruff, Terre Haute, IN, 2 May 1838, Wilford Woodruff Collection, CHL.)

162. Woodruff had been traveling with Townsend since 15 February 1838. (Woodruff, Journal, 15 Feb.–8 Mar. 1838.)

163. Camden lay just across Penobscot Bay from the Fox Islands. Northport and Belfast lay farther north along the west side of the bay. Frankfort, Hampden, and Bangor were situated along the Penobscot River. Woodruff's journal records his travels through various municipalities in Maine on the way to the sizable city of Bangor. Along the way there and back, Woodruff took small detours to preach in Searsmont and on the Isle au Haut. Woodruff wrote of preaching in the city hall in Bangor; in the Universalist chapel in Hampden; in schoolhouses in Camden, Searsmont, Belfast, Northport, Frankfort, Hampden, and the Isle au Haut; and at a "Mr. Bailey's" in Searsmont. (Woodruff, Journal, 13 Feb.–8 Mar. 1838.)

might mention, and the people heard with profound attention; and many are believing. I never saw more doors open for doing good, than at the present time in the State of Maine: But the Devil is stired up against me here on the Island.[164]

One Methodist priest has applied several times for a warrant to take me,[165] but the Officers, as yet, will not grant him any, for he cannot bring any accusation against me in truth or justice.

The most trouble I now have, is the stopping the papers. I have forwarded about 30 subscribers with the money, and now the press is burnt down,[166] and our enemies roar in the midst of the congregations,[167] and they set up these ensigns for signs.[168]

I expect the report of these things will come like a clap of thunder in the ears of the Saints upon these Islands and else where. They do not know it yet, but are wondering why these papers do not come. We have appointed a time to meet the church, and we shall lay all these things before them and trust in God for

---

164. Woodruff was on North Fox Island at this time. (Woodruff, Journal, 8–9 Mar. 1838.)

165. Woodruff wrote that North Fox Island had "a Baptist church & meeting house," while South Fox Island had "a small branch of the methodist church & a priest." Woodruff contended several times with "Mr William Douglass the Methodist Priest" from South Fox Island. When Woodruff began converting Baptists on North Fox Island, the Baptist minister, Gideon Newton, invited Douglass to preach there. Douglass preached against Mormonism, and Woodruff rebutted him. Woodruff later wrote, "I then followed Mr Douglass to his own Island, and commenced preaching to his Church, and Baptized a good share of his members." Woodruff also wrote that while he preached on South Fox Island, "the people came out by hundreds, to hear and filled the schoolhouses to overflowing." A late nineteenth-century local history of South Fox Island stated that the Mormon religion had "held sway for several years, during which time a number of the leading members of the hitherto prevailing faith were converted to its ranks." In January, Douglass had swayed some of Woodruff's converts, but Woodruff reclaimed them and had what he called a "serious interview" with Douglass. (Woodruff, Journal, 20 Aug. 1837; 11, 17, and 30 Sept. 1837; 28 Dec. 1837; 29 Jan.–1 Feb. 1838; Letter from Wilford Woodruff and Jonathan H. Hale, 18 Sept. 1837, in *JSP*, D5:454; "History of Wilford Woodruff," 27, Historian's Office, Histories of the Twelve, 1856–1858, 1861, CHL; *Brief Historical Sketch of the Town of Vinalhaven*, 59–60.)

166. Woodruff had sent in subscriptions to the church newspaper, the *Elders' Journal*. On the night of 15–16 January, the building in Kirtland where the church printed the *Elders' Journal* was burned to the ground with all its contents. JS and many other Latter-day Saints assumed that dissenters in Kirtland had set the fire. Dissenter Warren Parrish alleged that the building was burned down at the command of JS. Decades later, devout Latter-day Saint Benjamin F. Johnson recounted that Lyman Sherman, another loyal Saint living in Kirtland, set fire to the building after it had fallen into the hands of dissenters. (Woodruff, Journal, 20 Nov. and 31 Dec. 1837; 3 Jan. and 6 Feb. 1838; John Smith and Don Carlos Smith, Kirtland Mills, OH, to George A. Smith, Shinnston, VA, 15–18 Jan. 1838, George Albert Smith, Papers, CHL; Letter to the Presidency in Kirtland, 29 Mar. 1838, p. 58 herein; Warren Parrish, Kirtland, OH, 5 Feb. 1838, Letter to the Editor, *Painesville [OH] Republican,* 15 Feb. 1838, [3]; Johnson, "A Life Review," 24.)

167. Organized opposition on the islands and the mainland came primarily from the Baptists. (Thompson, "Wilford Woodruff's Missions to the Fox Islands," 108–114.)

168. See Psalm 74:4.

wisdom to direct us.[169] The Elders that are with me are expecting to go to their homes, and I shall be left to fight the battles alone.[170] Brethren, pray for me out of Zion, for I have a load to bear; but in the name of Elijah's God, I am determined to stand at my post. I feel as though the time of Jacob's trouble had began, but I know God will deliver him out of it, and fulfil his word.[171]

We are advising the Saints of God to go from this country to Zion, as soon as they can. I suppose this is right: many are preparing to go the following season.

Now we say to the Presidency of the church in Zion;[172] we do not expect to counsel you, nor any one there, let God be your counsellors. But we ask, can it not be consistent with the will of God and your feelings and circumstances, to soon publish the Elders' Journal from Zion,[173] that we may have one weapon, to cut away some of the deep gloom, that will be cast upon the minds of thousands of the Saints, by wicked men and devils, and false brethren. The traveling Elders feel the wait of these things, equally, if not more than those who are in Zion; for we are naked targets to the press and tongue, as we pass through the midst of the Gentiles.[174] O my God! have mercy and support us, I

---

169. Three days later, on the evening of 12 March 1838, Woodruff met with Latter-day Saints at the home of Malatiah Luce to "lay before them the situation of the church in Kirtland." Woodruff wrote that they "had a good meeting & these things did not move the faith of the Saints." (Woodruff, Journal, 12 Mar. 1838.)

170. Woodruff wrote in his journal that on 21 March 1838, Ball left North Fox Island "to return to his friends in the city of Boston." Ball was originally from Boston or Cambridge and still had family there, though he had moved to the Kirtland area. Townsend was from Buxton, Maine, where he lived with his wife and children. By 21 March, Townsend had already left and would not return until 11 April. As Woodruff noted in his diary, "I am now left to labour again alone upon these Islands." (Woodruff, Journal, 21 Mar. and 11 Apr. 1838.)

171. See Jeremiah 30:7.

172. The letter Woodruff had just received from an Elder Robbins in Kirtland informed him that JS and Sidney Rigdon had departed Kirtland for Far West. (Woodruff, Journal, 8 Mar. 1838.)

173. The first two issues of the *Elders' Journal*, dated October and November 1837, were published in Kirtland, with JS as the editor. Following JS's departure from Kirtland in January 1838 and the destruction of the printing office shortly thereafter, publishing operations ceased. An 1831 revelation designated Missouri as "the land of Zion" and commanded that William W. Phelps move to Independence, Missouri, to be a printer for the church. A year later, Phelps and others established a printing operation and began publishing a newspaper, *The Evening and the Morning Star*. When a mob razed the Mormon print shop, the Mormons continued the *Star* in Kirtland. In 1834, the *Star* was replaced by the *Latter Day Saints' Messenger and Advocate*, which in turn was replaced in 1837 by the *Elders' Journal*. Because the print shop in Kirtland had burned down and JS, the editor of the *Elders' Journal*, was moving to Missouri, Woodruff proposed that the church once again establish a newspaper in "the land of Zion." (Crawley, *Descriptive Bibliography*, 1:32–34, 47–49, 72–74; Revelation, 20 July 1831, in *JSP*, D2:5–12 [D&C 57].)

174. Latter-day Saints considered the vast majority of white Americans to be "Gentiles," or non-Israelites. However, Woodruff, like other Latter-day Saints, considered himself a descendant of Israel through Israel's son Joseph and through Joseph's son Ephraim. Woodruff had received a patriarchal blessing that identified him as a descendant of Joseph and "of the Blood of Ephraim." Woodruff believed that

pray, through the toils that are to come, that our garments may be washed white in the blood of the Lamb![175] for it is through tribulation that we inherit the blessing and overcome.[176]

Could the Elders' Journal be continued, it would be great relief to the feelings of all the faithful; for while our enemies are publishing against us, even in Kirtland,[177] we should also know what God is doing for his Saints.

Brethren, we pray you to consider this last clause, not for our sake alone, but for the sake of all the faithful that are scattered abroad. We do not make these remarks because we have any lack of confidence in you,—*No*, God forbid, we believe you have done, and will do all that lies in your power for [p. 35] the salvation of Israel; and for one, I pray God to take away my life, sooner than to suffer me to turn my back upon the faithful part of the church of Latter Day Saints, and Joseph whom God hath chosen to lead his people. O my soul mourns over the corruptions of the hearts of men! O how man will stumble in dark places,[178] when he neglects prayer and departs from his God! O ye Saints of Zion, watch and pray,[179] and keep the Celestial law,[180] which is safe!

That you may know the feelings of the undersigners of this page, we say to you before God, that we are in full fellowship with Joseph Smith jr. and the first Presidency of the church, and with all who still adhere to, and receive

---

his mission was "to search out the Blood of Ephraim & gather him from these Islands." (Book of Mormon, 1830 ed., i; "Israel Will Be Gathered," *The Evening and the Morning Star*, June 1833, [5]; Revelation, Sept. 1830–B, in *JSP*, D1:185–186 [D&C 28:8–9, 14]; Woodruff, Journal, 15 Apr. and 5 Sept. 1837; see also Woodruff, Journal, 20 Aug. and 28 Sept. 1837.)

175. See Revelation 7:14; and Book of Mormon, 1830 ed., 27, 259, 321, 567 [1 Nephi 12:10–11; Alma 13:11; 34:36; Ether 13:10].

176. See Revelation, 1 Aug. 1831, in *JSP*, D2:14 [D&C 58:4]; and Revelation, 24 Feb. 1834, in *JSP*, D3:460 [D&C 103:12–13].

177. In 1837 Warren Cowdery, who edited the *LDS Messenger and Advocate* in Kirtland, used the paper to critique the officers of the Kirtland Safety Society (including JS and Sidney Rigdon) for their mismanagement of the failed financial institution. In the month before Woodruff wrote this letter, Warren Parrish attacked JS and the church in one of the newspapers in nearby Painesville, Ohio. (Editorial, *LDS Messenger and Advocate*, July 1837, 3:535–541; Warren Parrish, Kirtland, OH, 5 Feb. 1838, Letter to the Editor, *Painesville [OH] Republican*, 15 Feb. 1838, [3].)

178. See Jeremiah 13:16.

179. See Matthew 26:41; and Mark 13:33.

180. According to a revelation JS dictated in 1834, "Zion cannot be built up unless it is by the principoles of the law of the Celestial kingdom." By "Celestial law," Woodruff probably meant the "Laws of the Church" that had been revealed in 1831, including the consecration of property. The Saints in and around Independence, Jackson County, Missouri, had attempted to live by this law of consecration prior to being driven out of their "centre place" in Jackson County. Now, after purchasing several tracts of land in Caldwell County, church leaders there were contemplating how to live the law of consecration again. (Revelation, 22 June 1834, in *JSP*, D4:73 [D&C 105:5]; Revelation, 9 Feb. 1831, in *JSP*, D1:251–252 [D&C 42:30–39]; Cook, *Joseph Smith and the Law of Consecration*, 29–39; Revelation, 20 July 1831, in *JSP*, D2:5–12 [D&C 57]; Minute Book 2, 6–7 and 23 Dec. 1837; see also 24n108 herein.)

their teachings and instructions; and we say, in the name of Jesus Christ, that we will uphold such by our prayers, faith, and influence,[181] at the risk of our fortunes, lives, and worldly honor.[182] "For life is but a name, when virtue and truth is gone."

We further believe, that judgment awaits the world speedily, Kirtland not excepted,[183] and we do believe that those who have dissented from the body of the church, will have cause to lament for their folly. We ask in the name of reason and revelation, who has power to take from Joseph, the keys delivered to him by the God of Abraham, Isaac, and Jacob, and deprive him of the work that God has said he should perform? We answer, none but God alone.[184] We believe the book of Mormon and Doctrine and Covenants, speaks too loud upon the subject,[185] to fall unfulfilled and to be made void, by those who have neglected prayer, and departed from the living God,[186] and sought to take honor unto themselves.[187] O ye Saints of God in Zion! we entreat you to uphold Joseph by prayer, faith, brotherly love, and charity:[188] for we testify, in the Spirit of God, that he will be brought off conquerer, and his enemies put to shame.[189]

Do you remember his toils and labors for your salvation? Nothing but a God has supported him to the present day. His perils are great, and the great-

---

181. See Instruction on Priesthood, between ca. 1 Mar. and ca. 4 May 1835, in *JSP*, D4:314 [D&C 107:22].

182. See the closing line of the United States Declaration of Independence.

183. Several JS revelations predicted millenarian judgment upon the world. One revelation, dictated in 1831, includes the Lord's intention to "retain a strong hold in the Land of Kirtland, for the space of five years in the which I will not overthrow the wicked, that thereby I may save some." Though Kirtland had been singled out as a stronghold, it was only temporarily so. (Revelation, 11 Sept. 1831, in *JSP*, D2:65 [D&C 64:21]; see also Revelation, ca. 7 Mar. 1831, in *JSP*, D1:274–280 [D&C 45].)

184. In an early revelation, JS was "chosen to do the work of the Lord." JS's revelations and writings indicated that the "keys" he had received allowed him to unlock the mysteries of heaven and divine authority. A recent revelation declared that "the keys which I have given him . . . shall not be taken from him untill I come." (Revelation, July 1828, in *JSP*, D1:8 [D&C 3:9–10]; Revelation, 23 July 1837, in *JSP*, D5:416 [D&C 112:15]; see also Matthew 16:19; Revelation, 30 Oct. 1831, in *JSP*, D2:93 [D&C 65:2]; Revelation, 15 Mar. 1832, in *JSP*, D2:208 [D&C 81:2]; and JS History, ca. Summer 1832, 1, in *JSP*, H1:10.)

185. The Book of Mormon includes prophecies of a latter-day prophet named Joseph, who would be "like unto Moses" and help restore the house of Israel in preparation for the second coming of Jesus Christ. Revelations in the Doctrine and Covenants affirm JS's divine calling. (Book of Mormon, 1830 ed., 66–68, 500 [2 Nephi 3:6–25; 3 Nephi 21:10–11]; see also Articles and Covenants, ca. Apr. 1830, in *JSP*, D1:121 [D&C 20:5–11].)

186. See Hebrews 3:12; and Articles and Covenants, ca. Apr. 1830, in *JSP*, D1:122 [D&C 20:32].

187. Warren Parrish and others in Kirtland had attempted to depose JS and either replace him with David Whitmer or lead the church themselves. (Historian's Office, Brigham Young History Drafts, 14; Backman, *Heavens Resound,* 327–329.)

188. See Revelation, Feb. 1831–A, in *JSP*, D1:258 [D&C 43:12]; and Instruction on Priesthood, between ca. 1 Mar. and ca. 4 May 1835, in *JSP*, D4:314 [D&C 107:22].

189. See Psalm 44:7.

est are among false brethren;[190] and we do entreat the Saints in Zion not to add to his wounds, by following the example of many in Kirtland.— Bear with us, ye Saints of God, while we exhort you to keep the Celestial law of God, while in the land of Zion. Be humble, be watchful, be prayerful.[191] Beware of pride, lest you fall like others.[192] We do not make these remarks for compliment sake, we feel what we say. Kirtland is and will be scourged, to fulfill revelation and prophecy;[193] it is all right, the hand of God is in it. God's work will not stop. He will work for, and with his Saints. God will redeem Jacob.[194] God will build up Zion.[195] The Lord will establish Jerusalem. And O ye Judges in Zion![196] that God may bestow wisdom and salvation upon you, is the prayer of

WILFORD WOODRUFF,
JAMES TOWNSEND, &
JOSEPH BALL.

———— ⌀ ————

Minutes, 15 March 1838

Source Note

Zion high council and bishopric, Minutes, Far West, Caldwell Co., MO, 15 Mar. 1838. Featured version copied [between 1 Oct. 1842 and 14 Sept. 1843] in Minute Book 2, pp. 108–109; handwriting of Hosea Stout; CHL. For more information on Minute Book 2, see Source Notes for Multiple-Entry Documents, p. 569 herein.

Historical Introduction

On 15 March 1838, JS met with the Zion high council and bishopric. Several developments had occurred since November 1837, when they had last met together. Most significantly, the rift between the presidency of the church in Missouri and the rest of the church

---

190. See 2 Corinthians 11:26.

191. See Book of Mormon, 1830 ed., 321, 576 [Alma 34:39; Moroni 6:4].

192. See Revelation, 2 Jan. 1831, in *JSP*, D1:233 [D&C 38:39].

193. The letter that Woodruff received the day before from Elder Robbins reported that JS and Rigdon had left Kirtland for Far West and that, as Woodruff wrote in his journal, "the faithful are to follow them for Kirtland will be scorged." Woodruff added: "Often have I herd Joseph Prophecy of these things for a year past." (Woodruff, Journal, 8 Mar. 1838.)

194. See Isaiah 44:23; Jeremiah 31:11; and Minutes and Prayer of Dedication, 27 Mar. 1836, in *JSP*, D5:205 [D&C 109:62].

195. See Psalm 102:16.

196. JS's revelations explained that Edward Partridge, the bishop of Zion, was "a Judge in Israel" and a "common judge," while the president of the high priesthood was a supreme church judge. In addressing this 3 March letter to Partridge, JS, and his counselors in the First Presidency, Woodruff was addressing the chief judges in Zion. (Revelation, 1 Aug. 1831, in *JSP*, D2:15 [D&C 58:17–18]; Revelation, 11 Nov. 1831–B, in *JSP*, D2:132–136 [D&C 107 (partial)].)

Ebenezer Robinson and Hosea Stout. The minutes for the 3 March 1838 meeting of the Zion high council and bishopric and the minutes for several subsequent meetings were taken by high council clerk
Ebenezer Robinson (left, photographed circa 1880s). Years later, in Nauvoo, Illinois, Robinson's loose-leaf
minutes were recorded in an official minute book by Hosea Stout (right, circa 1860). (Robinson image
courtesy Community of Christ Library-Archives, Independence, MO. Stout image: Church History
Library, Salt Lake City.)

leaders there had widened. By early February 1838, the presidency had been removed from
office and replaced by apostles Thomas B. Marsh and David W. Patten.[197] On 10 March, former presidency members William W. Phelps and John Whitmer were excommunicated.[198]
Then, on 14 March JS arrived in Far West, where he intended to take up residence.[199] After
fleeing Kirtland amid dissent and turmoil, he was determined to root dissent out of the
church. The day after his arrival, JS met in council with Missouri church leaders to address
matters relevant to the problem of dissent. In the first session of the meeting, JS reviewed the
minutes of previous council meetings. In the second session, the council members considered
the conduct of John Corrill, who was the bishop's agent and "keeper of the Lord's store
House."[200] The clerk for the meeting, Ebenezer Robinson, produced a brief overview of the
proceedings. His original minutes are apparently not extant; the featured version was recorded in Minute Book 2 by Hosea Stout in Nauvoo in 1842 or 1843.[201]

---

197. Letter from Thomas B. Marsh, 15 Feb. 1838, pp. 18–23 herein.
198. Minute Book 2, 10 Mar. 1838.
199. JS, Journal, Mar.–Sept. 1838, p. 16, in *JSP,* J1:237.
200. Minute Book 2, 22 May 1837; Minutes, 7 Nov. 1837, in *JSP,* D5:471.
201. Nauvoo High Council Minutes, 1 Oct. 1842.

Document Transcript

The High Council of Zion, together with the Bishoprick[202] met in Far West,[203] on ~~Saturday~~ Thursday March the 15th 1838, agreeable to appointment[204] and was organized as follows. President Joseph Smith jr took the charge of the Council[205]

Simeon Carter	No 1	Jared Carter	No 2[206]
Brigham Young[207]	" 3	Thomas Grover	" 4
Levi Jackman	" 5	Thomas Gates	" 6
Stephen Winchester[208]	" 7	Moses Martin[209]	" 8
George M. Hinkle	" 9	George W. Harris[210]	" 10
Elias Higbee	" 11	John Murdock	" 12

The Council opened by singing "This earth was once a garden place &c."[211] and prayer by Prest Joseph Smith jr.

The minutes of some previous Councils were read by the Clerk

First, The minutes of a Council held on Saturday the 24th of February 1838,[212] when it was voted— First

---

202. The Zion bishopric often met with the Zion high council. The high council had recently invited the bishopric to meet with the council to help resolve problems with presidency members William W. Phelps and John Whitmer, and the bishopric continued to meet with the council in subsequent gatherings. (Minute Book 2, 3 and 5–7 Apr. 1837; see also Minute Book 2, 11 June 1837–17 Mar. 1838.)

203. The high council and bishopric may have met in a schoolhouse, as they had on some occasions in 1837 and as they did on 24 February and 17 March 1838. (Minute Book 2, 29 July and 5 Aug. 1837; 24 Feb. and 17 Mar. 1838; see also JS, Journal, 6 Aug. 1838, in *JSP*, J1:297–298.)

204. The council presumably arranged this meeting on 10 March 1838, during the previous council meeting. (Minute Book 2, 10 Mar. 1838.)

205. A month earlier, Thomas B. Marsh, who was the president of the Quorum of the Twelve Apostles, and David W. Patten, who was the next most-senior apostle, had replaced the recently removed Zion presidency as temporary presidents. Marsh and Patten had expected to preside over the church in Zion until JS moved there. (Letter from Thomas B. Marsh, 15 Feb. 1838, p. 23 herein; JS, Journal, Mar.–Sept. 1838, p. 16, in *JSP*, J1:237.)

206. Carter was apparently substituting for Elisha Groves, who had moved from Far West; Carter soon replaced Groves permanently. (Minutes, 7–8 Apr. 1838, p. 73 herein.)

207. Young, a senior member of the Quorum of the Twelve Apostles, was apparently substituting for Calvin Beebe, who had moved from Far West. (Minute Book 2, 23 Dec. 1837; Minutes, 24 Mar. 1838, p. 47 herein; Minutes, 7–8 Apr. 1838, p. 73 herein.)

208. Winchester was substituting for George Morey. (See Minute Book 2, 10 and 17 Mar. 1838.)

209. Martin was substituting for Newel Knight. Martin had spoken strongly against the former members of the Zion presidency in their February trial. (Letter from Thomas B. Marsh, 15 Feb. 1838, p. 22 herein; see also Minute Book 2, 10 and 17 Mar. 1838.)

210. Harris was apparently substituting for Lyman Wight, who had moved from Far West; Harris soon replaced Wight permanently. (Minutes, 7–8 Apr. 1838, p. 73 herein.)

211. Hymn 23, *Collection of Sacred Hymns*, 29–30.

212. During the council meeting held on 24 February 1838, those present passed resolutions to regulate "the several Branches with in the bounds of this Stake." These measures were apparently designed

That the 6th article of the said minutes be null & void & also, that a new article be put in the place of it (which was done)—[213]

President Joseph Smith j[r] gave a history of the ordination of David Whitmer, which took place in July 1834, to be a leader, or a prophet to this Church, which (ordination) was on conditions that he (J. Smith jr) did not live to God himself.[214]

President J. Smith jr approved of the proceedings of the High Council, after hearing the minutes of the former Councils.[215]

The Council ajourned for one hour.

7-o'clock P.M. The Council and Bishoprick convened agreeably to adjournment and was [p. 108] organized, Joseph Smith jr presiding, when it was opened by prayer by John Murdock,[216] after which B[r] John Carrill [Corrill] made some

---

to stop the former members of the Zion presidency and those who sympathized with them from taking charge of any of the settlements around Far West. (Minute Book 2, 24 Feb. 1838.)

213. Article 6 recommended that all high priests, elders, and priests in the settlements around Far West "take the lead of all meetings" in their settlements. This article was replaced by the third resolution, which stated that high priests, elders, and priests were not to take the lead of meetings without the "invitation or consent of the Presiding officer of that branch," who was the branch-appointed teacher. The third resolution further stipulated that the presiding teacher had authority to object to any church officer "who may come among them, to officiate, who is not in good standing or a friend to the true cause of Christ" and that the presiding teacher should report to the high council anyone who was "unruly" or teaching "corrupt doctrine" in the settlement. (Far West Stake High Council Minutes, 24 Feb. 1838; Minute Book 2, 24 Feb. 1838.)

214. In February 1831, JS dictated a revelation for church members regarding his authority: "This ye shall know asshuredly that there is none other appointed unto you to receive commandments & Revelations untill he be taken if he abide in me. but Verily Verily I say unto you that none else shall be appointed unto this gift except it be through him for if it be taken from him he shall not have power except to appoint another in his stead."[a] JS ordained Whitmer the president of the church in Zion in 1834. Whitmer and others later recounted that JS had also ordained Whitmer as JS's successor,[b] and some of the dissidents in Kirtland sought to replace JS with Whitmer as church president. The minutes of the 10 March 1838 high council meeting, which JS was probably reviewing in this 15 March meeting, included a letter from Whitmer and his former counselors, which they signed as the Zion presidency, thus rejecting the decision of the 5–9 February general assembly that removed them from office. Furthermore, the letter rejected as illegal the actions planned for the 10 March high council meeting, including the excommunication of Phelps and John Whitmer.[c] (a. Revelation, Feb. 1831–A, in *JSP*, D1:258 [D&C 43:3–4]. b. Minutes and Discourse, ca. 7 July 1834, in *JSP*, D4:93; Whitmer, *Address to All Believers in Christ*, 55; [William E. McLellin], Editorial, *Ensign of Liberty*, Mar. 1847, 5–6; William E. McLellin, Kirtland, OH, to David Whitmer, 2 Dec. 1846, in *Ensign of Liberty*, Apr. 1847, 18–19; "The Successor of Joseph, the Seer," *Ensign of Liberty*, Dec. 1847, 43–44; see also Quinn, *Origins of Power*, 187–189. c. Historian's Office, Brigham Young History Drafts, 14; Minute Book 2, 10 Mar. 1838; Letter from Thomas B. Marsh, 15 Feb. 1838, pp. 18–22 herein.)

215. In addition to the minutes of the 24 February high council meeting, JS apparently reviewed the minutes of the 10 March 1838 meeting, in which William W. Phelps and John Whitmer were excommunicated.

216. Council meetings were often begun with a prayer by the moderator or by a presiding authority. As the oldest member of the Zion high council, Murdock was designated its president in 1836, although the Zion presidency presided over high councils when present, just as the church presidency had presided over Kirtland high council meetings when present. (See 23n104 herein; Minutes, 7 Nov. 1837, in *JSP*,

remarks respecting his former conduct, by way of confession, but not to the satisfaction of the Council, after which Thomas B. Marsh made a few remarks, followed by George M. Hinkle and others, when Bʳ Carrill made perfect satisfaction.²¹⁷

The Council adjourned untill tomorrow at 1 o'clock. Benediction by President Joseph Smith jr²¹⁸

Ebenezer Robinson Clk²¹⁹

———— ☙ ————

Motto, circa 16 or 17 March 1838

Source Note

JS and others, "Motto of the Church of Christ of <u>Latterday</u> <u>Saints</u>," [Far West, Caldwell Co., MO], [ca. 16 or 17 Mar. 1838]. Featured version copied with signatures of Thomas B. Marsh, David W. Patten, Brigham Young, Samuel Smith, George M. Hinkle, and John Corrill, [28 or 29 Mar. 1838], in JS, Journal, Mar.–Sept. 1838, pp. 16–17; signature of George W. Robinson added [28 or 29 Mar. 1838]; handwriting of George W. Robinson; CHL. Includes use marks. For more information on JS, Journal, Mar.–Sept. 1838, see Source Notes for Multiple-Entry Documents, p. 564 herein.

Historical Introduction

Within a few days of arriving at Far West, Missouri, JS composed a "Motto of the Church of Christ of <u>Latterday</u> <u>Saints</u>." Regarding the motto's creation, JS later related to his

---

D5:469; Minutes, 10 Nov. 1837, in *JSP,* D5:475; Minute Book 2, 6–7 Dec. 1837; and Letter from Thomas B. Marsh, 15 Feb. 1838, pp. 18–22 herein.)

217. Marsh took the lead in the 5 February trial to remove the Zion presidency from office. Hinkle and several other members of the high council spoke against the Zion presidency during the meeting. Some, like Edward Partridge, "spake against the proceedings of the meeting, as being hasty and illegal," but only Corrill "spake against the High Council." In a letter that Marsh sent to JS with the minutes of the 5–9 and 10 February meetings, he wrote, "We believe that brother Corrill intends to be [united] with you and us; although he was not with us in the meetings." (Letter from Thomas B. Marsh, 15 Feb. 1838, pp. 20, 21, 24 herein.)

218. The council apparently did not reconvene until 17 March 1838, and the minutes of that meeting do not mention JS attending. (Minute Book 2, 17 Mar. 1838.)

219. On 6 December 1837, Oliver Cowdery was appointed standing clerk of the high council, although he only recorded minutes for the meeting held the following day. Soon thereafter, Cowdery fell severely ill and remained so for several weeks, during which time John Whitmer served as clerk for a December meeting. After the members of the Zion presidency were removed from office and excommunicated, the deposed presidency sent a letter protesting their removal and Cowdery attested the letter as clerk of the high council. He was never officially removed from his position as high council clerk, but he did not function as such thereafter. Presumably for this reason, Robinson acted as clerk for this 15 March meeting as well as for council meetings earlier that month. Three weeks later, Robinson was officially appointed as the clerk of the high council. (Minute Book 2, 6–7 and 23 Dec. 1837; 20 Jan. 1838; 3 and 10 Mar. 1838; Letter from Oliver Cowdery, 21 Jan. 1838, in *JSP,* D5:504; Minutes, 6 Apr. 1838, p. 69 herein.)

scribe, George W. Robinson, that he arrived in Far West on 14 March 1838, that his younger brother Samuel arrived two or three days later—which would have been 16 or 17 March— and that "shortly after his [Samuel Smith's] arrival while walking with him & cirtain other bretheren the following sentements occured to my mind."[220] The motto was apparently written down during or soon after their walk and then signed by JS and the other men while they were still with him.

The date the original document was produced is uncertain, though it was most likely sometime between 16 and 29 March 1838. JS enclosed a copy of the motto with his 29 March letter to the presidency of the church in Kirtland, Ohio. In that letter, JS reported that Robinson had arrived the previous day and that the letter included "the folowing motto of the Church of Jesus Christ of Latter day Saints Recorded on Pages 16 & 17 of J Smith Jr Scriptory Record Book A."[221] The motto was indeed inscribed in the Scriptory Book on those pages and is in Robinson's handwriting, indicating that Robinson copied the motto into the Scriptory Book on 28 or 29 March and then the motto was copied from the Scriptory Book into the letter to the Kirtland presidency, perhaps by Robinson. If the motto had been composed within a few days of Robinson's arrival, he or JS might have dated the document. Instead, the copy of the motto in the Scriptory Book is introduced with a retrospective narrative, suggesting that the motto was composed closer to the arrival of Samuel Smith, around 16 or 17 March. Robinson's signature appears at the end of the motto in the Scriptory Book, to the side of the other signatures, suggesting that he added his signature to the others as he was transcribing the original motto into the Scriptory Book.

The motto is a patriotic declaration extolling republican virtues and condemning political vices. Following months of persecution, the threat of violence, and legal wrangling in Ohio, JS no doubt hoped that he, as well as the Latter-day Saints collectively, might enjoy the civil, political, and religious rights articulated in the Constitution of the United States. Such desires are reflected in the motto. The motto affirms JS's commitment to God, to principles of freedom and justice, to the Constitution, and to all "good and wholesome Law's." The motto also decries various forms of tyranny, including vexatious lawsuits.

Document Transcript

Motto of the Church of Christ of <u>Latterday</u> <u>Saints</u>.
The Constitution of our country formed by the Fathers of Liberty.
Peace and good order in society Love to God and good will to man.[222]
All good and wholesome Law's; And virtue and truth above all things
And Aristarchy[223] live forever!!!

---

220. JS, Journal, Mar.–Sept. 1838, pp. 15–16, in *JSP,* J1:236–237.

221. Letter to the Presidency in Kirtland, 29 Mar. 1838, p. 60 herein.

222. See Luke 2:14.

223. Webster's 1828 dictionary defines *aristarchy* as "a body of good men in power, or government by excellent men." ("Aristarchy," in *American Dictionary.*)

But Wo to tyrants, Mobs, Aristocracy, Anarchy and Toryism:²²⁴ And all those who invent or seek out unrighteous and vexatious lawsuits under the pretext or color of law or office, either religious or political.²²⁵

Exalt the standard of Democracy! Down [p. 16] with that of Priestcraft, and let all the people say Amen! that the blood of our Fathers may not cry from the ground against us.²²⁶

Sacred is the Memory of that Blood which baught for us our liberty.

Signed   Joseph Smith Jr.
Geo. W. Robinson²²⁷   Thomas B. Marsh
                                                              D[avid] W. Patten
                                                              Brigham Youngs [Young]
                                                              Samuel H. Smith
                                                              George M. Hinkle
                                                              John Corrill.—²²⁸

---

224. JS's sentiments are best understood in light of the brutal expulsion of the Latter-day Saints from Jackson County, Missouri, in 1833 and the internal and external conflicts at Kirtland. After JS and Sidney Rigdon were attacked by a mob in Hiram, Ohio, in 1832, they and other Saints in northeastern Ohio were confronted with numerous threats and some instances of mobbing and other violence.ᵃ Wording in the motto was echoed in JS's letter of 29 March 1838, identifying JS's former scribe Warren Parrish and other Kirtland dissenters, many of whom had been excommunicated, as "Aristocrats or Anarchys."ᵇ Parrish's group had held meetings to renounce JS and his teachings, and for months they had attempted to control meetings in the House of the Lord in Kirtland, even resorting to violence.ᶜ Use of *Tory* or *Toryism* in this context refers to what might be called "resident enemy sympathizers."ᵈ Sampson Avard later testified that in October 1838, during the Mormon conflict in Missouri, JS stated that Saints in Caldwell County who "did not take arms in defence of the Mormons of Davi[es]s should be considered as tories, and should take their exit from the county."ᵉ (a. Parkin, "Conflict at Kirtland," 248–263; Adams, "Grandison Newell's Obsession," 170–172, 177–180. b. See Letter to the Presidency in Kirtland, 29 Mar. 1838, p. 58 herein. c. Parkin, "Conflict at Kirtland," 314–317. d. "Tory," and "Toryism," in *American Dictionary*. e. Sampson Avard, Testimony, Richmond, MO, Nov. 1838, p. [5], State of Missouri v. JS et al. for Treason and Other Crimes [Mo. 5th Jud. Cir. 1838], in State of Missouri, "Evidence.")

225. Eber D. Howe, editor of the *Painesville (OH) Telegraph,* later recounted, "Many of our citizens thought it advisable to take all the legal means within their reach to counteract the progress of so dangerous an enemy in their midst, and many law suits ensued." A campaign of legal harassment against JS had been waged under the direction of Grandison Newell, a Mentor, Ohio, businessman. Ohio had a law intended "to prevent frivolous and vexatious suits," which applied in cases such as "malicious prosecutions" for which the damages were judged to be less than five dollars. (Howe, *Autobiography and Recollections,* 45; Petition to Arial Hanson, 7 Nov. 1836, in *JSP,* D5:306–312; Walker, "Kirtland Safety Society," 32–148; Backman, *Heavens Resound,* 321–323; An Act to Prevent Frivolous and Vexatious Suits [19 Dec. 1821], *Acts of a General Nature* [1821–1822], chap. 2; for the impact of Newell's actions on JS, see Letter to the Presidency in Kirtland, 29 Mar. 1838, pp. 56–61 herein.)

226. See Genesis 4:10–11; and Book of Mormon, 1830 ed., 113, 473 [2 Nephi 28:10; 3 Nephi 9:11].

227. Robinson was appointed general church recorder and clerk in Kirtland in September 1837 and again in Missouri on 6 April 1838. (Minutes, 17 Sept. 1837–A, in *JSP,* D5:443; Minutes, 6 Apr. 1838, p. 69 herein.)

228. Marsh, Patten, and Young were the three most senior members of the Quorum of the Twelve Apostles. After the Zion presidency was deposed in February 1838, Marsh and Patten were appointed

Minutes, 24 March 1838

Source Note

Zion high council, Minutes, Far West, Caldwell Co., MO, 24 Mar. 1838. Featured version cop-
ied [between 1 Oct. 1842 and 14 Sept. 1843] in Minute Book 2, pp. 110–114; handwriting of Hosea
Stout; CHL. For more information on Minute Book 2, see Source Notes for Multiple-Entry Documents,
p. 569 herein.

Historical Introduction

On 24 March 1838, the Zion high council in Far West, Missouri, met twice to conduct business. First, the council convened to address a charge that James W. Newberry
leveled against John Murdock for "unchristian-like conduct, in speaking reproachfully
of youngsters." Newberry was a twenty-year-old student at the school where Murdock
served as schoolmaster.[229] Murdock was also a member of the high council.[230] The dispute
arose after Murdock accused his students of misbehaving, and Newberry disapproved
of how Murdock had dealt with him. The aggrieved parties met with a council of elders, and one witness later explained in the high council meeting that Newberry and
Murdock had aired their grievances and come to a resolution. However, Newberry apparently remained upset and appealed his case to the high council. Because Murdock
was the defendant, his council duties were fulfilled by a substitute. The council deemed
this a "difficult case" and followed established procedures to appoint six counselors for
the case—three counselors to represent Newberry and three to represent Murdock.[231]
After hearing testimony from several witnesses, the high council decided that Newberry
had mistreated Murdock and that Murdock was not at fault. After a one-hour adjournment, the high council reconvened and decided that counselors who could not attend
meetings would resign their seats to those who could attend. As the clerk for the meeting, Ebenezer Robinson kept the minutes, which were later copied into Minute Book 2
by Hosea Stout.

Document Transcript

The High Council of Zion met pursuant to adjournment, Saturday March
24th 1838.[232]

---

presidents pro tempore. Young, who arrived in Missouri at or about the same time as JS, was appointed
to the new Zion presidency on 6 April 1838. JS's brother Samuel Smith, who had been a member of
the Kirtland high council, was with JS when JS conceived the motto. Hinkle and Corrill were
Missouri church officials. (Letter from Thomas B. Marsh, 15 Feb. 1838, p. 23 herein; Minutes, 6 Apr.
1838, p. 70 herein.)

229. Obituary for James Newberry, *Saints' Herald,* 20 Mar. 1895, 192.

230. Minutes, 3 July 1834, in *JSP,* D4:90; Minutes, 7 Nov. 1837, in *JSP,* D5:471.

231. Revised Minutes, 18–19 Feb. 1834, in *JSP,* D3:442 [D&C 102:13–14].

232. In the high council's previous meeting, the council planned to meet on 24 March at "9 o'clock."
(Minute Book 2, 17 Mar. 1838.)

Council ws organized as follows;

Joseph Smith jr. David W. Patten and Thos B. Marsh Presidents

Simeon Carter	no 1	Jared Carter	no 2
Calvin Beebee [Beebe]	" 3	Tho⁵ Grover	" 4
Levi Jackman	" 5	Solomon Hancock	" 6
George Morey	" 7	Newel Knight	" 8
George M. Hinkle	" 9	George W. Harris	" 10
Elias Higbee	" 11	Isaac Higbee	" 12²³³

The Council was opened by prayer by Presᵗ David W. Patten.

A Charge was prefered against John Murdock for unchristian-like conduct, in speaking reproachfully of youngsters, by James Newberry.

After a short deliberation it was considered a most difficult case, therefore Six Councellors were appointed to speak on the case, viz: George M. Hinkle, Elias Higbee and Simeon Carter, on the part of the Church and George W. Harris, Isaac Higbee, and Jared Carter on the part of the accused.

Jacob Gates testifies that Br Murdock was at his house, the subject of Spelling Schools, in the evening was introduced, which he disapproved of also, mentioned about a young man's undertaking to hug a girl in an evening meeting but mentioned no names, he disapproved of evening schools and meetings on account of the young people being light minded & tended to draw away their minds from their studdies²³⁴ [p. 110]

Sister Gates testifies that Bʳ Murdock was at her house and disapproved of evening schools &c she concurs with the testimony of her husband.

Bʳ Outhouse testifies that he labored with Bʳ Murdock together with Bʳ Newberry when Bʳ Murdock denied making a motion to show how James Newberry undertook to hug the girl.

He was ~~there~~ then ⟨cross⟩ examined ⟨and⟩ says Br. Murdock said in meeting that in making the motion to show how J. W. Newberry undertook to hug

---

233. Higbee was standing in for John Murdock, the defendant. Murdock resumed his usual position as the twelfth council member when the council reconvened at 6:00 p.m. (See Minute Book 2, 7 July 1834; 1 Aug. 1837; and 23 Dec. 1837.)

234. "Spelling schools" were spelling competitions between neighborhoods or ad hoc teams and were usually held in the evening at a local or neighboring schoolhouse. Spelling schools were largely social events, which provided an opportunity for youth to meet. These events were sometimes criticized as opportunities for flirtation and were associated with activities that some pious Protestants considered questionable, such as dancing, marching games, and sleigh rides. ("'Spelling Down': Old Times Revived," *Cambridge [MA] Chronicle,* 6 July 1872, [1]; Tatum, "Please Send Stamps," 100n47; Bohn, "Early Wisconsin School Teachers," 60; Loehr, "Moving Back from the Atlantic Seaboard," 95.)

the girl, he did not intend to hit Orlando Carter as hard as he did as he was the one to whom he made the motion.

Alonzo Herrick testifies that he was at school one day when the master & James Newberry got to disputing about hugging the girl, the boy denied undertaking to hug the girl & Mʳ Murdock made a motion to show how he done the thing when the boy said it was not so, he also says ⟨that⟩ he never heard Bʳ Murdock twit the boys of being with the girls, also, that he believes Bʳ Murdock used his best endeavors for the good of the school; also, saw one of the schollars shake his fist at the master; also, that he saw some verses in the hands of James W Newberry, Joseph Outhouse & Edward Prindall, which served to tantalize the master.

George P. Dydes testifies that the Elders were called together & Bʳ Murdock presented a case which was investigated, but he thought proper weight was not put upon the testimony

Edward Prindal testifies that he saw Bʳ Murdock make a motion to show how James Newberry undertook to hug the girl in meeting which James Newberry denied, saying he never done any such thing also that he heard the master say that he did not like to have spelling schools because there was too much [p. 111] going home with the girls also he shook his fist at the master because he thaught the master meddled with that which was none of his buisness in correcting them for going home with the girls, also, that he thinks James W. Newberry was not in the habit of running about more than common, also, that it was rumoured about by Bʳ Murdock one or two before being mentioned in school that some of the boys had hugged a girl in meeting. also, Bʳ Murdock said in a̶ the meeting of Elders that he had not taken the regular steps with James W. Newberry, and he was sorry that he had not.

A testimony was presented from Orlando Carter, in writing, which was read.

John Lowrie [Lowry] testifies he was at a meeting where Bʳ Murdock requested the Elders to take a seperate as he had a matter to have investigated, he made his statement to the Elders & in it he said that he had done wrong in speaking of the matter of James W. Newberry's hugging the girl in meeting before going to him and laboring, with him, for which he was sorry, also, testifies that he thought the young men did not treat Bʳ Murdock with that respect with which they ought.

Lyman Leonard ⟨testifies⟩ that he was at the meeting of the Elders before mentioned when Br Murdock and James W. Newberry laid before them their agrieveances and the matter was investigated. Br Murdock made confession, saying that he had done wrong in mentioning about the young man's attempting to hug the girl, before laboring with him. also, that a decision was had, and a settlement took place between the parties. also, that he did not approve of the treatment of the young men towards B^r Murdock and reproved them for it. also that the Court of Elders was called by mutual consent as far as he knew, and both made their statements.

Sister Leonard concurs with the testimony of her husband and that she was at the meeting in which [p. 112] the young man was accused of attempting to to hug the girl & she saw James Newberry wink and smile when the girl went to get water, which she did not like.

Elizabeth Legg testifies that she attended the school & she did not hear B^r Murdock twit the boys of going home with the girls, also, she saw the boys shake their fists at B^r Murdock when his back was turned, viz: James W. Newberry and Joseph Outhouse.

Simeon Carter testifies that he was pleased with the conduct of the young men while before him on account of their steadiness.[235]

James W. Newberry testifies that he did not have any hand in writing or composing the verses spoken of in Orlando Herrick's testimony.[236]

The Councellors made a few very appropriate remarks, all of whom thought the charge was not sustained, but rather the accuser was in the fault

Decided that the charge was not sustained, but B^r James W. Newberry was in the fault in treating B^r Murdock as he did.

The question was then put to the Council if they concur[r]ed with the decision if so to manifest it by saying aye. which was done unanimous.

Council adjourned one hour to meet at the Bishops office

Ebenezer Robinson Clk.

6 o'clock P.M. The council met pursuant to adjournment & was organized as follows;

Simeon Carter	nº 1	Elisha H. Groves	nº 2
Calvin Beebee	" 3	Thomas Grover	" 4
Levi Jackman	" 5	Solomon Hancock	" 6
George Morey	" 7	Newel Knight	" 8
G. M. Hinkle	" 9	George W. Harris	" 10
Elias Higbee	" 11	John Murdock	" 12

The Council opened by prayer by Solomon Hancock. [p. 113]

---

235. Simeon Carter was the father of Orlando Carter, who testified on behalf of Newberry. (Warr, History of the Carter Family, 39.)

236. Apparently a reference to Alonzo Herrick's testimony, given above.

The subject of absent Councillors was discussed when it was decided that those who can not attend the Councils, resign their seats and let others fill ~~their~~ them who will be able to attend punctually.[237]

Adjourned

Ebenezer Robinson Clk

———— ✌ ————

Questions and Answers, between circa 16 and circa 29 March 1838–A [D&C 113:1–6]

Source Note

"Quest. on Scripture," [Far West, Caldwell Co., MO], [between ca. 16 and ca. 29 Mar. 1838]. Featured version copied [ca. mid- or late Apr. 1838] in JS, Journal, Mar.–Sept. 1838, p. 17; handwriting of George W. Robinson; CHL. Includes use marks. For more information on JS, Journal, Mar.–Sept. 1838, see Source Notes for Multiple-Entry Documents, p. 564 herein.

Historical Introduction

Sometime in mid- or late March 1838, after JS arrived in Far West, Missouri, he apparently answered a series of questions regarding the prophecies in Isaiah chapters 11 and 52. The questions and answers were inscribed in JS's "Scriptory Book" by George Robinson. No authorship was attributed to the questions and answers, although some of the answers begin with "thus saith the Lord." JS's authorship is implied, in that some of the answers are couched in the language of revelation, similar to other revelations transcribed in the Scriptory Book.[238] Further, most of the documents transcribed in the book are explicitly JS documents.

When the questions and answers regarding the prophecies of Isaiah were copied into the multivolume manuscript history JS began in 1838, they were grouped under the heading "Questions on Scripture."[239] Following this format, the questions and answers were presented as a unified set when the history was later printed in the church's newspaper.[240] However, the five question-and-answer pairs were inscribed in the Scriptory Book under two headings: the first three pairs appear under the heading "Quest. on Scripture," while the remaining two appear under the heading "Questions by Elias Higby."[241] These headings are

---

237. In the quarterly conference held two weeks later, high council member John Murdock announced that "the seats of Elisha H. Groves, Calvin Bebee [Beebe], and Lyman Wight was vacant in consequence of their having moved away so far that they could not attend the council." (Minutes, 7–8 Apr. 1838, p. 73 herein.)

238. See Revelation, 11 Apr. 1838, pp. 81–82 herein [D&C 114]; and Revelation, 17 Apr. 1838, pp. 107–108 herein.

239. JS History, vol. B-1, 784–785.

240. "History of Joseph Smith," *Deseret News,* 5 Mar. 1853, [1]. This combined format was used again when Orson Pratt added the questions and answers to the 1876 edition of the Doctrine and Covenants. (Doctrine and Covenants 113, 1876 ed. [D&C 113].)

241. See Questions and Answers, between ca. 16 and ca. 29 Mar. 1838–B, pp. 54–56 herein [D&C 113:7–10].

comparable to the other headings in the Scriptory Book that were used to demarcate different document transcripts.[242] The first three questions, posed by an unidentified interlocutor, regard Isaiah chapter 11, while the other two questions, posed by Elias Higbee, concern Isaiah chapter 52. Additionally, whereas the first three questions were answered with "thus saith the Lord" responses, the other questions were not. These differences further suggest what seems to be indicated by the distinct headings: that the two sets of question-and-answer pairs were considered separate, albeit obviously related, texts.

The dating of these two texts is uncertain, but their location in the Scriptory Book suggests an approximate period of between 16 and 29 March 1838. The questions and answers follow a motto for the church, which JS composed at the earliest on 16 March, and are followed by several document transcripts that are arranged in roughly chronological order. These documents begin with two that JS produced in September 1837 in Kirtland, before he migrated to Far West.[243] This pair of Kirtland documents raises the possibility that some or all of the questions and answers also date back to the Kirtland period. However, the similarities in the format and the subject of the two sets of questions suggest that all of the questions were posed and answered in the same setting. Further, the fact that some of the questions were posed by Elias Higbee—who had been living in Caldwell County, Missouri, since 1836 and had been serving on the Zion high council in Far West[244]—indicates that the questions and answers date to the period after JS arrived in Far West on 14 March. Following the pair of Kirtland documents is JS's letter to the Kirtland presidency on 29 March 1838, strongly suggesting that the questions and answers were composed between 16 March and 29 March 1838.[245] As with the other documents inscribed in the Scriptory Book, Robinson probably transcribed the questions and answers from an earlier manuscript. If the questions and answers were composed following Robinson's arrival in Far West on 28 March, he could have dated the documents, which suggests they were composed earlier. While JS could have met with Higbee anytime between 16 and 29 March, the only known time they were together was during a meeting of the high council and bishopric on 24 March 1838, suggesting the possibility that the discussion took place after the meeting adjourned that evening.[246]

242. See JS, Journal, Mar.–Sept. 1838, pp. 16–32, CHL.

243. JS, Journal, Mar.–Sept. 1838, pp. 16–23, in *JSP*, J1:237–245; Motto, ca. 16 or 17 Mar. 1838, pp. 43–45 herein.

244. "Higbee, Elias," in Jenson, *LDS Biographical Encyclopedia,* 1:253; Minutes, 7 Nov. 1837, in *JSP*, D5:471.

245. When the questions and answers were transcribed into the manuscript history serially published as "History of Joseph Smith," they were placed between the church motto and a letter dated 29 March 1838. (JS History, vol. B-1, 784–785.)

246. Minutes, 24 Mar. 1838, pp. 46–47 herein. The minutes of the meeting do not include any of the questions. Two 1832 documents that follow a similar question-and-answer format appear to have been produced in more private settings with fewer people present. Another possibility is that this exchange took place while Higbee, Thomas B. Marsh, and John Corrill were escorting JS and his family on the final leg of their journey from Kirtland to Far West. (See Answers to Questions, between ca. 4 and ca. 20 Mar. 1832, in *JSP*, D2:208–213 [D&C 77]; Sample of Pure Language, between ca. 4 and ca. 20 Mar. 1832, in *JSP*, D2:213–215; and Letter to the Presidency in Kirtland, 29 Mar. 1838, pp. 57–58 herein.)

Isaiah chapter 11, the subject of the first set of questions, figures prominently in JS's revelations and writings. Within a few months of answering these questions, JS recounted in his manuscript history that when visited by the angel Moroni in 1823, Moroni "quoted the Eleventh Chapter of Isaiah saying that it was about to be fulfilled."[247] The Book of Mormon draws heavily on Isaiah's prophetic worldview and encourages readers to "search the prophecies of Isaiah."[248] Several times, the volume singles out the "great" writings of Isaiah from the writings of other Israelite prophets, and the volume quotes extensively from the book of Isaiah, including entire chapters.[249] For example, the Book of Mormon quotes Isaiah chapter 11 in its entirety and then quotes verses 4–9 again later on in the volume.[250] Furthermore, JS's subsequent revelations and writings repeat or allude to several verses in this chapter, applying them to the gathering of Israel in the last days.[251] Shortly before JS left Kirtland, a member of the First Quorum of the Seventy delivered a sermon there "on the gathering of the house of Israel," using Isaiah 11 as his text.[252]

Isaiah 11:1 contains the prophecy that a "rod" or a "branch" (a new shoot) would grow out of the "stem" (stump) or "roots" of Jesse, the father of the Israelite king David. The next four verses have traditionally been interpreted as further prophecy regarding what this David-like messianic figure would do for the children of Israel. However, the first two questions apparently assume that these verses describe the stem, or old stump, of Jesse rather than the rod or new branch growing out of the stem. The first question regards the identity of the stem of Jesse. Whereas the Christian exegetical tradition generally interprets the stem of Jesse as the Davidic dynasty, JS interpreted it as Jesus Christ.[253] In addition, whereas most Christians interpret the root of Jesse to be Christ, JS interpreted the root as a latter-day figure.[254] As evidenced in JS's earlier revelations regarding the Bible, including his revision, or "new translation," of the Bible, he considered himself a prophet similar to those in the Old Testament, with full authority to receive new revelation to interpret and clarify the writings of his

---

247. JS History, vol. A-1, 6, in *JSP*, H1:224 (Draft 2). Christian ministers and scholars generally interpreted the prophecies of Isaiah 11 as prophecies of Jesus Christ. While the Book of Mormon asserts that many of Isaiah's prophecies applied to the life and ministry of Jesus Christ, JS indicated Isaiah 11 was not yet fulfilled. (See, for example, Calvin, *Commentary on the Book of the Prophet Isaiah,* 1:371–389; Wesley, *Explanatory Notes upon the Old Testament,* 3:1978–1980; and Henry, *Exposition of the Old and New Testament,* 4:67–71.)

248. Book of Mormon, 1830 ed., 533 [Mormon 8:23].

249. See, for example, Book of Mormon, 1830 ed., 86–102 [2 Nephi chaps. 12–24].

250. Book of Mormon, 1830 ed., 98–99, 117–118 [2 Nephi chap. 21; 30:9–15].

251. Isaiah's prophecy in chapter 11, verse 11, of the gathering of Israel from many nations and from "the islands of the sea" is reflected in several JS writings.[a] Isaiah's prophecy in verse 12 of an ensign, or rallying flag, used to gather Israel is echoed in a September 1831 revelation.[b] His prophecy in verse 16 of a highway on which scattered Israel would return is alluded to in a 3 November 1831 revelation.[c] (*a.* See Revelation, 1 Nov. 1831–B, in *JSP*, D2:105 [D&C 1:1]; Revelation, 3 Nov. 1831, in *JSP*, D2:117 [D&C 133:8]; and Letter to Noah C. Saxton, 4 Jan. 1833, in *JSP*, D2:351. *b.* Revelation, 11 Sept. 1831, in *JSP*, D2:67 [D&C 64:42]. *c.* Revelation, 3 Nov. 1831, in *JSP*, D2:118 [D&C 133:27].)

252. Quorums of the Seventy, "Book of Records," 2 Jan. 1838, 38–39.

253. See, for example, Wesley, *Explanatory Notes upon the Old Testament,* 3:1978; and Henry, *Exposition of the Old and New Testament,* 4:67.

254. See Romans chaps. 8–12; Revelation 5:5; 22:16; and Henry, *Exposition of the Old and New Testament,* 4:69–70.

predecessors. The answers to the second and third questions, regarding the rod coming out of the stem of Jesse and the root of Jesse, suggest that JS or a similar latter-day figure would fulfill these prophecies. These answers came within the context of JS experiencing the fallout of apostasy in Kirtland and then engaging in a reassertion of his prophetic authority in the land of Zion.

Whereas the second set of questions was posed by Higbee, it is uncertain who posed the first set of questions. Although presumably not Higbee, it could have been another person present at the 24 March meeting, or it could have been JS, petitioning the Lord for revealed answers to his questions. It is also unknown who originally wrote down the questions and answers, though JS's revelations were usually written by someone else acting in the role of scribe.[255] Robinson probably had not yet arrived in Far West. Higbee, who served as a judge in Caldwell County and was soon called as a church historian, may have had some clerical duties. Although Robinson began the Scriptory Book in late March, with an account of JS's arrival in Far West and a copy of the motto, he apparently did not add anything further to the book until mid-April. Therefore, Robinson likely copied the questions and answers from a loose manuscript into the Scriptory Book, probably sometime in mid- or late April.

Document Transcript

Quest. on Scripture.

1st. Who is the stem of Jessee spoken of in the 1st. 2d. 3d. 4th. and 5th. verses of the 11th. Chap. of Isiah.

Ans. Verely thus saith the Lord It is Christ

Q. 2d. What is the Rod spoken of in the 1st. verse of the 11th. verse Chap. that shoud come of the stem of Jessee.

Ans. Behold thus saith ⟨the Lord⟩ it is a servant in the hands of Christ who is partly a decendant of Jessee as well as of Ephraim or of the house of Joseph,[256] on whome thare is Laid much power.[257]

---

255. "Revelations," *Ensign of Liberty,* Aug. 1849, 98–99; see also William E. McLellin, Independence, MO, to Joseph Smith III, [Plano, IL], July 1872, typescript, Letters and Documents Copied from Originals in the Office of the Church Historian, Reorganized Church, CHL; and Pratt, *Autobiography,* 65.

256. See JS's answer to the third question, regarding the "root of Jessee."

257. Isaiah's messianic prophecy of a rod to come out of the stem of Jesse explicates and immediately follows his prophecy that Judah's enemies would be cut down and that "Lebanon shall fall by a mighty one." JS's revelations and translations apparently offer further information regarding this "mighty one." The Book of Mormon, which is deeply rooted in the prophetic worldview of Isaiah, includes a prophecy by Lehi that his son Jacob's posterity would survive into the last days and accept the Book of Mormon. Lehi explained: "There shall raise up one, mighty among them, which shall do much good, both in word and in deed, being an instrument in the hands of God, with exceeding faith, to work mighty wonders, and do that thing which is great in the sight of God, unto the bringing to pass much restoration unto the House of Israel, and unto the seed of thy brethren." In 1832, in response to migration and settlement problems in Jackson County, Missouri, JS prophesied that, if needed, the Lord would "send on[e] mighty and strong" to "set in order the house of God and to arange by lot the inheritance of the saints." (Isaiah 10:34; Book of Mormon, 1830 ed., 68 [2 Nephi 3:24]; Letter to William W. Phelps, 27 Nov. 1832, in *JSP,* D2:319 [D&C 85:7].)

Qest 3.^{d.} What is the Root of Jessee spoken of in the 10th. verse of the 11th. Chap.

Ans. Behold thus saith the Lord; it is a decendant of Jessee as well as of Joseph[258] unto whom rightly belongs the Priesthood[259] and the kees of the Kingdom[260] for an ensign[261] and for the geathering of my people in the Last day.—[262] [p. 17]

--------- ∾ ---------

Questions and Answers, between circa 16 and circa 29 March 1838–B [D&C 113:7–10]

Source Note

"Questions by Elias Higby," [Far West, Caldwell Co., MO], [between ca. 16 and ca. 29 Mar. 1838]. Featured version copied [ca. mid- or late Apr. 1838] in JS, Journal, Mar.–Sept. 1838, p. 18; handwriting of George W. Robinson; CHL. Includes use marks. For more information on JS, Journal, Mar.–Sept. 1838, see Source Notes for Multiple-Entry Documents, p. 564 herein.

Historical Introduction

Sometime after JS arrived in Far West, Missouri, he apparently answered two sets of questions, one regarding Isaiah chapter 11 and the other, labeled "Questions by Elias Higby [Higbee]," relating to Isaiah chapter 52. The dating of these two sets of questions and answers is uncertain, but they were probably produced sometime between 16 and 29 March

---

258. In the tenth verse of chapter 11, Isaiah prophesies that the "root of Jesse" would "stand for an ensign of the people," while the eleventh and twelfth verses foretell that the Lord would set up "an ensign for the nations" and "assemble the outcasts of Israel." The thirteenth verse states that the enmity between Ephraim (the northern kingdom of Israel) and Judah (the southern kingdom) would be resolved. JS's answers to the second and third questions suggest that the "root of Jesse" spoken of in verse 10 would reunite Judah and the northern tribes in part by being a descendant of Joseph (through Ephraim) as well as of Judah (through Jesse).

259. In response to a question regarding another passage in Isaiah, JS explained that there is a hereditary right to the priesthood. (See Questions and Answers, between ca. 16 and ca. 29 Mar. 1838–B, pp. 54–56 herein [D&C 113:8].)

260. According to JS's revelations and writings, the "keys" he received allowed him to unlock the mysteries of heaven and divine authority. Mirroring language in Matthew 16:19, a revelation published in 1835 stated that the Lord conveyed the "keys of my kingdom" to JS and Oliver Cowdery by sending to them the New Testament apostles Peter, James, and John as heavenly messengers. JS's journal recounts a vision in 1836 in which Moses appeared to JS and Oliver Cowdery and delivered to them the "keys of the gathering of Israel from the four parts of the Eearth." In July 1837, JS dictated a revelation declaring that "the keys which I have given him [JS] . . . shall not be taken from him untill I come." (Revelation, ca. Aug. 1835, in *JSP*, D4:411 [D&C 27:12–13]; Visions, 3 Apr. 1836, in *JSP*, D5:228 [D&C 110:11]; Revelation, 23 July 1837, in *JSP*, D5:416 [D&C 112:15]; see also Revelation, 30 Oct. 1831, in *JSP*, D2:93 [D&C 65:2]; Revelation, 15 Mar. 1832, in *JSP*, D2:208 [D&C 81:2]; and JS History, ca. Summer 1832, 1, in *JSP*, H1:10.)

261. See Revelation, 11 Sept. 1831, in *JSP*, D2:67 [D&C 64:42].

262. Isaiah 11:10–16 contains a prophecy that the Israelites will be gathered to their homeland.

1838.[263] While JS could have met with Higbee, who was a member of the Zion high council, anytime during this period, the one time they were known to be together was during a meeting of the high council and bishopric on 24 March 1838, suggesting that Higbee may have posed his questions to JS after the meeting adjourned that evening.[264] The answers to the first set of questions, regarding Isaiah 11, begin with "thus saith the Lord." The revealed answers may have provoked Higbee to ask the questions about Isaiah 52:1–2, though the answers given to Higbee's questions do not include the same revelatory language. These verses regard the redemption of Zion and introduce Isaiah's suffering servant oracles, including the material in chapter 53, which is one of traditional Christianity's most important texts for Christianizing the Old Testament.[265] Isaiah 52:1–2 is quoted twice in the Book of Mormon,[266] and other passages in chapter 52 also appear in the book.[267] JS revelations also repeat or allude to verses in this chapter, using them to explain the gathering and reestablishment of the house of Israel in the latter days.[268]

Higbee posed two questions. The answers, presumably from JS, stated that those called of God in the last days would be given priesthood authority to gather scattered Israel home to Zion. These answers may have been considered as having special significance at this time because of JS's move to Missouri, the Saints' "Land of Zion."[269] Probably sometime in mid- or late April, George W. Robinson inscribed the questions and answers in the "Scriptory Book," probably from an earlier manuscript.[270]

Document Transcript

Questions by Elias Higby [Higbee]

1st. Q. What is ment by the command in Isiah 52d. chap 1st. verse which saith Put on thy strength O Zion and what people had I[sa]iah referance to

A. He had reference to those whome God should call in the last day's who should hold the power of Priesthood to bring again zion and the redemption of Israel.[271]

---

263. See Historical Introduction to Questions and Answers, between ca. 16 and ca. 29 Mar. 1838–A [D&C 113:1–6], pp. 50–53 herein.

264. Minutes, 24 Mar. 1838, pp. 46–47 herein.

265. See, for example, Calvin, *Commentary on the Book of the Prophet Isaiah*, 4:109–132; Wesley, *Explanatory Notes upon the Old Testament*, 3:2085–2088; and Henry, *Exposition of the Old and New Testament*, 4:241–248.

266. Book of Mormon, 1830 ed., 78, 498 [2 Nephi 8:24–25; 3 Nephi 20:36–37].

267. See Book of Mormon, 1830 ed., 31, 182, 187, 188, 215, 488, 498–499, 500, 501 [1 Nephi 13:37; Mosiah 12:21–24; 15:14–18, 29–31; 16:1; 27:37; 3 Nephi 16:18–20; 20:32, 34–35, 38–45; 21:8, 29].

268. See Revelation, 2 Jan. 1831, in *JSP*, D1:233 [D&C 38:42]; Revelation, 7 May 1831, in *JSP*, D1:303 [D&C 49:27]; Revelation, 3 Nov. 1831, in *JSP*, D2:116–117 [D&C 133:5]; and Revelation, 22–23 Sept. 1832, in *JSP*, D2:301–302 [D&C 84:98].

269. See Revelation, 20 July 1831, in *JSP*, D2:7, 12 [D&C 57:1–2, 14].

270. See Questions and Answers, between ca. 16 and ca. 29 Mar. 1838–A, pp. 50–54 herein [D&C 113:1–6].

271. JS asserted that the priesthood and church authority held by the ancient prophets and apostles had been lost in a great apostasy but had been restored to him and that the Church of the Latter Day

And to put on her strength is to put on the authority of the priesthood which she (zion) has a right to by lineage:[272] Also to return to that power which she had lost[273]

Ques. 2ᵈ· What are we to understand by zions loosing herself from the bands of her neck 2ᵈ· verse.

A. We are to understand that the scattered remnants are exorted to to return to the Lord from whence they have fal[l]en which if they do the promise of the Lord is that he will speak to them or give them revelation See 6ᵗʰ· 7ᵗʰ· and 8ᵗʰ· verses The bands of her neck are the curses of God upon her or the remnants of Israel in their scattered condition among the Gentiles.

———— ❧ ————

Letter to the Presidency in Kirtland, 29 March 1838

Source Note

JS, Letter, Far West, Caldwell Co., MO, to "the Presidency of the Church of Jesus Christ of Latter Day Saints in Kirtland," Kirtland Township, Geauga Co., OH, 29 Mar. 1838. Featured version copied [ca. mid- or late Apr. 1838] in JS, Journal, Mar.–Sept. 1838, pp. 23–26; handwriting of George W. Robinson; CHL. Includes use marks. For more information on JS, Journal, Mar.–Sept. 1838, see Source Notes for Multiple-Entry Documents, p. 564 herein.

Historical Introduction

About two weeks after JS's arrival in Far West, Missouri, he wrote the following letter to the presidency of the church in Kirtland, Ohio: William Marks, president, and John Smith and Reynolds Cahoon, assistant presidents.[274] In the letter, JS recounted the difficulties of the journey from Kirtland in the middle of winter, his safe arrival in Far West, and information regarding Rigdon and his family, who had stopped traveling for several days because of illness. JS and his family had pushed on, arriving in Far West on 14 March.

Saints was "the only true & living Church upon the face of the whole Earth," with a mission to gather and redeem the house of Israel. (JS History, ca. Summer 1832, 1–2, in *JSP*, H1:10–12; Revelation, 1 Nov. 1831–B, in *JSP*, D2:107 [D&C 1:30]; see also Revelation, 5 Jan. 1831, in *JSP*, D1:235–236 [D&C 39:11]; and Revelation, ca. Aug. 1835, in *JSP*, D4:410–412 [D&C 27:5–18].)

272. Some of JS's revelations and translations connect priesthood authority to lineal descent. (See Revelation, ca. June 1835, in *JSP*, D4:357–358 [D&C 68:14–21]; Revelation, 6 Dec. 1832, in *JSP*, D2:327 [D&C 86:8–10]; Instruction on Priesthood, between ca. 1 Mar. and ca. 4 May 1835, in *JSP*, D4:313, 318–319 [D&C 107:13–17, 69–76]; and "The Book of Abraham," *Times and Seasons*, 1 Mar. 1842, 3:704, 705 [Abraham 1:2, 27].)

273. JS's revelations and translations foretell the gathering of Israel and the establishment of Zion. (See, for example, Book of Mormon, 1830 ed., 499 [3 Nephi 21:1]; and Revelation, 24 Feb. 1834, in *JSP*, D3:460 [D&C 103:13].)

274. John Smith and Clarissa Lyman Smith, Kirtland, OH, to George A. Smith, Shinnston, VA, 1 Jan. 1838, George Albert Smith, Papers, CHL; Hepzibah Richards, Kirtland, OH, to Willard Richards, Bedford, England, 18–19 Jan. 1838, Willard Richards, Papers, CHL.

George W. Robinson, Rigdon's son-in-law, arrived two weeks later, on 28 March, with news that Rigdon would probably arrive soon.

JS's letter to the Kirtland presidency also reported that the problems with William W. Phelps and John Whitmer, former members of the Zion presidency, had been recently "a[d]justed" by apostles Thomas B. Marsh and David W. Patten in collaboration with the high council. JS conveyed expressions of friendship for those in Kirtland and relayed a vision he had seen of Marks, which JS interpreted as an indication that God would deliver Marks from his enemies. JS requested that the Saints migrating to Missouri bring seeds for vegetables, fruit trees, and hay and bring well-bred cattle and horses. With the letter, JS enclosed a copy of the "Motto of the Church of Christ of Latterday Saints," which he had composed for the church upon arriving in Far West.[275]

Although the original letter sent to the Kirtland presidency is apparently not extant, George W. Robinson made a copy of the letter in JS's "Scriptory Book." Robinson apparently made this transcript from a retained copy of the letter sometime in mid- or late April.[276]

Document Transcript

Far West March 29ᵗʰ A.D. 1838

To the ~~first~~ Presidency of the Church of Jesus Christ of Latter Day Saints in Kirtland

Dear & well beloved brotheren. Through the grace & mercy of our God, after a long & tedious journey of two months & one day,[277] I and my family arrived in th[e] City of Far West Having been met at Huntsville 120 Miles from this by brotheren with teams & money[278] to forward us on our Journey When within eight miles of the City of Far West We were met by an [p. 23]

---

275. Motto, ca. 16 or 17 Mar. 1838, pp. 44–45 herein.

276. The letter references the enclosure of the motto, stating that the motto was transcribed in the Scriptory Book. This indicates that the Scriptory Book, which begins in and is almost entirely in Robinson's handwriting, was started sometime between Robinson's arrival in Far West on 28 March and JS's composition of the letter on 29 March. Although Robinson began the book at this time, with an account of JS's arrival in Far West and a copy of the motto, he apparently did not add anything further to the book until the middle of April, at the time of the excommunications of Oliver Cowdery and David Whitmer. The title page of the Scriptory Book is dated 12 April 1838, the date of Cowdery's church trial, and editorial notes between the various documents that Robinson transcribed into the book explain how the events documented in the various transcripts led up to the excommunications of Cowdery and Whitmer. (JS, Journal, Mar.–Sept. 1838, pp. 15–32, in *JSP*, J1:236–257.)

277. JS's later history states that he and Rigdon left Kirtland on 12 January 1838 at "about 10 o'clock" at night and arrived "at 8 o clock of the morning of the 13th . . . in Norton Township, Medina County, Ohio." (JS History, vol. B-1, 780.)

278. After receiving word that JS and Rigdon were on their way, the Zion high council in Far West planned to send men with two wagons and $300 to meet the travelers and help them finish their journey. John Barnard met JS and his family at Huntsville, Missouri, and brought them in his carriage to his home in Caldwell County. (Minute Book 2, 24 Feb. 1838; Historian's Office, Brigham Young History Drafts, 17; JS, Journal, Mar.–Sept. 1838, p. 16, in *JSP*, J1:237.)

escort of bretheren from the city Who were T[homas] B. Marsh John Corril[l] Elias Higby [Higbee] & severel others of the faithfull of the West[279] Who received us with open armes and warm hearts and welcomed us to the bosom of their sosciety [society] On our arrival in the city we wire [were] greeted on every hand by the saints who bid us welcom; Welcome; to the land of their inheritance.[280] Dear bretheren you may be assured that so friendly a meeting & reception paid us Will [well] for our long seven years of servictude persecution & affliction in the midst of our enimies[281] in the land Kirtland[282] yea verily our hearts were full and we feel greatfull to Almighty God for his kindness unto us. The particulars of our Journey brotheren cannot weell be writen but we trust that the same God who has protected us will protect you also, and will sooner or later grant us the privilege of seeing each other face ⟨to⟩ face & of rehersing of all our sufferings[283] We have herd of the destruction of the printing office[284] which we presume to believe must have been occasioned by the Parrishites[285] or more properly the Aristocrats or Anarchys as we believe,[286] The saints here have provided a room for us[287] and daily necessary's which is brought in from all parts of the co. to make us comfortable, so that I have nothing to do but to attend to my spiritual concerns or the spiritual affairs of

---

279. These men from Far West met JS's party in Caldwell County at John Barnard's home, where the party had stopped for the night. (JS, Journal, Mar.–Sept. 1838, p. 16, in *JSP*, J1:237.)

280. In 1831, JS dictated revelations that designated Missouri as the "land of your [the Saints'] inheritance." (Revelation, 6 June 1831, in *JSP*, D1:332 [D&C 52:42]; Revelation, 14 June 1831, in *JSP*, D1:339 [D&C 55:5]; see also Revelation, 20 July 1831, in *JSP*, D2:7–12 [D&C 57].)

281. See Psalm 110:2.

282. JS moved to Kirtland in February 1831.[a] Several of JS's revelations referred to Kirtland Township or the Kirtland area as the "Land of Kirtland."[b] (a. JS History, vol. A-1, 92; [Matthew S. Clapp], "Mormonism," *Painesville [OH] Telegraph,* 15 Feb. 1831, [1]–[2]. b. See, for example, Revelation, 11 Sept. 1831, in *JSP*, D2:65 [D&C 64:21]; see also Bushman, *Rough Stone Rolling,* 191.)

283. En route to Missouri, JS, Rigdon, and their families endured severe cold and several difficult river crossings. (JS History, vol. B-1, 780; JS, Journal, 29 Dec. 1842, in *JSP*, J2:196–197; Historian's Office, Brigham Young History Drafts, 16–17.)

284. See 35n166 herein.

285. Warren Parrish had served as JS's personal scribe from fall 1835 to spring 1837 and was a member of the First Quorum of the Seventy. He had also served as the clerk of the Kirtland Safety Society and later as its cashier.[a] After questioning JS's leadership and decisions as president of the church, Parrish renounced church leaders and led a group of dissenters in an effort to establish a new church.[b] (a. Notice, ca. Late Aug. 1837, in *JSP*, D5:418–420; Staker, *Hearken, O Ye People,* 465–466, 480, 600. b. Introduction to Part 6: 20 Apr.–14 Sept. 1837, in *JSP*, D5:363–366; Backman, *Heavens Resound,* 327–329; Staker, *Hearken, O Ye People,* 535, 600.)

286. Within the prior two weeks, JS had composed a church motto, which denounced "tyrants, Mobs, Aristocracy, Anarchy and Toryism." (Motto, ca. 16 or 17 Mar. 1838, p. 45 herein.)

287. JS's Scriptory Book notes that upon arriving in Far West, his family was "immediately received under the hospitable roof of George W. Harris who treated us with all kindness possible." (JS, Journal, Mar.–Sept. 1838, p. 16, in *JSP*, J1:237.)

the Church The difficulties of the Church had been ajusted before arrival here by a Judicious High Council With T. B. Marsh & D[avid] W Patten who acted as Pres. Pro. Tem. of the Church of zion being appointed by the voice of the Council & Church W[m.] W. Phelps & John Whitmer having been cut off from the Church, D[avid] Whitmer remains as yit[288] The saints at this time are in union & peace & love prevails throughout, in a word Heaven smiles upon the saints in Caldwell. Various & many have been the falshoods writen from thence [p. 24] to this place, but have prevailed nothing,[289] We have no uneaseness about the power of our enimies in this place to do us harm Br Samuel H Smith & family arrived here soon after we did in go[o]d health. Br B[righam] Young Br D[aniel] S. Miles & Br L[evi] Richards[290] arrivd here when we did, They were with us on the last of our journey which ad[d]ed much to our sattisfaction,[291] They also are well They have provided places for their families & are now about to break the ground for seed,[292] Being under the hand of wicked vexatious Lawsuits[293] for seven years past my buisness was so dangerous that I was not able to leave it, in as good a situation as I had antisipated, but if there are any wrongs, They shall all be noticed so far as the Lord gives me ability & power to do so,[294] say to all the brotheren that I have not forgotten them, but remember them in my prayers, Say to Mother Beaman [Sarah Beman]

288. See Minute Book 2, 20 Jan. and 10 Mar. 1838; and Letter from Thomas B. Marsh, 15 Feb. 1838, pp. 18–23 herein.

289. For an example of correspondence from dissidents, see Lyman Cowdery, Kirtland, OH, to Oliver Cowdery, Richmond, MO, 21 Aug. 1838, photocopy, CHL.

290. Young was a member of the Quorum of the Twelve Apostles, Miles was a member of the Presidency of the Seventy, and Richards was a high priest. (Minutes, Discourse, and Blessings, 14–15 Feb. 1835, in *JSP*, D4:228; Quorums of the Seventy, "Book of Records," 6 Apr. 1837, 18; Stevenson, *Richards Family History*, 1:13.)

291. Young and others joined JS and his traveling party near Jacksonville, Illinois. (Historian's Office, Brigham Young History Drafts, 16.)

292. Young later recounted that he "purchased a small improvement on mill creek . . . and proceeded to fence in a farm." Miles owned land in Caldwell County. (Historian's Office, Brigham Young History Drafts, 17; Hamer, *Northeast of Eden*, 75, 88; see also Revelation, 17 Apr. 1838, pp. 107–108 herein.)

293. The church motto JS had composed within the prior two weeks denounced "vexatious lawsuits." (Motto, ca. 16 or 17 Mar. 1838, p. 45 herein.)

294. JS incurred several thousand dollars of debt while living in Kirtland, primarily as a result of building the Kirtland House of the Lord.[a] Prior to leaving for Missouri, he appointed William Marks and others to oversee efforts to pay church debts.[b] (a. See, for example, Statement of Account from John Howden, 29 Mar. 1838, pp. 61–65 herein; Statement of Account from Perkins & Osborn, ca. 29 Oct. 1838, pp. 252–261 herein; Agreement with Mead & Betts, 2 Aug. 1839, pp. 535–539 herein; and "Schedule Setting Forth a List of Petitioner[']s Creditors, Their Residence, and the Amount Due to Each," ca. 15–16 Apr. 1842, CCLA. b. See Pay Order to Edward Partridge for William Smith, 21 Feb. 1838, pp. 27–30 herein.)

that I remembr her,[295] Also Br Daniel Carter Br Stong & family[296] Br [Oliver] Granger & family,[297] Finally I cannot innumerate them all for the want of room I will just name Br Knights[298] the Bishop[299] &c. My best respects to them all ~~for the want of room~~ & I commend them and the Church of God in Kirtland to our Heavenly Father & the word of his grace,[300] which is able to make you wise unto Salvation[301] I would just say to Br. [William] Marks, that I saw in a vision while on the road that whereas he was closely persued by an innumerable concource of enimies and as they pressed upon him hard as if they were about to devour him, It ⟨&⟩ had seemingly attained some degre[e] of advantage over him But about this time a chariot of fire came and near the place and the Angel of the Lord put forth his hand unto Br. Marks & said [p. 25] unto him thou art my son[302] come <u>here,</u> and immediately he was caught up in the Chariot and rode away triumphantly out of their midst[303] and again the Lord said I will raise th[ee] up for a blessing unto many people Now the particulars of this whole matter cannot be writen at this time but the vision was evidently given to me that I might know that the hand of the Lord would be on his behalf

J Smith Jr

I transmit to you the fol[l]owing motto of the Church of Jesus Christ of Latter day Saints Recorded on Pages 16 & 17 of J Smith Jr Scriptory Record Book A.[304] We left Pres. [Sidney] Rigdon 30 miles this side of Parris [Paris] Illinois in consequence of the sickness of Br. G[eorge] W. Robinsons

---

295. Sarah Burt Beman was the widow of Alvah Beman, with whom the Smith family had been friends since before the organization of the church in 1830. (Noble and Noble, Reminiscences, [16]; Pratt, *Autobiography*, 117–118; "Mormonism—No. II," *Tiffany's Monthly*, Aug. 1859, 167.

296. Possibly Ezra Strong Sr. (1788–1877) or Harvey Strong (1803–1875). (Backman, *Profile*, 69; Reorganized Church of Jesus Christ of Latter Day Saints, Northwest Illinois District, Church Records, 1866–1870, pp. 4–5, microfilm 1,927,666; Berrien Co., MI, Death Records, 1867–1929, 1934–1967, vol. A, p. 158, microfilm 945,406, U.S. and Canada Record Collection, FHL.)

297. Granger, a member of the high council in Kirtland, was also a church agent working with Marks to help JS and Rigdon manage and settle debts. (See, for example, Power of Attorney to Oliver Granger, 27 Sept. 1837, in *JSP*, D5:460; and Grandison Newell, Assignment of Judgment to William Marks and Oliver Granger, Kirtland, OH, 1 Mar. 1838, Newel K. Whitney, Papers, BYU; see also "Memorandum O. Granger G Newell Assignment," Newel K. Whitney, Papers, BYU.)

298. Possibly Vinson Knight, a counselor in the Kirtland bishopric. Knight, like Granger and Bishop Newel K. Whitney, was probably involved in resolving financial problems that JS left behind in Kirtland.

299. Newel K. Whitney was the bishop in Kirtland.

300. See Acts 14:3; 20:32.

301. See 2 Timothy 3:15.

302. See Psalm 2:7; and Old Testament Revision 1, p. 1 [Moses 1:4].

303. See 2 Kings 2:11.

304. See Motto, ca. 16 or 17 Mar. 1838, pp. 43–45 herein.

wife,[305] on yesterday br. Robinson arrived here who informed us that his father in Law (S. Rigdon) was at Huntsville detained there on account of the ill health of his wife, They will probaly be here soon, Choice seeds of all kinds of fruit[306] also Choice breed of Cattle would be in much demand also, best blood of horses garden seeds of every description also hay seed of all sorts, all of these are much needed in this place

Verry respe[c]tfully I subscribe myself your servent in Christ our Lord & Savior

Joseph Smith Jr
Pres[t.] of the Church of
Jesus Christ of
Latterday Saints

———— ☙ ————

Statement of Account from John Howden, 29 March 1838

Source Note

John Howden, Statement of Account, [Painesville, Geauga Co., OH], for JS and Sidney Rigdon, 29 Mar. 1838; one page (possibly missing second page); handwriting of John Howden; CHL. Includes redactions and docket.

One leaf measuring 13 × 7⅞ to 8 inches (33 x 20 cm). The document includes a watermark: "L & C°". The bottom of the leaf appears to be machine cut, whereas the top and sides appear to be hand cut. Residue from a red adhesive wafer on the verso has no corresponding residue on the recto of the document, suggesting the wafer was not used to seal the document but to attach another leaf that is no longer extant. The document includes filing folds and a corresponding docket in unidentified handwriting: "John Houtans | Bills". Redactions were made in ink and graphite in unidentified handwriting. The document shows signs of moderate wear, and five strips of tape were applied to the verso to mend tears.

Howden may have given this statement to Oliver Granger or another church agent in 1838. At some point, Latter-day Saint Francis Clark acquired the statement.[307] This document and Clark's other papers apparently remained in his and then his descendants' custody until his great-granddaughter sold them. The papers were eventually purchased by Scallawagiana Books of Salt Lake City and then sold to Peter Crawley, a rare book and document collector. Crawley sold the papers to the Historical Department of the LDS church in 1982.[308]

---

305. George W. Robinson was married to Rigdon's daughter Athalia. JS's multivolume manuscript history recounts that JS left the Rigdon family at Terre Haute, Indiana, about twenty miles east, not west, of Paris. Similarly, Rigdon's son recounted that his family parted with JS in Indiana and then traveled to Paris. (JS History, vol. B-1, 780; Rigdon, "Life Story of Sidney Rigdon," 62.)

306. See Book of Mormon, 1830 ed., 18, 39, 540 [1 Nephi 8:1; 16:11; Ether 1:41; 2:3].

307. Clark joined the church in England and immigrated to the United States in 1841. (See Neibaur, Journal, 7 Mar. 1841.)

308. See full bibliographic entry for Statement of Account from John Howden, 29 Mar. 1838, in the CHL catalog.

Historical Introduction

On 29 March 1838, merchant John Howden of Painesville, Ohio, prepared this statement of debts that JS and Sidney Rigdon owed him, including debts they apparently assumed on behalf of other Latter-day Saints.[309] This statement was not the first that Howden produced for JS and Rigdon; on 1 January 1838, Howden wrote a statement identifying two debts: one that JS owed and one for which Rigdon had signed as a surety for Zebedee Coltrin and Sampson Avard.[310] JS's debt appears to have been paid by 29 March 1838, but Rigdon's remained unpaid.

The majority of the entries listed in this statement reference promissory notes that JS and other Latter-day Saints at Kirtland, Ohio, gave to Howden in 1837—probably for goods purchased from his Painesville store or for money borrowed from him. The first two items listed in the statement are promissory notes that JS, Rigdon, Hyrum Smith, John Johnson, and Edmund Bosley signed on 13 April 1837. Howden endorsed these notes and transferred them to other individuals, who in fall 1837 began lawsuits because the debts remained unpaid.[311] Other entries listed in the statement are debts for goods, horses, and property. The extant statement may be incomplete. The individual debts are not totaled at the end of the page, and the verso contains wafer residue, perhaps to attach a second leaf. Because a second page of the statement may be missing, it is impossible to know the overall status of JS's and Rigdon's accounts.

It appears that Howden included several of the unpaid promissory notes in this 29 March statement in an effort to settle the debts before the matters were tried in court. Lawsuits on four of the notes—the two 13 April 1837 promissory notes that JS and Rigdon were involved in, one from Reuben Hedlock, and the one that Rigdon had signed as a surety for Coltrin and Avard—were brought before the Geauga County Court of Common Pleas on 3 April 1838, a few days after this statement was compiled. In the trials against Coltrin and Hedlock, Howden informed the judge that the debts had been settled by mutual agreement outside of court before 3 April. In contrast, the debts for the 13 April 1837 promissory notes were not settled before being brought to trial—possibly because the debts involved Howden as well as those to whom he had transferred the notes.[312]

---

309. Howden operated a dry goods store on Main Street in 1836 and 1837. (See Advertisement, *Painesville [OH] Telegraph,* 4 Nov. 1836, [3]; Advertisement, *Painesville [OH] Republican,* 1 Dec. 1836, [4]; and Advertisement, *Painesville Republican,* 2 Feb. 1837, [4].)

310. JS's debt of $224 was listed on the January statement but not on the March statement, suggesting it had been paid. The promissory note for which Rigdon acted as a surety was included in the 29 March statement, suggesting that Coltrin or Avard had not paid it and that Howden may have requested that Rigdon pay the debt. (John Howden, Account Statement for JS and Sidney Rigdon, 1 Jan. 1838, JS Collection, CHL; Transcript of Proceedings, 3 Apr. 1838, Howden v. Coltrin [Geauga Co. C.P. 1838], Final Record Book U, pp. 612–613, microfilm 20,279, U.S. and Canada Record Collection, FHL.)

311. Transcript of Proceedings, 3 Apr. 1838, Bailey and Reynolds v. JS et al. (Geauga Co. C.P. 1838), Final Record Book V, p. 5, microfilm 20,280; Transcript of Proceedings, 3 Apr. 1838, Boynton and Hyde v. JS (Geauga Co. C.P. 1838), Final Record Book U, pp. 512–513, microfilm 20,279, U.S. and Canada Record Collection, FHL.

312. The terms of the court settlement with Howden are not known. (See Transcript of Proceedings, 3 Apr. 1838, Bailey and Reynolds v. JS et al. [Geauga Co. C.P. 1838], Final Record Book V, p. 5,

Howden probably sent the statement to Kirtland, where one of the church agents, likely Oliver Granger, took responsibility for repaying the debts on behalf of JS and Rigdon. Granger or another agent may have written to JS about the statement, but it is not known whether JS received or reviewed it. The statement bears no address or postal information, suggesting that if JS received it in Missouri, it was likely delivered by a Latter-day Saint courier. By October 1838, Howden considered all debts owed him by JS, Rigdon, and other Latter-day Saints to be paid, and he credited Granger for the timely resolution of his and other merchants' debts.[313]

Document Transcript

Sydney [Sidney] Rigdon & Joseph Smith Jun Esqr

In A/c with John W Howden <u>Dr</u>[314]

1838 March 29th

To Amt Two Notes dated April 13th 1837[315]——	16.50.	00
Int on Same—	99.	00
Amt Cost on the above Notes[316]	30.	00
protests[317]——	2.	00
Amt per centage[318] 2 ½ prct	43.	72
Amt Rigden & ~~Hedlock~~ ⟨[Zebedee] Coltrin⟩ Note[319]	496.	00

---

microfilm 20,280; Transcript of Proceedings, 3 Apr. 1838, Boynton and Hyde v. JS [Geauga Co. C.P. 1838], Final Record Book U, pp. 512–513; Transcript of Proceedings, 3 Apr. 1838, Howden v. Coltrin [Geauga Co. C.P. 1838], Final Record Book U, pp. 612–613; Transcript of Proceedings, 3 Apr. 1838, Howden v. Hedlock [Geauga Co. C.P. 1838], Final Record Book U, pp. 618–619, microfilm 20,279, U.S. and Canada Record Collection, FHL.)

313. See Letter of Introduction from John Howden, 27 Oct. 1838, p. 248 herein.

314. "Dr" is an abbreviation that indicates debits on an account—in this case, amounts JS and Rigdon owed Howden. (Jones, *Principles and Practice of Book-Keeping*, 20.)

315. JS, Rigdon, Hyrum Smith, Edmund Bosley, and John Johnson signed two promissory notes for Howden on 13 April 1837. Each note appears to have been for $825. Howden transferred one note to Nathaniel Bailey and Henry Reynolds and the other note to Ray Boynton and Harry Hyde. In late October 1837, both parties began lawsuits against JS and his associates for failure to pay the notes. (Transcript of Proceedings, 3 Apr. 1838, Bailey and Reynolds v. JS et al. [Geauga Co. C.P. 1838], Final Record Book V, p. 5, microfilm 20,280; Transcript of Proceedings, 3 Apr. 1838, Boynton and Hyde v. JS [Geauga Co. C.P. 1838], Final Record Book U, pp. 512–513, microfilm 20,279, U.S. and Canada Record Collection, FHL.)

316. The costs for this and other promissory notes are not identified and may be court fees or other legal fees associated with lawsuits for not paying the notes. (See Statement of Account from Perkins & Osborn, ca. 29 Oct. 1838, pp. 254–261 herein; and Statement of Account from Hitchcock & Wilder, between 9 July and 6 Nov. 1838, pp. 288–290 herein.)

317. This entry pertains to the cost of having a notary public create protests, or notices indicating non-payment; a protest declares that all parties are held responsible to the holder of the note for the amount due. ("Protest," in Bouvier, *Law Dictionary*, 2:307.)

318. It is not clear what this and other entries for percentages indicate; they may refer to a commission or to additional interest.

319. This entry refers to the note Rigdon signed for Coltrin and Avard. The amount due on 1 January 1838 was $488.87. When a writ for the case was issued in October 1837, Avard and Rigdon were not in

Cost——	13.	40
pr centage	12.	40
[Reuben] Hedlock Note[320] —— ⟨3237⟩[321]	257.	58
Cost——	13.	40
pr centge	6.	44
Cost on [Samuel] Newcomb Note[322]	13.	40
	2642.	34
Am^t O Grangr [Oliver Granger] Note[323]	600	
	3242.	34
dedu[c]t Bosly——[324]	1700	
	1542	34
Am^t paid Bosly	30	
	1572.	34
1838 Ma[r]ch 29th To Amt Mortgage[325]	270.	00

Kirtland, so the case proceeded against Coltrin alone. This fact may explain why Coltrin was listed along with Rigdon as a surety, whereas Avard was not. (John Howden, Account Statement for JS and Sidney Rigdon, 1 Jan. 1838, JS Collection, CHL; Transcript of Proceedings, 3 Apr. 1838, Howden v. Coltrin [Geauga Co. C.P. 1838], Final Record Book U, pp. 612–613, microfilm 20,279, U.S. and Canada Record Collection, FHL.)

320. This may be the note that Hedlock gave to Howden on 31 July 1837. That note was for $247.58; if this is the same note, it is unclear why an additional $10.00 was added. No documentation indicates that JS or Rigdon had any responsibility for Hedlock's note. However, with church members' departure from Kirtland, JS and Rigdon may have consolidated and personally assumed the outstanding debts of the Saints in an effort to repay the debts. In March 1837, JS assumed the debts of some church leaders. JS also acted as a surety on promissory notes that church members created, meaning he could be pursued for repayment in preference to the creators of the notes because of his prominence and assets. (See Transcript of Proceedings, 3 Apr. 1838, Howden v. Hedlock [Geauga Co. C.P. 1838], Final Record Book U, pp. 618–619, microfilm 20,279, U.S. and Canada Record Collection, FHL; and N. K. Whitney & Co., Daybook, 28–30 Mar. 1837, pp. 195–196.)

321. TEXT: Possibly "3037 ⟨3237⟩". This text is smaller, is written at a slight angle, and appears to the side of the column of monetary amounts.

322. Probably Samuel Newcomb, a Kirtland church member who acted as a surety on Hedlock's bail bond in the lawsuit Howden brought against Hedlock. (Transcript of Proceedings, 3 Apr. 1838, Howden v. Hedlock [Geauga Co. C.P. 1838], Final Record Book U, pp. 618–619, microfilm 20,279, U.S. and Canada Record Collection, FHL.)

323. Granger may have given this promissory note in his capacity as an agent for JS and Rigdon, or he may have been conducting his own business.

324. Likely Edmund Bosley. This amount indicates a credit to the account of JS and Rigdon, but it is not clear whether this credit was a result of Bosley paying Howden or of Howden owing money to Bosley and crediting it to the account of JS and Rigdon.

325. Granger mortgaged land to Howden on 29 March 1838. The mortgage record indicates that Howden paid Granger $3,022.50 for 103 acres in Kirtland. Granger likely made the arrangement as an agent for JS and Rigdon and mortgaged the property to Howden so Granger could obtain money to pay the outstanding debts of JS and other Kirtland church members. (Geauga Co., OH, Deed Record,

| 1 Note for Goods— | 50. 00 |
| 1 "   "   " & Horses & naggs | 210. 16 |

——— ❧ ———

Letter from David Thomas, 31 March 1838

Source Note

David Thomas, Letter, Pleasant Park, Carroll Co., MO, to JS, [Far West, Caldwell Co., MO], 31 Mar. 1838. Featured version copied [ca. mid- or late Apr. 1838] in JS, Journal, Mar.–Sept. 1838, pp. 26–28; handwriting of George W. Robinson; CHL. Includes use marks. For more information on JS, Journal, Mar.–Sept. 1838, see Source Notes for Multiple-Entry Documents, p. 564 herein.

Historical Introduction

David Thomas, a land speculator in Carroll County, Missouri, wrote to JS on 31 March 1838, suggesting that the Latter-day Saints purchase land in that area. Thomas, who had apparently met JS and his wife Emma Smith, offered to sell the Saints a part of his land near De Witt. Thomas also introduced JS to Henry Root, another Carroll County landowner who was interested in selling land to the Saints. Root reportedly visited with JS and Sidney Rigdon in the next few days. Later, church leaders met with Thomas and Root and eventually agreed to purchase land from Root at De Witt, where Latter-day Saints proceeded to settle.[326]

Document Transcript

Pleasent [Pleasant] Park Mo. March 31ˢᵗ 1838

Respected Sir

Permit me to introduce to your acquaintance Mr. Henry Root of Dewit [De Witt] near this place on Missouri river His buisness I am unacquainted with, Though any thing he may say to you, you may put the most implisit confidence in, as I have allways found him to be a man of truth & honor, neither have I ever [p. 26] known him to give a misrepresentation of any part, He is a merchant and I suppose doing a moderate buisness[.] his place is now, onley laid out about a year since a beautifull sight to the river, and a first rate landing[327] And Sir permit me to say to you, if you could make it convenient or for your advantage to settle in this County, I would let you have

1795–1921, vol. 25, pp. 665–666, 29 Mar. 1838, microfilm 20,241, U.S. and Canada Record Collection, FHL.)

326. See Sidney Rigdon, Testimony, Nauvoo, IL, 1 July 1843, pp. [2]–[3], Nauvoo, IL, Records, CHL; and [Rigdon], *Appeal to the American People,* 36–37; see also Perkins, "Prelude to Expulsion," 264–268; Baugh, "Call to Arms," 144–145; and LeSueur, "Missouri's Failed Compromise," 140–144.

327. Root owned part of the plat for De Witt, near the Missouri River. (Carroll Co., MO, Deed Records, 1819–1929, bk. A, pp. 234–238, 367–368, microfilm 959,374, U.S. and Canada Record Collection,

part of my land[.][328] There is yet to enter adjoining my land, as good land is in the world, I have no doubt you can do as weell here in forming a settlement and probaly better than any place in the state The facilities of the river will be of great servise t̶o̶ in settling this uper country[329] besid[e]s some of the knowing ones have aimed to uproot you,[330] but here you can break them down in turn,[331] I will join you in the speculation if necessary and if possible the church[.] I will have after paying for <u>1600</u> acres of land $4,000, If they pay me in Far West, enough give my respects to Mrs Smith & accept for yourself

a friends respect

David Thomas

Elder Joseph Smith Jr

N.B. P.S. Further I own a section of land in Monroe [County] near the forks of Salt river, and if necessary sell or make a settlement there I know of no man in the world I would rather entertain than yourself I would be glad if you would find whether my debt is secure in that place, and let me know Please to help me if you can do so without being oppressive to your feelings or interest these I do not wish you [to?] violate for me Mr. Root is my confidential friend anything [you?] may say to him is safe, if you cannot come [p. 27] a line from you at any time will be thankfully Received through the mail or otherwise D.T.

I expect Mr. Root is on the buisness which I have named to you in this, We have consulted on this buisness by others——

David Thomas

———— ∽ ————

FHL; Sidney Rigdon, Testimony, Nauvoo, IL, 1 July 1843, pp. [2]–[3], Nauvoo, IL, Records, CHL; [Rigdon], *Appeal to the American People,* 36; see also Perkins, "Prelude to Expulsion," 264–268.)

328. Thomas owned land a few miles west of De Witt. (Carroll Co., MO, Deed Records, 1819–1929, bk. A, pp. 418–419, microfilm 959,374, U.S. and Canada Record Collection, FHL.)

329. Far West and other Mormon settlements in Caldwell County were situated on Shoal Creek and its tributaries. Shoal Creek ran into the Grand River, which ran into the Missouri River at De Witt. (See Berrett, *Sacred Places,* 4:286; and Hamer, *Northeast of Eden,* 18–19, 30–31.)

330. A network of influential "old-settlers" in northwestern Missouri believed that the Latter-day Saints should be driven from the area or that their settlement should be confined to Caldwell County. (Anderson, "Clarifications of Boggs's Order," 30–39.)

331. Located at the confluence of the Grand and Missouri rivers, De Witt was a strategic site for facilitating Mormon participation in regional commerce. The Saints in the Far West area could haul agricultural products by wagon to Adam-ondi-Ahman, ship them on the Grand River to the De Witt landing, and from there send them on the Missouri River to other markets. (Riggs, "Economic Impact of Fort Leavenworth," 130.)

Minutes, 6 April 1838

Source Note

Zion high council, Minutes, Far West, Caldwell Co., MO, 6 Apr. 1838. Featured version published in Elders' Journal, *July 1838, 46–47. For more information on* Elders' Journal, *see Source Notes for Multiple-Entry Documents, p. 563 herein.*

Historical Introduction

On 6 April 1838, JS presided over and Ebenezer Robinson took the minutes for a meeting in Far West, Missouri, to commemorate the anniversary of the church's founding, to appoint new officers, and to perform ordinances. By 3 March 1838, when the Zion high council scheduled this meeting, members of the council knew that JS had departed Kirtland, Ohio, for Far West, and they probably expected that he would arrive before the meeting.[332] The Zion presidency had been removed in early February 1838. John Whitmer, who had been an assistant president, had also been removed from his positions as church historian and clerk.[333] The church in Missouri, therefore, required not only a new presidency but also a new historian and a new clerk. A written agenda for the meeting indicates that a plan for filling vacancies had been made. In the 6 April meeting, the Saints approved the recently appointed pro tempore presidency, two new historians, and two new clerks. These appointments completed the basic organizational structure of the church in Missouri, likely preparing the way for the business to be conducted in the church conference held the following two days. According to George W. Robinson's abbreviated minutes in the "Scriptory Book," this meeting was "a Conf. of the authorities of the Church of Latter day Saints Assembled at their first quarterly Conference in the City of Far West."[334] However, according to the official minutes of both the 6 April meeting and the 7–8 April meeting, published in the July issue of the *Elders' Journal,* the 6 April meeting was not part of the quarterly conference.[335] Nevertheless, the 6 April meeting included church business that was related to the conference that followed.

The 6 April meeting was planned to begin at 9:00 a.m. The meeting agenda states that the "doors [would] be opened" at that time and that a sexton would be appointed as a "door keeper," indicating that the meeting was held indoors. The meeting proceeded as outlined in the agenda. An hour-long intermission is noted in the middle of the meeting, suggesting the meeting adjourned for a midday meal and then extended into the afternoon. The first session concerned the new appointments, and the second session was devoted to ordinances: the sacrament of the Lord's Supper and the blessing of children. Minutes of the meeting were taken by Ebenezer Robinson, who had taken minutes at recent high council meetings and was appointed the clerk of the Missouri church during this 6 April

---

332. See Minute Book 2, 24 Feb. and 3 Mar. 1838.

333. See Letter from Thomas B. Marsh, 15 Feb. 1838, p. 22 herein. Whitmer was appointed historian in 1831. In an 1832 letter, JS referred to Whitmer as "the lord['s] clerk." (Revelation, ca. 8 Mar. 1831–B, in *JSP,* D1:286 [D&C 47:1, 3]; Minute Book 2, 9 Apr. 1831; Letter to William W. Phelps, 27 Nov. 1832, in *JSP,* D2:318 [D&C 85:1].)

334. Minutes, 6 Apr. 1838, in JS, Journal, Mar.–Sept. 1838, p. 29, in *JSP,* J1:250.

335. See Minutes, 7–8 Apr. 1838, pp. 71–74 herein.

meeting.[336] The minutes conclude with JS's name and his designation as "president," which may refer to his office in the church or his role in presiding over the meeting. JS's name as it appears in the extant minutes may represent his signature in the original minutes or in a fair copy, or Robinson may have added JS's name to the minutes because JS was the meeting's presiding authority. A fair copy of Robinson's original minutes was probably used by a typesetter to prepare the version of the minutes published in the July issue of the church's newspaper at the time, the *Elders' Journal*.[337]

Document Transcript

Far West, April 6th 1838.

Agreeable to a resolution passed the high council of Zion, March 3rd 1838,[338] the saints in Missouri assembled at this place,[339] to hold the anniversary of the church of Jesus Christ of Latter Day Saints[340] and to transact Church business.

The meeting was opened by singing and prayer by David W Patten—After which president Joseph Smith Jr read the order of the day as follows:—

> Doors will be opened at 9 o'clock A M and [p. 46] the meeting will commence by singing and prayer.
>
> A sexton will then be appointed for a door keeper and other services in the house of the Lord.[341]
>
> Two historians will then be appointed to write and keep the church history.
>
> Also a general recorder to keep the records of the whole Church, and be the clerk of the first presidency.[342]

---

336. See Minute Book 2, 10 and 17 Mar. 1838; Minutes, 15 Mar. 1838, p. 43 herein; and Minutes, 24 Mar. 1838, p. 50 herein.

337. Apparently, neither the original minutes nor a fair copy is extant.

338. The minutes of the 3 March meeting do not mention the scheduling of the 6 April 1838 meeting. (See Minute Book 2, 3 Mar. 1838.)

339. The vast majority of the Latter-day Saints in Missouri at this time were living in Far West and in several other smaller settlements in Caldwell County. A few Mormon settlements had also been established in Daviess County, and some Mormon families and individuals lived in surrounding counties in northwestern Missouri. (Berrett, *Sacred Places*, 4:286–289, 358–360, 499–512.)

340. The church had been organized eight years earlier, on 6 April 1830. (JS History, vol. A-1, 37–38, in *JSP*, H1:364–372 [Draft 2]; Articles and Covenants, ca. Apr. 1830, in *JSP*, D1:120–121 [D&C 20:1–12].)

341. The meeting may have been held in a schoolhouse, as previous council meetings had been. (See 18n78 herein.)

342. In addition to serving as the church historian, John Whitmer had been called by revelation to assist JS "in Transcribing all things" and to "keep the Church Record." JS had also referred to Whitmer as "the lord['s] clerk whom he has appointed to keep a hystory and a general church reccord of all things that transpire in Zion." (Revelation, ca. 8 Mar. 1831–B, in *JSP*, D1:286 [D&C 47:1, 3]; Letter to William W. Phelps, 27 Nov. 1832, in *JSP*, D2:318 [D&C 85:1]; see also Minute Book 2, 9 Apr. 1831.)

And a clerk will be appointed for the high Council, and to keep the Church records of this stake.[343]

And three presidents will be appointed to preside over this Church of Zion.[344]

After which an address will be delivered by the presidency:[345]

Then an intermission of one hour will take place;

When the meeting will again convene and open by singing and prayer;

The Sacrament will then be administered and the blessing of infants attended to;[346]

The meeting then proceeded to business[347] George Morey was appointed sexton and Dimick [B.] Huntington assistant;[348]

John Corrill and Elias Higbee were appointed historians;[349]

George W Robinson was appointed general Church Recorder and Clerk for the first Presidency;[350]

343. Oliver Cowdery had been appointed standing clerk of the high council but had fallen from favor. He had not served as the clerk for a high council meeting since December 1837. Ebenezer Robinson and others took minutes of meetings in early 1838. (See Minute Book 2, 6 Dec. 1837–10 Feb. 1838; and 43n219 herein.)

344. After the Zion presidency was removed in February 1838, apostles Thomas B. Marsh and David W. Patten were appointed as pro tempore presidents until the First Presidency arrived and became the presidency of the church in Missouri. JS, however, planned for the Saints in Zion to have their own presidency operating under the general church presidency. (Letter from Thomas B. Marsh, 15 Feb. 1838, p. 23 herein.)

345. This reference is to the First Presidency: JS, Rigdon, and Hyrum Smith. However, Hyrum Smith was still traveling from Kirtland and did not arrive until late May. (Hyrum Smith, Commerce, IL, to "the Saints Scattered Abroad," Dec. 1839, in *Times and Seasons,* Dec. 1839, 1:21.)

346. The Latter-day Saints used the term *the sacrament* to refer only to the sacrament of the Lord's Supper, the Eucharist, or communion.[a] The church's foundational "Articles and Covenants" stipulated that "every member of this church of Christ having children, are to bring them unto the elders before the church who are to lay hands on them in the name of the Lord, and bless them in the name of Christ."[b] (a. See Book of Mormon, 1830 ed., 575–576 [Moroni chaps. 4–5]; and Revelation, 7 Aug. 1831, in *JSP,* D2:32–33 [D&C 59:3, 9]. b. Articles and Covenants, ca. Apr. 1830, in *JSP,* D1:125 [D&C 20:70].)

347. According to George W. Robinson's abbreviated minutes in the Scriptory Book, the first item of business was recognizing JS and Rigdon as the presiding authorities over the meeting. (Minutes, 6 Apr. 1838, in JS, Journal, Mar.–Sept. 1838, p. 29, in *JSP,* J1:250.)

348. Morey had served as a doorkeeper in the House of the Lord in Kirtland. Huntington served as a constable in Far West. According to George W. Robinson's abbreviated minutes in the Scriptory Book, Morey and Huntington were appointed "door keepers" for the meeting. (JS, Journal, 29 Feb. 1836, in *JSP,* J1:191; Dimick Huntington, Reminiscences and Journal, [14]–[15]; Minutes, 6 Apr. 1838, in JS, Journal, Mar.–Sept. 1838, p. 29, in *JSP,* J1:250.)

349. Both Corrill and Higbee had some clerical or related experience. Corrill served as a financial agent for the church and as an occasional clerk. Higbee served as the presiding judge of Caldwell County. (Minute Book 2, 22 May 1837; George W. Pitkin, Testimony, Nauvoo, IL, 1 July 1843, p. 1, Nauvoo, IL, Records, CHL; see also Minute Book 2, 24 Feb. 1838; and Affidavit, 5 Sept. 1838, p. 225 herein.)

350. Robinson was appointed general church recorder and clerk in September 1837 in Kirtland. Robinson's abbreviated minutes of the 6 April meeting in the Scriptory Book describe his appointment

Ebenezer Robinson was appointed Church Clerk and Recorder for this stake of Zion and Clerk for the high Council;[351]

Thomas B Marsh was appointed President pro tempore of the Church in Zion, and Brigham Young and David W Patten his assistant Presidents:[352]

The meeting adjourned for one hour—and again opened by David W Patten—After which the bread and wine was administered, and 95 infants were brought forward and blessed—When on motion the meeting closed.

JOSEPH SMITH Jr.
President.

E. ROBINSON Clerk.

— ❧ —

Minutes, 7–8 April 1838

Source Note

Zion high council, Minutes, Far West, Caldwell Co., MO, 7–8 Apr. 1838. Featured version published as "Conference Minutes," in Elders' Journal, *July 1838, 47. For more information on* Elders' Journal, *see Source Notes for Multiple-Entry Documents, p. 563 herein.*

Historical Introduction

On 7–8 April 1838, JS presided over a conference in Far West, Missouri, and Ebenezer Robinson took minutes. This quarterly conference, the first one held that year, had been scheduled by the Zion high council on 3 March 1838. By that date, the council members knew that JS had departed Kirtland, Ohio, for Far West, and they probably expected that he would arrive in time for the conference.[353] On 6 April, the day prior to the conference's start, the church held a meeting in which a pro tempore presidency for the church in Zion and a number of other officers were appointed. According to the abbreviated minutes that George W. Robinson included in the "Scriptory Book," the 6 April meeting was "a Conf. of

---

slightly differently, stating he was "elected as general Church Clerk & Recorder to keep a record of the whole Church also as Scribe for the first Presidency." (Minutes, 17 Sept. 1837–A, in *JSP*, D5:443; Minutes, 6 Apr. 1838, in JS, Journal, Mar.–Sept. 1838, p. 29, in *JSP*, J1:250.)

351. Robinson had served as a clerk for previous meetings of the Zion high council in Far West. (Ebenezer Robinson, "Items of Personal History of the Editor," *Return,* July 1889, 104.)

352. Marsh, Patten, and Young were the three most senior members of the Quorum of the Twelve Apostles. Marsh and Patten had been living in Caldwell County for over a year. Young had helped JS travel to Missouri and had arrived in Caldwell County with him three weeks earlier. The appointment of Marsh, Patten, and Young as presidents was probably only temporary because as members of the Quorum of the Twelve Apostles (the church's traveling high council), they would eventually travel, proselytize, and supervise units of the church outside of Zion and its stakes. (Letter to the Presidency in Kirtland, 29 Mar. 1838, p. 59 herein; Instruction on Priesthood, between ca. 1 Mar. and ca. 4 May 1835, in *JSP*, D4:314–315 [D&C 107:23–37].)

353. See Minute Book 2, 24 Feb. and 3 Mar. 1838.

the authorities of the Church of Latter day Saints Assembled at their first quarterly Conference in the City of Far West."[354] However, the official minutes of both the 6 April meeting and the 7–8 April meeting, which were published in the July issue of the *Elders' Journal,* indicate the 6 April meeting was separate from the quarterly conference held 7–8 April.[355] Nevertheless, the appointments made in the 6 April meeting prepared the church administratively for the conference held the next two days.

The conference was another step in the reorganization of church leadership in the wake of the disaffection of church leaders in Ohio and Missouri. The conference was probably held indoors—as was the 6 April meeting—possibly in a schoolhouse or some other public building.[356] According to the minutes, at the beginning of the conference JS, Sidney Rigdon, and the Zion presidency "took the stand," suggesting there was a rostrum. Then, as was customary in conferences, the priesthood officers organized according to their quorums and councils. Next, JS "gave some instruction respecting the order of the day," after which the conference formally "opened" with singing and prayer. David W. Patten and Brigham Young, the assistants to Thomas B. Marsh in the pro tempore presidency of the church in Zion, offered the opening prayers at the sessions—and possibly conducted as well.[357] JS gave instruction during both days of the conference. The leaders of the priesthood quorums and councils reported on their respective organizations, and vacancies in the high council were filled. The minutes were taken by Ebenezer Robinson, who had taken minutes of recent high council meetings and was appointed as the clerk of the church in Zion during the 6 April meeting.[358] The minutes of the conference close by listing JS as "president," perhaps signifying that he was the head of the church or that he presided over the conference. JS may have signed the original minutes or a fair copy, although it is also possible that Robinson simply added JS's name as the presiding authority. A fair copy of the minutes was probably used to prepare the version published in the July issue of the *Elders' Journal,* the church's newspaper.[359]

Document Transcript

CONFERENCE MINUTES.

Agreeable to a resolution of the high council, assembled at Far West, on Saturday the 3rd of March 1838, the general authorities of the church met, to hold the first quarterly conference of the Church of Latter Day Saints Zion,[360] at Far West on the 7th of April 1838. Presidents J. Smith jr, S[idney] Rigdon,

---

354. Minutes, 6 Apr. 1838, in JS, Journal, Mar.–Sept. 1838, p. 29, in *JSP,* J1:250.

355. See Historical Introduction to Minutes, 6 Apr. 1838, p. 67 herein.

356. See 18n78 herein.

357. In some previous meetings, the officer conducting also gave the opening prayer. (Minutes, 7 Nov. 1837, in *JSP,* D5:469; Letter from Thomas B. Marsh, 15 Feb. 1838, p. 18 herein; Minutes, 15 Mar. 1838, p. 41 herein.)

358. Minute Book 2, 10 and 17 Mar. 1838; Minutes, 15 Mar. 1838, p. 43 herein; Minutes, 24 Mar. 1838, p. 50 herein; Minutes, 6 Apr. 1838, p. 70 herein.

359. Neither the original minutes nor a fair copy is apparently extant.

360. A written resolution from the conference referred to the meeting as "a general Conference of the ordained members." (Resolution, ca. 8 Apr. 1838, p. 76 herein.)

T[homas] B Marsh, D[avid] W. Patten, and B[righam] Young took the stand;[361] after which the several quorums, the high council, the high priests, the seventies the elders, the bishop, the priests, the teachers, and deacons, were organized by their Presidents.

President J. Smith jr. made some remarks, also gave some instruction respecting the order of the day. The conference was then opened by singing, "O God our hope in ages past"[362] and prayer by President B. Young.— Also a hymn was sung "how firm a foundation".[363] After which, President J. Smith, Jr. arose and addressed the congregation at considerable length, on some important items.— President Rigdon continued the subject for a length of time, after which, on motion, the meeting adjourned for the space of twenty minutes.

Pursuant to adjournment the conference convened, and opened by prayer by D. W. Patten who also made a few remarks respecting the twelve apostles. He spake of T. B. Marsh, Brigham Young, Orson Hyde, Heber C. Kimball, P[arley] P. Pratt, and O[rson] Pratt, as being men of God, whom he could reccommend with cheerful confidence. He spake somewhat doubtful of William Smith from something which he had heard respecting his faith in the work. He also spake of William E. McLellin, Luke Johnson, Lyman Johnson, and John F. Boynto,n as being men whom he could not reccommend to the conference.[364]

---

361. The men who "took the stand" were the available members of the First Presidency and the pro tempore Zion presidency. Whereas Rigdon had arrived in Far West, JS's other counselor, Hyrum Smith, had not yet arrived from Kirtland. Marsh, Patten, and Young had been appointed to the presidency of the church in Zion the previous day. (Hyrum Smith, Commerce, IL, to "the Saints Scattered Abroad," Dec. 1839, in *Times and Seasons,* Dec. 1839, 1:21; O'Driscoll, *Hyrum Smith,* 167–170; Minutes, 6 Apr. 1838, p. 70 herein.)

362. Hymn 86, *Collection of Sacred Hymns,* 116–117.

363. Hymn 82, *Collection of Sacred Hymns,* 111–112.

364. A month later, when McLellin was tried in a church disciplinary council in Far West, he stated that he "had no confidence in the heads of the Church, beleiving they had transgressed, and got out of the way, and consequently he left of[f] praying and keeping the commandments of God." In the September 1837 reorganization meeting in Kirtland, Luke Johnson, Lyman Johnson, and John F. Boynton were rejected as members of the Quorum of the Twelve Apostles and were apparently disfellowshipped. On that occasion, Rigdon explained "the starting point or cause of all the difficulty," cautioning the elders against "leaving their calling to persue any occupation derogatory to that calling, assuring them that if persued, God would let them run themselves into difficulties." Boynton, who was present, "attributed his difficulties & conduct to the failure of the bank"—the Kirtland Safety Society—"stating that the bank he understood was instituted by the will & revilations of God, & he had been told that it never would fail let men do what they pleased." A week after the September reorganization meeting, Boynton and the Johnsons "made confession to the Church," and it was "voted that they be received into the fellowship of the Saints and retain their office of Apostleship." However, after further problems, Luke Johnson and Boynton were excommunicated in December 1837. They joined with other leading dissenters to organize a new church in January 1838, which publicly denounced JS. In April 1838, a church trial was held for Lyman Johnson on charges of speaking against JS and other church leaders, failing to attend church meetings, violating the church's dietary

President John Murdock, then represented the high council. The report was favorable. He stated that the seats of Elisha H. Groves, Calvin Bebee [Beebe], and Lyman Wight was vacant in consequence of their having moved away so far that they could not attend the council.[365]

Thomas B. Marsh then nominated Jared Carter to fill the seat of Elisha H. Groves who was received unanimously.[366]

He then nominafed John P. Green[e], to fill the seat of Calvin Bebee, who was received unanimously.[367]

Also George W Harris, to fill that of Lyman Wight, who was received unanimously—[368] The presidency then ordained him to the office of high priest.

On motion the Conference adjourned to the 8th at 9 o'clock A M.

Sunday April the 8th;—— Pursuant to adjournment the Conference convened, and opened by singing and prayer by President B. Young.

President Joseph Smith Jr. made a few remarks respecting the Kirtland Bank—[369] Who was followed by Brigham Young, who gave a short history of his travels to Massachusetts and New York.[370]

---

code, committing fraudulent business dealings, instigating lawsuits against church members, and other offenses. He was removed from office and excommunicated. (JS, Journal, 11 May 1838, in *JSP*, J1:268; Minutes, 3 Sept. 1837, in *JSP*, D5:423–424; Minute Book 1, 10 Sept. 1837; John Smith and Clarissa Lyman Smith, Kirtland, OH, to George A. Smith, Shinnston, VA, 1 Jan. 1838, George Albert Smith, Papers, CHL; Letter to Wilford Woodruff, ca. 18 June 1838, p. 156 herein; Minutes, 13 Apr. 1838, pp. 96–101 herein.)

365. On 24 March 1838, the high council decided that council members unable to attend council meetings were to "resign their seats and let others fill them who will be able to attend punctually." Groves and Wight had moved to Daviess County, Missouri, and Beebe had moved to Clinton County, Missouri. (Minutes, 24 Mar. 1838, p. 50 herein; Elisha Groves, "An Account of the Life of Elisha Hurd Groves," 4, Obituary Notices and Biographies, CHL; JS, Journal, 18 May–1 June 1838, in *JSP*, J1:271; Calvin Beebe, Affidavit, Lee Co., Iowa Territory, 28 Oct. 1839, Mormon Redress Petitions, 1839–1845, CHL.)

366. Carter had served as the president of the high council in Kirtland and more recently as a substitute for Groves in the Zion high council. (Minute Book 1, 9 Sept. 1837; Minute Book 2, 10 Mar. 1838; Minutes, 15 Mar. 1838, p. 41 herein; Minutes, 24 Mar. 1838, p. 47 herein.)

367. Greene had served as a member of the high council in Kirtland. (Minutes, 13 Jan. 1836, in *JSP*, D5:140.)

368. Harris had recently substituted for Wight in the Zion high council. (Minute Book 2, 1 and 5 Aug. 1837; 10 and 17 Mar. 1838; Minutes, 15 Mar. 1838, p. 41 herein; Minutes, 24 Mar. 1838, p. 47 herein.)

369. The Kirtland Safety Society, often called the Kirtland Bank, collapsed in 1837, causing financial losses for the Mormon community in Kirtland, adding to the strain already felt from the financial panic of 1837. Because of these circumstances, along with doubts and resentment toward JS, some members became disaffected from the church. (Notice, ca. Late Aug. 1837, in *JSP*, D5:418–420; Introduction to Part 6: 20 Apr.–14 Sept. 1837, in *JSP*, D5:363–366; see also Staker, *Hearken, O Ye People*, chaps. 33–34.)

370. Young served two missions in 1837 to transact church business. (Historian's Office, Brigham Young History Drafts, 11–14; see also Richards, Journal, 13 Mar.–19 May and 11–12 June 1837.)

President Charles [C.] Rich, who is the president of the high priests in Zion; represented his quorum; he read the names of those who belonged to his quorum, the principal part of which were in good standing.

The seventies were represented, by presidents Daniel Miles, and Levi Hancock.

The quorum of Elders were represented by president Harvey Green— Their number was 124, in good standing.

President Joseph Smith Jr, next made a few remarks on the word of wisdom,[371] giving the reason of its coming forth, saying it should be observed.[372] On motion, the Conference adjourned for one hour.

The Conference convened, agreeable to adjournment, and opened by singing and prayer, after which Bishop [Edward] Partridge, represented the lesser priesthood,[373] and his council,— He gave an account of the incomes and outgoes of Church property which had passed through his hands.[374]

It was then motioned and seconded, and carrried that the first presidency be appointed to sign the licences of the official members of the church—[375] After which on motion, the Conference adjourned until the first Friday in July next.[376]

JOSEPH SMITH, Jr.
President.

Ebenezer Robinson, Clerk. [p. 47]

———— ∽ ————

---

371. The "word of wisdom"—the revelation containing the church's dietary code—proscribed the ingestion of distilled liquors, wine, coffee, tea, and tobacco. (See Revelation, 27 Feb. 1833, in *JSP*, D3:11–24 [D&C 89].)

372. Failure to observe the "word of wisdom" was one reason the members of the Zion presidency were removed from office in February 1838. (See Letter from Thomas B. Marsh, 15 Feb. 1838, p. 20 herein.)

373. That is, the Aaronic order of priesthood offices, which Partridge presided over. (Revelation, 22–23 Sept. 1832, in *JSP*, D2:296–297 [D&C 84:25–30]; Instruction on Priesthood, between ca. 1 Mar. and ca. 4 May 1835, in *JSP*, D4:313 [D&C 107:13–15].)

374. Between January and March, Partridge sold almost one hundred acres of land in Jackson County, Missouri, possibly to help fund land purchases and urgent settlement needs in Caldwell County, Missouri. Partridge also allotted land in the Far West plot, including to JS, Rigdon, and Hyrum Smith. These transactions may have been among those reported at this time. (Jackson Co., MO, Deed Records, 1827–1909, vol. F, pp. 107–108, 10 Jan. 1838; p. 109, 2 Feb. 1838; p. 110, 9 Mar. 1838, microfilm 1,017,980, U.S. and Canada Record Collection, FHL; Minute Book 2, 3 Mar. 1838.)

375. Resolution, ca. 8 Apr. 1838, p. 76 herein.

376. The church's founding "Articles and Covenants" instructed the elders of the church to meet in conference quarterly. (Articles and Covenants, ca. Apr. 1830, in *JSP*, D1:124; see also Revelation Book 1, p. 56, in *JSP*, MRB:83 [D&C 20:61].)

Resolution, circa 8 April 1838

Source Note

JS, Sidney Rigdon, and Hyrum Smith, Resolution, Far West, Caldwell Co., MO, [ca. 8 Apr. 1838], in License Record Book, Dec. 1837–May 1862, p. 19; handwriting of George W. Robinson; CHL. For more information on License Record Book, Dec. 1837–May 1862, see Source Notes for Multiple-Entry Documents, p. 567 herein.

Historical Introduction

On 8 April 1838, the second day of a quarterly church conference held in Far West, Missouri, the Saints passed a resolution that a member of the First Presidency should sign all licenses for the church's priesthood officers. The church issued licenses to its officers to use when traveling, providing proof that they were legitimate officers in good standing. At first, these licenses were handwritten; later, the church printed license forms upon which information, including the officer's name and the signatures of those authorizing the license, could be added by hand after the officer was ordained.[377] According to the licensing reforms adopted in 1836, all licenses were to be authorized with the signatures of the chairman and the clerk of the conference in which the officer was ordained. When this policy was established, JS was appointed as the church's licensing chairman, with Frederick G. Williams, who was a counselor in the First Presidency, appointed as the licensing clerk.[378] Later, David Whitmer, president of the church in Missouri, was appointed as the licensing chairman for licenses issued there, and William W. Phelps was appointed as the licensing clerk.[379] In February 1838, when the members of the Zion presidency were removed from office, they were also rejected as licensing officers. Apostles Thomas B. Marsh and David W. Patten were appointed to replace the Zion presidency as presidents pro tempore and to serve as licensing officers until JS's arrival.[380] When JS arrived in Missouri, he retained Marsh and Patten as presidents over the church in Zion, but JS and his counselors in the First Presidency assumed the role of licensing officers.[381] This resolution may have been part of the general effort to address the recent dissent of some church members against JS. The resolution ensured that only leaders who supported JS would receive valid licenses.

Sometime after the conference, George W. Robinson noted the resolution in a license record book. The record book begins with a note regarding the appointment of the committee that drafted the March 1836 licensing reforms. Because the 8 April resolution revised the reforms of 1836, Robinson may have added the note about the 8 April resolution in the record

---

377. See, for example, License for John Whitmer, 9 June 1830, in *JSP,* D1:142–146; License for Frederick G. Williams, 25 Feb. 1834, in *JSP,* D3:463–465; and License, 21 Mar. 1836, in *JSP,* D5:186–188.

378. Minutes, 3 Mar. 1836, in *JSP,* D5:181–185.

379. Minute Book 2, 6–7 Dec. 1837.

380. Letter from Thomas B. Marsh, 15 Feb. 1838, p. 23 herein.

381. See Minutes, 6 Apr. 1838, p. 70 herein.

book to clarify that the 1836 policy had been revised.[382] Robinson's note does not match the language of the resolution as recorded in the minutes of the conference, and the note adds the detail that Robinson was appointed as the licensing clerk. The note, therefore, is not a transcribed excerpt from the minutes of the conference but a documentary production in its own right. The note bears the date of 6 April 1838, when a meeting was held to commemorate the anniversary of the church's organization, to conduct church business, and to perform ordinances. However, the resolution was actually made on 8 April, during the two-day quarterly conference that followed the anniversary meeting. Although the formatting of the note—which presents the date on its own line like a dateline—seems to indicate that the resolution was passed on 6 April, the wording may be understood to mean that any other form of licensing would be considered fraudulent after 6 April—the start of meetings in which new leaders were appointed. The note regarding the resolution may also carry a 6 April date because church conferences that lasted more than one day were often dated in church records with only the first day of the conference.[383] Although the minutes of the two meetings identify only the 7–8 April meeting as the quarterly conference, in Robinson's note the anniversary meeting was considered part of the "general Conference." The minutes of the 7–8 April conference specify that the resolution was moved, seconded, and carried on 8 April.[384] Robinson probably inscribed the note shortly after the 7–8 April conference. The latest possible copying date was apparently 1 June 1838, the day he received the first new license and copied it into the record book just beneath the note.[385] This license and the licenses that follow in the record book manifest that the resolution of the conference was followed in the ensuing months.[386]

Document Transcript

Voted by a general Conference of the ordained members of the Church of Jesus Christ of Latter Day Saints, assembled in Far West Mo. April 6th 1838. That all licenses hereafter Should be Signed by one of the first Prests of the Church as Prest. & the general Recorder as Clerk. And all others, of course will be concidered fraud after this Date[387]

Far, West, Mo. April 6th 1838.

---

382. General Church Recorder, License Record Book, 1.

383. See, for example, Minutes, ca. 3–4 June 1831, in *JSP*, D1:317; Minute Book 2, 5–7 Apr. 1837; and Minutes, 4–5 May 1839, p. 444 herein.

384. This was one of the final resolutions passed in the conference, following a one-hour intermission that may have allowed for a midday meal. (See Minutes, 7–8 Apr. 1838, p. 74 herein.)

385. General Church Recorder, License Record Book, 19.

386. General Church Recorder, License Record Book, 19–32; see also License for Gardner Snow, 19 Jan. 1839, pp. 316–318 herein.

387. This phrasing may indicate that previously issued licenses were no longer valid. The licensing reforms of March 1836 included an article requesting all previous license holders to turn in their old licenses and receive new ones issued under the new regulations. (Minutes, 3 Mar. 1836, in *JSP*, D5:183.)

Joseph Smith Jr ⎫
Sidney Rigdon ⎬ Pre[ts.] of Said Church
Hyrum Smith[388] ⎭

Geo. W. Robinson } Recorder General.[389]

———— ℯ⁊ ————

Letter to John Whitmer, 9 April 1838

Source Note

JS and Sidney Rigdon, Letter, Far West, Caldwell Co., MO, to John Whitmer, [Far West, Caldwell Co., MO], 9 Apr. 1838; attested by Ebenezer Robinson. Featured version copied [ca. mid- or late Apr. 1838] in JS, Journal, Mar.–Sept. 1838, p. 28; handwriting of George W. Robinson; CHL. Includes use marks. For more information on JS, Journal, Mar.–Sept. 1838, see Source Notes for Multiple-Entry Documents, p. 564 herein.

Historical Introduction

On 9 April 1838, JS and Sidney Rigdon wrote to former church historian John Whitmer, requesting that he give them the writings he had been preparing since 1831 for a church history. When asked in 1831 to serve as the church's historian, Whitmer initially declined. However, after JS dictated a revelation appointing Whitmer to "keep the Church Record & History continually," Whitmer accepted a formal appointment to perform these duties.[390] Within a few months of his appointment, Whitmer began writing the history of the church.[391] In late 1832, JS referred to Whitmer in his role of church historian as "the lord['s] clerk."[392] Nevertheless, Whitmer remained somewhat uncertain about his roles, and JS had some concerns about Whitmer fulfilling his responsibilities. By the time of his excommunication on 10 March 1838, Whitmer had apparently written eighty-five manuscript pages recounting the history of the church up to that time.[393] These writings placed several revelation texts and

---

388. Although Hyrum Smith's name is affixed to this resolution as a member of the First Presidency of the church, he was not present at the conference. Smith, who was moving from Ohio to Missouri, departed Kirtland in March and did not arrive at Far West until late May. JS, Rigdon, or Robinson may have signed for Hyrum Smith in his absence. It is also possible that the inscribed names of the First Presidency do not represent signatures but that Robinson added the names to the written resolution to represent their authority as the presiding officers of the conference in which the resolution was passed or to represent their authority as the new licensing officers named in the resolution. (Hyrum Smith, Commerce, IL, to "the Saints Scattered Abroad," Dec. 1839, in *Times and Seasons,* Dec. 1839, 1:21; O'Driscoll, *Hyrum Smith,* 167–170.)

389. Robinson was appointed "general Church Recorder and Clerk for the first Presidency" in the 6 April 1838 anniversary and business meeting. (Minutes, 6 Apr. 1838, p. 69 herein.)

390. Whitmer, History, 24, in *JSP,* H2:36; Revelation, ca. 8 Mar. 1831–B, in *JSP,* D1:286 [D&C 47:3]; Minute Book 2, 9 Apr. 1831.

391. Whitmer, History, 1, in *JSP,* H2:12.

392. Letter to William W. Phelps, 27 Nov. 1832, in *JSP,* D2:318 [D&C 85:1].

393. See Historical Introduction to Whitmer, History, in *JSP,* H2:6–8.

other important documents in context and provided firsthand information regarding significant episodes in the church's history. However, as the 9 April letter suggests, Whitmer's writings may not have met JS's expectations.

Following Whitmer's excommunication, the church needed to fill his roles as church clerk, record keeper, and historian. In a meeting held 6 April 1838, the Latter-day Saints in Missouri appointed two new historians as well as two clerks.[394] This and other business conducted in the meeting organizationally prepared the church for the quarterly conference held over the next two days. Perhaps in response to business conducted at the 7–8 April conference, church leaders wrote letters on 9 April to address administrative matters. Edward Partridge sent a letter notifying Oliver Cowdery of his upcoming trial on 12 April, and John Murdock sent letters to Lyman Johnson and David Whitmer, notifying them of their upcoming trials on 13 April.[395] JS and Rigdon wrote the featured letter to Whitmer, criticizing his capabilities and performance as a church historian and requesting that he turn over his historical writing to the church. Whitmer evidently refused to relinquish his writings.[396] By the end of April 1838, JS, Rigdon, and their clerk, George W. Robinson, began writing a new history, which included much more detail than Whitmer's effort did.

Document Transcript

Far West April 9th 1838

Mr J[ohn] Whitmer

Sir. We were desireous of honouring you by giving publicity to your notes on the history of the Church of Latter day Saints,[397] after such corrections as we thought would be necessary; knowing your incompetency as a historian, and that your writings coming from your pen, could not be put to the press, without our correcting them, or elce the Church must suffer reproach; Indeed Sir, we never supposed you capable of writing a history; but were willing to let it come out under your name notwithstanding it would realy not be yours but ours.[398] We are still willing to honour you, if you can be made to know your

---

394. Minutes, 6 Apr. 1838, pp. 69–70 herein.

395. See Minutes, 12 Apr. 1838, pp. 87–89 herein; and Minutes, 13 Apr. 1838, pp. 97, 103 herein.

396. Although no written reply from Whitmer exists, his refusal to turn over his history is apparent from subsequent events, including the creation of a substitute history. A few years later, Whitmer offered to sell his history, which he titled the "Book of John Whitmer," to the church. By the time Whitmer offered to sell his history, JS's new history was well under way, and Whitmer's offer was declined. (JS, Journal, 27 Apr. 1838, in *JSP*, J1:260; John Whitmer, Far West, MO, to William W. Phelps, Nauvoo, IL, 8 Jan. 1844, JS Office Papers, CHL; Willard Richards, Nauvoo, IL, to John Whitmer, Far West, MO, 23 Feb. 1844, copy, Willard Richards, Papers, CHL; for an introduction to and a transcript of Whitmer's history, which is now owned by the Community of Christ church, see Whitmer, History, in *JSP*, H2:3–110.)

397. Besides his historical notes and manuscript history, Whitmer apparently had letters, membership rosters, minutes of meetings, and other documents. (Historical Introduction to Whitmer, History, in *JSP*, H2:5–9.)

398. Decades later, Ebenezer Robinson recounted that the church attempted to obtain Whitmer's historical writings and other church records before JS and Rigdon wrote the letter but that Whitmer refused

own interest and give up your notes, so that they can be corrected, and made fit for the press.[399] But if not, we have all the materials for another, which we shall commence this week to write[400]

	your humble Servents
Attest	Joseph Smith Jr
E[benezer] Robinson	Sidney Rigdon
Clerk[401]	Presidents of the whole
	Church of Latterday Saints

[p. 28]

——— ❧ ———

Promissory Note from Lorenzo Young, 9 April 1838

Source Note

Lorenzo Young, Promissory Note, Far West, Caldwell Co., MO, to JS, 9 Apr. 1838; handwriting of JS; signature of Lorenzo Young; notation of partial payment added in handwriting of JS; two pages; JS Collection, CHL.

One leaf measuring 4¼ × 7⅝ inches (11 × 19 cm). The document was folded for filing. Presumably, JS kept the note and it remained in church custody after his death, eventually becoming part of the JS Collection in the Historical Department of the LDS church.

Historical Introduction

On 9 April 1838, JS wrote a promissory note stating Lorenzo Young and Isaac Decker would repay forty dollars they had jointly borrowed from JS. Young signed the note on behalf of himself and Decker. The language of the note—stating that Young and Decker "have had" the borrowed money—suggests that they borrowed the money sometime before 9 April. According to an early biography of Isaac's wife, Harriet Wheeler Decker, Isaac had been a prosperous Ohio farmer before he impoverished his family in early 1837 in an attempt to ease JS's and Rigdon's financial difficulties. Decker and some other Saints

---

to relinquish the items. This failed attempt, which may have influenced the insulting tone of the subsequent letter from JS and Rigdon, may have been made by Ebenezer Robinson or George W. Robinson after the Zion high council meeting held on 6 April. (Ebenezer Robinson, "Items of Personal History of the Editor," *Return,* Sept. 1889, 133.)

399. When a mob razed the Mormon print shop in Independence, Missouri, in 1833, the church formed a new printing establishment in Kirtland, Ohio. Now that JS was living in Far West and loyal Saints in Kirtland were preparing to follow him, he may have planned to reestablish the church's printing operations in Missouri. (See Crawley, *Descriptive Bibliography,* 1:17–20.)

400. When JS, Rigdon, and Robinson started writing a new history, they had access to copies of JS's revelations, correspondence, and other documents, some of which were later incorporated in the history. (JS, Journal, 27 Apr. 1838, in *JSP,* J1:260; Historical Introduction to History Drafts, 1838–ca. 1841, in *JSP,* H1:192–194.)

401. Ebenezer Robinson had recently been appointed "Church Clerk and Recorder for this stake of Zion and Clerk for the high Council." (Minutes, 6 Apr. 1838, p. 70 herein.)

apparently feared the two church leaders would be forced to repay all notes issued by the recently closed Kirtland Safety Society.[402] Lorenzo Young befriended Isaac Decker and helped outfit his family for travel, and in late 1837 their families traveled together to Missouri.[403] The Decker and Young families stopped for the winter in Dublin, Indiana, where they were joined by Lorenzo's brother Brigham—one of the twelve apostles—and later by JS, Sidney Rigdon, and others. While the Young and Decker families were wintering in Indiana, Lorenzo Young traveled to Cincinnati and Isaac Decker traveled to Michigan, perhaps at JS's direction. Meanwhile, Brigham Young helped arrange a donation of $300 from a local Latter-day Saint, which allowed JS and the others to continue their journey. The Young and Decker families moved on with JS and the rest, with Brigham, Lorenzo, and Isaac later catching up to the company.[404] According to later biographies, soon after Lorenzo Young and Decker arrived in Missouri, JS directed them to settle their families in Daviess County, where Young bought a farm and Decker rented property.[405] Young and Decker may have traveled from residences in Daviess County to Far West, Caldwell County, to attend the quarterly conference held there 7–8 April.[406] The following day, Young signed the featured promissory note. Three months later, one or both of them made a partial payment on the debt, as noted on the back of the document, but apparently the remainder of the debt was never repaid.

Document Transcript

Far West April 9ᵗʰ 1838

I hereby certify that I in company with Isaac Decker have had forty dollers of Joseph Smith Jr which we are in Justice bound to pay to him when he calls for it with use[407]

—Lorenzo Young [p. [1]]

9ᵗʰ July 1838

Rec— on the within five dollers[408] [p. [2]]

———— ❧ ————

---

402. Decker was not alone in providing financial assistance. (See *JSP,* D5:420n292.)

403. Orson F. Whitney, "Pioneer Women of Utah," *Contributor,* July 1890, 323.

404. Historian's Office, Brigham Young History Drafts, 15–16.

405. Little, "Biography of Lorenzo Dow Young," 38; "History of Brigham Young," *Deseret News,* 3 Feb. 1858, 378; Orson F. Whitney, "Pioneer Women of Utah," *Contributor,* July 1890, 323.

406. See Minutes, 7–8 Apr. 1838, pp. 71–74 herein.

407. In this context, "use" apparently means usury, or interest. ("Usury," in *American Dictionary.*)

408. As was common practice, JS likely issued a receipt to Young and Decker for this partial payment; the receipt is apparently not extant. (See, for example, Receipt from Samuel Musick, 14 July 1838, p. 206 herein.)

Revelation, 11 April 1838 [D&C 114]

Source Note

Revelation, [Far West, Caldwell Co., MO], 11 Apr. 1838. Featured version copied [ca. mid- or late Apr. 1838] in JS, Journal, Mar.–Sept. 1838, p. 32; handwriting of George W. Robinson; CHL. Includes use marks. For more information on JS, Journal, Mar.–Sept. 1838, see Source Notes for Multiple-Entry Documents, p. 564 herein.

Historical Introduction

On 11 April 1838, JS dictated a revelation for David W. Patten, directing him to settle his business affairs and prepare for a mission. At the time, Patten and fellow apostle Brigham Young were serving as assistants to Thomas B. Marsh in the pro tempore presidency over the church in Missouri.[409] This appointment was apparently temporary because, as members of the Quorum of the Twelve Apostles, Marsh, Patten, and Young were eventually expected to travel, proselytize, and supervise the church conferences and branches outside of Zion and its stakes—that is, outside of the main church congregation in Missouri and any other places designated for gathering.[410] The previous summer, Patten had asked the Zion high council in Far West, Missouri, to relieve him of his debts and allow him to travel and preach.[411] Though the high council resolved to grant Patten's request, instead of embarking on a mission Patten soon departed for Kirtland with Marsh in an effort to reunite the Quorum of the Twelve Apostles. Shortly after they arrived in Kirtland, JS dictated a revelation for Marsh, the president of the quorum, directing him and the other apostles to purify themselves "and then go ye into all the world and preach my gospel unto every creature who have not received it."[412] At the same time, apostles Heber C. Kimball and Orson Hyde were beginning a mission in England. The missionaries wrote to their fellow Latter-day Saints in the United States with news of the hundreds of people in England who had joined the church.[413]

---

409. Minutes, 6 Apr. 1838, p. 70 herein.

410. See Minutes and Discourses, 27 Feb. 1835, in *JSP*, D4:252; Minutes and Discourse, 2 May 1835, in *JSP*, D4:301–302; Instruction on Priesthood, between ca. 1 Mar. and ca. 4 May 1835, in *JSP*, D4:314 [D&C 107:23]; and JS, Journal, 27 Mar. 1836, in *JSP*, J1:204.

411. Patten submitted the following written request: "I am in debt and want to go away, will the Church pay my debts and take me for the same. and let me go and preach the Kingdom of God." (Minute Book 2, 11 June 1837.)

412. Revelation, 23 July 1837, in *JSP*, D5:417 [D&C 112:28].

413. For example, letters from Kimball and Hyde were published in the church newspaper. News of the success in England was also reported by Joseph Fielding, who was also proselytizing there, in a letter to his sister Mary Fielding Smith, the wife of JS's brother Hyrum. (Heber C. Kimball, Preston, England, to Vilate Murray Kimball, Kirtland, OH, 2–6 Sept. 1837, in *Elders' Journal,* Oct. 1837, 4–7; Orson Hyde, Preston, England, to Marinda Nancy Johnson Hyde, Kirtland, OH, 14 Sept. 1837, in *Elders' Journal,* Nov. 1837, 19–22; Joseph Fielding, Preston, England, to Mary Fielding, Kirtland, OH, 2 Oct. 1837, Mary Fielding Smith, Collection, CHL; see also Heber C. Kimball, Preston, England, to Vilate Murray Kimball, Kirtland, OH, 12 Nov. 1837, Heber C. Kimball, Correspondence, CHL; and Allen et al., *Men with a Mission,* 20–53.)

The 11 April 1838 revelation to Patten, probably dictated in Far West,[414] stated that Patten would be sent on a mission the following spring and implied that he would go with the other apostles. Another revelation, received about three months later, specified that in 1839 the twelve apostles would "depart to go over the great waters and there promulge my gospel," suggesting they would serve a mission in Europe to follow up on the success of Kimball and Hyde's mission in England.[415] Patten, however, was killed in October 1838 in the conflict between the Latter-day Saints and other Missourians.

As JS dictated the 11 April revelation, it may have been inscribed by Patten, who was presumably present, or by George W. Robinson, the First Presidency's scribe. Robinson transcribed the original into JS's "Scriptory Book," probably in mid- or late April.[416]

Document Transcript

Revelation to D[avid] W. Patten. given April 11ᵗʰ· 1838 Verily thus Saith the Lord, it is wisdom in my Servant D. W. Patten, that he settle up all his buisness, as soon as he possibly, can, and make a disposition of his merchandise,[417] that he may perform a mission unto me next spring, in company with others even twelve including himself, to testify of my name and bear glad tidings unto all the world,[418] for verrily thus Saith the Lord that inasmuch as there are those among you who deny my name,[419] others shall be planted in their stead[420] and receive their bishoprick[421] Amen.———

——— ❧ ———

---

414. The copy of this revelation in JS's multivolume manuscript history specifies that the revelation was "given at Far West." (JS History, vol. B-1, 790.)

415. Revelation, 8 July 1838–A, pp. 179–180 herein [D&C 118:4]. The word *promulge* is an archaic form of *promulgate*. ("Promulge," in *Oxford English Dictionary*, 8:1458.)

416. Beginning with a revelation dated 26 April 1838, Robinson apparently kept the Scriptory Book regularly for some time, suggesting that he copied the 11 April revelation for Patten—which appears in chronological order among other April documents and journal entries—sometime in mid- or late April. (See JS, Journal, Mar.–Sept. 1838, pp. 32–34, in *JSP*, J1:257–260.)

417. Patten moved to Caldwell County, Missouri, by April 1837. In June the Zion presidency and high council gave Patten a lot in Far West. He may have been operating a business from this lot. (See Minute Book 2, 5–7 Apr. and 11 June 1837.)

418. See Isaiah 52:7; Luke 8:1; Book of Mormon, 1830 ed., 260 [Alma 13:22]; and Revelation, 13 Aug. 1831, in *JSP*, D2:47 [D&C 62:5].

419. See Revelation 3:8.

420. See Book of Mormon, 1830 ed., 135 [Jacob 5:44]; Revelation, 7 Dec. 1830, in *JSP*, D1:221 [D&C 35:18]; and Revelation, 11 Sept. 1831, in *JSP*, D2:66 [D&C 64:40]. In the quarterly conference held 7–8 April 1838, Patten represented the Quorum of the Twelve Apostles and reported he could not recommend that the conference participants sustain William E. McLellin, Luke Johnson, Lyman Johnson, or John F. Boynton as apostles. He also "spake somewhat doubtful of William Smith." (Minutes, 7–8 Apr. 1838, p. 72 herein.)

421. The term *bishoprick* was sometimes used in a generic sense to refer to any office. ("Bishopric," in *Oxford English Dictionary*, 1:879; see also Acts 1:20; and Psalm 109:8.)

Minutes, 12 April 1838

Source Note

Zion high council and bishopric, Minutes, Far West, Caldwell Co., MO, 12 Apr. 1838. Featured version copied [between 1 Oct. 1842 and 14 Sept. 1843] in Minute Book 2, pp. 118–126; handwriting of Hosea Stout; CHL. For more information on Minute Book 2, see Source Notes for Multiple-Entry Documents, p. 569 herein.

Historical Introduction

On 12 April 1838, JS testified in the church trial of Oliver Cowdery in Far West, Missouri. The rift between church leaders who were loyal to JS and those who were not had been widening for several months, beginning in Kirtland, Ohio, in 1837 and extending into Missouri later that year. The 12 April trial as well as another trial on 13 April represented the culmination of ecclesiastical efforts to cull dissent and division within the church. At the 12 April trial, JS testified that prior to Cowdery's dissension, he had been JS's "bosom friend." In 1829, Cowdery had served as JS's principal scribe for the Book of Mormon translation, and since that time the two men had jointly experienced visions, witnessed angelic visitations, and served as the church's first teachers and leading elders.[422] Further, in 1834 JS designated Cowdery as first assistant in the church presidency.[423] Despite these experiences, by 1837 Cowdery began to express displeasure with JS's leadership of the church.[424] As Cowdery noted in a letter included in the 12 April minutes, a central issue for him and others who opposed JS was the extent that the church and its leaders were involved in the "temporal interests" of its members. As another factor contributing to Cowdery's dissent, by summer 1837 he was deeply in debt, likely in part because he previously purchased wholesale goods for a mercantile firm he operated with JS and Sidney Rigdon.[425] In addition, as noted in his trial, Cowdery had insinuated since 1837 that JS was guilty of adultery. Nevertheless, in a 3 September 1837 conference of the church in Kirtland, Cowdery was accepted as one of the "assistant Councilors" in the First Presidency. The next day, JS wrote to church leaders in Missouri, warning them that although Cowdery had been "chosen as one of the Presidents or councilors" in the First Presidency, he had "been in transgression" and that if he did not "humble himself & magnify his calling . . . the church will soon be under the necessaty of raising their hands against him."[426] In October 1837, Cowdery moved to Missouri, where he

---

422. See "Printer's Manuscript of the Book of Mormon," in *JSP*, R3, Part 1, pp. xxiii–xxiv; Revelation, ca. Aug. 1835, in *JSP*, D4:411 [D&C 27:8, 12]; JS History, vol. A-1, 37–38, in *JSP*, H1:368–370 [Draft 2]; Articles and Covenants, ca. Apr. 1830, in *JSP*, D1:120 [D&C 20:1–3]; and JS, Journal, 3 Apr. 1836, in *JSP*, J1:219–222; see also Harper, "Oliver Cowdery as Second Witness," 73–89.

423. Account of Meetings, Revelation, and Blessing, 5–6 Dec. 1834, in *JSP*, D4:194.

424. See Historical Introduction to Letter from Thomas B. Marsh, 15 Feb. 1838, pp. 12–13 herein.

425. See, for example, John Whitmer, Far West, MO, to Oliver Cowdery and David Whitmer, Kirtland Mills, OH, 29 Aug. 1837, Western Americana Collection, Beinecke Rare Book and Manuscript Library, Yale University, New Haven, CT; and Statement of Account from Perkins & Osborn, ca. 29 Oct. 1838, p. 261 herein.

426. Letter to John Corrill and the Church in Missouri, 4 Sept. 1837, in *JSP*, D5:430.

evidently devoted much of his time to improving his dire financial situation.[427] He sold personal property in Jackson County, Missouri, and to bolster his emerging clerical and legal practice, he encouraged lawsuits against church members. Both of these activities were included in the high council's charges against Cowdery in the 12 April trial.

The sale of Jackson County land by Cowdery, John Whitmer, and William W. Phelps was the impetus for some of the earlier charges against the members of the Zion presidency. John Whitmer and Phelps, who had served as counselors to Zion president David Whitmer, were removed from office in early February.[428] Cowdery showed implicit support for the deposed Zion presidency by attesting a letter the former presidency members wrote to Thomas B. Marsh, protesting the trial of Phelps and John Whitmer.[429] On 7 April, Seymour Brunson submitted nine charges against Cowdery, most relating to accusations of misconduct and disloyalty to JS and the church. Two days later, church leaders wrote letters to Cowdery, David Whitmer, and Lyman Johnson—an apostle and frequent associate of the dissenters in Kirtland and Far West—informing them of their trials before the high council. Cowdery received his letter the day it was written. On 12 April, instead of attending his trial in person, Cowdery sent a letter to Bishop Edward Partridge that underscored Cowdery's opposition to the actions of the church and asked that he be allowed to withdraw his membership.

Cowdery's trial was held at Partridge's office in Far West.[430] The trial proceeded according to official instructions for trying "a president of the high priesthood" before a "common council of the church," which consisted of a bishop, acting as a "common judge," and twelve high priests.[431] In this case, Partridge conducted the case with the assistance of his counselors in the bishopric and the twelve members of the high council. The letter in which Cowdery requested to withdraw from the church was read to the bishopric and high council, and the court proceeded to investigate the charges. Most of the testimony centered on Cowdery's emerging legal practice, his accusations that JS had committed adultery, and his alleged connection to counterfeiters in Ohio. JS testified twice during the trial. As a result of the testimony JS and others offered, Partridge and his counselors decided to excommunicate Cowdery; the high council concurred. Minutes of the council meeting were taken by clerk Ebenezer Robinson. They were later copied into Minute Book 2 by Hosea Stout.

Document Transcript

The High Council and Bishoprick of Zion met according to appointment[432] in Far-West April 12ᵗʰ 1838 Edward Partridge Presiding

---

427. Whitmer, Daybook, 20 Oct. 1837.

428. Letter from Thomas B. Marsh, 15 Feb. 1838, pp. 19, 22 herein; Minute Book 2, 10 Mar. 1838.

429. David Whitmer et al., Far West, MO, to Thomas B. Marsh, Far West, MO, 10 Mar. 1838, in Minute Book 2, 10 Mar. 1838.

430. Synopsis of Oliver Cowdery Trial, 12 Apr. 1838, in *JSP*, J1:254.

431. Instruction on Priesthood, between ca. 1 Mar. and ca. 4 May 1835, in *JSP*, D4:318, 320 [D&C 107:74, 82–84].

432. The high council had last met on 24 March 1838. (Minutes, 24 Mar. 1838, pp. 46–50 herein.)

The Council was organized as follows;

Samuel H. Smith[433]	no 1	Jared Carter	no 2
Thomas Grover	" 3	Isaac Higbee[434]	" 4
Levi Jackman	" 5	Solomon Hancock	" 6
George Morey	" 7	Newel Knight	" 8
George M. Hinkle	" 9	George W. Harris	" 10
Elias Higbee	" 11	John Murdock	" 12

Voted unanimously that John Murdock be a President of the High Council,[435] whose duty it shall be to receive charges and give notice to the defendant, also, to call the Council together and organize them &c

The Council opened by prayer by E. Partridge

After some remarks by Edward Partridge, several charges were read by him prefered against Oliver Cowdery which are as follows;

"To the Bishop and Council of the Church of Jesus Christ of Latter day Saints in Missouri.

I do hereby prefer the following charges against President Oliver Cowdery.

1st, For stiring up the enemy to persecute the brethren by urging on vexatious Lawsuits and thus distressing the inocent.[436]

---

433. Samuel Smith was apparently substituting for Simeon Carter. (See Minutes, 24 Mar. 1838, p. 47 herein; and Minutes, 13 Apr. 1838, p. 96 herein.)

434. Higbee was apparently substituting for John P. Greene. (See Minute Book 2, 7–8 Apr. 1838; and Minutes, 13 Apr. 1838, p. 96 herein.)

435. See 23n104 herein.

436. In a 10 March 1838 letter to his brothers, Cowdery reported having "some four or five suits to attend to" at the April term of the circuit court in Caldwell County, Missouri.[a] The details of these cases are largely unknown because of the lack of extant court records. One of these cases may have been a suit on behalf of George Walters to redeem an 1836 promissory note from the First Presidency. In July 1838, Partridge testified that Cowdery promised to help Walters redeem the note in exchange for removing Cowdery's name as a debtor on the note.[b] Several church leaders, probably drawing on passages in the New Testament, the Book of Mormon, and JS's revelations, expressed the belief that it was immoral to sue other church members in a court of law.[c] For example, in 1837 the Quorum of the Seventy in Kirtland voted to "withdraw fellowship from all who are in a habit of promoting litigation among their brethren and still persist in so dooing."[d] It is likely that such beliefs, coupled with a general antipathy toward lawyers, motivated some of the ecclesiastical charges against Cowdery. (a. Oliver Cowdery, Far West, MO, to Warren Cowdery and Lyman Cowdery, Kirtland, OH, [10] Mar. 1838, in Cowdery, Letterbook, 92. b. Edward Partridge, Affidavit, Caldwell Co., MO, 12 July 1838, in Frampton, Justice of the Peace Docket Entry, CHL. c. See 1 Corinthians 6:1; Ashurst-McGee, "Zion Rising," 128–129; and Firmage and Mangrum, *Zion in the Courts,* 12–18; see also JS, Journal, 7 Mar. 1844, in *JSP,* J3:191–192. d. Quorums of the Seventy, "Book of Records," 32, 37.)

2$^{\underline{nd}}$, For seeking to destroy~~ing~~ the character of President Joseph Smith j^r, by falsly insinuating that he was guilty of adultry &c.[437]

3$^{\underline{rd}}$ For treating the Church with contempt by not attending meetings.[438]

4$^{\underline{th}}$ For virtually denying the faith by declaring that he would not be governed by any ecclesiastical authority nor Revelation whatever in his temporal affairs[439] [p. 118]

5th For selling his lands in Jackson County contrary to the Revelations.[440]

6th For writing and sending an insulting letter to President T[homas] B. Marsh while on the High Council, attending to the duties of his office, as President of the Council and by insulting the whole Council with the contents of said letter[441]

7$^{\underline{th}}$, For leaving the calling, in which God had appointed him, by

---

437. For information on Cowdery's accusations of adultery, see Historical Introduction to Letter from Thomas B. Marsh, 15 Feb. 1838, pp. 12–13 herein.

438. Similar charges were made against Lyman Johnson and David Whitmer. Though Cowdery was clerk of the high council, there is no record of him attending high council meetings after 7 December 1837. In early February 1838, Cowdery wrote to his brothers that the Zion presidency refused to attend the February general assembly meetings in which presidency members were removed from office. Although Cowdery's role was not yet in question at that date, he said he planned to only "attend one meeting, say what I think wisdom and leave them to their own damnation." (Minutes, 13 Apr. 1838, pp. 96, 102 herein; Minute Book 2, 6–7 Dec. 1837; Oliver Cowdery, Far West, MO, to Warren Cowdery and Lyman Cowdery, [Kirtland, OH], 4 Feb. 1838, in Cowdery, Letterbook, 84.)

439. In February 1838, Cowdery wrote to his brothers that he told a committee of the Zion high council, "If I had property, while I live and was sane, I would not be dictated, influenced or controlled, by any man or set of men by no tribunal of ecclesiastical pretences whatever." (Oliver Cowdery, Far West, MO, to Warren Cowdery and Lyman Cowdery, [Kirtland, OH], 4 Feb. 1838, in Cowdery, Letterbook, 84.)

440. Following the expulsion of the Saints from Jackson County in 1833, JS told Edward Partridge that "it is better that you should die in the ey[e]s of God, then that you should give up the Land of Zion." In 1835 three of the church's lots, held by Phelps and Cowdery, were seized by the county and sold at a sheriff's auction, apparently to cover the costs of the church's legal proceedings in that county. On 11 January 1838, Cowdery, Phelps, John Whitmer, and their wives signed a quitclaim deed to their remaining interest in those lots, for an amount Cowdery described as "a small sum." (Letter to Edward Partridge, 5 Dec. 1833, in *JSP*, D3:371; Letter to Edward Partridge, 10 Dec. 1833, in *JSP*, D3:378–379; Jackson Co., MO, Deed Records, vol. D, pp. 148–152, microfilm 1,017,979; Jackson Co., MO, Deed Records, vol. F, pp. 54–55, 11 Jan. 1838, microfilm 1,017,980, U.S. and Canada Record Collection, FHL; Oliver Cowdery, Far West, MO, to Warren Cowdery and Lyman Cowdery, [Kirtland, OH], 4 Feb. 1838, in Cowdery, Letterbook, 84.)

441. On 10 March 1838, David Whitmer, William W. Phelps, and John Whitmer wrote a letter to Thomas B. Marsh complaining about the way he and the high council had treated the three men. Cowdery apparently served as the scribe and added an attestation to the letter. The letter was delivered by Cowdery's nephew, Marcellus Cowdery, to the council at the trial for Phelps and John Whitmer. According to the minutes of the trial, "The letter was considered no more, nor less, than a direct insult, or contempt, cast upon the authorities of God, and the church of Jesus Christ." (Minute Book 2, 10 Mar. 1838.)

Revelation, for the sake of filthy lucre,[442] and turning to the practice of the Law.[443]

8ᵗʰ, For disgracing the Church by ~~lieing~~ being connected in the 'Bogus' buisness as common report says.[444]

9ᵗʰ· For dishonestly Retaining notes after they had been paid[445] and finally for leaving or forsaking the cause of God, and betaking himself to the beggerly elements of the world and neglecting his high and Holy Calling' contrary to his profession.

Far West April the 7ᵗʰ 1838. Seymour Brunson"

It was not considered a difficult case, therefore, ~~two~~ ⟨one⟩ spake on a side viz Samuel H. Smith on the part of the Church and Jared Carter on the part of the defendant.

A letter was then read by Edward Partridge from O. Cowdery which reads as follows:

Far. West M͟o April 12ᵗʰ 1838

Dear Sir.

I received your note of the 9ᵗʰ inst on the day of its date, containing a copy of nine charges prefered ~~against~~ ⟨before⟩ yourself and Council, against me, by Elder Seymour Brunson.

---

442. See 1 Timothy 3:3, 8; Titus 1:7, 11; and 1 Peter 5:2.

443. Cowdery had expressed interest in law since at least 1836. In 1837 he was elected as a justice of the peace in Kirtland, and by the time he moved to Far West later that year, he had commenced studying law in preparation for becoming a licensed lawyer. In March 1838, Cowdery informed his brothers that he had given legal advice on several cases and planned to apply for a license to practice law later that summer. Despite his intentions, in June 1838 Cowdery noted that he still "had little or no law practice to test my skill or talent." (Cowdery, Diary, 18 Jan. 1836; Kirtland Township Trustees' Minutes and Poll Book, 153–154; Oliver Cowdery, Far West, MO, to Warren Cowdery, 21 Jan. 1838, in Cowdery, Letterbook, 82–83; Oliver Cowdery, Far West, MO, to Warren Cowdery and Lyman Cowdery, Kirtland, OH, [10] Mar. 1838, in Cowdery, Letterbook, 92; Oliver Cowdery, Far West, MO, to Warren Cowdery and Lyman Cowdery, Kirtland Mills, OH, 2 June 1838, Lyman Cowdery, Papers, CHL.)

444. Aside from these minutes, few extant documents mention the allegations regarding counterfeiting. In 1839 Reed Peck, who had left the church and had not witnessed events in Kirtland firsthand, claimed that "very many credible persons in the [Kirtland Safety] Society have asserted that while the mony fever raged in Kirtland the leaders of the church and others were, more or less, engaged in purchasing and circulating Bogus money or counterfeit coin." Peck stated that JS and his followers traded accusations with Cowdery and other dissenters over who was responsible for the counterfeiting. (Reed Peck, Quincy, IL, to "Dear Friends," 18 Sept. 1839, pp. 17–18, Henry E. Huntington Library, San Marino, CA.)

445. In June 1838, a letter warning Cowdery to leave Caldwell County stated that he "brought notes with him [to Missouri] upon which he had received pay and had promised to destroy them[.] Since here he made an attempt to Sell them to Mr Arthur of Clay County." (Oliver Cowdery et al., Far West, MO, ca. 17 June 1838, at josephsmithpapers.org.)

I could have wished, that those charges might have been defered untill after my interview with President Smith; but as they are not, I must waive the <u>anticipated</u> pleasure with which I [p. 119] had flattered myself of an understanding on those points which are grounds of ~~difference~~ different opinions on some ~~church~~ Church regulations, and others which personally interest myself.

The fifth charge reads as follows: "For selling his lands in Jackson County contrary to the revelations" so much of this charge, "For selling his lands in Jackson County" I acknowledge to be true, and believe ~~a~~ that a large majority of this Church have already spent their Judgements on that act, and pronounced it sufficient to warrant a disfellowship; and also that you have concured in its correctness— consequently, have no good reason for supposing you would give any decision contrary

Now sir the lands in our Country are <u>allodial</u> in the strictest construction of that term, and have not the least shadow of <u>feudal</u> tenours attached to them, consequently, they may be disposed of by deeds of conveyance without the consent or even <u>approbation</u> of a superior.

The fourth charge is in the following words, "For virtually denying the faith by declaring that he would not be governed by any ecclesiastical authority nor revelation whatever in his temporal affairs."

With regard to this, I, think, I am warranted in saying, the Judgement is also passed as on the ~~fifth~~ matter of the fifth charge, consequently, I have no disposition to contend with the Council: this charge covers simply the doctrine of the fifth, and if I were to be controlled by other than my own judgement, in a compulsory manner, in my temporal interests. of course, could not buy or sell without the consent of some real or supposed authority. Whither that clause contains the precise words, I am not certain— I think howevere they were these "I will not be influenced, governed, or controlled, in my temporal interests by any ecclesiastical authority or pretended revelation [p. 120] what ever, contrary to my own judgement" such being still my opinion shall only remark that the three great principles of English liberty, as laid down in the books, are "the right of personal security; the right of personal liberty, and the right of private property"[446] My venerable ancestor was among that little band, who landed on the rocks of Plymouth in 1620— with him he brought those maxims, and a body of those laws which were the result and experience of many

446. Blackstone, *Commentaries,* 1:93–94.

centuries, on the basis of which now stands our great and happy Goverment:[447] and they are so interwoven in my nature, have so long been inculcated into my mind by a liberal and intelligent ancestry, that I am wholly unwilling to exchange them for any thing less liberal, less benevolent, or less free.

The very principle of which I conceive to be couched in an attempt to set up a kind of petty government, controlled and dictated by ecclesiastical influence, in the midst of this National and State Goverment. You will, no doubt say this is not correct; but the bare notice of those charges, over which you assume a right to decide, is, in my opinion, a direct attempt to make the secular power subservient to Church dictation— to the correctness of which I cannot in conscience subscribe— I believe that principle never did fail to produce Anarchy & confusion.

This attempt to controll me in my temporal interests, I conceive to be a disposition to take from me a portion of my Constitutional privileges and inherent rights— I only, respectfully, ask leave, therefore, to withdraw from a society assuming ~~these~~ they ⟨have⟩ such right.

So far as relates to the other seven charges, I [p. 121] shall lay them carefully away, and take such a course with regard to them, as I may feel bound by my honor, to answer to my rising posterity.

I beg you, sir, to take no view of the foregoing remarks, other than my belief on the outward government of this Church. I do not charge you, or any other person who differs with me on those points, of not being sincere; but such difference does exist, which I sincerely regret.

With considerations of the hi[gh]est respect, I am,
Your obedient servent.
O Cowdery.

Rev.
Edward Partridge
Bishop of the Church of Latter day Saints

John Carrill [Corrill] testifies that some time last fall Marcellus Cowdery came to him and requested him to pay certain notes, against Joseph Smith jr but

---

447. Presumably, Cowdery was referring to Edward Fuller, a signatory of the Mayflower Compact and Cowdery's fourth great-grandfather. However, since Cowdery's family had several lines tracing back to some of the earliest English colonies in North America, Cowdery may have been making a reference to his general family heritage. (Fuller, *Genealogy of Some Descendants of Edward Fuller,* 199; Mehling, *Cowdrey-Cowdery-Cowdray Genealogy,* 37.)

he declined, soon after a writ was served on him; he supposed that it was through the influence of O. Cowdery that the writ was served. From circumstances, he is of the impression that O. Cowdery has used his influence to urge on lawsuits, which have taken place of late in this place. Also, that O. Cowdery[448] said to him "the law is my theme.["]

John Anderson testifies that, from circumstances, he believes that O. Cowdery has been influential in causing lawsuits in this place, as a number more lawsuits have taken place since he came here than before

Dimic[k] B. Huntington. testifies, that O. Cowdery called to him one ~~day~~ evening as he was passing through the street, and said that he Smelt a Skunk (an enemy &c.[449]) and if he knew who it was he would put the screws to him. and also informed D. B Huntington if he [p. 122] heard any guns fired in town to put the screws (I.E. the law) to him who done it,[450] this was after he was appointed to attend the suits of the corporation. and also went on to urge lawsuits as even to issue a writ on the Sabbath day also,[451] that he heard him say that he intended to form a partnership with Donophon [Alexander Doniphan],[452] who is a man of the world and a wicked man

George M. Hinkle, testifies that O. Cowdery wanted to become a secret partner in the store as he would be able to collect the debts & act as an Aterny [Attorney] and thereby be able to get his fees or living which was verbally agreed to, when he traded a considerable and finally they got sick of him and got rid of him the best way they could, which they did do, but still solicited for buisness in the law line, and has frequently solicited for buisness in collecting debts, as he was an Aterny in the place, also testifies that he has seen him urge on lawsuits with others.

George W. Harris testifies that one evening last fall O. Cowdery was at his house together with Joseph Smith, jr, and Thomas B. Marsh, when a conversa-

---

448. Marcellus Cowdery was the son of Oliver Cowdery's brother Warren. (Mehling, *Cowdrey-Cowdery-Cowdray Genealogy,* 170.)

449. TEXT: While it appears that "&c." was canceled by wipe erasure, another possibility is that the ink was accidentally smudged, without the intent to cancel the text.

450. Possibly a reference to the Missouri statute prescribing punishment for individuals who "wilfully disturb the peace of any neighborhood or of any family, by loud and unusual noise, loud and offensive or indecent conversation, or by threatening, quarrelling, challenging or fighting." (An Act concerning Crimes and Their Punishments [20 Mar. 1835], *Revised Statutes of the State of Missouri* [1835], p. 204, art. 7, sec. 15.)

451. Huntington served as the constable in Far West, making him responsible for serving writs and legal instruments. Missouri law forbade serving writs on Sunday for civil suits. (Dimick Huntington, Reminiscences and Journal, [14]; An Act respecting Constables [17 Mar. 1835], *Revised Statutes of the State of Missouri* [1835], p. 116, sec. 7; An Act Regulating Writs and Process [16 Dec. 1834], *Revised Statutes of the State of Missouri* [1835], p. 625, sec. 3.)

452. Doniphan, who had defended the Latter-day Saints in western Missouri, had a legal practice in Liberty, Missouri. (Launius, *Alexander William Doniphan,* 12–23.)

tion took place between Joseph Smith jr & O. Cowdery, when he seemed to insinuate that Joseph Smith jr was guilty of adultery, but when the question was put, if he (Joseph) had ever acknowledged to him that he was guilty of such a thing; when he answered, No.[453] Also he believes him to be instrumental in causing so many lawsuits as had taken place of late

David W. Patten testifies, that he went to Oliver Cowdery to enquire of him if a certain story was true respecting J. Smith's committing adultery with a certain girl, when he turned on his heel and insinuated as [p. 123] though he was guilty; he then went on and gave a history of some circumstances respecting the adultery scrape stating that no doubt it was true. Also said that Joseph told him, he had confessed to Emma, Also that he has used his influence to urge on lawsuits.

Thomas B. Marsh testifies that while in Kirtland last summer, David W. Patten asked Oliver Cowdery if he Joseph Smith jr had confessed to his wife that he was guilty of adultery with a certain girl, when Oliver Cowdery cocked up his eye very knowingly and hesitated to answer the question, saying he did not know as he was bound to answer the question yet conveyed the idea that it was true. Last fall after Oliver came to this place he heard a conversation take place between Joseph Smith and Oliver Cowdery when J. Smith asked him if he had ever confessed to him that he was guilty of adultery, when after a considerable winking &c. he said <u>no</u>. Joseph then ⟨asked⟩ him if he ever told him that he confessed to any body, when he answered <u>no</u>.

Joseph Smith jr testifies that Ooliver Cowdery had been his bosom friend, therefore he entrusted him with many things.[454] He then gave a history respecting the girl buisness. Also that Oliver Cowdery took him one side and said, that he had come to the conclusion to get property and if he could not get it one way he would another, God or no God, Devil or no Devil, property he must ~~must~~ have and since that he has dealt dishonest with him [JS], that he has taken a printing press and type from Kirtland for which he was to give up some notes which he had against Joseph Smith jr and Sidney Rigdon which he did not do, nor has to this day.[455]

---

453. See 25n113 herein.

454. It is unclear precisely what information JS entrusted to Cowdery regarding JS's relationship with Fanny Alger. Later accounts variously claim that Cowdery performed a marriage ceremony between JS and Alger, was called upon by JS to mediate between JS and Emma Smith after the relationship with Alger was discovered, or had been taught the doctrine of plural marriage privately and took a plural wife contrary to JS's instructions. (See Bradley, "Relationship of Joseph Smith and Fanny Alger," 19–20, 28; and Hales, "Accusations of Adultery and Polygamy against Oliver Cowdery," 19–21.)

455. Cowdery obtained one of two presses in the Kirtland printing office and had the press and type shipped to Far West, where he gave them to John Whitmer and Phelps for "timbered land." (Elisha Groves, "An Account of the Life of Elisha Hurd Groves," 3–4, Obituary Notices and Biographies, CHL;

The Council adjourned one hour.

The Council convened according to adjournment opened by prayer by B[righam] Young. [p. 124]

Sidney Rigdon testifies that in January 1837 Oliver Cowdery offered to sell out his share in the printing office at Kirtland Ohio,[456] which they Joseph Smith jr & Sidney Rigdon bought and gave their notes, after which say in the spring following he wished to get a press & some of the type which they granted him on conditions that he should give up the notes above refered to, he ⟨then⟩ went into the office and took whatever he pleased & so completely strip[p]ed the office, as he (Rigdon) was informed by D. C. [Don Carlos] Smith, that there was scarcely enough left to print the "Elders Journal," whereas, before there was a sufficient quantity to print a weekly and monthly paper, the book of Covenants, Hymn Book, Book of Mormon &c.[457] but the notes he did not give up

F[rederick] G. Williams ⟨testifies⟩[458] that Oliver Cowdery told him that there was a certain man in the Church who could compound metal and make dies, that he could make money so that it could not be detected and if it was the case it was no harm to take that money and pass it. The man's name was Davis.[459] Also three men came to him to take out a writ to take some persons who had passed some Bogus (counterfeit) money[460] viz: John [F.] Boynton, Warren Parrish and Burton H. Phelps.[461] Also that it was reported that Oliver was

---

John Whitmer, Far West, MO, to Oliver Cowdery and David Whitmer, Kirtland Mills, OH, 29 Aug. 1837, Western Americana Collection, Beinecke Rare Book and Manuscript Library, Yale University, New Haven, CT.)

456. Cowdery procured the initial press for the Kirtland printing office in 1833 and was heavily involved with the office until 1837. (Crawley, *Descriptive Bibliography,* 1:33–34, 47–49, 51–52.)

457. The Kirtland printing office published the weekly *Northern Times,* the monthly *Latter Day Saints' Messenger and Advocate,* the 1835 edition of the Doctrine and Covenants, the 1835 *Collection of Sacred Hymns,* and the 1837 edition of the Book of Mormon.

458. In January 1838, Williams chaired a meeting attended by Cowdery, Phelps, David Whitmer, and others who opposed the actions of the Zion high council. Two months after the April trial, Cowdery claimed that Williams was preparing to leave the state with other dissenters. Given his apparent sympathy toward Cowdery and other dissenters, it is unclear why Williams chose to testify against Cowdery on this occasion. (Oliver Cowdery, Far West, MO, to Warren Cowdery and Lyman Cowdery, [Kirtland, OH], 4 Feb. 1838, in Cowdery, Letterbook, 85; Oliver Cowdery, Far West, MO, to Warren Cowdery and Lyman Cowdery, Kirtland Mills, OH, 2 June 1838, Lyman Cowdery, Papers, CHL.)

459. Probably Marvel Davis, who had operated a gunsmith shop in Kirtland. Davis had been excommunicated in January 1838 along with Warren Parrish and several other church members for "rising up in rebellion against the church." (Johnson, "A Life Review," 19; William Rockafellow, Affidavit, Russell, OH, 19 Mar. 1885, in *Naked Truths about Mormonism* [Oakland, CA], Apr. 1888, 2; Quorums of the Seventy, "Book of Records," 7 Jan. 1838, 39.)

460. The three men likely approached Williams because he was a justice of the peace in Kirtland from June 1836 to September 1837. (Kirtland Township Trustees' Minutes and Poll Book, 143, 155.)

461. Boynton and Parrish were prominent Kirtland dissenters.[a] Phelps, a constable in Geauga County, Ohio, had worked closely with Cowdery during Cowdery's term as justice of the peace.[b]

engaged in the Bogus money buisness. Also he did not disapprove of the principle of Davis' making the dies and money.

Joseph Smith j̲r̲ testifies that Mr Sapham[462] a man who did not belong to the church came to him and told him that ⟨a⟩ warrant was about to be isued against Oliver Cowdery for being engaged in making a purchase of Bogus money & dies to make the counterfeit money with. after which himself and President Rigdon went to see him, [p. 125] (Oliver) and talk with him about it, when he denied it after which they told him if he was guilty he had better leave the country; but if he was inocent to stand a trial & he should come out clear; but that night or the next he left the country.[463]

Sidney Rigdon concurs with the foregoing testimony.

John Carrill testifies that Oliver Cowdery has neglected attending meeting.

George W. Harris concurs in the same

The fourth and fifth charges were rejected by the Court. The 6th charge was withdrawn.

After some remarks by the Councellors, it was decided by the Bishop and his Council that the 1st, 2nd, & 3rd charges were sustained, the 7th was sustained also the 8th charge was sustained satisfactoryly by circumstancial evidence. The ninth charge was sustained. he was, therefore, considered no longer a member of the Church of Jesus Christ of Latter Day Saints.

Williams's testimony is ambiguous regarding whether Boynton, Parrish, and Phelps made the complaint or were accused of counterfeiting, but a later editorial in the church newspaper alleged that Parrish traveled to Tinker's Creek, Ohio, to buy a box of counterfeit coins and discovered upon his return that the box contained only sand and stones. The editorial also claimed that "Parrish stole the paper out of the institution, and went to buying bogus or counterfeit coin with it" and "was aided by his former associates."*c* (*a.* See, for example, "Mormonism," *Waldo Patriot* [Belfast, ME], 4 May 1838, [1]. *b.* See, for example, Cowdery, Docket Book, 2–5. *c.* Editorial, *Elders' Journal*, Aug. 1838, 58; see also Letter from Heber C. Kimball and Orson Hyde, between 22 and 28 May 1838, p. 147 herein.)

462. Possibly Jonathan Lapham, a lawyer and justice of the peace in Cuyahoga County, Ohio, who had taken an active role in anti-Mormon activities in the region. (See Howe, *Mormonism Unvailed*, 252; and "Hon. Jas. A. Brigg's Statement," *Naked Truths about Mormonism* [Oakland, CA], Jan. 1888, 4.)

463. In June 1838, a letter warning Oliver Cowdery to leave Caldwell County stated that "during the full Career of Oliver Cowdry and David Whitmiers Bogus money business . . . several gentlemen were preparing to commence a prosecution against Cowdry[.] He finding it out took with him Lyman E Johnson and fled to Far West with their familys." Aside from these allegations, little is known about Cowdery's departure for Missouri. Cowdery left Kirtland shortly after 15 September 1837, when he gave his justice of the peace docket book to Frederick G. Williams—likely in preparation for migrating to Missouri. Cowdery arrived in Far West on 20 October 1837. Eight years after the trial, in a letter to his brother-in-law, Cowdery vigorously denied having committed "crimes of theft, forgery, &c. Those which all my former associates knew to be false." (Oliver Cowdery et al., Far West, MO, ca. 17 June 1838, at josephsmithpapers.org; Cowdery, Docket Book, 227; Whitmer, Daybook, 20 Oct. 1837; Oliver Cowdery, Tiffin, OH, to Phineas Young, Nauvoo, IL, 23 Mar. 1846, CHL; see also An Act Providing for the Punishment of Crimes [7 Mar. 1835], *Acts of a General Nature* [1834–1835], pp. 39–40, secs. 28–32.)

The decision was sanctioned by the High Council

The Council adjourned untill tomorrow at 9 o'clock. Closed in prayer by Isaac Morley.

Ebenezer Robinson Clerk

—————— ⟡ ——————

Minutes, 13 April 1838

Source Note

Zion church presidency and high council, Minutes, Far West, Caldwell Co., MO, 13 Apr. 1838. Featured version copied [between 1 Oct. 1842 and 14 Sept. 1843] in Minute Book 2, pp. 126–133; handwriting of Hosea Stout; CHL. For more information on Minute Book 2, see Source Notes for Multiple-Entry Documents, p. 569 herein.

Historical Introduction

On 13 April 1838, JS participated in a meeting that the Zion presidency and high council held to consider the charges against Lyman Johnson and David Whitmer. Johnson had begun challenging JS's leadership by May 1837, when he and fellow apostle Orson Pratt filed charges with Bishop Newel K. Whitney, accusing JS of "lying & misrepresentation— also for extortion— and for— speaking disrespectfully against his brethren behind their backs."[464] The next month, Johnson and his fellow apostle and business partner, John F. Boynton, sought to dissuade apostle Heber C. Kimball from accepting a missionary appointment to England.[465] In a 3 September 1837 conference, Johnson, his brother Luke, and Boynton were rejected as apostles because of their opposition to the church.[466] The three men reconciled with the church a week later at another conference and were reinstated as apostles. Shortly afterward Johnson traveled with Oliver Cowdery to Far West.[467] While there, Johnson attended the November church conference, during which he was again sustained as an apostle.[468] However, by December, Johnson was meeting with Cowdery, David and John Whitmer, and other dissenters in Missouri to discuss their opposition to other church leaders. Johnson seems to have associated especially with Cowdery, and the two apparently planned to start a legal practice together.[469] In January 1838, Johnson attended a meeting with Cowdery, the Whitmer broth-

---

464. Charges against JS Preferred to Bishop's Council, 29 May 1837, in *JSP*, D5:397.

465. Kimball, "History," 55.

466. At least some of the difficulty between these men and the church revolved around the collapse of the economy in Kirtland, Ohio. During the meeting, Boynton attributed his opposition to "the failure of the bank." Although Sidney Rigdon rejected Boynton's explanation, Rigdon likewise thought the root of the conflict was related to economic concerns; he condemned Johnson and Boynton for operating a mercantile firm while neglecting their ecclesiastical responsibilities. (Minutes, 3 Sept. 1837, in *JSP*, D5:423–424.)

467. Minute Book 1, 10 Sept. 1837; Oliver Cowdery et al., Far West, MO, ca. 17 June 1838, at josephsmithpapers.org.

468. Minutes, 7 Nov. 1837, in *JSP*, D5:471.

469. Oliver Cowdery, Far West, MO, to Warren Cowdery and Lyman Cowdery, Kirtland, OH, [10] Mar. 1838, in Cowdery, Letterbook, 92.

ers, and other dissenters, during which they made plans to leave Far West because of their opposition to the high council there.[470] Johnson also continued to correspond with Warren Parrish and other Kirtland, Ohio, dissenters.[471] On 7 April 1838, apostle David W. Patten reported at a church conference that he could not sustain Johnson and four other members of the quorum.[472] Two days later, church leaders wrote to Johnson, Cowdery, and David Whitmer, reporting that charges had been made against them and that hearings would be held on 12 April for Cowdery and on 13 April for Johnson and Whitmer.[473]

Neither Johnson nor Whitmer attended the 13 April hearing, during which the high council and the Zion presidency investigated the charges against the two men. Instead, like Cowdery the day before, Johnson and Whitmer sent letters expressing their opposition to the charges and the council proceedings and indicating they were withdrawing from the church. The council deliberated over Johnson's case during two sessions, with JS testifying against Johnson during the first session. As a result of the testimony JS and others offered, the council excommunicated Johnson.

The council then turned to the case of David Whitmer. After he, John Whitmer, and William W. Phelps had been removed from the Zion presidency in February 1838, the three men had decried the decision. In a 10 March letter, the men argued that the procedures for removing them were "contrary to the principles of the revelations of Jesus Christ, and his gospel." Later in the day, the high council read the letter and excommunicated Phelps and John Whitmer.[474] No action was taken against David Whitmer until 9 April, when he was notified of his 13 April trial. During the trial, the council read the letter and determined that he should be excommunicated. As the final item of business during the meeting, the council revoked Cowdery's November 1837 assignment to help identify locations for new Latter-day Saint settlements.[475]

Minutes of the council meeting were taken by the high council clerk, Ebenezer Robinson. The minutes were copied into Minute Book 2 by Hosea Stout in 1842 or 1843.

Document Transcript

The High Council of Zion met in Far-West on Friday April 13th 1838[476]

Thomas B. Marsh, David W. Patten and Brygham [Brigham] Young Presiding. The Council was organized as follows:

| Simeon Carter | no. 1 | Jared Carter | no 2 |

---

470. Oliver Cowdery, Far West, MO, to Warren Cowdery and Lyman Cowdery, [Kirtland, OH], 4 Feb. 1838, in Cowdery, Letterbook, 85.

471. See, for example, Oliver Cowdery, Far West, MO, to Warren Cowdery and Lyman Cowdery, Kirtland, OH, 24 Feb. 1838, in Cowdery, Letterbook, 87; and Stephen Burnett, Orange Township, OH, to Lyman Johnson, 15 Apr. 1838, in JS Letterbook 2, pp. 64–66.

472. Minutes, 7–8 Apr. 1838, p. 72 herein.

473. Minutes, 12 Apr. 1838, pp. 87–89 herein.

474. Minute Book 2, 10 Mar. 1838.

475. See Travel Account and Questions, Nov. 1837, in *JSP*, D5:481.

476. The council met as planned in the 12 April 1838 high council meeting. (Minutes, 12 Apr. 1838, p. 94 herein.)

Thomas Grover	" 3.	John P. Green[e]	" 4
Levi Jackman	" 5	Solomon Hancock	" 6
George Morey	" 7	Newel Knight	" 8
George M. Hinkle	" 9	George ⟨W.⟩ Harris	" 10
Elias Higbee	" 11	John Murdock	" 12

The Council was opened by singing and prayer by President David W. Patten after which several charges were prefered, against Lyman [p. 126] Lyman E. Johnson which are as follows:

"To the Council of the Church of Christ of Latter day saints in Missouri.

I prefer the following charges before your honorable body against Lyman E. Johnson.

1st, For persecuting brethren by stiring up people to prosecute them, and urging on vexatious lawsuits against them and thereby bringing distress upon the inocent.[477]

2nd For virtually denying the faith of the Church of Christ of Latter Day saints, by vindicating the cause of the enemies of this Church, who are dissenters from us, now in Kirtland, and speaking reproachfully of the Church and High Council, by saying their proceedings were illegal and that he never would acknowledge them to be legal,[478] these assertions were without foundation and truth, also, treating the Church with contempt by absenting himself from meetings on the sabbath,[479] by not observing his prayers in the season thereof and by not observing the word of wisdom.[480]

3.rd For seeking to injure the character of Joseph Smith jr by reporting that he had a demand against him of One thousand dollars, when it was without foundation in truth

---

477. Drawing on passages in the New Testament, the Book of Mormon, and JS's revelations, several church leaders frequently expressed a belief that it was immoral to sue other church members in a court of law. (See 85n436 herein.)

478. Many of the dissenters in Missouri rejected the actions of the high council, especially the removal of the former Zion presidency and the subsequent excommunications of John Whitmer and Phelps. (Oliver Cowdery, Far West, MO, to Warren Cowdery and Lyman Cowdery, Kirtland, OH, [10] Mar. 1838, in Cowdery, Letterbook, 91.)

479. The last church meeting Johnson was recorded as attending was on 6 November 1837. Similar charges were made against Cowdery and David Whitmer. (Minutes, 6 Nov. 1837, in JSP, D5:467; Minutes, 12 Apr. 1838, p. 86 herein.)

480. A February 1833 revelation known as the "Word of Wisdom" contained a dietary code that counseled against using tobacco, alcohol, and "hot drinks"—widely interpreted as coffee and tea. John Whitmer noted in his daybook that Johnson and other dissenters purchased several pounds of coffee and tea during the later 1830s. (Revelation, 27 Feb. 1833, in JSP, D3:21 [D&C 89:7–9]; Whitmer, Daybook, [138].)

4th For laying voilent hands on our Brother Phineas Young, and by kicking and beating him, thereby throwing contempt on the Church of Christ of Latter Day Saints in Missouri

5th And by saying that he would appeal the suit between him & Brother Phineas Young and take it out of the County, saying that he could not get justice done him, thereby speaking reproachfully of the authority, of Caldwell County.

6th For telling a falshood.

7th For taking whiskey and making Weldon drink & then cheating him out of his property[481]

A[lanson] Ripley" [p. 127]

After which ~~at~~ a letter was read from the defendant by John Murdock[482] as follows:

"Far. West M͟o April 12th 1838

Sir[483] yours of the 9th ins͟t, containing a copy of six charges, prefered, before the Council by A. Ripley, against me has been received, and it appears to me to be a novel document, assuming a right to compel me under pain of religious sencure [censure] and excommunication not to appeal a lawsuit or change the venue of the same in which I am deeply interested, without the consent of a religious body.

This assumpsion of power being manifest in the fifth Charge, I should not condescend to put my constitutional rights at issue upon so disrespectful a point: as to answer any other of those charges until that is withdrawn & untill then shall withdraw myself from your society and fellowship.[484]

Yours

Lyman E. Johnson

---

481. According to George M. Hinkle's testimony in these minutes, Johnson traveled north, probably to Daviess County, Missouri, to purchase a farm from a member of the Weldon family. Johnson offered Mr. Weldon liquor and waited until he was drunk before introducing the potential purchase, hoping to obtain the land for a considerably lower price. Several members of the Weldon family were among the earliest white settlers in what eventually became Daviess County; it is unclear which individual Johnson allegedly defrauded. (See *History of Daviess County, Missouri,* 146–147, 179, 188–189, 811.)

482. The previous day, the high council voted "that John Murdock be a President of the High Council, whose duty it shall be to receive charges and give notice to the defendant, also, to call the Council together and organize them &c." Murdock was apparently already filling this role, at least in giving notice to defendants. (Minutes, 12 Apr. 1838, p. 85 herein.)

483. That is, Murdock.

484. Johnson's letter echoes many of the themes of constitutional rights and liberties that Cowdery expressed in his letter to the high council on 12 April 1838. Cowdery also asked to withdraw from the church. (Minutes, 12 Apr. 1838, pp. 87–89 herein.)

M.ʳ John Murdock

The case was not considered difficult, therefore, two spake on the case; viz Thomas Grover, on the part of the Church and John P. Green on the part of the defendant.

George M. Hinkle testifies he knew Lyman E. Johnson has been active in urging on lawsuits, also, that L. E. Johnson told him he had a note against him (Hinkle) which he procured in Clay County, which was not sa◊ the case, as he had no note of the description, therefore, he had lied.

Tho.ˢ Grover testifies that M.ʳ Gilbert[485] had a claim upon a piece of land, after which Lyman E. Johnson entered it from under him, after being told that M.ʳ Gilbert had a claim upon it.

Alonson Ripley testifies, that Lyman E Johnson had been told that there was a claim upon the piece of land which was refered to above, also he heard Lyman E Johnson say he had a note against J. Smith jr.

Simeon Carter testifies, that Lyman E. Johnson inquired of him if there was any land to be entered, when he told [p. 128] him he thought there was none except it was some which poor brethren had a claim on, and that it he must not enter that, as it was contrary to the decision of the High Council; afterwards he did enter a forty upon which one of the brethren had made some improvement.[486]

Arthur Morrison[487] testifies that it was the understanding that Lyman E. Johnson acted as an Atterney for Mr. Bennor[488] in commencing a suit against George M. Hinkle, & took a very active part in the case.

David W. Patten testifies, that Lyman E. Johnson had told him in conversation at different times, that while God sat upon his throne or his face the color it now was, he never would sanction the proceedings of the High Council

---

485. Possibly William Gilbert. (Johnson and Romig, *Index to Early Caldwell County, Missouri, Land Records,* 5, 75.)

486. According to federal law, settlers could apply for and secure a preemptive land claim from the federal government's land office, allowing the settlers to occupy and make improvements on government-owned land in areas where the land had not come up for sale. When a public sale was held, the person with the land claim had first rights to purchase the property. According to Carter's testimony, Johnson apparently usurped a poor Saint's preemption claim to a forty-acre piece of land. (Walker, "Mormon Land Rights," 14–17; Rohrbough, *Land Office Business,* 200–220.)

487. Morrison, a Latter-day Saint, was elected as a Caldwell County, Missouri, justice in August 1838, suggesting he had some association with the county court. (Arthur Morrison, Affidavit, Adams Co., IL, 1 Nov. 1839, Mormon Redress Petitions, 1839–1845, CHL; "Copy of the Record of Election of Justices," in *Complainant's Abstract of Pleading and Evidence,* 283.)

488. Possibly Elias or Henry Benner; both men were Latter-day Saint mill owners in Caldwell County. (Henry Benner, Affidavit, Adams Co., IL, 25 May 1839, Mormon Redress Petitions, 1839–1845, CHL; *History of Caldwell and Livingston Counties, Missouri,* 588.)

in this place, because he said they were ~~ittegal~~ illegal and as for coming to this Council he would not, also he used tea and coffee while living at D. W. Patten's and did not tend family prayers while living at his house, also had used his influence against certain brethren especially against the Smith family, also he had a correspondence with the dissenters at Kirtland and vindicated their cause and spoke against the First Presidents of the Church, also made light of the word of wisdom, also Lyman E Johnson reported he had a thousand dollar note against Joseph Smith jr

Joseph Smith jʳ testifies that he, Lyman E. Johnson vindicated the cause of the dissenters, both in publick and private and spoke against the saints while in Kirtland, also heard Lyman E. Johnson Say that while God sat upon his throne and his face was the color it is now was he never would sanction the proceedings of the Church and Council, in this place also Lyman E. Johnson told him he had a thousand dollar note against him (J. Smith) which was not the case, but the note which he pretended to have was one given to Joseph Smith jr while acting as [p. 129] cashier in the Kirtland Bank[489]

Absolon [Absalom] Scritchfield[490] testifies, that he has seen Lyman E. Johnson come to Mʳ [Samuel] Musick's (tavern) and drink liquor, say brandy.

George W. Harris testifies that he has neglected to attend meeting on the Sabbath days.

George Morey concurs with the above testimony.

The Council adjourned for one hour.

The Council convened agreeable to adjournment.

Opened in prayer by President B. Young.

Brigham Young, testifies that Phineas Young came to Bʳ. Green's a few mornings since,[491] with his head cut the blood running out of his ears, also his stomach was injured, & Phineas said Lyman E. Johnson had fought him; which was proved in court afterwards.

---

489. Johnson claimed he had a promissory note from JS for $1,000, but JS claimed the note was actually the record of a loan Johnson received from the Kirtland Safety Society in 1837. According to an April 1838 letter to Johnson from disgruntled church member Stephen Burnett, JS claimed that Johnson obtained a $2,000 loan from the Safety Society in 1837 and used the money to purchase land in Missouri. Existing financial records for the Safety Society show that Johnson secured smaller loans from the institution in January 1837; there is no evidence of a $1,000 or $2,000 loan in the records, which are incomplete. Records do indicate Johnson purchased a significant amount of land in Missouri during the time frame Burnett specified in his letter, suggesting that a loan of $1,000 or $2,000 may have existed. (Stephen Burnett, Orange Township, OH, to Lyman Johnson, 15 Apr. 1838, in JS Letterbook 2, p. 65; Kirtland Safety Society Accounts and Discounted Notes, Jan. 1837, JS Office Papers, CHL; Vilate Murray Kimball, Kirtland, OH, to Heber C. Kimball, Preston, England, ca. 10–12 Sept. 1837, Heber C. Kimball, Collection, CHL.)

490. See Minute Book 2, 6 Aug. 1834.

491. John P. Greene was the brother-in-law of Brigham and Phineas Young. (Greene, "Biographical Sketch of the Life and Travels of John Portenus Greene," 1.)

Minutes, 13 April 1838. Clerk Ebenezer Robinson took minutes at a council meeting in Far West, Missouri, on 13 April 1838. Four years later, in October 1842, the Nauvoo, Illinois, high council directed clerk Hosea Stout to copy Robinson's loose-leaf minutes into a minute book. It appears that Stout occasionally struggled to read Robinson's handwriting and may have introduced errors into the text. For example, Stout's handwriting became larger as he attempted to transcribe the name of an alcoholic drink mentioned in the minutes. Although Stout copied this word as "lumbórum," the number of characters, their shapes, and the context suggest that the word Robinson wrote in the original minutes may have been "laudanum," an alcoholic drink containing opium. Handwriting of Hosea Stout. Minute Book 2, p. 131, Church History Library, Salt Lake City. (Photograph by Welden C. Andersen.)

John P. Green concurs with the above testimony.

Dimic[k] B. Huntington, testifies that Lyman E. Johnson told him that he had given Phines Young a pounding, because he had given him the lie, and if any other man should give me the lie, he would not promise that he would not get the same sauce.

Also testifies that Lyman E. Johnson told him, previous, to a decision, being had by civil authority, that he would not begrudge paying five dollars for whipping a man as he did Phineas, but if the judgement was any wise high, he would change the venue and take it out of the County.

David W. Patten, testifies that Lyman E. Johnson told him that he would change the venue and take the suit out of the County, previous to the time that the warrant was issued.

George Morey, testifies that, previous to decision being given on the case of Phineas Young, Lyman E. Johnson told him he intended to get bail and take a change of venue and take it out of the County.

Thomas B. Marsh testifies that Lyman E. Johnson told him, that he had learned the [k]nack of [p. 130] travelling on Steam Boats without paying his fare, by slipping from place to place in the Boat when they were calling for the fare, and when they would ask him for his pay, he would tell them he had paid it, when he had not.

Edward Partridge, testifies that in purchasing a lot for father Smith, he turned out a note against Lyman E. Johnson, which he rather declined paying at the first presentation, but afterwards said, he had paid it taken it up when he had, therefore, told a falshood.

George M. Hinkle testifies that Lyman E. Johnson told him, after he returned from the North, when he purchased his farm of Weldon, the history is as follows: "Before we got there, as we understood, he was fond of liquor, so we got some, lumbórum,[492] (as Bump[493] called it) and went to Mʳ Weldon's and got him tolerably well shaved, before we introduced the trade, when we purchased a large farm with great improvements together with five hundred head of hogs, a good stock of horses and cattle, also, a flock of sheep, the ploughs belonging to the farm &c. for twenty-two hundred dollars and fifty dollars."

Thomas B. Marsh concurs with the above testimony, and also David W. Patten.

After some few appropriate remarks, by the Councellors, it was decided by the President that Lyman E Johnson be no longer considered a member of the Church of Christ of Latter Day Saints, nor a member of the Quorum of the twelve Apostles of the Lamb and also be given over to the buffetings of Satan[494] untill he learns to blaspheme no more against the authorities of God.

Ebenezer Robinson Clerk

A charge was then prefered against David Whitmer, by Alonson Ripley, as follows:

"To the High Council of the Church of Latter day Saints in Missouri. [p. 131]

I prefer the following charges before your Honorable body against David Whitmer.

---

492. TEXT: "lumbórum"—Latin for "of the loins"—is written in much larger and more deliberate characters, suggesting that Hosea Stout struggled to transcribe the word. Given the context, the number of characters, and the placement of the minims and ascenders, the original word he was trying to transcribe was likely *laudanum*—a mixture of liquor or wine and opium. ("Laudanum," in *American Dictionary*.)

493. Probably Jacob Bump, a Kirtland dissenter. (Historian's Office, Brigham Young History Drafts, 14.)

494. See Revelation, 1 Mar. 1832, in *JSP*, D2:199 [D&C 78:12]; Revelation, 26 Apr. 1832, in *JSP*, D2:237 [D&C 82:21]; and Revelation, 23 Apr. 1834, in *JSP*, D4:23 [D&C 104:9–10].

Charge First, For not observing the word of wisdom,[495] for un-christian-like conduct in neglecting to attend to meetings,[496] in uniting with, and possessing the same spirit with the Dissenters, in writing letters to the Dissenters in Kirtland unfavorable to the cause and to B<u>r</u> Joseph Smith jr.[497]

2<u>nd</u> 3<u>rd</u> For neglecting ⟨the⟩ ~~his~~ duties of his calling.

4th, For seperating himself from the cause and the Church while he has a name among us.

5 For signing himself President of the Church of Christ in an in-sulting letter to the High Council.[498]

A. Ripley."

---

495. In January 1838, the Zion presidency was charged with, among other things, failing to ad-here to the revealed dietary code known as the Word of Wisdom. According to the report of the com-mittee assigned to discuss the charges with the presidency, Phelps denied breaking the Word of Wisdom, while Cowdery and the Whitmers admitted to drinking tea or coffee, as "they did not con-sider them to come under the head of hot drinks." In February, Hinkle criticized David Whitmer for "persisting in the use of tea, coffee, and tobacco." Decades later, Whitmer identified the Word of Wisdom as one of the principal causes of dispute between himself and other church leaders in Far West. (Minute Book 2, 26 Jan. 1838; Letter from Thomas B. Marsh, 15 Feb. 1838, p. 20 herein; Gurley, "Questions Asked of David Whitmer," 1.)

496. The last church meeting Whitmer was recorded as attending was on 6 December 1837. Similar charges were made against Cowdery and Johnson. (Minute Book 2, 6–7 Dec. 1837; see also Minutes, 12 Apr. 1838, p. 86 herein.)

497. In June 1838, a letter directing David Whitmer, Cowdery, and other dissenters to leave Far West also accused the men of having "kept up continual correspondance with your gang of Marauders in Kirtland." No correspondence from Whitmer to Kirtland has been located; how-ever, during this period Cowdery and Johnson appear to have maintained regular correspondence with Kirtland dissenters, which suggests that Whitmer may have as well. An August 1837 letter from John Whitmer in Missouri to David Whitmer and Cowdery in Kirtland implies that correspondence was encouraged, if not already occurring: "Communicate to us any thing that you in your wisdom may think expedient." John Whitmer assured his brother and Cowdery that because Phelps was the post-master of Far West, "a letter can be addressed to him on any subject and no one know it." (Oliver Cowdery et al., Far West, MO, ca. 17 June 1838, at josephsmithpapers.org; John Whitmer, Far West, MO, to Oliver Cowdery and David Whitmer, Kirtland Mills, OH, 29 Aug. 1837, Western Americana Collection, Beinecke Rare Book and Manuscript Library, Yale University, New Haven, CT; see also Oliver Cowdery, Far West, MO, to Warren Cowdery and Lyman Cowdery, [Kirtland, OH], 4 Feb. 1838, in Cowdery, Letterbook, 87; Oliver Cowdery, Far West, MO, to Warren Cowdery and Lyman Cowdery, Kirtland, OH, 24 Feb. 1838, in Cowdery, Letterbook, 87; Stephen Burnett, Orange Township, OH, to Lyman Johnson, 15 Apr. 1838, in JS Letterbook 2, pp. 64–66; and Oliver Cowdery, Far West, MO, to Warren Cowdery and Lyman Cowdery, Kirtland Mills, OH, 2 June 1838, Lyman Cowdery, Papers, CHL.)

498. On 10 March 1838, the Whitmer brothers and Phelps wrote a letter to Marsh, complaining about the treatment they received from Marsh and the high council and signing the letter as presidents of the church in Zion. A similar charge was made against Cowdery, who attested to the three men's complaints and signed the letter as the clerk of the high council. (Minute Book 2, 10 Mar. 1838; Minutes, 12 Apr. 1838, p. 86 herein.)

After which a letter was read from D. Whitmer in words as follows:

"Far West M<u>o</u> April 13th 1838.

John Murdock

Sir I received a line from you bearing date the 9th inst, requesting me as a High Priest to appear before the High Council and answer to five several charges on this day at 12 o'clock.

You sir with a majority of this Church have decided that certain Councils were legal by which it is said I have been deprived of my office as one of the Presidents of this Church I have thought and still think they were not agreeable to the revelations of God, which I believe and by my now attending this Council, and a[n]swering to charges as a High Priest, should be acknowledgeing the correctness and legality of those former <u>assumed</u> Councils, which I shall not do.[499]

Believing as I verily do, that you and the leaders of the Councils have a determination to persue your unlawful course at all hazards, and bring others to your standard in violating of the revelations, to spare you any further trouble I hereby withdraw from your fellowship and communion— choosing to seek a place among the meek and humble, where the revelations of Heaven will be observed and the [p. 132] rights of men regarded.

David Whitmer."

After the reading of the above letter it was not considered necessary to investigate the case, as he had offered contempt to the Council by writing the above letter; but let the Councellors speak what they had to say ~~and~~ upon the case and pass decision

The councellors then made a few remarks in which they spoke warmly of the contempt offered to the Council in the above letter, therefore, thought he was not worthy a membership in the Church.

When Pres^t Marsh made a few remarks and decided that David Whitmer be no longer considered a member of the Church of Christ of Latter day Saints.

Voted by the high Council that Oliver Cowdery be no longer a Committeeman to search our locations for the geathering of the saints.

---

499. During the February 1838 proceedings in which Whitmer was removed from the Zion presidency, Murdock addressed criticism that the high council's treatment of the presidency aberrated from the rules of the church. According to Murdock, the council's actions were "perfectly legal, according to the instructions of President Joseph Smith jr." (Letter from Thomas B. Marsh, 15 Feb. 1838, p. 19 herein.)

Council adjourned untill tomorrow morning 9 o'clock. Closed in Benediction by President Joseph Smith jr

Ebenezer Robinson Clerk

--------- ❧ ---------

Minutes, 14 April 1838

Source Note

*Zion high council, Minutes, [Far West, Caldwell Co., MO], 14 Apr. 1838. Featured version cop-
ied [between 1 Oct. 1842 and 14 Sept. 1843] in Minute Book 2, pp. 133–135; handwriting of Hosea
Stout; CHL. For more information on Minute Book 2, see Source Notes for Multiple-Entry Documents,
p. 569 herein.*

Historical Introduction

On 14 April 1838, JS presided at a high council meeting to investigate a complaint against
Nathan West for his position regarding enforcement of the "Word of Wisdom," the church's
revealed dietary code. The church's position regarding this code had recently become more
rigid and had provoked some members to resist the church's involvement in temporal matters.
West's case had been tried earlier in a council of elders, who apparently ruled in his favor.
However, Truman Wait, the original complainant, appealed his case against West to the high
council on 27 March 1838. The high council members convened to hear the case on 14 April,
immediately following two days of disciplinary councils in which they had excommunicated
dissident church leaders.[500] In the trial against David Whitmer held the day before, one of the
charges was that Whitmer did not observe the Word of Wisdom.[501] Wait brought several witnesses to testify regarding statements West had allegedly made about the Word of Wisdom
and church authority. An hour-long adjournment noted in the meeting minutes suggests the
trial lasted several hours. In the end, JS ruled that West had merely "erred in spirit" and
should only be admonished. Meeting minutes, which included a transcript of the complaint,
were taken by high council clerk Ebenezer Robinson. The minutes were later copied into
Minute Book 2 by Hosea Stout.

Document Transcript

The High Council of Zion met agreeable to adjournment on Saturday the
14th of April 1838.[502]
Being organized as follows:
Joseph Smith jr Thomas B. Marsh and Brigham Yound [Young] Presiding.

---

500. See Minutes, 12 Apr. 1838, pp. 83–94 herein; and Minutes, 13 Apr. 1838, pp. 95–104 herein.
501. See Minutes, 13 Apr. 1838, p. 102 herein.
502. At the close of the meeting held the previous day, the high council "adjourned untill tomorrow
morning 9 o'clock." (Minutes, 13 Apr. 1838, p. 104 herein.)

Simeon Carter	N̲o̲ 1	Jared Carter	No. 2
Thomas Grover	" 3	Isaac Higbee	" 4[503]
Levi Jackman	" 5	Solomon Hancock	" 6
George Morey	" 7	Newel Knight	" 8
George M. Hinkle	" 9	George W. Harris	" 10
Elias Higbee	" 11	John Murdock	" 12

Council opened in prayer by Elder John Murdock.

An appealed case was then presented to the Council,[504] pending between Elders [Truman] Wait and [Nathan] West, from the Elders quorum, when the proceedings of the Elders quorum were read also the charges which reads as [p. 133] follows:

"Far West March 27th 1838.

To the High Council,

I, in appealing the case between me and Elder West, to the High Council, prefer the first charge contained in the original charges, namely; A spirit of dissension, in that he declared publickly that he did not believe in the vote of the General Assembly, last Nov̲ 7th, "not to support stores and shops selling spiritous liquors, tea, coffee, and tobacco." And also I shall bring any testimony I can find to the same effect and connect it with the foregoing charge.

And also, the first item of the second charge contained in the original, namely; Teaching incorrect doctrine in that he said the word of Wisdom did not concern our Spiritual Salvation.

Truman Wait, Complainant"[505]

The case was not considered difficult, therefore, two Councellors were to speak on the case, viz: George Morey, on the part of the Church, and Newel Knight, on the part of the part of the defendant.

Some remarks were made by the defendant, in which he acknowledged a part of the first charge.

---

503. Isaac Higbee was apparently standing in for John P. Greene. (See Minutes, 7–8 Apr. 1838, p. 73 herein; Minutes, 13 Apr. 1838, p. 96 herein; and Minute Book 2, 12 May 1838.)

504. When a bishop or another officer acted as a judge in a church trial, the decision could be appealed to a council consisting of the presidency of the high priesthood and twelve high priests acting as counselors. After JS moved to Missouri, the high council there regularly served as the twelve counselors to the First Presidency in these church courts, including in this case. (Instruction on Priesthood, between ca. 1 Mar. and ca. 4 May 1835, in *JSP*, D4:319 [D&C 107:78–80]; Minutes, 15 Mar. 1838, pp. 42–43 herein; Minutes, 24 Mar. 1838, p. 47 herein; see also Minutes, 21 Apr. 1838, p. 109 herein.)

505. For more information on the enforcement of the Word of Wisdom in Missouri at this time, see 20n88 herein.

Darwin Chase, testifies that he heard Nathan West say that he would not believe the decision of the High Council if it did not coincide with the Book of Covenants.[506]

Also, he heard Mᵣ West say that he did not covenant to not uphold stores and shops, which sold liquor, tea, coffee and tobacco, because he had already made as many covenants as he kept &c but if any persons had made any such covenants, he would say to them 'for God's sake to keep them.'

William Hulet, testifies that he heard Elder West say that if he had his mind made up on ~~any~~ ⟨a⟩ certain item of Revelation and the High Council should decide contrary to his mind upon that item, he would not believe the decision except they would bring proof to substantiate it.[507] Also that he never did hear Elder West say any thing against [p. 134] Joseph Smith jᵣ but heard him say that he considered him the Prophet as much as ever.

The Council adjourned one hour.

Council convend according to adjournment.

Silas Maynard, testifies, that he heard Elder West say one evening last winter that he did not acquiesce in the proceedings of the High Council and Church in cutting off W[illiam] W. Phelps & John Whitmer from the Presidents office.[508]

Thomas Grover, testifies, that at the General Confference last winter, when the case of W. W. Phelps & John Whitmer was investigated, Elder West voted to have them continue in the office of Presidents.[509]

Elder West confesses, that at the time of the Conference above refered to, he did think the move ~~too~~ too hasty and did not coincide with the proceedings of the Council at the time, but now saw the matter different and does coincide with them &c.[510]

Elder Wait, testifies that Elder West said in a Conference of Elders that he did not consider the word of Wisdom given by Commandment or Constraint.[511]

---

506. That is, the Doctrine and Covenants.

507. Hulet may have objected to West's lack of respect for high council decisions, perhaps based on an understanding that high council decisions were inspired by God. (See Darowski, "Seeking After the Ancient Order," 102–104.)

508. See Letter from Thomas B. Marsh, 15 Feb. 1838, pp. 18–23 herein.

509. In the "general assembly" meeting held in Far West, "the vote against David Whitmer, John Whitmer, and William W. Phelps was unanimous, excepting 8 or 10 and this minority only wished them to continue in offioe [office] little longer, or until Joseph Smith jr. came up." (Letter from Thomas B. Marsh, 15 Feb. 1838, p. 22 herein.)

510. When Phelps and Whitmer were tried for transgression in February 1838, the Zion bishopric and others believed that the proceedings were "hasty." (Letter from Thomas B. Marsh, 15 Feb. 1838, pp. 20–21 herein.)

511. The dietary code was presented to the Latter-day Saints "not by commandment or Constraint, but by Revelation & the word of wisdom shewing forth the order & will of God in the temporal salvation of all Saints." (Revelation, 27 Feb. 1833, in *JSP*, D3:20 [D&C 89:2].)

After a few remarks by the Councellors and parties it was decided by the President, that considering the case, Br. West had erred in spirit,[512] therefore, feel to admonish him, but do not find any thing in him worthy of death or bonds.[513]

Council adjourned untill next Saturday at 9 o'clock.

Closed in prayer by ~~President~~ B^r Harris.

Ebenezer Robinson Clerk

———— ❧ ————

Revelation, 17 April 1838

Source Note

Revelation, Far West, Caldwell Co., MO, 17 Apr. 1838. Featured version copied [ca. late Apr. 1838] in JS, Journal, Mar.–Sept. 1838, p. 32; handwriting of George W. Robinson; CHL. Includes use marks. For more information on JS, Journal, Mar.–Sept. 1838, see Source Notes for Multiple-Entry Documents, p. 564 herein.

Historical Introduction

On 17 April 1838, JS dictated a revelation for Brigham Young. A month earlier, JS and Young had arrived in Far West, Missouri, after having fled Kirtland, Ohio, with Young assisting JS in his travels.[514] On 6 April, Young was appointed to the pro tempore presidency of the church in Zion, which was centered in Far West.[515] The wording of the 17 April 1838 revelation suggests that Young's wife, Mary Ann, who was very sick, and their five children, including infant twins, had also arrived in Missouri.[516] He settled his family on property he purchased at Mill Creek, at least three miles from Far West,[517]

---

512. See Isaiah 29:24.

513. See Acts 23:29; 26:31.

514. Young fled for his life on 22 December 1837. JS fled Kirtland on 12 January 1838, later meeting up with Young en route to Missouri. (Historian's Office, Brigham Young History Drafts, 15–16.)

515. Minutes, 6 Apr. 1838, p. 70 herein.

516. Mary Ann was sick when she and her children departed Kirtland in the spring, and her sickness worsened from the fatigue of traveling. When the family arrived in Missouri, apparently by the time of this revelation, Brigham was reportedly so surprised by Mary Ann's appearance that he exclaimed to her, "You look as if you were almost in your grave." At the time, Young's children included daughters Elizabeth and Vilate (from Brigham's first wife, Miriam Works, who died in 1832), son Joseph, and infant twins Brigham Jr. and Mary. (Emmeline B. Wells, "Biography of Mary Ann Angell Young," *Juvenile Instructor,* 1 Jan. 1891, 18–19; Historian's Office, Brigham Young History Drafts, 17.)

517. Mill Creek is a tributary of Shoal Creek near Far West. Young's autobiography recounts: "I purchased a small improvement on mill creek, located my family and proceeded to fence in a farm. I bought several pieces of land and obtained deeds for them." It is uncertain which land at Mill Creek belonged to Young, but based on contemporary land records, his land was likely three to seven miles from Far West. Heber C. Kimball, Young's close friend and fellow apostle, later recounted that Young's farm was

but his ecclesiastical duties required his presence at the Missouri church's center. During the previous weeks, he had been involved in council meetings in Far West. For example, he had attended the 14 April 1838 high council meeting just three days prior to the revelation.[518]

This short revelation to Young, dictated by JS in Far West, directed Young to go to his home at Mill Creek and support his family. The revelation was probably dictated orally and written down by Young or, as was typical, by a scribe.[519] George W. Robinson transcribed the revelation into JS's "Scriptory Book," apparently in late April 1838.[520] Young's absence in subsequent council meetings held in Far West suggests that he followed the direction given in the revelation.[521]

Document Transcript

Revelation given to Brigham Young at Far West April 17[th] 1838. Verrily thus Saith the Lord, Let my Servant Brigham Young go unto the place which he has baught on Mill Creek and there provide for his family until an effectual door is op[e]ned[522] for the suport of his family untill I shall command [him] to go hence, and not to leave his family untill they are amply provided for[523] Amen.——

——— ☙ ———

"3 or 4 miles from the City on Mill creek." (Historian's Office, Brigham Young History Drafts, 17; Kimball, "History," 91; see also JS, Journal, Mar.–Sept. 1838, p. 16, in *JSP*, J1:237; *Illustrated Historical Atlas of Caldwell County, Missouri*, 7, 34, 40; U.S. Department of the Interior, *Geological Survey Topographic Map: Hamilton West, Missouri, Quadrangle*, 7.5 Minute Series, 2012; and Hamer, *Northeast of Eden*, 30, 34, 42.)

518. See Minutes, 7–8 Apr. 1838, p. 72 herein; Minutes, 13 Apr. 1838, p. 95 herein; and Minutes, 14 Apr. 1838, p. 104 herein.

519. See "Revelations," *Ensign of Liberty*, Aug. 1849, 98–99; see also William E. McLellin, Independence, MO, to Joseph Smith III, [Plano, IL], July 1872, typescript, Letters and Documents Copied from Originals in the Office of the Church Historian, Reorganized Church, CHL; and Pratt, *Autobiography*, 65.

520. Robinson began recording daily journal entries with the entry for 26 April 1838, suggesting that the 17 April revelation regarding Young had been copied into the journal by that time.

521. Aside from presiding over a 24 May 1838 council meeting, he was not mentioned as attending council meetings held during the next half year. (Minute Book 2, 14 Apr.–6 Oct 1838.)

522. See 1 Corinthians 16:9; Revelation, 12 Oct. 1833, in *JSP*, D3:324 [D&C 100:3]; and Revelation, 23 July 1837, in *JSP*, D5:416 [D&C 112:19].

523. Young and his fellow apostles had expected to travel abroad since the time their quorum was organized in 1835 with a commission to preach to all nations. In summer 1837, JS dictated a revelation to Thomas B. Marsh, the president of the Quorum of the Twelve Apostles, directing him to settle his business affairs and prepare for a mission. Apostles Heber C. Kimball and Orson Hyde were already proselytizing in England. On 11 April 1838, JS dictated a revelation directing apostle David W. Patten to prepare for a mission the following spring, apparently with his fellow apostles. (Instruction on Priesthood, between ca. 1 Mar. and ca. 4 May 1835, in *JSP*, D4:315 [D&C 107:33–35]; Revelation, 23 July 1837, in *JSP*, D5:414–417 [D&C 112]; Historical Introduction to Letter from Heber C. Kimball and Orson Hyde, between 22 and 28 May 1838, pp. 145–146 herein; Revelation, 11 Apr. 1838, p. 82 herein [D&C 114].)

Minutes, 21 April 1838

Source Note

Zion high council, Minutes, [Far West, Caldwell Co., MO], 21 Apr. 1838. Featured version copied [between 1 Oct. 1842 and 14 Sept. 1843] in Minute Book 2, pp. 135–137; handwriting of Hosea Stout; CHL. For more information on Minute Book 2, see Source Notes for Multiple-Entry Documents, p. 569 herein.

Historical Introduction

JS and the Zion high council met on 21 April 1838 to address many of the needs of the growing church in Far West, Missouri. After JS arrived in Missouri the previous month, he participated in the effort to remove dissenters from positions of leadership and, if necessary, from the church. This effort included the excommunications of Oliver Cowdery and David Whitmer in the council meetings held 12 and 13 April.[524] With the church in Zion largely reorganized and major dissenters cut off, the high council was now able to shift its attention to building up the church in Far West.

The meeting of 21 April probably began at 9:00 a.m., as determined during the previous high council meeting.[525] As indicated in the minutes, the meeting was held in a schoolhouse in Far West and began with a prayer by JS. Council meetings in Far West often began with a prayer by the presiding officer, suggesting that JS was conducting the meeting.[526] The council passed measures to improve the schoolhouse in which the council was meeting, to build one or more storehouses in which to keep consecrated goods, and to build houses for JS and Sidney Rigdon. The council also passed several measures related to reestablishing a church print shop and newspaper, having purchased a printing press and necessary supplies on 17 April.[527] Minutes of the meeting were taken by John P. Greene. They were later copied into Minute Book 2 by Hosea Stout.

Document Transcript

High Council met according to adjournment on Saturday the 21st of April 1838.

After singing a hymn, a prayer was offered by Br. Joseph Smith jr. [p. 135]

A charge was then prefered against Lyman Wight by John Anderson, which charge was put over until Thursday the 24th of May next, at 9 o'clock A.M.[528]

---

524. See Minutes, 12 Apr. 1838, pp. 83–94 herein; and Minutes, 13 Apr. 1838, pp. 94–104 herein.

525. Minutes, 14 Apr. 1838, p. 107 herein.

526. See, for example, Minutes, 7 Nov. 1837, in *JSP*, D5:469; Minutes, 15 Mar. 1838, p. 41 herein; and Minutes, 12 Apr. 1838, pp. 84–85 herein.

527. Cowdery had procured the printing equipment from the church in Kirtland, Ohio, and traded it to Whitmer for "timbered land" in Missouri. Whitmer sold the press and type to Marsh on 17 April 1838. (Minutes, 12 Apr. 1838, p. 91 herein; Whitmer, Daybook, 17 Apr. 1838, [133].)

528. Anderson charged Wight "for unjust deal and for abuse to me and for defamation of character." Wight had moved to Daviess County, Missouri, and probably required notice to attend the high council meeting to answer the charge. The charge was presented again on 24 May, but the investigation did not

1st Resolved, that the "Elder's Journal" be published monthly, as it was commenced.[529]

2nd Resolved that President Thomas B. Marsh be the publisher of the "Elders Journal."[530]

3rd Resolved, that the printing press, type, and furniture which was purchased of [*blank*] ⟨John Whitmer⟩ with all the furniture pertaining to the establishment, be sold by the Committee to Edward Partridge, and that he be authorized to pay for the same out of the avails of the City lots or donations[531]

4th Resolved, that Edward Partridge do not pay to W[illiam] W. Phelps and John Whitmer a certain mortgage, which they hold against him, and that this Council uphold him in not paying the the above mortgage.[532]

---

take place until late June. (Minute Book 2, 28–29 June 1838; Minutes, 7–8 Apr. 1838, p. 73 herein; JS, Journal, 18 May–1 June 1838, in *JSP*, J1:271.)

529. The *Elders' Journal,* the church newspaper edited by JS, commenced in Kirtland with two issues, dated October and November 1837. The printing shop was destroyed by fire shortly after JS fled to Missouri. Wilford Woodruff, a member of the First Quorum of the Seventy who was preaching in Maine, wrote a letter to Bishop Edward Partridge and the First Presidency on 9 March in which he pleaded that the *Elders' Journal* be revived. Correspondence between Marsh and Woodruff traveled in less than four weeks, suggesting that Woodruff's letter arrived in Far West sometime in early or mid-April. (John Smith and Don Carlos Smith, Kirtland Mills, OH, to George A. Smith, Shinnston, VA, 15–18 Jan. 1838, George Albert Smith, Papers, CHL; Letter from Wilford Woodruff et al., 9 Mar. 1838, pp. 36–37 herein; 33n155 herein.)

530. Marsh was listed as publisher of the October and November 1837 issues of the *Elders' Journal,* which were published in Kirtland. However, Marsh departed Kirtland for Far West shortly after the September 1837 reorganization conference, so it is unclear what role he played in the publication of these two issues. (Letter to Wilford Woodruff, ca. 18 June 1838, pp. 155–156 herein; Masthead, *Elders' Journal,* Oct. 1837, 16; Masthead, *Elders' Journal,* Nov. 1837, 32.)

531. As the bishop of Zion, Partridge received donations for the church. A 17 May 1837 bond governing the transfer of the Far West plat from William W. Phelps and John Whitmer to Partridge authorized him to use the funds from the sale of lots "for the benefit of the printing office or literary firm" as well as for other purposes. (Revelation, 9 Feb. 1831, in *JSP*, D1:251–252 [D&C 42:31–34]; Edward Partridge, Bond, Far West, MO, to William W. Phelps and John Whitmer, 17 May 1837, John Whitmer Family Papers, CHL; see also Minute Book 2, 5–7 Apr. 1837.)

532. Phelps and Whitmer purchased the land in Far West with money raised and borrowed with interest from church members. When Phelps and Whitmer agreed to turn over the land to Partridge, they made the transaction conditional on a mortgage and two bonds that required Partridge to pay them $1,450 and to take responsibility for their subscription of $2,000 for the House of the Lord in Far West. When the building plans fell through and others withdrew their subscriptions, Phelps and Whitmer withdrew theirs as well and sought payment in cash for the $2,000 and the $1,450. Because the original money was donated by church members for the cause of Zion or was still owed with interest and because the sale of public lands was supposed to support the church, the high council believed that Phelps and Whitmer had swindled the church. Partridge's last recorded payment on the mortgage occurred on 13 March 1838, although his estate made two additional payments in the 1840s. (Letter to Wilford Woodruff, ca. 18 June 1838, pp. 157–160 herein; see also Minute Book 2, 25 July 1836; 5–7 Apr. 1837; 10 Mar. 1838; "T. B. Marsh," [2], Historian's Office, Histories of the Twelve, 1856–1858, 1861, CHL; and

5th Resolved, that this Council authorize Edward Partridge to assist, in making houses on, and fencing the lots in this City which are appropriated to the use of Joseph Smith j^r and Sidney Rigdon, with the avails arising from the town plot.[533]

6th Resolved— that Edward Partridge make an appropriation of not more than one hundred dollars to this School house, out. of the avails of the town plot.

7th Resolved that this Council support Thomas B. Marsh as the publisher of the "Elders' Journal" and use their influence to obtain subscriptions for the same.

8th Resolved that this Council, the Bishop and his Council use their influence to cause the people to consecrate to the Lord for the support of the poor and needy.[534]

9th Resolved that the Bishop be authorized to obtain or build a sufficient store house or houses to recieve all the consecrations of the people,[535] to be paid for out of the avails of the town plot [p. 136]

10th Resolved that this High Council and Clerk publish the minits of the High Council, from time to time as they shall deem proper

11th Resolved that the afore said record Commence at the time of the last Council held in Clay County.[536]

Edward Partridge and Lydia Partridge, Mortgage, Far West, MO, to William W. Phelps and John Whitmer, 17 May 1837, John Whitmer Family Papers, CHL.)

533. On 3 March 1838, the high council authorized Partridge to give lots in Far West to JS, Rigdon, and Hyrum Smith. (Minute Book 2, 3 Mar. 1838.)

534. See Psalm 82:4; and Revelation, 4 Dec. 1831–B, in *JSP*, D2:152 [D&C 72:12].

535. The role of the storehouse in Zion was firmly established by revelation in the early 1830s.^a John Corrill was appointed "keeper of the Lord's store House" in May 1837, suggesting that the Latter-day Saints in Missouri already had a storage place. This resolution indicates that if the Saints did already have a storage place, it might have been inadequate to accommodate the increased donations anticipated as a result of the previous resolution.^b (a. Revelation, 9 Feb. 1831, in *JSP*, D1:251–252 [D&C 42:30–34]; Revelation, 20 May 1831, in *JSP*, D1:316 [D&C 51:13]; Revelation, 20 July 1831, in *JSP*, D2:11 [D&C 57:8]; Revelation, 1 Aug. 1831, in *JSP*, D2:16, 17 [D&C 58:24, 37]; Revelation, 4 Dec. 1831–B, in *JSP*, D2:152 [D&C 72:9–10]; Revelation, 30 Apr. 1832, in *JSP*, D2:243 [D&C 83:4–6]. b. Minute Book 2, 22 May 1837.)

536. The last extant set of minutes for a council meeting in Clay County, Missouri, is for 25 July 1836. These minutes conclude with a resolution to "search out land for the Church to settle upon &c." This resolution, which was part of the effort to relocate the Missouri Saints and provide land for new immigrants, resulted in the purchase of land along Shoal Creek for the settlement of Far West. Minutes from a 10 November 1837 council meeting were published in a Kirtland issue of the *Elders' Journal.* When publication of the paper recommenced in Far West, the first issue included a letter from Marsh that contained the minutes of a "general assembly" that the high council initiated, in which Zion church presidents William W. Phelps and John Whitmer were removed from office; the minutes of the 10 March 1838 council meeting in which Phelps and Whitmer were excommunicated; and the minutes of the 7–8 April 1838 quarterly conference, held "agreeable to a resolution of the high council," in which

Adjourned till Saturday the 28th inst

John P. Green[e] Clk pro. tem.—[537]

———— ❧ ————

Revelation, 26 April 1838 [D&C 115]

Source Note

Revelation, Far West, Caldwell Co., MO, 26 Apr. 1838. Featured version copied [ca. 26 Apr. 1838] in JS, Journal, Mar.–Sept. 1838, pp. 32–34; handwriting of George W. Robinson; CHL. Includes use marks. For more information on JS, Journal, Mar.–Sept. 1838, see Source Notes for Multiple-Entry Documents, p. 564 herein.

Historical Introduction

JS dictated a revelation on 26 April 1838 stating that the city of Far West, Missouri, "should be built up" by the gathering of the Saints and that they should build a temple there. Since the creation of Caldwell County in 1836, Latter-day Saints in Missouri and elsewhere had been gathering in Far West, the county's principal Mormon community, and in surrounding settlements. In early 1837, about a year before JS's arrival, Zion presidency members William W. Phelps and John Whitmer drew a plan for a temple and appointed a committee to superintend construction of the temple in Far West's central lot. In April 1837, the high council questioned the Zion presidency's authority to appoint such a committee and even to select the site for the city.[538] This problem was somewhat resolved, and several hundred Saints assembled to begin excavating for the temple foundation in July.[539] When JS and Sidney Rigdon visited Far West in November, they participated in a council meeting wherein the members resolved to expand the size of the existing city plat. This resolution suggests that JS and the other council members approved the location of the city and its central lot. Moreover, the council members apparently authorized the plan to build a temple and approved the location, but it was decided to suspend any construction work "till the Lord shall reveal it to be his will to be commenced."[540]

After JS moved to Caldwell County in March 1838 and helped root dissension out of the church, he and the high council turned their attention to developing Far West as the church's gathering center. On 21 April, they passed several resolutions to build

---

new officers were appointed. (Minute Book 2, 25 July 1836; Gentry and Compton, *Fire and Sword,* 28–36; Minutes, 10 Nov. 1837, *Elders' Journal,* Nov. 1837, 30–31; "Minutes of the Proceedings of the Committee of the Whole Church in Zion," *Elders' Journal,* July 1838, 44–46; "Minutes of High Council," *Elders' Journal,* July 1838, 46; "Conference Minutes," *Elders' Journal,* July 1838, 47.)

537. Greene, a member of the high council, was substituting for high council clerk Ebenezer Robinson. (Minutes, 6 Apr. 1838, p. 70 herein; Minutes, 7–8 Apr. 1838, p. 73 herein.)

538. Minute Book 2, 3 Apr. 1837; Letter to Wilford Woodruff, ca. 18 June 1838, pp. 157–160 herein.

539. Minute Book 2, 7 Apr. 1837; Letter from William W. Phelps, 7 July 1837, in *JSP,* D5:402–403.

540. Minutes, 6 Nov. 1837, in *JSP,* D5:467; Minutes, 10 Nov. 1837, in *JSP,* D5:475; see also Letter to Wilford Woodruff, ca. 18 June 1838, pp. 157–160 herein.

the community, including improving the schoolhouse used for community meetings, building one or more storehouses, and reestablishing the church press.[541] By this time, thousands of Saints were living in Far West and its vicinity and hundreds more were expected from Kirtland within the next few months.[542] The gathering of the Saints, especially with heavy migration from Ohio, would eventually require settlement beyond the bounds of Far West, and church leaders had already begun efforts to locate other sites for settlement.

JS's revelation of 26 April 1838 spoke to these recent developments. The revelation was addressed to JS, other church leaders, and all other members of the "Church of Jesus Christ of Latter Day Saints"—which the revelation specified was the new official name of the church. The revelation enjoined the church's leaders and members to continue gathering to Far West, to sanctify the city through consecrated living, and to build the temple. The Saints were instructed to begin work on the temple on 4 July and to build it according to a pattern that would be revealed to the First Presidency. When church members resided in Clay County earlier in the 1830s, no revelations had instructed the Saints to establish a city of gathering or to construct a temple there. The plan for the Saints in Missouri up until this time had been one of temporary settlement while waiting for a return to the "centre place" of Zion in Jackson County. The 26 April 1838 revelation marked a change in Mormon plans in Missouri. Though the Latter-day Saints were not in Zion's "centre place" at Independence and were not building "the City of Zion," they were commanded to build up *a* city of Zion with a temple.[543] The revelation concluded with a commandment to the Saints to build up Far West and to establish other communities "in the regions round about" as directed by their prophet.

The revelation was probably dictated orally and written down by a scribe, as was typical with JS's revelations.[544] George W. Robinson copied the revelation into JS's "Scriptory Book," apparently around the time JS dictated the revelation.[545] The Latter-day Saints followed the direction of the revelation by laying the cornerstones of the temple on 4 July 1838, whereupon Rigdon gave a speech in which he vigorously asserted the rights of the Latter-day Saints to settle wherever they pleased.[546]

---

541. See Minutes, 21 Apr. 1838, pp. 109–112 herein.

542. Backman, *Heavens Resound,* 354–355. The influx of Saints from Kirtland was at least in part the result of a 12 January 1838 revelation directing the First Presidency to move to Far West as soon as possible and for loyal Latter-day Saints to follow. (Revelation, 12 Jan. 1838–C, in *JSP,* D5:501–502.)

543. See Revelation, 20 July 1831, in *JSP,* D2:7–8 [D&C 57:1–3].

544. "Revelations," *Ensign of Liberty,* Aug. 1849, 98–99; see also William E. McLellin, Independence, MO, to Joseph Smith III, [Plano, IL], July 1872, typescript, Letters and Documents Copied from Originals in the Office of the Church Historian, Reorganized Church, CHL; and Pratt, *Autobiography,* 65.

545. Beginning with this 26 April revelation, the Scriptory Book appears to have been kept regularly, suggesting that the revelation was inscribed sometime in late April or early May. The revelation was later published in the church's newspaper at the time, the *Elders' Journal.* (JS, Journal, Mar.–Sept. 1838, pp. 32–38, in *JSP,* J1:257–264; "An Extract of Revelation," *Elders' Journal,* Aug. 1838, 52–53.)

546. JS, Journal, 4 July 1838, in *JSP,* J1:275–276; "Celebration of the 4th of July," *Elders' Journal,* Aug. 1838, 60; Discourse, ca. 4 July 1838, at josephsmithpapers.org.

Document Transcript

Revelation given in Far West, April 26⟨th⟩, 1838, Making known the will of God, concerning the building up of this place and of the Lord's house &c.

Verrily thus Saith the Lord unto you my Servant Joseph Smith Jr. and also my Servant Sidney Rigdon, and also my Servant Hyrum Smith, and your counselors who are and who shall be hereafter appointed,[547] and also unto my Servant Edward Partridge and his Councilors,[548] and also unto my faithfull Servants, who are of the High Council of my Church in zion (for thus it shall be called) and unto all the Elders and people of my Church of Jesus Christ of Latter Day Saints, Scattered abroad [p. 32] in all the world,[549] For thus shall my Church be called in the Last days even the Church of Jesus Christ of Latter Day Saints,[550] Verrily I say unto you all; arise and shine forth forth [551] that thy light may be a standard for the nations[552] and that thy gathering to-gether upon the land of zion and upon her stakes[553] may be for a

---

547. In the September 1837 reorganization conference held in Kirtland, JS presented the names of Sidney Rigdon and Frederick G. Williams as his counselors in the First Presidency, with Oliver Cowdery, Joseph Smith Sr., Hyrum Smith, and John Smith as "assistant councillors." The full group constituted "the heads of the Church." In the November 1837 reorganization conference held in Far West, Hyrum Smith replaced Williams as JS's second counselor in the First Presidency; the names of the other assistant counselors were not presented in that meeting. (Minutes, 3 Sept. 1837, in *JSP*, D5:422–423; Minutes, 7 Nov. 1837, in *JSP*, D5:469–470.)

548. Bishop Partridge's two counselors were Isaac Morley and Titus Billings. (Minutes, 7 Nov. 1837, in *JSP*, D5:471.)

549. See Nehemiah 1:8; Matthew 9:36; and Book of Mormon, 1830 ed., 216, 464, 496 [Mosiah 28:17; 3 Nephi 5:24; 20:13].

550. The first name used to identify the church that JS organized on 6 April 1830 was "the Church of Christ."*a* In 1834 a conference of church leaders changed the name to "The Church of the Latter Day Saints," perhaps to avoid confusion with other churches named Church of Christ.*b* On occasion, the two names of the church were combined as "the church of Christ of Latter Day Saints."*c* The Kirtland dissenters seem to have criticized church leaders for removing Christ's name from the formal name of the church. In a June 1838 letter, Thomas B. Marsh wrote that the dissenters "claimed, themselves to be the old standard, called themslves the Church of Christ, excluded that of saints, and set at naught Bʳ. Joseph and the whole Church, denounceing them as Heriticks." Restoring the name of Christ to the name of the church may have answered this criticism.*d* The name specified in the revelation, a combination of the two earlier names of the church, began to be used in the early months of 1838.*e* (*a.* Revelation, 6 Apr. 1830, in *JSP*, D1:130 [D&C 21:11]; Articles and Covenants, ca. Apr. 1830, in *JSP*, D1:120 [D&C 20:1]. *b.* Minutes, 3 May 1834, in *JSP*, D4:44. *c.* Doctrine and Covenants 5, 1835 ed. [D&C 102]; Minutes, *LDS Messenger and Advocate*, Feb. 1836, 2:266. *d.* Letter to Wilford Woodruff, ca. 18 June 1838, p. 156 herein. *e.* Letter from Thomas B. Marsh, 15 Feb. 1838, p. 18 herein; see also Letter to the Presidency in Kirtland, 29 Mar. 1838, p. 57 herein; JS, Journal, Mar.–Sept. 1838, p. 15, in *JSP*, J1:236; and Resolution, ca. 8 Apr. 1838, p. 76 herein.)

551. See Isaiah 60:1.

552. See Jeremiah 50:2; 51:27; and Revelation, ca. 7 Mar. 1831, in *JSP*, D1:276 [D&C 45:9].

553. JS dictated a revelation in 1831 that designated "the land of Missorie" as "the Land which I, have appointed & consecrated for the gethering of the Saints" and as "the Land of Zion." The term *stake*, used

defence and for a reffuge[554] from the storm[555] and from wrath when it shall be poured out without mixture upon the whole Earth,[556] Let the City Far West, be a holy and consecrated land unto me, and ⟨it shall⟩ be called ⟨most⟩ holy for the ground upon which thou standest is holy[557] Therefore I command you to build an house unto me for the gathering togeth~~er~~ing of my Saints that they may worship me,[558] and let there be a begining of this work; and a foundation and a preparatory work, this following Summer; and let the begining be made on the 4ᵗʰ day of July next;[559] and from that time forth let my people labour diligently to build an house, unto my name,[560] and in one year from this day, let them recommence laying the foundation of my house; thus let them from that time forth laibour diligently untill it shall be finished, from

---

by Saints to describe an approved place for gathering outside of the principal Mormon community in Missouri, derived from the biblical metaphor of Zion as a tent whose "curtains" were stretched out, with cords fastened to the ground by stakes. (Revelation, 20 July 1831, in *JSP*, D2:7, 12 [D&C 57:1, 14]; Isaiah 54:2–3; Revelation, 26 Apr. 1832, in *JSP*, D2:236 [D&C 82:13–14].)

554. See Psalm 59:16; see also Psalm 94:22.

555. See Isaiah 25:4.

556. See Revelation 14:10.

557. See Exodus 3:5; see also Acts 7:33. The Book of Mormon teaches that the Americas, like the land of Canaan in the Bible, are a "land of promise" and a "holy land."*ᵃ* JS dictated a revelation in 1831 specifically designating Missouri as a "land of promise."*ᵇ* In his 4 September 1837 letter to the Saints in Far West, JS began by blessing the name of the Lord, who "has delivered you many times from the hands of your enemies And planted you many times in an heavenly or holy place," implying that Far West was a holy place.*ᶜ* On 23 July 1838, Reynolds Cahoon wrote a letter to Newel K. Whitney, reporting: "It is said by some that Jacson Co. is where the gardon of Edon was[.] Far west is where Adam dwelt after he was driven from the gardin[.] Adam on-di Ahman is where he built an alter & blest his sons this I have not heard from Br. Joseph but expect it is his teachings."*ᵈ* (*a.* Book of Mormon, 1830 ed., 26, 143–144 [1 Nephi 12:1; Enos 1:10]. *b.* Revelation, 20 July 1831, in *JSP*, D2:7–8 [D&C 57:1–2]. *c.* Letter to John Corrill and the Church in Missouri, 4 Sept. 1837, in *JSP*, D5:427. *d.* Reynolds Cahoon, Far West, MO, to Newel K. Whitney, Kirtland, OH, 23 July 1838, CHL; see also Reed Peck, Quincy, IL, to "Dear Friends," 18 Sept. 1839, pp. 19–20, Henry E. Huntington Library, San Marino, CA; and Whitney, *Life of Heber C. Kimball*, 219–220.)

558. At the conclusion of the November 1837 reorganization conference in Far West, Rigdon "called upon the Lord" in prayer "to dedicate this land for the gathering of the Saints." Previous JS revelations directed the Latter-day Saints to build temples at Independence and Kirtland. (Minutes, 7 Nov. 1837, in *JSP*, D5:472; Revelation, 20 July 1831, in *JSP*, D2:7–8 [D&C 57:1–3]; Revelation, 27–28 Dec. 1832, in *JSP*, D2:345 [D&C 88:119]; Revelation, 1 June 1833, in *JSP*, D3:104–108 [D&C 95].)

559. The version of the revelation published in the August 1838 issue of the *Elders' Journal* has "and let there be a beginning of this work, and a foundation, and a preparatory work for the foundation, in this following season, and let this beginning be made on the 4th day of July next." An excavation for a cellar, measuring 110 by 80 feet, had been dug the previous summer. On 4 July 1838, church leaders laid the four cornerstones. ("An Extract of Revelation," *Elders' Journal*, Aug. 1838, 52; Letter from William W. Phelps, 7 July 1837, in *JSP*, D5:403; "Celebration of the 4th of July," *Elders' Journal*, Aug. 1838, 60.)

560. See 1 Kings 5:5; 8:19; Revelation, 2 Aug. 1833–B, in *JSP*, D3:206 [D&C 94:10]; and Revelation, 2 Aug. 1833–A, in *JSP*, D3:202 [D&C 97:15].

the Corner Stone thereof unto the top thereof, untill there shall not any thing remain that is not finished.

Verrily I say unto you let not my servant Joseph neither my Servant Sidney, neither my Servant Hyrum, get in debt any more for the building of an house unto my name.[561] But let my house be built unto my name according to the pattern which I will shew unto them,[562] and if my people build it not according to the pattern which I Shall shew unto their presidency, I will not accept it at their hands, But if my people do build it according to the pattern which I shall shew unto their presidency, even my servant Joseph and his Councilors; then I will accept it at [p. 33] the hands of my people,[563] And again; Verrily I say unto you it is my will, that the City Far West should be built up spedily,[564] by the gathering of my Saints, and also that other places should be appointed for stakes in the regions round about as they shall be manifested unto my Servant Joseph from time to time.[565] For behold I will be with him and I will Sanctify

---

561. JS and other Latter-day Saints had gone into debt to finance the construction of the temple in Kirtland, and eventually the temple had to be mortgaged. In 1838 JS was deeper in debt than ever before. (Robison, *First Mormon Temple*, 99–101; Mortgage to Mead, Stafford & Co., 11 July 1837, in *JSP*, D5:407–410; Madsen, "Tabulating the Impact of Litigation," 232–240.)

562. See Exodus 25:9; 2 Kings 16:10; Hebrews 8:5; and Revelation, 2 Aug. 1833–B, in *JSP*, D3:206, 207 [D&C 94:6, 12].

563. This directive followed the precedent set with the design of the temple in Kirtland. In 1833 JS dictated a revelation stating that the Lord would reveal the pattern of the Kirtland temple.[a] Within a few days, JS and his counselors in the church presidency reported a vision in which they saw a model of the temple.[b] Soon thereafter, they sent drawings of the model, which they called a "pattern," to the church in Jackson County to use in building a temple there.[c] (a. Revelation, 1 June 1833, in *JSP*, D3:107 [D&C 95:14]; see also Minutes, ca. 1 June 1833, in *JSP*, D3:104. b. Angell, Autobiography, 14–15; see also Truman Angell, Salt Lake City, Utah Territory, to John Taylor, 11 Mar. 1885, First Presidency [John Taylor] Correspondence, CHL; and Orson Pratt, in *Journal of Discourses*, 9 Apr. 1871, 14:273. c. Letter to Church Leaders in Jackson Co., MO, 25 June 1833, in *JSP*, D3:152; Plan of the House of the Lord, between 1 and 25 June 1833, in *JSP*, D3:145; see also Robison, *First Mormon Temple*, 9.)

564. See Revelation, 2 Aug. 1833–A, in *JSP*, D3:201 [D&C 97:11].

565. Earlier revelations directed the church to purchase land not only at Independence and other areas in Jackson County but also "in the adjoining Counties round about." The Saints may have interpreted these revelations to mean that church members could venture to new settlements outside of Caldwell County.[a] A committee was created in November 1837 to explore the land northward, searching for locations for additional settlements.[b] By April 1838, Lyman Wight moved north to Daviess County, and the church was considering settling Saints to the east in De Witt, Carroll County.[c] This expansion conflicted with the understanding of Missourians in neighboring counties that the Latter-day Saints would confine themselves to Caldwell County.[d] (a. Revelation, 20 July 1831, in *JSP*, D2:7–12 [D&C 57:3–6, 14]; Revelation, 16–17 Dec. 1833, in *JSP*, D3:395 [D&C 101:71]; Revelation, 22 June 1834, in *JSP*, D4:76 [D&C 105:28]. b. Travel Account and Questions, Nov. 1837, in *JSP*, D5:481; Minute Book 2, 6–7 Dec. 1837; Letter from Oliver Cowdery, 21 Jan. 1838, in *JSP*, D5:504–505. c. Minutes, 7–8 Apr. 1838, p. 73 herein; JS, Journal, 18 May–1 June 1838, in *JSP*, J1:271; Letter from David Thomas, 31 Mar. 1838, pp. 65–66 herein. d. See LeSueur, "Missouri's Failed Compromise," 113–144.)

Temple lot in Far West, Missouri. 1907. A revelation Joseph Smith dictated on 26 April 1838 stated that "the City Far West should be built up" and directed the Latter-day Saints to build a temple there. The Saints were unable to construct the temple because they were expelled from the state in early 1839. (Church History Library, Salt Lake City. Photograph by George Edward Anderson.)

him before the people for unto him have I given the Keys of this Kingdom and ministry[566] even so— Amen.

———— ✍ ————

Minutes, 28 April 1838

Historical Introduction

On 28 April 1838, JS participated in the trial of Aaron Lyon, which the Zion high council conducted in Far West, Missouri. Information about the case was captured in the trial's official minutes, which were kept by high council clerk Ebenezer Robinson, and in an account that George W. Robinson included in JS's "Scriptory Book." Both documents are presented here.

Lyon was the presiding high priest in the church branch at the settlement at Guymon's mill, about eight miles east of Far West.[567] One of the members living there was Sarah Jackson. She had moved from Illinois to Missouri in 1837 to settle with the Latter-day Saints, with the expectation that her husband would soon join her.[568] When her husband did not arrive within a few months, she asked Lyon "to inquire of the Lord concerning my husband and what was the cause of his not coming." Sometime later, the recently widowed Lyon told her he had received a revelation that her husband had died. On another occasion, Lyon told Jackson of a vision in which he saw her as his wife. Jackson initially expressed doubt about the validity of Lyon's vision, but the influential, much-older man coerced her to agree to marry him. However, in November 1837, before the wedding occurred, Jackson's husband arrived. Lyon attempted to excuse his actions by blaming the devil for giving him false revelations. Nevertheless, Jackson's husband brought charges against Lyon in an "elder's meeting." The verdict of the elders council, which is not known, was appealed to the high council. JS may have heard of the case in March 1838 from John Barnard, who was a member of the branch of the church at Guymon's mill.[569] As JS traveled from Kirtland, Ohio, to Far West, Barnard joined him in central Missouri, and they completed the journey together, stopping one night at Barnard's residence en route.[570] On 21 April, JS attended a high council meeting, during which the council members scheduled a meeting for 28 April, probably with the intention to review the Lyon appeal.[571] On 27 April, the day before the high council considered the

---

566. See Matthew 16:19. JS's revelations affirmed that God had given him the "keys" of the kingdom. (See, for example, Revelation, 11 Sept. 1831, in *JSP*, D2:63 [D&C 64:4–5]; Revelation, ca. Aug. 1835, in *JSP*, D4:411 [D&C 27:12–13]; and Questions and Answers, between ca. 16 and ca. 29 Mar. 1838–A, p. 54 herein [D&C 113:6].)

567. Foote, Autobiography, 24 Sept. 1838, 29.

568. Nothing further is known of Sarah Jackson, nor has her husband been identified.

569. See Hamer, *Northeast of Eden*, 59, 81.

570. See Historian's Office, Brigham Young History Drafts, 17; and JS, Journal, Mar.–Sept. 1838, p. 16, in *JSP*, J1:237; see also Riggs and Thompson, "Notorious Case of Aaron Lyon," 108–109.

571. The minutes of this meeting state that the high council was "adjourned till Saturday the 28th inst." (Minutes, 21 Apr. 1838, p. 112 herein.)

appeal, Jackson wrote a testimony regarding her interactions with Lyon in a letter to the high council.

On the morning of 28 April, JS, Sidney Rigdon, and George W. Robinson were invited to attend the high council meeting during which the trial would be held.[572] When the council was called to order and only ten of its members were present, JS and Rigdon were invited to participate. They joined the two counselors assigned to speak on behalf of the defendant and the plaintiff, respectively. After hearing testimony from Latter-day Saints in the branch at Guymon's mill, Rigdon argued for justice and JS argued for mercy. The council determined to retain Lyon as a member of the church but revoked his office in the priesthood.

Ebenezer Robinson prepared the official minutes of the council meeting most likely during the meeting or based on notes that he took during the meeting. His minutes were recorded in Minute Book 2 in 1842 or 1843 by Nauvoo high council clerk Hosea Stout. George W. Robinson wrote an account of the trial in JS's Scriptory Book. Robinson wrote the 28 April entry during the Scriptory Book's transition from a record of "scripts"—transcripts of letters, revelations, and other documents—to a journal for JS.[573] The account begins much like a journal entry, with a narrative of the invitation that JS, Rigdon, and George W. Robinson received to attend the trial. The account then moves into a summary of the trial; this summary is somewhat similar to the content and format of meeting minutes. At the conclusion of the account, Robinson signed it explicitly as "scribe," thus differentiating this entry from the ordinary journal entries that would follow and resembling more the discrete transcripts that he had previously inscribed in the Scriptory Book. Robinson's identification of his role as a scribe suggests he wrote the document for the First Presidency or for First Presidency members JS and Rigdon, who participated prominently in the trial. The format of the trial summary—comprising a narrative amalgamation of facts from witnesses' testimonies, followed by a dramatic recounting of the arguments made on behalf of justice and mercy—suggests that Robinson did not write the account during the trial. Rather, he likely wrote the account later in the day or within a few days of the trial.[574]

1. Ebenezer Robinson, Minutes in Minute Book 2
Source Note

Zion high council, Minutes, Far West, Caldwell Co., MO, 28 Apr. 1838. Featured version copied [between 1 Oct. 1842 and 14 Sept. 1843] in Minute Book 2, pp. 137–140, 157–159; CHL; handwriting of Hosea Stout. For more information on Minute Book 2, see Source Notes for Multiple-Entry Documents, p. 569 herein.

---

572. Several high council meetings had been held in Far West since JS's arrival. JS attended and presided over most but not all of these councils. For example, JS did not attend the 17 March meeting, at which Thomas B. Marsh presided. Also, on 13 April 1838, JS testified in the trial of Lyman Johnson, but Marsh presided over the meeting. (Minute Book 2, 17 Mar. 1838; Minutes, 13 Apr. 1838, pp. 95, 99 herein.)

573. The recording of document transcripts continued up through the entry for 26 April 1838, which consisted of a copy of JS's revelation on that date. The following entry, for 27 April, took the form of an ordinary journal entry. The entry for 28 April recounted the Lyon trial held that day. Daily entries for the next two weeks and sporadic entries over the next four months generally took the form of a journal. (JS, Journal, Mar.–Sept. 1838, in *JSP*, J1:225–320.)

574. Because Ebenezer Robinson likely wrote his minutes before George W. Robinson wrote his account, Ebenezer Robinson's minutes are presented first in this volume.

Document Transcript

The High Council of Zion met in Far-West April 28th 1838 agreeable to adjournment.

Thomas B. Marsh and David W. Patten Presiding[575]

The Council was organizid as followss;

Simion [Simeon] Carter	n⁰ 1	Jared Carter	no. 2
Levi Jackman	" 2 3	Zecheriah Wilson	" 4
Sidney Rigdon	" 5	Joseph Smith jr	" 6
George Morey	" 7	Newel Knight	" 8
George M. Hinkle	" 9	George W. Harris	" 10
Elias Higbee	" 11	John Murdock	" 12

After which it was voted that Joseph Smith j[r] and Sidney Rigdon act in the places of n⁰ 9 & 10.[576]

The Council was opened by in prayer by Pres[t] Marsh

An appealed case was presented pending between Jackson and Lyons [Aaron Lyon], when the minutes of an Elder's meeting was read by Councellor Hinkle in which the above case had been tried, also the charges and the appeal. The several charges were read when the accused confessed the 1st, 2nd 3rd 4th the 5th he denied also the 6th, 7th 8th, 9th, 10th & 11th.

The Case was considered difficult, therefore, 4 were to speak on it viz; George M. Hinkle and Sidney Rigdon on the part of the Church and George W. Harris and Joseph Smith jr on the part of the defendant.

The Council adjourned for one hour.

Council met agreeable to adjournment. [p. 137]

Opened in singing "This Earth was once a garden place"[577] &c and prayer by President David W. Patten.

Peter Dustan [Dustin] was appointed to fill the seat of No. 2 pro. tempore.

---

575. Marsh was the president pro tempore of the church in Zion, with David W. Patten and Brigham Young as assistant presidents. Young may have not attended the meeting because JS had recently dictated a revelation directing Young to go to his property at Mill Creek, where his family was residing, and to provide for them. (Minutes, 6 Apr. 1838, p. 70 herein; Revelation, 17 Apr. 1838, p. 108 herein.)

576. When cases were brought before the council, the counselors were numbered, and one or more odd-numbered counselors represented the plaintiff, with the same number of even-numbered counselors representing the defendant. For each odd-numbered counselor representing the plaintiff, the even-numbered counselor just higher in number represented the defendant. The responsibilities for representing the two parties seem to have rotated through the council. In the council meeting of 28 April, it was the duty of counselors 9 and 10—George M. Hinkle and George W. Harris—to represent the plaintiff and defendant. (See Minute Book 2, 10 Mar.–29 June 1838.)

577. This popular hymn, composed by William W. Phelps, is about Adam-ondi-Ahman. (Hymn 23, *Collection of Sacred Hymns*, 29–30.)

Voted by the High Council that the proceedings of the Elder's Conference held to investigate the case of J. Lemons [John Lemon] & S. Wixom are null and void, as they keept no regular minutes or records of them.[578]

Br. Best testifies that he heard Br Lyons prophecy at B[r] Wheeler's[579] that some one would be heard to mourn, after that Lyons told him that he had a wife selected and she was in the house, they were then at Br Curtis', and she was Sister [Sarah] Jackson and Lyons requested him to tell her that her husband was dead, also, Lyons told him, the Lord had shown her to him for his wife, also heard Lyons say that if she broke her covenant she would be miserable, because he had seen her future state, also, when he told Sister Jackson what Lyons requested him, she cried and said she hoped the Lord would be merciful to her in her afflictions

At another time, he heard Sister Jackson say that Lyons told her the Lord had revealed to him that she was to be his wife and she believed that she had a testimony that he told the truth. Sister Jackson had been absent from her husband about five months, but he returned soon after, which was some time in November last. Also, was knowing to Lyons walking to and from meetings with her, both in night and day time, as she lived at his house.

Shadrach Roundy— testifies that Lyons had some conversation with him respecting getting a wife, saying he was going to have a wife and that by revelation, because the Lord was going to let him have a wife with whom he could live in peace &c.[580]

At another time Lyons told him that he enquired of the Lord respecting a companion, when Sister Jackson was presented before him, when he said to the Lord "She is pregnant by another man", when the Lord replied "wait my time & [p. 138] it will all come right" Lyons generally took the lead of meetings in that Branch.

John P. Barnam [Barnard] testifies that, Lyons told him he had a revelation and it was of God, he should be married in a few days, but seemed to almost doubt of its truth, but soon after he enquired of the Lord to know whether it was of God or not, when the reply was, "I know all things", therefore Lyons Concluded it was of God, also that Lyons was a man of great influence in the Church, and when he spoke in the name of the Lord, the brethren had great confidence in it &c

---

578. The appeal of the case involving Lemons and Wixom was presented to the Zion high council on 10 March but was rescheduled for the 28 April council meeting. (Minute Book 2, 10 Mar. 1838.)

579. Probably John Wheeler, who owned land in the area. (Hamer, *Northeast of Eden,* 59, 93.)

580. Aaron Lyon's wife, Roxana Palmer Lyon, died in August 1836, leaving Aaron with "a family of children." (Obituary for Roxana Palmer Lyon, *LDS Messenger and Advocate,* Jan. 1837, 3:447–448.)

Thomas Guyman [Guymon] concurs in the testimony previously given,[581] also he heard Sister Jackson say she was afraid of the curses of God falling upon her, therefore she consented to have B^r Lyons but was soon sorry for it also after Lyons said her husband was dead she was considerably troubled about it and frequently requested the Church to pray for her husband that he might return &c. but after some time she expressed her fears that he was dead & was inclined to think she had a testimony to that effect, also Lyons told him Br. Best had given him liberty to come to his house to see Sister Jackson.

Br Jackson testifies that his wife was not pregnant when he returned. ⟨See Sister Jackson's letter on Pages 157 and 158 & 159⟩[582]

Br Benjamin[583] testifies that, Calvin Reed, a boy about 15 years of age,[584] said he had a revelation or vision, in which he saw Br Jackson dead or preaching to the spirits in prison &c.[585]

After some lengthy remarks by the Councellors, and very good instruction given by Councellor Smith, the accused made confession to the satisfaction of the Council, When it was decided that Br Lyon be retained in the Church, but his licence be taken from him, as it is ~~not~~ considered that ⟨he⟩ is not qualified to hold an office in this Church [p. 139]

The Council concured with the foregoing decision.

The Council adjourned untill two weeks from today. Closed in prayer by Sidney Rigdon.

Ebenezer Robinson Clerk

———— ❧ ————

---

581. Guymon was the owner of the local horse-powered mill. (Foote, Autobiography, 15 Sept. 1838, 29.)

582. TEXT: This insertion is enclosed in an inscribed rectangle. When Stout copied Sarah Jackson's testimony into Minute Book 2, he copied the testimony out of place and then noted that it "should have been inserted on Page 139." Her testimony is reproduced at the end of the minutes.

583. Possibly Nahum or Timothy Benjamin, both of whom lived near Guymon's mill. Nahum Benjamin owned land near Barnard. (Hamer, *Northeast of Eden*, 59, 81.)

584. Calvin Reed was Nahum Benjamin's nephew. Calvin's father, Tillison Reed, was the brother of Nahum Benjamin's wife, Judith Reed Benjamin. (Merrill, *History of Acworth*, 259.)

585. The New Testament states that between the death and resurrection of Jesus Christ, he "preached unto the spirits in prison." In 1832, JS and Rigdon affirmed this doctrine in their account of a vision of the postmortal kingdoms of heavenly glory. In the mid-1830s, this doctrine developed to include the idea of faithful men joining in this divine enterprise by preaching to "the spirits in prison" after they died. In her written testimony, Sarah Jackson recounted that Lyon told her that her husband was "preaching to the spirits in prison." Though it is unclear whether Reed related his own vision or a vision Lyon claimed he received, if Sarah Jackson had heard Reed recount a vision of his own in which her husband was dead and preaching to postmortal spirits, it may have helped her accept Lyon's claim that he had received a revelation to that effect. (1 Peter 3:18–20; Vision, 16 Feb. 1832, in *JSP*, D2:189 [D&C 76:73]; Patriarchal Blessing for Lorenzo Snow, 15 Dec. 1836, Lorenzo Snow, Papers, CHL; Woodruff, Journal, 3 Jan. 1837.)

Editorial Note

When Hosea Stout copied the minutes of the council meeting, he did not initially include the written testimony of Sarah Jackson. After copying minutes of further meetings, he found Jackson's letter and copied it under an explanatory heading: "The following letter of Sarah Jackson should have been inserted on Page 139, in the minutes of a Council, on the 28 of April 1838, but was not in consequence of its being mislaid and did not come to hand until the recording had been done thus far. (See Page 139.)" Stout copied the letter on pages 157–159 of Minute Book 2. The copy of the letter is appended here.[586]

"It came to pass in the year of our Lord 1837, That I having lately came into this work, my husband sent me to this country some ~~time~~ months previous to his coming. I was here some time and he did not come.

I, believing Elder [Aaron] Lyon to be a man of God, asked him to inquire of the Lord concerning my husband and what ~~had~~ was the cause of his not coming.

Some time after that, he held a prayer meeting [p. 157] at Br Wheelers, here he prophecied ~~that~~ and said some one now in the room shall be led to mourn before three weeks unless there was a speedy repentance, & who it was he did not know. So on returning from meeting, he told me, that he had inquired of the Lord, and that my husband was dead and preaching to the spirits in prison, and that I was the one that should be led to mourn.

The next morning, he passed by where I was and began to tell of his restlessness and that the Lord had appointed him a wife, by revelation, and he knew her name, and if he did not have her in less than six months he would never prophesy in the name of Jesus again.

At another time, he told me that he would tell me the whole of his mind, saying that when he inquired of the Lord, that the Lord told him that my husband was dead and preaching to the spirits in prison, and that I was presented before him, and that the Lord told him that I was to be his wife. "Lord is it so?" "Yes for I know all things." He said he went again to inquire of the Lord and I was presented before him again

"Why Lord she won't have me" "Yes she will" said the Lord, and if she don't I'll place another in her stead that shall be more beautiful to the eye than she is.

_____

586. Minute Book 2, 28 Apr. 1838, p. 157.

He told me that if I refused this I should be forever miserable, for he had a complete view of my future state and he would write it down, for he knew just how it would be. Said he you are young and I am old I am afraid some one will try to persuade you off.[587]

Moreover if this is not all true I will [p. 158] deny that there is a God in Heaven. I said I doubt it. He then accused me of unbelief saying when a man of truth told me any thing I was hard to believe when it is of God.

Furthermore he said he was then in the same spirit that he was when he cursed that man and he died, and when he saw the death of his wife, and that he had proved it by living testimony and why should you not as well believe me now as to believe that, for I would not tell you any thing to injure you, for them that are ordained to this high authority are ordained of God and you have as much right to believe me as to believe Paul; yes and ~~more~~ a better right for it is not handed down so far.

He said Br Joseph told him to be cautious who he cursed in the name of the Lord, for who he cursed was cursed, and who he blessed was blessed.

And at another time he told me the Lord had told him, that I did not care as much for him as he thought I did and that I need not try to hide any thing from him, for the Lord would reveal it to him.

And he led me to believe that the vengeance of God was about to be poured speedily upon me if I did not agree to his evil designs.

This ~~is~~ I ~~sent~~ send to the honorable High Council of Far-West as testimony against Elder Lyon as being true testimony.

Given under my hand, this 27th day of April 1838."

Sarah Jackson [5 lines blank] [p. 159]

11. George W. Robinson, Account in JS's "Scriptory Book"
Source Note

Zion high council, Minutes, [Far West, Caldwell Co., MO], 28 Apr. 1838. Featured version copied [ca. 28 Apr. 1838] in JS, Journal, Mar.–Sept. 1838, pp. 34–37; handwriting of George W. Robinson; CHL. Includes use marks. For more information on JS, Journal, Mar.–Sept. 1838, see Source Notes for Multiple-Entry Documents, p. 564 herein.

---

587. Lyon was fifty-five or fifty-six. (See Obituary for Aaron Lyon, *Times and Seasons*, Apr. 1840, 1:95.)

Document Transcript

Saturday 28ᵗʰ This morning Presᵗˢ Smith & [Sidney] Rigdon & myself, were invited ~~into~~ attend the High Council; and accordingly attended, the buisness before the high council, was the trial of ~~an~~ case appealed, from the branch of the Church, near gymans [Guymon's] horse mill; Whereas [*blank*] Jackson was plantiff, and Aaron Lyon defendant. Council called to order. T[homas] B. Marsh &. D[avid] W. Patten, Presiding, It appeared in calling the council to order, that some of the seats were vacated; the council then proceeded to fill those seats: &c. And as there appeared to be no persons to fill Said Seats, Eligible to that office; Presidents Smith & Rigdon, were strongly solisited to act as councilors, or to Preside, and let the then presiding officers sit on the council; &c. They accepted of the former proposal, and accordingly Presᵗ· Smith was choosen to act on the part of the defence, and to speak upon the case, togeth[er] with Geo. W. Harris. ~~and~~ Presᵗ· Rigdon, was chosen to act on the part of the prossecution, and to speak upon the case together with Geo. M. Hinkle, after the council was organized, and op[e]ned by prayer; the notorious case of Aaron Lyon, was called in question; after some arbitrarious⁵⁸⁸ speeches, to know whether witnesses should be admitted, to testify against A. Lyon, or whether he should have the privilege of confessing his own Sins, It was desided; that witnesses Should be admited, and also the writen testimo[p. 34]ny of the ~~said~~ wife of Said Jackson. Naw as to this man Lyon, it is a well known ⟨fact,⟩ and without contradiction, that he has been in transgression ⟨ever⟩ Since he first came into Kirtland, which is some four, or five years since,⁵⁸⁹ as appeared this day, by different witnesses, which are unimpeacible [unimpeachable]. Witnesses against ~~the~~ ⟨this⟩ man Lyon, were these 1,ˢᵗ Sarah Jackson, wife of said plantiff, Jackson. ~~one~~ ⟨an⟩⁵⁹⁰ Br. Best: also Br. [Shadrach] Roundy. Br John P. ~~Pound~~ Barnand [Barnard]: also Br. Thomas Girmon [Guymon]⁵⁹¹; also Br Benjamin, and the plantiff; Which testimony says, Whereas, the plantiff, had some time last season, sent his wife from Alton, Illinois, to

---

588. Noah Webster's dictionary of early American English lists one definition of *arbitrary* as "not governed by any fixed rules." ("Arbitrary," in *American Dictionary*.)

589. It is unclear when Lyon moved from Warsaw, New York, to Kirtland, but by summer 1833 he was planning to make the move. (Letter to Church Leaders in Jackson Co., MO, 6 Aug. 1833, in *JSP*, D3:237.)

590. TEXT: Possibly "and".

591. Best housed Jackson while she lived in the settlement at Guymon's mill. The other men were prominent members of the community: Roundy was a member of the Second Quorum of the Seventy, Barnard was a local landholder, and Guymon was the owner of the local mill. (Quorums of the Seventy, "Book of Records," 6; Foote, Autobiography, 15 Sept. and 7 Oct. 1838, 29.)

this country as he himself could not come, at that time, accordingly his wife Mrs Jackson, came and settled in the branch first above mentioned, Now ~~the~~ ⟨this⟩ man Lyon had settled in this branch also, and was their presiding high priest, and had gained to himself great influence in and ~~on~~ over that branch, and it also appears that ~~the~~ this man had great possessions, and (if we may judge from testimony given this day) calculates to keep them let the saints ~~of God's necessity~~ necessities be what they may, and it also appears that this man was in want of a wife (if actions bespeak the desires of any man) consequently set his wits to work to get one, he commences by getting (as he said,) revelations from God, that he must marry Mrs Jackson, or that she was the woman ~~for~~ to make his wife, and it appeared that these revilations were frequently received by him, and shortly introdused ~~them~~ to Mrs. Jackson, It also was manifested that the old man had sagasity enough to know; that unless he used his priestly office, ~~he~~ to assist him in accomplishing his designs, ⟨he would fail in the attempt;⟩ he therefore told Mrs. Jackson that he had ~~a~~ had a revelation from god that her husband was dead &c. and that She must concent to marry him, or she would be forever miserable; for he had seen her future state of existance, and that she must remember, that whom soever he blessed, would be blessed, and whom soever he cursed, would be cursed,[592] [p. 35] influencing her mind if possible, to believe his power was sufficient, to make her forever miserable; provided she complied not with his request. &c.[593] Accordingly, they came to an agreement, and were soon to be married, but fortunately or unfortunately for both parties previous to the ~~nuptial~~ arrival of the nuptial day, Behold!! to the asstonishment of our defendant, the husband of Mrs. Jackson arrived at home,[594] and consequently, disanuled the proceedings of the above alluded parties, the old gentleman Lyon, at this time (if not before,) knew verry well, that his god who gave ~~his~~ these revelations, (if ~~any~~ revelations he had,) must of course be no less than the devil, and in order to paliate the justice of his crime, sadled the

---

592. See Matthew 16:19; 18:18; see also Revelation, 24 Feb. 1834, in *JSP*, D3:461 [D&C 103:25].

593. JS had previously taught that "the order of the High priesthood is that they have power given them to seal up the Saints unto eternal life." This teaching was based on passages in the gospel of Matthew regarding the apostles' authority to bind things on earth and in heaven, as well as in JS revelations indicating that this authority included the power to bind or "seal" salvation or damnation—to bless or to curse. (Minutes, 25–26 Oct. 1831, in *JSP*, D2:82; see Matthew 18:18; 16:19; Book of Mormon, 1830 ed., 435 [Helaman 10:7]; Revelation, 1 Nov. 1831–A, in *JSP*, D2:101 [D&C 68:12]; Revelation, 1 Nov. 1831–B, in *JSP*, D2:105 [D&C 1:8]; and Revelation, 19 Jan. 1841, in Book of the Law of the Lord, 10 [D&C 124:93].)

594. Sarah Jackson's husband arrived in the area sometime in November, about five months after Sarah settled there.

Joseph Smith and Sidney Rigdon. On 28 April 1838, Joseph Smith (left, portrait by David Rogers, circa 1842) and Sidney Rigdon (right, photographed circa 1873) were invited to serve as substitutes in the Zion high council and to speak on opposing sides in the case of Aaron Lyon. The council was trying Lyon for attempting to coerce Sarah Jackson to marry him. Rigdon argued for administration of justice, while Smith argued for mercy. The high council revoked Lyon's priesthood license but did not excommunicate him. (Smith image courtesy Community of Christ Library-Archives, Independence, MO. Rigdon image: Church History Library, Salt Lake City; photograph by Irving Saunders, copy by studio of Alexander Fox and Charles W. Symons.)

whole burden upon the devil, that in scourging the person, who had previously befriended him, and counseled him in his former days; peradventure he might extricate himself from the Snare, of his own setting, and dictation. But, alass!! to[o] late for the old man, the testimony, being closed, and the Sword of Justice,[595] began to be unsheathed, which fell upon the old man like a scourge of ten thousand lashes, wielded by the hand of President S. Rigdon & George M. Hinkle, inspired by the spirit of justice, accompanied with a flow of elequence, which searched for the feelings, like the sting of so many scorpions,[596] which served to atone for past iniquity. there were no feelings that were not felt after, there were no sores that were not probed, there were no excuses rend[e]red that were not exceptionable. After Justice had

595. See Book of Mormon, 1830 ed., 397–398, 441 [Alma 60:29; Helaman 13:5].
596. See 1 Kings 12:14; and 2 Chronicles 10:14.

ceased to weild ~~his~~ ⟨its⟩ sword, Mercy then advanced to rescue its victom, which inspired the heart of President J. Smith J̲r̲, & Geo W. Harris who, with profound elequence ⟨&⟩ with ⟨a⟩ deep & sublime thought, with clemency of feeling, spoke in faivour of ~~mercy~~ the defendant, but in length of time, while mercy appeared to be doing her utmost, in contending against justice, the latter at last gained the ascendency, and took full ~~power over~~ ⟨possession of⟩ the mind of [p. 36] the speaker,[597] who leveled a voley of darts, which came upon the old man, like ⟨a⟩ huricanes upon the mountain tops, which seemingly, was about to sweep the victom entirely out of the reach of mercy, but amidst the clashing of the sword of Justice, mercy still claimed the victom,[598] and saved him still in the church of Jesus Christ of Latter Day Saints, and in this last kingdom[599] Happy is it for those whose sins (like this mans) goes before them to Judgement,[600] that they may yet repent and be saved in the Kingdom of our God. Council desided, that inasmuch as this man, had confessed his sins, and asked for, forgiveness, and promised to mark well the path of his feet,[601] and do, (inasmuch as lay in his power.) what God, Should ~~required~~ at his hand⟨s⟩. accordingly, it was decided, that he give up his license as High Priest, and stand as a member in the Church, this in consequence of his being concidered not capable of dignifying that office, &c[602] Council Adjourned

Geo. W. Robinson, <u>Scribe</u>

Prospectus for *Elders' Journal*, 30 April 1838

Source Note

Prospectus for Elder's Journal, *[Far West, Caldwell Co., MO], 30 Apr. 1838; one page; Wilford Woodruff, Journals and Papers, 1828–1898, CHL. Includes docket and archival marking.*

Bifolium measuring 16 × 10¼ inches (41 × 26 cm). The document was printed with varying type sizes and some bold type. The prospectus was double trifolded for mailing, and later it was refolded for

---

597. Ebenezer Robinson's minutes state that Lyon "made confession to the satisfaction of the Council" after "some lengthy remarks by the Councellors, and very good instruction given by Councellor Smith," suggesting that JS may be "the speaker" referred to here.

598. See Book of Mormon, 1830 ed., 339, 340 [Alma 42:23–24, 31].

599. JS's revelations framed the work of the Latter-day Saints as a final dispensation of the gospel in preparation for the second coming of Jesus Christ and a transition into the millennial kingdom of God. (See, for example, Revelation, 23 July 1837, in *JSP*, D5:417 [D&C 112:30–32].)

600. See 1 Timothy 5:24.

601. See Proverbs 4:26; and Hebrews 12:13.

602. Ebenezer Robinson's minutes indicate that the high council concurred in the decision, which, according to established practice, was likely presented by Marsh or by Marsh and Patten.

filing and was docketed. The prospectus has marked wear, with some partially separated folds. The document has undergone conservation.

Inscribed on the prospectus is a letter from Thomas B. Marsh to Wilford Woodruff, circa 18 June 1838.[603] The letter includes Marsh's signature and a Far West, Missouri, postmark. Woodruff likely donated the document to the Church Historian's Office as part of his collected papers, possibly during his tenure as assistant church historian (1856–1883) or as church historian (1883–1889).[604]

Historical Introduction

On 30 April 1838, a prospectus announcing the continuation of the *Elders' Journal,* the church's newspaper, was published in Far West, Missouri. The prospectus, which was composed in the first-person plural voice, was presumably published by JS and Thomas B. Marsh, whom the document identifies as the editor and publisher, respectively. The church initially established a publishing enterprise in 1831 in response to JS revelations naming individuals to assist in "the work of Printing" and directing that "a Printer unto the Church" be "planted in the Land of Zion."[605] The first church newspaper was published in Independence, Missouri. After the printing office there was destroyed in 1833, the church reestablished printing operations in Kirtland, Ohio. In April 1838, with JS, Sidney Rigdon, and others living in or relocating to Missouri, the church was once again setting up its printing operations there.

The *Elders' Journal* originally began in Kirtland. Before the newspaper's first issue was printed, a prospectus was published in the last two issues of the *Latter Day Saints' Messenger and Advocate,* the church's previous newspaper.[606] The launch of early American newspapers was often announced in a prospectus,[607] and the church followed this practice when beginning its newspapers.[608] The original prospectus for the *Elders' Journal* explained that the newspaper was "intended to be a vehicle of communication for all the elders of the church . . . through which they can communicate to others, all things pertaining to their mission" and to the growth of the church in America and abroad.[609] Accordingly, the two Kirtland issues—dated October and November 1837—consisted

---

603. See Letter to Wilford Woodruff, ca. 18 June 1838, pp. 152–162 herein.

604. "Contents of the Historian and Recorder's Office. G. S. L. City July 1858," 6, Historian's Office, Catalogs and Inventories, 1846–1904, CHL; Turley, "Assistant Church Historians," 20–21; see also Park, "Developing a Historical Conscience," 115–134.

605. Revelation, 14 June 1831, in *JSP,* D1:339 [D&C 55:4–5]; Revelation, 20 July 1831, in *JSP,* D2:11, 12 [D&C 57:11, 14].

606. "Prospectus," *LDS Messenger and Advocate,* Aug. 1837, 3:545–547; "Prospectus," *LDS Messenger and Advocate,* Sept. 1837, 3:571–574.

607. See, for example, "Prospectus of a New Country Paper," *Gazette of the United States and Daily Advertiser* (Philadelphia), 13 Oct. 1801, [2]; and "Prospectus of the American Spectator and Washington City Chronicle," *Western Intelligencer* (Hudson, OH), 21 Jan. 1830, [3].

608. See "Prospectus," *The Evening and the Morning Star,* Sept. 1834, 192; "Prospectus," *LDS Messenger and Advocate,* Aug. 1837, 3:545–547; and "Prospectus," *LDS Messenger and Advocate,* Sept. 1837, 3:571–574.

609. Leaders may have also envisioned the new publication as a means to document proselytizing efforts for historical purposes. The prospectus asserted the newspaper would be a vehicle to "transmit to succeeding generations an account of their religion, and a history of their travels, and of the reception which they met with in the nations." ("Prospectus," *LDS Messenger and Advocate,* Aug. 1837, 3:545, 546.)

mostly of letters from church elders.[610] In late December 1837 or early January 1838, the printing press and everything else in the printing office were seized by the sheriff in connection with legal action against JS and Rigdon. On 15 January, when the sheriff sold these items, which were still housed in the printing office, they came under the control of a group of dissenters from the church, who intended to use the printing office to publish materials opposing the church. That night, the office was set on fire and burned to the ground, with all its contents destroyed.[611] The production of the *Elders' Journal* and all other church publications ceased.

The need to resume publishing the church newspaper was expressed by Wilford Woodruff in an early March 1838 letter to Bishop Edward Partridge and the First Presidency. Woodruff, who was a member of the First Quorum of the Seventy and was preaching in Maine, pleaded that the *Elders' Journal* be revived in Missouri to assist missionaries in proselytizing efforts. Woodruff's letter likely arrived in Far West sometime in early or mid-April.[612] On 21 April, the Zion high council in Far West met and passed several resolutions related to reestablishing the church's printing operations. The council decided that the *Elders' Journal* would be "published monthly, as it was commenced"; that the high counselors would "support Thomas B. Marsh as the publisher" and "use their influence to obtain subscriptions"; and that they would publish in the newspaper some of the minutes of their council meetings.[613] The appropriateness of publishing the church's newspaper in Far West was affirmed five days later, when JS dictated a revelation stating that Far West was "most holy" and a place in "the land of zion" to build up a city for the gathering of the Saints.[614]

To announce the revival of the *Elders' Journal* and "arouse the Saints to energy in obtaining subscribers," a new prospectus was produced on 30 April 1838 in Far West. The prospectus was apparently printed on a press that had been used by the church in Kirtland, sold to Oliver Cowdery, brought to Missouri in 1837, and repurchased by the church.[615]

The authors of the prospectus expressed the hope that the traveling elders would use their influence to obtain subscribers. Copies of the prospectus may have been sent to many of the church's traveling elders. The copy of the prospectus featured here was sent to

---

610. See, for example, Heber C. Kimball, Preston, England, to Vilate Murray Kimball, Kirtland, OH, 2–6 Sept. 1837, in *Elders' Journal,* Oct. 1837, 4–7; and Orson Hyde, Preston, England, to Marinda Nancy Johnson Hyde, Kirtland, OH, 14 Sept. 1837, in *Elders' Journal,* Nov. 1837, 19–22.

611. "Sheriff Sale," *Painesville (OH) Telegraph,* 5 Jan. 1838, [3]; Hepzibah Richards, Kirtland, OH, to Willard Richards, Bedford, England, 18–19 Jan. 1838, Willard Richards, Papers, CHL; John Smith and Don Carlos Smith, Kirtland Mills, OH, to George A. Smith, Shinnston, VA, 15–18 Jan. 1838, George Albert Smith, Papers, CHL.

612. Subsequent correspondence between Marsh and Woodruff traveled in less than four weeks, suggesting Woodruff's letter to Partridge and the First Presidency did as well. (See 33n155 herein.)

613. Minutes, 21 Apr. 1838, pp. 110, 111 herein.

614. Revelation, 26 Apr. 1838, pp. 114–115 herein [D&C 115:6–7].

615. See 91n455 herein; and Minutes, 21 Apr. 1838, p. 110 herein.

Woodruff, who was still proselytizing in New England. Woodruff succeeded in obtaining several subscribers for the *Elders' Journal* and was probably not alone in responding to the call for subscriptions.[616] Meanwhile in Far West, the church was making progress toward recommencing the *Elders' Journal,* eventually publishing issues dated July and August 1838.[617]

The prospectus was reprinted in the first Missouri issue of the newspaper, dated July 1838. The reprinted version of the prospectus bears the date 26 April instead of 30 April.[618] The reprint may have been dated to match the date of JS's revelation regarding Far West as a new headquarters of the church.[619] In contrast, the original copy of the prospectus, which Marsh mailed to Woodruff, is dated 30 April and bears an 18 June postmark, showing that it significantly predates the version published in the newspaper.[620] The newspaper version differs from the version sent to Woodruff in a few ways, correcting the placement of the apostrophe in the periodical's title, fixing a misspelled word, modifying punctuation, and adding Far West as the place of publication; these differences indicate the prospectus printed in the newspaper was a corrected version of the original document.

Document Transcript

PROSPECTUS
FOR THE
ELDER'S JOURNAL,
Of the Church Of Jesus Christ, of Latter Day Saints.[621]

It is, we presume, generally known, that this paper was commenced in Kirtland, Ohio, in October last;[622] but by reason of the great persecution against the Saints in that place, the paper had to be stopped; and through the

---

616. See, for example, Woodruff, Journal, 22 and 31 July 1838.

617. In May, Rigdon was assigned to edit the letters that would be included in the *Elders' Journal.* In June the high council resolved that Marsh would be the "sole proprietor of the printing establishment." (Minute Book 2, 12 May and 23 June 1838.)

618. "Prospectus for the Elders' Journal," *Elders' Journal,* July 1838, 34.

619. See Revelation, 26 Apr. 1838, pp. 112–118 herein [D&C 115].

620. See Letter to Wilford Woodruff, ca. 18 June 1838, p. 162 herein.

621. TEXT: The first, third, and fourth lines are printed in bold. The two issues published in Kirtland bear the title *Elders' Journal of the Church of Latter Day Saints.* The prospectus featured here and the two issues published in Far West bear the title *Elders' Journal of the Church of Jesus Christ of Latter Day Saints,* reflecting the new and expanded name of the church. In contrast to the prospectus, both the Kirtland and the Far West issues use "Elders'" (plural possessive) instead of "Elder's" (singular possessive), indicating the journal belonged to the church elders as a group, as was explicit in the prospectus for the issues published in Kirtland. ("Prospectus," *LDS Messenger and Advocate,* Aug. 1837, 545–547; "Prospectus," *LDS Messenger and Advocate,* Sept. 1837, 3:571–574.)

622. Nameplate, *Elders' Journal,* Oct. 1837, 1.

craft of wicked men they got possession of the Printing Office,[623] and knowing they could not hold it, it was burned!![624]

The paper is now about to be resuscitated in this place;[625] to be conducted as set forth in the former prospectus.[626] It will be issued in a few weeks, and sent to the former subscibers, as previously stated.[627]

We send this prospectus to arouse the Saints to energy in obtaining subscribers. We hope the Elders abroad, will not fail to use their influence to give as general a circulation as possible.

The JOURNAL will be Edited by Joseph Smith jr., and Published by Thomas B. Marsh,[628] at Far West, Caldwell County, Missouri.

---

623. All of the contents in the printing office were seized by Sheriff Abel Kimball following a judgment against JS and Rigdon in a lawsuit they lost. Kimball then sold the goods in the office to pay for the judgment. Because the sale included not only the printing office's press but also its paper, printing was apparently halted. When the scheduled sale took place on 15 January, Vilate Murray Kimball wrote that the goods were bid off "in a very underhanded way." Don Carlos Smith, who had been running the printing office, was ready to purchase the office's holdings when the bidding began, "but before the hour arived they bid it off among them selves." The press was bought by Nathan Milliken, "one of the decenting party," perhaps with help from Grandison Newell. Kimball and John Smith suspected that Milliken purchased the press on behalf of a group of dissenters and excommunicated church members. Kimball wrote that the group intended to use the printing equipment to publish materials in opposition to the church. (Transcript of Proceedings, 24 Oct. 1837, Rounds v. JS [Geauga Co. C.P. 1837], Final Record Book U, pp. 362–364, microfilm 20,279, U.S. and Canada Record Collection, FHL; "Sheriff Sale," *Painesville [OH] Telegraph,* 5 Jan. 1838, [3]; Vilate Murray Kimball, Kirtland, OH, to Heber C. Kimball, Preston, England, 19–29 Jan. 1838, Heber C. Kimball, Collection, CHL; Hepzibah Richards, Kirtland, OH, to Willard Richards, Bedford, England, 18–19 Jan. 1838, Willard Richards, Papers, CHL; John Smith and Don Carlos Smith, Kirtland Mills, OH, to George A. Smith, Shinnston, VA, 15–18 Jan. 1838, George Albert Smith, Papers, CHL.)

624. The printing office was burned on the night of 15 January 1838. (See 35n166 herein.)

625. The version of the prospectus published in the July 1838 issue named Far West as the place of publication, which is affirmed in the nameplates and mastheads of the July and August issues.

626. "Prospectus," *LDS Messenger and Advocate,* Aug. 1837, 3:545–547; "Prospectus," *LDS Messenger and Advocate,* Sept. 1837, 3:571–574.

627. The original prospectus projected that one issue would be published each month. ("Prospectus," *LDS Messenger and Advocate,* Sept. 1837, 3:574.)

628. Similarly, the masthead of the Kirtland issues of the newspaper stated it was edited by JS and published by Marsh,[a] though both men spent October and November traveling to Far West and participating in church meetings.[b] The work of publishing the paper had evidently fallen to Don Carlos Smith, JS's younger brother.[c] The original prospectus for the *Elders' Journal* in Kirtland stated that it would be a forum for the church's elders while "traveling and proclaiming the gospel."[d] It was fitting therefore that the paper be published by Marsh; as president of the Quorum of the Twelve Apostles, he directed the work of all traveling elders outside of Zion and church stakes.[e] A revelation in July 1837 stated that Marsh would "send forth my word unto the ends of the earth" and that although Marsh was to remain in Zion, the Lord had a "great work" for him to do "in publishing my name among the children of men."[f] (a. Masthead, *Elders' Journal,* Oct. 1837, 16; Masthead, *Elders' Journal,* Nov. 1837, 32. b. Travel Account and Questions, Nov. 1837, in *JSP,* D5:480–482; "T. B. Marsh," [2], Historian's Office, Histories of the Twelve, 1856–1858, 1861, CHL. c. Masthead, *Elders' Journal,* Oct. 1837, 16; Masthead, *Elders' Journal,* Nov. 1837, 32; Minutes, 12 Apr. 1838, p. 92 herein; JS History, vol. C-1 Addenda, 12. d. "Prospectus," *LDS Messenger and Advocate,* Sept. 1837, 3:572. e. Instruction on Priesthood, between

Terms[629]—One dollar, per annum, paid in advance. All letters must be Post Paid, and directed to the Publisher.

April 30, 1838.[630]

———— ∽ ————

Discourse, 6 May 1838

Source Note

JS, Discourse, Far West, Caldwell Co., MO, 6 May 1838. Featured version transcribed [ca. 6 May 1838] in JS, Journal, Mar.–Sept. 1838, p. 38; handwriting of George W. Robinson; CHL. Includes use mark. For more information on JS, Journal, Mar.–Sept. 1838, see Source Notes for Multiple-Entry Documents, p. 564 herein.

Historical Introduction

In worship meetings held in Far West, Missouri, on Sunday, 6 May 1838, JS delivered two discourses, the first of which is featured here. Both discourses were summarized by George W. Robinson in the 6 May entry he made in JS's journal. In reporting on the first discourse, Robinson apparently attempted to capture some of JS's words. According to the summary of this discourse, JS advised the Saints against forming hasty judgments. This instruction was apparently motivated in part by a speech that an office-seeking politician had delivered to church members the previous day. Robinson provided less detail about the content of the second discourse, stating only that JS "dwelt some upon the Subject of Wisdom, & upon the word of Wisdom. &c." Robinson noted that JS delivered the second discourse in "the after part of the day," suggesting that JS gave the first discourse in the morning.[631] Robinson likely attended JS's morning discourse and reported on it from personal observation—his general method for making entries in the journal. He made daily entries in the journal from late April through mid-May, suggesting that he inscribed this report of JS's discourses on or within a few days after 6 May 1838.

Document Transcript

This day, President Smith. delivered a discourse. to the people. Showing, or setting forth the evils that existed, and would exist, by reason of hasty Judgement or dessisions upon any subject, given by any people. or in judgeing

---

ca. 1 Mar. and ca. 4 May 1835, in *JSP*, D4:315 [D&C 107:33–35]. *f.* Revelation, 23 July 1837, in *JSP*, D5:415 [D&C 112:4–6].)

629. TEXT: This word is printed in bold type.

630. TEXT: This line of text is printed in bold type. In the version of the prospectus printed in the first Missouri issue of the journal, the corresponding line is "Far West, Mo. April 26, 1838." ("Prospectus for the Elders' Journal," *Elders' Journal,* July 1838, 34.)

631. JS, Journal, 6 May 1838, in *JSP*, J1:266.

before they hear both sides of the question,[632] He also cautioned them against men men, who should come here whining and grouling about their money, because they had helpt the saints and bore some of the burden with others. and thus thinking that others, (who are still poorer and who have still bore greater burden than themselves) aught to make up their loss &c. And thus he cautioned them to beware of them for here and there they through [throw?] out foul insinuations, to level as it were a dart to ⟨the⟩ best interests of the Church, & if possible to destroy the Characters of its Presidency[633] He also instructed the Church, in the misteries of the Kingdom of God; giving them a history of the Plannets &c. and of Abrahams writings upon the Plannettary System &c.[634]

632. On 5 May, the First Presidency attended a political speech by John Wilson, a Whig candidate for the United States House of Representatives.[a] JS's Scriptory Book referred to Wilson as a "Federalist." The Federalist Party, which died out in the 1820s, had similarities to the new Whig Party, leading Democrats to accuse the Whigs of being aristocratic Federalists. Whigs were portrayed in this manner in the *Northern Times*—the Democratic newspaper published by the Latter-day Saints in Kirtland.[b] On 7 May, JS spent time with county judge Josiah Morin, the Democratic candidate for the Missouri Senate.[c] On 10 May, JS attended a political speech by Sidney Rigdon in which Rigdon discussed the policies of both parties. According to Robinson's account of the discourse, Rigdon was "endeavering to give an impartial hearing on both Sides of the question, In consequence of One Gen Willsons [John Wilson's] speech, delivered upon Politics in the same place, a short time previous to this: Who touched upon one side of the matter only." Robinson added that "the Politics of this Church (with but few exceptions onley,) are that of Democracy; which is Allso the feelings of the speaker who spoke this day, and all of the first presidency."[d] (*a.* JS, Journal, 5 May 1838, in *JSP*, J1:264; Shoemaker, *Missouri and Missourians,* 1:412; *Encyclopedia of the History of Missouri,* 6:484. *b.* Holt, *Rise and Fall of the American Whig Party,* 2–3; "The Election," *Northern Times,* 2 Oct. 1835, [2]; see also "Extract of a Letter to the Editor of the Telegraph," *Painesville [OH] Telegraph,* 17 Apr. 1835, [3]. *c.* JS, Journal, 7 May 1838, in *JSP*, J1:266–267. *d.* JS, Journal, 10 May 1838, in *JSP*, J1:267–268.)

633. This warning may have been particularly motivated by the continued presence of Oliver Cowdery and other dissenters who had moved from Kirtland to Far West, had been excommunicated, and remained among the Latter-day Saints. Cowdery evidently encouraged lawsuits against debtors in order to solicit business for his clerical or legal practice. Cowdery was excommunicated on 12 April in part for "stiring up the enemy to persecute the brethren by urging on vexatious Lawsuits and thus distressing the inocent." Cowdery was also cut off for "seeking to destroy the character of President Joseph Smith jr, by falsly insinuating that he was guilty of adultry." (Minutes, 12 Apr. 1838, pp. 84–94 herein; see also 93n463 herein; and *JSP*, J1:253n92.)

634. Astronomical material appeared in the Book of Abraham, which JS began translating in 1835. (Book of Abraham Excerpt, between ca. Early July and ca. 26 Nov. 1835, in *JSP*, D5:80 [Abraham 1:31]; see also "The Book of Abraham," *Times and Seasons,* 1 Mar. 1842, 3:703–706; 15 Mar. 1842, 3:719–722 [Abraham chaps. 1–5]; JS, Journal, 1 Oct. 1835, in *JSP*, J1:67; and JS History, vol. B-1, 622.)

Declaration to the Geauga County Court of Common Pleas, 7 May 1838

Source Note

Perkins & Osborn on behalf of JS, Declaration, JS for use of Granger v. Smalling and Coltrin [Geauga Co. C.P. 1838], Chardon, Geauga Co., OH, [7 May 1838]. Featured version copied [ca. 8 Nov. 1838] in Geauga County Court of Common Pleas Record, vol. V, pp. 501–502; handwriting of David D. Aiken; Geauga County Archives and Records Center, Chardon, OH.[635]

The declaration appears in the Geauga County Court of Common Pleas Record, volume V. The volume contains 330 leaves plus two front flyleaves and two back flyleaves measuring 16 × 10 inches (41 × 25 cm). The boards and spine are covered in brown leather. The bound volume measures 16¾ × 11½ × 2½ inches (43 × 29 × 6 cm). Gold letters on the spine read: "LAW RECORDS | COM. PLEAS | GEAUGA COUNTY | U". The spine also includes an inscription in black ink: "V". Page 1 is inscribed on the verso of the second front flyleaf. Entries in the volume span circa 3 April 1838–circa 16 April 1839. Each case entry is written in ink. Common Pleas Record, volume V, was microfilmed by the Micro-Photo Service Bureau of Cleveland, Ohio, in 1948. The volume was in the possession of the Geauga County, Ohio, Court of Common Pleas from the volume's creation until 1996, when it was transferred to the newly established Geauga County Archives and Records Center.

Historical Introduction

On 7 May 1838, JS through the law partnership Perkins & Osborn brought a declaration[636] to the Geauga County Court of Common Pleas in a lawsuit against Cyrus Smalling and John Coltrin.[637] Perkins & Osborn, comprising partners William Perkins and Salmon Osborn, had begun the lawsuit on JS's behalf on 28 February 1838 for an outstanding promissory note of $500 that JS received from Smalling and Coltrin on 30 September 1836.[638] At the time of issuing the promissory note, Smalling and Coltrin were church members; Smalling lived in Kirtland, Ohio, and Coltrin resided in nearby Strongsville.[639] The

---

635. Volumes of the Geauga County Court of Common Pleas Record have been microfilmed and made available at the Family History Library; some of these microfilm copies are titled Final Record Book.

636. In legal terminology, a declaration is a legal pleading identifying the cause of action. ("Declaration," in Bouvier, *Law Dictionary*, 1:293.)

637. Transcript of Proceedings, 6 Nov. 1838, JS for use of Granger v. Smalling and Coltrin (Geauga Co. C.P. 1838), Final Record Book V, p. 501, Geauga County Archives and Records Center, Chardon, OH.

638. Perkins & Osborn represented JS in at least four lawsuits in 1837 and continued to oversee litigation and to apprise him of outstanding debts after his departure from Kirtland in January 1838.[a] The original 30 September 1836 promissory note is apparently not extant. The due date of the note was not recorded in the court records, but the court proceedings imply that the period of repayment had elapsed by the end of February 1838.[b] (a. "Law Notice," *Painesville [OH] Telegraph*, 21 Feb. 1834, [3]. b. Transcript of Proceedings, 6 Nov. 1838, JS for use of Granger v. Smalling and Coltrin [Geauga Co. C.P. 1838], Final Record Book V, p. 501, Geauga County Archives and Records Center, Chardon, OH.)

639. Notice, *LDS Messenger and Advocate*, June 1836, 2:336; Minutes, 16 June 1836, in *JSP*, D5:248; Quorums of the Seventy, "Book of Records," 6 Apr. 1837, 17–19; 1830 U.S. Census, Strongsville, Cuyahoga Co., OH, 129.

reason for the promissory note is not specified in the court records.[640] The note may have been for mercantile goods; the firm Rigdon, Smith & Co. began operating a store in Chester, Ohio, in September 1836,[641] and JS may have operated a store in Kirtland.[642] It is also possible that the debt was for land Smalling and Coltrin purchased from JS.[643]

By February 1838, with the note past due, JS assigned it to Julius Granger, a brother of Oliver Granger.[644] In cases such as JS's against Smalling and Coltrin, in which the note had been assigned to another individual, the declaration clarified that the individual to whom it had been transferred should be paid on the note. Therefore, although JS brought the lawsuit, Granger was to be paid.[645]

A writ was issued on 28 February against Coltrin and Smalling, requiring them to appear before the court of common pleas on 3 April 1838. Local sheriff Abel Kimball found Smalling and served him a writ for the lawsuit. Coltrin could not be found and therefore was not prosecuted.[646] Smalling offered a plea, no longer extant, in response to the lawsuit, and on 3 April the court agreed to postpone the trial until the next term of court.[647]

---

640. Although the declaration mentions both goods purchased from JS and money lent by JS, these statements were formulaic and were included in most cases involving unpaid debts; they may not have reflected the transaction underlying the promissory note.

641. The firm Rigdon, Smith & Cowdery purchased wholesale goods in New York in 1836. These goods were then sold by the firm Rigdon, Smith & Co. While the two firms were related, it is not clear whether Oliver Cowdery was a partner in both. Chester, Ohio, was around six miles south of Kirtland. (John Newbould, Invoice, Buffalo, NY, for Rigdon, Smith & Cowdery, 17 June 1836; Mead, Stafford & Co., Invoice, New York City, for Rigdon, Smith & Cowdery, 8 Oct. 1836, JS Office Papers, CHL; Rigdon, Smith & Co., Store Ledger, 1–5; "Mormonism in Ohio," *Aurora* [New Lisbon, OH], 21 Jan. 1837, [3]; Notes Receivable from Chester Store, 22 May 1837, in *JSP*, D5:382–385.)

642. There is little documentation for the Kirtland store, and it is unknown whether it was operated by Rigdon, Smith & Co. or by JS alone. (Deed, 3 June 1841, in Lake Co., OH, Land Registry Records, bk. A, p. 513, CHL; Brigham Young, in *Journal of Discourses*, 8 Oct. 1855, 3:121.)

643. See, for example, Mortgage to Peter French, 5 Oct. 1836, in *JSP*, D5:293–299.

644. Julius Granger was living in Willoughby, Ohio, in 1836 and remained in the area until at least 1840. No records indicate that he was a member of the church. (Julius Granger, Agreement with Jared Carter et al., 7 Oct. 1836, Lord Sterling Papers, Lake County Historical Society, Painesville, OH; Geauga Co., OH, Probate Court, Marriage Records, 1806–1920, vol. C, p. 374, microfilm 873,461, U.S. and Canada Record Collection, FHL.)

645. "When a suit is brought in the name of one person for the use of another . . . the only object of naming the assignee in the suit, is to show who controls the suit, and to whom the officer may pay over the avails of the judgment." (Swan, *Practice in Civil Actions and Proceedings at Law*, 1:36.)

646. Transcript of Proceedings, 6 Nov. 1838, JS for use of Granger v. Smalling and Coltrin (Geauga Co. C.P. 1838), Final Record Book V, pp. 501–504, Geauga County Archives and Records Center, Chardon, OH. The reason for Coltrin's absence is not known; he may have been temporarily away from his home in Strongsville, Ohio, or he may have moved from the state.

647. By 1838, Smalling no longer had any ties to the church. He had been a leader among the dissenters in Kirtland, many of whom opposed JS's involvement in temporal affairs, and had been excommunicated from the church in late December 1837. No documentation indicates Coltrin's standing in the church in 1838. (John Smith and Clarissa Lyman Smith, Kirtland, OH, to George A. Smith, Shinnston, VA, 1 Jan. 1838, George Albert Smith, Papers, CHL.)

On 7 May, Perkins & Osborn filed the declaration with the Geauga County Court of Common Pleas in Chardon, Ohio. The declaration constituted JS's grounds for the suit and identified the parties and circumstances involved in the suit.[648] In the declaration, Perkins & Osborn reiterated Smalling and Coltrin's debt of $500 and indicated that the law partnership would prosecute for payment of the outstanding debt and for damages, amounting to $1,000.[649] Perkins & Osborn drafted the document using the language and structure from a legal form in general use in Ohio. This form likely included instructions to list "any sum sufficient to cover the real demand," which they calculated to be $1,000.[650]

As was common practice in contemporary declarations, the wording in the featured declaration suggests Perkins & Osborn were presenting several distinct counts against the defendants, such as "the price and value of goods . . . then and there bargained and sold," "for money then and there lent," "for money then and there paid by the plaintiff," and "for money found to be due from the defendant . . . on an account." The courts of Ohio treated these items collectively, stating that the "common counts thus made up are but one count."[651]

In response to the declaration, Smalling requested the opportunity to amend his original plea with the court—a request that the court granted. His amended plea, presented in August 1838, stated that he had not promised to pay the amount identified by JS in the declaration and that JS owed him an even greater amount to compensate for Kirtland Safety Society notes that Smalling apparently held but that had no value.[652] When the case was tried in November 1838, a jury concluded that Smalling was not responsible for repaying JS.[653]

---

648. See "Declaration," in Bouvier, *Law Dictionary,* 1:293–294.

649. In debt litigation, damages include not only the amount of unpaid promissory notes but also a penalty for nonpayment. ("Damages on Bills of Exchange," in Bouvier, *Law Dictionary,* 1:279.)

650. Swan, *Practice in Civil Actions and Proceedings at Law,* 1:203, 216–217.

651. Swan, *Practice in Civil Actions and Proceedings at Law,* 1:216–217, 217nA. In December 1834, the Ohio Supreme Court ruled on the case of *Nichols v. Poulson,* in which the plaintiff presented his case using language similar to what Perkins & Osborn used in the 7 May 1838 declaration. The Ohio court noted the different counts and stated, "There are several other distinct paragraphs, for other things [money owed], stated in the same manner. . . . All these paragraphs put together make but one count." (Hammond, *Cases Decided in the Supreme Court of Ohio,* 307.)

652. Smalling stated he had $1,500 in Kirtland Safety Society notes that could no longer be redeemed or circulated, and he wanted JS to repay the amount. Smalling was not alone in his demands for repayment. Others in northeastern Ohio believed JS and Rigdon should be held financially responsible for the unredeemed notes of the Safety Society. According to church member Samuel Tyler, a large group of Saints who traveled from Kirtland to Far West, Missouri, in summer 1838 was confronted in Willoughby and Mansfield, Ohio, by individuals who demanded payment for the Safety Society notes in their possession. (Transcript of Proceedings, 6 Nov. 1838, JS for use of Granger v. Smalling and Coltrin [Geauga Co. C.P. 1838], Final Record Book V, pp. 501–504, Geauga County Archives and Records Center, Chardon, OH; Tyler, Journal, 16 July 1838, 11.)

653. On 8 November, Perkins & Osborn, acting on behalf of JS, notified the court of the attorneys' intention to appeal the case to the Ohio Supreme Court, but it appears no appeal was made. (Geauga Co., OH, Court of Common Pleas, Journal N, p. 407, 8 Nov. 1838, Geauga County Archives and Records Center, Chardon, OH.)

The original declaration, likely written by Perkins or Osborn, is apparently not extant. The version featured here was copied into the Geauga County Court of Common Pleas Record by clerk David D. Aiken around 8 November 1838 as part of the transcript of the trial proceedings.

Document Transcript

The State of Ohio ⎱
Geauga County ⎰ ss   Court of Common Pleas vacation after
April Term 1838.[654]

Joseph Smith Jn[r.] for [p. 501] the use of[655] Julius Granger complains of Cyrus Smalling (the Sheriff of said County having returned not found as to John Coltrin against whom process in this cause was also issued) in a plea of the case for that whereas the said Cyrus Smalling & John Coltrin on the thirtieth day of September AD 1836 at Kirtland in the County of Geauga made their promissory note in writing and delivered the same to the said Joseph Smith Jr and thereby promised to pay to the said Joseph Smith Jr. five hundred dollars on demand with interest which period has now elapsed[656] and the said defendant and John Coltrin then & there in consideration of the premises[657] promised to pay the amount of said note to the said Joseph Smith Jr according to the tenor and effect thereof And also for that whereas the said Cyrus Smalling and John Coltrin on the thirtieth day of September AD eighteen hundred & thirty six at Kirtland aforesaid were indebted to the said Joseph Smith Jr in the sum of one thousand dollars for the price and value of goods then and there bargained and sold by the plaintiff to the defendant and the said John Coltrin at their request: And in the sum of one thousand dollars for the price and value of goods then and there sold and delivered by the plaintiff to the defendant and the said John Coltrin at their request: And in the sum of one thousand dollars for money then and there lent by the plaintiffs to the defendant and the said John Coltrin at their request:

---

654. The Ohio legislature scheduled three terms of court per year for each county court. The legislative records for Ohio in 1838 are not extant, so the exact dates of the 1838 terms cannot be determined. Based on the dates for the 1837 and 1839 terms of court, the April 1838 term for the Geauga County Court of Common Pleas likely occurred between 1 and 16 April. (An Act to Regulate the Times of Holding the Judicial Courts [4 Feb. 1837], *Acts of a General Nature* [1836–1837], p. 13, sec. 4; An Act to Regulate the Time of Holding the Judicial Courts [12 Feb. 1839], *Acts of a General Nature* [1838–1839], p. 14, sec. 4.)

655. The phrase "for the use of" indicates that JS had assigned the promissory note to Julius Granger. (See "Assignment," in Bouvier, *Law Dictionary,* 1:99.)

656. The interest was apparently set at 6.25 percent. In February 1838, the amount due on the note with interest was $531.25. (Transcript of Proceedings, 6 Nov. 1838, JS for use of Granger v. Smalling and Coltrin [Geauga Co. C.P. 1838], Final Record Book V, p. 501, Geauga County Archives and Records Center, Chardon, OH.)

657. The term *premises* has several legal definitions; in legal pleading, it means "that which is put before," or the previous statements. ("Premises," in Bouvier, *Law Dictionary,* 2:288.)

And in the sum of one thousand dollars for money then and there paid by the plaintiff for the use of the defendant and the said John Coltrin at their request: And in the sum of one thousand dollars for money then and there received by the defendant and the said John Coltrin for the use of the plff: And in the sum of one thousand dollars for money found to be due from the defendant and the said John Coltrin to the plaintiff on an account then and there stated between them: And whereas the defendant and John Coltrin afterwards on the thirtieth day of September AD 1836 in consideration of the premises then and there promised to pay the said several sums of money to the plaintiff on request: Yet they have disregarded their promises and have not nor have either of them paid the said several sums of money nor either nor any of them nor any part thereof; to the damage of the plaintiff one thousand dollars and thereupon he brings suit &c.

Perkins & Osborn Plffs. Atty[s.]

Questions and Answers, 8 May 1838

Source Note

JS, Questions and Answers, Far West, Caldwell Co., MO, 8 May 1838. Featured version published in Elders' Journal, *July 1838, 42–44. For more information on* Elders' Journal, *see Source Notes for Multiple-Entry Documents, p. 563 herein.*

Historical Introduction

On 8 May 1838, JS prepared responses to a collection of questions he and other church leaders were asked approximately six months earlier while traveling from Kirtland, Ohio, to Far West, Missouri. The leaders had embarked on the trip in September 1837 in order to locate new gathering places for the Saints and to organize church affairs in Far West. JS explained that on the journey, they held public meetings and were asked questions "daily and hourly . . . by all classes of people." Upon his return, JS prepared a list of twenty questions—ranging from how the gold plates were discovered to whether the church practiced polygamy—and then published the list in the November 1837 issue of the *Elders' Journal,* promising that the next issue would include answers to the queries.[658] The next issue was not published until July 1838, after JS relocated from Ohio to Missouri and the periodical was reestablished in Far West.[659]

JS's journal entry for 8 May 1838 notes that he spent "the after part of the day, in answering the questions proposed."[660] He may have begun developing answers at the time the questions were asked in late 1837, perhaps in the public meetings the church leaders

658. Travel Account and Questions, Nov. 1837, in *JSP,* D5:480–484.
659. See Prospectus for *Elders' Journal,* 30 Apr. 1838, pp. 128–133 herein.
660. JS, Journal, 8 May 1838, in *JSP,* J1:267.

held in towns and villages in Ohio, Indiana, and Missouri along the way to Far West. JS noted that the meetings "were tended with good success and generally allayed the prejudice and feeling of the people, as we judge from the treatment we received, being kindly and hospitably entertained."[661] Whatever the tone of JS's initial oral responses to interested non-Mormons, he adopted a playful attitude in his written answers for the Latter-day Saint audience of the July 1838 issue of the *Elders' Journal*. It is unknown whether JS or others continued working on the answers after 8 May 1838. Because the original document is apparently not extant, it remains unclear whether JS wrote the answers himself or relied on a scribe.

Document Transcript

In obedience to our promise, we give the following answers to questions, which were asked in the last number of the Journal.[662]

Question 1st. Do you believe the b[i]ble?

Answer. If we do, we are the only people under heaven that does. For there are none of the religious sects of the day that do.

Question 2nd. Wherein do you differ from other sects?

Answer. Because we believe the bible, and all other sects profess to believe their interpretations of the bible, and their creeds.[663]

Question 3rd. Will every body be damned but Mormons?

Answer. Yes, and a great portion of them, unless they repent and work righteousness.[664]

Question 4th. How, and where did you obtain the book of Mormon?

---

661. Travel Account and Questions, Nov. 1837, in *JSP*, D5:480–481.

662. See Travel Account and Questions, Nov. 1837, in *JSP*, D5:482–484.

663. In the antebellum United States, many Americans believed that creeds, or statements of official denominational belief, constricted rather than illuminated interpretation of the Bible. JS employed anticreedal rhetoric in an 1835 letter to Latter-day Saint elders, arguing that creeds impeded true understanding of scripture. Around the time that JS prepared the answers featured here, he described in his history the confusion he experienced as a teenager because "the teachers of religion of the different sects understood the same passage of Scripture so differently as to destroy all confidence in settling the question by an appeal to the Bible." JS recalled that after praying for guidance, he received a visitation from God the Father and Jesus Christ in 1820, during which Christ stated that the creeds of contemporary churches "were an abomination in his sight." (Hatch, *Democratization of American Christianity*, 81, 169, 215; Letter to the Elders of the Church, 30 Nov.–1 Dec. 1835, in *JSP*, D5:99; JS History, vol. A-1, 2–3, in *JSP*, H1:212, 214 [Draft 2]; see also Welch, "All Their Creeds Were an Abomination," 228–249.)

664. In November 1831, JS dictated a revelation declaring that "this Church . . . [is] the only true & living Church upon the face of the whole Earth with which I the Lord am well pleased." Baptism by the proper authority was required for membership in the church. The Book of Mormon also used the phrase "repent and work righteousness" to refer to those who entered into the "high priesthood." (Revelation, 1 Nov. 1831–B, in *JSP*, D2:107 [D&C 1:30]; 144n679 herein; Book of Mormon, 1830 ed., 259 [Alma 13:10].)

Answer. Moroni, the person who deposited the plates, from whence the book of Mormon [p. 42] was translated, in a hill in Manchester, Ontario County New York, being dead, and raised again therefrom, appeared unto me, and told me where they were; and gave me directions how to obtain them. I obtained them,[665] and the Urim and Thummim with them; by the means of which, I translated the plates; and thus came the book of Mormon.[666]

Question 5th. Do you believe Joseph Smith Jr. to be a prophet?

Answer. Yes, and every other man who has the testimony of Jesus. "For the testimony of Jesus, is the spirit of prophecy."— Rev. 19:10.

Question 6th. Do the Mormons believe in having all things common?

Answer. No.[667]

Question 7th. Do the Mormons believe in having more wives than one.

Answer. No, not at the same time.[668] But they believe, that if their companion dies, they have a right to marry again.[669] But we do disapprove of the custom which has gained in the world, and has been practised among us, to our great mortification, of marrying in five or six weeks, or even in two or three months after the death of their companion.

---

665. JS recounted that Moroni, the last prophet to write in the Book of Mormon, visited JS on the night of 21–22 September 1823. Moroni summarized the plates' contents and provided instructions regarding where to locate them. After visiting the location annually for four years, JS obtained the plates on 22 September 1827. (JS History, ca. Summer 1832, 4–5, in *JSP*, H1:13–15; JS History, 1834–1836, 62, 78–79, in *JSP*, H1:57, 71; Revelation, ca. Aug. 1835, in *JSP*, D4:410–411 [D&C 27:5].)

666. The Book of Mormon describes revelatory stones, or "interpreters," that could be used to "translate all records that are of ancient date."[a] JS recounted finding such instruments with the plates and using them to translate the record on the plates into English.[b] Extant documents suggest that the biblical term *Urim and Thummim* was first applied to the interpreters by William W. Phelps in 1833 and that JS adopted the term thereafter.[c] JS also used other seer stones to translate the plates.[d] After 1833, JS at times referred to seer stones as *Urim and Thummim*.[e] (a. Book of Mormon, 1830 ed., 172–173 [Mosiah 8:13]. b. "Urim and Thummim," in the glossary on the Joseph Smith Papers website, josephsmithpapers.org. c. "The Book of Mormon," *The Evening and the Morning Star*, Jan. 1833, [2]; Exodus 28:30; Leviticus 8:8; Numbers 27:21; "Printer's Manuscript of the Book of Mormon," in *JSP*, R3, Part 1, p. xix; JS, Journal, 9–11 Nov. 1835, in *JSP*, J1:89. d. See "Urim and Thummim," in the glossary on the Joseph Smith Papers website, josephsmithpapers.org. e. Woodruff, Journal, 27 Dec. 1841; Historian's Office, Brigham Young History Drafts, 60.)

667. "All things common" is a phrase in the Bible and the Book of Mormon that refers to communal arrangements among early Christians. Allegations frequently arose in the 1830s that the church's financial program constituted a "common stock" organization, in which property was owned jointly. Church members repeatedly denied this claim. (Acts 2:44; 4:32; Book of Mormon, 1830 ed., 514 [4 Nephi 1:3]; JS, Journal, 30 Oct. 1835, in *JSP*, J1:79; JS History, vol. A-1, 93; see also 143n675 herein.)

668. The question about plural marriage may have derived from rumors of an early plural marriage. However, monogamous marriage was still the general church rule and practice. (Historical Introduction to Letter from Thomas B. Marsh, 15 Feb. 1838, pp. 12–13 herein; Statement on Marriage, ca. Aug. 1835, in *JSP*, D4:477–478.)

669. The 1835 "Statement on Marriage" indicated that "in case of death," the surviving spouse was "at liberty to marry again." (Statement on Marriage, ca. Aug. 1835, in *JSP*, D4:478.)

We believe that due respect ought to be had, to the memory of the dead, and the feelings of both friends and children.[670]

Question 8th. Can they raise the dead.

Answer. No, nor any other people that now lives or ever did live. But God can raise the dead through man, as an instrument.[671]

Question 9th. What signs do Jo Smith give of his divine mission.

Answer. The signs which God is pleased to let him give: according as his wisdom thinks best: in order that he may judge the world agreably to his own plan.

Question 10. Was not Jo Smith a money digger.

Answer. Yes,[672] but it was never a very profitable job to him, as he only got fourteen dollars a month for it.[673]

Question 11th. Did not Jo Smith steal his wife.

Answer. Ask her; she was of age, she can answer for herself.[674]

---

670. In nineteenth-century America, relatives were expected to mourn for set periods of time after the death of a spouse, parent, or child; the length of mourning varied depending on a relative's age, gender, class, region, and relationship to the deceased individual. (Faust, *This Republic of Suffering,* 148; Hall, *Social Customs,* 255–264.)

671. Both the Bible and the Book of Mormon state that disciples of Christ are empowered to raise the dead. Early Latter-day Saints believed that raising the dead was among the spiritual gifts that were restored in the last days. When Brigham Young was ordained an apostle in 1835, for example, his ordination blessing indicated that "the Holy Priesthood [was] confirmed upon [him], that he may do wonders in the name of Jesus," including "rais[ing] the dead." (Minutes, Discourse, and Blessings, 14–15 Feb. 1835, in *JSP,* D4:229; see also Matthew 10:8; Luke 7:22; John chap. 11; Book of Mormon, 1830 ed., 493, 514 [3 Nephi 19:4; 4 Nephi 1:5]; and Bowman, "Raising the Dead," 79–83.)

672. Several of JS's contemporaries recounted his participation in treasure-seeking activities in the 1820s in locations ranging from the area of Manchester, New York, to the area of Harmony, Pennsylvania. (Trial Proceedings, Bainbridge, NY, 20 Mar. 1826, State of New York v. JS [J.P. Ct. 1826], in "The Original Prophet," *Fraser's Magazine,* Feb. 1873, 229–230; "A Document Discovered," *Utah Christian Advocate,* Jan. 1886, 1; see also JS History, vol. A-1, 7–8, in *JSP,* H1:234, 236–237 [Draft 2]; Bushman, *Rough Stone Rolling,* 48–52; and Vogel, "Locations of Joseph Smith's Early Treasure Quests," 197–231.)

673. JS was probably referring to his employment with Josiah Stowell in 1825, which involved searching for a rumored Spanish silver mine in Harmony, Pennsylvania. JS's mother, Lucy Mack Smith, recalled that Stowell sought out JS because "he was in possession of certain means, by which he could discern things, that could not be seen by the natural eye." These "means" included seer stones. JS's monthly wage of fourteen dollars was comparable to that of contemporary unskilled adult male laborers in the Harmony area, who earned about fifty cents a day. (JS History, vol. A-1, 7–8, in *JSP,* H1:234 [Draft 2]; Agreement of Josiah Stowell and Others, 1 Nov. 1825, in *JSP,* D1:345; Lucy Mack Smith, History, 1845, 95; Staker and Jensen, "David Hale's Store Ledger," 104.)

674. Emma Hale was twenty-two years old when she married JS in South Bainbridge (later Afton), New York, on 18 January 1827. Because her father, Isaac Hale, opposed the union, the claim arose that JS "stole" Emma. She stated in a February 1879 interview with her son Joseph Smith III, "I had no intention of marrying when I left home; but, during my visit at Mr. Stowell's, your father visited me there. My folks were bitterly opposed to him; and, being importuned by your father, aided by Mr. Stowell, who urged me to marry him, and preferring to marry him to any other man I knew, I consented. We went to Squire [Zachariah] Tarbell's and were married." (Isaac Hale, Affidavit,

Question 12th. Do the people have to give up their money, when they join his church.

Answer. No other requirement than to bear their proportion of the expenses of the church, and support the poor.[675]

Question 13th. Are the Mormons abolitionists.

Answer. No, unless delivering the people from priest-craft,[676] and the priests from the prower of satan, should be considered such.— But we do not believe in setting the Negroes free.[677]

Question 14th. Do they not stir up the Indians to war and to commit depredations.

Answer. No, and those who reported the story, knew it was false when they put it into circulation. These and similar reports, are pawned upon the people by the priests, and this is the reason why we ever thought of answering them.[678]

Harmony, PA, 20 Mar. 1834, in "Mormonism," *Susquehanna Register, and Northern Pennsylvanian* [Montrose, PA], 1 May 1834, [1]; Joseph Smith III, "Last Testimony of Sister Emma," *Saints' Herald,* 1 Oct. 1879, 289.)

675. In February 1831, a JS revelation outlined the "Laws of the Church of Christ," which included the principle of consecration, or donation, of personal and real property to the church. Latter-day Saints who consecrated their property were to receive a stewardship over property that met their needs. Consecrated property was intended to be used to support church financial programs and "to administer to the poor and needy." (Revelation, 9 Feb. 1831, in *JSP,* D1:252 [D&C 42:34]; see also Cook, *Joseph Smith and the Law of Consecration,* 29–42.)

676. See "Priestcraft," in *American Dictionary.*

677. Although many early Latter-day Saints came from northern states, where opposition to slavery was gaining ground, church leaders during the mid-1830s tended to favor the status quo on slavery and to oppose abolitionism. This approach partly stemmed from the July 1833 eruption of violence in Jackson County, Missouri, after vigilantes misunderstood an article in the church newspaper *The Evening and the Morning Star* that addressed the status of free blacks under Missouri law.[a] Further complicating the church's relationship with the institution of slavery, missionaries converted hundreds of individuals— including some slave owners—in Kentucky, Tennessee, and other southern states during the 1830s.[b] The declaration on government and law published in the 1835 edition of the Doctrine and Covenants contained a clause stating that missionaries should not baptize slaves without the master's consent.[c] In 1836, in response to a recent lecture by abolitionist John W. Alvord in Kirtland, JS published an editorial in the church periodical *Messenger and Advocate* disavowing abolitionism and even citing biblical references in defense of the institution of slavery.[d] (a. Letter from John Whitmer, 29 July 1833, in *JSP,* D3:186–198. b. Berrett, "History of the Southern States Mission," 68–123. c. Declaration on Government and Law, ca. Aug. 1835, in *JSP,* D4:484 [D&C 134:12]. d. Letter to Oliver Cowdery, ca. 9 Apr. 1836, in *JSP,* D5:236– 243; see also Reeve, *Religion of a Different Color,* 122–126.)

678. As early as 1831, allegations arose that Latter-day Saint missionaries were seeking to convert Indians and instigate Indian attacks on non-Mormons. These claims were based on Book of Mormon prophecies (echoing language in the biblical book of Micah) that the "remnant of the House of Jacob," which some Latter-day Saints interpreted as meaning converted Native Americans, would be "as a young lion among the flocks of sheep, who, if he goeth through, both treadeth down and teareth in pieces, and none can deliver."[a] In 1832 JS cautioned church members against discussing these prophecies, fearing that people outside of the church would believe that the Latter-day Saints were "putting up the Indians to

Question 15th. Do the Mormons baptize in the name of Jo Smith.

Answer. No, but if they did, it would be as valid as the baptism administered by the sectarian priests.[679]

Question 16th. If the Mormon doctrine is true what has become of all those who have died since the days of the apostles.

Answer. All those who have not had an opportunity of hearing the gospel, and being administered to by an inspired man in the flesh, must have it hereafter, before they can be finally judged.[680]

Question 17th. Does not Jo Smith profess to be Jesus Christ.

Answer. No, but he professes to be his brother, as all other saints have done, and now do.— Matthew, 12:49, 50— And he stretched forth his hand toward his disciples and said, Behold my mother and my brethren: For whosoever shall do the will of my father which is in heaven, the same is my brother, and sister, and mother.

Question 18th. Is there any thing in the Bible which lisences you to believe in revelation now a days.

---

slay" whites and that this conclusion would endanger "the lives of the Saints evry where."[b] Fears that the Saints were "tampering" with Indians contributed to opposition toward Latter-day Saint settlements in Jackson County, Missouri, in 1833 and Clay County, Missouri, in 1836, prompting church leaders to deny having any connection with Native Americans and stating that the Saints feared "the barbarous cruelty of rude savages" as other frontier whites did.[c] (a. Ezra Booth, "Mormonism—No. VI," *Ohio Star* [Ravenna], 17 Nov. 1831, [3]; Book of Mormon, 1830 ed., 496–497, 500 [3 Nephi 20:15–16; 21:11–12]; Micah 5:8. b. Letter to William W. Phelps, 31 July 1832, in *JSP*, D2:266. c. Isaac McCoy, "The Disturbances in Jackson County," *Missouri Republican* [St. Louis], 20 Dec. 1833, [2]–[3]; "Public Meeting," *LDS Messenger and Advocate,* Aug. 1836, 2:353–355; Letter to John Thornton et al., 25 July 1836, in *JSP,* D5:263–264; see also Reeve, *Religion of a Different Color,* 59–69.)

679. Passages in the Book of Mormon emphasize that baptism must be administered by proper authority. Soon after the church was organized in April 1830, JS dictated a revelation declaring that "old covenants"—meaning baptisms administered by officials in other churches—were invalid. Converts were therefore instructed to receive baptism into this "last covenant and this church," which God had caused "to be built up . . . even as in days of old." (Book of Mormon, 1830 ed., 200–201, 477–478, 479 [Mosiah 21:33–35; 3 Nephi 11:21–22; 12:1]; Revelation, 16 Apr. 1830, in *JSP*, D1:138, 138n150 [D&C 22:1–3].)

680. In 1832 JS and Sidney Rigdon reported receiving a vision of the afterlife. In this vision, they saw those "who died with out Law" and "the spirits of men kept in prison whom the son visited and preached the gospel" so that they "might be judged according to men in the flesh," a reference to 1 Peter 3:18–19 and 4:6. Four years later, JS reported that he received a vision of the "celestial kingdom of God, and the glory thereof," wherein he saw his deceased brother Alvin. JS recounted his amazement upon learning that Alvin was in that kingdom, even though Alvin had not been baptized. According to JS's account of the vision, the Lord declared, "All who have died with[out] a knowledge of this gospel, who would have received it, if they had been permitted to tarry, shall be heirs of the celestial kingdom of God." These visions indicated that salvation would ultimately be made available for all of humanity. (Vision, 16 Feb. 1832, in *JSP*, D2:189 [D&C 76:73]; JS, Journal, 21 Jan. 1836, in *JSP*, J1:167–168; see also Givens, *Wrestling the Angel,* 245–255.)

Answer. Is there any thing that does not authorize us to believe so; if there is, we have, as yet, not been able to find it.

Question 19th. Is not the cannon of the Scriptures full. [p. 43]

Answer. If it is, there is a great defect in the book, or else it would have said so.[681]

Question 20th. What are the fundamental principles of your religion.

Answer. The fundamental principles of our religion is the testimony of the apostles and prophets concerning Jesus Christ, "that he died, was buried, and rose again the third day, and ascended up into heaven;"[682] and all other things are only appendages to these, which pertain to our religion.

But in connection with these, we believe in the gift of the Holy Ghost,[683] the power of faith, the enjoyment of the spiritual gifts according to the will of God,[684] the restoration of the house of Israel,[685] and the final triumph of truth. [p. 44]

———— ✸ ————

Letter from Heber C. Kimball and Orson Hyde, between 22 and 28 May 1838

Source Note

Heber C. Kimball and Orson Hyde, Letter, Kirtland Township, Geauga Co., OH, to JS, Far West, Caldwell Co., MO, [between 22 and 28 May 1838]. Featured version copied [between 6 July and ca. late July 1838] in JS, Journal, Mar.–Sept. 1838, pp. 48–49; handwriting of George W. Robinson; CHL. For more information on JS, Journal, Mar.–Sept. 1838, see Source Notes for Multiple-Entry Documents, p. 564 herein.

---

681. Questions 18 and 19 and their answers reflect the complex debate over the biblical canon— that is, the authoritative list of divinely inspired scriptural books. Many nineteenth-century Protestants advocated the belief in a closed canon, whereas some other groups, such as the Latter-day Saints, contended that revelation was still possible and that the canon was open. The church's 1830 Articles and Covenants addressed this ongoing controversy with an allusion to Revelation 22:17–18. This commonly cited passage prohibits adding to or taking away from "the words of the prophecy of this book," which commentators interpreted variously as referring to the book of Revelation alone or the Bible as a whole. The Articles and Covenants stated that JS's revelations contained divine truth and neither added to nor diminished the book of Revelation or the Bible. (Bruce, *Canon of Scripture,* 17–24; Holland, *Sacred Borders,* 1–15, 26–29; Articles and Covenants, ca. Apr. 1830, in *JSP,* D1:123 [D&C 20:35].)

682. See Articles and Covenants, ca. Apr. 1830, in *JSP,* D1:122 [D&C 20:23–24].

683. See Revelation, Oct. 1830–B, in *JSP,* D1:207 [D&C 33:15]; and Revelation, 5 Jan. 1831, in *JSP,* D1:236 [D&C 39:23].

684. See Revelation, ca. 8 Mar. 1831–A, in *JSP,* D1:280 [D&C 46].

685. See Revelation, 5 Jan. 1831, in *JSP,* D1:235–236 [D&C 39:11].

Historical Introduction

In late May 1838, Heber C. Kimball and Orson Hyde wrote to JS to inform him of their recent return to Kirtland, Ohio, from their mission in England. Kimball and Hyde were members of the Quorum of the Twelve Apostles and had been appointed as traveling ministers and "special witnesses of the name of Christ, in all the world."[686] The two apostles started on their mission in June 1837, departing Kirtland with fellow missionaries Willard Richards and Joseph Fielding and traveling to New York City, where the four men were joined by a few other missionaries. In July the group of missionaries sailed from New York City to Liverpool, England, to begin what would be the first Mormon mission outside of North America.[687] Over the next nine months, Kimball, Hyde, and others proselytized and organized branches of the church in Preston and in a number of towns and villages in the Ribble Valley of Lancashire, where they enjoyed great success. By the end of their mission, over fifteen hundred people had joined the church.[688] Kimball and Hyde departed England in April 1838 and arrived in Kirtland on 21 May, only to find Kirtland rife with rumors about and antagonism toward JS. In their letter to JS, they wrote that they had arrived on "monday last," which indicates they wrote their letter sometime between 22 and 28 May.

In the letter, Kimball and Hyde briefly rehearsed their proselytizing activities in England, reported on the caustic atmosphere they encountered upon returning to Kirtland, and confirmed their steadfast loyalty to JS and the church. They also expressed their desire to move with their families to Missouri as soon as they could afford to do so, and they inquired regarding the spiritual well-being and harmony of the Saints in Far West, Missouri. Kimball, the more senior apostle and first signatory, may have inscribed the letter.

When George W. Robinson copied the letter from Kimball and Hyde into JS's journal, Robinson wrote that JS received the letter on 6 July 1838.[689] Robinson likely made the copy by late July; transcripts of this letter and a few other documents appear within a gap in regular journal keeping, with regular entries resuming late that month.[690] The original letter is apparently not extant.

Document Transcript

Dear Brother Joseph

In health peace & saf[e]ty we arrived in this place on monday last,[691] from the scene of our labor during the past year after a passage of 31 days.[692] We

---

686. See Instruction on Priesthood, between ca. 1 Mar. and ca. 4 May 1835, in *JSP*, D4:314 [D&C 107:23].

687. Thompson, *Journal of Heber C. Kimball*, 10–14.

688. Allen et al., *Men with a Mission*, 28–53.

689. JS, Journal, 6 July 1838, in *JSP*, J1:278–279.

690. See JS, Journal, 4–8 and 26–31 July 1838, in *JSP*, J1:275–296.

691. In an autobiographical sketch, Hyde noted that he and Kimball arrived at Kirtland on 21 May 1838, which was a Monday. ("History of Orson Hyde," 16, Historian's Office, Histories of the Twelve, 1856–1858, 1861, CHL; see also Fielding, Journal, 1837–1838, 75–76.)

692. Kimball and Hyde sailed from Liverpool on 20 April 1838 and arrived in New York City on 12 May 1838. (Thompson, *Journal of Heber C. Kimball*, 41–42.)

cannot give a full account of our labors now, but suffise it to say the standard of truth is reared on the other side of the great waters, and hundreds are now fi[gh]ting the good fight of faith,[693] beneath the shade of its glorious banner. We have fought in the name of the Lord Jesus, and under the shadow of the cross we have conquered, Not an enimy has risen up against us, but that has fallen for our sakes, Every thing we have done has prospered, and the God of the Holy Prophets[694] has been with us, and to him belongs the praise Our bretheren in the East are poor yet rich in faith[695] and the peace of our God[696] abides upon them, we have not interfeered with the priests at all except when we have been assalted by them,[697] We have preached repentance & baptism & baptism & repentance,[698] We have strictly attended to our own buisness and have let others alone We have experienced the truth of solomons words which are as follows When a mans ways please the Lord he maketh his enimies that they are at peace with him[699] our enimies have seen their entire insufficincy to stand against the power of truth manifest through us, and have gone away and left us in peacefull possession of [p. 48] the field, Concerning the Nicholatine Band of which you warned us against we would say God is not there, and we are not there, they deal in sand stone & bogus,[700] but we in faith hope & Charity[701] We have not means to situate our

---

693. See 1 Timothy 6:12.

694. See Revelation 22:6.

695. See James 2:5. Hyde observed that the converts in the Preston area were "mostly manufacturers and some other mechanics" who were "extremely poor, most of them not having a change of clothes decent to be babtized in." Kimball similarly wrote that the indigent masses of Preston were "the most poor people that I ever saw" and that "it is as much as they can do to live." (Orson Hyde, Preston, England, to Marinda Nancy Johnson Hyde, Kirtland, OH, 14 Sept. 1837, in *Elders' Journal*, Nov. 1837, 19; Heber C. Kimball, Preston, England, to Vilate Murray Kimball, Kirtland, OH, 2–6 Sept. 1837, in *Elders' Journal*, Oct. 1837, 5.)

696. See Colossians 3:15; Philippians 4:7; and Book of Mormon, 1830 ed., 242 [Alma 7:27].

697. Kimball and Hyde faced opposition from ministers in Preston. (Allen et al., *Men with a Mission*, 36, 41–42.)

698. One of JS's early revelations directed elders to "preach repentance & remission of sins by way of baptism." (Revelation, 14 June 1831, in *JSP*, D1:339 [D&C 55:2]; see also Articles of the Church of Christ, June 1829, in *JSP*, D1:371.)

699. See Proverbs 16:7.

700. Many of those estranged from the church were residing in Kirtland when Hyde and Kimball returned in May 1838. "Sand stone & bogus" may be an allusion to a story about dissenter Warren Parrish, who allegedly traveled to Tinker's Creek, Ohio, to buy a box of bogus, or counterfeit coin, and discovered upon his return that the box contained only "sand and stones." Parrish and others organized themselves into a new "Church of Christ," and JS apparently equated this group or at least some of the estranged church members at Kirtland with the heretical Nicolaitan sect mentioned in the New Testament. (Editorial, *Elders' Journal*, Aug. 1838, 58; Backman, *Heavens Resound*, 327–329; Revelation 2:6, 15; Revelation, 8 July 1838–E, p. 193 herein [D&C 117:11].)

701. See 1 Corinthians 13:13.

families in Far West at present and as we have not been chargable to the Church hitherto, we do not like to become a burthen to them in the extreme state of poverty to which they are reduced,[702] We can preach the gospel when the Lord is with us, and by it we can live, and the time will come when we shall have means to settle with the saints. Kirtland is not our home, it looks dolefull here, We shall go westward as soon as we can, the folks here tell many dark and pittifull tales about yourself & others. but the faults of our bretheren is poor entertainment for us, We have no accusation to bring for the Lord has shown us that he has taken the matter into his own hands, and every secret shall be braught to light[703] and every man chastened for his sins, untill he confess and forsake them[704] and then he shall fined mercy[705] Therefore we can say we are at peace with God and with all mankind, and if any creature has aught against us, we have naught against him, and we say forgive us for Christ sake, We should be glad to see all our bretheren of the Twelve, and we s[h]all as we can consistantly, our good wishes and best respects to them To yourself Bro. Sidney [Rigdon] and families, and to all the faithfull bretheren and sisters in Christ Jesus our Lord,[706] Will you or some other of the bretheren write us soon and let us know the true state of things in Far West, We have been gone allmost a year and have heard but very little, but we now hear much, We would like to know if a spirit of union prevails &c. &c. We are as ever your bretheren in the bonds of the everlasting covenant,[707]

To Pres^t J, Smith Jr.

H[eber] C. Kimball
Orson Hyde
We are one [p. 49]

———— ☙ ————

Letter from Don Carlos Smith, circa Late May 1838

Source Note

Don Carlos Smith, Letter, near Terre Haute, Vigo Co., IN, to JS, [Far West, Caldwell Co., MO], [ca. late May 1838]. Featured version copied [ca. July 1838] in JS, Journal, Mar.–Sept. 1838, pp. 50–51;

702. Elias Smith, who lived in Kirtland, wrote that some of the discord there resulted from the "extreme poverty" of the Latter-day Saints. (Kirtland Camp, Journal, 12–13.)

703. See Book of Mormon, 1830 ed., 118, 173 [2 Nephi 30:17; Mosiah 8:17].

704. See Revelation, 1 Aug. 1831, in *JSP*, D2:19 [D&C 58:43].

705. See 2 Timothy 1:18; and Book of Mormon, 1830 ed., 314 [Alma 32:13].

706. See Ephesians 1:1.

707. See Philemon 1:13; and Genesis 17:13.

handwriting of George W. Robinson; CHL. Includes use marks. For more information on JS, Journal, Mar.–Sept. 1838, see Source Notes for Multiple-Entry Documents, p. 564 herein.

Historical Introduction

While the extended Smith family was moving from Ohio to Missouri in mid-1838, Don Carlos Smith wrote to his brother JS regarding the journey. The move was in response to a revelation that JS had dictated in January, directing the members of the First Presidency and their families to leave Kirtland "as soon as it is praticable" and for their "faithfull friends" to "arise with their families also and get out of this place and gather themselves together unto Zion."[708] JS left Kirtland, Ohio, that night and was joined by his wife and children a few days later in Norton, Ohio. From there, they made their way to Far West, Missouri.[709] Hyrum Smith, JS's brother and a counselor in the First Presidency, departed Kirtland with his family in late March and arrived at Far West in late May.[710] Before leaving, he arranged for the Smiths still in Ohio to receive financial assistance for their move to Missouri. These arrangements, however, fell through, and the twenty-eight travelers, consisting of the extended Smith family and a few others, were underfunded when they departed Norton on 7 May 1838. Before the group was halfway to Caldwell County, they had spent over one hundred dollars and had only twenty-five dollars for the remainder of the journey. While the group was traveling through the vicinity of Terre Haute, Indiana, one of the horses became lame and the group stopped to care for it, providing an opportunity for Don Carlos Smith to write to JS.

Although the letter is undated, the timing of the letter can be estimated by correlating the group's month-long journey between Norton and the Mississippi River (as referenced in the reminiscences of Lucy Mack Smith and in the featured letter) with contemporaneous accounts of other Latter-day Saints traveling the same or nearly the same route.[711] The well-documented travels of the 1834 Camp of Israel expedition (later known as Zion's Camp) and of the 1838 "Kirtland Camp" migration suggest that the Smiths' group was likely in the vicinity of Terra Haute sometime between 24 and 28 May.[712] At the end of the letter, Don Carlos Smith wrote, "It is now dark and I close," suggesting that he wrote the letter in the twilight.

---

708. Revelation, 12 Jan. 1838–C, in *JSP*, D5:501, 502.

709. JS History, vol. B-1, 780.

710. Hyrum Smith, Commerce, IL, to "the Saints Scattered Abroad," Dec. 1839, in *Times and Seasons,* Dec. 1839, 1:21; O'Driscoll, *Hyrum Smith,* 167–170.

711. See, for example, JS History, vol. A-1, 477–479, addenda, 6–12; Travel Account and Questions, Nov. 1837, in *JSP,* D5:480–481; Hyrum Smith, Commerce, IL, to "the Saints Scattered Abroad," Dec. 1839, in *Times and Seasons,* Dec. 1839, 1:21; George A. Smith, Autobiography, 14–36; and Kirtland Camp, Journal, 6 July–2 Oct. 1838; see also Lucy Mack Smith, History, 1844–1845, bk. 15, [3]–[6]; and Plewe et al., *Mapping Mormonism,* 38–39.

712. The Camp of Israel traveled nearly the same route, crossing the Wabash River about fifteen miles north of Terre Haute; the Kirtland Camp traveled through Terre Haute. It took the Camp of Israel seventeen days to travel from Norton Township to the Wabash River, while it took the Kirtland Camp twenty-eight days to travel from Norton to Terre Haute—not counting the days

In the letter, Don Carlos Smith recounted the difficulty the Smith family experienced trying to fund their migration, and he also mentioned some of the problems the party encountered en route. Because of these challenges, he requested that JS or Hyrum Smith send money to help the travelers complete their journey. It is uncertain when JS received the letter. It should have reached Far West from near Terre Haute in about one to two weeks.[713] JS's scribe, George W. Robinson, copied the letter into JS's journal after a letter that JS received from Heber C. Kimball and Orson Hyde on 6 July and before a journal entry for 8 July 1838, suggesting JS received the letter sometime between 6 and 8 July.[714] These entries fall within a large gap in regular journal keeping, and Robinson apparently did not resume making regular entries until late July, which indicates that he may not have copied the letter from Don Carlos Smith before that time.[715] The original letter is apparently not extant.

JS may have responded to the letter by sending the requested financial assistance, just as the Saints in Missouri had sent him financial assistance to complete his journey.[716] The Smith party may have received such assistance when they arrived in Huntsville, Missouri. Lucy Mack Smith later recounted that upon arriving there, they rested in a home for a while and arranged for a buggy to transport her daughter Katharine Smith Salisbury, who was ill and lagging behind. Lucy further recounted that when the group moved on from Huntsville, they were able to pursue their journey "without any further difficulty."[717]

---

the camp members stopped to work for wages along the way.[a] The Camp of Israel spent eleven days traveling from the Wabash River to the Mississippi River, while the Kirtland Camp spent thirteen days traveling from Terre Haute to the Mississippi River.[b] Lucy Mack Smith recollected that her daughter Katharine Smith Salisbury gave birth after they crossed the Mississippi River; additional sources recall the birth as occurring 7 June.[c] This collection of information suggests that the Smith party—departing from Norton on 7 May and arriving at the Mississippi River by 7 June—would have reached Terre Haute before 25 May and would have left by 27 May. The letter was written "Nine Miles from Terre Haute"—either to the east or the west—adding approximately one day on either side. (a. JS History, vol. A-1, 478–479, addenda 8n4; "Camp of Israel Route, May–June 1834," in *JSP*, D4:55; Kirtland Camp, Journal, 11 July–7 Sept. 1838. b. JS History, vol. A-1, 483, addenda, 8n4; Kirtland Camp, Journal, 7–20 Sept. 1838. c. Lucy Mack Smith, History, 1844–1845, bk. 15, [4]; Solomon J. Salisbury, "Reminiscences of an Octogenarian," *Journal of History*, Jan. 1922, 18; "Records of Early Church Families," *Utah Genealogical and Historical Magazine,* Oct. 1935, 152.)

713. Mail between Kirtland and western Missouri generally required three to four weeks of travel time. (Hartley, "Letters and Mail between Kirtland and Independence," 176.)

714. Years later, the Latter-day Saints working on the history JS initiated in 1838 implied that both letters were received the same day. This assumption was likely based on the placement of the letters in JS's journal, not knowledge of when the letters arrived in Far West. However, both letters may well have arrived in the same delivery of mail. (JS History, vol. B-1, 801.)

715. JS, Journal, 4–8 and 26–31 July 1838, in *JSP*, J1:275–296.

716. JS was met in Huntsville, Missouri, by John Barnard, who had been sent from Caldwell County with money to assist JS and those with him in completing their journey. (See Historian's Office, Brigham Young History Drafts, 17; and JS, Journal, Mar.–Sept. 1838, p. 16, in *JSP*, J1:237.)

717. Don Carlos Smith, who went ahead of the main group, arrived in Far West by 8 July 1838, as did his wife, Agnes Coolbrith Smith, and possibly other members of the party. (Lucy

Document Transcript

Nine Miles from Terre Haute, Ind.

Bro. Joseph

I sit down to inform you of our situation at the present time. I started from Norton, Ohio,[718] the 7th of May, in company with Father, Wm. [Smith], Jenkins salsbury [Wilkins Jenkins Salisbury], Wm. McClerry [McCleary] & Lewis Rob[b]ins, and families,[719] also sister singly[720] is one of our number, we started with 15 horses seven wagons, & two cows, we have left two horses by the way sick one with a swelling in ⟨on⟩ his shoulder, a 3rd horse (as it were our dependance) was taken lame, last evening and is not able to travel, and we have stop[p]ed to docter him We were disappointed on every hand before we started, in getting money, we got no assistance whatever only as we have taken in sister singly and she has assisted us as far as her means extends, we had when we started, $75 dollars in money, we sold the 2 cows for $13.50 per cow we have sold of your goods to the amt of $45.74 and now we have only $25 dollars to carry 28 souls & 13 horses, 500 miles, we have lived very close and camped out knight, notwithstanding the rain & cold, & my babe only 2 weeks old when we started, Agness [Agnes Coolbrith Smith] is very feeble[721] Father & Mother are not well but very much fatigued, Mother has a severe cold,[722]

Mack Smith, History, 1844–1845, bk. 15, [5]–[6]; Deed to Samuel F. Whitney, 8 July 1838, pp. 200, 201 herein.)

718. New Portage, in Norton Township, had a strong branch of the church. Situated on the Ohio and Erie Canal, Norton was an important junction for Latter-day Saints traveling from Kirtland to Missouri.[a] For example, in 1834 groups of men from Kirtland and other places met in Norton to embark on the Camp of Israel.[b] In January 1838, after fleeing Kirtland, JS waited in Norton for his wife and children to join him on his journey to Far West.[c] Joseph Smith Sr. and Don Carlos Smith moved from Kirtland to Norton soon thereafter to avoid being arrested for performing marriages without being considered regularly ordained ministers. When the remainder of the extended Smith family was ready to move to Far West, they joined with Joseph Smith Sr. and Don Carlos Smith in Norton to pursue their journey together.[d] (a. *1833 Ohio Gazetteer*, 344. b. JS History, vol. A-1, 477–479; "Elder Kimball's Journal," *Times and Seasons*, 15 Jan. 1845, 6:771; Baldwin, Account of Zion's Camp, 8–9; McBride, Reminiscence, 2. c. JS History, vol. B-1, 780. d. Lucy Mack Smith, History, 1844–1845, bk. 15, [1]–[3].)

719. William Smith was Don Carlos Smith's brother. Wilkins Jenkins Salisbury and William McCleary were the husbands of Don Carlos's sisters Katharine and Sophronia. Lewis Robbins lived with Don Carlos Smith in Kirtland. (Robbins, Autobiographical Sketch, 3–4; Backman, *Profile*, 111.)

720. Possibly Margaret Leasure Singley (1791–1874). (Ambrosia Branch, Lee Co., Iowa Territory, Record Book, 4; Obituary for Margaret Leasure Singley, *True Latter Day Saints' Herald*, 1 Dec. 1874, 733.)

721. Don Carlos Smith's wife, Agnes Coolbrith Smith, gave birth to Sophronia Smith on 22 April 1838. Sophronia was apparently named after her aunt Sophronia Smith McCleary, who was also part of the group traveling with Don Carlos Smith. ("Family Record of Don C. Smith," in Smith Family Genealogy Record, CHL.)

722. Lucy Mack Smith later recounted that she "took a severe cold" after having to travel three days in wet clothing. By the time they reached the Mississippi River, she was "unable to sit up any length and could not walk without assistance." (Lucy Mack Smith, History, 1844–1845, bk. 15, [4].)

and it is nothing in fact but the prayer of faith[723] and the power of God, that will sustain them and bring them through, our carriage is good and I think we shall be braught through, I leave it with you and Hyram [Hyrum Smith] to devise some way to assist us to some more expence money, we have had un-accountable ~~road~~ ⟨bad⟩ roads, had our horses down in the mud, and broke of[f] one wagon tongue [p. 50] and fills,[724] and broke down the carriage twice and yet we are all alive and camped on a dry place for allmost the first time,[725] Poverty is a heavy load but we are all obliged to welter under it, it is now dark and I close, may the Lord bless you all and bring us together is my prayer Amen

All the arrangements that bro. Hyram left for getting money failed, they did not gain us one cent.

To J. Smith Jr.   Don C. Smith

———— ∽ ————

Letter to Wilford Woodruff, circa 18 June 1838

Source Note

Thomas B. Marsh on behalf of JS, Letter, Far West, Caldwell Co., MO, to Wilford Woodruff, Vinalhaven, Fox Islands, Waldo Co., ME, [ca. 18 June 1838]. Written on a copy of "Prospectus for the Elder's Journal, *of the Church of Jesus Christ, of Latter Day Saints"; handwriting and signatures of Thomas B. Marsh; four pages; Wilford Woodruff, Journals and Papers, CHL. Includes address in the handwriting of Thomas B. Marsh, a stamped postmark and manuscript postage in red ink, a docket in ink in the handwriting of Wilford Woodruff, and an archival call number in graphite.*

Bifolium measuring 16 × 10¼ inches (41 × 26 cm). The letter was written on a published prospectus for the Missouri issues of the *Elders' Journal.* The document was trifolded twice in letter style and then postmarked in red ink. The letter was later refolded for archival filing and then docketed. The folds are weakened and partially separated. Adhesive wafers that sealed the letter created holes in the paper when the letter was opened, resulting in some loss of inscription. The document has undergone some conservation.

In addition to the signatures of Thomas B. Marsh, the letter includes a docket in Wilford Woodruff's handwriting: "Thomas B Marsh | April 30. 1838". Woodruff apparently donated the letter to the LDS church as part of his collected papers, possibly during his tenure as assistant church historian (1856–1883) or church historian (1883–1889).[726]

---

723. See James 5:15.

724. "The thills are the two pieces of timber extending from the body of the carriage on each side of the last horse, by which the carriage is supported in a horizontal position." ("Thill," in *American Dictionary.*)

725. Lucy Mack Smith recounted traveling "thrugh marshes and quagmires on foot exposing our-selves to wet and cold." (Lucy Mack Smith, History, 1844–1845, bk. 15, [4].)

726. "Contents of the Historian and Recorder's Office. G. S. L. City July 1858," 6, Historian's Office, Catalogs and Inventories, 1846–1904, CHL; Turley, "Assistant Church Historians," 20–21; see also Park, "Developing a Historical Conscience," 115–134.

Historical Introduction

Sometime in mid- or late spring 1838, JS assigned Thomas B. Marsh to write a letter to Wilford Woodruff, who was proselytizing in the northeastern United States. In the letter, Marsh responded to a 9 March 1838 missive that Woodruff and two fellow missionaries addressed to Bishop Edward Partridge, JS and his counselors in the First Presidency, and the Saints in Missouri. Woodruff, the primary author of the letter, reported on his proselytizing efforts, challenges, and successes in the Fox Islands, located off the coast of Maine. He also requested that publication of the *Elders' Journal* be recommenced in Missouri because missionaries desperately needed church literature to counter false information being circulated about the church. Woodruff concluded by expressing loyalty to JS and the church and by admonishing the Saints in Missouri to avoid making the mistakes church members in Ohio had made.[727] It is unclear when Woodruff's letter arrived in Far West, Missouri, but later in the year, correspondence between Marsh and Woodruff traveled through the mail in less than four weeks, suggesting that this letter arrived sometime in early or mid-April.[728]

JS apparently read the letter or heard it read and assigned Marsh to reply. Marsh was president of the Quorum of the Twelve Apostles and therefore held ecclesiastical jurisdiction over the apostles, seventies, and all traveling elders—including Woodruff—which made Marsh an appropriate person to respond to Woodruff.[729] Marsh acknowledged that the letter had arrived "some day's since" and explained that the bishop and First Presidency had been busy with church affairs.

Marsh wrote to Woodruff on a copy of the prospectus for the Missouri issues of the *Elders' Journal*. The prospectus, which requested that traveling elders such as Woodruff enlist subscribers for the newspaper, was printed at the top of the recto of the first leaf of a bifolium, with Marsh's letter beginning below the prospectus.[730] Marsh ended his letter on the top half of the verso of the second leaf, slightly compressing his last few lines to leave room for the address, which he added after folding the letter as an envelope. As with the copy of the prospectus Marsh used, other copies of the prospectus may have been printed on bifolia, inscribed with personal notes, and then folded and mailed to Mormon missionaries who were proselytizing outside of Missouri. Marsh wrote the letter sometime between 30 April, which was the publication date of the prospectus, and 18 June, the date of the postmark stamped on the letter. The postscript Marsh added suggests he may have written the letter over more than one day, apparently completing it on or shortly before 18 June. Marsh may have written the letter at his home in Far West.[731]

The letter to Woodruff has two parts. The first part of the letter explains the disaffection of Warren Parrish and other Latter-day Saints in Kirtland. The second part of

---

727. See Letter from Wilford Woodruff et al., 9 Mar. 1838, pp. 34–39 herein.

728. See 33n155 herein.

729. Instruction on Priesthood, between ca. 1 Mar. and ca. 4 May 1835, in *JSP*, D4:315 [D&C 107:33–35]; Revelation, 23 July 1837, in *JSP*, D5:414–415 [D&C 112:1–10].

730. See Prospectus for *Elders' Journal*, 30 Apr. 1838, pp. 131–133 herein.

731. See 17n73 herein.

the letter explains Missouri church members' dissatisfaction with William W. Phelps and John Whitmer, as well as the excommunication of Phelps, John Whitmer, David Whitmer, Oliver Cowdery, and Lyman Johnson. Marsh concluded his letter by noting that with the excommunications, internal opposition had been removed from the church in Zion, that JS and Sidney Rigdon had moved to Zion, and that the *Elders' Journal* would soon be published again. Marsh's postscript describes the April revelation designating Far West as a holy place of gathering in which to build a city of Zion and a temple.

Because Marsh knew the church newspaper would soon be reestablished, he may have written the letter with the intention of responding to Woodruff personally and of publishing the letter in the newspaper to explain to a broader audience the recent developments in Kirtland and Far West. Or, Marsh may have determined after writing the letter that it could be published as a report on recent events. A revised version of the letter, apparently based on a retained copy, appeared in the July issue of the *Elders' Journal*.[732] Before mailing the letter, Marsh made some revisions that softened the antagonism he originally expressed toward the Kirtland dissenters, perhaps to make the letter more suitable for publication. Some of the substantive changes Marsh made in the version he sent to Woodruff do not appear in the *Elders' Journal* version, suggesting that Marsh further revised the letter to Woodruff after making the retained copy. Marsh also revised the retained copy before publishing it.

The letter, mailed on 18 June, probably reached the post office in Vinalhaven, Maine, in mid- or late July. The letter was apparently received by one of Woodruff's converts on the Fox Islands, as Woodruff had been on the mainland since late April. When he returned to the islands on 7 August 1838, he visited fellow Latter-day Saints Ephraim Luce, Stephen Luce, and a "Brother Sterretts," and one of them apparently gave Woodruff the letter.[733]

Document Transcript

Brother W[ilford] Woo⟨d⟩ruff.

Sir, your Letter of the 9ᵗʰ· of March, directed to Bishop [Edward] Partridge, Presidents Joseph Smith Jʳ·, Sidney Rigdon, ⟨and⟩ Hyram [Hyrum] Smith, and the Saints in zion, came safely ⟨to⟩ them, some day's since. And on account of the press of business now on their hands,[734] ⟨and the request of J Smi◊th Jʳ·,⟩

---

732. Thomas B. Marsh, [Far West, MO], to Wilford Woodruff, [Vinalhaven, ME], [ca. 18 June 1838], in *Elders' Journal*, July 1838, 36–38.

733. Woodruff left the Fox Islands on 28 April 1838. Regarding his return on 7 August, Woodruff wrote, "I received a letter from Elder Thomas B. Marsh from Zion in answer to the one I wrot to the Bishop & Presidency & Saints in Zion." The following day, Woodruff visited the post office to obtain further mail, which indicates that he received Marsh's letter from one of the members he visited before he went to the post office. (Woodruff, Journal, 28 Apr. and 7–8 Aug. 1838.)

734. JS spent most of late May and early June in Daviess County, surveying the land and directing the construction of houses. (JS, Journal, 18 May–5 June 1838, in *JSP*, J1:270–275.)

I have taken it upon me to answer it. You say, that you have heard of the deplorable state of things in Kirtland; and it gave me much Joy to learn by your letter, that you viewed those things in their true light.[735] Great has been the afflictions of the saints in that place, particularly our beloved Brotheren Joseph Smith J[r]., and S. Rigdon.

~~During~~ In the past summer; I Journeyed from this place in company with W[m] Smith, and D[avid] W. Patten, to Kirtland, for the purpose of meeting in Conference thare with the ~~12~~ ⟨twelve.⟩.[736] On our arrival, we soon learned the dificulties that then existed thare: these however ware all appearantly settled, preveious~~ly~~ to my leaving Kirtland: And ⟨W⟩ Parish [Warren Parrish], who has since become ~~so~~ ~~notoriously wicked~~ ⟨an unbeliever in ~~the book of Mormon,~~ reveiled religion,⟩, affected to repent and become sattisfied, with Br. Joseph and the Church: Others also did the same:[737] But this settlement was not of long duration. Soon after this, President Hyram Smith and I, left Kirtland for the upper Missouri:[738] and President Joseph Smith, President S. Rigdon, and ⟨Prest.⟩ W[m.] Smith,[739]

---

735. Letter from Wilford Woodruff et al., 9 Mar. 1838, pp. 34–39 herein.

736. After hearing reports of "much evil" regarding fellow apostles Luke Johnson, John F. Boynton, and Lyman Johnson, Marsh called for the apostles to meet in Kirtland on 24 July 1837 so he could help resolve problems and give counsel regarding the quorum's proselytizing plans. Marsh, William Smith, and Patten—who were members of the Quorum of the Twelve Apostles—departed Far West sometime in late May or June and arrived by 8 July 1837. (Thomas B. Marsh and David W. Patten, Far West, MO, to Parley P. Pratt, Toronto, Upper Canada, 10 May 1837, in JS Letterbook 2, pp. 62–63; "T. B. Marsh," [2], Historian's Office, Histories of the Twelve, 1856–1858, 1861, CHL; Mary Fielding, Kirtland, OH, to Mercy Fielding Thompson, Upper Canada, 8 July 1837, Mary Fielding Smith, Collection, CHL.)

737. At the reorganization conference held in early September 1837, members in Kirtland voted to retain in office JS and church leaders who were loyal to him. (See Minutes, 3 Sept. 1837, in *JSP*, D5:422–423.)

738. Marsh and Hyrum Smith left Kirtland in early September and arrived in Far West by mid-October 1837. (See Vilate Murray Kimball, Kirtland, OH, to Heber C. Kimball, Preston, England, ca. 10–12 Sept. 1837, Heber C. Kimball, Collection, CHL; and Power of Attorney to Hyrum Smith, 5 Sept. 1837, in *JSP*, D5:433–437.)

739. It is uncertain why Marsh inserted "Pres[iden]t" before William Smith's name. Smith was called "Pres[ident]" in two instances in JS's journal in 1836, but extant documents do not mention Smith, a member of the Quorum of the Twelve Apostles, being appointed president of any church council or quorum. It is possible that, like his brother Hyrum; his father, Joseph; and his uncle John, he was at some point included in the general church presidency, although there is no other evidence of him belonging to the presidency. The designation of Smith as "Pres[iden]t" was omitted in the version of the letter published in the July issue of the church newspaper. (JS, Journal, 28 Jan. and 6 Feb. 1836, in *JSP*, J1:174, 182; Minutes, 3 Sept. 1837, in *JSP*, D5:422; Thomas B. Marsh, [Far West, MO], to Wilford Woodruff, [Vinalhaven, ME], [ca. 18 June 1838], in *Elders' Journal*, July 1838, 36.)

soon followed us to Far West:[740] and during their absence, it seemes that ⟨M^{r.}⟩ Parish, J. F Bointon [John F. Boynton], Luke.— Johnson, Joseph Coe, and some others,[741] ~~plotted~~ ⟨united⟩ togeather in ~~for the overthrow~~ ⟨refuting the procedings⟩[742] of the Church.[743] President Smith and his company returned on or about the 10th. of December; soon after which this ~~gadian-ton~~[744] ⟨decenting [dissenting]⟩ band, openly, and publickly, renounced the Church of Christ of Latterday Saints, and claimed, themselves to be the old standard, called themslves the Church of Christ, ~~excluding~~ excluded that of saints, and set at naught B^{r.} Joseph and the whole Church, denounceing them as Hericks [p. [1]] How blind and infatuated are the minds of men, when once turned from Rigteousness to wickedness? They did not understand, that by taking upon them the name of Latter day Saints, did not do away that of the Church of Christ. Neither did they consider, that the ancient church, was the Church of Christ, and that they were Saints.[745] And again, it appears that they did not consider the Prophesy, of Daniel, which ⟨says⟩ ~~saith~~; "The <u>saints</u> shall take the King[d]om" &^c [746] "Again, "the Kingdom, and the greatness of the Kingdom, under the whole Heaven, was given to the people, (the <u>Saints</u>) of the most High" &^c [747] And the Saints here alluded to, were certainly Latterday Saints; inas much, as the above prophesy is to be fulfilled, in the Last days; and is yet future, as all professed readers of the bible will confess.[748] We have of late learned, that Parish, and

---

740. JS, Rigdon, William Smith, and Vinson Knight departed Kirtland for Far West on 27 September 1837. (Travel Account and Questions, Nov. 1837, in *JSP*, D5:480.)

741. Both John Smith and Vilate Kimball identified Parrish, Boynton, Johnson, Coe, and Martin Harris as "the Leaders" of the dissenting party. Smith also named Cyrus Smalling as a leader. (John Smith and Clarissa Lyman Smith, Kirtland, OH, to George A. Smith, Shinnston, VA, 1 Jan. 1838, George Albert Smith, Papers, CHL; Vilate Murray Kimball, Kirtland, OH, to Heber C. Kimball, Preston, England, 19–29 Jan. 1838, Heber C. Kimball, Collection, CHL.)

742. TEXT: Marsh apparently inserted "Prest." before "Wm. Smith", inserted "M^{r.}" before "Parish", and changed "for the overthrow" to "refuting the procedings" after the retained copy was made. Most of the other substantive revisions to the letter are reflected in the version of the letter published in the *Elders' Journal*.

743. Marsh apparently meant that this group intended to overturn the results of the September 1837 reorganization conference in which JS and members loyal to him were retained in their church offices. (See Minutes, 3 Sept. 1837, in *JSP*, D5:420–425.)

744. In the Book of Mormon, Gadianton was the founder of the "Gadianton robbers"—a secret society of political and religious dissenters who sought to obtain wealth and power through intrigue, murder, and war. (See Book of Mormon, 1830 ed., 411, 423, 427–428 [Helaman 2:8; 6:17–19; 7:21].)

745. See, for example, 1 Corinthians 14:33; see also Minutes, 3 May 1834, in *JSP*, D4:42–44.

746. Daniel 7:18.

747. Daniel 7:27.

748. The vision of Daniel culminated with all nations dissolving and with the people of God receiving everlasting dominion over the earth. (Daniel chap. 7.)

the most of this ~~wicked band~~ ⟨combination⟩, have openly renounced the Book of Mormon, and ⟨~~and~~⟩ be[c]ome deists[749]——I will now Leave Kirtland, and give you some acount of the movement of things here, as they are and have been.

You, undoubtedly, will remember the visit, which I, in company with Elder [Elisha] Groves, made to the Churches in Kentucky and Tennessee, in the summer of 1836. You also may reecollect, the nature and result, of our visit.[750] We came to solisit assistance, for <u>Poor</u> <u>bleeding</u> <u>zion</u>:[751] And we obtained, through the goodness of the Children of God, in those regeons, the sum of fourteen hundred and fifty dollars,[752] which we delivered unto Wm. Phelps & John Whitmer, on our arrival to this place.[753] But these men, instead of laying out the money for the benefit of <u>Poor</u> <u>bleeding</u> <u>zion</u>, purchased Land for their own emolument. They generally did their business, independant⟨ly⟩ of the aid, or council of ⟨either⟩ the bishop or High Council. This gave some uneasiness to the two authorities of zion: not only because they purchased land with Church funds, in their own name, for their own agrandisement,[754] but because they selected the place of the City Far West and appointed the spot for the House of the Lord to be built on, drew the plan of said house, and appointed and ordained a committee to build the same, without asking or seeking council, at the hand of either Bishop, High Council, or first presidency;[755] when it was well understood that these authorites wer

---

749. Early American Deists believed in a singular creator god and rejected all shades of polytheism, including Trinitarian theology. They tended to believe that the creator god was the architect of the universe, who after setting the stars and planets in motion withdrew from any further intervention. Deists rejected miracles, spiritual gifts, and any form of supernatural revelation, including those described in the Bible. They criticized classical Christian theology and espoused in its place a commonsense morality. (Holifield, *Theology in America,* 162–170.)

750. Woodruff had encountered Marsh while proselytizing in Kentucky in August and September 1836. (Woodruff, Journal, 29 Aug. and 2–4 Sept. 1836.)

751. Marsh and Groves were commissioned to raise money to help poor Latter-day Saints moving to Missouri. (Minute Book 2, 25 July 1836.)

752. This money was borrowed at 10 percent interest. ("T. B. Marsh," [2], Historian's Office, Histories of the Twelve, 1856–1858, 1861, CHL.)

753. When Marsh and Groves were commissioned to raise money, they were instructed to "put the same into the hands of the Zion Presidency." (Minute Book 2, 25 July 1836.)

754. Phelps and Whitmer purchased the original square mile for Far West in August 1836 and used the money raised by Marsh and Groves to purchase additional land in the vicinity in November 1836. Because the church was not incorporated in Missouri, church leaders could hold church property in their own names only. The use and administration of such property, however, was often subject to the deliberations of church councils. (Caldwell Co., MO, Original Land Entries, 1835–1859, p. 11, microfilm 2,438,695, U.S. and Canada Record Collection, FHL; Minute Book 1, 2 Apr. 1836.)

755. In November 1836, the Zion church presidency "selected and appointed Jacob Whitmer, Elisha H. Groves, and George M. Hinkle for a building committee to assist the Presidency to build the

⟨appointed⟩ for the purpose of counciling on all important matters pertaining to the saints of God.[756]

These two presidents also managed to get the town plott into their own hands,[757] that they ~~that they~~ might reap the avails ariseing from the sale of the lots. In consequence of these, with many other things, the Council met by themselves on the 3ᵈ· day of April 1837, and resolved to ~~meet on the 5~~ invite the two president⟨s⟩, the Bishop and his council, and the two apostles, namely T[homas] B. Marsh and D. W. Pattatten,[758] to meet with them, on the 5ᵗʰ· inst. to which time they adjourned.[759] Acordingly the above named authorites met, on the [p. [2]] 5ᵗʰ·, and after lbouring dilegently three days in succession, it was unanimously agreed upon, that the town ~~plott~~ Plat, with four eighties adjacent to the plat,[760] should be ~~given~~ at the disposal of the Bishop and his council the High Council, the two presidents, and the two

---

house of the Lord." In April 1837, the high council and the bishop and his counselors accepted the appointment of this committee and the Zion presidency's related plans. (Minute Book 2, 15 Nov. 1836 and 7 Apr. 1837.)

756. When the Zion high council was organized in 1834, JS told the council members "that he now had done his duty in organizing the High Council, through which Council the will of the Lord might be known on all importent occasions in the building up of Zion." (Minutes and Discourse, ca. 7 July 1834, in *JSP,* D4:93.)

757. Among their various holdings, Phelps and Whitmer owned the land for the platted town of Far West. Marsh may have been specifically referring to a map of Far West that was used for allotment—possibly a certified copy of the Far West plat. ("Description of Far West Plat," BYU Church History and Doctrine Department, Church History Project Collection, CHL.)

758. Most other members of the Quorum of the Twelve lived in Ohio or were on proselytizing missions. (See Thomas B. Marsh and David W. Patten, Far West, MO, to Parley P. Pratt, Toronto, Upper Canada, 10 May 1837, in JS Letterbook 2, pp. 62–63.)

759. According to the minutes of the meeting, the council prepared a list of questions for the two men, challenging the presidents' authority to unilaterally select and purchase the land for the new settlement, sell lots in the city plat for their own profit, designate the temple site, appoint a committee to help build the temple, and take other actions. Two of the questions focused on whether the land and proceeds from selling lots should remain in the hands of Phelps and Whitmer or whether some should be distributed to other church leaders as compensation for their services. (Minute Book 2, 3 Apr. 1837.)

760. The Far West plat was one mile square, constituting 640 acres, half of which were owned by Phelps and the other half by Whitmer. Between August 1836 and January 1837, Phelps and Whitmer purchased additional land in Caldwell County, including nineteen 80-acre tracts. Fourteen of these tracts were adjacent to or near the land platted for Far West. Of these fourteen, Phelps and Whitmer deeded to Edward Partridge the two tracts west of the town plat in sections 10 and 15, a tract located on the northeast corner of the plat in section 11, and a tract located about a half mile south of the plat in section 22 or section 23. ("Description of Far West Plat," BYU Church History and Doctrine Department, Church History Project Collection, CHL; Caldwell Co., MO, Original Land Entries, 1835–1859, p. 11, microfilm 2,438,695, U.S. and Canada Record Collection, FHL; Edward Partridge and Lydia Partridge, Mortgage, Far West, MO, to William W. Phelps and John Whitmer, 17 May 1837, John Whitmer Family Papers, CHL.)

apostles.[761] During this labour the two presidents acknoledged they were wrong, and they to all appearance, willingly suffered themselves to be corrected by the Council.

In the begining of May following, the Council again met, and resolved ~~to~~ to have the above named property transfered into the hands of the bishop,[762] as an equivalent to the <u>Poor</u> <u>bleeding</u> <u>zion</u> <u>money</u>,[763] and that the avails, of said land, should be thareafter applied to the benefit of the poor, and ~~the~~ other public purposes.[764] The business of the transfer of said property, was transacted by the two presidents, the Bishop and his council, and by some means they managed to bind the bishop in a ~~heavy~~ mortgage ⟨of three thousand four hundred and fifty dollars⟩ to apply two thousand dollars of the avails of the town plat ⟨which they had subscribed⟩ to the building of the House of worship,[765] which they intended to ~~build~~ ⟨have erected.⟩[766] Since that time, the affair of building the house has falen through.[767] Consequntly,

---

761. The minutes of the meeting clarify that this group would determine the disposition of the property. The minutes indicate the group included the high council, Bishop Partridge and his counselors, and the two apostles, but not Phelps and Whitmer. (Minute Book 2, 5–7 Apr. 1837.)

762. An undated resolution to this effect appears in a note following the minutes of a meeting on 5–7 April 1837. The land was transferred on 17 May 1837. (See Minute Book 2, 5–7 Apr. 1837; and Edward Partridge and Lydia Partridge, Mortgage, Far West, MO, to William W. Phelps and John Whitmer, 17 May 1837, John Whitmer Family Papers, CHL.)

763. The 640-acre plat and four additional 80-acre tracts totaled 960 acres. Purchased at the usual government fee of $1.25 per acre, the original value of this land totaled $1,200, which was $250 less than the $1,450 Marsh and Groves originally borrowed and delivered to Phelps and Whitmer in fall 1837. By this time, some of the lots would have included improvements that raised the original value of the parcels.

764. According to the conditions of the second of two bonds governing the transfer of the land from Phelps and Whitmer to Partridge, the proceeds from selling land were to be used to support poor Saints, purchase additional land for the church, build a house of the Lord in Far West, and establish a printing office. (Edward Partridge, Bond, Far West, MO, to William W. Phelps and John Whitmer, 17 May 1837, John Whitmer Family Papers, CHL.)

765. At some point prior to May 1837, Phelps and Whitmer each subscribed $1,000 to build a House of the Lord in Far West. The money was to be supplied through selling lots in the town. (Minute Book 2, 5–7 Apr. 1837.)

766. The transfer of the town plat and four 80-acre tracts from Phelps and Whitmer to Partridge was conditioned upon a mortgage and two bonds. The first bond required Partridge to pay Phelps and Whitmer $1,450 for the land and to take responsibility for their subscriptions of $1,000 each for building the House of the Lord. The second bond built on and was conditional upon the terms of the first bond and mortgage. This second bond restated the combined sum of $3,450 due to Phelps and Whitmer and established how the proceeds that Partridge earned from selling town lots could be used. The penalty for the first bond was $10,000, while the penalty for the second was $25,000. (Edward Partridge, Bonds, Far West, MO, to William W. Phelps and John Whitmer, 17 May 1837, John Whitmer Family Papers, CHL.)

767. The construction of the House of the Lord in Far West was postponed in November 1837. (Minutes, 6 Nov. 1837, in *JSP*, D5:467.)

many people have withdrawn ther subscription ~~to it~~, and these two men, claiming this two thousand dollars as their subscription, chuse to withdraw it, and put it into their own pockets. A small part of which has been already paid to W^m. W. Phelps.[768]

The Council, not feeling ⟨willing⟩ that the Church should be defrauded o[ut?] of two thousand dollars of her public funds,[769] and also know⟨ing⟩ that the Church in general as well as themselvs, had become dissatisfied with their conduct as Christians, in many things, appointed a committee to labour with them;[770] after which, they called the whole church in Zion togeathe[r], who almost unanimously voted them out of their presidenceal office.[771]

Not long after this, the Council saw cause to appoint a seccond committee, to wait on these men who still presisted in their opposition to the interests of the Church. After which, charges were prefered against them before the Council, which were substantiated, and they were ~~cut off~~ excommunicated.[772] Also, the Church has had much sorrow during the past winter, on account of the unfaithfulness of O. Cowdry [Oliver Cowdery], David Whitmer, and Lyman Johnson, and in consequence of this, and their opposition to our beloved Brothr Joseph Smith J^r., and the best interests of the Church of Jesus Christ, for presisting in the same, a number of Charges have been substantiated against them, before the Councils & bishop of the Church, and they have also been excluded from ~~the Church~~

----

768. Estate records for Edward Partridge list an undated payment of $187 to Phelps on a $2,000 debt owed to Phelps and Whitmer. (Account, Estate of Edward Partridge with John Whitmer, John Whitmer Family Papers, CHL.)

769. On 10 November 1837, four days after a conference of church officers voted to halt construction of the House of the Lord, priesthood holders at Far West voted that the funds generated from the sale of town lots would be "consecrated for the public benefit of the church— for building houses for public worship, or such other purposes as the church shall say." (Minutes, 10 Nov. 1837, in *JSP*, D5:475.)

770. In January 1838, members of the high council appointed George M. Hinkle, Thomas Grover, and George Morey to this committee. They visited the Zion presidency and Oliver Cowdery, who was functioning as the clerk for the Zion presidency and high council. The committee then reported to the high council regarding the sale of land in Jackson County and the Zion presidency's observance of the revealed dietary code known as the "Word of Wisdom." (Minute Book 2, 20 and 26 Jan. 1838.)

771. Meetings were held in February 1838 in Far West and in four outlying settlements. Based on the outcome of the meetings, David Whitmer and counselors William W. Phelps and John Whitmer were removed from the presidency of the church in Zion. (See Letter from Thomas B. Marsh, 15 Feb. 1838, pp. 22–23 herein.)

772. Phelps and John Whitmer were excommunicated in March 1838 for their financial dealings and related offenses. (Minute Book 2, 10 Mar. 1838.)

fellowship.[773] "How has the gold become dim the most fine gold changed"!!![774] But I mus[t] drop this subject for want of room. Suffice ⟨it⟩ to say Bretheren, J. Smith J[r.] & S. Rigdon are now with us,[775] the Church now flourishes, and the Saints rejoice, and the ⟨internal⟩ enemies of the Church are <u>down</u>. You will see by the above prospectes, that your anxious desires for the Journal are about to be granted.[776]

May the God of Abraham, Isaac, and Jacob, bless you,[777] and keep you unto his coming and Kingdom, Amen. My love to all the saints in those regeons.

Yours in the Love of God.

Thomas B. Marsh

Wilford Wooruff [p. [3]]

P. S. Since B[r.] Joseph came to this place, we have been favored with a lengthy revelation, in which many important items are shown forth.[778] First, that ~~he~~ the Church, shall hereafter be Called, "The Church of Jesus Christ of Latter day Saints" Second it ~~saith~~ ⟨says⟩ "Let the City Farwest be a holy and a consecrated land unto me, and it shall be called most holy, for the ground upon which thou standest is holy: Therefore, I command you to build an house unto me, for the geathering togeather of my Saints, that they may worship me" &[c] It also teaches, that the foundation or corner stone must be laid on the 4[th.] of July nex, and that a commencement must be made in this following season, and in one year from the 26[th.] of April last, the foundation must be again commenced, and from that time, to continue the worke untill it is finished. Thus we see that the Lord is more wise than men, for Phelps and Whitmer thought to commence it long before this,[779] but it was not the Lords time, tharefore, he overthrew it. and has appointed his own time. The plan is

---

773. Cowdery, Whitmer, and Johnson were excommunicated on a variety of charges in April 1838. (See Minutes, 12 Apr. 1838, pp. 84–94 herein; and Minutes, 13 Apr. 1838, pp. 95–104 herein.)

774. Lamentations 4:1.

775. JS and Rigdon arrived in Far West in March and April, respectively. (JS, Journal, Mar.–Sept. 1838, p. 16, in *JSP*, J1:237; JS History, vol. B-1, 786.)

776. Woodruff pleaded in his 9 March 1838 letter to church leaders that the *Elders' Journal* be recommenced in Missouri. (Letter from Wilford Woodruff et al., 9 Mar. 1838, p. 36 herein.)

777. This wording echoes language Woodruff used in his letter. (See Letter from Wilford Woodruff et al., 9 Mar. 1838, p. 38 herein.)

778. See Revelation, 26 Apr. 1838, pp. 112–118 herein [D&C 115].

779. Under the direction of the Zion presidency, Latter-day Saints in Far West began excavating for the House of the Lord in July 1837 and then began planning construction, but plans were postponed in November at the direction of the First Presidency. (Letter from William W. Phelps, 7 July 1837, in *JSP*, D5:402–403; Minutes, 6 Nov. 1837, in *JSP*, D5:467.)

to yet be shown to the first presidency,[780] and all the saints, in all the world, are commanded to assist in building the house

Thomas B. Marsh.—

Mᴿ· Wilford Woodruff
Vinalhaven.
Fox Islands
Me.
/[781] FAR WEST Mo.
JUNE 18
/[782] 23 [p. [4]]

———— ❦ ————

Minutes, 28 June 1838

Source Note

Minutes, Adam-ondi-Ahman, Daviess Co., MO, 28 June 1838. Featured version published in Elders' Journal, *Aug. 1838, 60–61. For more information on* Elders' Journal, *see Source Notes for Multiple-Entry Documents, p. 563 herein.*

Historical Introduction

On 28 June 1838, JS served as the chairman of a conference to organize a stake of Zion at Adam-ondi-Ahman in Daviess County, Missouri. Two months earlier, on 26 April 1838, a revelation had designated nearby Far West, in Caldwell County, as a holy place in which to build a city of Zion and a temple.[783] In addition, the revelation directed that "other places" should also "be appointed for stakes in the regions round about as they shall be manifested unto my Servant Joseph from time to time."[784] JS had long contemplated establishing multiple places of gathering in Missouri. In 1833, JS explained that when growth necessitated expansion beyond the original plat of the city of Zion in Jackson County, Missouri, the Saints could develop another plat "in the same way and so fill up the world in these last days."[785] By 1837 it was time to expand, and in September church leaders in Kirtland selected JS and Sidney Rigdon to go to Missouri and "appoint other Stakes or

---

780. JS's April 1838 revelation regarding Far West and the temple stated that the Latter-day Saints were to build the temple "according to the pattern which I Shall shew unto their presidency." (Revelation, 26 Apr. 1838, p. 116 herein [D&C 115:16].)

781. TEXT: Postmark stamped in red ink.

782. TEXT: Postage written in red ink in unidentified handwriting.

783. Revelation, 26 Apr. 1838, p. 115 herein [D&C 115:7–8].

784. Revelation, 26 Apr. 1838, p. 116 herein [D&C 115:18].

785. Plat of the City of Zion, ca. Early June–25 June 1833, in *JSP,* D3:128.

places of gathering" in addition to Far West.[786] After traveling to Missouri, JS and Rigdon met with local church officers, who affirmed the assignment to locate sites for future settlement and established a committee to assist in locating sites.[787] One of the committee members was Oliver Cowdery, who reported that he had found an abundance of sites for mills and settlements to the north.[788] Another committee member, Lyman Wight, soon settled with his family north of Far West on the Grand River in Daviess County.[789]

In the second half of May 1838, JS and several others traveled north to Daviess County to survey land for Latter-day Saint settlement, using church member Lyman Wight's home on the Grand River as a base of operations. On 21 May, the surveying party decided that instead of exploring further northward, they should focus on securing all the land they could on the Grand River, especially in the vicinity of Wight's farm, by a bluff they called Spring Hill. Around this time, JS dictated a revelation stating that Spring Hill "was called Adam Ondi Awmen, because said he it is the place where Adam shall come to visit his people."[790] The word *Awmen* (also spelled *Ahman, Ah Man,* and *Awman*) was not new to JS. In 1832 he produced a document titled "Sample of Pure Language," which stated *Awmen* was the name of God in the language of Adam.[791] In 1835 JS taught that Adam, before dying, had gathered "the residue of his posterity, who were righteous, into the valley of Adam-ondi-ahman, and there bestowed upon them his last blessing."[792] According to John Corrill, when JS applied this name to Spring Hill, he gave the following interpretation in English: "The valley of God, in which Adam blessed his children."[793] JS returned to Far West at the end of the month.[794]

In early June 1838, JS and others returned to Daviess County. According to JS's journal, the group "continued surveying and building houses &c for some time day after day."[795] The surveying culminated in the completion of a city plat for Adam-ondi-Ahman, likely by

---

786. Minutes, 17 Sept. 1837–B, in *JSP,* D5:445.

787. Travel Account and Questions, Nov. 1837, in *JSP,* D5:481; see also Minutes, 6 Nov. 1837, in *JSP,* D5:467.

788. Travel Account and Questions, Nov. 1837, in *JSP,* D5:481; Letter from Oliver Cowdery, 21 Jan. 1838, in *JSP,* D5:504–505.

789. Minutes, 7–8 Apr. 1838, p. 73 herein; Corrill, *Brief History,* 28, in *JSP,* H2:163; JS, Journal, 18 May–1 June 1838, in *JSP,* J1:271; Lyman Wight, Mountain Valley, TX, to Wilford Woodruff, [Salt Lake City], 24 Aug. 1857, p. 9, Historian's Office, Histories of the Twelve, 1856–1858, 1861, CHL.

790. JS, Journal, 18 May–1 June 1838, in *JSP,* J1:271–273; see also Swartzell, *Mormonism Exposed,* 11–12.

791. Sample of Pure Language, between ca. 4 and ca. 20 Mar. 1832, in *JSP,* D2:215; see also William W. Phelps, Kirtland, OH, to Sally Waterman Phelps, Liberty, MO, 26 May 1835, William W. Phelps, Papers, BYU.

792. Instruction on Priesthood, between ca. 1 Mar. and ca. 4 May 1835, in *JSP,* D4:317 [D&C 107:53].

793. Corrill, *Brief History,* 28, in *JSP,* H2:163; see also Letter to Stephen Post, 17 Sept. 1838, p. 242 herein.

794. JS returned to Far West on 24 May. On 28 May, JS was headed north of Far West to scout out further locations for settlement. He returned again to Far West on 1 June, the day before the birth of his son Alexander Hale Smith. (JS, Journal, 18 May–1 June 1838, in *JSP,* J1:271–273.)

795. JS, Journal, 4–5 June 1838, in *JSP,* J1:275.

John Smith. Circa 1852. Joseph Smith's uncle John Smith was appointed president of the Adam-ondi-Ahman stake of Zion on 28 June 1838. Reynolds Cahoon and Lyman Wight were appointed as his counselors in the presidency. (Church History Library, Salt Lake City. Photograph likely by Marsena Cannon.)

Adam-ondi-Ahman, Missouri. 2000. On 28 June 1838, Joseph Smith presided at the formal organization of Adam-ondi-Ahman as a stake of Zion. In 1835, Smith taught that Adam-ondi-Ahman was the location where Adam, the father of the human race, blessed his posterity before he died. In April 1838, Smith dictated a revelation identifying the location of Adam-ondi-Ahman and indicating that Adam, presumably in a resurrected state, would visit the Saints in Adam-ondi-Ahman. (© Intellectual Reserve, Inc. Photograph by Matthew Reier.)

the end of the month.[796] During this time, JS's uncle John Smith—a former member of the church presidency in Kirtland—arrived in Far West with six other families who had moved from Kirtland to be with the Latter-day Saints in Missouri. According to JS's history, JS "counseled them to settle at Adam ondiahman."[797] William Swartzell, who was already living there, reported that on 24 June the First Presidency "called a meeting" at Adam-ondi-Ahman to organize the church there. The meaning of "called" is unclear; Swartzell may have been referring to a circulated announcement about the organizational meeting to be held on 28 June, or he may have been describing the meeting itself, giving the wrong date.[798] Two days before the meeting, John Smith and those traveling with him arrived at Adam-ondi-Ahman.[799]

On the morning of 28 June 1838, JS served as the chairman at the "conference meeting," which convened near Wight's home. During the meeting, Adam-ondi-Ahman was organized as a stake with a presidency, a high council, and a temporary bishop. John Smith and other former officers in the presidency and bishopric of the Kirtland stake, which was being disbanded, were appointed to fill similar roles in the stake in Adam-ondi-Ahman. After these and other appointments, JS gave instruction to the new officers.

The minutes of the meeting close by listing JS as the chairman, possibly indicating that he approved of the minutes, and Isaac Perry and Lorenzo Barnes as the clerks.[800] At some point, the decision was made to publish the minutes in the *Elders' Journal*.[801] Sidney Rigdon, who had been appointed in May to edit articles for the paper, may have helped prepare the minutes for publication.[802] A fair copy was probably prepared for the printers to use in typesetting. The minutes were published in the August issue of the *Elders' Journal*.

Document Transcript

For the Elders Journal—
CONFERENCE MINUTES.

A conference meeting of Elders, and members, of the church of Christ of Latter Day Saints, was held in this place, this day, for the purpose of organziing this stake of Zion, called Adam-ondi-ahman. The meeting convened at 10 o'clock A. M. in the grove near the house of elder Lyman Wight.[803] President

---

796. JS History, vol. B-1, 799; see also "Record Book A," in Sherwood, Record Book, CHL.

797. John Smith, Journal, 16 June 1838; JS History, vol. B-1, addenda, 6nV.

798. Swartzell, *Mormonism Exposed*, 13. This passage in Swartzell's publication may be a retrospective expansion on his original journal entry. John Smith wrote in his journal that JS "called thelders to gether." (John Smith, Journal, 28 June 1838.)

799. John Smith, Journal, 26 June 1838.

800. Barnes was appointed clerk for the high council and the stake at the end of the conference.

801. The Zion high council had decided to publish meeting minutes in the *Elders' Journal* when deemed proper. Four sets of minutes were published in the July issue. (Minutes, 21 Apr. 1838, pp. 110, 111 herein; *Elders' Journal*, July 1838, 44–47.)

802. Minute Book 2, 12 May 1838; see also Minutes, 6 Aug. 1838, in JS, Journal, 6 Aug. 1838, in *JSP*, J1:298.

803. Meetings were held frequently in this grove.ᵃ Swartzell described it as "a grove, in the woods, adjoining brother White's house," that was "situated between Grand River and a large prairie, well timbered

Joseph Smith Jr. was called. to the chair, who explained the object [p. 60] of the meeting, which was to organize a Presidency, and High Council, to preside over this stake of Zion, and attend to the affairs of the church in Daviess county.[804] It was then motioned, seconded and carried, by the unanimous voice of the assembly, that Pr's John Smith, should act as President of the stake of Adam-ondi-ahman. Reynolds Cahoon was unanimously chosen 1st and Lyman Wight 2nd counsellors. After prayer, the Presidents proceded to the ordination of elder Wight as 2nd assistant counsellor.[805] Vinson Knight was then chosen acting Bishop pro tempore by the unanimous voice of the assembly.[806] President John Smith, then proceded to organize the high council. The counsellors were chosen according to the following order, by a unanimous vote. John Lemon 1st, Daniel Stanton 2nd, Mayhew Hillman 3rd, Daniel Carter 4th, Isaac Perry 5th, Harrison Sagers 6th, Alanson Brown 7th, Thomas Gordon 8th, Lorenzo Barnes 9th, George A. Smith 10th, Harvey Olmstead [Olmsted] 11th, Ezra Thayer 12th.[807]

After the ordination of the counsellors, who had not previously been ordained to the high priesthood.[808] President J. Smith Jr. made remarks by

and beautifully shaded" and that had several benches "made out of trees split in two."[b] Wight had purchased and was working Adam Black's farm,[c] which was situated on the floodplain between the bluffs and the river.[d] The grove was apparently within uncleared land along the riverside. (a. See John Smith, Journal, 1 and 8 July 1838; and Swartzell, *Mormonism Exposed*, 14. b. Swartzell, *Mormonism Exposed*, 17, 20; see also Berrett, *Sacred Places*, 4:439, 443–444. c. Lyman Wight, Testimony, Nauvoo, IL, 1 July 1843, p. 11, Nauvoo, IL, Records, CHL; Orange Wight, Reminiscences, 8. d. "Fractional Township 60 North of the Base Line Range 27. West of 5th Principal Meridian," Daviess Co., MO, 15 Sept. 1838; "Fractional Township 60 North of the Base Line Range 28 West of 5th Principal Meridian," Daviess Co., MO, 15 Sept. 1838, in *Public Land Survey Township Plats,* reel 47; Orange Wight, Adam-ondi-Ahman Diagram, CHL; Berrett, *Sacred Places,* 4:439.)

804. In addition to the church members in Adam-ondi-Ahman, groups of Saints had settled in southern Daviess County at Marrowbone Creek, Honey Creek, Lick Fork, and possibly other locations. (*History of Daviess County, Missouri,* 188–190; Berrett, *Sacred Places,* 4:358, 366–370, 493–496.)

805. John Smith and Reynolds Cahoon had previously served in the church presidency in Kirtland. (John Smith and Clarissa Lyman Smith, Kirtland, OH, to George A. Smith, Shinnston, VA, 1 Jan. 1838, George Albert Smith, Papers, CHL; Hepzibah Richards, Kirtland, OH, to Willard Richards, Bedford, England, 18–19 Jan. 1838, Willard Richards, Papers, CHL; see also Shurtleff and Cahoon, *Reynolds Cahoon,* 4.)

806. Knight previously served as a counselor to Bishop Newel K. Whitney in Kirtland. Knight may have been appointed as the temporary bishop pending Whitney's arrival. (Minutes, 13 Jan. 1836, in *JSP,* D5:140; Minutes, 3 Sept. 1837, in *JSP,* D5:420–425; see also Revelation, 8 July 1838–E, pp. 191–194 herein [D&C 117].)

807. The men were probably numbered by casting lots, as had been done at the organizations of the Ohio and Missouri high councils in 1834. The numbers were used in council meetings to determine speaking order. (Minutes, 17 Feb. 1834, in *JSP,* D3:437; Minutes and Discourse, ca. 7 July 1834, in *JSP,* D4:94.)

808. The high councils of the church were to be composed of high priests. George A. Smith later recounted that he was ordained a high priest on this occasion by John Lemon. John Smith noted in his journal that after the appointment of the presidency and high council, "the Council decides that I must live in the city and see to the affairs of the church." (George A. Smith, Autobiography, 71; John Smith,

way of charge to the Presidents and counsellors, instructing them in the duty of their callings, and the responsibility of their stations; exhorting them to be cautious and deliberate, in all their councils, and to be careful to act in righteousness in all things.[809] President John Smith, R. Cahoon and Lyman Wight, then made some remarks. Lorenzo Barnes was unanimously chosen clerk of this council and stake;[810] and after singing the well known hymn Adam-ondi-ahman,[811] the meeting closed by prayer by Pres. Cahoon, and a benediction by Pres. J. Smith Jr.[812]

Adam-ondi-ahman Mo.
Daviess Co. June 28 1838.

J. SMITH Jr. *Chairman.*

LORENZO BARNES
ISAAC PERRY.   } Clerks,

Journal, 28 June 1838; see also Revelation, 11 Nov. 1831–B, in *JSP,* D2:134–135 [D&C 107:79]; and Minutes, 17 Feb. 1834, in *JSP,* D3:436–437.)

809. JS offered similar instruction when he organized the high councils in Kirtland and Missouri in 1834. (Minutes, 17 Feb. 1834, in *JSP,* D3:437; Minutes, 19 Feb. 1834, in *JSP,* D3:446; Minutes and Discourse, ca. 7 July 1834, in *JSP,* D4:93.)

810. Barnes had previously been a schoolteacher. (Barnes, Reminiscences and Diaries, vol. 1, p. 2.)

811. Hymn 23, *Collection of Sacred Hymns,* 29–30. "Adam-ondi-Ahman" was written by William W. Phelps in 1835. ("Adam-ondi-Ahman," *LDS Messenger and Advocate,* June 1835, 1:144.)

812. The primary definition of *benediction* in Noah Webster's 1828 dictionary is "the act of blessing; a giving praise to God or rendering thanks for his favors; a blessing pronounced." ("Benediction," in *American Dictionary.*)

PART 2: 8 JULY– 29 OCTOBER 1838

Part 2 covers the period from July to October 1838. During July 1838, JS and his agents attempted to improve the church's financial standing and further develop Mormon settlements in Missouri, particularly Far West in Caldwell County, Adam-ondi-Ahman in Daviess County, and De Witt in Carroll County. In August the outbreak of violence between Latter-day Saints and other Missourians resulted in legal difficulties and opposition that led to further conflict in September and October. The expansion of the Mormon presence in northwestern Missouri and the resulting conflicts are the subject of many of the documents in part 2.

JS had spent much of June 1838 in Daviess County laying out and building Adam-ondi-Ahman, which was organized as a stake by the end of the month.[1] About the same time, the church purchased land in De Witt to serve as another place for the Saints to settle. Latter-day Saint George M. Hinkle moved from Far West to De Witt to help lead the Saints who would settle there.[2] Sometime in early or mid-July, JS moved into Hinkle's Far West home, which was located in the southwest quadrant of the town.[3] Several documents produced during the period of July to October 1838 were probably created in this home.

This period also saw the formation of the Society of the Daughter of Zion,[4] a private military group established in response to fears that church dissenters who were expelled from Caldwell County in mid-June would encourage residents of surrounding counties to oppose or even engage in mob violence against the Saints.[5] In late June or the first few days of July, Latter-day Saint men who had been active in the discussions leading to the

---

1. Minutes, 28 June 1838, p. 165 herein.

2. Murdock, Journal, 23 June 1838, 95; John Murdock, Affidavit, Adams Co., IL, 10 Jan. 1840, photocopy, Material relating to Mormon Expulsion from Missouri, 1839–1843, CHL.

3. Minute Book 2, 6 July 1838; "List of Names of the Church of Latter Day Saints Living in the S W Quarter of Far West," 25 Mar. 1838, p. [5], in Teachers Quorum Minutes, CHL.

4. The name was apparently a reference to militant imagery in the biblical book of Micah: "Arise and thresh, O daughter of Zion: for I will make thine horn iron, and I will make thy hoofs brass: and thou shalt beat in pieces many people: and I will consecrate their gain unto the Lord, and their substance unto the Lord of the whole earth." (Micah 4:13; see also Corrill, *Brief History*, 32, in *JSP*, H2:168.)

5. Reed Peck, Testimony, Richmond, MO, Nov. 1838, p. [63], State of Missouri v. JS et al. for Treason and Other Crimes (Mo. 5th Jud. Cir. 1838), in State of Missouri, "Evidence"; JS, Journal, 8 July 1838, in *JSP*, J1:284; see also Oliver Cowdery et al., Far West, MO, ca. 17 June 1838, at josephsmithpapers.org.

expulsion of dissenters formally organized the military group, which by the end of July was known as the Danite society.[6] The preamble to the society's constitution declared the intention of the Danites to defend the Saints' rights and religion.[7] John Corrill, who attended some of the Danites' early meetings but soon after left the church, recounted that the First Presidency attended one of the first meetings, during which JS introduced the officers and indicated that "they wanted to be prepared for future events." According to Corrill's account, JS also explained that "he wished to do nothing unlawful & if the people would let him alone they [the Latter-day Saints] would preach the gospel & live in peace."[8] Corrill and others who later testified against JS reported that at about the same time, JS delivered a public sermon in which he took a more aggressive stance. Abner Scovil recounted that JS told the audience, "If the people would let him alone he would conquer them by the sword of the Spirit, but if they would not he would beat the plow shears into swords & their pruning hooks into spears & conquer them."[9] Other accounts of this sermon similarly note that JS declared the Saints would no longer subject themselves to mob violence.[10] JS and the Danites were determined to defend the Saints, even threatening retribution against any mob that sought to oppress church members.

This stance was announced more broadly in an oration Sidney Rigdon delivered at the church-sponsored Independence Day celebration held at Far West's public square on 4 July 1838. A crowd of thousands—including both Latter-day Saints and other Missourians—gathered for this event, which JS presided over and which included the participation of various church, militia, and Danite officers. The celebration began with a parade, with contingents representing the Caldwell County militia and the Danite society, and also featured the laying of cornerstones for a temple, which indicated that the Saints intended to remain in the area.[11] Then Rigdon gave his oration, affirming the loyalty of the Latter-day Saints to the United States and to the principles of civil and religious liberty. After reviewing the history of violence against the Saints, Rigdon stated that the Saints intended to defend their rights against any future persecution. He concluded by declaring that although the Saints would never be the aggressors, if faced with further mob violence they not only would defend themselves but would also wage "a war of extermination" against their enemies.[12] Ebenezer Robinson, the clerk of the high council in Far West, recounted decades later that

---

6. JS, Journal, 27 July 1838, in *JSP,* J1:293. JS later stated that this name came from Judges chapter 18, which describes the Israelite tribe of Dan—the Danites—conquering territory. JS explained that he introduced the term *Danite* when alluding to Judges chapter 18 at a time "when the brethren prepared to defend themselves from the mob in Far West." (Nauvoo City Council Draft Minutes, 3 Jan. 1844, 36.)

7. See Constitution of the Society of the Daughter of Zion, ca. Late June 1838, at josephsmithpapers.org.

8. John Corrill, Testimony, Richmond, MO, Nov. 1838, p. [30], in State of Missouri, "Evidence."

9. Abner Scovil, Testimony, Richmond, MO, Nov. 1838, p. [50], in State of Missouri, "Evidence."

10. See, for example, John Corrill, Testimony, Richmond, MO, Nov. 1838, pp. [30]–[31]; George Walter, Testimony, Richmond, MO, Nov. 1838, p. [35]; George M. Hinkle, Testimony, Richmond, MO, Nov. 1838, p. [42], in State of Missouri, "Evidence"; see also Thomas B. Marsh and Orson Hyde, Affidavit, Richmond, MO, 24 Oct. 1838, copy, Mormon War Papers, MSA.

11. JS, Journal, 4 July 1838, in *JSP,* J1:275–278; "Celebration of the 4th of July," *Elders' Journal,* Aug. 1838, 60.

12. Discourse, ca. 4 July 1838, at josephsmithpapers.org.

Joe Smith's House.

Joseph Smith home in Far West, Missouri. Joseph Smith lived in at least three homes at Far West, Missouri: George W. Harris's house, the Samuel Musick tavern, and a house he purchased from fellow Latter-day Saint George M. Hinkle in June 1838. A state history published in 1877 included "a faithful picture" of one of Smith's homes in Far West—likely the last of the three—as it stood at the time. The accompanying historical sketch described the home as "a rude, old-fashioned, one-story frame building, with two rooms"; the home's distinguishing characteristic was "an unusually large and clumsy" chimney. The home was apparently torn down in the 1880s, but the site remained a place of historic pilgrimage for Latter-day Saints well into the twentieth century. One visitor retrieved this brick fragment from the remains of the chimney and subsequently donated it to the church in the 1930s. (Home image from C. R. Barns, ed., *The Commonwealth of Missouri: A Centennial Record* [St. Louis: Bryan, Brand & Co., 1877], 242. Brick image: Courtesy Church History Museum, Salt Lake City. Photograph by Alex D. Smith.)

when Rigdon concluded, JS "led off with the shout of Hosanna, Hosanna, Hosanna."[13] Robinson printed the oration in pamphlet form, and JS included a recommendation in the August issue of the *Elders' Journal* that the Latter-day Saints purchase the pamphlet.[14]

On 6 and 7 July, the church held its second quarterly conference of the year, and on 8 July, JS dictated five revelations related to the organization of church leadership and resources in Missouri. The first revelation named new apostles—John Taylor, John E. Page, Wilford Woodruff, and Willard Richards—to replace those who had been removed in the previous months for dissent and apostasy. The revelation also directed all members of the quorum to prepare for a mission "over the great waters" the following spring.[15] The second revelation addressed the subject of former church leaders who had been removed, excommunicated, and then rebaptized. This revelation directed that former church presidents Frederick G. Williams and William W. Phelps be ordained elders and that they travel, preach, and proselytize.[16] The third and fourth revelations dealt with church finances, outlining a plan for raising church revenue and directing that donations be managed by a council consisting of the First Presidency and other leaders.[17] The fifth revelation, concerning both finances and leadership, instructed William Marks and Newel K. Whitney to settle church finances in Kirtland, Ohio, and relocate to Missouri before winter in order to help lead the church there. Later that day, JS and his counselors in the First Presidency wrote a letter to Marks and Whitney, conveying the text of the revelation and encouraging Marks, Whitney, and all faithful Latter-day Saints in Kirtland to move to Missouri.[18]

At least the first three revelations were read to the congregation of Saints who attended the worship service held that day.[19] When JS and his counselors visited Adam-ondi-Ahman about two days later, they probably shared the new revelations with the Saints living there.[20] In response to the revelations, the Saints began donating personal property to the church, with the Danites helping gather the donations. On 26 July, JS convened a council of church leaders, as instructed in the fourth of the 8 July revelations, to determine how to manage the donations.[21]

During the remainder of July, the members of the First Presidency were "chiefly engaged in counciling and settling the emigrants to this land," according to George W. Robinson.[22] By

---

13. Robinson also recalled that the speech "was a carefully prepared document, previously written, and well understood by the First Presidency," suggesting that JS was involved in the speech's production. (Ebenezer Robinson, "Items of Personal History of the Editor," *Return,* Nov. 1889, 170.)

14. Selections from *Elders' Journal,* Aug. 1838, p. 216 herein.

15. Revelation, 8 July 1838–A, pp. 179–180 herein [D&C 118:4, 6].

16. Revelation, 8 July 1838–B, pp. 181–183 herein.

17. Revelation, 8 July 1838–C, pp. 183–189 herein [D&C 119]; Revelation, 8 July 1838–D, pp. 189–190 herein [D&C 120].

18. Revelation, 8 July 1838–E, pp. 191–194 herein [D&C 117]; Letter to William Marks and Newel K. Whitney, 8 July 1838, pp. 194–197 herein.

19. JS, Journal, 8 July 1838, in *JSP,* J1:284–288.

20. JS History, vol. B-1, 804.

21. Revelation, 8 July 1838–C, pp. 187–189 herein [D&C 119]; Revelation, 8 July 1838–D, p. 190 herein [D&C 120:1]; Minutes, 26 July 1838, pp. 207–208 herein; see also JS, Journal, 27 July 1838, in *JSP,* J1:293.

22. JS, Journal, 8 July 1838, in *JSP,* J1:284.

then, several thousand Saints had moved to Caldwell County, particularly to Far West.[23] A history the church published two years later in Nauvoo, Illinois, stated that by summer 1838, "there were from one hundred to one hundred and fifty dwelling houses erected in that place, six dry good stores in operation, one grocery and several mechanic shops. There were in the county, nearly or quite three hundred farms opened and several thousand acres under cultivation also, four saw and five grist mills doing good business."[24] The Mormon presence in Far West and in neighboring counties in northwestern Missouri was becoming a force to be reckoned with.

Violence between Mormons and non-Mormons in northwestern Missouri broke out in Gallatin, Daviess County, during the election held on 6 August 1838, with federal, state, and local offices on the ballot. William Peniston, a Whig candidate for the Missouri House of Representatives, wanted to limit the voting power of the Mormon population in the county. As Latter-day Saints approached the polls in Gallatin, Peniston persuaded a crowd of men that the Saints should not be permitted to vote. When one of the men attempted to strike a Latter-day Saint, a fight ensued. The Danites who were present rallied to defend themselves and other Saints against the mob. Although several on both sides were injured, no one was killed. Few, if any, church members voted.[25]

Reports of the riot reached Far West the following day, with exaggerated claims that two or three church members had been killed. Consistent with Rigdon's Independence Day declaration that the Saints would retaliate against mobs, the First Presidency, Danite commanders, and other church members in Caldwell County marched to Daviess County on 7 August. Upon arriving in Adam-ondi-Ahman, the church's main settlement in Daviess County, they learned that although several Saints were injured during the Gallatin affray, no one had been killed. They also heard rumors that Daviess County justice of the peace Adam Black was organizing anti-Mormon vigilantes with the intention of driving the Saints out of the county. The following day, more than one hundred armed Latter-day Saints rode to Black's residence to investigate the truth of the rumors. After an intense exchange, Black agreed to write and sign a statement pledging to leave the Saints alone and uphold the law.[26]

The Latter-day Saints left Black's home believing that the tense situation had been resolved, but Black immediately took legal action. He prepared an affidavit claiming that JS and Lyman Wight—who was the most well-known church member living in Daviess County—had led more than one hundred men to Black's residence, threatened his life, and forced him to sign an agreement against his will. Black went to neighboring Livingston County to rally support against the Saints, while Peniston and other allies went to Richmond, Ray County, Missouri, where they prepared a complaint repeating Black's claims and then presented it before Judge Austin A. King of Missouri's fifth judicial circuit. Based on the complaint, King issued a warrant for the arrest of JS and Wight. Daviess County sheriff

---

23. Berrett, *Sacred Places,* 4:288; *History of Caldwell and Livingston Counties, Missouri,* 118.

24. "A History, of the Persecution," *Times and Seasons,* Mar. 1840, 1:66, in *JSP,* H2:232; see also *History of Caldwell and Livingston Counties, Missouri,* 121.

25. See Historical Introduction to Affidavit, 5 Sept. 1838, pp. 219–222 herein; and Butler, "Short Account of an Affray," [1]–[4], CHL; see also LeSueur, "Mixing Politics with Religion," 184–208.

26. See Affidavit, 5 Sept. 1838, pp. 222–225 herein.

William Morgan went to Adam-ondi-Ahman to serve the warrant on Wight, but Wight reportedly rebuffed the sheriff. Morgan then went to Far West, where JS told the sheriff he was willing to submit to arrest but that he preferred to be tried in Caldwell County rather than in Daviess County. Morgan then traveled to Richmond to consult with King; when the sheriff returned to Far West, he reportedly acknowledged that he was outside of his jurisdiction and could not take JS. Rumors quickly circulated that the Latter-day Saint leaders were resisting arrest.[27]

At the beginning of September 1838, JS received word that a multicounty anti-Mormon vigilante force was forming to arrest him and Wight. In an attempt to defuse the rising tension, JS contacted King and obtained legal counsel from David R. Atchison, who was an attorney and also a major general in the Missouri militia. King arranged to preside over a preliminary hearing to be held just north of the border between Caldwell and Daviess counties. On 5 September, in preparation for the hearing, JS prepared an affidavit describing the 8 August confrontation at Black's home.[28] At the hearing, held 7 September, King found probable cause to believe that JS and Wight had committed a misdemeanor during the confrontation. The judge therefore held that the two men should appear at the next session of the Daviess County Circuit Court.[29] Following the hearing, JS and Rigdon met with Sterling Price and Edgar Flory, who had been sent by Chariton County citizens to investigate the situation. In response, the church leaders prepared an affidavit addressing rumors that the Latter-day Saints had been conspiring with Native Americans to attack other Missourians.[30]

Missouri vigilantes were not placated by the results of the 7 September hearing. Instead of dispersing, the vigilantes began taking Mormon captives and arranged to acquire militia rifles from Ray County to use in an attack on the Saints in Daviess County. On 9 September, upon learning of these developments, a company of ten Latter-day Saints under the command of William Allred intercepted the guns and arrested the men transporting the arms shipment. Around this time, JS and Rigdon wrote to King, seeking counsel. The judge replied on 10 September, assuring the church leaders that the detained Latter-day Saints would be released unharmed and insisting that JS and Rigdon release the arrested gunrunners. King also stated that he had advised Major General Atchison to call out two hundred militiamen to maintain order.[31] On 12 September 1838, Brigadier General Alexander Doniphan, acting under Atchison's orders, arrived in Far West and assumed custody of the gunrunners and the rifles.[32]

Doniphan proceeded to Daviess County, where he sought to resolve the impasse between the Mormons and the anti-Mormon vigilantes by meeting with representatives from both sides and arranging for a preliminary hearing on 18 September. On that date, Daviess County justices of the peace John Wright and Elijah Foley evaluated the evidence against

---

27. Historical Introduction to Affidavit, 5 Sept. 1838, pp. 220–221 herein; JS, Journal, 16–18 Aug. 1838, in *JSP*, J1:304.

28. Historical Introduction to Affidavit, 5 Sept. 1838, pp. 221–222 herein.

29. See Historical Introduction to Recognizance, 7 Sept. 1838, pp. 226–227 herein.

30. See Affidavit, 8 Sept. 1838, pp. 233–236 herein.

31. See Letter from Austin A. King, 10 Aug. 1838, pp. 239–240 herein.

32. See 239n386; 240n388 herein.

thirteen church members who were allegedly at Black's home on 8 August. Rather than defend themselves in the court's hostile environment, the Latter-day Saints agreed to appear before the next session of the Daviess County Circuit Court. Seeing that the militia intended to uphold the law, the vigilantes dispersed.[33]

However, the calm proved to be short lived. In October 1838, the conflict between the Saints and other Missourians reignited and then violently exploded.[34] During this period of conflict, JS produced few documents. Nevertheless, his representatives dealt with various financial matters on his behalf, which resulted in the production of several documents. Bishop Edward Partridge continued to manage financial affairs for JS and the church in Far West, while church agent Oliver Granger worked to resolve church debts in Kirtland. By late October, Granger had successfully settled the First Presidency's debts to four merchants in Painesville, Ohio, and was working with Ohio attorneys to assess remaining obligations. The corresponding financial documents, as well as revelations, correspondence, and legal papers, are featured in part 2.

———— ✑ ————

Revelation, 8 July 1838–A [D&C 118]

Source Note

Revelation, Far West, Caldwell Co., MO, 8 July 1838. Featured version copied [probably between Apr. and Sept. 1839], in Brigham Young, Journal, 4 May 1837–28 Mar. 1845, 105–106[b]; handwriting of Brigham Young; Brigham Young Office Files, CHL.

Brigham Young's journal for 4 May 1837–28 March 1845 is a pocket-size blank book measuring 5⅝ × 3¾ × ½ inches (14 × 10 × 1 cm). The text block consists of sixty-four leaves. The bound volume contains white pastedowns and two matching flyleaves, which Young inscribed, on each side of the text block. The volume was constructed using a tight-back binding, covered with red textured leather. At some point in the nineteenth century, two archival paper labels were pasted onto the spine of the volume. Young inscribed the volume using a number of media, including graphite and black, brown, and blue ink.

The journal was apparently used to help draft Young's history, which was serially published in the *Deseret News* starting in January 1858, suggesting the volume likely entered the custody of the Church Historian's Office sometime before 1858.[35] The journal may have been returned to Young in 1862. The volume was listed in a Historian's Office inventory in 1878 and has remained in continuous institutional custody since at least that time.[36]

---

33. See Robert Wilson, Gallatin, MO, to James L. Minor, Jefferson City, MO, 18 Mar. 1841, in *Document Containing the Correspondence,* 159–164; and Alexander Doniphan, "Camp on Grand River," MO, to David R. Atchison, 15 Sept. 1838, copy; David R. Atchison, Liberty, MO, to Lilburn W. Boggs, 20 Sept. 1838, copy, Mormon War Papers, MSA.

34. For further information regarding the "Mormon War" in Missouri in October 1838, see Introduction to Part 3: 4 Nov. 1838–16 Apr. 1839, pp. 265–270 herein.

35. See Historian's Office, Brigham Young History Drafts, CHL; and "History of Brigham Young," *Deseret News,* 27 Jan. 1858, 369.

36. Woodruff, Journal, 26 Feb. 1862; "Historian's Office Catalogue Book March 1858," [24]; "Index of Records and Journals in the Historian's Office 1878," [15], Historian's Office, Catalogs and Inventories, 1846–1904, CHL.

Historical Introduction

On Sunday, 8 July 1838, JS dictated five revelations in Far West, Missouri, each of which concerned church leadership or finances; one of these revelations regarded the Quorum of the Twelve Apostles. The quorum had not been immune to the dissent and disaffiliation that plagued the church in 1837 and 1838. Apostles Luke Johnson and John F. Boynton renounced the church in December 1837 and were consequently excommunicated by the high council.[37] In the quarterly conference held 7–8 April 1838, David W. Patten gave a report on the quorum and stated that he could not recommend Lyman Johnson or William E. McLellin.[38] Lyman Johnson, who may have sympathized with his brother Luke, was excommunicated for various transgressions on 13 April 1838.[39] McLellin, who had been troubled with the church and JS for some time, was "found in transgression" in a church trial held 11 May.[40] JS apparently began selecting replacements for disaffected members of the quorum before he departed Kirtland, Ohio, for Far West on 12 January 1838. For example, John E. Page and John Taylor had been designated as replacements for Luke Johnson and Boynton by early January 1838.[41]

Despite the turmoil in the church, most of the apostles remained loyal to JS or repaired their relationships with him, and many were serving missions or were expecting to serve in the near future.[42] Under JS's direction, apostles Heber C. Kimball and Orson Hyde undertook a dramatically successful mission to England from June 1837 to May 1838.[43] During the year prior to the dictation of this 8 July 1838 revelation, JS dictated revelations for senior apostles Thomas B. Marsh, David W. Patten, and Brigham Young, with each revelation mentioning or implying forthcoming proselytizing assignments. The revelation for Patten directed him to prepare to embark on a mission the following spring and implied that the other apostles would go with him.[44] On 6 July 1838, JS received a letter from Kimball and Hyde reporting on their return from England and the hundreds of new converts they had brought into the church.[45]

Two days later, in a leadership meeting held before the Sunday worship services for "the congregation of the saints," JS dictated this revelation regarding the Quorum of the Twelve Apostles. The Sunday leadership meeting was probably associated with the quarterly

---

37. Letter to Wilford Woodruff, ca. 18 June 1838, p. 156 herein; John Smith and Clarissa Lyman Smith, Kirtland, OH, to George A. Smith, Shinnston, VA, 1 Jan. 1838, George Albert Smith, Papers, CHL.

38. Minutes, 7–8 Apr. 1838, p. 72 herein.

39. Minutes, 13 Apr. 1838, p. 101 herein.

40. JS, Journal, 11 May 1838, in *JSP*, J1:268; see also Porter, "Odyssey of William Earl McLellin," 321–324.

41. John Smith and Clarissa Lyman Smith, Kirtland, OH, to George A. Smith, Shinnston, VA, 1 Jan. 1838, George Albert Smith, Papers, CHL; see also Hepzibah Richards, Kirtland, OH, to Willard Richards, Bedford, England, 18–19 Jan. 1838, Willard Richards, Papers, CHL; and Quorums of the Seventy, "Book of Records," 23 Jan. 1838, 40.

42. See Esplin, "Emergence of Brigham Young," chap. 6; and Shepard and Marquardt, *Lost Apostles,* chap. 6.

43. See Letter from Heber C. Kimball and Orson Hyde, between 22 and 28 May 1838, pp. 145–148 herein.

44. Revelation, 23 July 1837, in *JSP*, D5:415, 416 [D&C 112:7, 17]; Revelation, 11 Apr. 1838, p. 82 herein [D&C 114:1]; Revelation, 17 Apr. 1838, p. 108 herein.

45. See Letter from Heber C. Kimball and Orson Hyde, between 22 and 28 May 1838, pp. 145–148 herein.

conference held the previous two days.[46] When Thomas B. Marsh wrote about the leadership meeting to Wilford Woodruff, he recounted that "Prest. Joseph Smith Jr. and somome others ware assembled togeather to attend to some church business."[47] In JS's journal, George W. Robinson wrote that the revelation was "given to the Twelve Apostles"; however, Marsh was the only apostle present at the meeting. According to JS's journal, the meeting included "J smith Jr. S[idney] Rigdon, H[yrum] smith, E[dward] Partridge I, Morly [Isaac Morley] J[ared] Carter, S[ampson] Avard T[homas] B, Marsh & G[eorge] W, Robinson,"[48] all of whom held positions of leadership. JS, Rigdon and Hyrum Smith composed the First Presidency. Partridge was the bishop of Zion, and Morley was the first counselor in the bishopric.[49] Carter was the captain general of the Society of the Daughter of Zion (Danites), and Avard was the society's brigadier general.[50] Marsh was the pro tempore president of Zion and the president of the Quorum of the Twelve Apostles. Robinson, the church recorder and clerk as well as the scribe for the First Presidency, was probably present in a clerical capacity.[51]

In JS's journal, this revelation appears as the first of five revelations dictated on 8 July. JS's journal entry for 8 July introduces the first three revelations by stating they were read to the congregation that met later that day but does not specify whether the fourth and fifth revelations were read at the same time. The fifth revelation—addressed to William Marks, Newel K. Whitney, and Oliver Granger—was copied into a letter the First Presidency wrote later in the day to Marks and Whitney. The letter states that the revelation had been "rec[d.] this morning."[52] The order in which the revelations were copied into JS's journal suggests that all five revelations were dictated on the morning of 8 July, apparently in the leadership meeting mentioned in the introduction to the first revelation.[53]

In the letter that Marsh wrote to Woodruff, he explained that JS dictated this revelation "when it was thought proper to select those who ware designed of the Lord to fill the places of those of the twelve who had fallen."[54] As presented in JS's journal, the revelation was a direct

---

46. JS, Journal, 8 July 1838, in *JSP*, J1:284; Minute Book 2, 6–7 July 1838.

47. Thomas B. Marsh, Far West, MO, to Wilford Woodruff, Vinalhaven, ME, 14 July 1838, Wilford Woodruff, Journals and Papers, CHL.

48. JS, Journal, 8 July 1838, in *JSP*, J1:284.

49. Minutes, 7 Nov. 1837, in *JSP*, D5:469–471.

50. Reed Peck, Testimony, Richmond, MO, Nov. 1838, p. [56], State of Missouri v. JS et al. for Treason and Other Crimes (Mo. 5th Jud. Cir. 1838), in State of Missouri, "Evidence"; see also Reed Peck, Quincy, IL, to "Dear Friends," 18 Sept. 1839, pp. 46–47, Henry E. Huntington Library, San Marino, CA; JS, Journal, 7–9 Aug. 1838, in *JSP*, J1:299; and Constitution of the Society of the Daughter of Zion, ca. Late June 1838, at josephsmithpapers.org. Peck also wrote that Avard was "the most busy actor and sharpest tool of the Presidency." (R. Peck to "Dear Friends," 18 Sept. 1839, pp. 50–51.)

51. Minutes, 6 Apr. 1838, pp. 69, 70 herein.

52. Letter to William Marks and Newel K. Whitney, 8 July 1838, p. 195 herein.

53. The content of the revelations suggests that Robinson transcribed them in the order they were dictated. For example, a revelation explaining how to raise revenue for the church is immediately followed by a revelation identifying which church officers were to determine how to use the revenue. (See Revelation, 8 July 1838–C, pp. 183–189 herein [D&C 119]; and Revelation, 8 July 1838–D, pp. 189–190 herein [D&C 120].)

54. Thomas B. Marsh, Far West, MO, to Wilford Woodruff, Vinalhaven, ME, 14 July 1838, Wilford Woodruff, Journals and Papers, CHL.

response to the plea to "show unto us thy will O, Lord concerning the Twelve."[55] The revelation named new apostles—Taylor, Page, Woodruff, and Willard Richards—to replace those who had been removed, and it also directed all the members of the quorum to prepare for a mission "over the great waters" the following spring. This and the other 8 July revelations were probably transcribed by Robinson as JS dictated them.

The text of this 8 July revelation was read aloud in the worship meeting for all church members later in the day.[56] Marsh responded to the revelation by calling for a meeting the next day with Sidney Rigdon and the four other members of the quorum who were available in the area. They agreed to contact absent and newly appointed members of the quorum to inform them of their expected mission abroad.[57]

In addition to the copy of the revelation Robinson transcribed in JS's journal, copies were also made by Brigham Young, Wilford Woodruff, and Willard Richards.[58] A comparison of the copies suggests that Young's version most closely represents the wording of the original revelation; therefore, this version is featured here.[59] Young inscribed the revelation in a book that he intermittently used as a notebook and a journal. Contextual evidence suggests that Young copied the revelation between April 1839 and 12 October 1840. He apparently copied two other documents at the time that he copied the revelation.[60] One of these documents, a 30 March letter Orson Hyde wrote from Missouri to Young in Illinois indicates Young did not copy the revelation until at least April 1839, after receiving the letter from Hyde. Immediately following the three copied documents, Richards inscribed a page and a half of his own genealogical information. Just below this information, Young recorded a journal entry for 12 October 1840.[61] Because the genealogical information written by Richards included dates from 1839, Richards apparently inscribed it sometime after Young joined him in England in April 1840 but no later than 12 October 1840, when Young

55. JS, Journal, 8 July 1838, in *JSP*, J1:285.

56. This revelation, as well as other 8 July revelations, may also have been shared with the Saints in Adam-ondi-Ahman when JS, his counselors in the presidency, and Robinson visited the town about two days later. (JS History, vol. B-1, 804; see also JS, Journal, 26 July 1838, in *JSP*, J1:291.)

57. Minutes, *Elders' Journal,* Aug. 1838, 61. Within a week, Marsh wrote to Woodruff regarding Woodruff's appointment.[a] Decades later, Taylor recounted that a messenger brought him a letter of appointment from the First Presidency.[b] A notice in the *Elders' Journal* requested that Woodruff, Taylor, Richards, and Page "come immediately to Far West, to prepare for a great mission."[c] With the exception of Willard Richards, who was proselytizing in England, the newly appointed apostles were ordained and formally joined the quorum by April 1839.[d] The apostles left on their mission later that year and arrived in England in early 1840.[e] (a. Thomas B. Marsh, Far West, MO, to Wilford Woodruff, Vinalhaven, ME, 14 July 1838, Wilford Woodruff, Journals and Papers, CHL. b. Taylor, *Succession in the Priesthood,* 15. c. Notice, *Elders' Journal,* Aug. 1838, 62. d. Minute Book 2, 19 Dec. 1838; Woodruff, Journal, 26 Apr. 1839; see also Richards, Journal, 14 Apr. 1840. e. Allen et al., *Men with a Mission,* 67–83.)

58. Woodruff, "Book of Revelations," [9]–[10]; Richards, "Pocket Companion," 3–4.

59. Comparisons of the versions of the five 8 July 1838 revelations show that Robinson added introductory phrases and made other slight revisions to polish the texts when he copied them into JS's journal.

60. The three documents, in the order copied, are a 30 March 1839 letter from Orson Hyde, JS's 8 July 1838 revelation regarding the Quorum of the Twelve, and JS's 23 July 1837 revelation for Thomas B. Marsh. All three documents are apparently in the same ink, suggesting they were copied at the same time.

61. Young, Journal, 1837–1845, 12 Oct. 1840.

added the new journal entry.[62] Based on the reception of Hyde's letter and the inscription of Richards's genealogical information, it can be determined that Young copied the three documents sometime between April 1839 and 12 October 1840.

Other clues further narrow the likely time of copying to mid-1839. Young's journal entries between 14 September 1839 and September 1840 are inscribed in blue ink or in darker ink than that used for the 8 July revelation, suggesting he copied the revelation prior to 14 September. Additionally, Young used the volume on 14 July 1839 to record at least one person to contact when he arrived in England to proselytize,[63] suggesting that during summer 1839, Young was already planning to take his journal with him on his mission. At the time, other apostles, such as Wilford Woodruff, were copying JS revelations and discourses into personal volumes that they intended to bring on their mission.[64] It seems plausible that Young also copied relevant texts while preparing for the overseas mission and that he copied the featured revelation between April and mid-September 1839.

Document Transcript

Revelation given July 8th. 1838 at Far West Caldwell Co Mo[65]

Shew unto us thy will O Lord concerning the Twelve—

Ans—[66] Verily thus saith the Lord let a conference be held immediately let the Twelve be organized and let men be appointed to supply the place of those who are fallen let my servant Thomas remain for a ~~little~~ season in the Land of Zion to publish my word[67] let the remainder continue to prech from that hour and if they will do this in all lowliness of [p. 105] heart in meekness and pureness[68] and long suffering, I the Lord God give unto them a promise that I will provide for their families and an effectual door shall be opened for ~~their fami-lies~~ them from ~~lies~~ henceforth[69] and next spring let them depart to go over the

---

62. Young, Journal, 1837–1845, 6 Apr. 1840; Richards, Journal, 9 Apr. 1840.

63. Young, Journal, 1837–1845, 14 July 1839.

64. See, for example, Discourse, 27 June 1839, pp. 508–510 herein.

65. Robinson's version adds "in the presence of J smith Jr. S[idney] Rigdon, H[yrum] smith, E[dward] Partridge I, Morly [Isaac Morley] J[ared] Carter, S[ampson] Avard T[homas] B, Marsh & G[eorge] W, Robinson Making known the will of the Lord concerning the Twelve." (JS, Journal, 8 July 1838, in *JSP*, J1:284–285.)

66. TEXT: Young inscribed two dashes, one on top of the other, possibly intending an equal sign.

67. Thomas B. Marsh was the publisher of the church newspaper as well as "sole proprietor of the printing establishment." A year earlier, JS had dictated a revelation for Marsh directing him to "let thy habitation be known in Zion, and remove not thy house, for I the Lord have a great work for thee to do, in publishing my name among the children of men." (Minutes, 21 Apr. 1838, p. 110 herein; Prospectus for *Elders' Journal*, 30 Apr. 1838, p. 132 herein; Minute Book 2, 23 June 1838; Revelation, 23 July 1837, in *JSP*, D5:415 [D&C 112:6].)

68. Instead of "pureness," Woodruff's and Richards's versions have "humility." (Woodruff, "Book of Revelations," [9]; Richards, "Pocket Companion," 3.)

69. JS dictated a revelation in April directing Brigham Young to "provide for his family until an effectual door is op[e]ned for the suport of his family untill I shall command [him] to go hence." (Revelation, 17 Apr. 1838, p. 108 herein.)

great waters[70] and there promulge[71] my gospel the fulness thereof and to bear record of my name[72] let them take leave of my saints in the City Far West on the 26th day of April next on the building spot of my house saith the Lord[73] let my servant John Taylor and also my servant John E. Page [p. 106[a]][74] and also my servant Wilford Woodruff and also my servant Willard Richards be appointed to fill the places of those who have fallen and be officially notified of their appointment[75] [*11 lines blank*] [p. 106[b]][76]

70. Heber C. Kimball and Orson Hyde wrote a letter reporting their dramatic proselytizing successes in England, declaring that the church had been established "on the other side of the great waters." (Letter from Heber C. Kimball and Orson Hyde, between 22 and 28 May 1838, p. 147 herein.)

71. An archaic form of *promulgate*. ("Promulge," in *American Dictionary*.)

72. Three months earlier, on 11 April 1838, JS dictated a revelation directing Patten to settle his business affairs in order to go on a mission the following spring "in company with others even twelve including himself." On this mission, they were to "testify of my name and bear glad tidings unto all the world." (Revelation, 11 Apr. 1838, p. 82 herein [D&C 114:1].)

73. Four days prior to this revelation, the church dedicated the cornerstones for the Far West temple according to directions in a 26 April 1838 revelation. The revelation also instructed the Latter-day Saints to "recommence laying the foundation of my house" on 26 April 1839. The apostles apparently intended to depart from the temple site in connection with this recommencing of the temple's construction. Though the Latter-day Saints were expelled from Missouri in early 1839, some of the apostles returned to the temple site to formally begin their mission, as directed in the revelation. ("Celebration of the 4th of July," *Elders' Journal*, Aug. 1838, 60; Revelation, 26 Apr. 1838, pp. 115–116 herein [D&C 115:11]; Woodruff, Journal, 26 Apr. 1839.)

74. TEXT: Young numbered two manuscript pages as "106".

75. Robinson's version adds "even so Amen."[a] The calling of the new apostles may have been related to the apostolic mission "over the great waters" commanded in this revelation. John Taylor, an English native who lived in Upper Canada, had been instrumental in the conversion of the English Canadian missionaries who accompanied apostles Heber C. Kimball and Orson Hyde on their mission to England and who had helped arrange their original contacts there.[b] John E. Page was completing a successful mission in Upper Canada and was expected to travel to Missouri with a large group of newly converted Latter-day Saints.[c] Wilford Woodruff—a member of the First Quorum of the Seventy—was serving a successful mission in New England and had spent a few months preaching in the Fox Islands off the coast of Maine.[d] Woodruff and others saw great significance in preaching the gospel in and gathering the House of Israel from "the islands of the sea," as the Old Testament prophet Isaiah had prophesied and as JS's revelations had commanded.[e] Willard Richards had joined apostles Heber C. Kimball and Orson Hyde on their mission to England and continued proselytizing there after his companions returned to America.[f] (a. JS, Journal, 8 July 1838, in *JSP*, J1:285. b. Porter, "Beginnings of the Restoration," 20–33. c. "History of John E. Page," 1–2, Historian's Office, Histories of the Twelve, 1856–1858, 1861, CHL; John E. Page, Kirtland, OH, to "Dear brother in Christ," 24 Jan. 1837, in *LDS Messenger and Advocate*, Jan. 1837, 3:446–447; JS, Journal, 5 May 1838, in *JSP*, J1:264; Baugh, "Call to Arms," 158. d. Letter from Wilford Woodruff et al., 9 Mar. 1838, pp. 31–39 herein. e. See Isaiah 11:11; Revelation, 3 Nov. 1831, in *JSP*, D2:117 [D&C 133:8]; and Letter from Wilford Woodruff and Jonathan H. Hale, 18 Sept. 1837, in *JSP*, D5:451. f. See Historical Introduction to Letter from Heber C. Kimball and Orson Hyde, between 22 and 28 May 1838, p. 146 herein.)

76. TEXT: This is the second of two manuscript pages numbered "106".

Revelation, 8 July 1838–B

Source Note

Revelation, Far West, Caldwell Co., MO, 8 July 1838. Featured version copied [ca. Aug. 1838]; handwriting of Newel K. Whitney; one page; Revelations Collection, CHL. Includes docket.

Single leaf measuring 12⅜ × 7¾ inches (31 × 20 cm). The top and bottom edges have the square cut of manufactured paper. The right edge appears to have been torn from a bound volume. The left edge appears to have been hand cut. The verso contains a transcript of Revelation, 8 July 1838–C, also in the handwriting of Newel K. Whitney. The document was folded for filing and was docketed by Whitney: "A revelation relative | to Phelps & Williams | also Tithing the Church | July 8, 1838". Separations at folds have been repaired. The Historical Department of the LDS church cataloged this version of the revelation in the Revelations Collection in 1983.[77]

Historical Introduction

On Sunday, 8 July 1838, JS dictated five revelations, each of which concerned church leadership or finances; one of these revelations regarded former church leaders Frederick G. Williams and William W. Phelps. Williams had been a counselor to JS in the First Presidency—which also served as the church presidency in Kirtland, Ohio, through 1837— and Phelps had been a counselor in the church presidency in Missouri. Williams was sustained as a counselor in the September 1837 reorganization conference in Kirtland, Ohio, but was rejected in the November 1837 reorganization conference in Far West, Missouri. Soon after the November conference, Williams moved from Kirtland to Far West, where he remained involved in church service.[78] However, like Oliver Cowdery, Lyman Johnson, and some other Latter-day Saints who relocated to Far West, Williams sympathized with Phelps and John Whitmer in their conflict with the Zion high council in Far West.[79] Phelps and Whitmer were removed from office in early February 1838 and excommunicated in early March.[80] It seems that Williams aligned himself with JS and the church from that time until around late May or early June, when he apparently began associating again with Cowdery and other dissenters who had been excommunicated. At some point, Williams may also have been excommunicated, as he was later rebaptized and reconfirmed.[81]

In mid-June several Latter-day Saints in Caldwell County, Missouri, signed a letter warning Cowdery, David and John Whitmer, Phelps, and Johnson to move out of the county within three days or to expect "a more fatal calamity." The letter further stated, "We will have no more promises to reform as you have already made and in every instance violated your promises."[82] John Whitmer later recounted that at the First

---

77. Best, "Register of the Revelations Collection," 19.

78. Williams, *Life of Dr. Frederick G. Williams,* 493–515, 526–527.

79. Oliver Cowdery, Far West, MO, to Warren Cowdery, 21 Jan. 1838, in Cowdery, Letterbook, 80–83; Oliver Cowdery, Far West, MO, to Warren Cowdery and Lyman Cowdery, [Kirtland, OH], 4 Feb. 1838, in Cowdery, Letterbook, 83–86.

80. See Letter from Thomas B. Marsh, 15 Feb. 1838, p. 22 herein; and Minute Book 2, 10 Mar. 1838.

81. Williams, *Life of Dr. Frederick G. Williams,* 538–545.

82. Oliver Cowdery et al., Far West, MO, ca. 17 June 1838, at josephsmithpapers.org.

Presidency's instigation, George W. Robinson began suing the men named in the letter, as well as Williams, for debts. The inclusion of Williams in the lawsuits may indicate that he had been added to the group of men who were warned to leave. Robinson also initiated legal procedures to claim the men's belongings to pay the debts.[83] John Corrill, who also recounted these events, wrote that the circumstances "compelled others of the dissenters to confess and give satisfaction to the church."[84] Phelps quickly wrote church leaders about his good intentions and willingness to rectify any wrongs he had committed. Consequently, he was allowed to remain at Far West despite the unconditional language in the mid-June letter of warning.[85] Williams may have initiated reconciliation around the same time, and he also remained in Far West. The other men named in the letter of warning fled Caldwell County on 19 June.[86] Both Phelps and Williams were evidently rebaptized in late June.[87]

On 8 July, JS dictated five revelations in Far West, apparently in a leadership meeting addressing several items of church business.[88] The revelation featured here directed that Williams and Phelps should be ordained elders and travel, preach, and proselytize. The featured version of the revelation indicates the revelation was an answer to a question about the two men. Later in the day, the revelation was read to "the congregations of the saints," which may have included Williams and Phelps.[89] About a month later, on 5 August, Williams was reconfirmed a church member.[90] There is no evidence of either man being ordained an elder or of either departing on a proselytizing mission during the next few months.[91]

---

83. Whitmer, History, 86–87, in *JSP*, H2:97–98; see also JS, Journal, 4 July 1838, in *JSP*, J1:276–278.

84. Corrill, *Brief History*, 30, in *JSP*, H2:165.

85. In November, Phelps claimed that he had conformed to the church's expectations in order to protect his property. (William W. Phelps, Testimony, Richmond, MO, Nov. 1838, pp. [85], [87], State of Missouri v. JS et al. for Treason and Other Crimes [Mo. 5th Jud. Cir. 1838], in State of Missouri, "Evidence.")

86. Reed Peck, Quincy, IL, to "Dear Friends," 18 Sept. 1839, pp. 25–28, Henry E. Huntington Library, San Marino, CA; Whitmer, Daybook, 19 June 1838; see also Corrill, *Brief History*, 30, in *JSP*, H2:165.

87. Edward Partridge wrote to Newel K. Whitney on 24 July 1838, stating that Phelps and Williams "were baptized about 4 weeks since," indicating that they were baptized around 26 June. JS's journal notes that several people were confirmed as members of the church on 5 August 1838 and that "Br. F, G, Williams was among the number, who being rebaptized a few days since was this day confirmed." (Edward Partridge, Far West, MO, to Newel K. Whitney, Kirtland, OH, 24 July 1838, in Reynolds Cahoon, Far West, MO, to Newel K. Whitney, Kirtland, OH, 23 July 1838, CHL; JS, Journal, 5 Aug. 1838, in *JSP*, J1:296; see also Abner Scovil, Testimony, Richmond, MO, Nov. 1838, p. [50], in State of Missouri, "Evidence.")

88. See Historical Introduction to Revelation, 8 July 1838–A [D&C 118], pp. 176–179 herein.

89. In JS's journal, Robinson introduced the revelation as follows: "Revelation Given the same day, and at the same place, and read the same day in the congregations of the saints." (JS, Journal, 8 July 1838, in *JSP*, J1:285.)

90. JS, Journal, 5 Aug. 1838, in *JSP*, J1:296.

91. Phelps apparently remained in Far West. Williams's activity during this period is uncertain. A family biography of Williams states that sometime around October, he was with Phelps in Burlington, Iowa Territory, where Williams bought land for the church at JS's request. (See William W. Phelps,

Several versions of the revelation are extant. Robinson apparently copied the revelation into JS's journal sometime in mid- or late July.[92] When Robinson copied the revelation, he added a headnote stating that the revelation made known "the duty" of Williams and Phelps.[93] Copies were also made by Newel K. Whitney and Frederick G. Williams.[94] A comparison of these early manuscripts suggests that Whitney's version most closely represents the original wording of the revelation; therefore, Whitney's version is featured here.[95] Whitney may have copied the revelation from a copy that Oliver Granger brought to Kirtland in late July or early August 1838.[96]

Document Transcript

Revelation Given July 8. 1838 in Far West M⁰·

O Lord what is thy will concerning W W Phelps & F. G. Williams

Verily thus saith the Lord in consequence of their transgressions their former standing has been taken away from them⟨,⟩ and now⟨,⟩ if they will be saved⟨,⟩ let them be ordained as Elders in my ~~vineyard~~ Church to Preach my gospel⟨,⟩ and to travel abroad from land to land & from place to place to gather mine Elect unto me saith the Lord,[97] and let this be their labours from henceforth <u>Amen</u>

———— ❧ ————

Revelation, 8 July 1838–C [D&C 119]

Source Note

Revelation, Far West, Caldwell Co., MO, 8 July 1838. Featured version copied [ca. 8 July 1838]; handwriting of Edward Partridge; one page; Revelations Collection, CHL. Includes docket.

One leaf measuring 10⅛ × 7¾ inches (26 × 20 cm). The top and left edges have the square cut of manufactured paper, while the bottom and right edges are unevenly cut. The document was folded for filing, and it was docketed with "tithing", apparently by Edward Partridge. The document was later docketed with "July 1838" in graphite in unidentified handwriting. Separations at folds have been repaired.

Testimony, Richmond, MO, Nov. 1838, pp. [84]–[96], in State of Missouri, "Evidence"; and Williams, *Meet Dr. Frederick Granger Williams,* 120; compare Williams, *Life of Dr. Frederick G. Williams,* 549–563.)

92. See Historical Introduction to Revelation, 8 July 1838–D [D&C 120], p. 189 herein.

93. JS, Journal, 8 July 1838, in *JSP,* J1:285.

94. Revelation, 8 July 1838–B, copy, Revelations Collection, CHL.

95. For example, Whitney's version preserves what is presumably the original interrogatory, "O Lord what is thy will concerning W W Phelps & F. G. Williams," whereas Robinson's and Williams's versions provide a heading that is descriptive and more likely retrospective: "Revelation . . . Making known the duty" of the two men.

96. See Letter to William Marks and Newel K. Whitney, 8 July 1838, p. 195 herein.

97. See Matthew 24:31; Mark 13:27; and Revelation, Sept. 1830–A, in *JSP,* D1:179 [D&C 29:7].

The Historical Department of the LDS church cataloged this version of the revelation in the Revelations Collection in 1983.[98]

Historical Introduction

On Sunday, 8 July 1838, JS dictated five revelations, each of which concerned church leadership or finances; one of these revelations outlined a plan for raising church revenue. The subject of church finances was not new to the Saints. From the time the church was established, JS dictated revelations and instituted programs related to economic and social concerns. An 1831 revelation on "the Laws of the Church of Christ" directed the Latter-day Saints to consecrate their property to the church bishop and then manage stewardships of property or other responsibilities assigned to them.[99] Church members attempted to follow this program of consecration and stewardship in Jackson County, Missouri, but their attempts ended when they were driven out of the county in 1833.[100] In the early and mid-1830s, JS and other church leaders in Ohio engaged in a number of business and banking ventures, most of which ultimately failed.[101] The troubled situation of church finances was compounded by the nationwide panic of 1837 and the ensuing economic recession.[102] During this period, JS and Sidney Rigdon incurred several thousand dollars of debt.[103]

In the latter half of 1837, the bishops in Missouri and Kirtland, Ohio, took new steps to address the church's financial problems. In September, the church published an appeal from Bishop Newel K. Whitney and his counselors in Kirtland, calling on church members everywhere to "bring their tithes into the store house" to relieve church debts and to help establish the community of Saints in Missouri.[104] While this general request did not include recommended donation amounts, in December 1837 a committee composed of Edward Partridge, the bishop of Zion; Isaac Morley, the first counselor in the bishopric;

98. Best, "Register of the Revelations Collection," 19.

99. Revelation, 9 Feb. 1831, in *JSP*, D1:251–252 [D&C 42:30–36]; see also Revelation, 20 May 1831, in *JSP*, D1:315–316 [D&C 51:4–6]; and Questions and Answers, 8 May 1838, p. 141 herein. The Book of Mormon, which was translated a year before the church was organized, recounts that after the resurrected Christ visited people in the Americas, they "had all things common among them," as did some members of Christ's church in Jerusalem during New Testament times. (See Book of Mormon, 1830 ed., 507, 514 [3 Nephi 26:19; 4 Nephi 1:3]; and Acts 2:44; 4:32.)

100. See Cook, *Joseph Smith and the Law of Consecration*, 5–28.

101. See Parkin, "Joseph Smith and the United Firm," 4–66; "Joseph Smith Documents from April 1834 through September 1835," in *JSP*, D4:xxiii–xxiv; Introduction to Part 5: 5 Oct. 1836–10 Apr. 1837, in *JSP*, D5:285–293; Introduction to Part 6: 20 Apr.–14 Sept. 1837, in *JSP*, D5:363–366; and Historical Introduction to Notes Receivable from Chester Store, 22 May 1837, in *JSP*, D5:382–384.

102. "Editorial," *LDS Messenger and Advocate*, June 1837, 3:522; see also Lepler, *Many Panics of 1837*, 1–7.

103. See Statement of Account from John Howden, 29 Mar. 1838, pp. 61–65 herein; Statement of Account from Perkins & Osborn, ca. 29 Oct. 1838, pp. 252–261 herein; and Statement of Account from Hitchcock & Wilder, between 9 July and 6 Nov. 1838, pp. 285–290 herein.

104. Newel K. Whitney et al., *To the Saints Scattered Abroad, the Bishop and His Counselors of Kirtland Send Greeting* [Kirtland, OH: ca. Sept. 1837], copy at CHL; see also Newel K. Whitney et al., Kirtland, OH, to "the Saints scattered abroad," 18 Sept. 1837, in *LDS Messenger and Advocate*, Sept. 1837, 3:561–564.

Edward Partridge. One of the revelations Joseph Smith dictated on 8 July 1838 directed the Latter-day Saints to donate all their surplus property to the church. This property was "to be put into the hands of the bishop of my church of Zion," Edward Partridge. Bishop Partridge and his counselors worked closely with Joseph Smith and his counselors in the First Presidency and with the high council. This likeness of Partridge was made in 1884, evidently by adapting an image of Partridge's grandson Platte De Alton Lyman, and published as the frontispiece in the October issue of the *Contributor* that year. (Church History Library, Salt Lake City.)

and John Corrill, the appointed "keeper of the Lord's Storehouse,"[105] proposed that every head of household be asked to annually donate a certain percentage of net worth, with the percentage based on church needs for the year. To cover anticipated church expenses for 1838, the committee proposed a "tithing" of 2 percent. The committee believed that such a program would "be in some degree fullfilling the law of consecration."[106] In February 1838, when Thomas B. Marsh, the pro tempore president of Zion, wrote to JS about coming to Missouri, Marsh reported that the Saints there "seem to wish to have the whole law of God lived up to; and we think that the church will rejoice to come up to the law of consecration, as soon as their leaders shall say the word, or show them how to do it."[107] In April

---

105. Minutes, 7 Nov. 1837, in *JSP*, D5:471.
106. Minute Book 2, 6–7 Dec. 1837.
107. Letter from Thomas B. Marsh, 15 Feb. 1838, p. 24 herein.

a revelation called for Far West, Missouri, to be built up as a city of Zion with a temple but directed the presidency not to go into debt to build the Far West temple as they had when building the Kirtland temple.[108] The issue of JS's and Rigdon's debts was raised again in May when the two petitioned the high council to obtain compensation for their services in the church.[109] Debts continued to loom over JS and Rigdon, and on 8 July 1838 the first payment on a debt totaling over $4,000 was due to JS's attorneys.[110]

That day, JS dictated this revelation on tithing—apparently in a church leadership meeting held in Far West.[111] This revelation was the third dictated that day that George W. Robinson copied into JS's journal. A copy of the revelation states that JS dictated it in direct response to the petition, "Lord, show unto thy servents how much thou requirest of the properties of thy people for a Tithing?"[112] The resulting revelation called for the Latter-day Saints to consecrate all of their surplus property and thereafter to pay "one tenth of all their interest annually." Robinson, who was present at the leadership meeting, may have transcribed the revelation as JS dictated it.

The revelation was read later that day to a congregation of Latter-day Saints. Over the next few weeks, church members responded to the revelation by consecrating surplus property. According to the 27 July entry in JS's journal, "Some time past the brethren or saints have come up day after day to consecrate, and to bring their offerings into the store house of the lord, . . . They have come up hither Thus far, according to the ord[e]r of the Dan-Ites."[113] Officers in the Danite society had attended the leadership meeting in which JS apparently dictated this revelation, and members of the society were now helping gather the consecrated goods.[114] The success in collecting surplus property apparently did not last long. John Corrill, the keeper of the storehouse, recounted in 1839 that the Danites "set out to enforce the law of consecration; but this did not amount to much."[115] Brigham Young, who was serving in the pro tempore church presidency in

---

108. Revelation, 26 Apr. 1838, pp. 115, 116 herein [D&C 115:8, 13]; see also Discourse, 6 Apr. 1837, in *JSP*, D5:356–357.

109. JS, Journal, 12 May 1838, in *JSP*, J1:269; see also Minute Book 2, 12 May 1838. Ebenezer Robinson, the clerk for the high council, recounted decades later when he was antagonistic toward JS that the high council approved an annual stipend of $1,100 for each member of the presidency, that when church members heard of the decision they "lifted their voices against it," that the high council therefore revoked the decision, and that JS dictated the revelation on consecration and tithing "a few days after." As these decisions were not documented in extant high council minutes, Robinson's veracity regarding this episode is questionable. (Ebenezer Robinson, "Items of Personal History of the Editor," *Return,* Sept. 1889, 136–137; see also Minute Book 2, 24 May–6 July 1838.)

110. See Statement of Account from Hitchcock & Wilder, between 9 July and 6 Nov. 1838, p. 288 herein.

111. See Revelation, 8 July 1838–A, pp. 175–180 herein [D&C 118].

112. JS, Journal, 8 July 1838, in *JSP*, J1:288.

113. JS, Journal, 27 July 1838, in *JSP*, J1:293.

114. See Historical Introduction to Revelation, 8 July 1838–A [D&C 118], pp. 176–177 herein.

115. Corrill, *Brief History,* 46, in *JSP*, H2:193. Reed Peck wrote that "the business of consecration was immediately followed by the formation of four large firms," implying the strategy for church finances shifted from private donations to cooperative labor. According to JS's journal, agricultural firms were established in late August. JS, his counselors in the First Presidency, and the presidency's scribe, George W. Robinson, reportedly visited Adam-ondi-Ahman about two days after the 8 July 1838 leadership meeting and probably

Zion, recollected several years later that church members were sparing in what they considered surplus property.[116]

Robinson made a copy of the revelation in JS's journal, apparently sometime in mid- or late July 1838.[117] The revelation was also copied by other church leaders: Newel K. Whitney made one copy, and Edward Partridge made at least two copies.[118] A comparison of the copies by Robinson, Whitney, and Partridge suggests that one of Partridge's copies most closely represents the wording of the original revelation. This version is featured here.[119] Partridge was present when the revelation was dictated and probably made the featured copy shortly thereafter; the latest possible copying date is 27 May 1840, the day he died.

Document Transcript

Far West July 8th 1838

A revelation

Question O Lord show unto thy servants[120] how much thou requirest of the properties of thy people for a tithing?

Answer. Verily thus saith the Lord, I require all their surplus property,[121] to be put into the hands of the bishop of my church of Zion[122] for the building of

---

shared the new revelations with church leaders there. Lyman Wight, a counselor in the stake presidency at Adam-ondi-Ahman, preached on the principle of consecration on 22 July. (Reed Peck, Quincy, IL, to "Dear Friends," 18 Sept. 1839, pp. 51–52, Henry E. Huntington Library, San Marino, CA; JS, Journal, 20–21 Aug. 1838, in *JSP*, J1:305; JS History, vol. B-1, 804; Swartzell, *Mormonism Exposed,* 23–24.)

116. Brigham Young, in *Journal of Discourses,* 3 June 1855, 2:306–307.

117. Robinson copied the 8 July revelations into JS's journal as part of the entry for that day. This entry, which consists almost entirely of revelation transcripts, appears in a gap in regular journal keeping. Robinson apparently did not resume making regular journal entries until late July, indicating that he may not have copied the revelations into the journal before then.

118. Revelation, 8 July 1838–C, copies, Revelations Collection, CHL [D&C 119].

119. Partridge's two versions have a few variants. The variants in Partridge's version featured here match the wording in the version Robinson copied into JS's journal, which suggests that this wording represents the original transcript, whereas the wording in Partridge's other version deviates somewhat from the original. This other version appears to be the source from which Whitney's version was derived.

120. Instead of "show unto thy servants," Whitney's version has "shew unto us thy servants." (Revelation, 8 July 1838–C, copy, Revelations Collection, CHL.)

121. Property was apparently considered "surplus" if it could not be put to good use by the owner. In a council meeting held 26 July 1838, it was agreed that the First Presidency would "keep all their properties, that they can dispose of to their advantage and support, and the remainder be put into the hands of the Bishop or Bishops, agreeably to the commandments, and revelations." Brigham Young later shared his understanding that church members were asked to donate property, such as land and cattle, that they could not "make use of to advantage." (JS, Journal, 26 July 1838, in *JSP*, J1:291; Brigham Young, in *Journal of Discourses,* 3 June 1855, 2:306–307.)

122. Partridge was appointed in 1831 to receive donations and administer church property in Missouri. (Revelation, 4 Feb. 1831, in *JSP*, D1:244–245 [D&C 41:9–10]; Revelation, 9 Feb. 1831, in *JSP*, D1:251–252 [D&C 42:31–34]; Revelation, 1 Aug. 1831, in *JSP*, D2:15 [D&C 58:14–17]; see also Minutes, 7 Nov. 1837, in *JSP*, D5:471.)

mine house[123] and for the laying the foundation of Zion[124] and for the priesthood and for the debts of the presidency of my church and this shall be the beginning of the tithing of my people and after that those who have ~~been~~ thus been tithed shall pay one tenth[125] of all their interest annually[126] and this shall be a standing law unto them forever for my holy priesthood saith the Lord. Verily I say unto you it shall come to pass that all those who gather unto the land of Zion shall be tithed of their surplus properties and shall observe this law or they shall not be found worthy to abide among you[127] and behold I say unto you if my people observe not this law to keep it holy and by this law sanctify the land of Zion unto me[128] that my statutes

---

123. A revelation JS dictated in April 1838 directed that the Saints should construct a temple in Far West and that the First Presidency should not go into debt to fund the construction. JS and other church officers had ceremonially laid cornerstones for the temple four days prior to this revelation. (Revelation, 26 Apr. 1838, p. 116 herein [D&C 115:13]; "Celebration of the 4th of July," *Elders' Journal,* Aug. 1838, 60.)

124. See Isaiah 28:16.

125. Hebrews 7:4 states that the Old Testament patriarch Abraham "gave the tenth of the spoils," alluding to his donation of "tithes" to Melchizedek following the victory over Chedorlaomer. The Book of Mormon similarly states that Abraham "paid tithes of one-tenth part of all he possessed." Similar to the covenant that Abraham's grandson Jacob made with the Lord—"of all that thou shalt give me I will surely give the tenth unto thee"—JS and Oliver Cowdery signed a covenant in 1834 promising that if they were able to relieve themselves of their debts, they would "give a tenth, to be bestowed upon the poor in his church, or as he shall command." (Genesis 14:17–20; 28:22; Book of Mormon, 1830 ed., 260 [Alma 13:15]; JS, Journal, 29 Nov. 1834, in *JSP,* J1:46; see also Numbers 18:21–28.)

126. Edward Partridge, the bishop of Zion, was present on 8 July 1838 in the leadership meeting that was apparently the setting in which JS dictated this revelation. Two weeks later, Partridge wrote a letter to Newel K. Whitney, the bishop in Kirtland, in which Partridge explained that "the saints are required to give all their surplus property into the hands of the bishop of Zion, and after this first tithing they are to pay annually one tenth of all their interest. that is if a man is worth a $1000, the interest on that would be $60, and one/10. of the interest will be of course $6.— thus you see the plan."[a] Six percent was a common interest rate at the time.[b] Both Ohio and Missouri statutes fixed interest rates at six percent if no other rate was agreed upon.[c] (a. Edward Partridge, Far West, MO, to Newel K. Whitney, Kirtland, OH, 24 July 1838, in Reynolds Cahoon, Far West, MO, to Newel K. Whitney, Kirtland, OH, 23 July 1838, CHL. b. See, for example, Burritt, *Burritt's Universal Multipliers for Computing Interest,* 4. c. An Act Fixing the Rate of Interest [12 Jan. 1824], *Statutes of Ohio,* vol. 2, chap. 586, p. 1297, sec. 1; An Act Regulating Interest of Money [11 Dec. 1834], *Revised Statutes of the State of Missouri* [1835], p. 333, sec. 1.)

127. In the early 1830s, JS also dictated revelations regarding church members' observance of God's laws in the land of Zion. Three weeks prior to this 8 July 1838 revelation, prominent dissenters had been warned to leave the county. (Revelation, 1 Aug. 1831, in *JSP,* D2:15 [D&C 58:19]; Revelation, 11 Sept. 1831, in *JSP,* D2:66 [D&C 64:34–36]; Revelation, 22–23 Sept. 1832, in *JSP,* D2:298 [D&C 84:55–59]; Letter to William W. Phelps, 27 Nov. 1832, in *JSP,* D2:320 [D&C 85:9–11]; Oliver Cowdery et al., Far West, MO, ca. 17 June 1838, at josephsmithpapers.org.)

128. JS previously dictated revelations stating that the Saints would be sanctified by living the laws of God. (Revelation, Feb. 1831–A, in *JSP,* D1:258 [D&C 43:9]; Revelation, 27–28 Dec. 1832, in *JSP,* D2:338 [D&C 88:21, 34–35].)

and ⟨my⟩ judgements[129] may be kept thereon that it may be most holy, behold verily I say unto you it shall not be a land of Zion unto you[.] And this shall be an ensample unto all the stakes of Zion even so amen

———— ✧ ————

Revelation, 8 July 1838–D [D&C 120]

Source Note

Revelation, Far West, Caldwell Co., MO, 8 July 1838. Featured version copied [ca. July 1838] in JS, Journal, Mar.–Sept. 1838, 8 July 1838, p. 57; handwriting of George W. Robinson; CHL. Includes use marks. For more information on JS, Journal, Mar.–Sept. 1838, see Source Notes for Multiple-Entry Documents, p. 564 herein.

Historical Introduction

On Sunday, 8 July 1838, JS dictated five revelations, each of which concerned church leadership or finance; one of these revelations regarded the disposition of property donated to the church. The management of such property had evolved over the years. Initially, the disposition of property was within the purview of the church's bishops.[130] Then, from 1832 to 1834 the United Firm managed church assets.[131] In the mid-1830s, after presidencies and high councils were established in Ohio and Missouri, they also became involved in overseeing the use of church assets.[132] In 1837 William W. Phelps and John Whitmer, counselors in the Zion presidency, began making significant financial decisions without the input of the high council or the bishopric. High council members in particular resented the exclusion, and council members compelled Phelps and Whitmer to include the council and bishopric in future financial decisions.[133]

The 8 July 1838 revelation regarding the management of donated property was the fourth of the five revelations from that day that George W. Robinson copied into JS's journal. JS apparently dictated these revelations in a leadership meeting held in the morning before the day's worship services, and at some point in July, Robinson copied the revelations into JS's journal as part of the entry for 8 July. This entry, which consists almost entirely of revelation transcripts, appears in a gap in regular journal keeping. Robinson apparently did not resume making regular journal entries until late July, suggesting that he may not have copied the revelations into the journal before then.[134]

---

129. This passage echoes the phrasing in Deuteronomy that refers to the law of Moses, which the Israelites were commanded to live by in their promised land. (Deuteronomy 12:1; see also Deuteronomy 16:12.)

130. See Revelation, 9 Feb. 1831, in *JSP*, D1:251–252 [D&C 42:31–34]; and Revelation, 1 Aug. 1831, in *JSP*, D2:15 [D&C 58:17].

131. See "Joseph Smith Documents from April 1834 through September 1835," in *JSP*, D4:xxiii–xxiv; and Parkin, "Joseph Smith and the United Firm," 4–66.

132. See, for example, Minute Book 1, 2 Apr. 1836; and Minute Book 2, 7 Apr. 1837.

133. Minute Book 2, 3 and 5–7 Apr. 1837.

134. JS, Journal, 8 July 1838, in *JSP*, J1:281–291.

The third revelation directed the Latter-day Saints to consecrate surplus property to the church as "the beginning of the tithing of my people" and then to donate one-tenth of their interest annually.[135] Robinson's headnote for the fourth revelation, featured here, states that it was given in reference to "the disposition of the properties tithed, as named in the preceeding revelation." This short revelation directed that the donated property be managed by a council consisting of the First Presidency, Bishop Edward Partridge and his counselors in the Zion bishopric, and the Zion high council—all acting together under the inspiration of God. Whereas the first three 8 July revelations included in the journal entry for that day were read to the congregation of Saints at the worship service later in the day, it is unclear whether this fourth revelation was also read at that time. On 26 July 1838, the council that was called for in this revelation met as directed.[136]

Document Transcript

Revelation Given the same day July 8th 1838
Making known the disposition of the properties tithed, as named in the preceeding revelation—[137]

Verrily thus saith the Lord, the time has now come that it shall be disposed of, by a council composed of the first Presidency of my Church and of the Bishop and his council and by ⟨my⟩ high Council,[138] and ⟨by⟩ mine own voice unto them saith the Lord, even so Amen.

135. Revelation, 8 July 1838–C, p. 188 herein [D&C 119:3].

136. JS, Journal, 26 July 1838, in *JSP*, J1:291; see also Minute Book 2, 26 July 1838.

137. Another early manuscript copy of the revelation, in unidentified handwriting, also begins with the heading "Revelation given the same day." However, that copy has a different secondary headnote—"On the disposeal of the property of the Church"—which the unidentified scribe apparently inserted after copying the revelation. This difference suggests that Robinson added the headnote in the featured copy when he inscribed it in JS's journal—a practice he apparently followed with the other 8 July revelations when he copied them into the journal. (Revelation, 8 July 1838–D, copy, Revelations Collection, CHL.)

138. It is unclear whether the high council included the pro tempore Zion presidency at Far West, which ordinarily presided over the council,[a] or whether the First Presidency was to preside directly over the body of twelve counselors, as the presidency had in Kirtland.[b] When the Zion high council met on 31 August 1838, Sidney Rigdon and Hyrum Smith presided directly over the twelve counselors; the Zion presidency was apparently not present. This was the last high council meeting recorded before JS was taken prisoner by Missouri officials in November 1838.[c] (*a.* Minute Book 2, 3 July 1834–29 June 1838. *b.* Minute Book 1, 17 Feb. 1834–17 Sept. 1837. *c.* Minute Book 2, 31 Aug. 1838.)

Revelation, 8 July 1838–E [D&C 117]

Source Note

Revelation, Far West, Caldwell Co., MO, 8 July 1838. Featured version copied [between 8 July 1838 and 27 May 1840]; handwriting of Edward Partridge; two pages; Revelations Collection, CHL. Includes dockets.

Single leaf measuring 12½ × 7⅞ inches (32 × 20 cm). The document was folded for filing, and then Edward Partridge docketed the letter with "Revelation". Later, a graphite docket in unidentified hand-writing was added: "1838". Separations at folds have been repaired.

The Historical Department of the LDS church cataloged this version of the revelation in the Revelations Collection in 1983.[139]

Historical Introduction

On Sunday, 8 July 1838, JS dictated five revelations, each of which concerned church leadership or finances; one of these revelations was directed mainly to William Marks and Newel K. Whitney, with some information concerning Oliver Granger.[140] Following JS's departure from Kirtland, Ohio, in January 1838, Marks was designated to preside over the church there and to act as a financial agent for JS and Sidney Rigdon in arranging payment of their debts. Whitney was the bishop in Kirtland, overseeing the temporal operations of the church there. It was apparently expected that Marks and Whitney would quickly settle the church's affairs and then move to Missouri in accordance with the 12 January 1838 revela-tion directing faithful Saints to relocate there, and it seems that Whitney had been planning to move since at least June 1838.[141] Yet, neither Whitney nor Marks departed Kirtland with the "Kirtland Camp," a large group of emigrating Saints that left Kirtland on 6 July.[142] This revelation was the last of the 8 July revelations that George W. Robinson copied into JS's journal.[143] The content of this revelation suggests it may have come in response to informa-tion conveyed by Granger, a church financial agent and a member of the Kirtland high council, who arrived in Far West, Missouri, by 8 July 1838, probably on church business.[144]

JS apparently dictated this and the other 8 July revelations in the leadership meeting held prior to the Sunday worship services for the day.[145] In a letter to Marks and Whitney written the same day, the First Presidency specified that this revelation was received in the morning.[146]

---

139. Best, "Register of the Revelations Collection," 19.

140. Some of the content in the revelation can also be read as general direction. When George W. Robinson copied the revelation into JS's journal, he added a headnote stating, "Revelation Given to W^m. Marks, N[ewel] K, Whitney Oliver Granger & others. Given in Zion. <u>July 8th 1838</u>." (JS, Journal, 8 July 1838, in *JSP*, J1:289.)

141. On 23 July, Reynolds Cahoon responded to a 21 June letter in which Whitney asked several questions regarding travel to and the economy in Missouri. (Reynolds Cahoon, Far West, MO, to Newel K. Whitney, Kirtland, OH, 23 July 1838, CHL.)

142. Kirtland Camp, Journal, 6 July 1838.

143. JS, Journal, 8 July 1838, in *JSP*, J1:289.

144. The previous year, Granger was appointed an agent for JS. A letter the First Presidency wrote on 8 July indicates Granger was in Far West. (Power of Attorney to Oliver Granger, 27 Sept. 1837, in *JSP*, D5:460; Letter to William Marks and Newel K. Whitney, 8 July 1838, p. 195 herein.)

145. See Revelation, 8 July 1838–A, pp. 175–180 herein [D&C 118].

146. See Letter to William Marks and Newel K. Whitney, 8 July 1838, p. 195 herein.

The revelation directed Marks and Whitney to relocate to Missouri before winter. Once in Missouri, they were to preside over the Saints in their respective callings, Marks as president of the church in Missouri and Whitney as a bishop in Adam-ondi-Ahman. Granger was to return to Kirtland and continue to act as an agent for the First Presidency in settling remaining business affairs, thereby allowing Marks and Whitney to move to Missouri sooner.

The revelation, which is somewhat personal in nature, may not have been read during the worship services on 8 July, as were at least some of the other revelations dictated that day. JS and his counselors in the First Presidency included a transcript of the revelation in the letter they wrote to Marks and Whitney and encouraged the two men to follow the revelation's direction.[147]

George W. Robinson apparently copied the revelation into JS's journal sometime in mid- or late July.[148] Copies were also made by Edward Partridge, Newel K. Whitney, Lydia Granger, and James Mulholland, among others.[149] A comparison of the early copies suggests that Partridge's version most closely represents the wording of the original revelation.[150] Partridge was present when the revelation was dictated and probably made the copy shortly thereafter; the latest possible copying date is 27 May 1840, the day he died.

Document Transcript

A revelation given at Far West July 8th A.D. 1838

verily thus saith the Lord unto my servants[151] William Marks and N. K. Whitney, Let them settle up their business speedily and journey from the land of Kirtland, before I the Lord sendeth snow[152] again upon the ground. Let them awake and arise and come forth[153] and not tarry, for I the Lord commandeth it.— therefore if they tarry, it shall not be well with them.— Let them repent of all their sins, and all their covetous desires before me saith the Lord: ~~And whatsoever remaineth, let it remain in your hands~~ for what is property unto me saith the Lord. Let the properties at Kirtland be turned out for debts saith the Lord.[154] Let them go saith the Lord; and whatsoever remaineth, let it remain in your hands saith the Lord: for have I not the fowls of Heaven, and also the fish of the

---

147. Letter to William Marks and Newel K. Whitney, 8 July 1838, pp. 195–196 herein.

148. See Historical Introduction to Revelation, 8 July 1838–D [D&C 120], p. 189 herein.

149. See Revelation, 8 July 1838–E, copy, Revelations Collection, CHL; "Revelation Given 8 July 1838," BYU; Letter to William Marks and Newel K. Whitney, 8 July 1838, pp. 195–196 herein; and Revelation, 8 July 1838–E, in Book of the Law of the Lord, 56; see also Richards, "Pocket Companion," 102.

150. For example, the spelling of Adam-ondi-Ahman in Partridge's and Granger's versions seems to reflect an earlier, less refined spelling, copied from the original transcript. Some wording in Partridge's version apparently retains the original grammar, matched in other independent versions, whereas it was modified in Granger's version.

151. TEXT: Possibly "servant⟨s⟩".

152. Instead of "snow," Robinson's copy has "the snows." (JS, Journal, 8 July 1838, in *JSP,* J1:289.)

153. See Revelation, 3 Nov. 1831, in *JSP,* D2:117 [D&C 133:10].

154. Marks was engaged in selling Mormon property in order to pay the debts of JS and Rigdon. (See Pay Order to Edward Partridge for William Smith, 21 Feb. 1838, pp. 27–30 herein.)

sea, and the beasts of the mountains. Have I not made the earth?[155] Do I not hold
the destinies of all the armies of the nations of the earth? Therefore will I not
make the solitary places to bud and to blossom[156] and to bring forth in abundance saith the Lord. Is there not room enough upon the mountains of
Adamondi awman,[157] or[158] upon the plains of Olea Shinihah,[159] or the land[160]
where Adam dwelt, that you should not covet that which is but ~~but~~ the drop, and
neglect the more w[e]ighty matters.—[161] Therefore come up hither unto the land
of my people even Zion. Let my servant William Marks be faithful over a few
things, and he shall be ruler over many things.[162] Let him preside in the midst of
my people in the city Far West, and let him be blessed with the blessings of my
people.—[163] Let my servant N. K. Whitney be ashamed of the Nicolitans,[164] and
of all their secret abominations, and of all his littleness of soul before me saith the
Lord, and come up unto the land of Adam ondi awman and be a ~~man~~ bishop
unto my people saith the Lord, not in name but in deed saith the Lord.[165] And

---

155. See Genesis chap. 1.

156. See Isaiah 35:1.

157. Here and later in the revelation, Mulholland's copy uses the spelling "Adam Ondi Ahman."
According to John Corrill, when JS applied this name to Spring Hill, Missouri, he gave the English interpretation of the name as "the valley of God, in which Adam blessed his children." (Revelation, 8 July
1838–D, copy, Revelations Collection, CHL [D&C 117:8]; Corrill, *Brief History*, 28, in *JSP*, H2:163; see
also Letter to Stephen Post, 17 Sept. 1838, p. 242 herein.)

158. Instead of "or," Robinson's and Whitney's copies have "and." (JS, Journal, 8 July 1838, in *JSP*,
J1:289; Letter to William Marks and Newel K. Whitney, 8 July 1838, p. 196 herein.)

159. Robinson's copy uses the spelling "Olaha Shinehah." In JS's translation of the Book of
Abraham, the Lord shows Abraham a vision of the Lord's heavenly creations and names some of them:
"And he [the Lord] said unto me this is Shinehah, (which is the sun.) . . . And he said unto me, Olea,
which is the moon." (JS, Journal, 8 July 1838, in *JSP*, J1:289; "The Book of Abraham," *Times and Seasons*,
15 Mar. 1842, 3:719–720 [Abraham 3:13].)

160. Instead of "or the land," Robinson's and Whitney's copies have "or in the land." (JS, Journal,
8 July 1838, in *JSP*, J1:289; Letter to William Marks and Newel K. Whitney, 8 July 1838, p. 196 herein.)

161. See Matthew 23:23.

162. See Matthew 25:21, 23.

163. Kirtland president William Marks was apparently intended to replace Thomas B. Marsh, who
was serving as the pro tempore president of Zion. (Minutes, 6 Apr. 1838, p. 70 herein.)

164. Robinson's copy has "Nicholatine band." (JS, Journal, 8 July 1838, in *JSP*, J1:290; see also
147n700 herein.)

165. Ten days earlier, when a stake of Zion was organized in Adam-ondi-Ahman, Vinson Knight was
appointed the bishop pro tempore. It may have been intended that Knight, who had previously served as a
counselor to Bishop Whitney in Ohio, would be replaced by Whitney when Whitney arrived. However, that
plan may have changed with the revelation's chastisement of Whitney and its statement that he would serve
in Adam-ondi-Ahman as a bishop "not in name but in deed." Bishop Edward Partridge wrote to Whitney
about the revelation two weeks later, stating, "I some expect that you will have to take the tithing
at Adamondiahman the same as I have to here." (Minutes, 28 June 1838, p. 166 herein; Edward Partridge,
Far West, MO, to Newel K. Whitney, Kirtland, OH, 24 July 1838, in Reynolds Cahoon, Far West, MO, to
Newel K. Whitney, Kirtland, OH, 23 July 1838, CHL.)

again verily I say unto you I remember my servant Oliver Granger. Behold verily I say unto him, that his name shall be had in sacred rememberance from generation to generation forever and ever saith the Lord. Therefore let him contend earnestly for the redemption of the first presidency of my church saith the Lord; and when he falls he shall rise again; for his sacrifice shall be more sacred to me, than his increase saith [p. [1]] the Lord; therefore let him come up hither speedily unto the land of Zion, and in due time he shall be made a merchant unto my name saith the Lord for the benefit of my people:[166] therefore let no man despise[167] my servant Oliver Granger,[168] but let the blessings of my people be upon him forever and ever. Amen.

And again I say unto you let all the saints in the land of Kirtland remember the Lord their God, and mine house to preserve it holy, and to overthrow the money changers[169] in mine own due time said the Lord [*3/4 page blank*] [p. [2]]

———— ৩ ————

Letter to William Marks and Newel K. Whitney, 8 July 1838

Source Note

Sidney Rigdon, JS, and Hyrum Smith, Letter, Far West, Caldwell Co., MO, to William Marks and Newel K. Whitney, [Kirtland Township, Geauga Co., OH], 8 July 1838; copy, [ca. Aug. 1838]; handwriting of Newel K. Whitney; two pages; JS Collection, CHL. Includes redaction and docket.

One leaf measuring 12½ × 7¾ inches (32 × 20 cm). The top, right, and bottom edges of the leaf have the square cut of manufactured paper, whereas the left edge is uneven, suggesting it was cut from a blank book or a larger sheet. The letter includes redactions in graphite. The letter was folded for filing and docketed in graphite. In various places, the paper has separated at the folds. The document has undergone conservation.

It is not known how or when Whitney's copy came into the possession of the LDS church. The church's Historical Department processed the letter as part of the JS Collection in 1973.

Historical Introduction

On 8 July 1838, JS and his counselors in the First Presidency wrote a letter to William Marks and Newel K. Whitney, conveying a revelation JS dictated that morning. The revelation directed Marks and Whitney to relocate from Kirtland, Ohio, to Missouri before

---

166. A revelation JS dictated in 1831 appointed Sidney Gilbert to a similar position. (Revelation, 20 July 1831, in *JSP*, D2:11 [D&C 57:8–10].)

167. See 1 Corinthians 16:11; 1 Timothy 4:12; and Titus 2:15.

168. Granger may have been looked down on by others because of his partial blindness. He had lost much of his eyesight in 1827 from exposure to the cold. (JS History, vol. C-1 Addenda, 11.)

169. This phrasing is an allusion to John 2:13–16 and to attempts by creditors or dissenters to take control of the House of the Lord in Kirtland. (Hepzibah Richards, Kirtland, OH, to Willard Richards, Bedford, England, 18–19 Jan. 1838, Willard Richards, Papers, CHL.)

winter and then preside over the Saints—with Marks as the president of the church in Zion and with Whitney as a bishop in Adam-ondi-Ahman. To expedite their move, the revelation directed Oliver Granger, who had recently traveled from Kirtland to Far West, Missouri, to return to Kirtland and continue settling the debts of the First Presidency.[170]

In addition to including the full text of the revelation in the letter, the First Presidency expressed confidence that Marks and Whitney would follow the direction in the revelation. The presidency also encouraged all Latter-day Saints in Kirtland to migrate to Missouri. The letter may have been written on behalf of the First Presidency by Sidney Rigdon, the first signatory.

Marks and Whitney apparently received the letter, as the extant copy is in Whitney's handwriting. Marks and Whitney moved from Kirtland later in the year but did not reach northwestern Missouri before Missouri governor Lilburn W. Boggs called for the expulsion of the Latter-day Saints from the state.[171] As directed, Granger continued his efforts in Kirtland to settle the debts of the First Presidency.[172]

Document Transcript

Far W[e]st July 8, 1838
Pres.ᵗ William Marks and Bishop N K Whitny [Newel K. Whitney]
Gn.ᵗ We send you by the hand of br O[liver] Granger a revelation rec.ᵈ this morning which reads as follows[173]

> Verily thus saith the Lord unto my servants W.ᵐ Marks & N K Whitny let them settle up their businss speedily & Journy from the Land of Kirtland before ~~me~~ I the Lord sendeth snow again upon the ground, Let them awake & arise & come forth & not tarry for I the Lord commandeth it. Therefor if they tarry it shall not be well with them.
>
> Let them repent of all their sins & of all their covetous desires before me saith the Lord, For what is property unto me Saith the Lord. Let the

---

170. See Revelation, 8 July 1838–E, pp. 192–194 herein [D&C 117].

171. Whitney heard of the expulsion en route to Missouri and therefore waited for a time in St. Louis.ᵃ Marks left Kirtland in October, before he could have heard of the expulsion.ᵇ They eventually rejoined the Latter-day Saints in Commerce, Illinois, where Marks was appointed president of the stake and Whitney became bishop of the Middle Ward.ᶜ (a. [Elizabeth Ann Smith Whitney], "A Leaf from an Autobiography," *Woman's Exponent,* 15 Nov. 1878, 91. b. Geauga Co., OH, Deed Record, 1795–1921, vol. 27, pp. 149–150, 1 Oct. 1838, microfilm 20,242, U.S. and Canada Record Collection, FHL; Letter from William Perkins, 29 Oct. 1838, p. 251 herein. c. Minutes, 6 May 1839, pp. 450–451 herein; see also Minutes, *Times and Seasons,* Dec. 1839, 1:30–31.)

172. See Authorization for Oliver Granger, 13 May 1839, pp. 456–459 herein; JS History, vol. C-1 Addenda, 11–12; Thomas Griffith and John Seymour, Letter of Introduction, Painesville, OH, for Oliver Granger, 19 Oct. 1838, in JS Letterbook 2, p. 40; Horace Kingsbury, Letter of Introduction, Painesville, OH, for Oliver Granger, 26 Oct. 1838, in JS Letterbook 2, p. 40; and Letter of Introduction from John Howden, 27 Oct. 1838, pp. 246–249 herein.

173. See Revelation, 8 July 1838–E, pp. 191–194 herein [D&C 117].

properties of Kirtland be turned out for ~~debts~~ debt saith the Lord. Let
them go saith the Lord & whatsoever remaineth let it remain in your
hands saith the Lord. For have I not the fowls of Heaven & also the fish
of the sea & the beasts of the mountains, Have I not made the earth. do
I not hold the destinies of all the armies of the nations of the earth.
Therefore will I not make the solitary places to bud & to blossom & to
bring forth in abundance saith the Lord. Is there not room enough upon
the mountains of Adam ondi awman & upon the plains of Obashinihah
or Oleashinihah or in the Land ~~of~~ where Adam dwelt that you should
not covet that which is but the drop & neglect the more weighty matters— Therefore come up hither unto the Land of my people even
Zion— Let my serv.^t W^m marks be faithful over a few things & he shall
be ruler ~~of~~ over many things— Let him preside in the midst of my
(blank or omited)[174] in the city Far West & let him be blessed with the
blessings of my people Let my Servt N K Whitny be ashamed of
the Nicholatins & of all their secret abominations & of all his littleness
of soul before me saith the Lord & come up unto the Land of Adam
ondi awman & be a Bishop unto my people saith the Lord, Not in ~~name~~
Name but in deed saith the Lord— And again verily I say unto you I
remember my serv.^t, Oliver Granger behold verily I say unto him that his
name shall be had in sacred remembrence from generation to generation
for ever & ever saith the Lord. Therefore let him Contend earnestly for
the redemption of the first presidency of my church saith the Lord (over)
[p. [1]] and when he falls he shall rise again, for his sacrafice shall be
more sacred to me than his increase saith the Lord. Therefor let him
come up hither speedily unto the land of Zion & in due time he shall be
made a merchant unto my name saith the Lord for the benifit of my
people— Therefore let no man let no man despise my serv.^t oliver
Granger but the blessings of my people be on him forever & ever— And
again verily I say unto you let all my Serv^ts. in the land of Kirtland
remember the Lord their god & mine house also to preserve it holy & to
overthrow the money changers in mine own due time saith the Lord

By this you will understand the will of the Lord concerning you & will
doubtless act accordingly— It would be wisdom for all the Saints that Come this
Summer to come & make an effort to do so as ~~soon~~ it will be better for them[175]

---

174. The version of the revelation in JS's journal has "people" at this point in the text. (JS, Journal,
8 July 1838, in *JSP,* J1:289.)

175. A revelation JS dictated in January 1838 directed faithful church members in Kirtland to "gather
themselves together unto Zion." This revelation was read in the worship services held the day this letter was

If they cannot sel their property let them turn it out on the debts[176] & when the Lord lift us all up they will rise with the rest, but let none think to get property whenever they ~~get~~ ⟨Come⟩ here for there is none for them at present but there will be—[177] There is a note in the hands of Eth◇◇[178] Spencer it was money borrowd from a man by the name of Colgrove,[179] to put into the B[a]nk[180] if it is possible turn out property to satisfy it, as Spencer is almost dead about it— There need be no fear in the saints coming up here there are provisions or will be in great abundance of all kinds indeed there is a plenty now neither has there been a scarcity at any time since we come

We leave you in the hands of the Lord asking the blessings of salvation to rest upon you

Yo[r.] breth[n.] in Ch[ri]st Jesus
Sig[d.] { Sidn[e]y Rigdon
Joseph Smith Jr
Hyr[u]m Smith

[p. [2]]

———— ☙ ————

<hr>

written to Marks and Whitney. Another JS revelation, from April 1838, expressed the Lord's will that "the City Far West should be built up spedily, by the gathering of my Saints, and also that other places should be appointed for stakes in the regions round about." (Revelation, 12 Jan. 1838–C, in *JSP*, D5:502; JS, Journal, 8 July 1838, in *JSP*, J1:281–284; Revelation, 26 Apr. 1838, p. 116 herein [D&C 115:17–18].)

176. Several Latter-day Saints in Kirtland conveyed their property to Marks, who was to sell the property to pay the First Presidency's debts. (See Pay Order to Edward Partridge for William Smith, 21 Feb. 1838, pp. 27–30 herein.)

177. On 24 July 1838, Bishop Edward Partridge wrote a letter to Bishop Newel K. Whitney, stating it was unclear when the land in Daviess County, Missouri, would be for sale. Like other settlers in America's frontier states and territories, the Latter-day Saints in Daviess County intended to utilize the federal law protecting preemption rights when the land eventually came to market. (Edward Partridge, Far West, MO, to Newel K. Whitney, Kirtland, OH, 24 July 1838, in Reynolds Cahoon, Far West, MO, to Newel K. Whitney, Kirtland, OH, 23 July 1838, CHL; Walker, "Mormon Land Rights," 17–18, 28–34.)

178. TEXT: Possibly "Ether" or "Ethan". An Ethan Spencer paid sixty dollars' worth of Kirtland Safety Society notes to the institution in June 1837. The money may have been a payment for stock—although the stock ledger does not specify that Spencer held any stock—or Spencer may have been returning notes to the society, believing that JS might otherwise be required to redeem the notes. (Kirtland Safety Society, Stock Ledger, 227–228; Historical Introduction to Notice, ca. Late Aug. 1837, in *JSP*, D5:418–420; Staker, "Raising Money in Righteousness," 248n171.)

179. TEXT: Possibly "Colgrave" or "Colgroves". The reference is possibly to Nathaniel Colgrove of Claridon, Ohio, or Alanson Colgrove of Kingsville, Ohio. (1840 U.S. Census, Claridon, Geauga Co., OH, 180; Ashtabula Co., OH, Census Records, 1811–1835, microfilm 960,607, U.S. and Canada Record Collection, FHL.)

180. Probably a reference to the Kirtland Safety Society. This direction may have been part of an effort to financially bolster the institution. (See Notice, ca. Late Aug. 1837, in *JSP*, D5:418–420; and Staker, "Raising Money in Righteousness," 248n171.)

Deed to Samuel F. Whitney, 8 July 1838

Source Note

JS, Emma Smith, Don Carlos Smith, Agnes Coolbrith Smith, William Miller, and Phebe Scott Miller,
Quitclaim Deed for property in Kirtland Township, Geauga Co., OH, to Samuel F. Whitney, 8 July 1838.
Featured version copied 27 Oct. 1838 in Geauga County Deed Record, vol. 26, pp. 491–492; handwriting of
Ralph Cowles; signed by JS, Emma Smith, Don Carlos Smith, Agnes Coolbrith Smith, William Miller, and
Phebe Scott Miller; witnessed by William W. Phelps; certified by John Cleminson; Geauga County Archives
and Records Center, Chardon, OH.

The deed appears in Geauga County Deed Record, volume 26. The volume contains 320 leaves as
well as front and back flyleaves measuring 15⅝ × 10 inches (40 × 10 cm). At an unknown time, the original leather cover and spine were covered with cream canvas and maroon leather corners. Four false
raised bands demarcate five panels on the spine. The volume has a construction similar to other contemporaneous records housed at the Geauga County Archives and Records Center. The bound volume
measures 16½ × 10¾ × 3 inches (42 × 27 × 8 cm). The volume contains deeds recorded from 22 May to
20 December 1838. Each deed record is written in ink.

This volume was in the possession of the Geauga County, Ohio, Recorder's Office from its creation until 1996, when it was transferred to the newly organized Geauga County Archives and Records
Center.

Historical Introduction

On 8 July 1838, JS and several others signed a deed in Far West, Missouri, transferring
their rights to a tract of land in Kirtland, Ohio. This 239-acre property, located in the
southwest corner of Kirtland Township, was purchased from Peter and Sarah French[181] on
5 October 1836 by JS and Emma Smith, Don Carlos and Agnes Coolbrith Smith, William
and Caroline Grant Smith, and William and Phebe Scott Miller.[182] Also on 5 October, the
group signed a mortgage agreement to pay the Frenches $1,000 annually for thirteen years,
starting in April 1838, with a fourteenth and final payment due in 1851 for a smaller sum,
which may have represented a portion of the interest.[183] During fall 1836, JS individually
and jointly purchased a substantial amount of land throughout the Kirtland area. The
5 October 1836 transaction with the Frenches and one with Alpheus and Elizabeth Russell
on 10 October 1836 amounted to over 371 acres and were the largest land purchases JS was

---

181. This was the second substantial land transaction between church leaders and the Frenches. In
the first transaction, in 1833, church leaders purchased a large tract of land commonly referred to as the
French farm; the Kirtland House of the Lord was built on a section of this tract. (See Historical
Introduction to Minutes, 23 Mar. 1833–A, in *JSP*, D3:46–47.)

182. William Miller was born in Avon, New York, in 1814. He married Phebe Scott in May 1834 and
was baptized into the church on 28 October 1834. He first bought land in Kirtland in November 1834,
and he and Phebe moved there in fall 1835. They may have been involved in the 5 October 1836 transaction to help finance the purchase. William may also have been expected to act as an overseer since he
owned land in an adjacent lot. ("Miller, William," in Jenson, *LDS Biographical Encyclopedia*, 1:481–482;
Geauga Co., OH, Deed Record, 1795–1921, vol. 19, pp. 178–179, 1 Nov. 1834, microfilm 20,238, U.S. and
Canada Record Collection, FHL.)

183. See Mortgage to Peter French, 5 Oct. 1836, in *JSP*, D5:293–299.

involved in while residing in Kirtland.[184] In April 1837, JS and Emma Smith signed a quit-claim deed[185] giving William Marks, apparently acting as an agent for JS, their right to the land jointly purchased from the Frenches.[186]

On 5 February, Marks created a deed to sell land to Samuel F. Whitney, the younger brother of Newel K. Whitney.[187] Because Marks did not own the land—rather, he only held the rights he had acquired from JS and Emma Smith—this deed was a quitclaim deed rather than a standard warranty deed. In return for the land, Samuel F. Whitney provided Marks with "thirteen thousand dollars . . . paid in hand in obligations against Joseph Smith Jr" and others.[188] These obligations were likely the promissory notes that JS and the other purchasers gave to Peter and Sarah French in October 1836.[189] Since promissory notes were transferable, Whitney may have purchased them from the Frenches or received them as payment in another transaction. The 5 February 1838 quitclaim deed transferring the land to Samuel F. Whitney only provided him with the property rights that Marks held, not the rights of each of the original purchasers.

---

184. See Mortgage to Peter French, 5 Oct. 1836, in *JSP*, D5:293–299; and Geauga Co., OH, Deed Record, 1795–1921, vol. 23, pp. 539–540, 10 Oct. 1836, microfilm 20,240, U.S. and Canada Record Collection, FHL.

185. A warranty deed is one of the most common types of deed. It is used to convey or sell the title of land from one party to another when there is no lien or prior claim to the land. In contrast to a warranty deed, a quitclaim deed releases the owner's title to, interest in, and claims to a property and conveys these rights to another person. ("Quit Claim," and "Warranty," in Bouvier, *Law Dictionary*, 2:321, 486–487; Greenwood, *Researcher's Guide to American Genealogy*, 409, 410.)

186. The assumption that Marks was acting as an agent for JS rather than in his own financial interest is based on the fact that in early April 1837, shortly after Marks moved to Kirtland, JS and Sidney Rigdon transferred the church's printing office, which they owned, to Marks. On 7 and 10 April 1837, JS also transferred several important pieces of land to Marks, including the land purchased from French on 15 October 1836 and the lot on which the Kirtland temple had been built. On 11 July 1837, when JS, Sidney Rigdon, Oliver Cowdery, Hyrum Smith, Jared Carter, and Reynolds Cahoon mortgaged the temple to Mead, Stafford & Co., Marks did not seek personal compensation when he signed over to the firm the land on which the temple was built. (See Deed to William Marks, 10 Apr. 1837, in *JSP*, D5:357–362; Mortgage to Mead, Stafford & Co., 11 July 1837, in *JSP*, D5:404–410.)

187. Samuel F. Whitney moved to Kirtland by 1828.[a] He was not a member of the church and had acted antagonistically toward JS and other church members.[b] However, after Newel K. Whitney left Kirtland in 1838, Samuel managed Newel's Kirtland property and business affairs.[c] (a. "Died in Kirtland," *Deseret News*, 26 May 1886, 297; Kirtland Township Trustees' Minutes and Poll Book, 14 Oct. 1828, 61. b. Kirtland Township Trustees' Minutes and Poll Book, 29 Oct. 1831, 82; see also Warrant, 21 Oct. 1833, in *JSP*, D3:325–331. c. Newel K. Whitney, Power of Attorney to Samuel F. Whitney, 7 Nov. 1838; Samuel F. Whitney, Kirtland, OH, to Newel K. Whitney, Nauvoo, IL, 13 Jan. 1843, Newel K. Whitney, Papers, BYU.)

188. Geauga Co., OH, Deed Record, 1795–1921, vol. 25, pp. 570–571, 5 Feb. 1838, microfilm 20,241, U.S. and Canada Record Collection, FHL.

189. These promissory notes have not been located, but it was common practice for each of the promissory notes related to a mortgage or other purchase to be created, signed by the debtors, and then provided to the creditor at the time of the transaction. (See Mortgage to Mead, Stafford & Co., 11 July 1837, in *JSP*, D5:404–410.)

Under the 8 July quitclaim deed, JS and Emma Smith, Don Carlos and Agnes Smith, and William and Phebe Miller—all of the original purchasers other than William and Caroline Smith—transferred their interest in the land to Whitney. William Smith had turned over several pieces of land to Marks before moving to Missouri in early 1838 and may have given Marks a quitclaim deed for his portion of the property in exchange for land in Missouri.[190] The 8 July deed indicates that as part of the transaction, Whitney had agreed to pay $3,000, likely to Marks, for the right to the land. The deed identifies the sellers as "Joseph Smith Jr. & Others" and "Joseph Smith Jr. & Firm," suggesting that JS was considered the leader of the sale.

The content of revelations JS dictated on 8 July may have contributed to the execution of this deed on the same day. One of the revelations regarded the donation of surplus property and may have influenced JS and other Latter-day Saints newly settled in Missouri to discharge their Ohio land for the good of the church.[191] Another 8 July revelation, which instructed Marks and Newel K. Whitney to "settle up their businss speedily" and "let the properties of Kirtland be turned out for debt," also likely encouraged JS to execute the deed.[192] By signing the deed and confirming the sale of the land to Samuel F. Whitney, JS aided Marks in selling Kirtland property and providing funds to settle outstanding debts.

After the Smiths and Millers signed the deed on 8 July, Caldwell County judge William W. Phelps certified the deed and the release of the wives' dower rights.[193] The next day John Cleminson, clerk for the Caldwell County court, certified Phelps's authority by signing and sealing the document. The deed was then taken to Kirtland, probably by Oliver Granger, who had been instructed to return to Kirtland and manage church and business affairs there on behalf of the First Presidency.[194] In Kirtland the deed was given to Samuel F. Whitney, who brought it to Ralph Cowles, the Geauga County recorder in Chardon, Ohio. Cowles copied the deed into a Geauga County record book in October 1838. The original deed has not been located; the version featured here is the Geauga County record of the deed.

Document Transcript

Joseph Smith Jr. & Others To Samuel F Whitney

To all people to whom these presents shall come Greeting: Know Ye that we Joseph Smith Jr. & Emma Smith his wife Don C[arlos] Smith Agnes M Smith [Agnes Coolbrith Smith] his wife Wm Miller, Phebe Miller all of

---

190. See Historical Introduction to Pay Order to Edward Partridge for William Smith, 21 Feb. 1838, pp. 27–30 herein.

191. See Revelation, 8 July 1838–C, pp. 187–189 herein [D&C 119].

192. Letter to William Marks and Newel K. Whitney, 8 July 1838, p. 195 herein; see also Historical Introduction to Revelation, 8 July 1838–E [D&C 117], pp. 191–192 herein.

193. William W. Phelps was appointed a justice of the Caldwell County Court by Governor Lilburn W. Boggs on 4 February 1837. (Lilburn W. Boggs, Commission, Jefferson City, MO, to William W. Phelps, 4 Feb. 1837, William W. Phelps Commissions, CHL.)

194. See Letter to William Marks and Newel K. Whitney, 8 July 1838, pp. 195–196 herein.

Missouri State— For the consideration of three thousand dollars to us in hand paid by S. F. Whitney— received to our full satisfaction of— the State of Ohio Co. of Geauga, township of Kirtland— do remise release and forever quit claim unto the said S. F Whitney to his heirs assigns— and to heirs and assigns forever, the following described Tract piece parcel, or Lot of land lying situate in the township of Kirtland County of Geauga and the State of Ohio being in township number nine in the ninth Range of townships in the Connecticut Western Reserve so called— being in Co— Geauga, being known by the farm deeded by Peter French & Sarah French his wife— deeded to Joseph Smith Jr. Wᵐ Smith Don C Smith Wᵐ Miller, which deed being dated the fifth day of October AD. one thousand Eight hundred & thirty six— To have and to hold the above granted and bargained premises with the appurtenances thereof unto him the said S. F. Whitney his heirs and assigns forever to his and their own proper use and behoof. So that neither they the said Joseph Smith Jr. & Firm nor— heirs nor any other person or persons claiming under them or their administrators or assigns Shall at any time hereafter by any ways or means have claim or demand any right or title to the aforesaid premises or appurtenances or any part thereof, In witness whereof we have hereunto set our hands and seals the Eighth day of July in the year of our Lord One thousand Eight hundred and thirty Eight—

Joseph Smith Jr Seal[195]
Emma Smith Seal
Don C Smith Seal
Agnes M Smith Seal
William Miller Seal
Phebe Miller Seal

Signed Sealed and delivered in presence of
W[illiam] W Phelps

State of Missouri⎫
Caldwell County ss ⎬ July 8. A.D. 1838—

Personally appeared Joseph Smith Jr. Don C Smith and William Miller who acknowledged that they did sign and seal the foregoing instrument and that the same is their free act and deed I further certify that I did examine the said Emma Smith Agnes M. Smith and Phebe Miller separate and apart from their said husbands and did then and there make known to them the contents of the foregoing instrument and upon that examination they declared that

---

195. TEXT: All instances of "Seal" enclosed in hand-drawn representations of seals.

they did voluntarily sign seal and acknowledged the same and that they was still satisfied therewith[196]

William W. Phelps. President Judge[197] of Caldwell County Court— [p. 491]

    State of Missouri ⎤ ss.
    County of Caldwell ⎦

I John Cleminson Clerk of the County Court within and for the County aforesaid do certify that William W. Phelps before whom the foregoing acknowledgment appears to have been taken is the presiding Judge of the Caldwell County Court duly authorized and commissioned according to Law In testimoney whereof I have hereunto set my hand and seal affixed the seal of said Court at Far West this 9ᵗʰ day of July 1838

John Cleminson— Clerk

Ralph Cowles— Recorder

Received 25ᵗʰ and Recorded 27ᵗʰ of October A.D. 1838.

———— ℘ ————

Certificate from Elias Higbee, 9 July 1838

Source Note

Elias Higbee, Certificate, Caldwell Co., MO, to JS, Sidney Rigdon, and Hyrum Smith, 9 July 1838; one page; handwriting and signature of Elias Higbee; JS Collection, CHL. Includes docket.

Blue bifolium measuring 10 × 8 inches (25 × 20 cm). The document was folded for filing and was docketed. The document was presumably placed with JS's other papers after it was received and has remained in continuous institutional custody.

Historical Introduction

On 9 July 1838, Judge Elias Higbee wrote a certificate for JS, Sidney Rigdon, and Hyrum Smith, affirming that stolen goods had been recovered and verified as belonging to the three men and were thus being returned to them. Higbee was the presiding judge of Caldwell County as well as a member of the Zion high council in Far West, Missouri.[198] He stated in the certificate that the goods were "stolen or embezelled" from

---

196. This part of the deed released the dower rights the women legally had in the property after the deaths of their husbands. This release of rights required that the wives be questioned without their husbands present to ensure that the women understood the content of the deed and voluntarily accepted it. This procedure was followed in most instances in which a deed involved a married man. (An Act relating to Dower, [26 Jan. 1824], *Statutes of Ohio,* vol. 2, chap. 591, pp. 1314–1316; see also Mortgage to Peter French, 5 Oct. 1836, in *JSP,* D5:293–299.)

197. "President Judge" indicates Phelps held the highest judicial position in the county court. (An Act to Establish Courts of Record and Prescribe Their Powers and Duties [7 Mar. 1835], *Revised Statutes of the State of Missouri* [1835], p. 157, sec. 17.)

198. Minutes, 7 Nov. 1837, in *JSP,* D5:471; Parley P. Pratt, Testimony, Nauvoo, IL, 1 July 1843, p. 2, Nauvoo, IL, Records, CHL.

the men; were found in the possession of Sylvester Hulet, who was an elder in the church; and were seized from him.[199] Neither the certificate nor other extant documents provide details about the circumstances of the theft, the search warrant mentioned in the document, or the seizure of the goods. The language of the certificate closely follows that of the Missouri statute for recovering and returning "stolen or embezzled" goods. When an individual could produce "satisfactory proof of the title" to recovered property in the custody of a magistrate, the property would "be delivered to" the rightful owner after the owner paid "the necessary expenses incurred" by the magistrate in preserving the property. The magistrate would also issue a certificate documenting the transaction.[200] Higbee presumably produced the document in Caldwell County, his judicial jurisdiction, and most likely in Far West, the county seat. The certificate was apparently delivered to JS and the others in conjunction with the return of the goods.

Document Transcript

This is to certify that I have received satisfactory proof that a certain Lot of goods taken by virtue of a search warrant found in possession of Sylvester Hulitt [Hulet] are goods stolen or embezelled ⟨and⟩ are goods belonging to Joseph Smith Jun[r] Sidney Rigdon & others & Hiram [Hyrum] Smith[201] I therefore deliver the said Lot of goods unto Joseph Smith Jun[r.] & others as aforesaid that he & they take full possession of the same

Certified by me this 9th day of July AD 1838

Elias Higbee J.C.C.C.C.[202]

———— ☙ ————

199. Minute Book 2, 31 July–1 Aug. 1834.

200. An Act to Regulate Proceedings in Criminal Cases [21 Mar. 1835], *Revised Statutes of the State of Missouri* [1835], p. 500, art. 9, secs. 1–4, 6–8.

201. According to the statutes regarding stolen goods, a magistrate issued a warrant "upon complaint being made on oath, to any officer authorized to issue process for the apprehension of offenders, that any personal property has been stolen or embezzled, and that the complainant suspects that such property is concealed in any particular house, or place" and if the magistrate was satisfied that there were "reasonable grounds for such suspicion." The warrant was given to the sheriff or a constable. If the official recovered the stolen goods, he was to return them to the magistrate who issued the warrant. Therefore, JS, Rigdon, or Hyrum Smith apparently made a formal complaint to Higbee and indicated that they suspected the stolen goods were at Hulet's house. (An Act to Regulate Proceedings in Criminal Cases [21 Mar. 1835], *Revised Statutes of the State of Missouri* [1835], p. 500, art. 9, secs. 1–4; also 6.)

202. These initials represent Higbee's position. At the close of an affidavit made in September 1838, Higbee signed his name and identified himself as "one of the justices of the county court within and for Caldwell county." (Affidavit, 8 Sept. 1838, p. 236 herein; see also Affidavit, 5 Sept. 1838, pp. 222, 225 herein.)

Receipt from Samuel Musick, 14 July 1838

Source Note

Samuel Musick, Receipt, Far West, Caldwell Co., MO, to JS, 14 July 1838; handwriting of Edward Partridge; signature of Samuel Musick; one page; JS Collection, CHL.

One leaf measuring 2⅞–3 × 7½ inches (7–8 × 19 cm). The top and the left side of the recto are unevenly hand cut or torn. The document was folded, perhaps for transmission and storage. The document was presumably filed with JS's financial papers in Far West, Missouri, and has remained in continuous institutional custody. The Historical Department of the LDS church cataloged the receipt in the JS Collection in 1973.[203]

Historical Introduction

On 14 July 1838, Samuel Musick signed a receipt for rent that JS paid to lease Musick's tavern in Far West, Missouri. Musick, a native of Virginia, joined the church and moved to Missouri by 1834.[204] By November 1836, Musick apparently began operating the tavern.[205] The receipt mentions "an article"—presumably an article of agreement—between Musick and JS. However, because this article is apparently not extant, the specifics of JS's agreement with Musick are unclear. The receipt could be for a payment of an earlier promissory note for rent or could be for a scheduled payment as part of a rental contract. JS and others seem to have treated the tavern as JS's personal property, and several reminiscences suggest that JS may have purchased the tavern.[206] However, the language in the receipt suggests that if JS purchased the tavern, he had not done so by 14 July 1838.

When JS began renting the tavern, likely by May 1838, he apparently used it as a home for his family.[207] By 23 June, JS was apparently planning to move his family to

---

203. Johnson, *Register of the Joseph Smith Collection,* 10.

204. According to census records, during spring 1834 Samuel Musick's wife, Elizabeth, gave birth to a son in Missouri whom they named Teancum, after a soldier mentioned in the Book of Mormon. In 1835 Sally Waterman Phelps wrote a letter to her husband, William W. Phelps, in which she mentioned a "Bothe [Brother] Music" living with the Saints in Clay County, Missouri, but provided no other identifying information. (1850 U.S. Census, Ward 6, St. Louis, MO, 473[A]; 1860 U.S. Census, Pike, Stoddard Co., MO, 483; 1900 U.S. Census, Mansfield City, Wright Co., MO, 229B; Sally Waterman Phelps, Liberty, MO, to William W. Phelps, Kirtland, OH, 29 July 1835, William W. Phelps, Papers, BYU.)

205. Missouri law differentiated between licensed taverns, which were authorized to sell "wine or spirituous liquor," and private inns. The tavern operated by Musick and later by the Smiths was likely a licensed tavern. John Whitmer recorded purchasing brandy from Musick, and in June 1838 the high council in Far West instructed JS and other tavern keepers to no longer allow drinking at their establishments. In addition to regulating the sale and consumption of alcohol, Missouri law required innkeepers with tavern licenses to "find and provide . . . good and wholesome diet and lodging for travellers and other guests, and also provide and furnish sufficient stabling and provender for horses." (Musick Account, 30 Nov. 1836–18 May 1837, in Whitmer, Daybook; Minute Book 2, 23 June 1838; An Act to Regulate Inns and Taverns [18 Mar. 1835], *Revised Statutes of the State of Missouri* [1835], pp. 316, 317, 319, secs. 1–2, 13, 29.)

206. See, for example, Kimball, "History," 105–106; and Lucy Mack Smith, History, 1844–1845, bk. 15, [6].

207. In documents produced as late as 13 April 1838, the tavern was strictly associated with Musick, suggesting that JS began renting the building sometime after that date and before the featured receipt was issued on 14 July. Heber C. Kimball later wrote that JS purchased a house in Far West

George M. Hinkle's home in Far West. That day, Hinkle purchased property in De Witt, Missouri, with the intention of moving his family there, and the high council in Far West instructed Bishop Edward Partridge to "dispose of it [the tavern] as he pleases."[208] Two weeks later, the high council assigned Partridge to purchase Hinkle's Far West home for JS.[209]

Despite these arrangements, this 14 July receipt indicates that JS did not entirely relinquish control of the tavern. In late June or early July, JS turned over the tavern to his parents and extended family to serve as their home and a source of income. JS's mother, Lucy Mack Smith, later recalled that when the family arrived in Far West, they lived in "a small log house having but one room." Seeing that this was "a very inconveinient place for so large a family," she continued, JS proposed that she and Joseph Smith Sr. "take a large tavern house . . . and keep a tavern."[210] It is unclear when the extended Smith family moved into the Musick tavern, but records suggest the move may have occurred sometime between 23 and 28 June.[211] The Smith family maintained the tavern until they were expelled from Missouri.[212]

The 14 July receipt was prepared by Partridge, who helped manage JS's financial affairs after JS arrived in Far West in early 1838. Because of Partridge's role as bishop, he already had a number of financial responsibilities in the church, such as collecting donations, providing for impoverished members, and overseeing church lands. His management of JS's personal finances was likely seen as an outgrowth of these responsibilities.[213] In addition to preparing the receipt, Partridge likely engaged in the 14 July transaction with Musick on

---

"which had been formerly occupied as a public house." According to Kimball, JS later related that shortly after his family moved into the home, one of his children became very sick and JS performed several healing blessings for the child. Although there is no contemporaneous record of this event, JS's journal states that he spent much of 3 May 1838 "administering to the Sick," which may have included this incident. (Minutes, 13 Apr. 1838, p. 99 herein; Kimball, "History," 105–106; JS, Journal, 3 May 1838, in *JSP*, J1:264.)

208. Murdock, Journal, 23 June 1838, 95; John Murdock, Affidavit, Adams Co., IL, 10 Jan. 1840, photocopy, Material relating to Mormon Expulsion from Missouri, 1839–1843, CHL; Minute Book 2, 23 June 1838.

209. Minute Book 2, 6 July 1838.

210. JS's mother mentioned the tavern was "recently purchased from brother Gilbert," but she was apparently mistaken about the identity of the tavern's previous owner because there is no record of a Far West tavern owned by someone named Gilbert. Contemporaneous sources name only two taverns in Far West: the one operated by JS and one operated by church member John Burk. (Lucy Mack Smith, History, 1844–1845, bk. 15, [6]; Minute Book 2, 23 and 28–29 June 1838; see also *History of Caldwell and Livingston Counties, Missouri*, 121.)

211. On 23 June 1838, the high council in Far West appointed a committee to visit tavern keepers John Burk and JS to ensure that they keep "good orderly houses, and have no drinking, swearing, gambling, and debauchery carried on therein." On 28 June, the committee reported that "Mr J. Smith jr, Mr J. Burke *and families* manifested a perfect willingness to comply with the request of your Honorable body." The 23 June minutes do not mention the tavern keepers' families, but the 28 June minutes do, suggesting JS's extended family may have moved into the tavern between those dates. (Minute Book 2, 23 and 28–29 June 1838, italics added.)

212. Lucy Mack Smith, History, 1844–1845, bk. 16, [6].

213. Revelation, 4 Feb. 1831, in *JSP*, D1:244 [D&C 41:9]; see also Pay Order from Robert Snodgrass, 18 Sept. 1838, pp. 245–246 herein; and Receipt from Timothy Clark, Oct. 1838, pp. 262–263 herein.

JS's behalf since JS was in Adam-ondi-Ahman, Missouri, at the time.[214] Musick presumably signed the receipt and returned it to Partridge to keep on JS's behalf.

Document Transcript

Rec^{ed.} of Joseph Smith Jun. fifteen dollars 75/100 which is to apply upon an article which is given for the rent of my tavern house in Far West
Far West July 14th 1838 Samuel Musick LS[215]

———— ❧ ————

Minutes, 26 July 1838

Source Note

First Presidency, Zion high council, and Zion bishop's council, Minutes, [Far West, Caldwell Co., MO], 26 July 1838. Featured version copied [ca. 26 July 1838] in JS, Journal, Mar.–Sept. 1838, pp. 59–60; handwriting of George W. Robinson; CHL. Includes use marks. For more information on JS, Journal, Mar.–Sept. 1838, see Source Notes for Multiple-Entry Documents, p. 564 herein.

Historical Introduction

On 26 July 1838, JS met with several other church leaders to determine how to manage property that Latter-day Saints in Caldwell County, Missouri, had recently donated to the church. Earlier in the month, on 8 July, JS dictated a revelation calling for the Latter-day Saints to donate all of their surplus property to the church and thereafter to donate "one tenth of all their interest annually."[216] Later that day, JS dictated another revelation, directing that donated property be managed by a council consisting of the First Presidency and the Zion bishopric and high council, acting together under the inspiration of God.[217] In response to the revelation about making donations, the Saints began donating property of various kinds. On 26 July, the council of church leaders that was called for in the latter revelation met to determine how to manage these donations. The council likely convened in Far West, where JS and other church leaders were living at the time.[218] The council members agreed on several resolutions, most of which clarified the relationship between the First Presidency and the bishop in financial matters.

The minutes do not identify an appointed clerk for the council but contain the specificity of and are written in the style of formal minutes. George W. Robinson may have taken minutes at the meeting, which would explain why he inscribed them in JS's journal

---

214. Swartzell, *Mormonism Exposed*, 17–18.

215. TEXT: Inscription is surrounded by a hand-drawn representation of a seal. "L S" is an abbreviation for *locus sigilli*, which is Latin for "location of the seal."

216. Revelation, 8 July 1838–C, pp. 187, 188 herein [D&C 119:1, 4]. This direction adapted the church's original plan, presented in earlier revelations, for consecrating property. (See, for example, Revelation, 9 Feb. 1831, in *JSP*, D1:251–252 [D&C 42:30–39].)

217. Revelation, 8 July 1838–D, p. 190 herein [D&C 120].

218. See JS, Journal, 8–28 July 1838, in *JSP*, J1:288–294.

and why the minutes do not appear in Minute Book 2, where clerks typically recorded the minutes of high council and other meetings. Robinson inscribed the minutes in JS's journal likely on the day of or within a few days after the meeting, as they appear immediately before a series of daily journal entries, the first of which is dated 27 July 1838.[219]

Document Transcript

July 26th 1838 This day the first presidency, High Council, & Bishops Court,[220] ~~to~~ met to take into concideration, the disposing of the publick properties in the hands of the Bishop, in Zion, for the people of Zion have commenced liberally to consecrate agreeably to the revelations, and commandments of the Great I am[221] of their surpluss properties &c.

It was agreed that the first presidency keep all their properties, that they can dispose of to their advantage and support, and the remainder be put into the hands of the Bishop or Bishops,[222] agreeably to the commandments, and revelations,

1[st.] Mooved seconded & carried unanymously, That the first presidency shall have their expences defrayed in going to Adam Ondi Awman [Adam-ondi-Ahman], and also returning therefrom That the Bishop of Zion pay one half, and the Bishop of Adam Ondi Awman the other half[223]

2[nd.] Mooved seconded & carried unanymously— that all the traveling expences of the first presidency, shall be defrayed in traveling at any time or place [p. 59]

3[rd.] Mooved seconded & carried unanymously That the Bishop be authorized to pay orders coming from the east inasmuch as they will consecrate liberally, but this to be done under the inspection of the first presidency[224]

---

219. See JS, Journal, 26 July–10 Sept. 1838, in *JSP*, J1:291–319.

220. The "Bishops Court" consisted of the bishop and his counselors. (See Revelation, 8 July 1838–D, p. 190 herein [D&C 120].)

221. This name for Deity, taken from Exodus 3:14, also appears in several of JS's early revelations. (See Revelation, Sept. 1830–A, in *JSP*, D1:178 [D&C 29:1]; Revelation, 2 Jan. 1831, in *JSP*, D1:230 [D&C 38:1]; and Revelation, 5 Jan. 1831, in *JSP*, D1:235 [D&C 39:1].)

222. A month earlier, Vinson Knight was appointed the pro tempore bishop at Adam-ondi-Ahman, Missouri. Bishop Newel K. Whitney, still residing in Kirtland, Ohio, was expected to move to Missouri and act as a bishop there. (Minutes, 28 June 1838, p. 166 herein; Revelation, 8 July 1838–E, p. 193 herein [D&C 117:11].)

223. JS, his counselors in the First Presidency, and Robinson visited Adam-ondi-Ahman repeatedly during the previous two months. (JS, Journal, 18 May–5 June 1838, in *JSP*, J1:270–275; Minutes, 28 June 1838, pp. 162–167 herein; John Smith, Journal, 28 June 1838; JS History, vol. B-1, 804; see also Swartzell, *Mormonism Exposed*, 9–25.)

224. Many Latter-day Saints emigrating from Kirtland entrusted church leaders remaining there with the proceeds from selling the Saints' properties. In return, these Saints received pay orders written by William Marks on behalf of JS and Sidney Rigdon that stated the value of the Saints' donations. Upon arriving in Missouri, the Saints presented the pay orders to Bishop Edward Partridge to request repayment in

4th That the first presidency shall have the prerogative to say to the Bishop whose orders, shall or may be paid by him in this place or in his Jurisdiction. <u>carried unanimously</u>

5[th.] Mooved seconded and carried That the Bishop of Zion receive all consecrations,[225] east, west, & south, who are not in the Jurisdiction of a Bishop of any other stake.[226]

6th Mooved & carried, that we use our influence to put a stop to the selling of Liquor in the City Far West or in our midst, That our streets may not be filled with drunkeness[227] and that we use our influence to bring down the price of provisions.—[228]

7[th.] Mooved, seconded & carried unanimously that <u>br. W[m] W. Phelps,</u> be requested to draw up a petition to remove the county seat to Far West[229]

---

money or property. (Corrill, *Brief History*, 27, in *JSP,* H2:161; Reed Peck, Quincy, IL, to "Dear Friends," 18 Sept. 1839, pp. 14–15, Henry E. Huntington Library, San Marino, CA; Pay Order to Edward Partridge for William Smith, 21 Feb. 1838, pp. 27–30 herein; see also Receipt from Timothy Clark, Oct. 1838, pp. 262–263 herein; and Receipt from Sarah Burt Beman, 26 Jan. 1839, pp. 323–325 herein.)

225. See Revelation, 9 Feb. 1831, in *JSP,* D1:251–252 [D&C 42:33].

226. A month earlier, a stake was organized to the north at Adam-ondi-Ahman, with Vinson Knight as the pro tempore bishop. De Witt, the other stake planned in Missouri, had not been organized. (Minutes, 28 June 1838, p. 166 herein; Letter to Stephen Post, 17 Sept. 1838, p. 242 herein; R. Peck to "Dear Friends," 18 Sept. 1839, pp. 20–21; Rockwood, Journal, 14 Oct. 1838.)

227. The "Word of Wisdom," the church's revealed dietary code, proscribed "strong drink." In the reorganization conference held in Far West in November 1837, the congregation voted that they would not support "Stores and Shops selling spirituous liquors, Tea, Coffee or Tobacco." On 23 June 1838, the high council in Far West appointed a committee to visit local tavern keepers to ensure that they were keeping "good orderly houses, and have no drinking, swearing, gambling, and debauchery carried on therein." (Revelation, 27 Feb. 1833, in *JSP,* D3:20 [D&C 89:5]; Minutes, 7 Nov. 1837, in *JSP,* D5:472; Minute Book 2, 23 June 1838.)

228. The church's original communitarian plans in Missouri included a store that also functioned as a storehouse to help provision the Latter-day Saints.[a] Prices on the frontier could be significantly higher than elsewhere in the United States. In Missouri, according to historian Jeff Bremer, "almost all goods [were] sold at two to three times eastern prices."[b] Three days before this meeting, Reynolds Cahoon wrote from Far West to Newel K. Whitney in Kirtland with suggestions of what kinds of goods Whitney should bring to Missouri since it was possible to "transport them much Cheaper than you can git them hear." Cahoon's list included furniture, stoves, livestock, and plows, among other items.[c] (a. See Revelation, 20 July 1831, in *JSP,* D2:11 [D&C 57:8–10]; Revelation, 1 Aug. 1831, in *JSP,* D2:16, 17 [D&C 58:24, 37]; and Berrett, *Sacred Places*, 4:47–48. b. Bremer, *Store Almost in Sight*, 155. c. Reynolds Cahoon, Far West, MO, to Newel K. Whitney, Kirtland, OH, 23 July 1838, CHL; see also Editorial, *Elders' Journal*, July 1838, 34.)

229. This decision was reaffirmed within two weeks.[a] The legislation that organized Caldwell County in December 1836 included measures for establishing a seat of justice in April 1837.[b] It is not known whether these measures were followed. However, Far West served as the county's de facto if not official seat of justice because the town was the place where county justices Elias Higbee and William W. Phelps operated, where the office of county clerk John Cleminson was located, and where the circuit court was held a few days after this 26 July meeting.[c] The Latter-day Saints in Caldwell County, and apparently other Missourians as well, considered Far West the county seat.[d] (a. JS, Journal, 6 Aug. 1838, in *JSP,* J1:298. b. An Act to Organize the Counties of Caldwell and Daviess [29 Dec. 1836],

Discourse, 29 July 1838

Source Note

JS, Discourse, Adam-ondi-Ahman, Daviess Co., MO, 29 July 1838. Featured version published [ca. May 1840] in William Swartzell, Mormonism Exposed, 27. For more information on William Swartzell, Mormonism Exposed, see Source Notes for Multiple-Entry Documents, p. 578 herein.

Historical Introduction

On 29 July 1838, JS preached at a Sunday worship service held at Adam-ondi-Ahman, Missouri, regarding the spiritual manifestations and persecution he had experienced and his willingness to submit to the will of God. According to George W. Robinson, JS and Sidney Rigdon left Far West for Adam-ondi-Ahman on 28 July to "transact some important buisness" and assist in the settlement of recent immigrants from Upper Canada.[230] At least part of this business may have been the formal integration of the Danites at Adam-ondi-Ahman into the broader Danite organization, which was headquartered at Far West. According to William Swartzell, a Latter-day Saint who was living in Adam-ondi-Ahman and keeping a journal at the time, the Danites at Adam-ondi-Ahman met on 28 July and were placed under the command of a brigadier general and other officers.[231] JS and Rigdon presumably attended this meeting and may have addressed the men prior to their reorganization.[232]

Swartzell wrote that the next day, Rigdon and JS addressed the Saints during the worship service held at Lyman Wight's unfinished home at the foot of Tower Hill in Adam-ondi-Ahman.[233] Rigdon spoke first, taking Ephesians 4:4–13 as his text and expounding on the

---

Laws of the State of Missouri [1836–1837], pp. 46–47, sec. 3; see also An Act for Organizing Counties Hereafter Established [9 Dec. 1836], *Laws of the State of Missouri* [1836–1837], pp. 38–39, secs. 1–4; and An Act to Establish Judicial Circuits, and to Prescribe the Times and Places of Holding Courts [21 Jan. 1837], *Laws of the State of Missouri* [1836–1837], p. 57, sec. 23. *c.* Petitions for Habeas Corpus to Elias Higbee, Aug. 1838, George W. Robinson, Papers, CHL; Certificate of William W. Phelps's Oath of Office, 4 Apr. 1838, William W. Phelps Commissions, CHL; JS, Journal, 30–31 July 1838, in *JSP*, J1:294–296. *d.* Editorial, *Elders' Journal*, July 1838, 33; see also Greene, *Facts relative to the Expulsion*, 18; *Illustrated Historical Atlas of Caldwell County, Missouri*, 8, 10; and *History of Caldwell and Livingston Counties, Missouri*, 121, 259.)

230. JS, Journal, 28 July 1838, in *JSP*, J1:294.

231. Swartzell, *Mormonism Exposed*, 25–26.

232. Swartzell wrote that in two earlier Danite meetings held at Adam-ondi-Ahman, JS preached to the men. Swartzell also noted that on 28 July, the Danites at Adam-ondi-Ahman were organized "after considerable preaching, as usual"—suggesting that JS may also have addressed the Danites during this organizational meeting. John Smith, the president of the Adam-ondi-Ahman stake, noted in his journal that at least three Danite meetings had taken place by 4 August 1838, though he neglected to provide dates or additional details. (Swartzell, *Mormonism Exposed*, 17–18, 20–21, 25–26; see also Thompson, "Chronology of Danite Meetings in Adam-ondi-Ahman," 12; and John Smith, Journal, 4 Aug. 1838.)

233. Swartzell, *Mormonism Exposed*, 26; Berrett, *Sacred Places*, 4:376, 399–402. John Smith likewise noted in his journal the following week that JS and Rigdon held a meeting in Adam-ondi-Ahman "last Sabbath." (John Smith, Journal, 4 Aug. 1838.)

theme of "one Lord, one faith, one baptism." He criticized other Christian denominations for their lack of "those gifts which Jesus Christ gave to men when he ascended on high."[234]

JS spoke next, taking 1 Thessalonians 5:15–23 as his text, particularly the instruction to "despise not prophesyings." Much of JS's address, as captured by Swartzell, focused on JS's experiences—possibly drawing on the themes and events he had recently narrated in a new personal and church history. JS, Rigdon, and Robinson had begun work on the history in late April 1838, following the excommunication of John Whitmer, the previous church historian.[235] The draft of this history focused on JS's earliest visions, including his first vision of Deity and the persecution he faced after reporting the experience.[236] Though Swartzell's account of JS's 29 July sermon lacks detail, the material he recorded matches elements of JS's written history.

Swartzell apparently recorded JS's discourse in his journal on or within a few days of the worship service.[237] Part of his account is a summary, but he also captured, or attempted to capture, some of JS's words. Within a month of this meeting, Swartzell renounced the church and returned to his former home in Pekin, Ohio.[238] In spring 1840, Swartzell prepared his journal, which is no longer extant, for publication as part of an anti-Mormon exposé explaining his history with the church and warning about "one of the most extraordinary bands of fanatics that ever was known in the annals of human delusion."[239] While Swartzell added retrospective material to his journal before publication, it is fairly easy to distinguish these editorial comments and explanations from the rather ordinary entries of the original journal.[240] As a whole, Swartzell's historical account of events in Adam-ondi-Ahman matches well with contemporary sources. No evidence suggests that his account of JS's 29 July discourse was manufactured or embellished. In fact, on other occasions Swartzell reported that JS had preached but that Swartzell did "not recollect" JS's words.[241]

Document Transcript

Brother Joseph Smith then preached, and took his text in 1 Tessalonians, 5:15 to 23d verse. He preached on prophecy, and said that the Spirit of God had appeared to him, with wonderful *light* and *mystery*—in such a manner that we would not believe him, were he to tell us what he had seen;[242] and that he could

---

234. Swartzell, *Mormonism Exposed,* 26–27.

235. See Letter to John Whitmer, 9 Apr. 1838, pp. 77–79 herein.

236. JS, Journal, 30 Apr.–4 May 1838, in *JSP,* J1:263–264; see also "Joseph Smith's Historical Enterprise," in *JSP,* H1:xxii–xxiii; and Historical Introduction to History Drafts, 1838–ca. 1841, in *JSP,* H1:195.

237. Swartzell's journal has daily entries. His account of JS's 29 July 1838 discourse begins by stating that JS and Rigdon preached "to-day," suggesting that Swartzell wrote the entry later that day. (Swartzell, *Mormonism Exposed,* 26.)

238. Swartzell, *Mormonism Exposed,* 35–37.

239. Swartzell, *Mormonism Exposed,* [iii].

240. See, for example, Swartzell, *Mormonism Exposed,* 11, 13–14, 21.

241. Swartzell, *Mormonism Exposed,* 21.

242. JS seems to have been talking about his first vision of Deity. The history JS initiated in 1838 states that in 1820, the young JS prayed to know which church to join and in response "saw a pillar of light

Lyman Wight home and land in Adam-ondi-Ahman, Missouri. In February 1838, Lyman Wight purchased a small cabin and farm near the Grand River in Daviess County, Missouri. Within the next few months, he began building a larger home (left, photographed circa 1904) on the side of the bluffs overlooking the river. That summer, Joseph Smith spent considerable time at and near Wight's property (right, 1907), surveying the area for future church settlement. On 29 July, a congregation of Saints gathered in Wight's unfinished home, and Joseph Smith delivered a sermon recounting a vision he had received and the persecution he had suffered. (Both images: Church History Library, Salt Lake City. House photograph by James Ricalton. Land photograph by George Edward Anderson.)

not say what God did these things for.²⁴³ "But," said he, "I cannot help it.²⁴⁴ I know that all the world is threatening my life; but I regard it not, for I am willing to die at any time when God calls for me. I have been beaten, abused, stoned, persecuted, and have had to escape by day and by night.²⁴⁵ I have been sued at law, and have always proved myself innocent.²⁴⁶ I have had *twenty-one law-suits*.²⁴⁷ I am of age; and care not how long I live. Not my will be done, but thine, O Lord!"²⁴⁸

exactly over my head . . . which descended gradually untill it fell upon me. . . . When the light rested upon me I saw two personages [God and Jesus Christ] (whose brightness and glory defy all description) standing above me in the air." (JS History, vol. A-1, 3, in *JSP*, H1:214 [Draft 2].)

243. In accounts of his first vision of Deity, JS stated that God appeared to him in answer to his prayers for forgiveness of his sins and for guidance on which church to join. JS was told that his sins were forgiven and that he should not join any church; he also received "a promise that the fulness of the gospel should at some future time be made known" to him. In these accounts, JS did not disclose everything he saw and heard. For example, in the account written in the history he started in 1838, he added that "many other things did he [Jesus Christ] say unto me which I cannot write at this time." (JS History, ca. Summer 1832, 3, in *JSP*, H1:12–13; JS History, vol. A-1, 3, in *JSP*, H1:214 [Draft 2]; JS, "Church History," *Times and Seasons*, 1 Mar. 1842, 3:707, in *JSP*, H1:494.)

244. In the history JS began in 1838, he narrated his first vision of Deity using similar language: "Though I was hated and persecuted for saying that I had seen a vision, Yet it was true. . . . I knew it, and I knew that God knew it, and I could not deny it." (JS History, vol. A-1, 4, in *JSP*, H1:218 [Draft 2].)

245. JS was the victim of violence on a number of occasions during the 1820s and 1830s, including being beaten and tarred and feathered in Hiram Township, Ohio, in 1832. Threats of violence increased following the dissent that gripped the church in 1837. Mary Fielding reported that in fall 1837, JS and Rigdon escaped from a mob while traveling near Painesville, Ohio—presumably in the daytime. On 12 January 1838, JS dictated a revelation instructing the members of the First Presidency and their families to leave Kirtland, Ohio, because of their enemies there. JS and Rigdon fled Kirtland that night. (JS History, vol. A-1, 205–208; Mary Fielding, [Kirtland, OH], to Mercy F. Thompson, [Upper Canada], [between ca. Aug. and Sept. 1837], Mary Fielding Smith, Collection, CHL; Revelation, 12 Jan. 1838–C, in *JSP*, D5:501–502; JS History, vol. B-1, 780; Introduction to Part 1: 15 Feb.–28 June 1838, p. 3 herein.)

246. JS was never convicted in a criminal trial, with the possible exception of an 1826 trial in South Bainbridge, New York, in which he was charged with being a "disorderly person." This charge was related to JS's employment with Josiah Stowell in 1825, during which JS used a seer stone in an attempt to find buried treasure. Accounts of the trial are contradictory, variously stating or suggesting that JS was discharged, found guilty, acquitted, or allowed (and encouraged) to escape and leave the area. (See Trial Proceedings, Bainbridge, NY, 20 Mar. 1826, State of New York v. JS [J.P. Ct. 1826], in "The Original Prophet," *Fraser's Magazine*, Feb. 1873, 229–230; Oliver Cowdery, "Letter VIII," *LDS Messenger and Advocate*, Oct. 1835, 2:201; W. D. Purple, "Joseph Smith, the Originator of Mormonism," *Chenango Union* [Norwich, NY], 2 May 1877, [3]; and [Abram W. Benton], "Mormonites," *Evangelical Magazine and Gospel Advocate*, 9 Apr. 1831, 120.)

247. JS appears to have been the defendant in at least thirty legal cases prior to July 1838, six of which were criminal rather than civil cases. Other cases against JS may have been brought before local justices of the peace who were not required to keep records, who neglected to keep records, or whose records have been lost. (See, for example, John C. Dowen, Statement, 2 Jan. 1885, Collection of Manuscripts about Mormons, 1832–1954, Chicago History Museum; see also "Legal Chronology of Joseph Smith," in Madsen et al., *Sustaining the Law*, 461–479.)

248. See Luke 22:42.

Discourse, 12 August 1838

Source Note

JS, Discourse, Adam-ondi-Ahman, Daviess Co., MO, 12 Aug. 1838. Featured version published [ca. May 1840] in William Swartzell, Mormonism Exposed, *32–33. For more information on William Swartzell,* Mormonism Exposed, *see Source Notes for Multiple-Entry Documents, p. 578 herein.*

Historical Introduction

On 12 August 1838, JS delivered a discourse at a Sunday worship service held at Adam-ondi-Ahman, Daviess County, Missouri, regarding the troubles between the Saints and other Missourians. The members of the First Presidency stopped at Adam-ondi-Ahman on their way from Far West, Caldwell County, Missouri, to the "Forks of Grand River" in Daviess County, where they intended to counsel with a company of Canadian Saints who settled there instead of at Adam-ondi-Ahman, where they had been instructed to settle.[249]

This stop in Adam-ondi-Ahman occurred amid the increasing turmoil between the Saints and other residents of Missouri. On 30 July, non-Mormons held a public meeting at Carrollton, the seat of Carroll County, and passed resolutions calling for the Saints to leave the county. Those at the meeting also sent a committee to De Witt, a settlement in the county, to demand that the Saints leave by 7 August.[250] On that day, the committee reported in another public meeting at Carrollton that the Saints were determined to stay and that "they would apply to the Far West for assistance" if needed. In response to this report, the citizens of Carroll County began seeking allies in neighboring counties and requesting "aid to remove Mormons, abolitionists, and other disorderly persons" from the county.[251]

Troubles were also increasing in Daviess County, Missouri. On 6 August, a riot broke out at the election poll in Gallatin, and on 8 August, Latter-day Saints confronted Adam Black, a justice of the peace, who was reportedly organizing anti-Mormon vigilantes to take action against the Saints. Rumors of conflict with the Latter-day Saints spread to the surrounding counties, fueling fears that the Saints were in rebellion against the state.[252] On 9 and 10 August, residents at public meetings in Richmond, Ray County, called for an investigation of the confrontation with Black and for a peaceful resolution of hostilities. The Richmond citizens appointed a three-man committee to travel to Daviess and Caldwell counties and gather information regarding the conflict.[253] According to William Swartzell, a Latter-day Saint living in Adam-ondi-Ahman, on 11 August the committee

---

249. JS, Journal, 11 Aug. 1838, in *JSP*, J1:302; see also JS, Journal, 6 Aug. 1838, in *JSP*, J1:297.

250. "The Mormons in Carroll County," *Missouri Republican* (St. Louis), 18 Aug. 1838, [2]. The committee was appointed to deliver its message to prominent non-Mormons at De Witt, but the committee apparently addressed the Saints there as well. (Murdock, Autobiography, 37.)

251. "The Mormons in Carroll County," *Missouri Republican* (St. Louis), 18 Aug. 1838, [2].

252. See Introduction to Part 2: 8 July–29 Oct. 1838, pp. 173–174 herein.

253. "Mormon War," *Missouri Republican* (St. Louis), 3 Sept. 1838, [2]; "Public Meeting," *Missouri Republican*, 3 Sept. 1838, [2].

traveled to the town, where JS had stopped on his way to the Canadian Saints' settlement. The committee, JS, and about one hundred other Latter-day Saints met "at the usual place of meeting for worship"—likely the grove near Lyman Wight's first cabin.[254] The committee then went to Wight's unfinished home and met privately with Wight and JS.[255]

The next day, JS addressed a congregation of Saints in Adam-ondi-Ahman.[256] According to Swartzell, the meeting was held in the morning in the same place that JS met the committee the day before; it is unclear whether Swartzell was referring to the public meeting grounds or to Wight's unfinished home, where JS had preached two weeks earlier.[257] JS gave a discourse in which he exhorted the Saints in Adam-ondi-Ahman "to be of good cheer," assuring them that they were not in danger but also admonishing them to be prepared to travel to De Witt in Carroll County to rescue the Saints living there.

William Swartzell apparently recorded the discourse in his journal within a few days after JS gave the sermon.[258] While the majority of Swartzell's account is a summary, he also captured, or attempted to capture, some of JS's words. Swartzell's original journal is apparently not extant; however, after he left the church, he published the journal as part of an anti-Mormon exposé.[259]

Document Transcript

The Prophet exhorted the [p. 32] brethren to be of good cheer,[260] and not to be "scared at trifles,"[261] "that he would tell them when danger was near—that at

---

254. Swartzell, *Mormonism Exposed,* 32; 165n803 herein.

255. The timing of the committee's movements is somewhat unclear. According to George W. Robinson, a public meeting was held in Far West on the evening of 11 August in response to the committee's visit. Robinson initially dated the meeting minutes as 13 August in JS's journal but then revised the date to 11 August. Further, Robinson's minutes indicate the committee came from Ray County, whereas Swartzell's entry identifies the committee as coming from Clay County. Given the discrepancies in the accounts, there are many possibilities regarding the details of the visit: Robinson may have incorrectly dated the committee's visit; or the committee may have visited Far West on 11 August in hopes of conferring with JS, who had already left for Daviess County, and may have caught up to him at Adam-ondi-Ahman later in the day; or the committee may have split up and visited Caldwell and Daviess counties simultaneously; or the committee at Adam-ondi-Ahman may have been a separate committee sent from Clay County and not mentioned in other extant documents. (JS, Journal, 11 Aug. 1838, in *JSP,* J1:302–303; Swartzell, *Mormonism Exposed,* 32.)

256. This meeting may have been the usual Sunday worship service; however, Swartzell wrote that "the congregation was called together" specifically by JS for a morning meeting, perhaps so that JS could travel to the Forks of Grand River later that day. (Swartzell, *Mormonism Exposed,* 32; JS, Journal, 12 Aug. 1838, in *JSP,* J1:303.)

257. See Discourse, 29 July 1838, pp. 209–212 herein.

258. Swartzell's journal has daily entries. Also, his account of JS's 12 August 1838 discourse states that it was delivered in a meeting held "this morning," suggesting that Swartzell wrote the entry that day.

259. For more on the reliability of Swartzell's published journal, see Historical Introduction to Discourse, 29 July 1838, pp. 209–210 herein.

260. See, for example, Mark 6:50; John 16:33; Acts 27:22; Book of Mormon, 1830 ed., 453 [3 Nephi 1:13]; and Revelation, 1 Nov. 1831–A, in *JSP,* D2:101 [D&C 68:6].

261. JS may have been drawing from "The Hunters of Kentucky," a popular song celebrating Andrew Jackson and the American victory over the British in the 1815 Battle of New Orleans. The

present he did not even anticipate such a thing[262]—for us to hold ourselves in readiness at a moment's warning, well armed and equipped, to go down to Carroll county and rescue brother [George M.] Hinkle,[263] who is in a suffering condition; and that they must expect to endure trials there."

——————— ❧ ———————

Selections from *Elders' Journal,* August 1838

Source Note

Selections from Elders' Journal, *Aug. 1838, 54, 62. For more information on* Elders' Journal, *see Source Notes for Multiple-Entry Documents, p. 563 herein.*

Historical Introduction

The *Elders' Journal,* which published two issues in Kirtland, Ohio, in 1837 before the church's printing office was destroyed, was reestablished in Far West, Missouri, in 1838, after JS and most other church leaders migrated from Kirtland to Far West. Thomas B. Marsh was the proprietor of the newspaper, and JS was the editor, though the amount and nature of JS's involvement and editorial oversight is unclear.[264] By May 1838, JS and Sidney Rigdon began working on material for the first Far West issue, dated July 1838.[265] Ultimately,

---

song reported: "Jackson he was wide awake, / And wasn't scared at trifles, / For well he knew what aim we take / With our Kentucky rifles." ("The Hunters of Kentucky," in Burton, *Burton's Comic Songster,* 52.)

262. Following the 12 August worship meeting at Adam-ondi-Ahman, the First Presidency proceeded to the Mormon settlement at the "forks of Grand river." After a worship service held at Anson Call's home, JS spoke privately with some of the men in the settlement. Years later, Call recounted that JS instructed them to relocate to Adam-ondi-Ahman or Far West because "there was going to be difficulties." (JS, Journal, 12 Aug. 1838, in *JSP,* J1:303; Call, Autobiography, 10.)

263. JS and the high council in Far West had sent Hinkle to settle De Witt, downriver from Adam-ondi-Ahman at the confluence of the Grand and Missouri rivers. Charles Hales, a Latter-day Saint living in De Witt, later wrote that Hinkle served as the "president of the Branch." The First Presidency intended to establish a stake of Zion in De Witt. (Murdock, Autobiography, 37; "Biographies of the Seventies of the Second Quorum," 208; Letter to Stephen Post, 17 Sept. 1838, p. 242 herein; Reed Peck, Quincy, IL, to "Dear Friends," 18 Sept. 1839, pp. 20–21, Henry E. Huntington Library, San Marino, CA; see also Rockwood, Journal, 14 Oct. 1838.)

264. See Selections from *Elders' Journal,* Oct. 1837, in *JSP,* D5:460–463; Historical Introduction to Selections from *Elders' Journal,* Nov. 1837, in *JSP,* D5:484–485; Minutes, 21 Apr. 1838, p. 110 herein; and Prospectus for *Elders' Journal,* 30 Apr. 1838, p. 132 herein. JS was identified as the editor of the November 1837 issue of the paper even though he was away from Kirtland from 27 September to approximately 10 December. (Editorial, *Elders' Journal,* Nov. 1837, 27; Letter to Wilford Woodruff, ca. 18 June 1838, p. 156 herein; Vilate Murray Kimball, Kirtland, OH, to Heber C. Kimball, Preston, England, 19–29 Jan. 1838, Heber C. Kimball, Collection, CHL.)

265. See JS, Journal, 8 May 1838, in *JSP,* J1:267. In May, Sidney Rigdon was assigned to edit the letters that would be included in the *Elders' Journal.* (Minute Book 2, 12 May 1838; see also Minute Book 2, 23 June 1838.)

two issues were published in Missouri, dated July 1838 and August 1838. The July issue included letters to and from church elders serving proselytizing missions, as well as articles, minutes of meetings, and other items.[266] The August issue contained similar material, including an editorial by JS and a letter that the First Presidency commissioned George W. Robinson to write to Latter-day Saints who had not yet gathered to Missouri. The August issue also included an obituary for Ethan Barrows Jr., who died in mid-August 1838,[267] indicating that the issue was published sometime in the second half of the month or later.

The first editorial JS prepared for the August 1838 issue of the *Elders' Journal* encouraged Latter-day Saints to acquire personal copies of the sermon that First Presidency member Sidney Rigdon delivered on 4 July 1838 at an Independence Day celebration,[268] which JS presided over.[269] Decades later, Ebenezer Robinson apparently stated that JS reviewed the sermon in advance.[270] In the address, Rigdon recounted the principles of freedom on which the United States government was founded, and he affirmed church members' allegiance to the nation but also declared the Saints' intention to vigorously defend their rights. A copy of the sermon appeared by early August in the *Far West,* a newspaper published in Liberty, Missouri.[271] Additionally, Robinson published the sermon in pamphlet form, entitled *Oration Delivered by Mr. S. Rigdon, on the 4th of July, 1838.*[272] To encourage Latter-day Saints to secure copies of the pamphlet, JS prepared the featured editorial for publication in the August issue of the *Elders' Journal.* No manuscript of the editorial is known to exist; the printed version is reproduced here.

———— ❧ ————

Document Transcript

In this paper, we give the procedings which were had on the fourth of July, at this place, in laying the corner stones of the temple, about to be built in this city.[273]

The oration delivered on the occasion, is now published in pamphlet form:[274] those of our friends wishing to have one, can get it, by calling on

---

266. See, for example, Questions and Answers, 8 May 1838, pp. 139–145 herein.

267. The obituary in the *Elders' Journal* states that Barrows died on 15 August, but his father's later autobiography gives the date of 18 August. (Obituary for Ethan Barrows Jr., *Elders' Journal,* Aug. 1838, 64; "The Journal of Ethan Barrows," *Journal of History,* Jan. 1922, 46; see also "The Journal of Ethan Barrows," *Journal of History,* Oct. 1922, 451–452.)

268. See Historical Introduction to Discourse, ca. 4 July 1838, at josephsmithpapers.org.

269. "Celebration of the 4th of July," *Elders' Journal,* Aug. 1838, 60.

270. Ebenezer Robinson, "Items of Personal History of the Editor," *Return,* Nov. 1889, 170–171.

271. JS, Journal, 1–3 Aug. 1838, in *JSP,* J1:296.

272. See Crawley, *Descriptive Bibliography,* 1:80.

273. "Celebration of the 4th of July," *Elders' Journal,* Aug. 1838, 60.

274. See Discourse, ca. 4 July 1838, at josephsmithpapers.org.

Ebenezer Robinson, by whom they were printed. We would reccommend to all the saints to get one, to be had in their families, as it contains an outline of the suffering and persecutions of the Church from its rise. As also the fixed determinations of the saints, in relation to the persecutors, who are, and have been, continually, not only threatening us with mobs, but actually have been putting their threats into execution; with which we are absolutely determined no longer to bear, come life or come death, for to be mob[b]ed any more without taking vengeance, we will not.[275]

EDITOR.

[. . .] [p. 54] [. . .]

———— ❧ ————

Editorial Note

The August issue of the *Elders' Journal* also included a letter "to the Saints gathering into Zion." The letter was presumably written in expectation of a large group of Latter-day Saints arriving from Kirtland, Ohio, as well as the continued gathering to Missouri of newly converted Saints from throughout the United States and abroad.[276] The letter was written by George W. Robinson at the direction of the First Presidency, for whom Robinson was a scribe.

Robinson likely wrote the letter sometime in July or August 1838 at Far West, Missouri, where he and the presidency lived. In the letter, he admonished Latter-day Saints preparing to gather to Missouri that, upon arriving, they should give their names to the recorders for the stakes in which they settled. Robinson also assured that, contrary to rumors, food was and would be plentiful. The letter was conveyed to the Latter-day Saints by being published in the *Elders' Journal*, which was mailed to Saints throughout the United States and possibly to Saints in British North America and England.

———— ❧ ————

275. Rigdon concluded the sermon with a warning: "That mob that comes on us to disturb us; it shall be between us and them a war of extermination, for we will follow them, till the last drop of their blood is spilled, or else they will have to exterminate us; for we will carry the seat of war to their own houses, and their own families, and one party or the other shall be destroyed." Although the Latter-day Saints would "never be the agressors" or "infringe upon the rights" of others, they would no longer permit aggressors to infringe on the rights of the Saints. (See Discourse, ca. 4 July 1838, at josephsmithpapers.org; and Revelation, 6 Aug. 1833, in *JSP*, D3:226–227 [D&C 98:31].)

276. In JS's journal entry for 28 July 1838, Robinson noted that a large group of "Cannadian bretheren" had recently arrived in Missouri. In the entry for 29 July, Robinson wrote that "a large majority of the saints in Kirtland have and are arriving here every day." In this entry, Robinson also noted that apostles Orson Hyde and Heber C. Kimball had returned from their mission to England with the news that more than one thousand there had joined the church. It was reasonable to assume that at least some would migrate to the United States. (JS, Journal, 28–29 July 1838, in *JSP*, J1:294.)

To the Saints gathering into Zion:—

It is of importance that they should return their names to the recorders of the different stakes, in order that their names may be had in the general Church record.— Many have come and have settled at a distance without returning their names to the recorders of the stakes, in which they have settled. Thus rendering it very difficult for the general church record to be kept.[277]

It is expected that all the saints coming up to this land, or gathering into Zion; will have their names recorded on the records of the respective stakes, where they may settle.[278]

We further say to the saints gathering, that the rumors which have gone abroad of the scarcity of provisions in this part of the country, is absolutely FALSE—there is a great abundance, and the present appearance for corn, was never surpassed in any part of the United States.[279]

Therefore you need not fear, but gather yourselves together unto this land,[280] for there is, and will be an abundance.[281]

---

277. The church's founding "Articles and Covenants" included directions for reporting membership "so that there can be kept a regular list of all the names of the members of the whole church in a book." A "general" record book used in Far West began with such a list of members. (Articles and Covenants, ca. Apr. 1830, in *JSP*, D1:126 [D&C 20:81–82]; "Names of the Members of the Church in Missouri," 2–14.)

278. The April 1838 revelation designating Far West a holy city of Zion also directed "that other places should be appointed for stakes in the regions round about as they shall be manifested unto my Servant Joseph from time to time."*a* After surveying and directing settlement in Adam-ondi-Ahman, Missouri, JS organized a stake there in June.*b* JS similarly directed settlement in De Witt, Missouri, suggesting that he intended to organize a stake there as well.*c* (*a*. Revelation, 26 Apr. 1838, p. 116 herein [D&C 115:18]. *b*. Minutes, 28 June 1838, pp. 165–167 herein. *c*. See Letter from David Thomas, 31 Mar. 1838, pp. 65–66 herein; Letter to Stephen Post, 17 Sept. 1838, p. 242 herein; Rockwood, Journal, 14 Oct. 1838; and Perkins, "Prelude to Expulsion," 261–280.)

279. The previous issue of the *Elders' Journal* included an editorial written in May that reported extensive cultivation generally and stated, "Hundreds of acres of corn have been planted already, in our immediate neighborhood; and hundreds of acres more are now being planted." The editorial claimed that "no part of the world can produce a superior to Caldwell County." On 24 July 1838, Bishop Edward Partridge in Missouri wrote to Bishop Newel K. Whitney in Ohio that whereas the wheat crop had been average, "the corn looks uncommonly prosperous." (Editorial, *Elders' Journal,* July 1838, 33–34; Edward Partridge, Far West, MO, to Newel K. Whitney, Kirtland, OH, 24 July 1838, in Reynolds Cahoon, Far West, MO, to Newel K. Whitney, Kirtland, OH, 23 July 1838, CHL; see also Swartzell, *Mormonism Exposed,* 39.)

280. See Revelation, 24 Feb. 1834, in *JSP*, D3:461 [D&C 103:22].

281. In the July issue of the *Elders' Journal,* an editorial written in May likewise anticipated an "abundant harvest." On 24 July 1838, Bishop Edward Partridge wrote a letter to Bishop Newel K. Whitney in Ohio, noting there was "no danger of the saints starving." However, there was significant scarcity in Adam-ondi-Ahman in July 1838. William Swartzell wrote that there was "complaining among the poor for food and water." (Editorial, *Elders' Journal,* July 1838, 34; Edward Partridge, Far West, MO, to Newel K. Whitney, Kirtland, OH, 24 July 1838, in Reynolds Cahoon, Far West, MO, to Newel K. Whitney, Kirtland, OH, 23 July 1838, CHL; Swartzell, *Mormonism Exposed,* 18–19.)

Done by order of the first presidency,

GEO. W. ROBINSON, SCRIBE.

—————— ల్ఫ ——————

Affidavit, 5 September 1838

Source Note

JS, Affidavit, Far West, Caldwell Co., MO, 5 Sept. 1838; handwriting of Elias Higbee and George W. Robinson; signature of JS; certified by Elias Higbee; three pages. Featured version inserted in Sidney Rigdon and others (including JS), "To the Publick"; JS Collection, CHL.

Bifolium measuring 12½ × 7⅞ inches (32 × 20 cm), with forty very faded lines per page. The affidavit was folded for filing. The lack of official filing notations suggests that the featured version of the affidavit was not submitted to the Daviess County Circuit Court. In 1839, the featured copy was inserted in "To the Publick," a petition draft that was prepared by Sidney Rigdon and others in Illinois and was published in 1840 as *An Appeal to the American People*.[282] The affidavit, along with "To the Publick," has likely remained in continuous institutional custody.

Historical Introduction

On 5 September 1838, JS prepared an affidavit describing his involvement in a confrontation between a group of armed Latter-day Saint men and Adam Black, a justice of the peace in Daviess County, Missouri. The confrontation occurred in response to rumors of a fight between Latter-day Saints and other Missourians at an election held on 6 August 1838 in Gallatin, the seat of Daviess County. Reports indicated two church members were killed, and this news prompted JS and dozens of Latter-day Saint men to travel from Far West, Caldwell County, Missouri, to Daviess County to investigate.[283] At Adam-ondi-Ahman in Daviess County, the men learned that no one had been killed, although several on both sides were severely injured. There were also reports that Adam Black—who in 1837 had helped lead an attempt to expel Latter-day Saints from Daviess County[284]—was again assembling vigilantes to move against the Saints. On 8 August, JS and more than one hundred Latter-day Saint men visited Black's residence, where after a heated exchange

---

282. [Rigdon], *Appeal to the American People,* 26–28.

283. Sidney Rigdon recalled that Josiah Morin, a Democratic candidate from Daviess County and a friend to the Latter-day Saints, reported the election-day affray to church leaders in Far West, although he was not at the polls when the fighting broke out. John P. Greene indicated that several messengers brought word of the fracas. (Sidney Rigdon, JS, et al., Petition Draft ["To the Publick"], pp. 12[a]–[12b]; Greene, *Facts relative to the Expulsion,* 19.)

284. Adam Black, Certificate, 27 July 1838, copy; William Bowman, Certificate, no date, copy; John Brassfield, Certificate, no date, copy, Record Group 233, Records of the U.S. House of Representatives, National Archives, Washington DC; "A History, of the Persecution," *Times and Seasons,* Mar. 1840, 1:65–66, in *JSP,* H2:230–232; JS, Journal, 7–9 Aug. 1838, in *JSP,* J1:300; Samuel Brown, Affidavit, Caldwell Co., MO, 5 Sept. 1838, pp. 11[a]–[11b], in Sidney Rigdon, JS, et al., Petition Draft ("To the Publick").

Black wrote and signed a statement indicating he would uphold the Constitution and the Saints' rights.[285]

On 10 August, Black's ally William Peniston and other Daviess County citizens visited Richmond, Missouri, and presented a complaint against JS and Lyman Wight to Judge Austin A. King. In the complaint, Peniston and three others claimed that JS, Wight, and more than one hundred other Latter-day Saints had surrounded Black's home and compelled him, under the threat of death, to sign an agreement, the contents of which Peniston and the others did not disclose.[286] Peniston and his companions also asserted that five hundred armed Latter-day Saints—"whose movements and conduct are of a highly insurrectionary and unlawful character"—had assembled in Daviess County "to take revenge for some injuries or immaginary injuries done to some of their friends."[287] Based on these allegations, King issued a warrant to arrest JS and Wight, with Daviess County sheriff William Morgan assigned to complete the task.[288]

When the sheriff went to Wight's home in Adam-ondi-Ahman, Wight reportedly refused arrest, arguing that "the law had never protected him"—presumably referring to the failure of civil authorities to protect the Saints in Jackson County, Missouri, in late 1833. Furthermore, Wight allegedly said "that the whole state of Missouri could not take him."[289] Morgan, who opted against taking Wight by force, then proceeded to Far West, where he presented JS with the warrant on 16 August 1838. According to JS's journal, which George W. Robinson was keeping, JS informed the sheriff that although he was willing to submit to arrest, "he wished to be tried in his own County as the Citisens of Daviess County were highly exasperated toward him." Morgan left Far West without serving the warrant, stating that he needed to consult with King. Upon returning to Far West, Morgan declined to arrest JS, apparently because Morgan believed he was not authorized to act outside of Daviess County.[290] Meanwhile, Black, Peniston, and others advertised that "the leaders of the banditti"—a reference to the Latter-day Saints—"have not, and say they will

---

285. JS, Journal, 7–9 Aug. 1838, in *JSP*, J1:298–301; Adam Black, Complaint, Daviess Co., MO, 28 Aug. 1838, copy, Mormon War Papers, MSA.

286. Wight was probably named along with JS because Wight was widely considered the leader of the Latter-day Saints in Daviess County. (See 498n335 herein.)

287. William Peniston et al., Complaint, Ray Co., MO, 10 Aug. 1838, State of Missouri v. JS et al. for Riot (Mo. 5th Jud. Cir. 1838), microfilm 959,084, U.S. and Canada Record Collection, FHL. Black, who wrote a similar statement on 8 August 1838, was apparently not in Richmond on 10 August. Along with Peniston, three other men—William Bowman, Wilson McKinney, and John Netherton—signed the 10 August complaint. (Adam Black, Affidavit, Daviess Co., MO, 8 Aug. 1838, in "Public Meeting," *Missouri Republican* [St. Louis], 3 Sept. 1838, [2].)

288. Warrant, Ray Co., MO, 10 Aug. 1838, State of Missouri v. JS et al. for Riot (Mo. 5th Jud. Cir. 1838), microfilm 959,084, U.S. and Canada Record Collection, FHL. King did not identify a charge in the warrant. In April 1839, a Daviess County grand jury indicted JS, Wight, and other Latter-day Saint men for causing a riot at Black's home. (Indictment, [Honey Creek Township, MO], [ca. 10] Apr. 1839, State of Missouri v. JS et al. for Riot [Daviess Co. Cir. Ct. 1839], Historical Department, Nineteenth-Century Legal Documents Collection, CHL.)

289. "Mormon War," *Missouri Republican* (St. Louis), 3 Sept. 1838, [2]; see also Historical Introduction to Letter from William W. Phelps, 6–7 Nov. 1833, in *JSP*, D3:336–339.

290. JS, Journal, 16–18 Aug. 1838, in *JSP*, J1:304–305; see also Petition to Elias Higbee, ca. 16 Aug. 1838, at josephsmithpapers.org. Morgan was apparently unaware of a Missouri statute that permitted him

not be taken nor submit to the laws of the land." Black's allies called upon vigilantes in neighboring counties to become the law's "executors," setting 7 September as the day appointed to arrest JS and Wight.[291]

On 2 September, rumors reached JS that men were gathering from eleven counties to arrest him and Wight. Robinson noted in JS's journal, "This looks a leettle to[o] much like mobocracy, it foretells some evil intentions," suggesting that the Saints believed Black and his allies ultimately intended to expel church members from Daviess County.[292] Prompted by these reports, JS contacted attorney and militia commander David R. Atchison for assistance. On 4 September, Atchison met with JS in Far West and promised to "do all in his power to disperce the mob" and to represent JS and Wight in court. The two church leaders agreed to submit to arrest, and Atchison arranged a preliminary hearing with King to be held near the boundary between Caldwell and Daviess counties on 6 September, a date probably chosen to preempt the vigilantes' plan to arrest JS on 7 September.[293]

In preparation for the hearing, on 5 September JS composed this affidavit with Robinson and Elias Higbee, who was a justice of the Caldwell County court.[294] In the affidavit, JS described the rumors of violence at the Gallatin polls, the subsequent expedition of Latter-day Saint men from Caldwell County to Daviess County, and the Saints' peaceful intentions at Black's home. Higbee inscribed the first two pages and parts of the third page of the document, while Robinson wrote other portions of the third page. Both Higbee and Robinson made changes to the document as they wrote, but some alterations may have been made at a later time.[295] After the affidavit was completed, JS signed the document and Higbee certified it. Although JS may have intended to submit the affidavit to Judge King, no extant evidence indicates the affidavit was filed with the court.[296] However, the

---

to work through a local magistrate to serve the warrant. (An Act to Regulate Proceedings in Criminal Cases [21 Mar. 1835], *Revised Statutes of the State of Missouri* [1835], p. 475, art. 2, secs. 4–5.)

291. "Public Meeting," *Missouri Republican* (St. Louis), 3 Sept. 1838, [2]; "The Mormons," *Missouri Argus* (St. Louis), 6 Sept. 1838, [1]; "Mormons Once More," *Hannibal (MO) Commercial Advertiser,* 25 Sept. 1838, [1]; "Mormon Troubles," *Missouri Republican,* 19 Sept. 1838, [2].

292. JS, Journal, 2 Sept. 1838, in *JSP,* J1:312–313.

293. JS, Journal, 4 and 6 Sept. 1838, in *JSP,* J1:314, 316; Austin A. King, Ray Co., MO, to William Morgan, Daviess Co., MO, 4 Sept. 1838, William Morgan, Papers, CHL.

294. Although JS referred to himself as a "deponent" in the document, the format more closely matches that of an affidavit—a sworn statement. A deposition is an official transcript of a witness's testimony before a "competent tribunal," with the witness "answer[ing] all the interrogatories." ("Affidavit" and "Deposition," in Bouvier, *Law Dictionary,* 1:63, 313.)

295. Higbee and Robinson may have made additional changes to the affidavit in 1839, when they assisted Sidney Rigdon in preparing a history of the conflicts between the Latter-day Saints and other Missourians. The published history includes a version of the affidavit that incorporates Higbee's and Robinson's changes. Since it is unknown when each change was made, each has been reproduced here. (Sidney Rigdon, JS, et al., Petition Draft ["To the Publick"], pp. 15[a]–[15c]; [Rigdon], *Appeal to the American People,* 26–28.)

296. It is possible that a fair copy of the affidavit was made and submitted to King in 1838 and filed the following year in the Daviess County Circuit Court with other documents pertaining to the case. In 1974, when the contents of the case files were microfilmed, the affidavit was missing. (See Source Note for Recognizance, 7 Sept. 1838, p. 225 herein.)

four witnesses who testified on JS's behalf at the hearing likely conveyed the content of the affidavit to the judge.[297]

Document Transcript

/[298]State of Missouri ⎱ ss
Caldwell County ⎰

Before me Elias Higbee, one of the Justices of the County Court, within and for the County of Caldwell aforesaid. Personally came Joseph Smith Jun[r] who being duly sworn according to Law, deposeth and saith, "That on the 7th day of August 1838, being informed that an affray had taken place in Davies[s] County ~~on~~ at the Election, in the town of Gallatin, in the which ~~some~~ two persons were killed, and one person badly wounded, and fled to the woods to save his life, all of which were ⟨said to be⟩ persons belonging to the Society of ~~Mormons so Called~~ ⟨the Church of Latter day Saints⟩ And further, said— informant stated "that those persons who committed the outrage, would not suffer ~~said~~ the bodies of those who had been killed, to be taken of[f] the ground and buried. These reports with others, ~~concerning the affair~~ one of which was, that the ~~Mormons~~ ⟨saints⟩ ~~so called~~ had not the privelege of voting at the polls, as other citizens.[299] Another was, that those opposed to the ~~Mormons~~ ⟨saints⟩ were determined to drive them from Davies County,[300] and Also that ~~the persons~~ they were Arming & strengthening their forces, and preparing for a battle; & that the ~~Mormons~~ ⟨saints⟩ were preparing & making ready to stand in self defence.[301] These reports,

---

297. The four defense witnesses were Robinson, Dimick B. Huntington, Gideon Carter, and Adam Lightner. (JS, Journal, 7 Sept. 1838, in *JSP*, J1:317.)

298. TEXT: Elias Higbee handwriting begins.

299. Latter-day Saint John D. Lee recalled that by August 1838, "the two political parties [Democrat and Whig] were about equally divided in Daviess county, and that the Mormons held the balance of power, and would turn the scale which ever way they desired." Before the 6 August election, rumors spread that the Daviess County Whigs, realizing the Latter-day Saints would likely vote for the Democrats, planned to stop the Saints from voting. Just before the outbreak of fighting in Gallatin, a Missourian declared that when the Saints resided in Clay County, they were permitted to vote "no more than the dam[n] negros." (Lee, *Mormonism Unveiled*, 56; Samuel Brown, Affidavit, Caldwell Co., MO, 5 Sept. 1838, pp. 11[a]–[11b], in Sidney Rigdon, JS, et al., Petition Draft ["To the Publick"].)

300. John Butler, who was present at the Gallatin polls and heard Peniston speak, later recounted that Peniston claimed "he had headed a company to order the Mormons, off of there farmes & possessions." This action was presumably part of a mid-1837 effort to intimidate church members into leaving the county. (Butler, "Short Account of an Affray," [1], CHL; see also Sidney Rigdon, Far West, MO, to Sterling Price, 8 Sept. 1838, draft, CHL.)

301. Latter-day Saint William Swartzell noted that armed church members "assembled at Adam-on-Diammon, for the purpose of resisting an attack that was hourly expected." Women and children were gathered together and guarded in expectation of a siege. (Swartzell, *Mormonism Exposed*, 28.)

having excited, the feelings of the citizens of "Far West" and vicinity, I was invited with others, by D^r [Sampson] Avard & some others,[302] to go out to Davies[s] County, to the scene of these Outrages; they having previously ~~having~~ determined to go out and learn the facts concerning said reports. Accordingly ~~a~~ some of the citizens,— myself among the number, went out, two; three, and four, in companys, As ~~we~~ they got ready. The reports and exitement continued untill several of those small companys, through the day, were induced to follow the first,[303] who were all eager to learn the facts concerning this matter: we arived in the evening, at the house of Lyman Wight, about 3 miles from Gallatan, the scene of the reported outrages; here we learned the truth concerning the said affray, which had been considerably exageated [exaggerated], yet, there had been a serious Outrage committed. We there learned that the mob ~~were~~ was collected at [p. [1]] Mill Port, to a considerable number, and that Adam Black was at their head, and were to attack the ~~Mormons~~ ⟨saints⟩ the next day, at the place where we then were, called Adam Ondiahman, this report, we ~~esteemed to be worthy of~~ ⟨gave were inclined⟩ ~~some~~ to believe might be true. As this Adam Black who was said to be their leader, had been but a few months before engaged in endeavoring to drive those, of the society, who— had settled in that vicinity, from the County. This fact, had become notorious, from the fact that said Black had personally Ordered several of the said society to leave the County. The next Morning, we dispacthed a committee to said Black's to asscertain the truth of these reports, and ⟨to know⟩ what his intentions were, and as we understood he was a peace officers, we wished to know what we might expect from him, the Committee returned, in a short time, with an unfavorable report, that Mr Black instead of giving them any— assurance of preserving the peace, insulted them and gave them no satisfaction.[304]

---

302. See Sampson Avard, Testimony, Richmond, MO, Nov. 1838, pp. [2]–[3], State of Missouri v. JS et al. for Treason and Other Crimes (Mo. 5th Jud. Cir. 1838), in State of Missouri, "Evidence"; and Baugh, "Call to Arms," 103–107. Avard was a Danite general, subordinate only to the First Presidency and Captain General Elias Higbee. Robinson recorded in JS's journal that "the bretheren from all parts of the County, followed after and continued to come and join us and before we arrived at Col. [Lyman] Wights we had quite a large company." This company was led by the First Presidency, "General Higbee," and "Gen. Avard." (Reed Peck, Quincy, IL, to "Dear Friends," 18 Sept. 1839, pp. 45, 47, 63, Henry E. Huntington Library, San Marino, CA; Constitution of the Society of the Daughter of Zion, ca. Late June 1838, at josephsmithpapers.org; JS, Journal, 7–9 Aug. 1838, in *JSP,* J1:299.)

303. Robinson recorded in JS's journal that "some 15 or 20 men started from this place [Far West] armed and equipt for our defence the bretheren from all parts of the County, followed after and continued to come and join us." (JS, Journal, 7–9 Aug. 1838, in *JSP,* J1:299.)

304. Black later indicated that on 6 August 1838, Wight and about seventeen other Latter-day Saint men visited the Black residence to discuss the violence at the Gallatin polls and "to get him [Black] to sign an obligation, binding him . . . to do them justice as justice of the peace." Black refused,

⟨being desirous to know the feelings of Mr. Black for myself,⟩ ~~About the time the committee returned we a number of us who were~~ ⟨and being⟩ in want of good water, and, understanding there were none nearer than Mr— Blacks spring[305] ⟨myself with several others⟩ Mounted our horses ~~myself among the number~~ and rode up to Mr Blacks fence, Dr Avard with one or two others, who had rode ahead, went into M^r. Black's house, myself and some others went to the spring for water. I was shortly after, sent for ⟨by Mr. Black,⟩ and invited into the house, Being introduced to M^r. Black, by Dr Avard, M^r. Black ~~invited me to take a chair~~ ⟨he asked me to be seated,⟩ we then commenced a conversation, on the subject of the late ~~ordeal~~ dificulties and present exitement. I found M^r. Black ~~considerable~~ quite hostile in his feelings, towards ~~the Mormons~~ ⟨saints⟩; but assured us that he did not belong to the mob, neither would he take any part with them, but said he was bound ⟨by his oath⟩ to ~~keep~~ support the Constitutition of the United States, and the Laws of the State of Missouri. Deponent then asked him, if he would make said statements in writing, so as to refute the arguments of those who had afirmed that he (Black) was one of the leaders of the mob? M^r. Black answered in the affirmative, ~~that~~ accordingly, he did so; which writing is in the possession of the deponent."[306] [p. [2]] /[307] The deponent further states, "that no violence was offered to any individual, in his presence or ~~under~~ ⟨within⟩ his knowledge and that no insulting language was given ~~on~~ by either ~~hand~~ ⟨party⟩; except on the part of Mr^s. Black, who while Mr. Black was engaged in making out the ⟨above named⟩ writing (which he made with his own hand) gave to this deponent and others of the ~~Mormon~~ sosciety

---

stating that "if his oath and the laws of the country did not bind him, a written obligation would be no more binding." When Black suggested that the Saints file legal charges against those who attacked them on 6 August, Wight apparently declined, citing Missouri officials' past failures to protect the Saints. The committee left feeling insulted, while Black felt threatened. (Robert Wilson, Gallatin, MO, to James L. Minor, Jefferson City, MO, 18 Mar. 1841, in *Document Containing the Correspondence,* 159–161.)

305. Hyrum Smith later affirmed that the spring was one reason for the visit to Black's home. (Hyrum Smith, Testimony, Nauvoo, IL, 1 July 1843, p. 2, Nauvoo, IL, Records, CHL.)

306. Black recalled that thirty minutes after the first committee departed, more than 150 armed Latter-day Saint men surrounded his home and "blocked up his doors." Avard apparently entered the house first and accused Black of intending to lead a mob against the Saints. Avard allegedly threatened to kill Black if he refused to sign the agreement to uphold the law. At Black's request, JS then entered the home to defuse the situation. Black, "seeing the situation of his family," agreed to write a statement certifying that he would "suport the consticution of this State & of the united State[s] . . . and so long as they [the Latter-day Saints] will not mol[e]st me I will not molest them." (Robert Wilson, Gallatin, MO, to James L. Minor, Jefferson City, MO, 18 Mar. 1841, in *Document Containing the Correspondence,* 161–162; Taylor, *Short Account of the Murders,* 2.)

307. TEXT: Elias Higbee handwriting ends; George W. Robinson begins.

highly insulting Language, and false accusations, which were calculated in their nature to greatly irritate, if possible the feelings of the bystanders belonging to said ~~Mormon~~ sosciety, in Language like ~~this~~ this, being asked by the deponent, if she knew any thing in the Mormon people derogatory to the character of Gentlemen? /[308]She answered in the negative; but said she did not know, but the object of their visit was to steal something from them. After Mʳ Black had executed the writing, deponent asked Mr Black if ⟨he had⟩ ~~there were~~ any unfreindly feelings towards the— deponent, and if he had not treated him genteelly, /[309]he answered in the affermative.[310] your deponent then took leave of said Black, and repaired to the house of Lyman Wight. The next day we returned to "Far West," And further, this deponent saith not.

Joseph Smith Jr

/[311]Sworn to and subscribed, this fifth day of September AD 1838.

Elias Higbee J. C. C. C. C.[312] [p. [3]]

———— ✌ ————

Recognizance, 7 September 1838

Source Note

Recognizance, [Daviess Co., MO], 7 Sept. 1838, State of Missouri v. JS et al. for Riot (Mo. 5th Jud. Cir. 1838); handwriting of Austin A. King; signatures of JS, Lyman Wight, Edward Partridge, and James Durfee; certified by Austin A. King; notation by Robert Wilson, [Honey Creek Township, Daviess Co., MO], 1 Mar. 1839; two pages; BYU. Includes dockets and possible redactions in unidentified handwriting.

Single leaf measuring 12½ × 7⅝ inches (32 × 19 cm). The document was folded for filing. Austin A. King kept the document until 1 March 1839, when it was filed in the Daviess County Courthouse. By 1974 at the latest, the document was removed from the courthouse and entered private possession.[313] On 1 May 1990, Brigham Young University's Harold B. Lee Library purchased the recognizance, and since then the document has remained in the library's possession.[314]

---

308. TEXT: George W. Robinson handwriting ends; Elias Higbee begins.

309. TEXT: Elias Higbee handwriting ends; George W. Robinson begins.

310. Black later conceded that JS did not use threatening language and that when Black asked JS whether he supported Avard's threats, JS replied that he did not. (Robert Wilson, Gallatin, MO, to James L. Minor, Jefferson City, MO, 18 Mar. 1841, in *Document Containing the Correspondence,* 161–162.)

311. TEXT: George W. Robinson handwriting ends; Elias Higbee begins.

312. The initials indicate Higbee's position as "one of the justices of the county court within and for Caldwell county." (Affidavit, 8 Sept. 1838, p. 236 herein; see also Certificate from Elias Higbee, 9 July 1838, p. 203 herein.)

313. In 1974, when the contents of the case files were microfilmed, the recognizance was missing.

314. Case File for Recognizance, 7 Sept. 1838, State of Missouri v. JS et al. for Riot (Mo. 5th Jud. Cir. 1838), BYU.

Historical Introduction

On 7 September 1838, Judge Austin A. King of Missouri's fifth judicial circuit wrote this recognizance (a legal instrument), which required JS and Lyman Wight to appear at the next session of the circuit court in Daviess County, Missouri.[315] The recognizance was the result of a preliminary hearing held on 7 September in Daviess County to evaluate a complaint that William Peniston and three other church opponents made the prior month.[316] These men stated that JS and Wight assembled 500 armed Latter-day Saint men in early August, intending "to commit great violence to many of the citisens of Davis County." The complaint further alleged that on 8 August, JS, Wight, and 120 of the armed men threatened the life of Adam Black, a Daviess County justice of the peace, forcing him "to sign a paper writing of a verry disgraceful character."[317]

King presided at the 7 September hearing to evaluate the allegations. During the hearing, held just north of the boundary between Caldwell and Daviess counties,[318] Peniston acted as the prosecutor, while David R. Atchison defended JS and Wight.[319] Atchison also calmed the crowd that had assembled to harass the Latter-day Saint prisoners.[320] Though no record of the witnesses' testimonies is extant, the testimony of the prosecution's sole witness, Adam Black, was likely consistent with Peniston's complaint and Black's prior statements on the matter.[321] However, Sterling Price and Edgar Flory, non-Mormons who attended the hearing, subsequently reported that Black conceded,

---

315. See "Recognizance," in Bouvier, *Law Dictionary,* 2:329.

316. JS, Journal, 7 Sept. 1838, in *JSP,* J1:316–318.

317. William Peniston et al., Complaint, Ray Co., MO, 10 Aug. 1838, State of Missouri v. JS et al. for Riot (Mo. 5th Jud. Cir. 1838), microfilm 959,084, U.S. and Canada Record Collection, FHL.

318. JS and Wight's attorney, David R. Atchison, initially requested that King schedule the hearing for 6 September 1838, likely to preempt an anticipated 7 September rendezvous of anti-Mormon vigilantes who were intent on seizing the Latter-day Saint leaders. The hearing was scheduled to be held at the home of Latter-day Saint Waldo Littlefield, near the boundary between Daviess and Caldwell counties, so that JS could quickly return to Caldwell County if trouble arose.[a] However, on 6 September neither Peniston nor Black appeared, leading King to postpone the hearing one day, subpoena Black as a witness, and move the hearing to John Raglin's home, located within a half mile north of the boundary between the counties.[b] (a. JS, Journal, 4 Sept. 1838, in *JSP,* J1:314; Austin A. King, Ray Co., MO, to William Morgan, Daviess Co., MO, 4 Sept. 1838, William Morgan, Papers, CHL; "Mormons Once More," *Hannibal [MO] Commercial Advertiser,* 25 Sept. 1838, [1]; "Public Meeting," *Missouri Republican* [St. Louis], 3 Sept. 1838, [2]; "The Mormons," *Missouri Argus* [St. Louis], 6 Sept. 1838, [1]; "Mormon Troubles," *Missouri Republican,* 19 Sept. 1838, [2]. b. JS, Journal, 6–7 Sept. 1838, in *JSP,* J1:316; Subpoena, [6] Sept. 1838, State of Missouri v. JS et al. for Riot [Mo. 5th Jud. Cir. 1838], microfilm 959,084, U.S. and Canada Record Collection, FHL; George A. Smith, Autobiography, 110; Berrett, *Sacred Places,* 4:497.)

319. JS, Journal, 4 and 7 Sept. 1838, in *JSP,* J1:314, 316.

320. Dibble, "Philo Dibble's Narrative," 89.

321. See William Peniston et al., Complaint, Ray Co., MO, 10 Aug. 1838, State of Missouri v. JS et al. for Riot (Mo. 5th Jud. Cir. 1838), microfilm 959,084, U.S. and Canada Record Collection, FHL; Adam Black, Affidavit, Daviess Co., MO, 8 Aug. 1838, in "Public Meeting," *Missouri Republican* (St. Louis), 3 Sept. 1838, [2]; and Adam Black, Complaint, Daviess Co., MO, 28 Aug. 1838, copy, Mormon War Papers, MSA.

"Mr. Smith may have said that he [Black] would not be forced to sign" the document.[322] The defense witnesses—George W. Robinson, Dimick B. Huntington, Gideon Carter, and Adam Lightner—likely offered testimony that was consistent with the affidavit JS made two days earlier.[323] Price and Flory concluded, "Mr. Smith proves that he assured Mr. Black that he should not be forced to sign any instrument of writing but that he requested it as a favor."[324]

After hearing the testimony, King ruled there was sufficient evidence that JS and Wight committed a misdemeanor at Black's home on 8 August 1838 and that the case would proceed to a grand jury hearing. King then wrote the featured recognizance, which obligated the two Latter-day Saint leaders to appear before the next session of the Daviess County Circuit Court in November 1838. Latter-day Saints Edward Partridge and James Durfee served as sureties on the recognizance to ensure that JS and Wight appeared in court.[325] The four men signed the recognizance, and then King certified and docketed it.

Subsequent events did not permit JS and Wight to appear before the circuit court in November. By then, both men were in state custody on charges of treason and other crimes allegedly committed during the conflict between church members and other Missourians in October 1838.[326] On 1 March 1839, King delivered the recognizance to Robert Wilson, clerk for the Daviess County Circuit Court, who docketed the document and filed it with the court. JS and Wight fulfilled the conditions of the recognizance when they appeared before the circuit court in April 1839 to answer charges that indicted the Latter-day Saint leaders and thirteen other church members for riot.[327]

---

322. "The Mormon Difficulties," *Niles' National Register* (Washington DC), 13 Oct. 1838, 103.

323. See Affidavit, 5 Sept. 1838, pp. 219–225 herein. Robinson, Huntington, and Carter may have been chosen to testify because of their connections with the Danite society. Robinson was a Danite colonel, as well as the First Presidency's scribe; Huntington was captain of the Danite guard. Extant sources do not explicitly indicate whether Carter was a Danite, but his brother, Jared, was captain general of the society for a time.[a] In addition, early names for the society—the "Brother of Gideon" and the "gideonites"— were perhaps connected with Gideon Carter in addition to chapter 8 of the book of Judges.[b] Lightner, who was not a member of the church, may have provided testimony regarding JS's character. Lightner was married to Latter-day Saint Mary Rollins Lightner.[c] (*a.* JS, Journal, 7–9 Aug. 1838, in *JSP,* J1:299; Reed Peck, Quincy, IL, to "Dear Friends," 18 Sept. 1839, pp. 34–35, 38, 45, Henry E. Huntington Library, San Marino, CA; Dimick Huntington, Reminiscences and Journal, [14]–[15]. *b.* William Phelps, Testimony, Richmond, MO, Nov. 1838, p. [86]; Robert Snodgrass, Testimony, Richmond, MO, Nov. 1838, p. [35], State of Missouri v. JS et al. for Treason and Other Crimes [Mo. 5th Jud. Cir. 1838], in State of Missouri, "Evidence"; Whitmer, History, 86, 95–96, in *JSP,* H2:97, 108. *c.* JS, Journal, 7 Sept. 1838, in *JSP,* J1:317; "Mary Elizabeth Rollins Lightner," *Utah Genealogical and Historical Magazine,* July 1926, 198.)

324. "The Mormon Difficulties," *Niles' National Register* (Washington DC), 13 Oct. 1838, 103.

325. See "Surety," in Bouvier, *Law Dictionary,* 2:421. Partridge may have acted as a surety for JS and Wight because in Partridge's role as bishop, he managed the church's finances and properties.[a] Durfee may have acted as a surety because he owned four hundred acres, which made him one of the fifteen largest landowners in Caldwell County, Missouri.[b] (*a.* Revelation, 4 Feb. 1831, in *JSP,* D1:244–245 [D&C 41:9–11]; Revelation, 9 Feb. 1831, in *JSP,* D1:250 [D&C 42:10]; Revelation, 20 May 1831, in *JSP,* D1:315–317 [D&C 51]. *b.* Hamer, *Northeast of Eden,* 56, 84.)

326. See Introduction to Part 3: 4 Nov. 1838–16 Apr. 1839, pp. 270–274 herein.

327. Daviess Co., MO, Circuit Court Record, Apr. 1839, bk. A, 71, 77, Daviess County Courthouse, Gallatin, MO; Indictment, [Honey Creek Township, MO], [ca. 10] Apr. 1839, State of

Document Transcript

Be it remembered that on this ⟨7ᵗʰ⟩ 8ᵗʰ day of September 1838 personally appeared before me Austin A King Judge of the 5ᵗʰ Judicial circuit Joseph Smith Jr. Lyman Wight Edward Pa[r]tridge and James Durfee and acknowledge themselves to be indebted to the state of Missouri in that is to say the said Wight & Smith in the Sum of five hundred dollars each & the said Patridge & Durfee in the sum of two hundred & fifty dollars each,³²⁸ to be levied of their respective good chattles lands & armements, to be void if the above named Smith & Wight comply with the conditions under written,— The conditions of this recognance is such that the said Wight & Smith do make their personal appea⟨ance⟩ at the next term of the Daviess circuit court to be holden on the 1ˢᵗ Thursday after the 4ᵗʰ monday in November next³²⁹ to answer to an indictment to be prefered against them for a misdemeanor³³⁰ and not depart this court without [p. [1]] them this recognizance to be void else to remain in full force

/³³¹**Joseph Smith Jr**
Lyman Wight
Edward Partridge
James Durfey

/³³²The above recognizance taken and certified subscribed before me the undersigned judge of the 5ᵗʰ Judicial circuit on the day & year above

Austin A King
Judge &c³³³

Missouri v. JS et al. for Riot (Daviess Co. Cir. Ct. 1839), Historical Department, Nineteenth-Century Legal Documents Collection, CHL. Because JS and Wight escaped from state custody on 16 April 1839, the case did not proceed to a full trial. (See Historical Introduction to Promissory Note to John Brassfield, 16 Apr. 1839, pp. 422–426 herein.)

328. Missouri law permitted magistrates to set recognizance amounts "not exceeding one thousand dollars." (An Act to Regulate Proceedings in Criminal Cases [21 Mar. 1835], *Revised Statutes of the State of Missouri* [1835], p. 472, art. 1, sec. 4.)

329. That is, 29 November 1838. Missouri law specified that the fifth circuit would hold a session in Daviess County "on the first Thursdays after the fourth Mondays in March, July and November." (An Act to Establish Judicial Circuits, and to Prescribe the Times and Places of Holding Courts [21 Jan. 1837], *Laws of the State of Missouri* [1836–1837], p. 57, sec. 23.)

330. Perhaps riot, a misdemeanor for which the two men were later indicted. (An Act concerning Crimes and Their Punishments [20 Mar. 1835], *Revised Statutes of the State of Missouri* [1835], p. 202, art. 7, sec. 6; see also Indictment, [Honey Creek Township, MO], [ca. 10] Apr. 1839, State of Missouri v. JS et al. for Riot [Daviess Co. Cir. Ct. 1839], Historical Department, Nineteenth-Century Legal Documents Collection, CHL.)

331. TEXT: Austin A. King handwriting ends; individual signatories begin.

332. TEXT: Individual signatories end; Austin A. King handwriting begins.

333. Missouri law required the magistrate to certify recognizances. (An Act to Regulate Proceedings in Criminal Cases [21 Mar. 1835], *Revised Statutes of the State of Missouri* [1835], p. 477, art. 2, sec. 29.)

⟨State⟩
⟨vs⟩[334]
J. Smith Jr. &
L. Wight—
<u>Recognizance</u>[335]

/[336]475
<u>15</u>
2375
<u>475</u>
71.25
/[337]Filed in my office the 1ˢᵗ· March 1839
R[obert] <u>Wilson</u> <u>Clerk</u> [p. [2]]

———— ℰↄ ————

Land Patent, 7 September 1838

Source Note

United States General Land Office, Washington DC, Land Patent, for JS, 7 Sept. 1838; printed form with handwriting of two unidentified scribes; signature of Martin Van Buren by Martin Van Buren Jr. and signature of Joseph S. Wilson; Land Entry Case File 7874, Record Group 49, Records of the Bureau of Land Management, National Archives and Records Administration, Washington DC. Includes seal and docket.

One leaf measuring 16 × 10 inches (41 × 25 cm). The document was folded for transmission or filing. A paper seal attached to the bottom right corner of the recto contains the image of an eagle circumscribed by the words "United States General Land Office". The form was apparently filled out by an unidentified recorder in the United States General Land Office in Washington DC and then sent to the land office in Lexington, Missouri, where JS could obtain the document. However, the patent was never retrieved, and thus it remained filed in the Lexington land office. By 1922 all land offices in Missouri had closed, and the Bureau of Land Management assumed custody of Missouri land office documents. In 1945 the records were transferred to the National Archives and Records Administration in Washington DC.[338]

Historical Introduction

On 7 September 1838, three land patents were finalized in Washington DC, granting JS the title to approximately 560 acres of land in the vicinity of Far West, Missouri. Two years

---

334. TEXT: Insertion in graphite in unidentified handwriting.

335. TEXT: King wrote this docket sideways on the right-hand side of the verso.

336. TEXT: Austin A. King handwriting ends; unidentified handwriting begins. These clerical annotations, which presumably are calculations of clerk fees and other costs, were written upside down on the verso.

337. TEXT: Unidentified handwriting ends; Robert Wilson begins. Wilson wrote his docket upside down at the bottom of the verso. Missouri law required the magistrate to deliver recognizances to the circuit court clerk "on or before the first day of the next term." (An Act to Regulate Proceedings in Criminal Cases [21 Mar. 1835], *Revised Statutes of the State of Missouri* [1835], p. 477, art. 2, sec. 29.)

338. Holding Report for Record Group 49, Records of the General Land Office, 7 Aug. 1945, Records of the Bureau of Land Management, National Archives, Washington DC.

earlier, in June and September 1836, JS directed agents to apply on his behalf for three patents—land titles from the federal government indicating he owned the specified land.[339] After the agents completed the applications at the regional land office in Lexington, Missouri, the applications were sent to the United States General Land Office in Washington DC for approval. The General Land Office was responsible for processing hundreds of thousands of patents and other federal land claims; because of severe understaffing, it was not uncommon for land patent approval to be delayed a year or more, as was the case with JS's application.[340] His three patents were prepared at the same time and originally dated 7 November 1837, but this date was knife erased in each document and replaced with the date of 7 September 1838. It is not known why the date was changed. It is also unclear whether Martin Van Buren Jr., the secretary signing on behalf of President Martin Van Buren, endorsed the patents in November 1837 or September 1838.

It is also unknown when the finalized patents were sent back to the land office in Lexington. Apparently, Missouri patent applications submitted to the General Land Office over a span of several months were processed by the general office and then returned to the Lexington office in one group. Transmitting the patents from Washington DC to Lexington likely took around a month, meaning that if the three patents were sent in September 1838, they likely did not reach Missouri before October.[341] News that patents had arrived probably spread through word of mouth or announcements in local newspapers.[342] Given JS's focus on the conflict with Missourians that began in early October, it is unlikely that he traveled to Lexington to obtain the patents if they had arrived by that time.[343] Since many Saints applied for land in Caldwell County, Missouri, in summer and fall 1836, their patents were likely processed and returned along with JS's; therefore, it is possible that one or two men were sent to Lexington to collect all of the patents that had arrived for the Latter-day Saints. Since the patent featured here remained in the possession of the Lexington land office, it was likely overlooked when JS's other patents were apparently obtained from the Lexington office.[344] The featured patent, also called a final

---

339. See Application for Land Patent, 22 June 1836, in *JSP,* D5:253–258; Register's Office Receipt to JS, Lexington, MO, 8 Sept. 1836, Land Entry Case File no. 8667, in Record Group 49, Records of the Bureau of Land Management, National Archives, Washington DC; and Land Patents for JS, Caldwell Co., MO, nos. 7873, 8667, General Land Office Records, Bureau of Land Management, U.S. Department of the Interior.

340. Rohrbough, *Land Office Business,* 65–66, 234, 262–267, 298.

341. The General Land Office apparently hired couriers to carry money and financial records between the regional land offices and the general office in Washington DC, but it is not known whether couriers carried land records. Transmission through the postal system may have taken a month or longer. Contemporary correspondence between individuals in Washington DC and Missouri took three to four weeks to arrive. (See, for example, E. A. Lampkin, Carrollton, MO, to Thomas G. Bradford, Washington DC, 8 Sept. 1838, Thomas G. Bradford, Correspondence, CHL.)

342. Rohrbough, *Land Office Business,* 77.

343. See Bill of Damages, 4 June 1839, pp. 496–501 herein.

344. Redress petitions made by Latter-day Saints in 1839 and 1840 indicate that Saints who had purchased land patents in Caldwell County in 1836 had the patents, also called certificates or duplicates, which proved their ownership of the land. (Simeon Carter, Affidavit, Lee Co., Iowa Territory, 2 Jan. 1840, Mormon Redress Petitions, 1839–1845, CHL; Johnson, *Mormon Redress Petitions,* xxviii–xxix; Bill of Damages, 4 June 1839, p. 505 herein.)

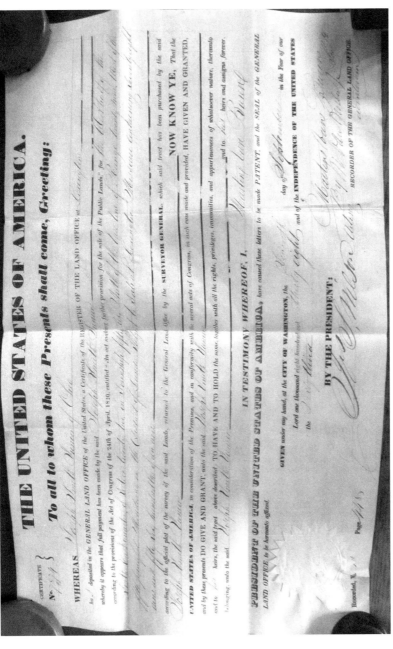

Land patent, Caldwell County, Missouri. In June 1836, John Corrill applied to purchase federal land for Joseph Smith in what became Caldwell County, Missouri. Smith's patent, or title, for this land was approved by the General Land Office in Washington DC in September 1838 and was then sent to the local land office in Lexington, Missouri. A delay of one to two years was common because of the understaffing and consequent backlog of work in the General Land Office. Handwriting of two unidentified scribes; signature of Martin Van Buren by Martin Van Buren Jr. and signature of Joseph S. Wilson. Land Patent, 7 Sept. 1838, Records of the Bureau of Land Management, National Archives and Records Administration, Washington DC.

certificate, is the only one of JS's three patents still extant and is representative of the other two land patents.[345]

Document Transcript

THE UNITED STATES OF AMERICA.

CERTIFICATE⎫
  N⁰· __7874__ ⎬

To All to whom these Presents shall come, Greeting:

WHEREAS __Joseph Smith Junior of Ohio__ [346] *ha_s_ deposited in the* GENERAL LAND OFFICE *of the United States, a Certificate of the* REGISTER OF THE LAND OFFICE[347] *at* __Lexington__ *whereby it appears that full payment has been made by the said* __Joseph Smith Junior__ *according to the provisions of the Act of Congress of the 24th of April, 1820, entitled "An act making further provision for the sale of Public Lands," for* __the West half of the South East quarter, of Section twenty two, in Township fifty six, North of the base line of Range twenty nine, West of the fifth principal Meridian, in the District of Lands, Subject to Sale at Lexington Missouri containing seventy eight acres and fifty six, hundereth of an acre__ *according to the official plat of the survey of the said Lands, returned to the General Land Office by the* SURVEYOR GENERAL, *which said tract has been purchased by the said* __Joseph Smith Junior__

NOW KNOW YE, *That the* UNITED STATES OF AMERICA, *in the consideration of the Premises, and in conformity with the several acts of Congress, in such case made and provided,* HAVE GIVEN AND GRANTED, *and by these presents* DO GIVE AND GRANT, *unto the said* __Joseph Smith Junior__ *and to* __his__ *heirs, the said tract above described:* TO HAVE AND TO HOLD *the same, together with all the rights, privileges, immunities, and appurtenances of whatsoever nature, thereunto belonging, unto the said* __Joseph Smith Junior__ *and to* __his__ *heirs and assigns forever.*

IN TESTIMONY WHEREOF, I, __Martin Van Buren__ PRESIDENT OF THE UNITED STATES OF AMERICA, *have caused these letters to be made patent, and the SEAL of the GENERAL LAND OFFICE to be hereunto fixed.*

---

345. The Bureau of Land Management's records contain filed copies of all three JS patents, indicating that all were received and processed by the General Land Office. (See Land Patents for JS, Caldwell Co., MO, nos. 7873, 7874, 8667, General Land Office Records, Bureau of Land Management, U.S. Department of the Interior.)

346. When John Corrill applied for the patent on behalf of JS in June 1836, JS was living in Kirtland, Ohio. (See Application for Land Patent, 22 June 1836, in *JSP*, D5:253–258.)

347. The application for this land patent consisted of two documents: a certificate from the register in the local land office and a receipt from the receiver. (See Application for Land Patent, 22 June 1836, in *JSP*, D5:253–258.)

GIVEN *under my hand, at the* CITY OF WASHINGTON, *the* __Seventh__ *day of* ~~November~~ ⟨September⟩ *in the Year of our Lord one thousand eight hundred and* __thirty seven~~ ⟨eight⟩~~__ *and of the* INDEPENDENCE OF THE UNITED STATES *the* __Sixty ~~second~~ ⟨third⟩__

BY THE PRESIDENT: __Martin Van Buren__

By __M[artin] Van Buren Jr Sec__^y [348]

__Jos S. Wilson Acting__ *RECORDER OF THE GENERAL LAND OFFICE.* ⟨ad interim⟩

Recorded, V. __18__ Page __448__ [349]

——— ℰℐ ———

Affidavit, 8 September 1838

Source Note

JS and Sidney Rigdon, Affidavit, [Caldwell Co., MO], 8 Sept. 1838; certified by Elias Higbee. Featured version published in "The Mormon Difficulties," Niles' National Register (Washington DC), 13 Oct. 1838, 103.

"The Mormon Difficulties" appears in an issue of the *Niles' National Register* containing sixteen pages measuring 11⅞ × 8⅛ inches (30 × 21 cm). Each page of the issue contains three columns of printed text, with each column measuring 2½ inches (6 cm) wide. In the mid-nineteenth century, the featured copy was bound together with the twenty-five other issues in volume 55 and with an index and title page, creating a book measuring 11⅞ × 8⅛ × ¾ inches (30 × 21 × 2 cm). The volume was rebound sometime in the mid-twentieth century. This and other volumes of the *Niles' National Register* were acquired by the Utah Territorial Library before 1852.[350] In 1890, the Utah Territory legislature directed that some items in the territorial library be transferred to the University of Deseret, which was later renamed the University of Utah; the volume has remained in the university's custody.[351]

Historical Introduction

On 8 September 1838, JS and Sidney Rigdon prepared an affidavit in Caldwell County, Missouri, for Sterling Price and Edgar Flory, who were sent from Chariton County, Missouri, to investigate tensions between church members and vigilantes in northwestern Missouri. While in Caldwell County, Price and Flory asked about allegations that the Saints were conspiring with American Indians to "commit depredations" against white Missourians who were not members of the church.[352] Latter-day Saints had a special affinity toward Indians, believing them to be descendants of a Book of Mormon

---

348. Martin Van Buren Jr. apparently began working as a personal secretary for his father, President Martin Van Buren, in 1837, writing and copying the president's correspondence. (Cole, *Martin Van Buren,* 343; West, *Calendar of the Papers of Martin Van Buren,* 306, 341, 344, 346, 358, 370.)

349. TEXT: Seal of the General Land Office affixed here.

350. *Catalogue of the Utah Territorial Library,* 60.

351. An Act Providing for and Regulating the Utah Territorial Library [13 Mar. 1890], *Laws of the Territory of Utah,* p. 99, sec. 3.

352. "The Mormon Difficulties," *Niles' National Register* (Washington DC), 13 Oct. 1838, 103.

people known as the Lamanites.[353] The Saints believed that converted Indians would help build the New Jerusalem, or city of Zion, which an 1830 JS revelation indicated would be established "among the Lamanites."[354] A revelation in July 1831 identified Zion as being located in Jackson County, Missouri,[355] near the border separating Euro-American settlements from territory set aside for Indians.[356]

The Saints also believed that the Lamanites would play a key role in the calamities preceding the second coming of Jesus Christ. According to the Book of Mormon, the "remnant of Jacob [Lamanites], shall be among the Gentiles [European Americans], yea, in the midst of them, as a lion among the beasts of the forest, as a young lion among the flocks of sheep, who, if he go through, both treadeth down and teareth in pieces, and none can deliver."[357] Realizing that such ideas could produce a hostile reaction among non-Mormons, church leaders discouraged the Saints from speaking openly of these beliefs.[358]

Though Latter-day Saints proselytized among indigenous peoples in the 1830s, few of them joined the church.[359] Nevertheless, allegations repeatedly arose during the decade that church members were allying with Indians to attack European Americans. These charges contributed to the Saints' expulsion from Jackson County in 1833 and from Clay County, Missouri, in 1836.[360] During the 1836 crisis, church leaders in Kirtland, Ohio, unsuccessfully attempted to defuse the situation with a statement that dismissed the allegations as the "subtle purposes of those whose feelings are embittered against" the church. The church

---

353. According to the Book of Mormon, the Lamanites were Hebrews who migrated from Jerusalem to the Americas around 600 BC. (See "Printer's Manuscript of the Book of Mormon," in *JSP*, R3, Part 1, p. xi; and Ashurst-McGee, "Zion Rising," chap. 4.)

354. Book of Mormon, 1830 ed., 501 [3 Nephi 21:23]; Revelation, Sept. 1830–B, in *JSP*, D1:185–186 [D&C 28:9]; see also Walker, "Seeking the Remnant," 1–33.

355. Revelation, 20 July 1831, in *JSP*, D2:7–8 [D&C 57:1–3].

356. Under the 1830 Indian Removal Act, Indians were required to relocate from their land in the eastern United States to land west of the Mississippi River. In December 1832, an article in the church's Independence, Missouri, newspaper celebrated the federal government's relocation policy as a "marvelous" fulfillment of prophecy, allowing the descendants of the Lamanites to gather together and help build Zion. (Satz, *American Indian Policy*, 64–87; "The Indians," *The Evening and the Morning Star*, Dec. 1832, [6].)

357. Book of Mormon, 1830 ed., 500 [3 Nephi 21:12]; see also Book of Mormon, 1830 ed., 488, 500 [3 Nephi 16:15; 20:16–17]; Micah 5:8; Pratt, *Mormonism Unveiled*, 15; Pratt, *Voice of Warning*, 188, 191–192; and Underwood, *Millenarian World of Early Mormonism*, 79–81.

358. For example, when two Indians attended a church meeting in Jackson County in 1833, a white church member informed the visitors that "the time would soon come when they should embrace the Gospel and also that if we will not fight for our selves the Indians will fight for us." Responding to a report of this exchange, First Presidency member Frederick G. Williams conceded that "all this may be true" but cautioned the Missouri Saints that "it is not needful that it should be spoken for it is of no service to the saints and has a tendency to stir up the people to anger." (Frederick G. Williams, Kirtland, OH, to "Dear Brethren," 10 Oct. 1833, in JS Letterbook 1, p. 59; see also Letter to William W. Phelps, 31 July 1832, in *JSP*, D2:266.)

359. See Taylor, "Telling Stories about Mormons and Indians," 115–123, 181–187.

360. Ezra Booth, "Mormonism—No. VI," *Ohio Star* (Ravenna), 17 Nov. 1831, [3]; Isaac McCoy, "The Disturbances in Jackson County," *Missouri Republican* (St. Louis), 20 Dec. 1833, [2]; "Public Meeting," *LDS Messenger and Advocate*, Aug. 1836, 2:354.

leaders insisted the Saints in Missouri were determined "to be among the first to repel any [Indian] invasion, and defend the frontier from all hostilities."[361]

As tensions between the Saints and other Missourians escalated in August 1838, church members were once again accused of conspiring with Indians.[362] By 1 September, former Latter-day Saint Nathan Marsh prepared a statement in Chariton County indicating he had firsthand knowledge of the rumored alliance. Marsh claimed he had heard Latter-day Saint preachers teach that "the time had arrived, when the flying Angel should pass through the land accompanied by the Indians, to accomplish the work of destruction." He further stated that JS publically announced he had fourteen thousand men, whom Marsh presumed to be Indians, ready to answer JS's call. According to Marsh, "all classes" of Latter-day Saints were "rejoicing . . . that the time had arrived, when all the wicked should be destroyed from the face of the earth, & that the Indians would be the principal means by which this object would be accomplished."[363] On 1 September, Chariton County citizens Daniel Ashby, James Keyte, and Sterling Price forwarded Marsh's statement to Missouri governor Lilburn W. Boggs and suggested that he call out the state militia to suppress the insurrection allegedly being planned by Latter-day Saints and Indians.[364]

About the same time that Marsh made his statement, vigilantes in Daviess County, Missouri, called on Chariton County and other counties to send volunteers to help arrest JS and Lyman Wight.[365] In a meeting on 3 September 1838, Chariton County citizens decided not to send troops but instead to appoint Price, who was a member of the Missouri House of Representatives, and Flory, another county resident, as an investigative committee to verify the allegations made against the Latter-day Saints.[366] Price and Flory attended a preliminary hearing in Daviess County on 7 September, during which Judge Austin A. King

---

361. Letter to John Thornton et al., 25 July 1836, in *JSP,* D5:264.

362. The 1838 allegations stemmed from a poorly understood intertribal meeting held on Indian lands late that summer. As one Missourian stated, "There are strong aprehensions also of hostilities by the Indians from the cherokees having built a large council house and inviting all the other tribes, and holding secret consultations." In reality, the Cherokees called the conference to promote peaceful relations among the Indian nations that were thrown together in the wake of the 1830 Indian Removal Act; the meeting's intent was not to plan attacks against white settlers. Nevertheless, European Americans in the state ascribed sinister intentions to the Cherokees, consistent with previous scares in the 1830s that resulted in faux Indian wars in Missouri. (E. A. Lampkin, Carrollton, MO, to Thomas G. Bradford, Washington DC, 8 Sept. 1838, Thomas G. Bradford, Correspondence, CHL; Foreman, *Advancing the Frontier,* 195–200; McCandless, *History of Missouri,* 2:55–57; "A Long Letter, and a View of Franklin County in 1838," *Republican Tribune* [Union, MO], 24 Mar. 1922, 1, 8; see also Historical Introduction to Affidavit, 5 Sept. 1838, pp. 219–222 herein.)

363. Nathan Marsh, Statement, no date, in Daniel Ashby et al., Brunswick, MO, to Lilburn W. Boggs, 1 Sept. 1838, copy, Mormon War Papers, MSA.

364. Daniel Ashby et al., Brunswick, MO, to Lilburn W. Boggs, 1 Sept. 1838, copy, Mormon War Papers, MSA. Another former Latter-day Saint, John Sapp, made a statement similar to Marsh's three days later in Carroll County. (John Sapp, Affidavit, Carroll Co., MO, 4 Sept. 1838, in Joseph Dickson, Carrollton, MO, to Lilburn W. Boggs, 6 Sept. 1838, copy, Mormon War Papers, MSA.)

365. See Historical Introduction to Affidavit, 5 Sept. 1838, pp. 220–221 herein; and Historical Introduction to Letter from Austin A. King, 10 Sept. 1838, p. 237 herein.

366. "The Mormon Difficulties," *Niles' National Register* (Washington DC), 13 Oct. 1838, 103; Eiserman, "Sterling Price," 117–118.

evaluated the charges against JS and Wight relating to the Saints' confrontation with anti-Mormon Adam Black on 8 August.[367] After the hearing, Price and Flory concluded that Black's accusations against the Saints were exaggerated, and the two men wanted to meet with Latter-day Saint leaders "to learn the facts of this great exitement."[368]

On 8 September, JS and Rigdon met in Far West, Missouri, with Price, Flory, and David R. Atchison, who was acting as JS's attorney. After hearing about "this whole matter, the present state of exitement and the cause of all this confusion," Price and Flory "expressed their fullest sattisfaction upon this matter," agreeing that the Saints "had been outrageously imposed upon."[369] Following the meeting, JS and Rigdon prepared an affidavit denying Marsh's claims and affirming the Saints' allegiance to Missouri and the United States. Elias Higbee, a judge in the Caldwell County court, certified the document. After Price and Flory received the affidavit and returned to Keytesville, the Chariton County seat, they described their findings in a written report dated 10 September. The report, which included a copy of the affidavit, may have been first published as a handbill or in a local newspaper, perhaps explaining why the report and affidavit appeared in the 22 September 1838 issue of the *Columbia Patriot,* a newspaper published in Boone County, Missouri, approximately sixty miles southeast of Keytesville. Copies of the 22 September issue of the newspaper are apparently not extant. On 13 October, the *Niles' National Register* reprinted the report and affidavit; the *Register*'s version of the affidavit is featured here.[370]

Document Transcript

"We hereby certify that we have learned that a Mr. Nathan Marsh has certified that the people some time called Mormons have ingratiated themselves with the Indians, for the purpose of getting the Indians to commit depredations upon the people of this state, which certificate of Marsh (as represented to us) is utterly false. We have never had any communication with the Indians on any subject; and we, and all the Mormon church, as we believe, entertain the same feelings and fears towards the Indians that are entertained by other citizens of this state. We are friendly to the constitution and laws of this state and of the United States, and wish to see them enforced.

JOSEPH SMITH, jr.
SIDNEY RIGDON."

Sworn to and subscribed before me this 8th day of September, A.D. 1838.

ELIAS HIGBEE.

One of the justices of the county court within and for Caldwell county.

--------- ❧ ---------

367. See Historical Introduction to Recognizance, 7 Sept. 1838, pp. 226–227 herein.

368. JS, Journal, 7 Sept. 1838, in *JSP,* J1:317–318; "The Mormon Difficulties," *Niles' National Register* (Washington DC), 13 Oct. 1838, 103.

369. JS, Journal, 8 Sept. 1838, in *JSP,* J1:318.

370. "The Mormon Difficulties," *Niles' National Register* (Washington DC), 13 Oct. 1838, 103.

Letter from Austin A. King, 10 September 1838

Source Note

Austin A. King, Letter, Richmond, Ray Co., MO, to JS and Sidney Rigdon, Far West, Caldwell Co., MO, 10 Sept. 1838; handwriting of Austin A. King; three pages; JS Collection, CHL. Includes address, dockets, and use marks.

Bifolium measuring 7½ × 6⅛ inches (19 × 16 cm). The letter was trifolded and addressed for mailing. In 1844, church clerks included excerpts of the letter in JS's manuscript history.[371] Later, the letter was refolded for filing, and Leo Hawkins docketed the verso of the second leaf in the 1850s as part of his clerical duties in the Church Historian's Office. Andrew Jenson, an employee in the Church Historian's Office, later wrote in graphite on the verso of the second leaf: "Mentioned in | history A. J.", suggesting the letter has remained in continuous institutional custody.

Historical Introduction

On 10 September 1838, Judge Austin A. King wrote a letter to JS and Sidney Rigdon, offering counsel to them in the midst of rising tensions between the Saints and anti-Mormon vigilantes. After the Saints' confrontation with antagonist Adam Black on 8 August 1838, King issued an arrest warrant for JS and Lyman Wight. When neither of the men was arrested in the following days, Black and his allies argued that the two Latter-day Saint leaders were resisting arrest and defying the law. Using this argument, Black and his associates called on neighboring counties to send volunteers by 7 September to effectuate the arrest; in response, men from eleven counties began gathering. JS received news of this development on 2 September, and his scribe, George W. Robinson, noted in JS's journal that "the whole uper Missouri is all in an uproar and confusion."[372] Hoping to calm the situation, JS and Wight appeared at a preliminary hearing on 7 September in Daviess County, at which King ruled there was probable cause to believe that the two men had committed a misdemeanor at Black's home; therefore, King ordered the two men to appear at the next session of the Daviess County Circuit Court.[373]

Although the Saints believed that King gave the ruling "to pasify as much as possible the feelings of the mobers,"[374] the anti-Mormon vigilantes continued to call for assistance, arguing that other Latter-day Saints who were present at Black's residence on 8 August were defying the law and resisting arrest. On 28 August, Black named sixteen men who he claimed had threatened his life and forced him to sign an agreement "not to molest the people called Mormons." Furthermore, Black alleged, the group of men stated that "they would not submit to the laws."[375] In response, William Dryden, a justice of the peace in Daviess County, issued an arrest warrant for these sixteen Latter-day Saints. When special deputy Nathaniel Blakely

---

371. Historian's Office, JS History, Draft Notes, 10 Sept. 1838; JS History, vol. B-1, 823; Jessee, "Writing of Joseph Smith's History," 441.

372. Historical Introduction to Affidavit, 5 Sept. 1838, pp. 237–239 herein; JS, Journal, 2 Sept. 1838, in *JSP,* J1:313.

373. JS, Journal, 2–7 Sept. 1838, in *JSP,* J1:312–317; Historical Introduction to Recognizance, 7 Sept. 1838, pp. 226–227 herein.

374. JS, Journal, 7 Sept. 1838, in *JSP,* J1:317.

375. Adam Black, Complaint, Daviess Co., MO, 28 Aug. 1838, copy, Mormon War Papers, MSA.

attempted to serve the warrant, he was purportedly "driven by force" from Adam-ondi-Ahman, which convinced Dryden that "the power of the County is wholy unable to execute any civil or Criminal process" against the Latter-day Saints. "They also declare that they are independent," Dryden stated, and they "hold in utter contempt the institutions of the Country in which they live."[376] George A. Smith, one of the Latter-day Saints named in the arrest warrant, later stated that legal officials had "all possible chance to arrest me that could be desired." Smith claimed that rather than serve the warrant, Morgan "endeavored to excite the people of the State, by reporting we would not submit to the law."[377]

As tensions rose, the anti-Mormon vigilantes began harassing Latter-day Saints in outlying areas of Daviess County and started seizing church members as prisoners.[378] In planning an attack on Adam-ondi-Ahman, opponents of the Saints arranged to transport forty-five state-owned Jäger rifles and ammunition—apparently without authorization—from Ray County to Daviess County.[379] Hearing of the shipment, Caldwell County sheriff George Pitkin "deputized William Allred to go with a company of men and to intercept" the gunrunners. Allred and ten Latter-day Saint cavalrymen seized the guns on 9 September and arrested the three individuals who were transporting the rifles—John Comer of Ray County and Allen Miller and William McHaney of Daviess County. The Mormon men took the prisoners, guns, and ammunition to Far West, Caldwell County, where the firearms were distributed to Latter-day Saints.[380] The following morning Albert Petty, a Caldwell County justice of the peace, presided at a preliminary hearing to assess charges against Comer, Miller, and McHaney for "abetting the mob" by "carying the guns and amunition to those murderers," as George W. Robinson recounted in JS's journal.[381] Although Petty denied the three men bail, he granted their request to adjourn the hearing so they could obtain counsel.[382]

As these events developed, JS and Sidney Rigdon sent two letters to King, requesting assistance and advice. Although these missives are apparently not extant, King's response suggests that JS and Rigdon's letters informed the judge of the anti-Mormon vigilantes' movements; of the identities of Latter-day Saints—an "Umpstead" and an "Owens"—who had been taken captive; and of the situation with Comer, Miller, McHaney, and the

---

376. The sixteen Latter-day Saints whom Black named in his 28 August 1838 complaint are Alanson Brown, John Butler, "Dr. Gourze," Cornelius P. Lott, Abram Nelson, Hiram Nelson, Harvey Olmstead, Ephraim Owens, Harlow Redfield, Alanson Ripley, George A. Smith, Riley Stewart, Andrew Thor, Amos Tubbs, James Whitacer, and John Woods. Dryden recounted the Saints' alleged resistance to arrest in a 15 September 1838 petition to Missouri governor Lilburn W. Boggs. Dryden also sent Black's complaint and the warrant to Boggs. The original complaint is apparently not extant; a copy is in the Missouri State Archives. No copies of the warrant have been located. (Adam Black, Complaint, Daviess Co., MO, 28 Aug. 1838, copy; William Dryden, Petition, Daviess Co., MO, 15 Sept. 1838, copy, Mormon War Papers, MSA.)

377. George A. Smith, Autobiography, 110.

378. See Baugh, "Call to Arms," 127–132.

379. "Citizens of Daviess and Livingston Counties," Daviess Co., MO, to Lilburn W. Boggs, 12 Sept. 1838, copy; Alexander Doniphan, "Camp on Grand River," MO, to David R. Atchison, 15 Sept. 1838, copy, Mormon War Papers, MSA; George W. Pitkin, Testimony, Nauvoo, IL, 1 July 1843, p. 1, Nauvoo, IL, Records, CHL.

380. George W. Pitkin, Testimony, Nauvoo, IL, 1 July 1843, p. 1, Nauvoo, IL, Records, CHL.

381. JS, Journal, 9–10 Sept. 1838, in *JSP*, J1:318–319.

382. George W. Pitkin, Testimony, Nauvoo, IL, 1 July 1843, p. 1, Nauvoo, IL, Records, CHL.

captured rifles. King received JS and Rigdon's second letter on 10 September, probably in the afternoon or evening, after a courier carried it the approximately thirty-five miles from Far West to Richmond. King responded to both letters later that day, explaining that militia commander David R. Atchison would intervene with state militia to defuse the tension, that the Latter-day Saints taken by the vigilantes would be released unharmed, and that the gunrunners taken by the Mormon posse should also be released. Given the urgency of the situation and the lack of postal markings on the letter, it is likely that King sent the letter by courier, with JS and Rigdon perhaps receiving the letter on 11 September.

Document Transcript

Richmond
Sept. 10th 1838.

Gentlemen,

I recd your communication yesterday by Mr Morrison & another today

To the one on yester I can say Mr Morrison[383] has gone to Genl. [David R.] Atchison, who I presume will do his duty. in reference to dispersing the armed force on grand river, I hope great forbearance will be used in giving any cause for collission until he can act—[384] In reference, to your last [p. [1]] I have assurance that Umpstead will not be hurt, and that he shall be turned loos, I was assured before I recd yours that Owens was not Shot at nor was there any intention to hurt him or it could have been done— he shall be turned loos unmolested,[385] I advise you to turn those three men loos and let them receive kind treatment,[386]

---

383. "Mr Morrison" was perhaps Arthur Morrison, a Latter-day Saint and a Caldwell County judge. (Arthur Morrison, Affidavit, Adams Co., IL, 1 Nov. 1839, Mormon Redress Petitions, 1839–1845, CHL; see also Corrill, *Brief History,* 35, in *JSP,* H2:173–174.)

384. Before writing to JS and Sidney Rigdon on 10 September, King wrote to Atchison, advising the commander of the state's Third Division to call out at least two hundred militiamen to enforce the law and avert any disturbances in Daviess County. (Austin A. King, Richmond, MO, to David R. Atchison, 10 Sept. 1838, copy, Mormon War Papers, MSA.)

385. "Umpstead" was possibly Harvey or Moses Olmstead, while "Owens" was probably Ephraim Owen, who later described being accosted by five vigilantes in Daviess County. Umpstead and Owens may have been Mormon scouts gathering intelligence on the vigilantes. (See H. W. Lile et al. to David R. Atchison, 10 Sept. 1838, in Austin A. King, Richmond, MO, to David R. Atchison, 10 Sept. 1838, copy, Mormon War Papers, MSA; Harvey Olmstead, Affidavit, Hancock Co., IL, 14 May 1839, Mormon Redress Petitions, 1839–1845, CHL; JS et al., Memorial to U.S. Senate and House of Representatives, 28 Nov. 1843, in Records of the U.S. Senate, Committee on the Judiciary, Records, 1816–1982, National Archives, Washington DC; Memorial of Ephraim Owen Jr., H.R. Doc. no. 42, 25th Cong., 3rd Sess. [1838]; and Corrill, *Brief History,* 35, in *JSP,* H2:173.)

386. King was referring to Comer, Miller, and McHaney, who were in the custody of Caldwell County civil authorities. According to Rigdon, testimony in the hearing on 12 September 1838 established that Comer stole the guns with the intention to arm the vigilantes, who were "collecting for the purpose of driving the saints from their homes." Miller and McHaney were considered Comer's accomplices. Later that day, Brigadier General Alexander Doniphan arrived in Far West with orders from Atchison to resolve the situation. Deeming the detention of the men illegal, Doniphan sent Comer to Atchison in

as to the guns they were in the care of Capt [William] Pollard[387] of this vicinity, whether they [p. [2]] went by his authority or permission, I am unable to
say,— I am at a loss to give any advice about them, If Capt Pollard or any one
for him will go after them under a pledge to return them to this place I will
write to you again The guns belong to the Government, & they shall not
through any agency of mine be taken from you to be converted & used for
illegal purposes.[388]

I am respectfully
A[ustin] A. King [p. [3]]

✉

Mssrs Smith & [Sidney] Rigdon
Far West.
Mo

———— ℰℐ ————

Letter to Stephen Post, 17 September 1838

Source Note

*JS and Sidney Rigdon, Letter, Far West, Caldwell Co., MO, to Stephen Post, Bloomfield Township,
Crawford Co., PA, 17 Sept. 1838; handwriting of George W. Robinson; three pages; Stephen Post, Papers,
CHL. Includes address, postal stamp, and wafer seal.*

Bifolium measuring 12⅝ × 7⅞ inches (32 × 20 cm). The letter was trifolded and gatefolded before
being sealed with a red wafer and addressed for mailing. A hole along one of the folds, apparently caused
by rodents, obscures text on both sides of the first leaf. The letter was retained by Stephen Post's family
until his grandson Edward O. Post donated the letter and other correspondence to the LDS church in
July 1971.[389]

Historical Introduction

On 17 September 1838, JS and Sidney Rigdon wrote to church member Stephen Post,
answering several questions he posed in a letter that is apparently not extant. Post was baptized in 1835 and was ordained to the office of elder and then seventy in 1836.[390] After a brief

---

Ray County and then transported Miller and McHaney to Daviess County, where Doniphan released
them on a promise of good behavior. (Sidney Rigdon, JS, et al., Petition Draft ["To the Publick"], 20[a]–
[20b]; Historian's Office, JS History, Draft Notes, 12 Sept. 1839; Alexander Doniphan, "Camp on Grand
River," MO, to David R. Atchison, 15 Sept. 1838, copy, Mormon War Papers, MSA.)

387. See *History of Ray County, Mo.,* 274.

388. After Alexander Doniphan learned that the Latter-day Saints had distributed the rifles among
themselves, on 12 September 1838 he ordered that the weapons be collected. All but three of the forty-five
rifles were located and transferred to Atchison's camp in Ray County. (Alexander Doniphan, "Camp on
Grand River," MO, to David R. Atchison, 15 Sept. 1838, copy, Mormon War Papers, MSA.)

389. Evans, *Register of the Stephen Post Papers,* 3.

390. Post, Journal, 14 July 1835; 27 Jan. and 13 Feb. 1836; Quorums of the Seventy, "Book of Records," 9.

stay in Kirtland, Ohio, during winter 1835–1836, Post returned to his home in Crawford County, Pennsylvania, which was relatively close to church headquarters in Kirtland, likely enabling him to regularly receive news about the church via traveling elders and the church's newspapers.[391] In 1836–1838 he spent considerable time preaching in surrounding neighborhoods and towns.[392] On 1 August 1838, after the vast majority of Ohio Saints had moved to Missouri, Post wrote to JS, seemingly in preparation to move to Missouri. In his letter, Post apparently requested news about the church and clarification of some doctrines. Post's letter likely arrived in Far West by late August, when a doctrinal treatise he wrote—and probably enclosed in his letter to JS—was published in the *Elders' Journal*.[393] As JS explained in the reply to Post's letter, JS was too busy to respond immediately to Post's missive, possibly because of ongoing legal difficulties stemming from the 8 August confrontation with Adam Black.[394]

JS prepared his response to Post on 17 September, with George W. Robinson acting as scribe. Although the entire letter is written in first-person singular, Rigdon signed the document along with JS. The letter contains several copying errors, such as repeated and canceled words, suggesting that the version Robinson sent to Post is a copy of a draft that is no longer extant. Robinson added his name as scribe before folding and addressing the letter. The missive was not mailed until 3 October; Post presumably received it sometime in late October or early November.

Document Transcript

<u>Far West Sept 17th 1838</u>

Stephen Post

    Sir.

    I proceed to answer your communication of the 1st August which I should have answered before had it not been for the press of buisness on my mind etc. The Journal is isued from this place it commenced I think in May.[395] As to your

---

391. Post, Journal, 30 Nov. 1835–4 Apr. 1836; see also, for example, Post, Journal, 6 Feb. and 25 Apr. 1837.

392. Post, Journal, 13 Apr. 1836–2 Sept. 1838.

393. Stephen Post, "Reflections on the Order of God and Effects Flowing from It," *Elders' Journal*, Aug. 1838, 49–50. The August edition of the *Elders' Journal* was published sometime after 15 August 1838. (See Historical Introduction to Selections from *Elders' Journal*, Aug. 1838, p. 216 herein.)

394. See Historical Introduction to Affidavit, 5 Sept. 1838, pp. 219–222 herein; Historical Introduction to Recognizance, 7 Sept. 1838, pp. 226–227 herein; and Historical Introduction to Letter from Austin A. King, 10 Sept. 1838, pp. 237–239 herein.

395. In his letter, Post apparently asked about the status of the *Elders' Journal*. He probably had not yet received the first issue of the *Elders' Journal* published at Far West, Missouri, dated July 1838, but he may have had access to the 30 April 1838 prospectus announcing the resumption of the paper. He was likely interested in the paper as a way to remain connected with other believers, and he may also have been interested in writing for the newspaper. When sending his 1 August letter to JS, Post apparently enclosed a theological treatise on the order of God that he presumably wrote for publication in the paper. (See Prospectus for *Elders' Journal*, 30 Apr. 1838, pp. 128–133 herein; and

information relative to Elders in foreign lands it is correct Elders [Orson] Hyde & Kimble [Heber C. Kimball] with several others in company have visited Great Britton, Elders Hyde & Kimbal have returned they are here[396] you will probaly se[e] their narative, which I think they are about to publish in pamphlet form.[397] They have been very successfull have baptized between one & two thousands, ordained some 40 Elders besides other officers necessary.[398] Other Stakes have been appointed but not by a committee appointed as you supposed, for the Lord has said that no stake shall be concidered a stake of Zion unless appointed, dedicated, and set apart, by the first presidency,[399] One of these is situated about 30 miles north of this place on [Gr]and[400] river, which is nearly as large as this place at this time ~~One~~ This is called Adam Ondi Awman [Adam-ondi-Ahman], or the place where Adam dwelt.[401] One at the mouth of Grand river called Dewitt it was a gentile city plott and named by them that is about 40 ~~miles~~ miles East of this place &c. &c. &c.[402]

Stephen Post, "Reflections on the Order of God and Effects Flowing from It," *Elders' Journal,* Aug. 1838, 49–50.)

396. Kimball arrived in Far West on 22 July 1838, and Hyde arrived sometime between then and 29 July. (Reynolds Cahoon, Far West, MO, to Newel K. Whitney, Kirtland, OH, 23 July 1838, CHL; JS, Journal, 29 July 1838, in *JSP,* J1:294; see also Letter from Heber C. Kimball and Orson Hyde, between 22 and 28 May 1838, pp. 145–148 herein.)

397. JS was likely referring to the *Journal of Heber C. Kimball,* published in 1840. Publication of this pamphlet was likely delayed because of the 1838 conflict with Missourians and the expulsion of the Latter-day Saints from Missouri in winter 1838–1839. (See Robert B. Thompson, ed., *Journal of Heber C. Kimball, an Elder of the Church of Jesus Christ of Latter Day Saints* [Nauvoo, IL: Robinson and Smith, 1840].)

398. Under the direction of Hyde and Kimball, over fifteen hundred individuals were baptized in England. Although the exact number of elders is unknown, Joseph Fielding stated that when the two apostles departed, at least seventy-seven men had been ordained to priesthood offices. (Allen et al., *Men with a Mission,* 52–53; Fielding, Journal, 1837–1838, 59.)

399. On 17 September 1837, a conference of elders at Kirtland resolved "it was necessary that there be more Stakes of Zion appointed in order that the poor might have a place to gather to." The elders therefore requested that JS and Sidney Rigdon "go & appoint other Stakes or places of gathering." The next day, the bishopric at Kirtland wrote a memorial likewise calling upon JS and Rigdon to organize additional stakes for the Saints. In response, JS and Rigdon appointed a committee in November to locate sites for settlement in Missouri. This decision was published in the November 1837 issue of the *Elders' Journal,* which Post likely read. A revelation on 12 January 1838 clarified that stakes must be appointed and dedicated by the First Presidency. (Minutes, 17 Sept. 1837–B, in *JSP,* D5:445; Newel K. Whitney et al., *To the Saints Scattered Abroad, the Bishop and His Counselors of Kirtland Send Greeting* [Kirtland, OH: ca. Sept. 1837], copy at CHL; Newel K. Whitney et al., Kirtland, OH, to "the Saints scattered abroad," 18 Sept. 1837, in *LDS Messenger and Advocate,* Sept. 1837, 3:561–564; Travel Account and Questions, Nov. 1837, in *JSP,* D5:481; Revelation, 12 Jan. 1838–B, in *JSP,* D5:499.)

400. TEXT: "[*Page torn*]and".

401. JS taught that Adam-ondi-Ahman was where Adam and Eve lived after their expulsion from the Garden of Eden. JS organized a stake at Adam-ondi-Ahman on 28 June 1838. (See Minutes, 28 June 1838, pp. 165–167 herein.)

402. Although JS identified De Witt as a stake in this letter, it is unknown whether a stake was ever formally organized there. A month after this letter was written, Latter-day Saint Albert P. Rockwood

The house of the Lord is the next question,[403] The celler is dug the corner stones were laid July 4ᵗʰ 1838.[404] Next comes the work of the gathering. As to this, there are thousands gathering this season [p. [1]] The road is full companies of frequently 10, 20 & 30 ⟨wagons⟩ arrives, some almost daily[405] One company which is the camp[406] is close here with one hundred wagons John E Page report says is comming less than one hundred miles of this place, with 64 wagons and the road is litterly lined with wagons between here and Ohio.[407] The work of the gathering is great. all the saints should gather as soon as possible, urge all the saints to gather immediately if they possibly can.[408] The chance is great for purchasing lands here land is very cheap the old settlers will sell for half price yes, for quarter price they are determined to get away. Congress land is plenty[409] and good land can be had for property other than money, such as horses

wrote that "De Witt was not an appointed stake of Zion." (See Rockwood, Journal, 14 Oct. 1838; see also Reed Peck, Quincy, IL, to "Dear Friends," 18 Sept. 1839, pp. 20–21, Henry E. Huntington Library, San Marino, CA.)

403. Post may have asked about the construction of a House of the Lord in Missouri because of his noteworthy experience during the 1836 dedication of the House of the Lord in Kirtland. In his journal, Post described his experience as a "pentecost" like that described in Acts, chapter 2, of the New Testament. Post wrote, "Angels of God came into the room, cloven tongues rested upon some of the servants of the Lord like unto fire, & they spake with tongues & prophesied." (Post, Journal, 27–31 Mar. 1836.)

404. The Saints commenced work on the cellar in summer 1837. They continued until November, when JS directed church members to cease constructing the House of the Lord. A revelation on 26 April 1838 instructed the Saints to resume construction, and on 4 July 1838 JS presided over the dedication of the cornerstones. (Letter from William W. Phelps, 7 July 1837, in *JSP,* D5:402–403; Minutes, 6 Nov. 1837, in *JSP,* D5:467; Revelation, 26 Apr. 1838, p. 115 herein [D&C 115:8]; "Celebration of the 4th of July," *Elders' Journal,* Aug. 1838, 60.)

405. During spring and summer 1838, several small companies of Latter-day Saints journeyed from Ohio to join the main body of Saints in Missouri. (See Rockwood, Journal, 14 Oct. 1838.)

406. TEXT: Possibly "comp[any]".

407. At the time JS dictated this letter, Page was leading a company of Saints from Upper Canada to Missouri. While on the road, Page's company joined with a larger company of Saints traveling to Missouri from Kirtland. This larger company, known as the "Kirtland Camp," contained over five hundred Saints. At some point, Page likely wrote to JS about the progress of this large company and other groups Page met on the way. On 17 September, the day JS replied to Post, the Kirtland Camp passed through Jacksonville, Illinois—approximately two hundred miles from Far West. The company did not arrive at its final destination of Adam-ondi-Ahman until 4 October 1838. (Page, Journal Synopsis, [1]–[2]; Kirtland Camp, Journal, 13 Mar.–2 Oct. 1838; Tyler, Journal, 4 Oct. 1838, 74–75.)

408. On 26 April 1838, JS dictated a revelation directing that "the City Far West should be built up spedily, by the gathering of my Saints," and that JS should appoint further locations for gathering. (See Revelation, 26 Apr. 1838, p. 116 herein [D&C 115:17–18].)

409. JS was likely referring to land patents granted by the federal government's General Land Office. In 1836 JS and many other Latter-day Saints began acquiring patent titles for land in Caldwell County. JS's own application was approved just ten days prior to the date of this letter, though the news had not yet reached JS. (See Application for Land Patent, 22 June 1836, in *JSP,* D5:253–258; and Land Patent, 7 Sept. 1838, pp. 229–233 herein.)

wagons goods of all kinds &c, &c, Andiana [Indiana] and Illinois State Banks will buy Congress lands,[410] Eastern money can be exchanged on the road, with ease.[411] You next ask what is the cause of the papers stoping it was because the office was burnt down, by the decenters [dissenters] from the faith in Kirtland,[412] As to Mechanical branches, all kinds are needed, & would do well,[413] As to the Stick of Joseph in the hand of Ephraim,[414] I will merely say suppose yourself to be an Ephraimite, and suppose all this church to be, of the blood of Ephraim[415] and the book of Mormon to be a record of Manasseh[416] which would of course [be a re]cord[417] of Joseph, Then suppose you being an Ephraimite, Should take the record of Joseph in your hand, would not then the stick of Joseph ~~of Joseph~~ be in the hand of Ephraim. solve this mistery and se[e].[418]

The persecutors of the saints are not asleep in Missouri but God is near as to communicate his will unto us, I can write no more at present, I would say ~~say~~ may [p. [2]] the Lord bless you and all the faithful and enable you to come up to Zion with songs of everlasting joy[419] upon your head is the prayer of your unworthy servant and brother in the Lord Even so Amen,

---

410. JS was discussing a type of land speculation that increased in the western United States in the mid-1830s. In 1839, land speculator and recent Latter-day Saint convert Isaac Galland explained to a friend that the Illinois courts in particular expressed a preference for patent titles over other legal claims. "Patents are therefore in demand," Galland reported, "and you may venture to purchase all that you can get at a fair price." (Isaac Galland, Chillicothe, OH, to Samuel Swasey, North Haverhill, NH, 22 July 1839, CCLA; see also Rohrbough, *Land Office Business,* 221–249.)

411. By the late 1830s, many banks in the eastern United States had expanded their spheres of influence westward, and most western banks depended on eastern capital for financial stability. (Bodenhorn, *History of Banking in Antebellum America,* 185–189, 193–195; Knodell, "Interregional Financial Integration," 291.)

412. See Introduction to Part 7: 17 Sept. 1837–21 Jan. 1838, in *JSP,* D5:441–442; and 35n166 herein.

413. In later census records, Post was identified as a blacksmith, suggesting that he may have asked JS about the prospect of blacksmithing in Missouri. (1850 U.S. Census, Rome Township, Crawford Co., PA, 270[A].)

414. See Ezekiel 37:19. Post recorded using this passage in a sermon nearly four months prior to his letter to JS. (Post, Journal, 15 Apr. 1838.)

415. Ephraim was one of two sons of Joseph, son of Jacob, in the Old Testament. Several JS revelations in 1831 associated descent from Ephraim with membership in the church. (See, for example, Revelation, 11 Sept. 1831, in *JSP,* D2:66 [D&C 64:36]; Revelation, 29 Oct. 1831, in *JSP,* D2:92 [D&C 66]; Revelation, 3 Nov. 1831, in *JSP,* D2:118 [D&C 133:30–34]; and Mauss, "In Search of Ephraim," 145–147.)

416. The Book of Mormon states that the Nephites and the Lamanites were descendants of Manasseh, a son of Joseph in the Old Testament. (See Book of Mormon, 1830 ed., 248 [Alma 10:3].)

417. TEXT: "[*Page torn*]cord".

418. The Book of Mormon and JS's revelations taught that the prophecy in Ezekiel chapter 37 of the Old Testament, which mentions the "stick of Joseph," was a reference to the writings of the Nephites in the Book of Mormon. (See Book of Mormon, 1830 ed., 67 [2 Nephi 3:11–12]; and Revelation, ca. Aug. 1835, in *JSP,* D4:410–411 [D&C 27:5].)

419. See Isaiah 35:10; Revelation, ca. 7 Mar. 1831, in *JSP,* D1:280 [D&C 45:71]; Revelation, 29 Oct. 1831, in *JSP,* D2:91 [D&C 66:11]; and Minutes and Prayer of Dedication, 27 Mar. 1836, in *JSP,* D5:203 [D&C 109:39].

Stephen Post

Joseph Smith Jr.
Sidney Rigdon
George W. Robinson
<u>Scribe</u> [p. [3]]

/[420]25

✉

<u>Elder</u>
Stephen Post.
Bloomfield Crawford <u>Co.</u>
P. a.
/[421] FAR WEST MO
OCT. 3,

——— ∾ ———

Pay Order from Robert Snodgrass, 18 September 1838

Source Note

Robert Snodgrass, Pay Order, to JS and Edward Partridge, [Far West, Caldwell Co., MO], 18 Sept. 1838; handwriting probably of Robert Snodgrass; one page; JS Collection, CHL.

Single leaf measuring 2⅛–2¼ × 7⅝ inches (6 × 19 cm). The top and right edges of the recto have the square cut of manufactured paper, whereas the left and bottom edges were unevenly hand cut. The document was trifolded, likely for transmission.

Little is known about the pay order's custodial history. The document was presumably filed with JS's financial papers in Far West, Missouri, and has remained in continuous institutional custody. In 1973 the Historical Department of the LDS church cataloged the pay order in the JS Collection.[422]

Historical Introduction

On 18 September 1838, Latter-day Saint Robert Snodgrass wrote a pay order near Far West, Missouri, requesting that JS and Edward Partridge pay the unspecified holder of the note $28.93 on behalf of Snodgrass. Snodgrass purchased land in Clay County, Missouri, in 1836.[423] By 1838 he had moved to Caldwell County, Missouri, where he purchased land and built a mill approximately three miles from Far West. This mill was one of the closest to Far West, and the Saints depended on it to grind their grain.[424]

A pay order, such as the one Snodgrass produced, authorized the bearer of the order (the person receiving payment) to be paid by the individual named in the order rather than

---

420. TEXT: Postage in unidentified handwriting.

421. TEXT: Postmark stamped in red ink.

422. Johnson, *Register of the Joseph Smith Collection,* 10.

423. Bushman, *Index of the First Plat Book of Clay County, Missouri,* 14. Snodgrass joined the church in 1834 in Indiana. (John Gregg, Sugar Creek, IN, to Oliver Cowdery, [Kirtland, OH], 12 Aug. 1834, in *The Evening and the Morning Star,* Sept. 1834, 192.)

424. Murdock, Journal, ca. Nov. 1838, 106; Gentry and Compton, *Fire and Sword,* 454–455.

by the creator of the order. The amount would then be charged against the creator's account, with the creator later reimbursing the person making the payment, or would be credited against any debt the individual providing payment owed the creator.[425] No extant documents indicate whether Snodgrass repaid JS and Partridge, but Snodgrass may have done so by deducting the amount from an account that JS or Partridge had at Snodgrass's mill. The order Snodgrass created is the only extant pay order in the records from Far West, although such requests for payment may have been relatively common, especially among individuals who did business with the church.

Document Transcript

this Spt 18th 1838

Mr. Edward partridge[426] and Joseph Smith please to let the ~~Beared~~ Bearer have twenty Eight Dollars Ninety three Cents you will oblige your friend Robert Snodgrass

———— ❧ ————

Letter of Introduction from John Howden, 27 October 1838

Source Note

John Howden, Letter of Introduction, Painesville, Geauga Co., OH, for Oliver Granger, on behalf of JS and Sidney Rigdon, 27 Oct. 1838. Featured version copied [between 29 May and 30 Oct. 1839] in JS Letterbook 2, p. 41; handwriting of James Mulholland; JS Collection, CHL. For more information on JS Letterbook 2, see Source Notes for Multiple-Entry Documents, p. 566 herein.

Historical Introduction

On 27 October 1838, John Howden wrote a letter of introduction attesting to JS's and Sidney Rigdon's honorable character and to Oliver Granger's satisfactory settlement of debts JS and Rigdon owed to Howden. While living in Kirtland, Ohio, JS, Rigdon, and other church members had purchased goods on credit from Howden, a merchant in Painesville, Ohio, and the debts were left unpaid as the Saints moved to Missouri throughout 1838.[427] Because JS and Rigdon abruptly departed Ohio in January 1838, some people evidently thought the two men were attempting to defraud Howden and other

---

425. "Bearer," in Bouvier, *Law Dictionary*, 1:124. Bouvier stated, "If a bill note be made payable to bearer, it will pass by delivery only, without endorsement; and whoever fairly acquires a right to it, may maintain an action against the drawer or acceptor."

426. Partridge was likely named first in the order because as bishop in Far West, he managed various financial affairs for the church. (Revelation, 4 Feb. 1831, in *JSP*, D1:244 [D&C 41:9]; Minutes, 7 Nov. 1837, in *JSP*, D5:471.)

427. See Statement of Account from John Howden, 29 Mar. 1838, pp. 61–65 herein. Howden operated a dry goods store on Main Street in Painesville in 1836 and 1837. It is not clear whether the store was still functioning in 1838. (See Advertisement, *Painesville [OH] Telegraph*, 4 Nov. 1836, [3];

creditors.[428] JS and Rigdon repaid several creditors and avoided litigation on outstanding debts by appointing Granger, William Marks, and others to settle these matters.[429] Granger began acting as an agent for JS and Rigdon in Ohio in 1837.[430] He traveled to Missouri in 1838 and was in Far West on 8 July when JS dictated a revelation concerning the church's finances in Ohio. This revelation directed Marks and Newel K. Whitney to move to Missouri; when they did so, the responsibility for settling Ohio debts shifted solely to Granger.[431]

In his role as an agent, Granger settled debts owed to Howden and other creditors.[432] On 19 October, Painesville merchants Thomas Griffith and John Seymour gave Granger a letter of introduction stating that his efforts "in settling the claims, accounts &c against the former Citizens of Kirtland Township" had "done much credit to himself, and all others that committed to him the cares of adjusting their business with this community."[433] On 26 October, Horace Kingsbury—a Painesville resident and disaffected member of the church[434]—wrote a letter commending Granger's "management in the arrangement of the unfinished business" of church members. Kingsbury also stated that Granger's work in "redeeming their [church members'] pledges and thereby sustaining their integrity" had "entitled him to my highest esteem, and ever grateful recollection."[435] Howden's letter of introduction written on 27 October contained similar praise for Granger and by extension for JS and the church. The letter from Howden is representative of the letters from Kingsbury and from Griffith and Seymour. All three letters were written in mid- or late

---

Advertisement, *Painesville [OH] Republican,* 1 Dec. 1836, [4]; and Advertisement, *Painesville Republican,* 2 Feb. 1837, [4].)

428. Painesville merchants Thomas Griffith and John Seymour later stated that Granger's actions confirmed "there was no intention on their [JS and Rigdon's] part of defrauding their Creditors," suggesting that some people previously suspected JS and Rigdon of fraud. (Thomas Griffith and John Seymour, Letter of Introduction, Painesville, OH, for Oliver Granger, 19 Oct. 1838, in JS Letterbook 2, p. 40.)

429. See Pay Order to Edward Partridge for William Smith, 21 Feb. 1838, pp. 27–30 herein.

430. See Historical Introduction to Notice, ca. Late Aug. 1837, in *JSP,* D5:418–420.

431. See Revelation, 8 July 1838–E, pp. 191–194 herein [D&C 117].

432. See Statement of Account from John Howden, 29 Mar. 1838, pp. 61–65 herein.

433. Thomas Griffith and John Seymour, Letter of Introduction, Painesville, OH, for Oliver Granger, 19 Oct. 1838, in JS Letterbook 2, p. 40. Griffith and Seymour operated a dry goods store in Painesville in 1836 and 1837. In October 1837, JS and Rigdon were brought to court for not paying four promissory notes (totaling $147) they had given to Griffith and Seymour. (Advertisement, *Painesville [OH] Republican,* 12 Jan. 1837, [4]; Transcript of Proceedings, 24 Oct. 1837, Seymour and Griffith v. JS and Rigdon [Geauga Co. C.P. 1837], Final Record Book U, p. 383, microfilm 20,279, U.S. and Canada Record Collection, FHL.)

434. Kingsbury apparently became disaffected from the church in 1837. It is unclear what business Granger settled with Kingsbury by October 1838, but it may have related to land transactions or Kingsbury's involvement with the Kirtland Safety Society. (JS History, vol. B-1, 767; Vilate Murray Kimball, Kirtland, OH, to Heber C. Kimball, Preston, England, ca. 10–12 Sept. 1837, Heber C. Kimball, Collection, CHL; Historical Introduction to Kirtland Safety Society Notes, 4 Jan.–9 Mar. 1837, in *JSP,* D5:331–333.)

435. Horace Kingsbury, Letter of Introduction, Painesville, OH, for Oliver Granger, 26 Oct. 1838, in JS Letterbook 2, p. 40.

October and were probably solicited by Granger, perhaps in response to direction from JS, to verify the credibility of JS, Rigdon, and Granger.[436]

On 27 October, the same day Howden produced the letter of introduction, Missouri governor Lilburn W. Boggs ordered the state militia to expel the Saints from the state. Within a matter of days, JS was arrested in Far West, Missouri.[437] It is unlikely that JS received this and the other letters of introduction during his nearly six-month incarceration. Granger probably kept the letters and gave them to JS at a later point, possibly when both men were in Illinois in spring 1839.[438] The original letter Howden wrote is severely damaged, with sections on the left side and at the top of the document missing.[439] JS's scribe, James Mulholland, copied the letter into JS Letterbook 2 sometime between 29 May and 30 October 1839.[440] Because that copy is complete, it is featured here.

Document Transcript

To all whom it may Concern.

This may certify that during the year of Eighteen hundred and thirty-seven I had dealings with Messrs Joseph Smith Jr and Sidney Rigdon together with other members of the society,[441] to the amount of about three thousand dollars, And during the spring of Eighteen Hundred and thirty eight, I have received my pay in full of Col Oliver Granger to my satisfaction.[442] And I would here remark that it is due Messrs Smith & Rigdon & the society generally, to say that they have ever dealt honorable and fair with me, And I have received as good treatment from them as I have received from Any other society in this vicinity: And so far as I have been correctly informed, And made known of ~~their~~ them business transactions generally they have so far as I can judge been honorable and honest, And have made every exertion to arrange & settle their affairs; & I would further state that

---

436. JS's history characterized the letters of recommendation for Granger as evidence that JS was not attempting to defraud creditors. (JS History, vol. B-1, 837.)

437. See Lilburn W. Boggs, Jefferson City, MO, to John B. Clark, Fayette, MO, 27 Oct. 1838, copy, Mormon War Papers, MSA; and Introduction to Part 3: 4 Nov. 1838–16 Apr. 1839, pp. 270–272 herein.

438. See Minutes, 4–5 May 1839, pp. 444–445 herein.

439. See John Howden, Letter of Introduction, Painesville, OH, for Oliver Granger et al., 27 Oct. 1838, JS Office Papers, CHL.

440. Mulholland copied his own 29 May 1839 letter to Edward Partridge on page 15 of JS Letterbook 2, making that the earliest likely copying date for documents he subsequently copied but that had dates preceding 29 May. The latest that Mulholland could have copied the letter was 3 November 1839, the day he died, though the latest likely copying date is 30 October, after which illness presumably precluded scribal duties. (Emma Smith, Nauvoo, IL, to JS, Washington DC, 6 Dec. 1839, Charles Aldrich Autograph Collection, State Historical Society of Iowa, Des Moines; Obituary for James Mulholland, *Times and Seasons,* Dec. 1839, 1:32.)

441. That is, the Church of Jesus Christ of Latter Day Saints.

442. Granger was previously a colonel in the New York militia. (JS History, vol. C-1 Addenda, 11; Historian's Office, Obituary Notices of Distinguished Persons, 10.)

the closing up of my business with said society has been with their agent Col Granger appointed by them for that purpose; And I consider it highly due, Col Granger from me here to state that he has acted truly And honestly with me in all his business ~~transactions~~ with me, and has accomplished more than I could have reasonably expected. And I have also been made acquainted with his business in this section, And wherever he has been called upon to act, he has done so, And with good management he has accomplished And effected a close of a very large amount [of] business for said society, And as I believe to the entire satisfaction of all concerned.

John W Howden

Pain[e]sville Geauga Co Ohio Oct— 27th 1838

——— ℰ℘ ———

Letter from William Perkins, 29 October 1838

Source Note

William Perkins, Letter, Painesville, Geauga Co., OH, to JS, Far West, Caldwell Co., MO, 29 Oct. 1838; handwriting of William Perkins; two pages; JS Collection, CHL. Includes enclosures.

Single leaf measuring 6⅛ × 8 inches (16 × 20 cm), with nineteen printed lines per page. The top edge was apparently hand cut, whereas the other edges have the square cut of manufactured paper. The leaf was folded for transmission or filing. Docketing by William Clayton on one of the enclosures indicates the letter and the enclosure—a statement of account for JS and other church members—was added to JS's office papers in Nauvoo, Illinois, as early as 1842, suggesting continuous institutional custody thereafter.[443]

Historical Introduction

On 29 October 1838, William Perkins of the Ohio law firm Perkins & Osborn wrote a letter to JS to introduce account statements listing unpaid legal fees and other debts. Perkins and his law partner, Salmon Osborn, began providing legal advice to JS and other church members, as well as defending them in several lawsuits, in 1837. Perkins and Osborn continued to act as JS's attorneys after his January 1838 move to Missouri.[444]

In this letter to JS, Perkins mentioned that he was aware of the conflict between the Latter-day Saints and other Missouri residents; that he had been in contact with Oliver Granger and William Marks, both of whom acted as agents for JS and the church to pay debts in Kirtland, Ohio; and that he had prepared an account statement at Granger's request.[445] Perkins also asked that his fees be paid, and he explained how he calculated the

---

443. See Source Note for Statement of Account from Perkins & Osborn, ca. 29 Oct. 1838, p. 252 herein. Clayton served as a clerk and scribe for JS in Nauvoo from 1842 to 1844. (Clayton, Diary, 10 Feb. 1842; Clayton, History of the Nauvoo Temple, 18, 30–31; JS, Journal, 29–30 June 1842, in *JSP*, J2:71–73.)

444. See Declaration to the Geauga County Court of Common Pleas, 7 May 1838, pp. 135–139 herein.

445. Marks and Granger began acting as agents for JS in 1837 and continued in that capacity during 1838. (See Historical Introduction to Deed to William Marks, 10 Apr. 1837, in *JSP*, D5:358–359;

charges for representing JS, Sidney Rigdon, Newel K. Whitney, Frederick G. Williams, Horace Kingsbury, and Warren Parrish in the lawsuits that Samuel Rounds brought against the men in 1837 for issuing notes from the unincorporated Kirtland Safety Society.[446] The cases against Whitney, Williams, Kingsbury, and Parrish were dismissed before coming to trial, whereas JS and Rigdon were tried in absentia in October 1837, found guilty, and fined $1,000 each.[447] Because the legal representation and fees varied by case, Perkins noted that he charged each individual based on the proportion of time he spent on a case. By 1838 Kingsbury had become disaffected from the church and Parrish had been excommunicated; both remained in Geauga County, Ohio.[448] As a result, Perkins did not include their fees in JS's account statement.

Perkins's letter to JS was accompanied by several enclosures. One enclosure was the account statement listing the debts of JS and other church members to the law firm Perkins & Osborn. This account statement also includes information on several outstanding promissory notes that New York merchants asked Perkins & Osborn to collect payment on.[449] Perkins's letter also mentions enclosures, apparently not extant, intended for Marks and George W. Robinson.

It is unknown how the letter was transmitted or when JS received it. Neither the letter nor the account statement bears addressing or other postal markings, but a wrapper, now missing, may have. JS was taken into state custody on 31 October 1838 in Far West, Missouri, and remained imprisoned until April 1839.[450] While JS was imprisoned, Granger apparently kept the letter and account statement. The filing docket indicates that JS eventually received the documents, perhaps when Granger and JS were both in Illinois in spring 1839.

Historical Introduction to Notice, ca. Late Aug. 1837, in *JSP*, D5:418–420; Pay Order to Edward Partridge for William Smith, 21 Feb. 1838, pp. 27–30 herein; and Revelation, 8 July 1838–E, pp. 191–194 herein [D&C 117].)

446. For more on Rounds's lawsuits, see Introduction to Part 5: 5 Oct. 1836–10 Apr. 1837, in *JSP*, D5:285–293.

447. Transcripts of Proceedings, 24 Oct. 1837, Rounds v. Parrish; Rounds v. Williams; Rounds v. Whitney; Rounds v. Kingsbury; Rounds v. Rigdon; Rounds v. JS (Geauga Co. C.P. 1837), Final Record Book U, pp. 353–364, microfilm 20,279, U.S. and Canada Record Collection, FHL.

448. Kingsbury apparently became disaffected and distanced himself from the church in 1837. Parrish was excommunicated in late December 1837. (JS History, vol. B-1, 767; Vilate Murray Kimball, Kirtland, OH, to Heber C. Kimball, Preston, England, ca. 10–12 Sept. 1837, Heber C. Kimball, Collection, CHL; John Smith and Clarissa Lyman Smith, Kirtland, OH, to George A. Smith, Shinnston, VA, 1 Jan. 1838, George Albert Smith, Papers, CHL.)

449. On 1 September 1837, Perkins apparently oversaw the negotiations between New York mercantile firms and JS and his associates. The New York firms had sold wholesale goods to the Kirtland-area mercantile firms Rigdon, Smith & Cowdery and Cahoon, Carter & Co. The Kirtland firms provided promissory notes as payment but were unable to pay many of the notes when they became due. (See William Perkins, Painesville, OH, to Reuben McBride, 23 July 1867, copy, in Franklin D. Richards, Liverpool, England, to Brigham Young, 27 Aug. 1867, Brigham Young Office Files, CHL; and Historical Introduction to Power of Attorney to Oliver Granger, 27 Sept. 1837, in *JSP*, D5:457–459; see also Statement of Account from Perkins & Osborn, ca. 29 Oct. 1838, pp. 254–261 herein; and 260n497 herein.)

450. See Introduction to Part 3: 4 Nov. 1838–16 Apr. 1839, pp. 270–271 herein.

Document Transcript

Pain[e]sville Oct 29. 1838

Joseph Smith ᴶʳ Esq

Dea[r] Sir

At Suggestion of our friend Mr Grangir [Oliver Granger] we send you Statement of our accᵗ & demnds— You know I threw my whole influence, industry & whatever talents I have faithfully into your affairs— do something for me, "The labourer is worthy of his hire"⁴⁵¹

In the Quis tam Suits of Rounds, we have charged the differ[e]nt individuals according as we thought was about right in proportion to our Services— I spent a great deal of time & labour in my office in those suits, & though unsuccessfull it was no fault of ours you know. [Warren] Parrish rebelled & we have a judgᵗ against him for his proportion & presume it will be collected—⁴⁵²

I have heard much of your troubles⁴⁵³ & take an interest in your welfare & believed you must [p. [1]] prevail, not withstanding all persecutions—

I recᵈ Mr Rigdons [Sidney Rigdon's] eloquent & spirrted 4ᵗʰ of July address fr[om?] mail,⁴⁵⁴ please present my compliments to him & well wishes for his prosperity— We have a small amount aga[i]nst Mr [William] Marks, which he will recognize, It escaped our recollection when he left—⁴⁵⁵

Yours truly

Wᵐ L Perkins

P.S. We also send an account against Mr George W Robinson & one to G W. Robinson⁴⁵⁶ [p. [2]]

---

451. Luke 10:7.

452. Parrish apparently had not paid his portion of the legal fees in the Rounds lawsuits. To obtain Parrish's payment, Perkins & Osborn brought a claim against him, likely through the justice of the peace court since the debt was small—under one hundred dollars.

453. Ohio newspapers published several articles referencing the Missouri situation. (See, for example, "The Mormons," *Daily Herald and Gazette* [Cleveland, OH], 13 Sept. 1838, [2]; "Mormon Difficulties," *Daily Herald and Gazette*, 10 Oct. 1838, [2]; and "Mormon Campaign," *Painesville [OH] Republican,* 11 Oct. 1838, [1].)

454. In his discourse, Rigdon emphasized the Saints' loyalty to the United States, reviewed the violence against the Saints, and stated that church members would defend themselves against future violence. (Discourse, ca. 4 July 1838, at josephsmithpapers.org.)

455. Marks left Kirtland earlier in the month. (Geauga Co., OH, Deed Record, 1795–1921, vol. 27, pp. 149–150, 1 Oct. 1838, microfilm 20,242, U.S. and Canada Record Collection, FHL.)

456. Perkins probably listed both versions of Robinson's name because Robinson's debts to Perkins & Osborn involved notes in which his first name was written out and other notes in which his first and middle initials were used.

Statement of Account from Perkins & Osborn, circa 29 October 1838

Source Note

William Perkins on behalf of Perkins & Osborn, Statement of Account, Painesville, Geauga Co., OH, for JS and others, [ca. 29 Oct. 1838]; handwriting of William Perkins; seven pages; JS Collection and JS Office Papers, CHL. Includes docket.

Two bifolia measuring 12⅞ × 8 inches (33 × 20 cm), with thirty-nine printed lines per page. One horizontal line and five vertical lines were drawn on the rectos to mirror the format of a financial ledger. The pages were folded for filing. The second verso in the first bifolium contains a docket in the handwriting of William Clayton: "Perkins & Osburns | Bill | against Joseph Smith".

The docket indicates the statement was filed with JS's papers in Nauvoo, Illinois, as early as 1842, with continuous institutional custody thereafter.[457] When Clayton filed the pages in JS's Nauvoo office, the pages were out of order, with the first bifolium, which begins with a statement for JS, placed after the second, which begins with a statement for Oliver Cowdery. The two bifolia were separated during the era when documents were filed by name and subject in the Church Historian's Office. The first bifolium, containing JS's and Sidney Rigdon's accounts, was placed in the JS Collection. The second bifolium, which begins with an entry for Oliver Cowdery, was placed in the Nauvoo and Pre-Nauvoo Collection; in 2012, the bifolium was cataloged as part of the JS Office Papers.

Historical Introduction

Around 29 October 1838, William Perkins prepared a statement of the accounts that JS and other church members had with Perkins & Osborn, a Painesville, Ohio, law partnership comprising Perkins and Salmon Osborn.[458] Perkins probably prepared the statement on or within a few days of 29 October 1838, when he wrote a letter to JS introducing the statement.[459] Many of the debts listed on the statement resulted from church members' endeavors beginning in summer 1836 to further develop Kirtland, Ohio, through buying and selling land, pursuing mercantile ventures, and organizing a bank called the Kirtland Safety Society. These efforts were hampered, however, by several factors. The bank was never able to obtain a charter; after operating as an uncharted financial institution, it closed by fall 1837 because of underfunding and intense opposition that led to distrust, bank runs, and litigation.[460] The ambitious plans to expand Kirtland were also hindered by the national financial panic of 1837, which resulted in decreased land values and made it

---

457. William Clayton served as a recorder and scribe for JS in Nauvoo from 1842 to 1844. (Clayton, Diary, 10 Feb. 1842; Clayton, History of the Nauvoo Temple, 18, 30–31; JS, Journal, 29–30 June 1842, in *JSP*, J2:71–73.)

458. Perkins prepared another undated statement that appears to be an earlier rendering of several of the mercantile debts included in this October 1838 statement. In the other undated statement, Perkins included notes indicating he had written to New York merchants, asking for instructions on their unpaid promissory notes, and was awaiting their reply. In the October 1838 statement featured here, Perkins identified who was in possession of the notes and who should be paid. (Perkins & Osborn, "Demands in Hands of Perkins & Osborn," between 1 Sept. 1837 and 28 Oct. 1838, JS Office Papers, CHL.)

459. See Letter from William Perkins, 29 Oct. 1838, p. 251 herein.

460. See Introduction to Part 5: 5 Oct. 1836–10 Apr. 1837, in *JSP*, D5:285–293.

difficult for individuals who had purchased land or goods on credit to pay their debts. In turn, these problems led to litigation by unpaid creditors.[461]

Perkins's October 1838 statement includes three parts. The first part lists the legal fees that JS, Sidney Rigdon, and others owed Perkins & Osborn for representing the men in various lawsuits, including the cases Samuel Rounds brought against them for issuing notes for the Kirtland Safety Society.[462] Also included in the first section of the statement are promissory notes that JS, Rigdon, Jared Carter, and Oliver Cowdery gave Perkins & Osborn. The statement also indicates that Reynolds Cahoon had refused to provide Perkins & Osborn with a promissory note, asserting that JS was responsible for payment. Perkins did not specify the reason for the promissory notes. However, JS, Rigdon, Carter, Cowdery, and Cahoon were involved in mercantile firms in the Kirtland area and may have owed Perkins & Osborn for helping renegotiate debts in September 1837.

The second section of the statement enumerates the debts, in the form of promissory notes, that the Kirtland-area mercantile firms Rigdon, Smith & Cowdery and Cahoon, Carter & Co. owed to the New York mercantile firms John A. Newbould, Mead & Betts, Holbrook & Ferme, and Halsted, Haines & Co.[463] The New York merchants had hired Perkins & Osborn to collect the overdue payments or, if necessary, initiate lawsuits to obtain the money owed. The debts enumerated in the second section were the result of a 1 September 1837 arrangement in which Perkins helped the two Kirtland-area firms renegotiate their unpaid debts with the four New York firms. The principals for the debts to three of the firms were Carter, Cahoon, and Hyrum Smith. JS and twenty-eight other individuals signed the promissory notes as sureties, promising to pay if the principals did not.

The third section lists other debts Perkins was aware of. For example, the section includes lawsuits that New York merchant Hezekiah Kelley brought against Rigdon, Smith & Cowdery and Cahoon, Carter & Co. Neither firm purchased goods from Kelley, but a promissory note the firms created and signed was endorsed by the original recipient and given to Kelley as payment for an unrelated transaction.[464]

---

461. See "Joseph Smith Documents from October 1835 through January 1838," in *JSP*, D5:xix–xxxvi; Introduction to Part 6: 20 Apr.–14 Sept. 1837, in *JSP*, D5:363–366; and Notes Receivable from Chester Store, 22 May 1837, in *JSP*, D5:382–385.

462. Transcript of Proceedings, 24 Oct. 1837, Rounds v. JS (Geauga Co. C.P. 1837), Final Record Book U, pp. 362–364; Transcript of Proceedings, 24 Oct. 1837, Rounds v. Rigdon (Geauga Co. C.P. 1837), Final Record Book U, pp. 359–362, microfilm 20,279, U.S. and Canada Record Collection, FHL.

463. The mercantile firm Rigdon, Smith & Cowdery was a partnership that Sidney Rigdon, JS, and Oliver Cowdery began by June 1836. The mercantile firm Cahoon, Carter & Co., which included Reynolds Cahoon, Jared Carter, and Hyrum Smith, was selling goods by June 1835. The mercantile efforts of Cahoon, Carter, and Smith appear to be related to their endeavor to construct and finance the House of the Lord in Kirtland. (See John Newbould, Invoice, Buffalo, NY, for Rigdon, Smith & Cowdery, 17 June 1836; Mead, Stafford & Co., Invoice, New York City, for Rigdon, Smith & Cowdery, 8 Oct. 1836, JS Office Papers, CHL; Advertisement, *Northern Times,* 2 Oct. 1835, [4]; and Minutes, 6 June 1833, in *JSP*, D3:115.)

464. Transcript of Proceedings, 5 June 1837, Kelley v. Rigdon et al. (Geauga Co. C.P. 1837), Final Record Book U, pp. 97–99; Transcript of Proceedings, 5 June 1837, Kelley v. Cahoon et al. (Geauga Co. C.P. 1837), Final Record Book U, pp. 100–101, microfilm 20,279, U.S. and Canada Record Collection, FHL. Promissory notes were transferrable financial instruments. An individual or company could receive a promissory note and then endorse it and transfer it to another individual or company for payment.

According to the amounts listed in this statement, JS personally owed around $196 to Perkins & Osborn, while Rigdon personally owed $97.[465] Additionally, the two men owed around $2,740 as members of the firm Rigdon, Smith & Cowdery.[466] Perkins did not specify a time frame for paying these debts; the purpose of the statement was to inform JS of his and others' debts and to request payment.[467] The promissory notes given to New York merchants in September 1837 and due a year later totaled around $4,000. The next set of promissory notes, due in March 1839, amounted to around $4,100. In September 1839, another payment was due, amounting to around $4,230 (not including interest).[468] Oliver Granger, acting as an agent for JS and Rigdon, had already settled several debts stemming from when JS and Rigdon lived in Kirtland.[469] Granger's efforts to pay the debts owed to the New York merchants continued into 1839, when a new agreement was reached.[470]

It is not known how the statement, which was enclosed in Perkins's 29 October letter to JS, was transmitted or when JS received it. Neither Perkins's letter nor its extant enclosures bear addressing or other postal markings, although a wrapper, no longer extant, may have had such notations. Granger, who was in Kirtland in October 1838 settling accounts,[471] apparently obtained the letter and statement and kept them while JS was imprisoned from 31 October 1838 to 16 April 1839. JS eventually received the letter and statement, as indicated by a filing docket by William Clayton.

Document Transcript

Joseph Smith Jr
To Perkins & Osborn Dr[472]

1838 [1837][473]		
March	To Retainer & Term fee[474]	$5 00

---

465. As calculated in this statement, JS personally owed Perkins & Osborn $159.50 for the firm's services. He was credited $23.01 for money lent and goods purchased, and he was then required to pay Cahoon's note for $51.34. With these additions plus a year of interest, JS's costs amounted to around $191.00. JS also likely paid the retainer fee of $5.00 for a lawsuit Timothy Martindale initiated.

466. The debts JS and Rigdon owed jointly in connection with the mercantile firm Rigdon, Smith & Cowdery were for the judgment and damages in the Kelley lawsuit, totaling $2,083.47, and for a promissory note given to John Ayer for $442.12, which totaled $506.49 after twenty-five months of simple interest at 7 percent.

467. See Letter from William Perkins, 29 Oct. 1838, pp. 249–251 herein.

468. Amounts were not recorded for the promissory notes given to John A. Newbould, due eighteen months and twenty-four months after September 1837.

469. See Letter of Introduction from John Howden, 27 Oct. 1838, pp. 246–249 herein.

470. See Agreement with Mead & Betts, 2 Aug. 1839, pp. 535–539 herein.

471. See Historical Introduction to Letter of Introduction from John Howden, 27 Oct. 1838, pp. 246–248 herein.

472. "Dr" is an abbreviation that indicates a debit on a financial account. (Jones, *Principles and Practice of Book-Keeping*, 20.)

473. The date of 1838 was a scribal error by Perkins, who was writing in 1838. Parallel entries under Rigdon's name are dated March 1837.

474. The term fee was the amount Perkins & Osborn charged for legal services during that term of court. A term fee of five to ten dollars was common; as a frontier lawyer, Abraham Lincoln generally

T[erm][475]	Rounds Qui tam vs. you[476]	
June T[477]	" hearing on demurrer[478] & Term fee	5 00
	" going to Kirtland in May for you & consulting in sundry Cases	10 00
	Expenses same time .19¢ horse & wagon ~~paid $2~~	2 19
	" fees on Newells [Grandison Newell's] Complaint before [Edward] Flint[479]	15 00
June T	" fees on same in Court of Com. Pleas	35 00
28	" Consultation at Kirtland	3 00
July 27	" defending you successfuly in three suits before Flint, Kingsbury & [Lewis] Miller[480]	10 00
	" Retainer Barker use of Bump vs you[481]	5 00

---

charged such amounts. (See "The Law Practice of Abraham Lincoln: A Narrative Overview," in Benner and Davis, *Law Practice of Abraham Lincoln;* and Pratt, *Personal Finances of Abraham Lincoln,* 25–57.)

475. The March 1837 term of the Geauga County Court of Common Pleas began on 21 March. (An Act to Regulate the Times of Holding the Judicial Courts [4 Feb. 1837], *Acts of a General Nature* [1836–1837], p. 13, sec. 4.)

476. A qui tam court case is a lawsuit in which the plaintiff sues on his or her own behalf as well as on behalf of the state for the monetary amount permitted by statute. In this case, Rounds was suing for himself and for the state of Ohio. ("Qui Tam," in Bouvier, *Law Dictionary,* 2:320; Transcript of Proceedings, 24 Oct. 1837, Rounds v. JS [Geauga Co. C.P. 1837], Final Record Book U, pp. 362–364, microfilm 20,279, U.S. and Canada Record Collection, FHL.)

477. The June 1837 term of court began on 5 June. (An Act to Regulate the Times of Holding the Judicial Courts [4 Feb. 1837], *Acts of a General Nature* [1836–1837], p. 13, sec. 4.)

478. A demurrer is a legal document given to the court to indicate that the "objecting party *will not proceed* with the pleading, because no sufficient statement has been made on the other side; but will wait the judgment of the court whether he is bound to answer." ("Demurrer," in Bouvier, *Law Dictionary,* 1:307, italics in original.)

479. On 13 April 1837, Newell brought a complaint against JS to Justice of the Peace Flint in Painesville, Ohio, accusing JS of directing two men to murder Newell. Flint held a court of inquiry in early June 1837, and the case was then brought before the Geauga County Court of Common Pleas on 10 June. After disparate witness testimonies, JS was acquitted and discharged. (Transcript of Proceedings, 5 June 1837, State of Ohio on Complaint of Newell v. JS [Geauga Co. C.P. 1837], Final Record Book T, pp. 52–53, microfilm 20,279; Geauga Co., OH, Court of Common Pleas, Journal N, p. 225, 10 June 1837, microfilm 20,271, U.S. and Canada Record Collection, FHL.)

480. Flint and Miller were justices of the peace in Painesville; the cases referenced here were probably trials in the justice of the peace court. Kingsbury's identity is unknown, but he may have been a justice of the peace in Painesville. Two prominent Kingsbury families lived in Painesville in the 1830s, but extant records do not list a justice with the surname of Kingsbury. (See Historical Introduction to Letter from Newel K. Whitney, 20 Apr. 1837, in *JSP,* D5:367–369; Transcript of Proceedings, 25 Apr. 1835, State of Ohio v. JS [J.P. Ct. 1835], Lewis Miller, Docket Book, 332, Henry E. Huntington Library, San Marino, CA; and *History of Geauga and Lake Counties, Ohio,* 20, 22, 41.)

481. This case involved a promissory note JS and Cowdery gave to William Barker in July 1836 and that Barker later transferred to Jacob Bump. Barker claimed the note had not been fully paid by July 1837, but he discontinued the lawsuit when the case was brought before the court in October 1837. (See Transcript

28	" time & trouble with Holbrook about watch[482]	1 00
Augt	" Consultation & advice with Knights respecting Whitneys deed[483]	2 00
16	" 3 pair of shoes returned by [William] Perkins	3 31
Sept 15	" fees State vs Ritch on your complaint before [Oliver] Cowdery[484]	6 00
	Horse & wagon & expenses	2 00
Oct. T[485]	" trial Rounds Qui Tam against you	25 00
	" drawing bill of Exceptions for writ of Error[486]	10 00
		139 50
Dec[r]	" fees several suits against you at Columbus—[487]	5 00
	" ~~fee~~ " in Underwood Bald & Spencer against you[488]	

of Proceedings, 24 Oct. 1837, Barker for use of Bump v. JS and Cowdery [Geauga Co. C.P. 1837], Final Record Book U, p. 237, microfilm 20,279, U.S. and Canada Record Collection, FHL.)

482. The identity of Holbrook is not clear. Holbrook may have been a sheriff. JS's history recounts that litigation in Painesville prevented him from leaving on a trip to Canada in late July 1837. In response to a writ the sheriff served, JS gave the sheriff his watch as security that JS would appear before the court. Alternatively, the Holbrook mentioned in the account statement may have been Chandler or Joseph Holbrook; both men were church members living in Kirtland. (JS History, vol. B-1, 767, addenda, 6nS; Backman, *Profile,* 36.)

483. Geauga County deed records do not list a land transaction between the Knights and the Whitneys.

484. On 12 September 1837, JS brought a complaint against Abram Ritch—a constable in Geauga County—to Cowdery, who was a justice of the peace in Kirtland Township in 1837. JS accused Ritch of "unlawful oppression by color of office." (Docket Entry, 12 Sept. 1837, State of Ohio v. Ritch [J.P. Ct. 1837], in Cowdery, Docket Book, 224.)

485. The October 1837 term of court began on 24 October. (An Act to Regulate the Times of Holding the Judicial Courts [4 Feb. 1837], *Acts of a General Nature* [1836–1837], p. 13, sec. 4.)

486. A bill of exception is a written statement objecting "to the decision of the court on a point of law, which, in confirmation of its accuracy, is signed and sealed by the judge or court who made the decision." According to Bouvier's *Law Dictionary,* "The object of the bill of exceptions, is to put the question of law on record for the information of the court of error having cognizance of such cause." A writ of error directs a judge who has rendered a final judgment to either reexamine the case or send it to a higher court to address an allegation of an error in proceedings. Both writs represent the preliminary steps for making an appeal. ("Bill of Exception," in Bouvier, *Law Dictionary,* 1:129; "Writ of Error," in Bouvier, *Law Dictionary,* 2:501.)

487. Nothing is known about the suits referenced here. These suits may represent cases before a Columbus justice of the peace or suits brought before the Ohio Supreme Court. In the nineteenth century, Ohio circuit court cases that were appealed had to be brought before the state's supreme court justices, who did not review the cases until December, when the justices met in Columbus. No extant records of the proceedings of the Ohio Supreme Court include cases involving JS. (An Act to Regulate the Times of Holding the Judicial Courts [4 Feb. 1837], *Acts of a General Nature* [1836–1837], pp. 11–13, secs. 1–4.)

488. Cowdery had purchased engraved plates and bank notes for the Kirtland Safety Society from the firm Underwood, Bald, Spencer & Hufty in fall 1836. In June 1837 the engraving firm began a lawsuit against Rigdon, JS, and fourteen others for payment on the $1,450 owed to the firm. (Transcript of Proceedings, 16 Apr. 1839, Underwood et al. v. Rigdon, JS, et al. [Geauga Co. C.P. 1839], Final

	and others now pending	}15 00
		$159 50
1837	Contra Cr[489]	
May	By cash to Perkins at Kirtland	$5.00
Jun 28	" bill of shoes of Knights [Vinson Knight][490]	8.14
	" spade	1.50
July 27	" Cash to Perkins $1.00 d[itt]o to [Salmon] Osborn $1.	2.00
Augt 16	" 2 pr of shoes to Perkins $1.81 } for shoes } 2 Blk books for P&O $1.50 } Returned }	3.31
26	" a saw to Perkins 10/	1.25

	" by iron Chest[491] at N.Y. Bill & transportation }
	  the Bill never handed us, nor have }
	  we the keys to the little drawer— }	

	To Interest on ballance one year——[p. [1]]	

[*page [2] blank*]

	Sidney Rigdon	
1837	To Perkins & Osborn Dr	
March T	To Retainer & Term fee Rounds Qui Tam vs you	$5 00
June T	" Hearing on demurrer & Term fee	5 00
Oct T	" trial Same case	25 00
	" Bill of Exceptions same case for writ of Error	10 00
Dec*r	" fees several suits vs you at Columbus	5 00

1838 April	" fees Retainer Term fees & taking depositi[o]ns }
	  in suit against Newell discontinued }
	  by order of your agent }
		15 00

		$65 00
	Interest one year——	

Record Book X, pp. 34–36, microfilm 20,281, U.S. and Canada Record Collection, FHL; see also Historical Introduction to Kirtland Safety Society Notes, 4 Jan.–9 Mar. 1837, in *JSP*, D5:331–333.)

489. "Cr" is an abbreviation used to indicate credits on an account. Several of the entries in this section indicate that Perkins and Osborn purchased goods from one of the Kirtland-area stores in which JS was a partner but that instead of paying for the goods, the attorneys deducted the cost from JS's account with Perkins & Osborn. (Jones, *Principles and Practice of Book-Keeping*, 20.)

490. Knight was a clerk at the store run by the firm H. Smith & Co. He may also have occasionally clerked in stores run by Rigdon, Smith & Co. and may have written the bill listed here or accepted it as payment from Perkins & Osborn. (See Bailey Hewitt, Receipt, Kirtland, OH, to Sidney Rigdon et al., 27 Sept. 1836, JS Office Papers, CHL; and H. Smith & Co. Ledger, in Trustees Land Book A, CHL.)

491. The term *iron chest* is another name for a safe. The iron chest referenced in the account may be one of several safes that agents for the mercantile firm Rigdon, Smith & Cowdery bought in October 1836 from New York merchant Jesse Delano, who patented the first fireproof safe in 1826. (*Digest of Patents*, 58; Jesse Delano, Invoice, New York City, for JS and Oliver Cowdery, 15 Oct. 1836, JS Office Papers, CHL.)

Joseph Smith Jr & others

1837	To Perkins & Osborn Dr	
March	To Retainer & Term fee T[imothy] D. Martindale vs you[492]	⟨$⟩5.00
Sept 11	" Note of Jo.ˢ Smith Jr & S. Rigdon of this date	154 00
	Interest on the same——— note on demᵈ & Int———	

Fred[eric]ᵏ· G. Williams

1837	To Perkins & Osborn Dr	
March T	To Retainer & Term Rounds Qui tam vs you	⟨$⟩5.00
June T	" hearing on Dem[urre]ʳ & Term fee	5 00
Oct T	" to term fee & preparation for trial discontinᵈ	10 00
		$20 00

Interest one year———

Newel K. Whitney

1837	To Perkins & Osborn Dr	
March T	To Retainer & Term fee Rounds Qui Tam vs you	$5 00
June T	" Hearing on Demʳ & Term	5 00
Oct T.	" Term & preparation for trial discontᵈ	10 00
		$20 00

[p. [3]]
[*page [4] blank*]

Oliver Cowdery

1837	To Perkins & Osborn Dʳ	
July 14	To your note of this date on demᵈ & Int—	$51 34
	Interest on the same	

Jared Carter

1837	To Perkins & Osborn Dʳ	
Sept 11	To your note of this date on demᵈ & Int	$51 34
	Interest on the same	

[Reynolds] Cahoon refuses to give us his note says it ought to be pᵈ by Mr S[mith][493]

---

492. This June 1837 case involved nonpayment of a $5,000 promissory note that Kirtland land owner Timothy Martindale received from JS, Newel K. Whitney, Reynolds Cahoon, and John Johnson. The note was apparently for land JS and his associates bought from Martindale, and payment was due 1 January 1837. When the case came to trial in June 1837 it had already been settled by the two parties, and the case was therefore discontinued. (Transcript of Proceedings, 5 June 1837, Martindale v. JS et al. [Geauga Co. C.P. 1837], Final Record Book U, pp. 106–108, microfilm 20,279, U.S. and Canada Record Collection, FHL; see also Letter from Newel K. Whitney, 20 Apr. 1837, in *JSP*, D5:366–370.)

493. TEXT: This text was written vertically on the left side of the page.

Mr Smith will recollect that we were to have R Cahoons note for same amount of same date, & the understanding was if he would not give it Mr Smith would give his. it is Cahoons proportion of the Com[mission]^s on extending Credit & taking notes for the largr debts so we state his acc^t

	Reynolds Cahoon	
1837	To Perkins & Osborn D^r	
Sept 11	To am^t of Com^s [Commissions] &c	$51 34
	Interest on the same from date—	

Statement of demands in our hands for collection

Jo^s Smith Jr & 31 others[494] notes to Halsted & Hain[e]s[495] dated Sept 1. 1837

1 at one year from date for $2251.77

1 at 18 $\underline{mo}$ "   "   "   2323.66

1 at 24 $\underline{mo}$ "   "   "   2395.37

Interest from time they fall due

To Mead & Betts[496] same date

1 at one year ——— for ——— $1177.20

1 " 18 ^{mo} ———   " ——— 1213.87

1 " 24 ^{mo} ———   " ——— 1251.54

Interest from time they fall due [p. [5]]

[*page [6] blank*]

Demd^s in our hands for collection cont$^{\underline{d}}$

Three notes to J[ohn] A Newbould[497] dated Sept 1. 1837 against Jo.^{s} Smith Jr & 31 others

---

494. The extant promissory notes for Halsted, Haines & Co. have thirty-three signatures, including JS's. (See Hyrum Smith et al., Promissory Note, Kirtland, OH, to Halsted, Haines & Co., 1 Sept. 1837, photocopy, CHL.)

495. The mercantile firm Halsted, Haines & Co. included several members of the Halsted family— William Halsted, Matthias Halsted, and James Halsted—as well as Richard Haines and Richard Thorne. The firm sold wholesale dry goods in New York City from the 1830s to the 1890s. (Transcript of Proceedings, 16 Apr. 1839, Halsted, Haines & Co. v. JS et al. [Geauga Co. C.P. 1839], Final Record Book W, pp. 384–386, microfilm 20,280, U.S. and Canada Record Collection, FHL; Williams, *New-York Annual Register,* 507; *Northeastern Reporter,* 900–901.)

496. The mercantile firm Mead & Betts consisted of Francis Betts and Matthew Mead. They sold wholesale dry goods in Buffalo, New York, in 1836. Granger made an agreement with the firm to resolve outstanding debts in August 1839. (*Directory for the City of Buffalo* [1836], 45, 109; Mead & Betts, Invoice, Buffalo, NY, for Cahoon, Carter & Co., 18 June 1836, JS Office Papers, CHL; Agreement with Mead & Betts, 2 Aug. 1839, pp. 535–539 herein.)

497. This firm, which was operated by John Newbould in Buffalo, New York, sold hardware in the mid-1830s.^{a} He brought lawsuits against Rigdon, Smith & Cowdery and Cahoon, Carter & Co. for unpaid promissory notes in 1837.^{b} In JS's 1842 schedule of debts, he included an entry for $669.97 owed to Newbould; this amount appears to include the debts owed by Rigdon, Smith & Cowdery and by Cahoon, Carter & Co.^{c} (*a.* John Newbould, Invoice, Buffalo, NY, for Rigdon, Smith & Cowdery, 17 June

1 at 12 $^{\underline{mo}}$ from date $282.36

The other two notes are not in our hands but Newbould has them, our mem$^{\underline{os}}$ do not show the amn^{t} but they are just as much larger as this note would be by ~~deducting~~ ⟨discounting⟩ one years Int from this & adding for the 2^{d} note 18 $^{\underline{mos}}$ Int to the ballance & 24 $^{\underline{mos}}$ for the 3^{d} note—

The notes taken to Holbrook & Firme [Ferme][498] are not in our hands, the first is in his,[499] & the two others he has sold ⟨to creditors⟩— their several amou[n]ts are as follows

1 at 12 $^{\underline{mo}}$ from Sept 1. 1837 for $269.81
1 " 18 "   "   " "   "   "   278.42
1 " 24 "   "   " "   "   "   <u>287.05</u>   <u>835 28</u>
Int after due
Judg[men]^{t} of H[ezekiah] Kelley vs Smith & others[500]
   Term of June 1837 Da^{s} [Damages][501] $2083.47
   Costs——
   Increase Costs
Same against Carter & oth[e]rs $2083.47
   Costs——
   Increase costs

1836; John Newbould, Invoice, Buffalo, NY, for Cahoon, Carter & Co., 17 June 1836, JS Office Papers, CHL; *Directory for the City of Buffalo* [1836], 114; *Directory for the City of Buffalo* [1837], 103. *b.* Transcript of Proceedings, 24 Oct. 1837, Newbould v. Rigdon et al. [Geauga Co. C.P. 1837], Final Record Book U, pp. 351–353; Transcript of Proceedings, 24 Oct. 1837, Newbould v. Cahoon et al. [Geauga Co. C.P. 1837], Final Record Book U, pp. 364–366, microfilm 20,279, U.S. and Canada Record Collection, FHL. *c.* "Schedule Setting Forth a List of Petitioner[']s Creditors, Their Residence, and the Amount Due to Each," ca. 15–16 Apr. 1842, CCLA.)

498. The mercantile firm Holbrook & Ferme consisted of partners Edward Holbrook and John Ferme. They sold hardware in New York City in the 1830s. (*Longworth's American Almanac* [1836], 331; Holbrook and Ferme v. Vibbard and Garrett, 2 Scammon 465–468 [Chicago Mun. Ct. 1840].)

499. Probably Edward Holbrook or John Ferme.

500. In this case, Perkins and Osborn acted as lawyers for Kelley, a New York City merchant. The lawyers prosecuted two lawsuits for him—one against Cahoon, Carter & Co. and the other against Rigdon, Smith & Cowdery—regarding the same unpaid promissory note. Cahoon, Carter & Co. had given Rigdon, Smith & Cowdery a promissory note for $2,014.74 on 18 June 1836. Rigdon, Smith & Cowdery endorsed this note and transferred it to John Ayer, who endorsed the note and transferred it to A. C. Demerrit; in turn, Demerrit endorsed the note and gave it to Kelley for payment. In March 1837, the note had not been paid, and Kelley began lawsuits against both Cahoon, Carter & Co. and Rigdon, Smith & Cowdery. (Transcript of Proceedings, 5 June 1837, Kelley v. Rigdon et al. [Geauga Co. C.P. 1837], Final Record Book U, pp. 97–99; Transcript of Proceedings, 5 June 1837, Kelley v. Cahoon et al. [Geauga Co. C.P. 1837], Final Record Book U, pp. 100–101, microfilm 20,279, U.S. and Canada Record Collection, FHL.)

501. Damages in debt litigation include not only the cost of the unpaid promissory note but a penalty for nonpayment. ("Damages on Bills of Exchange," in Bouvier, *Law Dictionary,* 1:279.)

These are for the same dem^d Jud^t are against the makers in our suit, & against the endor[s]ers in the other, If the Da^s & Costs in one are paid & the Costs in the other, that is all which we Can Dem^d We have levied on several little bits of lands in Kirtland— hope they will bring something— [p. [7]]

Sidney Rigdon

~~1837~~ 1836	To Orrin Terry⁵⁰² Dr	
~~Jun 25~~ Oct 18	To one barrel Liver Oil 36 Gals ~~$28~~— at 28¢ for 31½ Galls	⟨$⟩ 32 00

Interest fr[o]m 18 Oct 1836 at 7 p ct—
Rigdon Smith & Cowderys⁵⁰³ note
to John V. Ayer⁵⁰⁴ Endorsed to & the property
of Geo. W. Bucknell Jn^r dated Sept. 16. 1836
at 3 ^mo payable in Buffalo N. York   442 12
    Int after due at 7 per cent———[p. [8]]

——— ☙ ———

---

502. Another statement of demands from Perkins & Osborn indicated this debt was owed to an Oliver Terry.^a It is not clear whether Rigdon purchased the oil from Orrin Terry or Oliver Terry. Orrin Terry was a Buffalo, New York, merchant who sold hides, oil, leather goods, and wholesale groceries in the 1830s and 1840s.^b Purchasing agents for the Kirtland-area stores, likely Cowdery and Hyrum Smith, traveled to New York to purchase goods and could have purchased oil for Rigdon at Orrin Terry's store.^c Oliver Terry was a merchant who did business in Hartford, Connecticut, from the 1830s to the 1850s. Rigdon may have ordered the oil from Oliver Terry and had it shipped to Kirtland.^d (a. Perkins & Osborn, "Demands in Hands of Perkins & Osborn," between 1 Sept. 1837 and 28 Oct. 1838, JS Office Papers, CHL. b. *Directory for the City of Buffalo* [1837], 131; Walker, *Walker's Buffalo City Directory,* 213. c. See Ames, Autobiography, [12]; and Cyrus Smalling, Kirtland, OH, to "Dear Sir," 10 Mar. 1841, in Lee, *Mormons,* 13–14. d. "New Flour Store," *Independent Press* [Hartford, CT], 7 July 1834, [4]; 1850 U.S. Census, Hartford, Hartford Co., CT, 625.)

503. The firm Rigdon, Smith & Cowdery purchased wholesale goods in New York in 1836. These goods were then sold by the firm Rigdon, Smith & Co. While the two firms were related, it is not clear whether Oliver Cowdery was a partner in both. (John Newbould, Invoice, Buffalo, NY, for Rigdon, Smith & Cowdery, 17 June 1836; Mead, Stafford & Co., Invoice, New York City, to Rigdon, Smith & Cowdery, 8 Oct. 1836, JS Office Papers, CHL; Rigdon, Smith & Co., Store Ledger, 1; "Mormonism in Ohio," *Aurora* [New Lisbon, OH], 21 Jan. 1837, [3]; Notes Receivable from Chester Store, 22 May 1837, in *JSP,* D5:382–385.)

504. Ayer was a cobbler and wholesale merchant in Buffalo, New York, in 1836 and 1837. The mercantile firm Cahoon, Carter & Co. purchased shoes from Ayer in June 1836. In late 1836, Ayer apparently bought stock in the Bank of Monroe in Monroe, Michigan, and may have informed JS and Rigdon, in their role as officers of the Kirtland Safety Society, about the opportunity to purchase stock in the Bank of Monroe or may have sold them a portion of the stock he had purchased. (*Directory for the City of Buffalo* [1836], 40; John Ayer, Invoice, Buffalo, NY, for Cahoon, Carter & Co., 16 June 1836, JS Office Papers, CHL; "Bank of Monroe," *Daily Cleveland Herald,* 7 Feb. 1837, [2]; "Monroe Bank," *Painesville [OH] Telegraph,* 24 Feb. 1837, [3]; see also Bank of Monroe, Account Statement, [Monroe, MI], for Kirtland Safety Society, ca. Apr. 1837, CHL; and Introduction to Part 5: 5 Oct. 1836–10 Apr. 1837, in *JSP,* D5:285–293.)

Receipt from Timothy Clark, October 1838

Source Note

Timothy Clark, Receipt, Far West, Caldwell Co., MO, to Edward Partridge on behalf of JS, Oct. 1838; handwriting of Edward Partridge; signature of Timothy Clark; one page; JS Collection, CHL. Includes docket.

One leaf measuring 3½ × 7¾ inches (9 × 20 cm). The bottom of the leaf is unevenly hand cut. Partridge docketed the leaf, and at some point it was folded, perhaps for transmission and storage. The document has undergone conservation, which involved gluing mesh to the recto and verso of the leaf.

Little is known of the document's custodial history. Presumably, the document was filed with JS's financial papers in Far West, Missouri, and has remained in continuous institutional custody. The Historical Department of the LDS church cataloged the receipt in the JS Collection in 1973.[505]

Historical Introduction

In October 1838, Latter-day Saint Timothy Clark signed a receipt acknowledging payment on an order that was issued on JS's behalf in Kirtland, Ohio.[506] The order was originally given to church member John Tanner, likely in exchange for money or land he gave to William Marks to help the church with its debts. In return, Marks, who was acting as an agent for JS in Kirtland, provided Tanner with the order. Tanner could then take the order to Far West, Missouri, where the order would be exchanged for money or land through Bishop Edward Partridge.[507] Partridge was overseeing church finances while JS was traveling to areas of conflict to aid the Saints and gather men to fight against Missouri vigilantes.[508]

The order Marks gave to Tanner is similar to the many other orders Marks created in early 1838 as Latter-day Saints transferred their property to him before leaving Ohio.[509] Although Tanner's order is apparently not extant, the description of it in the receipt indicates the order was for one hundred dollars. Tanner presumably sold the order to Clark in Far West sometime between July and October 1838.[510] Clark apparently presented the order

---

505. Johnson, *Register of the Joseph Smith Collection*, 10.

506. Clark, who apparently sometimes went by his middle name of Baldwin, was born in Connecticut in 1778 and married Mary Keeler in 1802. Shortly after he joined the church in spring 1835, Clark and several members of his family moved to Clay County, Missouri, and from there to Caldwell County, Missouri. (Clark, "Timothy Baldwin Biography"; Rich, Journal, 7 May 1835.)

507. See Corrill, *Brief History*, 27, in *JSP*, H2:161; Reed Peck, Quincy, IL, to "Dear Friends," 18 Sept. 1839, pp. 14–15, Henry E. Huntington Library, San Marino, CA; Historical Introduction to Pay Order to Edward Partridge for William Smith, 21 Feb. 1838, pp. 27–30 herein; and Receipt from Sarah Burt Beman, 26 Jan. 1839, pp. 323–325 herein.

508. See Historical Introduction to Receipt from Samuel Musick, 14 July 1838, pp. 204–206 herein; Bill of Damages, 4 June 1839, pp. 496–500 herein; JS History, vol. B-1, 836–837; and Sarah Head, Statement, ca. 22 Jan. 1845, Historian's Office, JS History Documents, 1839–1860, CHL.

509. See Historical Introduction to Pay Order to Edward Partridge for William Smith, 21 Feb. 1838, pp. 27–30 herein.

510. The Tanner family left Kirtland in spring 1838 and arrived in Far West by early July 1838. (Elizabeth Tanner, Autobiography, [2]; "Sketch of an Elder's Life," 14–15.)

to Partridge, who paid Clark $27.50 on JS's behalf and wrote the receipt featured here. Clark then signed and returned the receipt to Partridge to retain as proof of payment.[511]

Document Transcript

Rec<u>d.</u> of Joseph Smith Junr. by the hand of Edward Partridge twenty seven dollars & fifty cents, which is to apply on an order which was given by William ~~his agent~~ Marks, his agent to John Tanner on E. Partridge of $100, which I bought of said Tanner
Far West Oct<u>r.</u> 1838
    Timothy B Clark LS[512] [p. [1]]
                    T. B. Clark's
                    Receipt $27.50
                 in favor of J. S. Jun [p. [2]]

---

511. The $27.50 was likely a partial payment. It is not clear whether a portion of the note was paid before Tanner sold the note to Clark.

512. TEXT: Inscription is surrounded by a hand-drawn representation of a seal. "LS" is an abbreviation of *locus sigilli*, which is Latin for "location of the seal."

PART 3: 4 NOVEMBER 1838–
16 APRIL 1839

Part 3 covers JS's time in state custody—primarily in the Clay County jail in Liberty, Missouri—from his arrest on 31 October 1838 to his escape on 16 April 1839. His incarceration was based on charges stemming from crimes allegedly committed during the October 1838 conflict between the Latter-day Saints and other Missourians.

In mid-September 1838, Brigadier General Alexander Doniphan and his militia troops successfully disbanded and dispersed vigilantes in Daviess County, Missouri. However, under the leadership of William Austin, the vigilantes refocused their efforts on the small Mormon settlement at De Witt, Carroll County, Missouri. In late September, the vigilantes announced that the Saints had until 1 October to leave De Witt. Unwilling to abandon their property, the Saints endured a ten-day siege in early October, under the leadership of church member and colonel George M. Hinkle. During the siege, JS traveled from Far West, Missouri, to De Witt to rally church members. Ultimately, civil and militia authorities refused to intervene, and the outnumbered Saints had little choice but to evacuate the town and relocate to Far West.[1] During the journey, at least two female church members died and were buried in unmarked graves.[2]

Emboldened by this victory, the anti-Mormon vigilantes acquired a cannon and moved their operations back to Daviess County, hoping to drive out the Saints living there. JS and other church leaders determined that the failure of state authorities to protect the Saints necessitated aggressive self-defense. On 16 October, about three hundred Latter-day Saint men from Caldwell County marched to Adam-ondi-Ahman.[3] Over the next few weeks,

---

1. See Bill of Damages, 4 June 1839, pp. 496–497 herein; "The Mormons in Carroll County," *Missouri Republican* (St. Louis), 18 Aug. 1838, [2]; Alexander Doniphan, "Camp at Grand River," MO, to David R. Atchison, Richmond, MO, 15 Sept. 1838, copy; David R. Atchison, Boonville, MO, to Lilburn W. Boggs, Jefferson City, MO, 5 Oct. 1838, copy, Mormon War Papers, MSA; and Murdock, Journal, Oct. 1838, 100–102.

2. Latter-day Saint Morris Phelps recalled that two women died during the move—"one by the infirmity of old age the other in child birth." Contemporary accounts do not give the women's names; however, later sources identify the elderly woman's surname as Downey and the younger woman's surname as Jensen. (Phelps, Reminiscences, [8]; Isaac Leany, Affidavit, Quincy, IL, 20 Apr. 1839, photocopy, Material relating to Mormon Expulsion from Missouri, 1839–1843, CHL; Daniel Avery, Affidavit, Lee Co., Iowa Territory, 5 Mar. 1840, Mormon Redress Petitions, 1839–1845, CHL; Judd, "Reminiscences of Zadoc Knapp Judd," 7; *History of the Church,* 3:159.)

3. See Rockwood, Journal, 19 Oct. 1838; and Foote, Autobiography, 21 Oct. 1838, 30.

Latter-day Saints and anti-Mormons engaged in vigilante actions in the absence of civil and militia responses to the rising tensions. According to John Corrill, the Mormon vigilantes intended "to fall upon and scatter the mob wherever they could find them collected" and "to destroy those places that harbored them." On 18 October, David W. Patten, an apostle and a member of the pro tempore Zion presidency, led a targeted raid on Gallatin, the county seat. Lyman Wight, a member of the Adam-ondi-Ahman stake presidency and a veteran of the War of 1812, directed a similar raid on Millport. Seymour Brunson, a high priest who served in the War of 1812, led a third raid on Grindstone Fork. The Mormon forces dispersed the anti-Mormons, destroyed buildings—including a store, a mill, and several houses—and confiscated property as wartime appropriations.[4] JS reportedly sent a letter to Far West announcing the Saints' victory.[5] A few days later, Patten and his men secured the cannon that their enemies had brought to Daviess County. John Smith, president of the Adam-ondi-Ahman stake, noted in his journal on 22 October that "we have Driven most of the enemy out of the co[unty]."[6]

JS and the other Caldwell County men returned to Far West on 22 October.[7] For the remainder of the month, chaos reigned in Daviess County, with both Mormons and anti-Mormons burning homes and confiscating property. Latter-day Saint Benjamin Johnson recalled, "It should not be supposed because we sought to repel mob violence and were compelled to forage for food when hemmed in on all sides by a mob who had driven us from homes . . . that we were common robbers because we took as by reprisal with which to keep from starvation our women and children. Ours was a struggle for our lives and homes; and a more conscientious, noble, and patriotic spirit never enthused man than that which animated our leaders in this just defense of our rights."[8] Meanwhile, anti-Mormon vigilantes under the command of Cornelius Gilliam, operating out of neighboring counties, led targeted strikes on Mormon homes in outlying areas of Daviess County, taking prisoners, burning buildings, and confiscating goods.[9]

---

4. Corrill, *Brief History*, 35–38, in *JSP*, H2:174–178; Lyman Wight, Testimony, Nauvoo, IL, 1 July 1843, pp. 16–19, Nauvoo, IL, Records, CHL; John Smith, Journal, 16–18 Oct. 1838; Historical Introduction to Agreement with Jacob Stollings, 12 Apr. 1839, pp. 417–419 herein; see also Baugh, "Call to Arms," 190–206. When Jacob Stollings's store in Gallatin was burned, so were records belonging to the post office and treasurer's office, both of which were housed in the store. While there is no evidence that the Saints targeted the records, reports of the arson quickly circulated. (Patrick Lynch, Testimony, Richmond, MO, Nov. 1838, p. [113], State of Missouri v. JS et al. for Treason and Other Crimes [Mo. 5th Jud. Cir. 1838], in State of Missouri, "Evidence"; Thomas B. Marsh and Orson Hyde, Richmond, MO, to Lewis Abbott and Ann Marsh Abbott, Far West, MO, 25–30 Oct. 1838, in JS Letterbook 2, p. 18.)

5. This letter is apparently not extant. Sampson Avard claimed that JS and Sidney Rigdon exchanged several missives during the October 1838 expedition, but later witnesses described the contents of only one letter. Rigdon purportedly read the letter to about two hundred church members in Caldwell County. (Sampson Avard, Testimony, Richmond, MO, Nov. 1838, p. [6]; George M. Hinkle, Testimony, Richmond, MO, Nov. 1838, pp. [44]–[45]; James C. Owens, Testimony, Richmond, MO, Nov. 1838, p. [48]; Nathaniel Carr, Testimony, Richmond, MO, Nov. 1838, pp. [48]–[49], in State of Missouri, "Evidence.")

6. John Smith, Journal, 21–22 Oct. 1838.

7. Historian's Office, JS History, Draft Notes, 22 Oct. 1838.

8. Johnson, "A Life Review," 37; see also Foote, Autobiography, 21 Oct. 1838, 30.

9. Bill of Damages, 4 June 1839, p. 501 herein; Letter to the Church in Caldwell Co., MO, 16 Dec. 1838, p. 303 herein; Sidney Rigdon, JS, et al., Petition Draft ["To the Publick"], pp. 29[a]–[31b].

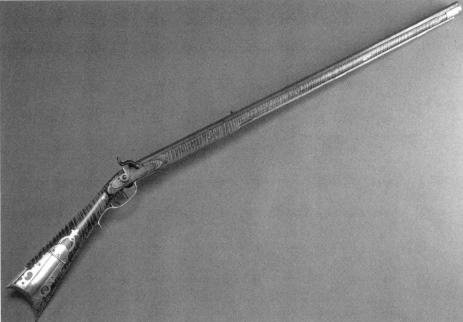

David W. Patten's rifle and powder horn. David W. Patten, an apostle and a member of the pro tempore Zion presidency, was a commander of the Mormon defense forces during the October 1838 conflict in Missouri. He led companies in the raid on Gallatin in Daviess County, the seizure of a cannon from anti-Mormons in Livingston County, and the skirmish with the Ray County militia along Crooked River just south of Caldwell County. He was wounded in the skirmish at Crooked River and died shortly thereafter. (Courtesy Church History Museum, Salt Lake City.)

Reports of Latter-day Saint military operations spread quickly throughout northwestern Missouri. Several non-Mormon eyewitnesses prepared affidavits on 21 and 22 October, describing what they had seen.[10] Likewise, apostles Thomas B. Marsh and Orson Hyde, who had recently defected from the church because they opposed the preemptive strikes in Daviess County, described the military operations in an affidavit prepared on 24 October in Richmond, Ray County, Missouri.[11] These affidavits were forwarded to Missouri governor Lilburn W. Boggs, and the information contained in them was circulated in the press.[12]

Anticipating a prolonged conflict, JS and other Latter-day Saint leaders prepared Far West to be the "head quarters of the Mormon war," as church member Albert P. Rockwood described it. These preparations included engaging the "armies of Isreal" in drills and forming special companies to build new cabins, gather food and wood, monitor the movements of anti-Mormon vigilantes, and assist families living outside of Far West to move to the city. Rockwood wrote that these companies were "called Danites because the Prophet Daniel has said they shall take the kingdom and possess it for-ever."[13] At a meeting held at the home of Sidney Rigdon on 24 October, the command structure for the Mormon forces was solidified. Lyman Wight and Seymour Brunson would command the infantry and cavalry, respectively, in Daviess County, while George M. Hinkle and David W. Patten would perform the same duties in Caldwell County. Wight, Brunson, and Patten had led the targeted strikes in Daviess County on 18 October, while Hinkle was the commanding colonel of the Caldwell County regiment of the state militia.[14]

---

10. See 500n346 herein.

11. Thomas B. Marsh and Orson Hyde, Affidavit, Richmond, MO, 24 Oct. 1838, copy, Mormon War Papers, MSA.

12. William Peniston, Daviess Co., MO, to Lilburn W. Boggs, 21 Oct. 1838, copy; R. S. Mitchell et al., Richmond, MO, to Lilburn W. Boggs, 23 Oct. 1838, copy, Mormon War Papers, MSA; 322n303 herein.

13. Rockwood, Journal, 22 Oct. 1838. Rigdon, who remained in Far West during the Daviess County military operations, organized the special companies on 20 October. Although the name Danite was still in use in October 1838, it is unclear how the small, secretive, oath-bound society founded in early summer 1838 was related to the large force that included all able-bodied Mormon men that fall. It is possible the Danite society became the special companies operating in the fall, with the senior leadership and overall structure changing during the transition. (Burr Riggs, Testimony, Richmond, MO, Nov. 1838, pp. [76]–[77]; Addison Greene, Testimony, Richmond, MO, Nov. 1838, p. [110]; William W. Phelps, Testimony, Richmond, MO, Nov. 1838, pp. [92]–[93], in State of Missouri, "Evidence"; Rockwood, Journal, 15 and 22–23 Oct. 1838; see also Shurtliff, Autobiography, 125, 131; and Call, Statement, Bountiful, Utah Territory, 30 Dec. 1885, CHL.)

14. See Sampson Avard, Testimony, Richmond, MO, Nov. 1838, p. [8]; George Walters, Testimony, Richmond, MO, Nov. 1838, pp. [37]–[38]; George M. Hinkle, Testimony, Richmond, MO, Nov. 1838, pp. [40]–[41], in State of Missouri, "Evidence." It is unclear how the October "armies of Israel," or "Danites," related to the Caldwell County regiment of the state militia. Hinkle's leadership in both organizations suggests there was some overlap between the two organizations. In late October 1838, Caldwell County judge Elias Higbee—who had served as the captain general of the Danites—ordered Hinkle to call out the Caldwell regiment "to defend the citizens against mobs." However, Hinkle claimed that when he issued the call, his officers told him "they cared nothing for their commissions—that the organization of the Danite band had taken all power out of their hands." (George M. Hinkle, Testimony, Richmond,

In late October, non-Mormon vigilantes targeted church members living near the borders of Caldwell County. Ostensibly fearing a Mormon invasion of Ray County, Captain Samuel Bogart of the state militia sought and received authorization "to range the line between Caldwell & Ray County."[15] The militiamen exceeded this authorization, harassing church members living near the border between Caldwell and Ray counties, burning at least one Latter-day Saint cabin, and capturing three Mormon men—Addison Greene, Nathan Pinkham Jr., and William Seely, two of whom were probably scouts. Patten, apparently operating under the commission he received the day before to command cavalry in Caldwell County, led a contingent of about sixty Mormon cavalry to rescue the prisoners. At dawn on 25 October, Patten's men exchanged gunfire with Bogart's company of thirty-five men near Crooked River, two miles south of the Caldwell County border, resulting in the deaths of three Latter-day Saints—Patten, Patterson Obanion, and Gideon Carter—as well as Missourian Moses Rowland.[16] On 30 October, more than two hundred anti-Mormon vigilantes attacked the settlement at Hawn's Mill in eastern Caldwell County, where approximately thirty Latter-day Saint families had gathered. The vigilantes, many of whom were members of the Daviess and Livingston county militias operating without authorization from their superior officers, apparently instigated the attack in retaliation for the Mormon military operations in Daviess County earlier in the month. As women and children fled the mill amidst gunfire, at least one woman was injured in the hand. Latter-day Saint men and some boys assumed a defensive position in an unfinished blacksmith shop, which quickly turned into a death trap. The vigilantes killed—in some cases, brutally—ten Latter-day Saint men and boys and fatally injured seven others. Another thirteen men and boys were wounded. None of the vigilantes were killed.[17] In the wake of the killings, the survivors interred the dead in a nearby well, which became a mass grave.[18]

On 27 October, in response to exaggerated reports of the Saints' Daviess County operations and the Crooked River engagement, Boggs issued an order accusing church

MO, Nov. 1838, p. [40], in State of Missouri, "Evidence"; see also JS, Journal, 7–9 Aug. 1838, in *JSP*, J1:299.)

15. David R. Atchison, Liberty, MO, to Samuel Bogart, 23 Oct. 1838, p. [26], in State of Missouri, "Evidence."

16. Rockwood, Journal, 25 Oct. 1838; Charles C. Rich, Statement, ca. Feb. 1845, Historian's Office, JS History Documents, 1839–1860, CHL; Pratt, *History of the Late Persecution,* 35–36; Thorit Parsons, Testimony, Richmond, MO, Nov. 1838, p. [119], in State of Missouri, "Evidence"; Sidney Rigdon, Testimony, Nauvoo, IL, 1 July 1843, p. [12], Nauvoo, IL, Records, CHL; Reed Peck, Quincy, IL, to "Dear Friends," 18 Sept. 1839, p. 95, Henry E. Huntington Library, San Marino, CA; see also Baugh, "Call to Arms," 218–252. The skirmish occurred in a six-mile by twenty-four-mile strip of unincorporated land known as the Buncombe Strip, which was "attached to Ray for Civil & Military purposes only." (Sashel Woods and Joseph Dickson, Carrollton, MO, to John B. Clark, [ca. 25] Oct. 1838, copy, Mormon War Papers, MSA; Alexander Doniphan, Jefferson City, MO, to William W. Phelps, Shoal Creek, MO, 8 Jan. 1837, William W. Phelps, Collection of Missouri Documents, CHL; see also *History of Caldwell and Livingston Counties, Missouri,* 104–105.)

17. Joseph Young and Jane Bicknell Young, Affidavit, ca. 1839, pp. [38b]–39[a]; David Lewis, Affidavit, ca. 1839, pp. [40c]–[40d], in Sidney Rigdon, JS, et al., Petition Draft ["To the Publick"]; Baugh, "Call to Arms," chap. 9, appendixes I–J.

18. Amanda Barnes Smith, Affidavit, Quincy, IL, 18 Apr. 1839, Historian's Office, JS History Documents, 1839–1860, CHL; see also Radke-Moss, "Mormon Women as Healers, Concealers, and Protectors," 30–33.

members of being "in the attitude of an open and armed defiance of the laws," of waging "war upon the people of this state," and of committing "outrages . . . beyond all description." Claiming that "the Mormons must be treated as enemies and must be exterminated or driven from the state if necessary," Boggs ordered the state militia to "operate against the Mormons."[19] Major General Samuel D. Lucas assembled eighteen hundred troops in Caldwell County and on 30 October established his headquarters approximately one mile south of Far West. The following day, Lucas met with Hinkle and a delegation of Saints, presenting conditions for peacefully resolving the crisis: JS and several other church leaders were required to submit to arrest and prosecution. The Mormon participants in the conflict were required to surrender their weapons and sign over their property to pay for debts they owed to other Missourians and for the damages incurred during the conflict. Further, all Latter-day Saints were required to leave the state.[20]

Upon the delegates' return to Far West, they presented JS and other church leaders with a copy of Boggs's 27 October 1838 order.[21] According to Lyman Wight, Hinkle then informed the church leaders that Lucas "desired an interview" with JS, Sidney Rigdon, Wight, Parley P. Pratt, and George W. Robinson and that they would "be released that night or the next morning early." Evidently, the delegation did not inform JS and the others that they would be Lucas's prisoners when they entered the camp.[22] For his part, Lucas viewed the men as hostages to be held until Hinkle decided whether to comply with the conditions. If he did, the prisoners were to be held for trial; if he rejected the

---

19. Lilburn W. Boggs, Jefferson City, MO, to John B. Clark, Fayette, MO, 27 Oct. 1838, copy, Mormon War Papers, MSA. Noah Webster's 1828 *American Dictionary* defines *exterminate* as "literally, to drive from within the limits or borders" but also "to destroy utterly." Corrill feared that the militia would interpret Boggs's order as "authority from the executive to exterminate, with orders to cut off our [the Saints'] retreat . . . [the] innocent as well as guilty; so of course there was no escape for any." ("Exterminate," in *American Dictionary*; Corrill, *Brief History*, 42, in *JSP*, H2:185.)

20. Samuel D. Lucas, "near Far West," MO, to Lilburn W. Boggs, 2 Nov. 1838, copy, Mormon War Papers, MSA. The other members of the delegation included John Corrill, Reed Peck, John Cleminson, and William W. Phelps, all previously trusted church leaders who had become critical of the Danites and the Saints' October military operations in Daviess County. Accounts differ regarding whether Latter-day Saints Seymour Brunson and Arthur Morrison were part of the delegation. (Corrill, *Brief History*, 40–41, in *JSP*, H2:182–184; R. Peck to "Dear Friends," 18 Sept. 1839, pp. 104–111; George M. Hinkle, Buffalo, Iowa Territory, to William W. Phelps, Nauvoo, IL, 14 Aug. 1844, in *Ensign*, Aug. 1844, 30–32; Berrett, *Sacred Places*, 4:300–301.)

21. Corrill, *Brief History*, 40–41, in *JSP*, H2:185–186; R. Peck to "Dear Friends," 18 Sept. 1839, p. 111.

22. Lyman Wight, Journal, in *History of the Reorganized Church*, 2:260; Rockwood, Journal, 31 Oct. 1838; Brigham Young, Testimony, Nauvoo, IL, 1 July 1843, p. 2, Nauvoo, IL, Records, CHL; Samuel D. Lucas, "near Far West," MO, to Lilburn W. Boggs, 2 Nov. 1838, copy, Mormon War Papers, MSA; Bill of Damages, 4 June 1839, p. 501 herein. The men were likely arrested at least in part because of their leadership positions. Rigdon was a member of the First Presidency,[a] while Wight was a counselor in the presidency of the stake at Adam-ondi-Ahman and was considered by many Missourians to be the leader of the Latter-day Saints in Daviess County.[b] Robinson was clerk for the First Presidency,[c] and Pratt was an apostle who participated in the skirmish at Crooked River.[d] (a. Minutes, 7 Nov. 1837, in *JSP*, D5:469. b. Minutes, 28 June 1838, p. 166 herein; Alexander Doniphan, "Camp on Grand River," MO, to David R. Atchison, 15 Sept. 1838, copy, Mormon War Papers, MSA. c. Minutes, 6 Apr. 1838, p. 69 herein. d. Minutes, 7 Nov. 1837, in *JSP*, D5:471; Pratt, *History of the Late Persecution*, 33–36.)

conditions, the prisoners would be released and the militia would prepare to subdue Far West by force. On 1 November, Hinkle formally accepted the terms, and Lucas paraded his captives through the streets of Far West.[23] As several documents in part 3 attest, JS passionately argued that Hinkle and the other delegates had deceived and betrayed him.[24] Later, in response to these accusations, Hinkle claimed he surrendered only with JS's authorization.[25] On the same day as the surrender, 1 November, Hyrum Smith and Amasa Lyman were arrested and confined with the other prisoners.[26] That evening, Lucas reportedly held an ad hoc court martial in which JS and the six other Latter-day Saint prisoners were sentenced to death. Only the protest of Doniphan stopped the executions from proceeding.[27]

In Far West and Adam-ondi-Ahman, as well as at Hawn's Mill, state militiamen and anti-Mormon vigilantes ransacked the homes of the Latter-day Saints, stole food and other property, and harassed church members.[28] Disaffected Mormons who served as informants for the militia taunted the Saints.[29] Former apostle William E. McLellin ransacked JS's home in Far West. Not long afterward, Hinkle, the previous owner of the Smiths' home, stole items from the property and expelled Emma and her children from the premises.[30] In the midst of the chaos, anti-Mormon men committed multiple acts of sexual

---

23. Samuel D. Lucas, "near Far West," MO, to Lilburn W. Boggs, 2 Nov. 1838, copy, Mormon War Papers, MSA.

24. See Letter to Emma Smith, 4 Nov. 1838, p. 280 herein; Letter to the Church in Caldwell Co., MO, 16 Dec. 1838, pp. 300–301 herein; and Petition to George Tompkins, between 9 and 15 Mar. 1839, p. 344 herein.

25. George M. Hinkle, Buffalo, Iowa Territory, to William W. Phelps, Nauvoo, IL, 14 Aug. 1844, in *Ensign,* Aug. 1844, 30–32. Similarly, after Corrill and Peck left the church, they defended their role in the negotiations, arguing that JS fully understood Lucas's demands. (Corrill, *Brief History,* 41, in *JSP,* H2:184; R. Peck to "Dear Friends," 18 Sept. 1839, pp. 115–116.)

26. Lyman Wight, Journal, in *History of the Reorganized Church,* 2:260; Hyrum Smith, Commerce, IL, to "the Saints Scattered Abroad," Dec. 1839, in *Times and Seasons,* Dec. 1839, 1:21. Hyrum Smith was a member of the First Presidency, while Amasa Lyman was captain of a company of Mormon scouts sent to patrol the southern border of Caldwell County; at least one of the scouts was captured by Captain Samuel Bogart's Ray County militiamen just before the Crooked River battle. (Minutes, 7 Nov. 1837, in *JSP,* D5:469–470; Amasa Lyman, Affidavit, in [Rigdon], *Appeal to the American People,* 84; Addison Greene, Testimony, Richmond, MO, Nov. 1838, p. [110], in State of Missouri, "Evidence.")

27. Lyman Wight, Journal, in *History of the Reorganized Church,* 2:260–261; Eliza R. Snow, Caldwell Co., MO, to Isaac Streator, Streetsborough, OH, 22 Feb. 1839, photocopy, CHL; Hyrum Smith, Testimony, Nauvoo, IL, 1 July 1843, pp. 23–25, Nauvoo, IL, Records, CHL; see also Baugh, "Call to Arms," 336–339.

28. See Baugh, "Call to Arms," 359–368. During November 1838, the militia confined church members to Caldwell and Daviess counties, impeding the Saints from claiming their lands at the land office in Lexington, Lafayette County, during the period allotted under the preemption law. Consequently, other Missourians—many of whom participated in the conflict—claimed the Saints' lands. (See Walker, "Mormon Land Rights," 32–46.)

29. See Kimball, "History," 88; Pratt, *History of the Late Persecution,* 41; and T. B. Foote, Nephi, Utah Territory, to Editor of the *Deseret News,* 28 May 1868, Historian's Office Correspondence Files, CHL.

30. See Declaration to the Clay County Circuit Court, ca. 6 Mar. 1839, pp. 337–338 herein; and 348n444 herein.

violence, including rape, against Latter-day Saint women.[31] In addition, militiamen near Far West struck Latter-day Saint William Carey's head with a rifle, causing his death.[32] Carey may have been the last of about forty Mormons who were killed or died from exposure during the conflict.[33] As demonstrated in several documents in part 3, JS and other church members considered these individuals to be martyrs for the cause of Zion.[34]

On 2 November, JS and the other prisoners were permitted to obtain provisions and bid an emotional good-bye to their families before being taken to Jackson County, Missouri.[35] Lucas assigned Brigadier General Moses Wilson and three hundred state militiamen from Jackson County to escort the prisoners the fifty miles to Independence, the headquarters for the militia's Fourth Division. Upon arriving in Independence on 4 November, the prisoners were placed first in a large and comfortable log home and subsequently at Noland's Inn, rather than in the Jackson County jail.[36] Five days later, Lucas moved the prisoners to Richmond, where Major General John B. Clark assumed custody of them, having received an order from Boggs to oversee the entire campaign to quell the Mormon "rebellion," including through prosecuting the "ring leaders." In Richmond, JS and his fellow prisoners were placed in chains in a vacant log house near the unfinished courthouse.[37] Clark also confined forty-six other Latter-day Saint men to the courthouse on charges stemming from their alleged roles in the October 1838 operations in Daviess County.[38]

---

31. *American Slavery as It Is,* 191–192; Murdock, Journal, 29 Oct. 1838, 103–104; Hyrum Smith, Testimony, Nauvoo, IL, 1 July 1843, pp. 13, 24, Nauvoo, IL, Records, CHL; see also Radke-Moss, "Beyond Petticoats and Poultices."

32. Greene, *Facts relative to the Expulsion,* 14; Hyrum Smith, Testimony, Nauvoo, IL, 1 July 1843, pp. 9–10, Nauvoo, IL, Records, CHL.

33. John B. Clark, Jefferson City, MO, to Lilburn W. Boggs, 29 Nov. 1838, copy, Mormon War Papers, MSA; "Letter from the Editor," *Missouri Republican* (St. Louis), 7 Dec. 1838, [2]; see also Rockwood, Journal, 11 Nov. 1838.

34. See, for example, Letter to Emma Smith, 4 Nov. 1838, p. 280 herein; Letter to Edward Partridge and the Church, ca. 22 Mar. 1839, pp. 392–393 herein; and Letter from Alanson Ripley, 10 Apr. 1839, pp. 412–413 herein; see also Grua, "Memoirs of the Persecuted," chap. 1.

35. See Bill of Damages, 4 June 1839, p. 502 herein; and Letter to Edward Partridge and the Church, ca. 22 Mar. 1839, p. 395 herein.

36. Samuel D. Lucas, "near Far West," MO, to Lilburn W. Boggs, 2 Nov. 1838, copy, Mormon War Papers, MSA; Parley P. Pratt, Independence, MO, to Mary Ann Frost Pratt, Far West, MO, 4 Nov. 1838, Parley P. Pratt, Letters, CHL; Lyman Wight, Journal, in *History of the Reorganized Church,* 2:295–296; Historical Introduction to Receipt from William Collins, 8 Feb. 1839, p. 325 herein.

37. Lilburn W. Boggs, Jefferson City, MO, to John B. Clark, 1 Nov. 1838, copy; Lilburn W. Boggs, Jefferson City, MO, to John B. Clark, 6 Nov. 1838, copy; Samuel D. Lucas, Independence, MO, to Lilburn W. Boggs, 7 Nov. 1838, copy; John B. Clark, Richmond, MO, to Lilburn W. Boggs, 10 Nov. 1838, copy; John B. Clark, Jefferson City, MO, to Lilburn W. Boggs, 29 Nov. 1838, copy, Mormon War Papers, MSA; Lyman Wight, Journal, in *History of the Reorganized Church,* 2:296–297; Sidney Rigdon, JS, et al., Petition Draft ("To the Publick"), p. 44[a].

38. Clark arrived in Far West on 4 November 1838, intent on identifying Latter-day Saints who participated in the recent military operations in Daviess County and who could be charged with crimes. The major general's key informant was Avard, a former Danite leader, who agreed to provide names and testify for the state in exchange for immunity from prosecution. At the conclusion of Clark's investigation in Far West, he detained forty-six Latter-day Saints and brought them to Richmond on 9 November—the

On 10 November 1838, Clark asked Austin A. King of the fifth judicial circuit to preside at a criminal court of inquiry in Richmond.[39] From 12 to 29 November, Judge King evaluated testimony that the prisoners had committed treason and other crimes during the October 1838 conflict. A charge of treason, which is legally defined as "levying war" against the United States (or a state) or "giving aid" to its enemies, can be established only if two witnesses testify of the same "overt act" or the defendant confesses to the crime in court.[40] Forty-two witnesses, many of whom were disaffected church members, testified for the prosecution, which contended that JS and other church leaders had begun planning an insurrection against the state of Missouri as early as spring 1838, with the implementation starting that fall. Former Danite general Sampson Avard was the prosecution's key witness.[41] Although the prisoners submitted the names of dozens of potential defense witnesses, ultimately only seven testified, largely because of the intimidation of court officials.[42] During the course of the proceedings, eleven more Latter-day Saint men were charged, bringing the total to sixty-four defendants.[43] The

----

same day JS and his companions arrived from Independence. (John B. Clark, Richmond, MO, to Lilburn W. Boggs, 10 Nov. 1838, copy; John B. Clark, Jefferson City, MO, to Lilburn W. Boggs, 29 Nov. 1838, copy, Mormon War Papers, MSA; see also Berrett, *Sacred Places,* 4:243–249.)

39. John B. Clark, Richmond, MO, to Lilburn W. Boggs, 10 Nov. 1838, copy; John B. Clark, Jefferson City, MO, to Lilburn W. Boggs, 29 Nov. 1838, copy, Mormon War Papers, MSA; see also Madsen, "Joseph Smith and the Missouri Court of Inquiry," 93–136.

40. If convicted of treason against the state, the penalty was death or incarceration in the "penitentiary for a period not less than ten years." (See U.S. Constitution, art. 3, sec. 3; Missouri Constitution of 1820, art. 13, sec. 15; An Act concerning Crimes and Their Punishments [20 Mar. 1835], *Revised Statutes of the State of Missouri* [1835], p. 166, art. 1, sec. 1; and Madsen, "Joseph Smith and the Missouri Court of Inquiry," 93–136.)

41. Witnesses for the prosecution included Sampson Avard, Charles Blackley, Samuel Bogart, Elisha Cameron, Nathaniel Carr, John Cleminson, James Cobb, Asa Cook, John Corrill, Wyatt Cravens, Freeburn Gardner, Addison Greene, George M. Hinkle, Andrew Job, Jesse Kelley, Samuel Kimble, Timothy Lewis, John Lockhart, Patrick Lynch, Joseph McGee, Jeremiah Myers, Nehemiah Odle, Thomas Odle, James Owens, Reed Peck, Morris Phelps, William W. Phelps, Addison Price, John Raglin, Allen Rathburn, Burr Riggs, Abner Scovil, Benjamin Slade, Robert Snodgrass, William Splawn, John Taylor, James Turner, George Walters, John Whitmer, Ezra Williams, George Worthington, and Porter Yale. (Testimonies, Richmond, MO, Nov. 1838, pp. [2]–[113], [122]–[123], in State of Missouri, "Evidence.")

42. Hyrum Smith later stated that, per King's instructions, the prisoners identified sixty potential defense witnesses. Although the judge apparently subpoenaed these individuals, only the following seven testified for the defense: Jonathan Barlow, Ezra Chipman, Arza Judd Jr., Thorit Parsons, Delia Pine, Malinda Porter, and Nancy Rigdon. Multiple Latter-day Saints described officers of the court harassing potential witnesses or not permitting them to testify. (Hyrum Smith, Testimony, Nauvoo, IL, 1 July 1843, pp. 18–19; George Pitkin, Testimony, Nauvoo, IL, 1 July 1843, pp. 1–2, Nauvoo, IL, Records, CHL; Murdock, Journal, Nov. 1838, 105–106; Malinda Porter, Testimony, Richmond, MO, Nov. 1838, p. [115]; Delia F. Pine, Testimony, Richmond, MO, Nov. 1838, pp. [116]–[117]; Nancy Rigdon, Testimony, Richmond, MO, Nov. 1838, pp. [117]–[118]; Jonathan Barlow, Testimony, Richmond, MO, Nov. 1838, pp. [118]–[119]; Thorit Parsons, Testimony, Richmond, MO, Nov. 1838, pp. [119]–[120]; Ezra Chipman, Testimony, Richmond, MO, Nov. 1838, pp. [120]–[121]; Arza Judd Jr., Testimony, Richmond, MO, Nov. 1838, p. [121], in State of Missouri, "Evidence.")

43. The eleven men were Samuel Bent, Ebenezer Brown, Jonathan Dunham, King Follett, Clark Hallett, Sylvester Hewlett, Joel Miles, James Newberry, Morris Phelps, James Rollins, and William Wightman. (Trial Proceedings, Richmond, MO, Nov. 1838, pp. [1]–[2], [34], [61], [70], [100], in State of Missouri, "Evidence.")

defendants later alleged that the hearing was significantly marred by procedural and substantive problems.[44]

At the conclusion of the hearing, King ruled there was probable cause to believe that JS, Wight, Hyrum Smith, Alexander McRae, and Caleb Baldwin had committed treason in Daviess County during the conflict and that Rigdon had committed the same offense in Caldwell County. As treason was a nonbailable offense and neither Daviess nor Caldwell county had a jail, these men were confined in the Clay County jail in Liberty to await a spring trial.[45] The judge also ruled there was probable cause to believe that Pratt and four other Latter-day Saint men had participated in the murder of Moses Rowland in the Crooked River skirmish; because murder was also nonbailable, King committed these prisoners to the Ray County jail to await trial.[46] Finally, King found probable cause to believe that twenty-four other defendants had committed arson, burglary, robbery, and larceny. The judge admitted them to bail on the condition that they appear before the Daviess County Circuit Court during the spring term.[47] The remaining prisoners were discharged for lack of evidence.[48]

On 1 December 1838, JS and his companions arrived in Liberty, the seat of Clay County, and were incarcerated in the county jail, an imposing edifice with four-foot-thick walls made of limestone and oak. The jail had only one entrance: double iron doors at the landing of a short flight of stairs. The doors opened to a room containing two windows, each with vertical iron bars preventing entrance or escape. A trapdoor in the floor opened into the jail's dungeon, a 14- by 14½-foot space that was 6½ feet from stone floor to ceiling. Two windows, 2 feet wide and 6 inches high, with a heavy iron bar running horizontally through each, provided the only natural light.[49] The prisoners were guarded by Clay County

---

44. Petition to George Tompkins, between 9 and 15 Mar. 1839, pp. 345–346 herein; see also Madsen, "Joseph Smith and the Missouri Court of Inquiry," 93–136.

45. Ruling, Richmond, MO, Nov. 1838, p. [124], in State of Missouri, "Evidence"; An Act to Regulate Proceedings in Criminal Cases [21 Mar. 1835], *Revised Statutes of the State of Missouri* [1835], p. 475, art. 2, sec. 8; Mittimus, Richmond, MO, 29 Nov. 1838, State of Missouri v. JS et al. for Treason and Other Crimes (Mo. 5th Jud. Cir. 1838), JS Collection, CHL.

46. King ruled there was probable cause to believe that Pratt, Darwin Chase, Luman Gibbs, Morris Phelps, and Norman Shearer had committed murder. (Ruling, Richmond, MO, Nov. 1838, pp. [124]–[125], in State of Missouri, "Evidence.")

47. The following prisoners were admitted to bail: Samuel Bent, Daniel Carn, Jonathan Dunham, Jacob Gates, George Grant, Clark Hallett, James Henderson, Francis M. Higbee, John Higbee, Jesse Hunter, George Kimball, Joel Miles, Ebenezer Page, Edward Partridge, David Pettegrew, Thomas Rich, Alanson Ripley, Ebenezer Robinson, George W. Robinson, James Rollins, Sidney Turner, Washington Voorhees, William Wightman, and Joseph Younger. (Trial Proceedings, Richmond, MO, Nov. 1838, pp. [125]–[126], in State of Missouri, "Evidence.")

48. These men included Martin Allred, William Allred, Ebenezer Brown, John Buchanan, Moses Clawson, Benjamin Covey, Sheffield Daniels, John Earl, Elisha Edwards, King Follett, David Frampton, George W. Harris, Anthony Head, Chandler Holbrook, Sylvester Hulet, Benjamin Jones, Amasa Lyman, Silas Maynard, Isaac Morley, James Newberry, Elijah Newman, Zedekiah Owens, Daniel Shearer, Allen Stout, John Tanner, Daniel Thomas, Alva Tippets, Andrew Whitlock, and Henry Zabrisky. (Trial Proceedings, Richmond, MO, Nov. 1838, pp. [108]–[109], [123], in State of Missouri, "Evidence.")

49. "Clay County, Missouri," *Historical Record,* Dec. 1888, 7:670; "Liberty Jail," *Liahona, the Elders' Journal,* 18 Aug. 1914, 122; see also Jessee, "Prison Experience," 25.

sheriff and jailer Samuel Hadley and his deputy, Samuel Tillery.[50] Through the winter of 1838–1839, the prisoners slept on dirty straw mattresses and subsisted on a coarse diet.[51] However, the prisoners spent some of their time in the upper story of the jail, eating meals and meeting with visitors.[52] Emma Smith, for example, visited JS in the jail three times before she departed from the state.[53] In addition, they were occasionally permitted to leave the jailhouse under supervision of a guard.[54]

The main body of the church endured the winter in Caldwell County.[55] On 10 December 1838, Edward Partridge and other church leaders wrote an extensive petition to the Missouri legislature, providing the Saints' perspective on the recent conflict and requesting that the legislature rescind Boggs's expulsion order. While acknowledging that some church members were guilty of unlawful behavior, especially during the October "difficulties in Daviess Co[unty]," the petitioners argued that such crimes should be understood in the context of past wrongs inflicted on the Saints. Partridge and the others also queried why the Saints were charged with crimes when not one vigilante was arrested for the murders committed at Hawn's Mill.[56] In early 1839, it became apparent that the legislature would not intervene on behalf of the Saints;[57] consequently, church leaders in Far West organized the evacuation of the eight to ten thousand Latter-day Saints living in Missouri.[58] Faced with insufficient supplies, inclement weather, and disease, many church members suffered considerably during the journey of nearly two hundred miles to Quincy, Illinois, a town along the Mississippi River. The residents of Quincy welcomed the Latter-day Saint refugees, providing food, shelter, and work.[59] During this mass migration, there

---

50. Mittimus, Richmond, MO, 29 Nov. 1838, State of Missouri v. JS et al. for Treason and Other Crimes (Mo. 5th Jud. Cir. 1838), JS Collection, CHL; Woodson, *History of Clay County, Missouri,* 333.

51. See Letter to Isaac Galland, 22 Mar. 1839, p. 380 herein; and Bill of Damages, 4 June 1839, p. 504 herein.

52. Alexander McRae, "Incidents in the History of Joseph Smith," *Deseret News,* 2 Nov. 1854, [1]; George A. Smith, Autobiography, 123–125; see also Jessee, "Prison Experience," 26.

53. See 375n641 herein; and *History of the Reorganized Church,* 2:309, 315.

54. William T. Wood, "Mormon Memoirs," *Liberty [MO] Tribune,* 9 Apr. 1886, [1]; Andrew Jenson et al., "Liberty Jail," *Deseret News,* 3 Oct. 1888, 608.

55. By late November 1838, in compliance with the orders of state militia officers, the Saints in Daviess County had evacuated the county and resettled in Caldwell County. (See Introduction to Part 3: 4 Nov. 1838–16 Apr. 1839, p. 265 herein.)

56. Edward Partridge et al., Petition, Far West, MO, to the Missouri State Legislature, 10 Dec. 1838, copy, Edward Partridge, Papers, CHL.

57. The legislature briefly considered the petition but chose not to take action. (See *Journal, of the House of Representatives, of the State of Missouri,* 19 Dec. 1838, 128; and Gentry and Compton, *Fire and Sword,* 460–461.)

58. Eliza R. Snow, Caldwell Co., MO, to Isaac Streator, Streetsborough, OH, 22 Feb. 1839, photocopy, CHL; Elias Smith, Far West, MO, to Ira Smith, East Stockholm, NY, 11 Mar. 1839, Elias Smith Correspondence, CHL; Heber C. Kimball, Far West, MO, to Joseph Fielding, Preston, England, 12 Mar. 1839, in Compilation of Heber C. Kimball Correspondence, CHL; see also LeSueur, *1838 Mormon War in Missouri,* 29, 35–36; and Leonard, *Nauvoo,* 31, 671–672n33.

59. See Hartley, "Winter Exodus from Missouri," 6–40; and Bennett, "Study of the Mormons in Quincy," 83–105.

Clay County jail. 1878. Erected in 1833, the Clay County jail in Liberty, Missouri, was a two-story edifice with double doors, iron-barred windows, and four-foot-thick walls of stone and timber. From 1 December 1838 to 6 April 1839, Joseph Smith and his fellow prisoners were confined primarily to the jail's dungeon, although they were occasionally permitted to take meals or receive visitors in the upper story and to temporarily leave the jail under guard. Most of the documents in part 3 of this volume were produced in the Clay County jail. (Church History Library, Salt Lake City.)

was little to no correspondence between the body of the church and the prisoners left behind in Missouri.

Eager to join the Saints leaving Missouri, the prisoners pursued various options to obtain their freedom. In late January 1839, the prisoners petitioned the Clay County court for habeas corpus, a legal remedy that permitted incarcerated individuals to challenge their imprisonment; the court granted the petition. At the hearing held on 22 January 1839 to evaluate the reasons for the prisoners' detention, Clay County justice Joel Turnham reviewed the testimony from the November 1838 hearing before Judge King, listened to statements from the prisoners, and heard arguments from prosecution attorney William Wood and defense attorneys Alexander Doniphan and Peter Burnett; Turnham apparently did not permit additional witnesses to testify for the defendants. He released Rigdon on bail but remanded JS and the other prisoners to jail.[60] After this setback, the prisoners tried to escape. While receiving visitors in the jail's upper room on 7 February, Hyrum Smith attempted to force his way out through the exterior doors. The

---

60. None of the documents from this hearing are extant. (See Sidney Rigdon, Testimony, Nauvoo, IL, 1 July 1843, pp. [22]–[24], Nauvoo, IL, Records, CHL; Burnett, *Recollections and Opinions,* 53–55; *History of the Reorganized Church,* 2:315–316; Letter to Isaac Galland, 22 Mar. 1839, p. 379 herein; and Bill of Damages, 4 June 1839, pp. 503–504 herein.)

jailer and guards quickly apprehended Hyrum and the other prisoners who tried to follow him.[61] In early March, the prisoners endeavored to escape by digging through the
wooden inner wall of the dungeon. However, before they could remove the outer limestone block, the handles of their augers broke; they sought outside assistance, and their
plan was discovered.[62] With the failure of this second escape attempt, the prisoners again
pursued legal remedies. In mid-March, the men prepared petitions for writs of habeas
corpus. The justices of the Missouri Supreme Court refused the petitions, despite expressing sympathy for the imprisoned Saints.[63]

Although physically separated from the main body of the church, JS maintained
family ties and directed church affairs through letters. During his time in state custody,
he wrote at least five letters to his wife Emma Smith, expressing his love and affection for
her and their children. These missives are rare examples of JS's surviving holographic letters.[64] One letter from Emma to JS is extant. In addition to personal missives, JS wrote
more formal letters to church leaders and the Saints at large, providing leadership at a
time when the church community was seriously threatened. In late March, JS dictated
two lengthy general epistles to church members in Quincy and elsewhere, offering in-
sight into the meaning of the Saints' recent persecutions, reflections on past missteps,
and guidance on reestablishing church communities. Portions of these epistles were
presented in the voice of Deity in a manner similar to that in JS's revelations. Two of the
revelation-like sections addressed the significance of suffering and promised that JS and
the Saints would be divinely vindicated. Another section contained counsel on the righteous use of priesthood power. When composing these more formal letters, JS relied on
his fellow prisoners to act as scribes. Alexander McRae served as the primary scribe for
the two general epistles, with Caleb Baldwin assisting. JS reviewed and made corrections
to both of these epistles.

---

61. Samuel Tillery, Testimony, Liberty, MO, 11 Feb. 1839, State of Missouri v. Ripley et al. (J.P. Ct.
1839), Clay County Archives and Historical Library, Liberty, MO; Alexander McRae, "Incidents in the
History of Joseph Smith," *Deseret News*, 2 Nov. 1854, [1]; *History of the Reorganized Church*, 2:316.

62. Hyrum Smith described the early March 1839 escape attempt thus: "We made a hole through the
logs in the lower room & through the stone wall all but the out side stone which was suffitiently large
to pass out when it was pushed out but we were hindred for want of handles to the augurs[.] the
logs were so hard that the handles would split & we had to make new ones with our fire wood[.] we
had to bore the hole for the shank with my penknife which delayed time in spite of all we could
do." According to Lyman Wight, the prisoners reached out to a man named Shoemaker, who "felt
so tickled to think that he was our assistant that he made a confidant of Doctor Moss. The thing
leaked out, and there were ten guards called for." (Hyrum Smith, Liberty, MO, to Mary Fielding
Smith, Quincy, IL, 16 Mar. 1839, Mary Fielding Smith, Collection, CHL; Lyman Wight, Journal,
in *History of the Reorganized Church*, 2:317; Letter to the Church and Edward Partridge, 20 Mar. 1839,
p. 364 herein.)

63. See Historical Introduction to Petition to George Tompkins, between 9 and 15 Mar. 1839, pp. 341–
344 herein.

64. As JS explained in a May 1834 letter to Emma Smith, he saw writing to her "with [his] own hand"
as fulfilling part of his "dut[i]es of a Husband and Father," a sentiment that reflected nineteenth-century
cultural assumptions about handwriting and intimacy. (Letter to Emma Smith, 18 May 1834, in *JSP*,
D4:50; Thornton, *Handwriting in America*, 81.)

JS preferred correspondence to be transmitted to and from the jail by couriers rather than through the postal service. The identities of only a handful of couriers have been preserved, but presumably most were church members or other trusted individuals. When the main body of the church was in Missouri, the couriers would have traversed the approximately forty miles between Liberty and Far West, which probably took a day or two. As church members relocated to Illinois, the couriers would have traveled the approximately two hundred miles between Liberty and Quincy, a distance probably covered in about a week.[65]

On 6 April, the prisoners and their guards departed the Clay County jail for Gallatin, where they were scheduled to appear at a session of the Daviess County Circuit Court.[66] Around 10 April, a grand jury indicted JS and several other Saints for treason and other crimes allegedly committed during the previous summer and fall. The court then granted the prisoners a change of venue from Daviess County to Boone County, where they believed their chances for a fair trial would be better. The prisoners may also have believed they could escape from custody en route to their new destination. The prisoners did just that on 16 April 1839, evidently with the guards' complicity, and made their way to Illinois, arriving on 22 April.[67] Prior to learning of the escape, several church members in Quincy wrote to JS, apparently in response to the general epistles he sent in late March. Knowing that the prisoners had been moved from Liberty and that they would probably receive a change of venue, the Saints may not have sent these letters to Missouri, preferring to wait for additional information on JS's whereabouts.

Correspondence between JS and the Saints, as well as legal documents produced during his incarceration, compose the majority of documents in part 3. Also included are financial and other documents that JS's representatives produced on his behalf during this period. In Far West, Bishop Partridge continued to manage JS's financial affairs, while First Presidency scribe George W. Robinson issued priesthood licenses.[68] In Ohio, church agent Oliver Granger worked with attorney Reuben Hitchcock to assess JS's remaining debts.[69]

———— ⌘ ————

---

65. Only JS's final missive to Emma, written just before his early April 1839 departure from the jail, was sent to Illinois through the postal system. (See Letter to Emma Smith, 4 Apr. 1839, pp. 401–406 herein.)

66. The grand jury hearing was held approximately one mile southeast of Gallatin proper, on the property of Elisha B. Creekmore, since Daviess County lacked a courthouse. (See Leopard et al., *History of Daviess and Gentry Counties,* 75; and Berrett, *Sacred Places,* 4:485.)

67. Hyrum Smith, Diary, 6–16 Apr. 1839; Historical Introduction to Promissory Note to John Brassfield, 16 Apr. 1839, pp. 422–426 herein.

68. See Receipt from Sarah Burt Beman, 26 Jan. 1839, pp. 323–325 herein; and License for Gardner Snow, 19 Jan. 1839, pp. 316–318 herein.

69. See Statement of Account from Hitchcock & Wilder, between 9 July and 6 Nov. 1838, pp. 285–290 herein.

Letter to Emma Smith, 4 November 1838

Source Note

JS, Letter, Independence, Jackson Co., MO, to Emma Smith, Far West, Caldwell Co., MO, 4 Nov. 1838; handwriting of JS (signature now missing); three pages; JS Materials, CCLA. Includes address, wafer seals, and redactions.

Bifolium measuring 12½ × 7¾ inches (32 × 20 cm), with thirty-five printed lines per page. The document was trifolded twice in letter style, sealed with wafers, and addressed. Later, the letter was refolded, perhaps for filing. JS's signature was subsequently cut from the second leaf.[70] The leaves eventually became separated and were reattached with staples. At some point, the two leaves were numbered in graphite. The letter likely remained in the Smith family's possession until it was transferred, on an unknown date, to the custody of the Reorganized Church of Jesus Christ of Latter Day Saints (now Community of Christ).[71]

Historical Introduction

Following JS's late October 1838 arrest in Far West, Missouri, he wrote to his wife Emma Smith on 4 November 1838.[72] JS and his fellow prisoners—Sidney Rigdon, Hyrum Smith, Lyman Wight, George W. Robinson, Parley P. Pratt, and Amasa Lyman—arrived in Independence, Missouri, around noon on 4 November in the midst of a severe storm.[73] The prisoners were lodged in a large "old log house" situated on Maple Street, immediately north of Independence's public square and courthouse.[74] In the evening, the prisoners were "provided with Paper and writing Materials and Candles,"[75] and JS wrote the following letter to Emma Smith, recounting the prisoners' reception in Independence and expressing anxiety for her welfare. The absence of a postmark suggests the letter was hand delivered. JS may have sent the letter by way of a "Mr Collins," who on 7 November carried a letter from inmate Parley P. Pratt to his wife, Mary Ann Frost Pratt, in Far West.[76] By the time Emma Smith received this letter, she and her children had likely been evicted from their residence and were probably staying at the home of George and Lucinda Pendleton Harris in Far West.[77]

---

70. According to Richard Howard, former historian for the Reorganized Church of Jesus Christ of Latter Day Saints, a high-ranking church official in the early twentieth century cut JS signatures from documents—a common practice at the time. (Richard Howard, email to Rachel Killebrew, 5 Jan. 2015, copy in editors' possession.)

71. See R. Howard to R. Killebrew, 5 Jan. 2015.

72. For more information on JS's arrest and move from Far West to Independence, see Introduction to Part 3: 4 Nov. 1838–16 Apr. 1839, pp. 270–272 herein.

73. Parley P. Pratt, Independence, MO, to Mary Ann Frost Pratt, Far West, MO, 4 Nov. 1838, Parley P. Pratt, Letters, CHL.

74. Lyman Wight, Journal, in *History of the Reorganized Church*, 2:295–297.

75. P. Pratt to M. Pratt, 4 Nov. 1838.

76. P. Pratt to M. Pratt, 4 Nov. 1838; Lyman Wight, Journal, in *History of the Reorganized Church*, 2:295.

77. In 1842 Emma Smith testified that following JS's arrest, George M. Hinkle, the previous owner of the Smiths' house in Far West, entered the home, stole Smith family possessions, and "used Coersive measures to drive Witness [Emma Smith] and her Family therefrom, the Premises & House." She also explained, "I went with my Children to the House of George W. Harris in Far West Missouri." (Minute Book 2, 6 July 1838; Emma Smith, Deposition, Nauvoo, IL, 22 Apr. 1842, JS v. George M. Hinkle [Lee Co. Dist. Ct. 1842], CHL.)

Document Transcript

November 4th 1838

Indipendace [Independence] Jackson Co— Mo—

My dear and beloved companion, of my bosam, in tribulation, and affliction, I woud inform you that I am well, and ~~I am~~ that we are all of us in good spirits as regards our own fate, we have been protected by the Jackson County boys, in the most genteel manner,[78] and arrived here in ⟨the⟩ midst of a splended perade, ~~this~~ a little after noon,[79] instead ⟨of⟩ going to goal [jail][80] we have a good house provided for us and the kind[e]st treatment, I have great anxiety about you, and my lovely children, my heart morns ⟨and⟩ bleeds for the brotheren, and sisters, and for the slain ⟨of the⟩ people of God, ~~I~~ Colonal, [George M.] Hinkle, proved to be a trator, to the Church,[81] he is worse than a hull who betraid the army at detroit,[82] he decoyed ⟨us⟩ unawares God reward him, ~~I~~ Johon Carl [John Corrill] ~~told ⟨general Willson⟩ was a going~~ told general, [Moses] Wilson, that he was a going to leave the Church,[83] general Willson says he thinks much less of him now then before, why I mention this is to have you careful not to trust them, if we are permited to ~~be~~ stay any time here, we ⟨have⟩ obtained a promice that ~~they~~ we may have our families brought to us,[84] what God may ~~do~~ do for us I do not know but I hope for the best always in all

---

78. Parley P. Pratt confirmed that the "oficers and troops, of Jackson County; have Behaved with that Respect, honor and kindness towards us." (P. Pratt to M. Pratt, 4 Nov. 1838.)

79. Parley P. Pratt recalled, "It was now past noon, and in the midst of a great rain. But hundreds crowded to witness the procession, and to gaze at us as we were paraded in martial triumph through all the principal streets—our carriages moving in the centre, while the brigade on horseback were formed in front and rear, and the bugles sounded a blast of triumphant joy." (Pratt, *History of the Late Persecution*, 46.)

80. Jackson County's first jail was built in 1827; it housed Latter-day Saint prisoners during the 1833 conflict. (*History of Jackson County, Missouri,* 639–640; Parley P. Pratt et al., "'The Mormons' So Called," *The Evening and the Morning Star,* Extra, Feb. 1834, [2].)

81. For more on Hinkle's role in the negotiations that led to JS's arrest, see Introduction to Part 3: 4 Nov. 1838–16 Apr. 1839, pp. 270–271 herein.

82. William Hull (1753–1825) was a Revolutionary War veteran, territorial governor of Michigan, and brigadier general of the army in the northwest United States during the War of 1812. On 16 August 1812, while quartered at Fort Detroit, Hull surrendered to a much smaller British force. In the wake of the capitulation, other perceived traitors in the war were condemned as being "worse than Hull." (Taylor, *Civil War of 1812,* 154–173, 196.)

83. Previously a trusted church leader in Missouri, Corrill became disaffected in summer 1838. In his history, Corrill suggested that it was his disillusionment with the Danites, the Saints' October 1838 military operations in Daviess County, and JS's leadership that led him to leave the church in winter 1838. (See, for example, Corrill, *Brief History,* 29–32, 36–37, 40, 46, 48, in *JSP,* H2:165–169, 175–178, 183, 193–194, 196–197; see also 301n167 herein.)

84. Parley P. Pratt wrote to his wife, "If we should Stay Long In this place, General Willson, has Promised us that our families shall Be guarded to us and Protected." (P. Pratt to M. Pratt, 4 Nov. 1838.)

circumstances although I go unto death, I will trust in God, what outrages may be committed by the mob I know not, but expect there will be but little ⟨or⟩ no restraint[85] Oh may God have mercy on us, [p. [1]] when we arrived at the river last night an express came to gene[r]al Willson from geneal [John B.] Clark of Howard County claiming the right of command ordering us back where ⟨or what place⟩ God only knows, and there is some feelings betwen the offercers,[86] I do not know where it will end, it ⟨is⟩ said by some that general Clark, is determined to ~~exterminating~~ exterminate[87] God has spared some of us thus far perhaps he will extend mercy in some degree toward us ⟨yet⟩[88] some of the people of this place have told me that some of the mormans may settle in this county as others ⟨men⟩ do[89] ~~the peg~~ I have

---

85. Michael Arthur, who was not a member of the church but was friendly to the Saints, indicated that "small companies" of armed men were "constantly strolling up and down Caldwell county . . . insulting the women in any and every way; and plundering the poor devils [Latter-day Saints] of all the means of subsistence." (Michael Arthur, Liberty, MO, to "Respected Friends," 29 Nov. 1838, copy, Mormon War Papers, MSA; see also Introduction to Part 3: 4 Nov. 1838–16 Apr. 1839, p. 269 herein.)

86. In early November 1838, Major General Samuel D. Lucas and Major General John B. Clark disputed who held ultimate command in the field and therefore was responsible for the Latter-day Saint prisoners. Lucas claimed that when he and his men approached Far West in late October, he believed he was the ranking officer in the field and thus was fully authorized to negotiate the peace terms with Colonel George M. Hinkle and to arrest the Mormon leaders on 31 October 1838. In a subsequent letter to Governor Lilburn W. Boggs, Lucas explained he was unaware that the governor had given Clark command over all the militia forces. On 2 November, Lucas ordered Brigadier General Moses Wilson and his men to take the prisoners to Lucas's headquarters in Independence.[a] Upon hearing this news, Clark, who had not yet reached Far West, ordered Lucas on 3 November to reroute the prisoners to Clark's headquarters in Richmond.[b] Although both men were major generals, Lucas argued that his "grade of Office" was superior to Clark's, leading Lucas to disregard Clark's 3 November order, as he "could not under any circumstances, be commanded by a Junior Major Genl."[c] On 6 November, Lucas received confirmation in Independence that Boggs had indeed appointed Clark as the commanding officer, and Lucas agreed to give the prisoners to Clark.[d] (a. Samuel D. Lucas, Independence, MO, to Lilburn W. Boggs, 5 Nov. 1838, copy, Mormon War Papers, MSA. b. John B. Clark, Richmond, MO, to Samuel D. Lucas, 3 Nov. 1838, copy, Mormon War Papers, MSA. c. Samuel D. Lucas, Independence, MO, to Lilburn W. Boggs, 7 Nov. 1838, copy, Mormon War Papers, MSA; S. Lucas to L. Boggs, 5 Nov. 1838. d. S. Lucas to L. Boggs, 7 Nov. 1838; John B. Clark, Richmond, MO, to Lilburn W. Boggs, 10 Nov. 1838, copy, Mormon War Papers, MSA.)

87. For more information on Governor Lilburn W. Boggs's 27 October 1838 order to Major General John B. Clark, see Introduction to Part 3: 4 Nov. 1838–16 Apr. 1839, pp. 270–271 herein.

88. When the prisoners left Far West for Independence, Clark was not in the city yet, and it was unclear whether he would adopt Lucas's terms or interpret the governor's order more forcefully. Clark ultimately retained most of Lucas's stipulations. However, after viewing "the situation of their women and children, and the inclemency of the weather," Clark decided to "modify the terms" and allow the Saints to "remain until their convenience suited them in the spring." (J. Clark to L. Boggs, 10 Nov. 1838.)

89. At Far West on 5 November 1838, Major General John B. Clark delivered a speech in which he reportedly encouraged the Saints to "become as other citizens," by which he meant "to scatter abroad and never again organize with Bishops, Presidents, &c." Judge Austin A. King shared the belief that the problems between the Latter-day Saints and their Missouri neighbors were rooted in the Saints' practice of gathering. "If the Mormons would disperse and not gather into exclusive communities of their own, I

some hopes that something may turn out for good to the afflicted saints,[90] I want you to stay where you are untill you here from me again, I may send for you to bring you to me, I cannot learn much for certainty in the situation that I am in, and can only pray for deliverance, untill it is meeted out, and take every thing as it comes, with ~~patient~~ patience and fortitude, I hope you will be faithful and true to every trust, I cant write much in my situation, conduct all matters as your circumstances and necesities require, may God give you wisdom and prudance and sobriety which ⟨I⟩ have every reason to believe you will, those little ⟨childrens⟩ are subjects of my meditation continually, tell them that Father is yet alive, God grant that he may see them again Oh Emma for God sake [p. [2]] do not forsake me nor the truth but remember, if I do ⟨not⟩ meet you again in this life may God grant that we may ⟨may we⟩ meet in heaven, I cannot express my feelings, my heart is full, Farewell Oh my kind and affectionate Emma I am yours forever your Husband and true friend

[Joseph Smith Jr.][91]

To Mrs Emma Smith
Far West, Mo
Coldwell Co. Mo— [p. [3]]

———— ✂ ————

Letter to the Citizens of Jackson County, 5 November 1838

Source Note

JS, Hyrum Smith, Parley P. Pratt, Amasa Lyman, George W. Robinson, Lyman Wight, and Sidney Rigdon, Letter, Independence, Jackson Co., MO, to the "citizens of Jackson County," MO, 5 Nov. 1838. Featured version published in Daily Commercial Bulletin *(St. Louis), 19 Nov. 1838, p. [2].*

Issue containing four pages, with six printed columns per page. This issue was photographed on microfilm on 14 April 1976 by the State Historical Society of Wisconsin. The microfilm copy, which is the version featured in this volume, has remained in institutional custody.

Historical Introduction

On 5 November 1838, JS and his fellow prisoners—Sidney Rigdon, Hyrum Smith, Lyman Wight, George W. Robinson, Parley P. Pratt, and Amasa Lyman—wrote a letter

---

think with the exception of a few of their leaders, the people might be reconciled to them." These sentiments also existed among some residents of Jackson County, from which the Latter-day Saints had been expelled in fall 1833. (Greene, *Facts relative to the Expulsion,* 27; Editorial Note, in *JSP,* H2:282–283; Austin A. King, Richmond, MO, to Lilburn W. Boggs, 23 Dec. 1838, copy, Mormon War Papers, MSA.)

90. See Romans 8:28; Revelation, 12 Oct. 1833, in *JSP,* D3:325 [D&C 100:15]; and Revelation, 6 Aug. 1836, in *JSP,* D5:278 [D&C 111:11].

91. TEXT: At a subsequent date, JS's signature was cut from the second leaf.

to the citizens of Jackson County, Missouri, expressing gratitude for the treatment the prisoners received from the citizens and the state militia's Fourth Division. On 2 November 1838, the prisoners, Brigadier General Moses Wilson, and three hundred militiamen departed Far West, Caldwell County, Missouri, for Independence, Jackson County, the headquarters of Wilson's superior, Major General Samuel D. Lucas. The prisoners likely did not expect a positive experience in Jackson County, given the violent expulsion of the Saints from the county in 1833, church leaders' arrest in late October 1838, the threat of execution, and the militia's occupation of Far West.[92]

Upon the prisoners' arrival in Independence on 4 November, rather than being confined in the county jail, they were lodged in a large log house situated on the north side of the public square. Their militia guards provided good food, prepared comfortable sleeping quarters, and permitted guests to visit the prisoners. According to Wight, the day after their arrival the Latter-day Saint prisoners "were at liberty to go where we pleased about through the town," including to the place church leaders had designated for a temple in 1831.[93] As Parley P. Pratt wrote to his wife, Mary Ann Frost Pratt, "Were it not for the absence of Our families we Should allmost forget that we were Prisoners."[94]

In the prisoners' 5 November 1838 letter, they expressed their "unfeigned gratitude" to Jackson County's citizens, to Lucas and Wilson, and to the militia for the unexpected kindness and civility. The prisoners may have believed that the letter would cultivate favor among the county's residents and encourage the good treatment to continue.

Because the original letter is apparently not extant, it is unknown which of the prisoners penned the letter. Upon its completion, JS and the other men signed it. Addressed to the "citizens of Jackson County," the letter may have been intended for publication, perhaps as a broadside or in a local newspaper. However, it is unclear whether the letter circulated in Jackson County—either in manuscript form or in print—after it was completed. The earliest known publication of the letter was on 10 November 1838 in the *Boon's Lick Democrat,* a newspaper published in Fayette, Howard County, Missouri, more than one hundred miles east of Independence. As published, the letter was titled "a card"; it is unknown whether this title was editorially supplied or if it was original to the letter. The editors of the *Boon's Lick Democrat* stated in an introductory note that the letter "furnishes a refutation of the reports which have reached here from various sources and that some of General Lucas's command, after their arrival at Far West, had been guilty of many flagrant and nameless outrages upon the persons of some of their Mormon prisoners."[95] Although this issue of the *Boon's Lick*

---

92. Introduction to Part 3: 4 Nov. 1838–16 Apr. 1839, p. 272 herein.

93. Letter to Emma Smith, 4 Nov. 1838, p. 280 herein; Lyman Wight, Journal, in *History of the Reorganized Church,* 2:295–296; Revelation, 20 July 1831, in *JSP,* D2:8 [D&C 57:3].

94. Parley P. Pratt, Independence, MO, to Mary Ann Frost Pratt, Far West, MO, 4 Nov. 1838, Parley P. Pratt, Letters, CHL; see also Pratt, *History of the Late Persecution,* 46–47.

95. Notice, *Daily Commercial Bulletin* (St. Louis), 19 Nov. 1838, [2]. Major General John B. Clark later reported, "Hearing at Richmond that some of the guard left by Genl Lucas at Far West were killing prisoners and commiting other excesses I left my troops and went in advance riding all night in order to check such things." Although Clark concluded that such reports were exaggerated, he was unwilling to "vouch for the troops before [his] arrival" on 4 November. Pratt echoed several Latter-day Saints who claimed that after Lucas's troops disarmed the Saints, "the brutal mob were now turned

Democrat has not been located, the letter and introductory note were reprinted in the 19 November 1838 issue of the St. Louis *Daily Commercial Bulletin;* that version of the letter is featured here.

Document Transcript

A CARD.

To the citizens of Jackson County:

It is with feelings of no ordinary kind that the undersigned take this method of tendering their most unfeigned gratitude to you for the kind treatment and great attention they have received at your hands since they were committed to your charge as prisoners: having received every degree of kindness that could be expected at the hands of a magnanimous and honourable people. This, gentlemen, is not designed as flattery, but a debt that they feel they owe to you. We hope that Generals [Samuel D.] Lucas and [Moses] Wilson, and all the officers and privates under their command, will receive this expression of our feelings, as due to them from us, in return for the kind treatment received at their hands. Gentlemen, we found you friends at a time when we most needed them; and since the time arrived at this village, we have not received the first insult from any individual. Gentlemen, we are prisoners in your hands, and such has been your magnanimity, that while we remain prisoners, we shall desire to continue in your care.

For your prosperity in this life, and rest eternal in that which is to come, you have the sincere desire and devout prayer of your prisoners in tribulation.

JOSEPH SMITH, Jr.
HYRAM [Hyrum] SMITH,
P[arley] P. PRATT,
AMASA LYMAN,
GEORGE W. ROBINSON,
LYMAN WIGHT,
SIDNEY RIGDON.

Independence, Nov. 5th, 1838.

——— ❧ ———

loose to ravage, steel, plunder and murder without restraint. Houses were rifled, and women ravished, and goods taken as they pleased." (John B. Clark, Jefferson City, MO, to Lilburn W. Boggs, 29 Nov. 1838, copy, Mormon War Papers, MSA; Pratt, *History of the Late Persecution,* 42; see also Historical Introduction to Declaration to the Clay County Circuit Court, ca. 6 Mar. 1839, pp. 335–336 herein; and Hyrum Smith, Commerce, IL, to "the Saints Scattered Abroad," Dec. 1839, in *Times and Seasons,* Dec. 1839, 1:22–23.)

Statement of Account from Hitchcock & Wilder, between 9 July and 6 November 1838

Source Note

Reuben Hitchcock on behalf of Hitchcock & Wilder, Statement of Account, [Painesville, Geauga Co., OH?], [between 9 July and 6 Nov. 1838]; handwriting of Reuben Hitchcock; two pages; JS Collection, CHL.

Bifolium measuring 12½ × 8 inches (32 × 20 cm), with thirty-eight printed lines per page. The document was folded for transmission and filing. The upper right corner of the recto is missing, apparently from damage by a rodent.

Historical Introduction

Sometime between July and November 1838, Reuben Hitchcock of the law firm Hitchcock & Wilder, located in Painesville, Ohio, produced a statement listing the debts that JS, Sidney Rigdon, and other church members owed to various individuals and businesses in New York and Ohio, including Hitchcock and his partner, Eli Wilder.[96] Some of the debts in the statement arose from promissory notes that New York merchants received from the Kirtland, Ohio, mercantile firms Rigdon, Smith & Cowdery and Cahoon, Carter & Co.[97] These two firms bought a large amount of wholesale goods on credit from merchants in Buffalo and New York City in 1836 and struggled to repay the debts when the promissory notes were due in 1837.[98] Because some of the notes were now past due, the New York merchants could bring lawsuits against the Kirtland firms. The statement also lists fees, probably attorney's fees, that JS and others owed Hitchcock & Wilder because of litigation the firm successfully brought against JS and his associates on behalf of other individuals in 1837. Further, the statement includes a judgment resulting from the lawsuits that Samuel Rounds brought against JS, Rigdon, and four other Latter-day Saints for issuing notes from the Kirtland Safety Society, an

---

96. Hitchcock was a prosecuting attorney in Geauga County, Ohio, in the 1830s. Wilder was a young lawyer from Connecticut who moved to Ohio in 1837. Hitchcock and Wilder formed their law firm in July 1837 in Painesville. (*History of Geauga and Lake Counties, Ohio,* 23, 61; Curtiss-Wedge, *History of Goodhue County, Minnesota,* 96; "Law Notice," *Painesville [OH] Telegraph,* 21 July 1837, [2].)

97. The mercantile firm Rigdon, Smith & Cowdery was a partnership comprising Sidney Rigdon, JS, and Oliver Cowdery that began by June 1836 and purchased wholesale goods in New York in 1836. These goods were then sold by the firm Rigdon, Smith & Co., which operated at least one store, located in Chester, Ohio. The exact relationship between the two firms is unclear.[a] The mercantile firm Cahoon, Carter & Co. included Reynolds Cahoon, Jared Carter, and Hyrum Smith; the firm was selling goods in Kirtland by June 1835. Cahoon, Carter, and Smith's mercantile efforts appear to be related to their assignment to supervise funding for the construction of the House of the Lord in Kirtland.[b] (a. See J. F. Scribner, Invoice, Buffalo, NY, for Rigdon, Smith & Cowdery, 16 June 1836, JS Office Papers, CHL; Rigdon, Smith & Co., Store Ledger, 1; "Mormonism in Ohio," *Aurora* [New Lisbon, OH], 21 Jan. 1837, [3]; and Notes Receivable from Chester Store, 22 May 1837, in *JSP,* D5:382–385. b. See Advertisement, *Northern Times,* 2 Oct. 1835, [4]; and Minutes, 6 June 1833, in *JSP,* D3:115.)

98. See Invoices, June and Oct. 1836, JS Office Papers, CHL. For more information on the Kirtland firms' efforts to repay New York merchants, see Statement of Account from Perkins & Osborn, ca. 29 Oct. 1838, pp. 252–261 herein.

"The following is a list of the claims in collection against the different firms in which Rigdon & Smith were concerned & also where any of the members of the firm are held, exclusive of notes on land contracts.

John Hitchcock & Son
vs
Calhoon Carter & Co.

Note for $1130.49 due Feby 27. 1838 —
No suit commenced on it

Mead Stafford & Co.
vs
Joseph Smith Jr
Sidney Rigdon
Hiram Smith
Reynolds Cahoon
Jared Carter
Oliver Cowdery

Three Notes —
One for $1377.01 due July 8. 1838
One for $1464.54 " July 8. 1839
One for $1552.22 " July 8. 1840
No suit commenced

Otis Eaton
vs
Russell Potter
Reuben McBride
Hiram Smith
Reynolds Cahoon

Note given to Frazier & Eaton
& indorsed to Pltff —
Note dated April 15. 1837 for $539.00
with interest from date &
due six months from date
Suit commenced Costs probably   15.00

Jonathan F. Scribner
vs
Cahoon Carter & Co

Acct for Goods bought in
Buffalo June 15th 1836 — due Decr 15. 1836 — $867.71
Interest @ 7 pr ct —
Suit Costs about —   12.00

Jonathan F. Scribner
vs
Rigdon Smith & Cowdery

Acct for Goods bot in Buffalo June 15
1836 due Decr 15. 1836 $794.65
Int at 7 pr ct —
Suit commenced — Costs about   12.00

Charles Crosby
vs
Hiram Smith

Note for $237.19 — Due Feby 14. 1838
No suit commenced —

Hitchcock & Wilder —

Statement of account from attorneys. In fall 1838, the Painesville, Ohio, law partnership Hitchcock & Wilder created a statement listing outstanding debts owed by Joseph Smith and other Latter-day Saints. This statement, as with many of Smith's other papers, was not adequately preserved and was subsequently damaged. A rodent ate part of the upper left corner of this document, leaving teeth marks on the back. Handwriting of Reuben Hitchcock. Statement of Account from Hitchcock & Wilder, between 9 July and 6 Nov. 1838, JS Collection, Church History Library, Salt Lake City.

unchartered financial institution.[99] JS and Rigdon personally incurred some of the debts listed in this statement; in other cases, they may have acted as sureties for fellow church members' promissory notes, meaning JS and Rigdon were liable for the repayment of the notes.[100]

The statement is undated, but its entries suggest the time frame in which it was created. The statement lists three promissory notes that were part of a mortgage agreement with Mead, Stafford & Co., with the first payment due 8 July 1838. The notes were listed as unpaid on the statement, suggesting the statement was created after the 8 July due date. The statement also references a lawsuit initiated by Otis Eaton that was dismissed when it came to trial on 6 November 1838. Since the statement lists the lawsuit as a current case, the statement likely predates the November trial.[101] Therefore, Hitchcock presumably prepared the statement between 9 July and 6 November 1838, likely at the request of Oliver Granger, who was charged with settling the debts of JS, Rigdon, and other Latter-day Saints.[102]

Granger likely received the document while he was in Ohio in fall 1838.[103] The document does not bear addressing or postal markings, suggesting that Granger did not send the statement to JS in Missouri. Granger likely kept the statement for use in his efforts to resolve the unpaid claims.

---

99. In February 1837, Rounds sued JS, Rigdon, Newel K. Whitney, Frederick G. Williams, Horace Kingsbury, and Warren Parrish because of their involvement in the Kirtland Safety Society. Ultimately, only JS and Rigdon were brought to trial, and in October 1837 they were found guilty and fined $1,000 each. After the case concluded, Rounds transferred the judgment to Grandison Newell, an opponent of JS and the church. Acting as agents for JS and Rigdon, William Marks and Granger signed an agreement with Newell and on 1 March 1838 paid him $1,600. Hitchcock was likely unaware of the agreement between Newell and the agents and therefore still considered the original debt unresolved. (See Historical Introduction to Kirtland Safety Society Notes, 4 Jan.–9 Mar. 1837, in *JSP*, D5:331–333; Introduction to Part 5: 5 Oct. 1836–10 Apr. 1837, in *JSP*, D5:285–293; Transcript of Proceedings, 24 Oct. 1837, Rounds v. JS [Geauga Co. C.P. 1837], Final Record Book U, pp. 362–364; and Transcript of Proceedings, 24 Oct. 1837, Rounds v. Rigdon [Geauga Co. C.P. 1837], Final Record Book U, pp. 359–362, microfilm 20,279, U.S. and Canada Record Collection, FHL; see also Walker, "Kirtland Safety Society," 32–148.)

100. For example, JS and other church members acted as sureties when they signed promissory notes that Reynolds Cahoon, Jared Carter, and Hyrum Smith created on 1 September 1837 to renegotiate their outstanding debts with New York mercantile firms. (See JS et al., Promissory Note, Kirtland, OH, to Holbrook & Ferme, 1 Sept. 1837, photocopy, CHL; JS et al., Promissory Note, Kirtland, OH, to Holbrook & Ferme, 1 Sept. 1837, BYU; Hyrum Smith et al., Promissory Note, Kirtland, OH, to Halsted, Haines & Co., 1 Sept. 1837, photocopy, CHL; and Hyrum Smith et al., Promissory Notes, Kirtland, OH, to Halsted, Haines & Co., 1 Sept. 1837, Brigham Young Office, Halsted, Haines & Co. File, CHL.)

101. See Transcript of Proceedings, 6 Nov. 1838, Eaton v. Potter et al. [Geauga Co. C.P. 1838], Final Record Book W, pp. 149–152, microfilm 20,280, U.S. and Canada Record Collection, FHL.

102. Granger apparently took the same proactive approach in requesting information from Hitchcock & Wilder as he did with the law firm Perkins & Osborn. (See Letter from William Perkins, 29 Oct. 1838, p. 251 herein.)

103. See Historical Introduction to Letter of Introduction from John Howden, 27 Oct. 1838, pp. 246–248 herein.

Document Transcript

The following is a list of the claims [*page damaged*] collection against the different firms in which Rigdon & Smith were concerned & also where any of the members of the firm are held,[104] exclusive of notes on land contracts

John Hitchcock & Son[105]	Note for $1130.49 due Feby 27.
vs	~~1837~~ 1838—[106]
<u>Cahoon Carter & Co</u>	No suit commenced on it—
Mead Stafford & Co	Three notes—[107]
vs	one for $1377.01 due July 8. 1838—
Joseph Smith Jr	one for $1464.54 " July 8. 1839—
Sidney Rigdon	one for $1552.22 " July 8. 1840—
Hiram [Hyrum] Smith	
Reynolds Cahoon	No suit commenced—
Jared Carter	
<u>Oliver Cowdery</u>	
Otis Eaton	Note given to Frazier ~~Potter~~ Eaton
vs	& indorsed to Pl[ainti]ff—[108]

---

104. "Where any of the members of the firm are held" refers to promissory notes and other financial obligations held against JS and Rigdon.

105. John Hitchcock was a merchant in New York City in 1836. His sons James and John also worked in mercantile firms; it is unclear which son is referred to here. (*Longworth's American Almanac* [1836], 328; *Longworth's American Almanac* [1839], 333; New York Co., NY, Record of Wills, 1665–1916, vol. 89, pp. 344–347, 18 Mar. 1844, microfilm 874,571, U.S. and Canada Record Collection, FHL.)

106. This promissory note was apparently signed on 27 May 1837, replacing a previous promissory note that Cahoon, Carter & Co. gave John Hitchcock for goods purchased in 1836. (Hitchcock & Wilder, Statement of Account, between ca. 3 Apr. and 6 Nov. 1838, JS Collection, CHL; George W. Shields, Invoice, New York City, for John Hitchcock & Son, 12 Oct. 1836; John Hitchcock & Son, Invoice, [New York City], for Cahoon, Carter & Co., ca. Oct. 1836, JS Office Papers, CHL.)

107. In an effort to resolve their debts with the New York City mercantile firm Mead, Stafford & Co., JS and others signed a mortgage agreement with Zalmon Mead, Robert Mead, and Jonas Stafford on 11 July 1837, mortgaging the House of the Lord in Kirtland to the mercantile firm. The mortgage was written by Hitchcock, who was likely acting as the lawyer representing Mead, Stafford & Co. in the transaction. To fulfill the terms of the mortgage, JS and the other signers promised to pay the firm around $4,400; the first payment was due 8 July 1838. (See Historical Introduction to Mortgage to Mead, Stafford & Co., 11 July 1837, in *JSP,* D5:404–407.)

108. Frazier Eaton joined the church by May 1835. Although he lived in New York, it appears he visited Ohio and attended church meetings there. In 1837 he endorsed a promissory note he received from Russell Potter, Reuben McBride, Hyrum Smith, and Reynolds Cahoon, and then he transferred the note to Otis Eaton. Frazier and Otis Eaton appear to be related, though the specific familial connection is not known. They lived near one another in Hancock County, Illinois, in 1840, and both moved to Rushford, New York, before Frazier's death. (See Record of the Twelve, 22 May 1835; JS, Journal, 14 Dec. 1835, in *JSP,*

Russell Potter Reuben McBride Hiram Smith Reynolds Cahoon	Note dated April 15. 1837 for $539.00 with interest from date & due six months from date Suit commenced Costs probably 15.00[109]
Jonathan F. Scribner[110] vs Cahoon Carter & Co	Acct for Goods bought in Buffalo Jun 15th 1836— due Dec' 15. 1836— $867.71[111] Interest @ 7 pr ct— Sued. Costs about— 12.00
Jonathan F. Scribner vs Ri[g]don Smith. & Cowdery	Acct for Goods bot in Buffalo June 15 1836 due Dec' 15. 1836 $796.65[112] Int at 7 pr ct— Suit commenced— Costs about 12.00
Charles Crosby vs Hiram Smith	Note for $237.19— Due Feby 14. 1838[113] No suit commenced—

J1:122; 1840 U.S. Census, Hancock Co., IL, 208; 1850 U.S. Census, Rushford, Allegany Co., NY, 347[B], 358[B]; and Cemetery Records of Allegany County, New York, p. 5, microfilm 17,521, U.S. and Canada Record Collection, FHL.)

109. Otis Eaton brought a lawsuit against Potter, McBride, Smith, and Cahoon for not paying the promissory note Frazier Eaton endorsed to Otis. (See Transcript of Proceedings, 6 Nov. 1838, Eaton v. Potter et al. [Geauga Co. C.P. 1838], Final Record Book W, pp. 149–152, microfilm 20,280, U.S. and Canada Record Collection, FHL.)

110. In 1836 and 1837, Scribner was an "Importer and Wholesale and Retail Dealer in Fancy and Staple Hardware" in Buffalo, New York. (J. F. Scribner, Invoice, Buffalo, NY, for Rigdon, Smith & Cowdery, 16 June 1836, JS Office Papers, CHL; *Directory for the City of Buffalo* [1836], 133.)

111. Scribner brought a lawsuit against the firm Cahoon, Carter & Co. in 1837 for not paying a promissory note for goods purchased from him. (Transcript of Proceedings, 3 Apr. 1838, Scribner v. Cahoon et al. [Geauga Co. C.P. 1838], Final Record Book U, pp. 584–585, microfilm 20,279, U.S. and Canada Record Collection, FHL.)

112. Scribner brought a lawsuit against the firm Rigdon, Smith & Cowdery for not paying a promissory note for goods purchased from him. In September 1837, Granger apparently tried to settle the debt outside of court, but he was unsuccessful and the lawsuit went to trial the next month. (See Historical Introduction to Power of Attorney to Oliver Granger, 27 Sept. 1837, in *JSP*, D5:457–459; Transcript of Proceedings, 20 Oct. 1840, Scribner v. Rigdon et al. [Geauga Co. C.P. 1840], Final Record Book X, pp. 530–532, microfilm 20,281, U.S. and Canada Record Collection, FHL.)

113. This note is for fifteen acres of land in Kirtland that Hyrum Smith mortgaged to Crosby on 11 July 1837, the same day the Kirtland House of the Lord was mortgaged to Mead, Stafford & Co. Since this debt is not directly connected to JS or Rigdon, it is unclear why the debt is included on the statement. (Geauga Co., OH, Deed Record, 1795–1921, vol. 24, pp. 230–231, 11 July 1837, microfilm 20,240, U.S. and Canada Record Collection, FHL.)

Hitchcock & Wilder— [p. [1]]

[*page damaged*] also judgments as follows—

Samuel D. Rounds
   qui tam ~~vs~~
        vs   Debt $1000.
   <u>Joseph Smith Jr</u>   Costs—
                        Interest from Oct 24. 1837

      Same   Debt $1000.
         vs   Costs—
   <u>Sidney Rigdon</u>   Interest from Oct 24. 1837
                        Reuben Hitchcock [p. [2]]

———— ☙ ————

Letter to Emma Smith, 12 November 1838

Source Note

JS, Letter, Richmond, Ray Co., MO, to Emma Smith, Far West, Caldwell Co., MO, 12 Nov. 1838; handwriting and signature of JS; three pages; JS Materials, CCLA. Includes address, wafer seal, and redactions.

Bifolium measuring 12½ × 7½ inches (32 × 19 cm). The document was trifolded twice in letter style, sealed with an adhesive wafer, and addressed. Later, the leaves became separated and were numbered in graphite. The upper left and right corners of each leaf contain a small hole, perhaps indicating the use of a fastening device. The upper left corners of the leaves were fastened together with staples. Adhesive tape was later applied to both leaves. The letter likely remained in the Smith family's possession until transferred to the archives of the Reorganized Church of Jesus Christ of Latter Day Saints (now Community of Christ).[114]

Historical Introduction

On 12 November 1838, JS wrote to his wife Emma Smith from Richmond, Missouri. He and six other church leaders—Sidney Rigdon, Hyrum Smith, Lyman Wight, George W. Robinson, Parley P. Pratt, and Amasa Lyman—were in the custody of Missouri state officials. After spending five days in Independence, Missouri, the prisoners were transported to Richmond on 9 November. In Richmond, they and forty-six other Latter-day Saint defendants were scheduled to appear before Judge Austin A. King at a criminal court of inquiry, or preliminary hearing, to determine whether the state possessed sufficient evidence to hold a full trial on charges of treason and other crimes allegedly committed during the recent conflict.[115] For the remainder of the month, JS and his companions were held in "an old log

---

114. See Richard Howard, email to Rachel Killebrew, 5 Jan. 2015; Rachel Killebrew, email to David W. Grua, 26 June 2015, copies in editors' possession.

115. See Introduction to Part 3: 4 Nov. 1838–16 Apr. 1839, p. 272 herein.

house," while the forty-six other prisoners were confined in the unfinished Ray County Courthouse.[116]

The day the hearing was scheduled to begin—12 November—JS wrote this letter to Emma, perhaps from the log house jail or the county courthouse. He acknowledged receipt of an apparently nonextant missive from Emma, expressed his love and affection for her, wrote personal notes for each of their children, and included a prayer that he would be reunited with his family. He also described the loyalty and unity among the Latter-day Saint prisoners, affirmed his innocence, and explained that attorneys Amos Rees and Alexander Doniphan had agreed to represent him and his companions. JS noted that Lieutenant Colonel Sterling Price was screening the prisoners' correspondence, which may have influenced how JS crafted his letter. JS indicated that a "Brother Babbitt," whose identity remains uncertain, would carry the letter to Far West.

Document Transcript

November 12ᵗʰ 1838 Richmond

My Dear Emma.

we are prisoners in chains, and under strong guards, for Christ sake[117] and for no other causes although there has been things that were unbeknown to us, and altogether beyond our controal, that might seem, to the mob to be a pretext, for them to persacute us,[118] but on examination, I think that the authorities, will discover our inocence, and set us free, but if this blessing cannot be ~~done~~ obtained, I have this consolation that I am an innocent man, let what will befall me, I recieved your letter which I read over and over again, it was a sweet morsal to me, Oh God grant that I may have the privaliege of seeing once more my lovely Family, in the injoyment, of the sweets of liberty, and sotiaial life, to press them to my bosam and kissng their lovely cheeks would fill my heart with

---

116. Lyman Wight, Journal, in *History of the Reorganized Church,* 2:296–297; see also Berrett, *Sacred Places,* 4:243–249.

117. See Luke 21:12.

118. JS was perhaps referring to the information Sampson Avard shared with John B. Clark. Based on Avard's information, Clark concluded that the Latter-day Saints "have societies formed under the most binding covenants in form, & the most horrid oaths to circumvent the laws & put them at defiance, & to plunder and burn & murder & divide the spoils for the use of the Church—This is what they call the Danite Club or Society." Clark argued that the prisoners had committed treason, murder, arson, larceny, and other crimes during the October conflict, all "under the counsel of Joseph Smith jr, the prophet." On 16 December 1838, JS expressed his concerns about Avard and others: "We have learned also since we have been prisoners that many false and pernicious things which were calculated to lead the saints far astray and to do them great injury as coming from the Presidency, taught by Dʳ Avard, and we have reason to fear many other designing and corrupt characters like unto himself, which the Presidency never knew of being taught in the Church." (John B. Clark, Richmond, MO, to Lilburn W. Boggs, 10 Nov. 1838, copy, Mormon War Papers, MSA; Letter to the Church in Caldwell Co., MO, 16 Dec. 1838, p. 306 herein.)

unspeakable ~~great~~ grattitude, tell the chilldren that I am alive and trust I shall come and see them before long, comfort their hearts all you can, and try to be comforted yourself, all you can, there is no possible dainger but what we shall be set at Liberty if Justice can be ⟨and⟩ done ⟨and⟩ that you know as well as myself, the tryal will begin today for some of us, Lawyer Rice [Amos Rees] and we expect [Alexander] Doniphan, will plead our cause, we could ⟨git⟩ no others in time for the tryal, they are able man and ⟨will⟩ do well no doubt,¹¹⁹ Brother Robison [George W. Robinson] is chained next to me he ~~he~~ has a true heart and a firm mind, Brother Whight [Lyman Wight], is next, Br. [Sidney] Rigdon, next, Hyram [Hyrum Smith], next, Parely [Parley P. Pratt], next, Amasa [Lyman], next, and thus we are bound together in chains as well as the cords of everlasting love, we are in good spirits and rejoice that we are counted worthy to be persicuted for christ sake,¹²⁰ tell little Joseph, he must be a good boy, and Father loves him ⟨with⟩ a perfect love, he is the Eldest must not hurt those that ⟨are⟩ smaller then him, but cumfort them tell little Frederick, Father, loves him, with all his heart, he is a lovely boy [p. 1] Julia is a lovely little girl, I love hir also She is a promising child, tell her Father wants her to remember him and be a good girl, tell all the rest that I think of them and pray for them all, Br Babbit¹²¹ is waitting to carry our letters, for us ~~the~~ colonal ⟨price [Sterling Price]⟩¹²² is inspecting them therefore my time is short ⟨the⟩ little ~~baby~~ Elexander [Alexander] is on my mind continualy Oh my affectionate Emma, I want you to remember that I am ⟨a⟩ true and faithful friend, to you and the chilldren, forever, my heart is intwined around you[r]s forever and ever, Oh may God bless you all amen ~~you~~ I am your husband and am in bonds and tribulation &c

　　to Emma Smith} Joseph Smith Jr

　　P S write as often as you can, and if possible come and see me, and bring the chilldren if possible, act according to your own feelings ⟨and⟩ best

---

119. Alexander Doniphan and Amos Rees also represented the Saints during their Jackson County difficulties in 1833. (William T. Wood et al., Independence, MO, to William W. Phelps et al., 28 Oct. 1833, William W. Phelps, Collection of Missouri Documents, CHL; Agreement with Amos Rees and Alexander Doniphan, 28 Nov. 1838, at josephsmithpapers.org.)

120. See Acts 5:41.

121. At least two Latter-day Saint men by the name of Babbitt were in Missouri in 1838: siblings Almon and John. (Johnson, "A Life Review," 48.)

122. Price and his men guarded the Latter-day Saint prisoners in Richmond. (Pratt, *Autobiography,* 216, 228.)

Judgement, and indeavour to be comforted, if possible, and I trust that all will turn out for the bist. yours, J.S. [p. [2]]

✉

/[123]Mrs Emma Smith
Far West

Dear
Affectionate
Affection [p. 3]

——— ☙ ———

Letter to Emma Smith, 1 December 1838

Source Note

JS, Letter, Liberty, Clay Co., MO, to Emma Smith, Far West, Caldwell Co., MO, 1 Dec. 1838; handwriting and signature of JS; two pages; CHL. Includes address, docket, and possible dealer marking.

One loose leaf measuring 9¾ × 7¾ inches (25 × 20 cm). The document was trifolded twice in letter style and addressed but not sealed. The document was later refolded, possibly for filing. A docket in unidentified handwriting reads: "Joe Smith Jr | Mormon". A possible dealer marking in unidentified handwriting reads: "#090". The docket and possible dealer marking are both in graphite and appear to have been inscribed at the same time. The letter has undergone conservation work. Emma Smith presumably received the letter, and it likely remained in the Smith family's possession for some time before it was acquired by a third party. The Historical Department of the LDS church purchased the letter from David G. Phillips Co. of North Miami, Florida, in 1979; David G. Phillips Co. represented the estate of E. N. Sampson of Clearwater, Florida.[124]

Historical Introduction

On the evening of 1 December 1838, JS wrote a short letter to his wife Emma Smith, informing her that he and his fellow prisoners had been safely transported from Richmond, Missouri, to the Clay County jail in Liberty, Missouri.[125] The men had been in Richmond for a criminal court of inquiry, at which Judge Austin A. King of the fifth judicial circuit ruled there was probable cause to believe that JS, Hyrum Smith, Lyman Wight, Alexander McRae, and Caleb Baldwin had committed treason in Daviess County, Missouri, and that Sidney Rigdon had committed the same offense in Caldwell County, Missouri. Because treason was

---

123. TEXT: Address block in unidentified handwriting.
124. Kenneth R. Laurence, North Miami, FL, to Robert D. Bingham, Salt Lake City, 15 Jan. 1979; Donald T. Schmidt, Salt Lake City, to Kenneth R. Laurence, North Miami, FL, 23 Jan. 1979, Donald T. Schmidt, Correspondence, CHL; Minutes, 25 Jan. 1979, Historical Department File, 1970s–1980s, CHL. In 1975, rare documents dealer Steve Barnett informed officials in the church's Historical Department that the letter was in private possession. It was purchased on 24 January 1979. (Steve Barnett, Provo, UT, to Dean Jessee, [Salt Lake City], 2 Sept. 1975, photocopy, CHL.)
125. See also Mittimus, Richmond, MO, 29 Nov. 1838, State of Missouri v. JS et al. for Treason and Other Crimes (Mo. 5th Jud. Cir. 1838), JS Collection, CHL.

a nonbailable offense and neither Daviess nor Caldwell County had a jail, King committed the prisoners to the Clay County jail to await their trials in the spring.[126]

In this 1 December letter, JS did not detail the outcome of the court of inquiry, which suggests that he had previously conveyed that information to his wife. He noted in this letter that Samuel Bogart, captain of the Ray County militia, would deliver the letter to her in Far West.[127]

Document Transcript

December 1st 1838

My Dear companion I take this oppertunity to inform you that I we arrived in Liberty and commited to Joal [jail] this Evening but we are all in good spirits Captain bogard [Samuel Bogart] will hand you this line my respects to all remain where you are at preasant

yours &c—

Joseph Smith Jr [p. [1]]

⊠

To Emma Smith
Far West

———— ☙ ————

Letter to the Church in Caldwell County, 16 December 1838

Source Note

JS, Letter, Liberty, Clay Co., MO, to the church in Caldwell County, MO, 16 Dec. 1838. Featured version copied [between 16 Dec. 1838 and ca. May 1839]; handwriting of Zina Huntington; seven pages; JS Collection, CHL. Includes use marks, docket, and possible redactions.

Two biofolia measuring 12½ × 8 inches (32 × 20 cm). The bifolia were folded for filing. Later, they were fastened with two staples in the upper left corner; the staples were subsequently removed. The document has undergone conservation.

The copied letter was in Zina Huntington's possession from the time of inscription until late 1839 or early 1840, when it was evidently used as a source text for the published version of the letter in the April 1840 issue of the *Times and Seasons*.[128] In the 1840s, church clerk William Clayton docketed the verso of

---

126. For more information on the November 1838 hearing, see Introduction to Part 3: 4 Nov. 1838–16 Apr. 1839, pp. 273–274 herein.

127. Bogart presumably commanded the guards who transported the prisoners to the Clay County jail. (Pratt, *History of the Late Persecution,* 34–36.)

128. Huntington's copy and the *Times and Seasons* version share about fifty variants that are not found in other versions. In one case, the *Times and Seasons* incorporated wording regarding Sampson Avard that was inserted between lines of text in Huntington's copy. (See JS, Liberty, MO, to the Church in Caldwell Co., MO, 16 Dec. 1838, in *Times and Seasons,* Apr. 1840, 1:82–86.)

Letter to Emma Smith. During his time in Missouri state custody in winter 1838–1839, Joseph Smith wrote at least five letters to his wife Emma Smith including this short missive informing her of his arrival at the Clay County jail on 1 December 1838. Whereas Smith dictated official correspondence to scribes, he personally penned the letters to his wife, depicted here in an 1842 portrait by David Rogers. Handwriting of Joseph Smith. Letter to Emma Smith, 1 Dec. 1838, Church History Library, Salt Lake City. (Smith image courtesy Community of Christ Library-Archives, Independence, MO.)

the second leaf of the second biofolium: "Epistle from J. Smith | Liberty Jail— to the | Church of J. C. L. D. S | Decr 16— 1838." The document has apparently remained in continuous institutional custody.[129]

Historical Introduction

On 16 December 1838, JS composed a letter from the Clay County jail in Liberty, Missouri, to the Latter-day Saints in Caldwell County, Missouri, as well as "all the Saints who are scattered abroad." By 16 December, JS had been in state custody for more than six weeks and had undergone a seventeen-day criminal court of inquiry, or preliminary hearing, that resulted in his imprisonment in Liberty. There he awaited a spring 1839 trial on charges of treason and other crimes.[130] Filled with indignation toward those he perceived were the cause of his imprisonment and dismayed at his doleful circumstances and the thought of spending the winter in jail, JS vented his emotions in this lengthy letter to the church. JS apparently patterned the letter after New Testament epistles, opening with a salutation, expressing prayers for church members, commenting on difficulties the church faced, and concluding with a blessing.[131] He also quoted liberally from the Bible and other scriptures and placed the Saints' predicament within the context of the long history of persecution against God's people.

Much of the letter condemns dissenters—the devil's "emissaries." JS contended that they cooperated with the Saints' enemies during the recent conflict and were therefore responsible for the deaths of several Latter-day Saints, for JS's arrest and incarceration, and for the expulsion of church members from the state. JS focused his ire on the delegation that had negotiated with Major General Samuel D. Lucas on 31 October 1838: George M. Hinkle, John Corrill, Reed Peck, William W. Phelps, and John Cleminson. JS argued that the delegation had betrayed him, resorting to deception to lure him into the enemies' camp. Additionally, JS asserted that several other dissenters—including Oliver Cowdery, David and John Whitmer, and Thomas B. Marsh—had spread false rumors that endangered the church. JS also contended that the teachings of Sampson Avard, a former Danite general, were not authorized by the First Presidency. In the letter, JS also stated that the many dissenters who testified for the prosecution at the November 1838 hearing had "borne false witness" against the Mormon prisoners.

Further, JS condemned the anti-Mormon forces that fought against the Latter-day Saints. He argued that religious and civil elites—whom he compared to Sadducees, Pharisees, and other opponents of Jesus Christ in the New Testament—instigated mob violence against church members. JS denied committing the crimes for which he and other Mormons were imprisoned, including treason and murder, and argued instead that the church's enemies were guilty of these offenses.

---

129. Church clerk Thomas Bullock used this copy as a source text for an amalgamated version of the 16 December 1838 letter he inscribed in JS's manuscript history in the mid-1840s. The document was included in the Joseph Smith Collection circa 1970. (Historian's Office, JS History, Rough Draft Notes, 16 Dec. 1838; JS History, vol. C-1, 868–873.)

130. See Introduction to Part 3: 4 Nov. 1838–16 Apr. 1839, pp. 272–274 herein.

131. See Doty, *Letters in Primitive Christianity,* 27–47.

Although much of the letter is colored by JS's indignation toward the church's opponents, portions of the epistle also reflect confidence that God would vindicate the
Saints. Comparing the dissenters to Haman, Balaam, Korah, and Job's false friends—
biblical figures who sought to hinder and persecute God's people—JS reassured church
members that just as the Lord rescued his ancient followers from their oppressors, he
would deliver his latter-day people. Perhaps responding to dissenters who challenged JS's
prophetic leadership, JS also included in the letter the text of a revelation that declared he
retained the "keys," or the divine authority, that had been given to him. Near the close of
the letter, JS promised the Saints that although Zion appeared to be dead, it would ultimately be revitalized.

It is unclear how JS produced the original letter, which is not extant. JS probably
discussed the major themes of the epistle with his fellow prisoners—which perhaps explains the frequent use of the first-person plural in the letter—although he alone signed the
document. Close examination of extant copies indicates that two distinct textual tradi-
tions—one based on a rough draft, the other based on a revised draft—may have originated from inside the jail. Assuming that the textual production of the 16 December 1838
letter was similar to that of the circa 22 March 1839 general epistle, JS likely dictated a
rough draft, which then was edited and revised under his direction. One or more subsequent drafts would have then been made to incorporate the changes, and both versions
would have been sent out of the jail, presumably to increase circulation of the letter's content among the Saints.[132]

JS's scribe, James Mulholland, copied the rough draft or an intermediary version into
a church record book, probably before moving to Illinois in spring 1839.[133] Latter-day Saint
Zina Diantha Huntington likely copied a revised version or an intermediary copy prior to
her move to Illinois in May.[134] Consistent with the proposed scenario regarding the letter's

---

132. Two drafts of the circa 22 March 1839 general epistle are extant. JS dictated the first draft, corrected and revised it, and then had a fair copy made that reflected the changes. Despite differences
between the drafts, JS evidently sent both versions of the circa 22 March epistle to the Saints, presumably to broaden circulation. (See Historical Introduction to Letter to Edward Partridge and the Church,
ca. 22 Mar. 1839, pp. 389–391 herein; see also Hall, *Ways of Writing*, 32–33.)

133. See JS, Liberty, MO, to the Church in Caldwell Co., MO, 16 Dec. 1838, in "General," Record
Book, 101–108. There are two indications that Mulholland copied the letter before moving from Missouri
to Illinois. First, Mulholland inscribed the letter in the record book that was JS's primary journal in
Missouri in 1838. After Mulholland copied the letter into the record book, it remained unused until the
mid-1840s. When Mulholland copied JS's Missouri-era correspondence in Illinois, he used a different
record book, JS Letterbook 2. Second, George W. Robinson probably corrected Mulholland's transcript
while the two men were working together in Missouri, perhaps when Robinson corrected Mulholland's
copy of a revelation in the Missouri journal that Robinson was keeping for JS. There is no indication that
Robinson functioned as JS's scribe after leaving Missouri. (See Source Note for Journal, Mar.–Sept. 1838,
in *JSP*, J1:225; JS, Journal, Mar.–Sept. 1838, pp. 72–74, in *JSP*, J1:306–309; Mulholland, Journal, 22 Apr.
1839; and 438n46 herein.)

134. Huntington arrived in Commerce, Illinois, on 16 May 1839. Although it is possible that
Huntington copied the epistle after her removal to Illinois, her own illness and the death of her mother
makes it unlikely. Her copy includes an interlineal insertion regarding Sampson Avard that was later incorporated into the version of the letter published in the *Times and Seasons,* indicating that April 1840 is the last
possible copying date. (Zina Huntington Young, Autobiographical Sketch, 10; Oliver Huntington, "History

production, the differences between the copies made by Mulholland and Huntington reflect conscious editing decisions rather than routine copying errors. The variants include shortened phrases, modernized word forms (for example, "seeth" changed to "sees"), altered diction (for example, "God" changed to "the Lord" and "state" changed to "government"), deleted slang phrases, and improved grammatical constructions. In a few cases, entire phrases and sentences in Mulholland's copy are absent from Huntington's copy; for example, Huntington's copy does not include "We stood in our own defence and we believe that no man of us acted only in a just a lawful and righteous retaliation against such marauders." Given that Huntington's copy likely represents the textual tradition of the most polished version produced under JS's direction, it is featured here. Significant variants in Mulholland's version are noted in annotation.

As demonstrated by the multiple copies that have survived, the epistle circulated broadly among the Saints in manuscript form.[135] In a 14 May 1839 letter, Latter-day Saint David Foote included an eleven-line quotation from the revised version of the 16 December 1838 epistle to support his assertion that JS's willingness to suffer for his religion proved his sincerity and his status as a prophet.[136] A revised version of the 16 December letter was published in the April 1840 issue of the *Times and Seasons*, substantially increasing the letter's circulation.[137]

Document Transcript

Liberty Jail Missouri. Dec 16th 1838

To the church of latter day saints[138] in Caldwell county and the saints scattered abroad[139] and are persecuted and made desolate[140] and are afflicted in divers manners for christ's sake and the gospel's, and whose perils are greatly

---

of Oliver Boardman Huntington," 47–48, 52–54; JS, Liberty, MO, to the Church in Caldwell Co., MO, 16 Dec. 1838, in *Times and Seasons,* Apr. 1840, 1:85.)

135. At a later date, Phebe Carter Woodruff made an incomplete copy of the letter that reflected the rough draft's textual tradition. Although Woodruff's copy closely parallels Mulholland's, her copy contains some copying errors—for example, writing "mental" instead of "mutual" and "starve" instead of "strive." She also omitted some words and short phrases, apparently inadvertently. A few variants may have been editorial decisions, such as changing words (for example, revising "evidence" to "witness") and adding phrases that were probably not in the original letter, such as the heading "An Epistle given to the church of Latter-day Saints in Caldwell County Missouri by Jesus Christ through Joseph Smith jr. while in Liberty jail." For unknown reasons, Woodruff did not complete the copy. According to a note written on the letter's wrapper, Phebe's husband, Wilford Woodruff, donated the copy to the Church Historian's Office on 27 May 1857. (JS, Liberty, MO, to the Church in Caldwell Co., MO, 16 Dec. 1838, JS Collection, CHL.)

136. David Foote, Adams Co., IL, to Thomas Clement and Betsey Foote Clement, Dryden, NY, 14 May 1839, CHL.

137. JS, Liberty, MO, to the Church in Caldwell Co., MO, 16 Dec. 1838, in *Times and Seasons,* Apr. 1840, 1:82–86.

138. In April 1838, JS dictated a revelation announcing that the church's official name was changing from the Church of the Latter Day Saints to the Church of Jesus Christ of Latter Day Saints. The former name was evidently still used at times after the dictation of the revelation. (Revelation, 26 Apr. 1838, p. 114 herein [D&C 115:4].)

139. See James 1:1.

140. See Jeremiah 12:11; Ezekiel 6:6; and Job 16:7.

augmented by the wickedness and corruption of false brethren.[141] May grace, mercy, and peace, be and abide with you[142] and notwithstanding all your sufferings we assure you that you have our prayers and fervent desires for your welfare both day and night.[143] We believe that, that God who sees us in this solitary place[144] will hear our prayers & reward you openly.[145] Know assuredly dear brethren that it is for the testimony of Jesus that we are in bonds and in prison.[146] But we say unto you that we consider our condition better, (notwithstanding our suffering) than those who have persecuted us and smitten us and ⟨borne⟩ ~~bear~~ false witness against us,[147] and we most assuredly believe that those who bear false witness against us ⟨do⟩ seem to have a great triumph over us for the present. But we want you to remember Haman and Mordecai you know that Haman could not be satisfied so long as he saw Mordecai at the king's gate, and he sought the life of Mordecai and the people of the jews. But the Lord so ordered that Haman was hanged upon his own gallows.[148] So shall it come to pass with poor Haman in the last days. Those who have sought by their unbelief and wickedness and by the principle of mobocracy to destroy us and the people of God by killing and scattering them abroad and wilfully and maliciously delivering us into the hands of murderers desiring us to be put to death thereby having us dragged about in chains and cast into prison,[149] and for what cause; it is because we were honest men and were determined to defend the lives of the saints at the expense of our own. I say unto you that those who have thus vilely treated us like Haman shall be hanged upon their own gallows, or in other words shall fall into their own gin and trap and ditch which they have prepared for us and shall go backward and stumble and fall,[150] and their names shall be blotted out,[151] and God shall reward them according to all their abominations. Dear brethren do not think that our hearts faint as though some strange thing had happened unto us[152] for we have seen and been

---

141. See 2 Corinthians 11:26.

142. See 2 Timothy 1:2; and Titus 1:4.

143. See Book of Mormon, 1830 ed., 320 [Alma 34:27].

144. See Mark 1:35.

145. See Matthew 6:6.

146. Being imprisoned "for the testimony of Jesus" is a nonbiblical phrase frequently used in the early nineteenth century by authors of religious texts. (See, for example, Clarke, *New Testament*, 777; and *Abridgment of the Book of Martyrs*, 176, 563.)

147. See Exodus 20:16.

148. See Esther chaps. 2–8.

149. See Matthew 4:12; Luke 23:19; John 3:24; and Book of Mormon, 1830 ed., 17, 200, 298 [1 Nephi 7:14; Mosiah 21:23; Alma 26:29].

150. See Psalms 7:15; 140:5.

151. See Psalm 69:28.

152. See 1 Peter 4:12.

assured of all these things beforehand, and have an assurance of a better hope[153] than that of our persecutors. Therefore God has made our shoulders broad that we can bear it.[154] We glory in our tribulation because we know that God is with us,[155] that he is our friend and that he will save our souls.[156] We do not care for those that kill the body they cannot harm our souls; we ask no favors at the hands of mobs nor of the world, nor of the devil nor of his emissaries the dissenters.[157] We have never dissembled nor will we for the sake of our lives. Forasmuch then as we know that we have been endeavoring with all our mights, minds, and strength [p. [1]] to do the will of God and all things whatsoever he has commanded us.[158] And as to our light speeches from time to time they have nothing to do with the fixed principle of our hearts.[159] Therefore it sufficeth us to say that our souls were vexed from day to day.[160] We refer you to Isaiah who considers those who make a man an offender for a word and lay a snare for them that reproveth in the gate.[161] We believe the old prophet verily told the truth. We have no retraction to make, we have reproved in the gate and men have laid snares for us we have spoken words and men have made us offenders, and notwithstanding all this our minds are not darkened[162] but feel strong in the Lord. But behold the words of the savior, if the light which is in you become darkness behold how great is that darkness.[163] Look at the dissenters. And again if you were of the world the world would love its own[164] Look at M[r] [George M.] Hinkle. A wolf in sheep's clothing.[165] Look at

---

153. See Hebrews 7:19.

154. Mulholland's copy has "God hath made broad our shoulders for the burden," while Foote's quotation has "God has made our shoulders broad that we can resist." (JS, Liberty, MO, to the Church in Caldwell Co., MO, 16 Dec. 1838, in "General," Record Book, 102; David Foote, Adams Co., IL, to Thomas Clement and Betsey Foote Clement, Dryden, NY, 14 May 1839, CHL.)

155. See Romans 5:3.

156. See Matthew 10:28; and Luke 12:4.

157. In Mulholland's copy, this phrase is followed by "and those who love and make and swear falsehoods, to take away our lives." (JS, Liberty, MO, to the Church in Caldwell Co., MO, 16 Dec. 1838, in "General," Record Book, 102.)

158. See Revelation, May 1829–A, in *JSP*, D1:54 [D&C 11:20].

159. Instead of "principle," Mulholland's copy has "purposes" and Woodruff's copy has "principles." (JS, Liberty, MO, to the Church in Caldwell Co., MO, 16 Dec. 1838, in "General," Record Book, 102; JS, Liberty, MO, to the Church in Caldwell Co., MO, 16 Dec. 1838, JS Collection, CHL.)

160. See 2 Peter 2:8.

161. Isaiah 29:21.

162. See Doctrine and Covenants 36:1, 1835 ed. [D&C 10:2].

163. See Matthew 6:23; compare Book of Mormon, 1830 ed., 482–483 [3 Nephi 13:23].

164. See John 15:19.

165. See Matthew 7:15; compare Book of Mormon, 1830 ed., 484 [3 Nephi 14:15]. For more information on Hinkle's role in the arrest of JS, see Introduction to Part 3: 4 Nov. 1838–16 Apr. 1839, pp. 270–271 herein. Although no evidence indicates Hinkle associated with other dissenters prior to the 31 October 1838 negotiations with Major General Samuel D. Lucas, Hinkle had been critical of JS's

his brother John Corrill Look at the beloved brother Reed Peck who[166] aided him in leading us, as the savior was led, into the camp as a lamb prepared for the slaughter and a sheep dumb before his shearer so we opened not our mouth[167] But these men like Balaam being greedy for a reward sold us into the hands of those who loved them, for the world loves his own.[168] I would remember W[illiam] W. Phelps who comes up before us as one of Job's comforters.[169] God suffered such kind of beings to afflict Job, but it never entered into their hearts that Job would get out of it all.[170] This poor man who professes to be much of a prophet has no other dumb ass to ride but David Whitmer to forbid his madness when he goes up to curse Israel, and this ass not being of the same kind of Balaams therefore the angel notwithstanding appeared unto him yet he could not penetrate his understanding sufficiently so but what he brays out cursings instead of blessings. Poor ass whoever lives to see it will see him and his rider perish like those who perished in the gainsaying of Core, or after

leadership of the Mormon military operations against anti-Mormon vigilantes. He also testified for the prosecution at the November 1838 hearing. (George M. Hinkle, Testimony, Richmond, MO, Nov. 1838, pp. [38]–[45], State of Missouri v. JS et al. for Treason and Other Crimes [Mo. 5th Jud. Cir. 1838], in State of Missouri, "Evidence.")

166. Woodruff's copy has "took him by the hand and" here. (JS, Liberty, MO, to the Church in Caldwell Co., MO, 16 Dec. 1838, JS Collection, CHL.)

167. See Isaiah 53:7; Acts 8:32; and Book of Mormon, 1830 ed., 186 [Mosiah 14:7; 15:6]. Corrill and Peck accompanied Hinkle during the negotiations with Lucas on 31 October 1838. Corrill and Peck later claimed their dissent began with the expulsion of David and John Whitmer, Oliver Cowdery, and Lyman Johnson from Far West in June 1838. Corrill and Peck were also critical of the Danite society and the Saints' military operations during the Daviess County expedition in October 1838. Both testified for the prosecution at the November 1838 hearing. (John Corrill, Testimony, Richmond, MO, Nov. 1838, pp. [29]–[34]; Reed Peck, Testimony, Richmond, MO, Nov. 1838, pp. [55]–[64], in State of Missouri, "Evidence"; Corrill, Brief History, 29–30, 32, 36–38, in JSP, H2:165–166, 168–169, 175–179; Reed Peck, Quincy, IL, to "Dear Friends," 18 Sept. 1839, pp. 29, 34–36, 41–42, 50–51, 56–57, 84–92, 106, 108, Henry E. Huntington Library, San Marino, CA.)

168. See Numbers chap. 22. Hinkle later denied receiving "Missouri gold"—meaning a bribe—for his role in the surrender and arrest of JS. (George M. Hinkle, Buffalo, Iowa Territory, to William W. Phelps, Nauvoo, IL, 14 Aug. 1844, in Ensign, Aug. 1844, 30–32.)

169. Instead of "comforters," Mulholland's copy has "destroyers." Phelps was also a member of the delegation that met with Lucas on 31 October 1838. Phelps had been excommunicated in March 1838 but was rebaptized in late June or early July. However, he later said that he opposed JS's and Rigdon's alleged efforts to circumvent lawsuits. According to Latter-day Saint Burr Riggs, Rigdon identified Phelps in late July as a dissenter whose influence needed to be curbed. Like Hinkle, Corrill, and Peck, Phelps opposed the church's October 1838 military operations in Daviess County. He testified for the prosecution at the November 1838 hearing. (JS, Liberty, MO, to the Church in Caldwell Co., MO, 16 Dec. 1838, in "General," Record Book, 102; R. Peck to "Dear Friends," 18 Sept. 1839, p. 108; Minute Book 2, 10 Mar. 1838; Edward Partridge, Far West, MO, to Newel K. Whitney, Kirtland, OH, 24 July 1838, in Reynolds Cahoon, Far West, MO, to Newel K. Whitney, Kirtland, OH, 23 July 1838, CHL; William W. Phelps, Testimony, Richmond, MO, Nov. 1838, pp. [84], [87]; Burr Riggs, Testimony, Richmond, MO, Nov. 1838, pp. [73]–[74], in State of Missouri, "Evidence.")

170. See Job 2:11–13.

the same condemnation.[171] Now as for these and the rest of their company we will not presume to say that the world loves them but we presume to say that they love the world and we classify them in the error Balaam and in the gainsaying of Core and with the company of Cora [Korah] and Dathan and Abiram.[172] Perhaps our brethren may say because we thus write that we are offended at those characters, if we are, it is not for a word neither because they reproved in the gate. But because they have been the means of shedding innocent blood. Are they not murderers then at heart?[173] Are not their consciences seared as with a hot iron?[174] We confess that we are offended [p. 2] but the saviour said that offences must come but woe unto them by whom they come,[175] and again blessed are ye when all men shall revile you and speak all manner of evil against you falsely for my sake, rejoice and be exceeding glad for great is your reward in heaven for so persecuted they the prophets which were before you.[176] Now dear brethren if any men ever had reason to claim this promise we are the men, for we know that the world not only hates us[177] but ~~but~~ speak all manner of evil of us falsely for no other reason than because we have been endeavoring to teach the fulness of the gospel of Jesus Christ after we were bartered away by Hinkle and were taken into the militia camp we had all the evidence we could have wished for that the world hated us and that most cordially too. If there were priests of all the different sects they hated us,[178] if there were Generals they hated us, if there were Colonels they hated us, and the soldiers and officers of every kind hated us, and the most profane blasphemers and drunkards & whoremongers hated us, they all hated us most cordially.[179] And now what did they hate us for, purely because of the testimony of Jesus Christ. Was it because we were liars? We know that it has been reported by some but it has been reported falsely Was it because we have

171. See Numbers chap. 16; and Jude 1:11.

172. See Numbers chap. 16; 26:9; Deuteronomy 11:6; and Psalm 106:17.

173. See Book of Mormon, 1830 ed., 46 [1 Nephi 17:44].

174. See 1 Timothy 4:2.

175. See Matthew 18:7; and Luke 17:1.

176. Matthew 5:11–12; compare Book of Mormon, 1830 ed., 480 [3 Nephi 12:11–12].

177. See John 15:18.

178. Hyrum Smith testified in 1843 court proceedings that on 1 November 1838, about twenty priests "of the different religious denominations" participated in a court-martial in the militia camp, during which the prisoners were condemned to death. The execution was averted through the intervention of Brigadier General Alexander Doniphan. (Hyrum Smith, Testimony, Nauvoo, IL, 1 July 1843, p. 14, Nauvoo, IL, Records, CHL; see also Introduction to Part 3: 4 Nov. 1838–16 Apr. 1839, p. 271 herein.)

179. In Pratt's 1839 history, he recounted that he, JS, and the other prisoners "were marched into camp surrounded by thousands of savage looking beings, many of whom were painted like Indian warriors," and that their captors "set up a constant yell, like so many blood hounds let loose on their prey, as if they had achieved one of the most miraculous victories which ever dignified the annals of the world." (Pratt, *History of the Late Persecution,* 40.)

committed treason against the government in Daviess County or of burglary, or of larceny or arson,[180] or any other unlawful act in Daviess county. We know that certain priests and certain lawyers and certain judges[181] who are the instigators aiders and abettors of a certain gang of murderers and robbers who have been carrying on a scheme of mobocracy to uphold their priestcraft against the saints of the last days for a number of years and have tried by a well contemplated and premeditated scheme to put down by physical power a system of relig[i]on that all the world by all their mutual attainments and by any fair means whatever were not able to resist. Hence, mobbers were encouraged by priests and Levites, by the Pharisees, Sadducees, and Essenees, and the Herodians,[182] and the most ruthless, abandoned, and debauched, lawless inhuman and the most beastly set of men that the earth can boast of; and indeed a parallel cannot be found any where else; to gather together to steal to plunder to starve and to exterminate and burn the houses of the Mormons these are the characters that by their treasonable and avert acts have desolated and laid waste Daviess County[183] these are the characters that would fain make all the world believe that we are guilty of the above named acts. But they represent us [p. 3] falsely;[184] we say unto you that we

180. For more information on the criminal charges against JS and other Mormons, see Introduction to Part 3: 4 Nov. 1838–16 Apr. 1839, p. 271 herein.

181. Religious, political, and legal elites had been the foremost opponents of the Saints in Missouri since the early 1830s. The 1830s was the decade with the highest level of mob violence in the United States prior to the Civil War. Rigdon later reported that some of the most active instigators of mob violence against the Mormons in 1838 were Presbyterian minister Sashel Woods, Methodist minister Samuel Bogart, attorneys Thomas C. Burch and Amos Rees, state senator Cornelius Gilliam, and a Judge Smith of the Daviess County Circuit Court. (Grimsted, "Rioting in Its Jacksonian Setting," 361–397; Anderson, "Clarifications of Boggs's Order," 27–83; Sidney Rigdon, JS, et al., Petition Draft ["To the Publick"], pp. 16–17[a], 22[a], 26[a], [27b], [31b].)

182. In Mulholland's copy, this phrase is followed by "and every other E and ite agging on." The term "agging on" was a nineteenth-century variant of the slang term "egging on."[a] The New Testament mentions the Pharisees, Sadducees, and Herodians—all Jewish groups—often in the context of persecuting Jesus. Although the Essenes are not mentioned in the Bible, information on this Jewish group was included in a widely circulated nineteenth-century theological dictionary.[b] (a. JS, Liberty, MO, to the Church in Caldwell Co., MO, 16 Dec. 1838, in "General," Record Book, 104; see "A Provincial Vocabulary," 421; "Suit for Alleged Malpractice," 120; and "Relation of Plumbing to Public Health," 24. b. See, for example, Matthew 16:1; Mark 12:13; Luke 20:27; and "Essenes," in Buck, *Theological Dictionary,* 132; see also Stemberger, *Jewish Contemporaries of Jesus,* 1–4; and Meier, "Historical Jesus and the Historical Herodians," 740–746.)

183. Following the October 1838 expulsion of the Saints from De Witt, Carroll County, Missouri, anti-Mormon vigilantes announced they would remove the Mormons from Daviess County. Heeding the call, troops under Cornelius Gilliam and other vigilante leaders began harassing Latter-day Saints in outlying areas of the county, forcing some to flee their homes and seek refuge in Adam-ondi-Ahman and Far West, Missouri. These activities continued through early November. (Greene, *Facts relative to the Expulsion,* 20–21; Sidney Rigdon, JS, et al., Petition Draft ["To the Publick"], pp. 29[a]–[31b].)

184. In Mulholland's copy, this phrase is followed by "We stood in our own defence and we believe that no man of us acted only in a just a lawful and righteous retaliation against such marauders." (JS, Liberty, MO, to the Church in Caldwell Co., MO, 16 Dec. 1838, in "General," Record Book, 104; for more

have not committed treason, nor any other unlawful act in Daviess County was it for murder in Ray county against mob-militia who was a wolf in the first instance[185] hide and Hair, teeth, and legs, and tail, who afterwards put on a militia sheepskin with the wool on, who can sally forth in the day time into the flock and snarl & show his teeth, and scatter and devour the flock and satiate himself upon his prey, and then sneak back into the brambles in order that he might conceal himself in his well tried skin with the wool on. We are well aware that there is a certain set of priests & satellites and mobbers that would fain make all the world believe that we are the dogs that barked at this howling wolf that made such havoc among the sheep who when he retreated howled and bleated at such a desperate rate that if one could have been there he would have thought that all the wolves whether wrapped up in sheep skins or goat skins or any other skins and in fine all the beast of the forest were awfully alarmed and catching the scent of innocent blood they sallied forth with a tremenduous howl and crying of all sorts and such a howling and such a tremenduous havoc never was known such a piece of inhumanity and relentless cruelty and barbarity cannot be found in all the annals of history. These are the characters that would make the world believe that we had committed murder by making an attack upon this howling wolf while we were at home and in our beds and asleep and knew nothing of that transaction any more than we know what is going on in China while we are within these walls. Therefore we say again unto you we are innocent of these things they have represented us falsely Was it for committing adultery, we are aware that false slander has gone abroad for it has been reiterated in our ⟨ears⟩.[186] These are falsehoods also.

---

information on the Latter-day Saints' October 1838 strikes against anti-Mormons in Daviess County, see Introduction to Part 3: 4 Nov. 1838–16 Apr. 1839, pp. 265–269 herein.)

185. The "wolf" was probably Captain Samuel Bogart of the Ray County militia, whose troops engaged in a skirmish with Latter-day Saint men at Crooked River near the Ray County–Caldwell County border on 25 October 1838. Neither JS nor his fellow prisoners were present for the fight, during which Missourian Moses Rowland was killed, although JS met the returning Mormon men about six miles south of Far West soon after to administer healing blessings to the wounded. In the November 1838 preliminary hearing, Judge Austin A. King did not find probable cause to believe that JS was involved in Rowland's death, although the press identified JS as an accessory to the killing both before and after the fact and a Ray County grand jury subsequently indicted him as an accessory, after the fact, to murder. (Introduction to Part 3: 4 Nov. 1838–16 Apr. 1839, p. 269 herein; Sampson Avard, Testimony, Richmond, MO, Nov. 1838, p. [21]; Morris Phelps, Testimony, Richmond, MO, Nov. 1838, p. [28]; Austin A. King, Ruling, Richmond, MO, Nov. 1838, pp. [124]–[125], in State of Missouri, "Evidence"; Baugh, "Call to Arms," 245–246; "The Mormon Prisoners," *Daily Herald and Gazette* [Cleveland, OH], 29 Dec. 1838, [2]; Indictment, Richmond, MO, Apr. 1839, State of Missouri v. Pratt et al. [Ray Co. Cir. Ct. 1839], Boone Co., MO, Circuit Court Records, 1839, State Historical Society of Missouri, Columbia.)

186. TEXT: "ears" was written over a knife-erased word, perhaps "allso." Allegations of adultery may have derived from rumors of an early plural marriage. (Historical Introduction to Letter from Thomas B. Marsh, 15 Feb. 1838, pp. 12–13 herein; Minutes, 12 Apr. 1838, p. 91 herein.)

Renegadoes, mormon dissenters are running through the world and spreading various foul and libelous reports against us thinking thereby to gain the friendship of the world because they know that we are not of the world and that the world hates us;[187] therefore they make a tool of these fellows[188] by them they do all the injury they can and after that they hate them worse than they do us because they find them to be base traitors and sycophants.[189] ~~God~~ Such characters God hates we cannot love them the world hates them and we sometimes think the devil ought to be ashamed of them. We have heard that it has been reported by some that some of us should have said that we not only dedicated our property but our families also to the Lord, and satan taking advantage of this has transfigured it into lasciviousness such as a community of wives [p. 4] which is an abomination in the sight of God.[190] When we consecrate our property to the Lord it is to administer to the wants of the poor and needy for this is the law of God[191] it is not for the purpose of the rich those who have no need and when a man consecrates or dedicates his wife and children he does not give them to his brother or to his neighbor for there is no such law for the law of God is thou shalt not commit adultery[192] thou shalt not covet thy neighbor's wife.[193] He that looketh upon a woman to lust after her has committed adultery already in his heart.[194] Now for a man to consecrate his property and his wife & children to the Lord, is nothing more nor less than to feed the hungry, clothe the naked, visit the widow and the fatherless, the sick, and the afflicted, and do all he can to administer to their relief in their afflictions,[195] and for him and his house to serve the Lord.[196] In order to do this he and all his house must be virtuous and shun every appearance of evil.[197] Now if any person has represented any

---

187. See John 15:19.

188. Instead of "make a tool of these fellows," Mulholland's copy has "make a toast of these characters" and Woodruff's copy has "make a fool of these characters." (JS, Liberty, MO, to the Church in Caldwell Co., MO, 16 Dec. 1838, in "General," Record Book, 105; JS, Liberty, MO, to the Church in Caldwell Co., MO, 16 Dec. 1838, JS Collection, CHL.)

189. Instead of "base traitors and sycophants," Woodruff's copy has "liars traitors all around."

190. The phrase "community of wives," derived from English translations of Plato's *Republic,* was used in the early nineteenth century to describe communal groups in which men shared relationships with women in addition to sharing property. ("Nicolaitans," in Buck, *Theological Dictionary,* 312; "Polygamy," in *Encyclopaedia Americana,* 10:230; *Memoirs of Matthias the Prophet,* 12.)

191. See Revelation, 9 Feb. 1831, in *JSP,* D1:245–256 [D&C 42:1–72]; and Cook, *Joseph Smith and the Law of Consecration,* 5–28.

192. See Exodus 20:14; and Revelation, 9 Feb. 1831, in *JSP,* D1:251 [D&C 42:24].

193. See Exodus 20:17.

194. See Matthew 5:28; compare Book of Mormon, 1830 ed., 481 [3 Nephi 12:28].

195. See Book of Mormon, 1830 ed., 165 [Mosiah 4:26]; and James 1:27.

196. See Joshua 24:15.

197. See 1 Thessalonians 5:22.

thing other wise than what we now write he or she is a liar and have represented us falsely. And this is another manner ~~of~~ of evil which is spoken against us falsely. We have learned also since we have been in prison that many false and pernicious things which were calculated to lead the saints far astray and to do great injury ⟨have been taught by Dr. [Sampson] Avard⟩ as coming from the Presidency ~~taught by Dr Avard~~ and we have reason to fear ⟨that⟩ many ⟨other ~~things~~⟩ designing and corrupt characters like unto himself ⟨have been teaching many things⟩[198] which the presidency never knew of being taught in the church by any body untill after they were made prisoners, which if they had known of, they would have spurned them and their authors from them as they would the gates of hell.[199] Thus we find that there has been frauds and secret abominations and evil works of darkness going on leading the minds of the weak and unwary into confusion and distraction, and palming it all the time upon the presidency while mean time the presidency were ignorant as well as innocent of these things, which were practicing in the church in their name and were attending to their own family concerns, weighed down with sorrow, in debt, in poverty, in hunger assaying to be fed yet finding themselves receiving deeds of charity but inadequate to their subsistence, and because they received those deeds they were envied and hated by those who professed to be their friends But notwithstanding

---

198. TEXT: These insertions are in a different ink and perhaps in different handwriting.

199. Avard was an influential Danite general during the first few months after the society was organized in summer 1838. He led the movement to expel dissenters from Far West in June, received public recognition as a general in the Fourth of July parade in Far West, and assumed a prominent role in the expedition to Daviess County in August.[a] To achieve the purpose of the society—to silence internal dissent and defend the church from vigilante attacks[b]—Avard reportedly advocated unquestioned obedience to the First Presidency, lying, stealing, killing, and resistance to the law.[c] According to Reed Peck, after some Danites objected to Avard's teachings, the First Presidency attended a meeting "to show the society that what he [Avard] was doing was according to their direction or will." Avard, however, "did not explain to the presidency what his teachings had been in the society."[d] John Corrill reported that Avard's more extreme proposals were known only to a few Danite leaders and that the First Presidency denied knowledge of the proposals.[e] At some point after the August expedition to Daviess County, JS removed Avard from leadership, although Avard apparently continued to exercise influence outside of the society's leadership structure.[f] Perhaps embittered by his demotion, Avard was the key witness for the state in the November 1838 hearing.[g] (a. Oliver Cowdery et al., Far West, MO, ca. 17 June 1838, at josephsmithpapers.org; "Celebration of the 4th of July," *Elders' Journal,* Aug. 1838, 60; JS, Journal, 7–9 Aug. 1838, in *JSP,* J1:299; Affidavit, 5 Sept. 1838, pp. 222–225 herein. b. See Introduction to Part 2: 8 July–29 Oct. 1838, p. 170 herein. c. Corrill, *Brief History,* 30–32, in *JSP,* H2:166–169; R. Peck to "Dear Friends," 18 Sept. 1839, pp. 38–52; Phelps, Reminiscences, 6–7. d. Reed Peck, Testimony, Richmond, MO, Nov. 1838, p. [56], in State of Missouri, "Evidence." e. Corrill, *Brief History,* 30–32, in *JSP,* H2:166–167. f. Sampson Avard, Testimony, Richmond, MO, Nov. 1838, p. [6], in State of Missouri, "Evidence"; Phelps, Reminiscences, 9; Lyman Wight, Journal, in *History of the Reorganized Church,* 2:298. g. Sampson Avard, Testimony, Richmond, MO, Nov. 1838, pp. [2]–[23], in State of Missouri, "Evidence"; John B. Clark, Jefferson City, MO, to Lilburn W. Boggs, 29 Nov. 1838, copy, Mormon War Papers, MSA; see also Nimer, "Sampson Avard," 37–60.)

we thus speak we honor the church when we speak of the church, as a church, for their liberality, kindness, patience, and long suffering, and their continued kindness towards us. And now brethren we say unto you, what can we enumerate more; is not all manner of evil of every description spoken against us falsely, yea, we say unto [p. 5] unto you falsely; we have been misrepresented and misunderstood and belied and the purity of our hearts have not been known. And it is through ignorance, yea, the very depth of ignorance is the cause of it, and not only ignorance but gross wickedness on the part of some and hypocrisy also who by a long face and sanctified prayers and very pious sermons had power to lead the minds of the ignorant and unwary and thereby obtain such influence that when we approached their iniquities the devil gained great advantage & would bring great sorrow upon our heads and in fine we have waded through an ocean of tribulation, and mean abuse practiced upon us by the ill bred and ignorant such as Hinkle, Corrill, and Phelps, Avard, Reed Peck, [John] Cleminson,[200] and various others who are so very ignorant that they cannot appear respectable in any decent and civilized society, and whose eyes are full of adultery and cannot cease from sin.[201] Such characters as [William E.] McLellin,[202] John Whitmer, D. Whitmer,[203] O[liver] Cowdery,[204] Martin Harris,[205] who are too mean to mention and we had liked to have forgotten

---

200. Cleminson was another member of Hinkle's delegation. According to Peck, Cleminson opposed the expulsion of Cowdery and others from Far West in June 1838, as well as the church's October 1838 military operations in Daviess County. Cleminson testified for the prosecution at the November 1838 hearing, stating that JS ordered Cleminson, who was the clerk for the Caldwell County Circuit Court, not to issue warrants in "vexatious" suits against church leaders. (R. Peck to "Dear Friends," 18 Sept. 1839, pp. 29, 37, 84, 108; John Cleminson, Testimony, Richmond, MO, Nov. 1838, p. [51], in State of Missouri, "Evidence.")

201. See 2 Peter 2:14.

202. McLellin's actions and stance toward the church were considered in a disciplinary council on 11 May 1838. Extant records do not indicate whether the apostle was excommunicated at that time, but during the meeting he relinquished his license and withdrew from the church. (See Historical Introduction to Declaration to the Clay County Circuit Court, ca. 6 Mar. 1839, p. 335 herein.)

203. John and David Whitmer were excommunicated in March and April 1838. Both were expelled from Far West in June, along with Oliver Cowdery and Lyman Johnson. Heber C. Kimball claimed that the Whitmers accompanied Major General Lucas to Far West and helped identify church leaders, who were later charged with crimes. John Whitmer also testified against JS at the November 1838 hearing. (See Introduction to Part 1: 15 Feb.–28 June 1838, pp. 9–10 herein; Minutes, 13 Apr. 1838, p. 103 herein; Kimball, "History," 88; and John Whitmer, Testimony, Richmond, MO, Nov. 1838, pp. [97]–[99], in State of Missouri, "Evidence.")

204. Cowdery, previously an "assistant councilor" in the First Presidency, was excommunicated in April 1838 and expelled, along with other dissenters, from Far West in June. (See Minutes, 12 Apr. 1838, p. 93 herein; and Introduction to Part 1: 15 Feb.–28 June 1838, pp. 9–10 herein.)

205. Harris was the only dissenter named in the letter who was not in Missouri in 1838. He was still in Kirtland, Ohio, where he had been a member of the high council. In 1837 he joined with other dissenters who opposed church control over temporal affairs, and the Kirtland high council excommunicated him in December 1837. He was among the founders and financial backers of the "Church of Christ," a

them. [Thomas B.] Marsh[206] & [Orson] Hyde[207] whose hearts are full of corruption, whose cloak of hypocrisy was not sufficient to shield them or to hold
them up in the hour of trouble, who after having escaped the pollutions of the
world through the knowledge of God and become again entangled and overcome the latter end is worse than the first.[208] But it has happened unto them
according to the words of the savior, the dog has returned to his vomit, and the
sow that was washed to her wallowing in the mire.[209] Again if we sin wilfully
after we have received the knowledge of the truth, there remaineth no more
sacrifice for sin, but a certain fearful looking ⟨for⟩ of judgement and fiery indignation to come which shall devour these adversaries. For he who despiseth
Moses' law died without mercy under two or three witnesses of how much
more severe punishment suppose ye shall he be thought worthy who hath sold
his brother and denied the new and everlasting covenant by which he was

---

short-lived organization created in 1838 and composed primarily of dissenters. (Stephen Burnett, Orange
Township, OH, to Lyman Johnson, 15 Apr. 1838, in JS Letterbook 2, pp. 64–66; John Smith and Clarissa
Lyman Smith, Kirtland, OH, to George A. Smith, Shinnston, VA, 1 Jan. 1838, George Albert Smith,
Papers, CHL; Marquardt, "Martin Harris," 10–15.)

206. Marsh, president of the Quorum of the Twelve Apostles, strongly supported JS during the 1837–
1838 problems that resulted in the removal of the Missouri church presidency. Marsh subsequently became
president pro tempore of the church in Missouri. His support may have wavered when other church leaders
sided with Lucinda Pendleton Harris in a dispute with Marsh's wife, Elizabeth Godkin Marsh. Although he
opposed the June expulsion of the dissenters from Far West, he remained president of the Twelve and president pro tempore of the church in Missouri until late October, when he dictated an affidavit describing the
Danite society and the Saints' military operations against the Daviess County vigilantes. On 25 October,
Marsh explained in a letter to his sister, Ann Marsh Abbott, and her husband, Lewis Abbott, his decision to
leave the church "for conscience sake, and that alone," and he alleged that JS and Sidney Rigdon were permitting theft, arson, and other crimes in Daviess County. (Letter from Thomas B. Marsh, 15 Feb. 1838,
pp. 18–26 herein; Cook, "Thomas B. Marsh Returns to the Church," 394–396; R. Peck to "Dear Friends,"
18 Sept. 1839, pp. 22–23; Thomas B. Marsh and Orson Hyde, Affidavit, Richmond, MO, 24 Oct. 1838, copy,
Mormon War Papers, MSA; Thomas B. Marsh and Orson Hyde, Richmond, MO, to Lewis Abbott and
Ann Marsh Abbott, Caldwell Co., MO, 25–30 Oct. 1838, in JS Letterbook 2, p. 18; see also Esplin,
"Emergence of Brigham Young," 340–343.)

207. Hyde, a member of the Quorum of the Twelve Apostles, returned from his mission to England
in mid-1838 and settled in Far West. He opposed the church's military operations against the anti-
Mormon vigilantes in Daviess County and filed an affidavit on 24 October that supported Marsh's more
detailed affidavit of the same date. Hyde subsequently wrote a letter to a friend in which he explained that
he left the church "fully beleiving, that God is not with them, and is not the mover of their schemes and
projects." (Letter from Heber C. Kimball and Orson Hyde, between 22 and 28 May 1838, p. 146 herein;
Thomas B. Marsh and Orson Hyde, Affidavit, Richmond, MO, 24 Oct. 1838, copy, Mormon War Papers,
MSA; Thomas B. Marsh and Orson Hyde, Richmond, MO, to Lewis Abbott and Ann Marsh Abbott,
Caldwell Co., MO, 25–30 Oct. 1838, in JS Letterbook 2, p. 19; see also Esplin, "Emergence of Brigham
Young," 336.)

208. See 2 Peter 2:20.

209. Although JS ascribed these words to Jesus Christ, the phrase comes from 2 Peter 2:22, which in
turn quotes Proverbs 26:11. (See also Book of Mormon, 1830 ed., 468 [3 Nephi 7:8].)

sanctified calling it an unholy thing and doing despite to the spirit of grace.[210] And again we say unto you that inasmuch as there be virtue in us and the holy priesthood hath been conferred upon us, and the keys of the kingdom hath not been taken from us,[211] for verily thus saith the Lord[212] be of good cheer for the keys that I gave unto ⟨you⟩ are yet with you Therefore we say unto you dear brethren in the name of the Lord Jesus Christ, we deliver these characters unto the buffetings of satan untill the day of redemption[213] that they may be dealt with according to their works [p. 6] and from henceforth their works shall be made manifest.[214] And now dear and well beloved brethren and when we say brethren we mean those who have continued faithful in christ men, women, and children, we feel to exhort you in the name of the Lord Jesus, to be strong in the faith of the new and everlasting covenant, and nothing frightened at your enemies. For what has happened unto us is an evident token to them of damnation but unto us of salvation and that of God.[215] Therefore hold on even unto death, for he that seeks to save his life shall ~~loose~~ lose it but he that loseth his life for my sake and the gospels shall find it sayeth Jesus Christ.[216] Brethren from henceforth let truth and righteousness prevail and abound in you and in all things be temperate, abstain from every appearance of evil, drunkenness, and profane language, and from every thing which is unrighteous or unholy; also from enmity, and hatred, and covetousness and from every unholy desires. Be honest one with another, for it seemeth that some have come short of these things, and some have been uncharitable & have manifested greediness because of their debts towards those who have been persecuted & dragged about with chains without cause and imprisoned. Such persons God hates and they shall have their turn of sorrow in the rolling of the great wheel for it rolleth and none can hinder.[217] Zion shall yet live

---

210. See Hebrews 10:26–29.

211. See Matthew 16:18–19; Revelation, ca. Aug. 1835, in *JSP*, D4:411–412 [D&C 27:13]; and Revelation, 26 Apr. 1838, pp. 116–118 herein [D&C 115:19].

212. In Mulholland's copy, this phrase is followed by "Fear not, but." (JS, Liberty, MO, to the Church in Caldwell Co., MO, 16 Dec. 1838, in "General," Record Book, 107.)

213. See Revelation, 1 Mar. 1832, in *JSP*, D2:199 [D&C 78:12]; and Revelation, 23 Apr. 1834, in *JSP*, D4:23 [D&C 104:9–10].

214. See 1 Corinthians 3:13.

215. See Philippians 1:28.

216. See Mark 8:35.

217. JS was perhaps alluding to the *rota fortunae,* or wheel of fortune, a concept that is rooted in ancient philosophy and that entered Anglo-American culture through Chaucer's *Canterbury Tales,* Shakespeare's plays, and other sources. Such texts reference the idea that an individual's prospects can rise and fall according to the dictates of fate and providence. (Robinson, "Wheel of Fortune," 207–216; Chapman, "Wheel of Fortune in Shakespeare's Historical Plays," 1–7.)

though she seemeth to be dead. Remember that whatsoever measure you meet out to others it shall be measured to you again.[218] We say unto you brethren be not afraid of your adversaries contend earnestly against mobs, and the unlawful works of dissenters and of darkness. And the very God of peace shall be with you[219] and make a way for your escape[220] from the adversary of your souls[221] we commend you to God and the word of his grace[222] which is able to make us wise unto salvation.[223] Amen.

Joseph Smith Jun. [p. 7]

———— ৎ১ ————

Letter to Heber C. Kimball and Brigham Young, 16 January 1839

Source Note

Sidney Rigdon, JS, and Hyrum Smith, Letter, Liberty, Clay Co., MO, to Heber C. Kimball and Brigham Young, Far West, Caldwell Co., MO, 16 Jan. 1839. Featured version copied [between ca. May 1839 and ca. 27 Aug. 1841]; handwriting of Vilate Murray Kimball, Robert B. Thompson, and Heber C. Kimball; two pages; Kimball Family Correspondence, CHL. Includes docket and use marks.

Bifolium measuring 12 × 7¾ inches (30 × 20 cm), with thirty-nine printed lines per page. The document contains needle holes in the center fold and browning along the outer edges, suggesting that the pages were originally bound in a blank book. Before the bifolium was removed, two texts were inscribed on the first leaf: a portion of Heber C. Kimball's autobiography was inscribed on the recto, which is paginated "23",[224] and a copy of Missouri governor Lilburn W. Boggs's expulsion order of 27 October 1838 was inscribed on the verso. After the leaves were extracted from the blank book, the bifolium was folded, apparently for storage, and the 16 January 1839 letter was copied on the recto and verso of the second leaf. One of the resulting folds was used as a left margin on the recto of the second leaf. At some point, the two leaves were separated. Pinholes near the center fold may indicate the leaves were refastened with pins. The leaves were later inscribed with graphite use marks, refolded for filing, and docketed by Thomas Bullock: "Jan 16. 39 | Joseph, Sidney & Hyrum | to | Heber and Brigham | cop^d".

This copy of the letter apparently remained in Kimball's possession, except for when Thomas Bullock copied it into an expanded version of Kimball's autobiography, likely in the late 1850s or in the 1860s.[225] After Kimball's death in 1868, the letter was passed down to his descendants, who evidently maintained possession of the letter until 1973, when Spencer W. Kimball donated it to the Historical Department of the LDS church.[226]

---

218. See Matthew 7:2; and Mark 4:24; compare Book of Mormon, 1830 ed., 483 [3 Nephi 14:2].

219. See Romans 15:33.

220. See 1 Corinthians 10:13.

221. See Psalm 71:13.

222. See Acts 20:32.

223. See 2 Timothy 3:15.

224. See Kimball, "Journal and Record," 30.

225. Kimball, Autobiography, 64a.

226. Helen Mar Kimball Whitney, "Scenes and Incidents in Nauvoo," *Woman's Exponent,* 1 Jan. 1882, 114; Instrument of Gift, 11 July 1973, in Case File for Kimball Family Correspondence, CHL.

Historical Introduction

On 16 January 1839, JS, Sidney Rigdon, and Hyrum Smith wrote from the Clay County jail in Liberty, Missouri, to Heber C. Kimball and Brigham Young—the two senior apostles in Far West, Missouri—directing them to manage church affairs temporarily while the First Presidency remained imprisoned. In early January 1839, Kimball and Young had sent a letter, apparently no longer extant, to the First Presidency, requesting guidance on when the apostles should begin moving their families out of Missouri. Some Latter-day Saints had left Missouri in November and December 1838 to comply with the expulsion order that Governor Lilburn W. Boggs issued on 27 October 1838; however, the majority of church members, including Kimball, Young, and their families, remained in Caldwell County, waiting for spring.[227]

In this 16 January letter, the First Presidency directed Kimball and Young to remain with their families in Missouri until the presidency was released from jail, because the Quorum of the Twelve Apostles was temporarily responsible for managing church affairs and proselytizing efforts. When the quorum was established in 1835, it presided over the church outside of Zion and its stakes, under the direction of the First Presidency. In early 1838, the senior apostles—Thomas B. Marsh, David W. Patten, and Brigham Young—were appointed to a pro tempore presidency over the church in Missouri.[228] After Marsh disaffected and Patten died in October, Young was the only remaining member of the Missouri presidency.[229] The impending migration of church members out of Missouri signaled the necessary suspension of regular church organization in the state, and the Zion high council, over which Young presided, met for the last time on 16 January, the date of this letter.[230] As indicated in the letter, with the First Presidency imprisoned and unable to direct day-to-day affairs, senior apostles Kimball and Young were to assume leadership of the church.

In the letter, the First Presidency instructed Kimball and Young to ordain individuals previously called as apostles, thereby rebuilding the quorum, which had been depleted during the crises of 1837 and 1838. By late spring 1838, four apostles had been excommunicated or otherwise removed from office for disaffection, reducing the quorum to eight members.[231] The October 1838 conflict in Missouri further diminished the council's ranks, with Thomas B. Marsh and Orson Hyde withdrawing from church

---

227. See Hartley, "Winter Exodus from Missouri," 6–40.

228. Instruction on Priesthood, between ca. 1 Mar. and ca. 4 May 1835, in *JSP*, D4:314, 315 [D&C 107:23, 33]; Minutes, 6 Apr. 1838, p. 70 herein; see also Esplin, "Emergence of Brigham Young," chap. 7.

229. Thomas B. Marsh and Orson Hyde, Affidavit, Richmond, MO, 24 Oct. 1838, copy, Mormon War Papers, MSA; Pratt, *History of the Late Persecution*, 35–36.

230. Minute Book 2, 16 Jan. 1839.

231. The Kirtland, Ohio, high council identified apostles John F. Boynton and Luke Johnson as leading dissenters in December 1837, and the council probably excommunicated the two men at that time. The Far West high council excommunicated Lyman Johnson for apostasy in April 1838. Apostle William E. McLellin was tried a month later by a bishop's council in Missouri and may have been removed from his office around that time. (John Smith and Clarissa Lyman Smith, Kirtland, OH, to George A. Smith, Shinnston, VA, 1 Jan. 1838, George Albert Smith, Papers, CHL; Minutes, 13 Apr. 1838, p. 101 herein; JS, Journal, 11 May 1838, in *JSP*, J1:268.)

fellowship and with David W. Patten dying in a military engagement at Crooked River.[232] Around the same time, William Smith fell out of favor after criticizing JS.[233] Brothers Parley P. and Orson Pratt remained in good standing in the quorum, but the former was imprisoned and the latter was in St. Louis.[234] In mid-December 1838, Young and Kimball ordained John Taylor and John E. Page to the apostleship in Far West.[235] The 16 January letter instructed Young and Kimball to ordain others who had been appointed to the apostleship but not yet ordained, to fill the remaining vacancies, and to appoint the oldest remaining member of the original quorum as president of the quorum.

In addition, the presidency addressed the twelve apostles' responsibility "to build up the church, and regulate all the affairs of the same, in all nations."[236] In prior years, new converts were encouraged to gather to Kirtland, Ohio, or to church settlements in Missouri. However, in early 1838 a revelation encouraged the Saints in Kirtland to immigrate to Missouri,[237] and conflicts later that year in Missouri meant it was no longer an option for gathering. In the absence of a central gathering place, the presidency indicated that new converts should remain in their homes for the time being, except for English converts who chose to "take their chance with the saints here"; these converts were encouraged to "send wise men before them and buy out" the Kirtland area for settlement. The presidency also reminded Kimball and Young that they and the other apostles were to depart from the Far West temple site on 26 April 1839 for a mission to Great Britain.

Like some of JS's other letters written in the jail, this missive invokes scriptural language and was apparently patterned after New Testament epistles, with a greeting, counsel on specific items, and a concluding blessing.[238] It is unknown who inscribed the original letter, which is apparently not extant; Rigdon, who was the first signatory, may have written it.[239] JS may have inscribed the postscript, which he was the first to initial. How the letter was transmitted from Liberty to Far West is unknown, although it is possible that the First Presidency entrusted the letter to Bishop Edward Partridge, who visited the jail on 16–17 January 1839.[240] A copy of the letter was made as early as May 1839. The first ten lines were copied by Robert B. Thompson, who began performing scribal work for Kimball

---

232. See 308nn206–207 herein; and Introduction to Part 3: 4 Nov. 1838–16 Apr. 1839, p. 269 herein.

233. Woodruff, Journal, 13 Feb. 1859; Minutes, 4–5 May 1839, p. 446 herein.

234. "History of Orson Pratt," 22, Historian's Office, Histories of the Twelve, 1856–1858, 1861, CHL.

235. Minute Book 2, 19 Dec. 1838. A July 1838 revelation appointed Taylor and Page to fill vacancies in the quorum, but the outbreak of conflict delayed their ordinations. (Revelation, 8 July 1838–A, p. 180 herein [D&C 118:6].)

236. Instruction on Priesthood, between ca. 1 Mar. and ca. 4 May 1835, in JSP, D4:315 [D&C 107:33].

237. Revelation, 12 Jan. 1838–C, in JSP, D5:501–502.

238. See Doty, Letters in Primitive Christianity, 27–47.

239. On previous occasions when Rigdon acted as scribe, he signed the document first. (See, for example, License for Edward Partridge, ca. 4 Aug. 1831–ca. 5 Jan. 1832, in JSP, D2:29; Vision, 16 Feb. 1832, in JSP, D2:192 [D&C 76]; and Charges against Missouri Conference Preferred to Joseph Smith, ca. Mar. 1832, in JSP, D2:229.)

240. History of the Reorganized Church, 2:315.

in May 1839.²⁴¹ For unknown reasons, Kimball copied the next four lines and one word of the fifth line. Kimball's wife, Vilate Murray Kimball, copied the remainder of the letter. Thompson died on 27 August 1841; therefore, at least his portion of the copy was inscribed by that date.²⁴²

Document Transcript

/²⁴³Liberty Jany 16ᵗʰ 1839

Broˢ H[eber] C Kimball and B[righam] Young

Joseph Smith Jr Sidney Rigdon and Hyram [Hyrum] Smith prisoners for Jesus sake²⁴⁴ sends greeting.

In obedience to your request in your letter we say to you as follows. It is not wisdom for you to go out of Caldwell with your Families yet for a little season untill we are out of Prison after which time you may act your pleasure. but though you take your Families out of the state yet it will be necessary /²⁴⁵for you to Return and leave as before designed on the 26 of April.—²⁴⁶ In as much as we are in prison and for a litt[l]e season if need be the managment of the affairs of the church devolves on you that is the twelve ⟨the⟩²⁴⁷ gathering. /²⁴⁸the gathering of necessity stopt.—²⁴⁹ but the convertion

---

241. Kimball, "History," 51; Robert B. Thompson, Nauvoo, IL, to Heber C. Kimball, London, 5 Nov. 1840, Heber C. Kimball, Collection, CHL; Thompson, *Journal of Heber C. Kimball;* Kimball, *Heber C. Kimball,* 67–78.

242. "Death of Col. Robert B. Thompson," *Times and Seasons,* 1 Sept. 1841, 2:519. Heber C. Kimball was away from Nauvoo, Illinois, from late 1839 through July 1841 on a mission to England, returning to Illinois on 1 July, approximately two months prior to Thompson's death. While in England, Kimball continued working on his autobiography, a portion of which was copied in unidentified handwriting on the first leaf of the bifolium that the 16 January 1839 letter was copied on. These circumstances suggest that the letter may have been copied after Kimball's July 1841 return to Illinois. (Kimball, "Journal and Record," 30; Clayton, Diary, 3 Sept. and 24 Nov. 1840; Heber C. Kimball, Nauvoo, IL, 4 Aug. 1841, Letter to the Editor, *Times and Seasons,* 16 Aug. 1841, 2:511.)

243. TEXT: Robert B. Thompson handwriting begins.

244. See Philemon 1:1; and 2 Corinthians 4:5.

245. TEXT: Robert B. Thompson handwriting ends; Heber C. Kimball begins.

246. On 8 July 1838, JS dictated a revelation directing the twelve apostles to undertake a mission "over the great waters," where they were to promulgate "my gospel the fulness thereof and to bear record of my name." The apostles were to "take leave of my saints in the City Far West on the 26ᵗʰ· day of April next on the building spot of my house." (Revelation, 8 July 1838–A, pp. 179–180 herein [D&C 118:4–5].)

247. TEXT: Insertion in the handwriting of Vilate Murray Kimball.

248. TEXT: Heber C. Kimball handwriting ends; Vilate Murray Kimball begins.

249. Early revelations commanded Latter-day Saints to gather in church communities to seek protection from the calamities expected before the Second Coming and to build the ideal Christian society. At various times during the 1830s, Missouri and Ohio functioned as the church's primary gathering places, although opposition forced church members to abandon both locations by the end of the decade. At the time of this letter, Quincy, Illinois, the largest settlement on the Illinois side of the Mississippi River, was becoming a de facto refuge for Latter-day Saints migrating from Missouri. (Revelation, Sept. 1830–A, in *JSP,* D1:179 [D&C 29:8]; Revelation, 20 July 1831, in *JSP,* D2:7–12 [D&C 57]; Minutes, 17 Feb.

of the world need not stop. but under wise management can go on more rapidly than ever. wher[e] churches are built let them continue where they are until a door is open to do other wise. and let every Elder ocupy his own ground. and when he builds a church let him preside over it. and let not others run in to trouble him.[250] and thus let every man prove himself unto God that he is worthy. If we live we live, and if we die for the testimony of Jesus we die. but whether we live or die let the work of God go on.[251] Let the churches in England continue there, till further orders. till a door cac [can] be opened for them. except they choose to come to America. and take their chance with the saints here.[252] if they do that, let them come, and if they choose to come the[y] would do well to send wise men before them and buy out Kirtland,[253] and the regions round about. or they may settle whare they can till things may alter. It will be necessary for you to get the twelve togather ordain such as have not ben ordained, or at least such of them as you can get.[254] and proceed to regulate the Elders as the Lord may give you wisdom.[255] We nominate George A Smith and Lyman Sherman to take the

---

1834, in *JSP*, D3:436–437; Revelation, 12 Jan. 1838–C, in *JSP*, D5:500–502; Albert P. Rockwood, Quincy, IL, to Luther Rockwood, Holliston, MA, 30 Jan. 1839, Albert Perry Rockwood, Mormon Letters and Sermons, 1838–1839, Western Americana Collection, Beinecke Rare Book and Manuscript Library, Yale University, New Haven, CT; Bennett, "Study of the Mormons in Quincy," 83–105.)

250. In the 1830s, temporary branches were established for church members who resided outside of the Saints' main gathering places in Ohio and Missouri. Traveling elders often presided over new branches, although as the congregations grew and became more established, local elders and high priests were frequently appointed as presiding authorities. In 1835 JS stated that "no Elder has a right to go into any branch of the church and appoint meetings or regulate the Church without the consent or advic[e] of the presiding Elder of said branch." (Minute Book 2, 3 Dec. 1832; Letter to the Church in Thompson, OH, 6 Feb. 1833, in *JSP*, D3:3–6; Minutes and Discourse, 2 May 1835, in *JSP*, D4:302; Plewe et al., *Mapping Mormonism*, 40–43.)

251. See Romans 14:8.

252. In 1837, Kimball and Hyde were called as the church's first missionaries to England. By the time they left England in April 1838, more than fifteen hundred new converts were organized into at least twenty branches. (Allen et al., *Men with a Mission*, 23–53.)

253. Although persecution forced the majority of Latter-day Saints to abandon Kirtland for Missouri in 1838, a few church members stayed in the area after the mass departure. Given Kirtland's former prominence, it remained a logical destination for Saints gathering during 1839 and thereafter. (Bitton, "Waning of Mormon Kirtland," 455–464.)

254. On 8 July 1838, JS dictated a revelation that appointed Taylor, Page, Wilford Woodruff, and Willard Richards to fill vacancies in the Quorum of the Twelve Apostles. Taylor and Page were not ordained until 19 December 1838 because of the outbreak of conflict in Missouri. The ordinations of Woodruff and Richards were delayed even further because the men were away on missions. (Revelation, 8 July 1838–A, p. 180 herein [D&C 118:6]; Historical Introduction to Letter to Wilford Woodruff, ca. 18 June 1838, pp. 153–154 herein; Willard Richards, History, [1], Historian's Office, Histories of the Twelve, 1856–1858, 1861, CHL; Minute Book 2, 19 Dec. 1838.)

255. The 1835 instruction on priesthood designated the Quorum of the Twelve Apostles as a "travelling, presiding high council" with authority "to build up the church, and regulate all the affairs of the

place of Orson Hyde and Thomas B Marsh[256] Brethren fear not, but be strong in the Lord and in the power of his [p. [1]] might.[257] What is man that the servent of God should fear him. or the son of man that he should tremble at him.[258] Neither think strang[e] concerning the firy trials with which we are tried as though some strange thing had hapened unto us.[259] Remember that all have ben pertakers of like afflictions.[260] Therefore rejoice in our afflictions by which you are perfected and through which the captain of our salvation was perfected also.[261] Let your hearts and the hearts of all the saints be comforted with you,[262] and let them rejoice exceedingly for great is our reward in heaven. for so perciduted the wicked the prophets which were before us.[263]

America will be a Zion to all that choose to come to it.—[264] And if the churches in foren countries wish to come let them do so.— Say to Br P[arley] P Pratt that our feelings accord with his. he is as we are, and we as he. may peace rest upon him in life and in death.—[265] Brethren pray for us, and cease not. till our deliverence comes. which we hope may come. we hope we say, for our famalies sake.— Let the elders preach nothing but the first principles of the Gospel.[266] and let them publish our afflictions. the injustice and cruelty thereof

---

same" outside of Zion and its stakes. The quorum's responsibilities included inquiring about the conduct and teachings of traveling elders and verifying their good standing in the church. (Instruction on Priesthood, between ca. 1 Mar. and ca. 4 May 1835, in *JSP*, D4:315 [D&C 107:33]; Record of the Twelve, 4–9 May 1835.)

256. For information on the disaffection of Hyde and Marsh, see 308nn206–207 herein.

257. See Ephesians 6:10.

258. See Psalms 8:4; 144:3; and Hebrews 2:6.

259. See 1 Peter 4:12.

260. See 2 Timothy 1:8.

261. See Hebrews 2:10.

262. See Revelation, 6 Aug. 1833, in *JSP*, D3:224 [D&C 98:1]; Revelation, 12 Oct. 1833, in *JSP*, D3:325 [D&C 100:15]; and Revelation, 16–17 Dec. 1833, in *JSP*, D3:390 [D&C 101:16].

263. See Matthew 5:12; compare Book of Mormon, 1830 ed., 480 [3 Nephi 12:12].

264. This statement reflects the Book of Mormon's references to the "promised land," which JS explained in 1833 was the "land of America." (Letter to Noah C. Saxton, 4 Jan. 1833, in *JSP*, D2:354; Revelation, 20 July 1831, in *JSP*, D2:7–8, 12 [D&C 57:1–2, 14]; see also Book of Mormon, 1830 ed., 26, 143–144 [1 Nephi 12:1; Enos 1:10].)

265. After the November 1838 court of inquiry, Parley P. Pratt was incarcerated in Richmond, Missouri, where he awaited trial on murder charges stemming from his involvement in the battle at Crooked River. The language here suggests that Pratt had recently written or otherwise sent word to the prisoners in Liberty. (Ruling, Richmond, MO, Nov. 1838, pp. [124]–[125], State of Missouri v. JS et al. for Treason and Other Crimes [Mo. 5th Jud. Cir. 1838], in State of Missouri, "Evidence"; see also Baugh, "Final Episode of Mormonism in Missouri," 1–34.)

266. In 1837 the church newspaper *Messenger and Advocate* identified "faith, repentance, baptism, remission of sin, and . . . the reception of the Holy Ghost" as the five "first principles of the gospel." (A. Cheney, "The Gospel," *LDS Messenger and Advocate*, May 1837, 3:498–500; see also Letter to the Elders

upon the house tops.[267] Let them write it and publish it in all the papers where they go. charge them perticularly on this point—[268]

Brethren we remain yours in hope of Eternal life[269]

Sidney Rigdon

Joseph Smith Jr

Hyrum Smith

N. B. Appoint the oldest of those of those twelve who were firs[t] appointed, to be the President of your Quorum.—[270]

J S

S R

H S [p. [2]]

⟨Jan 16. 39⟩
⟨Joseph, Sidney & Hyrum to Heber and Brigham⟩

———— ☙ ————

License for Gardner Snow, 19 January 1839

Source Note

JS, License, Far West, Caldwell Co., MO, for Gardner Snow, 19 Jan. 1839; printed form with additions in handwriting of George W. Robinson; signature of George W. Robinson and signature of JS by George W. Robinson; notation by and signature of George W. Robinson; two pages; Ella M. Bennett Collection, CHL. Includes docket.

Single leaf measuring 3 × 8 inches (8 × 20 cm). The right edge of the recto has the square cut of manufactured paper. The top, bottom, and left edges have been unevenly cut. The license was folded for filing, and "G. Snows | License" was docketed on the verso, possibly by Gardner Snow. The license remained in the possession of Snow's descendants until 1986, when it was donated to the Historical Department of the LDS church.[271]

---

of the Church, 2 Oct. 1835, in *JSP,* D5:7–15; Hebrews 5:12; Book of Mormon, 1830 ed., 193 [Mosiah 18:20]; and Revelation, ca. Summer 1829, in *JSP,* D1:90 [D&C 19:21].)

267. See Matthew 10:27.

268. Following the late 1833 expulsion of the Saints from Jackson County, Missouri, JS dictated a revelation commanding the Saints to seek redress from government officials. These efforts included appealing to the general public for justice, a tactic that JS reaffirmed later in 1839 as part of the strategy to obtain redress for the Saints' losses in 1838 and 1839. (Revelation, 16–17 Dec. 1833, in *JSP,* D3:396 [D&C 101:86–89]; "An Appeal," *The Evening and the Morning Star,* Aug. 1834, 183–184; Letter to Edward Partridge and the Church, ca. 22 Mar. 1839, p. 397 herein.)

269. See Titus 1:2; 3:7.

270. The letter here reiterates JS's instructions to the Quorum of the Twelve Apostles on 2 May 1835. Young and Kimball were the oldest members of the quorum. Young was born 1 June 1801, while Kimball was born 14 June 1801. The First Presidency may not have known which of the men was older. (Minutes and Discourse, 2 May 1835, in *JSP,* D4:301.)

271. Acquisition Sheet and Instrument of Gift, 20 Dec. 1986, in Case File for Ella M. Bennett Collection, CHL.

Historical Introduction

In January 1839, Gardner Snow received a new elder's license attesting to his priesthood office and his good standing in the church.[272] Snow was appointed as an elder in winter 1834, and in 1836 he was ordained as a seventy.[273] Although Snow already possessed an elder's license,[274] church members passed a resolution at an April 1838 conference in Far West, Missouri, specifying that priesthood officers should obtain new licenses, signed by a member of the First Presidency and the general church recorder. All licenses previously issued would be considered invalid following the conference.[275]

Circumstances did not permit Snow to obtain a new license until early 1839. He was in Kirtland, Ohio, at the time of the April 1838 conference and did not arrive in Missouri until fall.[276] By that time, the conflict with anti-Mormon vigilantes had disrupted the First Presidency's ability to issue new licenses.[277] Although JS and his counselors in the First Presidency were incarcerated during the winter in Liberty, Missouri, general church recorder George W. Robinson resumed producing routine documents such as priesthood licenses in late December 1838.[278] On 19 January 1839, Robinson completed and issued the following license to Snow in Far West. Likely in Robinson's capacity as the First Presidency's scribe, he signed JS's name on his behalf.

Document Transcript

To whom it may concern:

This certifies that Gardner Snow has been received into the church of Jesus Christ of Latter Day Saints,[279] organized on the sixth of April, in the year of our Lord one thousand eight hundred and thirty, and has been ordained

---

272. Articles and Covenants, ca. Apr. 1830, in *JSP*, D1:124 [D&C 20:64].

273. Gardner Snow, Autobiographical Sketch, 1874, in Patriarchal Blessings, 124:3; Quorums of the Seventy, "Book of Records," 20 Dec. 1836, 10.

274. Elder's License for Gardner Snow, Kirtland, OH, 11 July 1836, Ella M. Bennett Collection, CHL.

275. See Minutes, 7–8 Apr. 1838, p. 74 herein; and Resolution, ca. 8 Apr. 1838, p. 76 herein.

276. Following Snow's arrival in Missouri with the Kirtland Camp in October 1838, he temporarily settled in Adam-ondi-Ahman before the state militia forced him and other Saints to relocate to Caldwell County in late November 1838. (Kirtland Camp, Journal, 13 Mar. and 2 Oct. 1838; Robert Wilson, Adam-ondi-Ahman, MO, to John B. Clark, 14 Nov. 1838, copy; Robert Wilson, Keytesville, MO, to John B. Clark, 25 Nov. 1838, copy, Mormon War Papers, MSA; Gardner Snow, Autobiographical Sketch, 1874, in Patriarchal Blessings, 124:3.)

277. A church record book shows that George W. Robinson issued new licenses from April to September 1838. No entries for new licenses were recorded in October and November. (General Church Recorder, License Record Book, 32; see also Introduction to Part 3: 4 Nov. 1838–16 Apr. 1839, pp. 265–271 herein.)

278. When Robinson resumed issuing licenses in late December, he recorded the date of each license on the flyleaf of the church record book. (General Church Recorder, License Record Book.)

279. See Articles and Covenants, ca. Apr. 1830, in *JSP*, D1:123 [D&C 20:37]. Gardner Snow was baptized into the church by Orson Pratt on 18 June 1833 in Vermont. (Orson Pratt, Journal, 18 June 1833.)

a_n Elder_,[280] according to the rules and regulations of said church;[281] and is duly authorised to preach the gospel, agreeably to the authority of that office.[282]

Given by the direction of a general conference of the authorities of said church, assembled in the City of Far West, Missouri, the sixth of April, in the year of our Lord one thousand eight hundred and thirty eight.

   Geo. W. Robinson Clerk.   _Joseph Smith Jr._ President. [p. [1]]

/[283]Given and recorded in Far West M[o.] January 19 1839 in License Record Book A. Page 47[284]

G. W. Robinson
Gen Recorder

———— ⁊ ————

Memorial to the Missouri Legislature, 24 January 1839

Source Note

[JS and others], Memorial, Liberty, Clay Co., MO, to Missouri legislature, Jefferson City, Cole Co., MO, 24 Jan. 1839. Featured version copied [between 27 June and 30 Oct. 1839] in JS Letterbook 2, pp. 66–67; handwriting of James Mulholland; JS Collection, CHL. For more information on JS Letterbook 2, see Source Notes for Multiple-Entry Documents, p. 566 herein.

Historical Introduction

On 24 January 1839, JS and his fellow prisoners in the Clay County jail composed a memorial to the Missouri legislature, requesting a change of venue for their impending trials.[285] Nearly two months had passed since Judge Austin A. King of the fifth judicial circuit ruled there was probable cause to believe that JS, Hyrum Smith, Lyman Wight,

---

280. In the 1830s, seventies were issued elder's licenses.

281. Articles and Covenants, ca. Apr. 1830, in *JSP*, D1:124 [D&C 20:60].

282. Articles and Covenants, ca. Apr. 1830, in *JSP*, D1:124 [D&C 20:42].

283. TEXT: Preprinted form ends; George W. Robinson handwriting begins.

284. In March 1836, members at a church conference resolved that a clerk should record licenses in a record book "and that said recording clerk be required to endorse a certificate under his own hand and signature on the back of said licences, specifying the time when & place where such license was recorded, and also a reference to the letter and page of the Book containing the same." Although Robinson wrote on Snow's license that it was recorded on page 47 of License Record Book, December 1837–May 1862, the last copied license was recorded in September 1838 on page 32. When Robinson resumed issuing licenses in December 1838, he apparently did not simultaneously copy the new licenses into the record book, opting instead to create a list of issued licenses, including the name, office, date of issuance, and page number, on the flyleaf of the record book. The list suggests that Robinson anticipated recording Snow's license in the book on page 47, but he apparently was unable to do so given the Saints' exodus from the state. (Minutes, 3 Mar. 1836, in *JSP*, D5:182–183; General Church Recorder, License Record Book, 32.)

285. A memorial is "a petition or representation made by one or more individuals to a legislative body." ("Memorial," in Bouvier, *Law Dictionary*, 2:111; see also Missouri Constitution of 1820, art. 13, sec. 3.)

Alexander McRae, and Caleb Baldwin had committed treason against the state of Missouri in Daviess County. King also ruled there was probable cause to believe that Sidney Rigdon had committed the same offense in Caldwell County.[286] The 24 January memorial was the second one the prisoners wrote to the legislature that month. Although the first memorial is apparently not extant, the second one evidently builds upon arguments presented in the first memorial. The second memorial alleges that two obstacles impeded the prisoners from receiving a fair trial within the fifth judicial circuit. First, the memorialists, as they called themselves, argued that the recent conflict had a significant impact on the "upper Counties"—those counties within the fifth judicial circuit—rendering the task of finding an impartial jury essentially impossible.[287] Daviess County, where the trial for JS, Hyrum Smith, Wight, McRae, and Baldwin was to be held, had been a seedbed for anti-Mormon sentiment since 1837, and the antagonism had only grown stronger in the wake of the 1838 conflict.[288] Latter-day Saints in Caldwell County, where Rigdon was to be tried, were leaving the state and rapidly being replaced by new arrivals, many of whom were hostile to the Saints.[289]

Second, the memorialists argued that King, the presiding officer of the fifth judicial circuit, was antagonistic toward the Latter-day Saints and had been since the 1833 conflict between church members and anti-Mormon vigilantes in Jackson County. The prisoners contended that King's public statements during the 1838 crisis and its aftermath demonstrated his bias against the Saints. JS later wrote that during the November 1838 hearing, the judge had been motivated by "shear prejudice and the Spirit of persecution and malice and prepossision against him [JS] on account of his religeon."[290]

Missouri law permitted a change of venue "to the circuit court of another county"—presumably within the same judicial circuit—when "the minds of the inhabitants of the county in which the cause is pending are so prejudiced against the defendant that a fair trial cannot be held therein." For JS and his fellow prisoners, the other counties in the fifth judicial circuit were hardly better options than Daviess and Caldwell counties.[291] For the prisoners' trials to be moved out of the fifth circuit, either the Missouri legislature would need to amend the law or the defense would need to show that the presiding judge had a conflict of interest.[292]

---

286. Ruling, Richmond, MO, Nov. 1838, p. [124], State of Missouri v. JS et al. for Treason and Other Crimes (Mo. 5th Jud. Cir. 1838), in State of Missouri, "Evidence."

287. When the prisoners wrote the memorial, the fifth judicial circuit included Daviess, Livingston, Carroll, Ray, Clay, Clinton, and Caldwell counties. (An Act to Establish Judicial Circuits, and to Prescribe the Times and Places of Holding Courts [21 Jan. 1837], *Laws of the State of Missouri* [1836–1837], p. 56, sec. 12.)

288. Anderson, "Clarifications of Boggs's Order," 30–42.

289. See Walker, "Mormon Land Rights," 35–46.

290. Petition to George Tompkins, between 9 and 15 Mar. 1839, p. 345 herein.

291. An Act to Regulate Proceedings in Criminal Cases [21 Mar. 1835], *Revised Statutes of the State of Missouri* [1835], pp. 486–487, art. 5, sec. 16. Many of the anti-Mormon vigilantes who participated in the 1838 conflict hailed from counties within the fifth judicial circuit. (See JS, Journal, 2 Sept. 1838, in *JSP*, J1:312–313.)

292. An Act to Regulate Proceedings in Criminal Cases [21 Mar. 1835], *Revised Statutes of the State of Missouri* [1835], p. 486, art. 5, sec. 15.

The prisoners, likely with the assistance of their attorney, Peter Burnett, wrote the memorial featured here on 24 January 1839. For reasons that remain unclear, none of the Latter-day Saints' names appear in the document, either in the body of the document or as signatories.[293] The first two paragraphs refer to JS and his companions in the third-person plural. Beginning with the third paragraph and continuing for the remainder of the document, the memorial is written in first-person plural, directly representing the memorialists' perspective. The initial portion may have been written by Burnett, who visited the jail several times in January 1839 and who added a postscript to the memorial.[294] It is also possible that the prisoners wrote the memorial in multiple stages and neglected to maintain a consistent voice throughout. In the postscript, Burnett requested that Clay County representative James M. Hughes, whom the memorial was addressed to, present the memorial to the legislature.[295]

It is unknown whether the memorial was transmitted to Hughes, who began a leave of absence from the legislative session on 28 January.[296] Clay County's other representative, David R. Atchison, presumably assumed the task of representing the prisoners' interests before the legislature. Although it is unclear whether Atchison formally submitted the memorial to the house of representatives,[297] he did introduce a bill on 25 January that amended the existing statute to permit a change of venue "from one circuit to another, when the people in the circuit, where the indictment is found, are so prejudiced against the defendant that a fair trial cannot be had."[298] Both the house and the senate passed the bill—apparently without controversy—and Boggs signed it into law on 13 February 1839.[299] The original memorial is apparently not extant. James Mulholland inscribed a copy, using the original or a retained copy, in JS Letterbook 2 sometime between 27 June and 30 October 1839.[300]

---

293. It is possible that the prisoners named themselves in the memorial written a few days earlier and saw no need to include their names in the 24 January memorial.

294. *History of the Reorganized Church*, 2:315.

295. James Madison Hughes (1809–1861) was an attorney and Clay County representative in 1839. He represented Missouri in the United States Congress from 1843 to 1845. (*Biographical Directory of the United States Congress, 1774–2005*, 1296.)

296. The leave of absence was granted on 25 January 1839. (*Journal, of the House of Representatives, of the State of Missouri*, 25 Jan. 1839, 298.)

297. Atchison may not have submitted the memorial because of lawmakers' ongoing debates about whether to appoint a committee to investigate the causes of the conflict. (See Gentry and Compton, *Fire and Sword*, 485–496.)

298. *Journal, of the House of Representatives, of the State of Missouri*, 25 Jan. 1839, 289; An Act to Amend an Act concerning Criminal Proceedings [13 Feb. 1839], *Laws of the State of Missouri* [1839], p. 98.

299. *Journal, of the House of Representatives, of the State of Missouri*, 26 and 28 Jan. 1839; 13 Feb. 1839, 305, 320, 321–322, 466. Although the prisoners ultimately obtained a change of venue in April 1839, it was granted on different procedural grounds than in the February 1839 act. (See Historical Introduction to Promissory Note to John Brassfield, 16 Apr. 1839, p. 422 herein.)

300. Mulholland copied JS's 27 June 1839 letter to Jacob Stollings on page 50 of JS Letterbook 2, making that the earliest possible copying date for the documents that followed, including the 24 January 1839 memorial. For information on the latest likely copying date, see 248n440 herein.

Document Transcript

To the Hon The Legislature of Missouri

Your memorialists having a few days since, Solicited your attention to the same subject, would now respectfully submit to your Honorable body a few additional facts in support of their prayer.

They are now in imprisonment imprisoned Under a charge of Treason against the State of Missouri, And their lives and fortunes and characters[301] being suspended upon the result of the trial on the criminal charges preferred against them, your Hon. body will excuse them for manifesting the deep concerns they feel in relation to their trials for a crime so enormous as that of treason[302]

It is not our object to complain—to asperse any one. All we ask is a fair and impartial trial. We ask the sympathies of no one, we ask sheer justice—tis all we expect— and all we merit, but we merit that— We know the people of no county in this State to which we would ask our final trials to be sent are prejudiced in our favour. But we believe that the state of excitement existing in most of the upper Counties is such that a jury would be improperly influenced by it. But that excitement, and the prejudice against us in the counties comprising the fifth Judicial court circuit are not the only obstacle we are compelled to meet.

We know that much of that prejudice against us is not so much to be attributed to a want of honest motive among the citizens, as it is to wrong information

But it is a difficult task to change opinions once formed, The other [p. 66] obstacle which we candidly consider are of the most weighty, is the feeling which we believe is entertained by the Hon, A[ustin] A, King against us, and his Consequent incapacity to do us impartial justice. It is from no disposition to speak disrespectfully of that high officer that we lay before your Hon. Body the facts we do, but simply that the Legislature may be apprised of our real Condition. We look upon Judge King as like all other

---

301. Likely an allusion to the United States Declaration of Independence, which reads: "And for the support of this Declaration, with a firm reliance on the protection of divine Providence, we mutually pledge to each other our Lives, our Fortunes and our sacred Honor."

302. Because treason was a nonbailable offense, Judge King committed JS and his fellow prisoners to the Clay County jail to await their trials in spring 1839. The penalty for treason against the state was death or incarceration in the "penitentiary for a period not less than ten years." (An Act to Regulate Proceedings in Criminal Cases [21 Mar. 1835], *Revised Statutes of the State of Missouri* [1835], p. 475, art. 2, sec. 8; Letter to Emma Smith, 1 Dec. 1838, p. 294 herein; An Act concerning Crimes and Their Punishments [20 Mar. 1835], *Revised Statutes of the State of Missouri* [1835], p. 166, art. 1, sec. 1.)

mere men, liable to be influenced by his feelings, his prejudices, and his previously formed opinions

We consider his reputation as being partially if not entirely committed against us.

He has written much upon the subject of our late difficulties in which he has placed us in the wrong— These letters have been published to the world[303] He has also presided at an excited public meeting as chairman and no doubt sanctioned all the proceedings.[304] We do not complain of the citizens who held that meeting. They were entitled to that privilege.

But for the Judge before whom the very men were to be tried for a capital offense, to participate in an expression of condemnation of these same individuals is to us at least apparently wrong, and we cannot think that we should after such a course on the part of the Judge have the same chance of a fair and impartial trial— as all admit we ought to have.[305]

---

303. On 24 October 1838, King sent Boggs a detailed account of the Saints' Daviess County expedition, which culminated with the 18 October raids of Gallatin and Millport. "Until lately I thought the Mormons wer disposed to act only on the defensive," King stated, "but their recent conduct shows that they are the aggressors, & that they intend to take the law into their own hands." The judge asked Boggs to intervene. "The country is in great commotion and I can assure you that either with or without authority, something will shortly have to be done." King's report was probably based on statements made by Latter-day Saint dissenters and other Missouri residents who claimed to have witnessed the Saints' activities.[a] Although the memorial references multiple letters, only King's 24 October 1838 letter seems to have circulated in the press. The *Missouri Watchman,* published in Jefferson City, the state capital, printed King's letter on 29 October, and it was widely discussed and reproduced thereafter.[b] (a. Austin A. King, Richmond, MO, to Lilburn W. Boggs, 24 Oct. 1838, copy; Charles R. Morehead et al., Statement, Richmond, MO, 24 Oct. 1838, copy; Thomas B. Marsh and Orson Hyde, Affidavit, Richmond, MO, 24 Oct. 1838, copy, Mormon War Papers, MSA. b. "Mormon Troubles," *Adams Sentinel* [Gettysburg, PA], 19 Nov. 1838, [3]; "Letter from Judge King," *Missouri Republican* [St. Louis], 2 Nov. 1838, [2]; "Letter from Jud[g]e King," *Missouri Argus* [St. Louis], 8 Nov. 1838, [1].)

304. On 26 December 1838, King presided at a public meeting in Ray County, where citizens condemned a letter that Clay County resident Michael Arthur wrote to his state legislators. Arthur, who was sympathetic to the Saints, criticized "devils in the form of human beings inhabiting Davis, Livingston and a part of Ray Counties" who were harassing the defenseless Saints in Far West. Arthur hoped that the legislature would authorize the formation of a small guard, numbering about twenty-five men, to protect Caldwell County from marauders. King opposed Arthur's proposal on the grounds that such a guard would undermine civil authority. Those at the public meeting defended the actions of Ray County citizens and claimed the governor's expulsion order was necessary to maintain public order. ("Public Sentiment," *Jeffersonian Republican* [Jefferson City, MO], 19 Jan. 1839, [1]; Michael Arthur, Liberty, MO, to "Respected Friends," 29 Nov. 1838, copy; Austin A. King, Richmond, MO, to Lilburn W. Boggs, 23 Dec. 1838, copy, Mormon War Papers, MSA.)

305. In early January 1839, the Missouri legislature debated the propriety of King chairing an "anti-Mormon meeting," as the *Daily Missouri Republican* described it, when he was scheduled to preside at the prisoners' trials. Although a few legislators shared the *Republican*'s disapproval, the debate "ended where

We believe that the foundation of the feeling against us which we have reason to think Judge King entertains, may be traced to the unfortunate troubles which occurred in Jackson County some few years ago. In a battle between the mormons and a portion of the Citizens of that County, Mr Brassell [Hugh Breazeale], the brotherinlaw of Judge King, was killed.[306] It is natural that the Judge should have some feeling against us, whether we were right or wrong in that controversy. We mention these facts not to disparage Judge King— We believe that from the relation he bears to us, he would himself prefer that our trials should be had in a different circuit, and before a different court,

Many other reasons and facts we might mention but we forebear.

Liberty Jail, Jan 24th 1839   L.[307]

James M. Hughes Esqr

Mem, House Rep,

Jefferson City Mo—

Will you be so good as to present this to the house. The Community here would, I believe have no objections for the trial of these men being transferred to St. Louis.

J <u>M. H.</u>

P. H. (B.) [Peter H. Burnett] [p. 67]

———— ❧ ————

Receipt from Sarah Burt Beman, 26 January 1839

Source Note

Joseph B. Noble on behalf of Sarah Burt Beman, Receipt, for Edward Partridge on behalf of JS and Sidney Rigdon, Far West, Caldwell Co., MO, 26 Jan. 1839; handwriting of Edward Partridge; signature of Joseph B. Noble; two pages; JS Collection, CHL. Includes docket.

Single leaf measuring 3½ × 7⅞ inches (9 × 20 cm). The receipt was folded for carrying and storage. It has undergone conservation work. Since the time of its reception, the receipt has apparently remained in the possession of the LDS church.

---

it began, without any result." (News Item, *Daily Missouri Republican* [St. Louis], 8 Jan. 1839, [2]; "Letter from the Editor," *Daily Missouri Republican*, 10 Jan. 1839, [2].)

306. Breazeale married Austin A. King's sister, Amanda, in 1827 and was killed on 4 November 1833 in a skirmish between Latter-day Saints and anti-Mormon vigilantes intent on expelling church members from Jackson County. (Roane Co., TN, Marriage Records, 1801–1962, Dec. 1801–Sept. 1838, p. 7, microfilm 560,087, U.S. and Canada Record Collection, FHL; "The Outrage in Jackson County," *The Evening and the Morning Star,* Dec. 1833, 118.)

307. Mulholland may have written the first "L" of "Liberty Jail" in the middle of the page before deciding to inscribe the prisoners' location on the left side of the page.

Historical Introduction

On 26 January 1839, Bishop Edward Partridge created the following receipt in Far West, Missouri, showing that Latter-day Saint Joseph B. Noble had received a payment of $220.37 on behalf of his mother-in-law, Sarah Burt Beman.[308] In creating this receipt, Partridge acted on behalf of JS and Sidney Rigdon of the First Presidency, who were imprisoned in Liberty, Missouri.[309] The receipt represents the completion of the final step in a financial process that began in Kirtland, Ohio, before Beman migrated to Missouri in July 1838.[310] First, on 26 April 1838, Beman and some of her relatives deeded to church agent Oliver Granger 130 acres, likely to help alleviate the church's debts.[311] Second, on the same day, church agent William Marks issued Beman one or more orders totaling the value Granger assigned to the donation—$1,700—which authorized her to receive the equivalent of that amount in land or cash from Partridge in Missouri. The third and final step in the process was to receive payment, which Beman did at least three times—for $300.00 on 22 August 1838, $63.44 on 9 January 1839, and $220.37 on 26 January 1839. On each occasion, Partridge wrote a receipt confirming that Beman received payment.[312] The third receipt, featured here as representative of similar documents, was signed on Beman's behalf by Noble, suggesting Beman was not present when the payment was received.

Document Transcript

<u>$220.37</u> Rec^{d.} of Joseph [Sm]ith[313] Jun, and Sidney Rigdon by the hand of Edward Partridge two hundred and twenty dollars and 37/100 which ⟨is⟩ to apply on an order given by them through their agent Wm. Marks in my favor on E. Partridge Sarah Beman

---

308. Joseph B. Noble married Mary Beman on 11 September 1834. (Noble and Noble, Reminiscences, [10]–[12], [14].)

309. JS and Rigdon held many of the church's debts in their own names. (See, for example, Statement of Account from John Howden, 29 Mar. 1838, pp. 61–65 herein; and Statement of Account from Perkins & Osborn, ca. 29 Oct. 1838, pp. 252–261 herein; for information on Partridge's role in handling financial affairs, see Historical Introduction to Pay Order to Edward Partridge for William Smith, 21 Feb. 1838, pp. 27–30 herein.)

310. Helen Mar Kimball Whitney, "Closing Paragraph of Life Incidents," *Woman's Exponent*, 15 June 1881, 9.

311. Geauga Co., OH, Deed Record, 1795–1921, vol. 25, pp. 663–664, 26 Apr. 1838, microfilm 20,241, U.S. and Canada Record Collection, FHL. For information on the use of donations to the church, see Historical Introduction to Pay Order to Edward Partridge for William Smith, 21 Feb. 1838, pp. 27–30 herein.

312. It is unknown whether Marks issued a single order or multiple orders that totaled $1,700, as the order(s) have apparently not survived. However, the 9 January 1839 receipt created when Beman received payment from Partridge confirms that Marks issued the corresponding order(s) on 26 April 1838. The fact that the three extant receipts total only $583.81 suggests that Beman did not redeem the entire $1,700 or that additional receipts are not extant. (Sarah Burt Beman, Receipt, Far West, MO, for JS and Sidney Rigdon, 22 Aug. 1838; Sarah Burt Beman, Receipt, Far West, MO, for JS and Sidney Rigdon, 9 Jan. 1839, JS Collection, CHL.)

313. TEXT: "[*Page torn*]ith".

By

Far West Jany. 26th 1839 J. B. Noble L S^314 [p. [1]]
S. Beman's
Receipt $220.37

——— ℰↄ ———

Receipt from William Collins, 8 February 1839

Source Note

William Collins, Receipt, for JS and Lyman Wight, Liberty, Clay Co., MO, 8 Feb. 1839; handwriting of Lyman Wight; signature of William Collins; one page; JS Collection, CHL.

Single leaf measuring 3 × 7¼ inches (8 × 18 cm). The right edge of the recto has the straight cut of manufactured paper, while the top, bottom, and left edges have been unevenly cut. The receipt was folded for filing. From its reception, the document has presumably remained in the possession of the LDS church.

Historical Introduction

On 8 February 1839, William Collins visited JS and Lyman Wight while they were imprisoned in Liberty, Clay County, Missouri; during the visit, Collins signed a receipt in return for receiving money owed. The payment probably stemmed from debts incurred during the prisoners' stay in Independence, Jackson County, Missouri, in early November 1838. JS recalled that the men "had to pay for [their] own <u>board</u>" during their time in Independence even though they were prisoners of Major General Samuel D. Lucas.[315] Wight explained that the detainees stayed two nights in "Knowlten's hotel," likely referring to Noland's Inn, a tavern operated by Smallwood Noland. Wight also noted that Lucas permitted the prisoners to move freely throughout Independence and that they even "traded some" at local establishments.[316] According to Wight, "a gentleman by the name of Collins" accompanied the detainees just west of town to the lot the Saints had purchased in 1831 as the site for a temple.[317] The prisoners likely turned to Collins for help in covering their expenses while in Independence, becoming indebted to him.[318]

---

314. TEXT: Signature and "L S" in handwriting of John B. Noble. "L S" is surrounded by a hand-drawn representation of a seal. "L S" is an abbreviation of *locus sigilli*, which is Latin for "location of the seal."

315. Bill of Damages, 4 June 1839, pp. 502–503 herein.

316. Lyman Wight, Journal, in *History of the Reorganized Church*, 2:296; Deatherage, *Early History of Greater Kansas City*, 240; see also *History of Jackson County, Missouri*, 826.

317. Wight reported that Collins "presumed the place did not look as it would had we [the Saints] been permitted to have remained in this county." (Lyman Wight, Journal, in *History of the Reorganized Church*, 2:295–296.)

318. A "Mr Collins" also delivered a letter from Parley P. Pratt to his wife, Mary Ann Frost Pratt, in Far West, Missouri. Jackson County land records indicate a William Collins owned at least thirty acres in the county. (Parley P. Pratt, Independence, MO, to Mary Ann Frost Pratt, Far West, MO, 4 Nov. 1838, Parley P. Pratt, Letters, CHL; Jackson Co., MO, Deed Records, 1827–1909, bk. C, pp. 280–281, 2 Jan. 1834;

Collins visited the Clay County jail on 8 February to receive payment.[319] After JS and Wight reimbursed Collins, Wight wrote this receipt, which Collins signed to confirm he had been paid in full.

Document Transcript

Liberty February the 8 1839

Recd of Lyman Wight & Joseph Smith an order for $93 25 cts in full for a Saddle[320] and Board at Nolands and trade at Robbets[321] in Jackson County.—

W[m.] Collins

Liberty February 1839[322]

——————— ☙ ———————

Letter from Edward Partridge, 5 March 1839

Source Note

Edward Partridge, Letter, Quincy, Adams Co., IL, to JS and others, Liberty, Clay Co., MO, 5 Mar. 1839. Featured version copied [between 22 Apr. and 30 Oct. 1839] in JS Letterbook 2, pp. 3–4; handwriting of James Mulholland; JS Collection, CHL. For more information on JS Letterbook 2, see Source Notes for Multiple-Entry Documents, p. 566 herein.

Historical Introduction

On 5 March 1839, Bishop Edward Partridge wrote to JS and the other Latter-day Saint prisoners in Liberty, Missouri, explaining recent developments regarding land dealer Isaac Galland's offer to sell land to the church and relating the situation of church mem-

---

bk. D, pp. 43–44, 9 May 1835; bk. D, pp. 504–505, 17 Nov. 1836, microfilm 1,017,979; bk. E, p. 506, 6 Mar. 1838; bk. F, pp. 237–238, 9 Jan. 1839, microfilm 1,017,980, U.S. and Canada Record Collection, FHL.)

319. Wight recalled that while the prisoners were in the Clay County jail they were required "to pay the most extravagant price" for their board in Independence or have their property seized. The prisoners evidently reimbursed Collins with an order that he could use to obtain repayment elsewhere—presumably from Bishop Edward Partridge in Far West. (Lyman Wight, Testimony, Nauvoo, IL, 1 July 1843, pp. 26–27, Nauvoo, IL, Records, CHL; Pay Order to Edward Partridge for William Smith, 21 Feb. 1838, pp. 27–30 herein; Receipt from Sarah Burt Beman, 26 Jan. 1839, pp. 323–325 herein.)

320. The prisoners may have purchased the saddle for one of the two horses they were permitted to ride from Independence to Richmond, Missouri. The horses had allegedly been stolen from Latter-day Saints by the militia and then loaned to the prisoners for this trip. In 1842, Latter-day Saints Elias Higbee, Hyrum Smith, and Henry G. Sherwood each estimated the value of a saddle at forty to fifty dollars. (Hyrum Smith, Testimony, Nauvoo, IL, 1 July 1843, p. 16, Nauvoo, IL, Records, CHL; Elias Higbee, Deposition, Nauvoo, IL, 22 Apr. 1842; Hyrum Smith, Deposition, Nauvoo, IL, 22 Apr. 1842; Henry G. Sherwood, Deposition, Nauvoo, IL, 22 Apr. 1842], JS v. George M. Hinkle [Lee Co. Dist. Ct. 1842], CHL.)

321. Perhaps David Roberts, a Jackson County merchant. (1840 U.S. Census, Jackson Co., MO, 68; see also Jackson Co., MO, Deed Records, 1827–1909, bk. D, pp. 119–120, 1 Oct. 1835, microfilm 1,017,979; bk. E, pp. 408–410, 15 Sept. 1837, microfilm 1,017,980, U.S. and Canada Record Collection, FHL.)

322. TEXT: "Liberty February 1839" is written upside down.

bers who had recently relocated to Illinois. In January 1839, as it became apparent that the Missouri legislature would not reverse Governor Lilburn W. Boggs's expulsion order, the Latter-day Saints organized an exodus from the state.[323] Quincy, Illinois, became a magnet for church members because it was the closest sizeable settlement to where the Saints had lived in Missouri.[324]

As Latter-day Saints poured into western Illinois, church leaders appointed Israel Barlow and David Rogers as a committee to seek "shelter from the inclemency of the season" in "the up river country" of Illinois as well as in Iowa Territory. In early February 1839, Barlow and Rogers examined about forty empty buildings in Commerce, located at the bend of the Mississippi River in western Illinois. They then crossed the river and looked at the barracks of the abandoned Fort Des Moines in Iowa Territory.[325] They also met with Isaac Galland, who offered to sell the church twenty thousand acres of land within what was known as the "Half-Breed Tract" in Lee County, Iowa Territory,[326] for two dollars per acre, paid in twenty annual installments without interest.[327]

Upon their return to Quincy, Barlow and Rogers attended a meeting at which they reported on their trip. They spoke "very favourably" of Galland's offer to church leaders and suggested that the land was "every way suited for a Location for the church." William Marks, who presided at the meeting, favored the purchase, "providing that it was the will of the Lord that we should again gather together." Marks suspected that the church's practice of gathering was a major cause of the previous conflicts with anti-Mormons in Missouri and Ohio. Partridge, who was also at the meeting, stated that "it was better to scatter into different parts and provide for the poor which will be acceptable to God." The council voted to table the issue for the time being.[328] In mid-February 1839, word of Galland's offer reached JS, who sent a letter to church leaders in Quincy, apparently expressing support for the purchase.[329]

---

323. See Hartley, "Saints' Forced Exodus from Missouri," 347–356.

324. See Bennett, "Study of the Mormons in Quincy," 83–105.

325. Rogers, Statement, [1], CHL.

326. An 1824 treaty between the United States and the Sac and Fox nation set aside about 119,000 acres of land between the Mississippi and Des Moines rivers, just south of Fort Madison, for the mixed-race children of white soldiers and Sac and Fox women. Galland, representing the New York Land Company, obtained the land in 1836. (Treaty with the Sock and Fox Indians [4 Aug. 1824], *Public Statutes at Large,* vol. 7, p. 229, art. 1; Cook, "Isaac Galland," 264–265.)

327. Rogers, Statement, [1], CHL; Quincy Committee, Minutes, ca. 9 Feb. 1839, Far West Committee, Minutes, CHL.

328. Quincy Committee, Minutes, ca. 9 Feb. 1839, Far West Committee, Minutes, CHL.

329. Church leaders at Quincy forwarded their minutes to church leaders in Missouri, and the minutes were incorporated into the records of the Far West removal committee, which had been appointed to oversee the exodus of church members from the state. It is likely that JS learned of Galland's offer through those minutes or from an oral report from members of the Far West removal committee, who frequently visited the jail. JS's letter, which is apparently not extant, was referenced by Partridge in the letter featured here. (Quincy Committee, Minutes, ca. 9 Feb. 1839, Far West Committee, Minutes, CHL; see also Letter to the Church and Edward Partridge, 20 Mar. 1839, p. 367 herein.)

Sidney Rigdon arrived in Quincy on 16 February 1839, following his release from the Clay County jail on bail.[330] Sometime during the week of 17–23 February, Rigdon and other church leaders visited Commerce in hopes of discussing the potential land purchase with Galland, but he was not at home.[331] As Partridge noted in the letter featured here, Rigdon and other church leaders were hesitant to make the purchase, although they thought it might be advisable in the future. The arrival of JS's mid-February 1839 letter, even with its positive endorsement of the purchase, did little to change their minds. On 26 February, Galland wrote to Rogers, discussing the church's potential purchase of Galland's properties in Iowa Territory and in Commerce and offering to render any assistance the Saints required as they left Missouri. He also noted that Iowa Territory officials were supportive of the proposal that church members locate there.[332]

Galland's letter probably arrived in Quincy in late February or early March 1839, at which point church leaders decided to forward it and other documents to JS in Liberty, with Rogers acting as courier.[333] Among the documents was Partridge's 5 March letter, which not only summarized the developments regarding Galland's land offer but also described the generous reception the Latter-day Saints received in Quincy and updated the prisoners on the status and well-being of their families. Rogers left Quincy on 10 March and, after stopping in Far West, arrived in Liberty on the evening of 19 March.[334] Partridge's letter directly contributed to at least three subsequent letters that JS and the other prisoners wrote.[335] Partridge's original letter is apparently not extant, but it was copied by James Mulholland into JS Letterbook 2 between 22 April and 30 October 1839.[336]

---

330. In late January 1839, Rigdon was granted a writ of habeas corpus and was released from prison on bail. As a member of the First Presidency and a recent inmate with JS, Rigdon provided additional leadership to the Saints in Illinois. (Introduction to Part 3: 4 Nov. 1838–16 Apr. 1839, p. 276 herein; Editorial, *Quincy [IL] Whig*, 23 Feb. 1839, [1].)

331. Isaac Galland, Commerce, IL, to David Rogers, [Quincy, IL], 26 Feb. 1839, in JS Letterbook 2, p. 3.

332. I. Galland to D. Rogers, 26 Feb. 1839, in JS Letterbook 2, pp. 1–3.

333. Partridge likely selected Rogers to act as courier for three reasons. First, Rogers had personal knowledge of the negotiations with Galland. Second, Rogers had recently moved to Illinois from New York and was not known in Missouri; therefore, he could pass through the state unrecognized in the wake of Governor Lilburn W. Boggs's expulsion order. Third, Partridge assigned Rogers to sell church-owned property in Jackson County, Missouri, and Rogers would be traveling to Missouri to accomplish that assignment. (Rogers, Statement, [1], CHL.)

334. Rogers, Statement, [1], CHL; Far West Committee, Minutes, 17 Mar. 1839; Hyrum Smith, Liberty, MO, to Mary Fielding Smith, Quincy, IL, 19 Mar. 1839, Mary Fielding Smith, Collection, CHL.

335. See Letter to the Church and Edward Partridge, 20 Mar. 1839, pp. 356–372 herein; Letter to Isaac Galland, 22 Mar. 1839, pp. 376–388 herein; and Letter to Edward Partridge and the Church, ca. 22 Mar. 1839, pp. 388–401 herein.

336. Mulholland began to "write for the Church" on 22 April 1839, and Partridge's letter was one of the first documents Mulholland inscribed in Letterbook 2. For information on the latest likely copying date, see 248n440 herein.

Document Transcript

Quincy Ill. March 5th 1839

Beloved Brethren

Having an opportunity to send direct to you by br [David W.] Rogers, I feel to write a few lines to you. Pre$^{t\cdot}$ [Sidney] Rigdon, Judge [Elias] Higbee, I[srael] Barlow and myself went to see D^{r} [Isaac] Galland week before last.[337] brn, Rigdon, Higbee, and myself are of opinion that it is not wisdom to make a trade with the Doct$^{r\cdot}$ at present, possibly it may be wisdom to effect a trade hereafter.[338] The people receive us kindly here, they have contributed near $100 cash besides other property for the relief of the suffering among our people.[339] Brother Joseph's wife lives at Judge Clevelands [John Cleveland's], I have not seen her but I sent her word of this opportunity to send to you.[340] Br Hyrum [Smith]'s wife lives not far from me, I have been to see her a number of times, her health was very poor when she arrived but she has been getting better, she knows of this opportunity to send.[341] I saw Sister [Harriet Benton] Wight soon after her arrival here, all were well, I understand that she has moved out about two miles with Father [Isaac Higbee] & John Higbee who are fishing this spring.[342]

---

337. That is, during the week of 17–23 February 1839.

338. Although Higbee initially favored accepting Galland's offer in February 1839, he changed his mind when Partridge voiced opposition. Rigdon's reasons for opposing the purchase in February remain unclear. (Quincy Committee, Minutes, ca. 9 Feb. 1839, Far West Committee, Minutes, CHL.)

339. Latter-day Saint Elizabeth Haven wrote in late February 1839 that the people of Quincy donated between $400 and $500 to assist church members, perhaps in cash and other contributions. "God has opened their hearts to receive us," she noted. "We are hungry and they feed us, naked and clothe us." The Quincy Democratic Association held a number of meetings in February 1839 resolving to help the refugee Mormons find employment, shelter, and supplies. (Elizabeth Haven, Quincy, IL, to Elizabeth Howe Bullard, Holliston, MA, 24 Feb. 1839, Barlow Family Collection, CHL; "Proceedings in the Town of Quincy," *Quincy [IL] Argus,* 16 Mar. 1839, [1]; "The Mormons, or Latter Day Saints," *Quincy Argus,* 16 Mar. 1839, [2]; see also Bennett, "Study of the Mormons in Quincy," 83–105.)

340. John Cleveland and his wife, Sarah Kingsley Cleveland, lived on a farm approximately four miles east of Quincy. (Woodruff, Journal, 3 May 1839; Oliver Huntington, "History of Oliver Boardman Huntington," 47.)

341. The prisoners' family members were invited to send letters with Rogers. Mary Fielding Smith was living at the home of a "Father Dixon," likely Charles Dixon, roughly a half mile from the residence of Joseph Smith Sr. and Lucy Mack Smith. Mary Fielding Smith noted on 11 April 1839 that she had been ill for the past "4 or 5 months," during which she had been "intirely unable to take care of household affairs." Despite several attempts, she was unable to communicate with Rogers before he left for Missouri. Other family members had more success in sending letters with Rogers. (Letter from Don Carlos Smith and William Smith, 6 Mar. 1839, p. 333 herein; Mary Fielding Smith, [Quincy, IL], to Hyrum Smith, 11 Apr. 1839, Mary Fielding Smith, Collection, CHL; see also Letter from Emma Smith, 7 Mar. 1839, pp. 338–340 herein.)

342. The Higbee family owned and operated a seine, a type of fishing net. (Letter from Edward Partridge, 13–15 June 1839, p. 507 herein; Higbee, Journal and Reminiscences, [12]; "British Channel Fisheries," *Tait's Edinburgh Magazine,* Mar. 1834, 125.)

Sister [Eunice Fitzgerald] McRae is here living with B^r Henderson and is well I believe she knows of this opportunity to send. B^r [Caleb] Baldwin's family I have not seen, and do not know that she has got here as yet, She may however be upon the other side of the river the ice has run these three days past so that there has been no crossing, the weather is now moderating and the crossing will soon commence again.

This place is full of our people, yet they are scattering off nearly all the while. I expect to start tomorrow for Pittsfield, Pike Co, Ill, about 45 miles, S. E from this place.[343] B^r Geo. W. Robinson told me this morning that he expected that his [p. 3] Father in law,[344] Judge Higbee, and himself would go on a farm about 20 miles N, E from this place.[345] Some of the leading men have given us, (that is our people) an invitation to settle in and about this place, many no doubt will stay here.

Brn, I hope that you will bear patiently the privations that you are called to endure— the Lord will deliver in his own due time. Your letter respecting the trade with Galland was not received here untill after our return from his residence at the head of the shoals or rapids. If br Rigdon were not here we might (after receiving your letter) come to a different conclusion respecting that trade. There are some here that are sanguine that we ought to ~~accept~~ trade with the Doct^r.[346] Bishop [Newel K.] Whitney[347] and Knights [Vinson Knight][348] are not here, and have not been here as I know of. B^r [Isaac] Morley[349] and [Titus] Billings[350] have settled some 20 or 25 miles N of this place for the present. A

---

343. Partridge likely intended to visit several Latter-day Saint families that had settled in Pike County, Illinois, after migrating from Missouri in early 1839. (See Burgess, Autobiography, 5–6; Silas S. Smith, Autobiographical Sketch, 1; Osborn, Reminiscences and Journal, 14–15; and Berrett, *Sacred Places,* 3:229–230.)

344. That is, Rigdon.

345. See Letter from Elias Higbee, 16 Apr. 1839, p. 429 herein.

346. Although it is unknown whom Partridge was referring to, in February 1839 Wandle Mace expressed full support of the purchase. (Quincy Committee, Minutes, ca. 9 Feb. 1839, Far West Committee, Minutes, CHL.)

347. Whitney was appointed as a bishop in 1831. While en route from Ohio to Missouri in late 1838, Whitney and his family heard of the Saints' troubles in Missouri and temporarily stopped in Carrollton, Illinois. (Revelation, 4 Dec. 1831–A, in *JSP,* D2:150 [D&C 72:7–8]; Historical Introduction to Letter to Newel K. Whitney, 24 May 1839, p. 474 herein.)

348. Knight was called as a bishop in Missouri in June 1838. As of February 1839, he was still in Missouri. (Minutes, 28 June 1838, p. 166 herein; Vinson Knight, Spencerburg, MO, to William Cooper, Perrysburg, NY, 3 Feb. 1839, Vinson Knight, Letters, CHL.)

349. Morley was appointed as a counselor to Bishop Partridge in 1831. During the winter of 1838–1839, Morley moved his family to Hancock County, Illinois. (Minutes, ca. 3–4 June 1831, in *JSP,* D1:327; Cox, "Brief History of Patriarch Isaac Morley," 4.)

350. Billings was appointed as a counselor to Bishop Partridge in 1837. Fearing possible arrest for his participation in the skirmish at Crooked River, near Ray County, Missouri, on 25 October 1838, Billings

B^r Lee who lived near Hawn's Mill died on the opposite side of the river a few days since, B^r Rigdon preached his funeral sermon in the Courthouse.[351]

It is a general time of health here, We greatly desire to see you, and to have you enjoy your freedom. The Citizens here are willing that we should enjoy the privileges guaranteed to all civil people without molestation.

I remain your brother in the Lord.

E[dward] Partridge

To Joseph Smith Junr and others⎫
confined in Liberty Jaol.   ⎬
Mo.   ⎭

———— ⁊ ————

Letter from Don Carlos Smith and William Smith, 6 March 1839

Source Note

Don Carlos Smith, Letter with postscript by William Smith, Quincy, Adams Co., IL, to JS and Hyrum Smith, Liberty, Clay Co., MO, 6 Mar. 1839. Featured version copied [between 29 May and 30 Oct. 1839] in JS Letterbook 2, pp. 38–39; handwriting of James Mulholland; JS Collection, CHL. Includes endorsement. For more information on JS Letterbook 2, see Source Notes for Multiple-Entry Documents, p. 566 herein.

Historical Introduction

On 6 March 1839, Don Carlos Smith wrote to his brothers JS and Hyrum Smith, who remained imprisoned in Liberty, Missouri, to inform them of the well-being of their family members. Small groups of the extended Smith family had departed Far West, Missouri, for Illinois throughout the previous winter. Samuel Smith, who feared being arrested because of his participation in the skirmish at Crooked River on 25 October 1838, hurriedly departed Caldwell County before the state militia occupied Far West on 1 November. He soon settled in Quincy, Illinois, and his wife, Mary Bailey Smith, and their children followed him later.[352] William Smith left Missouri for Illinois sometime in December 1838 or January 1839.[353] On 7 February 1839, Emma Smith and her children left Far West, arriving about a week later in Illinois.[354] The largest group of the Smiths comprised Joseph Smith Sr., Lucy Mack Smith,

---

fled Caldwell County before the state militia occupied Far West on 1 November 1838, relocating to Lima, Illinois. (Minute Book 2, 1 Aug. 1837; Lorenzo D. Young, Statement, ca. 1894, CHL; Billings and Shaw, "Titus Billings," 20.)

351. The identity of Brother Lee is unknown. The *Quincy Whig* noted that Rigdon preached at the funeral service of an unnamed Latter-day Saint on 27 February 1839. (Editorial, *Quincy [IL] Whig*, 2 Mar. 1839, [2].)

352. Lucy Mack Smith, History, 1844–1845, bk. 17, [1].

353. Lucy Mack Smith, History, 1844–1845, bk. 16, [8].

354. Far West Committee, Minutes, 7 Feb. 1839; Historian's Office, JS History, Draft Notes, 6–7 and 15 Feb. 1839.

several of their children—Sophronia Smith McCleary, Katherine Smith Salisbury, Don Carlos Smith, and Lucy Smith—and their children's families. The group departed Far West in mid-February and arrived in Quincy later that month.[355] Hyrum Smith's wife, Mary Fielding Smith, apparently left Far West in a separate party in mid-February with her new-born son, named Joseph F., and Hyrum's five children from his first marriage: Lovina, John, Hyrum, Jerusha, and Sarah. They likewise arrived in Quincy later that month.[356]

In late February or early March 1839, church leaders in Quincy decided to send a batch of correspondence and other documents to JS concerning land purchases and other matters. Family members of the prisoners were invited to write letters to be included in the packet.[357] In his letter, Don Carlos Smith related news of the various branches of the Smith family, in particular the health of Mary Fielding Smith, who had contracted a "severe cold" in late 1838. Because she had been essentially bedridden since that time, she relied heavily on her sister Mercy Fielding Thompson and family friend Hannah Grinnels to care for her and Hyrum's children.[358] After Don Carlos concluded the letter, his brother William Smith appended a brief note explaining why he had not visited JS and Hyrum in Liberty and expressing his wishes for their liberation.

David Rogers, the Latter-day Saint chosen to carry the letters to Missouri, left Quincy on 10 March 1839 and arrived in Liberty on the evening of 19 March.[359] JS expressed gratitude for Don Carlos's letter when composing a general epistle to the church on 20 March 1839.[360] Don Carlos's original letter, which is apparently not extant, was copied into JS Letterbook 2 by James Mulholland sometime between 29 May and 30 October 1839.[361]

Document Transcript

Quincy Illinois March 6th 1839
Brethren Hyrum [Smith] and Joseph,
Having an opportunity to send a line to you, I do not feel disposed to let it slip unnoticed. Father's family have all arrived in this state,[362] except you two,

---

355. Historian's Office, JS History, Draft Notes, 14 Feb. 1839; Lucy Mack Smith, History, 1844–1845, bk. 16, [9], [12]; see also Woodruff, Journal, 16 Mar. 1839.

356. Thompson, Autobiographical Sketch, 5; Hyrum Smith, Liberty, MO, to Hannah Grinnels et al., 16 Mar. 1839, Hyrum Smith, Papers, BYU; "Recollections," *Juvenile Instructor*, 4 Mar. 1871, 37.

357. Historical Introduction to Letter from Edward Partridge, 5 Mar. 1839, p. 328 herein.

358. Mary Fielding Smith, Commerce, IL, to Joseph Fielding, June 1839, in Tullidge, *Women of Mormondom*, 256; Thompson, Autobiographical Sketch, 5; Hyrum Smith, Liberty, MO, to Hannah Grinnels et al., 16 Mar. 1839, Hyrum Smith, Papers, BYU; O'Driscoll, *Hyrum Smith*, 177–178n7.

359. Rogers, Statement, [1], CHL; Hyrum Smith, Liberty, MO, to Mary Fielding Smith, Quincy, IL, 19 Mar. 1839, Mary Fielding Smith, Collection, CHL; see also Historical Introduction to Letter from Edward Partridge, 5 Mar. 1839, p. 328 herein.

360. Letter to the Church and Edward Partridge, 20 Mar. 1839, p. 365 herein.

361. Mulholland copied his own 29 May 1839 letter to Edward Partridge on page 15 of JS Letterbook 2, making that the earliest likely copying date for documents he subsequently copied but that had dates preceding 29 May. For information on the latest likely copying date, see 248n440 herein.

362. Samuel Smith, who arrived in Quincy in late 1838, arranged for his parents—Joseph Smith Sr. and Lucy Mack Smith—to stay in the home of Quincy resident Archibald Williams. Joseph Smith Sr. and

And could I but see your faces, this side of the Mississippi, and know and realize that you had been delivered from your enemies, it would certainly light up a new gleam of hope in our bosoms; nothing could be more satisfactory, nothing could give us more joy.

Emma and Children are well, they live three miles from here, and have a tolerable good place.[363] Hyrum's children and mother Grinolds [Hannah Grinnels] are living at present with father; they are all well, Mary [Fielding Smith] has not got her health yet, but I think it increases slowly. She lives in the house with old Father Dixon, likewise B[r] [Robert B.] Thompson and family; they are probably a half mile from Father's; we are trying to get a house, and to get the family together, we shall do the best we can for them, and that which we consider to be most in concordance with Hyram's feelings. One thing I would say (not however to the disrespect of Sister [Mercy Fielding] Thompson) which is ~~that~~ this, the family would do better without her than with her; which I am confident you will regulate when you come. One reason for so saying, is that I do not think that she is a suitable person to govern the family.[364] Father and Mother stood their journey remarkably, they are in tolerable health, Samuel [Smith]'s wife has been sick ever since they arrived, W[m] [Smith] has removed 40 miles from here,[365] but is here now, and says he is anxious to have you liberated, and see you enjoy liberty once more. My family is well, my health has not been good for about two weeks, and for 2 or 3 days the toothache has been my tormentor. It all originated from a severe cold.

Lucy Mack Smith were joined by their children Sophronia Smith McCleary, Samuel Smith, Katherine Smith Salisbury, Don Carlos Smith, and Lucy Smith, along with their respective families. (Lucy Mack Smith, History, 1844–1845, bk. 16, [9], [12]; George Miller, St. James, MI, to "Dear Brother," 22 June 1855, in *Northern Islander* [St. James, MI], 9 Aug. 1855, [1]; Asbury, *Reminiscences of Quincy, Illinois,* 153; see also Woodruff, Journal, 16 Mar. 1839.)

363. Emma Smith and her children resided with John and Sarah Kingsley Cleveland, some four miles east of Quincy. (Letter from Edward Partridge, 5 Mar. 1839, p. 329 herein; Woodruff, Journal, 3 May 1839; Oliver Huntington, "History of Oliver Boardman Huntington," 47.)

364. Upon their arrival in Quincy, Hyrum Smith's family was evidently separated between two households, with Hyrum's five children from his deceased wife, Jerusha Barden Smith, staying with their Smith grandparents in the home of Archibald Williams. Family friend Hannah Grinnels was also living at Williams's residence and likely cared for the children. Mary Fielding Smith, Joseph F., and Thompson stayed with a Father Dixon, probably Charles Dixon. The separation was partly logistical, because Mary probably needed to remain with her sister, who had been caring for Mary and Joseph F., and there likely was insufficient room for everyone in the Williams's residence. Don Carlos also alluded to undisclosed difficulties regarding family dynamics that likely contributed to the separation. (Hyrum Smith, Liberty, MO, to Hannah Grinnels et al., 16 Mar. 1839, Hyrum Smith, Papers, BYU; Thompson, Autobiographical Sketch, 3, 5; Dixon, *History of Charles Dixon,* 16, 60; see also Letter from Don Carlos and Agnes Coolbrith Smith, 11 Apr. 1839, pp. 414–417 herein; and Esplin, "Hyrum Smith," 122–163.)

365. William Smith settled his family in Plymouth, Illinois, located roughly forty miles northeast of Quincy. (Lucy Mack Smith, History, 1844–1845, bk. 16, [8]; JS, Journal, 15–17 June 1839, in *JSP,* J1:341.)

Dear Brethren, we just heard that the Governor says that he is a going to set you all at liberty;[366] I hope it's true, other letters that you will probably recieve, will give you information concerning the warm feeling of the people here towards us,[367] After writing these hurried lines in misery I close by leaving the Blessings of God with you—[368] and praying for your health, prosperity and restitution to liberty. This from a true friend and brother.

Don C[arlos] Smith

J, Smith Jr, H Smith.

Bro Hyrum & Joseph,— I should have called down to Liberty to have seen you, had it not have been for the multiplicity of business that was on my hands & again I thought perhaps that the people might think [p. 38] that the Mormons would rise up to liberate you; consequently too many going to see you might make it worse for you; but we all long to see you, and have you come out of that lonesome place. I hope you will be permitted to come to your families before long, do not worry about them, for they will be taken care of; all we can do will be done, ~~farther~~ further than this we can only wish, hope, desire, and pray for your deliverance.

Wm Smith

Joseph Smith Jr, Liberty Mo.

———— ❧ ————

Declaration to the Clay County Circuit Court, circa 6 March 1839

Source Note

John A. Gordon on behalf of JS, Declaration, to Clay County Circuit Court, Liberty, Clay Co., MO, [ca. 6 Mar.] 1839, JS v. McLellin (Clay Co. Cir. Ct. 1839); handwriting probably of John A. Gordon; signature of John A. Gordon; two pages; Clay County Archives and Historical Library, Liberty, Missouri. Includes dockets.

Bifolium measuring 12½ × 7⅝ inches (32 × 19 cm), with thirty-five printed lines (now very faded) per page. The document was folded for filing. The verso of the second leaf includes several dockets in unidentified handwriting: "Joseph Smith Jr. | vs. | William E. McCLeland | Trespass on the case | Damage $500 | The clerk will issue | process"; "Sheriff fee $1.00 | 3rd Day"; "22 March"; and "1839." An "8"—likely an archival marking—is stamped on the verso. At some point, the leaves became separated.

---

366. Mary Fielding Smith later noted that "many false reports" circulated among the Saints in Illinois regarding the prisoners' release from jail. (Mary Fielding Smith, [Quincy, IL], to Hyrum Smith, 11 Apr. 1839, Mary Fielding Smith, Collection, CHL.)

367. See Letter from Edward Partridge, 5 Mar. 1839, pp. 329–331 herein.

368. See Book of Mormon, 1830 ed., 397 [Alma 60:25].

The declaration remained in the possession of the Clay County Circuit Court from March 1839 until circa 1979, when it was transferred to the Clay County Archives and Historical Library.[369]

Historical Introduction

In early March 1839, attorney John A. Gordon wrote a declaration on JS's behalf, initiating a civil lawsuit against William E. McLellin in the circuit court in Clay County, Missouri.[370] McLellin was one of the original apostles called in 1835; however, in May 1838 he confessed that "he had no confidence in the heads of the Church" and that he had stopped "praying and keeping the commandments." At this time, McLellin gave up his preaching license and withdrew from the church.[371] JS's declaration against McLellin alleges that on 1 September 1838 while in Clay County, McLellin obtained books, fabric, and other goods—worth a total of $500—belonging to JS. Although JS repeatedly asked McLellin to return the materials, the former apostle disposed of the items on 10 September.

The details of the situation are unclear. One possible scenario is that the items in question were goods being temporarily stored in Clay County—the location of a major Missouri River landing—prior to being moved to Caldwell County, Missouri.[372] These goods may have been inventory from stores that JS co-owned in Ohio or items purchased elsewhere.[373] However, aside from the March 1839 declaration, no evidence suggests that JS had such goods in Clay County on 1 September 1838.

Several sources describe a different scenario, in which McLellin ransacked JS's home in Caldwell County in early November 1838, when the state militia occupied the county and JS was in jail. One observer described McLellin as "the leader of a clan who went about from house to house, plundering the poor saints, and insulting both male and female."[374] According to James Mulholland, who was living with Emma Smith and the Smith children at the time, McLellin entered JS's home and stole linen, cashmere, but-

---

369. See Clay County Archives and Historical Library, "About Us."

370. Although the document does not use the word *declaration*, when Clay County sheriff Samuel Hadley executed the summons, he referred to the document as a declaration, and it follows the usual format for declarations. Land records show that McLellin purchased property in Caldwell County in late 1837. McLellin's wife, Emeline Miller McLellin, recalled that the family resided in Caldwell County for only a few months in 1838 before moving to Clay County, where the family had previously resided. The McLellins were apparently in Clay County by June 1838. (Summons, 6 Mar. 1839, JS v. McLellin [Clay Co. Cir. Ct. 1839], Clay County Archives and Historical Library, Liberty, MO; Johnson and Romig, *Index to Early Caldwell County, Missouri, Land Records,* 121; Porter, "Odyssey of William Earl McLellin," 323; [William E. McLellin], Editorial, *Ensign of Liberty,* Mar. 1847, 9.)

371. JS, Journal, 11 May 1838, in *JSP,* J1:268; Porter, "Odyssey of William Earl McLellin," 314–324.

372. Berrett, *Sacred Places,* 4:212–213; Woodson, *History of Clay County, Missouri,* 313. Latter-day Saint William Swartzell noted on 24 May 1838 that the Mormons primarily used the landing near Richmond, Ray County, Missouri, to receive goods. (Swartzell, *Mormonism Exposed,* 9.)

373. A May 1837 inventory of a store that JS co-owned in Chester, Ohio, listed items similar to those that McLellin allegedly took, including various types of tools, fabric, and buttons; books on history, geography, arithmetic, and Hebrew grammar; and a polyglot Bible. (Bill of Goods in Chester Store, 20 May 1837, JS Collection, CHL; see also Bill of Goods in Chester Store, 19–24 May 1837, JS Office Papers, CHL; and Notes Receivable from Chester Store, 22 May 1837, in *JSP,* D5:382–385.)

374. Ebenezer Page, Letter to the Editor, *Zion's Reveille,* 15 Apr. 1847, 55.

tons, books, a harness, and various other items; this list aligns with the declaration's list of stolen goods.[375] Phoebe Babcock Patten, widow of apostle David W. Patten, similarly accused McLellin of "plundering and Robbing" her home after "the surrender of arms" on 1 November. When Patten asked McLellin why he was acting "contrary to law," he allegedly responded that "there is no law now, but mob law."[376]

The declaration may have been intentionally vague regarding how McLellin acquired JS's goods because of the type of suit that Gordon initiated for JS—a trover—which permitted the plaintiff "to recover the value of personal chattels, wrongfully converted by another to his own use."[377] JS's suit may have been a transitory action, which does not require specifying the venue in which the theft occurred.[378] As explained in an influential nineteenth-century legal dictionary, "In a transitory action, the plaintiff may lay the venue in any county he pleases; that is, he may bring suit wherever he may find the defendant, and lay his cause of action to have arisen there, even though the cause of action arose in a foreign jurisdiction."[379] JS was therefore permitted to bring suit in Clay County, where both he and McLellin were living in March 1839. In cases that do not require the venue to be specified, the plaintiff is required to state the time of the event "in general" only. The exact timing is not considered material, which may explain why the declaration states that McLellin acquired JS's goods on 1 September 1838 rather than in November 1838.[380]

Following the required format for declarations, the document names the parties and the court, recites the allegations, identifies the type of suit, and specifies the damages the plaintiff sought.[381] In addition, per legal requirements, the declaration states that JS previously possessed the goods as his property and that McLellin allegedly acquired the goods improperly. Also as required by law, the declaration describes how McLellin allegedly converted the goods for his use.[382]

Gordon, who practiced law in Clay County, may have written the declaration in the upper room of the Clay County jail, where JS and his fellow prisoners were occasionally permitted to receive visitors.[383] Although Gordon did not date the declaration, he likely composed and submitted it by 6 March 1839, when the clerk of the Clay County Circuit Court issued a summons requiring McLellin to appear to answer the charges.[384] At the

---

375. James Mulholland et al., Complaint, [Far West, MO], Statements against William E. McLellin et al., CHL.

376. Phoebe Babcock Patten et al., Complaint against William E. McLellin, [Far West, MO], 1838, Statements against William E. McLellin et al., CHL; see also Butler, Autobiography, 26.

377. "Trover," in Bouvier, Law Dictionary, 2:454.

378. "Action," in Bouvier, Law Dictionary, 1:53.

379. "Venue," in Bouvier, Law Dictionary, 2:467.

380. "Declaration," in Bouvier, Law Dictionary, 1:293.

381. See "Declaration," in Bouvier, Law Dictionary, 1:293–294.

382. See "Trover," in Bouvier, Law Dictionary, 2:454–455; and Troubat and Haly, Practice in Civil Actions and Proceedings, 2:40–46.

383. History of Clay and Platte Counties, Missouri, 580; see also Alexander McRae, "Incidents in the History of Joseph Smith," Deseret News, 2 Nov. 1854, [1].

384. Summons, 6 Mar. 1839, JS v. McLellin (Clay Co. Cir. Ct. 1839), Clay County Archives and Historical Library, Liberty, MO.

April 1839 term of the Clay County Circuit Court, McLellin pleaded not guilty and filed a motion requiring JS to post security for the court costs. The court dismissed the suit on 21 August 1839 because JS, who by that time had escaped from custody, did not appear to post the security.[385]

Document Transcript

State of Missouri

Clay Circuit Court

Clay County to wit: April Term 1839[386]

Joseph Smith jr. complains of William E McCleland [McLellin] being in the custody of &c of a plea of trespass on the case.[387] For that whereas the said plaintiff heretofore to wit: on the first day of September in the year of our Lord eighteen hundred and thirty eight at the county of Clay aforesaid was lawfully possessed as of his own property of certain goods and chattles to wit of a Library of books part of which were in the Hebrew and Syriac languages the balance in the English language treating of history, divinty and general Literature twenty yards of broadcloth— ⟨20 yards of silk⟩ and forty yards of calico with various other articles of ⟨Great⟩ value to wit of the value of five hundred dollars lawful money of Missouri And being so possessed thereof he the said plaintiff afterterwards to wit on the day and year first above mentioned at the Clay county aforesaid casually lost the said library of books cloth calico and other articles out of his possession and the same afterwards to wit on the day and year last aforesaid at the county aforesaid came to the possession of the said defendant by finding.[388] Yet the said defendant well knowing the said library of books— cloth calico and other articles to be the property of the said plaintiff and of right to belong and [p. [1]] appertain to him but contriving and fraudulently intending craftily and and subtilly to deceive and defraud the said plaintiff in this behalf hath not as yet delivered the said library of books, cloth calico or other articles or any part thereof to the said plaintiff (although often requested so to do) but so to do hath hitherto wholly refused and still refuses, And afterwards to wit on the tenth day of September in the year eighteen hundred and thirty eight

---

385. Clay Co., MO, Circuit Court Records, 1822–1878, vol. 2, p. [279], 18 Apr. 1839; p. 298, 20 Apr. 1839; p. [315], 21 Aug. 1839, Clay County Archives and Historical Library, Liberty, MO.

386. The Clay County Circuit Court term was scheduled to start on 15 April 1839. (An Act to Establish a Judicial Circuit out of the Second and Fifth Judicial Circuits [31 Jan. 1839], *Laws of the State of Missouri* [1839], p. 34, sec. 5.)

387. "Trespass on the case" is a legal writ that permits an individual to sue for damages for wrongs committed. Trover is a specific type of trespass on the case. (See "Writ of Trespass on the Case," in Bouvier, *Law Dictionary*, 2:503–504.)

388. "Trover signifies finding." ("Trover," in Bouvier, *Law Dictionary*, 2:454.)

at the county of Clay aforesaid converted and disposed of the said library of books, cloth calico and other articles to his the said defendants own use to the damage of the said plaintiff of five hundred dollars and therefore he brings suit &c

J[ohn] A. Gordon
<u>At Pltff</u> [p. [2]]

———— ↻ ————

Letter from Emma Smith, 7 March 1839

Source Note

Emma Smith, Letter, Quincy, Adams Co., IL, to JS, Liberty, Clay Co., MO, 7 Mar. [1839]. Featured version copied [between 29 May and 30 Oct. 1839] in JS Letterbook 2, p. 37; handwriting of James Mulholland; JS Collection, CHL. For more information on JS Letterbook 2, see Source Notes for Multiple-Entry Documents, p. 566 herein.

Historical Introduction

On 7 March 1839, Emma Smith wrote the following letter to JS, who remained imprisoned in Missouri, updating him on her situation since her departure from Far West, Missouri, the previous month. Accompanied by Latter-day Saint Stephen Markham, Emma and her children left Far West on 7 February 1839 and arrived in Illinois in mid-February.[389] She and her children found lodging in the home of John and Sarah Kingsley Cleveland, about four miles east of Quincy, Illinois.[390] In late February or early March 1839, church leaders in Quincy decided to send important documents to JS, and family members of the prisoners were invited to send letters with the courier.[391] In this 7 March letter, which Emma likely wrote in the Clevelands' residence, she expressed her feelings upon leaving her imprisoned husband and described the sufferings of the Latter-day Saint refugees during their winter migration to Illinois.

Church leaders in Quincy chose Latter-day Saint David Rogers to deliver the letters and other documents to the Missouri prisoners. Rogers left Quincy on 10 March and arrived in Liberty on the evening of 19 March.[392] JS acknowledged receipt of his wife's letter and expressed profound gratitude for it in his 20 March 1839 general epistle to the church.[393] The following day, he wrote a personal response to her letter.[394] Emma Smith's original

---

389. Far West Committee, Minutes, 7 Feb. 1839; Historian's Office, JS History, Draft Notes, 6–7 and 15 Feb. 1839.

390. See 329n340 herein.

391. See Historical Introduction to Letter from Edward Partridge, 5 Mar. 1839, p. 328 herein.

392. Rogers, Statement, [1], CHL; Historical Introduction to Letter from Edward Partridge, 5 Mar. 1839, p. 328 herein.

393. Letter to the Church and Edward Partridge, 20 Mar. 1839, p. 365 herein.

394. See Letter to Emma Smith, 21 Mar. 1839, pp. 372–375 herein.

letter, which is apparently not extant, was copied into JS Letterbook 2 by James Mulholland between 29 May and 30 October 1839.[395]

Document Transcript

Quincy March 7th

Dear Husband

Having an opportunity to send by a friend I make an attempt to write, but I shall not attempt to write my feelings altogether, for the situation in which you are, the walls, bars, and bolts, rolling rivers, running streams, rising hills, sinking vallies and spreading prairies that separate us, and the cruel injustice that first cast you into prison and still holds you there,[396] with many other considerations, places my feelings far beyond description.

Was it not for conscious innocence, and the direct interposition of divine mercy, I am very sure I never should have been able to have endured the scenes of suffering that I have passed through, since what is called the Militia, came in to Far West, under the ever to be remembered Governor's notable order; an order fraught with as much wickedness as ignorance and as much ignorance as was ever contained in an article of that length;[397] but I still live and am yet willing to suffer more if it is the will of kind Heaven, that I should for your sake.

We are all well at present, except Fredrick who is quite sick.

Little Alexander who is now in my arms is one of the finest little fellows, you ever saw in your life, he is ⟨so⟩ strong that with the assistance of a chair he will run all round the room.

I am now living at Judge [John] Cleveland's four miles from the village of Quincy. I do not know how long I shall stay here. I want you to write an answer by the bearer. I left your change of clothes with H. C. Kimbal [Heber C. Kimball] when I came away, and he agreed to see that you had clean clothes as often as necessary.[398]

---

395. Mulholland copied his own 29 May 1839 letter to Edward Partridge on page 15 of JS Letterbook 2, making that the earliest likely copying date for documents he subsequently copied but that had dates preceding 29 May. For information on the latest likely copying date, see 248n440 herein.

396. For more information on the events leading to JS's arrest and imprisonment, see Introduction to Part 3: 4 Nov. 1838–16 Apr. 1839, pp. 265–271 herein.

397. For more information on the expulsion order that Missouri governor Lilburn W. Boggs issued on 27 October 1838 and the state militia's occupation of Far West, see Introduction to Part 3: 4 Nov. 1838–16 Apr. 1839, pp. 269–272 herein.

398. Whereas most of the Saints had left Missouri, Kimball was instructed to remain in Far West to assist the prisoners until their release. (Heber C. Kimball, Far West, MO, to Vilate Murray Kimball, Quincy, IL, 2 Apr. 1839, Heber C. Kimball, Collection, CHL; Alanson Ripley, Statements, ca. Jan. 1845, Historian's Office, JS History Documents, 1839–1860, CHL.)

No one but God, knows the reflections of my mind and the feelings of my heart when I left our house and home, and allmost all of every thing that we possessed excepting our little Children, and took my journey out of the State of Missouri, leaving you shut up in ~~jail~~ that lonesome prison. But the ~~reflection~~ recollection is more than human nature ought to bear, and if God does not record our sufferings and avenge our wrongs on them that are guilty,[399] I shall be sadly mistaken.

The daily sufferings of our brethren in travelling and camping out nights, and those on the other side of the river would beggar the most lively description.[400]

The people in this state are very kind indeed, they are doing much more than we ever anticipated they would;[401] I have many more things I could like to write but have not time and you may be astonished at my bad writing and incoherent manner, but you will pardon all when you reflect how hard it would be for you to write, when your hands were stiffened with hard work, and your heart convulsed with intense anxiety. But I hope there is better days to come to us yet, Give my respects to all in that place that you respect, and am ever your's affectionately.

Emma Smith

Joseph Smith Jr [p. 37]

———— ✧ ————

Petition to George Tompkins, between 9 and 15 March 1839

Source Note

Alanson Ripley, Heber C. Kimball, William Huntington, Joseph B. Noble, and JS, Petition, Liberty, Clay Co., MO, to George Tompkins, [Jefferson City, Cole Co., MO], between 9 and 15 Mar. 1839; handwriting of Alexander McRae, with insertions by Elias Smith and JS; signatures of Alanson Ripley, Heber C. Kimball, William Huntington, Joseph B. Noble, and JS; certified by Abraham Shafer, with additional signatures of Alanson Ripley, Heber C. Kimball, William Huntington, Joseph B. Noble (now missing), and JS (now missing); attestation [probably Far West, Caldwell Co., MO] by Elias Smith, with

---

399. See Romans 12:19.

400. Church members began leaving Far West in significant numbers in January and February 1839. They traveled through snow and other hazards, and upon reaching the Mississippi River, some found that they had to wait up to two weeks before the river thawed sufficiently to cross safely by boat. According to one estimate, as many as one hundred families camped on the Missouri side of the river in late February. (Hartley, "Saints' Forced Exodus from Missouri," 354–364; see also Introduction to Part 3: 4 Nov. 1838–16 Apr. 1839, pp. 275–276 herein.)

401. The citizens of Quincy provided temporary shelter, basic assistance, and employment for the Mormon refugees. (See Bennett, "Study of the Mormons in Quincy," 88–95; and Hartley, "Saints' Forced Exodus from Missouri," 366–370.)

additional signatures of Amasa Lyman, Henry G. Sherwood, James Newberry, Cyrus Daniels, and Erastus Snow; seven pages; JS Collection, CHL. Includes dockets.

Two bifolia measuring 12⅛ × 7½ inches (31 × 19 cm). Alexander McRae inscribed the petition on the first bifolium and the first leaf of the second bifolium. Justice of the Peace Abraham Shafer then wrote a certification on the verso of the first leaf of the second bifolium. The petition was folded for carrying, and Alexander McRae docketed it. Elias Smith then inscribed the attestation on the recto of the second leaf of the second bifolium, probably in Far West, Missouri. The second bifolium was then refolded and docketed again in unidentified handwriting. Subsequently, JS's signature on the verso of the first leaf of the second bifolium was removed and Joseph B. Noble's signature was partially removed. The two leaves of the second bifolium became separated at a later time. The document has marked brittleness and separation at the folds.

The petition was carried to Jefferson City, Missouri, twice—in late March and early April 1839—by Latter-day Saints intent on submitting the petition to the Missouri Supreme Court. Both times, the court rejected the petition, and the lack of official filing notations suggests that the court never assumed custody of the document. The petition was then apparently taken to Illinois, where it likely served as the source text for two copies of the petition made by church members in Illinois in 1839. The document evidently left the church's possession soon thereafter.[402] Wilford Wood, a collector of manuscripts and artifacts related to the LDS church, acquired the petition in the mid-twentieth century and subsequently donated it to the Church Historian's Office.[403]

Historical Introduction

In mid-March 1839, JS and his fellow prisoners sought release from the Clay County jail in Liberty, Missouri, by petitioning the Missouri Supreme Court for writs of habeas corpus, a common law writ. When a writ of habeas corpus is issued, the officer (usually a sheriff or jailer) who has custody of the prisoner must bring the prisoner before the court, with the judge examining whether the incarceration is legal.[404]

---

402. James Sloan copied the featured version of the petition sometime between late April 1839 (when the petition likely arrived in Illinois from Missouri) and early June 1839. Sloan's copy was apparently included in a package of documents that John P. Greene took with him when he left Quincy, Illinois, on 5 June 1839 with an assignment to collect donations for Latter-day Saint refugees. Greene published the documents—including Sloan's copy of the petition—later that month in Cincinnati, Ohio.[a] Additionally, James Mulholland copied the featured version into JS Letterbook 2 sometime between 29 May and 30 October 1839.[b] (*a.* JS et al., Petition, Liberty, MO, between 9 and 15 Mar. 1839, copy, JS Collection, CHL; Historical Introduction to Letter from John P. Greene, 30 June 1839, p. 513 herein; Greene, *Facts relative to the Expulsion,* 31–33. *b.* JS et al., Petition, Liberty, MO, ca. 15 Mar. 1839, in JS Letterbook 2, pp. 21–24; see also 339n395 herein.)

403. A typescript note in the document's file in the Joseph Smith Collection states the document came from Wood. In 1937 he purchased from Charles Bidamon (Emma Smith's stepson) several historically significant documents, including two petitions that had belonged to JS. The church later purchased some of the Bidamon documents from Wood, possibly including the petition featured here. (Wilford C. Wood, Statement, Wilmette, IL, 10 July 1937, reel 16, fd. 7-J-b-2; David O. McKay to Arthur Winter, 21 July 1937, reel 16, fd. 7-J-b-2, Wilford C. Wood Collection of Church Historical Materials, CHL; see also "Documents Obtained by Wilford Wood," *Deseret News,* 21 July 1937, 13.)

404. "Habeas Corpus," in Bouvier, *Law Dictionary,* 1:454–456; Walker, "Habeas Corpus in Early Nineteenth-Century Mormonism," 5–8.

In January 1839, the prisoners petitioned Justice Joel Turnham of the Clay County court for a writ of habeas corpus, resulting in a hearing on 22 January. For unclear reasons, Turnham released Rigdon on bail on 30 January 1839; the justice remanded the remaining prisoners to the Clay County jail. Subsequently, the prisoners tried to escape. In early February, Hyrum Smith attempted to flee the jail when the door was left open, but he was quickly recaptured. In early March, the prisoners tried to dig through the dungeon walls, but when they sought outside help, the plot was discovered.[405]

Following the failed attempt to escape in March 1839, the Latter-day Saint prisoners opted to again pursue a writ of habeas corpus. On 9 March, Hyrum Smith wrote a petition to Judge Austin A. King, but the prisoners apparently did not submit the petition.[406] Rather, they decided to write individual petitions directed to the Missouri Supreme Court in mid-March 1839.[407] Since JS's petition is undated, it is uncertain when it was written. Many of the document's arguments were first articulated in Hyrum Smith's 9 March petition, suggesting that JS started his petition on that date or soon after.[408] JS's petition was completed by 15 March at the latest, when Clay County justice of the peace Abraham Shafer certified it.

Alexander McRae, one of the prisoners, served as scribe for the version featured here, which contains errors normally associated with copying, suggesting that he worked from an earlier draft. JS's petition is written in the first-person plural, with JS and four other Latter-day Saints cosigning the document. JS perhaps believed that including the signatures of multiple individuals swearing to the truth of the facts in the petition would strengthen his arguments. At the beginning of the featured version, McRae named Alanson Ripley, Heber C. Kimball, Daniel Shearer, William Huntington, and Jenkins Salisbury as the petition's cosigners, apparently expecting these men would visit the jail to sign the petition.[409] However, when Ripley, Kimball, and Huntington, along with Joseph B. Noble, visited the jail on 15 March, they were not accompanied by Shearer and Salisbury.[410] Therefore, Shearer's and Salisbury's names were crossed out, and Noble's name was added. Whether Ripley, Kimball, Huntington, and Noble contributed anything to JS's petition, other than their signatures, is unknown.

The prisoners apparently received little or no assistance from their attorneys in preparing this and other March petitions, relying instead on the Missouri habeas corpus statute

---

405. See Introduction to Part 3: 4 Nov. 1838–16 Apr. 1839, pp. 276–277 herein.

406. Hyrum Smith, Petition, Liberty, MO, 9 Mar. 1839, CHL.

407. Hyrum Smith, Petition, Liberty, MO, 15 Mar. 1839, CHL; Lyman Wight, Petition, Liberty, MO, 15 Mar. 1839, CHL; Caleb Baldwin, Petition, Liberty, MO, 15 Mar. 1839, CHL; Alexander McRae, Petition, Liberty, MO, 15 Mar. 1839, CHL.

408. Hyrum Smith, Petition, Liberty, MO, 9 Mar. 1839, CHL.

409. As Ripley later recalled, he and Kimball were "appointed by the church to visit the Brethren as often as possible who were in jail at liberty and also to importune at the feet of the judges" for the release of the prisoners. (Alanson Ripley, Statements, ca. Jan. 1845, Historian's Office, JS History Documents, 1839–1860, CHL; see also Heber C. Kimball, Far West, MO, to Vilate Murray Kimball, Quincy, IL, 2 Apr. 1839, Heber C. Kimball, Collection, CHL.)

410. In his diary, Hyrum Smith named Ripley, Kimball, Huntington, Noble, and Buell as the only visitors to the jail on 15 March 1839. (Hyrum Smith, Diary, 15 Mar. 1839.)

as a guide.[411] As required by the statute, JS's petition identifies JS as the person unlawfully imprisoned, the Missouri Supreme Court as the court to grant the writ, King as the judge who incarcerated the petitioner, and the Clay County jail as the location of imprisonment. The petition also includes facts concerning the imprisonment, claims of procedural irregularities that occurred during the November 1838 hearing, and substantive reasons that JS should not be charged with treason.[412]

Once McRae completed the version featured here, JS made minor changes to the text, mostly restoring words that McRae inadvertently omitted as he copied. Then Ripley, Kimball, Huntington, Noble, and JS signed the document, after which Justice Shafer certified the petition.[413] Shafer probably visited the jail to certify the document since the prisoners were likely not permitted to leave the jail given their recent escape attempts.[414] Following the certification, Ripley, Kimball, Huntington, Noble, and JS signed the document again. Ripley then carried JS's petition to Far West, where it was read by the church committee charged with overseeing the Saints' departure from the state. Committee member Elias Smith drafted an attestation—a statement affirming the truth of the facts given—which he then signed along with Amasa Lyman, Henry G. Sherwood, James Newberry, Cyrus Daniels, and Erastus Snow. Perhaps at this time, Elias Smith corrected the cosigners' names on the recto of the first leaf, canceling Shearer's and Salisbury's names and adding Noble's and JS's names.

On 18 March, the removal committee appointed Kimball and Theodore Turley to take the prisoners' petitions to the Missouri Supreme Court in Jefferson City.[415] Attorney Alexander Doniphan evidently gave Kimball and Turley a letter of introduction, but Clay County sheriff and jailer Samuel Hadley apparently refused to give them a copy of the mittimus—King's incarceration order from 29 November 1838—which, according to law, had to accompany petitions for writs of habeas corpus.[416] The supreme court judges—Mathias McGirk, George Tompkins, and John C. Edwards—"seemed to be friendly" to Kimball and Turley but ultimately would not accept the petitions "in conseqence of a lack of the order of Commitment."[417] Kimball and Turley subsequently

---

411. Letter to the Church and Edward Partridge, 20 Mar. 1839, pp. 364–365 herein. Hyrum Smith made notes on the habeas corpus statute in the back of his diary. (Hyrum Smith, Diary, CHL.)

412. An Act to Regulate Proceedings on Writs of Habeas Corpus [6 Mar. 1835], *Revised Statutes of the State of Missouri* [1835], p. 297, art. 1, secs. 1–3; see also Madsen, "Joseph Smith and the Missouri Court of Inquiry," 102–115.

413. Missouri law required petitions to "be verified by the oath of the applicant, or some other competent person," such as a justice of the peace. (An Act to Regulate Proceedings on Writs of Habeas Corpus [6 Mar. 1835], *Revised Statutes of the State of Missouri* [1835], p. 297, art. 1, sec. 4.)

414. William T. Wood, an attorney living in Clay County, recalled that the prisoners were occasionally permitted to leave the jail under supervision of a guard. However, as JS noted in his 15 March 1839 letter to Presendia Huntington Buell, the Clay County jailer was especially vigilant following the prisoners' escape attempt in early March. (William T. Wood, "Mormon Memoirs," *Liberty [MO] Tribune,* 9 Apr. 1886, [1]; Letter to Presendia Huntington Buell, 15 Mar. 1839, p. 354 herein.)

415. Far West Committee, Minutes, 17–18 Mar. 1839.

416. Theodore Turley, Memoranda, ca. Feb. 1845, Historian's Office, JS History Documents, 1839–1860, CHL; An Act to Regulate Proceedings on Writs of Habeas Corpus [6 Mar. 1835], *Revised Statutes of the State of Missouri* [1835], p. 297, art. 1, sec. 5.

417. Hyrum Smith, Diary, 30 Mar. 1839; see also Theodore Turley, Memoranda, ca. Feb. 1845, Historian's

met with King, and Kimball later recalled that the judge "was mad at us, for presenting his illegal papers to the Supreme Judges: he treated us very roughly."[418] Based on this meeting, however, King apparently instructed Sheriff Hadley to give Kimball and Turley a copy of the mittimus.[419] In early April, JS sent Erastus Snow to Jefferson City, presumably with JS's petition, the petitions of the other prisoners, and the copy of the mittimus. "I saw the Judges," Snow noted, "but they would do nothing about it." Snow did not give the judges' reasons for rejecting the petitions.[420] Although the March petitions for writs of habeas corpus were not granted, JS and the other prisoners remained in the Clay County jail only a few more weeks. On 6 April 1839, they were moved to Gallatin, Missouri, to appear before the Daviess County Circuit Court.[421]

Document Transcript

/[422]To the honorable Judge [George] Thompkins ~~of~~ or either of the Judges of the supream court for the state of Missouri.

Your petitioners Alanson Ripl[e]y Heber C. ~~Kim~~ Kimble [Kimball] ~~Daniel Shearer~~ ⟨Joseph B. Noble⟩[423] William [D.] Huntington ~~Jinkins Salsbury~~ [blank] ⟨& Joseph Smith jr⟩[424] beg leave respectfully to represent to your honor that Joseph Smith Jr is now unlawfully confined and restrained of his liberty in Liberty jail Clay County (Mo) that he has been restrained of his liberty near five months your petitioners clame that the whole transaction which has been the cause of his confinement ~~was~~ ⟨is⟩ unlawfull from the first to the Last he was taken from his home by a fraude being practised upon him by a man by the name of George M Hinkle and one or two others thereby your petitioner ~~was forced~~ respectfully show that he was forced contrary to his wishes and without knowing the cause into the camp which was commanded by General Lucus [Robert Lucas] of Jackson County[425] and

---

Office, JS History Documents, 1839–1860, CHL; and Heber C. Kimball, Far West, MO, to Vilate Murray Kimball, Quincy, IL, 2 Apr. 1839, Heber C. Kimball, Collection, CHL. Tompkins (1780–1846) served on the Missouri Supreme Court from 1824 until 1845; McGirk (ca. 1783–1842), from 1821 to 1841; and Edwards (1804–1888), from 1837 to 1839. (Bay, *Reminiscences of the Bench and Bar of Missouri*, 30–31, 536–537; Ellsberry, *Cemetery Records of Montgomery County, Missouri*, 1:41; *Biographical Directory of the United States Congress, 1774–2005*, 1005.)

418. Kimball, "History," 99.

419. See Mittimus, Richmond, MO, 29 Nov. 1838, State of Missouri v. JS et al. for Treason and Other Crimes (Mo. 5th Jud. Cir. 1838), JS Collection, CHL.

420. Snow, Journal, 1838–1841, 47–48. According to Missouri law, courts could not grant writs of habeas corpus for nonbailable offenses, such as treason. (An Act to Regulate Proceedings on Writs of Habeas Corpus [6 Mar. 1835], *Revised Statutes of the State of Missouri* [1835], p. 297, art. 1, sec. 6.)

421. Hyrum Smith, Diary, 6 Apr. 1839.

422. TEXT: Alexander McRae handwriting begins.

423. TEXT: Cancellation and insertion in the handwriting of Elias Smith.

424. TEXT: Cancellation and insertion in the handwriting of Elias Smith.

425. For more information on Hinkle and the role of his delegation in JS's arrest, see Introduction

from thence to Ray County sleeping on the ground and suffering many insults and inguries and deprivations which were calculated in there natures to brake ⟨**down**⟩[426] the spirits and constitution of the most robust and hardy of mankind he was put in chains imediatly on his being landed in Richmund and there underwent a long and tedious expartie examination[427] not only was it expartie but your petitioners solemly declair that it was a mock examination that there was not the least shaddow of honor or justice or law administered to ward him but Shear prejudice and the Spirit of persecution and malice and prepossision against him on account of his religeon that the whole examination was an inquisatory examination your petitioners show that the said Joseph Smith jr was deprived of the privilage of being examined before the [p. [1]] court as the ⟨law⟩ directs[428] that the witnesses on the part of the State were taken by force of armes and thereatned [threatened] with extermination imediate Death and were brought without subpoena[429] or warent under this awfull and glaring anticipation of being exterminated if they did not swear something against ~~your petitioner~~ ⟨him⟩ to please the mob or his pirsecuters and those ~~persecuters~~ witnesses were compeled to swear at the musil [muzzle] of the gun and that some of them have ackno[w]ledged since

---

to Part 3: 4 Nov. 1838–16 Apr. 1839, pp. 270–271 herein.

426. TEXT: Insertion in the handwriting of JS.

427. An *ex parte* examination is one-sided, with evidence presented on behalf of only one party. Of the hearing, Latter-day Saint Morris Phelps recounted, "I was soon called on [to be] a witness on the part of the mob. In giving in my testimony I was sworn in I was first stop[p]ed by the prosecuting At[t]orney then by the Judge saying to me we do not want to here [hear] any testimony on that side of the question (meaning in favor of Joseph & Hyrum Smith and others of the prisenors)." ("Ex parte," in Bouvier, *Law Dictionary*, 1:384; Phelps, Reminiscences, 1.)

428. Missouri magistrates were required by law to inform the accused of the charges against him or her, to state that the prisoner had the right "to refuse to answer any question," and to permit the defendant to consult with an attorney before answering. The magistrate was then required to examine the defendant "without oath, in relation to the offence charged," and without any prosecution or defense witnesses present. The defendant's testimony was then required to be committed to writing and made subject to his or her review for accuracy. According to the hearing record, after the prosecution finished examining its witnesses, "the Court informed the prisoners that it would now proceed to take their examination without oath in relation to the offences charged, and the said Defendents declined making any statement." (An Act to Regulate Proceedings in Criminal Cases [21 Mar. 1835], *Revised Statutes of the State of Missouri* [1835], p. 476, art. 2, secs. 13–17; Trial Proceedings, Richmond, MO, Nov. 1838, p. [114], State of Missouri v. JS et al. for Treason and Other Crimes [Mo. 5th Jud. Cir. 1838], in State of Missouri, "Evidence.")

429. JS may not have been aware that King issued subpoenas for at least some witnesses. (Subpoena, Richmond, MO, for Porter Yale and Stephen Yale, 11 Nov. 1838, photocopy; Subpoena, Richmond, MO, for Henry Wood et al., 15 Nov. 1838, photocopy, State of Missouri v. JS et al. for Treason and Other Crimes [Mo. 5th Jud. Cir. 1838], Daviess Co., MO, Legal Documents, BYU; Subpoena, Richmond, MO, for James Blakely et al., 21 Nov. 1838, State of Missouri v. JS et al. for Treason and Other Crimes [Mo. 5th Jud. Cir. 1838], CHL; George M. Hinkle, Buffalo, Iowa Territory, to William W. Phelps, Nauvoo, IL, 14 Aug. 1844, in *Ensign*, Aug. 1844, 31.)

which your petitio[n]ers[430] do testify and are able to prove that they did swear fals and that they did it in order to save ~~there~~ their lives and your petitioners testify that all the testimony that had any tendancy or bearing of criminality against said Joseph Smith Jr ⟨is fals⟩[431] we are personly acquainted with the circumstances and being with him most of the time and being presant at the times spoken ~~by~~ of by them therefore we know that ~~there~~ their testimony was fals and if he could have had a fair and impartial and lawfull examination before that Court and could have been allowed the privilidge of interducing [introducing] his witnesses ⟨he could have disproved evry thing that was against him⟩ but the Court suffered him to be intimodated ⟨~~he could have disaproved evry thing that was against him~~⟩ some of them in the presants of the Court and they were driven also and hunted and some of them intirly [entirely] driven out of the State[432] and thus ~~your petitioner~~ ⟨he was⟩[433] not able to have a fair tryal that the spirit of the Court was tryranicle [tyrannical] and overbearing and the whole transaction of his treatment during ~~his~~ the examination was calculated to ~~convinced~~ your petitioners that it was a religeous persecution proscribing him in the liberty of consience which is garenteed to him by the Constitution of the United States and the State of Missouri[434] that a long catalogue of garbled testimony was permited by the Court perporting to be the religeous sentiment of the said Joseph Smith Jr, which testimony was false and your petitioners know that it was false and can prove also that it was false because the [p. [2]] witnesses testified that those sentiments were promulged[435] on surtain days and in the presants of large Congrigations and your petitioners can ⟨prove⟩ by those congrations that the said Joseph Smith Jr did not promulge such ridiculas and absurd sentiments for his religon as was ~~testify~~ testified of and admited before the honorable Austin. A. King. and at the same time those things had ~~not~~ bearing on the case that the said Joseph Smith Junior was ⟨pretended⟩ ~~said~~[436] be Charged with[437] and after the

---

430. TEXT: "petitio[*page torn*]ers".

431. TEXT: Insertion in the handwriting of JS.

432. For more information on the defense witnesses, see Introduction to Part 3: 4 Nov. 1838–16 Apr. 1839, pp. 273–274 herein.

433. TEXT: Cancellation and insertion in the handwriting of JS.

434. U.S. Constitution, amend. 1; Missouri Constitution of 1820, art. 13, sec. 4.

435. An archaic form of *promulgate*. ("Promulge," in *American Dictionary*.)

436. TEXT: Insertion and cancellation in the handwriting of JS.

437. JS and his fellow petitioners were perhaps referring to the testimonies of several witnesses regarding Mormon interpretations of the kingdom of God and Daniel chapters 1–7. George M. Hinkle, for example, stated that "the general teachings of the presidency were that the Kingdom they were setting up, was a temporal as well as a Spiritual Kingdom—that it was the little stone spoken of by Daniel . . . that the time had come when this Kingdom was to be set up by forcible means, if necessary." Hinkle also noted that "it was taught the times had come when the riches of the Gentiles were to be conse-

examination the said prisoner was committed to the ~~gail~~ jail for treason against the state of Missouri where as the said Joseph Smith Jr did not levy war against the state of Missouri neither did he commit any overt acts neither did he aid or abet an~y~ enemy against the State of Missouri during the time that he is charged with having done so[438] and further your petitioners have yet to learn that the State has an enimy neither is the proof evident nor the presumtion ~~grate~~ great in its most malignant form upon the face of the testimony on the part of the ⟨**State**⟩[439] expartee as it is in its nature that the said prisoner ⟨**has**⟩[440] ~~has not~~ committed the slightest degree of treason or any other act of transgression against the laws of the state of ~~the MO~~ Missouri and yet said prisoner has been committed to Liberty jail Clay County (Mo) for treason he has continually offered bail to any amount that could be required[441] not withstanding your petitioners alledge that he ought to have been acquited your petitioners also alledges that the commitment was ⟨an⟩ illegal commitment for the law requires that a coppy of the testimony should be put in the hands of the jailor which was not done[442] your petitioners alledge that the prisoner has been denied the privilage of the law in a writ of habeas corpus by the judges of this county whether they have prejudged the [p. [3]] case of the prisoner or whither they are not willing to administer law and justice to the prisoner or that they are intimidated by the high office of judge King who only acted in the case of the prisoners as a committing magistrate a consurvitor of the peace or by the threats of a lawless mob your petitioners are not able to say[443] but it is a fact

---

crated to the true Israel," referring to a revelation dictated by JS on 9 February 1831. (George M. Hinkle, Testimony, Richmond, MO, Nov. 1838, p. [42]; John Corrill, Testimony, Richmond, MO, Nov. 1838, p. [31]; Robert Snodgrass, Testimony, Richmond, MO, Nov. 1838, p. [35], in State of Missouri, "Evidence"; Revelation, 9 Feb. 1831, in *JSP*, D1:252 [D&C 42:39]; see also Whittaker, "Book of Daniel in Early Mormon Thought," 155–199.)

438. Both the United States and the Missouri constitutions define *treason* as levying war, which involves either committing an overt act against the government or giving aid and comfort to enemies of the state. (See Introduction to Part 3: 4 Nov. 1838–16 Apr. 1839, p. 273 herein.)

439. TEXT: Insertion in the handwriting of JS.

440. TEXT: Cancellation and insertion in the handwriting of JS.

441. Because treason was a nonbailable offense, Judge King had committed JS and his fellow prisoners to the Clay County jail to await their trials in spring 1839. (See Introduction to Part 3: 4 Nov. 1838–16 Apr. 1839, p. 274 herein.)

442. In cases wherein defendents were committed to prison for nonbailable offenses, Missouri law required magistrates to deliver to the jailer the warrant of commitment and a certified copy of the prisoners' and the witnesses' testimonies. (An Act to Regulate Proceedings in Criminal Cases [21 Mar. 1835], *Revised Statutes of the State of Missouri* [1835], p. 477, art. 2, sec. 29.)

443. Peter Burnett recalled that considerable opposition existed in Clay County regarding Turnham's decision to issue the writ of habeas corpus, with some contending that Turnham, as a county judge, could not review the ruling of King, the circuit judge. Missouri law permitted any "court of record in term," judges of the supreme or circuit courts, and "any justice of the county court" to receive petitions for writs of habeas

that they do not come forword boldly and administer the law to the relief of the prisoner and further your petitioners alledge that imidiately after the prisoner was taken his family was frightened and driven out of their house and that too by the witnesses on the part of the state ~~your petitioners respectfully show~~ and plundered of their goods that the prisoner was rob[b]ed of a verry fine horse Saddle and bridle and other property of conciderable amount[444] that they (the witnesses) in conection with the mob have finally succeeded by vile threatning and foul abuse in driving the family of the prisoner out of the State with little or no means[445] and without a protector and ~~there~~ their verry subsistance depends on the liberty of the prisoner[446] and your petitioners alledge that he is not guilty of any crime whereby he should be restrained of his liberty from a pursonal knoledge having been with him and being personly acquainted with the whole of the difficulties betwean the mormons and their pursicuters and that he has never acted at any time only in his own defence and that two on his own ground property and possisions that the prisoner has never ⟨**commanded**⟩[447] any military company nor held any military authority neither any other office real or pretended in the state of Missouri except that of a religeous teacher[448] that he never has born armes in the military ranks and in all such cases has acted as a private

---

corpus. Turnham "would do whatever he determined to do in defiance of all opposition." In contrast, Doniphan apparently told Lyman Wight that the judge "remanded [the prisoners] for fear he should offend Judge King." Furthermore, Turnham's assistant Meacham Curtis remembered the judge stating that "he would have acquitted the prisoners" if not "for fear that they would be assassinated by a furious mob." (Burnett, *Recollections and Opinions,* 54–55; An Act to Regulate Proceedings on Writs of Habeas Corpus [6 Mar. 1835], *Revised Statutes of the State of Missouri* [1835], p. 297, art. 1, sec. 2; Lyman Wight, Journal, in *History of the Reorganized Church,* 2:323; Meacham Curtis, Affidavit, Bandera, TX, 23 July 1878, in *Saints' Herald,* 15 Aug. 1878, 256.)

444. In a deposition Emma Smith made for an 1842 lawsuit against George M. Hinkle, she stated that following JS's 31 October 1838 arrest, Hinkle entered the Smiths' home in Far West and stole "a Horse, Saddle, Bridle Martingales & two Horse Blankets," as well as dry goods, clothing, and furniture, valued at $400. She also reported that Hinkle, who testified against JS in November 1838, "used Coersive measures to drive Witness [Emma Smith] and her Family therefrom, the Premises & House." (Emma Smith, Deposition, Nauvoo, IL, 22 Apr. 1842, JS v. George M. Hinkle [Lee Co. Dist. Ct. 1842], CHL.)

445. Emma Smith left Far West on 7 February 1839 for Quincy, Illinois. (Historian's Office, JS History, Draft Notes, 6–7 Feb. 1839; Far West Committee, Minutes, 7 Feb. 1839; see also Letter from Emma Smith, 7 Mar. 1839, pp. 339–340 herein.)

446. JS's petition may have drawn upon language from his brother's petition. Hyrum Smith, in his 9 March 1839 petition for a writ of habeas corpus, stated that "the family of your petitioner has been robbed of many of theyr valuable effects and have been obliged to leave the state without a protector or without a knowledge of where to go or without means of subsistance." (Hyrum Smith, Petition, Liberty, MO, 9 Mar. 1839, CHL.)

447. TEXT: Insertion in the handwriting of JS.

448. Hyrum Smith's 9 March 1839 petition also indicated "that he never has done military service nor commanded anny company at any time but has lawfully ben Exempt from all sutch service in all his life time." (Hyrum Smith, Petition, Liberty, MO, 9 Mar. 1839, CHL.)

charactor and as an individual how then ⟨**can**⟩[449] your petitioners would ask can it be posible that the prisoner has committed treason the prisoner has had nothing to do in Davis County only on his own buisines as an individual[450] ~~that this council testifyed of~~ that the testimony of Doctor Avard concerning a councyl held at James Slowns was false[451] your petitioners do solomly declair that there was no such councyl that your petitioners [p. [4]] ware with the prisoner and there was no such vote nor conversastion as Doctor Avard swore too[452] that Doctor Avard also swore false concerning a constitution as he said was introduced among the danit[e]s[453] that the prisoner had nothing to do with burning[454] in Davis County[455] that the prisoner made publick proclimation against such

---

449. TEXT: Insertion in the handwriting of JS.

450. In his 9 March 1839 petition, Hyrum Smith similarly stated "that he only went to Davis County to preserve his property from being destroyed by the mob." JS later stated that he went to Daviess County in October 1838 in part to protect his own property. (Hyrum Smith, Petition, Liberty, MO, 9 Mar. 1839, CHL; Bill of Damages, 4 June 1839, pp. 498–499 herein.)

451. Hyrum Smith, in his 9 March 1839 petition, similarly stated "that he knew nothing of the Council spoken of by Docttor arverd [Sampson Avard] in Cald weld [Caldwell] County nor in Davis County at James Sloans." JS evidently stayed at James Sloan's boarding house when visiting Daviess County. (Hyrum Smith, Petition, Liberty, MO, 9 Mar. 1839, CHL; Johnson, "A Life Review," 31.)

452. Sampson Avard claimed he was present at a council meeting held in Daviess County on 17 October 1838 during which JS instructed several church leaders that they should defend their rights "and that we should be free & Independent. and that as the state of Missouri & the U[nited] states would not protect us. It was time then we should rise as the saints of the most high God & protect ourselves & take the Kingdom. . . . he considered the U states rotten [and] he compared the Mormon church to the little stone spoken of by the Prop^t Daniel." According to Avard, JS also said that "the state . . . should be destroyed by this little stone." The council then voted unanimously to approve the measures. (Sampson Avard, Testimony, Richmond, MO, Nov. 1838, pp. [6]–[7], in State of Missouri, "Evidence.")

453. Avard testified that the constitution was created soon after the Danites were organized in June 1838 and that JS and Rigdon "adopted" the document "as their rule & guide in future." It was then read "article by article to the Danite band and unanimously adopted by them." John Corrill and John Cleminson, both of whom attended early meetings of the society, later testified that they had no memory of hearing the constitution being read to the group. (Sampson Avard, Testimony, Richmond, MO, Nov. 1838, p. [9]; John Corrill, Testimony, Richmond, MO, Nov. 1838, p. [34]; John Cleminson, Testimony, Richmond, MO, Nov. 1838, p. [54], in State of Missouri, "Evidence"; Constitution of the Society of the Daughter of Zion, ca. Late June 1838, at josephsmithpapers.org.)

454. In Hyrum Smith's 9 March 1839 petition, he stated "that he knew nothing of the burning in Davies County nor the plundering only by report." (Hyrum Smith, Petition, Liberty, MO, 9 Mar. 1839, CHL.)

455. During the October 1838 conflict in Daviess County, Latter-day Saint vigilantes set fire to buildings believed to be used by their enemies. Although no witnesses at the November 1838 hearing alleged that JS directly participated in these activities, several stated that he directed the expeditions from Adam-ondi-Ahman. Two witnesses claimed they saw JS observing from a distance as a house in Millport burned. In April 1839, a Daviess County grand jury named JS in two arson indictments stemming from the burnings in Gallatin and Millport. (Introduction to Part 3: 4 Nov. 1838–16 Apr. 1839, pp. 265–266 herein; Sampson Avard, Testimony, Richmond, MO, Nov. 1838, p. [7]; George M. Hinkle, Testimony, Richmond, MO, Nov. 1838, p. [39]; John Cleminson, Testimony, Richmond, MO, Nov. 1838, pp. [52], [54]; Charles Blakely, Testimony, Richmond, MO, Nov. 1838, p. [78]; James Cobb, Testimony, Richmond, MO,

things that the prisoner did oppose Doctor Avard and George M Hinkle against vile measures with the mob[456] but was threatned by them if he did not let them alone that the prisoner did not have any thing to do with what is called Bogarts Battle for he knew nothing ~~to do with~~ of it untill it was all over that he was at home and in the bosome of his own family during the time of that whole transaction[457] and in fine your petitioner alledge that he is held in confinement without cause and under an unlawfull and tyranicle oppression and that his health and constitution and life depends on being liberated from his confinement[458] your petitioners aver that they can disprove evry item of testimony that has any tendency of criminality against the prisoner for they know it themselvs and can bring many others also to prove the same therefore your petitioners prays your ⟨**honor**⟩[459] to grant to him the states writ of habeus Corpus directed to the jailor of Clay county (Mo)[460] commanding him forthwith to bring before you the body of the prisoner so that his case may be heard before your honor and the situationed of the prisoner be concidered and adjusted according to law and justice as it shall be pressented before your honor and as in duty bound your petitioners will

---

Nov. 1838, p. [79], in State of Missouri, "Evidence"; Baugh, "Call to Arms," 190–206; Indictment, [Honey Creek Township, MO], ca. 10 Apr. 1839, State of Missouri v. Gates et al. for Arson [Daviess Co. Cir. Ct. 1839], microfilm 959,084, U.S. and Canada Record Collection, FHL; Indictment, [Honey Creek Township, MO], ca. 10 Apr. 1839, State of Missouri v. Baldwin et al. for Arson [Daviess Co. Cir. Ct. 1839], Historical Department, Nineteenth-Century Legal Documents Collection, CHL.)

456. Sampson Avard admitted in his November 1838 testimony that he was removed as a Danite general and assigned to work as a surgeon. The reassignment may have resulted from Danite officers' opposition to Avard's teachings that the society would "waste away the Gentiles [non-Mormons] by robbing and plundering them of their property" in order to "build up the Kingdom of God." According to Morris Phelps, this opposition caused Avard to lose his influence among church leaders and the general church membership. No extant evidence suggests that Hinkle advocated harsh measures against vigilantes. Hinkle claimed that during the Daviess County expedition in October, he attempted to persuade JS to use his influence to stop the burning and plundering but that JS argued there was no other way to stop the vigilantes. (Sampson Avard, Testimony, Richmond, MO, Nov. 1838, p. [6]; George M. Hinkle, Testimony, Richmond, MO, Nov. 1838, pp. [38]–[39], in State of Missouri, "Evidence"; Phelps, Reminiscences, 7–9.)

457. Upon receiving word of the 25 October 1838 skirmish at Crooked River two miles south of the Caldwell County border, JS left Far West to pray over and to bless the wounded. At the November 1838 hearing, JS was not implicated in Rowland's death, but a Ray County grand jury later named him as an accessory to the murder for helping those who were directly involved in the skirmish to escape. (See Introduction to Part 3: 4 Nov. 1838–16 Apr. 1839, p. 269 herein; and 304n185 herein.)

458. In his 9 March 1839 petition, Hyrum Smith stated "that his health is fast declining in consequence of his confinement and his verry life depends upon your honors giving him his liberty." (Hyrum Smith, Petition, Liberty, MO, 9 Mar. 1839, CHL.)

459. TEXT: Insertion in the handwriting of JS.

460. Likely Samuel Hadley, who was the Clay County sheriff and jailer, or Samuel Tillery, who was the deputy jailer. (Mittimus, Richmond, MO, 29 Nov. 1838, State of Missouri v. JS et al. for Treason and Other Crimes [Mo. 5th Jud. Cir. 1838], JS Collection, CHL; Woodson, History of Clay County, Missouri, 333.)

ever p[ray. And further y]our[461] petitioners testify that [p. [5]] the said Joseph Smith Jr did make a publick proclamation in Far West in favor of the militia of the State of Missouri and of its laws and also of the constitution ~~of the constitution~~ of the United States that he has ever been a warm friend to his country and did use all his influance for peace that he is a peaceable and quiat citizen and is not worthy of death of stripes Bond, or imprisonment.[462] the above mentioned speach was delivered on the day before the surrender[463] at Far West.

/[464]Alanson Riply
Heber C. Kimball
Wm Huntington
Joseph. B. Noble
Joseph Smith Jr

/[465]State of Missouri⎱
County of Clay ⎰ ss

This day personally appears before me Abraham Shafer a Justice of the peace within & for the aforesaid County Alanson Ripley Heber. C. Kimball William Huntington Joseph B. Noble and Joseph Smith J^un. who being duly sworn doth depose & say that the matters & ~~parts~~ things set ~~fourth~~ forth in the foregoing Petition upon their own knowledge are true in substance and in fact & so far as set forth upon this information of others they believe to be true

Sworn & subscribed to⎫
this 15th. day of March ⎬
1839 before me   ⎪
Abraham Shafer J. P.   ⎭

/[466]Alanson Riply
Heber C Kimball
W^m. Huntington
[Joseph B. Noble]
[Joseph Smith Jr.][467] [p. [6]]

---

461. TEXT: The bottom left corner of the page is cut off. The missing text is supplied from Sloan's 1839 copy of the petition. (JS et al., Petition, Liberty, MO, 15 Mar. 1839, copy, JS Collection, CHL.)

462. See Acts 23:29; 26:31.

463. Reed Peck recalled that when he, Corrill, and Hinkle reported to JS the results of the delegates' 31 October 1838 meeting with Lucas, JS stated "that it would not do to resist the Militia of the state acting under the order of the Governor, He also said that the church must comply with whatever the officers required." (Reed Peck, Testimony, Richmond, MO, Nov. 1838, p. [62], in State of Missouri, "Evidence"; Reed Peck, Quincy, IL, to "Dear Friends," 18 Sept. 1839, p. 116, Henry E. Huntington Library, San Marino, CA.)

464. TEXT: Alexander McRae handwriting ends; signatories begin.

465. TEXT: Abraham Shafer handwriting begins.

466. TEXT: Abraham Shafer handwriting ends; individual signatories begin.

467. TEXT: The bottom right corner of the page is cut off. The missing text is supplied from Sloan's 1839 copy of the petition. (JS et al., Petition, Liberty, MO, 15 Mar. 1839, copy, JS Collection, CHL.)

/⁴⁶⁸WE the undersigned being ⟨many of us⟩, personally ~~with~~ acquainted with the said Joseph Smith jr and the circumstances connected with his imprisonment do concur in the ⟨petition &⟩ testimony of the above named individuals as most of the ~~things~~ transactions therein mentioned we know from personal knowldge to be correctly set forth and from information of others believe the remainder to be true

/⁴⁶⁹Amasa Lyman
H[enry] G Sherwood
James Newber[r]y
Cyrus Daniels
Erastus Snow
Elias Smith

Joseph Smith Jᵘⁿ ⁴⁷⁰ [p. [7]]

Joseph Smith jr
Petition⁴⁷¹

———— ☙ ————

Letter to Presendia Huntington Buell, 15 March 1839

Source Note

JS, Letter, Liberty, Clay Co., MO, to Presendia Huntington Buell, Clay Co., MO, 15 Mar. 1839. Featured version copied [16 Dec. 1854]; handwriting of Thomas Bullock; two pages; inserted in JS History, 1838–1856, vol. C-1, p. 898; Historian's Office, History of the Church, 1839–ca. 1882, CHL. Includes docket and redactions.

Single leaf measuring 12½ × 8 inches (32 × 20 cm), with thirty-five printed lines per page. The top, bottom, and right edges have the square cut of manufactured paper; the left edge is unevenly cut. After the document was folded for filing, Thomas Bullock added a docket. At an unknown date, a wafer was used to attach the top right corner of the verso to page 898 of JS History, 1838–1856, volume C-1. The top right corner of both the recto and the verso of the letter were inscribed in graphite with "898". At some point, cellophane tape was applied where the paper had torn away from the adhesive wafer.

Little is known about the custodial history of the original letter, which is apparently not extant. It presumably remained in Buell's possession for much of her life. On 16 December 1854, Buell temporarily loaned it to Thomas Bullock, a clerk in the Church Historian's Office, for copying. Bullock's copy was likely filed in the Church Historian's Office for some time before it was inserted into volume C-1, as

---

468. TEXT: Abraham Shafer handwriting ends; Elias Smith begins.

469. TEXT: Elias Smith handwriting ends; individual signatories begin.

470. TEXT: This docket was written vertically at the bottom right corner of the page in unknown handwriting, apparently after the attestation was inscribed and the petition was refolded.

471. TEXT: This docket was written in the middle of the page by Alexander McRae, apparently after Shafer added the certification but before the attestation was inscribed and the petition was refolded.

evidenced by wear along the copy's folds. It was added to that volume by 1905.[472] Volume C-1 has remained in the custody of the Church Historian's Office and successor institutions since its creation, as noted in inventories of church records.[473]

Historical Introduction

On 15 March 1839, JS wrote from the jail in Clay County, Missouri, to Presendia Huntington Buell, a Latter-day Saint who was also living in the county.[474] Hyrum Smith noted in his journal that earlier in the day, Buell visited the jail with her father, William Huntington, as well as Alanson Ripley, Heber C. Kimball, and Joseph B. Noble. Presumably, the purpose of the visit was for the four men to sign JS's petition for a writ of habeas corpus. While there, Buell requested to converse with the prisoners privately, but the jailer would not permit it.[475]

On the afternoon or evening of 15 March 1839, after the visitors departed and the petition was completed, JS wrote this letter to Buell. While imprisoned in Liberty, JS often relied on his fellow prisoners to act as scribes for lengthy documents created for a general church audience or for the government, but he personally wrote short communications to his wife Emma.[476] Because the original letter to Buell is apparently not extant, it is unknown who acted as the scribe. However, at the conclusion of this letter, JS stated that "I wanted to communicate something and I wrote this," suggesting he penned the letter himself. Believing that Buell desired counsel as to whether she and her husband, Norman Buell, should remain in Missouri or gather with the Saints in Illinois, JS advised the latter. He also offered encouragement, quoted liberally from scripture, and expressed his desire to once again be with church members and teach them the gospel. The address, "To Mʳˢ· Norman Buel | Clay Cᵒ· | Mᵒ·," suggests that JS completed the letter after Buell left the jail and that he had someone carry the letter to her home.

A copy of the letter was made on 16 December 1854 by Thomas Bullock.[477] Bullock's inclusion of the address at the bottom of the letter strongly suggests that Bullock had access to the original letter rather than a subsequent copy. In 1877, Latter-day Saint writer Edward Tullidge published a copy of the letter. It is unknown whether he copied the original letter or a subsequent version.[478] Bullock's version is featured here be-

---

472. See *History of the Church,* 3:285.

473. See "Schedule of Church Records. Nauvoo 1846," [1]; "Inventory. Historians Office. G. S. L. City April 1. 1857," [1]; "Index of Records and Journals in the Historian's Office 1878," [6], Historian's Office, Catalogs and Inventories, 1846–1904, CHL.

474. "A Venerable Woman," *Woman's Exponent,* 15 Jan. 1883, 123; 1 Mar. 1883, 147.

475. Hyrum Smith, Diary, 15 Mar. 1839; Petition to George Tompkins, between 9 and 15 Mar. 1839, p. 351 herein; Tullidge, *Women of Mormondom,* 209–210.

476. See, for example, Petition to George Tompkins, between 9 and 15 Mar. 1839, pp. 340–352 herein; Letter to Edward Partridge and the Church, ca. 22 Mar. 1839, pp. 388–401 herein; Letter to Emma Smith, 4 Nov. 1838, pp. 279–282 herein; and Letter to Emma Smith, 21 Mar. 1839, pp. 372–375 herein.

477. Historian's Office, Journal, 16 Dec. 1854, 17:252.

478. Tullidge, *Women of Mormondom,* 210–212.

cause it was presumably copied much earlier (when the original may have been more legible), because it is unknown whether Tullidge's published version depended upon an intermediate printer's manuscript, and because Tullidge may have edited his version for publication. Significant textual variants between Bullock's and Tullidge's versions are noted in annotation.

Document Transcript

Liberty Jail March 15[th.] 1839

Dear Sister

My heart rejoiced at the friendship you manifested in requesting to have conversation with us but the Jailer[479] is a very Jealous man for fear some one will leave[480] tools for us to get out with[481] he is under the eye of the Mob continually and his life is at Stake if he grants us any privileges he will not let us converse with any one alone Oh what a joy it would be to us to see our friends it would have gladdened my heart to have the privilege of conversing with you but the hand of tyrany is upon us but thanks be to God it cannot last always and he that sitteth in the heavens will laugh at their calamity and mock when their fear cometh[482] We feel Dear Sister that our bondage is not of long duration I trust that I shall have the chance to give such instructions as are communicated to us before long I suppose you wanted some instruction for yourself[483] and also give us some information and administer consolation to us and to find out what is best for you to do I think that many of the brethren if they will be pretty still can stay in this country until the indignation is over and past but I think it would be better for brother Buel [Norman Buell] to leave and go with the rest of the Brethren if he keep the faith[484] and at any rate for thus speaketh the Spirit concerning him I want him and you to know that I am your true friend I was glad to see you no tongue can tell what inexpressible Joy it gives a man to see the face of one who has been a friend after having been inclosed in the walls of a prison for five months[485] it seems to me that

---

479. Likely Samuel Hadley, who was the Clay County sheriff and jailer, or Samuel Tillery, who was the deputy jailer. (See Introduction to Part 3: 4 Nov. 1838–16 Apr. 1839, pp. 274–275 herein.)

480. Instead of "leave," Tullidge's version has "have." (Tullidge, *Women of Mormondom,* 210.)

481. For information on the prisoners' attempts to escape, see Introduction to Part 3: 4 Nov. 1838–16 Apr. 1839, pp. 276–277 herein; and Lyman Wight, Journal, in *History of the Reorganized Church,* 2:317.

482. See Psalm 2:4; and Proverbs 1:26.

483. Instead of "I suppose you wanted some instruction for yourself," Tullidge's version has "and as you wanted some instruction from us." (Tullidge, *Women of Mormondom,* 210.)

484. Norman Buell became disaffected from the church in 1838 or early 1839. He and Presendia remained in Missouri instead of joining the general church exodus from the state in 1839. (Kimball, Reminiscences, [2]; "A Venerable Woman," *Woman's Exponent,* 15 Mar. 1883, 155; "A Venerable Woman," *Woman's Exponent,* 1 Apr. 1883, 163.)

485. JS was arrested on 31 October 1838. He spent November in Independence and Richmond,

my heart will always be more tender after this than ever it was before my heart bleeds continually when I contemplate the distress of the Church Oh that I could be with them I would not shrink at toil and hardship to render them comfort and consolation I want the blessing once more to lift my voice in the midst of the Saints I would pour out my soul to God for their instruction it has been the plan of the Devil to hamper me and distress me from the beginning to keep me from explaining myself to them and I never have had opportunity to give them the plan that God has revealed to me[486] for many have run without being sent[487] crying tidings my Lord[488] and have done much injury[489] to the Church giving the Devil[490] more power over those that walk by sight and not by faith[491] [*blank*][492] will only give us that knowledge to understand the minds of the Ancients for my part I think I never could have felt as I now do if I had not suffered the wrongs that I have suffered all things shall work together for good to them that love God[493] [p. [1]] Beloved Sister we see that perilous times have truly come[494] and the things which we have so long expected have at last began to usher in but when you see the fig tree begin to put forth its leaves you may know that the Summer is nigh at hand[495] there will be a short work on the Earth it has now commenced[496] I suppose there will soon be perplexity all over the Earth[497] do not let our hearts faint when these things come[498] upon us for they must come or the word cannot be fulfilled I

Missouri, and was then transferred to Liberty, where he had been imprisoned since 1 December. (Letter to Emma Smith, 4 Nov. 1838, pp. 279–282 herein; Letter to Emma Smith, 12 Nov. 1838, pp. 290–293 herein; Letter to Emma Smith, 1 Dec. 1838, pp. 293–294 herein.)

486. The Book of Mormon and some of JS's revelations in the 1830s use *plan of salvation, plan of redemption,* and similar phrases to encompass the concepts of the fall of Adam, the atonement of Jesus Christ, faith, repentance, baptism, and the gift of the Holy Ghost. Although JS's early teachings suggest that the plan of salvation also includes a premortal existence, additional saving ordinances, and a doctrine of deification known as "exaltation," it was not until the 1840s in Illinois that he fully elaborated on this expanded plan. (Book of Mormon, 1830 ed., 79, 257, 338 [2 Nephi 9:6; Alma 12:24; 42:8]; Letter to the Church, ca. Feb. 1834, in *JSP,* D3:414; Instruction on Priesthood, 5 Oct. 1840, JS Collection, CHL; Givens, *Wrestling the Angel,* 257–315.)

487. See Jeremiah 23:21.

488. See 2 Samuel 18:31.

489. Instead of "done much injury," Tullidge's version has "have caused injury." (Tullidge, *Women of Mormondom,* 211.)

490. Instead of "Devil," Tullidge's version has "adversary." (Tullidge, *Women of Mormondom,* 211.)

491. See 2 Corinthians 5:7.

492. Tullidge's version has "Our trouble" here. (Tullidge, *Women of Mormondom,* 211.)

493. See Romans 8:28.

494. See 2 Timothy 3:1.

495. See Matthew 24:32.

496. See Romans 9:28.

497. See Luke 21:25.

498. See Matthew 24:6; and Luke 21:9.

know that something will soon take place to stir up this generation to see what they have been doing and that their fathers have inherited lies and they have been led captive by the Devil to no profit[499] but they know not what they do[500] do not have any feelings of enmity towards any Son or Daughter of Adam I believe I shall be let out of their hands some way or another and shall see good days we can not do any thing only stand still and see the Salvation of God[501] he must do his own work[502] or it must fall to the ground we must not take it in our hands to avenge our wrongs Vengeance is mine saith the Lord and I will repay[503] I have no fears I shall stand unto death God being my helper[504] I wanted to communicate something and I wrote this &c Write to us if you can

J. Smith J^{r.}

To Mrs. Norman Buel [Presdendia Huntington Buell]
Clay C^{o.} M^{o.} [p. [2]]

———— ‹› ————

Letter to the Church and Edward Partridge, 20 March 1839

Source Note

JS, Hyrum Smith, Lyman Wight, Caleb Baldwin, and Alexander McRae, Letter, Liberty, Clay Co., MO, to the church and Edward Partridge, Quincy, Adams Co., IL, 20 Mar. 1839; handwriting of Alexander McRae and Caleb Baldwin, with insertions by JS; signatures of JS, Hyrum Smith, Lyman Wight, Caleb Baldwin, and Alexander McRae; seventeen pages; Revelations Collection, CHL. Includes redaction and docket.

Four bifolia and one leaf measuring 9¾ × 7¾ inches (25 × 20 cm), each with twenty-eight printed lines (now mostly faded). The letter was trifolded for mailing, and the final leaf may have once had a conjugal leaf bearing an address, as do most of JS's letters written in the Clay County jail. The recto of the first bifolium's first leaf was paginated with "1" twice—in the top right corner and the top left corner. One of the numbers appears to be original, and the other is apparently redactive. JS's clerk William Clayton docketed the letter sometime in the 1840s. At some point, the bifolia were fastened together with two staples, which have since been removed. The document has undergone conservation.

The *Times and Seasons* published an edited version of the letter in July 1840.[505] Church clerk Thomas Bullock copied the letter into JS's manuscript history in 1845.[506] The letter was included in

499. See Jeremiah 16:19; and Book of Mormon, 1830 ed., 255, 334–335 [Alma 12:11; 40:13].

500. See Luke 23:34.

501. See Exodus 14:13.

502. See Book of Mormon, 1830 ed., 111 [2 Nephi 27:21].

503. See Romans 12:19; and Book of Mormon, 1830 ed., 524, 533 [Mormon 3:15; 8:20].

504. See Psalm 30:10; and Hebrews 13:6.

505. See "Copy of a Letter, Written by J. Smith Jr. and Others, While in Prison," *Times and Seasons,* May 1840, 1:99–104.

506. See JS History, vol. C-1, 900–906; and Jessee, "Writing of Joseph Smith's History," 441.

inventories for the Church Historian's Office circa 1904, and the letter was cataloged in the Revelations Collection in 1983, indicating the letter has remained in continuous institutional custody since its reception.[507]

Historical Introduction

In the Clay County, Missouri, jail on 20 March 1839, JS dictated a letter addressed to Bishop Edward Partridge; church members in Quincy, Illinois; and the Saints "scattered abroad." The letter was the second general epistle JS directed to the church while in the jail, with the first missive composed on 16 December 1838.[508] As the main body of Latter-day Saints was relocating from Missouri to Illinois and Iowa Territory, JS apparently envisioned writing a series of general epistles in March 1839 to offer guidance and instruction in the wake of the catastrophic changes of the previous year.[509] The immediate catalyst for the 20 March letter was the arrival of Latter-day Saint David Rogers the previous evening.[510] Rogers brought the prisoners a packet that contained letters from their families and friends, a letter from Illinois land speculator Isaac Galland, and "the documents and papers sent by the authorities at Quincy."[511]

Stylistically, the 20 March letter is reminiscent of the apostle Paul's epistles in the New Testament. Paul frequently named his companions in opening greetings and utilized the first-person plural voice even though he was the primary author of the letters.[512] In a similar fashion, the 20 March 1839 letter opens with greetings from JS "in company with his fellow prisoners"; the body of the letter consistently employs the first-person plural—"we," "our," and "us"—with the exception of one portion presented in the voice of Deity; and all the prisoners signed the letter. JS was the principal author,[513] although conversations with the other

---

507. See "Index to Papers. in the Historians Office," ca. 1904, p. 3; "Letters to and from the Prophet," ca. 1904, p. 1, Historian's Office, Catalogs and Inventories, 1846–1904, CHL; and the full bibliographic entry for the Revelations Collection in the CHL catalog.

508. Letter to the Church in Caldwell Co., MO, 16 Dec. 1838, pp. 294–310 herein.

509. Near the conclusion of this 20 March letter, JS and his fellow prisoners wrote, "We shall continue to offer further reflections in our next epistle." A short time later, the men wrote another general epistle, stating: "We continue to offer further reflections to Bishop Partridge and to the church of Jesus Christ of Latter day saints." The prisoners concluded this letter with a note that "we shall continue our reflections in our next." However, the prisoners apparently did not write another letter prior to their departure from the Clay County jail on 6 April 1839. (Letter to Edward Partridge and the Church, ca. 22 Mar. 1839, pp. 391, 401 herein; Hyrum Smith, Diary, 6 Apr. 1839.)

510. Hyrum Smith, Liberty, MO, to Mary Fielding Smith, Quincy, IL, 19 Mar. 1839, Mary Fielding Smith, Collection, CHL.

511. It is unknown which "documents and papers" the leaders in Quincy sent, but in JS's March 1839 general epistles, he indicated awareness of discussions documented in two sets of minutes, one dated 9 March 1839 and the other undated, which Rogers may have delivered to the jail. (See Rogers, Statement, [1], CHL; see also Letter to Edward Partridge and the Church, ca. 22 Mar. 1839, p. 392 herein; Minutes, 9 Mar. 1839, in JS Letterbook 2, p. 49; Far West Committee, Minutes, 17 Mar. 1839; and Minutes, no date, in JS Letterbook 2, p. 48.)

512. See, for example, 1 Corinthians 1:1; 2 Corinthians 1:1; Philippians 1:1; and Doty, *Letters in Primitive Christianity*, chap. 2; see also Letter to the Church in Caldwell Co., MO, 16 Dec. 1838, pp. 294–310 herein; and Letter to Heber C. Kimball and Brigham Young, 16 Jan. 1839, pp. 310–316 herein.

513. Letter to Emma Smith, 21 Mar. 1839, p. 373 herein.

prisoners may have contributed to the letter's ideas and themes.[514] It is unknown who acted as scribe for the dictation draft, which is apparently not extant. The version featured here, which contains errors usually associated with copying, was inscribed by Alexander McRae and Caleb Baldwin. After McRae finished copying the last portion of the letter, JS and the other men signed the copy. At some point, JS made minor corrections and additions.[515]

Following the opening greeting, the epistle contains an extended meditation on the Latter-day Saints' recent sufferings and the prisoners' frustrations in jail. This part of the missive includes a prayer in which JS pleads with God to deliver the Saints from their oppressors. The subject of the letter appears to shift with the acknowledgment of receiving letters from Edward Partridge, Don Carlos Smith, and Emma Smith, but this narrative actually continues the meditation on the meaning of persecution, revealing that reading the letters dissolved feelings of bitterness and opened JS's heart to receive inspiration. Then, the voice of the letter transitions from that of the prisoners to that of the Lord providing an answer to the letter's earlier prayer, explaining the deeper significance of the Saints' persecutions and pronouncing judgments against the church's enemies.

The second part of the letter addresses challenges the church faced in moving forward, such as deciding where the Saints should settle. JS declined to either approve or reject Isaac Galland's offer to sell land to the church; instead, JS said that church leaders in Quincy should make that decision in future conferences and should forward minutes of the proceedings to JS for approval. The letter also advises the Quincy church leaders to eschew "an aspiring spirit" that had previously prevailed over "milder councils," causing much suffering and death among the Saints. Additionally, the epistle contains counsel on how to seek revelation and guidance; this counsel is followed by strong affirmation that persecution would not hinder the work of God. Like other missives JS composed in the Clay County jail, this letter incorporates multiple biblical allusions.[516] Near the close, the letter signals that another general epistle was forthcoming.

Although the letter's greeting is directed to the church in general and to Partridge in particular, JS sent the missive to his wife Emma because he wanted her "to have the first reading of it." In a letter he wrote to her the following day, he informed her, "I have sent an Epistle to the church," suggesting the epistle had already left the jail.[517] The letter was probably carried from the jail by a church member, perhaps Alanson Ripley, who Hyrum Smith noted was visiting the jail on 20 March and was "going to start back this after noon" to Far West,

---

514. For example, Hyrum Smith wrote about a major theme in the general epistle—persecution and its significance—in March 1839 letters to his wife, Mary Fielding Smith. The brothers may have discussed the subject in the jail. On the evening of 20 March, Lyman Wight noted in his journal that while JS was "writing an epistle to the church," Wight and Caleb Baldwin were writing letters to their families, which suggests the two men had minimal or no involvement in preparing the epistle, at least at that time. (Hyrum Smith, [Liberty, MO], to Mary Fielding Smith, Quincy, IL, [ca. Mar. 1839], Hyrum Smith Collection, CHL; Hyrum Smith, Liberty, MO, to Mary Fielding Smith, Quincy, IL, 16 Mar. 1839; Hyrum Smith, Liberty, MO, to Mary Fielding Smith, [Quincy, IL], 20 Mar. 1839, Mary Fielding Smith, Collection, CHL; Lyman Wight, Journal, in *History of the Reorganized Church,* 2:323.)

515. The first draft was apparently discarded after it was copied, as was common practice.

516. See Letter to the Church in Caldwell Co., MO, 16 Dec. 1838, pp. 294–310 herein; and Letter to Heber C. Kimball and Brigham Young, 16 Jan. 1839, pp. 310–316 herein.

517. Letter to Emma Smith, 21 Mar. 1839, p. 373 herein.

Alexander McRae and letter to the church. During his confinement in the Clay County jail, Joseph Smith wrote three general epistles to the church, offering comfort and prophetic counsel to the displaced Saints. In composing these epistles, Smith relied heavily on his fellow prisoners, particularly Alexander McRae (photographed circa 1880), who transcribed Smith's dictation, assisted in revising the transcripts, and made polished copies to send to the Saints. Handwriting of Alexander McRae and Caleb Baldwin, with insertions by Joseph Smith. Letter to the Church and Edward Partridge, 20 Mar. 1839, Revelations Collection, Church History Library, Salt Lake City. (McRae image: Church History Library, Salt Lake City.)

Missouri. Ripley told the prisoners that he could send their letters to Illinois "a mediately by some of the brethren."[518] It remains unclear who transported the missive from Missouri to Illinois or when it arrived in Quincy. On 10 April 1839, Sidney Rigdon and Ripley wrote separate letters to JS and the other prisoners; both messages contain possible allusions to the general epistle, suggesting church members had received and read the epistle by that date.[519] On 11 April, Mary Fielding Smith wrote to her husband, Hyrum Smith, stating she had read the epistle and that it was "food to the hungrey." The 20 March epistle circulated widely among the Latter-day Saints in the months after its arrival in Illinois, as indicated by the extant copies in the handwriting of Partridge and Albert Perry Rockwood. In addition, the *Times and Seasons* published an edited version in 1840, extending the letter's circulation to the Saints "scattered abroad."[520]

Document Transcript

/[521]Liberty Jail Clay County Mo March 20th 1839.
To the church of Latterday saints at Quincy Illinois and scattered abroad[522] and to Bishop [Edward] Partridge in particular. your humble servant Joseph Smith Jr prisoner for the Lord Jesus Christ's sake and for the saints[523] taken and held by the power of mobocracy under the exterminating reign of his excelancy the Governer Lilburn W. Boggs in company with his fellow prisoners and beloved Brethren Caleb Baldwin Lymon [Lyman] Wight. Hyram [Hyrum] Smith and Alexander McRae. Send unto you all greeting. May the grace of God the father and of our Lord and savior Jesus Christ rest upon you all and abide with you for ever.[524] May knoledge be multiplied unto you by the

---

518. Hyrum Smith, Liberty, MO, to Mary Fielding Smith, [Quincy, IL], 20 Mar. 1839, Mary Fielding Smith, Collection, CHL. Wight reported that Ripley returned to the jail on 22 March 1839 and took the prisoners' "package of letters for Quincy." It is unclear whether Ripley went to Far West on 20 March and then returned to Liberty two days later or whether he remained in Liberty during that period. (Lyman Wight, Journal, in *History of the Reorganized Church,* 2:323.)

519. See Letter from Sidney Rigdon, 10 Apr. 1839, pp. 406–409 herein; and Letter from Alanson Ripley, 10 Apr. 1839, pp. 409–414 herein.

520. Mary Fielding Smith, [Quincy, IL], to Hyrum Smith, 11 Apr. 1839, Mary Fielding Smith, Collection, CHL; JS, Liberty, MO, to the Church and Edward Partridge, Quincy, IL, 20–25 Mar. 1839, copy, CHL; JS et al., Liberty, MO, to the Church and Edward Partridge, Quincy, IL, 20 Mar. 1839, copy, Albert Perry Rockwood, Mormon Letters and Sermons, 1838–1839, Western Americana Collection, Beinecke Rare Book and Manuscript Library, Yale University, New Haven, CT; "Copy of a Letter, Written by J. Smith Jr. and Others, While in Prison," *Times and Seasons,* May 1840, 1:99–104. Portions of the 20 March 1839 letter were canonized in the 1876 edition of the Doctrine and Covenants. (Doctrine and Covenants 121, 1876 ed. [D&C 121].)

521. TEXT: Alexander McRae handwriting begins.

522. See James 1:1.

523. See Philemon 1:1, 9; and Ephesians 3:1.

524. See Colossians 1:2; Philippians 1:2; and Book of Mormon, 1830 ed., 566, 585 [Ether 12:41; Moroni 9:26].

meorcy of God.[525] And may faith and virtue and knoledge and temperance and patience and Godliness and Brotherly kindness and charity be in you and abound that you may not be baron in anything nor unfrutefull.[526] Forasmuch as we know that the most of you are well acquainted with the rongs and the high toned injustice and cruelty that is practiced upon us whereas we have been taken prisoners charged falsly with evry kind of evil and thrown into prison inclosed with strong walls surrounded with a strong guard who continually watch day and knight as indefatigable as the devil is in tempting and laying snayers for the people of God.[527] Therefore dearly and beloved Brethren we are the more ready and willing to lay claim to your fellowship and love. For our curc[p. 1]umstances are calculated to awaken our spirits to a sacred rememberance of evry thing and we think that yours are also and that nothing therefore can seperate us from the love of God,[528] and fellowship one with another and that evry species of wickedness and cruelty practised upon us will only tend to bind our harts together and seal them together in love[529] we have no need to say to you that we are held in bonds without cause neither is it needfull that you say unto us we are driven from our homes and smitten without cause. We mutually unders[t]and that if the inhabitance of the state of Missouri had let the saints alone and had been as deserable of peace as they ware there would have been nothing but peace and quiatude [quietude] in this ⟨State⟩ unto this day we should not have been in this hell surrounded with demonds if not those who are damned, they are those who shall be damned and where we are compeled to hear nothing but blasphemo[u]s oaths and witness a seen of blasphemy and drunkeness and hypocracy and debaucheries of evry description. And again the ~~cry~~ cries of orphans and widdows would ⟨not⟩ have assended up to God. the blood of inocent women and children yea and of men also would not have cried to God against them ⟨**it**⟩[530] would ⟨**not**⟩[531] have stained the soyl of Missouri.[532] but oh! the unrelenting hand the inhumanity and murderous disposition of this people it shocks all nature it beggers and defies all discription. it is a tail [tale] of [p. 2] wo a lamentable tail yea a sorrifull tail too much to tell too

---

525. See 2 Peter 1:2.

526. See 2 Peter 1:5–8.

527. See Book of Mormon, 1830 ed., 250 [Alma 10:17].

528. See Romans 8:35, 39.

529. See Colossians 2:2.

530. TEXT: Insertion in the handwriting of JS.

531. TEXT: Insertion in the handwriting of JS.

532. See Genesis 4:10–11. For more information on Latter-day Saint casualties during the 1838 conflict, see Introduction to Part 3: 4 Nov. 1838–16 Apr. 1839, pp. 269–272 herein.

much for contemplation too much to think of for a moment too much for
human beings it cannot be found among the hethans it cannot be found among
the nations where Kings and tyrants are inthroned it cannot be found among the
savages of the wilderness yea and I think it cannot be found among the wild
and ferocious beasts of the forist that a man should be mangled for sport[533]
women be ~~violated~~ ⟨rob[b]ed⟩ of all that they have their last morsel for subsistance and then be violated[534] to gratify the ~~hells~~ ⟨hellish⟩ desires of the mob
and finally left to perish with their helpless of[f]spring clinging around their
necks but this is not all after a man is dead he must be dug up from his grave
and mangled to peaces for no other purpose than to gratify their splean
against the religeon of god. They practise ⟨these⟩ things upon the saints who
have done them no rong who are inocent and virtuous who loved the Lord
their god and were willing to forsaik all things for ~~his~~ ⟨Christ⟩ sake[535] these
things are awfull to relait [relate] but they are verily true it must needs bee
that offences come, but WO! to them by whom they come.[536] O God where
art thou and where is the pavilion that covereth thy hiding place[537] how long
shall thy hand be stayed and thine eye yea thy pure eye behold from ~~from~~ the
etearnal heavens the rongs of thy people and of thy servants [p. 3] and thine
ear be penetrated with their cyes [cries] yea o Lord how long shall they
suffer these rongs and unlawfull oppressions before thine hart shall be softened towards them and thy bowels be moved with compassion to-words them.
O Lord God almity maker of heaven earth and seas and of all things that in
them is[538] and who controleth and subjecteth the devil and the dark and
benig[h]ted dominion of shayole. Streach forth thy hand let thine eye pierce
let thy pavilion be taken up let thy hiding place no longer be covered[539] let
thine ear be inclined[540] let thine hart be softened and thy bowels moved with

---

533. David Lewis, a survivor of the Hawn's Mill massacre on 30 October 1838, later stated that vigilante Jacob Rogers used "an oald peace of a sythe blade" and "hacked down and hacked into peaces"
Latter-day Saint Thomas McBride. (David Lewis, Affidavit, ca. 1839, pp. [40c]–[40d], in Sidney Rigdon,
JS, et al., Petition Draft ["To the Publick"]; see also Joseph Young and Jane Bicknell Young, Affidavit,
ca. 1839, p. [38d], in Sidney Rigdon, JS, et al., Petition Draft ["To the Publick"].)

534. "Violated" was a nineteenth-century euphemism for sexual assault or rape. Several individuals
reported that anti-Mormon vigilantes harassed and raped Latter-day Saint women during the 1838 conflict.
(Block, *Rape and Sexual Power in Early America*, 111–112; see, for example, *American Slavery as It Is*, 191–192;
Murdock, Journal, 29 Oct. 1838, 103–104; Hyrum Smith, Testimony, Nauvoo, IL, 1 July 1843, pp. 13, 24,
Nauvoo, IL, Records, CHL.)

535. See Matthew 19:29.

536. See Matthew 18:7.

537. See Psalms 18:11; 27:5.

538. See Exodus 20:11.

539. See Revelation, 16–17 Dec. 1833, in *JSP*, D3:396 [D&C 101:89].

540. See Psalm 102:2.

compassion toward us let thine anger be kindle against our enemi[e]s and in the fury of thine hart with thy sword avenge us of our rongs remember thy suffering saint oh our God and thy servants will rejoyce in thy name for ever.[541] Dearly and beloved Brethren we see that peralas [perilous] times have come as was testified of[542] we may look then with most purfect asshurance for the roling in of all those things that have been written and with more confidence than ever before lift up our eyes to the luminary of day and say in our harts soon thou wilt vail thy blushing face he that said let there be light, and there was light[543] hath spoken this word, and again thou moon thou dimmer light thou luminary of night shall ~~trurn~~ ⟨turn⟩ to blood[544] we see that evry thing is fulfilling and the time shall soon come when the son of man shall [p. 4] descend in the clouds of ⟨heaven,⟩[545] our harts do not shrink neither are our spirits altogether broken at the grievious yoak which is put upon us We know that God will have our oppressors in derision[546] that he ~~laf~~ ⟨will laugh⟩ at their calamity and mock when their fear comith[547] oh that we could be with you Brethren and unbosome our feeling to you we would tell that we should have been at ⟨liberated⟩ the time Elder [Sidney] Rigdon was on the writ of habeas corpus had not our own lawyers interpreted the law contrary to what it reads against ⟨us,⟩ which prevented us from introducing our evidence before the mock court,[548] they have done us much harm ⟨from⟩ the begining they have of late acknoledged that the law was misconstrewed and tantalised our feelings with it and have intirally [entirely?] forsaken us and have forfeited their oaths and their bonds and we have a come back on them for they are co-workers with the mob.[549] As nigh as we can learn the publick mind has been for a long time turning in our favor and the majority is now friendly[550]

---

541. See Psalm 89:16.

542. See 2 Timothy 3:1.

543. See Genesis 1:3.

544. See Joel 2:31; Revelation 6:12; and Revelation, Sept. 1830–A, in *JSP*, D1:180 [D&C 29:14].

545. See Daniel 7:13; Matthew 24:30; and Mark 14:62.

546. See Psalms 2:4; 59:8.

547. See Proverbs 1:26.

548. On 22 January 1839, JS and his fellow prisoners appeared before Justice Joel Turnham of the Clay County court on a writ of habeas corpus. On 30 January, after reviewing the evidence, Turnham released Rigdon on bail but remanded the remaining prisoners to jail. (See Introduction to Part 3: 4 Nov. 1838–16 Apr. 1839, p. 276 herein; Letter to Isaac Galland, 22 Mar. 1839, p. 379 herein.)

549. On 23 March 1839, Hyrum Smith noted that "the Lawyers came in to see us today for the first time for many weeks they appear to be more friendly than usual." (Hyrum Smith, Liberty, MO, to Mary Fielding Smith, Quincy, IL, 23 Mar. 1839, Mary Fielding Smith, Collection, CHL.)

550. Hyrum Smith wrote on 16 March 1839 that "the people here seem to be friendly. . . . the Spirit of the people seems to be in our favour." (Hyrum Smith, Liberty, MO, to Mary Fielding Smith, Quincy, IL, 16 Mar. 1839, Mary Fielding Smith, Collection, CHL.)

and the lawyers can no longer browbeat us by saying that this or that is a matter of publick oppinion for publick oppinion is not willing to brook it for it is begining to look with feelings of indignation against our oppresors and to say that the mormons were not in the fault in the least we think that truth honor and virtue and inocence will eventually come out tryumphant we should have taken a habeas corpus before the high Judge and escaped [p. 5] the mob in a sumerary way but unfortunatly for us the timber of the wall being verry hard our auger handles gave out and hindered us longer than we expected we applied to a friend and a verry slight uncautious act gave rise to some suspition and before we could fully succeed our plan was discovered we had evry thing in readiness but the last stone and we could have made our escape in one minute and should have succeeded admirably had it not been for a little imprudance or over anxiety on the part of our friend.[551] The sheriff and jailor[552] did not blame us for our attempt it was a fine breach and cost the county a round sum[553] but publick oppinion says that we ought to have been permitted to have made our escape that then the disgrace would have been on us, but now it must come on the state. that there cannot be any charge sustained against us and that the conduct of the mob, the murders committed at hawns mill, and the exterminating order of the Governer,[554] and the one sided rascally proceedings of the Legislature has damned the state of Missouri to all eternity I would just name also that Genl. [David R.] Atchison has proved himself to be as contemtible as any of them[555] we have tryed for a long time to

---

551. For more information on the March 1839 escape attempt, see Introduction to Part 3: 4 Nov. 1838–16 Apr. 1839, pp. 276–277 herein.

552. Samuel Hadley was the Clay County sheriff and jailer, while Samuel Tillery was the deputy jailer. (See Introduction to Part 3: 4 Nov. 1838–16 Apr. 1839, pp. 274–275 herein.)

553. The cost of repairing the breach may have been included in the $480 that Clay County later charged Daviess County for interning the Mormon prisoners since Daviess County lacked a jail. (*History of Daviess County, Missouri*, 205, 247, 249.)

554. For more information on the expulsion order that Missouri governor Lilburn W. Boggs issued on 27 October 1838, see Introduction to Part 3: 4 Nov. 1838–16 Apr. 1839, pp. 269–270 herein.

555. The prisoners' frustration with the Missouri legislature stemmed from its decision to table the Latter-day Saints' 10 December 1838 petition for relief, as well as from its failure to appoint a committee of state representatives and senators to investigate the causes of the recent conflict. The bill to create the committee was tabled in the House of Representatives on 4 February 1839 because of opposition from representatives of counties that contained significant numbers of anti-Mormon vigilantes. Atchison, the Clay County representative who introduced the original legislation, did not speak against the motion to table the bill, believing the motion would pass regardless of his opposition. His subsequent failure to revive the bill was criticized in the press as being "a complete surrender of the position he has maintained during the whole session on this subject." Although Atchison told the press that his actions had been misconstrued, the prisoners apparently based their assessment on negative newspaper reports or suspected he had an ulterior motive. (Edward Partridge et al., Petition, Far West, MO, to the Missouri State Legislature, 10 Dec. 1838, copy, Edward Partridge, Papers, CHL; *Journal, of the House of*

get our lawyers to draw us some petitions to the supream Judges of this state. but they uterly refused we have examined the law[556] and drawn the petitions ourselvs and have obtained abundance of proof to counter act all the testimony [p. 6] that was against us, so that if the supream Judge dose [does] ⟨not grant⟩ us our liberty he has got to act without cause contrary to honor evidence law or justice[557] shearly to please the devil but we hope better things and trust that before many days God will so order our case that we shall be set at liberty and take up our habitation with the saints we received some letters last evening one from Emma[558] one from Don C[arlos] Smith[559] and one from Bishop Partridge[560] all breathing a kind and consoling spirit we were much gratified with there contence [contents] we had been a long time without information and when we read those letters they were to our ~~soles~~ ⟨souls⟩[561] as the gentle air, ⟨is⟩ refreshing but our joy was mingled with greaf because of the suffering of the poor and much injured saints and we need not say to you that the flood gates of our harts were hoisted and our eyes were a fountain of tears but those who have not been inclosed in the walls of a prison without cause or provication can have but a little ideah how sweat [sweet] the voice of a friend is one token of friendship from any sorce whatever awakens and calles into action evry simpathetick feeling it brings up in an instant evry thing that is pas[s]ed it sesses [seizes?] the presant with a vivasity of lightning it grasps after the future with the fearsness [fierceness] of a tiger it rhetrogrades from one thing to an other untill finally all enmity malice and hatred and past diferances misunderstandings and mis[p. 7]managements lie slain victoms at the feet of hope and when the hart is sufficiently contrite ~~and~~ ⟨then⟩ the voice of inspiration

Representatives, of the State of Missouri, 19 Dec. 1838 and 4 Feb. 1839, 128, 367; "Letter from the Editor," *Daily Missouri Republican* [St. Louis], 8 Feb. 1839, [2]; David R. Atchison, Jefferson City, MO, 10 Feb. 1839, Letter to the Editor, *Daily Missouri Republican,* 20 Feb. 1839, [2]; Gentry and Compton, *Fire and Sword,* 457–462, 485–496.)

556. Hyrum Smith kept notes on the Missouri habeas corpus statute in the back of his diary. (See Hyrum Smith, Diary, CHL; and An Act to Regulate Proceedings on Writs of Habeas Corpus [6 Mar. 1835], *Revised Statutes of the State of Missouri* [1835], pp. 297–298, art. 1.)

557. On 15 March 1839, the prisoners wrote petitions for writs of habeas corpus, with the intent to submit the petitions to the Missouri Supreme Court. JS's petition, which was cosigned by several Latter-day Saints from Far West, stated that the "petitioners aver that they can disprove evry item of testimony that has any tendency of criminality against the prisoner for they know it themselvs and can bring many others also to prove the same." This statement suggests that the prisoners intended to introduce new witnesses to prove JS's innocence. (Petition to George Tompkins, between 9 and 15 Mar. 1839, p. 350 herein; see also 342n407 herein.)

558. Letter from Emma Smith, 7 Mar. 1839, pp. 338–340 herein.

559. Letter from Don Carlos Smith and William Smith, 6 Mar. 1839, pp. 331–334 herein.

560. Letter from Edward Partridge, 5 Mar. 1839, pp. 326–331 herein.

561. TEXT: Correction in the handwriting of JS.

steals along and whispers my son pease be unto thy soul thine advirsity and thy afflictions shall be but a small moment[562] and then if thou indure it well God shall exalts the[e] on high thou shalt tryumph over all they foes thy friends do stand by the[e] and they shall hail the[e] again with warm harts and friendly hands thou art ~~yet~~ not yet as Job thy friends do not contend again[st] the[e] ~~the~~ neither charge the[e] with transgretion as they did Job[563] and they ⟨who⟩ do ~~the~~ charge the[e] with transgretion[564] there hope shall be blasted and there prospects shall melt away as the hory frost melteth before the burning rays of the rising sun and also that God hath set to his hand and seal to change the times and seasons[565] and to blind their minds that they may not understand his marvilos workings[566] that he may prove them also and take them in there own craftiness[567] also because their harts are corrupt and the thing which they are willing to bring upon others and love to have others suffer may come upon them⟨selvs⟩ to the verry utmost that they may be disappointed also and their hopes may be cut off[568] and not many years hence that they and their pasterity shall be swept from under heaven saith God that not one of them [p. 8] is left to stand by the wall[569] cursed are all those that shall lift up the heal[570] against mine anointed saith the Lord and cry they have sin[n]ed when they have not sined before me saith the Lord but have done that which was meat in mine eyes and which I commanded them but those who cry transgresion do it becaus they are the servants of sin[571] and are the children of disobediance[572] themselvs and those who swear false against my servants that they might bring them unto bondage and death. Wo unto them because they have offended my little ones they shall be severed from the ordinances of mine house[573] their basket shall not be full their houses and their barnes shall famish and they themselvs shall be dispised by those that flattered them they shall not have right to the priesthood nor their posterity after them from generation to generation it had been better for them that a millstone had been hanged about

---

562. See Isaiah 54:7.

563. See Job chaps. 4–5, 8, 11, 15, 18, 20, 22, 25, 32–37.

564. This section likely refers to Latter-day Saints who dissented from the church in 1838 and opposed JS. (See Letter to the Church in Caldwell Co., MO, 16 Dec. 1838, pp. 300–302 herein.)

565. See Daniel 2:21.

566. See 2 Corinthians 4:4.

567. See Job 5:13.

568. See Job 8:14.

569. See 1 Kings 16:11.

570. See Psalm 41:9; and John 13:18.

571. See John 8:34; and Romans 6:17.

572. See Colossians 3:6; and Ephesians 2:2; 5:6.

573. See Ezekiel 43:11; 44:5; and Isaiah 56:7.

their necks and they ~~having~~ drownd in the depth of the see[574] wo unto all those that discomfort my people and drive and murder and testify against them[575] saith the Lord of host a generation of viper[576] shall not escape the damnation of hell behold mine eyes seeth and knoweth all their works[577] and I have in reserve a swift judgement in the season thereoff for them all for there is a time appointed ~~for~~ ⟨to⟩ evry man [p. 9] according ~~their~~ ⟨as his⟩ work shall be[578] and now beloved Brethren we say unto [you?] that in asmuch as ~~good~~ ⟨God⟩ hath said that he would have a tried people that he would purge them as gold[579] now we think that this time he has chosen his own crusible wherein we have been tryed and we think if we get through with any degree of safty and shall have kept the faith that it will be a sign to this generation all together sufficient to leave them without excuse[580] and we think also that it will be a tryal of our faith equal to that of Abraham and that the antionts [ancients] will not have were off [whereof] to bo[a]st over us in the day of judgment as being called to pass through heavier afflictions that we may hold an even waight in the balances with them but now after having suffered so grate a sacrifis and having pased through so grate a scene of sorrow we trust that a Ram may be caught in the thicket[581] speedily to releave the sons and daughters of Abraham from their ~~grate~~ ⟨**great**⟩ [582] anxiety and to light up the lamp of salvation[583] upon their countinances that they may hold ~~up~~ ⟨on⟩ now after having gone so far unto everlasting life. Now brethren conserning the places for the location of the saints we cannot counsyl you as we could if we were presant with you and ⟨as⟩ to the things that ware writen heartofore [heretofore] we did not concider them any thing verry binding[584] therfore we now say once for all that we think it most proper that the general affairs of the

---

574. See Matthew 18:6; Mark 9:42; and Luke 17:2.

575. See, for example, information on the prosecution witnesses at the November 1838 hearing. (Introduction to Part 3: 4 Nov. 1838–16 Apr. 1839, pp. 273–274 herein.)

576. See Matthew 3:7; 12:34; 23:33; and Luke 3:7.

577. See Isaiah 66:18; and Revelation 3:8, 15.

578. See Job 7:1.

579. See Zechariah 13:9; and Malachi 3:3.

580. See Romans 1:20; and Revelation, 16–17 Dec. 1833, in *JSP*, D3:397 [D&C 101:93].

581. See Genesis 22:13.

582. TEXT: Insertion in the handwriting of JS.

583. See Isaiah 62:1.

584. This statement likely refers to church leaders' ongoing deliberations regarding whether to purchase land and vacant buildings from Isaac Galland in Lee County, Iowa Territory, and at Commerce, Illinois, to provide shelter for the Latter-day Saints emigrating from Missouri. After JS learned about early negotiations in mid-February 1839, he wrote to church leaders in Quincy, expressing support for the purchase. On 5 March, Bishop Edward Partridge explained in a letter to JS that church leaders were hesitant to make the purchase. (Letter from Edward Partridge, 5 Mar. 1839, pp. 329–330 herein.)

church which are nessisary [p. 10] to be concidered while your humble servant remains in bondage s[h]ould be transacted by a general conferance of
the most faithfull and the most respictible of the authorities of the church
and a minute of those transactions may be kept and fowarded from time to
time to your humble servant and if there should be any corrections by the
word of the word of the Lord they shall be f[r]eely transmitted and your
humble servant will approve all the things what soever is acciptable unto
God if any thing thing should have been sejusted [suggested] by us or any
names mentioned ex[ce]pt by commandment or thus saith the Lord we do
not concider it binding. therefore our harts shall not be greaved if diferant
arraingments should be entered into the nevertheless we would sejest the propriety of being awar[e] of an aspiring spirit which spirit has oftentimes urged
men fowards to make foul speaches and influaance the church and to reject
milder councils and has eventually by ⟨been⟩ the means been of bringing
much death and sorrow upon the church we would say be awar of pride also
for well and truly hath the wise man s[a]id that pride goeth before distruc-
tion and a haughty spirit before a fall[585] /[586]and Again outward appearance is
not always a Criterean for us to Judge our fellow man[587] but the lips betray
the haughty and over barinng immginations of the heart, by his words by
⟨and⟩ his deeds let him be scan[n]ed[588] [p. 11] flaterly also is a deadly poison
an a frank an ⟨a frank and⟩ open Rebuke provoketh a good man to Emulation
and in the hour of trouble he will be your best friend, but on the other-hand
it will draw out all the corruption of a corrupt heart And lying and the poison of asps shall be under their tongues[589] and they do cause the pure in
heart to be cast in to prison because they want them out of thare way, A
fanciful and flowely and heated immagination be aware of because the things
of God Are of deep import and time and expeariance and car[e]ful and pon-
durous and solom though[ts] can only find them out. thy mind O Man, if
thou wilt lead a soul unto salvation must streach [stretch] as high as the
utmost Heavens, and sink sear[c]h in to and contemplate the loest ⟨lowest⟩[590]
consideatins [considerations] of the darkest abyss, and Expand upon the broad
considerations of Eternal Expance, he must commune with God. how much
more dignifide and noble are the thoughts of God, than the vane immagination

---

585. See Proverbs 16:18.

586. TEXT: Alexander McRae handwriting ends; Caleb Baldwin begins.

587. See 1 Samuel 16:7.

588. Webster's 1828 dictionary defines *scanned* as "critically sifted or examined." ("Scanned," in *American Dictionary*.)

589. See Romans 3:13.

590. TEXT: Correction in the handwriting of JS.

of the human heart, none but fools, will triful [trifle], with the souls of men, how vane and trifling, have ben our spirits, our Conferencs our Coun[c]ils our— private Meetings our pri[v]ate as well as public Conversations to low to mean to vulgar [p. 12] to condecending, for the dignifide Characters of the Cald and Chosen of God, according to the purposes of his word will from befo[re] the foundation of the world.⁵⁹¹ to hold the keys, of the mistres [mysteries] of those things that have ben kept hid from the foundation untill now,⁵⁹² for ⟨of⟩ which som have tasted a little and which many of them are to be pored down from heaven upon the heads of babes, yea the weak, obscure and dispizable ones of this earth. tharefore We beseath of you bretheren, that bare ⟨you bear⟩⁵⁹³ with those [w]ho do not feel themselves more worthey than yourselves, while we Exort one another, to a reffermation [reformation?], with one an all. both old and young. teachers and taugt both high and low rich and poor—bond and free. Male and female. let honesty and sobriety, and cander and solemnity, and virtue, and pureness, and Meekness, and simplisity, Crown our heads in every place, and in fine becom as little Children⁵⁹⁴ without mallice guile or high packrichy Hypokrisy:⁵⁹⁵ and now Bretheren after your tribulations if you do this— things, and exercise fervent prayer,⁵⁹⁶ and faith in the sight of God Always, he shall give unto you knowledge [p. 13] /⁵⁹⁷by his holy spirit yea by the unspeakable gift of the holy-Ghost⁵⁹⁸ that has not been revealed since the world was untill now which our fathers have wated with anxious expectation to be revealed in the last times which their minds were pointed to by the Angels as held in reserve for the fullness of their glory a time to come in the which nothing shall be with held whither there be one god or many god's⁵⁹⁹ they shall be manifest all thrones and dominions principalities and powers⁶⁰⁰ shall be revealed and set forth upon all who have indured valiently for the gospel of Jesus Christ and also if there be bounds set to the heavens or to the seas or to the dry land or to the sun moon or starrs all the times of their revolutions all their appointed days month and years and all the Days of their days, months and years and all their glories laws and set

---

591. See John 17:24; Ephesians 1:4; and 1 Peter 1:20.

592. See Book of Mormon, 1830 ed., 547 [Ether 4:15].

593. TEXT: Deletion and insertion in the handwriting of JS.

594. See Matthew 18:3.

595. See 1 Peter 2:1.

596. See James 5:16.

597. TEXT: Caleb Baldwin handwriting ends; Alexander McRae begins.

598. See 2 Corinthians 9:15.

599. See 1 Corinthians 8:5.

600. See Colossians 1:16.

times shall be reveald[601] in the days of the dispensation of the fullness of times[602] according to that which was ordaind in the midst of the councyl of the eternal God of all other Gods before this world was[603] that should be reserved unto the finishing and the end thereoff ~~where~~ ⟨when⟩ evry man shall enter into his eternal presants and into his imortal rest[604] but I beg leave to say unto you Brethren that ignorance supe[r]stition and bigotry placing itself where it ought not is often times in the way of the prosperity of this church [p. 14] like the torant of rain from the mountains that floods the most pure and christle stream with mire and dirt and filthyness and obscures evry thing that was clear before and all hurls along in one general deluge but time tethers ⟨**wethers**⟩[605] tide and notwithstanding we are roled in for the time being by the mire of the flood the next surge peradventure as time roles on may bring us to the fountain as clear as cristal and as pure as snow while all the filthiness flood wood and rubbish is left is left and purged out by the way. How long can rowling watters reamin impure what power shall stay the heavens as well might man streach forth his puny arm to stop the Missouri River in its decread cours or to turne it up stream as to hinder the Almighty from pooring down knoledge from ⟨heaven⟩ upon the heads of the Latter day saints what is Boggs or his murderous party but wimbling willows upon the shore to catch the flood wood as will might we argue that watter is not watter because the the mountain torants send down mire and riles the cristle stream altho afterwords ren[d]ers it more pure than before Or that fire is not fire because it is of a quenchable nature by pooing [pouring] on the flood, as to say that our cause is down because runegadoes lyers preasts theavs and murderers who are all alike tenatious of their crafts and creeds have poord [p. 15] down from their spiritual wickednes in hig[h] places and from their strong holds of the divin[e] a flud of dirt and mire and

---

601. This language is reminiscent of JS's 1835 translation of Egyptian papyri, in which "the system of astronomy was unfolded" and "the formation of the planetary System" was explained. The 1835 "Grammar & A[l]phabet of the Egyptian Language" contains references to "the moon, the earth and the sun in their annual revolutions" and God setting "bounds" on the ocean and the lights of heavens during the Creation. (JS, Journal, 1 Oct. and 16 Dec. 1835, in *JSP*, J1:67, 124; "Grammar and A[l]phabet of the Egyptian Language," pp. 25, 27, 30, Kirtland Egyptian Papers, ca. 1835–1836, CHL.)

602. See Ephesians 1:10.

603. Psalm 82 and other Bible passages reference a divine council comprising a head God and a group of heavenly beings. JS's revelations and teachings in the 1830s expanded upon the biblical concept of Satan's fall from heaven, which implies a premortal heavenly council. It was not until the 1840s, however, that JS fully explained what he called the "council in heaven" and the "plurality of Gods." (Revelation 12:7; Isaiah 14:12; Old Testament Revision 1, p. 6 [Moses 4:1–4]; Revelation, Sept. 1830–A, in *JSP*, D1:181 [D&C 29:36–39]; Thomas Bullock, JS Sermon Notes, 16 June 1844, JS Collection, CHL; see also Mullen, *Divine Council*, 226–244; and Brown, *In Heaven as It Is on Earth*, 271–272.)

604. See Psalm 95:11; and Hebrews 4:1.

605. TEXT: Insertion in the handwriting of JS.

filthiness and vomit upon our heads no God forbid. hell may poor forth its rage like the burning lavy [lava] of mount vesuvias or of Etna or of the most terible of the burning mountains and yet shall mormonism stand. watter, fire, truth, and god are all the same truth is mormonism God is the author of it he is our shield[606] it is by him we received our birth, it was by his voice that we were called to in a dispensation of his gospel in the begining of the fullness of tim[e]s it was by him we received the book of mormon and it was by him that we remain unto this day and by him we shall remain if it shall be for our glory and in his almighty name we are determined to indure tribulation[607] as good soldiers unto the end but brethren we shall continue to offer further reflections in our next epistle you will learn by the time you have read this and if you do not learn it you may learn it that walls and ⟨iron⟩ doors ⟨and screaking hinges⟩ is only calcu and half scard to death Guards and jailors grining like some damned spirit lest an inocent man should make his escape to bring to light the damnible deeds of a murderous mob is cal[c]ulated in its verry nature to make the sole of an honist man feel stronger than the powers of hell. But we must bring our epistle to a close [p. 16] we send our respects to Fathers, Mothers, wives, and children, Brothers, and Sisters. we hold them in the most sacred rememberance I send this epistle to Emma that She may have the first parusal of it[608] we feel to inquire after Elder Rigdon if he has not forgotten us it has not been signified to us by his pen scrawl. Brother George W Robinson also[609] and Elder [Reynolds] Cahoon we remember him but would like to jog his memory a little on the fable of the bair and the two friends who mutually agreed to stand by each other[610] and prehaps it would not be amis to mention Unkle John [Smith][611] and various others, a word of consolation and a blessing would

---

606. See 2 Samuel 22:3; Psalm 84:9; and Proverbs 30:5.

607. See 2 Thessalonians 1:4.

608. JS may have stricken this line before sending the letter, since he subsequently wrote a separate missive informing Emma Smith that she should "have the first reading" of the letter. It is also possible that Emma or someone else struck this line after Emma read the letter. (Letter to Emma Smith, 21 Mar. 1839, p. 373 herein.)

609. Released on bail, Rigdon left the Clay County jail on 5 February 1839. His family, presumably including his son-in-law George W. Robinson, left Far West for Illinois soon thereafter, arriving in Quincy on 16 February. (Hyrum Smith, Diary, 15 Mar. 1839; *History of the Reorganized Church,* 2:316; Editorial, *Quincy [IL] Whig,* 23 Feb. 1839, [1]; Rigdon, "Life Story of Sidney Rigdon," 153–158.)

610. In Aesop's fable of the bear and the two travelers, two men agree to support each other during their travels. When a bear approaches them in the forest, one of the men climbs a tree, leaving his companion to play dead on the ground. The bear sniffs the man on the ground and then leaves him alone. The other man climbs down the tree and asks his friend what the bear told him. The friend replies that the bear advised him to "not ever make a Journey with Friends of this Kind." (Clarke, *Fabulae Aesopi Selectae,* 48.)

611. Cahoon and John Smith were in the presidency of the stake at Adam-ondi-Ahman, Missouri. Cahoon left Far West for Quincy on 4 February 1839. Smith left soon after and arrived in Illinois on

not come amiss from any body while we are being so closly whispered by the Bair but we feel to excuse evry body and evry thing. Yea the more readily when we contemplate that we are in the hands of a wors than a Bair for a the Bair would not pray upon a dead carcus. Our respects and love and fellowship to all the virtious saints we are your Brethren and fellow sufferers and prisoners of Jesus Christ for the gospels sake[612] and for the hope of glory which is in us.[613] Amen.

/[614]**Joseph Smith Jr**
Hyrum Smith
Lyman Wight
Caleb Baldwin
Alexander. M[c.]Rae. [p. 17]

—————— ☙ ——————

Letter to Emma Smith, 21 March 1839

Source Note

JS, Letter, Liberty, Clay Co., MO, to Emma Smith, Quincy, Adams Co., IL, 21 Mar. 1839; handwriting and signatures of JS; three pages; JS Collection, CHL. Includes address.

Bifolium measuring 9⅝ × 7⅝ inches (24 × 19 cm). The letter was addressed and trifolded twice in letter style. Needle holes along the center fold suggest that at some time the letter was sewn to other documents. The letter has undergone conservation.

Emma Smith presumably received the letter in Illinois and kept it for some time; it later left the Smith family's possession. Around 1901, the letter was acquired by Iowa antiques collector Charles Birge.[615] Subsequently, custody of the letter was transferred to autograph collector Frederick Peck, who retained the letter until his death in 1947.[616] The letter was in the possession of Mary Benjamin, an autograph dealer and editor of the *Collector*,[617] from an unknown date until circa 1953, when custody was transferred to physician Charles W. Olsen, an eminent collector of Abraham Lincoln memorabilia.[618] Olsen donated the letter to the LDS church in 1961.[619]

---

28 February 1839. (Minutes, 28 June 1838, p. 166 herein; Cahoon, Autobiography, 47; John Smith, Journal, 24 Oct. 1838–3 June 1839.)

612. See Mark 8:35; and 1 Corinthians 9:23.

613. See Romans 5:2; Colossians 1:27; and Book of Mormon, 1830 ed., 130, 286 [Jacob 4:11; Alma 22:14].

614. TEXT: Alexander McRae handwriting ends; individual signatories begin.

615. Joseph Smith III, Lamoni, IA, to "Dear Sirs," Keokuk, IA, 1 July 1901, photocopy, CHL; "Notable Deaths," *Annals of Iowa*, Jan. 1904, 316; "Joseph Smith," *Collector*, Nov. 1903, 3–4.

616. Lazare, *American Book-Prices Current* (1947), 581; *Frederick S. Peck Collection of American Historical Autographs*, Foreword, 70.

617. Dickinson, *Dictionary of American Antiquarian Bookdealers*, 12–13.

618. "Doctor Prizes Copy of Paper Freeing Slaves," *Chicago Daily Tribune*, 5 May 1946, part 3, p. 10; Obituary for Charles W. Olsen, *Chicago Daily Tribune*, 3 Dec. 1962, part 3, p. 20.

619. Memorandum, 14 June 1961; David O. McKay, Salt Lake City, to Charles W. Olsen, Chicago, IL, 21 June 1961, in David O. McKay, Diary Entries, 21–22 June 1961, CHL.

Historical Introduction

On 21 March 1839, JS wrote a letter from the Clay County jail to his wife Emma Smith, who was in Quincy, Illinois. This letter, the fourth extant missive he wrote to her during his imprisonment in winter 1838–1839, was partly a response to her 7 March letter, in which she reflected upon her forced departure from the Smiths' Missouri home and upon the family's situation in Illinois.[620] In his letter, JS offered her encouragement and commented on her living situation, the health of their children, and the pain of his separation from the family. JS also included instructions on copying and transmitting the 20 March 1839 general epistle to the church. Additionally, he proposed that church members develop a "bill of damages" documenting their losses in Missouri, to be used in seeking redress from the federal government.

JS wrote two pages and then closed and signed the letter. Afterward, he inscribed a third page and then closed and signed the letter again. The missive may have been included in the "package of letters for Quincy" that church member Alanson Ripley picked up at the jail on 22 March 1839.[621] It is unknown how the letter was carried from Missouri to Illinois, although the lack of postal markings suggests a courier carried the letter.

Document Transcript

Liberty Jail Clay Co Mo 1839 March 21st
Affectionate Wife
I have sent an Epistle to the church[622] directed to you because I wanted you to have the first reading of it and then I want Father and Mother to have a coppy of it keep the original yourself as I dectated the matter myself and shall send an other as soon as posible[623] I want to be with you very much but the powers of mobocra[c]y is to many for me at preasant I would ask if Judge cleaveland [John Cleveland] will be kind enough to let you and the children tarry there[624] untill can learn somethng futher concerning my ~~lot~~ fate I will reward him well if he will and see that you do not suffer fo[r][625] any thing I shall have a little mony left when I come my

---

620. See Letter to Emma Smith, 4 Nov. 1838, pp. 279–282 herein; Letter to Emma Smith, 12 Nov. 1838, pp. 290–293 herein; Letter to Emma Smith, 1 Dec. 1838, pp. 293–294 herein; and Letter from Emma Smith, 7 Mar. 1839, pp. 338–340 herein.

621. Lyman Wight, Journal, in *History of the Reorganized Church,* 2:323.

622. See Letter to the Church and Edward Partridge, 20 Mar. 1839, pp. 356–372 herein.

623. See Historical Introduction to Letter to Edward Partridge and the Church, ca. 22 Mar. 1839, pp. 389–390 herein.

624. John and Sarah Kingsley Cleveland provided Emma Smith and her children with lodging after the Smiths arrived in Quincy in mid-February 1839. (Letter from Emma Smith, 7 Mar. 1839, p. 339 herein; Historian's Office, JS History, Draft Notes, 15 Feb. 1839.)

625. TEXT: "fo[*page torn*]".

Dear Emma I very well know your toils[626] **and simpathise with you if God will spare my life once more to have the privelege of takeing care of you I will ease your care and indeavour to cumfort your heart [p. [1]] I wa[n]t the you to take the best care of the family you can which I believe you will do all you can I was sorry to learn that Frederick [Smith] was sick**[627] **but I trust he is well again and that you are all well I want you to try to gain time and write to me a long letter and tell me all you can and even if old major is alive yet**[628] **and what those little pratlers say that cling around you[r] neck do you tell them I am in prison that that their lives might be saved**[629] **I want all the church to make out a bill of damages and apply to the united states Court as soon as possible**[630] **howeveve[r] they will find out what can be done themselves**[631] **you expressed my feelings concerning the order**[632] **and I blieve that there is a way to git redress for such things but God ruleth all things after the council of his own will**[633] **my trust is in him**[634] **the salvation of my soul is of the most importants to me for as**

626. In her 7 March 1839 letter to JS, Emma Smith referred to "the scenes of suffering that I have passed through, since what is called the Militia, came in to Far West" after Missouri governor Lilburn W. Boggs issued the expulsion order. She also described the pain she felt when leaving the Smiths' Missouri home. JS was perhaps also referring to the hardships Emma had faced in Illinois without his support. (Letter from Emma Smith, 7 Mar. 1839, pp. 339–340 herein.)

627. In her 7 March 1839 letter, Emma Smith noted, "We are all well at present, except Fredrick who is quite sick." (Letter from Emma Smith, 7 Mar. 1839, p. 339 herein.)

628. Old Major was the Smith family's white English mastiff. (See "The Memoirs of President Joseph Smith," *Saints' Herald,* 6 Nov. 1934, 1414; and Davis, *Story of the Church,* 252.)

629. On 31 October 1838, Major General Samuel D. Lucas demanded that JS and other church leaders submit to arrest; otherwise, the three thousand militiamen under Lucas's command would attack Far West, Missouri. (Samuel D. Lucas, "near Far West," MO, to Lilburn W. Boggs, 2 Nov. 1838, copy, Mormon War Papers, MSA.)

630. In a general epistle written to the church soon after this letter to Emma Smith, JS proposed that a committee be appointed "to take statements and affidafets" documenting the losses and abuses the Latter-day Saints had experienced in Missouri, with the intention of submitting the documents to the government. (Letter to Edward Partridge and the Church, ca. 22 Mar. 1839, p. 397 herein.)

631. In February 1839, church leaders in Quincy, Illinois, began laying the groundwork for pursuing redress for their losses, including through appointing a committee "to draught a petition to the general Government stating our Grievances and one likewise presented to the citizens for the same object." The minutes of this February meeting were evidently sent to Far West and incorporated into the records of the Far West removal committee. Church leaders in Far West may have informed JS of these efforts. (Quincy Committee, Minutes, ca. 9 Feb. 1839, Far West Committee, Minutes, CHL; see also Historical Introduction to Letter from Edward Partridge, 5 Mar. 1839, pp. 326–328 herein.)

632. Emma Smith described Governor Boggs's expulsion order of 27 October 1838 as follows: "The ever to be remembered Governor's notable order; an order fraught with as much wickedness as ignorance and as much ignorance as was ever contained in an article of that length." (Letter from Emma Smith, 7 Mar. 1839, p. 339 herein.)

633. See Revelation, 1 Aug. 1831, in *JSP,* D2:15 [D&C 58:20].

634. See Psalm 91:2; and Hebrews 2:13.

much as I know for a certainty of Eternal things if the heveans linger it is nothing to ⟨me⟩ I must stear my bark safe which I intend to do I want you to do the same yours forever Joseph Smith Jr

Emma Smith [p. [2]]

I wa[n]t you ⟨to⟩ have the Epistole coppyed immedeately[635] and let it go to the Bretheren firs[t] into the hands of Father for I want the production for my record[636] if you lack for mony [o]r fo[r][637] bread do let me know it as soon as possible[638] my nerve trembles from long confinement but if you feel as I do you dont care for the imperfections of my writings for my part a word of consolation from any sourse is cordially recieved by us me I feel like Joseph in Egyept doth my friends yet live[639] if they live do they remember me have they regard for me if so let me know it in time of trouble[640] my Dear Emma do you think that my being cast into prison by the mob of renders me less worthy of your friendsship no I do not think so but when I was in prisen and ye viseted me inasmuch as you have don it to the least ⟨of⟩ these you have don it to me these shall enter into life Eternal[641] but no more

your Husband J Smith Jr [p. [3]]

Mrs— Emma Smith
Quincy
Ilinois

———— ℰℐ ————

635. Extant copies of the 20 March 1839 epistle are in the handwriting of Edward Partridge and Albert Perry Rockwood. (JS, Liberty, MO, to the Church and Edward Partridge, Quincy, IL, 20–25 Mar. 1839, copy, CHL; JS et al., Liberty, MO, to the Church and Edward Partridge, Quincy, IL, 20 Mar. 1839, copy, Albert Perry Rockwood, Mormon Letters and Sermons, 1838–1839, Western Americana Collection, Beinecke Rare Book and Manuscript Library, Yale University, New Haven, CT.)

636. JS was perhaps referring to the history that he began in April 1838. (JS, Journal, 27 and 30 Apr. 1838, in *JSP*, J1:260, 263–264; Historical Introduction to History Drafts, 1838–ca. 1841, in *JSP*, H1:193.)

637. TEXT: "[*Page torn*]r fo[*page torn*]".

638. The prisoners apparently had some money in the jail, presumably provided by individuals in Far West. While imprisoned, Hyrum Smith sent twenty dollars to his wife, Mary Fielding Smith, in Quincy. (Hyrum Smith, Liberty, MO, to Mary Fielding Smith, Quincy, IL, 23 Mar. 1839, Mary Fielding Smith, Collection, CHL; see also Kimball, "History," 100–101.)

639. See Genesis 43:7, 27; 45:3.

640. See Psalms 27:5; 37:39; and Revelation, July 1828, in *JSP*, D1:8 [D&C 3:8].

641. See Matthew 25:36, 40, 46. Emma Smith visited JS three times in the Clay County jail: on 8–9 and 20–22 December 1838 and on 21 January 1839. (*History of the Reorganized Church*, 2:309, 315.)

Letter to Isaac Galland, 22 March 1839

Source Note

JS, Letter, Liberty, Clay Co., MO, to Isaac Galland, [Commerce, Hancock Co., IL], 22 Mar. 1839. Featured version published in Times and Seasons, *Feb. 1840, pp. 51–56. For more information on* Times and Seasons, *see Source Notes for Multiple-Entry Documents, p. 572 herein.*

Historical Introduction

On 22 March 1839, JS wrote from the Clay County jail in Liberty, Missouri, to land speculator Isaac Galland in Commerce, Illinois. The month before, Galland met with church members Israel Barlow and David Rogers regarding his offer to sell the church twenty thousand acres of land in Lee County, Iowa Territory, for Latter-day Saint refugees.[642] Later in the month, on 26 February 1839, Galland wrote a letter to Rogers, expressing sympathy for the suffering church members and offering to assist them in any way possible.[643] In late February or early March, likely after reading Galland's letter, church leaders in Quincy, Illinois, assigned Rogers to deliver the letter and other important documents to JS. Rogers left soon thereafter, arriving in Liberty on 19 March 1839.[644] The following day, JS wrote a general epistle to the church, encouraging church leaders in Illinois to exercise their discretion in whether to accept Galland's offer. Before making a decision, however, church leaders were to consult with "the most faithfull and the most respicible of the authorities of the church" at general conferences.[645]

Soon after completing the general epistle on 20 March 1839, JS wrote to Galland, apparently responding to items in Galland's February missive to Rogers. Galland had inquired about the status of Rogers's "captive brethren in Missouri" and whether JS had yet been released. Galland had also conceded that he had "little knowledge . . . as yet of the doctrines, order or practice of the church."[646] In JS's response, he described the Saints' sufferings and the prisoners' misfortunes. He also gave an extended description of Latter-day Saint beliefs about the Bible, revelation, authority, and other "leading items of the gospel." JS concluded the letter by stating his intention to purchase Galland's land upon being released from prison. This statement indicates that JS's thinking had changed since writing the 20 March general epistle to the church.[647]

---

642. Rogers, Statement, [1], CHL; Quincy Committee, Minutes, ca. 9 Feb. 1839, Far West Committee, Minutes, CHL.

643. Isaac Galland, Commerce, IL, to David Rogers, [Quincy, IL], 26 Feb. 1839, in JS Letterbook 2, pp. 1–3.

644. Historical Introduction to Letter from Edward Partridge, 5 Mar. 1839, p. 328 herein; Letter to the Church and Edward Partridge, 20 Mar. 1839, p. 365 herein; Hyrum Smith, Liberty, MO, to Mary Fielding Smith, Quincy, IL, 19 Mar. 1839, Mary Fielding Smith, Collection, CHL.

645. Letter to the Church and Edward Partridge, 20 Mar. 1839, pp. 367–368 herein.

646. Isaac Galland, Commerce, IL, to David Rogers, [Quincy, IL], 26 Feb. 1839, in JS Letterbook 2, p. 2.

647. In contrast to the general epistle of 20 March 1839, which encouraged church leaders in Quincy to decide whether to purchase Galland's land, the second general epistle strongly encouraged church leaders "to secure to themselves the contract of the Land which is proposed to them by Mr. Isaac Galland." In this

JS, who was the only signatory of the letter, likely dictated it to one of his fellow prisoners, perhaps Alexander McRae, who performed most of the scribal duties for JS's extended compositions in March 1839.[648] The missive may have been included in the "package of letters for Quincy" that the prisoners gave church member Alanson Ripley when he visited the jail on 22 March 1839.[649] How the letter was carried to Galland in Illinois is unknown. The land speculator's immediate reaction to the letter is also unknown; extant records do not indicate whether he reserved the land for the Saints, but the land in question was available when JS arrived in Illinois on 22 April 1839, and soon afterward the church bought the land.[650] Additionally, the letter probably influenced Galland's decision to join the church in July 1839.[651]

The original letter is apparently not extant. However, a transcript of the letter was printed in the February 1840 issue of the *Times and Seasons;* this printed copy is the version featured here.[652]

Document Transcript

Liberty jail, Clay co. Mo. March 22nd, 1839.

Mr. Isaac Galland; Dear Sir:

I have just been privileged with a perusal of a letter, put into my hands by Mr. D[avid] W. Rogers, which letter was directed to him, dated February 26th, 1839. and signed, Isaac Galland.[653] The contents of said letter expresses a sympathy and a good feeling towards the people and church of the Latter Day Saints, which I have the high honor, of being their religious leader; I say high

second epistle, written about the same time that JS completed the letter to Galland, JS described Galland as a "man of honor and a friend to humanity." (Letter to Edward Partridge and the Church, ca. 22 Mar. 1839, pp. 391–392 herein; see also Letter to the Church and Edward Partridge, 20 Mar. 1839, pp. 356–372 herein.)

648. See Petition to George Tompkins, between 9 and 15 Mar. 1839, pp. 340–352 herein; Letter to the Church and Edward Partridge, 20 Mar. 1839, pp. 356–372 herein; and Letter to Edward Partridge and the Church, ca. 22 Mar. 1839, pp. 388–401 herein. In contrast, around this time JS wrote two short letters to Emma Smith in his own hand. (See Letter to Emma Smith, 21 Mar. 1839, pp. 372–375 herein; and Letter to Emma Smith, 4 Apr. 1839, pp. 401–406 herein.)

649. Lyman Wight, Journal, in *History of the Reorganized Church,* 2:323.

650. The church purchased land from Galland in Commerce and Lee County in April, May, and June 1839. (JS, Journal, 24 Apr.–3 May 1839, in *JSP,* J1:336; Minutes, 24 Apr. 1839, p. 438 herein; Agreement with George W. Robinson, 30 Apr. 1839, pp. 441–442 herein.)

651. JS baptized Galland and ordained him an elder on 3 July 1839. (JS, Journal, 3 July 1839, in *JSP,* J1:345.)

652. Other letters JS wrote from the Clay County jail were substantially edited before being published in the *Times and Seasons,* suggesting that the letter to Galland may have also been edited. At a minimum, the editors likely added citations to JS's several references to the Bible since JS might not have had a Bible in the jail. (See Historical Introduction to Letter to the Church in Caldwell Co., MO, 16 Dec. 1838, pp. 297–298 herein; Historical Introduction to Letter to the Church and Edward Partridge, 20 Mar. 1839, p. 360 herein; and Historical Introduction to Letter to Edward Partridge and the Church, ca. 22 Mar. 1839, p. 391 herein.)

653. See Isaac Galland, Commerce, IL, to David Rogers, [Quincy, IL], 26 Feb. 1839, in JS Letterbook 2, pp. 1–3.

honor, more especially, because I know them to be an honorable, a virtuous, and an upright people. And that honor, vir[p. 51]tue, and righteousness is their only aim and object in this life. They are sir, a much injured, and abused people; and are greatly belied as to their true character. They have been fallen upon by a gang of ruffians and murderers, three times, in the state of Missouri; and entirely broken up, without having committed the first offence: or without there being the least shadow in the very slightest degree of evidence, that they have done ought of any thing derogatory to the laws, or character, of the state of Missouri.[654] And this last time of their being broken up; it is either my misfortune, or good fortune, (for I rather count it good fortune to suffer affliction with the people of God,)[655] in connection with others of my brethren, to be made a severe sufferer, by the hands of the above mentioned *rascals:* they are supported by some portions of the authorities of the State, either in consequence of prejudices, excited by foul calumnies, or else they themselves, are the fathers and instigators, of the whole diabolical and murderous proceeding.

I am bold to say sir, that a more nefarious transaction never has existed, since the days of Yore; than that which has been practiced upon us.— Myself and those who are in prison with me, were torn from our houses, with our wives and children clinging to our garments,[656] under the awful expectation of being exterminated.[657] At our first examination, the mob found one or two persons, of low and worthless character, whom they compelled, at the peril of their lives, to swear some things against us: which things, if they had been even true, were nothing at all, and could not have so much as disgraced any man under

---

654. Prior to the 1838 conflict, the Latter-day Saints in Missouri were forced to relocate on two occasions. In late 1833, vigilantes violently expelled church members from Jackson County. In 1836, non-Mormons asked church members in Clay County to leave to avoid a repeat of the Jackson County expulsion. (See Historical Introduction to Letter from William W. Phelps, 6–7 Nov. 1833, in *JSP,* D3:336; and Historical Introduction to Letter to John Thornton et al., 25 July 1836, in *JSP,* D5:258–260; see also LeSueur, "Missouri's Failed Compromise," 113–144.)

655. See Hebrews 11:25.

656. Joseph Smith III recalled that when JS "was brought to the house by an armed guard I ran out of the gate to greet him, but was roughly pushed away from his side by a sword in the hand of the guard and not allowed to go near him. My mother, also, was not permitted to approach him and had to receive his farewell by word of lip only." ("The Memoirs of President Joseph Smith," *Saints' Herald,* 6 Nov. 1934, 1414; see also Letter to Edward Partridge and the Church, ca. 22 Mar. 1839, p. 395 herein; and Pratt, *History of the Late Persecution,* 42–43.)

657. "Being exterminated" likely refers to the order that Missouri governor Lilburn W. Boggs issued on 27 October 1838 that "the Mormons must be treated as enemies and must be exterminated or driven from the state if necessary." Lucy Mack Smith, JS's mother, recalled the anxiety she and Joseph Smith Sr. felt after JS was arrested. After hearing several gunshots, they concluded that their son had been murdered. (Lilburn W. Boggs, Jefferson City, MO, to John B. Clark, Fayette, MO, 27 Oct. 1838, copy, Mormon War Papers, MSA; Lucy Mack Smith, History, 1844–1845, bk. 16, [2].)

heaven.[658] Nevertheless, we could have proved, by more than five hundred witnesses, that the things were false. But the Judge employed an armed force, and compelled us to abandon the idea of introducing witnesses, upon the peril of the lives of the witnesses.[659] Under such circumstances, sir, we were committed to this jail, on a pretended charge of treason, against the State of Missouri, without the slightest evidence to that effect.[660] We collected our witnesses the second time, and petitioned a habeas corpus: but were thrust back again into prison, by the rage of the mob;[661] and our families robbed, and plundered: and families, and witnesses, thrust from their homes, and hunted out of the State, and dare not return for their lives.[662] And under this order of things, we, held in confinement, for a pretended trial: whereas we are to be tried by those very characters who have practiced those things, yea the very characters who have murdered some hundred men, women and children,[663] and have sworn to have our lives also; and have made public proclamation that these men must and should be hung, whether they were innocent, or guilty.[664] Such men too, sir, have made this proclamation, as general [David R.] Atchison, who is considered one of the most prominent men in the State. This is according to the information I have

---

658. For more information on witnesses for the prosecution, see Introduction to Part 3: 4 Nov. 1838–16 Apr. 1839, pp. 273–274 herein.

659. Hyrum Smith recalled that the prisoners submitted the names of sixty potential defense witnesses; only seven ultimately testified. Several Latter-day Saints recounted that officers of the court harassed and abused defense witnesses, discouraging individuals from testifying. (See 273n42 herein.)

660. For more information on the November 1838 court of inquiry and the treason charge against JS, see Introduction to Part 3: 4 Nov. 1838–16 Apr. 1839, pp. 273–274 herein.

661. On 22 January 1839, JS and the other prisoners appeared before Clay County justice Joel Turnham on a writ of habeas corpus. On 30 January, Turnham released Rigdon on bail but remanded the remaining prisoners to the Clay County jail. Attorney Peter Burnett recalled that there was considerable opposition in Clay County to Turnham's decision to issue the writ of habeas corpus and allow the hearing. (See Introduction to Part 3: 4 Nov. 1838–16 Apr. 1839, p. 276 herein.)

662. JS's home was ransacked during the state militia's occupation of Far West, Missouri, in early November 1838. The other prisoners' homes may have also been vandalized. The prisoners' families were part of the forced exodus of the Latter-day Saints in spring 1839. (Historical Introduction to Declaration to the Clay County Circuit Court, ca. 6 Mar. 1839, pp. 335–337 herein; Pratt, *History of the Late Persecution*, 42; Letter from Edward Partridge, 5 Mar. 1839, pp. 329–331 herein.)

663. TEXT: The *Times and Seasons* editors added a footnote here: "He was thus imformed by the Missourians." For more information on the Latter-day Saint casualties during the October 1838 conflict, see Introduction to Part 3: 4 Nov. 1838–16 Apr. 1839, p. 269 herein.

664. Judge Austin A. King, who presided at the November 1838 hearing, reportedly stated in public that JS should be executed, regardless of whether he was convicted. On another occasion, King issued an arrest warrant for JS and Lyman Wight following a confrontation on 8 August 1838 with Adam Black, a Daviess County justice of the peace. King was then quoted as saying he was "in hopes that joseph smith jun & Lyman Wight would not be taken & tried acording to law so that they could have the pleasure of taking their scalps." (Warner Hoopes, Affidavit, Pike Co., IL, 14 Jan. 1840, Record Group 233, Records of the U.S. House of Representatives, National Archives, Washington DC; see also Affidavit, 5 Sept. 1838, pp. 219–225 herein.)

received, which I suppose to be true.[665] Their plea sir, is that the State will be ruined, if the Mormon leaders are liberated, so that they can publish the real facts, of what has been practised upon them.

We are kept under a strong guard, night and day, in a prison of double walls and doors, proscribed in our liberty of conscience, our food is scant, uniform, and coarse; we have not the privilege of cooking for ourselves, we have been compelled to sleep on the floor with straw, and not blankets sufficient to keep us warm; and when we have a fire, we are obliged to have almost a constant smoke. The Judges have gravely told us from time to time that they knew we were innocent, and ought to be liberated, but they dare not administer the law unto us, for fear of the mob.[666] But if we will deny our religion, we can be liberated. Our lawyers have gravely told us, that we are only held now by the influence of long faced Baptists; how far this is true, we are not able to say: but we are certain that our most vehement accusers, are the highest toned professors of religion. On being interogated what these men have done? their uniform answer is, we do not know, but they are false teachers, and ought to die. And of late boldly and frankly acknowledge, that the religion of these men, is all that they have against them. Now sir, the only difference between their [p. 52] religion, and mine, is, that I firmly believe in the prophets and apostles, Jesus Christ, being the chief cornerstone.[667] And speak as one having authority among them, and not as the scribes,[668] and am liberal in my sentiments towards all men, in matters of opinion, and rights of conscience, whereas they are not.[669] But enough of this. I feel highly gratified to learn of a man who had sympathy, and feelings of friendship towards a suffering, and an injured, and an innocent people: if you can do them any good, render them any assistance, or protection, in the name of suffering humanity, we beseech you, for God's sake, and humanity's sake, that you will do it.[670] If you should see

---

665. For information on the prisoners' frustrations with and suspicions of Representative Atchison of Clay County, see 364n555 herein.

666. Meacham Curtis, assistant to Justice Turnham, remembered Turnham stating that "he would have acquitted the prisoners" in January 1839 if not "for fear that they would be assassinated by a furious mob." (Meacham Curtis, Affidavit, Bandera, TX, 23 July 1878, in *Saints' Herald,* 15 Aug. 1878, 256.)

667. See Ephesians 2:20.

668. See Matthew 7:29; and Mark 1:22.

669. Around the time JS wrote this letter to Galland, JS wrote a general epistle to the church, in which he described his thoughts on religious liberty and the denial of that right to the Latter-day Saints. (Letter to Edward Partridge and the Church, ca. 22 Mar. 1839, pp. 388–401 herein.)

670. JS was probably responding to statements Galland made in his 26 February 1839 letter: "I wish to serve your cause in any matter which providence may afford me the opportunity of doing, And I therefore request that you feel no hesitancy, or reluctance in communicating to me your wishes, at all times, and on any subject." Galland also wrote, "Accept dear Sir, for yourself, and in behalf of your church and people, assurance of my sincere sympathy in your sufferings and wrongs, and deep

Dungeon of Clay County jail. Circa 1940s. Joseph Smith noted in his 22 March 1839 letter to Isaac Galland that the prisoners were confined "in a prison of double walls and doors." He complained of eating "coarse" food and of being "compelled to sleep on the floor with straw" and without sufficient blankets. (Church History Library, Salt Lake City. Photograph by Otto Done.)

Gov. [Robert] Lucas, I wish you would have the kindness to state to him, the contents of this letter; as we know him from information to be a man of character and a gentleman.[671] I would be glad therefore, if it were possible that he, and not only him, but every other patriotic, and humane man, should know

solicitude for your immdediately releif from present distress, and future triumphant conquest over every enemy." (Isaac Galland, Commerce, IL, to David Rogers, [Quincy, IL], 26 Feb. 1839, in JS Letterbook 2, pp. 2, 3.)

671. Lucas served as governor of Ohio from 1832 to 1836, when the church was headquartered in Kirtland, Ohio. In 1838 he was appointed the first governor of Iowa Territory. In Galland's 26 February 1839 letter, he reported on Lucas's views toward the Latter-day Saints: "He respects them now as good and virtuous citizens, and feels disposed to treat them as such." (Ryan, *History of Ohio,* 177; Isaac Galland, Commerce, IL, to David Rogers, [Quincy, IL], 26 Feb. 1839, in JS Letterbook 2, p. 1; see also Letter to Edward Partridge and the Church, ca. 22 Mar. 1839, pp. 391–392 herein.)

the real facts of our sufferings: and of the unjust and cruel hand that is upon us. I have been in this State one year, the 12th, day of this month;[672] I have never borne arms at any time. I have never held any office, civil or military in this State. I have only officiated as a religious teacher, in religious matters, and not in temporal matters. The only occasion I have given, was to defend my own family, in my own door yard, against the invasions of a lawless mob: and that I did not at the expense of any man's life: but risked my own in defence of an innocent family,[673] consisting of a wife, five children,[674] hired servants[675] &c. My residence was in Far West. I was surrounded with a noble, generous, and enterprising society, who were friendly to the laws, and constitution of our country: they were broken up without cause, and my family now as I suppose, if living, are in Quincy, Illinois.[676]

We are informed that the prisoners in Richmond jail, Ray county, are much more inhumanly treated than we are;[677] if this is the case, we will assure you,

---

672. On 12 January 1838, JS departed Ohio for Missouri. By 12 March, JS had crossed into Missouri, and he arrived in Far West on 14 March, after traveling approximately eight hundred miles. (See JS, Journal, Mar.–Sept. 1838, p. 16, in *JSP*, J1:237; Letter to the Presidency in Kirtland, 29 Mar. 1838, p. 57 herein; JS History, vol. B-1, 831.)

673. JS presented a similar idea in his mid-March 1839 petition for a writ of habeas corpus: "The prisoner has never commanded any military company nor held any military authority neither any other office real or pretended in the state of Missouri except that of a religeous teacher that he never has born armes in the military ranks and in all such cases has acted as a private charactor and as an individual how then can . . . it be posible that the prisoner has committed treason the prisoner has had nothing to do in Davis County only on his own buisines as an individual?" (Petition to George Tompkins, between 9 and 15 Mar. 1839, pp. 348–349 herein.)

674. JS and Emma Smith were the parents of Julia Murdock (adopted), Joseph III, Frederick, and Alexander Smith. The fifth child JS referred to may have been Johanna Carter, an orphan who was apparently living with the Smiths in Far West. (See Letter to Emma Smith, 4 Apr. 1839, p. 404 herein.)

675. In 1838 Jonathan Barlow was "apointed Steward in the hous of President Joseph Smith." Barlow's duties entailed feeding and watering horses, cutting wood, and completing other odd jobs. The identities of JS's other hired servants in Missouri remain elusive. (Israel Barlow, Autobiographical Statement, no date, Barlow Family Collection, CHL; Jonathan Barlow, Testimony, Richmond, MO, Nov. 1838, p. [118], State of Missouri v. JS et al. for Treason and Other Crimes [Mo. 5th Jud. Cir. 1838], in State of Missouri, "Evidence"; see also Jonathan Barlow, Testimony, Liberty, MO, 12 Feb. 1839, State of Missouri v. Ripley et al. [J.P. Ct. 1839], Clay County Archives and Historical Library, Liberty, MO.)

676. JS's wife Emma Smith and brother Don Carlos Smith sent letters to JS noting that Emma and the children arrived in Illinois in mid-February 1839 and found lodging with John and Sarah Kingsley Cleveland about four miles from Quincy, although Emma added that "I do not know how long I shall stay here." Emma also informed her husband that their son Frederick was "quite sick." As JS and Emma had already lost four children, JS may have feared for Frederick's life. (Letter from Don Carlos Smith and William Smith, 6 Mar. 1839, p. 333 herein; Letter from Emma Smith, 7 Mar. 1839, p. 339 herein.)

677. In November 1838, Judge King ruled there was probable cause to believe that Parley P. Pratt, Norman Shearer, Darwin Chase, Luman Gibbs, and Morris Phelps murdered Moses Rowland during the skirmish at Crooked River, near Ray County, Missouri, on 25 October 1838. King ordered the men

that their constitutions cannot last long, for we find ours wearing away very fast: and if we knew of any source whereby aid and assistance could be rendered unto us, we should most cordially petition for it: but where is liberty? Where is humanity? Where is patriotism? Where has the genius of the pedistal of the laws and constitution of our boasted country fled? Are they not slain victims at the feet of prejudice, to gratify the malice of a certain class of men, who have learned that their craft and creed cannot stand against the light of truth, when it comes to be investigated?— hence they resort to the vilest of the vile means, and to foul calumnies, and to physical force to do what? To deprive some fifty thousand, of the right of citizenship, and for what?[678] because they are blasphemers? no: For this is contrary to their practice, as well as faith. Was it because they were tavern haunters, and drunkards? no. This charge cannot be substantiated against them as a people; it was contrary to their faith.[679] And finally was it for any thing? no sir, not for any thing, only, that Mormonism is truth; and every man who embraced it felt himself at liberty to embrace every truth: consequently the shackles of superstition, bigotry, ignorance, and priestcraft,[680] falls at once from his neck; and his eyes are opened to see the truth, and truth greatly prevails over priestcraft; hence the priests are alarmed, and they raise a hu-in-cry, down with these men! heresy! heresy! fanaticism! false prophet! false teachers! away with these men! crucify them! crucify them![681] And now sir, this is the sole cause of the persecution against the Mormon people, and now if they had been Mahomedans,[682]

---

to be held for trial in the Ray County jail. As with the prisoners in Clay County, those in Ray County spent time confined in the jail's small dungeon. Phelps noted that the conditions were filthy, the lighting was poor, the guards were abusive, and most visitors were turned away or closely watched. "Most of the time we had plenty to eat," Phelps recalled, "but it was verry ruff, cornbread and bacon, was our principal diate." The prisoners did have some privileges, including permission for their wives to stay in the jail. Although the conditions in the Ray County jail were not comfortable, it is unclear why JS believed the prisoners there were treated more severely than were the prisoners in the Clay County jail. (Ruling, Richmond, MO, Nov. 1838, pp. [124]–[125], in State of Missouri, "Evidence"; Phelps, Reminiscences, [20]–[23]; Parley P. Pratt, Richmond, MO, to Mary Ann Frost Pratt, Far West, MO, 1 Dec. 1838, Parley P. Pratt, Letters, CHL; see also Baugh, "Final Episode of Mormonism in Missouri," 1–34.)

678. There were approximately eight to ten thousand Latter-day Saints in Missouri in 1838. (Elias Smith, Far West, MO, to Ira Smith, East Stockholm, NY, 11 Mar. 1839, Elias Smith Correspondence, CHL; Heber C. Kimball, Far West, MO, to Joseph Fielding, Preston, England, 12 Mar. 1839, in Compilation of Heber C. Kimball Correspondence, CHL; LeSueur, *1838 Mormon War in Missouri,* 35; Leonard, *Nauvoo,* 671–672n33.)

679. JS dictated a revelation in 1833 proscribing the consumption of wine and "strong drinks"—apparently distilled liquors—although "wine of your own make" was permitted for the sacrament of the Lord's Supper. (Revelation, 27 Feb. 1833, in *JSP,* D3:20–21 [D&C 89:5–6].)

680. See "Priestcraft," in *American Dictionary.*

681. See Mark 15:13–14; Luke 23:21; and John 19:6.

682. "Mahomedans" was a name Europeans used when referring to Muslims. JS's advocacy for religious toleration of Muslims reflected the views of Thomas Jefferson and other national leaders who

Hottentots,[683] or Pagans;[684] or in fine sir, if their religion was as false as hell, what right would men have to drive them from their homes, and their country, or to exterminate them, so long as their religion did not interfere with the civil rights of men, according to the laws of our country? None at all. But the mind naturally being curious wants to know what those sentiments are, that are so at varience with the priests of the age, and I trust you will bear with me, while I offer to you a few of my reflections on this subject, and if they should not meet your mind, it may open a door for an exchange of ideas, and in the exercise of a proper liberality of spirit, it may not be unprofitable.

In the first place, I have stated above [p. 53] that Mormonism is truth, in other words the doctrine of the Latter Day Saints, is truth; for the name Mormon, and Mormonism, was given to us by our enemies,[685] but Latter Day Saints was the real name by which the church was organized.[686] Now sir, you may think that it is a broad assertion that it is truth; but sir, the first and fundamental principle of our holy religion is, that we believe that we have a right to embrace all, and every item of truth, without limitation or without being circumscribed or prohibited by the creeds or superstitious notions of men,[687] or by the dominations of one another, when that truth is clearly demonstrated to our minds, and we have the highest degree of evidence of the same; we feel ourselves bound by the laws of God, to observe and do strictly, with all our

---

contended that religious liberty should extend beyond traditional Christian groups to include adherents of Islam. (See Spellberg, *Thomas Jefferson's Qur'an*, 3–11.)

683. "Hottentots" was the name Dutch settlers gave to the Khoikhoi, a pastoralist indigenous people of southern Africa. One nineteenth-century gazetteer claimed that they had no recognizable religion prior to the arrival of Europeans. (Brookes, *New Universal Gazetteer*, 384–385; Thompson, *History of South Africa*, 10–11, 37.)

684. Europeans and European Americans in the eighteenth and nineteenth centuries used the term *pagan* to describe the religions of the indigenous peoples of the Americas and Africa. Some European Americans argued that these religions deserved legal toleration. (Pointer, "Native Freedom," 169–194.)

685. As early as June 1830, an outside observer noted that because JS's followers "believe in the Book of Mormon, they bear the name Mormonites." In the 1830s, journalists called the religion "Mormonism," with church members referred to as "Mormonites" and "Mormons." (Quinn, "First Months of Mormonism," 331; see also "Western Tartary Fifty Years Ago," *Maryland Gazette* [Annapolis], 7 Apr. 1831, [1]; "Forbearance of the Abolitionists," *Liberator* [Boston], 29 Aug. 1835, 139; and Editorial, *Sun* [Baltimore], 10 June 1837, [1].)

686. In 1830 the church was organized as the "Church of Christ." Four years later, the name was changed to the "Church of the Latter Day Saints." In April 1838, JS dictated a revelation that combined the two names as the Church of Jesus Christ of Latter Day Saints. (See 114n550 herein; and Revelation, 26 Apr. 1838, p. 114 herein [D&C 115:3–4].)

687. Presumably, JS was referring to the various statements of belief that had been adopted periodically throughout the history of Christianity, such as the fourth-century Nicene Creed and later Protestant statements, including the 1784 Methodist Articles of Religion. These statements were intended to define a group's doctrine, usually in contradistinction from other groups. (See Welch, "All Their Creeds Were an Abomination," 228–249.)

hearts, all things whatsoever is manifest unto us by the highest degree of testimony that God has committed us, as written in the old and new Testament, or
any where else, by any manifestation, whereof we know that it has come from
God: and has application to us, being adapted to our situation and circumstances; age, and generation of life; and that we have a perfect, and indefeasible
right, to embrace all such commandments, and do them; knowing, that God
will not command any thing, but what is peculiarly adapted in itself, to ame-
liorate the condition of every man under whatever circumstances it may find
him, it matters not what kingdom or country he may be in. And again, we
believe that it is our privilege to reject all things, whatsoever is clearly manifested to us that they do not have a bearing upon us. Such as, for instance, it is
not binding on us to build an Ark, because God commanded Noah to build
one.— It would not be applicable to our case; we are not looking for a flood.[688]
It is not binding on us to lead the children of Israel out of the land of Egypt,
because God commanded Moses.[689] The children of Israel are not in bondage
to the Egyptians, as they were then; our circumstances are very different. I
have introduced these for examples: and on the other hand, "Thou shalt not
kill. Thou shalt not steal. Thou shalt not commit adultery. Thou shalt not bare
false witness against thy neighbor. Thou shalt not covet thy neighbor's wife,
nor his ox, nor his ass, nor his man servant, nor his maid servant, nor any
thing that is thy neighbors."[690]

These sentiments we most cordially embrace, and consider them binding on
us because they are adapted to our circumstances. We believe that we have a
right to revelations, visions, and dreams from God, our heavenly Father; and
light and intelligence, through the gift of the Holy Ghost, in the name of Jesus
Christ, on all subjects pertaining to our spiritual welfare; if it so be that we keep
his commandments, so as to render ourselves worthy in his sight. We believe that
no man can administer salvation through the gospel, to the souls of men, in the
name of Jesus Christ, except he is authorized from God, by revelation, or by
being ordained by some one whom God hath sent by revelation, as It is written
by Paul, Romans 10:14, "and how shall they believe in him, of whom, they have
not heard? and how shall they hear without a preacher? and how shall they
preach, except they be sent?"[691] and I will ask, how can they be sent without a
revelation, or some other visible display of the manifestation of God. And
again, Hebrews, 5:4, "And no man taketh this honor unto himself, but he that

---

688. See Genesis chaps. 6–8.
689. See Exodus chap. 14.
690. Exodus 20:13–17.
691. Romans 10:14–15.

is called of God, as was Aaron."— And I would ask, how was Aaron called, but by revelation?

And again we believe in the doctrine of faith, and of repentance, and of baptism for the remission of sins, and the gift of the Holy Ghost, by the laying on of hands, and of resurrection of the dead, and of eternal judgment.[692] We believe in the doctrine of repentance, as well as of faith; and in the doctrine of baptism for the remission of sins as well as in the doctrine of repentance; and in the doctrine of the gift of the Holy Ghost by the laying on of hands, as well as baptism for the remission of sins; and also, in like manner, of the resurrection of the dead, and of eternal judgment. Now all these are the doctrines set forth by the apostles, and if we have any thing to do with one of them, they are all alike precious, and binding on us. And as proof, mark the following quotations. Mark 16 chap., 15–16 verses, "and he said [p. 54] unto them go ye into all the world and preach the gospel to every creature, and he that believeth and is baptized shall be saved, but he that believeth not shall be damned." Hear you will see the doctrine of faith: and again, Acts 2nd chap. 28 verse, "Then Peter said unto them repent and be baptized every one of you in the name of Jesus Christ for the remission of sins, and ye shall receive the gift of the Holy Ghost."[693] Hear you see the doctrine of repentance and baptism for the remission of sins, and the gift of the Holy Ghost, connected by the promise inseperably. Now I want you to consider the high standing of Peter; he was now being endowed with power from on high and held the keys of the kingdom of heaven. Mathew 16th chap. 19th verse, ["]and I will give unto you the keys of the kingdom of heaven, and whatsoever thou shalt bind on earth shall be bound in heaven, and whatsoever thou shalt loose on earth shall be loosed in heaven." This was the character, Sir, that made the glorious promise of the gift of the Holy Ghost, predicated upon the baptism for the remission of sins: and he did not say that it was confined to that generation, but see further: Act[s] 2nd chap. 39th verse, "for the promise is unto you, and your children, and to all who are afar off, even as many as the Lord our God shall call." Then, Sir, if the callings of God extend unto us, we come within the perview of Peter's promise. Now where is the man who is authorized to put his finger on the spot and say, thus far shalt thou go and no farther: there is no man. Therefore let us receive the whole, or none. And again, concerning the doctrine of the laying on of hands. Act[s] 8th chap. 14th to 17th verse. Now when the apostles, which were at Jerusalem, heard that Samaria had received the word of God, they sent unto them Peter and John; who, when they were

692. See Hebrews 6:1–2.
693. Although cited as Acts 2:28, the quoted language comes from Acts 2:38.

come down, prayed for them, that they might receive the Holy Ghost; for as yet he was fallen upon none of them, only they were baptized in the name of the Lord Jesus.— Then laid they their hands upon them, and they received the Holy Ghost.— Acts 19th chap. 5th–6th verses.— When they heard this, they were baptized in the name of the Lord Jesus.— And when Paul had laid his hands upon them, the Holy Ghost came on them; and they spake with tongues and prophesied. We discover by these, the doctrine of the laying on of the hands.— And for the doctrine of the resurrection of the dead and of eternal judgment: Hebrews 6th chap. 2nd verse, of the doctrine of baptism, and of laying on of the hands, and of reserrection of the dead, and of eternal judgment. I consider these to be some of the leading items of the gospel, as taught by Christ and his apostles, and as received by those whom they taught. I wish you would look at these, carefully and closely, and you will readily perceive that the difference between me and other religious teachers, is in the bible; and the bible and them for it: and as far as they teach the gospel of Jesus Christ, as it is verily written, and are inspired, and called as was Aaron, I feel myself bound to bow with all defference to their mandates and teachings; but see Gallations, 1st chap. 6th to 10th verse. I marvel that you are so soon removed from him that called you into the grace of Christ, unto another Gospel;[694] but there be some that trouble you, and would pervert the gospel of Christ. But though we, or an angel from heaven, preach any other gospel unto you than that which we have preached unto you, let him be accursed. As we said before, so say I now again, if any man preach any other gospel unto you than that ye have received, let him be accursed. For do I now persuade men or God? or do I seek to please men? for if I yet pleased men, I should not be the servant of Christ. Further, the 11–12 verses. But, I certify you, brethren, that the gospel which was preached of me is not after man; for I neither received it of man, neither was I taught it, but by the revelation of Jesus Christ.

Please Sir, to pardon me for having obtruded thus lengthy upon your feelings, as you are a stranger to me; and I know nothing of you, only what I have read in you[r] letter, and from that I have taken the liberty which I have. Be assured Sir, that I have the most liberal sentiments, and feelings of charity towards all sects, parties, and denominations; and the rights and liberties of concience, I hold most sa[p. 55]cred and dear, and dispise no man for differing with me in matters of opinion.

Accept Dear Sir, my best wishes for your welfare, and desire for further acquaintance, I close my letter, by giving you some quotations which you will have the goodness to read.

---

694. The quotation here omits the beginning of verse 7: "Which is not another."

The second epistle of Paul to Timothy, 1:5–7. 2:10–14. 4:2–7. Ephesians 4:10–18. 1st Corinthians 12:1–31. 8:3–6. Ephesians 4:1–8. The 1st Epistle of John 1: Mathew, 3:13–17. St. John 3:1[–]16. 10:1–50.[695] 28:18–20.[696] St. Luke 24:45–53. If you wish another address on this subject, you have only to let me know, and it shall be attended to.

Yours truly,

JOSEPH SMITH, Jr.

N. B. If Bishop [Edward] Partridge, or if the church have not made a purchase of your land, and if there is not any one who feels a particular interest in making the purchase, you will hold it in reserve for us; we will purchase it of you at the proposals that you made to Mr. [Israel] Barlow. We think the church would be wise in making the contract, therefore, if it is not made before we are liberated, we will make it.[697]

Yours &c.

JOSEPH SMITH, Jr.

———— ☙ ————

Letter to Edward Partridge and the Church, circa 22 March 1839

Source Note

JS, Hyrum Smith, Lyman Wight, Caleb Baldwin, and Alexander McRae, Letter, [Liberty, Clay Co., MO], to Edward Partridge and the church, Quincy, Adams Co., IL, [ca. 22 Mar. 1839]; handwriting of Alexander McRae, with insertions by JS; signatures of JS, Hyrum Smith, Lyman Wight, Caleb Baldwin, and Alexander McRae; nine pages; Revelations Collection, CHL. Includes address and dockets, with a redaction in graphite.

Three bifolia measuring 12½ × 7¾ inches (32 × 20 cm). The document was trifolded twice in letter style for mailing and was then addressed. The final leaf has marked soiling, and there is separation at the folds, with some loss of paper. Likely after being damaged at the folds, the bifolia were fastened with staples; subsequently, the staples were removed. The document has undergone conservation more than once. When cellophane tape was removed, the paper was damaged, reducing the legibility of portions of the document. Mold and then bleaching to remove the mold have caused the ink to fade, further reducing legibility.

The *Times and Seasons* published an edited version of the letter in July 1840.[698] Church clerk Thomas Bullock copied the letter into JS's multivolume manuscript history in 1845.[699] The letter was

---

695. John 10 has only 42 verses.

696. The biblical book of John has only 21 chapters. This reference was perhaps a printing error, with the intended reference being John 18:18–20 or Matthew 28:18–20.

697. Around the time that JS composed this letter, he wrote a general epistle to the church, in which he stated, "The church would do well to secure to themselves the contract of the Land which is proposed to them by Mr. Isaac Galland." (Letter to Edward Partridge and the Church, ca. 22 Mar. 1839, pp. 391–392 herein.)

698. "An Extract of a Letter Written to Bishop Partridge," *Times and Seasons,* July 1840, 1:131–134.

699. JS History, vol. C-1, 907–912; Jessee, "Writing of Joseph Smith's History," 441.

included in inventories for the Church Historian's Office in about 1904, and it was cataloged in the Revelations Collection in 1983, indicating continuous institutional custody.[700]

Historical Introduction

Around 22 March 1839, JS composed this epistle in the Clay County jail in Liberty, Missouri. Addressed to Bishop Edward Partridge and the church, the letter offered counsel on a range of issues. The epistle was the second letter JS wrote to the church in March 1839, and he evidently planned to write additional general epistles that month, offering guidance and comfort to the church after the devastating setbacks of 1838 and amid church members' forced removal from Missouri in early 1839. The first epistle, addressed to the church in general and Partridge in particular, was drafted on 20 March 1839 and included meditations on persecution and the church's divine destiny. At the conclusion of the missive, JS stated that the prisoners' intent was to "continue to offer further reflections in our next epistle."[701] This undated letter appears to be the promised sequel. JS was the primary author of the epistle, although the other prisoners may have assisted in its composition. Like the 20 March 1839 epistle, the undated letter shifts between three rhetorical perspectives: the first-person plural of all the prisoners, the first-person singular of JS, and the voice of Deity directed to JS. Each prisoner signed the letter.[702]

Dating the letter presents significant challenges. On 21 March 1839, JS informed Emma Smith, "I have sent an Epistle to the church," presumably referring to the 20 March letter. He then told her that he intended to "send an other as soon as posible," likely referring to this undated epistle.[703] The undated letter could have been written anytime between 21 March and 6 April, the day the prisoners left Liberty for Gallatin, Missouri, to appear before the Daviess County Circuit Court.[704] However, JS likely wrote it around 22 March, the day he composed a letter to land speculator Isaac Galland, who had offered to sell the church land in Illinois and Iowa Territory. In the 20 March 1839 epistle, JS deferred

---

700. See "Index to Papers. in the Historians Office," ca. 1904, p. 3; "Letters to and from the Prophet," ca. 1904, p. 1, Historian's Office, Catalogs and Inventories, 1846–1904, CHL; and the full bibliographic entry for the Revelations Collection in the CHL catalog.

701. Letter to the Church and Edward Partridge, 20 Mar. 1839, p. 371 herein.

702. See Historical Introduction to Letter to the Church and Edward Partridge, 20 Mar. 1839, pp. 357–358 herein.

703. Letter to Emma Smith, 21 Mar. 1839, p. 373 herein.

704. The letter's closing indicates that JS and his companions were still prisoners. The letter does not reference leaving the Clay County jail, meaning the letter was likely written before the prisoners departed Liberty on 6 April 1839. It is possible, though not likely, that it was written toward the end of their stay in Liberty rather than around 22 March. Hyrum Smith generally noted in his journal when correspondence arrived and was sent out. He did not write in his journal between 20 and 29 March, and his journal entries from 30 March to 6 April do not mention JS composing a general epistle to the church. When church clerks copied the undated letter into JS's manuscript history in 1845, they inserted the epistle between entries for 25 March and 4 April 1839, dates associated with the departure of Heber C. Kimball and Theodore Turley from Liberty for Jefferson City, Missouri, and their later return to Liberty. (Hyrum Smith, Diary, 30 Mar.–6 Apr. 1839; Historian's Office, JS History, Draft Notes, 25 Mar.–4 Apr. 1839; see also Historical Introduction to Petition to George Tompkins, between 9 and 15 Mar. 1839, pp. 341–344 herein.)

to the judgment of church leaders in Quincy, Illinois, regarding whether to accept Galland's offer. JS's thinking evidently changed by the time he wrote the letter to Galland on 22 March. In that letter, JS remarked that "the church would be wise in making the contract" and requested that Galland reserve the land for the Saints.[705] JS used similar language in the undated epistle, stating that "the church would do well to secure to themselves" Galland's land offer.[706]

In the epistle, JS revisited other major themes of the 20 March 1839 letter and also included new insights. In the earlier epistle, JS reflected on lessons learned from past mistakes; in the undated missive, JS further contemplated previous errors and suggested ways to avert similar problems in the future. The second epistle also contained an extended meditation on the righteous use of priesthood power; during the meditation, the perspective transitioned from the combined voice of JS and his companions addressing a general church audience to the voice of Deity addressing JS with regard to his future influence. After reviewing JS's recent arrest, forced separation from his family, and incarceration, the divine voice assured JS that his suffering would provide necessary experience. The letter then returned to the voice of JS and his companions, alternating between first-person singular and first-person plural. The epistle also instructed the Saints to prepare affidavits describing their losses in Missouri, to be submitted to government officials. The letter then concluded with an extended affirmation of the inspired nature of the United States Constitution and the principle of religious liberty.[707]

JS presumably dictated the rough draft of the epistle, which is in the handwriting of Alexander McRae, who acted as scribe for other lengthy documents produced in the jail.[708] This draft contains corrections by JS. When it was completed, each of the prisoners signed the epistle before it was folded in letter style and addressed to JS's wife Emma Smith in Quincy.[709] For reasons that remain unclear, McRae then produced a fair copy that incorporated JS's revisions to the rough draft. After McRae and JS made additional minor corrections to the fair

---

705. JS's thinking may have changed because he had given Galland's 26 February 1839 letter greater thought than he had before writing the 20 March missive. (Letter to Isaac Galland, 22 Mar. 1839, p. 388 herein.)

706. Isaac Galland, Commerce, IL, to David Rogers, [Quincy, IL], 26 Feb. 1839, in JS Letterbook 2, p. 1.

707. Portions of the undated epistle were subsequently canonized in sections 121–123 of the 1876 edition of the Doctrine and Covenants.

708. See Petition to George Tompkins, between 9 and 15 Mar. 1839, pp. 340–352 herein; and Letter to the Church and Edward Partridge, 20 Mar. 1839, pp. 356–372 herein.

709. Parley P. Pratt recalled that when JS dictated documents, "each sentence was uttered slowly and very distinctly, and with a pause between each, sufficiently long for it to be recorded, by an ordinary writer, in long hand." McRae's script in the rough draft is notably looser than in other documents he inscribed for JS in the jail, especially the fair copy of the letter, and may be the result of dictation. Although both the rough draft and the fair copy were written on paper of the same size, the relative tightness of McRae's script in the fair copy enabled him to fit an additional two to three words per line, reducing the length of the document by two pages. This draft contains the type of error commonly made by scribes who mishear similar-sounding words. For example, McRae wrote "thine elder one." When correcting the manuscript, JS canceled "one" and inserted "son." (Pratt, *Autobiography*, 48; JS et al., [Liberty, MO], to Edward Partridge and the Church, Quincy, IL, [ca. 22 Mar. 1839], Revelations Collection, CHL.)

copy, the prisoners signed it, and then it was folded and addressed to Emma Smith. The fair copy is featured here because it appears to be the most complete version of the letter sent to Illinois.[710]

The undated general epistle may have been among the "package of letters" that church member Alanson Ripley obtained from the jail on 22 March 1839.[711] Alternatively, if the letter was not yet completed at the time of Ripley's visit, other visitors to the jail in late March and early April, including Heber C. Kimball and Theodore Turley, may have been entrusted with the letter.[712] The letter was presumably delivered to Emma Smith, as it was addressed to her.[713] On 11 April 1839, Hyrum Smith's wife, Mary Fielding Smith, indicated that both the 20 March 1839 epistle and the undated letter had arrived in Quincy. "We have seen the Epistols to the Church and read them several times," she wrote to her husband. "They seem like food for the hungrey we have taken great pleasure on perusing them."[714] The undated epistle evidently was circulated widely among church members in Illinois, as indicated by the early copies that Edward Partridge and Albert Perry Rockwood made. An edited version of the letter was published twice in 1840—in church newspapers in Nauvoo, Illinois, and in Liverpool, England—further increasing the letter's circulation.[715]

Document Transcript

Continued to the church of Latter-day-saints.

We continue to offer further reflections to Bishop [Edward] Partridge and to the church of Jesus Christ of Latter day saints whom we love with a fervent love and do always bear them in mind in all our prayers to the throne of God. It still seems to bear ~~heavy~~ heavily in our minds that the church would do ~~will~~ well to secure to themselves the contract of the Land which is proposed to them

---

710. Both the rough draft and the fair copy were folded, addressed, and carried to Illinois, but it is unknown whether they were transported together.

711. Lyman Wight, Journal, in *History of the Reorganized Church*, 2:323.

712. Hyrum Smith, Diary, 30 Mar.–4 Apr. 1839. Heber C. Kimball, Theodore Turley, and Alanson Ripley were associated with the removal committee, a group charged with assisting the prisoners in Liberty and with organizing the Latter-day Saint exodus from Missouri. Ripley departed Missouri in early April and could have taken the undated letter to Illinois. (Far West Committee, Minutes, 26 Jan. 1839; Alanson Ripley, Statements, ca. Jan. 1845, Historian's Office, JS History Documents, 1839–1860, CHL; Letter from Alanson Ripley, 10 Apr. 1839, p. 411 herein; see also Far West Committee, Minutes, 7 Apr. 1839.)

713. Just as JS had wanted Emma Smith "to have the first reading" of the 20 March 1839 epistle, he likely wanted her to be the first to read the undated epistle. (Letter to Emma Smith, 21 Mar. 1839, p. 373 herein.)

714. Mary Fielding Smith, [Quincy, IL], to Hyrum Smith, 11 Apr. 1839, Mary Fielding Smith, Collection, CHL.

715. See JS, Liberty, MO, to the Church and Edward Partridge, Quincy, IL, 20–25 Mar. 1839, copy, CHL; JS et al., Liberty, MO, to the Church and Edward Partridge, Quincy, IL, 20 Mar. 1839, copy, Albert Perry Rockwood, Mormon Letters and Sermons, 1838–1839, Western Americana Collection, Beinecke Rare Book and Manuscript Library, Yale University, New Haven, CT; "An Extract of a Letter Written to Bishop Partridge," *Times and Seasons,* July 1840, 1:131–134; and "Letter from Elder Jos. Smith," *LDS Millennial Star,* Dec. 1840, 195–199.

by Mr. Isaac Galland and to cultivate the friendly feelings of that gentleman in as much ~~shall~~ as he shall prove himself to be a man of honor ~~humanity~~ and a friend to humanity. We really think that his letter breaths that kind of spirit if we can judge correctly.[716] And Isaac Van Allen Esq[r.] the attorney Gen[l.] of Iawa Territory that peradventure such men may be wrought upon by the providence of God to do good unto his people.[717] Governer [Robert] Lucas also.[718] We suggest the ideah of praying fervantly for all men who manifest any degree of sympathy for the suffering children of God. We think that peradventure the united States survayor of the Iowa Territory may be of grate benefeit to the church[719] if it be the will of God to this end[720] if ritiousness ~~shall~~ should be manifested as the girdle of our loins.[721] It seems to be deeply impresed upon our minds that the saints ought to lay hold of evry door ~~shall~~ that shall seem to be opened ~~for~~ unto them[722] to obtain foot hold on the Earth and be a ~~make~~ making all the preparation⟨s⟩ that is within the power of posibles for the terible storms that are now gethering in the heavens with darkness and gloominess and thick darkness as spoken of by the prophets[723] which cannot be now of a long time lingering for there seems to be a whispering that the angels of heaven[724] who have been intrusted with the ~~council~~ counsel of these matters for the last days have taken ~~council~~ counsel together: and among the rest of the general affairs that have to be transacted in their honorable ~~council~~ counsel they have taken cognisance of the testimony of those who were murdered at Hawns Mills and also those who

---

716. For more information on Galland's offer to sell property in Iowa Territory and Commerce, Illinois, to the church, see Historical Introduction to Letter from Edward Partridge, 5 Mar. 1839, p. 327 herein; and Historical Introduction to Letter to the Church and Edward Partridge, 20 Mar. 1839, p. 358 herein.

717. In his letter dated 26 February 1839, Galland reported that Van Allen (1816–1839) had recently stated he would endeavor to protect the Latter-day Saints "from insult or violence." (Isaac Galland, Commerce, IL, to David Rogers, [Quincy, IL], 26 Feb. 1839, in JS Letterbook 2, p. 2.)

718. For more information on Lucas, governor of Iowa Territory, see 408n837 herein.

719. Albert Ellis (1800–1885) was appointed the first surveyor general of Iowa Territory. In late February or early March 1839, Ellis met with church leaders in Quincy and offered to identify sites in Iowa Territory where the Latter-day Saints could settle. Further, Ellis stated that after the Saints selected a site, he would submit a petition to the United States Congress, "requesting that the entire tract be given to" the Saints. The minutes for the undated meeting with Ellis were included in the packet of documents Rogers delivered to the prisoners on 19 March 1839. (Wisconsin Bureau of Vital Statistics, Registration of Deaths, ca. 1862–1907, vol. I, p. 64, microfilm 1,311,649, U.S. and Canada Record Collection, FHL; *Report and Collections of the State Historical Society of Wisconsin*, 207, 208; Minutes, no date, in JS Letterbook 2, p. 48.)

720. JS inserted "to this end" in the rough draft.

721. See Isaiah 11:5.

722. The rough draft had "the saints," which JS canceled; he then inserted "unto them."

723. See Zephaniah 1:15.

724. JS inserted "of heaven" in the rough draft.

were martered with D[avid] W. Patten. and else where and[725] have passed some [p. 1] decisions peradventure in favour of the saints and[726] those who were called to suffer without cause these decisions will be made known in there time and they will take into concideration all those things that offend. We have a fervant desire that in your general conferences that evry thing should be discused with a grate deal of care and propriety lest you grieve the Holy Spirit[727] which shall be poured out at all times upon your heads[728] when you are exercised with those principals of ritiousness that are agreeable to the mind of God and are properly affected one toward an other and are carefull by all means to remember those ⟨who⟩ are in bondage and in heaviness and in deep affliction for your sakes and if there are any among you who aspire after their own aggrandisement and seek their own oppulance while thier brethren are groaning in poverty and are under sore trials and temptations they can not be benefeited by the intersesion of the Holy Spirit ⟨which⟩ maketh intersesion for us ~~daily~~ day and knight with groning that cannot be uttered.[729] We ought at all times to be verry carefull that such high mindedness never have place in our hearts but condesend to men of low estate and with all long suffering bear the infermities of the weak. Behold there are ma[n]y called but few are chosen.[730] And why are they not chosen? Because their hearts are set so much upon the things of this world and aspire to the honors of men that they do not learn this one lesson that the rights of priesthood are inseperably connected with the powers of heaven and that the powers of heaven connot be controled nor handled only upon the principals of rightiousness. That they may be confered upon us it is true but when we undertake to cover our sins[731] or to gratify our pride or vain ambition or to exercise controle or dominion or compulsion upon the souls of the children of men in any degree of unritiousness behold the heavens withdraw themselves the spirit of the Lord is grieved [p. 2] and when it has withdrawn <u>Amen</u> to the <u>priesthood</u> or the authority of that man behold ere he is aware he is left unto himself to kicken against the pricks to persecute the saints and to fight against God.[732] We have learned by sad experiance that it is the nature and disposition of almost all men as soon as they get a little authority as they suppose they will imediately begin to

---

725. JS inserted "else where and" in the rough draft.

726. JS inserted "the saints and" in the rough draft.

727. See Ephesians 4:30.

728. See Isaiah 32:15; Ezekiel 39:29; and Book of Mormon, 1830 ed., 164 [Mosiah 4:20].

729. See Romans 8:26–27.

730. See Matthew 20:16; 22:14.

731. See Psalm 32:1; Romans 4:7; and 1 Peter 4:8.

732. See Acts 26:14.

[e]xercise⁷³³ unritious dominion. hence ma[n]y⁷³⁴ [are]⁷³⁵ called but few are ch[osen.]⁷³⁶ [No power or in]f[luence]⁷³⁷ can or ought to be maintained by ⟨[vi]rt[ue]⟩⁷³⁸ of the Priesthood only by persuasion by long suffering by gentleness and meekness and by love unfaigned⁷³⁹ by kindness by pure knowledge which shall greatly enlarge the soul⁷⁴⁰ without hypocrisy and without guile reproving be-times with sharpness when moved upon by the Holy Ghost and then showing forth afterwords an increas of love toward him whom thou hast reproved lest he esteem the[e] to be his enimy that he may know that thy faithfulness is stronger than the cords of death thy bowells also being full of charity towards all men and to the household of faith⁷⁴¹ and virtue garnish thy thoughts unceasingly then shall thy confidence wax strong in the presants of God, and the doctrins of the Priesthood shall destill upon thy soul as the dews from heaven the Holy Ghost shall be thy constant companion and thy septer an unchanging septer of ritiousness⁷⁴² and truth and thy dominion shall be an everlasting dominion⁷⁴³ and without compulsory means it shall flow [un]to⁷⁴⁴ thee for ever and ever. The ends of the Earth⁷⁴⁵ shall [enq]uire⁷⁴⁶ after thy na[me]⁷⁴⁷ and fools shall have thee in deri[s]ion⁷⁴⁸ and hell shall rage against thee while the pure in heart⁷⁴⁹ and the wise and the noble and the virtious shall seek ~~council~~ counsel and authority and bless-ings constantly from under thy hand and thy people shall never be turned against thee by the testimony of traitors⁷⁵⁰ and although their influance shall cast the[e] into trouble and into bars and walls thou shalt be had in honor and

---

733. TEXT: "[*Page torn*]xercise".

734. TEXT: "ma[*page torn*]y".

735. TEXT: "[*Page torn*]". Here and in the rest of the document, missing text was supplied from the rough draft of this letter. (JS et al., [Liberty, MO], to Edward Partridge and the Church, Quincy, IL, [ca. 22 Mar. 1839], Revelations Collection, CHL.)

736. TEXT: "ch[*page torn*]". See Matthew 20:16; 22:14.

737. TEXT: "[*Page torn*]f[*page torn*]".

738. TEXT: "[*Page torn*]rt[*page torn*]".

739. See 2 Corinthians 6:6; and 1 Peter 1:22.

740. See Book of Mormon, 1830 ed., 315 [Alma 32:28].

741. See Galatians 6:10.

742. See Hebrews 1:8.

743. See Daniel 4:34; 7:14.

744. TEXT: "[*Page torn*]to".

745. See Isaiah 52:10; Psalm 65:5; Job 37:3; Acts 13:47; and Book of Mormon, 1830 ed., 524 [Mormon 3:18].

746. TEXT: "[*Page torn*]uire".

747. TEXT: "na[*page torn*]".

748. TEXT: "deri[*page torn*]ion".

749. See Matthew 5:8; Book of Mormon, 1830 ed., 128 [Jacob 3:2]; and Revelation, 2 Aug. 1833–A, in *JSP,* D3:202 [D&C 97:21].

750. For more information on the prosecution witnesses at the November 1838 hearing, see Introduction to Part 3: 4 Nov. 1838–16 Apr. 1839, pp. 273–274 herein.

but for a small moment and thy voice shall be more terable in the midst of thine enemies than the fierce Lion because of thy ritiousness and [p. 3] thy God shall stand by the[e] for ever and ever. If thou art called to pass through tribulation. If thou art in perals among fals brethren. If thou art in perals amongst robbers. If thou art in perals by land or by sea.[751] If thou art accused with all maner of fals accusations. If thine enimies fall upon the[e]. If they tear the[e] from the society of thy father and mother and brethren and Sisters.[752] And if with a drawn sword thine enimies tear the[e] from the bosome of thy Wife and of thine offsprings and thine El[d]er son[753] although but six years of age shall cling to thy garments and shall say my Father my Father why cant you stay with us Oh my Father what are the men going to do with you. And if then he shall be thrust from the[e] by the sword[754] and thou be draged to prison and thine enimies prowl around the[e] like wolves for blood of the Lamb and if thou shouldest be cast into the pit[755] or into the hands of murderers and the sentantce of death pased upon thee.[756] If thou be cast into the deep. If the billowing surge conspire against thee.[757] If fierce wind become thine enimy. If the heavens gether blackness and all the elements combine to hedge up the way and above all if the verry jaws of hell shall gap open her mouth wide after ⟨thee⟩ know thou my son that all these things shall give thee experiance and shall be for thy good.[758] The son of man hath desended below them all art thou greater than he? Therefore hold on thy way and the priesthood shall remain with thee for their bounds are set they cannot pass. ~~Thee~~ Thy days are known and thy years shall not be numbered less. therefore fear not what man can do[759] for God shall be with you[760] for ever and ever. Now brethren I would suggest for the concidereration of the conference of its being carefully and wisely understood by the ⟨counsel⟩ or conferences that our brethren

---

751. See 2 Corinthians 11:26.

752. Lucy Mack Smith later recalled that when JS was arrested, the Smith family feared he would be shot. (Lucy Mack Smith, History, 1844–1845, bk. 16, [2].)

753. The rough draft had "one," which JS canceled; he then inserted "son."

754. Joseph Smith III recalled that when JS "was brought to the house by an armed guard I ran out of the gate to greet him, but was roughly pushed away from his side by a sword in the hand of the guard and not allowed to go near him. My mother, also, was not permitted to approach him and had to receive his farewell by word of lip only." ("The Memoirs of President Joseph Smith," *Saints' Herald,* 6 Nov. 1934, 1414.)

755. See Genesis 37:20, 22, 24; 2 Samuel 18:17; Revelation 20:3; and Book of Mormon, 1830 ed., 557 [Ether 9:29].

756. For more information on the 1 November 1838 court-martial, in which JS and other church leaders were sentenced to death, see Introduction to Part 3: 4 Nov. 1838–16 Apr. 1839, p. 271 herein.

757. See Jonah 2:3.

758. JS inserted "and shall be for thy good" in the rough draft.

759. See Book of Mormon, 1830 ed., 582 [Moroni 8:16].

760. See Genesis 48:21.

scattered abroad[761] who understand the spirit of the gethering that [p. 4] they
fall into the places of refuge and saf[e]ty that God shall open unto them
betwean Kirtland and Far West. Those from the East and from the West and
from far ~~country~~ countries let them fall in some where betwean those two
boundries in the most safe and quiet places they can find and let this be the
presant understanding untill God shall open a more effectual door for us for
further conciderations.[762] And again we further suggest for the concideration of
the counsel that there be no organizations of large bodies upon common stock
principals in property[763] or of large companies of firms[764] untill the Lord shall
signify it in a proper manner as it opens such a dreafull [dreadful] field for the
averishous and the indolent and corrupt hearted to pray upon the inocent and
virtious and honist[765] We have reason to believe that many things were introduced among the saints before God had signified the times and not withstanding the principles and plans may have ⟨been⟩ good yet aspiring men or in other
word men ⟨who⟩ had not the substance of Godliness[766] about them perhaps
undertook to handle edg tools children you know are fond of tools while they
are not yet able to use them. Time and experiance however is the only safe
remidy against such evils there are many teachers but perhaps not many

---

761. See Matthew 9:36; John 11:52; and James 1:1.

762. On 16 January 1839, the First Presidency wrote in a letter to senior apostles Heber C. Kimball
and Brigham Young that "the gathering of necessity [had] stopt" but that, pending further developments,
the Latter-day Saints could consider gathering to "Kirtland, and the regions round about." (Letter to
Heber C. Kimball and Brigham Young, 16 Jan. 1839, pp. 313–314 herein.)

763. JS inserted "in property" in the rough draft.

764. In 1831 JS dictated a revelation that outlined the "Laws of the Church of Christ" for consecrating, or donating, property to the church to assist the poor. In the 1830s, church leaders used several
strategies to administer these laws, with varying degrees of success. During summer 1838, the church
organized multiple firms designed to combine the resources and organize the labor of the burgeoning
Latter-day Saint population in Missouri. According to church member Luman Shurtliff, he "was
attached with all [he] possessed" to "a cooperative Firm" led by Isaac Morley, a counselor in the Far
West bishopric, and the firms were divided into companies of ten men. Property was apparently leased
to the church rather than transferred outright. The firms were designed to facilitate agricultural
production; coordinate the construction of homes, a temple, and other church buildings; and stimulate
manufacturing to help the church achieve economic independence. Laborers were paid one dollar per
day and were given access to the church's storehouses for provisions. Although JS taught that participation in the firms was voluntary, dissenters John Corrill and Reed Peck later stated that Sampson
Avard and other Danites resorted to coercion to enforce participation. (Revelation, 9 Feb. 1831, in *JSP*,
D1:245 [D&C 42:1–72]; JS, Journal, 27 July and 20–21 Aug. 1838, in *JSP*, J1:293, 305; Shurtliff,
Autobiography, 119; Rockwood, Journal, 6 Oct. 1838; Corrill, *Brief History*, 45–46, in *JSP*, H2:193–194;
Reed Peck, Quincy, IL, to "Dear Friends," 18 Sept. 1839, pp. 34–35, 53–55, Henry E. Huntington
Library, San Marino, CA; see also Historical Introduction to Revelation, 8 July 1838–C [D&C 119],
pp. 184–187 herein.)

765. JS inserted "and virtious and honest" in the rough draft.

766. See 2 Timothy 3:5.

Fathers.⁷⁶⁷ There are times comming when God will signify many things which are expediant for the well being of the saints but the times have not yet come but will come as fast as there can be found place and reseptions for them. And again we would suggest for your concideration the propriety of all the saints gethering up ~~the~~ ⟨a⟩ knowledge of ⟨all⟩ the facts and suffering and abuses put upon them by the people of this state and also of all the property and amount of damages which they have sustained both of character and personal ⟨Injuries as will as real property⟩ ~~property~~ and also the names of all persons that have had a hand in their oppressions as far as they can get hold of them and find them out. and perhaps a committe can be appointed to find out these [p. 5] things and to take statements and affidafets and also to gether up the libilous publications that are afloat and all that are in the magazines and in the Insiclopedias [encyclopedias] and all the libillious ~~history~~ histories that are published and that ⟨are⟩ writing and by whom and present the whole concatination of diabolical rascality and nefarious and murderous impositions that have been practised upon this people that we may not only publish to all the world but present them to the heads of the government in all there dark and hellish⁷⁶⁸ hugh [hue?] as the last effort which is injoined on us by our heavenly. Father before we can fully and completely claim that promise which shall call him forth from his hiding place and also the whole nation may be left without excuse⁷⁶⁹ before he can send forth the power of his mighty arm.⁷⁷⁰ It is an imperious duty that we owe to God to angels with whom we shall be brought to stand and also to ourselves to our wives and our children who have been made to bow down with grief sorrow and care under the most damning hand of murder tyranny and oppression supported and urged on and upheld by the influance of that spirit which hath so strongly rivited the creeds of the fathers⁷⁷¹

---

767. See 1 Corinthians 4:15.

768. JS inserted "and hellish" in the rough draft.

769. See Romans 1:20; and Revelation, 27–28 Dec. 1832, in *JSP*, D2:342 [D&C 88:82].

770. See Psalm 89:13. These instructions to document and publicize the Saints' persecutions reiterated directions in an 1833 revelation to petition Missouri judges, the Missouri governor, and the president of the United States for redress following the 1833 expulsion of Latter-day Saints from Jackson County, Missouri. The revelation promised that if these officials denied the Saints' petitions, "the Lord [would] arise and come forth out of his hiding place & in his fury vex the nation." In late 1833 and in 1834, church members petitioned the aforementioned officials, as well as the American people in general, but the Saints received no relief. (Revelation, 16–17 Dec. 1833, in *JSP*, D3:395–397 [D&C 101:81–92]; Historical Introduction to Letter, 30 Oct. 1833, in *JSP*, D3:332–335; Jennings, "Importuning for Redress," 15–29; see also Letter to Heber C. Kimball and Brigham Young, 16 Jan. 1839, pp. 310–316 herein.)

771. On 22 March 1839, JS wrote in a letter to Galland that the Latter-day Saints opposed "creeds or superstitious notions of men," presumably referring to official statements of belief that various religious groups had adopted throughout the history of Christianity. JS explained that such creeds violated "the first and fundamental principle of our holy religion," and he asserted that the Saints had the "right to

who have inherited lies[772] upon the harts of the children[773] and filled the world with confusion and has been growing stronger and stronger and is now the verry ~~mein~~ main spring of all corruption and the whole Earth grones under the wait of its iniquity.[774] it is an iron yoke[775] it is a strong band[776] they are the verry hand cuffs and chains and shackles and fetters of hell Therefore it is an imperious duty that we owe not only to our own wives and children but to the widdows and fatherless whose husbands and fathers have been murdered under its iron hand which dark and blackning deeds are enough to make hell itself shudder and to stand aghast and pale and the hands of the verry devil tremble and palsy and also it is an imper[p. 6]ious duty that we owe to all the rising generation and to all the pure in heart which there ⟨are⟩ many yet on the Earth among all sects parties and de[no]minations who are blinded by the suttle craftiness of men whereby they ly in wait to decieve[777] and only kept from the truth because they know not where to find it therefore that we should waist and ware out our lives in bringing to light all the hidden things of dark-ness[778] wherein we know them and they are truly manifest from heaven. These should then be attended to with greate earnestness let no man counts them as small things for there is much which lieth in futurity pertaining to the saint which depends upon these things you know brethren that a verry large ship is benefeited verry much by a verry small helm in the time of a storm by being kept work ways with the wind and the waves Therefore dearly beloved ~~beloved~~ brethren let us cheerfully do all things ⟨that⟩ lieth in our power and then may we stand still with the utmost asurance to see the salvation of God[779] and for his arm to be revealed.[780] And again I would further suggest the impro-priety of the organization of bands or companies by covenant or oaths by penal-ties ⟨or ~~secrecy~~ secrecies⟩ but let the time past of our experiance and sufferings by the wickedness of Doctor [Sampson] Avard suffise[781] and let our covenant be that

---

embrace all, and every item of truth, without limitation or without being circumscribed." (Letter to Isaac Galland, 22 Mar. 1839, p. 384 herein.)

772. See Jeremiah 16:19.

773. See Malachi 4:6.

774. See Romans 8:21–22; and *Works of the Rev. Isaac Watts,* 3:208.

775. See Deuteronomy 28:48; and Jeremiah 28:13–14.

776. See Isaiah 28:22.

777. See Ephesians 4:14.

778. See 1 Corinthians 4:5.

779. See Exodus 14:13.

780. See Isaiah 53:1.

781. In June 1838, the Society of the Daughter of Zion (later known as the Danite band) was orga-nized in Caldwell County in response to internal and external opposition to the church. Former Danite leader Sampson Avard claimed in his testimony before Judge Austin A. King in November 1838 that JS suggested the "band should be bound together by a covenant." However, it remains unclear what

of the everlasting covenant as is contained in the Holy writ[782] and the things that God hath revealed unto us. Pure friendship always becomes weakened the verry moment you undertake to make it stronger by penal oaths and secrecy. Your humble servant or servants intend from henceforth to disapprobate every thing that is not in accordance with the fulness of the gospel of Jesus Christ[783] and is not of a bold and frank and an upright nature they will not hold their peace as in times past when they see iniquity begining to rear its head for fear of traitors or the concequences that shall flow ⟨**follow**⟩[784] by reproving those who creap in unawares that they may get something to distroy the flock. We believe that the experiance of the saints in times past has been sufficient that they will from [p. 7] henceforth be always ready to obey the truth without having mens persons in admiration because of advantage it is expadiant that we should be aware of such things. And we ~~should~~ ought always to be aware of those prejudices which sometimes so strangly presented themselves and are so congenial to human nature against our nieghbors friends and brethren of the world who choose to differ with us in opinion and in matters of faith. Our religeon is betwean us and our God. Their religeon is betwean them and their God. There is a ty[785] from God that should be exercised towards those of our faith who walk uprightly which is peculiar to itself but it is without prejudice but gives scope to the mind which inables us to conduct ourselves with grater liberality to-wards all others that are not of our faith[786] than what they exercise towards one another these principals approximate nearer to the mind of God because it is like God or God like. There is a principal also which we are bound to be exercised with that is in common with all men such as governments and laws and regulations in the civil conserns of life This principal guarentees to all parties sects and denominations and classes of religeon equal coherant and indefeasible rights they are things that pertain to this life therefore all are alike

role—if any—JS played in formulating the oath that Avard recited in court: "In the name of Jesus Christ the son of God, I do solemnly obligate myself, ever to conceal & never to reveal the secret purposes of this society called the daughter of Zion; Should I ever do the same I hold my life as the forfeiture." John Corrill, who was critical of the society, believed that the Danites swore additional oaths to support each other whether "right or wrong," to correct wrongs internally rather than relying on the law, to uphold the First Presidency without question, and to eliminate dissent in the church. (Sampson Avard, Testimony, Richmond, MO, Nov. 1838, pp. [2]–[3], State of Missouri v. JS et al. for Treason and Other Crimes [Mo. 5th Jud. Cir. 1838], in State of Missouri, "Evidence"; Corrill, *Brief History*, 30–31, in *JSP*, H2:166–167; see also R. Peck to "Dear Friends," 18 Sept. 1839, pp. 39–41; and 306n199 herein.)

782. See Genesis 17:13; Ezekiel 16:60; Hebrews 13:20; and Revelation, 16–17 Dec. 1833, in *JSP*, D3:392 [D&C 101:39].

783. See Book of Mormon, 1830 ed., 23, 487 [1 Nephi 10:14; 3 Nephi 16:10].

784. TEXT: Insertion in the handwriting of JS.

785. In the rough draft, "which belongs" was canceled here.

786. In the rough draft, JS inserted "that are not of our faith."

interested they make our responcibilities one towards another in matters of corruptible things while the former principals do not distroy the latter but bind us stronger and make our responcibilities not only one to another but unto God[787] also hence we say that the constitution of the unitid States is a glorious standard it is founded in the wisdom of God.[788] it is a heavenly banner it is to all those who are privilaged with the sweats of its liberty like the cooling shades and refreshing watters of a greate rock in a thirsty and a weary land[789] it is like a greate [p. 8] tree under whose branches men from evry clime can be shielded from the burning rays of an inclemant sun. We brethren are deprived of the protection of this glorious principal by the cruelty of the cruel by those who only look for the time being for pasterage like the beasts of the field only to fill themselves and forget that the mormons as well as the presbitarians and those of evry other class and description have equal rights to partake of the fruite of the greate tree of our national liberty[790] but notwithstanding we see what we see and we feel what we feel and know what we know. Yet that fruite is no less presious and delisious to our taist we cannot be weaned from the milk neither can we be drawn from the breast neither will we deny our religeon because of the hand of opresion but we will hold on untill death we say say that God is true that the constitution of the united States is true that the

---

787. This language parallels the famous rhetoric of religious liberty that Thomas Jefferson used in his *Notes on the State of Virginia*. In the late eighteenth century, governments at the state and federal levels began passing laws and constitutional provisions such as the 1786 Virginia Statute for Religious Freedom and the First Amendment to the Constitution of the United States. These laws and provisions, prompted largely by growing religious diversity, guaranteed the free exercise of religion first to white Protestants of all sects and gradually to white non-Protestants. This extension of religious liberty involved disestablishing previously privileged churches and ensuring that all churches enjoyed equal rights. These significant legal changes were paralleled by cultural changes, with white Americans beginning to accept coexistence with members of diverse religious groups. Although religious prejudice did not disappear, as the experience of many Catholics, Latter-day Saints, Jews, and other religious minorities attested, the formal granting of religious liberty gave rise to an unprecedented sense of ecumenism and pluralism in American society. (Jefferson, "Notes on the State of Virginia," 93–97; An Act for Establishing Religious Freedom [16 Jan. 1786], in Hening, *Statutes at Large*, 84–86; U.S. Constitution, amend. I; see also Beneke, *Beyond Toleration*, 6–10.)

788. Many Americans in the late eighteen century and early nineteenth century interpreted the ratification of the United States Constitution in 1787 as providential, arguing that God inspired the framers as they drafted the charter, guiding them to make the United States an "asylum for liberty." In 1833 JS dictated a revelation affirming that God "established the constitution of this Land by the hands of wise men" whom he "raised up unto this very purpose." (Guyatt, *Providence and the Invention of the United States*, 142–146; Revelation, 16–17 Dec. 1833, in *JSP*, D3:395 [D&C 101:80].)

789. See Exodus 17:6; Numbers 20:10–11; and Book of Mormon, 1830 ed., 44 [1 Nephi 17:29].

790. "Tree of liberty" was a common nineteenth-century phrase used to describe the United States and its Constitution; the tree's branches extended to provide equal protection for all. (See, for example, Knox, *Essays, Moral and Literary*, 3:317; and "Charm of the Word Liberty," 247.)

bible is true that the book of mormon is true ⟨that⟩ the book ⟨of⟩ covenants[791] are true that Christ is true that the ministering angels sent forth from God are true and that we know that we have an house not made with hands eternal in the heavens[792] whose ~~building~~ builder and maker is God[793] a consolation which our oppressors cannot feel when fortune or fate shall lay its iron hand on them as it has on us. Now we ask what is man?[794] Remember brethren that time ⟨and⟩ chance hapeneth to all men.[795] We shall continue our reflections in our next.[796] We subscribe ourselves your sinsear [sincere] friends and brethe[r]en[797] in the bonds of the everlasting gospel[798] prisoners of Jesus Christ[799] for the sake of the gospel[800] and the saints. We pronounce the blessing of heaven[801] upon the heads of the saints who seek to serve God with an undevided hearts[802] in the name of Jesus Christ Amen.

[803] **Joseph Smith Jr**
Hyrum Smith
Lyman Wight
Caleb Baldwin
Alexander. McRae. [p. 9]

Mrs. Emma Smith
Quincy I^{ll.}

——— ❧ ———

Letter to Emma Smith, 4 April 1839

Source Note

JS, Letter, Liberty, Clay Co., MO, to Emma Smith, Quincy, Adams Co., IL, 4 Apr. 1839; handwriting and signature (now missing) of JS; three pages; JS Papers, Beinecke Rare Book and Manuscript Library, Yale University, New Haven, CT. Includes address, wafer seal, and redactions.

791. That is, the Doctrine and Covenants.

792. See 2 Corinthians 5:1.

793. See Hebrews 11:10.

794. See Psalms 8:4; 144:3; and Hebrews 2:6.

795. See Ecclesiastes 9:11.

796. No subsequent epistle from the prisoners has been located.

797. TEXT: "brethe[*page torn*]en".

798. See Philemon 1:13; and Revelation 14:6.

799. See Philemon 1:9.

800. See Mark 8:35.

801. See Genesis 49:25.

802. "Serve God with an undivided heart" was a common nineteenth-century saying. (See, for example, Morison, *Family Prayers,* 196; and Doubleday, "Wife of President Edwards," 137.)

803. TEXT: Original signatures of JS, Hyrum Smith, Lyman Wight, Caleb Baldwin, and Alexander McRae.

Bifolium measuring 12¾ × 7½ inches (32 × 19 cm). The letter was addressed, trifolded twice in letter style, sealed with an adhesive wafer, and postmarked. At some point, the leaves became separated and the wafer became detached. Later, JS's signature was cut out, resulting in loss of text on the recto of the second leaf. The top of the recto of the second leaf was inscribed in graphite with "Letter of Joseph Smith | Prophet of the | Mormons", likely by a document dealer. The document has undergone conservation.

The letter was presumably in Emma Smith's possession for some time after she received it. Eventually it came into the possession of Oliver R. Barrett, a noted collector of Abraham Lincoln memorabilia, who owned the document at the time of his death in 1950. The same year, Parke-Bernet Galleries of New York City sold the letter and other selected manuscripts from Barrett's collection.[804] The letter was later acquired by William Robertson Coe, who donated it with his extensive Americana collection to Yale University in the early 1950s.[805]

Historical Introduction

On 4 April 1839, JS wrote to his wife Emma Smith in Quincy, Illinois, as he contemplated his imminent departure from the jail in Liberty, Clay County, Missouri, after months of incarceration. On 31 March, the prisoners' lawyer, Peter Burnett, had visited them in the jail and likely informed them that guards would soon transport the men from Liberty to Gallatin in Daviess County, Missouri, where a grand jury hearing for the eleventh judicial circuit was scheduled to begin on 8 April.[806] Burnett may have also told the prisoners that they would have the right to petition the court to change the venue of their upcoming trial to another Missouri county.[807]

JS summarized these updates in this letter to his wife. He also expressed his profound desire to be reunited with her and their children, and he offered her counsel regarding their family. As with previous letters JS penned to Emma from the jail, he wrote this 4 April letter himself rather than dictating it to a scribe. Instead of sending the missive to Illinois with a courier, as he apparently did with earlier letters to his wife, JS opted to send it through the postal service on 5 April 1839.[808] It probably arrived sometime before 11 April.[809]

---

804. Lazare, *American Book-Prices Current* (1951), xxiii, 599; Sandburg, *Lincoln Collector*, 3–8.

805. Withington, *Catalogue of Manuscripts in the Collection of Western Americana*, 244.

806. Hyrum Smith, Diary, 31 Mar. 1839; Ruling, Richmond, MO, Nov. 1838, p. [124], State of Missouri v. JS et al. for Treason and Other Crimes (Mo. 5th Jud. Cir. 1838), in State of Missouri, "Evidence"; An Act to Prescribe the Times of Holding Courts in the Eleventh Judicial Circuit [12 Feb. 1839], *Laws of the State of Missouri* [1839], p. 36.

807. On 4 April 1839, Hyrum Smith named in his journal six Missouri counties—Audrain, Monroe, Shelby, Clark, Lewis, and Marion—presumably as potential destinations for the venue change. (Hyrum Smith, Diary, 4 Apr. 1839.)

808. See Letter to Emma Smith, 4 Nov. 1838, pp. 279–282 herein; Letter to Emma Smith, 12 Nov. 1838, pp. 290–293 herein; and Letter to Emma Smith, 21 Mar. 1839, pp. 372–375 herein.

809. This assumption is based on the speed that contemporary correspondence was delivered through the mail. Hyrum Smith sent a letter, postmarked 5 April 1839, from the Liberty post office to his wife, Mary Fielding Smith, in Quincy. In her 11 April 1839 letter to her husband, she added an undated postscript acknowledging receipt of his missive. (Hyrum Smith, Liberty, MO, to Mary Fielding Smith, Quincy, IL, 23 Mar. 1839; Mary Fielding Smith, [Quincy, IL], to Hyrum Smith, 11 Apr. 1839, Mary Fielding Smith, Collection, CHL.)

Window bars from Clay County jail. The upper room of the Clay County jail in Liberty, Missouri, had two windows that were a foot and a half square, each with five vertical iron bars. The dungeon had two windows, each two feet by six inches, with a horizontal twenty-one-inch iron bar. As Joseph Smith noted in his 4 April 1839 letter to Emma Smith, he and his fellow prisoners would often "peak throu the greats [grates] of this lonesome prision." (Courtesy Church History Museum, Salt Lake City. Photograph by Alex D. Smith.)

Document Transcript

Liberty, Jail, Clay. Co., Mo, April, 4ᵗʰ, 1839.

Dear— and affectionate— Wife.

Thursday night I sat down just as the sun is going down, as we peak throu the greats of this lonesome prision,[810] to write to you, that I may make known to you my situation. It is I believe ⟨it is⟩ now about five months and six days since I have bean under the <u>grimace</u>, of a guard night and day, and within the walls grates and screeking of iron dors, of a lonesome dark durty prison.[811] With immotions known only to God, do I write this letter, the contemplations, of the mind under these circumstances, defies the pen, or tounge, or Angels, to discribe, or paint, to the human ~~mind~~ being, who never experiance what I we experience. This night we expect; is the last night we shall try our weary joints and bones on our dirty straw couches in these walls, let our case hereafter be as it may, as we expect to start tomorrow, for Davi[es]s Co— for our trial,[812] We shall have a change of Venue to some of the lower counties, for the final <u>trial</u>, as our <u>Lawyers</u> generaly say, if

---

810. For a description of the Clay County jail, see Introduction to Part 3: 4 Nov. 1838–16 Apr. 1839, pp. 274–275 herein.

811. JS and his fellow prisoners were incarcerated in the Clay County jail on 1 December 1838. JS was arrested on 31 October 1838, which may be the date he was using as the basis for his calculation of "five months and six days." (Letter to Emma Smith, 1 Dec. 1838, p. 294 herein.)

812. The prisoners departed on 6 April 1839 for Gallatin. (Hyrum Smith, Diary, 6 Apr. 1839.)

law can be adheared to in Davis, as it grants us the privaliege.⁸¹³ But you are awere of what we may expect, of beings that ⟨have⟩ conducted as they have. We lean of on the arm of Jehovah,⁸¹⁴ and none else, for our deliverance, and if he dont do it, it will not be done, you may be assured, for there is great thirsting for our blood, in this state; not because we are guilty of any thing: but because they say these men ⟨will⟩ give an account of what has been done to them; the wrongs they have sustain if it is known, it ⟨will⟩ ruin the State.⁸¹⁵ So the mob party have sworn, to have our lives, at all hasards, but God will disappoint them we trust, We shall be moved from this at any rate and we are glad of it let what will become of ⟨us⟩ we cannot ⟨get⟩ into a worse hole [p. [1]] then this is, we shall not stay here but one night besides this ⟨if that⟩ thank ⟨if that⟩ God, we shall never cast a lingering wish after liberty in clay county mo. Mo. we have enough of it to last forever, may God reward fals swearers according to their works, is all I can wish them.⁸¹⁶ My Dear Emma I think of you and the children continualy, if I could tell you my tale, I think you would say it was altogether enough for once, to grattify the malice of hell that I have suffered. I want ⟨to⟩ see little Frederick, Joseph, Julia, and Alexander, Joana,⁸¹⁷

---

813. The prisoners began seeking a change of venue as early as January 1839. On 24 January, the prisoners argued in a memorial to the Missouri legislature that they could not receive a fair trial within the fifth judicial circuit. Their petition led to a revised Missouri statute that permitted changes of venue between circuits. Ultimately, the prisoners received a change of venue on different grounds: the legislature reorganized the state's second and fifth judicial circuits, with Daviess County becoming part of the newly created eleventh circuit. The judge appointed to the eleventh circuit was Thomas Burch, who previously served as the prosecuting attorney in the prisoners' case. In cases in which the judge previously served as counsel, Missouri law mandated a change of venue. (Historical Introduction to Memorial to the Missouri Legislature, 24 Jan. 1839, pp. 319–320 herein; Historical Introduction to Promissory Note to John Brassfield, 16 Apr. 1839, pp. 422–426 herein.)

814. See 2 Chronicles 32:8.

815. In a 22 March 1839 letter to Isaac Galland, JS similarly commented that the church's enemies believed "the State will be ruined, if the Mormon leaders are liberated, so that they can publish the real facts, of what has been practised upon them." (Letter to Isaac Galland, 22 Mar. 1839, p. 380 herein.)

816. For more information on the prosecution witnesses at the November 1838 hearing, see Introduction to Part 3: 4 Nov. 1838–16 Apr. 1839, pp. 273–274 herein.

817. Probably Johanna Carter (1824–1847), a Latter-day Saint orphan who apparently lived with JS's family in the 1830s.ᵃ Johanna's mother, Elizabeth Kenyon Carter, died in 1828.ᵇ Her father, John Sims Carter, was a participant in the Camp of Israel expedition who died in 1834 in Missouri.ᶜ Johanna's stepmother, Jerusha Carter, died in 1835.ᵈ Johanna may have been living with the Smiths on 29 January 1836, when she and her sisters received patriarchal blessings from Joseph Smith Sr.ᵉ She possibly was staying with the Smiths in November 1838 in Far West, Missouri.ᶠ The inclusion of Johanna in this letter's list of children suggests that JS considered her one of his "five children," a reference he made in his 22 March 1839 letter to Isaac Galland.ᵍ (a. JS, Journal, 29 Jan. 1836, in *JSP*, J1:177; see also Smart, *Mormon Midwife*, 71–72. b. "Elizabeth Carter," in General Index to Vital Records of Vermont, Early to 1870, microfilm 27,502, U.S. and Canada Record Collection, [FHL]. c. "Afflicting," *The Evening and the Morning Star*,

and old major.[818] And as to yourself if you want to know how much I want to see you, examine your feelings, how much you want to see me, and judge for ⟨you[r]self⟩, I would gladly go ⟨walk⟩ from here to you barefoot, and bareheaded, and half naked, to see you and think it great pleasure, and never count it toil, but do not think I am babyish, for I do not feel so, I bare with fortitude all my oppression, so does do those that are with me, not one of us have flinched yet, I want you ⟨should⟩ not let those little fellows, forgit me, tell them Father loves them with a perfect love, and he is doing all he can to git away from the mob to come to them, do teach them all you can, that they may have good minds, be tender and kind to them, dont ⟨be⟩ fractious to them, but listen to their wants, tell them Father says they must be good children, ⟨and⟩ mind their mother, My Dear Emma there is great respo[n]sibility resting upon you, in preserveing yourself in honor, and sobriety, before them, and teaching them right things, to form their young and tender minds, that they begin in right paths, and not git contaminated when young, by seeing ungodly examples, I soppose you see [p. [2]] the need of my council, and help, but as ⟨a⟩ combinnation ⟨of⟩ things have conspired to place me where I am, and I know it ⟨is⟩ not my fault, and further if my voice and council, had been heeded I should not have been here, but I find no fault with you, att all I know nothing but what you have done the best you could, if there is any thing it is known to yourself, you must be your own judge, on that subject: and if ether of done us have done wrong it is wise in us to repent of it, and for God sake, do not b[e][819] so foolish as to yield to the flattery of the Devel, faslshoods, and vainty, in this hour of trouble, that our affections be drawn, away from the right objects, those preasious things, God has given us will rise up in judgement against us in the day of judgement against us if we do not mark well our steps, and ways. My heart has often been exceeding sorrowful when I have thought of these thing[s][820] for many considerations, one thing let [me?][821] [adm]onished you by way of my duty, do not [be?][822] self willed, neither harber a spirit of revevenge: and again remember that he who is my enemys,

July 1834, 176. *d.* "Jerusha Carter," in General Index to Vital Records of Vermont, Early to 1870, microfilm 27,502, U.S. and Canada Record Collection, FHL. *e.* JS, Journal, 29 Jan. 1836, in *JSP,* J1:176–178. *f.* See Caroline Clark et al., Complaint against William E. McLellin, no date, Statements against William E. McLellin et al., CHL. *g.* Letter to Isaac Galland, 22 Mar. 1839, p. 382 herein.)

818. Old Major was the Smiths' dog, a white English mastiff. (See "The Memoirs of President Joseph Smith," *Saints' Herald,* 6 Nov. 1934, 1414; and Davis, *Story of the Church,* 252.)

819. TEXT: "b[*page torn*]".

820. TEXT: "thing[*page torn*]".

821. TEXT: Page torn because of loss of seal.

822. TEXT: Page torn because of loss of seal.

is yours also, and never give up an old tried friend, who has waded through all manner of toil, for your sake, and throw him away becaus fools may tell ⟨you⟩ he ⟨has⟩ some <u>faults</u>; these things have accured to ⟨me⟩ as I have been writing, I do speak of ⟨them⟩ because you do not know them, but because I want to stir up your pure mind by way of <u>rememberance</u>: all feelings of diss[at]isfaction is far from my heart, I wish to act upon that principle of <u>generosity</u>, that will acquit myself in the preasance of [*page cut*]823 through the mercy of God You[rs?] [Joseph Smith Jr.]824 [p. [3]]

✉

Mrs. Emma Smith   /825 25
Quincy Ilinois
/826 LIBERTY Mo.
APR 5

——— ∽ ———

Letter from Sidney Rigdon, 10 April 1839

Source Note

Sidney Rigdon, Letter, Quincy, Adams Co., IL, to JS, Hyrum Smith, Caleb Baldwin, Lyman Wight, and Alexander McRae, [Liberty, Clay Co., MO], 10 Apr. 1839. Featured version copied [between 22 Apr. and 30 Oct. 1839] in JS Letterbook 2, pp. 4–5; handwriting of James Mulholland; JS Collection, CHL. For more information on JS Letterbook 2, see Source Notes for Multiple-Entry Documents, p. 566 herein.

Historical Introduction

On 10 April 1839, Sidney Rigdon wrote from Illinois to JS and his fellow prisoners in Missouri, updating them on the church's evolving plans to obtain redress for loss of life and property in Missouri. Rigdon arrived in Illinois from Missouri in mid-February 1839 and rented a farm in Big Neck Prairie, about thirty miles northeast of Quincy, Illinois.827 Despite the distance, he reportedly preached in Quincy frequently, "always to large audiences."828 While there, he also met with prominent citizens, who raised funds for the Latter-day Saint refugees.829 According to church member Elizabeth Haven, by late

---

823. TEXT: The dot of an *i* and possibly the top of an ascender are visible above the clipped portion.

824. TEXT: JS's signature was cut out of this letter at an unknown date.

825. TEXT: Postage rate written in brown ink in unidentified handwriting.

826. TEXT: Postmark stamped in red ink.

827. Editorial, *Quincy (IL) Whig*, 23 Feb. 1839, [1]; Letter from Elias Higbee, 16 Apr. 1839, p. 429 herein; Rigdon, "Life Story of Sidney Rigdon," 153–158; *Portrait and Biographical Record of Adams County, Illinois*, 180, 278.

828. Asbury, *Reminiscences of Quincy, Illinois*, 153.

829. "The Mormons," *Quincy (IL) Whig*, 16 Mar. 1839, [1]; "Proceedings in the Town of Quincy," *Quincy (IL) Argus*, 16 Mar. 1839, [1].

February 1839 Rigdon was planning to visit Washington DC to "plead at the feet of the President according to revelation"—a reference to a revelation JS dictated in 1833.[830] On 23 February, Rigdon wrote to United States attorney general Felix Grundy, inquiring about initiating a suit in federal court against the state of Missouri and private citizens who committed violence against the Saints in 1838.[831] Rigdon's 10 April letter to JS and the other prisoners demonstrates that Rigdon's "plan of operation" had evolved to include not only suing Missouri and sending a delegation to Washington but also assigning Latter-day Saints to lobby state legislatures to support Rigdon's proposal that the state of Missouri be "impeached" for lacking a republican form of government.

Rigdon's 10 April letter was likely a partial response to JS's general epistle dated 20 March 1839. Rigdon apparently had not written to the prisoners after his departure from the jail in Clay County, Missouri, in early February, causing them "to inquire after Elder Rigdon" and to note that "if he has not forgotten us it has not been signified to us by his scrawl."[832] In his 10 April letter, Rigdon referenced twice his unfailing friendship with the prisoners, and he emphasized he was busy laboring on behalf of them and the church.

Rigdon noted that a "Bʳ Mace"—perhaps Quincy resident Wandle Mace[833]—would carry the letter to Missouri, but it is unknown whether Mace actually did so. About the time that Rigdon completed his letter, word reached Quincy that the prisoners had been moved from the Clay County jail.[834] Rigdon may have waited to send his letter until receiving further news on the prisoners' location. The original letter is apparently not extant; James Mulholland copied it or a retained copy into JS Letterbook 2 sometime between late April and 30 October 1839.[835]

Document Transcript

Quincy Ill, April 10ᵗʰ 1839

To the Saints in prison, Greeting.

In the midst of a crowd of business I haste to send a few lines by the hand of Bʳ Mace our Messenger.

---

830. Elizabeth Haven, Quincy, IL, to Elizabeth Howe Bullard, Holliston, MA, 24 Feb. 1839, Barlow Family Collection, CHL; Revelation, 16–17 Dec. 1833, in *JSP*, D3:396 [D&C 101:88–89].

831. Sidney Rigdon, Quincy, IL, to Felix Grundy, [Washington DC], 23 Feb. 1839, Record Group 233, Records of the U.S. House of Representatives, National Archives, Washington DC.

832. Letter to the Church and Edward Partridge, 20 Mar. 1839, p. 371 herein; Hyrum Smith, Diary, 15 Mar. 1839.

833. Mace, Autobiography, 29–30.

834. After Mary Fielding Smith completed a letter to her husband, Hyrum Smith, on 11 April 1839, she attempted to send the missive with a courier, but it was returned because it was not known where the prisoners would be. After the letter was given back to her, she added a postscript, presumably on or soon after 11 April, explaining the situation. (Mary Fielding Smith, [Quincy, IL], to Hyrum Smith, 11 Apr. 1839, Mary Fielding Smith, Collection, CHL.)

835. Mulholland began to "write for the Church" on 22 April 1839, and Rigdon's letter was one of the first documents Mulholland inscribed in Letterbook 2. For information on the latest likely copying date, see 248n440 herein.

We wish you to know that our friendship is unabating and our exertions for your delivery, and that of the Church unceasing. For this purpose we have laboured to secure the friendship of the Governor of this State with all the principal men in this place. In this we have succeeded beyond our highest anticipations. Governor [Thomas] Carlin assured us last evening, that he would lay our case before the Legislature of this State and have the action of that body upon it; and he would use all his influence to have an action [p. 4] which should be favorable to our people. He is also getting papers prepared, signed by all the noted men in this part of the country to give us a favourable reception at Washington,[836] whither we shall repair forthwith after having visited the Governor of Iowa of whose friendship we have the strongest testimonies.[837]

We leave Quincy this day to visit him.[838] Our plan of operation is to impeach the State of Missouri on an item of the Constitution of the United States; That the general government shall give to each State a Republican form of government.[839] Such a form of Government does not exist in Missouri and we can prove it.

Governor Carlin and his Lady[840] enter with all the enthusiasm of their natures into this work, having no doubt but we can accomplish this object.

Our plan of operation in this work is to get all the Governors in their next messages to have the subject brought before the legislatures and we will have a man at the Capital of each State to furnish them with the testimony on the subject; and we design to be at Washington to wait upon Congress

---

836. See Samuel Holmes et al., Letter of Introduction, Quincy, IL, for Sidney Rigdon, 8 May 1839, in JS Letterbook 2, p. 44; and Samuel Leech, Letter of Introduction, Quincy, IL, for Sidney Rigdon, 10 May 1839, in JS Letterbook 2, p. 44.

837. The governor of Iowa Territory, Robert Lucas, served as governor of Ohio when the church was headquartered in Kirtland, Ohio. In early March 1839, Rigdon learned of a letter that land speculator Isaac Galland wrote to church member David Rogers on 26 February, in which Galland reported that Lucas believed the Latter-day Saints "were good Citizens of the State of Ohio" and that they should be treated as such. (Isaac Galland, Commerce, IL, to David Rogers, [Quincy, IL], 26 Feb. 1839, in JS Letterbook 2, p. 1; Minutes, 9 Mar. 1839, in JS Letterbook 2, p. 49.)

838. Presumably as a result of a mid-April 1839 meeting with church leaders in Burlington, Iowa Territory, Governor Lucas wrote Rigdon two letters of introduction dated 22 April 1839, both of which were for Rigdon to use when lobbying in Ohio and Washington DC. (Robert Lucas, Burlington, Iowa Territory, to Sidney Rigdon, 22 Apr. 1839, in JS Letterbook 2, p. 42; Robert Lucas, Letter of Introduction, Burlington, Iowa Territory, for Sidney Rigdon, 22 Apr. 1839, in JS Letterbook 2, pp. 42–43; Robert Lucas, Letter of Introduction, Burlington, Iowa Territory, for Sidney Rigdon, 22 Apr. 1839, in JS Letterbook 2, p. 43.)

839. See U.S. Constitution, art. 4, sec. 4.

840. That is, Rebecca Hewitt Carlin. (Madison Co., IL, Births, Marriages, Deaths, 1813–1916, Marriage Record, bk. 6, p. 1, microfilm 1,306,457, U.S. and Canada Record Collection, FHL.)

and have the action of that body on it also; all this going on at the same time, and have the action of the whole, during one session.

Br G[eorge] W. Robinson will be engaged all the time between this and the next sitting of the Legislatures in taking affidavits and preparing for the tug of war, while we will be going from State to State visiting the respective Governors to get the case mentioned in their messages to legislatures so as have the whole going on at once. You will see by this that our time is engrossed to overflowing.[841]

The Bishops of the Church[842] are required to ride and visit all scattered abroad, and collect money to carry on this great work. Be assured brethren that operations of an all important character are under motion, and will come to an issue as soon as possible.

Be assured that our friendship is unabated for you and our desires for your deliverance intense. May God hasten it speedily is our prayer day and night.

Yours in the bonds of affliction

Sidney Rigdon

J Smith Jr
H[yrum] Smith
C[aleb] Baldwin
L[yman] Wight
A[lexander] McRae [p. 5]

———— ☙ ————

Letter from Alanson Ripley, 10 April 1839

Source Note

Alanson Ripley, Letter, Quincy, Adams Co., IL, to JS, Hyrum Smith, Caleb Baldwin, Alexander McRae and Lyman Wight, [Liberty, Clay Co., MO], 10 Apr. 1839. Featured version copied [between 29 May and 30 Oct. 1839] in JS Letterbook 2, pp. 16–17; handwriting of James Mulholland; JS Collection, CHL. For more information on JS Letterbook 2, see Source Notes for Multiple-Entry Documents, p. 566 herein.

---

841. Rigdon was perhaps alluding to the instructions in JS's circa 22 March 1839 general epistle that the Saints should document and publicize their losses in Missouri. Robinson, who was Rigdon's son-in-law, was probably conducting these activities in his capacity as general church clerk and recorder as well as secretary to the First Presidency. Rigdon may have also referenced Robinson's activities as an indirect response to the prisoners' complaint in JS's 20 March 1839 general epistle that Robinson had not written to them following his departure from Missouri. (Letter to Edward Partridge and the Church, ca. 22 Mar. 1839, p. 397 herein; Letter to the Church and Edward Partridge, 20 Mar. 1839, p. 371 herein.)

842. That is, Newel K. Whitney, Edward Partridge, and presumably Vinson Knight; the latter served as an acting bishop in 1838.

Historical Introduction

On 10 April 1839, Latter-day Saint Alanson Ripley wrote from Quincy, Illinois, to JS and his fellow prisoners in the Clay County jail in Liberty, Missouri. In late 1838, Ripley was appointed by church leaders in Far West, Missouri, to attend to the prisoners' needs and "to importune at the feet of the judges" for the prisoners' release. During the next few months, Ripley worked to fulfill this assignment.[843] In early February 1839, he and four other church members apparently assisted the prisoners in an unsuccessful attempt to escape.[844] In mid-March, Ripley assisted with and signed JS's petition to the Missouri Supreme Court for habeas corpus.[845] At the end of the month, he traveled to Liberty again to report that "all was well & the [prisoners' families] were well also."[846] Upon his return to Caldwell County, Missouri, in early April, Ripley was told by the committee helping church members move out of Missouri that he needed to leave immediately for Illinois since anti-Mormons were threatening violence. Because of this need to seek "safty by leaving the State," Ripley was "compelled to abandon the idea of importuning at the feet of the judges" and to "leave the prisoners in the hands of God."[847]

On 10 April 1839, soon after his arrival in Quincy, Ripley wrote this letter to the prisoners. After summarizing Sidney Rigdon's developing plans to pursue justice for wrongs that Latter-day Saints had suffered in Missouri, Ripley explained his hurried departure from the state and offered to return to Missouri and continue supporting the prisoners. Ripley indicated that he was aware that the prisoners might obtain a change of venue after being indicted by a grand jury in Daviess County and suggested that, if desired, he would intercept them and their guards en route to the next destination. After Ripley completed the main body of his letter, he added two postscripts relaying brief words of greeting from other Latter-day Saints in Quincy. It is unknown whether Ripley's 10 April missive was sent to Missouri, because Saints in Quincy were aware that the prisoners had been moved from the jail in Liberty.[848] Although the original letter is apparently not extant, James Mulholland copied it or a retained copy into JS Letterbook 2 sometime between 29 May and 30 October 1839.[849]

---

843. Alanson Ripley, Statements, ca. Jan. 1845, Historian's Office, JS History Documents, 1839–1860, CHL.

844. Ripley, Jonathan Barlow, David Holeman, William D. Huntington, and Erastus Snow were later arrested and charged as accomplices to the escape attempt. (Samuel Tillery, Testimony, Liberty, MO, 11 Feb. 1839; Alanson Ripley, Testimony, Liberty, MO, 12 Feb. 1839, State of Missouri v. Ripley et al. [J.P. Ct. 1839], Clay County Archives and Historical Library, Liberty, MO.)

845. Petition to George Tompkins, between 9 and 15 Mar. 1839, p. 351 herein; Hyrum Smith, Diary, 15 Mar. 1839.

846. Hyrum Smith, Diary, 31 Mar. 1839.

847. Alanson Ripley, Statements, ca. Jan. 1845, Historian's Office, JS History Documents, 1839–1860, CHL.

848. See Historical Introduction to Letter from Sidney Rigdon, 10 Apr. 1839, pp. 406–407 herein.

849. Mulholland copied his own 29 May 1839 letter to Edward Partridge on page 15 of JS Letterbook 2, making that the earliest likely copying date for documents he subsequently copied but that had dates preceding 29 May. For information on the latest likely copying date, see 248n440 herein.

Document Transcript

Quincy Ill. April 10[th.] 1839

Dear brethren in Christ Jesus,[850]

It is with feelings in no small moment that I take ~~up~~ pen in hand to address you the prisoners of Jesus Christ[851] and in the same faith of the gospel with myself who are holden by the cords of malice and of hellish plottings against the just, and of the lifting up the heel against the Lords anointed,[852] but they shall soon fall and not rise again, for their destruction is sure, for no power beneath the Heavens can save them.— President [Sidney] Rigdon is wielding a mighty shaft against the whole kidney of foul calumniators and mobocrats of Missouri. Yesterday he spent part of the day with Governor [Thomas] Carlin of this State the President told him, that he was informed that Governor [Lilburn W.] Boggs was calculating to take out a bench warrant for himself[853] and others, and then make a demand of his Excellency for them to be given up to be taken back to Missouri for trial, And he was assured by that noble minded hero,[854] that if M[r] Boggs undertook that thing he would get himself insulted; he also assured him that the people called Mormons should find a permanent protection in this state, he also solicited our people one and all to settle in this state, and if there could be a tract of country that would suit our convenience he would use his influence for congress to make a grant of it to us, to redress our wrongs, and make up our losses.[855]

We met last night in council of the whole and passed some resolutions with respect to sending to the City of Washington.[856] We are making every exertion possible that lays in our power to accomplish that grand object, upon which hangs our temporal salvation, and interwoven with this our Eternal Salvation; and so closely allied to each other are they, that I

---

850. See Ephesians 1:1.

851. See Philemon 1:1, 9; and Ephesians 3:1.

852. Ripley was probably alluding to language in JS's 20 March 1839 general epistle: "Cursed are all those that shall lift up the heal against mine anointed." (Letter to the Church and Edward Partridge, 20 Mar. 1839, p. 366 herein [D&C 121:16]; see also Psalm 41:9; and John 13:18.)

853. That is, Sidney Rigdon.

854. That is, Thomas Carlin.

855. See Letter from Sidney Rigdon, 10 Apr. 1839, p. 408 herein.

856. The council meeting was perhaps held in response to the instruction in JS's 20 March 1839 general epistle that while he remained imprisoned, "a general conferance of the most faithfull and the most respictible of the authorities of the church" should manage "the general affairs of the church." The meeting's resolutions probably dealt with Rigdon's plan to seek redress from the federal government for the Saints' losses in Missouri. (Letter to the Church and Edward Partridge, 20 Mar. 1839, pp. 367–368 herein; Letter from Sidney Rigdon, 10 Apr. 1839, pp. 408–409 herein.)

want to see the head connected with the body again and while we are enjoying one, let us be ripening for the other: But my heart says where is he whose lips used to whisper the words of life[857] to us? Alas! he is in the hands of Zions enemies. Oh Lord crieth my heart will not heaven hear our prayers and witness our tears? Yes saith the spirit thy tears are all bottled up,[858] and shall speedily be rewarded with the deliverence of thy dearly beloved brethren.

But when I see the fearful apprehensions of some of our brethren it causes me to mourn, one instance of which I will mention. When I arrived at Far West, I made my mind known to some of the community, and I told them that I wanted that they should send a messenger to the gaol [jail] to communicate with you, but I was denied the privelege. They said that the Presidency was so anxious to be free once more, that they would not consider the danger that the Church was in. They met in council and passed resolutions that I myself, A[lanson] Ripley, A[masa] M. Lyman, [Jonathan] W Barlow[859] should leave Far West for Quincy forthwith:[860] But my spirits have been grieved ever since, So that I can hardly hold my peace. They are so afraid of bears,[861] that they hardly remember [p. 16] that there is a god in Israel,[862] that can blast the hellish desires and base designs of that infernal

---

857. See Revelation, 22–23 Sept. 1832, in *JSP*, D2:300 [D&C 84:85].

858. See Psalm 56:8.

859. Like Ripley, Lyman and Barlow assisted the prisoners. Lyman signed the attestation of JS's March 1839 petition for a writ of habeas corpus, affirming the truth of the claims in the document. During a visit Barlow and other men made to the jail on 7 February 1839, the prisoners attempted to escape, and the visitors were subsequently charged with assisting in the unsuccessful attempt. (Petition to George Tompkins, between 9 and 15 Mar. 1839, p. 352 herein; Jonathan Barlow, Testimony, Liberty, MO, 12 Feb. 1839, State of Missouri v. Ripley et al. [J.P. Ct. 1839], Clay County Archives and Historical Library, Liberty, MO.)

860. Ripley probably returned to Far West in early April 1839, after visiting the prisoners on 31 March.[a] It is not known when the Far West removal committee—the council referred to here—passed the resolution ordering Ripley, Lyman, and Barlow to depart for Illinois. The committee's minutes for 1–4 April were likely among the records that were stolen or destroyed by anti-Mormon vigilantes later that month.[b] On 6 April, anti-Mormons ordered the remaining Latter-day Saints to leave Far West immediately. The removal committee's 6 April minutes indicate that a planned visit to Liberty was abruptly canceled and Henry G. Sherwood was ordered to go to Illinois immediately for help. During the same meeting, the committee may have instructed Ripley, Lyman, and Barlow to go to Illinois, but this direction is not mentioned in the minutes.[c] Lyman and Barlow presumably departed Far West sometime in April, about the same time as Ripley, and settled in Quincy. (*a.* Hyrum Smith, Diary, 31 Mar. 1839. *b.* Kimball, "History," 101. *c.* Far West Committee, Minutes, 6 Apr. 1839.)

861. Ripley was perhaps alluding to JS's 20 March general epistle, which alluded to Aesop's fable of the bear and the two travelers. (Letter to the Church and Edward Partridge, 20 Mar. 1839, p. 371 herein.)

862. See 1 Samuel 17:46.

banditti whose hands have been embrued in the blood of martyrs and Saints: who wish to destroy the Church of God. But their Chain is short, there is but just enough left to bind their own hands with.

Dear Brethren I am at your service and I wait your Council at Quincy and shall be happy to grant you the desires of your hearts; I am ready to act. Please to give me all the intelligence that is in your power. If you take a change of venue please to let me know what county you will come to and when as near as possible and what road you will come, for I shall be an Adder in the path.[863] Yes My Dear Brethren God Almighty will deliver you, fear not, for your redemption draweth near,[864] the day of your deliverance[865] is at hand. Dear Brethren I have it in my heart to lay my body in the sand or deliver you from your bonds, and my mind is intensely fixed on the latter. Dear Brethren, you will be able to judge of the Spirit that actuates my breast, for when I realise your sufferings my heart is like wax before the fire,[866] but when I reflect upon the cause of your afflictions it is like fire in my bones,[867] and burns against your enemies to the bare hilt, and I never can be satisfied while there is one of them to piss against a wall,[868] or draw a sword or spring a trigger; for my sword never has been sheathed in peace; for the blood of D[avid] W. Patten and those who were butchered at Hawn's Mill crieth for vengeance from the ground[869] therefore hear it, Oh ye Heavens, and record it, Oh! ye recording angels, bear the tidings ye flaming seraphs, that I from this day declare myself the avenger of the blood[870] of those innocent men, and of the innocent cause of Zion and of her prisoners, and I will not rest untill they are as free who are in prison as I am.

Your families are all well and in good spirits.[871] May the Lord bless you all, Amen. B^rs A Lyman & W Barlow join in saying our hearts are as thy heart. Br Joseph if my Spirit is wrong, for God's Sake Correct it.

---

863. See Genesis 49:17. In quoting part of Jacob's blessing for his son Dan, Ripley was perhaps invoking the ethos of the Danite society, which was informally named after the Israelite tribe of Dan. (See Introduction to Part 2: 8 July–29 Oct. 1838, pp. 169–170 herein; and Nauvoo City Council Draft Minutes, 3 Jan. 1844, 36; see also Historical Introduction to Constitution of the Society of the Daughter of Zion, ca. Late June 1838, at josephsmithpapers.org.)

864. See Luke 21:28; and Revelation, 7 Dec. 1830, in *JSP*, D1:223 [D&C 35:26].

865. See Revelation, 5 Jan. 1831, in *JSP*, D1:235 [D&C 39:10].

866. See Psalm 22:14.

867. See Jeremiah 20:9; and Lamentations 1:13.

868. See 1 Kings 14:10; and 1 Samuel 25:22, 34.

869. See Genesis 4:10; and Revelation 6:10.

870. See Deuteronomy 19:12; and Joshua 20:3, 5, 9.

871. See Letter from Edward Partridge, 5 Mar. 1839, pp. 329–330 herein; and Letter from Don Carlos Smith and William Smith, 6 Mar. 1839, pp. 332–333 herein.

Brethren be of good cheer, for we are determined as God liveth[872] to rescue you from that hellish crowd or die in the ~~attempt~~ furrow. We shall come face foremost.

A Ripley.

N. B.

S. B. Crockett,

(I have been once driven but not whipped)

Br B[righam] Young's sends his best ~~compliments~~ respects to you all.[873]

A.R.

J— S— Jr
H— S— [Hyrum Smith]
C— B [Caleb Baldwin]
A— M^cR [Alexander McRae]
L— W. [Lyman Wight] [p. 17]

———— ✑ ————

Letter from Don Carlos and Agnes Coolbrith Smith, 11 April 1839

Source Note

Don Carlos Smith, Letter with postscript by Agnes Coolbrith Smith, Quincy, Adams Co., IL, to Hyrum Smith and JS, Liberty, Clay Co., MO, 11 Apr. 1839. Featured version copied [between 29 May and 30 Oct. 1839] in JS Letterbook 2, pp. 39–40; handwriting of James Mulholland; JS Collection, CHL. For more information on JS Letterbook 2, see Source Notes for Multiple-Entry Documents, p. 566 herein.

Historical Introduction

On 11 April 1839, Don Carlos Smith wrote from Quincy, Illinois, to his brother Hyrum Smith in the jail in Clay County, Missouri; Don Carlos's wife, Agnes Coolbrith Smith, added a postscript addressed to Hyrum and JS. In the letter, Don Carlos provided an update on Hyrum's family, who had departed Far West, Missouri, earlier in the year and settled in the vicinity of Quincy.

This letter was the second one Don Carlos sent to the prison. In his 6 March letter, he noted that Hyrum's wife, Mary Fielding Smith, continued to suffer with a "severe cold." He also reported that she and her infant son were staying with her sister Mercy Fielding Thompson and Mercy's husband, Robert B. Thompson, and that Hyrum's five children from his deceased wife, Jerusha Barden Smith, were staying with Hyrum's parents.

---

872. See 1 Kings 18:10; 2 Samuel 2:27; and Job 27:2.

873. Young departed Far West for Illinois in mid-February 1839. After experiencing some delays, he and his family arrived in Quincy in mid-March. (Historian's Office, Brigham Young History Drafts, 20; Knight, History, 1085–1086; Emmeline B. Wells, "Biography of Mary Ann Angell Young," *Juvenile Instructor*, 1 Jan. 1891, 19.)

Don Carlos also suggested there were problems with family dynamics.[874] This troublesome news was exacerbated because Hyrum had not received direct communication from Mary. According to the contents of the featured letter, Hyrum apparently replied to Don Carlos in late March, expressing anxiety and asking for additional information about his family. Don Carlos responded with this 11 April letter, reassuring his brother that Mary's health was improving and that the tensions in the family were partially relieved. Don Carlos also asked Hyrum to convey words of encouragement to JS and the other prisoners—Lyman Wight, Caleb Baldwin, and Alexander McRae. Agnes then added a short postscript addressed to Hyrum and JS, expressing her faith in divine providence and referring to the well-being of Hyrum's and JS's children.

As with the letters Sidney Rigdon and Alanson Ripley wrote to the prisoners on 10 April 1839, it is unknown whether Don Carlos and Agnes's 11 April letter was carried to Missouri immediately or held until the Saints received further information about the prisoners' anticipated change of venue.[875] The original letter is apparently not extant; however, James Mulholland copied the letter into JS Letterbook 2 sometime between 29 May and 30 October 1839.[876]

Document Transcript

Quincy April 11ᵗʰ 1839

Brother Hyrum [Smith], after reading a line from you to myself, and one to Father which awakens all the feelings of tenderness and brotherly affection that one heart is capable of containing, I sit down in haste to answer it; My health and that of my family is tolerable good, Mother and Lucy [Smith] have been very sick but are getting better.[877] Your family are in better health now than at any other period since your confinement: Mary [Fielding Smith] is getting tolerable good health,[878] she is doing the best she can for the good and enjoyment of the children; the family are all together and seem to be contented. Lovina is a good girl and has quite a <u>motherly</u> <u>care</u> for the children, and takes considerable interest in the welfare of her mother.[879] As respects you[r]

---

874. See Letter from Don Carlos Smith and William Smith, 6 Mar. 1839, pp. 331–334 herein.

875. See Historical Introduction to Letter from Sidney Rigdon, 10 Apr. 1839, pp. 406–407 herein.

876. Mulholland copied his own 29 May 1839 letter to Edward Partridge on page 15 of Letterbook 2, making that the earliest likely copying date for documents he subsequently copied but that had dates preceding 29 May. For information on the latest likely copying date, see 248n440 herein.

877. Soon after arriving in Illinois, Lucy Mack Smith and her daughter Lucy fell ill with "a very severe case of Cholera." (Lucy Mack Smith, History, 1844–1845, bk. 17, [2].)

878. After being essentially bedridden for "4 or 5 months," Mary Fielding Smith wrote to her husband on 11 April 1839—the same date as the featured letter—noting that her health was rapidly improving. (Mary Fielding Smith, [Quincy, IL], to Hyrum Smith, 11 Apr. 1839, Mary Fielding Smith, Collection, CHL.)

879. Lovina, the oldest daughter of Hyrum and Jerusha Barden Smith, was born on 16 September 1827. (Hyrum Smith Family Bible.)

fears concerning Mary, you may put them to rest:[880] I believe that she is your friend, and desires to promote your happiness; I have no fault to find with Mary, for she has had a long fit of sickness, and where there has been a lack of wisdom, had she been well and had her own way, there would in all probability been no call for the observations that I made in my letter to you.[881] I think it will be wisdom for Sister [Mercy Fielding] Thompson to remain where she is at present.[882] The course that we have pursued I think has proved advantageous to her. Brother Hyram I am in hopes that my letter did not increase your trouble, for I know that your affliction is too great for human nature to bear, and if I did not know that there was a God in Heaven, and that his promises are sure and faithful, and that he is your friend in the midst of all your trouble,[883] I would fly to your relief and either be with you in prison, or see you breathe free air, air too that had not been inhaled ~~by~~ and corrupted by a pack of ruffians who trample upon virtue and innocence with impunity and are not even satisfied with the property and blood of the Saints, but must exult over the dead. You both have my prayers, my influence, and warmest feelings with a <u>fixed</u> <u>determination</u> if it should so be, that you should be destroyed, to <u>avenge</u> your blood four fold. Joseph must excuse me for not writing to him at this time Give my love to all the prisoners, write to me as often as you can, and do not be worried about your families; Your's in affliction as well as in peace.

Don C[arlos] Smith [p. 39]

Beloved Brethren Hyrum and Joseph, by the permit of my companion I write a line to show that I have not forgotten you, neither do I forget you for my prayer is to my Heavenly Father for your deliverance; It seems as though the Lord was slow to hear[884] the prayers of the Saints, but the Lord's ways, are not

---

880. On 19 March 1839, when church member David Rogers brought the prisoners letters from family and friends, Hyrum Smith was distraught that there was nothing from his wife, Mary Fielding Smith. The next day, he wrote to Mary: "If you have forsaken me you could also send me word then I should know what to depend upon." (Hyrum Smith, Liberty, MO, to Mary Fielding Smith, [Quincy, IL], 20 Mar. 1839, Mary Fielding Smith, Collection, CHL.)

881. In his 6 March 1839 letter to Hyrum Smith and JS, Don Carlos Smith expressed his opinion about either Mary Fielding Smith or Mercy Fielding Thompson: "The family would do better without her than with her; which I am confident you will regulate when you come. One reason for so saying, is that I do not think that she is a suitable person to govern the family." Don Carlos's language is too vague to determine with certainty which woman he was referring to. (Letter from Don Carlos Smith and William Smith, 6 Mar. 1839, p. 333 herein; see also Esplin, "Hyrum Smith," 122–163.)

882. As of 11 April 1839, Mercy Fielding Thompson, Robert B. Thompson, and their daughter, Mary Jane, lived "in a small House in Quincy" with Mary Fielding Smith; her five-month-old son, Joseph F. Smith; and her five stepchildren, who had evidently relocated from their grandparents' residence. (Mary Fielding Smith, [Quincy, IL], to Hyrum Smith, 11 Apr. 1839, Mary Fielding Smith, Collection, CHL.)

883. See Psalm 138:7.

884. See Book of Mormon, 1830 ed., 180, 199 [Mosiah 11:24; 21:15].

like our ways,[885] therefore he can do better than ourselves; you must be comforted Bro H & J. and look forward for better days; your little ones are as playful as little lambs, be comforted concerning them, for they are not cast down as and sorrowful as we are; their sorrows are but momentary, and ours continual. May the Lord bless, protect, and deliver you from all your enemies, and restore you to the bosom of your families, is the prayer of A. M. [Agnes Coolbrith] Smith.

Hyrum Smith, Liberty Mo.

———— ❧ ————

Agreement with Jacob Stollings, 12 April 1839

Source Note

Jacob Stollings, Agreement with JS, Gallatin, Daviess Co., MO, 12 Apr. 1839. Featured version copied [between June and 30 Oct. 1839] in JS Letterbook 2, p. 50; handwriting of James Mulholland; JS Collection, CHL. For more information on JS Letterbook 2, see Source Notes for Multiple-Entry Documents, p. 566 herein.

Historical Introduction

On 12 April 1839, merchant Jacob Stollings of Gallatin, Missouri, entered into an agreement with JS, stating that Stollings would forgive Latter-day Saint debts to his store if JS would recover account books stolen from the store. The books were taken in mid-October 1838, during the conflict between Latter-day Saints and anti-Mormons. Earlier in October, Latter-day Saints were expelled from De Witt in Carroll County, Missouri, making it clear that civil authorities would not protect church members from extralegal violence. Having forced the Saints from De Witt, anti-Mormon Missourians turned their attention to Latter-day Saints in Adam-ondi-Ahman and other settlements in Daviess County. In response, church leaders in Far West, Caldwell County, decided to engage in aggressive self-defense rather than rely on unpredictable militia troops for protection. In John Corrill's words, the Saints planned "to scatter the mob" and "to destroy those places that harbored them" in Daviess County, particularly Gallatin, which was the county seat and a vigilante haven.[886]

On 18 October 1838, apostle David W. Patten led about eighty Latter-day Saint men to Gallatin to expel anti-Mormon vigilantes, burn buildings owned by vigilantes and their sympathizers, and confiscate essential goods as wartime appropriations.[887] Latter-day Saint

---

885. See Isaiah 55:8–9.

886. Corrill, *Brief History*, 35–38, in *JSP*, H2:174–179; Introduction to Part 3: 4 Nov. 1838–16 Apr. 1839, pp. 265–266 herein.

887. Andrew Job, Testimony, Richmond, MO, Nov. 1838, p. [70]; George Worthington, Testimony, Richmond, MO, Nov. 1838, p. [100]; Ezra Williams, Testimony, Richmond, MO, Nov. 1838, p. [109], State of Missouri v. JS et al. for Treason and Other Crimes (Mo. 5th Jud. Cir. 1838), in State of Missouri, "Evidence"; Lyman Wight, Testimony, Nauvoo, IL, 1 July 1843, p. 16, Nauvoo, IL, Records, CHL.

Morris Phelps, a participant in the expedition, stated that the town's residents scattered when they recognized the Mormons. The Saints targeted Stollings's grocery store since it was believed to be a "place of rendezvous" for anti-Mormons.[888] The store clerk, Patrick Lynch, later testified that he escaped the building just as the Latter-day Saints approached. From a secluded position, he watched the men secure the building and move goods into the street.[889] The Mormons then apparently burned the store.[890] Oliver Huntington, a Latter-day Saint living at Adam-ondi-Ahman at the time, later recalled that as he watched from a distance, he observed smoke "rising towards Heaven." When the men returned to Adam-ondi-Ahman, Huntington saw that goods confiscated from the store were deposited in Bishop Vinson Knight's home.[891]

Presumably among the goods were a ledger, three daybooks, and "one day book of Groceries." Lynch later testified that he searched for the ledger, three day books, and promis-

---

888. Phelps, Reminiscences, 9–10. Although Phelps did not disclose his participation in the Gallatin expedition, several witnesses at the November 1838 hearing identified him as among the men who were present. (See, for example, Sampson Avard, Testimony, Richmond, MO, Nov. 1838, p. [21]; George M. Hinkle, Testimony, Richmond, MO, Nov. 1838, p. [40]; and John Cleminson, Testimony, Richmond, MO, Nov. 1838, p. [52], in State of Missouri, "Evidence.")

889. Patrick Lynch, Testimony, Richmond, MO, Nov. 1838, pp. [112]–[113], in State of Missouri, "Evidence."

890. William W. Phelps, who was disaffected from the church, claimed he heard JS and other church leaders making plans in Adam-ondi-Ahman "to take the goods out of the Store at Gallatin, bring them to Diahmon & burn the store."[a] Although several individuals said they saw the building burning, none could definitively state that a Latter-day Saint had lit the fire.[b] Morris Phelps later claimed that Sampson Avard, a Latter-day Saint who participated in the expedition, had "in his rage hurled a pine brand into it [the store] which melted it to ashes." However, Phelps then backtracked: "Others have said that the mob burnt it in order to have a pretext or cause of action against the Mormons. But the particulars of these things remain yet to be determined. Allowing this to be the Mormons;— The reader will bear in mind the many extream which they have been driven to by loss of property, by the sufferings of their Women and children; their houses frequently burnt their women and children turned into the snow." Phelps conceded that "many had become much enraged and perhaps carried some things beyond the bounds of wisdom as other men frequently do when driven to desperation."[c] (a. William W. Phelps, Testimony, Richmond, MO, Nov. 1838, p. [91], in State of Missouri, "Evidence." b. William Morgan, Affidavit, Daviess Co., MO, 21 Oct. 1838, copy, Mormon War Papers, MSA; Sampson Avard, Testimony, Richmond, MO, Nov. 1838, p. [7]; Patrick Lynch, Testimony, Richmond, MO, Nov. 1838, p. [113]; Joseph McGee, Testimony, Richmond, MO, Nov. 1838, p. [103]; George W. Worthington, Testimony, Richmond, MO, Nov. 1838, p. [101], in State of Missouri, "Evidence." c. Phelps, Reminiscences, 10, 11.)

891. Oliver Huntington, "History of Oliver Boardman Huntington," 21–22. Latter-day Saint dissident Reed Peck testified at the November 1838 hearing that just before the October expedition to Gallatin, JS gave a speech "in refference to stealing," stating that "in a general way he did not approve of it" but that under certain circumstances it was necessary, such as when the "Saviour & his disciples stole corn in passing thro' the corn fields for the reason that they could not otherwise procure anything to eat." William W. Phelps testified that JS gave the speech because "when they went out to war it was necessary to take spoils to live on." Jeremiah Myers, a Latter-day Saint who participated in the expedition, explained that the goods removed from Stollings's store were "considered consecrated property & that they were to be dealt out by the bishop to those who stood in need." (Reed Peck, Testimony, Richmond, MO, Nov. 1838, p. [57]; William W. Phelps, Testimony, Richmond, MO, Nov. 1838, p. [89]; Jeremiah Myers, Testimony, Richmond, MO, Nov. 1838, p. [69], in State of Missouri, "Evidence"; see also Matthew 12:1–8; Mark 2:23–28; and Luke 6:1–5.)

sory notes estimated to be worth $300 in Adam-ondi-Ahman but was unsuccessful, although he did find in Knight's home some promissory notes from non-Mormon customers.[892] Stollings, likely also searching for the missing items, apparently ransacked the Smith residence in Far West following JS's arrest.[893]

In the November 1838 preliminary hearing, no witnesses placed JS in Gallatin during the expedition on 18 October; several witnesses testified that he remained in Adam-ondi-Ahman to direct the Mormons' several military operations in Daviess County.[894] Nevertheless, around 10 April 1839 a Daviess County grand jury indicted JS, as well as other Latter-day Saints, for burning Stollings's store, stealing items from Lynch, and committing other crimes in the county.[895]

On 12 April 1839, Stollings met with JS and proposed to forgive the debts that Latter-day Saints had incurred when trading in his store in 1838 if JS would assist in locating the missing account books. After the meeting, Stollings produced a formal statement of the agreement, which he noted "shall be a receipt in full to all intents and purposes," indicating the agreement would also be considered a receipt if the books were returned within four months. By the time Stollings completed the written agreement, JS and the other prisoners had been temporarily moved to Adam-ondi-Ahman while their guards prepared to transport the men to Boone County on a change of venue.[896] Stollings therefore sent the agreement and a cover letter to JS in Adam-ondi-Ahman.[897] The agreement evidently remained in JS's possession during the prisoners' escape from Missouri a few days later and their journey to Illinois.[898] The agreement was copied into JS Letterbook 2 by James Mulholland sometime between June and 30 October 1839; the original is apparently not extant.[899]

---

892. Patrick Lynch, Testimony, Richmond, MO, Nov. 1838, p. [113], in State of Missouri, "Evidence."

893. Emma Smith et al., Complaint against Jacob Stollings, 1839, Statements against William E. McLellin et al., CHL.

894. See Introduction to Part 3: 4 Nov. 1838–16 Apr. 1839, p. 266 herein; and 349n455 herein.

895. See Robert Wilson, Gallatin, MO, to James L. Minor, Jefferson City, MO, 18 Mar. 1841, in *Document Containing the Correspondence,* 156–159. Sampson Avard testified before the grand jury regarding both indictments. Lynch, Allen Rathbun, George Worthington, and John Stokes likewise testified concerning the larceny indictment. No record of their testimonies is extant. The grand jury indicted several Latter-day Saint men for breaking into and removing property from Stollings's store, but JS was not named as a defendant in that indictment. (Indictment, [Honey Creek Township, MO], ca. 10 Apr. 1839, State of Missouri v. Gates et al. for Arson [Daviess Co. Cir. Ct. 1839], microfilm 959,084, U.S. and Canada Record Collection, FHL; Indictment, [Honey Creek Township, MO], ca. 10 Apr. 1839, State of Missouri v. JS et al. for Larceny [Daviess Co. Cir. Ct. 1839], Daviess County Courthouse, Gallatin, MO; Indictment, [Honey Creek Township, MO], ca. 10 Apr. 1839, State of Missouri v. Baldwin et al. for Burglary [Daviess Co. Cir. Ct. 1839], Historical Department, Nineteenth-Century Legal Documents Collection, CHL.)

896. During the April 1839 circuit court hearing, Judge Thomas Burch approved the prisoners' request for the trial to be moved to a different circuit court, on the grounds that Burch had served as the prosecuting attorney in the November 1838 hearing and was therefore biased. (Historical Introduction to Promissory Note to John Brassfield, 16 Apr. 1839, p. 422 herein.)

897. Hyrum Smith, Diary, 12 Apr. 1839.

898. See Historical Introduction to Promissory Note to John Brassfield, 16 Apr. 1839, p. 424 herein.

899. Mulholland copied a document dated June 1839 onto page 48 of the letterbook, making June the earliest Mulholland likely copied documents on subsequent pages. For information on the latest likely copying date, see 248n440 herein.

Document Transcript

Gallitan, Davies County Mo

April 12th 1839

Know all men by these presents.

That I Jacob Stollings have this day agreed with Joseph Smith Jr to release all members of the Mormon Church from any and all debts due to me from them for goods sold to them by me at Gallitin during the year 1838 on the following condition viz: that said Joseph Smith Jr return or cause to be returned to me the following books— one Ledger— three day books, and one day book of Groceries which was taken from my store in Gallitin when said store was burned,

And if said books are returned to me within four months this shall be a receipt in full to all intents and purposes against any debt or debts due from Said Mormons to me on said books, but if not returned, this is to be null and void. Given under my hand this day and date before written.

Jacob Stollings

Attest ◊⁹⁰⁰ Lynch

———— ☙ ————

Letter from Jacob Stollings, circa 12 April 1839

Source Note

Jacob Stollings, Letter, Gallatin, Daviess Co., MO, to JS, Adam-ondi-Ahman, Daviess Co., MO, ca. 12 Apr. 1839. Featured version copied [between June and 30 Oct. 1839] in JS Letterbook 2, p. 50; handwriting of James Mulholland; JS Collection, CHL. For more information on JS Letterbook 2, see Source Notes for Multiple-Entry Documents, p. 566 herein.

Historical Introduction

Jacob Stollings, a merchant in Gallatin, Daviess County, Missouri, wrote a letter to JS around 12 April 1839, introducing a written version of a verbal agreement between the two men. Stollings and JS made the agreement in Gallatin on 12 April, around two days after a Daviess County grand jury indicted JS for crimes he had allegedly committed during the 1838 conflict, including stealing items from and burning Stollings's store on 18 October. Several account books had apparently been removed from his store that day, and the agreement specified that Stollings would forgive Latter-day Saints of the debts

---

900. TEXT: The initial before "Lynch" is somewhat unclear. Though it is almost certainly a "P," indicating Patrick Lynch, the letter may possibly be a "J" for Joshua Lynch, who also lived in Daviess County in 1839. (1850 U.S. Census, District 27, Daviess Co., MO, 365[B]; Lynch, *Life and Times of Joshua W. Lynch Descendants,* 4; Daviess Co., MO, Deed Records, 1838–1902, vol. A, p. 25, 30 July 1839, microfilm 954,887, U.S. and Canada Record Collection, FHL.)

they owed for purchasing goods from him in 1838 if JS would recover the merchant's account books.[901]

Stollings wrote this letter to introduce the enclosed agreement and to offer to compensate anyone who returned the books. Stollings probably wrote the letter the same day as or within a day or two after writing the formal agreement. He addressed the letter to JS in "Diamon" (a common shortened name for Adam-ondi-Ahman, Missouri), which indicates that Stollings penned the missive after JS and the other prisoners departed Gallatin on 12 April for Adam-ondi-Ahman but probably before 14 April, when the prisoners departed Adam-ondi-Ahman for Boone County on a change of venue.[902] It is unknown whether Stollings delivered the letter and the enclosed agreement or whether he relied on a courier. JS received the letter and took it with him when he and his fellow prisoners escaped from Missouri a few days later.[903] On 27 June 1839, about ten weeks after Stollings wrote the letter, JS responded from his new residence in Illinois.[904] Stollings's letter was copied into JS Letterbook 2 by James Mulholland sometime between June and 30 October 1839; the original letter is apparently not extant.[905]

Document Transcript

Dear Sir Enclosed I send you the receipt which I promised and if you will pay the necessary attention to it, and it will be a benefit to the Church and to me, and I think with a little attention on your part they can be produced, and any person who will deliver them at any point in the State so I can get them, I will compensate them well, as I know you feel deeply interested in the welfare of the Church, and when you consider that it will add to their character and look upon it in a proper light, you will spare no pains in assisting me in the recovery of those books.

Your's &c in haste
Jacob Stollings

Joseph Smith Jr Diamon [Adam-ondi-Ahman]

———— ∽ ————

---

901. See Historical Introduction to Agreement with Jacob Stollings, 12 Apr. 1839, pp. 417–419 herein; Introduction to Part 3: 4 Nov. 1838–16 Apr. 1839, p. 266 herein.

902. Hyrum Smith, Diary, 12–14 Apr. 1839.

903. See Historical Introduction to Promissory Note to John Brassfield, 16 Apr. 1839, p. 424 herein.

904. Letter to Jacob Stollings, 27–28 June 1839, pp. 511–512 herein.

905. Mulholland copied a document dated June 1839 onto page 48 of the letterbook, making that the earliest likely copying date for documents inscribed on subsequent pages. For information on the latest likely copying date, see 248n440 herein.

Promissory Note to John Brassfield, 16 April 1839

Source Note

JS, Promissory Note, MO, to John Brassfield, 16 Apr. 1839; handwriting of Alexander McRae and JS; probable signature of JS (now missing); one page; JS Collection, CHL.

Single leaf measuring 4 × 7½ inches (10 × 19 cm). The left and top edges have the square cut of manufactured paper. The right and bottom edges are unevenly torn. The document was folded for carrying and filing. The bottom right portion, where one or more signatures would have appeared, was subsequently torn off. A portion of the first letter of a signature remains, possibly a "J". The promissory note was likely in the possession of John Brassfield until it was redeemed, whereupon it passed into possession of the LDS church.

Historical Introduction

On 16 April 1839, a promissory note was made for John Brassfield, one of the men guarding JS and his fellow prisoners in Missouri. Textual and historical evidence indicate that JS and one or more of his companions issued this note, promising to pay Brassfield $150. Around six days earlier in Gallatin, Missouri, JS and his fellow prisoners were indicted by a grand jury for crimes they allegedly committed during the conflict between Latter-day Saints and other Missourians in 1838.[906] Following the indictments, presiding judge Thomas Burch granted the prisoners a change of venue from Daviess County to Columbia, Boone County, Missouri, on the grounds that Burch had served as the prosecuting attorney during the November 1838 preliminary hearing.[907]

---

906. JS was indicted for riot, treason, larceny, receipt of stolen goods, and two incidents of arson.[a] The riot indictment stemmed from an 8 August 1838 confrontation at the home of Adam Black, a Daviess County justice of the peace whom church members accused of leading a mob against the Latter-day Saints.[b] The remaining indictments were for alleged crimes committed during the October 1838 Daviess County expedition, which the Latter-day Saints launched in the wake of church members' expulsion from Carroll County, Missouri. The two arson indictments stemmed from fires in Gallatin and Millport, Missouri, both of which the Saints suspected were anti-Mormon vigilante havens.[c] (a. Daviess Co., MO, Circuit Court Record, Apr. 1839, bk. A, 57–58, Daviess County Courthouse, Gallatin, MO; Robert Wilson, Gallatin, MO, to James L. Minor, Jefferson City, MO, 18 Mar. 1841, in *Document Containing the Correspondence*, 156–159. b. See Affidavit, 5 Sept. 1838, pp. 219–225 herein; Recognizance, 7 Sept. 1838, pp. 225–229 herein; and Indictment, [Honey Creek Township, MO], [ca. 10] Apr. 1839, State of Missouri v. JS et al. for Riot [Daviess Co. Cir. Ct. 1839], Historical Department, Nineteenth-Century Legal Documents Collection, CHL. c. Indictment, [Honey Creek Township, MO], [ca. 10] Apr. 1839, State of Missouri v. Baldwin et al. for Arson [Daviess Co. Cir. Ct. 1839], Historical Department, Nineteenth-Century Legal Documents Collection, CHL; Indictment, [Honey Creek Township, MO], [ca. 10] Apr. 1839, State of Missouri v. Gates et al. for Arson [Daviess Co. Cir. Ct. 1839], microfilm 959,084, U.S. and Canada Record Collection, FHL; see also 349n455 herein.)

907. Daviess Co., MO, Circuit Court Record, Apr. 1839, bk. A, 67–70, Daviess County Courthouse, Gallatin, MO. The prisoners began seeking a change of venue as early as January 1839. On 24 January, the prisoners argued in a memorial to the Missouri legislature that they could not receive a fair trial within the fifth judicial circuit. Their petition led to a revised Missouri statute that permitted changes of venue between circuits. However, the prisoners ultimately received a change of venue on different grounds. In late January 1839, the Missouri legislature reorganized the state's second and fifth judicial circuits, moving Daviess County from the fifth circuit to the newly created eleventh circuit, with Burch as the circuit's judge.

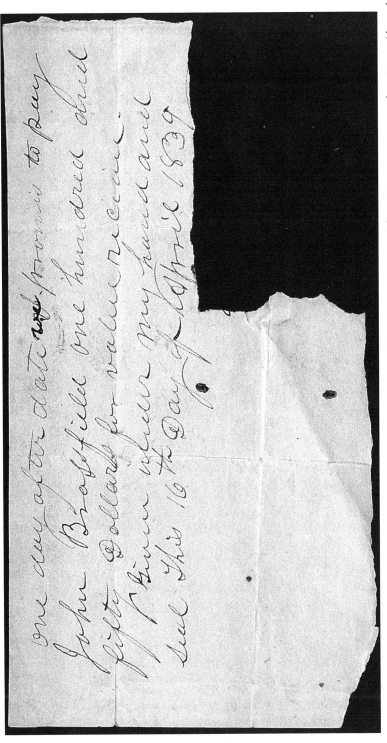

Promissory note for John Brassfield. On 16 April 1839, the day Joseph Smith and his companions escaped from Missouri state custody, prisoner Alexander McRae wrote this promissory note pledging that one of the prisoners—presumably Smith—would pay guard John Brassfield $150 for an unspecified transaction. After McRae wrote the note, Smith crossed out "I" and inserted "we," indicating that at least one of the other prisoners joined Smith in promising to pay Brassfield. Later, when Brassfield received payment, the note was voided by tearing any signatures from the document. The remnant of one letter—possibly a "J"—is visible at the tear. Handwriting of Alexander McRae and Joseph Smith. Promissory Note to John Brassfield, 16 Apr. 1839, JS Collection, Church History Library, Salt Lake City.

Daviess County sheriff William Morgan was tasked with transporting JS, Hyrum Smith, Lyman Wight, Caleb Baldwin, and Alexander McRae from Gallatin to Columbia, a journey of approximately 150 miles. Morgan selected four guards—William Bowman, Wilson McKinney, John Brassfield, and John Pogue—to assist him.[908] Hyrum Smith wrote in his journal that the guards were "verry lenient and kind."[909] On 12 April 1839, the group left Gallatin for Adam-ondi-Ahman, seven miles away, where they stayed two nights at Bowman's home, presumably to prepare for the remainder of the journey.[910] They then traveled another seven miles to Millport and spent the night of 14 April at the residence of Josiah Morin. On 15 April, the party continued the journey, staying the night at the home of a "Mr. Cox." The next day, the group progressed another nineteen miles toward Boone County and camped by a stream that Lyman Wight called Yellow Creek.[911] That night, the prisoners escaped.

On 16 April 1839—the last day of travel with the guards—McRae, who wrote letters on behalf of JS and the other prisoners while in the Clay County jail, wrote a promissory note for a financial transaction between one of the prisoners—presumably JS—and Brassfield. Sometime after McRae wrote the note, JS changed the wording of the note from "I" to "we," suggesting that the prisoner who originated the note was joined in the transaction by at least one other prisoner. These individuals agreed to pay Brassfield $150 for an undisclosed "value receive[d]"—the standard phrase used in promissory notes to indicate goods or services obtained. Comparable promissory notes usually set the due date as weeks or months after the date the note was issued, allowing time for the maker of the note to acquire the money needed to pay the note. In contrast, the note for Brassfield matured "one day after date," meaning he could redeem the note as early as 17 April.[912]

The nature of the $150 "value receive[d]" is unclear; contemporary documents indicate multiple possibilities. Hyrum Smith later stated that the guards sold the prisoners two

---

Missouri law mandated a change of venue "to the circuit court of some county in a different circuit" when the judge previously served as counsel in the case. (Historical Introduction to Memorial to the Missouri Legislature, 24 Jan. 1839, pp. 318–320 herein; An Act to Establish a Judicial Circuit out of the Second and Fifth Judicial Circuits [31 Jan. 1839], *Laws of the State of Missouri* [1839], p. 34, sec. 3; Bay, *Reminiscences of the Bench and Bar of Missouri,* 487; An Act to Regulate Proceedings in Criminal Cases [21 Mar. 1835], *Revised Statutes of the State of Missouri* [1835], p. 486, art. 5, sec. 15.)

908. Execution of Order, 6 July 1839, State of Missouri v. JS et al. for Larceny [Daviess Co. Cir. Ct. 1839], Daviess Co., MO, Circuit Court Records, 1839, State Historical Society of Missouri, Columbia. Starting in summer 1837, Bowman and Brassfield participated in anti-Mormon efforts to expel the Latter-day Saints from Daviess County. (Adam Black, Certificate, 27 July 1838, copy; William Bowman, Certificate, no date, copy; John Brassfield, Certificate, no date, copy, Record Group 233, Records of the U.S. House of Representatives, National Archives, Washington DC.)

909. Hyrum Smith, Diary, 14 Apr. 1839.

910. Bowman was living in the home that Lyman Wight built and previously owned. The travelers left a day behind schedule because of rain. (Hyrum Smith, Diary, 12–14 Apr. 1839.)

911. The exact location of the campsite is unknown, but it may have been in Chariton County or Linn County. (Hyrum Smith, Diary, 14–16 Apr. 1839; Lyman Wight, Testimony, Nauvoo, IL, 1 July 1843, p. 32, Nauvoo, IL, Records, CHL; Baugh, "We Took Our Change of Venue," 66, 79n39.)

912. Chitty, *Practical Treatise on Bills of Exchange,* 17–23; see also Promissory Note to Jason Brunell, 14 Sept. 1837, in *JSP,* D5:439–440; and Promissory Note to Jonathan Burgess, 17 Aug. 1836, in *JSP,* D5:280.

horses in exchange for a promissory note and some of the prisoners' extra clothing.[913] The men may have considered $150 a fair price for a horse, as that was the value of a horse JS owned in northwestern Missouri in 1838, and the note may have been for one of the two horses purchased.[914] It is also possible that the "value receive[d]" represented payment for facilitating the escape: on 16 April the party stopped for the night at an isolated location,[915] and the guards reportedly became intoxicated and fell asleep—possibly on purpose.[916] Hyrum Smith noted cryptically in his journal that the group intended "to stay all knight but did not stay all knight"; instead, the prisoners "left them"—presumably referring to the guards.[917] Rumors quickly circulated that the prisoners bribed the guards to allow the escape.[918] An 1843 note in JS's journal states that Brassfield "helped Joseph to escape from the missourians."[919] Also in 1843, Hyrum Smith recounted that Sheriff Morgan was informed by Judge Burch "never to carry us [the prisoners] to Boon County," suggesting that some Missouri officials were complicit in the escape.[920]

It also remains unclear when the promissory note was paid.[921] Brassfield may have visited the Saints in Illinois in mid-1839 to redeem the note. On 4 June 1839, Bishop Vinson Knight recorded in his account book a $150 debit for JS for "cash p[ai]d Brass Field"; however, it is

---

913. Hyrum Smith, Testimony, Nauvoo, IL, 1 July 1843, pp. 25–26, Nauvoo, IL, Records, CHL; Lyman Wight, Testimony, Nauvoo, IL, 1 July 1843, p. 32, Nauvoo, IL, Records, CHL; see also Rogers, Statement, [2], CHL.

914. Hyrum Smith, Deposition, Nauvoo, IL, 22 Apr. 1842; Elias Higbee, Deposition, Nauvoo, IL, 22 Apr. 1842; Lyman Wight, Deposition, Nauvoo, IL, 22 Apr. 1842, JS v. George M. Hinkle [Lee Co. Dist. Ct. 1842], CHL; see also Statement of Account from John Howden, 29 Mar. 1838, p. 65 herein.

915. Lyman Wight, Testimony, Nauvoo, IL, 1 July 1843, p. 32, Nauvoo, IL, Records, CHL; Baugh, "We Took Our Change of Venue," 66, 79n39.

916. Bill of Damages, 4 June 1839, p. 504 herein; Hyrum Smith, Testimony, Nauvoo, IL, 1 July 1843, pp. 25–26, Nauvoo, IL, Records, CHL.

917. Hyrum Smith, Diary, 16 Apr. 1839; Hyrum Smith, Testimony, Nauvoo, IL, 1 July 1843, p. 26; Lyman Wight, Testimony, Nauvoo, IL, 1 July 1843, p. 32, Nauvoo, IL, Records, CHL. Avoiding main roads and constrained by the necessity of sharing two horses among five men, JS and his fellow escapees arrived in Quincy, Illinois, on 22 April 1839. (Hyrum Smith, Diary, 16–19 Apr. 1839; JS, Journal, 16 and 22–23 Apr. 1839, in *JSP*, J1:336.)

918. William W. Phelps, Far West, MO, to Sally Waterman Phelps, St. Louis, 1 May 1839, CHL; see also Kimball, "History," 101–102. Church member David Rogers recalled that he encountered Brassfield within days of the prisoners' escape and that Brassfield related to Rogers "the particulars of their escape, and how they stole two of his Horses." One of Brassfield's companions stated, perhaps referring to the promissory note, that the prisoners "would have stolen more if they had have had more money." (Rogers, Statement, [2]–[3], CHL.)

919. JS, Journal, 28 Feb. 1843, in *JSP*, J2:279.

920. Hyrum Smith, Testimony, Nauvoo, IL, 1 July 1843, p. 26; Lyman Wight, Testimony, Nauvoo, IL, 1 July 1843, p. 32, Nauvoo, IL, Records, CHL; see also Stevens, *Centennial History of Missouri*, 2:119.

921. Apostle Heber C. Kimball recalled that in late April 1839, shortly after the prisoners' escape and while Kimball was still in Missouri, an unidentified man "presented an order drawn on me by Joseph Smith for $500⁰⁰ saying it was for horses furnished him." If the unidentified man was Brassfield, as the reference to furnishing horses may suggest, Kimball misremembered the financial instrument—calling it an order rather than a note—and he misremembered the amount of the note presented to him. It is possible that multiple promissory notes were made on or shortly before 16 April 1839, only one of which has been located. (Kimball, "History," 102.)

not certain what this entry referred to.[922] If it did not refer to John Brassfield and the featured promissory note, Brassfield may have redeemed the note on 28 February 1843, when he visited JS in Nauvoo, Illinois, and apparently stayed the night at JS's residence.[923] JS's son Joseph Smith III, who was ten years old at the time of Brassfield's visit, later recalled that the man came "for the purpose of collecting the amount of the bribe for which they [the guards] had allowed the prisoners to escape." Joseph Smith III remembered the amount being $800. He also recalled that his father gave Brassfield a "cream-colored or 'clay-bank' horse" to replace one used during the flight from Missouri.[924] At whatever time the note was paid, it was evidently returned to JS. As was customary, it was probably at this point that the note was canceled by tearing off the signature(s) to preclude the possibility of the note being redeemed again.[925] Because the signature area of the note was torn off, it is unclear how many of the prisoners signed the note.

Document Transcript

one day after date I ⟨we⟩[926] promis to pay John Brassfield one hundred and fifty Dollars for value receive.

Given under my hand and Seal This 16th Day of April 1839

[Joseph Smith Jr.][927]

———— ☙ ————

Letter from Elias Higbee, 16 April 1839

Source Note

Elias Higbee, Letter, Quincy, Adams Co., IL, to JS and others, "Liberty or elsewhere," MO, 16 Apr. 1839. Featured version copied [between 22 Apr. and 30 Oct. 1839] in JS Letterbook 2, p. 6; handwriting of James Mulholland; JS Collection, CHL. For more information on JS Letterbook 2, see Source Notes for Multiple-Entry Documents, p. 566 herein.

Historical Introduction

On 16 April 1839, Latter-day Saint Elias Higbee wrote from Illinois to JS and his fellow prisoners in Missouri, expressing sympathy for their situation and recalling the persecutions that he experienced with the men during the escalation of hostilities the previous year. During the 1838 conflict, Higbee played a prominent role in both an official and an un-

---

922. In addition, on 1 July 1839, Knight noted twenty dollars in "cash hold to pay Brassfield." (Knight, Account Book, 1, 3.)

923. JS, Journal, 28 Feb. 1843, in *JSP,* J2:279.

924. "The Memoirs of President Joseph Smith," *Saints' Herald,* 13 Nov. 1934, 1454.

925. Cancellation voided the promissory note, indicating that it had been paid in full. ("Cancellation," in Bouvier, *Law Dictionary,* 1:151; Chitty, *Practical Treatise on Bills of Exchange,* 214.)

926. TEXT: Cancellation and insertion in the handwriting of JS.

927. TEXT: Although the signature area was removed, still visible is a portion of the first letter— possibly a "J"—of the first (or perhaps only) signatory's name.

official military capacity. On various occasions, Higbee exercised his authority as a Caldwell County judge to call on the county's regiment of the state militia "for the defence of the citizens" against anti-Mormon vigilantes.[928] Higbee was also the Danites' captain general—the society's ranking officer—subject only to the First Presidency's executive authority. As such, he was an influential figure in multiple military operations during the conflict between Latter-day Saints and other Missourians in 1838.[929] His participation in the October 1838 skirmish at Crooked River forced him to flee from Far West, Missouri, in November or December, after which he relocated to the vicinity of Quincy, Illinois, to be with other Latter-day Saint refugees.[930] On 15 April 1839, he met with Emma Smith in Quincy, which may have prompted him to write to JS and the other prisoners the following day. In this letter, Higbee not only expressed sympathy for the prisoners' plight but also conveyed his confidence that divine providence was guiding the course of events in Missouri.

It is unknown whether Higbee's letter was carried to Missouri. His opening salutation indicates he was aware that the prisoners were probably no longer in the jail in Liberty, Missouri, suggesting that he may have kept the letter until receiving further information regarding their location.[931] Even if Higbee sent the letter to Missouri, the prisoners did not likely receive it there because they escaped from custody the day the letter was written and they arrived in Quincy a week later.[932] JS likely received the letter sometime after arriving at Quincy. The original letter is apparently not extant; JS's scribe, James Mulholland, copied it into JS Letterbook 2 sometime between 22 April and 30 October 1839.[933]

Document Transcript

Quincy April 16th 1839

To Joseph Smith Jr and others, prisoners in Liberty or elsewhere Greeting

Dear Brethren in affliction, Through the mercy and providence of God, I am here alive and in tolerable health, as also are all of your families as far

---

928. Affidavit, 5 Sept. 1838, pp. 222–225 herein; Sidney Rigdon, Testimony, Nauvoo, IL, 1 July 1843, p. [9]; George W. Pitkin, Testimony, Nauvoo, IL, 1 July 1843, p. 1; Parley P. Pratt, Testimony, Nauvoo, IL, 1 July 1843, p. 2, Nauvoo, IL, Records, CHL.

929. Reed Peck, Quincy, IL, to "Dear Friends," 18 Sept. 1839, pp. 45–47, Henry E. Huntington Library, San Marino, CA; Constitution of the Society of the Daughter of Zion, ca. Late June 1838, at josephsmithpapers.org; JS, Journal, 7–9 Aug. 1838, in *JSP*, J1:299; Nathaniel Carr, Testimony, Richmond, MO, Nov. 1838, p. [48], State of Missouri v. JS et al. for Treason and Other Crimes (Mo. 5th Jud. Cir. 1838), in State of Missouri, "Evidence."

930. See 428n937 herein.

931. See Historical Introduction to Letter from Sidney Rigdon, 10 Apr. 1839, pp. 406–407 herein.

932. See Promissory Note to John Brassfield, 16 Apr. 1839, pp. 422–426 herein.

933. Mulholland began to "write for the Church" on 22 April 1839, and Higbee's letter was one of the first documents Mulholland inscribed in Letterbook 2. For information on the latest likely copying date, see 248n440 herein.

as I know,[934] having heard from them lately, and having seen sister Emma yesterday.

Brethren I have sorrow of heart when I think of your great sufferings by that ungodly mob which has spread such desolation and caused so much suffering among us. I often reflect on the scenes which we passed through together, the course we pursued, the concillings we had, the results which followed, when harassed, pressed on every side, insulted and abused by that lawless banditti; and am decidedly of opinion that the hand of the great God hath controlled the whole business for purposes of his own which will eventually work out good for the Saints;[935] (I mean those who are worthy of that name,) knowing that your intentions and the intentions of all the worthy saints have been pure and tending to do good to all men, and to injure no man in person or property except we were forced to it in defence of our lives.

Brethren, I am aware that I cannot wholly realize your sufferings neither can any other person who has not experienced the like affliction,[936] but I doubt not for a moment, neither have I ever doubted for a moment, but that the same God which delivered me from their grasp, (though narrowly) will deliver you. I staid near Far West for about three weeks being hunted by them almost every day, and as I learned they did not intend to give me the chance of a trial but put an end to me forthwith I sent for my horse and left the wicked clan and come off.[937]

---

934. See Letter from Edward Partridge, 5 Mar. 1839, pp. 329–331 herein; Letter from Don Carlos Smith and William Smith, 6 Mar. 1839, pp. 332–334 herein; and Letter from Don Carlos and Agnes Coolbrith Smith, 11 Apr. 1839, pp. 415–417 herein.

935. See Romans 8:28.

936. On 4 April 1839, JS stated in a letter to Emma Smith, "With immotions known only to God, do I write this letter, the contemplations, of the mind under these circumstances, defies the pen, or tounge, or Angels, to discribe, or paint, to the human being, who never experiance what we experience." It is possible that when Higbee saw Emma Smith on 15 April 1839, she shared the letter with him; if so, Higbee may have been alluding to JS's statement. (Letter to Emma Smith, 4 Apr. 1839, p. 403 herein.)

937. As the state militia approached Far West in late October 1838, the Latter-day Saint troops that fought in the skirmish at Crooked River on 25 October were advised to flee to avoid being captured and executed without a legal trial. Most of the men departed Far West just before the militia's occupation of the town on 1 November. During that month, Samuel Bogart of Ray County, who commanded the non-Mormon troops in the Crooked River fight, actively pursued remaining Latter-day Saints, presumably including Higbee. Higbee may have remained in the area longer than most others because his son, Francis, had been arrested and charged with various crimes allegedly committed during the recent conflict. At the conclusion of the November 1838 court of inquiry held in Richmond, Missouri, Judge Austin A. King agreed to release Francis on bail if he would consent to appear at the spring session of the Daviess County Circuit Court to answer charges of "Arson, Burglary, Robbery and Larceny." Assuming Elias Higbee waited for his son, they presumably fled from Missouri in late November or early December. (Baugh, "Call to Arms," 326–329; Ruling, Richmond, MO, Nov. 1838, p. [125], in State of Missouri,

Francis [Higbee] is with his uncle in Ohio.[938] I received a letter lately from him, he is strong in the faith. I now live in the Big neck Prairie, on the same farm with President [Sidney] Rigdon[939] who is here with me and waiting for me with his riding dress on to go home, so I must necessarily close, praying God to speedily deliver you and bless you.

From yours in the bonds of the everlasting love,[940]

Elias Higbee. [p. 6]

"Evidence"; Samuel Bogart, Elkhorn, MO, to the Postmaster, Quincy, IL, 22 Apr. 1839, CHL; see also Lewis, Autobiography, 36.)

938. It is not known which uncle Francis Higbee stayed with in Ohio; he had multiple aunts and uncles on both sides of his family living in the Cincinnati area in the late 1830s. (See Higbee, Journal and Reminiscences, [20]–[21]; Clermont Co., OH, Marriage Records, 1801–1910, vol. 1, p. 142, 27 Aug. 1820, microfilm 327,559; vol. 2, p. 71, 11 Dec. 1823, microfilm 327,560, U.S. and Canada Record Collection, FHL; and 1840 U.S. Census, Springfield, Clermont Co., OH, 231, 237.)

939. Big Neck Prairie was located in Illinois, approximately thirty miles northeast of Quincy. (Rigdon, "Life Story of Sidney Rigdon," 157–158; *Portrait and Biographical Record of Adams County, Illinois,* 278.)

940. See Jeremiah 31:3; Philemon 1:13; and Book of Mormon, 1830 ed., 582 [Moroni 8:17].

PART 4: 24 APRIL–
12 AUGUST 1839

Part 4 of this volume, spanning from mid-April to mid-August 1839, covers the period of organization and growth that followed the Latter-day Saints' relocation from Missouri to Illinois and Iowa Territory. After nearly six months of imprisonment in Missouri, JS and his fellow prisoners escaped from state custody. They arrived in Quincy, Illinois, on 22 April 1839, where JS was reunited with his wife and children, who had moved to Quincy in February.[1] The town had become a central refuge for Latter-day Saints forced to leave Missouri. Several church leaders who settled there, including Edward Partridge and William Marks, had overseen the relocation of church members and corresponded with church leaders still in Far West, Missouri, in early 1839. The residents of Quincy offered assistance to the impoverished Saints, generously donating money and goods when church leaders requested help, providing shelter for the Latter-day Saint refugees, and offering to sell them land on favorable terms.[2]

Partridge and others in Quincy had corresponded with JS during his incarceration, keeping him apprised of church matters and seeking his counsel. In a March letter addressed to Partridge, JS advised the church leaders in Quincy to purchase land from Isaac Galland, a land speculator with acreage in Illinois and Iowa Territory.[3] Around the same time, JS wrote to Galland with a request to hold the land until JS and the other prisoners were released from jail.[4] Two days after arriving in Quincy, JS attended a council meeting at which he, Vinson Knight, and Alanson Ripley were appointed to a committee to visit land in Iowa Territory, apparently to identify locations for Latter-day Saint communities.[5] The committee members left Quincy the next day, 25 April, and traveled to the area around Commerce, Illinois, and parts of Lee County, Iowa Territory.

---

1. JS, Journal, 22–23 Apr. 1839, in *JSP*, J1:336; see also Historical Introduction to Promissory Note to John Brassfield, 16 Apr. 1839, pp. 422–426 herein; and Letter from Emma Smith, 7 Mar. 1839, p. 339 herein.

2. See "Proceedings in the Town of Quincy," *Quincy (IL) Argus,* 16 Mar. 1839, [1]; Letter from Edward Partridge, 5 Mar. 1839, p. 329 herein; George Miller, St. James, MI, to "Dear Brother," 22 June 1855, in *Northern Islander* (St. James, MI), 9 Aug. 1855, [1]; and Tillson, *History of the City of Quincy, Illinois,* 68.

3. Historical Introduction to Letter from Edward Partridge, 5 Mar. 1839, pp. 326–328 herein; Letter to Edward Partridge and the Church, ca. 22 Mar. 1839, pp. 391–392 herein.

4. Letter to Isaac Galland, 22 Mar. 1839, p. 388 herein.

5. Minutes, 24 Apr. 1839, p. 438 herein.

On 30 April, members of the land committee and other individuals acting for the church made the church's first land transactions in Illinois. Since the church was not yet an incorporated and legally recognized institution in the state, church leaders and church agents arranged to purchase the land in their own names. In the first land transaction on 30 April, Ripley arranged to buy approximately 130 acres on the Commerce peninsula from Hugh White, an early landowner in the Commerce area, for $5,000.[6] This purchase included White's house, which JS and his family would move to in May. In the second land purchase on 30 April, George W. Robinson, who was acting on behalf of the First Presidency, agreed to pay $9,000 to Isaac Galland for 47 acres of land on the Commerce peninsula as well as the rights to operate a ferry across the Mississippi River between Commerce and Montrose, Iowa Territory, southwest of Commerce.[7] Establishing a ferry allowed the Saints residing in Illinois and Iowa Territory to control transportation between their settlements. Although Robinson made arrangements to purchase the land in his own name, an agreement he made the same day with JS, Sidney Rigdon, and Hyrum Smith identified the three members of the First Presidency as the sureties guaranteeing payment to Galland.[8] These transactions may have taken place in the Commerce area, where both White and Galland were living at the time.[9]

In addition to helping secure land for the Saints, JS oversaw other church business. On 4–5 May, he presided at a general conference for all church members, and on 6 May he presided at a conference meeting for church leaders. During the general conference, the assembled church members considered various issues facing the church. One of the most pressing concerns was how to address the Saints' expulsion from Missouri. The congregation approved Sidney Rigdon's proposal to travel to Washington DC and appeal to the federal government for intervention on the Saints' behalf. To document what the Saints in Missouri had suffered, Almon Babbitt, Erastus Snow, and Robert B. Thompson were appointed as a committee to collect libelous reports about the church. Those at the conference also endorsed the mission of the Quorum of the Twelve Apostles to Europe, as directed in a revelation JS had dictated the previous year, and sustained new church leaders.[10] John P. Greene was directed to go to New York City; along the way, he was to solicit funds from church members to aid those impoverished by the Missouri expulsion. Oliver Granger was instructed to oversee the maintenance of and mortgage payments for

---

6. Hancock Co., IL, Bonds and Mortgages, 1840–1904, vol. 1, pp. 31–32, 30 Apr. 1839, microfilm 954,776, U.S. and Canada Record Collection, FHL.

7. See Agreement with George W. Robinson, 30 Apr. 1839, pp. 439–442 herein; Hancock Co., IL, Deed Records, 1817–1917, vol. 12 G, p. 247, 30 Apr. 1839, microfilm 954,195, U.S. and Canada Record Collection, FHL.

8. See Agreement with George W. Robinson, 30 Apr. 1839, pp. 441–442 herein.

9. These transactions may also have occurred around the same time of day on 30 April. Galland and Vinson Knight, the third member of the land committee, acted as witnesses to White's bond for Ripley; Knight also signed Robinson's agreement with the First Presidency as a witness. (See Hancock Co., IL, Bonds and Mortgages, 1840–1904, vol. 1, pp. 31–32, 30 Apr. 1839, microfilm 954,776, U.S. and Canada Record Collection, FHL; and Agreement with George W. Robinson, 30 Apr. 1839, p. 442 herein.)

10. Minutes, 4–5 May 1839, pp. 444–447 herein; see also Revelation, 8 July 1838–A, pp. 175–180 herein [D&C 118].

the House of the Lord in Kirtland, Ohio; preside over church affairs there; and continue in his previous assignment to resolve church debts. In conjunction with the appointments made during the conference, authorizations were prepared for Greene, Granger, Babbitt, Snow, and Thompson. Also during the conference, the members passed a resolution to encourage converts in the eastern United States to move to Kirtland.[11]

On 10 May, JS and his family moved from Quincy to the southern portion of the Commerce peninsula.[12] In several letters, JS encouraged his friends and fellow Saints to likewise move to the area, and he even selected lots for some to purchase. As the month progressed, JS and other church leaders continued their efforts to secure land for the church. Because church leaders needed additional funds for their previous and ongoing land acquisition, Stephen Markham was appointed to "gather up And receive such means in money or otherwise" to help the church.[13] Before Granger returned to Kirtland, he spent time discussing business matters with JS and completing various tasks as a church agent.[14] For example, in late May he arranged to purchase over two thousand acres of land in Iowa Territory from Galland.[15] Although many Saints moved to Commerce and Montrose, some Saints, including Bishop Partridge, remained in Quincy. As a church leader charged with helping the poor, Partridge corresponded with JS regarding the needs of the Saints living in Quincy.[16]

As JS and other church leaders worked to establish communities for the Saints in Illinois and Iowa Territory, they also confronted the aftermath of their forced expulsion from Missouri, such as by approving Rigdon's proposal to request federal intervention in Missouri. Although Rigdon's plan originally included soliciting support from governors to "impeach the State of Missouri," it is not clear what he, JS, or other church leaders hoped to achieve through federal intervention.[17] They may have hoped to obtain redress through regaining possession of their confiscated lands in Missouri or receiving monetary reparations.[18] As part of their efforts to document such losses, church members were asked to produce affidavits or redress petitions that identified personal damages resulting from the expulsion. In June, JS produced a petition describing his experiences in Missouri, enumerating his personal losses, and requesting redress. In contrast to the majority of the Saints' redress petitions, which are brief, JS's petition is an eight-page narrative. This document provides the most detail of any account regarding JS's experiences while imprisoned in Clay County, Missouri.[19]

---

11. See Minutes, 6 May 1839, pp. 449–451 herein.

12. JS, Journal, 10 May 1839, in *JSP*, J1:338.

13. Authorization for Stephen Markham, 27 May 1839, p. 481 herein; see also Letter to Father Bigler, 27 May 1839, p. 483 herein.

14. JS, Journal, 13–14 May 1839, in *JSP*, J1:339.

15. Lee Co., IA, Land Records, 1836–1961, vol. 1, pp. 507–510, 29 May 1839, microfilm 959,238, U.S. and Canada Record Collection, FHL.

16. See Letter from Edward Partridge, 27 May 1839, p. 486 herein; Letter to Edward Partridge, 29 May 1839, p. 487 herein; and Letter from Edward Partridge, 13–15 June 1839, pp. 506–508 herein.

17. Letter from Sidney Rigdon, 10 Apr. 1839, p. 408 herein.

18. By the time JS, Rigdon, and others left for Washington DC in October 1839, their focus was primarily on obtaining monetary compensation for the Latter-day Saints' collective losses. (JS et al., Petition, Washington DC, to United States Congress, Washington DC, ca. 29 Nov. 1839, JS Collection, CHL.)

19. See Bill of Damages, 4 June 1839, pp. 492–505 herein.

Additional issues related to Missouri arose when Lyman Wight published two letters in the *Quincy Whig* in May 1839. The letters, which Wight had written while imprisoned with JS, condemned the Democratic leadership in Missouri for not aiding the Saints during the Missouri conflict and for not helping them afterward.[20] Concerned that Wight's accusations would offend Democrats in Quincy or politicians in Washington DC, Latter-day Saint Robert B. Thompson wrote to JS about Wight's letters. The First Presidency responded to Wight's letters by writing to the editors of the *Quincy Whig,* explaining that the church intended to remain politically neutral and did not blame a specific party for the Saints' treatment in Missouri. JS also wrote a letter to Wight in late May, acknowledging Wight's right to publish his opinion but asking him to be cautious and to clarify that he was not speaking for the church.[21]

During this time JS also corresponded with individuals still in Missouri. In late May, JS dictated a letter to William W. Phelps, who had been excommunicated from the church and remained in Far West, informing him that his assistance was no longer needed in settling Missouri business.[22] In June, JS wrote to Missouri merchant Jacob Stollings, explaining that JS was unable to locate the merchant's stolen property, which was taken during the 1838 conflict.[23]

JS spent part of June instructing and counseling the Quorum of the Twelve Apostles and selected members of the Quorums of the Seventy as they prepared for their mission to Europe.[24] In 1837 and 1838, apostles Heber C. Kimball and Orson Hyde completed a dramatically successful mission to England, and in July 1838 JS dictated a revelation directing the apostles to commence a mission "over the great waters."[25] At the 6 May conference meeting, church leaders appointed thirteen members of the Quorums of the Seventy and five high priests to accompany the apostles on their mission. In preparation for the mission, the First Presidency signed recommendations for the apostles.[26] The Quorums of the Seventy resolved to create similar recommendations for the seventies who would be proselytizing with the apostles.[27]

From 15 to 26 June, JS traveled with his family to visit his brothers who were living in other areas of Illinois. JS, his wife, and their children stayed first with William Smith in Plymouth, Hancock County, Illinois, and then traveled to McDonough County, where Don Carlos Smith and Samuel Smith were living with their families. This visit was JS's first

---

20. See Lyman Wight, Quincy, IL, 1 May 1839, Letter to the Editors, *Quincy (IL) Whig,* 4 May 1839, [2]; and Lyman Wight, Quincy, IL, 7 May 1839, Letter to the Editors, *Quincy Whig,* 11 May 1839, [2]. The letters were originally addressed to the editors of the *Louisville (KY) Journal* and to Missouri senator Thomas Hart Benton, respectively.

21. See Letter from Robert B. Thompson, 13 May 1839, pp. 462–464 herein; Letter to the Editors, 17 May 1839, pp. 466–467 herein; and Letter to Lyman Wight, 27 May 1839, pp. 484–485 herein.

22. See Letter to William W. Phelps, 22 May 1839, pp. 468–469 herein.

23. Letter to Jacob Stollings, 27–28 June 1839, pp. 511–512 herein; see also Agreement with Jacob Stollings, 12 Apr. 1839, p. 420 herein.

24. See Recommendation for Brigham Young, 3 June 1839, p. 491 herein.

25. See Revelation, 8 July 1838–A, pp. 179–180 herein [D&C 118:4].

26. See Recommendation for Brigham Young, 3 June 1839, pp. 490–491 herein.

27. Quorums of the Seventy, "Book of Records," 12 May 1839, 71–72.

Expulsion from Missouri. After Missouri governor Lilburn W. Boggs issued the expulsion order on 27 October 1838, thousands of Saints left their homes during winter 1838–1839. These refugees temporarily settled in locations throughout Illinois and Iowa Territory, with many church leaders gathering in and around Quincy, Illinois. C. C. A. Christensen depicted the expulsion of the Saints in his painting *Leaving Missouri,* the eleventh scene in his Mormon Panorama, circa 1878. (Courtesy Brigham Young University Museum of Art, Provo, UT; gift of the grandchildren of C. C. A. Christensen, 1970.)

opportunity to see Samuel "since [JS's] deliverance from prison." During these travels, JS preached to several large congregations, addressing in particular the "coming forth of the Book of Mormon."[28]

JS and his immediate family returned to Commerce on 26 June, and on 27 June he presided at the third day of council meetings that the Quorum of the Twelve Apostles was holding in Montrose and Commerce. At this and subsequent meetings in late June and early July, JS instructed the departing missionaries on topics such as discernment of spirits, the doctrine of election, the importance of unity and humility, and the priesthood.[29] Intending to depart in early July, several of the apostles gave farewell addresses on 7 July.[30] However, their departures were delayed by malaria, which struck several of the apostles, their families, and many other Saints in Commerce and Montrose. In the midst of this crisis, JS and Emma helped care for the sick, bringing some into the Smith home and traveling to others throughout

---

28. JS, Journal, 15–26 June 1839, in *JSP,* J1:340–343.

29. See Discourse, 27 June 1839, p. 510 herein; Discourse, 2 July 1839, pp. 516–521 herein; Discourse, between ca. 26 June and ca. 2 July 1839, pp. 521–526 herein; and Discourse, between ca. 26 June and ca. 4 Aug. 1839–A, pp. 540–548 herein.

30. See Discourse, 7 July 1839, pp. 526–528 herein.

Commerce. JS also fell ill in mid-July[31] but recovered on 22 July, and he and other elders gave blessings of healing to ailing Saints, many of whom quickly recovered.[32]

During the summer, JS was also occupied with land acquisition. On 2 July, JS and others visited sections of the approximately sixteen thousand acres around Montrose that church agent Vinson Knight had recently purchased from Galland.[33] In August, JS and his counselors in the First Presidency arranged to buy additional land for the Saints. In one of the two transactions that month, JS, Sidney Rigdon, and Hyrum Smith signed a bond to purchase around four hundred acres in the Commerce peninsula from land speculator Horace Hotchkiss and his partners, John Gillet and Smith Tuttle.[34] The same day, the First Presidency arranged to purchase ninety acres that Hotchkiss had agreed to purchase from William White.[35] These transactions provided the church leaders with a substantial amount of land in and around Commerce, which the church could then sell to Saints moving to the area.

———— ✑ ————

Minutes, 24 April 1839

Source Note

Minutes, Quincy, Adams Co., IL, 24 Apr. 1839; handwriting of James Mulholland; two pages; Historian's Office, General Church Minutes, CHL. Includes redactions and docket.

One leaf measuring 9⅞ × 8 inches (25 × 20 cm). The document was folded in half vertically and then folded twice horizontally to pocket size. The top center of the recto contains a "2" in the handwriting of James Mulholland, indicating these minutes were the second of four sets of minutes that Mulholland recorded and numbered in 1839.[36] A docket on the recto, in the handwriting of Thomas Bullock, reads: "April 24. 1839 | Minutes of Conference". Bullock worked in the Church Historian's Office between 1842 and 1856, and he likely filed the minutes during that period, suggesting the document has been in continuous institutional custody since at least 1856. The minutes were placed in the General Church Minutes collection with other loose church minutes created by the general church scribe and other clerks affiliated with the Church Historian's Office.

Historical Introduction

After escaping from custody in Missouri, JS arrived in Quincy, Illinois, on 22 April 1839.[37] Two days later, on 24 April, he chaired a council meeting in Quincy to discuss

---

31. Historian's Office, Brigham Young History Drafts, 25–26.

32. See Historical Introduction to Discourse, 28 July 1839, pp. 534–535 herein.

33. See JS, Journal, 2 July 1839, in *JSP*, J1:344; and Historical Introduction to Discourse, 2 July 1839, pp. 516–518 herein.

34. See Bond from Horace Hotchkiss, 12 Aug. 1839–A, pp. 553–556 herein; and Promissory Note to John Gillet and Smith Tuttle, 12 Aug. 1839, pp. 556–557 herein.

35. See Bond from Horace Hotchkiss, 12 Aug. 1839–B, pp. 557–559 herein; and Promissory Note to Horace Hotchkiss, 12 Aug. 1839, pp. 559–560 herein.

36. When Mulholland copied the minutes of a 26 April 1839 meeting of the Quorum of the Twelve Apostles, he inscribed a "1" on the copy. (Historian's Office, General Church Minutes, 26 Apr. 1839.)

37. JS, Journal, 16 and 22–23 Apr. 1839, in *JSP*, J1:336. For more information on JS's escape, see Historical Introduction to Promissory Note to John Brassfield, 16 Apr. 1839, p. 424 herein.

church affairs. The first item of business was to review and approve a document that apostle John Taylor prepared, in which he expressed gratitude for Quincy residents' generosity in assisting the Saints. Taylor also disavowed "disorderly persons" in the area who claimed to be church members but in reality had been excommunicated or had no ties to the church. Taylor was concerned that they were abusing Quincy residents' charity by incurring debts without intending to repay them and that the church would unfairly be "charged with dishonesty" because these "wicked and designing people" were arriving with the Latter-day Saint refugees. Taylor also worried that these individuals' habits, such as drinking and swearing, would degrade the reputation of the church in the Quincy area. Quincy residents had welcomed impoverished Saints to the area, providing food, housing, and funds, and the church council hoped to maintain good relations. The council approved Taylor's document, and Taylor sent a copy to the editors of the *Quincy Argus* for publication.[38]

Next, the council members passed two resolutions concerning the settlement of church members in Illinois and Iowa Territory. First, the council members resolved that a committee composed of JS, Vinson Knight, and Alanson Ripley should immediately visit land in Iowa Territory for possible purchase. The three men acted on this resolution the following day, 25 April 1839, when they left to inspect tracts along the Mississippi River in Iowa Territory and Illinois;[39] this trip led to land purchases in both areas.[40] Second, the council members resolved that as many church members as possible should move north from Quincy to Commerce, Illinois. JS soon moved his family to a "small Log house" about one mile south of Commerce, on the eastern banks of the Mississippi River on land purchased from Hugh White.[41] In addition to these matters, the council members passed several resolutions regarding administrative matters.

The minutes indicate that Alanson Ripley served as clerk for the council meeting, and he presumably took minutes during the meeting. The minutes featured here were inscribed by James Mulholland, who probably copied Ripley's minutes, which are no longer extant. Mulholland's version contains three clarifying notes that Robert B. Thompson, who likely attended the 24 April meeting, added at a later time, possibly when he became general church recorder and clerk. The minutes, including Thompson's insertions, were copied into JS Letterbook 2 by Howard Coray in 1840.[42]

---

38. John Taylor, Quincy, IL, to "the Editor of the Argus," Quincy, IL, 1 May 1839, CHL. The letter was not printed in the newspaper.

39. See JS, Journal, 24 Apr.–3 May 1839, in *JSP*, J1:336.

40. On 30 April 1839, church agents purchased approximately 189 acres in the Commerce, Illinois, area from Isaac Galland and Hugh White. On 21 May, JS and others went on a scouting trip to investigate land in Iowa Territory; this trip eventually resulted in the purchase of 18,920 acres of land from Galland. (Hancock Co., IL, Deed Records, 1817–1917, vol. 12 G, p. 247, 30 Apr. 1839, microfilm 954,195; Hancock Co., IL, Bonds and Mortgages, 1840–1904, vol. 1, pp. 31–32, 30 Apr. 1839, microfilm 954,776; Lee Co., IA, Land Records, 1836–1961, vol. 1, pp. 507–510, 29 May 1839, microfilm 959,238; vol. 2, pp. 3–6, 13–16, 26 June 1839, microfilm 959,239, U.S. and Canada Record Collection, FHL; Historian's Office, JS History, Draft Notes, 25 Apr.–4 May 1839; Alanson Ripley, Statements, ca. Jan. 1845, Historian's Office, JS History Documents, 1839–1860, CHL; Woodruff, Journal, 21 May 1839.)

41. JS, Journal, 10 May 1839, in *JSP*, J1:338; Historian's Office, JS History, Draft Notes, 10 May 1839. For more information on White, see Introduction to Part 4: 24 Apr.–12 Aug. 1839, p. 432 herein.

42. See Minutes, 24 Apr. 1839, in JS Letterbook 2, pp. 139–140.

Document Transcript

Met in Council on the 24th day of April— (1839) President Joseph Smith J[r] was called to the chair, and B[r] A[lanson] Ripley chosen Clerk.

After prayer by the Chairman, Elder J. P. Green [John P. Greene] arose and explained the object of the meeting.

A document intended for publication was handed in, touching certain things relative to disorderly persons who have or may represent themselves as belonging to our Church; which document was approved by the council.

After which It was Resolved

1[rst] That President, J, Smith J[r] Bishop Knights [Vinson Knight], and B[r] A Ripley visit the Iaway Territory immediately [43]

2nd Resolved— That the advice of of this conference to the Brethren in general is, that as many of them as are able, move on to the north[44] as soon as they possibly can.

3rd Resolved— That all the prisoners[45] [p. [1]] be received into fellowship.

4th Resolved— That Brother [James] Mulholland[46] be appointed Clerk, pro, tem.

5th Resolved— That Father Smith's case relative to his circumstances be referred to the Bishops.[47]

6th Resolved— That B[r] [David W.] Rogers receive some money for remuneration for his Services.[48] [p. [2]]

———— ⚭ ————

43. TEXT: Thompson later added "for the purpose of making locations for the Church".

44. TEXT: Thompson later added "(to Commerce)".

45. JS, Hyrum Smith, Lyman Wight, Alexander McRae, and Caleb Baldwin escaped from Missouri custody on 16 April 1839. (Historical Introduction to Promissory Note to John Brassfield, 16 Apr. 1839, p. 424 herein.)

46. Mulholland, who had started keeping JS's journal in September 1838, was a natural choice as a temporary clerk. (JS, Journal, 3 Sept. 1838, in *JSP*, J1:324–325.)

47. Many members of the Smith family, including Joseph Smith Sr., Lucy Mack Smith, and Don Carlos Smith and his family, fled Missouri on 14 February 1839 under considerable duress. Upon relocating to Quincy, Illinois, many of them were housed in temporary residences. The reference to the bishops in this resolution may pertain to the Smiths' housing situation or general need for assistance. (Historian's Office, JS History, Draft Notes, 14 Feb. 1839; Lucy Mack Smith, History, 1844–1845, bk. 16, [12], bk. 17, [2]; Woodruff, Journal, 16 Mar. 1839; George Miller, St. James, MI, to "Dear Brother," 22 June 1855, in *Northern Islander* [St. James, MI], 9 Aug. 1855, [1].)

48. TEXT: Thompson later added "in transacting business for the church in Missouri". David Rogers, who had previously served on a committee to examine lands for purchase in Iowa, was sent to oversee the sale of church properties in Jackson County, Missouri. (Far West Committee, Minutes, 17 Mar. 1839.)

Agreement with George W. Robinson, 30 April 1839

Source Note

George W. Robinson, Agreement, [probably Commerce, Hancock Co., IL], with JS, Sidney Rigdon, and Hyrum Smith, 30 Apr. 1839; handwriting of George W. Robinson; signature of George W. Robinson; witnessed by Vinson Knight; two pages; Newel K. Whitney, Papers, BYU. Includes endorsement and docket.

One leaf measuring 7½ × 6¾ inches (19 × 17 cm). The document was folded for transmission and filing, and it has marked wear and water damage. William Clayton wrote a docket on the verso: "Geo. W. Robinson | Power of Attorney | for the Church".

This manuscript, along with many other personal and institutional documents that Newel K. Whitney kept, were inherited by his daughter Mary Jane Whitney, who married Isaac Groo. The documents were passed down within the Groo family until 1969, when the family began donating documents to the Harold B. Lee Library at Brigham Young University; the last documents were donated in 1974.[49]

Historical Introduction

On 30 April 1839, church members acting on behalf of the First Presidency purchased several tracts of land in the vicinity of Commerce, Illinois.[50] One of these transactions was arranged by George W. Robinson, who agreed to purchase land from Isaac Galland.[51] Galland owned a significant amount of land in Illinois and Iowa Territory, and in February 1839 he offered to sell his land to the church.[52] The 30 April purchase from Galland included land around Commerce as well as the rights that the Illinois legislature had granted Galland in a special charter to run a hotel and establish a ferry between Commerce and Montrose, Iowa Territory.[53] Though acting for the First Presidency, Robinson agreed to the land purchase in his own name, with JS, Sidney Rigdon, and Hyrum Smith acting as sureties for the payment to Galland.

The same day Robinson purchased the land, he created and signed an agreement, featured here, between himself and the First Presidency. The agreement references a power of attorney and contains language specific to bonds, with Robinson acknowledging that he was acting as an agent for JS, Rigdon, and Hyrum Smith in this transaction.[54] The

---

49. Andrus et al., "Register of the Newel Kimball Whitney Papers, 1825–1906," 5–6.

50. Because the church was not incorporated, church business was conducted in the names of individual church leaders and agents; these transactions were understood to be church business.

51. For more information on the land transactions, see Introduction to Part 4: 24 Apr.–12 Aug. 1839, pp. 431–436 herein.

52. See Historical Introduction to Letter to Isaac Galland, 22 Mar. 1839, pp. 376–377 herein; and Historical Introduction to Minutes, 24 Apr. 1839, pp. 436–437 herein.

53. The land specified in this agreement included the 47.17 acres that constituted the farm on which Galland lived and two fractional sections of land, one north of and one south of Commerce on the bank of the Mississippi River. The fractional sections were likely intended for ferry operations. (Hancock Co., IL, Deed Records, 1817–1917, vol. 12 G, p. 247, 30 Apr. 1839, microfilm 954,195, U.S. and Canada Record Collection, FHL; An Act to Incorporate the Commerce Hotel Company [28 Feb. 1839], Enrolled Laws of 1839, Secretary of State, Enrolled Acts of the General Assembly, Illinois State Archives, Springfield.)

54. The phrasing of the 30 April agreement suggests that Robinson previously received a power of attorney authorizing him to purchase the land for the church. (See also Hancock Co., IL, Deed Records,

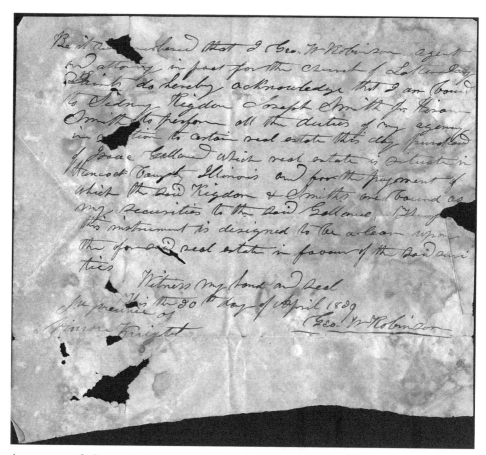

Agreement with George W. Robinson. On 30 April 1839, George W. Robinson purchased land from speculator Isaac Galland. Though he purchased the land as an agent of the First Presidency, he did not specify that in the deed. Consequently, on the day of the purchase, Robinson wrote and signed an agreement with the First Presidency to clarify that if the established payments were made and Robinson received title to the land, ownership of the land would be transferred to the presidency. Agreement with George W. Robinson, 30 April 1839, Newel K. Whitney, Papers, L. Tom Perry Special Collections, Harold B. Lee Library, Brigham Young University, Provo, UT.

agreement, according to Robinson, created a lien on the land he purchased from Galland. Robinson indicated that the lien was "in favour of the said surities," meaning JS, Rigdon, and Hyrum Smith.[55] Unlike a standard contract, Robinson's document does not specify the terms of the agreement or the consequences if he failed to meet the requirements, but it was likely understood that he would transfer the property to the First Presidency once he received the title to the land. It appears that the agreement was used to ensure the church's ownership of the land, because Robinson purchased the land in his name rather than specifying that he was acting as an agent for the members of the First Presidency, who should have been designated the principals in the transaction with Galland. Creating a lien, as Robinson apparently did in the agreement, prevented him from selling the land without church leaders' authorization.[56]

Robinson inscribed and signed the document, and then Vinson Knight signed the document as a witness. In December 1840, Hancock County clerk Chauncey Robison certified the document and recorded it in the county's Book of Bonds and Mortgages.

Document Transcript

/[57]Be it re[me]mbered[58] that I Geo. W Robinson agent and attorney in fact for the Church of Latter Day Saints[59] do hereby acknowledge that I am bound to Sidney Rigdon Joseph Smith Jr. Hiram [Hyrum] Smith to perform all the duties of my agency in r[ela]tion[60] to certain real estate this day purchased of

---

1817–1917, vol. 12 G, p. 247, 30 Apr. 1839, microfilm 954,195, U.S. and Canada Record Collection, FHL; and Historian's Office, JS History, Draft Notes, 1 May 1839.)

55. A lien is created when property is offered as payment for a debt or when one party issues to another party the right to detain property under specified circumstances. The lien Robinson established appears to be an example of the latter use. Since neither Robinson nor the First Presidency held the title to the land involved in the lien, the encumbrance apparently would be in force when Robinson eventually acquired the land. Traditionally, when a lien was made, the creator of the lien held the title to the property involved in the lien. (See "Lien," in Bouvier, *Law Dictionary*, 2:43; and Butts, *Business Man's Assistant*, 53.)

56. JS's history noted that the transaction between Robinson and Galland occurred with the "express understanding that he should deed it to the church, when the church had paid for it, according to their obligation in the contract." Robinson eventually deeded the land to JS on 24 March 1841 and transferred the ferry rights to JS on 5 August 1841. (Historian's Office, JS History, Draft Notes, 1 May 1839; Hancock Co., IL, Deed Records, 1817–1917, vol. I, p. 331, 24 Mar. 1841, microfilm 954,598; vol. N, pp. 403–404, 5 Aug. 1841, microfilm 954,600, U.S. and Canada Record Collection, FHL.)

57. TEXT: George W. Robinson handwriting begins.

58. TEXT: "re[*hole in paper*]mbered". Text supplied from Hancock Co., IL, Bonds and Mortgages, 1840–1904, vol. 1, p. 82, 30 Apr. 1839, microfilm 954,776, U.S. and Canada Record Collection, FHL.

59. On 26 April 1838, JS dictated a revelation that changed the official name of the church from the Church of the Latter Day Saints to the Church of Jesus Christ of Latter Day Saints. Hence, the name used here is anachronistic though not new. In a letter JS wrote in late 1838 to the church in Caldwell County, he also used "Church of Latter day Saints." (Revelation, 26 Apr. 1838, p. 114 herein [D&C 115:4]; Letter to the Church in Caldwell Co., MO, 16 Dec. 1838, p. 298 herein.)

60. TEXT: "r[*hole in paper*]tion". Text supplied from Hancock Co., IL, Bonds and Mortgages, vol. 1, 1840–1904, p. 82, 30 Apr. 1839, microfilm 954,776, U.S. and Canada Record Collection, FHL.

Isaac Galland which real estate is situate in Hancock County Illinois and for the payment of which the said Rigdon & Smiths are bound as my securities to the said Galland, Theref[ore][61] this instrument is designed to be a lean upon the aforesaid real estate in favour of the said surities.

Witness my hand and seal
This the 30th day of April 1839

Geo. W Robinson

In presence of
Vinson Knight[62] [p. [1]]

/[63]State of Illinois⎤
Hancock County⎦

Recorders Office 22 December 1840

I hereby Certify that the Within instrument Was this day filed in my Office for Record and duly recorded in Book of Mortgages & Bonds Page 82 Numbered 75—

Chauncey Robison
Recorder

Fees 37½ Paid

/[64]the Bond of Geo W Robinson
Power Atorny [p. [2]]

———— ❧ ————

Minutes, 4–5 May 1839

Source Note

General Conference Minutes, Quincy, Adams Co., IL, 4–5 May 1839; handwriting of James Mulholland; four pages; Historian's Office, General Church Minutes, CHL. Includes docket.

Two leaves measuring 9¾ × 7¾ inches (25 × 20 cm). The top left corner of the first page bears an embossed seal with the profile of a man. Above and to the left of the seal, James Mulholland added a "3", indicating these minutes were the third of four sets of minutes that Mulholland recorded and numbered in 1839.[65] It appears that the document was folded and filed with the minutes of a meeting on 6 May 1839 in Quincy, Illinois. A docket written by Thomas Bullock reads: "May 4. 1839 | Minutes of Conference". Bullock worked in the Church Historian's Office between 1842 and 1856,

---

61. TEXT: "Theref[*hole in paper*]". Text supplied from Hancock Co., IL, Bonds and Mortgages, vol. 1, 1840–1904, p. 82, 30 Apr. 1839, microfilm 954,776, U.S. and Canada Record Collection, FHL.

62. TEXT: Signature of Vinson Knight.

63. TEXT: George W. Robinson handwriting ends; Chauncey Robison begins.

64. TEXT: Chauncey Robison handwriting ends; unidentified begins.

65. Mulholland inscribed a "1" on minutes of a 26 April 1839 meeting and a "2" on minutes of a 24 April 1839 meeting. (Historian's Office, General Church Minutes, 24 and 26 Apr. 1839.)

and he likely filed the minutes during that period, suggesting the document has been in continuous institutional custody since at least 1856. The minutes were placed in the General Church Minutes collection with other loose church minutes created by the general church scribe and other clerks affiliated with the Church Historian's Office.

Historical Introduction

On 4–5 May 1839, JS presided over a general church conference held near Quincy, Illinois. He had recently escaped from incarceration in Missouri, and this general conference was the first meeting he attended in which the full membership of the church in Illinois was present.[66] The conference consisted of three sessions, held on Saturday midday, Sunday morning, and Sunday afternoon at the Presbyterian campground approximately two miles north of Quincy.[67]

The first session began with an emotional address by JS. Following his remarks, important issues were brought before the body of the church regarding operations, leadership, and settlement. The minutes featured here record the resolutions adopted by the assembled Saints in the Saturday and Sunday morning sessions, approving the church's recent purchase of land in Iowa Territory and appointing new ecclesiastical leaders. The members also resolved that a committee should collect libelous reports and that a delegation should submit affidavits to the federal government in Washington DC to seek redress for the persecution and losses church members experienced in Missouri. Additional resolutions included sanctioning the meeting that the Quorum of the Twelve Apostles held in Far West, Missouri, on 26 April 1839 and the intended mission of the quorum to Europe. The congregation also decided to suspend Orson Hyde and William Smith from the Quorum of the Twelve Apostles but to allow them to speak at the next general conference of the church to address their conduct in Missouri in 1838.

Two additional resolutions concerned Kirtland, Ohio. Oliver Granger was directed to oversee the House of the Lord and manage church affairs there, and Saints in the eastern United States were instructed to migrate to Kirtland. The majority of church members had moved from Kirtland to Missouri by summer 1838, but some church members remained in Kirtland. At the start of that year, church leaders had expressed their intention to retain land in Kirtland for Saints moving from the eastern United States,[68] and this intention was supported in the May 1839 general conference.

During the final session of the conference, on Sunday afternoon, the First Presidency and apostles provided instruction that is not included in the extant minutes. Before the conference was adjourned, the congregation was reminded that the next general conference would be held in October 1839 in Commerce, Illinois, signaling the impending move of the church to newly purchased land in the vicinity. The minutes were recorded by James Mulholland, the appointed clerk for the conference.

---

66. See Minutes, 24 Apr. 1839, p. 438 herein.

67. Woodruff, Journal, 4 May 1839.

68. John Smith and Don Carlos Smith, Kirtland Mills, OH, to George A. Smith, Shinnston, VA, 15–18 Jan. 1838, George Albert Smith, Papers, CHL; see also Historical Introduction to Pay Order to Edward Partridge for William Smith, 21 Feb. 1838, pp. 27–30 herein.

Document Transcript

Minutes of a General conference held by The Church of the Latter Day
Saints, at the Presbyterian Camp Ground Near Quincy, Adams County,
Illinois, on Saturday the 4th of May 1839.

At a quarter past eleven oclock, the meeting was called to order And
President Joseph Smith Jr appointed Chairman, A hymn was then sung,
When President Smith addressed a few observations on the state of his own
peculiar feelings, after having been so long separated from his brethren[69] &c
&c and then proceeded to open the meeting by prayer, When after some
pr[e]liminiary remarks by Elders J. P. Green [John P. Greene] and President
[Sidney] Rigdon, concerning a certain purchase of Land in the Iaway Territory,
made for the Church, by the Presidency[70]

The following Resolutions were unanimously agreed to.

1rst. Resolved, that Almand [Almon] Babbitt, Erastus Snow, and Robert, B
Thom[p]son be appointed a travelling committe to gather up and obtain all the
libelous reports and publications which have been circulated against our
Church, as well as other historical matter connected with said Church which
they can possibly obtain.[71]

2nd Resolved, That Bishop Knights [Vinson Knight] be appointed or
received into the Church in full Bishopric.[72]

---

69. According to a later reminiscence of Edward Stevenson, who was nineteen years old at the time
of the meeting, JS stood in silence on an open wagon for an unusual amount of time before he began
to speak. According to Stevenson, JS began his discourse by expressing his emotions upon being
reunited with the Saints: "To look over this Congregation of Latter Day Saints who have been driven
from their homes and still in good faith without homes as pilgrims in a strange land and to realize that
my life has been spared to behold your faces again seemed to me so great a pleasure that the present
scene was so great a sattisfaction that words seemed only a vague expression of my soul's grattitude."
(Stevenson, Autobiography, 129–130.)

70. At this time, the church was considering purchasing land from Isaac Galland in Iowa Territory.
Although no deed records indicate purchases were completed before the conference, Vinson Knight, a land
agent for the church, apparently purchased shares in a "Half Breed Land Company" from Galland on 1 May
1839. These shares entitled Knight to purchase land in the "Half-Breed Tract" in Lee County, Iowa Territory,
when the land was sold at public auction. (Kilbourne, *Strictures, on Dr. I. Galland's Pamphlet*, 9; see also
Minutes, 24 Apr. 1839, p. 438 herein; Alanson Ripley, Statements, ca. Jan. 1845, Historian's Office, JS History
Documents, 1839–1860, CHL; and Woodruff, Journal, 21 May 1839.)

71. While imprisoned in Liberty, Missouri, in winter 1838–1839, JS suggested that a committee
be formed to gather anti-Mormon publications. JS later clarified that Babbitt and Snow were to gather
anti-Mormon publications and other historical materials and that Thompson was to use these materials to draft a history that refuted libelous claims. Because of illness and other church assignments,
Thompson was unable to complete the history before dying in 1841. (Letter to Edward Partridge and the
Church, ca. 22 Mar. 1839, p. 397 herein; Snow, Journal, 1838–1841, 50–54; Authorization for Almon
Babbitt et al., ca. 4 May 1839, p. 448 herein.)

72. Knight was appointed as acting bishop at Adam-ondi-Ahman, Missouri, on 28 June 1838, before
the Saints were forced to leave Missouri. The term "full Bishopric" may indicate he was appointed at

3rd Resolved that this Conference does entirely sanction [p. [1]] the purchase lately made for the Church, in the Iaway Territory, as also the agency thereof.

4ᵗʰ Resolved, That Elder Grainger [Oliver Granger] be appointed to go to Kirtland and take the Charge and oversight of the House of the Lord and preside over the general affairs of the Church in that place.[73]

5ᵗʰ Resolved That the advice of this conference to the Brethren living in the Eastern States is, for them to move to Kirtland and the vicinity thereof, and again settle that place as a stake of Zion.[74] ⟨provided that they may feel so inclined, in preference to their moving further west⟩[75]

6ᵗʰ Resolved, That George, A. Smith be ordained to ⟨take⟩ the place of Thomas B. Marsh, as one of the twelve.[76]

7ᵗʰ Resolved that this conference are entirely satisfied with and do give their Sanction to the proceedings of the conference of the twelve and their

---

this meeting to serve in an official capacity instead of as an acting bishop. In the October 1839 general conference, Knight was appointed as one of Commerce's three bishops. (See Minutes, 28 June 1838, p. 166 herein; and Minutes, 5–7 Oct. 1839, in *Times and Seasons,* Dec. 1839, 1:30–31.)

73. Granger acted as an agent for JS and Rigdon in September 1837, and after the two men departed Kirtland in January 1838, Granger worked with William Marks to manage and settle outstanding debts. In July 1838, Granger was officially appointed to be an agent for the church and to resolve the church's financial obligations in Ohio. He oversaw the sale of various properties and succeeded in paying off some of the church's debt. This 4 May 1839 resolution gave Granger additional responsibilities over the church in Kirtland, and on 6 May, JS provided Granger with a signed certificate to take with him to Kirtland to indicate his position and authority there. (Authorization for Oliver Granger, 6 May 1839, p. 453 herein; see also JS History, vol. B-1, 837; and Geauga Co., OH, Deed Record, 1795–1921, vol. 25, pp. 552–553, 2 Sept. 1837; pp. 661–665, 28 and 29 Mar. 1838; 26 and 30 Apr. 1838; vol. 26, p. 477, 16 Oct. 1838, microfilm 20,241; vol. 30, p. 175, 24 Feb. 1838, microfilm 20,242, U.S. and Canada Record Collection, FHL.)

74. Writing in January 1838, John Smith and Don Carlos Smith referenced Kirtland as a stopping point for Saints migrating from the eastern United States. When conflict in Missouri intensified in fall 1838, Kirtland may have become a place for Saints who were migrating from the East to settle instead of traveling on to Missouri. In a January 1839 letter to apostles Heber C. Kimball and Brigham Young, JS suggested that before church members arrived from England, agents should "buy out Kirtland, and the regions round about. or they may settle whare they can till things may alter." (John Smith and Don Carlos Smith, Kirtland Mills, OH, to George A. Smith, Shinnston, VA, 15–18 Jan. 1838, George Albert Smith, Papers, CHL; Letter to Heber C. Kimball and Brigham Young, 16 Jan. 1839, p. 314 herein; see also Authorization for Oliver Granger, 6 May 1839, pp. 452–454 herein.)

75. This advice to settle Kirtland was included, nearly verbatim, in a certificate JS provided to Granger to take with him to Kirtland. (See Authorization for Oliver Granger, 6 May 1839, pp. 452–454 herein.)

76. Marsh withdrew from the church in October 1838 after months of disagreement with JS and other Saints. JS appointed George A. Smith on 16 January 1839 to fill this position, and he was ordained at the 26 April 1839 meeting of the Quorum of the Twelve Apostles in Far West, Missouri; the resolution mentioned here in the minutes constituted a ratification of the earlier appointment and ordination. (Letter to Heber C. Kimball and Brigham Young, 16 Jan. 1839, p. 314 herein; Historian's Office, General Church Minutes, 26 Apr. 1839; Revelation, 8 July 1838–A, p. 180 herein [D&C 118:6]; for more information on Marsh's disaffection, see 308n206 herein.)

friends, held on the Temple Spot at Far West Missouri, on Friday the 26th April last.[77]

8th Resolved That, ~~they~~ ⟨we⟩ also sanction the act of the coun[c]il held same date at same place, in cutting off from the commun[io]n of said church, certain persons mentioned in the minutes thereof.[78]

9th Resolved that Elders Orson Hyde, and Wm Smith be allowed the privilege of appearing personally before the next general conference of the church to give an account of their conduct, and that in the mean time, they be both suspended from exercising the functions [p. [2]] of their office.[79]

10th Resolved, That the Conference do sanction the mission intended by the twelve to Europe, and that they will do all in their power to enable them to go.[80]

11th Resolved, That the subject of Elder Rigdon's going to Washington be adjourned untill tomorrow.

12th Resolved, That the next general conference be held on the First Saturday in October next, at Commerce At the house of Elder Rigdon—[81]

13th. That we now adjourn untill tomorrow at 10 oclock AM

Joseph Smith Jr} President

---

77. On 26 April 1839, twelve men, including five of the twelve apostles, gathered at the temple lot in Far West. In addition to ordaining Wilford Woodruff and George A. Smith as apostles, the men recommenced "laying the foundation" of the temple, as directed in a revelation JS dictated 26 April 1838. They also symbolically began their mission to Europe, as instructed in a revelation dictated 8 July 1838. (Historian's Office, General Church Minutes, 26 Apr. 1839; Revelation, 26 Apr. 1838, p. 115 herein [D&C 115:11]; Revelation, 8 July 1838–A, pp. 179–180 herein [D&C 118:4–5].)

78. Before the 26 April 1839 meeting at the temple lot in Far West, the apostles and other priesthood officers held a meeting in the home of Samuel Clark, during which they excommunicated thirty-one people. (Kimball, "History," 102; Historian's Office, General Church Minutes, 26 Apr. 1839.)

79. This action suspended Hyde and William Smith from the Quorum of the Twelve Apostles. Disturbed by Mormon military operations against vigilantes in Daviess County, Missouri, in October 1838, Hyde left the church. He and Marsh filed an affidavit on 24 October 1838 describing and denouncing the military activities.[a] In March 1839, Hyde wrote to Brigham Young, expressing contrition and his desire to rejoin the Saints, but he was not restored to his place in the Quorum of the Twelve until 27 June 1839.[b] Young recounted that William Smith spoke publicly against JS before relocating from Missouri to Illinois.[c] On 25 May 1839, JS and the Quorum of the Twelve discussed Smith's case and restored him to the quorum.[d] Because Hyde and William Smith were accepted back into fellowship before the 5 October 1839 conference, they did not give public accounts of their conduct, as resolved in this May general conference. Instead, their reinstatements were announced.[e] (a. Thomas B. Marsh and Orson Hyde, Affidavit, Richmond, MO, 24 Oct. 1838, copy, Mormon War Papers, MSA; 308nn206, 207 herein. b. Orson Hyde, New Franklin, MO, to Brigham Young, 30 Mar. 1839, in Young, Journal, 1837–1845, 100–104; Kimball, "History," 103–104; JS, Journal, 27 June 1839, in JSP, J1:343; see also Bergera, "Personal Cost of the 1838 Mormon War," 139–144. c. "Hearken, O Ye Latter-Day Saints," Deseret News, 23 Aug. 1865, 372; Woodruff, Journal, 13 Feb. 1859. d. Woodruff, Journal, 25 May 1839. e. Minutes, 5–7 Oct. 1839, in Times and Seasons, Dec. 1839, 1:30.)

80. Each of the apostles was expected to go on the mission, with the exception of suspended apostles Hyde and William Smith.

81. The conference was held in Commerce on Saturday, 5 October 1839. (Minutes, 5–7 Oct. 1839, in Times and Seasons, Dec. 1839, 1:30–31.)

J[ames] Mulholland} Clerk

Sunday the fifth, met according to adjournment at 10 AM Meeting or Conference opened as usual by prayer singing &c &c When it unanimously Resolved— That this conference do send a delegate to the City of Washington to lay our case before the general Government and that President Rigdon be appointed to that office.[82]

2nd Resolved— That Almond Babbit be sent to Springfield Ill, clothed with authority and required to set to rights the church in that place in every way which may become necessary according to the order of the Church of Jesus Christ.[83] [p. [3]]

3rd Resolved— That Col. Lyman Wight be appointed to receive the affidavits which are to be sent to the City of Washington.[84]

After which, the afternoon was spent, in hearing instruction from the Presidency, and those of the twelve present.

When at 5 oclock P.M. Conference adjourned, according to the resolution of Saturday. viz untill first Saturday in October next, at Commerce Ill.

Joseph Smith Jr
Chairman
James Mulholland} Clerk [p. [4]]

———— ☙ ————

Authorization for Almon Babbitt and Others, circa 4 May 1839

Source Note

JS, Authorization, for Almon Babbitt, Erastus Snow, and Robert B. Thompson, Quincy, Adams Co., IL, [ca. 4 May 1839]. Featured version copied [between 29 May and 30 Oct. 1839], in JS Letterbook 2, p. 47;

---

82. This resolution ratified Rigdon's proposal that the church send delegations to visit U.S. state capitals and Washington DC to lobby Congress "to impeach the State of Missouri on an item of the Constitution of the United States; That the general government shall give to each State a Republican form of government." This plan was part of the broader effort to obtain redress for the Saints' losses in Missouri. Although Rigdon accompanied JS, Elias Higbee, and others to Washington DC in winter 1839–1840, illness precluded him from joining the delegation in meetings with President Martin Van Buren and various congressmen. (Letter from Sidney Rigdon, 10 Apr. 1839, p. 408 herein; U.S. Constitution, art. 4, sec. 4; Bushman, *Rough Stone Rolling*, 391–398; Van Wagoner, *Sidney Rigdon*, 265–272; see also Letter to Edward Partridge and the Church, ca. 22 Mar. 1839, p. 397 herein.)

83. A later report from Babbitt's brother-in-law attested that Babbitt relocated to Springfield by October 1839, but no information on his management of the church there has been located. (Johnson, "A Life Review," 51, 58.)

84. See Lyman Wight, Mountain Valley, TX, to Wilford Woodruff, [Salt Lake City], 24 Aug. 1857, p. 10, Historian's Office, Histories of the Twelve, 1856–1858, 1861, CHL; and "Inventory of Bills," Mormon Redress Petitions, 1839–1845, CHL.

handwriting of James Mulholland; JS Collection, CHL. For more information on JS Letterbook 2, see
Source Notes for Multiple-Entry Documents, p. 566 herein.

Historical Introduction

At a general church conference held in Quincy, Illinois, on 4–5 May 1839, Almon Babbitt, Erastus Snow, and Robert B. Thompson were appointed to collect anti-Mormon publications and then publish a history that detailed the church's difficulties in Missouri, in part to refute anti-Mormon claims.[85] This appointment corresponded with a letter JS wrote while incarcerated in Liberty, Missouri, proposing that a committee be formed "to gether up the libilous publications that are afloat" in order to "publish to all the world" the suffering of the Saints.[86] At the general conference in which Babbitt, Snow, and Thompson were appointed to this task, JS directed Babbitt and Snow to collect anti-Mormon publications while traveling and preaching. They were to send collected materials to Thompson, who would write the history of the church members' experiences.[87]

Following the conference, JS signed the featured authorization for Babbitt, Snow, and Thompson to use while they fulfilled their duties. Presumably, each man received a copy, but personal copies of the authorization have not been found. James Mulholland copied the authorization into JS Letterbook 2 between 29 May and 30 October 1839; that version is featured here.[88]

Document Transcript

This is to certify—that at a general conference held at Quincy Adam's County Illinois, by the Church of Jesus Christ of Latter Day Saints, on Saturday the 4th of May 1839.

President Joseph Smith Jr Presiding

It was Resolved

That Almond Babbit [Almon Babbitt], Erastus Snow and Robert B. Thompson be appointed a traveling committee to gather up and obtain all the libelous reports and publications which have been circulated against ~~our~~ Church— as well as other historical matter connected with said church which they can possibly obtain.[89]

---

85. Minutes, 4–5 May 1839, p. 444 herein.

86. Letter to Edward Partridge and the Church, ca. 22 Mar. 1839, p. 397 herein.

87. Although the authorization designated Thompson as a member of the "traveling committee," he was apparently not expected to travel but rather to compose the history based on what Babbitt and Snow compiled. (Snow, Journal, 1838–1841, 50–54.)

88. Mulholland copied his own 29 May 1839 letter to Edward Partridge on page 15 of JS Letterbook 2, making that the earliest likely copying date for documents he subsequently copied but that had dates preceding 29 May. For information on the latest likely copying date, see 248n440 herein.

89. Although Snow gathered a few affidavits describing the difficulties in Missouri, the committee was apparently unable to obtain additional material or complete the proposed history. (Snow, Journal, 1838–1841, 57–65, 75.)

Joseph Smith Jr Chairman[90]
James Mulholland Clerk[91]

3 Copies, one for each of the Committee. [p. 47]

──────── ☙ ────────

Minutes, 6 May 1839

Source Note

Minutes, Quincy, Adams Co., IL, 6 May 1839; handwriting of James Mulholland; two pages; Historian's Office, General Church Minutes, CHL.

Single leaf measuring 9¾ × 8 inches (25 × 20 cm). The document was trifolded for filing and transmission. A vertical tear of 2½ inches begins at the middle of the top edge of the leaf. The top left of the recto contains a "4" in the handwriting of James Mulholland, indicating these minutes were the last of four sets of minutes that Mulholland recorded and numbered in 1839. The document shows signs of wear. It appears that these minutes were folded with the minutes for a 4–5 May 1839 meeting. Thomas Bullock likely filed both documents in the Church Historian's Office when he worked there from 1842 to 1856, suggesting continuous institutional custody since at least 1856. The document, as well as a rough copy, was placed in the General Church Minutes collection with other loose church minutes gathered from files in the Historical Department of the LDS church.

Historical Introduction

From 4 to 7 May 1839, JS presided at several meetings in Quincy, Illinois. On 4 and 5 May, he convened the first general conference of the church since before his incarceration in Missouri. On 6 and 7 May, JS met with members of the Quorum of the Twelve Apostles and "others."[92] The minutes featured here record the events of a 6 May 1839 meeting of church leaders held at Edward Partridge's residence.[93]

James Mulholland acted as the scribe, taking minutes for the meeting; after preparing a rough draft of the minutes, he prepared a fair copy. The rough draft terms the meeting "a

───────────────────

90. JS was appointed chairman of the conference held 4–5 May 1839. (Minutes, 4–5 May 1839, p. 444 herein.)

91. At a conference held on 24 April 1839, Mulholland was appointed clerk pro tempore. His appointment evidently continued through the May 1839 general conference. (Minutes, 24 Apr. 1839, p. 438 herein; Minutes, 4–5 May 1839, p. 447 herein.)

92. It is unclear who attended the meetings. At the time, the Quorum of the Twelve had ten members; two of them, Orson Hyde and William Smith, had been suspended from office on 4 May 1839, meaning they likely did not attend the 6 and 7 May meetings. Parley P. Pratt was still imprisoned in Missouri. The remaining seven—Heber C. Kimball, John E. Page, Orson Pratt, George A. Smith, John Taylor, Wilford Woodruff, and Brigham Young—were in Quincy and may have attended the meetings. As for the "others" who attended, Woodruff recorded that "several of the Brethren attended this conference that was wounded by the Missouri mob," including Isaac Leany. Woodruff also mentioned that Joseph Young had recently escaped Missouri violence and that "although the balls flew around him like hail stones, yet he was not wounded," suggesting that Young was also present at the meeting. (Minutes, 4–5 May 1839, p. 446 herein; JS, Journal, 4–7 May 1839, in *JSP*, J1:338; Woodruff, Journal, 6 May 1839.)

93. Woodruff, Journal, 6 May 1839; Young, "Incidents," 169.

Conference."[94] The fair copy, featured here, originally labeled the gathering as a "Council," but at a later date that word was stricken and replaced with "Conference." The label of "Conference" was repeated in later iterations of the minutes, such as those copied in JS's multivolume manuscript history and Heber C. Kimball's autobiography.[95] The 6 May conference was apparently an extension of the general conference held the previous two days; whereas the meetings on 4–5 May were for all church members, the 6 May meeting was attended by church leaders only.[96]

Those at the 6 May meeting discussed matters closely related to resolutions passed at the general conference. Leaders at the 6 May meeting also passed resolutions regarding church administration in Commerce, Illinois, and in New York, as well as the imminent mission of the Quorum of the Twelve Apostles to Europe. Thirteen members of the Quorums of the Seventy, along with five high priests, were approved to join the Quorum of the Twelve Apostles on the mission.

The primary difference between Mulholland's two versions of the minutes is that the fair copy contains spelling corrections and standardized formatting; consequently, the fair copy is featured here. Substantive changes are noted in annotation.

Document Transcript

At a ~~Council~~ ⟨Conference⟩ meeting, held in the town of Quincy Ill on Monday the 6th of May 1839.

President Joseph Smith Jr Presiding.

The following resolutions were unanimously agreed to.

1rst Resolved— That the families of Elder [William] Marks,[97] Elder Grainger [Oliver Granger][98] and Bishop N[ewel] K. Whitney[99] be kept here amongst us for the time being.

2nd Resolved— That Elder Marks be hereby appointed to preside over the Church at Commerce, Ill.[100]

---

94. Historian's Office, General Church Minutes, 6 May 1839.

95. See JS History, vol. C-1, 935; and Kimball, "History," 103.

96. JS, Journal, 4–6 May 1839, in *JSP*, J1:338. In contrast to other records, Kimball's history states that the 6 May meeting was part of the general conference. (Kimball, "History," 103–104; see also Woodruff, Journal, 6 May 1839; and Quorums of the Seventy, "Book of Records," 12 May 1839, 72.)

97. Marks relocated from Kirtland, Ohio, to Quincy in early 1839 and was appointed president of the Quincy congregation in February 1839. (Quincy Committee, Minutes, ca. 9 Feb. 1839, Far West Committee, Minutes, CHL.)

98. During the conference held on 4–5 May, Granger was appointed to return to Kirtland to oversee the House of the Lord and manage church affairs there. (Minutes, 4–5 May 1839, p. 445 herein.)

99. During fall 1838, Whitney and his family moved from Ohio, intending to settle in Missouri. However, they stopped in Carrollton, Illinois, after learning of the expulsion order that Missouri governor Lilburn W. Boggs issued 27 October. While Whitney traveled, first to Kirtland and later to Quincy, his family remained in Carrollton. The Whitney family apparently had not moved to Quincy by the time of this meeting. ([Elizabeth Ann Smith Whitney], "A Leaf from an Autobiography," *Woman's Exponent*, 15 Nov. 1878, 91; Letter to Newel K. Whitney, 24 May 1839, pp. 473–475 herein.)

100. Marks was previously the stake president in Kirtland. In October 1839, Commerce was

3rd Resolved— That Bishop Whitney go also to Commerce and there act in unison with the other Bishops of the Church.[101]

4th Resolved— That brother [Theodore] Turleys gun Smith's tools shall remain for the general use of the Church untill his return from Europe.

5th Resolved— That the following of the Seventies have the sanction of this Council that they accompany the twelve to Europe.[102] viz:

Theodore Turley		
George Pitkin	Lorenzo Youngs [Young]	W[m] Burton
Bates Nobles [Joseph B. Noble]	Samuel Mullinar [Mulliner]	Lorenzo Barn[e]s
Charles Hubbard	Wil[l]ard Snow	Milton Holmes
John Scott	John Snider	Abra[ha]m, O, Smoot.

also the following [p. [1]] High Priests viz: Henry, G, Sherwood, John Murdock, Winslow Farr William Snow, Hirum [Hiram] Clark.

6[th] Resolved— That it be observed as a general rule that those of the Seventies who have not yet preached shall for the future not be sent on foreign missions.[103]

7th Resolved— That Elder J. P. Green [John P. Greene] be appointed to go to the city of New York, and preside over the Churches there, and in the regions round about.[104]

Adjourned till tomorrow at. 10 o'clock A. M.[105] [p. [2]]

———— ✧ ————

organized as a stake and Marks was appointed president of the stake. (Minutes, 5–7 Oct. 1839, in *Times and Seasons,* Dec. 1839, 1:30.)

101. Other bishops included Edward Partridge and Vinson Knight, both of whom relocated from Missouri to Illinois.

102. In the general conference on 4–5 May, the congregation approved plans for the Quorum of the Twelve Apostles to embark on a mission to Europe. (Minutes, 4–5 May 1839, pp. 445–446 herein.)

103. The rough draft of these minutes states, "Resolved that it be observed as a general rule that those of the above named Seventies who have not yet preached shall for the future not be sent on foreign missions, except &c &c some honorable exc[eptions]." Of the Seventies appointed to join the Quorum of the Twelve in Europe, four are not identified in extant documents as having previously served missions: Pitkin, Hubbard, Scott, and Mulliner. It is unclear how or why exceptions were made; Scott and Mulliner were converts from Canada with possible ties to England, which may have led to their assignment. (Historian's Office, General Church Minutes, 6 May 1839.)

104. The same day as this meeting, a certificate was produced for Greene that declared he was authorized to preside over church affairs in the region. (See Authorization for John P. Greene, ca. 6 May 1839, pp. 454–456 herein.)

105. Minutes from the meeting held the next day have not been located.

Authorization for Oliver Granger, 6 May 1839

Source Note

JS, Authorization, for Oliver Granger, 6 May 1839, Quincy, Adams Co., IL; handwriting of James Mulholland; signature of JS; one page; CHL. Includes docket.

One leaf measuring 10⅞ × 7¾ inches (28 × 20 cm). The authorization was folded for transmission and filing. The document has undergone conservation work to fix tearing along the folds. The top section of the leaf is missing; although the text of the authorization is intact, the missing section may have contained a title. The verso contains a docket in unidentified handwriting: "Conference | Recommend to | O. Granger".

The document came into the possession of Phineas Kimball Jr., who was the brother-in-law of Oliver Granger's daughter Sarah Granger Kimball and who appears to have retained this and other documents belonging to Granger. The authorization was passed down in the family to Phineas Kimball Jr.'s granddaughter Margaret Rheinburger Burke. At the time of her death, the document was given to her stepdaughter Sylvia Burke Van Blarcom, who sold it to a collector. The Church History Library acquired the document in January 2011.[106]

Historical Introduction

On 6 May, JS signed an authorization for Oliver Granger, instructing him to travel to Kirtland, Ohio, take charge of the House of Lord there, and preside over church affairs in the region. Granger was assigned these tasks during the first session of a general conference the church held on 4–5 May 1839. He had been acting as an agent for JS and the church since 1837.[107] In July 1838, JS dictated a revelation directing Granger to go to Kirtland to "contend earnestly for the redemption of the first presidency."[108] By October 1838, Granger had resolved debts with several Painesville, Ohio, merchants and was working to resolve other debts that JS and fellow church leaders owed.[109]

Granger continued to manage church affairs in Kirtland in 1839, traveling between that area and Illinois. Several Saints living in Illinois, including JS, still held property in the Kirtland area and provided Granger with powers of attorney and other agreements allowing him to manage their property.[110] Granger was also running a

---

106. See the full bibliographic entries for Authorization for Oliver Granger, 6 May 1839, and Authorization for Oliver Granger, 1 Nov. 1839, in the CHL catalog.

107. Granger and Jared Carter purchased stock from JS and other stockholders in the Kirtland Safety Society in June 1837 and in so doing took responsibility for the debts of the institution. Granger was also given a formal power of attorney by JS and Sidney Rigdon on 27 September 1837 to resolve their debts with Buffalo, New York, merchant Jonathan F. Scribner. (Historical Introduction to Notice, ca. Late Aug. 1837, in *JSP*, D5:418–420; Historical Introduction to Power of Attorney for Oliver Granger, 27 Sept. 1837, in *JSP*, D5:457–459.)

108. Revelation, 8 July 1838–E, p. 194 herein [D&C 117:13].

109. See Historical Introduction to Letter of Introduction from John Howden, 27 Oct. 1838, pp. 246–248 herein; and Historical Introduction to Letter from William Perkins, 29 Oct. 1838, pp. 249–251 herein.

110. For example, on 15 April 1839 Granger received two powers of attorney, one from Aaron Johnson and another from John W. Clark, to rent out their houses and land in Kirtland. On 7 May, William Marks provided Granger with powers of attorney for two Kirtland buildings that Marks

store in Kirtland by 1839, although it is not clear whether this store was a new venture or a continuation of one of the earlier mercantile firms that church members had established.[111]

The responsibilities assigned to Granger at the 4–5 May general conference highlighted the church's continued presence in Ohio and expanded his earlier assignment to resolve financial matters there. During the conference, the congregation also resolved that Latter-day Saints living in the eastern United States should be encouraged to move to the Kirtland area, if they preferred to settle there rather than in Illinois or Iowa Territory, and again recognized Kirtland as a stake of Zion. This information was included in Granger's authorization because of his assignment to preside in Kirtland and perhaps also because the information provided important direction for Saints in the eastern United States with whom Granger might communicate.

The authorization featured here was written on 6 May and may have been produced as part of a meeting of church leaders held that day. One week after James Mulholland wrote this authorization and JS signed it, the First Presidency created a lengthier authorization that provided further detail regarding Granger's assignment in Ohio and expressed the church leaders' confidence and trust in him.[112] Granger may have carried both authorizations with him or may have taken only the latter.

Document Transcript

This is to Certify that at a General Conference held at Quincy, Adam's County, Illinois,[113] by the Church of Jesus Christ of Latter Day Saints, on Saturday the 4th May 1839.[114]

President Joseph Smith Jr presiding

It was Resolved, That Elder ⟨Oliver⟩ Grainger [Granger] be appointed to go ⟨to⟩ Kirtland and take the Charge and oversight of the House of the Lord and preside over the general affairs of the Church in that place.[115]

It was also Resolved— That the advice of this conference to the Brethren living in the Eastern States, is, ~~to~~ for them to move to Kirtland and the vicinity

---

owned. (John W. Clark, Power of Attorney, to Oliver Granger, 15 Apr. 1839; Aaron Johnson, Power of Attorney, to Oliver Granger, 15 Apr. 1839; William Marks, Power of Attorney, to Oliver Granger, 7 May 1839, Hiram Kimball Collection, CHL.)

111. William Marks, Power of Attorney, to Oliver Granger, 7 May 1839, Hiram Kimball Collection, CHL.

112. See Authorization for Oliver Granger, 13 May 1839, pp. 456–459 herein.

113. Minutes of the conference specify that the meeting was held at the "Presbyterian Camp Ground," two miles north of Quincy. (Minutes, 4–5 May 1839, p. 444 herein; Woodruff, Journal, 4 May 1839.)

114. The conference continued on Sunday, 5 May 1839. (See Minutes, 4–5 May 1839, p. 446 herein.)

115. The wording of this sentence is almost the same as that of the fourth resolution recorded in the minutes for the general conference session on 4 May 1839. (See Minutes, 4–5 May 1839, p. 445 herein.)

thereof, and again settle that place as a stake of Zion, provided that they may feel so inclined in preference to their moving further Westward.[116]

Joseph Smith Jr} Chairman
James Mulholland}, Clerk

Given at Quincy Illinois 6th May 1839.

———— ❧ ————

Authorization for John P. Greene, circa 6 May 1839

Source Note

JS, Authorization, for John P. Greene, Quincy, Adams Co., IL, [ca. 6 May 1839]. Featured version copied [between 29 May and 30 Oct. 1839] in JS Letterbook 2, p. 45; handwriting of James Mulholland; JS Collection, CHL. For more information on JS Letterbook 2, see Source Notes for Multiple-Entry Documents, p. 566 herein.

Historical Introduction

Following a conference meeting held in Quincy, Illinois, on 6 May 1839, JS signed an authorization for high priest John P. Greene, reflecting the conference's resolution that he travel to New York City "and preside over the Churches there, and in the regions round about."[117] A branch was organized in the city in early 1838 by missionary Parley P. Pratt, and subsequent growth in the area required experienced leadership.[118] Greene's previous appointments in the church prepared him to oversee the church in the eastern United States. After being baptized in April 1832, Greene presided over branches in New York and Ohio; served on the Kirtland, Ohio, high council; and proselytized in New York, Ohio, and Canada. He later moved to Far West, Missouri, where he served on the high council. Following the 1838 conflict between church members and other Missourians, he migrated to Illinois, where he became a principal liaison between the Saints and the Democratic Association of Quincy, an organization composed of influential non-Mormons who raised money for the indigent Saints.[119]

---

116. The wording of this sentence is almost the same as that of the fifth resolution recorded in the minutes for the general conference session on 4 May 1839. In the minutes, the phrase "provided that they may feel so inclined, in preference to their moving further west" was inserted at a later time by Mulholland, who inscribed both the minutes and this certificate. It may be that this idea originated during the creation of this certificate and was then copied into the 4 May 1839 minutes. The concept of maintaining or rebuilding Kirtland as a stake of the church, rather than calling all the Saints to gather to one location, was not new. The location where the main body of the church would settle became uncertain during the Missouri troubles and the Saints' flight to Illinois, perhaps contributing to church leaders' continued interest in Kirtland. (Minutes, 4–5 May 1839, p. 445 herein; Letter to Heber C. Kimball and Brigham Young, 16 Jan. 1839, p. 314 herein.)

117. Minutes, 6 May 1839, p. 451 herein.

118. New York City Branch History, [1]; see also Givens and Grow, *Parley P. Pratt,* 120–129.

119. Greene, "Biographical Sketch of the Life and Travels of John Portenus Greene," 1–2; Minutes, 7–8 Apr. 1838, p. 73 herein; Greene, *Facts relative to the Expulsion,* iii–iv, 8–9; Bennett, "Study of the

Greene's authorization was inscribed by James Mulholland, who also recorded the minutes for the 6 May meeting at which Greene received his appointment. Mulholland began the authorization with a slightly altered version of the resolution inscribed in the meeting minutes. The authorization also includes more information on Greene's appointment and a description of his character. Additionally, the authorization directs Greene to collect donations to assist Latter-day Saint refugees who recently migrated from Missouri. JS, who presided at the 6 May meeting, signed the original authorization, which is apparently not extant. Mulholland inscribed a copy in JS Letterbook 2 sometime between 29 May and 30 October 1839.[120]

In summer and fall 1839, Greene gave public presentations in Ohio and New York on the Saints' sufferings and raised money for Mormon refugees.[121] Upon his arrival in New York City in August 1839, he met with church members and presented his "letter from the Presidency of the church . . . recommending Elder Green[e] as a man of God, and worthy of all confidence." The New York Saints sustained Greene as their president. At a conference held later that month in Monmouth County, New Jersey, Greene met with representatives of church branches in New Jersey, New Hampshire, Massachusetts, and Pennsylvania. Greene presented to them his authorization from the First Presidency, and the representatives sustained him as their president.[122]

Document Transcript

At a conference Meeting held by the Church of Jesus Christ of Latter Day Saints in the Town of Quincy Adams County Ill, on Monday the 6th day of May 1839.[123]

Joseph Smith Jr Presiding

It was unanimously Resolved—

That Elder John P. Green[e] be appointed to go to the City of New York and preside among the Saints in that place, and in the regions round about, and regulate the affairs of the Church according to the laws and doctrines of said Church, and he is fully authorized to receive donation moneys, by the liberality of the Saints, for the assistance of the poor among us who

---

Mormons in Quincy," 87–91. By November 1839, there were about two hundred Latter-day Saints in New York City and surrounding areas in the state. (New York City Branch History, [6].)

120. Mulholland copied his own 29 May 1839 letter to Edward Partridge on page 15 of JS Letterbook 2, making that the earliest likely copying date for documents he subsequently copied but that had dates preceding 29 May. For information on the latest likely copying date, see 248n440 herein.

121. Letter from John P. Greene, 30 June 1839, pp. 513–516 herein; Pratt, *Late Persecution of the Church,* 159–163.

122. New York City Branch History, [5]; "Conference Minutes," *Times and Seasons,* Jan. 1840, 1:44; John P. Greene, Monmouth Co., NJ, to Don Carlos Smith and Ebenezer Robinson, Nauvoo, IL, 10 Sept. 1839, in *Times and Seasons,* Dec. 1839, 1:28–29; Greene, "Biographical Sketch of the Life and Travels of John Portenus Greene," 4.

123. This meeting was held in conjunction with a general conference of the church on 4–5 May 1839. (Minutes, 6 May 1839, p. 450 herein.)

have been persecuted and driven from their homes in the State of Missouri,[124] And from our long acquaintance with Elder Green, and with his experience and knowledge of the laws of ~~God~~ the kingdom of God, we do not hesitate to recommend him to the Saints as one in whom they may place the fullest confidence, both as to their Spiritual welfare as well as to the strictest integrity in all temporal concerns, with which he may be intrusted

And we beseech the Brethren in the name of the Lord Jesus to receive this Brother in behalf of the poor with readiness, and to abound unto him in a liberal manner, for "in as much as ye have done it unto the least of these, ye have done it unto me".[125]

Yours in the bonds of the everlasting gospel[126] though no longer a prisoner in the hands of the Missourians;

And still faithful with the Saints

Joseph Smith Jr

Chairman— &c—[127]

───────── ❧ ─────────

Authorization for Oliver Granger, 13 May 1839

Source Note

JS, Sidney Rigdon, and Hyrum Smith, Authorization for Oliver Granger, Commerce, Hancock Co., IL, 13 May 1839. Featured version copied [between 29 May and 30 Oct. 1839] in JS Letterbook 2, pp. 45–46; handwriting of James Mulholland; JS Collection, CHL. For more information on JS Letterbook 2, see Source Notes for Multiple-Entry Documents, p. 566 herein.

Historical Introduction

During a general conference of the church on 4–5 May 1839, the Saints in Quincy, Illinois, resolved to send Oliver Granger to Kirtland, Ohio, to oversee the House of the Lord and church affairs in the region. On 6 May, JS and his counselors in the First Presidency prepared an authorization for Granger to carry with him to Kirtland.[128] While transacting

---

124. For information on Latter-day Saint refugees, see Introduction to Part 3: 4 Nov. 1838–16 Apr. 1839, pp. 275–276 herein.

125. Matthew 25:40.

126. See Philemon 1:13; and Revelation 14:6.

127. JS was appointed chairman of the general conference held 4–5 May 1839. (Minutes, 4–5 May 1839, p. 444 herein.)

128. Minutes, 4–5 May 1839, p. 445 herein; Authorization for Oliver Granger, 6 May 1839, p. 453 herein.

"various business" with Granger a week later in Commerce, the First Presidency wrote a second authorization, featured here.[129]

The 13 May authorization is longer than the 6 May authorization and is addressed to members of the church. The authorization expresses the First Presidency's confidence in Granger's integrity and ability to resolve the business concerns of the church. The authorization also expands the duties mentioned in the 6 May authorization, instructing him to oversee a broad set of church affairs in Ohio. These duties included acting as an agent for the church and collecting funds from church members. The authorization cites a revelation JS dictated in July 1838 concerning Granger's responsibilities and uses language from the revelation to appoint him as a church agent and bless him for his integrity and work on the church's behalf.

The authorization was copied into JS Letterbook 2 by James Mulholland between 29 May and 30 October 1839.[130] The original is apparently not extant, but its format was likely similar to that of the 6 May authorization and another authorization written for Granger on 1 November 1839, both of which were inscribed on loose leaves.[131]

Granger left for Kirtland sometime after 29 May 1839, when he acted as an agent in purchasing land in Iowa Territory from Isaac Galland.[132] Granger continued to travel between Kirtland and Commerce, managing JS's and the church's affairs in Ohio and the eastern United States, until his death in 1841.[133]

Document Transcript

Commerce Ill, 13th May 1839

Joseph Smith Jr, Sidney Rigdon, and Hyrum Smith; Presiding Elders of the Church of Jesus Christ of Latter Day Saints; do hereby certify And solemnly declare unto all the Saints scattered abroad, And send unto them greeting.[134] That we have always found President Oliver Granger to be a man of the most strict integrity and moral virtue, and in fine to be a man of God.

---

129. JS, Journal, 13–14 May 1839, in *JSP*, J1:339. The business may have included arranging for Granger to purchase land for the church in Lee County, Iowa Territory, from Isaac Galland.

130. Mulholland copied his own 29 May 1839 letter to Edward Partridge on page 15 of JS Letterbook 2, making that the earliest likely copying date for documents he subsequently copied but that had dates preceding 29 May. For information on the latest likely copying date, see 248n440 herein.

131. See JS et al., Authorization for Oliver Granger, Quincy, IL, 1 Nov. 1839, photocopy, CHL.

132. See Lee Co., IA, Land Records, 1836–1961, vol. 1, pp. 507–510, 29 May 1839, microfilm 959,238, U.S. and Canada Record Collection, FHL.

133. See Agreement with Mead & Betts, 2 Aug. 1839, p. 538 herein. For additional examples of Granger's actions and responsibilities as a church agent, see William Marks, Power of Attorney for Oliver Granger, 7 May 1839; John Newbould, Agreement with Oliver Granger, ca. 2 Aug. 1839; JS, Articles of Agreement with Oliver Granger, 29 Apr. 1840, Hiram Kimball Collection, CHL; JS, Nauvoo, IL, to Oliver Granger, Kirtland, OH, [23] July 1840, in JS Letterbook 2, pp. 159–161; and Nauvoo High Council Minutes, 12 Apr. 1840.

134. See James 1:1.

We have had long experience and acquaintance with Br Granger, we have entrusted vast business concerns to him which have been managed skilfully to the support of our Characters and interest,[135] as well as that [p. 45] of the Church, And he is now authorized by a general Conference[136] to go forth and engage in vast ~~business~~ and important concerns as an agent for the Church, that he may fill a station of usefulness in obedience to the commandments of God, which was given unto him July 8th 1838— which says, "Let him (meaning Br Granger) Contend earnestly for the redemption of the First Presidency of my Church saith the Lord."[137]

We earnestly solicit the Saints scattered abroad to strengthen his hands with all their might,[138] and to put such means into his hands as shall enable him to accomplish his lawful designs And purposes, according to the commandments, and according to the instructions which he shall give unto them. And that they intrust him with moneys, lands, chattles And goods, to assist him in this work, And it shall redound greatly to the interest and welfare, peace and satisfaction of my Saints Saith the Lord God. For this is an honorable agency which I have appointed unto him Saith the Lord; And again Verily thus saith the Lord, I will lift up my servant Oliver, And beget for him a great name on the earth and among my people,[139] because of the integrity of his soul; therefore let all my Saints abound unto him with all liberality[140] and long suffering, and it shall be a blessing on their heads.[141]

We would say unto the Saints abroad, Let our hearts abound with grateful acknowledgements unto God our Heavenly Father, who hath called us unto his holy calling,[142] by the revelation of Jesus Christ[143] in these last days, and has so mercifully stood by us, And delivered us out of the seventh trouble which happened unto us in the State of Missouri.[144]

---

135. See Historical Introduction to Letter of Introduction from John Howden, 27 Oct. 1838, pp. 246–248 herein.

136. See Minutes, 4–5 May 1839, p. 445 herein.

137. Revelation, 8 July 1838–E, p. 194 herein [D&C 117:12–13].

138. See Nehemiah 6:9; and Job 4:3.

139. See Genesis 12:2; and 1 Chronicles 17:8. An 8 July 1838 revelation included a similar promise to Granger. (See Revelation, 8 July 1838–E, p. 194 herein [D&C 117:12].)

140. See 2 Corinthians 8:2.

141. See Proverbs 10:6.

142. See 2 Timothy 1:9; and Book of Mormon, 1830 ed., 259 [Alma 13:5].

143. See Galatians 1:12; 1 Peter 1:13; and Revelation 1:1.

144. See Job 5:19. The authorization may be referencing the general exodus of church members from Missouri or the recent escape of JS and others from incarceration and their safe arrival in Illinois. For more information on these events, see Introduction to Part 3: 4 Nov. 1838–16 Apr. 1839, pp. 275–278 herein.

May God reward our enemies according to their works.[145] We request the prayers of all the Saints. Subscribing ourselves, their humble brethren in tribulation[146] in the bonds of the everlasting Gospel.[147]

Joseph Smith Jr
Sidney Rigdon
Hyrum Smith

———— ❧ ————

Letter from Robert B. Thompson, 13 May 1839

Source Note

Robert B. Thompson, Letter, Quincy, Adams Co., IL, to "the Presidency of the Church of Jesus Christ of Latter Day Saints" (including JS), [Commerce, Hancock Co., IL], 13 May 1839. Featured version copied [between 22 May and 30 Oct. 1839] in JS Letterbook 2, pp. 7, 10–11; handwriting of James Mulholland; JS Collection, CHL. For more information on JS Letterbook 2, see Source Notes for Multiple-Entry Documents, p. 566 herein.

Historical Introduction

On 13 May 1839, Latter-day Saint Robert B. Thompson wrote a letter to the First Presidency, expressing his concern that two letters church member Lyman Wight had written and recently published in local newspapers might cause difficulties with the non-Mormon population in western Illinois and with government officials in Illinois and Washington DC. After the Saints' expulsion from Missouri, most church members were destitute. In early 1839, many gathered to Quincy, Illinois, and the surrounding area, where they were met with generosity. Residents of Quincy collected donations on behalf of church members, opened their homes to them, and offered them desperately needed loans.[148]

The editors of both local newspapers, the *Quincy Whig* and the *Quincy Argus,* published articles discussing the conflict in Missouri, the political repercussions of that conflict, and the treatment of the Saints.[149] On 4 and 11 May 1839, the *Quincy Whig* published letters

---

145. See Matthew 16:27; and 2 Timothy 4:14.

146. See Revelation 1:9.

147. See Philemon 1:13; and Revelation 14:6.

148. For more information on the generosity of Quincy residents, see Letter from Edward Partridge, 5 Mar. 1839, p. 329 herein; "Proceedings in the Town of Quincy," *Quincy (IL) Argus,* 16 Mar. 1839, [1]; George Miller, St. James, MI, to "Dear Brother," 22 June 1855, in *Northern Islander* (St. James, MI), 9 Aug. 1855, [1]; and Tillson, *History of the City of Quincy, Illinois,* 68.

149. See Editorial, *Quincy (IL) Whig,* 23 Feb. 1839, [1]; News Item, *Quincy (IL) Argus,* 2 Mar. 1839, [2]; "Proceedings in the Town of Quincy," and "The Mormons, or Latter Day Saints," *Quincy Argus,* 16 Mar. 1839, [1]–[2]; "The Mormons," *Quincy Whig,* 16 Mar. 1839, [1]; Isaac Galland, Commerce, IL, 12 Apr. 1839, Letter to the Editors, *Quincy Argus,* 20 Apr. 1839, [1]; "The Quincy Argus an Enemy of Missouri," *Quincy Whig,* 27 Apr. 1839, [1]; and "The Mormons," *Quincy Argus,* 11 May 1839, [2].

that Wight wrote during his imprisonment with JS in the Clay County jail in Liberty, Missouri.[150] The letters described the violence the Saints endured in Missouri and condemned Democratic officials in Missouri for their failure to protect the Saints and to redress the Saints for their losses.[151] The editors of the *Quincy Whig* may have printed Wight's letters partly to undermine local Democrats, who the editors believed were pandering to the Saints for political gain. However, because the Quincy Democratic Association helped facilitate the Saints' warm reception there, Thompson feared that Wight's letters might offend the church's benefactors in Quincy.[152] Thompson was also likely sensitive to Wight's attack on Democrats because Thompson supported the party and worked as an editor for the Democratic *Quincy Argus*.[153]

On 12 May, Thompson met with church leaders in Quincy and raised his concerns about Wight's letters. The church leaders shared these concerns and appointed a committee to meet with Wight and dissuade him from further politicizing how the Saints were treated in Missouri. The next morning, Thompson wrote the letter featured here to the members of the First Presidency, who were in Commerce, Illinois. Thompson expressed concern that Wight's statements would be misconstrued as representing the views of the church as a whole, potentially upsetting local interests in Quincy and leading to a repeat of the Missouri violence. Thompson called upon the First Presidency to "correct the publick mind on this subject, And as a Church disavow all connexions with politics."

The original letter from Thompson to JS is no longer extant. The version featured here was copied, presumably from the original, into JS Letterbook 2 by James Mulholland sometime between 22 May and 30 October 1839.[154]

---

150. On 1 May 1839, Wight sent the *Quincy Whig* a letter containing extracts of a letter he wrote to the *Louisville Journal* on 2 April 1839. On 4 May, the *Whig* published the letter, in which Wight assailed Democratic leaders in Missouri. On 7 May 1839, he sent the newspaper a letter consisting of extracts from a 30 March 1839 letter he sent to Thomas Hart Benton, a United States senator from Missouri. The *Whig* published the condensed letter on 11 May 1839 and included Wight's introduction to the letter, in which he criticized the Democratic leaders of Missouri. Wight represented himself as one who had "heretofore been a strong advocate" of the Democratic Party. (Lyman Wight, Quincy, IL, 1 May 1839, Letter to the Editors, *Quincy [IL] Whig*, 4 May 1839, [2]; Lyman Wight, Quincy, IL, 7 May 1839, Letter to the Editors, *Quincy Whig*, 11 May 1839, [2].)

151. Lyman Wight, Quincy, IL, 1 May 1839, Letter to the Editors, *Quincy (IL) Whig*, 4 May 1839, [2]; Lyman Wight, Quincy, IL, 7 May 1839, Letter to the Editors, *Quincy Whig*, 11 May 1839, [2].

152. See "Proceedings in the Town of Quincy," *Quincy (IL) Argus*, 16 Mar. 1839, [1].

153. Thompson's wife, Mercy Fielding Thompson, later recounted that in November 1838, her husband and many male church members were "threatened and persued by a Mob" and fled from Far West, Missouri, arriving in Quincy sometime in January 1839. By the time his family arrived in late February, Thompson had secured housing and a position with the *Quincy Argus*. (Mercy Fielding Thompson, "Robert B. Thompson Biography," Nov. 1854, Historian's Office, JS History Documents, 1839–1860, CHL; Thompson, Autobiographical Sketch, 2–3, 5.)

154. Mulholland began to "write for the Church" on 22 April 1839, and Thompson's letter was one of the first documents Mulholland inscribed in Letterbook 2. For information on the latest likely copying date, see 248n440 herein.

which have been inserted in the Quincy Whig, I am aware that upon a cursory view of these, nothing very objectionable may appear; yet if they are attentively considered, there will be found very great objections to them indeed: For instance in condemning the Democracy of Missouri why condemn that of the whole union, and why use such epithets as "Demagogue" to T. H. Benton for not answering his letter when it is very probable that he had not received it. Yesterday I was waited upon by Mr Morris who asked me what was intended by such publications, and why we should come out against the democracy of the Nation, when they were doing all in their power to assist us; It was something which he could not understand And wished to know if we as a people countenanced such proceedings. I told him for my part, I was sorry that his letters had ever made their appearance; and believed that such a course was at variance with the sentiments of the greater part of our people. Yesterday, I brought the subject before the authorities of the Church who are here, where it was manifest that his conduct was not fellowshipped and the brethren wished to disavow all connexion with such proceedings and appointed a committee to wait on Brother Wight to beg of him not to persist in the course, which if not nipt in the bud will probably bring persecution with all its horrors upon an innocent people by the folly and imprudence of one individual.

From information I understand that the feelings of the Governor are very much hurt by the course which is pursued. I think we ought to correct the Publick mind on this subject, and as a Church disavow all connexions with politics; by such a course we may in some measure counteract the baneful influence which his letters have occasioned: But if such a course which he (Bro Wight) has adopted, be continued (as I understand that he intends to do) it will block up our way and we can have no reasonable prospect of obtaining justice from the authorities of the Union whom we wantonly condemn before we have made application.

The same feelings are beginning to be manifested in Springfield by those who have been our friends there. The Whigs are glad of such weapons and make the most of them. — You will probably think that I am a little too officious but I feel impressed with the subject, I feel for my brethren; The tears of widows, the cries of orphans & the moans of the distressed are continually present in my mind and I want to adopt and continue a course which shall be beneficial to us — — but if through the imprudence and conduct of Isolated individuals 3 – 4 – or 5 years hence our altars should be thrown down our homes destroyed, our brethren slain, our wives widows and our children orphans, your unworthy unworthy brother wishes to lift up his hands before God and appeal to him and say, thou who knowest all things, knowest that I am innocent in this matter. I am with great respect, Gent. Yours in the Bonds of Christ.

R. B. Thompson

Excuse haste &c
I have not time to copy } (N. B Postcript other side.)

Traces of a missing leaf in JS Letterbook 2. In 1839, scribe James Mulholland copied Joseph Smith's correspondence into Letterbook 2. Between pages 7 and 10 of the book, Mulholland used adhesive wafers to tip in a loose leaf that he numbered as pages 8 and 9. This leaf included copies of two April 1839 letters written to Smith by former church members William W. Phelps and Jacob Scott. This leaf was later removed from the letterbook, perhaps after Phelps and Scott were restored to membership in the church; only the wafer residue indicates where the leaf had been added. JS Letterbook 2, p. 10, JS Collection, Church History Library, Salt Lake City.

Document Transcript

To the Presidency of the Church of Jesus Christ of Latter Day Saints,
Greeting.

I beg leave to call your attention to a subject of considerable importance
to our Church, and which if not attended to is calculated (in my humble
opinion) to raise a prejudice in the minds of a considerable portion of
the community, and destroy those benevolent and philanthropic feelings
which have been manifested towards us as a people by a large portion of
this community:[155] I have reference to the Letters of Bro Lyman Wight
[p. 7] which have been inserted in the Quincy Whig, I am aware that upon
a Cursory view of these, nothing very objectionable may appear; yet if
they are attentively considered there will be found very great objections
to them indeed: for instance in condemning the Democracy of Missouri[156]
why condemn that of the Whole Union, And why use such epithets as
"Demagogue"[157] to T[homas] H. Benton[158] for not answering his letter when
it is very probable that he had not received it. Yesterday I was waited upon
by M‘ Morris[159] who asked me what was intended by such publications,
And why we should come out against the democracy of the nation,
when they were doing All in their power to assist us; It was something which
he could not understand And wished to know if we as a people countenanced such proceedings. I told him for my part, I was sorry that his letters had ever made their appearance, and believed that such a course was at

---

155. The Quincy Democratic Association organized multiple committees, undertook fact-finding
missions, communicated with Sidney Rigdon and possibly others, and publicly called upon citizens of
Quincy to set aside prejudice, disregard rumors concerning the refugee Saints, and aid the starving new-
comers. ("Proceedings in the Town of Quincy," *Quincy [IL] Argus,* 16 Mar. 1839, [1].)

156. That is, the government officials in Missouri who belonged to the Democratic Party.

157. In his letter to Benton, Wight described the "wicked mis-rule of Democracy" and how the
opposition that "commenced in 1832" was "fanned by enthusiastic demagogues; until they have succeeded
in driving at least five or six thousand inhabitants" from Missouri. He questioned why Missouri representatives and senators, especially Benton, did not address the persecution. Wight later echoed these sentiments in his letter to the editors of the *Louisville Journal.* (Lyman Wight, Quincy, IL, 1 May 1839, Letter
to the Editors, *Quincy [IL] Whig,* 4 May 1839, [2]; Lyman Wight, Quincy, IL, 7 May 1839, Letter to the
Editors, *Quincy Whig,* 11 May 1839, [2].)

158. In 1821 Benton became the first United States senator to represent the newly admitted state of
Missouri. Originally a member of the Democratic-Republican Party, he joined the Democratic Party in
1825 when the Democratic-Republicans disbanded. (Meigs, *Life of Thomas Hart Benton,* 133, 260, 262;
Biographical Directory of the United States Congress, 1774–2005, 646; Arrington and Bitton, *Mormon
Experience,* 98–99.)

159. Likely Isaac N. Morris, editor of the *Quincy Argus,* where Thompson worked as an editor.
("Death of Hon. Isaac N. Morris," *Daily Quincy [IL] Herald,* 30 Oct. 1879, 3.)

variance with the sentiments of the greater part of our people. Yesterday I brought the subject before the authorities of the Church who are here, where it was manifest that his conduct was not fellowshipped And the brethren wished to disavow all connexion with such proceedings and appointed a committee to wait on Brother Wight to beg of him not to persist in the course, which if not nipt in the bud will probably bring persecution with all its horrors upon an innocent people by the folly and imprudence of one individual.

From information I understand that the feelings of the Governor[160] are very much hurt by the course which is pursued. I think we ought to correct the publick mind on this subject, And as a Church disavow all connexions with politics; by such a course we may in some measure counteract the baneful influence which his letters have occasioned: But if such a course which he (Bro Wight) has adopted, be continued (as I understand that he intends to do) it will block up our way and we can have no reasenable prospect of obtaining justice from the authorities of the Union[161] whom we wantonly condemn before we have made application.

The same feelings are beginning to be manifested in Springfield by those who have been our friends there.[162] The Whigs are glad of such weapons and make the most of them.— You will probably think that I am a little too officious but I feel impressed with the subject, I feel for my brethren; The tears of widows, the cries of orphans & the moans of the distressed are continually present in my mind And I want to adopt and continue a course which shall be beneficial to us——— but if through the imprudence And Conduct of Isolated individuals 3- 4- or 5 years hence our altars should be thrown down[163] our Homes destroyed, our brethren slain, our wives widows and our Children orphans, your unworthy unworthy brother wishes to lift up his

---

160. Thomas Carlin, a Democrat, served as the governor of Illinois from 1838 to 1842.

161. By spring 1839, church leaders were gathering accounts of the violence against the Saints in Missouri and enumerating the Saints' losses there, in preparation for seeking redress in Washington DC. The Saints directed their petitions for redress to United States president Martin Van Buren, who was a Democrat, as were the majority of the Saints. (Letter to Edward Partridge and the Church, ca. 22 Mar. 1839, p. 397 herein; Minutes, 4–5 May 1839, p. 444 herein; Bill of Damages, 4 June 1839, pp. 492–505 herein.)

162. In May 1839, roughly forty community leaders in Springfield signed a declaration denying the Latter-day Saints permission to use the Christian Church's building in Springfield. One of the signers, Illinois congressman John T. Stuart, later helped publicize the Saints' complaints in Washington DC. (Washington, *They Knew Lincoln,* 199–200; Miller, *Lincoln and His World,* 317–318.)

163. See 1 Kings 19:10.

hands before God[164] and appeal to him and say, thou who knowest all things,[165] knowest that I am innocent in this matter. I am with great respect, Gen⟨t⟩. Yours in the Bonds of Christ.[166]

R[obert] B. Thompson.

Excuse haste &c &c} I have not time to Copy}

(N.B Postcript other side. J. M. [James Mulholland]) [p. 10][167]

P.S. If you do not intend to be in Quincy this week would you favor us with your opinions on this subject &c &c.

R B. T.

Quincy, Monday Morning
13th May 1839.

———— ⌔ ————

Letter to the Editors, 17 May 1839

Source Note

Sidney Rigdon, JS, and Hyrum Smith, Letter, Commerce, Hancock Co., IL, to the editors of the Quincy Whig, *Quincy, Adams Co., IL, 17 May 1839. Featured version copied [between 27 May and 30 Oct. 1839] in JS Letterbook 2, pp. 14–15; handwriting of James Mulholland; JS Collection, CHL. For more information on JS Letterbook 2, see Source Notes for Multiple-Entry Documents, p. 566 herein.*

Historical Introduction

On 17 May 1839, the First Presidency wrote a letter to the editors of the *Quincy Whig,* responding to Lyman Wight's letters recently published in that newspaper. Wight's letters described the violence the Saints experienced in Missouri and expressed disappointment that Missouri senator Thomas Hart Benton and other Democratic officials had not helped the Saints. After the letters were published, Robert B. Thompson wrote to the First Presidency, warning of the dangers Wight's letters posed, particularly to the relationship between church members and Democrats in Illinois.[168] In response, the First Presidency wrote to the *Whig,* stating that Wight did not speak with authority for

---

164. See Genesis 14:22.

165. See John 16:30.

166. See Philemon 1:13.

167. TEXT: The pagination of this copy of the letter does not include the numbers *8* and *9* because Mulholland inserted a loose leaf, which he numbered *8* and *9,* into JS Letterbook 2 using adhesive wafers. For more information on JS Letterbook 2, see Source Notes for Multiple-Entry Documents, p. 566 herein.

168. See Letter from Robert B. Thompson, 13 May 1839, pp. 460–464 herein. Thompson was concerned that Wight's letters would incite political rivalries and jeopardize the warm reception and much-needed aid being provided to church members in Quincy, Illinois. At least one other politically based paper, the *Daily Missouri Republican,* took note of Wight's letter in the *Whig* and contested some of his claims about leaders in Missouri. (See Editorial, *Daily Missouri Republican* [St. Louis], 4 June 1839, [2].)

the church, affirming the church's political neutrality, and explaining that no single political party in Missouri was to blame for the Saints' suffering there. Sidney Rigdon, the first signatory, may have composed this 17 May letter on behalf of the First Presidency. Alternatively, Rigdon or another individual may have inscribed the letter as JS dictated it.

In the days that followed, JS dictated letters to Thompson and Wight, expressing sentiments similar to those found in the letter to the editors.[169] When the 17 May letter from the First Presidency was printed in the *Whig* on 25 May, an editorial preceded the letter. Titled "Difference of Opinion," the editorial acknowledged that Wight did not speak for the church, questioned the First Presidency's conclusion that all political parties were equally responsible for the Saints' persecution, and defended Wight's sentiments, arguing that Democrats shouldered most of the blame for events in Missouri.[170] Soon thereafter, on 1 June, the Democratic *Quincy Argus* republished the First Presidency's letter along with a letter from John P. Greene, Reynolds Cahoon, and Robert B. Thompson, who indicated their agreement with the sentiments in the First Presidency's letter.[171] In response to the First Presidency's letter, Wight wrote a letter that was printed in the 1 June issue of the *Quincy Whig*. Wight stated in the letter, "Having discovered a note in your last number, signed Smith and Rigdon, which stated that our difficulties originated by all Parties, and that they did not wish to make a political question of it, neither do I, but duty prompts me to tell the truth."[172] He then continued to publish articles criticizing Missouri's Democratic leaders.[173]

The original letter from the First Presidency is apparently not extant. James Mulholland copied the text, likely from a retained copy of the letter, into JS Letterbook 2 between 27 May and 30 October 1839.[174] Mulholland's copy is featured here. The versions of the letter published in the *Quincy Whig* on 25 May 1839 and in the *Quincy Argus* on 1 June 1839 are similar to Mulholland's version. The editors of the *Whig* made a few changes to the text before publishing it, standardizing capitalization and punctuation. Significant differences between the versions are noted in annotation.

---

169. See Letter to Robert B. Thompson, 25 May 1839, pp. 477–479 herein; and Letter to Lyman Wight, 27 May 1839, pp. 483–485 herein.

170. "Difference of Opinion," *Quincy (IL) Whig,* 25 May 1839, [1].

171. Sidney Rigdon et al., Commerce, IL, 17 May 1839, Letter to the Editors, *Quincy (IL) Argus,* 1 June 1839, [1]; John P. Greene et al., Letter to the Editors, *Quincy Argus,* 1 June 1839, [2].

172. Lyman Wight, Quincy, IL, 30 May 1839, Letter to the Editors, *Quincy (IL) Whig,* 1 June 1839, [2]. The letter published 1 June was not the first in which Wight expressed remorse for the results of his letters. A week before the First Presidency's letter appeared in the *Whig,* the editors published a note from Wight in which he expressed regret that members of the church had been "assailed in round language" because of the personal opinions he presented in his letters. (Lyman Wight, Letter to the Editors, *Quincy Whig,* 18 May 1839, [2].)

173. See Lyman Wight, "Missouri-ism," *Quincy (IL) Whig,* 18 May 1839, [1]; Lyman Wight, "Missouri-ism, No. II," *Quincy Whig,* 1 June 1839, [1]; Lyman Wight, "Missouri-ism, No. III," *Quincy Whig,* 8 June 1839, [2]; and Lyman Wight, "Missouri-ism, No. IV," *Quincy Whig,* 22 June 1839, [1].

174. Mulholland copied this letter into JS Letterbook 2 after letters dated 27 May 1839, making that the earliest likely copying date. For information on the latest likely copying date, see 248n440 herein.

Document Transcript

Commerce May 17th 1839.

To the Editors of the Quincy Whig

Gentlemen— Some letters in your paper have appeared over the signature of Lyman Wight in relation to our affairs with Missouri.[175]

We consider it is Mr Wright's[176] privilege to express his opinion in relation to political or religious matters, and we profess no authority in the case whatever; but we have thought, and do still think, that it is not doing our cause justice to make a political question of it in any manner whatever. We have not at any time thought that there was any political party as such chargeable with the Missouri [p. 14] barbarities, neither any religious society as such: They were committed by a Mob Composed of all parties regardless of all difference of opinion either political or religious.

The determined stand in this State, and by the people of Quincy in particular made against the lawless outrages of the Missouri Mobbers by all parties in politics And religion have entitled them equally to our thanks and our profoundest regard,[177] And such, Gentlemen, we hope they will always receive from us.—— Favours of this kind ought to be engraven ~~in~~ on the rock to last forever.[178] We wish to say to the public through your paper, that we disclaim any intention of making a political question of our difficulties with Missouri, believing that we are not justified in so doing. We ask the aid of all parties both in politics and religion to have justice done us, And obtain redress.[179] We think, Gentlemen in so saying we have the feelings of our people generally, however individuals may differ, and we wish you to

---

175. See Lyman Wight, Quincy, IL, 1 May 1839, Letter to the Editors, *Quincy (IL) Whig*, 4 May 1839, [2]; and Lyman Wight, Quincy, IL, 7 May 1839, Letter to the Editors, *Quincy Whig*, 11 May 1839, [2].

176. The version of this letter published in the *Quincy Whig* spells Wight's name correctly. (Sidney Rigdon et al., Commerce, IL, 17 May 1839, Letter to the Editors, *Quincy [IL] Whig*, 25 May 1839, [1].)

177. The Quincy Democratic Association, a key public supporter of Latter-day Saint refugees, raised funds and collected supplies to support church members who fled Missouri. (Elias Higbee et al., "To the Quincy Democratic Association," *Quincy [IL] Argus*, 16 Mar. 1839, [1].)

178. See Job 19:24. In the version of this letter published in the *Quincy Whig*, this sentence is set in italics, perhaps reflecting emphasis included in the original letter. (Sidney Rigdon et al., Commerce, IL, 17 May 1839, Letter to the Editors, *Quincy [IL] Whig*, 25 May 1839, [1].)

179. The version of this letter published in the *Quincy Whig* adds "of our grievances." Around 22 March 1839, JS instructed church members to draft affidavits describing their suffering in Missouri, preparatory to seeking redress from the federal government. During the general conference of the church on 4–5 May 1839, Sidney Rigdon was appointed to lead a delegation to Washington DC to present the church's claims. (Sidney Rigdon et al., Commerce, IL, 17 May 1839, Letter to the Editors, *Quincy [IL] Whig*, 25 May 1839, [1]; Letter to Edward Partridge and the Church, ca. 22 Mar. 1839, p. 397 herein; Minutes, 4–5 May 1839, p. 447 herein; see also Historical Introduction to Bill of Damages, 4 June 1839, pp. 492–495 herein.)

consider the letters of Lyman Wight as the feelings And views of an individual but not of the society as such.

We are satisfied that our people as a body disclaim all such sentiments And feel themselves equally bound to both parties in this State, as far as kindness is concerned, and good will, And also believe that all political parties in Missouri are equally guilty.—— Should this note meet the public eye through the medium of your paper it will much oblige your humble servants.

Sidney Rigdon
Joseph Smith Jr
Hyrum Smith.

———— ❧ ————

Letter to William W. Phelps, 22 May 1839

Source Note

JS, Letter, Commerce, Hancock Co., IL, to William W. Phelps, [Far West, Caldwell Co., MO], 22 May 1839. Featured version copied [between 22 May and 30 Oct. 1839], in JS Letterbook 2, p. 7; handwriting of James Mulholland; JS Collection, CHL. For more information on JS Letterbook 2, see Source Notes for Multiple-Entry Documents, p. 566 herein.

Historical Introduction

On 22 May 1839, JS wrote William W. Phelps a letter that reflects the distance that had developed between the men during the previous two years. In September 1837, JS sent church members in Missouri a revelation declaring that Phelps and John Whitmer had "done those things which are not pleasing in my sight" and that unless they repented "they shall be removed out of their places."[180] In early February 1838, Phelps and the other members of the Missouri church presidency were removed from office following accusations that they misused funds and acted contrary to JS's revelations.[181] Phelps refused to repent and was excommunicated on 10 March 1838.[182] When he and other dissenters were ordered to leave Far West, Missouri, Phelps desired to stay, so he agreed to provide restitution to any he had wronged and "to conform to the rules of the church in all things, knowing [he] had a good deal of property in the county."[183] Soon thereafter, Phelps was

---

180. Revelation, 4 Sept. 1837, in *JSP*, D5:433.

181. See Letter from Thomas B. Marsh, 15 Feb. 1838, pp. 22–23 herein.

182. Minute Book 2, 10 Mar. 1838.

183. William W. Phelps, Testimony, Richmond, MO, Nov. 1838, pp. [85], [87], State of Missouri v. JS et al. for Treason and Other Crimes (Mo. 5th Jud. Cir. 1838), in State of Missouri, "Evidence." Those who left in response to threats included Oliver Cowdery, David and John Whitmer, and Lyman Johnson. (See Oliver Cowdery et al., Far West, MO, ca. 17 June 1838, at josephsmithpapers.org; and JS, Journal, 4 July 1838, in *JSP*, J1:276.)

rebaptized, and on 8 July JS dictated a revelation signaling that Phelps should be ordained an elder.[184]

On 31 October 1838, Phelps and others negotiated the surrender of Far West.[185] As with others who dissented, Phelps did not approve of church members' raids in Daviess County, which he considered illegal, and threats against nonconformists. At a court of inquiry in November 1838, he testified against JS and sixty-three other Mormon defendants.[186] He was excommunicated again on 17 March 1839 during a church conference in Quincy, Illinois.[187]

It is unclear how much communication Phelps had with church leaders after this excommunication. In addition to a letter he wrote to JS on 14 April 1839, which is no longer extant,[188] Phelps also wrote to John P. Greene in Quincy on 23 April 1839. In that letter, Phelps expressed interest in helping Joseph Smith Sr. sell his lands in Missouri—something Phelps had apparently promised Hyrum Smith he would assist with.[189] In JS's reply to the 23 April letter, he asked that Phelps not conduct any business on behalf of JS or his family; he also stated that he wished to cut off all further contact with Phelps. The original letter is apparently not extant; the featured version is a copy that James Mulholland inscribed into JS Letterbook 2 between 22 May and 30 October 1839.[190]

Document Transcript

Commerce Illinois May 22nd 1839

Sir

In answer to yours of 23rd April to John P Green[e] we have to say that we shall feel obliged by your not making yourself officious concerning any part of our business in future. We shall be glad if you can make off a living by minding your own affairs, and we desire (so far as you are concerned) to be left to manage yours as well as ~~you~~ we can. We would much rather loose our properties,[191] than be molested by such interference, and as we consider that we

---

184. Edward Partridge, Far West, MO, to Newel K. Whitney, Kirtland, OH, 24 July 1838, in Reynolds Cahoon, Far West, MO, to Newel K. Whitney, Kirtland, OH, 23 July 1838, CHL; Revelation, 8 July 1838–B, p. 183 herein.

185. See Corrill, *Brief History*, 40–41, in *JSP*, H2:182–184; and Samuel D. Lucas, "near Far West," MO, to Lilburn W. Boggs, 2 Nov. 1838, copy, Mormon War Papers, MSA.

186. William W. Phelps, Testimony, Richmond, MO, Nov. 1838, pp. [84]–[96]; Trial Proceedings, Richmond, MO, Nov. 1838, pp. [1]–[2], [34], [61], [70], [100], in State of Missouri, "Evidence."

187. "Extracts of the Minutes of Conferences," *Times and Seasons*, Nov. 1839, 1:15.

188. Mulholland copied the 14 April 1839 letter from Phelps on a loose leaf of paper and attached the page in JS Letterbook 2 using adhesive wafers. Mulholland included the added leaf in his pagination of the letterbook, numbering the pages "8" and "9." At some point, the loose leaf was removed from the letterbook and is apparently no longer extant. (See JS Letterbook 2, p. 384.)

189. William W. Phelps, Far West, MO, to John P. Greene, Quincy, IL, 23 Apr. 1839, in JS Letterbook 2, p. 7.

190. Mulholland began to "write for the Church" on 22 April 1839, and the letter to Phelps was one of the first documents Mulholland inscribed in Letterbook 2. For information on the latest likely copying date, see 248n440 herein.

191. Phelps's letter to Greene explained that a recent flood damaged a dam and that further flooding

have already experienced much over officiousness at your hand, Concerning men and things pertaining to our concerns, we now request once for all, that you will avoid all interference in our business or affairs, from this time henceforth And for ever. Amen.

Joseph Smith Jr.

W[illiam] W. Phelps.

——— ❧ ———

Letter to George W. Harris, 24 May 1839

Source Note

JS, Letter, Commerce, Hancock Co., IL, to George W. Harris, Quincy, Adams Co., IL, 24 May 1839. Featured version copied [between 25 May and 30 Oct. 1839] in JS Letterbook 2, pp. 11–12; handwriting of James Mulholland; JS Collection, CHL. For more information on JS Letterbook 2, see Source Notes for Multiple-Entry Documents, p. 566 herein.

Historical Introduction

On 24 May 1839, JS addressed three letters to close associates, requesting that they move to Commerce, Illinois. One of these letters was directed to Latter-day Saint George W. Harris, whose family provided lodging to JS, his wife Emma Smith, and their children when they arrived in Missouri on 14 March 1838.[192] By the time this letter was written, the church had purchased land in the Commerce area and JS had relocated there, moving into a house formerly owned by Hugh White.[193] In the letter, JS discussed Harris's potential move from Quincy, Illinois, to Commerce. JS also noted he was reserving a piece of land for Harris; his wife, Lucinda Pendleton Harris; and their children. This lot was located across the street from a lot for JS and adjacent to a lot JS was reserving for John and Sarah Kingsley Cleveland.[194]

It is not known when the Harris family moved to Commerce, but George W. Harris was appointed to the high council there in October.[195] Although the original letter is ap-

---

would decrease the value of land owned by Joseph Smith Sr. and others. Therefore, Phelps requested power of attorney in order to sell the property "before it is all lost." (William W. Phelps, Far West, MO, to John P. Greene, Quincy, IL, 23 Apr. 1839, in JS Letterbook 2, p. 7.)

192. The length of time the Smiths stayed with the Harris family is unknown, but the Smiths may have left the home by 3 May. (JS, Journal, Mar.–Sept. 1838, p. 16, in *JSP*, J1:237; Historical Introduction to Receipt from Samuel Musick, 14 July 1838, pp. 204–206 herein.)

193. JS, Journal, 10 May 1839, in *JSP*, J1:338; Woodruff, Journal, 18 May 1839; Alanson Ripley, Statements, ca. Jan. 1845, Historian's Office, JS History Documents, 1839–1860, CHL. As an agent for the church, Alanson Ripley purchased land from White in the Commerce area on 30 April 1839. (See Introduction to Part 4: 24 Apr.–12 Aug. 1839, pp. 431–432 herein.)

194. The Clevelands eventually owned a lot in block 147, located diagonally across the street from JS. (Trustees Land Book A, White Purchase Index, block [147], lot 2; Trustees Land Book B, 250.)

195. Minutes, 5–7 Oct. 1839, *Times and Seasons,* Dec. 1839, 1:30. Harris eventually owned property four blocks northeast of JS's lot. (Trustees Land Book B, 250, 252.)

parently not extant, it was likely dictated to James Mulholland, who was the scribe for another letter JS dictated that day.[196] Mulholland inscribed a copy of the letter to Harris in JS Letterbook 2 sometime between 25 May and 30 October 1839.[197]

Document Transcript

Commerce Ill, May 24th 1839

Dear Sir

I write you to say that I have selected a Town lot for you just across the street from my own,[198] and immediately beside yours one for M[r] [John] Cleveland [p. 11] as to getting the temporary house erected which you desired, I have not been able to find any person willing to take hold of the job, and have thought that perhaps you may meet with some person at Quincy who could take it in hand.

Business goes on with us in quite a lively manner[199] and we hope soon to have the acquisition of Brother [George W.] Harris and family, with other friends to assist us in our arduous, but glorious undertaking. Our families are all well And as far as we have knowledge all things are going on quietly and smoothly.

Yours &c &c

Joseph Smith Jr

M[r] G. W. Harris
    Quincy, Ill.

———— ✌ ————

Letter to John and Sarah Kingsley Cleveland, 24 May 1839

Source Note

JS and Emma Smith, Letter, Commerce, Hancock Co., IL, to John Cleveland and Sarah Kingsley Cleveland, Quincy, Adams Co., IL, 24 May 1839. Featured version copied [between 25 May and 30 Oct. 1839] in JS Letterbook 2, p. 12; handwriting of James Mulholland; JS Collection, CHL. For more information on JS Letterbook 2, see Source Notes for Multiple-Entry Documents, p. 566 herein.

---

196. Letter to Newel K. Whitney, 24 May 1839, pp. 473–475 herein.

197. Mulholland copied this letter into JS Letterbook 2 after a letter dated 25 May 1839, making that the earliest likely copying date for this letter to Harris. For information on the latest likely copying date, see 248n440 herein.

198. The lot JS referenced here was in block 155 in Commerce. (Trustees Land Book B, 263.)

199. JS's journal entry for 20–24 May 1839 notes that he was "at home" and "employed dictating letters and attending to the various business of the Church." (JS, Journal, 20–24 May 1839, in *JSP,* J1:339.)

Historical Introduction

On 24 May 1839, JS and his wife Emma Smith wrote a letter to John and Sarah Kingsley Cleveland, inviting them to move from Quincy, Illinois, to Commerce, Illinois. The Clevelands had generously lodged Emma and the Smith children when they arrived in Quincy in mid-February 1839.[200] In late April, after JS escaped custody in Missouri, he joined his family in the Cleveland home, where the Smiths lived until moving to Commerce on 9–10 May.[201]

In the 24 May letter to the Clevelands, JS and Emma mentioned they had selected lots of land in Commerce for the Clevelands to purchase, with one of the lots located across the street from the Smiths' lot. The previous month, the church had purchased land in the Commerce area; by mid-May, JS was apparently selecting lots for his friends and their families.[202] JS likely chose the specific lots for the Clevelands to show appreciation for the Clevelands' hospitality and friendship.[203] Extant records indicate that the Clevelands purchased the recommended plots of land by 1841; it is unclear whether the family moved to Commerce before that time.[204]

The original letter to the Clevelands, which both JS and Emma apparently signed, is not extant. James Mulholland inscribed a copy in JS Letterbook 2 between 25 May and 30 October 1839.[205]

---

200. Letter from Emma Smith, 7 Mar. 1839, p. 339 herein; Historian's Office, JS History, Draft Notes, 6–7 and 15 Feb. 1839; Letter from Edward Partridge, 5 Mar. 1839, p. 329 herein. Emma Smith wrote in a 7 March 1839 letter to JS that she and their children were living at the Clevelands' home but that she was not sure how long they would stay there. In his memoirs, Joseph Smith III recalled that the Clevelands housed and cared for the Smith family.[a] Sarah Cleveland joined the church by 1836; John Cleveland was never baptized but was sympathetic to the church's doctrine and was generous to church members.[b] The Clevelands were also kind to other Latter-day Saints; while housing Emma Smith and her children, the Clevelands also provided lodging for Phebe Brooks Rigdon (wife of Sidney Rigdon), her children, and Dimick B. Huntington. The Clevelands also helped the rest of Huntington's family move to Illinois.[c] (a. "The Memoirs of President Joseph Smith," *Saints' Herald*, 6 Nov. 1934, 1416. b. Compton, *In Sacred Loneliness*, 275–277; Lee, *Mormonism Unveiled*, 144. c. "The Memoirs of President Joseph Smith," *Saints' Herald*, 6 Nov. 1934, 1416; Dimick Huntington, Reminiscences and Journal, [20]–[21]; Oliver Huntington, "History of Oliver Boardman Huntington," 44–45.)

201. JS, Journal, 22 Apr.–10 May 1839, in *JSP*, J1:336–338; Woodruff, Journal, 3 May 1839.

202. Woodruff, Journal, 18 May 1839; Alanson Ripley, Statements, ca. Jan. 1845, Historian's Office, JS History Documents, 1839–1860, CHL.

203. The same day as writing this letter, JS addressed letters to close associates George W. Harris and Newel K. Whitney. In those letters, he likewise encouraged the men and their families to relocate near the Smiths in Commerce. (See Letter to George W. Harris, 24 May 1839, pp. 469–470 herein; Letter to Newel K. Whitney, 24 May 1839, pp. 473–475 herein; Trustees Land Book A, White Purchase Index, block [147], lot 2; and Trustees Land Book B, 250.)

204. Cleveland and Cleveland, *Genealogy of the Cleveland and Cleaveland Families*, 1:754; Trustees Land Book A, White Purchase Index, block [147], lot 2; Trustees Land Book B, 250, 265.

205. Mulholland copied this letter into JS Letterbook 2 after a letter dated 25 May 1839, making that the earliest likely copying date for this letter to the Clevelands. For information on the latest likely copying date, see 248n440 herein.

Document Transcript

Commerce Ill, 24th May 1839

Dear M^r [John] & M^{rs} [Sarah Kingsley] Cleveland,

We write you in order to redeem our pledge which we would have done before now, but that we have been in the midst of the bustle of business of various kinds ever since our arrival here,[206] we however beg to assure you And your family that we have not forgotten you, but remember you all, as well as the great kindness and friendship which we have experienced at your hands. We have selected a lot for you just across the street from our own beside M^r [George W.] Harris', And in the orchard[207] according to the desire of Sister Cleveland And also one on the river adapted to Mr Clevelands trade.[208] The various business attendant on settling a new place goes on here at present briskly while all around and concerning us goes on quietly and smoothly as far as we have knowledge. It would give us great pleasure to have you all here along with us, which we hope to enjoy in a short time.

I have also remembered Rufus Cleveland to the Surveyor,[209] And am happy to ⟨be⟩ able to say that the land in Ioway far exceeds my expectations, both as to richness of soil, and beauty of locations more so than any part of Missouri which I have seen.[210] We desire to have Mr Cleveland And his brother come up here as soon as convenient and see our situation, when they can judge for themselves, And we shall be happy to see them And give them all information in our power. Father Smith and family Arrived here Yesterday,

---

206. See JS, Journal, 20–24 May 1839, in *JSP*, J1:339.

207. No maps or other records of the Commerce area mention any orchards in the vicinity. The "orchard" referred to here perhaps consisted of a small garden or a few trees.

208. It is unclear what trade is referred to here. Cleveland worked as a farmer and wagon maker but may also have engaged in other mercantile activities. (See Cleveland and Cleveland, *Genealogy of the Cleveland and Cleaveland Families,* 1:754; 1850 U.S. Census, Eden, Schuyler Co., IL, 361[B]; and Gregg, *History of Hancock County, Illinois,* 579–580.)

209. Rufus Cleveland was John Cleveland's brother. The identity of the surveyor mentioned here is unknown. The letter may be referring to a county surveyor or to Alanson Ripley, who surveyed land in Commerce for the church. (Cleveland and Cleveland, *Genealogy of the Cleveland and Cleaveland Families,* 1:310, 757; Alanson Ripley, Statements, ca. Jan. 1845, Historian's Office, JS History Documents, 1839–1860, CHL.)

210. Three days earlier, on 21 May 1839, JS and a small number of other Saints inspected Iowa Territory lands that Isaac Galland was selling. (Woodruff, Journal, 21 May 1839; JS History, vol. C-1, 930–932; see also Lee Co., IA, Land Records, 1836–1961, vol. 1, pp. 507–510, 29 May 1839, microfilm 959,238; and vol. 2, pp. 3–6, 13–16, 26 June 1839, microfilm 959,239, U.S. and Canada Record Collection, FHL.)

his health rather improves.[211] We all join in wishing our sincere respects to each And every of you, And remain your very sincere friends.

Joseph Smith Jr
Emma Smith

Judge Cleveland[212] & Lady
   Quincy Ill. [p. 12]

——— ℰↄ ———

Letter to Newel K. Whitney, 24 May 1839

Source Note

JS, Letter, Commerce, Hancock Co., IL, to Newel K. Whitney, Carrollton, Greene Co., IL, 24 May 1839; handwriting of James Mulholland and unidentified scribe; signature of JS; one page; JS Collection, CHL. Includes address, postal markings, and endorsement.

One leaf measuring 10 × 7⅞ inches (25 × 20 cm). The document was trifolded for mailing. The remnant of a red adhesive wafer used to seal the letter remains on the recto and verso of the leaf. The document has undergone conservation.

The custodial history for this document is unknown. The lack of docketing suggests it was acquired by the Church Historian's Office in the twentieth century. Newel K. Whitney was custodian of a multitude of documents related to church affairs, many of which were passed down to descendants. The earliest known donation by Whitney descendants occurred in 1912.[213] The letter was included in a registry for the JS Collection in 1973.[214]

---

211. Although Joseph Smith Sr. appears to have enjoyed better health in May 1839, he was ill on the journey from Far West, Missouri, and remained sick for much of 1839. It is unclear which members of the extended Smith family were living in Commerce by this time. The party traveling with JS's parents from Far West included Sophronia Smith McCleary, husband William McCleary, and her child from her first marriage, Maria Stoddard; Katharine Smith Salisbury, husband Wilkins Jenkins Salisbury, and children Lucy, Solomon, and Alvin; Don Carlos Smith, wife Agnes Coolbrith Smith, and daughters Agnes and Sophronia; and Lucy Smith. On their arrival in Illinois, this group apparently stayed in Archibald Williams's home in Quincy. Soon thereafter, the families of Samuel and Don Carlos Smith traveled roughly sixty miles northeast to reside for a time on the property of church member George Miller near Macomb, Illinois. (George Miller, St. James, MI, to "Dear Brother," 22 June 1855, in *Northern Islander* [St. James, MI], 9 Aug. 1855, [1]; Lucy Mack Smith, History, 1844–1845, bk. 16, [9]–[12], bk. 17, [5]; Lucy Mack Smith, History, 1845, 36.)

212. Several contemporary sources refer to John Cleveland as a judge. However, according to extant records, he never held that position in Illinois, where he lived the majority of his life. The appellation is perhaps connected to his father, Gardner Cleveland, who may have served as a judge in New York. (See Letter from Emma Smith, 7 Mar. 1839, p. 339 herein; Dimick Huntington, Statement, ca. 1854–1856, Historian's Office, JS History Documents, 1839–1860, CHL; Oliver Huntington, "History of Oliver Boardman Huntington," 44–45; and Cleveland and Cleveland, *Genealogy of the Cleveland and Cleaveland Families,* 1:310, 754.)

213. Orson F. Whitney, Salt Lake City, to Joseph F. Smith, Salt Lake City, 1 Apr. 1912, Whitney Family Documents, CHL.

214. Johnson, *Register of the Joseph Smith Collection,* 8.

Historical Introduction

On 24 May 1839, JS dictated a letter for Newel K. Whitney, encouraging him and his family to relocate to Commerce, Illinois. Whitney and his family had remained in Kirtland, Ohio, after the majority of the Saints departed for Missouri in July 1838. A revelation JS dictated on 8 July directed Whitney, who was previously the church's bishop in Kirtland, to assist in settling the church's and the First Presidency's financial matters in the area and then join the body of the church in Missouri.[215] That fall, Whitney began moving his family to Missouri. En route, the Whitneys learned of the expulsion of church members from that state and, rather than continuing on, temporarily settled in Carrollton, Illinois.[216]

It is uncertain how long the Whitneys remained in Carrollton. The few records indicating where the Whitneys were residing in 1839 do not provide a clear chronology of their movements. On 6 May 1839, JS held a council meeting in Quincy, Illinois, during which church leaders resolved that Whitney should go to Commerce and his family should "be kept" in Quincy among church members.[217] It is unlikely that Whitney had moved his family to Quincy by that time, though Whitney may have traveled there. Sometime in spring 1839, likely after the 6 May council meeting, Whitney and his eldest son traveled to Commerce, where JS instructed Whitney that "as quickly as practicable" he should "join the Saints" there. While Whitney and his son were absent from their family, an anti-Mormon in Carrollton recognized Elizabeth Ann Smith Whitney and the five children who remained with her. Learning that the man intended to incite a mob against the family, Elizabeth Ann and the children fled from the town.[218] They headed for Quincy, meeting Newel K. Whitney and the eldest son on the way.[219] Though it is not clear exactly when the family fled from Carrollton, they likely arrived in Quincy by summer.

On 24 May, the same day JS dictated the featured letter to James Mulholland, JS addressed similar letters to George W. Harris and, in partnership with his wife Emma Smith, to John and Sarah Kingsley Cleveland, encouraging them to move to Commerce and informing them that he had selected land for them.[220] Each of these letters was recorded in JS Letterbook 2 by Mulholland.

JS's letter to Whitney was mailed to Carrollton, likely because JS was unaware of the Whitneys' sudden departure, which may have occurred around the time the letter was sent. A docket on the back of the letter indicates it arrived at the post office in Montrose, Iowa

---

215. See Revelation, 8 July 1838–E, pp. 191–194 herein [D&C 117]; and Letter to William Marks and Newel K. Whitney, 8 July 1838, pp. 194–197 herein.

216. [Elizabeth Ann Smith Whitney], "A Leaf from an Autobiography," *Woman's Exponent,* 15 Nov. 1878, 91.

217. Minutes, 6 May 1839, p. 450 herein.

218. Elizabeth Ann Smith Whitney recalled that "a man named Bellows, who had formerly known my husband in Kirtland, recognized us as the Mormon Bishop's family, and determined to have us mobbed and driven from the town." ([Elizabeth Ann Smith Whitney], "A Leaf from an Autobiography," *Woman's Exponent,* 15 Nov. 1878, 91.)

219. [Elizabeth Ann Smith Whitney], "A Leaf from an Autobiography," *Woman's Exponent,* 15 Nov. 1878, 91.

220. See Letter to George W. Harris, 24 May 1839, pp. 469–470 herein; and Letter to John and Sarah Kingsley Cleveland, 24 May 1839, pp. 470–473 herein.

Territory, on 29 May 1839. Whitney received the letter on 4 June 1839 at an unknown location. Soon after, on 16 June, Whitney arrived in Commerce.[221]

Document Transcript

/[222] Commerce Ill, 24th May 1839

Dear Sir

This is to inform you that Elder Grainger [Oliver Granger] has succeeded in obtaining the house which he had in contemplation when you left here,[223] and as we feel very anxious to have the society of Bishop [Newel K.] Whitney and his family here, we hope that he will make every exertion, consistent with his own business and convenience to come up to us here in ⟨at⟩ Commerce as soon as possibly in his power.

Joseph Smith Jr

Bishop. N. K. Whitney. [p. [1]]

✉

Mr Newel K. Whitney
/[224] Carrollton
Greene Co
Ill.
18¾

/[225] Montrose I.T.
May 29[th.]

⟨Recd 4 June from Jo Smith Jr⟩[226]

———— ☙ ————

---

221. JS, Journal, 16 June 1839, in *JSP,* J1:341. Whitney's family did not join him in Commerce until spring 1840. ([Elizabeth Ann Smith Whitney], "A Leaf from an Autobiography," *Woman's Exponent,* 15 Nov. 1878, 91; Orson F. Whitney, "The Aaronic Priesthood," *Contributor,* Jan. 1885, 130–131.)

222. TEXT: James Mulholland handwriting begins.

223. During a general conference on 4–5 May 1839 in Quincy, Oliver Granger was tasked with returning to Kirtland to direct church affairs and settle financial matters there. On 13–14 May, JS recorded in his journal that he "transacted various business" with Granger. The house mentioned here was perhaps part of the business transactions or a result of them. Granger may have obtained the home for the Whitneys in his capacity as a church agent.[a] However, since the Whitneys did not move to Commerce until spring 1840, this house may have been given to another church member. According to Elizabeth Ann Smith Whitney's later recollection, the family initially rented a home from Hiram Kimball upon relocating to Commerce.[b] (a. Minutes, 4–5 May 1839, p. 444 herein; JS, Journal, 13–14 May 1839, in *JSP,* J1:339. b. [Elizabeth Ann Smith Whitney], "A Leaf from an Autobiography," *Woman's Exponent,* 15 Nov. 1878, 91.)

224. TEXT: James Mulholland handwriting ends; unidentified begins.

225. TEXT: Postage and postal marking in red ink, now faded.

226. TEXT: Endorsement in handwriting of Newel K. Whitney.

Note, circa 24 May 1839

Source Note

JS, Note, Commerce, Hancock Co., IL, ca. 24 May 1839. Featured version copied [between 29 May and 30 Oct. 1839] in JS Letterbook 2, p. 47; handwriting of James Mulholland; JS Collection, CHL. For more information on JS Letterbook 2, see Source Notes for Multiple-Entry Documents, p. 566 herein.

Historical Introduction

On or around 24 May 1839, JS created a note approving recent items of church business in Commerce, Illinois. First, he sanctioned a statement from the Quorum of the Twelve Apostles concerning recent proceedings of the Quorums of the Seventy, which acted under the direction of the Twelve.[227] Consequently, the apostles, who acted under the direction of the First Presidency, brought the proceedings of the seventies to JS for review.

Second, JS indicated his approval of the proposed mission of the apostles to Europe. During the general conference of the church on 4–5 May 1839 and a meeting for leaders on 6 May, the Saints approved resolutions that the apostles, along with some seventies and high priests, should embark on a mission to Europe.[228] Seven of the apostles—Brigham Young, Heber C. Kimball, Orson Pratt, John Taylor, John E. Page, Wilford Woodruff, and George A. Smith—had recently returned from Far West, Missouri, where on 26 April 1839 they met at the temple site, as directed by revelation, in preparation for undertaking their transatlantic mission.[229]

The date of JS's note is uncertain. James Mulholland dated the note 24 May 1839 when he copied it into JS Letterbook 2. JS's journal indicates that JS dictated letters and "attend[ed] to the various business of the Church" from 20 to 24 May, which aligns with Mulholland's dating.[230] However, the journal entry dated 25 May states that JS "met in conference with the twelve, and others of the church."[231] Because the text of the note suggests it was drafted as a result of a council meeting or conference, the note was perhaps created in response to proceedings of the 25 May conference, for which there are no minutes. JS's original note, which is apparently not extant, may have been misdated, or

---

227. Instruction on Priesthood, between ca. 1 Mar. and ca. 4 May 1835, in *JSP*, D4:315 [D&C 107:34].

228. Minutes, 4–5 May 1839, p. 446 herein; Minutes, 6 May 1839, p. 451 herein.

229. Historian's Office, General Church Minutes, 26 Apr. 1839; Letter to Heber C. Kimball and Brigham Young, 16 Jan. 1839, p. 313 herein; see also Revelation, 8 July 1838–A, pp. 179–180 herein [D&C 118:4–5].

230. JS, Journal, 20–24 May 1839, in *JSP*, J1:339.

231. JS, Journal, 25 May 1839, in *JSP*, J1:339. Woodruff indicated that on 25 May, five of the twelve apostles traveled from Montrose, Iowa Territory, to Commerce and "spent the day in Council with Joseph." While no minutes from that council meeting are extant, various sources indicate that the meeting included the reinstatement of William Smith to full fellowship, discussion of the recent publication of Lyman Wight's letters in the *Quincy Whig*, and considerable instruction from JS. (Woodruff, Journal, 24–25 May 1839; Letter to Lyman Wight, 27 May 1839, pp. 483–485 herein; *JSP*, J1:339n25.)

Mulholland may have made an error when he copied the note into the letterbook.[232] Several elements in the text indicate JS authored the note. These elements include the note's reference to "myself"; the inclusion of JS's full name—possibly a signature in the original—after the first approved item; and his initials at the end of the second approved item. It is unknown whether he drafted the original himself or dictated it to a scribe. It appears that Mulholland copied the original note when he inscribed the text in Letterbook 2 between 29 May and 30 October 1839.

Document Transcript

May 24ᵗʰ 1839 Commerce Ill.

Statement made by the Twelve of the proceedings of the Seventies, Satisfactorily to myself and therefore Sanctioned.[233]

Joseph Smith Jr

Presiding Elder of the Church of Jesus Christ of Latter Day Saints.

Also approve of the Twelve going to England &c,[234] J. S.

———— ☙ ————

Letter to Robert B. Thompson, 25 May 1839

Source Note

JS, Hyrum Smith, and Sidney Rigdon, Letter, Commerce, Hancock Co., IL, to Robert B. Thompson, [Quincy, Adams Co., IL], 25 May 1839. Featured version copied [between 25 May and 30 Oct. 1839] in JS Letterbook 2, p. 11; handwriting of James Mulholland; JS Collection, CHL. For more information on JS Letterbook 2, see Source Notes for Multiple-Entry Documents, p. 566 herein.

---

232. Mulholland copied his own 29 May 1839 letter to Edward Partridge on page 15 of JS Letterbook 2, making that the earliest likely copying date for documents he subsequently copied but that had dates preceding 29 May. For information on the latest likely copying date, see 248n440 herein.

233. The Quorums of the Seventy met in council on 12, 14, and 19 May 1839. The proceedings mentioned in this note could have been a report of any or all of these meetings, since members of the Twelve were present at all three. At these meetings, participants discussed regulations for foreign and domestic missions, the necessity for quorum members to keep their families in order, and financial support for the presidents of the Seventy. The apostles may have presented to JS the seventies' 12 May resolutions to select some of their members to accompany the apostles on the mission to Europe and to provide those men with letters of recommendation. (Quorums of the Seventy, "Book of Records," 71–78.)

234. A revelation JS dictated on 8 July 1838 directed the apostles to go on a mission "over the great waters" in 1839. It appears that the elders intended to travel first to England, where Kimball and others preached in 1837, and from there expand their proselytizing to other European countries. Woodruff used "England" and "Europe" interchangeably when referring to the missionaries' destination, and James Mulholland addressed a letter of recommendation to his Irish relatives for "those of the European Mission who shall visit Ireland." JS's journal entry on 7 July describes the 1839 mission broadly as "this most important mission. viz to the nations of the earth, and the Islands of the sea." (Revelation, 8 July 1838–A, pp. 179–180 herein [D&C 118:4]; Woodruff, Journal, 4 May 1839; 8 and 17 June 1839; James Mulholland, Letter of Introduction, Commerce, IL, 10 July 1839, CHL; JS, Journal, 7 July 1839, in *JSP*, J1:345; see also Recommendation for Heber C. Kimball, between 2 and 13 June 1837, in *JSP*, D5:397–401.)

Historical Introduction

On 25 May 1839, JS and his counselors in the First Presidency wrote a letter responding to the 13 May letter of Latter-day Saint Robert B. Thompson, who expressed concern regarding letters that church member Lyman Wight had recently published in the *Quincy Whig*. Wight's letters condemned Missouri Democratic officials, and Thompson feared that Wight's statements would be interpreted as representing the church's position and would therefore have serious repercussions for the Saints.[235] After reading Thompson's letter, the First Presidency wrote a letter to the editors of the *Quincy Whig* on 17 May to clarify the church's position.[236]

On 25 May, JS attended a council meeting with other church leaders and discussed Thompson's concerns. The council members agreed that they did not approve of Wight "making the subject of our sufferings a political question" but that he had written with good intentions. Later in the day, the First Presidency wrote the letter featured here; though addressed to Thompson, JS expected the letter would also be published. The presidency suggested that Thompson use the letter to assuage the concerns of Quincy residents. Two days later, JS dictated a letter to Wight regarding his publications and their potential consequences for the Saints.[237]

The original 25 May letter to Thompson is not extant, but James Mulholland copied it into JS Letterbook 2 between 25 May and 30 October 1839.[238] The letter was also printed in the 15 June 1839 issue of the *Quincy Argus,* with some standardization of capitalization and punctuation and one difference in wording, which is noted in annotation.[239]

Document Transcript

Commerce, Hancock Co Ill 25,<u>th</u> May 1839

Dear Sir

In answer to your's of the 13th Inst. to us concerning the writings of Col, Lyman Wight[240] on the subject of our late sufferings in the State of Missouri; we wish to say that as to A statement of our persecutions being brought before the world as a political question, we entirely disapprove of it.

Having however great confidence in Col, Wight's good intentions And considering it to be the indefeisible right of every free man to hold his own opinion in politics as well as to religion, we will only say that we consider it to

---

235. For more information on Wight's letters and Thompson's concerns, see Historical Introduction to Letter from Robert B. Thompson, 13 May 1839, pp. 459–460 herein.

236. Letter to the Editors, 17 May 1839, pp. 466–467 herein.

237. Letter to Lyman Wight, 27 May 1839, p. 485 herein.

238. Mulholland may have copied the letter the day it was composed. For information on the latest likely copying date, see 248n440 herein.

239. Joseph Smith et al., Commerce, IL, to Robert B. Thompson, [Quincy, IL], 25 May 1839, in *Quincy (IL) Argus,* 15 June 1839, [2].

240. Wight was elected as a colonel when the Caldwell County militia was organized in August 1837. (Lyman Wight, Testimony, Nauvoo, IL, 1 July 1843, p. 10, Nauvoo, IL, Records, CHL.)

be unwise as it is unfair to charge any one party in politics, or Any one sect of religionists with having been our oppressors, since we so well know that our persecutors in the State of Missouri were of every sect, And of all parties both religious and political: And as Brother Wight disclaims having spoken evil of any administration save that of Missouri, we presume that it need not be feared that men of sense will now suppose him wishful to implicate any other.— We consider that in making these remarks we express the sentiments of the Church in general as well as our own individually, and also when we say in conclusion that we feel the fullest confidence, that when the subject of our wrongs has been fully²⁴¹ investigated by the authorities of the United States, we shall receive the most perfect justice at their hands; whilst our unfeeling oppressors shall be brought to condign punishment with the approbation of a free and an enlightened people without respect to sect or party.²⁴²

We desire that you may make whatever use you may think proper of this letter, And remain Your Sincere friends And Brethren.

Joseph Smith Jr
Hyrum Smith
Sidney Rigdon

Elder R[obert] B. Thompson.

———— ☙ ————

Authorization for Stephen Markham, 27 May 1839

Source Note

JS, Authorization for Stephen Markham, Commerce, Hancock Co., IL, 27 May 1839. Featured version copied [between 29 May and 30 Oct. 1839] in JS Letterbook 2, pp. 46–47; handwriting of James Mulholland; JS Collection, CHL. For more information on JS Letterbook 2, see Source Notes for Multiple-Entry Documents, p. 566 herein.

Historical Introduction

On 27 May 1839, JS signed an authorization for Stephen Markham to act as a church agent. In this role, Markham was to solicit funds from Latter-day Saints in order to pay

---

241. Instead of "fully," the *Quincy Argus* version of this letter has "fairly." (Joseph Smith et al., Commerce, IL, to Robert B. Thompson, [Quincy, IL], 25 May 1839, in *Quincy [IL] Argus,* 15 June 1839, [2].)

242. Around 22 March 1839, JS instructed church members to draft affidavits describing their suffering in Missouri, preparatory to seeking redress from the federal government. At the general conference of the church on 4–5 May 1839, Sidney Rigdon was appointed to go to Washington DC and present the church's claims. (Letter to Edward Partridge and the Church, ca. 22 Mar. 1839, p. 397 herein; Minutes, 4–5 May 1839, p. 447 herein; Historical Introduction to Bill of Damages, 4 June 1839, pp. 492–495 herein.)

for the church's recent land purchases. Because the church was not incorporated in Illinois, these purchases were made by individual church leaders and designated church agents. Acting for the church, Alanson Ripley bought 130 acres near Commerce, Illinois, from Hugh White on 30 April.[243] Also on that day, George Robinson made an agreement on behalf of the church to purchase around 59 acres in Illinois from Isaac Galland.[244] Additionally, JS's journal and the minutes of the general conference on 4–5 May indicate that land had been purchased in Iowa Territory; however, what the journal entry and meeting minutes call a purchase apparently consisted of Vinson Knight making arrangements to later purchase land from Galland when it was sold at public auction.[245] The church's earliest deeds for land in Iowa Territory were signed on 29 May when church agent Oliver Granger purchased land from Galland.[246] The authorization featured here indicates that Markham was assigned to visit church members in and around Quincy, Illinois, to obtain funds for the church.[247]

Because the original document is not extant, it is not known who inscribed the original; however, JS likely signed it. Markham presumably took the authorization with him during his fund-raising endeavors. James Mulholland copied the authorization into JS Letterbook 2 sometime between 29 May and 30 October 1839.[248]

Document Transcript

Commerce Hancock Co. Ill.
27th May 1839

To the Church of Jesus Christ of Latter Day Saints
　Greeting
　From our knowledge of the great sacrifices made by the bearer Br Stephen Mark[h]am in behalf of the welfare of us and the Church generally, And from the great trust which we have often times reposed in him, and as often found him trustworthy, not seeking [p. 46] his own aggrandizement, but

---

243. Hancock Co., IL, Bonds and Mortgages, 1840–1904, vol. 1, pp. 31–32, 30 Apr. 1839, microfilm 954,776, U.S. and Canada Record Collection, FHL.

244. Hancock Co., IL, Deed Records, 1817–1917, vol. 12 G, p. 247, 30 Apr. 1839, microfilm 954,195, U.S. and Canada Record Collection, FHL; see also Agreement with George W. Robinson, 30 Apr. 1839, pp. 441–442 herein.

245. Kilbourne, *Strictures, on Dr. I. Galland's Pamphlet*, 9; see also JS, Journal, 24 Apr.–3 May 1839, in *JSP*, J1:336; and 444n70 herein. Knight purchased a substantial amount of land from Galland a month later, on 26 June 1839. (Lee Co., IA, Land Records, 1836–1961, vol. 2, pp. 3–6, 13–16, 26 June 1839, microfilm 959,239, U.S. and Canada Record Collection, FHL.)

246. Minutes, 4–5 May 1839, pp. 444–445 herein; Isaac Galland, Deed to Oliver Granger, 29 May 1839, Hiram Kimball Collection, CHL; Lee Co., IA, Land Records, 1836–1961, vol. 1, pp. 507–510, 29 May 1839, microfilm 959,238, U.S. and Canada Record Collection, FHL.

247. One of these Saints was a "Father Biggler." (See Letter to Father Bigler, 27 May 1839, p. 483 herein.)

248. Mulholland copied his own 29 May 1839 letter to Edward Partridge on page 15 of JS Letterbook 2, making that the earliest likely copying date for documents he subsequently copied but that had dates preceding 29 May. For information on the latest likely copying date, see 248n440 herein.

rather that of the Community:[249] We feel warranted in commissioning him to go forth Amongst the faithful, as our agent to gather up And receive such means in money or otherwise as shall enable ~~him~~ us to meet our engagements which are now about to devolve upon us, in consequence of our purchases here for the Church,[250] and we humbly trust that our brethren generally will enable him to come to our assistance before our credit shall suffer on this account.

Joseph Smith Jr

P. E.[251]

———— ↄ ————

Letter to Father Bigler, 27 May 1839

Source Note

JS and Vinson Knight, Letter, Commerce, Hancock Co., IL, to Father Bigler, Quincy, Adams Co., IL, 27 May 1839. Featured version copied [between 27 May and 30 Oct. 1839] in JS Letterbook 2, p. 13; handwriting of James Mulholland; JS Collection, CHL. For more information on JS Letterbook 2, see Source Notes for Multiple-Entry Documents, p. 566 herein.

Historical Introduction

On 27 May 1839, JS and Vinson Knight wrote a letter addressed to "Father Biggler"—likely a member of the Bigler family in Quincy, Illinois—asking him to loan money to the church. Knight had recently been appointed a bishop, an assignment that involved overseeing church financial matters.[252] JS and Knight were also members of a committee appointed to select and purchase land for the church. The church had recently bought land in Illinois

---

249. In previous months, Markham served on a committee to oversee the safe removal of the Saints from Missouri, and he personally escorted JS's family to Quincy. He also was responsible for obtaining powers of attorney and selling the land of Saints who left Missouri during the exodus. (Far West Committee, Minutes, 29 Jan. 1839; 1 and 21 Feb. 1839; Historian's Office, JS History, Draft Notes, 6–7 and 15 Feb. 1839.)

250. JS was likely referencing the 30 April land transactions the church made in Illinois with Hugh White and Isaac Galland, as well as planned purchases in Iowa Territory. The land purchases on 30 April left the church with large financial obligations, but the due dates for paying these debts are unknown. Alanson Ripley provided White with promissory notes amounting to $5,000, but the bond for the purchase does not indicate when the notes were due. George W. Robinson's agreement with Galland stipulated a payment of $18,000. When the deed for the land was recorded in the Hancock County deed book on 29 June, the payment for the land was listed as $9,000. No schedule of promissory notes was outlined in the 30 April agreement or the 29 June deed. (Hancock Co., IL, Bonds and Mortgages, 1840–1904, vol. 1, pp. 31–32, 30 Apr. 1839, microfilm 954,776; Hancock Co., IL, Deed Records, 1817–1917, vol. 12 G, pp. 247–248, 30 Apr. and 29 June 1839, microfilm 954,195, U.S. and Canada Record Collection, FHL.)

251. Likely an abbreviation for "Presiding Elder." (See Note, ca. 24 May 1839, p. 477 herein.)

252. Minutes, 4–5 May 1839, p. 444 herein.

and was planning to purchase land in Iowa Territory.[253] Struggling to obtain the necessary funds for these purchases, JS and Knight requested that Bigler loan the church five or six hundred dollars.

James Mulholland copied the letter into JS Letterbook 2 sometime between 27 May and 30 October 1839.[254] At the bottom of the letter, Mulholland identified the recipient as "Mr John Biggler, Quincy Ill.," but there is no evidence of a John Biggler residing in Commerce or Quincy at the time of this letter. The 1844 rough draft notes of JS's manuscript history repeat the name John in connection with this 1839 letter and include a margin notation reading "Letter to J. Bigler."[255] When the letter was copied into the manuscript history in spring 1845, scribe Thomas Bullock changed the name to Mark Bigler, suggesting that someone with firsthand knowledge of the original 1839 letter or of the Bigler family informed Bullock that Bigler's forename was Mark.[256]

Mark Bigler was the patriarch of the Bigler family living in Quincy in 1839. The Biglers joined the church in Virginia in 1837, and in March 1838 Mark and Susanna Ogden Bigler's oldest son, Jacob Bigler, traveled to Far West, Missouri, to purchase land. During this trip, he became acquainted with JS. The majority of the Bigler family moved to Far West by fall 1838, but they left in February 1839 to escape the conflict in Missouri, settling soon after in Quincy. Mark Bigler, who remained in Harrison County, Virginia (later West Virginia), to settle business, joined his family in Quincy in spring 1839.[257] Although it is unclear whether JS knew Mark Bigler, Jacob Bigler helped JS and his family move from Quincy to Commerce in May 1839.[258]

JS and Knight likely wrote the letter in JS's home at Commerce, Illinois.[259] The original letter is not extant, and it is unknown who acted as scribe; JS may have dictated the letter to Knight. The letter was given to Stephen Markham, who traveled to Quincy as part of his assignment to collect money from church members.[260] It is not known whether Mark Bigler or another member of the Bigler family loaned funds in response to JS's letter.[261]

---

253. Agreement with George W. Robinson, 30 Apr. 1839, pp. 441–442 herein. During the 4–5 May general conference, church members approved a resolution to purchase land in Iowa Territory, but no extant documents indicate that this purchase had taken place by 27 May. According to extant records, the church's earliest purchase of land there was made by church agent Oliver Granger on 29 May 1839. (Minutes, 4–5 May 1839, p. 445 herein; Lee Co., IA, Land Records, 1836–1961, vol. 1, pp. 507–508, 29 May 1839, microfilm 959,238, U.S. and Canada Record Collection, FHL.)

254. Mulholland may have copied the letter the day it was composed. For information on the latest likely copying date, see 248n440 herein.

255. Historian's Office, JS History, Draft Notes, 27 May 1839.

256. JS History, vol. C-1, 946; Historian's Office, Journal, 3 May 1845, 1:38. For information on the creation of JS's manuscript history, see Historical Introduction to History Drafts, 1838–ca. 1841, in *JSP*, H1:192–203.

257. Bigler, Autobiographical Sketch, 1; Bathsheba Bigler Smith, Autobiography, 2–3, 6.

258. Bigler, Autobiographical Sketch, 1; Lucy Mack Smith, History, 1844–1845, bk. 17, [6].

259. See JS, Journal, 27 May–8 June 1839, in *JSP*, J1:340.

260. See Authorization for Stephen Markham, 27 May 1839, pp. 479–481 herein.

261. Mark Bigler died in Quincy on 23 September 1839. (Bigler, Autobiographical Sketch, 1.)

Document Transcript

Commerce Hancock Co Ill, 27ᵗʰ May 1839

Father Biggler

Dear Sir

We have thought well to write you by Brother Markam [Stephen Markham], on the subject of our purchase of lands here, in order to stir up Your pure mind to a remembrance[262] of the situation in which we have been placed by the act of the councils of the Church having appointed us as a Committee to transact business ⟨here⟩ for the Church. We have as is known to the Church in general; made purchases, And entered into contracts And promised payments of monies for all which we now stand responsible.[263]

Now as money seems to come in too slowly in order that that we may be able to meet our obligations— we have determined to call upon the liberality of Father Biggler through the agency of Bʳ Markam, And request that he will place in his hands for us, the sum of five or six hundred dollars for which he shall have the security of the said Committee, also, through the agency of Bʳ Markham, And the thanks of the Church besides.

Joseph Smith Jr
V[inson] Knight.

Mʳ John Biggler, Quincy Ill.

——— ☙ ———

Letter to Lyman Wight, 27 May 1839

Source Note

JS, Letter, Commerce, Hancock Co., IL, to Lyman Wight, Quincy, Adams Co., IL, 27 May 1839. Featured version copied [between 27 May and 30 Oct. 1839] in JS Letterbook 2, pp. 13–14; handwriting of James Mulholland; JS Collection, CHL. For more information on JS Letterbook 2, see Source Notes for Multiple-Entry Documents, p. 566 herein.

Historical Introduction

On 27 May 1839, JS composed a letter to Lyman Wight regarding two letters Wight had recently published in the *Quincy Whig*. In Wight's letters, he assailed Missouri officials, particularly Democratic politicians, for failing to aid the Latter-day Saints. Robert B. Thompson,

---

262. See 2 Peter 3:1.

263. Because the church was not incorporated in Illinois, church business was conducted in the names of individual church leaders and agents, but these transactions were understood as church business. The recent land purchases were unanimously approved in priesthood councils and a general conference of the church. (See Minutes, 24 Apr. 1839, p. 438 herein; and Minutes, 4–5 May 1839, p. 445 herein.)

who informed JS about Wight's letters, feared that Wight's anti-Democratic sentiments would offend residents of Quincy, Illinois, and harm the church's efforts in seeking federal redress for their losses in Missouri.[264] According to Thompson, church leaders in Quincy had appointed a committee to dissuade Wight from blaming Democrats for the church's problems in Missouri.[265] In response to the situation, on 17 May the First Presidency wrote a letter to the editors of the *Quincy Whig*. In the letter, the First Presidency affirmed Wight's freedom of expression but clarified that Wight spoke for himself, not the church, and that the mistreatment of the Saints in Missouri should not be turned into a political matter.[266]

In this 27 May letter to Wight, JS explained that in response to Thompson's and other church members' concerns, he and other church leaders had discussed Wight's letters in a council meeting and drafted a letter disapproving of Wight's statements. JS wrote that he and other church leaders did "not at all approve" of Wight's course of action, which had made "the subject of our sufferings a political question." Despite this rebuke, JS stressed his belief that Wight had acted with good intentions and was a man of integrity. JS also discussed the potential consequences of Wight's political assertions, and while JS did not ask Wight to stop writing, JS did urge caution and requested that Wight avoid writing as though he spoke for the church. Five days after JS wrote this letter, the *Quincy Whig* published another letter from Wight, in which he referenced the First Presidency's 17 May letter to the editors of the newspaper. Wight stated that he did not "wish to make a political question" of the Missouri troubles, but he dismissed the church leaders' earlier guidance and insisted that he must show who was responsible for the Saints' suffering.[267] The original letter JS sent to Wight is apparently not extant. The text featured here was copied by James Mulholland into JS Letterbook 2 between 27 May and 30 October 1839.[268]

Document Transcript

Commerce Ill, 27th May 1839

Dear Sir

Having last week received a letter from Br. R[obert] B, Thompson concerning your late writings in the Quincy Whig, and understanding thereby that the Church in general at Quincy were rather uneasy concerning these matters we have thought best to consider the matter of course, And accordingly

---

264. See Historical Introduction to Letter from Robert B. Thompson, 13 May 1839, pp. 459–460 herein; see also Lyman Wight, Quincy, IL, 1 May 1839, Letter to the Editors, *Quincy (IL) Whig*, 4 May 1839, [2]; and Lyman Wight, Quincy, IL, 7 May 1839, Letter to the Editors, *Quincy Whig*, 11 May 1839, [2].

265. Letter from Robert B. Thompson, 13 May 1839, pp. 462–464 herein.

266. See Letter to the Editors, 17 May 1839, pp. 466–467 herein; and Letter to Robert B. Thompson, 25 May 1839, pp. 478–479 herein.

267. Lyman Wight, Quincy, IL, 30 May 1839, Letter to the Editors, *Quincy (IL) Whig*, 1 June 1839, [2]; see also Letter to the Editors, 17 May 1839, pp. 466–467 herein.

268. Mulholland may have copied the letter on the day it was written. For information on the latest likely copying date, see 248n440 herein.

being in Council on Saturday last,[269] the subject was introduced, And discussed at some length, when an answer to Br Thompson's letter was agreed to, And sanctioned by the Council, which answer I expect will be published, and of course you will have an opportunity to see it.[270] It will be seen by that letter that we do not [p. 13] at all approve of the course which you have thought proper to take in making the subject of our sufferings a political question, at the same time you will percieve that we there express, what we really feel, that is, a confidence of your good intentions in so doing. And (as I took occasion to state to the Council) knowing your integrity of principle and steadfastness in the cause of Christ, I feel not to exercise even the privilege of Council on the subject save only to request that you will endeavour to bear in mind the importance of the Subject, And how easy it might be to get into ~~difficulty~~ a misunderstanding with the brethren concerning it, And though last, not least that whilst you continue to go upon your own credit, you will also steer clear of making the Church appear as either supporting or opposing you in your politics, lest such a course may have a tendency to bring about persecution on the Church where a little wisdom And caution may avoid it.

I do not know that there is any occasion for my thus cautioning you in this thing, but having done so, I hope it will be well taken And that all things shall eventually be found to work together for the good of the Saints.[271] I should be happy to have you here to dwell amongst us, And am in hopes soon to have that pleasure. I was happy to receive your favour of the 20ᵗʰ Inst[272] And to observe the contents, And beg to say in reply that I Shall attend to what you therein suggest, And shall feel pleasure at all times to answer any request of yours, And attend to them also in the best manner possible. With every possible feeling of love and friendship for an old fellow prisoner,[273] and brother in the Lord. I remain Sir,

Your Sincere Friend
Joseph Smith Jr

Col, Lyman Wight
    Quincy Ill.

—————— ❦ ——————

269. That is, 25 May 1839.

270. Letter to Robert B. Thompson, 25 May 1839, pp. 478–479 herein; see also Joseph Smith et al., Commerce, IL, to Robert B. Thompson, [Quincy, IL], 25 May 1839, in *Quincy (IL) Argus,* 15 June 1839, [2].

271. See Romans 8:28.

272. This 20 May 1839 correspondence from Wight to JS is apparently not extant.

273. Wight was imprisoned with JS in Missouri from November 1838 to April 1839.

Letter from Edward Partridge, 27 May 1839

Source Note

Edward Partridge, Letter, Quincy, Adams Co., IL, to JS, Commerce, Hancock Co., IL, 27 May 1839.
Featured version copied [between 27 May and 30 Oct. 1839] in JS Letterbook 2, p. 15; handwriting of
James Mulholland; JS Collection, CHL. For more information on JS Letterbook 2, see Source Notes for
Multiple-Entry Documents, p. 566 herein.

Historical Introduction

On 27 May 1839, Bishop Edward Partridge, who was living near Quincy, Illinois, sent a
brief letter to JS, who had relocated to Commerce, Illinois, on 10 May.[274] Partridge included
with his message another letter that he was informed was for JS. Because of JS's recent move,
it was possible that mail was still being sent to him in Quincy. On 29 May 1839, James
Mulholland replied to Partridge on JS's behalf, clarifying that JS was not the intended recipient of the forwarded letter.[275] Partridge's original letter to JS is apparently not extant, but
Mulholland copied it into JS Letterbook 2 between 27 May and 30 October 1839.[276]

Document Transcript

Quincy Ill, May 27th 1839

Beloved brother

Sister Bronson[277] has just handed me the enclosed letter which she wished
me to forward to you, She and B[r] H.[278] both say they expect that it is for you—
but if it proves not to be your letter you can rectify the mistake. Br W. C.[279] I
expect is up that way somewhere, I send by B[r] Fisher.[280] Br [George W.] Harris'
daughter[281] is thought to be rather on the mend, but she is yet very low.

---

274. JS and his family left Quincy on 9 May and arrived in Commerce on 10 May. (JS, Journal,
10 May 1839, in *JSP*, J1:338.)

275. See Letter to Edward Partridge, 29 May 1839, p. 487 herein.

276. Mulholland may have copied the letter the day it was composed. For information on the latest
likely copying date, see 248n440 herein.

277. Probably Harriet Gould Brunson. She and her husband, Seymour Brunson, lived in Far West,
Missouri, before relocating to Quincy. Seymour Brunson left Missouri in 1838, after Far West was occupied
by the state militia. Harriet Gould Brunson and their children remained in Far West until early 1839; they
joined Seymour in Quincy in late February or early March. They stayed in Quincy for a few months before
continuing on to Commerce. (Brunson, Autobiography, 11–13; Rich, Autobiography and Journal, 40.)

278. Probably George W. Harris, since the letter later refers to "Br Harris." (See Letter to George W.
Harris, 24 May 1839, p. 470 herein.)

279. Possibly William Cahoon, who left Far West in early February 1839 and temporarily settled in
Quincy. Sometime in mid- to late March, he moved in with a family by the name of Travis and remained
with them until relocating to Montrose, Iowa Territory, in fall 1839. (Cahoon, Autobiography, 46–47.)

280. Possibly Edward Fisher, who served on the high council in Lee County, Iowa Territory, beginning in October 1839. (Minutes, 5 Oct. 1839, in JS Letterbook 2, p. 198.)

281. Probably George W. Harris's stepdaughter Lucinda Wesley Morgan, then age fourteen. JS was
a close friend with the Harris family and lived with them briefly in 1838 in Far West. (Blessing for

Your's in the hope of immortality[282]
E[dward] Partridge

Pres[t] J Smith Jr
    Commerce Ill

———— ✑ ————

Letter to Edward Partridge, 29 May 1839

Source Note

James Mulholland on behalf of JS, Letter, Commerce, Hancock Co., IL, to Edward Partridge, Quincy, Adams Co., IL, 29 May 1839. Featured version copied [between 29 May and 30 Oct. 1839] in JS Letterbook 2, p. 15; handwriting of James Mulholland; JS Collection, CHL. For more information on JS Letterbook 2, see Source Notes for Multiple-Entry Documents, p. 566 herein.

Historical Introduction

On 29 May 1839, James Mulholland wrote to Bishop Edward Partridge on behalf of JS. Two days earlier, Partridge had forwarded a letter to JS that individuals in Quincy believed was intended for JS.[283] In this 29 May letter to Partridge, Mulholland indicated that JS was not the letter's intended recipient. The forwarded letter is apparently not extant, and nothing about its contents is known. The original 29 May letter is also apparently not extant; however, Mulholland copied the letter into JS Letterbook 2 between 29 May and 30 October 1839.[284]

Document Transcript

Commerce Hancock Co Ill, 27 29th May 1839
Bishop [Edward] Partridge—— Dear Sir
I have been directed by President Smith to return you the enclosed letter,[285] as upon examination he has found it ⟨to be⟩ not for the person whom you thought it was for. We are all well, and still remember the brethren at Quincy And elsewhere.— I am Sir Your's &c &c

James Mulholland

M[r] Edw[d] Partridge Quincy Ill. [p. 15]

———— ✑ ————

Lucinda Wesley Morgan, in Patriarchal Blessings, 3:8; Compton, *In Sacred Loneliness*, 45; JS, Journal, Mar.–Sept. 1838, p. 16, in *JSP*, J1:237; Letter to George W. Harris, 24 May 1839, p. 470 herein.)

282. See Alexander Campbell, Bethany, VA, to W. Jones, 26 Mar. 1835, in *Millennial Harbinger* (Bethany, WV), 1 July 1835, 228; "Man," in Buck, *Theological Dictionary*, 257; and New Testament Revision 2, part 2, p. 137 [Joseph Smith Translation, 1 Timothy 6:16].

283. See Letter from Edward Partridge, 27 May 1839, p. 486 herein.

284. Mulholland may have copied the letter the day it was composed. For information on the latest likely copying date, see 248n440 herein.

285. The letter referred to here is apparently not extant.

Discourse, 1 June 1839

Source Note

JS, Discourse, Quincy, Adams Co., IL, 1 June 1839. Featured version copied [ca. 1 June 1839] in Quorums of the Seventy, "Book of Records," pp. 79–80; handwriting of Elias Smith; First Council of the Seventy Records, CHL.

Blank book containing seventy-three leaves measuring about 7½ × 6 inches (19 × 15 cm). The volume was originally bound with at least two sheets of endpaper in the front of the volume and one sheet in the back. Little is known about the original binding; in the mid-twentieth century, the volume was rebound in a machine-sewn tight-back case binding with faux leather cloth. The rebound volume measures 7⅞ × 6⅜ × ⅝ inches (20 × 16 × 2 cm). The front cover of the volume is inscribed with "RECORD OF SEVENTIES | 1835–1843" in gold tooling.

The volume is inscribed in brown ink, and the second sheet of original endpaper is titled "BOOK OF RECORDS" with stylized capital letters. At some point another scribe added "OF SEVenties" in graphite, partially with similarly stylized letters. Elias Smith likely began the volume shortly after being appointed "clerk of the seventies" on 9 April 1837. After copying membership lists and minutes from the journal of Hazen Aldrich that dated back to December 1836,[286] Smith used the volume to record minutes he took; the last entry is dated 2 June 1839. Circa 1841, Smith—then serving as the bishop of the church in Iowa Territory[287]—began using unnumbered pages following the quorum minutes to record the membership of the branch of the church in Nashville, Iowa Territory. On a few other pages, he inscribed dates of significant family events and other information. As evidenced by these later entries, the volume apparently remained in Smith's possession until at least 1843; the volume was included in Church Historian's Office inventories by March 1858.[288]

Historical Introduction

On 1 June 1839, JS delivered a discourse at a meeting of the Quorums of the Seventy in Quincy, Illinois.[289] In addition to the seventies, JS's counselors in the First Presidency and several members of the Quorum of the Twelve Apostles were present. After the meeting was called to order and opened with a prayer, those in attendance relocated to a grove of trees about a mile outside of Quincy because of the large number present.[290] JS then gave a sermon instructing the seventies on what to preach, the nature of stewardship, and the need to account for money donated to them. His statements on donations were likely prompted by the seventies' plans to appoint a committee to care for the poor. Apostle Wilford Woodruff noted in his journal that JS explained that the plan was unnecessary because "bishops were the authorities that God had appointed for that purpose & that

---

286. Quorums of the Seventy, "Book of Records," 9.

287. Elias Smith, Journal, 12 and 18 July 1840.

288. "Historian's Office Inventory G. S. L. City March 19. 1858," [3], Historian's Office, Catalogs and Inventories, 1846–1904, CHL.

289. Although the seventies met at least weekly in Quincy in 1839, the earliest extant minutes of such a meeting are from 5 May 1839. (Quorums of the Seventy, "Book of Records," 65–84.)

290. Quorums of the Seventy, "Book of Records," 1 June 1839, 79. The grove was sometimes referred to as the Presbyterian Camp Ground. One visitor to the grove in June 1839 described it as a shaded "little patch of 'timber'" that comfortably seated 150 people. The grove had a "small rude platform, erected for a pulpit" and contained wood planks and logs for the audience. ("The Mormons," *Greensborough [NC] Patriot*, 17 Sept. 1839, [1].)

they should procede according to that order."[291] Hyrum Smith then addressed the council, echoing JS's directions to the seventies. He asked them to "remember the bishops of the church in their travels, and on all proper occasions when it could with propriety be done, to solicit aid for the poor and send that which they might receive to the Bishop or Bishops to be by them appropriated according to the laws of the church." Those in attendance then reviewed quorum matters, including proselytizing and charges brought against members of the quorums, after which the meeting was adjourned until the next morning.[292]

Two brief accounts of JS's discourse are extant: Woodruff's notes in his journal and the official minutes recorded by Elias Smith, clerk for the Quorums of the Seventy. Smith's account, apparently based on notes taken during the meeting and then inscribed in a record book for the quorums, is featured here. These minutes are somewhat more complete than Woodruff's journal account, which is secondhand and does not mention Hyrum Smith's discourse or any other aspect of the meeting. According to Woodruff's journal, Woodruff was in Montrose, Iowa Territory, some fifty miles from Quincy, on 1 June, the day of the discourse.[293] He copied notes on JS's discourse into his journal after his entry for 17 June and noted that the 1 June meeting was "principly for the benefit of the Seventies."[294]

Document Transcript

President Joseph Smith Jun gave the seventies much instruction about what things they should teach and the manner of communicating the gospel to the children of men and on ma[n]y other subjects especially enjoining it upon the elders to keep and render a just account of all monies put [p. 79] into their hands for any purpose whatever which account should be rendered to the bishop of the church,[295] and spoke at great length on the subject of every steward being just[296] who has any thing entrusted to his charge and be able at all times to give an account ⟨of⟩ his stewardship[297]

——— ‿ ———

291. Woodruff, Journal, 17 June 1839.

292. Quorums of the Seventy, "Book of Records," 1 June 1839, 80–83.

293. Woodruff, Journal, 30 May–1 June 1839.

294. Woodruff, Journal, 17 June 1839.

295. See Revelation, 9 Feb. 1831, in *JSP*, D1:251–252 [D&C 42:32]; and Revelation, 4 Dec. 1831–B, in *JSP*, D2:152–153 [D&C 72:9–23].

296. See Revelation, 20 May 1831, in *JSP*, D1:317 [D&C 51:19].

297. See Revelation, 11 Nov. 1831–A, in *JSP*, D2:131 [D&C 69:5]; and Revelation, 4 Dec. 1831–A, in *JSP*, D2:150 [D&C 72:1–8].

Recommendation for Brigham Young, 3 June 1839

Source Note

Sidney Rigdon, Hyrum Smith, and JS, Recommendation for Brigham Young, Quincy, Adams Co., IL, 3 June 1839. Featured version copied [between 5 and 8 June 1839]; handwriting of James Mulholland; signatures of Sidney Rigdon, Hyrum Smith, and JS; one page; JS Collection, CHL. Includes docket.

Single leaf measuring 9⅞ × 6¾ inches (25 × 17 cm). The recommendation was presumably cut from a larger leaf; the sides are unevenly cut and vary slightly in width. The verso contains a docket in the handwriting of Willard Richards, who was appointed JS's private secretary in December 1842: "June 3ᵈ 1839 | B. Young's Letter. Commendation | from | Joseph Smith Jr. | S.— R.— | H.— S". The docket suggests that the recommendation was filed in JS's papers between 1841, when Brigham Young returned from a mission, and 1854, after which Richards no longer worked in the Church Historian's Office.

Historical Introduction

In early June 1839, the First Presidency issued a recommendation to Brigham Young, who was acting president of the Quorum of the Twelve Apostles, in preparation for his approaching mission to Europe.[298] Almost a year earlier, on 8 July 1838, JS dictated a revelation directing the Quorum of the Twelve Apostles to embark on a mission "over the great waters" and to depart from the temple site in Far West, Missouri, on 26 April 1839.[299] The apostles traveled to Missouri and met in Far West on 26 April as directed, but they did not immediately leave for Europe. Instead, they returned to Quincy and soon afterward moved north with their families to Commerce, Illinois, and to Montrose, Iowa Territory. There they participated in various church councils in preparation for their mission.

Throughout the 1830s, those assigned to represent the church as proselytizing elders received licenses and recommendations from church leaders.[300] No extant documents describe the creation of the recommendations for the apostles' 1839 mission to Europe. The earliest extant recommendation for this mission is a draft that bears the date 3 June 1839.[301] This dating suggests that the draft was created while members of the First Presidency were visiting the Saints in Quincy from around 30 May until 5 June. After the presidency returned to Commerce on 5 June, James Mulholland, who did not travel to Quincy with the presidency, revised the draft recommendation, adding the salutation "To The Saints scattered abroad to the Nations of Europe and to the World.—" and noting when and where

---

298. With the disaffection of Thomas B. Marsh, Young became acting president of the quorum. (See Letter to the Church in Caldwell Co., MO, 16 Dec. 1838, p. 308 herein.)

299. Revelation, 8 July 1838–A, pp. 179–180 herein [D&C 118:4–5].

300. The 1830 "Articles and Covenants" of the church state that each man ordained to a priesthood office was to carry a certificate with him as he traveled, proving that he was authorized to "perform the duty of his calling." In March 1836, church authorities adopted resolutions regarding the granting and recording of licenses. (Articles and Covenants, ca. Apr. 1830, in *JSP*, D1:124 [D&C 20:63–64]; Minutes, *LDS Messenger and Advocate,* Feb. 1836, 2:266–268; Minutes, 3 Mar. 1836, in *JSP*, D5:181–185.)

301. It is unclear who inscribed the draft of the recommendation. Although the draft bears the name of Brigham Young, it likely was not prepared specifically for him but was used as a template, with Young's name as a placeholder. (See Recommendation for Brigham Young, 3 June 1839, Brigham Young Office Files, CHL.)

the recommendation was created.[302] Mulholland incorporated these revisions when he made a copy of the recommendation for Young, featured here, which the members of the First Presidency signed. After creating Young's recommendation, Mulholland created similar recommendations for other members of the Quorum of the Twelve Apostles who were leaving for the European mission.[303] Mulholland dated this copy 3 June, the date of the draft, but likely inscribed the copy between 5 and 8 June.[304]

Document Transcript

To the Saints scatterred abroad to the Nations of Europe and to the World—

Be it known unto you that Elder Brigham Young is fully authourised to preach the gospel of Jesus Christ and his testimony can be relied on he is a man of unexceptionable character and received his authourity and Preisthood from under the hands of the Presiding authourities of the Church of Jesus Christ of Latter Day Saints[305] who were called by actual revelation from God[306] therefore God will bless him and bear record by his power thereby confirming his word[307] and ministry thus testifieth your humble servants.—

Sidney Rigdon
Hyrum Smith
Joseph Smith Jr

Quincy Ill ⎫
June 3$\underline{\text{d}}$, 1839 ⎭

——————— ℰↄ ———————

---

302. JS, Journal, 27 May–8 June 1839, in *JSP,* J1:340; Recommendation for Brigham Young, 3 June 1839, Brigham Young Office Files, CHL.

303. Besides the two copies of Young's recommendation, only three recommendations are extant— ones for Heber C. Kimball, Wilford Woodruff, and George A. Smith. However, similar documents were likely produced for each apostle leaving for the European mission. The recommendations for Kimball, Woodruff, and George A. Smith are in Mulholland's handwriting, suggesting they were not made until after the First Presidency returned to Commerce. These recommendations include the revisions Mulholland made to Young's recommendation, suggesting Mulholland inscribed the copy of Young's recommendation before inscribing the other apostles' recommendations. (Recommendation for Heber C. Kimball, 3 June 1839, Helen Vilate Bourne Fleming, Collection, CHL; Recommendation for Wilford Woodruff, 3 June 1839; Recommendation for George A. Smith, 3 June 1839, JS Collection, CHL.)

304. Wilford Woodruff received his recommendation on 8 June. (Woodruff, Journal, 8 June 1839.)

305. Young was appointed to the Quorum of the Twelve Apostles on 14 February 1835 and ordained by Oliver Cowdery, David Whitmer, and Martin Harris. (Minutes, Discourse, and Blessings, 14–15 Feb. 1835, in *JSP,* D4:228; Kimball, "Journal and Record," 22.)

306. Revelation, June 1829–B, in *JSP,* D1:70, 72 [D&C 18:27].

307. See Mark 16:20.

Bill of Damages, 4 June 1839

Source Note

JS, Bill of Damages, Quincy, Adams Co., IL, 4 June 1839; handwriting of Robert B. Thompson; eight pages; JS Collection, CHL. Includes redactions, use marks, docket, and archival marks.

Two bifolia measuring 12¼ × 7½ inches (31 × 19 cm). The document was folded for transmission and perhaps for filing. At some point, its leaves were numbered in graphite. In the 1840s or early 1850s, church historian Willard Richards docketed the upper left corner of the first leaf: "Joseph's Bill of Damages | vs. Missouri June 4 | 1839".[308] Later, the two bifolia were fastened together with a staple, which was subsequently removed. The document has marked soiling and some separation along the folds. An archival marking—"d 155"—was inscribed in the upper right corner of the first leaf.

Following its completion, the bill of damages was temporarily in the possession of Robert B. Thompson and other church scribes, who in June and July 1839 revised and expanded the document for publication.[309] The bill of damages was possibly among the documents a Latter-day Saint delegation carried to Washington DC in winter 1839–1840. If so, the document was included with the "additional documents" that were in the custody of the Senate Judiciary Committee from 17 February 1840 to circa 24 March 1840, after which the documents were retrieved by the church delegation.[310] The document has probably remained in continuous institutional custody since that time, as indicated by Thomas Bullock's inscription of a copy in JS History, 1838–1856, volume C-1, in 1845 and by the docket and archival marking that were subsequently added to the document.[311]

Historical Introduction

On 4 June 1839, JS prepared a bill of damages describing his suffering and losses during the 1838 conflict in Missouri and his subsequent imprisonment. This document was one of several hundred that Latter-day Saints prepared in an effort to seek redress from the federal government for their losses in Missouri. In March 1839, while JS was imprisoned in the Clay County jail in Liberty, Missouri, he wrote to the Saints in Illinois, instructing them to document "all the facts and suffering and abuses put upon them by the people of this state [Missouri] and also of all the property and amount of damages which they have sustained."[312] JS explained in a letter to his wife Emma Smith that after documenting the damages, church members should "apply to the united states Court."[313] The Saints

---

308. Richards served as church historian from December 1842 until his death in 1854. (JS, Journal, 21 Dec. 1842, in *JSP*, J2:191; Orson Spencer, "Death of Our Beloved Brother Willard Richards," *Deseret News*, 16 Mar. 1854, [2].)

309. The scribes may have added the use marks when preparing the document for publication. (See Historical Introduction to "Extract, from the Private Journal of Joseph Smith Jr.," July 1839, in *JSP*, H1:468.)

310. *Journal of the Senate of the United States*, 17 Feb. 1840, 179; 23 Mar. 1840, 259–260; Elias Higbee, Washington DC, to JS, [Commerce, IL?], 24 Mar. 1840, in JS Letterbook 2, p. 105; see also Bushman, *Rough Stone Rolling*, 391–394.

311. Jessee, "Writing of Joseph Smith's History," 441; JS History, vol. C-1, 948–952. Bullock may have added the use marks after he finished copying the document in 1845, and Richards may have added the docket around the same time. The archival marking was added in the twentieth century.

312. Letter to Edward Partridge and the Church, ca. 22 Mar. 1839, p. 397 herein.

313. Letter to Emma Smith, 21 Mar. 1839, p. 374 herein.

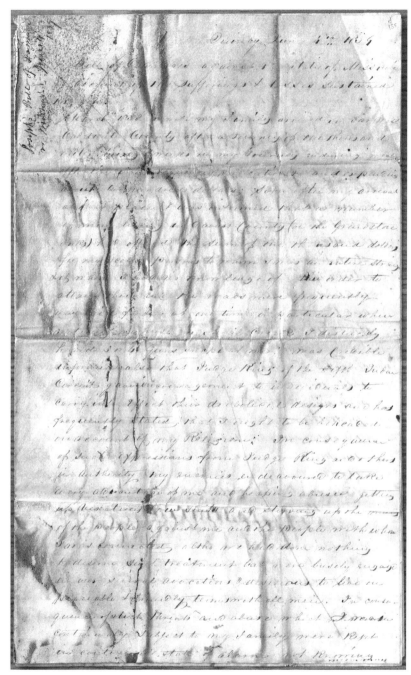

Bill of Damages, 4 June 1839. While imprisoned in Clay County, Missouri, in March 1839, Joseph Smith dictated an epistle encouraging church members to write affidavits documenting their suffering and losses in Missouri. After he escaped to Illinois, Smith worked with scribe Robert B. Thompson to compose an extended account of Smith's own suffering and losses, which he estimated to total $100,000. This bill of damages was presumably among the hundreds of affidavits brought to Washington DC in 1839–1840 as part of the church's efforts to obtain redress from the federal government. Bill of Damages, 4 June 1839, JS Collection, Church History Library, Salt Lake City.

subsequently altered this strategy, deciding in early May to send Sidney Rigdon to Washington DC to present Congress with church members' claims for redress.[314] That month, Latter-day Saints began in earnest to write affidavits, most of which were sworn before local government officials, describing church members' suffering and detailing the loss of life and property.[315]

JS prepared his bill of damages on 4 June 1839 during a visit to church members in Quincy, Illinois.[316] JS's regular scribe, James Mulholland, was not in Quincy at the time, so Robert B. Thompson assisted JS with the document.[317] Thompson had prior experience as a scribe for the church and had recently been assigned to write a history of the church's persecutions in Missouri. This assignment may have contributed to JS's decision to work with Thompson on the bill of damages.[318] The earliest extant version of the manuscript, featured here, is lengthy and fairly polished, suggesting there was at least one earlier draft.

The bill of damages begins with a brief description of JS's travels from Kirtland, Ohio, to Missouri and his experiences in Missouri during summer 1838. The document then focuses on the October 1838 conflict with anti-Mormons in Missouri, including the expulsion of the Latter-day Saints from Carroll County and the Saints' aggressive military operations to defend themselves in Daviess County. In his description of the operations, JS highlighted the participation of state militia leaders—Brigadier Generals Alexander Doniphan and Hiram Parks as well as Colonel George M. Hinkle of the Caldwell County regiment of the state militia—while deemphasizing the actions of the Latter-day Saints' "armies of Israel."[319] The bill also covers the state militia's occupation of Far West, as well as the incarceration of JS and others during winter 1838–1839, including unfair treatment of the prisoners, their attempts to obtain habeas corpus hearings, and their escape to Illinois in April 1839. The document concludes with a list of damages and expenses totaling $100,000. Unlike the vast majority of affidavits that Latter-day Saints made in 1839, JS's bill of damages was not sworn before a government official.

In June and July 1839, Thompson penciled in changes to the text of the bill of damages, apparently in preparation for publication. Since these changes were probably made for a purpose distinct from the intention of the original document, these revisions are not reproduced here. Thompson's changes, as well as other revisions and additions, were included in

---

314. Historical Introduction to Letter from Sidney Rigdon, 10 Apr. 1839, pp. 406–407 herein; Minutes, 4–5 May 1839, p. 447 herein.

315. See, for example, James Newberry, Affidavit, Adams Co., IL, 7 May 1839; Joseph Dudley, Affidavit, Adams Co., IL, 11 May 1839; Phebee Simpson Emmett, Affidavit, Adams Co., IL, 14 May 1839, Mormon Redress Petitions, 1839–1845, CHL.

316. JS, Journal, 27 May–8 June 1839, in *JSP*, J1:340.

317. Mulholland was in Commerce, Illinois, during JS's visit to Quincy in late May and early June 1839. (JS, Journal, 27 May–8 June 1839, in *JSP*, J1:340; Mulholland, Journal, 19 May–8 June 1839.)

318. "Extracts of the Minutes of Conferences," *Times and Seasons,* Nov. 1839, 1:15; Authorization for Almon Babbitt et al., ca. 4 May 1839, p. 448 herein; Snow, Journal, 1838–1841, 50–54.

319. For more information on the "armies of Israel," see Introduction to Part 3: 4 Nov. 1838–16 Apr. 1839, p. 268 herein.

the bill of damages when it was published as "Extract, from the Private Journal of Joseph Smith, Jr." in the July 1839 issue of the church periodical *Times and Seasons*.[320]

Document Transcript

Quincy June 4ᵗʰ 1839

Bill of Damages against the state of Missouri & Account of the sufferings & losses sustained therein.

March ⟨16.ᵗʰ⟩ 1838 I with my Family arrived in Far West Caldwell County after a Journey of one thousand miles being 8 weeks on my Journey[321] enduring great affliction in consequence of persecution &c and expending about two ⟨or 3⟩ hundred dollars.[322] Soon after my arrival at that place I was informed that a number of men living in Daviess County (on the Grindstone Forks) had offered the sum of one thousand dollars for my <u>scalp</u> persons to whom I was an entire strange[r] & of whom I had no knowledge of[323] ~~the~~ In order to attain their end the roads were frequently way laid for &c at one time in particular when watering my horse in Shoal Creek I distinctly heard 3 or 4 Guns snaps at me! was credible informed also that Judge [Austin A.] King of the Fifth Judicia[l] Circuit gave encouragement to individuals to carry into effect their diabolical designs and has frequently stated that I ought to be beheaded on account of my Religion:[324] In consequence of such expressions

320. "Extract, from the Private Journal of Joseph Smith Jr.," *Times and Seasons,* July 1839, 1:2–9, in *JSP,* H1:468–488.

321. JS departed Kirtland on 12 January 1838 and arrived in Far West on 14 March; the distance was approximately eight hundred miles. (JS, Journal, Mar.–Sept. 1838, p. 16, in *JSP,* J1:237; Letter to the Presidency in Kirtland, 29 Mar. 1838, p. 56 herein; JS History, vol. B-1, 831.)

322. By the time JS's party reached Dublin, a small town near Columbus, Ohio, the group was "destitute of money." In Dublin a "brother Tomlinson" sold his farm "and readily delivered to [JS] three hundred dollars which supplied [the group's] wants." JS later recounted that when his group reached Paris, Illinois, tavern keepers refused to admit the Latter-day Saints, relenting only when the traveling party threatened to obtain lodging through force. ("Incidents of Joseph Smith's Journal," ca. 1845, [1], Historian's Office, JS History Documents, 1839–1860, CHL; JS, Journal, 29 Dec. 1842, in *JSP,* J2:196–197.)

323. American colonial governments offered "scalp bounties" as a reward for killing Indians; the practice of scalping opponents continued into the nineteenth century. According to Brigadier General Parks, during the 1838 conflict "Morman scalps" were "much in demand" among anti-Mormons. Grindstone Fork, a small settlement in western Daviess County, served as a headquarters for vigilantes during the conflict. (Axtell and Sturtevant, "Unkindest Cut," 469–472; Taylor, *Civil War of 1812,* 192; Hiram Parks, Carroll Co., MO, to David R. Atchison, Booneville, MO, 7 Oct. 1838, copy, Mormon War Papers, MSA; Berrett, *Sacred Places,* 4:462.)

324. JS was perhaps referring to the legal difficulties stemming from the confrontation between armed Mormon men and Adam Black on 8 August 1838. Latter-day Saint Warner Hoopes recalled that when King issued a warrant to arrest JS and Lyman Wight, "Judge King & others said they ware in hopes that joseph smith jun & Lyman Wight would not be taken & tried acording to law so that they could have the pleasure of taking their scalps." (See Historical Introduction to Affidavit, 5 Sept. 1838, pp. 219–222 herein;

from Judge King and others in authority my enemies endeavoured to take every
advantage of me and heaping abuses getting up vexatious law suits and stirring
up the minds of the people against me and the people with whom I was connected altho we had done nothing to deserve such treatment but were busely
[busily] engagd in our several avocations & desireous to live on peaceable &
Friendly terms with all men. In consequence of such threats and abuse which
was I was continually subject to my Family were Kept in continuall state of
alarm not knowing[325] [p. [1]] what would befall me from day to day, particularly
when I went from home: on the Latter part of Septer 1838 I went to the lower
part of the County of Caldwell for the purpose of laying out selecting a location for a Town when on my Journey I was ment [met] by one of our Friends
with a message from Duet [De Witt] in Carrol[l] County stateing that our
Brethren who had settled in that place were & had for some time been surrounded by a mob who had threatned their lives and had shot several times at
them:[326] Immediately on hearing theis strange Intelligence I made preparations
to start in order if possible to all[a]y the feelings of oppositions if not to make
arrangements with those individuals of whom we had made purchases and to
whom I was responsible and holding for the part of the purchase money:[327] I
arrived there on the [*blank*] day[328] and found the accounts which I heard ⟨were⟩
correct: Our people were surrounded by a mob their provisions nearly
exhausted[329] messages were immedediately sent to the Governor requesting

and Warner Hoopes, Affidavit, Pike Co., IL, 14 Jan. 1840, Record Group 233, Records of the U.S. House of
Representatives, National Archives, Washington DC.)

325. TEXT: Below "knowing," Robert B. Thompson inserted the following letters: "mormmnes". The
letters, which are in the same ink as the rest of the document and were therefore probably inscribed con-
temporaneously, apparently do not pertain to the sentence above the insertion.

326. In June 1838, church leaders purchased nearly half of the lots in De Witt and encouraged
church members to settle there. The Latter-day Saint population in the area increased quickly. By late
July, a Carroll County committee decided that if the Saints would not leave voluntarily, they would be
expelled from the county. Although the acceleration of hostilities in Daviess County in August and
September temporarily diverted the attention of anti-Mormons in Carroll County, by late September
the seventy to eighty Latter-day Saint families living in De Witt were again threatened with expulsion.
Vigilantes gave church members in De Witt until 1 October to leave the county and "threatened if not
gone by that time to exterminate them without regard to age or sex and destroy their chattels, by
throwing them in the river." (Murdock, Journal, 23 June 1838, 95; "The Mormons in Carroll County,"
Missouri Republican [St. Louis], 18 Aug. 1838, [2]; Citizens of De Witt, MO, to Lilburn W. Boggs,
Jefferson City, MO, 22 Sept. 1838, copy, Mormon War Papers, MSA; see also Baugh, "Call to Arms,"
143–163; and Perkins, "Prelude to Expulsion," 266.)

327. The Saints purchased their De Witt property from land speculators David Thomas and Henry
Root with a $500 note endorsed by Bishop Edward Partridge. (See Letter from David Thomas, 31 Mar.
1838, pp. 65–66 herein; and Murdock, Journal, 23 June 1838, 95.)

328. JS departed Far West for De Witt on 5 October 1838 and arrived the following day with thirty
to forty men. (JS, Journal, 5 Oct. 1838, in *JSP*, J1:330; Rockwood, Journal, 14 Oct. 1838.)

329. After it became apparent that the Latter-day Saints would not leave De Witt, Missouri, by the

protection but instead of lending any assistance to the oppressed he stated that the Quarrel was between the Mormons and the mob and that they must fight it out:[330] Being now almost entirely destitute of provisions and having suffered great distress and some of the Brethren having died in consequence of their privations & sufferings and I had then the pain of beholding some of my Fellow creatures perish in a strange land from the cruelty of ~~of~~ a mobs— seeing no prospect of relief the Brethren agreed to leave that place and seek a shelter elsewere; after having their houses burnt down their cattle driven away and much of their property destroyed[331]——— [p. [2]]

Judge King was also petitioned to afford us some assistance: He sent a company ~~off~~ of about 100 men but instead of affording us any relief we were told by General [Hiram] Parks that he could afford none in consequence of the greater part of his Company under their officers Capt. Sam[l] Bogard [Bogart] having mutinized[332] about 70 waggons left Duet for Caldwell and duri[n]g their Journey were continually insulted by the mob who threatened to destroy us: in our Journey several of our Friends died and had to be interred withou[t] a Coffin & under such Circumstances which were extreemly distressing:[333] Immediately on my arrival ~~of~~ at Caldwell ~~we are~~ I was informed ~~by~~ that General Donaphan [Alexander Doniphan] from Clay County that a company of about 800 were marching towards a settlement of our Brethren in Daviess County and he advised that ~~thee~~ we should immediately go to protect

---

appointed day—1 October 1838—as many as three hundred vigilantes from Carroll and other Missouri counties besieged the settlement. Latter-day Saint John Murdock noted that the vigilantes "continued to harrass us day & night by shooting at our people in the woods in cornfields in town & into our camps." (Hiram Parks, Carroll Co., MO, to David R. Atchison, Booneville, MO, 7 Oct. 1838, copy, Mormon War Papers, MSA; Murdock, Journal, 1 Oct. 1838, 100.)

330. See Corrill, *Brief History*, 36, in *JSP*, H2:176; and Sidney Rigdon, Testimony, Nauvoo, IL, 1 July 1843, p. [3], Nauvoo, IL, Records, CHL.

331. Rigdon later noted that the Latter-day Saints in De Witt were "suffering for food and every comfort of life, in consequence of which there was much sickness and many died." John Murdock recorded that the Saints agreed to leave De Witt on 10 October 1838. (Sidney Rigdon, Testimony, Nauvoo, IL, 1 July 1843, p. [3], Nauvoo, IL, Records, CHL; John Murdock, Lima, IL, to Sister Crocker et al., 21 July 1839, CHL; see also Murdock, Journal, Oct. 1838, 102.)

332. The Latter-day Saints in De Witt petitioned King for assistance in early October 1838. Parks apparently learned of the Saints' plight independently on 3 October; the following day, he led two militia companies, one of which was commanded by Captain Bogart, to De Witt. Parks found the anti-Mormon vigilantes were waiting for additional reinforcements before launching a direct attack on church members. He told church member John Murdock that Parks "could do nothing because of the mob spirit in his men." (Murdock, Journal, Oct. 1838, 102; David R. Atchison, Booneville, MO, to Lilburn W. Boggs, Jefferson City, MO, 5 Oct. 1838, copy; Hiram Parks, Carroll Co., MO, to David R. Atchison, Booneville, MO, 7 Oct. 1838, copy, Mormon War Papers, MSA; John Murdock, Lima, IL, to Sister Crocker et al., 21 July 1839, CHL.)

333. See Murdock, Journal, 13–15 Oct. 1838, 102–103; see also Sidney Rigdon, Testimony, Nauvoo, IL, 1 July 1843, p. [5], Nauvoo, IL, Records, CHL.

our Brethren in Daviess County[334] (in what he called Whites town[335]) untill he should get the malitia to put them down ~~immediately a company~~ a company of malitia ⟨to the number of sixty⟩ who were ~~going~~ on their rout to that place he ordered back beleiving ⟨as he said⟩ that they were not to be depended upon and to use his own language were "damned" rotten hearted"[336] Colonel ~~Hinckle~~ ~~aggreeably~~ aggreable to the advise of General Doniphan[337] a number of our Brethren volunteered to go to Daviess to render what assistance they could[338] ⟨My labors having been principally expended in Davies county w[h]ere

---

334. On 13 October 1838, Bogart stated that "the Daviess & Livingston C° people and many from others, are on their way to Daviess County with one field piece, with the determination to prevent there [the Latter-day Saints] settling in that County at all hazards." The anti-Mormon vigilantes also evidently intended to expel church members already living in Daviess County. JS and other church leaders may have learned of the vigilantes' plans before the church leaders' return to Far West on 14 October 1838. Doniphan, who apparently arrived in Far West on 15 October, may have confirmed reports of the vigilantes' plans or may have informed JS of the size of the force. As John Corrill recalled, it was "believed by all . . . that the next day there would be eight hundred [vigilantes] to commence operations" in Daviess County. (Samuel Bogart, Elkhorn, MO, to Lilburn W. Boggs, 13 Oct. 1838, copy, Mormon War Papers, MSA; Corrill, *Brief History*, 36–38, in *JSP*, H2:176–178; Sidney Rigdon, JS, et al., Petition Draft ["To the Publick"], pp. 28[a]–[28b].)

335. Likely Adam-ondi-Ahman, the principal Latter-day Saint settlement in Daviess County. Doniphan perhaps called the settlement "Whites town" because Lyman Wight was one of the first church members to move there, his home served as the headquarters for surveying and platting the town, and he was considered the town's leader before Adam-ondi-Ahman was organized as a stake on 28 June 1838. At that time, Wight was appointed a counselor in the presidency of the stake. (JS, Journal, 18 May–1 June 1838, in *JSP*, J1:270–275; Minutes, 28 June 1838, p. 166 herein; see also Berrett, *Sacred Places*, 4:399–402, 416, 438–444.)

336. The company was probably composed of Colonel William Dunn's state militia troops, whom Parks sent to Daviess County. Parks confirmed that Doniphan disbanded Dunn's men. (Hiram Parks, Richmond, MO, to David R. Atchison, 21 Oct. 1838, copy, Mormon War Papers, MSA.)

337. Rigdon recalled that Doniphan advised church leaders in Caldwell County to go to Daviess County "in very small parties, without arms, so that no legal advantage could be taken of them." Rigdon explained that "no considerable number of men armed can pass out of one county into or through another county" without authorization from the civil authorities of the other county. (Sidney Rigdon, Testimony, Nauvoo, IL, 1 July 1843, pp. [8], [9], Nauvoo, IL, Records, CHL.)

338. On 16 October 1838, approximately 300 men from Caldwell County, including JS, arrived in Daviess County. Although Hinkle was colonel of the Caldwell County regiment of the state militia and a respected military leader among the Saints, it is unclear what role he played in the Mormons' October military operations in Daviess County, as Latter-day Saints David Patten, Lyman Wight, and Seymour Brunson were the principal field commanders during the targeted strikes on Gallatin, Millport, and Grindstone Fork. In the November 1838 hearing, following Hinkle's disaffection from the church, he claimed that he "went down [to Daviess County] without being attached to any company, or without having any command," and that he openly opposed the burning of buildings and the confiscation of non-Mormon goods. Despite subsequently claiming that he opposed these tactics, Hinkle reportedly accepted the position of commander of infantry in the Caldwell County division of the "armies of Israel" on 24 October in Far West. (John Smith, Journal, 16 Oct. 1838; Foote, Autobiography, 21 Oct. 1838, 30; George M. Hinkle, Testimony, Richmond, MO, Nov. 1838, pp. [40]–[41]; Sampson Avard, Testimony, Richmond, MO, Nov. 1838, [6]; George Walters, Testimony,

I intended to take up my residence & having a house in Building & having of other prosperty[339] there I hastened up to that place[340] &⟩ While I was there a number of the Brethrens Houses were burnt and depredations were continually committed such as driving off Horses, Cattle Sheep &c &c Being deprived of shelter & ⟨others⟩ having no safety in their Houses which were scattering and ~~continualy~~ ⟨being alarmed⟩ at the approach of the mobs: they had to flock togeth[er][341] ~~and~~ their sufferings were ~~under~~ very great in consequence of their defenceless situation being exposed to the [p. [3]] weather which was extreemly cold a large Snow Storm having just fallen:[342] In this state of affairs General Parks arrived at Daviess[343] and was at the House of Colonel [Lyman] Wight went [when] the intelligence was brought that the mob were burning Houses &c and also when women and childrren were flocking into the village for safety: Colonel Wight ⟨who held a commission 59th Regiment under his command⟩[344] asked him what steps should be taken He told him that he must immediately call out his men and go and put them down: Immediately preparations were made to raise a force to Quell the mob, and ~~unto~~ and ascertaining ~~what~~ that we were determined to bear such treatment no longer, but to make a vigourous effort to subdue them and likewise being informed of the orders of General Parks, broke up their encampment and fled

---

Richmond, MO, Nov. 1838, pp. [37]–[38], State of Missouri v. JS et al. for Treason and Other Crimes [Mo. 5th Jud. Cir. 1838], in State of Missouri, "Evidence"; for more information on the Latter-day Saint raids in Daviess County in October 1838, see the Introduction to Part 3: 4 Nov. 1838–16 Apr. 1839, pp. 266–269 herein.)

339. TEXT: Possibly "prospects".

340. A church-sponsored land survey in May 1838 allocated JS 320 acres in Adam-ondi-Ahman, as well as other land in Daviess County, in anticipation of obtaining legal title through preemption. According to William Swartzell, who was then living in Adam-ondi-Ahman, on 26 July 1838 Latter-day Saint men were "employed in getting out logs for brother Joseph Smith's house." (JS, Journal, 19 and 21 May 1838, in *JSP*, J1:270–271; "Record Book A," in Sherwood, Record Book, CHL; Berrett, *Sacred Places*, 4:456–458; Walker, "Mormon Land Rights," 14–20, 29–31; Swartzell, *Mormonism Exposed*, 25.)

341. See Elisha H. Groves, Affidavit, Columbus, IL, 6 May 1839; Solomon Chamberlin, Statement, no date; Urban Stewart, Affidavit, Montrose, Iowa Territory, 7 Jan. 1840, Mormon Redress Petitions, 1839–1845, CHL; and Hyrum Smith, Testimony, Nauvoo, IL, 1 July 1843, p. 6, Nauvoo, IL, Records, CHL.

342. About six inches of snow fell on 17 October 1838. (Foote, Autobiography, 21 Oct. 1838, 30.)

343. According to Park's account, he arrived on 18 October 1838, after the Latter-day Saints' military operations commenced. (Hiram Parks, Richmond, MO, to David R. Atchison, 21 Oct. 1838, copy, Mormon War Papers, MSA.)

344. Wight was commissioned as a colonel of the Caldwell County regiment of the state militia when he resided in the county in 1837. Wight's commission did not give him authority in the Daviess County regiment of the state militia, which was commanded by Colonel William Peniston, an antagonist of the Latter-day Saints. (Lyman Wight, Mountain Valley, TX, to Wilford Woodruff, [Salt Lake City], 24 Aug. 1857, p. 5, Historian's Office, Histories of the Twelve, 1856–1858, 1861, CHL; William Peniston, Daviess Co., MO, to Lilburn W. Boggs, 21 Oct. 1838, copy, Mormon War Papers, MSA; Baugh, "Call to Arms," 385.)

some of the inhabitants in the immediate neighbourhood who seeing no prospect of driving us by force resorted to stratagem and actually set fire to their own Houses after having removed their property and effects[345] and then sent sent information to Governor stating that our Brethren were committing depredations and destroying their property burning houses &c &[346]

On the retreat of the mob from Daviess County I return home to Caldwell on my arrival there I understood that a mob had commenced hostilities in the Borders of Caldwell had taken some of our People prisoners burnt some houses and had done considerable damage— Immediately Captain [David W.] Patten under who was ordered out by ⟨leutenant⟩ Colonel Hinckle [George M. Hinkle] to go against them[347] and about day light next morni[n]g came up with them: upon the approach of our people they fired upon them and after discharging their pieces fled with great precipitation. In this affray Capt Patten fell a victim to that spirit of mobocracy which has prevailed to ⟨Donophan " " 1st " " " "⟩

⟨Parks Brigadier General 2nd Brigade 3 Division of the Missouri Malitia⟩[348] [p. [4]] such an extent: along with 3 2 others other were sever[e]ly wounded:

---

345. Scholars of the 1838 conflict estimate that between twenty-five and fifty Daviess County buildings were burned, mostly by Latter-day Saint vigilantes. Warren Foote, a sympathetic non-Mormon who later joined the church, recounted that in response to the Saints' military operations in Daviess County, some Missourians "set their own houses afire, and ran into the adjoining counties, and declared that the 'Mormons' had driven them out, and burned their houses &c. This they done to excite the people against the Mormons, in order to get them to join them in their persecutions." (Baugh, "Call to Arms," 215; LeSueur, *1838 Mormon War in Missouri,* 124; Foote, Autobiography, 21 Oct. 1838, 30–31; see also Hyrum Smith, Testimony, Nauvoo, IL, 1 July 1843, p. 7, Nauvoo, IL, Records, CHL; Corrill, *Brief History,* 38, in *JSP,* H2:179; and Pulsipher, "Zerah Pu[l]siphers History," 8.)

346. On 21 October 1838, Daviess County sheriff William Morgan and Colonel William Peniston wrote descriptions of the recent Latter-day Saint military operations. The following day, other Daviess County residents dictated affidavits to Justice of the Peace Adam Black, who forwarded the statements to Governor Lilburn W. Boggs. (William Morgan, Affidavit, Daviess Co., MO, 21 Oct. 1838, copy; William Peniston, Daviess Co., MO, to Lilburn W. Boggs, 21 Oct. 1838, copy; Thomas Martin, Affidavit, 22 Oct. 1838, copy; James Stone, Affidavit, 22 Oct. 1838, copy; Samuel Venable, Affidavit, 22 Oct. 1838, copy; Jonathan J. Dryden, Affidavit, 22 Oct. 1838, copy, Mormon War Papers, MSA.)

347. On 23 October 1838, Ray County militia commander Captain Bogart received authorization to "range the line" between Ray County and Caldwell County. Bogart evidently exceeded his authorization by entering Caldwell County, harassing Latter-day Saints, and taking Mormon prisoners. According to Parley P. Pratt and Rigdon, Hinkle was not present when news of Bogart's actions reached Far West. Hinkle claimed that he was at his home at the time and was unaware of these developments until the following morning. Pratt recounted that Captain John Killian, who commanded the Far West men in Hinkle's absence, ordered Patten and his men to go to Crooked River. Apparently Patten also led the company at Crooked River in his capacity as a cavalry commander in the church's "war department." (See Introduction to Part 3: 4 Nov. 1838–16 Apr. 1839, p. 269 herein; Pratt, *History of the Late Persecution,* 33; Sidney Rigdon, Testimony, Nauvoo, IL, 1 July 1843, pp. [12]–[13], Nauvoo, IL, Records, CHL; and George M. Hinkle, Testimony, Richmond, MO, Nov. 1838, pp. [40]–[41], in State of Missouri, "Evidence.")

348. TEXT: The line of text identifying Parks's office, brigade, and division was apparently inserted

On the day after this affray Capten Patten sent for me to pray for him which I request I complied with[349] & then returned to my home: There continued to be great commotion in the County caused by the conduct of the mob who were continually bur[ni]ng Houses Driving off Horses Cattle &c and taking prisoners & threatning death to all the <u>mormons</u> amongst the Cattle <u>driven</u> off <u>were</u> <u>Two</u> <u>cows</u> of mine:[350] ~~about~~ on the 28th of October a large company of malitia— were seen approaching to Far West and encampd about 1 mile from the Town— The next day I was waited upon by Colonel Hinckle who stated that the officers of the malitia requested an interview with us in order to come to some amicable settlement of the difficulties which then subsisted they the officers not wishing under the present circumstances to carry into effect the exterminating orders they had received:[351] I immediately complied with the request and in company with Messrs. [Sidney] Rigdon [George W.] Robinson [Lyman] Wight [Parley P.] Pratt & ~~Am[a]sa Lyman & Hiran [Hyrum] Smith~~ my ~~Brother~~ proceeded to meet the officers of the malitia: But instead of treating us with with respect and as persons desiring ~~to treat for peace~~ ⟨accommodate matters⟩. we were to our astonishment we were delivered up as prisoners of war and taken into the camp as such—

It would be in vain for me to give any idea of the Scence [scene] which now presented itself in the camp The Hideous yells of more than a thousand infuriated beings whose desires was to wreck [wreak] their vengance upon me and the rest of my Friends was truly awfull and enough to appal the stoutest heart. In the eve[n]ing we had to lye down on the cold ground surrounded by a Strong guard[352] we petitioned the officers to know [p. [5]] ⟨why⟩

---

before the line of text identifying Doniphan's office, brigade, and division; the ditto marks refer to the text below.

349. Latter-day Saint Morris Phelps reported that JS "went to the wounded and pronounced a blessing on them & prayed for them to be healed & saved." (Morris Phelps, Testimony, Richmond, MO, Nov. 1838, p. [28]; Sampson Avard, Testimony, Richmond, MO, Nov. 1838, pp. [21]–[22], in State of Missouri, "Evidence.")

350. Hyrum Smith testified in court proceedings in 1843 that anti-Mormon vigilantes under Cornelius Gilliam harassed Latter-day Saints in Caldwell County throughout September and October 1838. In addition, Smith stated that militia troops under the command of Major General Samuel D. Lucas entered the county in late October and physically assaulted several Latter-day Saints. (Hyrum Smith, Testimony, Nauvoo, IL, 1 July 1843, pp. 9–10, Nauvoo, IL, Records, CHL.)

351. For more information on Governor Boggs's expulsion order issued on 27 October 1838 and Major General Lucas's negotiations with Hinkle, see Introduction to Part 3: 4 Nov. 1838–16 Apr. 1839, pp. 270–271 herein.

352. "This proved to be a dismal night on account of the rain," Wight recalled. "The hideous screeches and screaming of this wretched, murderous band would have made a perfect dead silence with the damned in hell." (Lyman Wight, Journal, in *History of the Reorganized Church*, 2:260.)

we were thus treated but they utterly refused to hold any conversation with us: The next day ~~a~~ they held a Court Martial upon us and sentenced me with the rest of the prisoners to be shot: which sentence was to be carried into effect on Friday morning in the public Square as they say an Ensample to the rest of the members⟨: but through the kind providence of God their murderous sentence was not carried into Execution⟩[353]

The Malitia then went ~~and saluted~~ to my house and drove my Family out of Doors under sanction of General [John B.] Clark and carried away all my property[354] Having oppertunity of speaking to General [Moses] Wilson and on asking him the cause of such strange proceedings told him that I was a Democrat had allways being a supporter of the Constitution he answered "I know that and that is the reason why I want to kill you or have you killed:[″][355] ~~They~~ We were led into Public Square and after considerable Entreaty we were permitted to see our Family's being attended with a strong guard. I found my Family in Tears expect that they had carried into Effect their sentences:[356] they clung to my garments with weeping requesting to hav an ⟨private⟩ interview with my wife & in an ajoining room but was refused when taking my departure from ~~me~~ my Family it was ~~an~~ almost ~~more~~ to painful for me, my child clung to me and were thrust away at the point of the swords of the soldiery—[357] We were then removed to Jackson County under the care of general Wilson and during our stay in there we had to sleep on the floor with nothing but a ~~a~~ mantle for our coverings and a stick of

---

353. For more information on the court-martial, see Introduction to Part 3: 4 Nov. 1838–16 Apr. 1839, p. 271 herein.

354. For more information on the Missouri militia's occupation of Far West and the treatment of the Smith family and property, see Introduction to Part 3: 4 Nov. 1838–16 Apr. 1839, pp. 271–272 herein; Historical Introduction to Declaration to the Clay County Circuit Court, ca. 6 Mar. 1839, pp. 335–337 herein; and 348n444 herein.

355. Most Latter-day Saints, including JS, supported the Democratic Party in the 1838 election. Wight stated that Wilson was a Democrat. (JS, Journal, 10 May 1838, in *JSP*, J1:268; Lyman Wight, Quincy, IL, 30 May 1839, Letter to the Editors, *Quincy [IL] Whig*, 1 June 1839, [2]; see also LeSueur, "Mixing Politics with Religion," 184–208.)

356. Lucy Mack Smith, JS's mother, recalled that after JS was arrested, she and Joseph Smith Sr. heard several gunshots and concluded that JS had been murdered. (Lucy Mack Smith, History, 1844–1845, bk. 16, [2].)

357. Joseph Smith III remembered that when JS "was brought to the house by an armed guard I ran out of the gate to greet him, but was roughly pushed away from his side by a sword in the hand of the guard and not allowed to go near him. My mother, also, was not permitted to approach him and had to receive his farewell by word of lip only." ("The Memoirs of President Joseph Smith," *Saints' Herald,* 6 Nov. 1934, 1414; see also Letter to Edward Partridge and the Church, ca. 22 Mar. 1839, p. 395 herein.)

wood for our pillow and had to pay for our own <u>board</u>:[358] While we were in Jackson General Clark with his troops arrived in Caldwell and sent an order for our return[359]—— [p. [6]] holding out the inducement that we were to be reinstated to our former priviledges: but instead of being taken to Caldwell we were taken to Richmond w[h]ere we immured in Prison and bound in— Chains.[360] After we were thus situated we were under the charge of Colonel [Sterling] Price of Chariton County who suffered us to be abused in every manner[361] which the people thought propper: our situation at this time was truly painful: we were taken before the Court of inquiry but in consequence of the proceedi[n]g of the mob and there threats we were not able to get such witnesses as would have been servicable. Even those we had were abused by the states attorney ~~in~~ at the Court and were not permitted to be examind by the Court as the laws direct[362]——

We were committed to Liberty Jail and petitio[n]ed to Judge [Joel] Turnham for a writ of Habeas Corpus but ~~on account~~ owening [owing] to the prejudice of the Jailor all communication was entirely cut off however at lengthe we succeeded in getting a petition conveyed to the Judge but he neglected ⟨to⟩ pay~~ing~~ any attention to it for Fourteen days and kept us in suspence: he then ordered us to appear before him but he utterly refused to hear any

---

358. In early November 1838, Wilson transported the Latter-day Saint prisoners from Far West to Lucas's militia headquarters in Independence, Missouri, where the prisoners stayed from 4 to 8 November 1838, first in a large house and then in a hotel. Wight later said that the prisoners were required to "pay the most extravagant price" for their stay in the hotel. (Introduction to Part 3: 4 Nov. 1838–16 Apr. 1839, p. 272 herein; Receipt from William Collins, 8 Feb. 1839, pp. 325–326 herein; Lyman Wight, Testimony, Nauvoo, IL, 1 July 1843, p. 27, Nauvoo, IL, Records, CHL.)

359. Major General Lucas initially ignored Clark's 3 November 1838 order to transport the prisoners from Independence to Richmond, the location of Clark's headquarters. After Lucas received confirmation on 6 November that Governor Boggs had placed Clark in command of the entire militia operation, Lucas arranged for the prisoners to be moved to Richmond, where a preliminary hearing was held to evaluate charges against the prisoners for crimes allegedly committed in the 1838 conflict. (See 281n86 herein; and Introduction to Part 3: 4 Nov. 1838–16 Apr. 1839, p. 272 herein.)

360. When the prisoners arrived in Richmond, Missouri, on 9 November 1838, they were placed in a room in "an old log house." They were bound together the following day "with three trace chains and seven padlocks . . . until [they] were all chained together about two feet apart." For the remainder of the month, they remained chained together and slept on the floor. (Lyman Wight, Journal, in *History of the Reorganized Church,* 2:296–297; Pratt, *History of the Late Persecution,* 52.)

361. Pratt described one night when the prisoners "listened for hours to the obscene jests, the horrid oaths, the dreadful blasphemies and filthy language of guards" as they "recounted to each other their deeds of rapine, murder, robbery, etc." committed against the Latter-day Saints in Caldwell County. (Pratt, *History of the Late Persecution,* 52; Pratt, *Autobiography,* 228, 229.)

362. Hyrum Smith recalled that the prisoners submitted the names of sixty potential defense witnesses; only seven ultimately testified. Several Latter-day Saints recounted that officers of the court harassed and abused the defense witnesses. (See 273n42 herein.)

of our witnesses which we had been at great trouble in providing— Our
Laweys [lawyers] likewise refused to act being afraid of the people:[363] ⟨We
likewise petitioned to Judge King and to the Judges of the Supreme Court
but ~~withe the same success~~—[364] they utterly refused——⟩[365]

Our vittuals were of the coarsest kind and served up in a manner which
was disgusting[366] after bearing up under repeated injuries we were removed
to Davies County under a strong guard[367] we were then arraigned before the
grand Jury who were mostly intoxicated: who indicted ~~us~~ me and the the rest
of my companions for Treason[368] [p. [7]] we then got a change of venue
to Boone County[369] and were on our way to that place on second evening
after our departure our Guards getting intoxicated ~~with~~ I & thought it a
favourable time to Effect our Escape from ~~a state~~ such men whose aim was
only to destroy our lifes, and to abuse us in every manner that wicked men
could invent accordingly we took advantage of their situation and made our
Escape[370] and after enduring considerable Fatigue & suffering hunger &

---

363. For more information on the January 1839 habeas corpus hearing, see Introduction to Part 3:
4 Nov. 1838–16 Apr. 1839, p. 276 herein.

364. TEXT: The line running through "with the same success" may not signify a cancellation; instead,
the line may be intended to separate the insertion from the main text.

365. On 9 March 1839, Hyrum Smith wrote a petition for a writ of habeas corpus; though directed
to King, it apparently was never submitted. In mid-March, JS and the other prisoners wrote separate petitions directed to the Missouri Supreme Court, but the requests were denied. (Hyrum Smith, Petition,
Liberty, MO, 9 Mar. 1839, CHL; Historical Introduction to Petition to George Tompkins, between
9 and 15 Mar. 1839, pp. 341–344 herein.)

366. Wight recalled that the prisoners were fed "with a scanty allowance, on the dregs of coffee and
Tea from the [jailer's] own Table and fetching the provisions in a basket in which the chickens had
roosted the night before without being cleaned." (Lyman Wight, Testimony, Nauvoo, IL, 1 July 1843,
p. 30, Nauvoo, IL, Records, CHL.)

367. From 6 to 8 April 1839, Clay County sheriff and jailer Samuel Hadley, deputy jailer Samuel
Tillery, and several other men escorted the prisoners from Liberty to Gallatin for a session of the Daviess
County Circuit Court. (Hyrum Smith, Diary, 6–8 Apr. 1839.)

368. The men were indicted around 10 April 1839 for treason against the state of Missouri. (Daviess
Co., MO, Circuit Court Record, Apr. 1839, bk. A, 58, Daviess County Courthouse, Gallatin, MO;
Indictment, [Honey Creek Township, MO], ca. 10 Apr. 1839, State of Missouri v. Gates et al. for Treason
[Daviess Co. Cir. Ct. 1839], Historical Department, Nineteenth-Century Legal Documents Collection,
CHL; see also Baugh, "We Took Our Change of Venue," 61–65.)

369. The defendants obtained a change of venue from Daviess County to Boone County because
Judge Thomas Burch served as prosecuting attorney during the November 1838 court of inquiry. Under
Missouri law, defendants were permitted a change of venue if the judge previously served as a lawyer in
the case. (See Historical Introduction to Promissory Note to John Brassfield, 16 Apr. 1839, p. 422
herein.)

370. The prisoners and their guards departed Gallatin on 12 April 1839. On 16 April, the party
stopped for the night, likely near Yellow Creek in Chariton County, where the prisoners escaped, evidently with the complicity of the guards. (See Historical Introduction to Promissory Note to John
Brassfield, 16 Apr. 1839, p. 424 herein.)

weariness Expecting that our enemies would be in persuit we arrived in the Town of Quincy Illinois amidst the congratulations of our Friends & the Joy of our Familys.[371] I have been here for several weeks as it is known to people in the State of Missouri but they knows they had no Justice in their Crusade against ~~us~~ me have not to my knowledge taken the first step to have me arrested[372]——

The Loss of Property which I have sustained is as follows—

Lossess sustained in Jackson County Davies County: Caldwell County including Lands: ⟨Houses⟩ Horses: Harness &c ~~Hogs~~ Cattle Hogs & Books & store Goods

Expences while in Bonds: of moneys paid out Expences of moving out of the State & damages sustained by ⟨False imprisonment⟩ threatnings: intimidation Exposure &c &c &c &c &c [p. [8]]

$100,000

———— ∾ ————

Letter from Edward Partridge, 13–15 June 1839

Source Note

Edward Partridge, Letter, Quincy, Adams Co., IL, to JS, Commerce, Hancock Co., IL, 13–15 June 1839. Featured version copied [between 27 June and 30 Oct. 1839] in JS Letterbook 2, pp. 68–69; handwriting of James Mulholland; JS Collection, CHL. For more information on JS Letterbook 2, see Source Note for Multiple-Entry Documents, p. 566 herein.

Historical Introduction

Bishop Edward Partridge wrote a letter to JS on 13–15 June 1839, responding to a letter from JS. In the response, Partridge noted that several church members were in need of assistance and that he was unable to help them because he had minimal funds and no prospects of earning money. JS likely received this letter on 26 June, when he returned to Commerce, Illinois, after an eleven-day trip to visit his brothers in other areas of the state.[373] The letter was possibly delivered by Vinson Knight, who arrived in Commerce from Quincy, Illinois, on 17 June.[374] As a bishop in the church, Knight was aware of church members' financial needs and may have traveled to Commerce to seek assistance for the

---

371. JS and his fellow prisoners arrived in Quincy on 22 April 1839. (JS, Journal, 22–23 Apr. 1839, in *JSP*, J1:336.)

372. JS was apparently unaware that in early June 1839, Missouri officials began the process of extraditing the escaped Latter-day Saint prisoners. (Austin A. King, Richmond, MO, to Lilburn W. Boggs, Jefferson City, MO, 7 June 1839, copy, Mormon War Papers, MSA; Thomas C. Burch, Keytesville, MO, to James L. Minor, Jefferson City, MO, 24 June 1839, Mormon Collection, Missouri History Museum Archives, St. Louis.)

373. JS, Journal, 15–26 June 1839, in *JSP*, J1:341–343; see also Editorial Note, in *JSP*, J1:341.

374. JS, Journal, 17 June 1839, in *JSP*, J1:341.

Quincy Saints. The original letter is not extant, but Mulholland copied the letter into Letterbook 2 between 27 June and 30 October 1839.[375]

Document Transcript

Quincy June 13th 1839

Prest, Smith

Sir

Your letter in Answer to my note to bishop [Vinson] Knight I recieved by the hand of br Harris,—[376] Respecting the cattle I had promised three or four yoke to Father Myers,[377] I did expect br Shearer[378] would have sent the cattle down immediately or I should not have been quite so willing to have accommodated him with some to moved with. Some of our poor brethren wished me to furnish them teams to move up to Iowa[379] with and I promised them that when the teams returned I should, they were very anxious to get up in time to get in a little garden, And were not my plans frustrated I could have accommodated them greatly to their satisfaction, the br[ethre]n that I allude to are the blind brethren,[380] who say that they had as lieve[381] live in tents there as here, it is now too late to think of making gardens and what is best for them brn to do I know not.—

I had promised some money as soon as I could sell a yoke of cattle, I know of nothing else I have that I can raise money with at this time, and they are getting to be dull sale to what they were.

---

375. Mulholland copied this letter into JS Letterbook 2 after a letter dated 27 June 1839, making that the earliest likely copying date for this letter from Partridge. For information on the latest likely copying date, see 248n440 herein.

376. Probably George W. Harris. The letter from JS to Partridge is not extant. (See Letter to George W. Harris, 24 May 1839, p. 470 herein; and Letter from Edward Partridge, 27 May 1839, p. 486 herein.)

377. Probably Jacob Myers Sr., a millwright. In spring 1839, he and his family moved from Caldwell County, Missouri, to Payson, Illinois, approximately fourteen miles southeast of Quincy. (Foote, Autobiography, vol. 2, pp. 114–117.)

378. Possibly Daniel Shearer or his brother Joel Shearer. (Daniel Shearer, Affidavit, Quincy, IL, 7 May 1839, Mormon Redress Petitions, 1839–1845, CHL; Chase, "Events in the Life of Daniel Shearer," 1–2.)

379. The Latter-day Saints in Iowa Territory were primarily living around Montrose, across the Mississippi River from Commerce, Illinois. In July they began to establish a new settlement at "Blefens point," later called Nashville. (Woodruff, Journal, 20 May 1839; 28 June 1839; 2 July 1839; JS, Journal, 2 July 1839, in *JSP*, J1:344.)

380. Later records indicate that some individuals living in the Commerce area were blind. (See Nauvoo City Council Minute Book, 17 Feb. 1842, 60; and Relief Society Minute Book, 2 Sept. 1843.)

381. "Lieve" is an alternate spelling of "lief," which is an adverb meaning "gladly; willingly; freely." ("Lieve," and "Lief," in *American Dictionary*.)

Sister Meeks[382] has been quite sick but she is getting better, she has nothing to eat only what she is helped to, a number of other poor here I think need assistance Wid[ow] Sherman[383] for one but if you think that all the means should be kept up there I have nothing to say only that I do not believe it to be my duty to stay here living on expence where I can earn nothing for myself, nor do anything to benefit others.

As I before stated I have promised some money as soon as I can raise it, I have not at this time two dollars in the world $1- 44 is all I owe for my rent And for making clothes for some of the twelve, And some other things, I am going into the room, br Harris leaves to save rent, what it is best for me ⟨to do⟩ I hardly know, hard labor I cannot perform,[384] light labor I can but I know of no chance to earn any thing, at any thing that I can stand it to do— It is quite sickly here five were buried in four days, br More's[385] Child Sis Louisa P and And br Pettigrews [David Pettegrew's] son Hiram 18 or 19 years of age[386] the other two were children of the world.[387]

I spoke to br I[saac] Higbee about his siene [seine] he said that he would speak to his brother about it, He said he thought that they would sell it, or

382. Possibly the wife of Garland Meeks, a seventy from the Kirtland, Ohio, area. Sister Meeks was also discussed on 14 April 1839 in a meeting about moving indigent Saints from Missouri to Illinois. (List of Priesthood Licenses, *LDS Messenger and Advocate,* Sept. 1836, 2:383; Woodruff, Journal, 3–4 Apr. 1837; Quorums of the Seventy, "Book of Records," 6 Feb. 1838, 41; Far West Committee, Minutes, 14 Apr. 1839.)

383. Probably Delcena Johnson Sherman, the widow of church leader Lyman Sherman. Her husband died in Far West, Missouri, around February 1839, and she apparently moved to Quincy by March 1839. (Kimball, "History," 98; Johnson, "A Life Review," 49–51.)

384. Partridge may have been weakened by malaria, which was raging in the Quincy area. Or, as Orson F. Whitney related in 1884, Partridge may have been weak or ill because of his imprisonment in Richmond, Missouri, in winter 1838–1839. In a prayer Partridge wrote in January 1839, he described the jail where he and several other Saints were held for several weeks: "The cold northern blast penetrated freely; our fires were small, and our allowance for wood, and for food, scanty; they gave us, not even, a blanket to lie upon; our beds were the cold floor." (Orson F. Whitney, "The Aaronic Priesthood," *Contributor,* Oct. 1884, 9; Edward Partridge, Prayer, Jan. 1839, Edward Partridge, Papers, CHL.)

385. A few men with the surname of Moore were members of the church in Nauvoo, Illinois, by 1842: Andrew Moore, Harvey Moore, and William Moore. Of these three, Andrew Moore is the only one known to have lived in Quincy in 1839, but his extant reminiscences do not mention the death of a child in 1839. Alternatively, it is possible Partridge was referring to James Moses, whose son John died in Quincy in 1839. (Nauvoo, IL, Tax List, district 3, 1842, pp. 187, 211, 222, 227, microfilm 7,706, U.S. and Canada Record Collection, FHL; Moore, Reminiscences, 28–29; Huntington, Cemetery Records, [1].)

386. David Pettegrew fled from Far West on 19 January 1839 and eventually settled in Quincy, where his family joined him around 15 April. He recorded in his autobiography that his son Hiram, age eighteen, became sick soon thereafter and died on 10 June 1839. (Pettegrew, "History," 34; Obituary for Hiram Pettegrew, *Times and Seasons,* Feb. 1840, 1:63.)

387. That is, children whose parents were not church members. (See Luke 16:8.)

they would come up in the fall and fish awhile but to lend it he thought it would not be best as those unaccustomed to fish in the rivers would [p. 68] be apt to tear it to pieces,[388] You percieve that I have not means to get you twine at present therefore I presume that you will not blame me for not doing it.

15th—— Were I well I would go up to Commerce with br [Newel K.] Whitney And settle with the Committee & br [David W.] Rogers[389] and see what is best to do—probably may come next week.[390]

If br [Stephen] Markham[391] could sell one yoke of cattle and let me have the avails of them I should be glad, and I think it best to let two yoke that are up there go to father Myers, As to team to move up some of the poor, do as you think best

I remain yours— E[dward] Partridge

Prest J. Smith Jr
   M[r] Joseph Smith Jun
   Commerce, Hancock Co. Ill.

———— ∾ ————

Discourse, 27 June 1839

Source Note

JS, Discourse, Commerce, Hancock Co., IL, 27 June 1839. Featured version copied [between 27 June and 8 Aug. 1839] in Wilford Woodruff, "Book of Revelations," pp. [19]–[20]; handwriting of Wilford Woodruff; CHL. For more information on Wilford Woodruff, "Book of Revelations," see Source Notes for Multiple-Entry Documents, p. 575 herein.

Historical Introduction

On 27 June 1839, JS delivered a discourse in a meeting of the Quorum of the Twelve Apostles held at Commerce, Illinois. The quorum members had met the previous two days, first in Montrose, Iowa Territory, and then in Commerce, debating the meaning of various

---

388. In a letter to JS on 5 March 1839, Partridge noted that Isaac Higbee Sr. and his son John Higbee moved two miles from Quincy to fish for the spring. At the time of Partridge's 13 June letter, it appears that two of Isaac Sr.'s sons—Isaac Jr. and John—were engaged in the fishing endeavor. (Letter from Edward Partridge, 5 Mar. 1839, p. 329 herein; Higbee, Journal and Reminiscences, [14]–[15].)

389. The committee Partridge mentioned may be the committee assigned to oversee the sale of land in Jackson County, Missouri. (See Minutes, 24 Apr. 1839, p. 438 herein; and Far West Committee, Minutes, 17 Mar. 1839.)

390. No records indicate whether Partridge made the proposed visit to Commerce, but he and his family apparently moved there in early July 1839. (Partridge, History, ca. 1839.)

391. Markham was appointed as a church agent on 27 May 1839. (See Authorization for Stephen Markham, 27 May 1839, pp. 480–481 herein.)

scriptures and discussing whether former apostle Orson Hyde should be readmitted into the quorum.[392] JS was absent at the time of the 25 June meeting, visiting his brothers in other areas of Illinois.[393] He returned to Commerce on 26 June, but it is not known whether he attended the quorum meeting that day. The 27 June meeting, which JS presided at, was the first of several council meetings in June and early July in which JS instructed the apostles as they prepared for their mission abroad.[394]

During the 27 June meeting, Hyde confessed his sins and was restored to full fellowship in the church and in the Quorum of the Twelve Apostles.[395] Following Hyde's reinstatement, JS instructed the apostles on the nature of ministering angels and the devil. Apostle Heber C. Kimball later described JS's instructions around this time as "unfolding keys of knowledge to detect Satan" when he appears as a ministering angel. Kimball noted that the instructions would "preserve us in the favor of God."[396] JS's and Sidney Rigdon's account of an 1832 vision identified Satan as a fallen angel,[397] and JS revelations had warned the Saints about the devil and other evil spirits.[398] In this 27 June discourse, JS provided tangible means of distinguishing between Satan and angels sent by God. Apostle Wilford Woodruff, who attended the meeting, noted in his journal that JS presented this instruction "to the Twelve for there benefit in there experience & travels in the flesh."[399]

Woodruff took notes on the discourse and then copied them into his "Book of Revelations" notebook, which he took with him when he left Illinois on 8 August to start his mission abroad. While in England, Woodruff lent his notebook to fellow missionary Willard Richards, who copied this discourse into another notebook, which he called a "Pocket Companion."[400] Woodruff also copied the discourse into his 1839 journal. In the journal account, which Woodruff apparently made sometime after he wrote his "Book of Revelations" account, Woodruff expanded on and reorganized the content in the earlier account. Because the account in Woodruff's "Book of Revelations" is the earliest extant version, it is featured here; significant differences between Woodruff's notebook and journal accounts are noted in annotation.

---

392. Woodruff, Journal, 25–26 June 1839. In October 1838, Hyde left the church and signed an affidavit describing the Saints' military operations against vigilantes in Daviess County, Missouri. (See 308n207 herein.)

393. JS traveled to Plymouth, Illinois, to visit William Smith and then went to Macomb, Illinois, to see Don Carlos and Samuel Smith. (JS, Journal, 15–26 June 1839, in *JSP*, J1:341–343; see also Editorial Note, in *JSP*, J1:341.)

394. See Allen et al., *Men with a Mission,* 59–60.

395. Woodruff, Journal, 27 June 1839; JS, Journal, 27 June 1839, in *JSP*, J1:343.

396. Kimball, "History," 106.

397. Vision, 16 Feb. 1832, in *JSP*, D2:186 [D&C 76:25–27]. Likewise, in the influential *Theological Dictionary,* which summarizes Protestant theology, minister Charles Buck described the devil as "a fallen angel" and the leader of fallen angels. Although both Buck and JS discussed the expulsion of angels from heaven as a result of sin, only JS characterized this expulsion in terms of a premortal council. ("Angel," and "Devil," in Buck, *Theological Dictionary,* 17, 116.)

398. See Revelation, ca. 8 Mar. 1831–A, in *JSP*, D1:282 [D&C 46:7]; and Revelation, 9 May 1831, in *JSP*, D1:306 [D&C 50:2]; see also JS History, vol. A-1, 93.

399. Woodruff, Journal, 27 June 1839.

400. Richards, "Pocket Companion," 9–10.

Document Transcript

[*Drawing of a key.*] As there are many[401] keys to the kingdom of God[402] the following one[403] will detect Satan[404] when he transforms himself nigh unto an angel of light[405] When Satan appears [p. [19]] in the form of a personage unto man & reaches out his hand unto him & the man takes hold of his hand & feels no substan[c]e he may know it is Satan for an angel of God (which is an angel of light) is a Saint with his resurrected body[406] & when he appears unto man[407] & offers him his hand[408] & the man feels a substance[409] when he takes hold of it as he would in shaking hands with his neighbour he may know it is a Angel of God.[410] & should a Saint appear unto man whose body is not resur-rectd he will never offer him his hand for it would be against the law by which they are governd[411] & by observing this key[412] we may detect Satan that he decieve us not

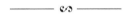

---

401. Instead of "as there are many," Woodruff's journal version has "among the vast number of the." (Woodruff, Journal, 27 June 1839.)

402. Woodruff's journal version adds "Joseph presented." (Woodruff, Journal, 27 June 1839.)

403. Woodruff's journal version adds "to the Twelve for there benefit in there experience & travels in the flesh which is as follows." (Woodruff, Journal, 27 June 1839.)

404. Instead of "Satan," Woodruff's journal version has "the devel." (Woodruff, Journal, 27 June 1839.)

405. See 2 Corinthians 11:14; and Book of Mormon, 1830 ed., 79 [2 Nephi 9:9].

406. See Luke 24:39–40, 42–43; and Matthew 27:52–53. Although theologians debated about the substance of angels, Charles Buck's *Theological Dictionary* noted that "the more general opinion is, that they are substances entirely spiritual, though they can at any time assume bodies, and appear in human shape." Like JS, eighteenth-century Swedish mystic Emmanuel Swedenborg described the corporality of angels and established his religious knowledge and authority by claiming to converse with angels face-to-face. Swedenborg also considered angels not as purely spiritual creations but as individuals who had at one time lived on earth. ("Angel," in Buck, *Theological Dictionary*, 17; *Brief Account of the Life of the Hon. Emanuel Swedenborg*, 20–24; McDannell and Lang, *Heaven*, 188–189; Park, "Early Mormon Angelology," 5–9.)

407. Woodruff's journal version adds "face to face in personage." (Woodruff, Journal, 27 June 1839.)

408. Instead of "offers him his hand," Woodruff's journal version has "reaches out his hand unto the man." (Woodruff, Journal, 27 June 1839.)

409. Woodruff's journal version describes the angel of God having a physical substance and then describes the devil's lack of physical substance. (Woodruff, Journal, 2 July 1839.)

410. Woodruff's journal version adds "& he should place all Confidence in him such personages or angels are Saints with there resurrected Bodies." (Woodruff, Journal, 27 June 1839.)

411. Instead of "it would be against the law by which they are governed," Woodruff's journal version has "this is against the law given him." (Woodruff, Journal, 27 June 1839.)

412. Instead of "by observing this Key," Woodruff's journal version has "in keeping in mind these things." (Woodruff, Journal, 27 June 1839.)

Letter to Jacob Stollings, 27–28 June 1839

Source Note

JS, Letter, Commerce, Hancock Co., IL, to Jacob Stollings, [Gallatin, Daviess Co., MO], 27–28 June 1839. Featured version copied [between 28 June and 30 Oct. 1839] in JS Letterbook 2, p. 50; handwriting of James Mulholland; JS Collection, CHL. For more information on JS Letterbook 2, see Source Notes for Multiple-Entry Documents, p. 566 herein.

Historical Introduction

On 27 June 1839, JS wrote to Jacob Stollings, a Missouri merchant, providing an update on an agreement the two men made just before JS's escape from Missouri in mid-April 1839. The agreement regarded account books that were apparently taken from Stollings's store during the Latter-day Saint military operations in Gallatin, Missouri, on 18 October 1838. In the April agreement, Stollings and JS established that if JS assisted in recovering the account books within four months, Stollings would forgive debts that church members incurred as customers at his store during 1838.[413]

After JS relocated to Commerce, Illinois, he wrote this letter to Stollings on 27 June, reporting that the account books had not been located. JS suggested that Stollings ask Sampson Avard—who had helped raid the store and presumably still lived in Missouri—regarding the whereabouts of the books. The next day, on 28 June, JS added a postscript to the letter, stating that someone reported seeing Avard with the books but did not know where they were now.

JS may have written the letter with the expectation that Stollings would recover the books from Avard and would then forgive the debts that church members owed him. Because the original letter is apparently not extant, it is unknown whether JS wrote the letter or relied on a scribe. It is also unknown whether or by what means the letter was sent, whether it reached Stollings, and how he reacted to it if he received it. James Mulholland copied the original letter or a retained copy into JS Letterbook 2 sometime between 28 June and 30 October 1839.[414]

Document Transcript

Commerce Ill, June 27th 1839

Sir

In answer to yours concerning those books I have to say that I have made enquiry concerning them as far as I consider there is any prospect of obtaining them for you, and not having been able to trace them in the least degree I have determined to give up the pursuit, I would recommend you to enquire after

---

413. Historical Introduction to Agreement with Jacob Stollings, 12 Apr. 1839, pp. 417–419 herein; Letter from Jacob Stollings, ca. 12 Apr. 1839, p. 421 herein.

414. Mulholland may have copied the the letter the day it was completed. For information on the latest likely copying date, see 248n440 herein.

them of Dr. [Sampson] Avard, as the only chance I know of at present.[415] Your's &c &c J. S. Jr

Mr Jacob Stollings. P. S. Since writing the above I have ascertained of one man (who told me) that he saw Dr Avard have the Books,[416] but what he did with them he knows not.

J S

June 28 [p. 50]

———— ∾ ————

Letter from John P. Greene, 30 June 1839

Source Note

John P. Greene, Letter, Cincinnati, Hamilton Co., OH, to JS, Sidney Rigdon, and Hyrum Smith, Commerce, Hancock Co., IL, 30 June 1839. Featured version copied [between ca. Dec. 1839 and ca. Apr. 1840] in JS Letterbook 2, pp. 75–76; handwriting of Robert B. Thompson; JS Collection, CHL. For more information on JS Letterbook 2, see Source Notes for Multiple-Entry Documents, p. 566 herein.

Historical Introduction

On 30 June 1839, John P. Greene wrote the following letter from Cincinnati, Ohio, to the First Presidency, describing his recent public presentations on the church's difficulties in Missouri. He conducted the presentations as part of an assignment he received the previous month to preside over the church in New York City and surrounding regions and to collect donations for the Saints migrating from Missouri to Illinois and Iowa Territory.[417] In preparation for his assignment, Greene acquired a letter of introduction on 8 May 1839 from Illinois governor Thomas Carlin, United States senator Richard Young from Illinois,

---

415. Following the state militia's occupation of Far West, Missouri, beginning on 1 November 1838, Avard renounced the church, and he was a key witness for the prosecution in the November 1838 hearings. In spring 1839, when the main body of the church migrated to Illinois, Avard remained in Missouri. On 17 March 1839, he was excommunicated in absentia at a church conference in Quincy, Illinois. Avard and his family relocated to Madison County, Illinois, by mid-1840. (306n199 herein; Reed Peck, Quincy, IL, to "Dear Friends," 18 Sept. 1839, pp. 123–124, Henry E. Huntington Library, San Marino, CA; "Extracts of the Minutes of Conferences," *Times and Seasons,* Nov. 1839, 1:15; 1840 U.S. Census, Ridge Prairie, Madison Co., IL, 99; 1850 U.S. Census, Township 3 N R 6 W, Madison Co., IL, 474[B].)

416. In his November 1838 testimony, Avard acknowledged his participation in the expedition to Gallatin, Missouri, on 18 October 1838, although he offered no specifics regarding his activities. Latter-day Saint Morris Phelps, who also participated in the Saints' activities in Gallatin, later recalled that "Sampson Avard in his rage hurled a pine brand into it [Stollings's store] which melted it to ashes." (Sampson Avard, Testimony, Richmond, MO, Nov. 1838, pp. [5]–[7], State of Missouri v. JS et al. for Treason and Other Crimes [Mo. 5th Jud. Cir. 1838], in State of Missouri, "Evidence"; Phelps, Reminiscences, 10; see also 418n888 herein.)

417. Minutes, 6 May 1839, p. 451 herein; Authorization for John P. Greene, ca. 6 May 1839, pp. 455–456 herein.

and other prominent Illinois citizens; in the letter, these individuals attested to Greene's upright character.[418] On 5 June, Greene left Quincy, Illinois, for Cincinnati, where he used the letter of introduction to set up a series of public meetings to request assistance for impoverished Saints.[419] In his presentations, Greene described his and other church members' sufferings in Missouri. Prominent Cincinnati residents spoke in support of Greene's claims, and committees passed resolutions condemning Missouri state officials, expressing support for the Saints, and encouraging Greene to publish his documentation, which he did later that month.[420] At the end of June, Greene wrote this letter to the First Presidency to report on the positive results of the June meetings. Greene's original letter is apparently not extant, but JS's clerk Robert B. Thompson copied it into JS Letterbook 2 sometime between December 1839 and April 1840.[421]

Document Transcript

Cincinnati, June 30th 1839

Hon[rd] & Ever respected Brother & also to Pres[ts]. S[idney] Rigdon & H[yrum] Smith

Sirs

It is with great satisfaction that I address you at this time, Altho I have been detained in this place much longer than I intended— but I very believe the Lord has directed my way since I left Quincy— when I first came to Cincinnati the doors seemed all colosed [closed] for about a week before I could get a hearing & at that time but very few came out:[422] for some said the Mormons deserved all that Missouri had done to them and others believed what the priests said:[423] But some came out & heard as they said the

---

418. Samuel Holmes et al., Letter of Introduction for John P. Greene, 8 May 1839, in JS Letterbook 2, pp. 41–42; Greene, *Facts relative to the Expulsion,* iii.

419. Greene, "Biographical Sketch of the Life and Travels of John Portenus Greene," 4.

420. See Greene, *Facts relative to the Expulsion.*

421. Thompson was hired to be JS's clerk after previous clerk James Mulholland died on 3 November 1839. Emma Smith complained that as of 6 December, Thompson had "not done any thing at all in the business," which suggests he did not copy Greene's letter until later in December, at the earliest. Thompson probably copied Greene's 30 June 1839 letter into the book by April 1840, when scribe Howard Coray began "copying a huge pile of letters into a book," presumably where Thompson left off in JS Letterbook 2. (Obituary for James Mulholland, *Times and Seasons,* Dec. 1839, 1:32; Emma Smith, Nauvoo, IL, to JS, Washington DC, 6 Dec. 1839, Charles Aldrich Autograph Collection, State Historical Society of Iowa, Des Moines; Coray, Autobiographical Sketch, 17.)

422. On 12 June 1839, Greene showed a small group his 8 May 1839 letter of introduction and documentary evidence for his claims. Those in attendance encouraged Greene to present his information at a public meeting. ("Mormons," *Liberty Hall and Cincinnati Gazette,* 20 June 1839, [4].)

423. Reverend W. H. Channing, writing for the Unitarian publication *Western Messenger,* argued after hearing Greene's presentation that "the fear, jealousy, envy and hatred felt against" the Saints in Missouri stemmed from a belief that "the Mormons were deluded, obstinate, zealous, exclusive in their faith" and led by men who "were thought to be speculators on the credulity of the ignorant." Furthermore, "they were a large and growing community, allied together both by necessity and choice, and *withal*

tale of woe for themselves,— the Lord helping me to tell the things in quite a systematic course & the people with Doctors Lawyers Priests & Drunkards all opened their ears eyes & mouth & then there hearts were accessible, and when I had done credulity had no place in the Colledge[424] M[r]— [Thomas] Morris Esqr & M[r] W[m] Greene Esq with others spoke freely on the Subject, and declared they believed all that I had stated to the letter.—[425] then appropriate resolutions were adopted—[426] the meeting was then adjourned for one week so as to be accomodated with the House but when the week came the house could not be occupied by us & the friends of liberty got there eyes pealed— & to See the Spirit of opposition & I think that all the wrath of man will yet work for our good.[427] At the meeting I was advised to publish my documents— a committee was appointed of the Citizens to examine the proof that was affixed on that subject. This Committee after examining my papers requested me to publish: and accepted their invitation;[428] I have

---

prosperous." Channing concluded that this was "*an explanation, but no justification.*" (Channing, "Outrages of Missouri Mobs on Mormons," 213, italics in original; see also Fluhman, *"A Peculiar People,"* 51–66.)

424. At a public meeting held at Cincinnati College's chapel on 17 June 1839, Greene recounted the suffering of the Saints, which one newspaper opined "has hardly a parallel even in the persecution of the primitive Christians." Greene vividly described women and children leaving bloody footprints in the snow, as well as vigilantes murdering young boys and an elderly man at Hawn's Mill. ("Mormon Meeting," *Albany [NY] Journal,* 28 June 1839, [2]; "Public Meeting," in Greene, *Facts relative to the Expulsion,* 42.)

425. Morris was an attorney and Ohio senator from 1833 to 1839. He was apparently in Missouri sometime during summer and fall 1838 and inquired into the causes of the conflict. His investigation convinced him that the Saints were industrious citizens, that none of them had been charged with crimes, and "that their religion gave offence to a mob." William Greene was an attorney and an outspoken abolitionist. At the meeting on 17 June 1839, he chaired the committee designated to evaluate John P. Greene's claims and to offer recommendations. (*Biographical Directory of the United States Congress, 1774–2005,* 1622; "Mormon Meeting," *Albany [NY] Journal,* 28 June 1839, [2]; Hamlin, "Selections from the William Greene Papers," 3; "Public Meeting," in Greene, *Facts relative to the Expulsion,* 42.)

426. The committee passed six resolutions that condemned the vigilantes' extralegal activities and Missouri government officials' failure to protect the Saints. The committee also promised to support "the surviving sufferers" financially and to help them regain their rights. Further, the committee members argued "that the story of wrongs done the Mormon people . . . ought to be spread before the American people and the world." ("Public Meeting," in Greene, *Facts relative to the Expulsion,* 42.)

427. It is unclear what Greene was referring to here. In spite of opposition, this meeting was held in the Cincinnati College chapel, the same location as the previous week's meeting. ("Mormon Meeting," in Greene, *Facts relative to the Expulsion,* 42.)

428. After some debate, those at the meeting accepted the committee's preamble, which condemned the Missouri vigilantes' violation of the Saints' constitutional rights, and approved four resolutions that commended the citizens of Quincy for "their generous defence and aid of the Mormons." Those attending also called for additional donations from Cincinnati residents for the Saints' relief and "approve[d] of the attempt of John P. Greene, to make known the history of his people's wrongs to the whole nation, through addresses and publications." ("Mormon Meeting," in Greene, *Facts relative to the Expulsion,* 42–43.)

compiled the whole documents with an appendix & it is now in the press a pamphlet of more than forty pages (of which I will send you as soon as they are out of press)[429] the Sound of Mormon representative in Cincinnati makes a great fuss here and also a far off the fifth day after I arrived in Cincinnatti my arrival was announced in the City of N York in one of the most noted papers of the Union, with strong terms of disapprobation of the [p. 75] administration of Missouri & also a very pathetic invitation for the Mormon representative to soon appear on the Sea Board that the Citizens of the East might have an oppertunity to sympathize with them in their afflictions.[430] At the same time the "Mo Republican["] complains very bitterly of the Editors of Cincinnatti for their sympathies expressed for the Mormons & also accuse them of that wicked & notorious crime (which deserved all the abuse that Mo had given them) their leader Jo Smith pretended to hold converse with the Deity[431] So we see that the people are stirred up for some reason— But Dear Sirs this course of things will have the desired Effect— it awakens up the attention of the people to hear and read and know for themselves & when ever these things are laid before them every honest man must believe them from the very nature of things & the former reffuse of lies are swept away[432] the Missourians appear in her own garb of Mobocracy while the Mormons are strip[p]ed of that dark sable mantle of all manner crime & wickedness which has come from th[e] pulpit and the press; & the credulity of the people allows them to believe the truth: and the church does appear in its own native plain[n]ess with⟨out⟩ partiality and without hypocracy[433] but I must bid you adieu for the present, but I will write you again & I wish you to write to me at philadelphia or New York and express your mind and feelings on this subject.

---

429. Greene's pamphlet included a memorial that Bishop Edward Partridge and other Latter-day Saints wrote on 10 December 1838 for the Missouri legislature; a copy of Governor Lilburn W. Boggs's 27 October 1838 expulsion order; and affidavits, petitions, and other materials describing the persecutions. According to family tradition, Greene printed as many as five thousand copies. (Greene, *Facts relative to the Expulsion*, 10–16, 21–24, 26–38; Greene, "Biographical Sketch of the Life and Travels of John Portenus Greene," 4.)

430. It is unknown which newspaper requested that Greene visit New York City in June 1839. On 16 September 1839, Greene attended a public meeting in that city, presenting an overview of the Saints' sufferings in Missouri. After various New York citizens gave speeches, the meeting's attendees approved resolutions that condemned the treatment of the Saints in Missouri and called for donations, which were subsequently collected by a committee. ("Meeting on Behalf of the Mormons," *New-York Spectator*, 19 Sept. 1839, [3].)

431. No extant evidence suggests that the *Missouri Republican* published such a response to Greene in June 1839. It is possible that the paper's editor was in Cincinnati and made these comments verbally.

432. See Isaiah 28:17.

433. See James 3:17.

I am Yours in the Covenant of the Gospel of Christ

J. P. Green [John P. Greene]

Joseph Smith Jr ⎫
  Sidney Rigdon ⎬ Pres
  Hyrum Smith ⎭

N B Excuse all the imperfections of this scrawl & ever pray for me as I do for you

J. P. G. [p. 76]

———— ☙ ————

Discourse, 2 July 1839

Source Note

JS, Discourse, Montrose, Lee Co., Iowa Territory, 2 July 1839. Featured version copied [between 2 July and 8 Aug. 1839] in Wilford Woodruff, "Book of Revelations," pp. [21]–[26]; handwriting of Wilford Woodruff; CHL. For more information on Wilford Woodruff, "Book of Revelations," see Source Notes for Multiple-Entry Documents, p. 575 herein.

Historical Introduction

On 2 July 1839, JS delivered a discourse regarding the cooperation and humility required of the apostles. The morning of 2 July, JS and several others traveled to Iowa Territory to visit land that Bishop Vinson Knight had recently purchased for the church.[434] After this visit, JS and his counselors in the First Presidency went to the home of apostle Brigham Young in Montrose, Iowa Territory, where the presidency met with the Quorum of the Twelve Apostles, the apostles' wives, and members of the Quorums of the Seventy. This meeting was one of several convened to instruct the apostles and several of the seventies who were preparing to leave for a proselytizing mission in Europe. The presidency gave blessings to three prospective missionaries and three of the women in attendance.[435] Hyrum

---

434. On 26 June, Knight purchased from Isaac Galland about sixteen thousand acres in the "Half-Breed Tract" in southern Iowa Territory. JS, accompanied by Sidney Rigdon, Hyrum Smith, Newel K. Whitney, Vinson Knight, Wilford Woodruff, and possibly other Montrose Saints, visited Nashville, Illinois, which Woodruff called "Blefens point," apparently named after F. P. Blevins, an Iowa Territory landowner. (JS, Journal, 2 July 1839, in *JSP*, J1:344; Lee Co., IA, Land Records, 1836–1961, vol. 2, pp. 3–6, 13–16, 26 June 1839, microfilm 959,239, U.S. and Canada Record Collection, FHL; Woodruff, Journal, 2 July 1839; Elias Smith, Journal, 24 June 1839; F. P. Blevins, Agreement with Alanson Ripley, Nashville, Iowa Territory, 28 June 1839, JS Office Papers, CHL.)

435. The presidency gave blessings to Wilford Woodruff and George A. Smith of the Quorum of the Twelve Apostles; Theodore Turley of the Quorum of the Seventy; and Mary Ann Angell Young, Leonora Cannon Taylor, and Phebe Carter Woodruff, who were wives of apostles in attendance. According to Woodruff, the blessings promised that "if we were faithful we had the promise of again returning to the bosom of our families & being blesed on our mission." (Woodruff, Journal, 2 July 1839; JS, Journal, 2 July 1839, in *JSP*, J1:344.)

Wilford Woodruff's "Book of Revelations." In summer 1839, Joseph Smith instructed the members of the Quorum of the Twelve Apostles on several occasions in preparation for their mission abroad. Wilford Woodruff recorded this account of Joseph Smith's 2 July 1839 remarks, other discourses, and revelations about the apostles in a small notebook titled "Book of Revelations." Woodruff brought this notebook on his mission to England, where Willard Richards copied the contents into his "Pocket Companion" notebook. Wilford Woodruff, "Book of Revelations," pp. [24]–[25], Church History Library, Salt Lake City.

Smith then instructed the apostles and seventies, advising the men to preach about "the first principles of the gospel."[436] He also warned the men against "trifling with their office, and of holding on strictly to the importance of their mission & the authority of the priesthood."[437]

After Hyrum Smith spoke, JS addressed the group. Apostle Wilford Woodruff, who attended the meeting, recorded in his journal that JS "arose & presented some precious things of the kingdom unto us in the power of the Holy Ghost."[438] According to JS's journal, he gave those in attendance instructions "calculated to guard them against self-sufficiency, selfrighteousness & selfimportance."[439] In particular, JS taught the importance of forgiveness, humility, unity, and cooperation among the apostles. He concluded by urging the men to endure the coming hardships without betraying Christ or each other. JS perhaps felt the need to caution the apostles because disaffection during the previous two years had resulted in several apostles being excommunicated and replaced with men who were loyal to JS and the church.

Three versions of this discourse are extant. Woodruff took notes on the discourse and later copied the notes into his "Book of Revelations," a notebook in which he copied JS revelations and discourses.[440] In his notebook, Woodruff dated the discourse as 1 July 1839, but the context of the discourse places it on 2 July, when JS was in Montrose.[441] Woodruff brought his notebook on his mission to England, where fellow missionary Willard Richards borrowed the notebook and copied this and other discourses into his own notebook.[442] Woodruff also copied the discourse into his 1839 journal. In the journal version, he omitted the final section of the discourse, which addressed apostasy, and made other minor revisions. Woodruff's "Book of Revelations" version is featured here because it is the earliest and most complete and was likely copied between 2 July and 8 August, the date Woodruff and fellow apostle John Taylor departed for New York, en route to England. Significant differences between the two versions are noted in annotation.

Document Transcript

The following important items & plain & preciious principles were delivered unto the Twelve from Joseph in Montrose Ioway Territory July 1ˢᵗ [2nd] 1839

Ever keep in exercise the principle of mercy & be ready to forgive our brother on the first intimations of repentance & asking forgiveness, & should we

---

436. Woodruff, Journal, 2 July 1839; see also 315n266 herein.

437. JS, Journal, 2 July 1839, in *JSP*, J1:344.

438. Woodruff, Journal, 2 July 1839.

439. JS, Journal, 2 July 1839, in *JSP*, J1:344.

440. For more information on Woodruff's record keeping, see Wilford Woodruff, "Book of Revelations," in Source Notes for Multiple-Entry Documents, p. 575 herein.

441. Woodruff corrected the date when he copied his discourse notes into his 1839 journal. JS's journal records JS traveling to Montrose and holding a meeting there on 2 July. (Woodruff, Journal, 2 July 1839; JS, Journal, 2 July 1839, in *JSP*, J1:344.)

442. See Richards, "Pocket Companion," 10–15.

even forgive our brother or Even our Enemy [443] before they repent or ask forgiveness[444] our heavenly father would be equally as merciful unto us. Again let the
Twelve & all Saints[445] be willing to confess all ~~there~~ their Sins & not keep back
a part[446] & let the twelve be humble & not be exalted[447] & beware of pride[448]
& not seek to excell one above another but act for each others good & pray for
one & another & honour ~~over~~ our brother or make [p. [21]] honourable mention
of his name[449] & not backbite & devour our brother. why will not man learn
wisdom by precept[450] at this late agee of the world where we have such a cloud of
witnesses[451] & Examples before us[452] & not be oblieged to learn by sad experianc
[experience] every thing we know. must the new ones that are chosen to fill the
places of those that are fallen of the quorum of the Twelve[453] begin to exalt
themselves[454] untill they exhalt themselves[455] so high that they will soon tumble

---

443. See 1 Kings 8:50; Revelation, 11 Sept. 1831, in *JSP*, D2:63–64 [D&C 64:9]; and Revelation,
6 Aug. 1833, in *JSP*, D3:227 [D&C 98:39–45].

444. Instead of "before they repent or ask forgiveness," Woodruff's journal version has "before they
ask it." (Woodruff, Journal, 2 July 1839.)

445. Instead of "again let all the twelve & all saints," Woodruff's journal version has "& also we
ought to." (Woodruff, Journal, 2 July 1839.)

446. Instead of "be willing to confess all their Sins & not keep back a part," Woodruff's journal version has "be willing to repent of & confess all of our own sins & keep nothing back." (Woodruff, Journal,
2 July 1839.)

447. See Revelation, 23 July 1837, in *JSP*, D5:415–416 [D&C 112:10, 15].

448. See Revelation, Apr. 1830–A, in *JSP*, D1:131 [D&C 23:1]; Revelation, July 1830–C, in *JSP*,
D1:164 [D&C 25:14]; and Revelation, 2 Jan. 1831, in *JSP*, D1:233 [D&C 38:39].

449. Instead of "pray for one & another & honour our brother or make honourable mention of his
name," Woodruff's journal version has "honerably make mention of each other's name in our prayrs before
the Lord & before our fellow men." (Woodruff, Journal, 2 July 1839; see also Romans 1:9; Ephesians 1:16;
and 1 Thessalonians 1:2.)

450. See Book of Mormon, 1830 ed., 114 [2 Nephi 28:30].

451. Hebrews 12:1.

452. Instead of "at this late agee of the world where we have such a cloud of witnesses & examples
before us," Woodruff's journal version has "& example at this late age of the world." (Woodruff, Journal,
2 July 1839.)

453. A revelation JS dictated on 8 July 1838 appointed John E. Page, John Taylor, Wilford Woodruff,
and Willard Richards to replace former quorum members William E. McLellin, Luke Johnson, John F.
Boynton, and Lyman Johnson.*a* In a 16 January 1839 letter from the jail in Clay County, Missouri, JS
named George A. Smith as a replacement for Thomas B. Marsh, who withdrew from the church in
October 1838. George A. Smith was ordained an apostle in April 1839.*b* On 4 May 1839, William Smith
and Orson Hyde were suspended from the Quorum of the Twelve; Smith was restored to the quorum on
25 May, and Hyde was restored on 27 June 1839.*c* (*a*. Revelation, 8 July 1838–A, p. 180 herein [D&C
118:6]. *b*. Letter to Heber C. Kimball and Brigham Young, 16 Jan. 1839, pp. 314–315 herein; Woodruff,
Journal, 26 Apr. 1839; see also 308n206 herein. *c*. See Minutes, 4–5 May 1839, p. 446 herein; and
Woodruff, Journal, 25 May and 27 June 1839.)

454. See Psalms 66:7; 140:8.

455. Instead of "exhalt themselves," Woodruff's journal version has "get." (Woodruff, Journal, 2 July
1839.)

over & have a great fall & go wallowing through the mud & mire & darkness Judas like[456] to the buffatings of Satan[457] as several of the quorum of the Twelve have done or will they learn wisdom & be wise. (O God give them wisdom & keep them humble I pray [p. [22]]

When the Twelve or any other witnesses stand before the Congragations of the Earth & they preach in the power & demonstratio[n] of the spirit of God[458] & the people are asstonised [astonished] & confounded at the doctrin[459] & say that that man has preached a powerful discours a great sermon then let that man or those men take care that they do not asscribe the glory unto themselves but be careful that they are humble & asscribe the praise & glory to God & the Lamb for it is by the power of the Holy Priesthood & Holy Ghost they have power thus to speak:[460] what art thou O man but dust[461] & from wholm dost thou receive thy power & blessing but from God Then O ye Twelve <u>notice</u> this [*drawing of a key*] key & be wise for Christ-sake & your own sols sake [p. [23]]

Ye are not sent out to be taught but to teach.[462] let every word be seasoned with grace be vigilent be sober. it is a day of warning ⟨[exhorting]⟩[463] & not of many words.[464] act honest before God & man beware of gentile <u>Sophestry</u> such as bowing & scraping unto men in whom you have no confiden[c]e be honset open & frank, in all your intercourse with mankind.

O ye Twelve & all Saints profit by this important <u>Key</u> [*drawing of a key*] that in all your trials troubles, temptations; afflictions, bonds, imprisonments, & death see to it that you do not betray heaven, that you do not betray Jesus Christ, that you do not betray your Brethren, that you do not betray the Revelations of God, whether in the Bible Book of Mormon or Doctrins & Covenants or [p. [24]] any other that ever was or ever will be given & revealed unto man in this world or that which is to come,[465] yea in all your kick[i]ng &

---

456. See Luke 22:47–48; and Mark 14:43–44.

457. See Revelation, 1 Mar. 1832, in *JSP*, D2:199 [D&C 78:12]; Revelation, 26 Apr. 1832, in *JSP*, D2:237 [D&C 82:21]; and Revelation, 23 Apr. 1834, in *JSP*, D4:23 [D&C 104:9].

458. Instead of "spirit of God," Woodruff's journal version has "Holy Ghost." (Woodruff, Journal, 2 July 1839.)

459. See Matthew 7:28.

460. See Book of Mormon, 1830 ed., 121 [2 Nephi 33:1]; and Revelation, 1 Nov. 1831–A, in *JSP*, D2:101 [D&C 68:4].

461. See Genesis 2:7; and Romans 9:20–21.

462. See Revelation, Feb. 1831–A, in *JSP*, D1:258 [D&C 43:15].

463. TEXT: Transliteration from Pitman shorthand: "[k-s-o-r-t]," with the beginning "e" and the ending "ing" implied to render "exhorting."

464. See Revelation, 30 Aug. 1831, in *JSP*, D2:54 [D&C 63:58].

465. Instead of "any other that ever was or ever will be given & revealed unto man in this world or that which is to come," Woodruff's journal version has "any of the word of God." (Woodruff, Journal, 2 July 1839.)

floundering see to it that you do not this thing lest innocent Blood be found in your skirts[466] & you go down to hell. all other sins are not to be compared to sining against the Holy Ghost & proving a traitor to thy brethren[467] (A final [*drawing of a key*] key delivered from Joseph in the following language.) I will give you one of the keys of the mysteries of the kingdom. It is an Eternal principle that has existed with God from all Eternity that that man who rises up to condemn others & finding fault with the Church saying that they are out of the way while he himself is righteous, then know assuredly that that man is in the high road [p. [25]] to apostacy & if he does not repent will apostatize as God live, the principle is as correct as the one that Jesus put forth in saying that ~~that person~~ he who seeketh after a sign is an adulterous person[468] & that principle is ⟨Eternal⟩ undeviating & firm as the pillars of heaven for whenever you see a man seeking after a Sign you may set it down that he is an adulterous man.[469]

———— ☙ ————

Discourse, between circa 26 June and circa 2 July 1839

Source Note

JS, Discourse, Commerce, Hancock Co., IL, [between ca. 26 June and ca. 2 July 1839]. Featured version copied [between 2 July and 8 Aug. 1839], in Wilford Woodruff, "Book of Revelations," pp. [26]–[35]; handwriting of Wilford Woodruff, CHL. For more information on Wilford Woodruff, "Book of Revelations," see Source Notes for Multiple-Entry Documents, p. 575 herein.

Historical Introduction

In summer 1839, likely in late June or early July, JS gave a discourse at Commerce, Illinois, regarding various principles of the gospel, including faith, baptism, and the doctrine of election. This discourse was one of several JS addressed to members of the Quorum of the Twelve Apostles and the Quorums of the Seventy as they were preparing to proselytize in Europe.

JS began by addressing the principles of faith, repentance, baptism, and the gift of the Holy Ghost. Next, he discussed the gift of speaking in tongues, the resurrection, and eternal judgment. JS then explicated Peter's instruction on making one's "calling and election sure." JS connected this doctrine with Paul's discussion of the sealing power of the "holy

---

466. See Jeremiah 2:34.

467. Instead of "all other sins are not to be compared to sining against the Holy Ghost & proving a traitor to thy brethren," Woodruff's journal version has "we may ever know by this sign that there is danger of our being led to a fall & apostcy, when we give way to the devil so as to neglect the first known duty but whatever you do do not betray your <u>Friend</u>." (Woodruff, Journal, 2 July 1839, underlining in original.)

468. See Matthew 12:39; 16:4.

469. TEXT: Curlicued line, possibly written over illegible characters.

Spirit of promise" and Jesus's teaching about "another Comforter,"[470] explaining that the "first Comforter" is the Holy Ghost, received after baptism, whereas the "other Comforter" is Jesus Christ, received after one's calling and election is made sure.[471] A revelation JS dictated in 1832 identified the other Comforter as the "holy spirit of promise" and connected this Comforter with the promise of salvation and eternal life.[472] However, the revelation did not indicate the other Comforter was Jesus Christ; JS clarified the doctrine in this 1839 discourse. As a final topic, JS discussed the office of patriarch, which he equated with the New Testament role of evangelist.

Apostle Wilford Woodruff took notes during the discourse and copied them into his "Book of Revelations," a notebook he began keeping in 1839 to record JS revelations and discourses. Woodruff brought his notebook on his mission to England, where fellow missionary Willard Richards copied the discourse notes into his "Pocket Companion."[473] In 1845 Thomas Bullock copied the discourse into the addenda of JS's multivolume manuscript history.

JS may have given the discourse as early as 26 June, during meetings the Quorum of the Twelve Apostles held from 25 to 27 June. JS was absent from Commerce the first day of meetings but returned the following day.[474] Woodruff's journal describes the 26 June meeting as including "interesting remarks" on Ephesians chapter 1 and John chapter 14, particularly on "the other Comforter"—topics addressed in the discourse featured here.[475] It is also possible that the council discussed these topics without JS on 26 June and that he was asked to expand on the subject on 27 June or in meetings with the Quorum of the Twelve Apostles during the next few days. JS presided at the meeting held on 27 June and gave at least one discourse that day.[476] That was the date Bullock assigned the discourse when he copied it into the manuscript history. However, in Woodruff's notebook this discourse is preceded by accounts of JS discourses from 27 June and 2 July.[477] According to JS's journal, 2 July is the last date that JS met with the apostles before their scheduled departure for Europe in early July. Nevertheless, since the apostles did not begin departing until August, it is possible that JS delivered the discourse later in July or early in August, before Woodruff left for his mission on 8 August.[478]

---

470. See 2 Peter 1:10; Ephesians 1:13; and John 14:16.

471. Many Christian theologians in the late 1700s and early 1800s agreed that the Holy Ghost, or Holy Spirit, represented the Comforter mentioned in John 14:16, 26. (See, for example, "Christianity," and "Holy Ghost," in Buck, *Theological Dictionary,* 69, 170; Gill, *Complete Body of Doctrinal and Practical Divinity,* 1:238; Henry, *Exposition of the Old and New Testament,* 4:864–865; and Hawker, *Sermons on the Divinity,* 139.)

472. Revelation, 27–28 Dec. 1832, in *JSP,* D2:336–337 [D&C 88:1–5].

473. See Richards, "Pocket Companion," 15–22.

474. Woodruff's 26 June journal entry states that JS was not present when the council began; he may have arrived later during the meeting. It appears that 26 or 27 June was the first time JS met with the apostles and seventies to give them instruction in preparation for their mission. (Woodruff, Journal, 26 June 1839; JS, Journal, 26 June 1839, in *JSP,* J1:343.)

475. Woodruff, Journal, 26 June 1839.

476. Woodruff, Journal, 27 July 1839; Discourse, 27 June 1839, p. 510 herein.

477. JS History, vol. C-1, addenda, 8–9; Jessee, "Writing of Joseph Smith's History," 441.

478. JS, Journal, 2 July 1839, in *JSP,* J1:344–345. The apostles gave farewell addresses on 7 July, intending to leave soon after, but were delayed when the majority fell ill. (JS, Journal, 7 July 1839, in *JSP,* J1:345.)

Document Transcript

Other important items of doctrins from Joseph given in Commerce Ill. ~~The pure testimony of the servnts of God in all ages of the world is attended with the spirit of Revelation & prophecy, or in other words faith comes by hearing the word of God & the~~[479] [p. [26]]

On the doctrins of faith

Faith comes by hearing the word of God[480] through the testimony of the Servants of God that Testimony is always attended by the spirit of prophecy & Revelation.[481]

Repentance[482]

Is a thing that cannot be trifled with every Day. Daily transgression & daily repentance is not that which is pleasing in the sight of God

Baptism

Is a Holy ordinance preparatory to the reception of the Holy Ghost; It is the Channel & Key by which the Holy Ghost will be administered. The gift of the Holy Ghost by the laying ~~of~~ on of hands [p. [27]] cannot be received through the medium of any other principle <u>than the principle of righteousness</u> for if the proposals are not complied with it is of no use but withdraws[483]

Tongues

Were given for the purpose of preaching among those whose language is not undertstood as on the day of Pentecost[484] &c. & it is not necessary for tongues to be taught to the Church particularly, for any man that has the Holy Ghost can speak of the things of God[485] in his own tongue as well as to speak in another. for faith comes not by signs[486] but by hearing the word of God[487] [p. [28]] The doctrin of the Resurrection of the Dead and Eternal judgment are necisary to preach among the first principles of the gospel of Jesus Christ[488]

---

479. TEXT: Woodruff canceled this section with an *X* after apparently deciding to organize his notes by topic.

480. See Romans 10:17.

481. See Revelation 19:10; and Book of Mormon, 1830 ed., 232, 239, 340 [Alma 4:20; 6:8; 43:2].

482. TEXT: "Repentance" is double underlined.

483. See Letter to Edward Partridge and the Church, ca. 22 Mar. 1839, p. 393 herein [D&C 121:36].

484. See Acts 2:1–18; and Minutes, 8 Sept. 1834, in *JSP*, D4:165.

485. See Revelation, 9 Feb. 1831, in *JSP*, D1:251 [D&C 42:17]; and Revelation, 8 Mar. 1833, in *JSP*, D3:28–29 [D&C 90:11].

486. See Revelation, 30 Aug. 1831, in *JSP*, D2:50 [D&C 63:9].

487. Although elsewhere JS characterized speaking in tongues as a gift of the Spirit, in 1831 he endeavored to curb church members' excess use of it. (See Revelation, ca. 8 Mar. 1831–A, in *JSP*, D1:283 [D&C 46:24–25]; and *JSP*, D1:270n158.)

488. See Hebrews 6:1–2; Revelation, ca. Summer 1829, in *JSP*, D1:89–90 [D&C 19:1–24]; and 315n266 herein.

The Doctrin of Election

St Paul exhorts us to make our calling & Election shure.[489] This is that Sealing Power spoken of by Paul in other places See Ephe 1ˢᵗ 13–14. vs[490] that we may be sealed up unto the day of redemption, this principle ought (in its proper place) to be taught for God hath not revealed any thing to Joseph but what he will make known unto the Twelve[491] & even the least saint may know all things as fast as he is able to hear them for the day must come when no man need say [p. [29]] to his neighbour know ye the Son[492] for all shall know him (who remain) from the least to the greatest[493] How is this to be done. it is to be done by this sealing power & the other Comforter spoken of which will be manifest by Revelation. There is two comforters spoken of, the first Comforter is the Holy Ghost[494] the same as given on the day of Pentecost[495] & that all Saints recieve after faith, Repentance, & Baptism. This first Comforter or Holy Ghost has no other affect than pure intelligence It is more powerful in expanding the mind enlightening the understanding & storeing the intellect with present Knowledge of a man who is of the [p. [30]] litteral Seed of Abram[496] ~~that~~ than one that is a gentile though it may not have half as much visible affect upon the body for as the Holy Ghost falls upon one of the literal seed of Abram it is caml [calm] & serene & his Whole soul & body are only exercised by the Pure spirit of Intelligence. While the affect of the Holy Ghost upon a gentile is to purge out the old blood & make him actually of the seed of Abram That man that has none of the Blood of Abram (naturally) must have a new creation[497] by the Holy Ghost in such a case there may be more of a powerful affect upon the body & visible to the eye than upon an [p. [31]] Israelite while the Israelite at first might be far before the gentile in pure intelligence.[498] The other Comforter spoken off is a subject of great interest &

---

489. See 2 Peter 1:10.

490. See also 2 Corinthians 1:20–22; and Ephesians 4:30.

491. See Instruction on Priesthood, between ca. 1 Mar. and ca. 4 May 1835, in *JSP*, D4:314, 315 [D&C 107:23–24, 33]; and Revelation, 23 July 1837, in *JSP*, D5:417 [D&C 112:30].

492. Instead of "Son," Richards's version of the discourse has "Lord." (Richards, "Pocket Companion," 18.)

493. See Hebrews 8:11; Jeremiah 31:34; and Revelation, 22–23 Sept. 1832, in *JSP*, D2:301 [D&C 84:98].

494. See John 14:26; and Book of Mormon, 1830 ed., 582–583 [Moroni 8:26].

495. See Acts chap. 2.

496. See Genesis 17; 22:17–18.

497. See 2 Corinthians 5:17; Galatians 6:15; and Book of Mormon, 1830 ed., 214 [Mosiah 27:26].

498. Several early JS revelations emphasized the election of the literal descendants of Abraham and emphasized the need to gather the house of Israel. However, those who were not literally descendants of Abraham were not excluded from election. The Book of Mormon teaches that Gentiles who embrace the gospel are numbered with the house of Israel. A revelation JS dictated in September 1832 indicates that

perhaps understood by few of this generation. After a person hath faith in Christ, repents of his Sins & is baptized for the remission of his Sins & recieves the Holy Ghost (by the laying on of hands,) which is the first Comforter then let him continue to humble himself before God hungering & thirsting after righteousness[499] & living by every word of God,[500] & the Lord will soon say unto him Son thou shalt be exalted, &c.[501] When the Lord has thoroughly proved him & find that the man is determind to serve him at all hazard then the man will find [p. [32]] his calling & Election made sure then it will be his privilege to recieve the other <u>Comforter</u> which the Lord hath promised the Saints as is recorded in the testimony of St. John in the XIV <u>ch</u> from the 12 to the 27 <u>vers</u> note the 16-17-18-21:23 <u>verses</u> Now what is this other Comforter is it is no more or less than the <u>Lord</u> <u>Jesus</u> <u>Christ</u> himself & this is the sum & substance of the whole matter that when any man obtains this last Comforter he will have the personage of Jesus Christ to attend him or appear unto him from time to time Even he will manifest the Father unto him & they will take up there abode with him & the visions of the heavens will be opened unto him & the Lord will teach him face to face[502] & [p. [33]] he may have a perfect knowlededg of the mysteries of the kingdom of God.[503] & this is the state & place where the ancient Saints arived at when they had such glorious visions. Isaiah[504] Ezekiel,[505] John upon the Isle of Patmos,[506] St Paul in the third heavens[507] & all the Saints, who held communion with the general assembly & Church of the first born &c.[508] The spirit of Revelation[509] is in connexion with those blessings.

---

faithful men ordained to the priesthood "become the sons of Moses and of Aaron and the seed of Abraham and the church and kingdom and the elect of God." It was not until this 1839 discourse that JS mentioned the physical changes associated with Gentiles becoming the seed of Abraham. (Book of Mormon, 1830 ed., 513–514 [3 Nephi 30:2]; Revelation, 22–23 Sept. 1832, in *JSP*, D2:297 [D&C 84:34].)

499. See Matthew 5:6; and Book of Mormon, 1830 ed., 479 [3 Nephi 12:6].

500. See Matthew 4:4; Luke 4:4; Revelation, 22–23 Sept. 1832, in *JSP*, D2:298 [D&C 84:44]; and Revelation, 6 Aug. 1833, in *JSP*, D3:225 [D&C 98:11].

501. See Luke 15:31; and Revelation, 23 July 1837, in *JSP*, D5:415 [D&C 112:3].

502. See Exodus 33:11; and Old Testament Revision 1, pp. 1, 15 [Moses 1:2; 7:4].

503. See Matthew 13:11; Vision, 16 Feb. 1832, in *JSP*, D2:184, 191 [D&C 76:7, 114]; and Revelation, 8 Mar. 1833, in *JSP*, D3:28 [D&C 90:14].

504. See Isaiah chap. 6.

505. See Ezekiel chaps. 1, 40–47.

506. See Revelation 1:9–10.

507. See 2 Corinthians 12:1–4.

508. See Hebrews 12:23; Vision, 16 Feb. 1832, in *JSP*, D2:183, 188 [D&C 76:54]; Answers to Questions, between ca. 4 and ca. 20 Mar. 1832, in *JSP*, D2:212 [D&C 77:11]; Revelation, 27–28 Dec. 1832, in *JSP*, D2:337 [D&C 88:5]; and Instruction on Priesthood, between ca. 1 Mar. and ca. 4 May 1835, in *JSP*, D4:314 [D&C 107:19].

509. See Book of Mormon, 1830 ed., 232 [Alma 4:20]; and Revelation, Apr. 1829–B, in *JSP*, D1:46 [D&C 8:3].

A person may profit by noticeing the first intimations of the spirit of revelation for Instance when you feel pure intelligence flowing unto you it may give you sudden stoks [strokes] of Ideas that by noticing it you may find it fulfilled the same day or soon <u>ie</u> those things that were presented unto your mind by the [p. [34]] spirit of God will come to pass & thus by learning the Spirit of God & understanding it you may grow into the principle of Revelation untill you become perfe[c]ted in Christ Jesus.[510]

An Evangelist[511]

Is a patriarch even the oldest man of the Blood of Joseph or of the seed of Abram whare ever the Church of Christ is established in the Earth there should be a Patriarch[512] for the benefit of the posterity of the Saints, as it was with Jacob in given his patriarchal bles[s]ing unto his Sons &c.[513] [p. [35]]

———— ☙ ————

Discourse, 7 July 1839

Source Note

JS, Discourse, Commerce, Hancock Co., IL, 7 July 1839. Featured version copied [ca. 7 July 1839] in Wilford Woodruff, Journal, vol. 2, 1 Jan. 1838–31 Dec. 1839, p. [97]; handwriting of Wilford Woodruff; Wilford Woodruff, Journals and Papers, 1828–1898, CHL. For more information on Wilford Woodruff, Journal, vol. 2, 1 Jan. 1838–31 Dec. 1839, see Source Notes for Multiple-Entry Documents, p. 576 herein.

Historical Introduction

On Sunday, 7 July 1839, JS delivered a discourse at a meeting of Latter-day Saints at Commerce, Illinois. Church members in Commerce were joined by approximately one hundred Saints from Montrose, Iowa Territory, including Wilford Woodruff and his wife, Phebe Carter Woodruff, as well as many who were not members of the church.[514] The group had gathered to hear the farewell addresses of members of the Quorum of the Twelve Apostles and the Quorums of the Seventy who were leaving to proselytize in Europe. Those who spoke during the meeting included John E. Page, John Taylor, Wilford Woodruff, Orson Hyde, Brigham Young, Sidney Rigdon, and JS. Rigdon's address, which discussed the persecution and trials the apostles and seventies would face while proselytizing, was

---

510. See Colossians 1:28.

511. See Ephesians 4:11–13; and 2 Timothy 4:5. In 1835, JS taught that the Quorum of the Twelve Apostles was to appoint "evangelical ministers" for large branches of the church. (Instruction on Priesthood, between ca. 1 Mar. and ca. 4 May 1835, in *JSP*, D4:316 [D&C 107:39].)

512. Joseph Smith Sr. was ordained the church patriarch on 6 December 1834 and continued in that position until his death in 1840. (Historical Introduction to Blessing from Joseph Smith Sr., 9 Dec. 1834, in *JSP*, D4:200–202.)

513. See Genesis chap. 49.

514. JS, Journal, 7 July 1839, in *JSP*, J1:347.

him in testimony & rejoiced in having the privilege of once more addressing the body of the church
Brother Orson Hide followed me & he had the spirit in the spirit. Brother Brigham Young next
spoke & also bore testimony in the spirit. We was then addressed by President S. Rigdon & his
address was peculiarly adapted to the circumstances of the Twelve taking their leave of all
they hold dear on earth & set forth from their ordination to stand before the kings & rulers of the nations
of the earth to bear testimony unto them of the fulness of the everlasting gospel of Jesus
Christ his address was of such a nature in appealing to our affections, in parting with our wives and
children, & the peculiarity of our mission, the perils that we might meet with & the blessings that
we should receive, &c. that tears was brought from many eyes. Joseph addressed us in few
words. Is & S. remember brethren that if you are imprisoned Brother Joseph has been imprisoned
before you, if you are placed where you can only see your Brethren through the grates
of a window while in Irons because of the gospel of Jesus Christ remember Brother Joseph
has been in like circumstances also after other similar remarks the meeting closed & three
persons were Baptized & confirmed which ended the deeies of the day..

REFLECTIONS Surely this is an important day to behold a quorum of Twelve Apostles of the
Lamb of God organized in these last days to go forth once to the nations of the earth to prune
the vineyard once more for the last time that the Saving may be prepared for the second
of Christ & that Israel may be gathered & babylon fall & the earth once more cleansed from
its pollutions & with Ephraim steps from the face thereof ... May the Lord enable the
Twelve ever to humble themselves before & to passper in this hand, as the day is in the hands of the pattern
& may we ever realize that while we are in the service of God & doing his will that though we
may be sometimes by trials & threatened with death that the Lord is our deliverer & that he will
support us in every time of troublesome trial

Discourse notes in Wilford Woodruff's 1838–1839 journal. This 7 July 1839 discourse, which Joseph Smith gave to the apostles on perseverance, is one of many that Wilford Woodruff recorded. The block printing and illustrations on this page are characteristic of Woodruff's journaling. Woodruff's journals, with volumes spanning from 1833 to 1898, constitute one of the most important sources for contextualizing and understanding the life of Joseph Smith and the development of the Church of Jesus Christ of Latter-day Saints. Wilford Woodruff, Journal, 1 January 1838–31 December 1839, p. [97], Wilford Woodruff, Journals and Papers, Church History Library, Salt Lake City.

particularly poignant.[515] Woodruff recorded that Rigdon's address "was of such a nature in appealing to our affections, in parting with our wives, and children, & the peculiarity of our mission, the perils that we might meet with, & the blessings that we should receive, &c. that tears was brought from many eyes."[516]

After Rigdon spoke, JS addressed a similar topic: the potential imprisonment and injustice the missionaries might face while preaching. JS alluded to the circumstances he endured while imprisoned in Missouri and offered the apostles and seventies guidance on how to respond if they found themselves in similar situations.[517] Woodruff likely recorded the discourse in a daybook and shortly thereafter copied the discourse into his journal.[518] After recounting the day's events, Woodruff considered the messages of JS, Rigdon, and others who had spoken; he concluded his journal entry with a section labeled "Reflections," in which he wrote: "May we [the Twelve] ever realize that while we are in the service of God & doing his will, that though we may be surrounds by mobs & threatened with death that the Lord is our deliverer & that he will support us in every time of trouble & trial."[519]

Document Transcript

Joseph addressed us in few words & says remember brethren that if you are imprisiond Brother Joseph has been imprisiond before you, if you are placed whare you can ownly see your Brethren through the grates of a window while in Irons[520] because of the gospel of Jesus Christ remember Brother Joseph has been in like circumstances also after other similar remarks the meeting closed [p. [97]]

———— ᘒᓄ ————

Letter from Isaac Galland, 24 July 1839

Source Note

Isaac Galland, Letter, Chillicothe, Ross Co., OH, to JS, Sidney Rigdon, Hyrum Smith, Vinson Knight, and George W. Robinson, Commerce, Hancock Co., IL, 24 July 1839. Featured version copied [between

---

515. JS, Journal, 7 July 1839, in *JSP,* J1:345–347; Woodruff, Journal, 7 July 1839.

516. Woodruff, Journal, 7 July 1839.

517. See Letter to the Church and Edward Partridge, 20 Mar. 1839, pp. 360–361 herein; and Bill of Damages, 4 June 1839, pp. 503–505 herein.

518. Although Woodruff's notes on JS's discourse are brief, they contain more detail than does JS's journal, which merely states that JS "requested their [the missionaries'] prayers & promised to pray for them." (JS, Journal, 7 July 1839, in *JSP,* J1:347.)

519. Woodruff, Journal, 7 July 1839.

520. Several letters JS composed while imprisoned in Missouri mention being in chains or bonds and looking through grates of windows or doors. (See Letter to Emma Smith, 12 Nov. 1838, p. 292 herein; Letter to the Church in Caldwell Co., MO, 16 Dec. 1838, p. 299 herein; and Letter to Emma Smith, 4 Apr. 1839, p. 403 herein.)

5 Aug. and 30 Oct. 1839] in JS Letterbook 2, pp. 70–71; handwriting of James Mulholland; JS Collection, CHL. For more information on JS Letterbook 2, see Source Notes for Multiple-Entry Documents, p. 566 herein.

Historical Introduction

On 24 July 1839, land speculator and Latter-day Saint Isaac Galland wrote to JS and other church leaders in Illinois regarding Galland's recent travels and conversations with notable men about the church. Galland's relationship with the church began in February 1839 as a financial association.[521] In several transactions between 30 April and 26 June 1839, Galland sold church leaders land in Hancock County, Illinois—including the hotel in which he was living at Commerce—and in Lee County, Iowa Territory.[522] Likely influenced by interactions with JS and other Latter-day Saints, Galland was baptized and confirmed by JS on 3 July in Commerce. The same day, JS ordained him to the priesthood office of elder.[523] Within a day, Galland and his family left Illinois on a steam packet, having divested their western land holdings to the church and wanting to return to the East, where they were originally from.[524] The boat stopped in St. Louis, Missouri, before arriving in Chillicothe, Ohio, around 13 July. Galland and his family took up residence at a hotel, where Galland planned to live until he could purchase a home in the region.[525] He may have written the featured letter from this hotel.

In this 24 July 1839 letter addressed to the First Presidency, scribe George W. Robinson, and Bishop Vinson Knight (who acted as a church agent in many of the Iowa Territory land transactions),[526] Galland portrayed himself as an ardent advocate of and missionary for the church. However, a letter he had sent two days earlier to his friend Samuel Swasey, a New Hampshire politician, differed significantly in content and tone, suggesting that Galland was

---

521. See Historical Introduction to Letter from Edward Partridge, 5 Mar. 1839, pp. 326–328 herein; Letter to Isaac Galland, 22 Mar. 1839, pp. 377–388 herein; and Letter to Edward Partridge and the Church, ca. 22 Mar. 1839, pp. 391–392 herein.

522. Agreement with George W. Robinson, 30 Apr. 1839, pp. 441–442 herein; Hancock Co., IL, Deed Records, 1817–1917, vol. 12 G, p. 247, 30 Apr. 1839, microfilm 954,195; Lee Co., IA, Land Records, 1836–1961, vol. 1, pp. 507–510, microfilm 959,238; vol. 2, pp. 3–6, 13–16, 26 June 1839, microfilm 959,239, U.S. and Canada Record Collection, FHL.

523. JS, Journal, 3 July 1839, in *JSP*, J1:345; see also Letter to Isaac Galland, 22 Mar. 1839, pp. 377–388 herein.

524. According to Latter-day Saint Franklin D. Richards, Galland and his family left the region because his wife was opposed to the church. (Franklin D. Richards, Quincy, IL, to Phineas Richards and Wealthy Dewey Richards, 5 Aug.–5 Sept. 1839, typescript, Richards Family Collection, CHL; see also Isaac Galland, Chillicothe, OH, to Samuel Swasey, North Haverhill, NH, 22 July 1839, CCLA.)

525. Isaac Galland, Chillicothe, OH, to Samuel Swasey, North Haverhill, NH, 22 July 1839, CCLA. Shortly after Galland arrived in Chillicothe, an anonymous advertisement was published in a local newspaper, soliciting a house "for a small family." The advertisement indicated that all responses were to be given to Ely Bentley, the owner of the hotel where Galland was staying, located at the corner of Water and Walnut streets. According to the ad, Bentley would forward responses to the interested party, presumably Galland. ("House Wanted," *Scioto Gazette* [Chillicothe, OH], 1 Aug. 1839, [3]; "National Hotel," *Scioto Gazette*, 29 Aug. 1839, [3].)

526. See Lee Co., IA, Land Records, 1836–1961, bk. 2, pp. 3–6, 13–16, 26 June 1839, microfilm 959,239, U.S. and Canada Record Collection, FHL.

less committed to the church than his 24 July letter purports. In his letter to Swasey, Galland related a brief history of the Saints' expulsion from Missouri but did not mention his conversion or his association with the Saints beyond land transactions. Further, while Galland's letter to JS and others contained several expressions of confidence in the church, Galland's correspondence with Swasey included the prediction that once the Saints established themselves in Illinois, their success would "induce the surrounding thieves to rob them again; at which time they will no doubt have to renounce their religion; or submit to a repetition of similar acts of violence, and outrage, as have already been inflicted on them."[527]

Galland's letter to church leaders arrived in Commerce by 11 September 1839, when JS responded with an update on the affairs of the church.[528] Although Galland's original letter is apparently not extant, James Mulholland copied it and JS's response into Letterbook 2 sometime between 5 August and 30 October 1839.[529]

Document Transcript

Chillicothe July 24th 1839

My very dear friends

After a journey of 9 days we reached this city in health and safety. No very remarkable incident occurred during our voyage excepting that we were very near being capsised on our passage from Cincinnatti to Portsmouth by a tornado, which rendered the Boat unmanageable, And at the moment she was completely turned upon her beam ends And about to go over, bottom upwards, She struck the shore broadside, And soon afterwards began to right up again. Our voyage was rather pleasant than otherwise. I find the public mind awfully abused in relation both to the doctrines as well as manners and morals of the latter day Saints.[530]

We had on board as far as St Louis, a gentleman from Delaware a M[r] [Arnold] Naudain late a Senator in congress from that State,[531] I had Some

---

527. Isaac Galland, Chillicothe, OH, to Samuel Swasey, North Haverhill, NH, 22 July 1839, CCLA.

528. JS, Commerce, IL, to Isaac Galland, Kirtland, OH, 11 Sept. 1839, in JS Letterbook 2, pp. 71–73.

529. Mulholland copied Galland's letter after he recorded a 5 August 1839 letter to Isaac Russell on page 69 of JS Letterbook 2, making that the earliest likely copying date for Galland's letter. For information on the latest likely copying date, see 248n440 herein.

530. Newspapers across the country were continuing to publish articles about the causes and results of the 1838 Missouri conflict. Additionally, newspapers began publishing in April 1839 a letter supposedly written by Matilda Sabin Spalding Davison that revived the allegation that the Book of Mormon was based on a fictional manuscript titled "Manuscript Found," written by Davison's late husband, Solomon Spalding. For example, a newspaper published at Chillicothe—the *Scioto Gazette*—printed at least two stories on the Saints in the month before Galland's arrival. One condemned the reported beating and shooting of a church member in Iowa Territory, while the other summarized Davison's letter. ("The Mormon Bible," *Scioto Gazette* [Chillicothe, OH], 20 June 1839, [1]; "Inexcusable," *Scioto Gazette,* 27 June 1839, [2]; see also John Storrs, "Mormonism," *Boston Recorder,* 19 Apr. 1839, [1].)

531. Naudain served as a United States senator for Delaware from 1830 to 1836.[a] After his resignation from the Senate, Naudain apparently spent some time in the western United States and in 1837

Isaac Galland. In early July 1839, Isaac Galland—a land speculator and recent convert—moved with his family from Commerce, Illinois, to Ohio. Later that month, Galland wrote a letter to Joseph Smith and other church leaders, describing his journey and his conversations with notable gentlemen regarding the church. (Church History Library, Salt Lake City.)

conversation with him, to whom also I sold one copy of The Book of Mormon He is a gentleman of very pleasant manners— And of good moral principles And I was much pleased with the uncompromising aversion which he manifested in his address on the 4th Inst towards all mobs, and lawless acts of

contemplated moving to Illinois.[b] Like Galland, Naudain was a land speculator, and he owned significant tracts of land in Illinois, Indiana, and Iowa Territory. He was likely in Illinois because some of his property in Springfield, Illinois, had been seized and was pending auction in consequence of his failure to pay taxes.[c] (a. *Biographical Directory of the United States Congress, 1774–2005,* 1644. b. "Mr. Webster," *Sangamo Journal* [Springfield, IL], 24 June 1837, [2]. c. Gates, "Southern Investments in Northern Lands," 169; "Notice Is Hereby Given," *Sangamo Journal,* 12 July 1839, [3]; Arnold Naudain, Decatur, IL, to Richard F. Barrett, 20 July 1839, in *Sangamo Journal,* 26 July 1839, [2]; "Springfield," *Sangamo Journal,* 16 Aug. 1839, [1].)

violence,[532] he expressed the most painful apprehensions for the fate of our present form of government, And entreated every individual who had the least love for his country, or wish for its perpetuity; to rally ~~round~~ to the support of the majesty of its laws. And to use his influence in suppressing insubordination and lawlessness in whatever they may present themselves.[533]

I heard of Elder Green [John P. Greene] at Cincinnati, but do not know whether he was there at that time or not.[534] I have not yet done anything, except to vindicate the truth wherever I have heard it assailed, And on suitable occasions to introduce the subject as a topic of conversation

I have had several very friendly tho' rather argumentative interviews with a Dr [Benjamin] Carpenter[535] of this City who seems entirely absorbed in the doctrines of Emanuel Swedenburg [Swedenborg]—[536] I have conceded to him, that it is not impossible but that the Lord did reveal those spiritual interpretations of the scriptures to Swedenborg of which he asserts, but if so, it was certainly done to shame the metaphisical follies of the mother of harlots[537] And her daughters who had as well in the age in which the Baron[538]

---

532. TEXT: Possibly "violence;".

533. While Naudain may have been referring to the recent expulsion of the Saints from Missouri, his remarks were more likely an expression of a broader complaint about the alleged lawlessness of American politics. Members of the Whig Party, such as Naudain, often considered themselves advocates for law and order, in opposition to the dangerous populism of Jacksonian Democrats. For example, in January 1838, ardent Whig Abraham Lincoln gave an address during which he complained about "the increasing disregard for law which pervades the country," leading men to substitute "worse than savage mobs, for the executive ministers of justice." Lincoln implored his listeners not "to violate in the least particular, the laws of the country; and never to tolerate their violation by others." (Howe, *What Hath God Wrought,* 599; *Collected Works of Abraham Lincoln,* 1:109, 112.)

534. Greene passed through Cincinnati on his way east to preside over the church in New York. (See Minutes, 6 May 1839, p. 451 herein; Authorization for John P. Greene, ca. 6 May 1839, pp. 454–456 herein; and Letter from John P. Greene, 30 June 1839, pp. 512–516 herein.)

535. Carpenter was a doctor who served as editor of a local Whig newspaper, the *Scioto Gazette and Independent Whig,* from 1834 to 1835. ("Prospectus of the Scioto Gazette," *Scioto Gazette and Independent Whig* [Chillicothe, OH], 23 Apr. 1834, [2]; "Valedictory," *Scioto Gazette and Independent Whig,* 15 Apr. 1835, [3].)

536. Swedenborg, an eighteenth-century Swedish theologian and mystic, published numerous books describing his visions of the afterlife, relating conversations with angels, and expounding esoteric doctrines. After his death, some of his followers in England formed the New Jerusalem Church, or New Church, based on his teachings. A national Swedenborgian society called the New Jerusalem Church was organized in the United States in 1817, and a congregation of the New Jerusalem Church was organized in Carpenter's home in Chillicothe in 1838. (McDannell and Lang, *Heaven,* 181–184, 234–235; Ahlstrom, *Religious History of the American People,* 483–486; Smith, "Rise of the New Jerusalem Church in Ohio," 393.)

537. See Revelation 17:5.

538. In 1719, Swedenborg was elevated to the Swedish nobility. Because his status was roughly equivalent to that of an English baron, in the United States he was often referred to as Baron Swedenborg. (See Tafel, *Documents concerning the Life and Character of Emanuel Swedenborg,* 3, 32.)

wrote his metaphisical theology, as in the present age, ran to the most extravagant lengths of philosophising religion and obscuring every truth in the gospel, and the axioms of common sense; hence that they should have those follies to their full, like the hebrews who murmured in the wilderness for flesh, that they ~~might~~ ⟨should⟩ be ~~So~~ gorged with it, ~~And~~ ⟨that they might,⟩ die with it between their teeth—[539] their [p. 70] stomachs being already filled to overflowing, And so of the doctrines of the "New Jerusalem Church" if none but those who read And understand the many thousand metaphysical solutions of philisophical problems, which Swedenborg has published, can be saved, then truly must Heaven be content with a spare population until the ~~inhabitants~~ intellectual capacities of the human race are vastly improved— but if the wisdom of this world is foolishness with God, And if God has chosen a system of salvation which is to the greeks foolishness And is not taught in the wisdom of mens words,[540] then indeed must it be a vain effort to establish a system in lieu thereof, which is purely the wisdom of the wise— And which has for its whole charm the praise of being philosophically systematic.

I expect next week to set out for Akron and Kirtland And as I shall write immediately on my return to this place, or perhaps from one of the above places, I will now conclude by requesting that I may be favored with letters from as many of you as can take time to write me, I shall probably have something more interesting to write about when I write you again, give my best wishes and ~~my~~ Assurance of my sincere affection to all the brethren [a]nd believe me ever your's most sincerely—

I[saac] Galland

P. S. Please let me hear every matter of importance which relates to the success or hindrance, prosperity or adversity of the Church.

Yours truly
I. G

To J Smith Jr
S[idney] Rigdon
H[yrum] Smith
V[inson] Knight
G[eorge] W. Robinson &c
Commerce Hancock Co Illinois——

———— ∾ ————

539. See Numbers chap. 11.
540. See 1 Corinthians 1:17–31.

Discourse, 28 July 1839

Source Note

JS, Discourse, Commerce, Hancock Co., IL, 28 July 1839. Featured version copied [ca. 28 July 1839]
in JS, Journal, 1839, p. 10; handwriting of James Mulholland; JS Collection, CHL. For more information
on JS, Journal, 1839, see Source Notes for Multiple-Entry Documents, p. 565 herein.

Historical Introduction

On 28 July 1839, JS delivered a discourse in a Sunday worship service at Commerce,
Illinois. Beginning in late June, Latter-day Saints in and around Commerce and
Montrose, Iowa Territory, began contracting malaria carried by mosquitos in the nearby
swamplands.[541] The disease soon reached epidemic proportions in the area, and church
member Wandle Mace wrote in his autobiography that "Joseph and Emma his wife would
ride on horseback from place to place, visiting the sick anointing with oil and laying on
hands, and healing them."[542] JS and Emma Smith also cared for ill Latter-day Saints in the
Smith home, and soon their home and yard were filled with the sick.[543] Latter-day Saint
Zina Huntington recounted that in the Smiths' yard, "there were hundreds, lying in tents
and wagons, who needed care."[544] In July, after weeks of JS caring for the sick, including
his father and one of his sons, JS contracted the disease and was bedridden for several
days.[545] No meetings were held on Sunday, 21 July, "on account of much rain, and much
sickness," but several elders gave blessings to the sick.[546] On 22 July, according to apostle
Wilford Woodruff, "the power of God rested upon" JS, giving him the strength to leave
his sickbed and begin blessing and healing the infirm. He first blessed those in and around
his home, "commanding the sick in the name of Jesus Christ to arise and be made whole."
Then he, along with other elders of the church, traveled from house to house in Commerce,
"healing the sick as he went." JS and the elders then crossed the river to Montrose, where
several of the members of the Quorum of the Twelve Apostles and their families were living, and administered more healing blessings before returning to Commerce.[547] Woodruff

---

541. JS described Commerce in summer 1839 as a place that was "literally a wilderness" and was "so
unhealthy very few could live there." In his autobiography, John L. Butler recounted that JS described the
Commerce area as "a low marshy wet damp and nasty place." (Historian's Office, JS History, Draft
Notes, 11 June 1839; Butler, Autobiography, 33.)

542. Mace, Autobiography, 31. Mace's statement is ambiguous as to whether Emma was involved
in the blessings given to the sick. For more information on women performing healing blessings, see
Derr et al., *First Fifty Years of Relief Society*, xxiv–xxv, 55, 55n156; and Stapley and Wright, "Female
Ritual Healing in Mormonism," 1–11.

543. Historian's Office, Brigham Young History Drafts, 25–26; Editorial Note, in *JSP*, J1:348.

544. Tullidge, *Women of Mormondom*, 214.

545. Woodruff, Journal, 12 and 19 July 1839; "The Memoirs of President Joseph Smith," *Saints' Herald*,
20 Nov. 1934, 1479; Historian's Office, Brigham Young History Drafts, 25.

546. JS, Journal, 21 July 1839, in *JSP*, J1:348.

547. Woodruff, Journal, 22 July 1839; Historian's Office, Brigham Young History Drafts, 25–26; Mace,
Autobiography, 31.

noted that after the sick were blessed, they "leaped from their beds made whole by the power of God."[548]

On 28 July, Sunday meetings resumed, with Parley P. Pratt speaking in the morning and Orson Pratt speaking in the afternoon. After Orson Pratt spoke, JS gave a discourse encouraging the Saints to purify themselves and observe the sacrament of the Lord's Supper so that the sick among them might be healed. A brief account of JS's discourse was recorded in his journal by James Mulholland. The wording of the account suggests that it may have been dictated to Mulholland in retrospect.

Document Transcript

Sunday 28 meeting held as usual. [. . .] [p. 9] [. . .] I spoke & admonished the church individually to set his house in order,[549] to make clean the insid[e of] the platter,[550] and to meet on the next sabbath[551] to partake of sacrament in order that by our obedieence to the ordinances, we might be enabled to prevail with God against the destroyer,[552] and that the sick may be healed.

———— ☙ ————

Agreement with Mead & Betts, 2 August 1839

Source Note

Perkins & Osborn on behalf of Mead & Betts, Agreement with Oliver Granger [agent] on behalf of JS, Painesville, Geauga Co., OH, 2 Aug. 1839; handwriting of William Perkins; signature of Mead & Betts in unidentified handwriting, possibly Salmon Osborn; one page; Hiram Kimball Collection, CHL. Includes docket.

Single leaf measuring 12½ × 7½ inches (32 × 19 cm), with thirty-nine printed lines (now faded). The document was folded for carrying and filing. A docket in unidentified handwriting on the verso reads "Mead & Betts". The agreement was retained by Oliver Granger and later came into the possession of his daughter, Sarah Granger Kimball, and then other members of the Kimball family. This document and other papers in the possession of the Kimball family were donated to the Church History Department in 2013.[553]

---

548. Woodruff, Journal, 22 July 1839.

549. See 2 Kings 20:1; Isaiah 38:1; Revelation, 8 Mar. 1833, in *JSP,* D3:29 [D&C 90:18]; and Revelation, 6 May 1833, in *JSP,* D3:90 [D&C 93:43].

550. That is, to purify oneself from within. (See Matthew 23:25–26; and Luke 11:39.)

551. JS's journal states that he spent the rest of the week "among the sick, who in general are gaining strength, and recovering health," and that the next Sunday, 4 August 1839, JS "exhorted the Church at length, concerning the necessity of being righteous and clean at heart before the Lord." Wilford Woodruff described the 4 August Sunday service as a "meeting of prayer & fasting." (JS, Journal, 28 July–4 Aug. 1839, in *JSP,* J1:349; Woodruff, Journal, 4 Aug. 1839.)

552. The term *destroyer* was often used to refer to the devil. In his autobiography, Mace wrote of the spread of disease in Commerce and Montrose in summer 1839, noting that "it seemed, that all the powers of Satan, was at work to destroy this people." (Mace, Autobiography, 31.)

553. See the full bibliographic entry for the Hiram Kimball Collection in the CHL catalog.

Historical Introduction

On 2 August 1839, William Perkins of the law partnership Perkins & Osborn drafted on behalf of the mercantile firm Mead & Betts an agreement with Oliver Granger, who was acting as an agent for JS and the church. The purpose of the agreement was to resolve debts owed to Mead & Betts by the Kirtland, Ohio, mercantile firm Cahoon, Carter & Co., which was operated by church members Reynolds Cahoon, Jared Carter, and Hyrum Smith.[554] The debts were reflected in three promissory notes, which were signed by Cahoon, Carter, and Hyrum Smith as principals and by twenty-nine individuals, including JS, as sureties. The sureties were liable for the debts if the principals defaulted; however, instead of seeking payment from the three principals, Perkins pursued payment from all thirty-two signers. In the agreement, Granger arranged payment on behalf of JS and the other signers and not only on behalf of Cahoon, Carter, and Hyrum Smith.

The earliest documented transaction between a Latter-day Saint firm and Mead & Betts occurred in 1836, when Cahoon, Carter & Co. bought goods from the New York store.[555] The debts owed to Mead & Betts and to three other firms in New York—John A. Newbould, Holbrook & Ferme, and Halsted, Haines & Co.—were renegotiated on 1 September 1837 with the help of William Perkins.[556] Two Kirtland-area firms were involved in these renegotiations: Cahoon, Carter & Co. arranged to pay its outstanding debts to Mead & Betts and Halsted, Haines & Co., while Rigdon, Smith & Co. arranged repayment with Holbrook & Ferme.[557] Unfortunately, no information is extant on the arrangements with the firm John A. Newbould, but the amounts listed on invoices from the firm suggest that the 1 September agreement combined the debts owed by Cahoon, Carter & Co. and Rigdon, Smith & Co.[558] In the renegotiation with Mead & Betts, Hyrum Smith, Reynolds Cahoon, and Jared Carter were named the principals on the three promissory notes, each for over $1,000, and JS and twenty-eight other Latter-day Saints signed as sureties.[559]

---

554. Mead & Betts was composed of two partners, Matthew B. Mead and Francis Betts. They sold wholesale dry goods in Buffalo, New York, in 1836. (*Directory for the City of Buffalo* [1836], 45, 109.)

555. The firms may have started doing business together in 1835, when Cahoon, Carter & Co. was established. (Advertisement, *Northern Times,* 2 Oct. 1835, [4]; Mead & Betts, Invoice, Buffalo, NY, to Cahoon, Carter & Co., 18 June 1836, JS Office Papers, CHL; see also Historical Introduction to Statement of Account from Perkins & Osborn, ca. 29 Oct. 1838, pp. 252–254 herein.)

556. See Statement of Account from Perkins & Osborn, ca. 29 Oct. 1838, pp. 252–261 herein.

557. JS et al., Promissory Note, Kirtland, OH, to Holbrook & Ferme, 1 Sept. 1837, photocopy, CHL; JS et al., Promissory Note, Kirtland, OH, to Holbrook & Ferme, 1 Sept. 1837, BYU; Hyrum Smith et al., Promissory Note, Kirtland, OH, to Halsted, Haines & Co., 1 Sept. 1837, photocopy, CHL; Hyrum Smith et al., Promissory Note, Kirtland, OH, to Halsted, Haines & Co., 1 Sept. 1837, Brigham Young Office, Halsted, Haines & Co. File, CHL; see also Statement of Account from Perkins & Osborn, ca. 29 Oct. 1838, pp. 252–261 herein.

558. See Statement of Account from Perkins & Osborn, ca. 29 Oct. 1838, pp. 252–261 herein; John A. Newbould, Invoice, Buffalo, NY, to Cahoon, Carter & Co., 17 June 1836; and John A. Newbould, Invoice, Buffalo, NY, to Rigdon, Smith & Cowdery, 17 June 1836, JS Office Papers, CHL.

559. A copy of one of the three notes given to Mead & Betts was recorded in probate records used in lawsuits against the estates of JS and Hyrum Smith. (Hyrum Smith et al., Promissory Note, Kirtland,

Presumably, Perkins & Osborn directed the 2 August 1839 agreement to Oliver Granger because of his role as an agent for the First Presidency and for the church. In this role, Granger was instrumental in addressing outstanding financial matters. By October 1838, he had successfully settled several debts that the First Presidency and other church members owed to Painesville merchants.[560] In a May 1839 general conference of the church in Quincy, Illinois, Granger was directed to preside over church affairs in Kirtland and continue his efforts to resolve the First Presidency's debts.[561] In Granger's capacity as agent, he took responsibility for settling the outstanding debts to the four New York merchants specified in the 2 August agreement. His involvement suggests either that JS was willing to assume responsibility for the debts or that Perkins & Osborn was focusing primarily on JS in efforts to obtain payment.

It is not known which party initiated the 2 August agreement. Granger may have proactively approached Perkins & Osborn or the New York merchants in an effort to repay the debts. Alternatively, Perkins may have presented Granger with a compromise in which Mead & Betts would settle the debts without lawsuits if the firm received partial payment in land. Whatever the case, the terms of the agreement appear to be generous, allowing Granger a year to provide Mead & Betts with land valued at half the amount owed; in return, the New York firm would forgive the other half of the debt. However, the agreement was conditional upon the same arrangement being made between Granger and the three other New York mercantile firms—John A. Newbould, Holbrook & Ferme, and Halsted, Haines & Co. One other agreement, made with John A. Newbould, is extant. This agreement was also written by Perkins & Osborn and was apparently created around the same time as the featured agreement. In the Newbould agreement, the firm's agent, Charles Taylor, agreed to similar terms of repayment, indicating that Granger successfully negotiated with at least one of the three mercantile firms specified in the featured agreement.[562]

As JS's agent in Ohio, Granger retained the 2 August agreement with Mead & Betts, as well as other agreements to resolve JS's debts.[563] These agreements were apparently never filed with JS's other papers.

OH, to Mead & Betts, 1 Sept. 1837, Mead & Betts v. Estate of JS, Illinois State Historical Society, Circuit Court Case Files, CHL.)

560. See Historical Introduction to Letter of Introduction from John Howden, 27 Oct. 1838, pp. 246–248 herein; and Reuben Hitchcock, Receipt, Painesville, OH, to Oliver Granger, 30 Oct. 1838, Hiram Kimball Collection, CHL.

561. Minutes, 4–5 May 1839, p. 445 herein; see also Historical Introduction to Authorization for Oliver Granger, 6 May 1839, pp. 452–453 herein; Authorization for Oliver Granger, 13 May 1839, pp. 456–457 herein; and Revelation, 8 July 1838–E, p. 194 herein [D&C 117:13].

562. It is not clear whether Taylor was in Painesville when he signed the document or whether the agreement was sent to Newbould in New York and then returned to Ohio. (Charles Taylor for John A. Newbould, Agreement with Oliver Granger, ca. 2 Aug. 1839, Hiram Kimball Collection, CHL.)

563. Granger died in Kirtland in 1841. At the time of his death, he was still working to resolve financial matters for JS and the church, and he likely possessed relevant financial documents, such as the Mead & Betts agreement. (Obituary for Oliver Granger, *Times and Seasons,* 15 Sept. 1841, 2:550; JS History, vol. C-1 Addenda, 11.)

Document Transcript

As Attornies for Messrs Mead & Betts we have in our hands for collection thru several notes of hand of Messrs Joseph Smith Jr and thirty one others[564] of the Mormon Church to said Mead & Betts all dated Sept 1, 1837 viz

one at 12 mo for $1177.20
one at 18　"　"　1213.87
one at 24　"　"　1251.54

And by authority from Messrs Mead & Betts we hereby agree with Oliver Granger that if within one year from the first day of October next he shall pay or cause to be paid in cash or good farming land cultivated or wild, & if in lands by good warrantee deed or deeds with unencumbred title, located any where between the Atlantic Ocean and the western border of the State of Ohio,[565] fifty pr cent of the whole amount of said notes and the interest thereon, & shall pay or secure to the staisfaction of Perkins & Osborn their fees and charges in respect of said notes, and also the demands ~~have against~~ said Perkins & Osborn have against the members of said church or any of them for fees and legal services,[566] then the said Mead & Betts will deliver up to the said Granger or his order the said notes—[567] If paid in lands the same are to be ~~applied~~ appraised by good judicious freeholders being Township or county officers and not members of the Mormon Church so called at its real value in cash

It is expressly stipulated that this writing shall not be obligatory unless Messrs Halsted Haines & Co John A Newbould & Holbrook & Firm [Ferme] or those holding the notes given them come into the arrangement—[568]

Dated at Pain[e]sville this 2nd day of August 1839

Mead & Betts by Perkins & Osborn
their Attorneys

———— ☙ ————

564. Perkins & Osborn did not distinguish between the three principals and the twenty-nine sureties but rather indicated all thirty-two signers were equally liable for the repayment.

565. The agreement with John A. Newbould specifies land in Ohio or New York. (Charles Taylor for John A. Newbould, Agreement with Oliver Granger, ca. 2 Aug. 1839, Hiram Kimball Collection, CHL.)

566. See Statement of Account from Perkins & Osborn, ca. 29 Oct. 1838, pp. 252–261 herein.

567. By giving the promissory notes to Granger, the firm would relinquish its claim to the debts owed. Granger, as an agent for JS and the others, could then cancel the notes, such as by removing the signatures, to ensure the notes did not reenter circulation.

568. An agreement with John A. Newbould written circa 2 August 1839 shows that the firm accepted the same terms as those in this agreement with Mead & Betts and suggests that the other two mercantile firms perhaps also accepted the terms, though no written agreements for these firms have been located. Perkins may have written agreements for John A. Newbould, Holbrook & Ferme, and Halsted, Haines & Co. at the time he wrote the agreement for Mead & Betts. (Charles Taylor for John A. Newbould, Agreement with Oliver Granger, ca. 2 Aug. 1839, Hiram Kimball Collection, CHL.)

Whereas Joseph Smith Jr Oliver Granger both on the first day of September 1837 executed their three several promisory notes of that date viz

one at 12 mo for
one at 18 mo for $282.26
one at 24 mo for

all payable to my order — And whereas said Granger proposes within one year from this first day of October next to pay the one half of said Notes and interest thereon in lands — Now we agree that when the said Granger shall before said first day of October Eighteen Hundred and forty make or cause to be made to us a good indefeasible title by warrantee deed to good farming lands situate in either of the following States Eastern New York or Ohio ————

either Cultivated or wild, at the appraisal of judicious men, being trustees or select men of townships or county officers in the township or County where such lands shall be situate at their fair marketable value in cash, to the amount of one half of said demands, we will then discharge the said Notes
John A. Newbould
By Charles Taylor

Agreements with New York Merchants. In early August 1839, church agent Oliver Granger made agreements with four New York mercantile firms to renegotiate debts incurred by mercantile firms that Joseph Smith and other church leaders operated while living in Kirtland, Ohio. The payments had been renegotiated in 1837 but remained outstanding, and these 1839 agreements demonstrate Granger's continuing efforts to pay debts still owed by Joseph Smith and other Latter-day Saints. The agreements with two of the New York merchants are extant: one with John A. Newbould (image above) and one with Mead & Betts (see transcript on pp. 535–538 herein). Handwriting of William Perkins; signature of John A. Newbould by Charles Taylor. Agreement with Oliver Granger, circa 2 Aug. 1839, Hiram Kimball Collection, Church History Library, Salt Lake City.

Discourse, between circa 26 June and circa 4 August 1839–A

Source Note

JS, Discourse, [Montrose, Lee Co., Iowa Territory, or Commerce, Hancock Co., IL], [between ca. 26 June and ca. 4 Aug. 1839]. Featured version copied [between 13 Jan. 1840 and 20 Apr. 1841] in Willard Richards, "W. Richards Pocket Companion Written in England," pp. 63–73; handwriting of Willard Richards; Willard Richards, Journals and Papers, CHL. For more information on Willard Richards, "W. Richards Pocket Companion Written in England," see Source Notes for Multiple-Entry Documents, p. 577 herein.

Historical Introduction

In the "Pocket Companion" notebook that Willard Richards kept during his 1837–1841 mission in England, he included a discourse JS gave on the priesthood and other doctrinal matters. Although Richards did not identify the discourse as JS's, the majority of the entries in the pocket notebook are JS revelations or discourses that Richards copied without attributing them to JS. When this discourse was added to JS's multivolume manuscript history by Thomas Bullock in 1845, the discourse was ascribed to JS.[569]

Richards did not date this discourse when he copied it into his notebook, but JS probably gave the discourse in summer 1839, likely between late June and early August, as members of the Quorum of the Twelve Apostles and the Quorums of the Seventy prepared to leave for their mission to Europe. During late June and early July, JS addressed the apostles and seventies on several "keys of the Kingdom of God," including the discernment of spirits, the spirit of prophecy and revelation, humility and cooperation, and the doctrines of election and salvation.[570] The discourse featured here explores similar themes and was probably given around the same time.[571] In JS's history, Bullock placed this discourse after a JS sermon dated 2 July and added a heading to this discourse, explaining that JS gave it around the time of the 2 July sermon.[572] However, the discourse could have been given as late as 4 August, the last time the apostles and seventies met with JS before the first of the men left Commerce for their mission to Europe.[573] Although the apostles and seventies had intended to leave in early July, they were delayed when most of them and their families contracted malaria.[574] Because so many Saints were ill, few meetings were held in July. Sunday meetings resumed on 28 July, with JS and some

---

569. JS History, vol. C-1, addenda, 11; Jessee, "Writing of Joseph Smith's History," 441.

570. See Woodruff, Journal, 27 June 1839; Discourse, 27 June 1839, p. 510 herein; Discourse, between ca. 26 June and ca. 2 July 1839, pp. 523–526 herein; and Discourse, 2 July 1839, pp. 518–521 herein.

571. The featured discourse includes a discussion of how to discern between good and evil spirits. A discourse JS gave on 27 June was also on the topic of discerning spirits, and it is unclear whether JS revisited this subject in multiple discourses or whether the featured document is a different account of the 27 June discourse. (See Discourse, 27 June 1839, p. 510 herein.)

572. JS History, vol. C-1, addenda, 11.

573. JS, Journal, 4 Aug. 1839, in *JSP*, J1:349–350; Woodruff, Journal, 4 Aug. 1839.

574. See Historical Introduction to Discourse, 7 July 1839, pp. 526–528 herein; and Historical Introduction to Discourse, 28 July 1839, pp. 534–535 herein.

Contents

Willard Richards's "Pocket Companion." While serving a mission in England, Willard Richards inscribed several of Joseph Smith's revelations and discourses into a small notebook. He copied many of them from Wilford Woodruff's "Book of Revelations." The "Pocket Companion" also contains three undated discourses Smith gave in summer 1839, which Richards copied from the records of another missionary in England, possibly John Taylor. Willard Richards, "Pocket Companion," Willard Richards, Papers, Church History Library, Salt Lake City.

of the apostles speaking the next week, on 4 August. On 8 August, two of the apostles departed for Europe.[575]

Richards's copy of this discourse states that the priesthood authority Peter, James, and John gave to JS was the same that had been given to the ancient patriarchs beginning with Adam and that this authority was eternal. The discourse also expounds on the prophecies in Daniel chapter 7, the role of Adam, the gatherings that had and would yet take place in Adam-ondi-Ahman, and other signs prophesied to occur before the second coming of Jesus Christ.

Richards was not present when JS gave the discourse; he was proselytizing in England and apparently copied the discourse from one of the apostles or seventies who arrived in Britain starting in December 1839 and who brought an account of the discourse with them.[576] He copied this discourse into his "Pocket Companion" between January 1840 and April 1841, at around the same time he copied two other discourses: one on the parable of the sower in Matthew, chapter 13, and the other on John, chapter 14, and the steps necessary to gain salvation and eternal life.[577] As with the discourse featured here, the other two discourses were likely given between late June and early August, and Richards probably copied the discourses from the same source. Although the source Richards copied from is unknown, he may have copied from notes that apostle John Taylor made. Two parenthetical remarks included in Richards's copy of the featured discourse end with the initials "J. T."— presumably indicating the notes were interpolations made in the text by Taylor, who arrived in England in January 1840.

Document Transcript

The Priesthood was.

first given To Adam:[578] he obtained ~~to~~ the <u>first</u> <u>Presidency</u> & held the <u>Keys</u> of it, from genration to Generation; he obtained it in the creation before the world was formed as in Gen. <u>1, 26:28,</u>— he had dominion given him over every living Creature. He is Michael, the Archangel,[579] spoken of in the Scriptures,— Then to Noah who is Gabriel,[580] he stands next in authority to

---

575. Woodruff, Journal, 8 Aug. 1839.

576. See Richards, Journal, 16 Jan. and 9 Apr. 1840; "From England," *Times and Seasons,* May 1840, 1:110–111; and "From England," *Times and Seasons,* June 1840, 1:119–121. Apostles John Taylor and Wilford Woodruff arrived in England in January 1840; several other apostles arrived in April. Richards could have copied the discourse notes of one of these apostles anytime between their 1840 arrivals and his 1841 return to the United States.

577. See Discourse, between ca. 26 June and ca. 4 Aug. 1839–B, pp. 548–550 herein; and Discourse, between ca. 26 June and ca. 4 Aug. 1839–C, pp. 550–553 herein.

578. See Revelation, 22–23 Sept. 1832, in *JSP,* D2:295 [D&C 84:16]; and Book of Abraham Manuscript, ca. Summer–Fall 1835, p. 1 [Abraham 1:3].

579. See Revelation 12:7; and Jude 1:9; see also Revelation, 27–28 Dec. 1832, in *JSP,* D2:345 [D&C 88:112–115]. As early as 1833, church leaders identified Adam as Michael. (See Oliver Cowdery, Kirtland, OH, to John Whitmer, [Liberty, MO], 1 Jan. 1834, in Cowdery, Letterbook, 15.)

580. See Daniel 8:16; 9:21; and Luke 1:19, 26; see also Oliver Cowdery, Kirtland, OH, to John Whitmer, [Liberty, MO], 1 Jan. 1834, in Cowdery, Letterbook, 15.

Adam in the Priesthood; he was called of God to this office & was the Father of all living[581] in his day, & To him was Given the Dominion. These men held keys. first on earth, & then in Heaven.— The Priesthood is an everlasting principle & Existed with God from Eternity & will to Eternity, without beginning of days or end of years.[582] The Keys have to be brought from heaven whenever the Gospel is sent.— When they are revealed from Heaven it is by Adams Authority.

Dan VII Speaks of the Ancient of days, he means the oldest man, our Father Adam, Michael; he will call his children together. & hold a council with them.[583] to prepare them for the coming [p. 63] of the Son of Man.[584] He, (Adam) is the Father of the human family[585] & presides over the Spirits of all men, & all that have had the Keys must Stand before him in this grand Council. This may take place before some of us leave this stage of action, The Son of Man Stands before him & there is given him glory & dominion.— Adam delivers up his stewardship to Christ, that which was deliverd to him as holding the Keys of the Universe, but retains his standing as head of the human family.[586]

The Spirit of Man is not a created being; it existed from Eternity & will exist to Eternity. Any thing created cannot be Eternal & earth, water &c—[587] all these had their existence in an elementary state from Eternity.[588] Our Savior Speaks of Children & Says their angels always stand before my father.[589]

The father called all spirits before him at the creation of Man & organized them.[590] He (Adam) is the head. & was told to multiply.[591] The Keys were ⟨first⟩ given to him, ⟨& by him to others⟩ he will have to [p. 64] give an account of his Stewardship, & they to him. The Priesthood is everlasting. The Savior. Moses. & Elias— gave the Keys to Peter, James & John on the Mount when they were

---

581. See Genesis 3:20; and Old Testament Revision 1, p. 7 [Moses 4:26].

582. See Hebrews 7:3; Book of Mormon, 1830 ed., 259 [Alma 13:7–9]; and Revelation, 22–23 Sept. 1832, in *JSP*, D2:293–295 [D&C 84:1–17].

583. In 1838, JS identified Spring Hill, Missouri, as Adam-ondi-Ahman, "the place where Adam dwelt" and "where Adam shall come to visit his people, or the Ancient of days shall sit as spoken of by Daniel the Prophet." (Letter to Stephen Post, 17 Sept. 1838, p. 242 herein; JS, Journal, 19 May 1838, in *JSP*, J1:271.)

584. See Daniel 7:13.

585. See Old Testament Revision 1, p. 2 [Moses 1:34]; and Revelation, ca. Aug. 1835, in *JSP*, D4:411 [D&C 27:11].

586. See Revelation, 1 Mar. 1832, in Doctrine and Covenants 76:3, 1835 ed. [D&C 78:16].

587. TEXT: A vertical line was inscribed on the left and right sides of "&c".

588. See Revelation, 6 May 1833, in *JSP*, D3:89 [D&C 93:29–35].

589. See Matthew 18:10.

590. See Book of Mormon, 1830 ed., 258–259 [Alma 13:2–5].

591. See Old Testament Revision 1, p. 8 [Moses 5:2]; and Genesis 1:28.

transfigured before him.[592] The Priesthood is everlasting. without biginning of days or end of years, without Father. Mother &c.—[593]

If there is no change of ordinances there is no change of Priesthood. Wherever the ordinances of the Gospel are adminesterd there is the priesthood. How have we come at the Priesthood in the last days? ~~They~~ ⟨It⟩ came down, down in regular succession— Peter James & John had it given to them & they gave it up.— Christ is the Great High priest;[594] Adam next.— Paul speaks of ~~an~~ the Church coming to an innumerable company of Angels, to God the Judge of all, the spirits of Just men made perfect, to Jesus the mediator of the New Covenant.[595] &c Heb XII, 2 3. I saw Adam in the valley of Ah-dam ondi-ahman— he called together his children & blessed them with a Patriarchal blessing. The Lord appeared in their midst. & he (Adam) blessed them [p. 65] all & foretold what should befall them to the latest generation— See D.C. Sec III 28. 29 par.—[596] This is why Abraham blessd his posterity; he wanted to bring them into the presence of God. They looked for a city, &c,—[597] Moses Sought to bring the children of Israel into the presence of God.[598] through the power of the Priesthood, but he could not. In the first ages of the world they tried to establish the same thing— & there were Elias's[599] raised up who tried to restore these very glories but did not obtain them.[600] ⟨but⟩ (Enoch did for himself & those that were with ~~them~~ Him, but not for the world.[601] J. T.[602]) They prophecied of a day when this Glory would be revealed.—[603] Paul spoke of the Dispensation of the fulness of times. when

---

592. See Matthew 17:1–3.

593. See New Testament Revision 2, part 2, p. 139 [Joseph Smith Translation, Hebrews 7:3].

594. See Hebrews 4:14; and 9:11.

595. See Hebrews 12:22–24.

596. Instruction on Priesthood, between ca. 1 Mar. and ca. 4 May 1835, in *JSP*, D4:317 [D&C 107:53–57].

597. See Hebrews 11:8–10.

598. See Exodus chaps. 19–20; and Revelation, 22–23 Sept. 1832, in *JSP*, D2:295–296 [D&C 84:23–25].

599. The name Elias is a title JS applied to individuals in the Bible who had preparatory or restorative responsibilities, such as Noah, John the Baptist, and John the Revelator. (See Revelation, ca. Aug. 1835, in *JSP*, D4:411 [D&C 27:6–7]; New Testament Revision 1, p. 28 [Joseph Smith Translation, Matthew 11:13–15]; New Testament Revision 2, part 1, p. 32 [Joseph Smith Translation, Matthew 17:10–14]; New Testament Revision 2, part 2, p. 106 [Joseph Smith Translation, John 1:20–28]; and Answers to Questions, between ca. 4 and ca. 20 Mar. 1832, in *JSP*, D2:213 [D&C 77:14].)

600. TEXT: A line connects this insertion with the sentence following the parenthetical note.

601. See Old Testament Revision 1, pp. 16, 19 [Moses 7:18–19, 69].

602. Probably the initials for John Taylor. It is not clear why his initials were included here and in a second parenthetical note. The notes perhaps originated in a copy of the discourse that Taylor made.

603. See Isaiah 40:5; and 1 Peter 4:13.

God would gather together all things in one[604] &c ⟨&⟩, Those men to whom these Keys have been given will have to be there (I.E. when Adam shall again assemble his children of the Priesthood, & christ be in their midst) the Ancient of Days come &c &c J. T.) And they without us ~~could~~ ⟨cannot⟩ not be made perfect.[605] These men are in heaven, but their children [p. 66] are on Earth. Their bowels yearn over us.[606] God sends down men for this reason, Mat. 13.41. & the Son of man shall send forth his angels &c— All these authoritative characters will come down & join hands in hand in bringing about this work— The kingdom of heaven is like a grain of mustard seed. the mustard seed is Small but brings forth a large tree. ⟨and the fowls lodge in the branches⟩[607] The fowls are the Angels. the Book of Mormon perhaps. ~~these~~ thus[608] Angels come down combine together to gather their children, & gather them. We cannot be made perfect without them. nor they without us when these ⟨things⟩ are done the Son of man will descend. the ancient of Days sit.—[609] We may come to an innumerable compa[n]y of Angels have communion with & rece[i]ve instruction from. ⟨them.⟩—[610] Paul told about Moses's proceedings. Spoke of the Children of Israel being baptized.[611] &, he knew this. & that all the ordinances & blessings were in the church. Paul had these things; ⟨&⟩ we may have the fowls of heaven Lodge in the branches &c. The horn made war with the saints, ⟨&⟩ overcame them &c, until the Ancient of Days came, judgment was given to the Saints of the Most [p. 67] High, from the Ancient of Days— the time came that the saints possessed the kingdom—[612] this not only makes us ministers here but in Eternity. Salvation cannot come without Revelation, it is in vain for any one to minister without it.

No man is a minister of Jesus Christ. without being a Prophet. No man can be the minister of Jesus Christ, except he has the testimony of Jesus & this is the Spirit of Prophesy.[613] Whenever Sa[l]vation has been administered it has been by Testimony, Men of the present time testify of Heaven & of Hell, &

---

604. See Ephesians 1:10.

605. See Hebrews 11:40.

606. See Old Testament Revision 1, p. 17 [Moses 7:41].

607. See Luke 13:19; Matthew 13:31–32; and Mark 4:32.

608. TEXT: A curved line connects "angels." to "thus", thereby setting apart "the Book of Mormon perhaps".

609. See Daniel 7:13.

610. See Hebrews 12:22–23.

611. See 1 Corinthians 10:1–4.

612. See Daniel 7:21–22.

613. See Revelation 19:10.

have never Seen either & I will say that no man knows these things without this. Men profess to prophecy. I will prophecy that the signs of the coming of the Son of man are already commencd, one pestilence will dessolate after another. we shall soon have war & bloodshed.[614] The Moon will be turned ~~into~~ into blood,[615] I testify of these things. & that the coming of the Son of Man is nigh [p. 68] even at your doors,—[616] If our souls & our bodies are not looking forth for the coming of the Son of Man. & after we are dead if we are not looking forth. &c We shall be among those who are calling for the rocks to fall upon us[617] &c— The hearts of the children of men will have to be turned to the fathers. & the fathers to the children, living or dead, to prepare them for the coming of the Son of Man. If Elijah did not come the whole earth would be Smitten.[618] There will be here & there a stake &c. ⟨for the gathering of the saints⟩ Some may have cried peace. but the Saints & the world will have little peace from henceforth. Let this not hinder us from going to the Stakes, for God has told us to flee not dallying. or we shall be scattered. one here, another there, There your children shall be blessed & you in the midst of friends where you may be blessed. &c The gospel net gathers of every kind,[619] I prophecy that that man who tarries after he has an opportunity of going will be afflicted by the Devil. Wars are at [p. 69] hand we must not delay, but are not required to sacrifice. We ought to have the building up of Zion as our greatest object.— when wars come we shall have to flee to Zion.[620] The cry is to make haste. The last revelation says ye shall not have time to have gone over the Earth until these things come. It will come as did the Cholera.[621] war. & fires burning Earthquake one pestilence after another &c ~~until~~ until the Ancient of Days come then judgment will be given to the Saints.

---

614. See New Testament Revision 1, p. 56[a] [Joseph Smith—Matthew 1:36]; and Revelation, 25 Dec. 1832, in *JSP,* D2:330–331 [D&C 87].

615. See Joel 2:31; Acts 2:20; and Revelation, Sept. 1830–A, in *JSP,* D1:180 [D&C 29:14].

616. See Mark 13:29; Revelation, ca. 7 Mar. 1831, in *JSP,* D1:279 [D&C 45:63]; and Revelation, 30 Aug. 1831, in *JSP,* D2:54 [D&C 63:53].

617. See Revelation 6:16.

618. See Malachi 4:5–6; Book of Mormon, 1830 ed., 505 [3 Nephi 25:6]; Revelation, ca. Aug. 1835, in *JSP,* D4:411 [D&C 27:9]; and Visions, 3 Apr. 1836, in *JSP,* D5:228–229 [D&C 110:15].

619. See Matthew 13:47–50.

620. See Revelation, ca. 7 Mar. 1831, in *JSP,* D1:280 [D&C 45:68–69].

621. A cholera epidemic that began in India in 1817 reached the East Coast of the United States in 1832. Cholera killed tens of thousands in the United States in the 1830s as it spread across the country. In 1834 Oliver Cowdery described the epidemic as a pestilence signaling Christ's second coming. ("Answer," *The Evening and the Morning Star,* Sept. 1834, 189; see also Jortner, "Cholera, Christ, and Jackson," 237–238.)

Whatsoever you may hear about me or Kirtland, take no notice of.[622] for if it be a place of refuge the Devil will use his greatest efforts to trap the Saints. You must make yourselves acquainted with those men, who, like Daniel, pray three times a day to the house of the Lord.—[623] Look to the Presidency &c ⟨& rece[i]ve instruction⟩.— Every man who is afraid. covetous &c will be taken in a snare— The time is soon coming when no man will have any peace but in Zion & her Stakes.[624] [p. 70]

I saw men hunting the lives of their own sons, & brother murdering brother, women killing their own daughters & daughters seeking the lives of their mothers. I saw armies arrayed against armies I saw blood. desolations, & fires &c,— The Son of Man has said that the mother Shall be against the daughter, & the daughter against the mother &c,[625] &c.— These things are at our doors. They will follow the Saints of God from City To City—[626] Satan will rage & The Spirit of the Devil is now enraged. &c I know not how soon these things will take place, and with a view of them shall I cry peace? NO! I will lift up my voice & testify of them. How long you will have good crops. & the famin be kept. ⟨off⟩ I do not know. when the fig tree leaves, know then that the summer is night at hand.[627] we may look for Angel[s] &c. ⟨& receive their ministreting⟩ but we are to try the Spirits & prove them[628] ⟨for⟩ it is often the case that men. make a mistake in regard to these things.

God has so ordained that when he has communicated, ⟨by vision,⟩ no vision is to be taken but what you see by the seeing of the eye [p. 71] or what you hear by the hearing of the ear— When you see a vision &c pray for the interpretation if you get not this, shut it up—[629] There must be certainty. ⟨in this matter⟩ An open vision will manifest that which is more important. Lying spirits are going forth in the Earth.[630]

622. JS was likely referring to rumors spread by dissenters in Kirtland, Ohio. For example, Warren Parrish and others published articles and wrote letters defaming JS and the church. (See Warren Parrish, Kirtland, OH, 5 Feb. 1838, Letter to the Editor, *Painesville [OH] Republican,* 15 Feb. 1838, [3]; and Stephen Burnett, Orange Township, OH, to Lyman Johnson, 15 Apr. 1838, in JS Letterbook 2, pp. 64–66.)

623. See Daniel 6:10.

624. See Revelation, ca. 7 Mar. 1831, in *JSP,* D1:280 [D&C 45:69].

625. See Matthew 10:35.

626. See Matthew 23:34.

627. See Matthew 24:32–33; and New Testament Revision 1, p. 56[a] [Joseph Smith—Matthew 1:38].

628. See 1 John 4:1; and Discourse, 27 June 1839, p. 510 herein.

629. See Vision, 16 Feb. 1832, in *JSP,* D2:187 [D&C 76:47].

630. See 1 Kings 22:22; JS History, vol. B-1, 773; Travel Account and Questions, Nov. 1837, in *JSP,* D5:481; and John Smith and Don Carlos Smith, Kirtland Mills, OH, to George A. Smith, Shinnston, VA, 15–18 Jan. 1838, George Albert Smith, Papers, CHL.

There will be great manifestation of Spirit both false & true. &c. Being born again[631] comes by the Spirit of God through ordinances. An angel of God never has wings. Some will Say that they have seen a Spirit. that he offered them his hand. but they did not touch it. This is a lie. First it is contrary to the plan of God A spirit can not come but in glory. An angel has flesh and bones. we see not their glory. The devil may appear as an angel of light.[632] Ask God to reveal it. if it be of the Devil. he it be will of flee from you. if of God he will manifest himself or make it manifest.[633] we may come to Jesus ⟨& ask him⟩ he will know all about it.— If he comes to a little child, he will [p. 72] adapt himself to the ⟨Language &⟩ capacity of a little child— There is no Gold nor silver &c, it is false, all is plain in heaven; every Spirit or vision or singing is not of God. The Devil is an orator, &c: he is powerful: he took our Savior onto a pinnacle of the temple; ⟨&⟩ kept him in the Wilderness for forty days.[634] The gift of discerning Spirits will be given to the presiding Elder. pray for him &c. ⟨that he may have this gift⟩ Speak not in the gift of Tongues[635] without understanding it, or without interpretation, The Devil can speak in Tongues. The Adversary will come with his work, he can tempt all classes Can speak in English or Dutch.— Let no one speak in tongues unless he interpret except by the consent of the one who is placed to preside, then he may discern or interpret or another may.[636] Let us seek for the Glory of Abraham. Noah. Adam. the Apostles have communion with these things and then we shall be among that number when Christ comes. [p. 73]

———— ☙ ————

Discourse, between circa 26 June and circa 4 August 1839–B

Source Note

JS, Discourse, [Montrose, Lee Co., Iowa Territory, or Commerce, Hancock Co., IL], [between ca. 26 June and ca. 4 Aug. 1839]. Featured version copied [between 13 Jan. 1840 and 20 Apr. 1841] in Willard Richards, "W. Richards Pocket Companion Written in England," pp. 74–75; handwriting of

---

631. 1 Peter 1:23.

632. See 2 Corinthians 11:14; and Book of Mormon, 1830 ed., 79 [2 Nephi 9:9].

633. See Discourse, 27 June 1839, p. 510 herein.

634. See Matthew 4:1–5.

635. See 1 Corinthians 12:10; Revelation, ca. 8 Mar. 1831–A, in *JSP*, D1:283 [D&C 46:23]; Historical Introduction to Minutes, 22–23 Jan. 1833, in *JSP*, D2:379–380; and Minutes and Prayer of Dedication, 27 Mar. 1836, in *JSP*, D5:203 [D&C 109:36].

636. See Discourse, between ca. 26 June and ca. 2 July 1839, p. 523 herein.

Willard Richards; Willard Richards, Journals and Papers, CHL. For more information on Willard Richards, "W. Richards Pocket Companion Written in England," see Source Notes for Multiple-Entry Documents, p. 577 herein.

Historical Introduction

Likely between late June and early August 1839, JS gave a discourse on Jesus's parable of the sower, and between January 1840 and April 1841 apostle Willard Richards copied an account of the discourse into his "Pocket Companion," a notebook he kept during his 1837–1841 mission in England.[637] Although Richards did not identify this discourse as coming from JS, the majority of the entries in the pocket notebook are JS revelations and discourses that Richards copied without giving attribution. Richards was proselytizing in England in summer 1839 and thus was not present when JS gave this discourse to members of the Quorum of the Twelve Apostles and Quorums of the Seventy. After the apostles and seventies joined Richards in England to proselytize, he presumably copied one of their accounts of the discourse.[638]

This discourse explains several parables, including the parable of the sower, the parable of the treasure hidden in a field, and the parable of the wheat and tares, all of which are found in Matthew, chapter 13. As part of his explanation, JS discussed signs in these parables of the second coming of Christ. The notes for this discourse are more fragmentary than are accounts of other JS discourses that Richards copied. Apparently, Richards or the missionary who took the original notes focused on capturing main points rather than on documenting the complete text of the discourse. In this account, the content of selected verses in Matthew, chapter 13, is briefly mentioned, followed by JS's explanations of the verses.

Document Transcript

Parables.

Behold a sower went forth to Sow &c Our Savior is the sower; the people are the world; the harvest is the end of the world; the reapers are the angels The end of the world is not come, consequently the Harvest. The harvest cannot come without Angels; The Son of man is to send forth his Angels.[639] The Son of Man Said that the Saints shall Judge the world & Angels.—[640] God has revealed himself. when they come up before God they will be asked did this Angel perform this or that. that he was sent to do. if not they will be judged— The world judgd—

---

637. For a discussion of the dating of this discourse, see Historical Introduction to Discourse, between ca. 26 June and ca. 4 Aug. 1839–A, pp. 540–542 herein.

638. Richards may have copied an account written by John Taylor. (See Historical Introduction to Discourse, between ca. 26 June and ca. 4 Aug. 1839–A, p. 542 herein.)

639. See Matthew 13:36–43.

640. See 1 Corinthians 6:1–3.

Some fell among thorns &c—[641] God sows— The enemy comes & Sows parties divisions. heresies; Shall we kill them? NO. not till harvest— The end of the world. The Son of God will do as he ever has done from the beginning. Send forth his Angels. If the reapers do not come, the wheat cannot be Saved.[642] Nothing but the Kingdom being restored, can save the world. Like unto a treasure [p. 74] hid in a field.[643] This figure is a representation of the [kingdom][644] in the last days.

Michael = Adam. Noah. I am Gabriel— Well says I. Who are you? I am Peter, the Angel flying through the midst of heaven[645] Moroni[646] delivered the book of Mormon. The pearl of great price is the inheritance prepared for the Saints. Sell all you have got, purchase &c.[647] What is the end of the world? the destruction of the wicked. The Angels have begun to be revealed.[648] They shall bind up the testimony[649] Like unto a merchantman buying goodly Pearls A net that gathers of every kind.[650] The wheat gathered into barns; the tares left on the field to be burned.[651] The Net gathers in of every kind. Those who held Keys were more concerned about their children than themselves. It happens to be our Lot to live in a day when this takes place.

———— ⁊ ————

Discourse, between circa 26 June and circa 4 August 1839–C

Source Note

JS, Discourse, [Montrose, Lee Co., Iowa Territory, or Commerce, Hancock Co., IL], [between ca. 26 June and ca. 4 Aug. 1839]. Featured version copied [between 13 Jan. 1840 and 20 Apr. 1841] in Willard Richards,

---

641. See Matthew 13:7; Mark 4:7; and Luke 8:7.

642. See Matthew 13:28–30, 41; and Revelation, 6 Dec. 1832, in *JSP*, D2:326 [D&C 86:1–7].

643. See Matthew 13:44.

644. Missing text supplied from a version of this discourse in Nuttall, "Extracts," 27.

645. See Revelation 8:13.

646. The Book of Mormon identifies Moroni as the last prophet to write in the book and as being responsible for hiding the Book of Mormon plates. JS said that Moroni appeared to JS in an 1823 vision. (See Title Page of the Book of Mormon, ca. Early June 1829, in *JSP*, D1:65; Book of Mormon, 1830 ed., 531–532 [Mormon 8:1, 4, 14]; and JS History, vol. A-1, 7, in *JSP*, H1:230–232 [Draft 2]; see also Questions and Answers, 8 May 1838, pp. 140–141 herein.)

647. See Matthew 13:46.

648. See New Testament Revision 1, p. 26 [Joseph Smith Translation, Matthew 13:39–40].

649. See Isaiah 8:16.

650. See Matthew 13:45–46.

651. See Matthew 13:24–30.

"W. Richards Pocket Companion Written in England," pp. 63–73; handwriting of Willard Richards; Willard Richards, Journals and Papers, CHL. For more information on Willard Richards, "W. Richards Pocket Companion Written in England," see Source Notes for Multiple-Entry Documents, p. 577 herein.

Historical Introduction

In summer 1839, likely between late June and early August, JS delivered a discourse on John, chapter 14. Between 1840 and 1841, apostle Willard Richards copied an account of the discourse into his "Pocket Companion" notebook.[652] Richards did not ascribe this discourse to JS, but the majority of the entries in the pocket notebook are JS revelations and discourses that Richards copied without including attribution. At the time JS delivered the discourse to members of the Quorum of the Twelve Apostles and the Quorums of the Seventy, Richards was proselytizing in England. After the apostles and seventies began arriving in England in December 1839 to proselytize, Richards likely copied one of their accounts of the discourse.[653] He copied this discourse after two other undated discourses in his "Pocket Companion" notebook, likely between January 1840 and April 1841.[654]

The discourse expounds upon the roles of the two Comforters and the steps necessary to gain salvation and eternal life. Richards's copy captures key points in JS's discourse rather than the full text, and the wording of some portions of the account suggests that JS asked questions and then provided answers for the audience.[655] The topics in the discourse are similar to those in a discourse that JS gave in late June or early July 1839 and that Wilford Woodruff recorded. It is unclear whether JS discussed these topics in multiple discourses or whether the Richards and Woodruff accounts are of the same discourse.[656]

Document Transcript

It is the privilige of the children of God to come to God & get Revelation. XIV John Let not your heart be troubled &c, There are a great many Mansions in my Father's house. I am going to prepare one for you [p. 75] rather Better than common.[657] It is the privilege of the sons of God to inherit the same Mansion &c. When any person receives a vision of Heaven, he Sees things that he never thought of before.[658] if we should tell of different glories as Paul did.[659] in my fathers house are many Mansions.[660] every man that receives

---

652. For a discussion of the dating of this discourse, see Historical Introduction to Discourse, between ca. 26 June and ca. 4 Aug. 1839–A, pp. 540–542 herein.

653. Richards may have copied an account written by John Taylor. (See Discourse, between ca. 26 June and ca. 4 Aug. 1839–A, p. 542 herein.)

654. See Discourse, between ca. 26 June and ca. 4 Aug. 1839–A, pp. 540–548 herein; and Discourse, between ca. 26 June and ca. 4 Aug. 1839–B, pp. 548–550 herein.

655. See also Discourse, between ca. 26 June and ca. 4 Aug. 1839–B, pp. 548–550 herein.

656. See Discourse, between ca. 26 June and ca. 2 July 1839, pp. 521–526 herein.

657. See John 14:1–3.

658. See Isaiah 64:4; and Vision, 16 Feb. 1832, in *JSP*, D2:184 [D&C 76:10].

659. See 1 Corinthians 15:40.

660. See John 14:2.

the Gospel receives that inheritance that the Apostles did. Every one that hath seen me hath Seen the Father.[661] He that believeth, any person that believs the works that I do shall he do also & greater works.[662] The Father could not be glorified in the Son on any other principle than we coming to God. asking. receiving. heavens open visions &c.— they are done away because of unbelief— I will pray the Father & he shall send you another <u>Comforter</u>.[663] There is one Comforter & another Comforter[664] to abide with you forever, reach to things within the vail. know that you are Sealed. If you get it, it will stand [p. 76] by you forever. How is it to be obtained? Keep my commandme[n]ts & I will pray &c.— It is a privilege to view the son of man himself, he dwelleth with you & Shall be in you. his Spirit shall be in you.[665] I will not leave you comfortless, <u>I</u> will come to you, abide with you forevever, Seal you up to Eternal life. yet a little while & ye shall see me no more, but ye see me.—[666] He that hath my commandments & keepeth them. he it is that loveth me &c— I will manifest myself to him. If he does not he has not told the truth. I will put promises in your heart. that will not leave you ~~but~~ that will ~~not~~ Seal you up. we may come to the general assembly & church of the first born, Spirits of Just men made perfect, unto Christ. The innumerable company of Angels[667] are those that have been ressurrected from the dead. the Spirits of Just men made perfect are those without bodies.[668] It is our privilege to pray for & obtain these things. [p. 77]

How wilt thou manifest thyself to us & not to the world? evidently knowing that it would be so that he would manifest himself.

There was no cholera, no mobs before this came. I told them that rejoiced in Mobs that they Should have them, they have since come in torrents.[669] they

---

661. See John 14:9.

662. See John 14:12.

663. See John 14:16.

664. The two Comforters are also discussed in another discourse that Richards copied into his "Pocket Companion." (See Discourse, between ca. 26 June and ca. 2 July 1839, pp. 524–525 herein.)

665. See John 14:17; and Revelation, 27–28 Dec. 1832, in *JSP*, D2:339 [D&C 88:50].

666. See John 16:16–17.

667. See Hebrews 12:22–23; Vision, 16 Feb. 1832, in *JSP*, D2:189 [D&C 76:67]; and Revelation, 27–28 Dec. 1832, in *JSP*, D2:337 [D&C 88:5].

668. See Hebrews 12:22–23.

669. The 1830s witnessed a rise in the frequency and intensity of riots and mob violence in the United States, a trend that continued through the Civil War. Vigilantes endeavored to expel groups such as abolitionists, free blacks, gamblers, and Latter-day Saints from communities. In 1833, vigilantes in Jackson County, Missouri, enumerated Latter-day Saint offenses and called for the Saints' expulsion. In October 1833, opponents of the church in Ohio issued warrants "warning out" several Latter-day Saints residing in Kirtland, ostensibly for their impoverished condition but likely because of their unpopular religion. In 1836, Latter-day Saints were forced to leave Clay County, Missouri, where they had taken refuge after leaving Jackson County. In October 1838, Missouri governor Lilburn W. Boggs called for the expulsion of Latter-day Saints, backing efforts of Missouri vigilantes to drive the Latter-day Saints from

did not receive the testimony of the Servants of God.[670] If a man love me he will keep my words. & my father will love him. & we both me & my father will take our abode with him.[671] There are certain characters that walked with God.[672] saw him, conversed about heaven &c But the comforter that I will send. (not the other Comforter) shall teach you all things.— Who?— He that loveth me &c— This shall bring all things to remembrance whatsoever things I have said unto you.[673] he shall teach you until ye come to me & my father. God is not a respecter of persons.[674] we all [p. 78] have the Same privilige. Come to God weary him until he blesses you &c— we are entitled to the Same blessings. Jesus, Revelations, Just men, &c— Angels &c. &c. not Laying again the doctrine of Christ go on to perfection.[675] Obtain that holy Spirit of promise—[676] Then you can be sealed to Eternal Life.— [2/3 page blank] [p. 79]

---------- ᴏ⁄ᴏ ----------

Bond from Horace Hotchkiss, 12 August 1839–A

Source Note

Horace Hotchkiss, Bond for Property in Hancock Co., IL, to JS, Sidney Rigdon, and Hyrum Smith, 12 Aug. 1839. Featured version copied 4 Sept. 1839 in Hancock County Deed Record, 1817–1917, vol. 12 G, p. 299; unidentified handwriting. For more information on Hancock County Deed Record, 1817–1917, vol. 12 G, see Source Notes for Multiple-Entry Documents, p. 563 herein.

Historical Introduction

On 12 August 1839, Horace Hotchkiss prepared a bond for land in the northern part of the Commerce, Illinois, area that Hotchkiss and his partners, John Gillet and Smith Tuttle, agreed to sell to JS and his counselors in the First Presidency.[677] This transaction and

---

the state. (Grimsted, "Rioting in Its Jacksonian Setting," 361–368; Feldberg, *Turbulent Era*, 5–6; Historical Introduction to Letter from William W. Phelps, 6–7 Nov. 1833, in *JSP*, D3:336–339; "To His Excellency, Daniel Dunklin," *The Evening and the Morning Star*, Dec. 1833, 114; Historical Introduction to Warrant, 21 Oct. 1833, in *JSP*, D3:326–328; Historical Introduction to Letter to John Thornton et al., 25 July 1836, in *JSP*, D5:258–260.)

670. See Vision, 16 Feb. 1832, in *JSP*, D2:191 [D&C 76:101]; and Minutes and Prayer of Dedication, 27 Mar. 1836, in *JSP*, D5:203 [D&C 109:41].

671. See John 14:23.

672. See Genesis 5:24; and Old Testament Revision 1, p. 13 [Moses 6:39].

673. See John 14:26.

674. See Acts 10:34.

675. See Hebrews 6:1.

676. See Ephesians 1:13; Vision, 16 Feb. 1832, in *JSP*, D2:188 [D&C 76:53]; and Revelation, 27–28 Dec. 1832, in *JSP*, D2:337 [D&C 88:3].

677. Hotchkiss, Gillet, and Tuttle were land speculators from Connecticut who bought land in northwestern Illinois in 1836. Hotchkiss and Gillet purchased the land mentioned in this 12 August 1839 bond from Alexander White in June 1836. This land was originally set aside by the federal government as

another one that day with Hotchkiss and William White were the largest land purchases the church had made in Illinois.[678] The tract of land that Hotchkiss, Gillet, and Tuttle were selling consisted of approximately four hundred acres in and around the platted towns of Commerce and Commerce City, Illinois, minus the lots in the Commerce plat that had already been sold.[679]

In the bond, Hotchkiss (who was representing his partners Gillet and Tuttle) specified that he would provide JS, Sidney Rigdon, and Hyrum Smith with a warranty deed for the land if the men made the scheduled payments, which totaled $110,000. Half the amount was to be paid to Hotchkiss in the form of twenty promissory notes for $1,500 each, due annually for the next twenty years, with a final note for $25,000 due in 1859.[680] The other half was to be paid to Tuttle and Gillet jointly in the same manner. The annual payments of $1,500 likely represented interest, although they were not specified as such in the bond.[681] JS, Rigdon, and Hyrum Smith promised to make the scheduled payments by signing the forty-two promissory notes outlined in the bond.[682] The original bond is apparently not extant; the version featured here was copied into a Hancock County deed record book in September 1839. In 1843, the bond was canceled by mutual agreement, and most of the land was returned to Hotchkiss, Tuttle, and Gillet through a quitclaim deed.[683]

Document Transcript

3189
[Horace] Hotchkiss to Sidney Rigdon Joseph Smith & Hyrum Smith
Bond for Deed

---

bounty land to be sold to men who held a military commission during the War of 1812. (Hancock Co., IL, Deed Records, 1817–1917, vol. B, p. 322, microfilm 954,192, U.S. and Canada Record Collection, FHL; Anthony Hoffman, Rushville, IL, to John Reid, Argyle, NY, 1 Nov. 1833, Abraham Lincoln Presidential Library, Springfield, IL.)

678. In previous months, church agents had purchased smaller tracts of land in Illinois from Isaac Galland and Hugh White, as well as larger ones in Iowa Territory from Galland. (See, for example, Agreement with George W. Robinson, 30 Apr. 1839, pp. 439–442 herein. For information on the other 12 August 1839 land transaction, see Bond from Horace Hotchkiss, 12 Aug. 1839–B, pp. 557–559 herein.)

679. Gregg, *History of Hancock County, Illinois,* 955.

680. All of the notes are extant. (See Promissory Notes, 12 Aug. 1839, JS Collection, CHL, also available at josephsmithpapers.org.)

681. An 1841 report by unidentified church agents noted that "$3000 are now due to Mr Hotchkiss being the first payment of Int." An 1841 letter written by the Quorum of the Twelve Apostles and printed in the church newspaper listed $53,500 as the amount the church owed for its August 1839 land transactions with Hotchkiss; the letter also noted that interest was accumulating on the promissory notes. The $53,500 appears to combine the two 12 August 1839 bonds made with Hotchkiss, with $50,000 representing the principal for the bond featured here and $3,500 representing the amount specified in the second bond. Therefore, the annual payments of $1,500 mentioned in the featured bond likely represent interest payments. ("Report of the Agents of the Church for Buying and Selling Land in Nauvoo," ca. Jan. 1841, JS Office Papers, CHL; "An Epistle of the Twelve," *Times and Seasons,* 15 Oct. 1841, 2:568.)

682. See Promissory Note to John Gillet and Smith Tuttle, 12 Aug. 1839, pp. 556–557 herein.

683. JS et al., Quitclaim Deed, Nauvoo, IL, to Smith Tuttle et al., 7 July 1843, in Hancock Co., IL, Deed Records, 1817–1917, vol. 12 G, p. 299, microfilm 954,195, U.S. and Canada Record Collection, FHL.

Know all men by these presents that I Horace R Hotchkiss of the City and County of Newhaven and State of Connecticut for the Consideration herein after mentioned have this day sold and I do hereby bargain sell and confirm unto Sidney Rigdon Joseph Smith Jr and Hiram [Hyrum] Smith all of Commerce Hancock County and State of Illinois and further agree and bind myself to give unto the said Rigdon & Smiths a full indisputable & perfect title to the following property namely the North half of the North East quarter of Section number two in township Number Six North and Range number nine West of the fourth principal Meridian (Reserving therefrom four Rods Square Deeded to Mrs Cutler[684] for her husbands grave) also the south East fractional quarter of Section thirty five in township Seven North and Range nine West of the fourth principal meridian Also the West half of the South West quarter of Section thirty six in township Seven North and in Range nine West of the fourth principal Meridian— Also the South West fractional quarter of section number thirty five in township Seven North and in Range nine West of the fourth principal Meridian also the North East fractional ~~quarter~~ Section number thirty five in township number Seven and in Range nine West of the fourth principal Meridian[685] Reserving from the above property in this sale the following Lots as described in Alex Whites survey of the town of Commerce and Recorded upon the County Records at Carthage[686] to wit;— Lots 3— 4— 7 and 8 in block 3. Lot 4 in block 4. Lots 1— and 4 in block 5. Lots 2— 7 and 8 in Block 6. Lot 8 in block 10. Lots 1— 2— 3— 5— 7 and 8 in block 11 Lots 1— 2 and 3 in block 12 Lots 1— 2— 3 and 4 in block 13 also Lots 2— 3— 6 & 7 in block 14. and for the above property I have received as a consideration the following Notes namely Two Notes for twenty five thousand Dollars each payable in twenty year and forty Notes of Fifteen hundred Dollars each two of which are payable every twelve months for twenty years one half of the whole being drawn to my own order and the other half to the order of John Gillett and Smith Tuttle amounting to the sum of One hundred And Ten Thousand Dollars and dated this 12th day of Aug[t.] 1839

---

684. Probably Mary Ann Munson Cutler Whitney, who became postmistress of Commerce in 1834 after the death of her first husband, George Y. Cutler. She married Daniel G. Whitney in August 1838. (Munson, *Munson Record*, 810–811; Obituary for Mary Ann Munson Whitney, *Quincy [IL] Whig*, 10 July 1844, [3]; Blum, *Nauvoo*, 4.)

685. A section comprised 640 acres; a quarter section, 160 acres; a half of a quarter section, 80 acres. The term *fractional quarter* indicated that the acreage of the parcel was less than the standard 160 acres.

686. Hancock Co., IL, Plat Books, 1836–1938, vol. 1, pp. 10–11, 24 May 1834, microfilm 954,774, U.S. and Canada Record Collection, FHL. The Commerce plat was commissioned by Alexander White and Joseph B. Teas; the survey was performed by John Johnston.

Now if the said Rigdon and Smiths shall pay or cause to be paid the aforesaid Notes according to their tenor then I do hereby bind myself my heirs executors administrators and assigns to deliver the said Rigdon and Smiths or their assigns a perfect Absolute and Warrantee Deed of all the property described in this instrument (except the specific reservations) together with all the buildings and the appurtenances in any way thereunto belonging

⟨Fee $1.⟩[687] In Witness Whereof I have this 12th day of August 1839 set my hand and Seal

Recorded 4th Sept 1839

Horace R Hotchkiss

———— ☙ ————

Promissory Note to John Gillet and Smith Tuttle, 12 August 1839

Source Note

Sidney Rigdon, JS, and Hyrum Smith, Promissory Note, Commerce, Hancock Co., IL, to John Gillet and Smith Tuttle, 12 Aug. 1839; handwriting of Horace Hotchkiss; signatures of Sidney Rigdon, JS, and Hyrum Smith; one page; JS Collection, CHL. Includes notation.

One leaf measuring 2¾ × 7¼ inches (7 × 18 cm). The document was written on a larger sheet of paper with several other promissory notes; the notes were then cut into separate documents. All edges of the featured promissory note appear to be hand cut. A notation in unidentified handwriting was made in red ink: "Paid".

The promissory note was likely returned to JS in 1843 when the bond was canceled; it was then filed with his other papers in Nauvoo, Illinois. Presumably, this note has remained in continuous institutional custody since then.

Historical Introduction

On 12 August 1839, JS, Sidney Rigdon, and Hyrum Smith signed forty-two promissory notes at Commerce, Illinois, in connection with a bond to purchase Commerce-area land from Horace Hotchkiss and his partners, John Gillet and Smith Tuttle. The bond specified that forty-two payments were due over the next twenty years. From 1840 to 1859, two payments of $1,500 were due annually: one was to be paid to Hotchkiss, and the other was to be paid to Gillet and Tuttle. In 1859, two additional larger payments were due, each for $25,000, with one owed to Hotchkiss and the other owed to Gillet and Tuttle.[688] Hotchkiss wrote a promissory note for each of the payments due, and the First Presidency presumably returned the notes to Hotchkiss after signing them.

---

687. The fee was probably for entering the bond into the Hancock County record book.

688. See Bond from Horace Hotchkiss, 12 Aug. 1839–A, pp. 553–556 herein; and Promissory Notes, 12 Aug. 1839, JS Collection, CHL, also available at josephsmithpapers.org.

All of the notes are extant. The promissory note featured here is for the last payment of $1,500 owed to Gillet and Tuttle, due in 1859.[689] Although the word "Paid" was written on the promissory note, this note was not paid.[690] Rather, the agreement was amended in 1843, which voided this and other notes associated with the bond. At the time the agreement was amended, the promissory notes were presumably returned to the First Presidency.

Document Transcript

Commerce (Illinois) 12[th.] Aug 1839

Twenty years after date we promise to pay John Gillet and Smith Tuttle <u>Fifteen Hundred Dollars</u>[691] for[692] value rec[d.]

Paid

[693]Sidney Rigdon

Joseph Smith Jr

Hiram [Hyrum] Smith

———— ☙ ————

Bond from Horace Hotchkiss, 12 August 1839–B

Source Note

Horace Hotchkiss, Bond for Property in Hancock Co., IL, to JS, Sidney Rigdon, and Hyrum Smith, 12 Aug. 1839. Featured version copied 4 Sept. 1839 in Hancock County Deed Record, 1817–1917, vol. 12 G, pp. 299–300; unidentified handwriting. Includes cancellation notation. For more information on Hancock County Deed Record, 1817–1917, vol. 12 G, see Source Notes for Multiple-Entry Documents, p. 563 herein.

Historical Introduction

On 12 August 1839, Horace Hotchkiss produced a bond outlining the sale of 89½ acres in the vicinity of Commerce, Illinois, to JS, Sidney Rigdon, and Hyrum Smith. This bond is one of two that Hotchkiss prepared that day to formalize land transactions

---

689. On josephsmithpapers.org, a different letter of the alphabet is appended to the title of each of the twenty-one promissory notes for Gillet and Tuttle to differentiate the notes; the promissory note featured here is appended with "T."

690. See Historical Introduction to Bond from Horace Hotchkiss, 12 Aug. 1839–A, pp. 553–554 herein. Each of the forty-two promissory notes bears the notation "Paid" in the handwriting of an unidentified scribe. It is unknown when these notations were added. They may have been made when the bond was canceled in 1843. Alternately, the notations may have been added when the notes were filed by clerks in the Church Historian's Office in Utah Territory.

691. TEXT: "Fifteen Hundred Dollars" is double underlined.

692. TEXT: "Paid" is written vertically in red ink over "for", in unidentified handwriting.

693. TEXT: Original signatures of Sidney Rigdon, JS, and Hyrum Smith.

with the First Presidency.[694] The bond featured here was for land that Hotchkiss had arranged to purchase from William White but had not yet paid for. Hotchkiss agreed that JS and his counselors could buy the land, which he held a claim to, if they paid both him and White.[695] In connection with this bond, the First Presidency signed three promissory notes totaling $3,500. Two of the notes were for $1,250 each—one due in five years and another due in ten years—and were given to Hotchkiss.[696] The third note—for $1,000— was signed by the three men and given to White. No due date was specified for this note, but a receipt that White made indicates the note was paid by April 1840, and White gave the First Presidency a deed for the specified land several months later.[697] The two notes given to Hotchkiss were renegotiated on 23 October 1840, with JS and his counselors providing Hotchkiss a new promissory note for $2,500 due in eight months.[698] Because White had been paid and Hotchkiss's notes were renegotiated, the bond was officially canceled on 23 October 1840.[699]

Document Transcript

3190
[Horace] Hotchkiss to [Sidney] Rigdon & Smith
Bond

Know all men by these presents that ~~we~~ I Horace R Hotchkiss of the City and County of New-Haven and State of Connecticut for the consideration hereinafter named have this day sold and I do hereby sell bargain and confirm unto Sidney Rigdon Joseph Smith Jr and Hiram [Hyrum] Smith all of Commerce Hancock County and State of Illinois [p. 299] and I further agree and bind myself to give unto said Rigdon and Smiths an indisputable title to the following property namely the South half of the North East quarter of Section number two in township Six North and in Range nine West of the fourth principal Meridian (Reserving from this said tract of Land half of one Acre for a burying ground) Also about ten Acres running from the last described tract to the Mississippi River and bounded North on

694. For information on the other bond, which involved land that Hotchkiss, John Gillet, and Smith Tuttle owned jointly, see Bond from Horace Hotchkiss, 12 Aug. 1839–A, pp. 553–556 herein.

695. William White, Receipt, Commerce, IL, to JS, 23 Apr. 1840, JS Receipts and Accounts, CHL. Hotchkiss did not have the title to the land because he had not yet paid White. The bond featured here required the First Presidency to pay White as well as Hotchkiss in order to receive the title to the land.

696. See Promissory Note to Horace Hotchkiss, 12 Aug. 1839, pp. 556–557 herein.

697. William White, Receipt, Commerce, IL, to JS, 23 Apr. 1840, JS Receipts and Accounts, CHL.

698. See JS et al., Promissory Note, Nauvoo, IL, to Horace Hotchkiss, 23 Oct. 1840, JS Collection, CHL.

699. A bond was canceled when the terms were fulfilled or when the parties involved agreed to terminate it. In the case of the bond featured here, the payments had been made or arranged and White provided JS and his counselors with a deed indicating fulfillment of the agreement with White and Hotchkiss.

Charles Munson and South on Sidney Rigdon and for the above described property or Lots of Land I have received as a consideration two Notes of twelve hundred and Fifty Dollars each with interest one payable in Five years and the other payable in ten Years and Wm White of Commerce is also to receive from said Rigdon and Smiths One Thousand dollars to be paid in such manner as shall be satisfactory to said White. Now if the said Rigdon and Smiths shall pay or cause to be paid the aforesaid Notes according to their tenor and also the Thousand dollars to said Wm White then I do hereby bind myself my heirs executors administrators and assigns to deliver to said Rigdon and Smiths or their assigns a perfect and absolute Warrantee Deed of all the property (except half an acre) described in this instrument together with all the privileges and appurtenances thereunto in any way ~~appurtaining~~ belonging

⟨Fee $0.75⟩ In Witness Whereof I have hereunto set my hand & seal this 12th day of August 1839

Recorded 4th Sept 1839

Horace R Hotchkiss

Nauvoo 23 Octo 1840[700]

The Within Bond is hereby cancelled and Surrendered to Horace R Hotchkiss in consequence of getting a Deed from M^r. William White for the Same Land which is described in Said Bond.

Joseph Smith

Sidney Rigdon

(Recorded 27th oct 1840)

———— ❧ ————

Promissory Note to Horace Hotchkiss, 12 August 1839

Source Note

Sidney Rigdon, JS, and Hyrum Smith, Promissory Note, Commerce, Hancock Co., IL, to Horace Hotchkiss, 12 Aug. 1839; handwriting of Horace Hotchkiss; probable signatures of JS, Sidney Rigdon, and Hyrum Smith (now missing); one page; JS Collection, CHL.

One leaf measuring 3½ × 7¾ inches (9 × 20 cm), with ten printed lines. The top edge of the leaf was unevenly hand cut, presumably from a larger sheet of paper. The document was folded twice for transmission or filing. The note was likely returned to JS when it was voided, whereupon the signatures were removed and the note was filed with JS's other papers in Nauvoo, Illinois. Presumably, the note has remained in continuous institutional custody since then.

---

700. TEXT: The location and date were written vertically in the left margin.

Historical Introduction

On 12 August 1839, JS, Sidney Rigdon, and Hyrum Smith signed three promissory notes in connection with a bond for land they arranged to purchase that day from Horace Hotchkiss. This bond was one of two that the First Presidency entered into with Hotchkiss on 12 August for land in and around Commerce, Illinois.[701] Hotchkiss created the bonds for the two transactions; the bond associated with the three promissory notes was for land that Hotchkiss arranged to purchase from William White.[702] One of these promissory notes—for $1,000—was given to White. The two other notes—for $1,250 each—were payable to Hotchkiss; one was due in five years, and the other, featured here, was due in ten years. In April 1840, JS and his counselors paid White, who provided the men with a deed for the specified land. On 23 October 1840, the First Presidency renegotiated the two notes for Hotchkiss by combining the two payments into one new note for $2,500, due in eight months.[703] As part of this new agreement, the signatures of the First Presidency were removed from the featured promissory note, indicating the note had been voided.[704]

Document Transcript

Commerce (Illinois) 12[th.] August 1839

Ten Years after date we promise to pay Horace R Hotchkiss or order Twelve Hundred and fifty Dollars with interest for value received

[signatures removed][705]

---

701. The other bond was with Hotchkiss and his business partners, John Gillet and Smith Tuttle. (See Bond from Horace Hotchkiss, 12 Aug. 1839–A, pp. 553–556 herein.)

702. See Bond from Horace Hotchkiss, 12 Aug. 1839–B, pp. 557–559 herein.

703. JS et al., Promissory Note, Nauvoo, IL, to Horace Hotchkiss, 23 Oct. 1840, JS Collection, CHL. The 23 October 1840 promissory note was paid no later than October 1841 by James Ivins on behalf of JS. (Horace R. Hotchkiss, Fair Haven, CT, to JS, Nauvoo, IL, 11 Oct. 1841; Horace R. Hotchkiss, Fair Haven, CT, to JS, Nauvoo, IL, 9 Nov. 1841, JS Collection, CHL.)

704. When a promissory note was paid or canceled, the signatures on the note were removed to invalidate the note, ensuring it was no longer negotiable; the invalidated note could then serve as a receipt for payment. Signatures might also be removed to void a note that had been renegotiated. ("Cancellation," in Bouvier, *Law Dictionary,* 1:151; Chitty, *Practical Treatise on Bills of Exchange,* 303.)

705. TEXT: The bottom right corner, which contained signatures, was torn off. The note was evidently signed by JS, Sidney Rigdon, and Hyrum Smith—the purchasers named in the associated bond. (Bond from Horace Hotchkiss, 12 Aug. 1839–B, p. 558 herein.)

REFERENCE
MATERIAL

Source Notes for Multiple-Entry Documents

Many of the texts featured in this volume are drawn from early church record books and other sources that consist of or include multiple individual texts. The following notes provide bibliographical and physical descriptions of such sources, as well as information on provenance and custodial history. Providing this information for these multiple-entry sources here reduces repetition in the source notes that appear throughout the main body of the volume. Images of many of these sources are available at josephsmithpapers.org. Information specific to the individual texts featured in the main body of the volume can be found in the source notes and historical introductions preceding them.

Elders' Journal of the Church of Latter Day Saints, Volume 1, 1837–1838

Elders' Journal of the Church of Latter Day Saints (Kirtland, Geauga Co., OH, and Far West, Caldwell Co., MO), vol. 1, nos. 1–2, Oct.–Nov. 1837, and nos. 3–4, July–Aug. 1838; nos. 1–2 edited by JS (in Kirtland) and nos. 3–4 edited by JS (in Far West).

Each monthly issue featured sixteen octavo pages that measured 10⅛ × 6⅛ inches (26 × 16 cm). Each page was printed in two columns, with each column 2⅛ inches (5 cm) wide.

The copy used for transcription was bound at a later, unknown date with three volumes of an earlier Mormon newspaper—the *Latter Day Saints' Messenger and Advocate*—in a stamped brown leather binding with decorative gold tooling on the covers and spine. The spine also contains two gold-tooled inscriptions: "MESSENGER | & | ADVOCATE" and "W. WOODRUFF." The pages were trimmed to 9⅛ × 5½ inches (23 × 14 cm), and the edges and endpaper feature a marbled pattern in blue, tan, red, and yellow. The bound volume measures 9½ × 6 × 1⅜ inches (24 × 15 × 3 cm). It includes marginalia and archival notations and is held at the Church History Library. The bound volume belonged to Wilford Woodruff, though at least some of the loose issues of the *Messenger and Advocate* originally belonged to Ezra Carter, Woodruff's father-in-law. After Woodruff's death, the volume passed to his daughter, Clara Woodruff Beebe, who inscribed her name on a flyleaf and pasted on the inside of the front cover a book plate containing her name. The volume entered the custody of the Church Historian's Office before June 1964, when pencil markings on a flyleaf indicate the volume was accessed by office staff.

Elders' Journal, volume 1, is the source for seven featured texts in this volume.

Hancock County Deed Record, Volume 12 G

Hancock Co., IL, Recorder, Deed Record, vol. 12 G, 24 Apr.–7 Nov. 1839; 462 pages; Hancock County Recorder's Office, Hancock Co., IL. Includes notations and archival marking.

Volume containing 236 leaves measuring 17½ × 11 inches (44 × 28 cm). At an unknown time, the original leather binding was covered with white canvas. The spine of the canvas was stamped in black ink: "DEED RECORD | 12 G | HANCOCK COUNTY". The bound volume measures 18¼ × 12 × 3⅛ inches (46 × 30 × 8 cm). This volume has been in the continuous custody of the Hancock County, Illinois, Recorder's Office since the volume's creation.

This record book is the source for two featured texts in this volume.

JS, Journal, March–September 1838

JS, "The Scriptory Book—of Joseph Smith Jr.—President of The Church of Jesus Christ, of Latterday Saints In all the World," Journal, Mar.–Sept. 1838; handwriting of George W. Robinson and James Mulholland; sixty-nine pages; in "General," Record Book, ca. June– ca. Dec. 1838, verso of Patriarchal Blessings, vol. 5, CHL. Includes redactions and archival marking.

JS's "Scriptory Book" is recorded on pages 15–83 of a large record book entitled "General" that also includes a list of church members in Caldwell County, Missouri (pages 2–14), a copy of JS's 16 December 1838 letter from the jail in Liberty, Missouri (pages 101– 108), and an aborted record partially entitled "Recor" in unidentified handwriting (page 110). The book, which measures 13 × 8¼ × 1¾ inches (33 × 21× 4 cm), has 182 leaves of ledger paper that are 12½ × 7¾ inches (32 × 20 cm) and has thirty-seven blue lines per page. There are eighteen gatherings of various sizes, each of about a dozen leaves. The text block is sewn all along over three strips of vellum tape. The heavy pink endpapers at either end of the text block consist of a pastedown and two flyleaves pasted together. The text block edges are stained green. The volume has a hardbound ledger-style binding with a hollow-back spine and blue-striped cloth headbands that were glued on. The volume is bound in brown split-calfskin leather with blind-tooled decoration around the outside border and along the turned-in edges of the leather on the inside covers. At some point, the letter "G" was hand printed in ink on the front cover. The original leather cover over the spine—which appears to have been intentionally removed—may have borne a title or filing notation.

The journal is inscribed in brown ink and is almost entirely in the handwriting of George W. Robinson. James Mulholland's handwriting appears in a copy of the 23 July 1837 revelation for Thomas B. Marsh (D&C 112) on pages 72–74. Robinson added running heads throughout the journal to indicate the months of the entries on the page. The volume was later used in Nauvoo, Illinois, as a source for JS's multivolume manuscript history of the church. During the preparation of the history, redactions and use marks were made in graphite. Redactions in graphite and ink may have been made at other times as well.[1]

George W. Robinson, who was appointed the church's general clerk and recorder in Ohio in September 1837, arrived in Far West on 28 March 1838 and started writing in the journal within two days. He began writing on the first blank page following a previously inscribed roster of Latter-day Saints living in Caldwell County, Missouri.

The journal opens with a brief retrospective account, apparently dictated by JS, of his arrival in Far West on 14 March 1838. Following this account is a copy of a church

---

1. For a transcript and a more extended introduction to this document, see JS, Journal, Mar.–Sept. 1838, in *JSP*, J1:225–320.

motto JS had recently composed. A letter JS wrote on 29 March 1838 (copied on pages 23–26 of the journal) explicitly indicates that the motto had been inscribed in the journal by that date. Next in the journal are two sets of questions and answers about the book of Isaiah, followed by transcripts or summaries of nine documents, all but one of which are related to a seven-month series of events that culminated in the 12–13 April 1838 excommunications of Oliver Cowdery and David Whitmer. As indicated by the date on the title page of the journal—12 April 1838—Robinson apparently began transcribing these documents on the same day that Cowdery was excommunicated. It seems that Cowdery's trial was the motivating factor for transcribing these documents. Following these documents are copies of revelations that JS dictated in mid- and late April 1838.

After inscribing these revelations, Robinson recorded daily journal entries, beginning with an entry for 27 April 1838. By this point, Robinson was serving as a scribe to the First Presidency, and the journal focused not only on JS but also on his counselors in the church presidency. Frequently, but not consistently, Robinson accompanied JS and the presidency on trips away from Far West. However, Robinson likely did not carry the large journal with him on every occasion, and a number of entries may not have been recorded until after he returned to Far West. In the journal entries, Robinson referred to JS in the third person and to himself in the first person. Thus, words such as "I" and "myself" in the journal entries usually indicate Robinson rather than JS.

The pattern of record keeping became more varied after the First Presidency and Robinson traveled to Daviess County, Missouri, in early June. Robinson's daily entries lapsed as the Mormons laid out a city plot for a settlement at Adam-ondi-Ahman, began building homes, and organized a stake. Although Robinson's journal keeping for JS lapsed for most of June and July, he did note significant developments in three early July entries, in which he primarily copied correspondence and revelations. Robinson resumed writing regular journal entries on 26 July and remained relatively consistent through 10 September, when the journal ends. Following his entry for 10 September, Robinson inscribed the dateline for the following day, indicating the intention to continue record keeping. The abrupt end of Robinson's record probably related to his responsibilities as an officer in the Saints' defense forces. At the time this journal was set aside, brief entries were already being made by clerk James Mulholland in another journal.

The Scriptory Book is the source for fifteen featured texts in this volume.

JS, Journal, 1839

JS, "Minute Book. 1839 J. Smiths Journal Escape from Prison," Journal, Apr.–Oct. 1839; handwriting of James Mulholland; fifteen pages; JS Collection, CHL. Includes redactions and archival marking.

Makeshift notebook measuring 10 × 4 inches (25 × 10 cm). The journal was fashioned by folding in half lengthwise eight sheets of paper measuring 10 × 8 inches (25 × 20 cm), forming a notebook of sixteen leaves (thirty-two pages). Some inscriptions on the versos reach the end of a line and cross the gutter onto another leaf, indicating that the folded pages were not sewn during their original use. Wear on the first and last pages indicates that the pages were not bound for some time. The text of the journal is inscribed on the first fifteen pages in brown ink. The remaining seventeen pages are blank. At some point,

a sheet of blue stock measuring 10 × 16 inches (25 × 41 cm) was folded in half twice to create a cover that measures 10 × 4 inches; the notebook was then pamphlet bound with hand
stitching. On the front cover, James Mulholland wrote "Minute Book. | 1839 | J. Smiths
Journal | Escape from Prison", below which are seven decorative underlines in black ink.
Near the top of the back cover, the words "Joseph Smith's Journal | Escape from Prison
1839" were written sideways in black ink. This notation, in unidentified handwriting,
appears to be an early archival marking. Textual redactions and use marks made in graphite
were added later by scribes who used the journal to produce the multivolume manuscript
history of the church. This thin journal was probably among the miscellaneous documents
collectively listed in Nauvoo, Illinois, and early Utah inventories of church records.[2] The use
of the journal in connection with the manuscript history, early inventories, and recent
archival records indicates that this journal, like other JS journals, has remained in continuous church custody.[3]

JS's 1839 journal is the source for one featured text in this volume.

JS Letterbook 2, 1839–1843

*JS Letterbook 2, [1839–ca. summer 1843]; handwriting of Howard Coray, James
Mulholland, Robert B. Thompson, Willard Richards, John Fullmer, William Clayton, and
George Walker; 245 pages of letters, plus 26 pages of index and 83 pages of company records for
Rigdon, Smith & Co.; JS Collection, CHL. Includes redactions.*

This letterbook was inscribed in a large-size, commercially produced blank ledger
book measuring 14¼ × 9½ × 1¾ inches (36 × 24 × 4 cm) with leather-covered boards and
pastedowns of marbled paper. The letterbook contains endpaper in the front and back of
the volume and twenty-four gatherings of 10 leaves each, with the exception of the last
gathering, which contains 8 leaves, for a total of 238 leaves. The leaves, which measure 13½
× 8⅞ inches (34 × 23 cm), are ruled with eight vertical red lines and three interspersed
double red lines, thirty-nine horizontal blue lines, and one red double line at the bottom
or top of the page, depending on the way the ledger sits. The book was originally used as
a financial ledger for Rigdon, Smith & Co., beginning in September 1836; eighty-three
pages were inscribed with account information for customers of that firm. In April 1839,
the book was inverted and repurposed as a letterbook; the back of the book for the mercantile firm was used as the front of the letterbook. The cover of the letterbook side bears
a handwritten title: "Letters &c. | 1839 | AD." The title page contains the inscription
"Copies of Letters, &c. &c. | 1839, AD." The spine of the book has a strip of red leather
imprinted with "LEGER" in gilt lettering. A paper label from the Church Historian's
Office was attached to the spine; the label reads "LETTER 1838–43".

Pagination began anew with the letterbook, which contains 245 pages of inscribed letters. Apparently, in 1839 James Mulholland used adhesive wafers to tip in a single leaf
between pages 7 and 10. The leaf, containing copies of two 1839 letters, is no longer attached

---

2. "Schedule of Church Records. Nauvoo 1846," [1]; "Inventory. Historian's Office. 4th April 1855," [2];
"Historian's Office Inventory G. S. L. City March 19. 1858," [3], Historian's Office, Catalogs and
Inventories, 1846–1904, CHL.

3. See Johnson, *Register of the Joseph Smith Collection*, 7.

and may not be extant; however, the letters it contained are included in the volume's first index.[4] Mulholland numbered the pages he inscribed, starting with 0 and ending with 74. After Mulholland died in November 1839, Robert B. Thompson became JS's scribe and paginated the remainder of the book, from page 75 to 475. Thompson created the first index for the volume on page 472, listing the contents of pages 0–13. Thompson also created a second, larger index, spanning pages 370–392; this index includes twelve hand-cut index tabs, each containing two printed letters in alphabetical order, with the last tab containing "W Y".

The letterbook contains a mix of contemporaneous letters, earlier letters, church organizational records, and church business records. The first documents were inscribed by Mulholland, who was hired by JS to "write for the Church" after JS and others escaped from imprisonment in Missouri and reunited with the Saints in Illinois on 22 April.[5] It is likely that Mulholland began inscribing documents into the letterbook in late April 1839; the exact date is not known. The first several entries in the letterbook are copies of letters that JS or others apparently received while imprisoned in Missouri from late 1838 to spring 1839. On pages 7–15, Mulholland inscribed copies of May 1839 letters between JS and church leaders in Quincy and Commerce, Illinois, apparently soon after they were written or received.[6] Several of the documents Mulholland copied next were created during JS's imprisonment and relate to the 1838 Missouri difficulties or to Sidney Rigdon's plans to seek redress from the federal government for the Saints' losses and mistreatment in Missouri. Pages 35–40 contain Smith family correspondence from April 1837 and April 1839. Another section of earlier letters was copied beginning on page 52, including a letter written on 29 July 1833 by John Whitmer, with a postscript by William W. Phelps to Oliver Cowdery and JS; a 4 June 1834 letter from JS to Emma Smith; and a 17 June 1829 letter from Jesse Smith to Hyrum Smith. Following these letters are three 1837–1838 letters relating to dissent in Kirtland and then a copy of JS's 24 January 1839 petition to the Missouri legislature. Mulholland may have copied these documents at the time that JS's history began to be written or when the Saints began writing the history of the Missouri troubles, per JS's instructions in March and May 1839.[7] The recording of contemporaneous letters continued until February 1843, except for when Howard Coray inscribed minutes from three church meetings held in April and May 1839 onto pages 138–144, between entries for April and May 1840.

JS Letterbook 2 is the source for thirty featured texts in this volume.

License Record Book

General Church Recorder, License Record Book, Dec. 1837–May 1862; handwriting of Robert B. Thompson, James Sloan, George W. Robinson, Willard Richards, Oliver Cowdery, Hyrum Smith, Thomas Bullock, William W. Phelps, and at least one unidentified scribe; 146 pages; CHL. Includes Hebrew, redactions, index, and archival markings.

---

4. See JS Letterbook 2, p. 472.

5. JS, Journal, 22 Apr. 1839, in *JSP,* J1:336; Mulholland, Journal, 22 Apr. 1839.

6. JS, Journal, 20–24 May 1839, in *JSP,* J1:339.

7. See JS, Journal, 11 June 1839; 3 and 4–5 July 1839, in *JSP,* J1:340, 345.

The License Record Book of the general church recorder is a large blank book measuring 12¾ × 8 × 1 inches (32 × 20 × 3 cm). The book consists of ledger paper that is untrimmed on the fore edge, with thirty-eight blue horizontal lines printed on each page. The volume contains twelve gatherings of 12 leaves (24 pages), making a text block of 144 leaves. There are two sheets of endpaper and one pastedown in the front and back of the volume. The volume is bound with all-along sewing in a case binding that is supported with recessed cords and a tight-back spine. The exterior of the volume consists of square-edge boards with marbled decoration and a leather quarter binding. The spine is inscribed in faded ink: "LICENSE RECORDS BOOK A". Three archival labels were later pasted on the spine. One of the labels reads "CERTIFICATES OF MEMBERS" in ink, with the alternative title "Record of church members 182 Nauvo" added in smaller letters in graphite. The remnants of a label of similar design and material are located at the bottom of the spine; only a partial, illegible character is visible. Above this label was later added a smaller label with the archival notation "N 6861".

The volume was primarily inscribed in brown and black ink; a few entries were made in graphite, and later scribes, particularly Robert B. Thompson and James Sloan, used blue ink as well. Pages 1–135 have been numbered, with the exception of pages [57]–[60], which are unnumbered but were counted; two pages between pages 115 and 116, which were not counted; and a page between pages 126 and 127, which was the first and only page of an aborted record of seventies' licenses kept by George W. Robinson. Pages 2–6 are blank though numbered. The handwriting and ink in the first entry on each page often match that of the page number, indicating that the clerks paginated as they worked, with Oliver Cowdery numbering pages 1–18; Robinson, 19–55; Thompson, 56 and 61–85; Sloan, 86–115; Willard Richards, 116–133; and Thomas Bullock, 134–135. On pages 1–11, Cowdery and Robinson initially maintained an index of certificates recorded in the volume, alphabetized by the certificate recipient's name; each of the index pages contains two or three stylized letters inscribed on the first line in brown ink. In December 1838 and January 1839, Robinson used the two sheets of endpaper at the front of the volume to list the licenses he had signed. Interspersed among his 1838 entries, Robinson copied the transliterated Hebrew text for Psalm 37:4, switching the order of the two phrases in the verse.

Until Sloan began recording in this book in October 1841, many of the entries included the signature of the recorder as well as a scribal signature for JS, for another member of the First Presidency, or—in the case of Cowdery's entries—for William W. Phelps or David Whitmer. Sloan included only his own signature, a practice that Richards continued until November 1843, when he began omitting his signature. Bullock, Phelps, and at least one unidentified scribe apparently followed Richards's lead in not signing their entries.

On 6 December 1837, Cowdery was appointed the "Recording Clerk" for elders' licenses signed by the Zion (Missouri) church presidency.[8] Cowdery began copying licenses two days later. He may have had already been in possession of this volume, as the first page contains a copy of the minutes of a 26 February 1836 meeting in Kirtland, during which Cowdery, Orson Hyde, and Sylvester Smith were appointed as a committee "to draft rules and regulations concerning licenses." It is unclear when Cowdery copied these minutes into

---

8. Minute Book 2, 6–7 Dec. 1837.

the volume. Cowdery continued recording licenses in his capacity as recording clerk until 3 February 1838. On 10 February, the Zion high council and bishopric stripped Cowdery of his position as recording clerk because of his role in a dispute between the recently rejected Zion presidency and other church leaders.[9]

At some point prior to 1 June 1838, Cowdery transferred the record book to the leadership of the church, possibly to Robinson. At the April 1838 general conference of the church, Robinson had been appointed "general Church Recorder and Clerk for the first Presidency" and a resolution had been passed requiring all licenses to be signed by a member of the First Presidency, with Robinson acting as clerk.[10] From 1 June to the end of September 1838, he recorded licenses into the volume. Sometime in winter 1838–1839, Robinson recorded a list of certificates he gave between 24 December 1838 and 26 January 1839. Afterward, the record book was apparently not used until April 1840, when Hyrum Smith and Thompson began copying new licenses as "pro tem" recorders or clerks. By the end of May 1840, Robinson again took over recording licenses in the volume and continued to do so until at least July. On 3 October 1840, Thompson formally replaced Robinson as general church clerk; Thompson began recording licenses within two days after that appointment.[11] Thompson died in August 1841, and on 2 October Sloan was appointed at a general conference of the church to become the church clerk. Sloan began recording licenses the next day. On 30 July 1843, as Sloan prepared to leave for a mission, JS appointed Willard Richards as Sloan's replacement, and Richards recorded his first licenses that day.[12] Richards continued to record entries in the record book until 1846; beginning in 1844, other clerks in his employ—such as Phelps, Bullock, and at least one unidentified scribe—appear to have increasingly assumed responsibility for recording licenses. Bullock recorded the last licenses in Nauvoo, Illinois, on 5 February 1846. On 16 May 1862, Bullock recorded the final entry, under the heading "Great Salt Lake City".

Evidence indicates the volume has remained in continuous institutional custody. Beginning with Sloan in fall 1841, church recorders also used the volume, turned over and rotated 180 degrees, to record church membership information in Nauvoo, such as certificates received and an 1842 census of church members. The volume, identified as the 1842 census, appears in early church inventories.[13] Further, Bullock made his final license entry in Salt Lake City, Utah Territory.

The License Record Book is the source for one featured text in this volume.

Minute Book 2, 1838, 1842, 1844

Zion (Missouri) High Council and Nauvoo Stake High Council, "The Conference Minutes, and Record Book, of Christ's Church of Latter Day Saints," Minute Book 2, 6 Apr. 1838–[ca. June 1838], [ca. Oct. 1842], [ca. June 1844]; handwriting of Ebenezer Robinson, Hosea Stout,

---

9. Letter from Thomas B. Marsh, 15 Feb. 1838, p. 23 herein.

10. Minutes, 6 Apr. 1838, p. 69 herein; Minutes, 7–8 Apr. 1838, p. 74 herein.

11. Minutes, *Times and Seasons,* Oct. 1840, 1:185.

12. Richards, Journal, 30 July 1843.

13. "Schedule of Church Records. Nauvoo 1846," [1], Historian's Office, Catalogs and Inventories, 1846–1904, CHL.

Levi Richards, Joseph M. Cole, and an unidentified scribe; 178 pages, as well as indexing in tabbed pages at beginning of book; CHL. Includes tables, redactions, use marks, and archival marking.

The second of two texts inscribed in a ledger book. The paper, which is ruled both horizontally and vertically, measures 12½ × 7¾ inches (32 × 20 cm). The book contains 276 leaves, including the flyleaves in the front and back of the book. The bound book, which features a brown suede leather cover, measures 13 × 8½ × 1¾ inches (33 × 22 × 4 cm). The spine has a pasted red label with "LEDGER" in gold lettering. Following the four front flyleaves, the first twenty-four pages are tabbed index pages. The next seventy-three pages were used by Warren Parrish for various financial accounts he kept prior to his move to Kirtland, Ohio. Following a blank page, Minute Book 2 fills the next 187 pages, although there are some blank pages within and at the end of this record. The portion of the ledger in which Minute Book 2 is inscribed has its own pagination, all apparently done by Hosea Stout. Ebenezer Robinson's handwriting appears on the title page (the recto of the leaf preceding page 1) and on pages 1–37, 41–42, 44–52, and 55–93. Pages 38–40 are blank. Levi Richards's handwriting appears on pages 43 and 52–55. There is also unidentified handwriting in the middle of page 87. The inscription ends with minutes of the Nauvoo, Illinois, stake high council meetings held 1 and 15 June 1844, recorded by Joseph M. Cole on pages 178–185. The minutes were recorded with a quill pen, and all are in brown ink, except for some blue ink on pages 179–181. The remaining 251 pages of the book are blank. There were originally four back flyleaves; only two remain, and they are blank.

Minute Book 2 includes several redactions made in graphite, as well as some marking in blue pencil. At some point, the leather cover was decorated with blind tooling, and a paper sticker was pasted on the spine with "CONFERENCE MINUTES AND HIGH COUNCIL RECORDS OF FAR WEST" inscribed in unidentified handwriting. This sticker resembles several other such stickers found on early church record books. The volume may have been included in the Nauvoo exodus inventory as part of "Records of High Council."[14] It is listed in middle- and late-nineteenth-century inventories of the Historian's Office in Salt Lake City.[15] The Genealogical Society of Utah made a microfilm copy of the volume in 1954.[16] Church historian Joseph Fielding Smith took the volume with him to the Office of the First Presidency when he became church president in 1970 and kept it in his safe.[17] The book was returned to the Church History Department in 2008.[18]

---

14. "Schedule of Church Records. Nauvoo 1846," [1], Historian's Office, Catalogs and Inventories, 1846–1904, CHL.

15. See, for example, "Inventory. Historians Office. G. S. L. City April 1. 1857," [1]; and "Index of Records and Journals in the Historian's Office 1878," [4], Historian's Office, Catalogs and Inventories, 1846–1904, CHL.

16. Minute Book 2, microfilm, 2 Nov. 1954, CHL.

17. "Inventory of President Joseph Fielding Smith's Safe," 23 May 1970, First Presidency, General Administration Files, CHL; Francis M. Gibbons to Earl E. Olson, 1 Nov. 1974, CHL; see also Cannon and Cook, Far West Record, v. The volume, however, was made available for microfilming in 1974 and for scanned images in 2006. (Microfilm Operator's Report, 2 Nov. 1974, in Case File for Minute Book 2, CHL; Minute Book 2, microfilm, 1 Nov. 1974, CHL; Minute Book 2, CD, 2006, CHL; see also the full bibliographic record for Minute Book 2 in the CHL catalog.)

18. Church History Department Correspondence, 17 Oct. 2008, in Case File for Minute Book 2, CHL.

These archival records and archival marking on the book indicate continuous institutional custody.

Minute Book 2 includes minutes of the first church conferences held in New York in 1830 and in Ohio in 1831. The bulk of the minutes, however, are from meetings held in Missouri in Jackson, Clay, and Caldwell counties during the 1830s. The record also includes minutes of meetings held in Indiana and Illinois. JS was present at New York and Ohio meetings and was present at Missouri meetings when he visited there and after moving there in March 1838. This record of minutes concludes in 1839, with the exception of minutes for two high council meetings held in Nauvoo in 1844.

The minutes inscribed in Minute Book 2 are copies—most likely copies of copies. The original minutes of these early church conferences, councils, and other meetings were taken by John Whitmer and several other men who acted as clerks. Whitmer, who lived in Missouri and was the appointed church historian, may have collected and kept the minutes that he and other clerks had taken down. Ebenezer Robinson, who began functioning as the clerk of the Zion (Missouri) high council in Far West on 3 March 1838, was formally appointed to that position on 6 April 1838.[19] Immediately following his appointment, Robinson attempted to procure the records of the church in Far West from Whitmer, but Whitmer refused to relinquish them. In response, JS and Sidney Rigdon wrote a letter on 9 April 1838 demanding that Whitmer surrender his notes for the history he had been appointed to keep for the church.[20] Half a century later, Robinson recounted that although Whitmer ignored this demand to give up his historical notes, a "record" was obtained from Whitmer and brought to Robinson's house, and Robinson "copied the entire record into another book, assisted a part of the time, by Dr. Levi Richards."[21] That Robinson copied the record into "another book" seems to imply that Whitmer's record was also kept in a record book. That Minute Book 2 is dated 6 April 1838 (when Robinson was appointed clerk), begins in Robinson's handwriting, and includes handwriting from Richards indicates that it is the copy of the early minutes of the church that Robinson made from Whitmer's record. Robinson titled his copy of the record book "The Conference Minutes, and Record Book, of Christ's Church of Latter Day Saints." The minute book has been more commonly known by the shorter and less formal name "Far West Record."[22] Because of its importance in the 1830s and the frequency with which it is cited in the annotation of The Joseph Smith Papers, it has been designated with the short citation "Minute Book 2."

The minutes of the church's January 1831 conference, as recorded on page 2 of Minute Book 2, include a reference to a revelation recorded on page 80 of the "Book

---

19. Minute Book 2, 3 Mar. and 6 Apr. 1838.

20. This letter was attested by Robinson. (Letter to John Whitmer, 9 Apr. 1838, p. 79 herein.)

21. Ebenezer Robinson, "Items of Personal History of the Editor," Return (Davis City, IA), Sept. 1889, 133.

22. The book was referred to as "Far West record Book A" in JS's March–September 1838 journal, and was listed as "Far West Record" in mid-nineteenth-century archival records of the Church Historian's Office. A transcript of the minute book was also published under that name: Donald Q. Cannon and Lyndon W. Cook, eds., Far West Record: Minutes of the Church of Jesus Christ of Latter-day Saints, 1830–1844 (Salt Lake City: Deseret Book, 1983). (JS, Journal, 13 Apr. 1838, in JSP, J1:256; "Historian's Office Inventory G. S. L. City March 19. 1858," [1], Historian's Office, Catalogs and Inventories, 1846–1904, CHL.)

of Commandments." This indicates that Whitmer's record was a copy of the original minutes and was likely made sometime between 1833 and 1835 after printing of the Book of Commandments had begun and before the Doctrine and Covenants was published. If Whitmer had begun making his copy of the minutes after the publication of the Doctrine and Covenants, he would have been much more likely to reference that book than the unfinished printing of the Book of Commandments.[23] That Robinson made a copy of the minutes, rather than continuing Whitmer's record, suggests that Whitmer's record was returned to him. Whitmer left Far West on 19 June 1838. He remained in Missouri and never reestablished ties with the church in Illinois.[24] Robinson, therefore, apparently finished copying Whitmer's record of minutes by 19 June when Whitmer separated from the body of the Saints. In the lists of conference and council participants found in some of the minutes, some names are followed by parenthetical remarks regarding their excommunication or their disciplinary status. These parenthetical notes were evidently added by Whitmer when he copied the originals and were then copied from Whitmer's record by Robinson.

Minute Book 2 is the source for seven featured texts in this volume.

Times and Seasons

Times and Seasons *(Commerce, Hancock Co., IL, and Nauvoo, Hancock Co., IL), vol. 1, no. 1–vol. 2, no. 3 (July 1839–1 Dec. 1840), edited by Ebenezer Robinson and Don Carlos Smith; vol. 2, nos. 4–12 (15 Dec. 1840–15 Apr. 1841), edited by Don Carlos Smith; vol. 2, nos. 13–19 (1 May–2 Aug. 1841), edited by Don Carlos Smith and Robert B. Thompson; vol. 2, no. 20 (16 Aug. 1841), edited by Robert B. Thompson and Ebenezer Robinson; vol. 2, no. 21–vol. 3, no. 7 (1 Sept. 1841–1 Feb. 1842), edited by Ebenezer Robinson; vol. 3, nos. 8–24 (15 Feb.– 15 Oct. 1842), edited by JS; vol. 4, no. 1–vol. 6, no. 23 (15 Nov. 1842–15 Feb. 1846), edited by John Taylor.*

The *Times and Seasons* was a newspaper published in Commerce (later Nauvoo), Illinois. After the first installment in July 1839, it was published monthly from November 1839 to October 1840 and then semimonthly—generally on the first and fifteenth of each month—until the final issue on 15 February 1846.[25] Each issue was printed on sixteen octavo pages measuring around 9½ × 6 inches (24 × 15 cm); the exact size varied depending on how an issue was cut. Each page contained two columns of text; in the issues prior to 1 July 1841, both columns were 2⅛ inches wide; in the later issues, the columns were

---

23. Whitmer could not have copied these minutes before January 1833, the earliest that the third gathering of the Book of Commandments (which included page 80) could have been printed, and would likely not have copied them after mid-September 1835, when the referenced revelation was available in the published Doctrine and Covenants. (Historical Introduction to Book of Commandments, in *JSP*, R2:9n35; William W. Phelps, Kirtland Mills, OH, to Sally Waterman Phelps, Liberty, MO, 16–18 Sept. 1835, private possession, copy at CHL.)

24. Jenson, LDS Biographical Encyclopedia, 1:251–252.

25. Because of opposition to the newspaper or a lack of supplies, issues were not published for 1 November 1842, 15 November 1843, 1 and 15 December 1843, 15 June 1844, and the months of September and October 1845.

2¼ inches wide.[26] The type of paper used varied in composition between wood pulp and linen fibers depending on what was available at the time of publication.

The first of the newspaper's six volumes consisted of twelve issues and one reprint; the issues were dated July 1839 and then November 1839 through October 1840. The second through fifth volumes contained twenty-four issues each and were dated November 1840–15 October 1841, 1 November 1841–15 October 1842, 15 November 1842–1 November 1843, and 1 January 1844–1 January 1845, respectively. The sixth volume contained only twenty-three issues and ran from 15 January 1845 to 15 February 1846. Volumes 1–3 were paginated 1–958; the numbers 577–582 were used on the pages at the end of volume 2 and were repeated on the pages at the beginning of volume 3. Volumes 4–6 were paginated 1–1135. Other minor errors in page numbers were made throughout both sets of pagination.

The volumes used in *The Joseph Smith Papers* were bound into several text blocks at a later date. Volumes 1 and 2 were bound together in three-quarter binding with red textured leather and shell marbled paper. The edges have been trimmed and speckled brown. The bound item measures 9 × 5⅝ × 1⅜ inches (23 × 14 × 3 cm). Another copy of volume 1 and another copy of volume 2 were bound with volume 3 in a three-quarter case binding with black leather and textured cloth, measuring 9 × 6 × 2¼ inches (23 × 15 × 6 cm). Volumes 4 and 5 were bound individually but are identical in composition and materials, suggesting they were originally bound at around the same time. The edges of the two volumes have been trimmed with blue speckling. Both are bound with a three-quarter binding of textured black leather and shell marbled paper. Volume 4 measures 9¼ × 6 × 1 inches (23 × 15 × 3 cm), and volume 5 measures 8⅞ × 5⅞ × 1 inches (23 × 15 × 3 cm). Both were likely compiled in Nauvoo, as they each contain a title page and index. It is not clear where they were originally bound. Volume 6 is likewise bound individually, though with a three-quarter binding of brown calf leather and marbled paper; the paper has been significantly worn down. The pages have been trimmed, and the edges have uneven brown coloring. The volume measures 9¼ × 6 × ¾ inches (23 × 15 × 2 cm). The spine of each bound item has gold tooling, along with the name of the newspaper and the volumes contained in the binding. The spine of volume 6 also has decorative blind roll tooling.

With the exception of the final volume, all of the bound volumes were rebound one or more times and underwent significant conservation work during the nineteenth and twentieth centuries. Nearly all of the volumes contain diamond-shaped press marks on the paper, and all of the volumes include archival stamping and labels from the Church Historian's Office or other earlier owners. Volumes of the *Times and Seasons* have been in the possession of the Church Historian's Office since at least 1846; however, it is unclear whether any of the earliest-acquired copies are the ones featured in *The Joseph Smith Papers*.[27] There are no archival markings identifying the original owners of volumes 1–3. Volumes 4 and 5 apparently belonged to Latter-day Saint Robert Campbell until his death in 1872. By 11 December 1889, they were subsequently acquired by Andrew Jenson, an

---

26. In a few issues, the initial page contained a single column. (See, for example, *Times and Seasons,* 15 Nov. 1841, 3:577.)

27. "Schedule of Church Records. Nauvoo 1846," [1], Historian's Office, Catalogs and Inventories, 1846–1904, CHL.

employee in the Church Historian's Office, for his personal library. A partially removed label describing lending policies for an unidentified library suggests that volume 6 belonged to a lending library until Jenson acquired the volume by 1890. In 1930, the three volumes Jenson acquired were transferred to the Church Historian's Office, along with the rest of his library.[28]

The newspaper was established after the First Presidency and other church leaders in the Commerce, Illinois, area met in June 1839. They determined that Ebenezer Robinson and Don Carlos Smith should publish the newspaper. The church would provide the printing press, with Robinson and Smith paying the publication expenses and receiving all profits from the business.[29]

The press was first set up in the basement of a structure on the banks of the Mississippi River, and two hundred copies of the first issue were printed in July. Severe illness among the editors and their families prevented more copies from being printed. In November 1839, with the assistance of Lyman Gaylord and in a new structure on the northeast corner of Water and Bain streets, the first issue was printed again, redated November 1839. The yearly subscription fee for the newspaper was one dollar.[30] The paper listed its publication location as Commerce until the May 1840 issue, when the location was changed to Nauvoo.

With the second volume, begun 1 November 1840, the paper began to be issued semimonthly and the subscription price increased to two dollars per year.[31] The issues were dated the first and fifteenth of each month, but print runs were frequently a week or more late; in some cases, they were months behind schedule. On 14 December 1840, Robinson and Smith dissolved their partnership, and Smith became the sole editor of the next nine issues, beginning with the 15 December issue.[32] Robert B. Thompson joined Smith as a coeditor for the issues of 1 May 1841 through 2 August 1841.[33] After Smith's death on 7 August 1841, Robinson once again joined the paper, coediting the 16 August issue with Thompson.[34] Thompson died before the next issue was printed, leaving Robinson as the sole editor beginning with the September 1841 issue. In November 1841, Robinson moved the *Times and Seasons* printing office across the street to the northwest corner of Water and Bain streets.[35]

A revelation on 28 January 1842 directed the Quorum of the Twelve Apostles to take responsibility for the paper. John Taylor and Wilford Woodruff were assigned to act as editors, and Robinson sold the printing establishment to JS on 4 February 1842.[36] JS was identified as the editor of the paper for the issues of 15 February 1842 through 15 October

---

28. Jenson, Journal, 1 Feb. 1930.

29. Ebenezer Robinson, "Items of Personal History of the Editor," *Return,* May 1890, 257.

30. Ebenezer Robinson, "Items of Personal History of the Editor," *Return,* May 1890, 257–258; "To the Patrons of the Times and Seasons," *Times and Seasons,* Nov. 1839, 1:15–16.

31. *Times and Seasons,* 1 Nov. 1840, 2:193, 208.

32. "Dissolution," *Times and Seasons,* 15 Dec. 1840, 2:256.

33. "New Arrangement," *Times and Seasons,* 1 May 1841, 2:402.

34. "Death of General Don Carlos Smith," *Times and Seasons,* 16 Aug. 1841, 2:503.

35. "Death of Col. Robert B. Thompson," *Times and Seasons,* 1 Sept. 1841, 2:519; JS, Journal, 28 Jan. and 4 Feb. 1842, in *JSP,* J2:33, 38.

36. JS, Journal, 28 Jan. and 4 Feb. 1842, in *JSP,* J2:33, 38.

1842. In early December 1842, JS leased the printing office to Taylor and Woodruff, who had been heavily involved in editing and printing the paper throughout JS's tenure as editor.[37] Beginning with the first issue of volume 4, dated 15 November 1842, Woodruff was named as a publisher, with Taylor listed as a publisher and editor.

In January 1844, JS initiated the sale of the printing office to Taylor, but the transaction was not finalized prior to JS's death in June 1844.[38] Taylor remained the sole named editor for the remainder of the paper's publication, which concluded with the issue of 15 February 1846.

The *Times and Seasons* is the source for one featured text in this volume.

Wilford Woodruff, "Book of Revelations"

Wilford Woodruff, "Book of Revelations," [ca. 23 Dec. 1837–1860]; handwriting of Wilford Woodruff and Asahel H. Woodruff; 107 pages; CHL. Includes shorthand, drawings, redactions, and use marks.

Blank book measuring 6 × 4 × ⅜ inches (15 × 10 × 1 cm). At some point, the first leaf of the text block and the two leaves of endpaper at the beginning of the volume were excised from the volume. Ink is visible on the stub of the first leaf of the text block, indicating that at least the recto of that leaf contained text. The wear on the stubs suggests that the pages were cut from the volume while it was still in use. The remainder of the text block consists of fifty-five leaves, followed by two sheets of endpaper at the back of the volume. The book has a tight-back, quarter binding with cow leather. The remainder of the boards have been covered with yellow paper. Woodruff inscribed "Book of Revelations | W Woodruff" on the front cover of the volume.

Many of the entries contain Woodruff's usual textual flourishes and decorations, including stylized punctuation marks and curlicued lines separating entries. Additionally, Woodruff regularly drew a small key where the word "key" appeared in the text. Woodruff's handwriting varies widely in the volume, and often within texts, ranging from his flowing cursive to his more blocky print.

The volume was initially owned by Asahel H. Woodruff, who began using it as a diary or genealogical record sometime around December 1837. Asahel died in October 1838, and his brother Wilford Woodruff took possession of Asahel's "private letters, Journals, writing papers [and] Account Books" on 13 December 1838.[39] Presumably this volume was among Asahel's papers. In summer 1839, Wilford Woodruff began copying into the volume JS's revelations regarding the duties of the Quorum of the Twelve Apostles and JS's instructions for their upcoming mission to Europe. Aside from a later 1839 discourse by Parley P. Pratt, no further entries were made until 1841. The volume was perhaps transferred with Woodruff's other papers and journals to the Church Historian's Office by 1858, but in 1860 Woodruff used the volume to record bids to provide grain for

---

37. JS, Journal, 2 Dec. 1842, in *JSP*, J2:171; Crawley, *Descriptive Bibliography*, 1:92–94.

38. JS, Journal, 23 Jan. 1844, in *JSP*, J3:168.

39. Woodruff, Journal, 13 Dec. 1838.

the soldiers stationed at Camp Floyd that year. The volume appears in church inventories by 1878.[40] At some point after 1878, the record was given to his wife Sarah Brown Woodruff and was then passed down through the family until it was donated to church historian and recorder Joseph Fielding Smith sometime in the mid-twentieth century.[41] Smith apparently retained the volume among his papers, and it likely became part of the First Presidency's papers when Smith became church president in 1970, as happened with other historical records in his possession.[42] In 2010 the First Presidency transferred custody of Woodruff's "Book of Revelations" to the Church History Library.[43]

Wilford Woodruff's "Book of Revelations" is the source for three featured texts in this volume.

Wilford Woodruff, Journal

Wilford Woodruff, "Willford Woodruff's Journal Vol. 2. And a Synopsis of Vol. 1," Journal, 1 Jan. 1838–31 Dec. 1839; handwriting of Wilford Woodruff; 121 pages; Wilford Woodruff, Journals and Papers, CHL. Includes shorthand, drawings, redactions, and use marks.

Blank book measuring 3⅞ × 6¾ × ¾ (10 × 17 × 2 cm). The volume contains 126 leaves (252 pages). There are three flyleaves at the front and the back of the volume, with a fourth leaf at the front and back pasted to the boards. The journal has a tight-back, limp binding, supported by two strips of vellum tape. The boards and spine are covered with brown calf leather. The spine contains a gold-tooled inscription: "WOODRUFF' | JOURNAL | VOL. 2."

The rectos of all three flyleaves in the front were inscribed by Woodruff and contain a title page, a summary of statistics from Woodruff's first journal, and the subtitle "THE FIRST BOOK | OF | WILLFORD VOL. 2. | FOR | 1838". An unknown scribe later labeled the verso of the pastedown: "1st. | January 1st. 1838. | to | December 31st. 1839." Woodruff inscribed all of his journal entries in the first six gatherings of the book in brown ink; the remainder of the volume is blank. Woodruff decorated his entries with borders, drawings, flourishes, and symbols; it seems that he used some of the decorations to track information such as ordinances performed, meetings attended, and letters sent and received. This volume was the second journal Woodruff wrote in after his baptism in December 1833. The format of this journal—which begins with a brief personal history, followed by daily journal entries—appears to be patterned after his earlier journal. The volume contains daily journal entries from 1 January 1838 to 31 December 1839. These entries were apparently copied from earlier daybooks that Woodruff seems to have

---

40. Woodruff, Journal, 13 Dec. 1838; "Historian's Office Catalogue Book March 1858," [25]; "Index of Records and Journals in the Historian's Office, 1878," [14], Historian's Office, Catalogs and Inventories, 1846–1904, CHL.

41. Eunice W. Perry to Joseph Fielding Smith, no date, in Case File for Woodruff, "Book of Revelations," CHL.

42. See, for example, Source Note for Revelation Book 1, in *JSP*, MRB:4–5.

43. Brook P. Hales to Glenn N. Rowe, 28 June 2010, in Case File for Woodruff, "Book of Revelations," CHL.

written in regularly and that he expanded upon in his journal entries.[44] Woodruff caught up on his copying in the second journal by 8 August 1839, when he departed for a mission to England and left the journal with his wife, Phebe. Presumably, Woodruff copied the remaining entries for 1839 sometime following his return to the United States in 1841. He did not copy any entries beyond December 1839 into the volume, although he had inscribed only half the volume. He inscribed later entries in a different volume. A March 1858 catalog record in the Church Historian's Office indicates that Woodruff's "Private Papers" were in the possession of the office by that time, probably because of his position as assistant church historian.[45] A July 1858 inventory clarified that these papers included Woodruff's journals.[46] The journals likewise appear on later inventories, suggesting that the second volume has been in continuous institutional custody.[47]

Wilford Woodruff's journal is the source for one featured text in this volume.

Willard Richards, "Pocket Companion"

Willard Richards, "W Richards Pocket companion written in England," notebook, [between 13 Jan. 1840 and 20 Apr. 1841]; handwriting of Willard Richards; 102 pages; Willard Richards, Journals and Papers, CHL. Includes use marks, drawings, and archival markings.

Blank book measuring 6¼ × 4 × ⅜ inches (16 × 10 × 1 cm). The book contains seventy-six leaves in six gatherings. The first leaf of the first gathering is glued to the front board, and the last leaf of the last gathering is glued to the back board. Willard Richards's entries in the book are in brown ink. The volume contains stains and mold damage throughout. The volume's limp case binding is supported by two strips of vellum tape along a hollow-back spine. After the book was bound, brown leather—possibly sheepskin—was pasted along the boards and spine of the book. Richards inscribed "Pocket Companion" in ink on the cover of the volume. He similarly wrote "W Richards Pocket companion written in England" on the recto of the second leaf. The majority of the volume's content is a copy of apostle Wilford Woodruff's "Book of Revelations," which contains several JS revelations and discourses as well as a sermon by Parley P. Pratt. Richards copied the content at some point after 13 January 1841, when Woodruff arrived in England for a proselytizing mission with Richards and others. Richards next wrote nearly thirty pages of scriptural notes under the heading "The Subject of the Dispensation of the fullness of Times" and then copied additional instructions from JS, which he likely received from another missionary, possibly John Taylor. Afterward, Richards copied selections from JS's Bible revisions for Genesis and Matthew, followed by a passage from a revelation not included in Woodruff's "Book of Revelations." Richards apparently completed making entries in the volume by 20 April 1841,

44. Several daybooks from which Woodruff copied entries into this and other journal volumes are located in the Wilford Woodruff Collection, CHL.

45. "Historian's Office Catalogue Book March 1858," [25], Historian's Office, Catalogs and Inventories, 1846–1904, CHL.

46. "Contents of the Historian and Recorder's Office. G. S. L. City July 1858," 9, Historian's Office, Catalogs and Inventories, 1846–1904, CHL.

47. "Index of Records and Journals in the Historian's Office 1878," [14], Historian's Office, Catalogs and Inventories, 1846–1904, CHL.

when he boarded a ship to leave England. After Richards became church historian and recorder later in the 1840s, this volume and his other personal papers were included among the archival holdings of the church. An early inventory of church records includes a reference to "D⁂ private books & Papers," which likely included the "Pocket Companion."[48] The volume contains archival and use marks throughout, suggesting that at some point material was copied from the "Pocket Companion," likely by staff in the Church Historian's Office in the mid-1850s. The use of the volume in the Church Historian's Office suggests that the volume has been in continuous institutional custody.

Willard Richards's "Pocket Companion" is the source for three featured texts in this volume.

William Swartzell, *Mormonism Exposed*

William Swartzell, Mormonism Exposed, Being a Journal of a Residence in Missouri from the 28th of May to the 20th of August, 1838, together with an Appendix, Containing the Revelation concerning the Golden Bible, with Numerous Extracts from the "Book of Covenants," &c., &c., *Pekin, OH: By the author, [between 12 April and 4 May] 1840; forty-eight pages. The copy used for transcription is held at BYU.*

Printed pamphlet containing twenty-five leaves. The text block measures 8¼ × 5⅜ × ⅛ inches (21 × 14 × 0.3 cm). The leaves were bound in a single sheet of purple paper that was pasted to the spine. The bulk of the pamphlet consists of the typescript of a journal William Swartzell kept in 1838. The printed journal evidently contains several editorial changes from the nonextant original manuscript; these changes tend to be easily identified because they are explicitly marked as editorial insertions or because of changes in verb tense.[49] Notwithstanding these changes, Swartzell's journal appears to be an accurate, contemporaneous record of events in Missouri during summer 1838. Swartzell apparently finished preparing his journal for publication on 12 April 1840 in Pekin, Carroll County, Ohio.[50] Shortly thereafter, Swartzell or a representative took the manuscript to Pittsburgh, Pennsylvania, to copyright the manuscript and to contract with the printing office of Alexander Ingram. On 4 May 1840, Ingram printed an advertisement for the pamphlet in the *Daily Pittsburgh Gazette,* noting that the pamphlet was "just published, and for sale" at his 78 Market Street office.[51] Though the pamphlet was printed in Pittsburgh by Ingram, its copyright page states that it was published by the author.

William Swartzell, *Mormonism Exposed,* is the source for two featured texts in this volume.

---

48. "Schedule of Church Records. Nauvoo 1846," [1], Historian's Office, Catalogs and Inventories, 1846–1904, CHL.

49. See, for example, Swartzell, *Mormonism Exposed,* 6, 11, 13–14, 19–20, 24–25.

50. Swartzell, *Mormonism Exposed,* iv.

51. Swartzell, *Mormonism Exposed,* [i], [ii]; Notice, *Daily Pittsburgh Gazette,* 4 May 1840, [2].

Chronology for November 1837–October 1839

This brief chronology is designed as a reference tool for situating any particular document or group of documents among the more significant events of JS's life. It includes important journeys, births and deaths of immediate family members, selected revelations, developments in ecclesiastical organization, and other significant incidents. This chronology also includes a few key dates before and after the period covered in the volume. Readers wishing to conduct further research into events in JS's life may consult the documented chronology posted on the Joseph Smith Papers website, josephsmithpapers.org.

1837

November	7	JS presided at conference in which Frederick G. Williams was removed from presidency and Hyrum Smith was appointed in his place, Far West, Missouri.
December	late	Kirtland high council excommunicated twenty-eight dissenters, including Martin Harris, Warren Parrish, and apostles Luke Johnson and John F. Boynton, Kirtland, Ohio.

1838

January	12	JS and Sidney Rigdon departed Kirtland for Far West.
February	5–9	Zion presidency removed from office by general assembly of church, Caldwell County, Missouri.
	10	Resident apostles Thomas B. Marsh and David W. Patten appointed as pro tempore presidents of church in Zion by Zion high council and bishopric, Far West.
March	10	Former presidents William W. Phelps and John Whitmer excommunicated by church council, Far West.
	14	JS and family arrived at Far West from Kirtland.
	15	JS presided over church council and approved recent council decisions, including leadership changes, Far West.
April	4	Sidney Rigdon arrived at Far West from Kirtland.
	6	Thomas B. Marsh sustained as president pro tempore of church in Zion, with David W. Patten and Brigham Young appointed as assistant presidents. George W. Robinson appointed as general church recorder and clerk, as well as scribe for First Presidency; Ebenezer Robinson appointed recorder and clerk for Zion church and high council, Far West.
	12	Church council excommunicated Oliver Cowdery, Far West.

	13	Church council excommunicated David Whitmer and Lyman Johnson, Far West.
	21	Church council decided to reestablish church publication efforts, including *Elders' Journal* newspaper, Far West.
	26	JS dictated revelation in Far West commanding Saints to establish Far West as a city of Zion with a temple and to change name of church to the Church of Jesus Christ of Latter Day Saints.
	27	With Sidney Rigdon and George W. Robinson, JS commenced writing detailed history of the church, Far West.
May	18	JS departed Far West for Daviess County, Missouri, to select sites for new settlements.
	19	JS planned settlement at Spring Hill (soon renamed Adam-ondi-Ahman), Missouri.
	24	JS returned to Far West from surveying trip in Daviess County.
	27	Hyrum Smith arrived at Far West from Kirtland.
	28	JS and Hyrum Smith departed Far West for Daviess County to select further sites for new settlements.
June	1	JS returned to Far West from Daviess County.
	2	Alexander Hale Smith born to JS and Emma Smith, Far West.
	4	JS left Far West to continue surveying at Adam-ondi-Ahman, Missouri, for new settlement.
	ca. 16	JS returned to Far West from Adam-ondi-Ahman.
	17	Sidney Rigdon delivered "Salt Sermon," criticizing dissenters, Far West.
	19	Prominent dissenters Oliver Cowdery, David Whitmer, John Whitmer, and Lyman Johnson departed Far West.
	23	John Murdock and George M. Hinkle, acting under direction of JS and other church leaders, purchased lots for church settlement in De Witt, Missouri.
	28	JS organized stake at Adam-ondi-Ahman, with John Smith as president.
July	4	JS presided over Independence Day celebration, during which temple cornerstones were laid and Sidney Rigdon delivered public address declaring Latter-day Saints' intent to defend themselves from persecution, Far West.
	6	Zion high council approved purchase of George M. Hinkle's residence for use by JS and Smith family, Far West.
		About five hundred Saints constituting "Kirtland Camp" began their migration to Missouri from Kirtland.
	8	JS dictated revelations regarding church leadership and finances, Far West.
	mid	JS and others visited Daviess County.

26 JS met with church council to arrange financial affairs of church, Far West.

28–30 JS and Sidney Rigdon visited Adam-ondi-Ahman to help settle Mormon immigrants from Upper Canada.

August   6 Fighting broke out during attempt to prevent Latter-day Saints from voting in election, with men injured on both sides and rumors spread that Saints were killed, Gallatin, Missouri.

8 With large company of Danites and other Latter-day Saint men, JS visited Adam Black, Daviess County justice of the peace, demanding that he agree to abide and uphold the law, Grand River Township, Missouri.

9 JS and others returned to Far West from Daviess County.

10 Judge Austin A. King issued arrest warrant for JS and Lyman Wight based on their actions in the confrontation with Adam Black, Richmond, Missouri.

11 JS departed Far West on journey to "forks of Grand river," noncounty area northwest of Daviess County, to warn Canadian Latter-day Saints of danger from other Missourians; also visited Adam-ondi-Ahman.

13 JS returned to Far West from trip to Adam-ondi-Ahman and area northwest of Daviess County.

16 Sheriff William Morgan attempted to arrest JS with Judge Austin A. King's warrant, Far West; Morgan later reported that he could not serve the writ because he was outside of his jurisdiction.

September   1 JS and others visited residence of Waldo Littlefield in Honey Creek Township, Daviess County, and designated the area as site for new "city of Zion."

4 JS hired David R. Atchison and Alexander Doniphan as legal counsel, Far West.

6 JS and others visited residence of Waldo Littlefield in Honey Creek Township for preliminary hearing before Austin A. King on charges arising from confrontation with Adam Black. Black was not present, so they returned to Far West.

7 JS and Lyman Wight visited John Raglin farm for preliminary hearing before Austin A. King on charges arising from confrontation with Adam Black; JS and Wight gave bonds for later court appearance, Honey Creek Township.

9 Militia officers in Caldwell County arrested men transporting guns to anti-Mormon vigilantes in Daviess County and held men and guns in Far West.

18 Several church members appeared for preliminary hearing on charges arising from confrontation with Adam Black, giving bonds for later court appearance; Major General David R. Atchison dispersed anti-Mormon vigilantes, Netherton Springs, Missouri.

October	1	Anti-Mormon vigilantes prepared to attack Latter-day Saints living at De Witt.
	2	Members of "Kirtland Camp" arrived in Far West.
	5–13	JS led rescue party to defend besieged Latter-day Saints at De Witt; Missouri governor Lilburn W. Boggs refused to intervene; JS assisted with evacuation of De Witt Saints to Far West.
	15–16	After learning that anti-Mormon vigilantes intended to attack Latter-day Saints at Adam-ondi-Ahman, JS delivered a discourse in Far West declaring the Saints would defend themselves from opposition; JS helped recruit about three hundred Latter-day Saint men and joined them on their march to Daviess County.
	18–21	Perceiving that civil and militia authorities would not uphold the law, Mormon vigilantes launched preemptive strikes at anti-Mormon rendezvous points, burning buildings owned or used by anti-Mormons and others, confiscating goods as wartime appropriations, seizing a cannon intended to be used against Saints, and expelling opponents and others from Daviess County.
	22	JS returned to Far West from Adam-ondi-Ahman.
	24	In Richmond, Thomas B. Marsh and Orson Hyde signed affidavits criticizing Mormon vigilantes' operations in Daviess County.
	25	Armed Latter-day Saint men in Caldwell County attacked company of volunteers from Ray County, Missouri, regiment of state militia who had captured two Mormon scouts; three Latter-day Saints and one Ray County militiaman killed at Crooked River, near Ray County; JS remained in Far West but later that day visited Latter-day Saints as they returned from the skirmish, near Log Creek, Missouri.
	27	Governor Lilburn W. Boggs issued orders authorizing extermination or expulsion of Latter-day Saints from state, Jefferson City, Missouri.
	30	General Samuel D. Lucas and nearly two thousand troops approached Far West and encamped at Goose Creek, Rockford Township, Missouri.
		Armed anti-Mormon men from Livingston County, Missouri, attacked community of Latter-day Saints, killing seventeen and wounding fourteen, Hawn's Mill settlement, Grand River Township.
	31	General Samuel D. Lucas presented peace terms to Colonel George M. Hinkle, including the surrender of JS and four others; JS taken prisoner by state militia and spent night in Missouri state militia encampment at Goose Creek.
November	1	Colonel George M. Hinkle accepted terms of surrender from General Samuel D. Lucas; Missouri militia troops occupied Far West.
		In Missouri state militia encampment, Mormon prisoners sentenced to death by military court; Alexander Doniphan objected, thus preventing execution, Goose Creek.
	4	JS and fellow prisoners arrived in Independence, Missouri.

	8–9	JS and fellow prisoners transported from Independence to Richmond.
	12–29	JS and others appeared at court of inquiry before Judge Austin A. King for treason and other crimes allegedly committed in Daviess, Caldwell, and Ray counties; King ruled there was sufficient evidence to send cases to full trial, Richmond.
December	1	JS, Hyrum Smith, Sidney Rigdon, Lyman Wight, Caleb Baldwin, and Alexander McRae transported to and incarcerated in jail at Liberty, Missouri.

1839

January	22–29	Judge Joel Turnham held habeas corpus hearing for JS and fellow prisoners, Liberty.
	30	Sidney Rigdon released on bail but remained in jail a few more days as safety precaution, Liberty.
February		Large-scale evacuation of Latter-day Saints from Missouri to Illinois began.
	7	JS and fellow prisoners attempted to escape jail but failed, Liberty.
March	4	JS and fellow prisoners made second attempt to escape jail but failed, Liberty.
	20	JS dictated epistle from jail to exiled Latter-day Saints, offering them counsel and sympathy, Liberty.
	ca. 22	JS dictated second general epistle to Saints, including instructions to Edward Partridge and church members to record depredations and losses suffered in Missouri by the Saints, Liberty.
April	6–8	JS and fellow prisoners transported from Liberty to Gallatin to attend circuit court hearing on crimes allegedly committed in Daviess County.
	ca. 10	JS indicted by grand jury for treason and other charges but granted change of venue, Gallatin.
	12	JS and fellow prisoners departed Gallatin on journey to stand trial in Columbia, Missouri.
	16	JS and fellow prisoners escaped custody while en route to Columbia for trial, Chariton County, Missouri.
	22	JS arrived in Quincy, Illinois, and reunited with his wife and children, who were residing in home of John and Sarah Kingsley Cleveland, Quincy.
	24	JS presided over church meeting at Quincy.
	ca. 24	JS and others investigated land for Mormon settlement, traveling to Lee County, Iowa Territory, and then Hancock County, Illinois.
	26	Members of Quorum of the Twelve Apostles and others held council at temple site in Far West.
	30	Church agents made initial purchases of land for Mormon settlement in area of Commerce, Illinois.

May	3	JS and others returned to Quincy from Lee County and Hancock County.
	4–5	JS presided at general conference of church in which plans were made to present accounts of Missouri injustices to federal government, Quincy.
	9–10	JS and family moved from Quincy to log home at Commerce.
	29	Church agent Oliver Granger purchased land for Mormon settlement from Isaac Galland in Lee County.
	ca. 30	JS and others traveled from Commerce to Quincy.
June	3	First Presidency initiated recommendations for apostles preparing for European proselytizing mission, Quincy.
	5	JS and others returned to Commerce from Quincy.
	15–26	JS and family traveled to Plymouth County, Illinois, to visit JS's brother William Smith and then traveled to the area of Macomb, Illinois, to visit JS's brothers Don Carlos Smith and Samuel Smith.
	26	Church agent Vinson Knight purchased land in Lee County from Isaac Galland for Mormon settlement.
	27	JS provided instruction at conference held by Quorum of the Twelve Apostles, Commerce.
	late	Malaria epidemic began, lasting through the summer, Commerce, Illinois, and Montrose, Iowa Territory.
July		First issue of church newspaper *Times and Seasons* published, with date of July 1839, Commerce.
	2	JS and others crossed Mississippi River to Brigham Young's residence, where JS instructed Latter-day Saint men preparing to leave for European proselytizing mission, Montrose.
	22–23	JS involved in administering blessings of healing to sick Latter-day Saints in and around Commerce and Montrose.
August	8	John Taylor and Wilford Woodruff departed for England, initiating European proselytizing mission of Quorum of the Twelve Apostles, Commerce.
	12	JS, Sidney Rigdon, and Hyrum Smith purchased land from Horace Hotchkiss and partners John Gillet and Smith Tuttle, Commerce.
October	5–7	JS presided over general church conference at Commerce, establishing stake at Commerce and branch of stake in Lee County.
	29	JS and other church delegates departed Illinois for Washington DC to seek redress and reparations from federal government for Saints' property losses in Missouri.

Geographical Directory

This directory provides geographical descriptions of most of the places mentioned in this volume of *The Joseph Smith Papers*. It includes villages and towns, townships, counties and states, and waterways.

Each place is listed with a complete political location. Many entries also include information such as municipal history, population, and distinctive natural environments, as well as details more particular to the significance of the place within JS's documents dated between February 1838 and August 1839. Unless otherwise noted, all places were within the United States of America during this time period. Spellings of the time period have been used for proper nouns. In the state of New York, the terms *town* and *township* were used interchangeably during JS's lifetime; this geographical directory uses the term *township*. "LDS church" refers to the church established by JS in 1830 and later known as the Church of Jesus Christ of Latter-day Saints.

Map coordinates refer to the maps found on pages 598–610. Readers wishing to conduct further research may consult the documented Geographical Directory posted on the Joseph Smith Papers website, josephsmithpapers.org.

Adam-ondi-Ahman, Grand River Township, Daviess County, Missouri. Map 1: B-1; Map 4: B-2; Map 5: A-4; Map 6: B-2; Map 10. Settlement located in northwest Missouri. 1835 revelation identified valley of Adam-ondi-Ahman as place where Adam blessed his posterity after leaving Garden of Eden. While seeking new areas in Daviess Co. for settlement, JS and others surveyed site on which to build city centered on bluffs of Grand River near home and ferry of Latter-day Saint Lyman Wight, May 1838. JS announced area as gathering place for Saints, May 1838. First called Spring Hill; renamed May or June 1838 when JS identified area as Adam-ondi-Ahman and place where Adam will return prior to Second Coming (Latter-day Saint nickname was "Diahman"). Large groups of Saints, many from Kirtland, Ohio, began settling there, June 1838. Town connected to Far West by way of Daviess Co. seat, Gallatin, on road built by Saints. Soon became principal Mormon settlement in Daviess Co. Stake organized, 28 June 1838. Under pressure from vigilantes, Mormon settlers from outlying areas of Daviess Co. took refuge here. As population of 400 grew to over 1,000, houses filled to overflowing, and many lived in tents and wagons. Responding to threats, able-bodied Mormon men in area conducted raids from settlement, which served as seat of Mormon military operations in county, mid-Oct. 1838. After surrender of Far West, state militia arrived at Adam-ondi-Ahman, 8 Nov. 1838, and gave Mormons ultimatum: evacuate county within ten days, or remain, unarmed and unprotected, subject to vigilante retaliation. Town almost completely abandoned, by 20 Nov. 1838. Originally occupied lands offered at public sale and purchased by local residents, 24 Nov. 1838, part of which became new town of Cravensville, 1839.

Caldwell County, Missouri. Map 4: C-1; Map 5: B-4; Map 6. Located in northwest Missouri. Settled by whites, by 1831. Described as being "one-third timber and two-thirds prairie" in 1836. Created specifically for Latter-day Saints by Missouri state legislature, 29 Dec. 1836, in attempt to solve "Mormon problem." Major Mormon immigration followed. Population by summer 1838 between 5,000 and 7,000. Population by 1840 about 1,500. Included at least nineteen Mormon settlements. Expansion of Mormon settlement beyond county borders resulted in conflict and violence between Saints and other Missourians. Governor Lilburn W. Boggs ordered that Saints be exterminated or driven from state, 27 Oct. 1838. State militia arrested and imprisoned JS and other Mormon leaders and expelled remaining Saints from state. Almost all Caldwell Co. Saints evacuated, by spring 1839.

Chariton County, Missouri. MAP 4: C-3; MAP 5: C-6. Established 16 Nov. 1820. Village of Chariton named county seat, 1820. Keytesville named county seat, 1833. Population in 1830 about 1,800. Population in 1836 about 3,500. In Aug. 1831, while en route from Independence to Kirtland, JS met ten other elders in county. JS also dictated at least one revelation in county. While being transported from Gallatin to Boone for trial, JS and four others allowed by captors to escape near Yellow Creek possibly in county, 16 Apr. 1839.

Cincinnati, Hamilton Co., Ohio. MAP 1: C-5; MAP 3: D-1. Area settled largely by emigrants from New England and New Jersey, by 1788. Village founded and surveyed adjacent to site of Fort Washington, 1789. First seat of legislature of Northwest Territory, 1790. Incorporated as city, 1819. Developed rapidly as shipping center after opening of Ohio and Erie Canal, 1832. Seventh most populous city in U.S., by 1833. Port of entry and county seat. Population in 1820 about 9,600; in 1830 about 25,000; and in 1840 about 46,000. Four missionaries to American Indians preached in city en route from Kirtland, Ohio, to Missouri, by Jan. 1831. JS visited city, June 1831, meeting with Campbellite minister Walter Scott. JS revelations directed him, Sidney Rigdon, and Oliver Cowdery to preach in city while traveling from Independence, Missouri, to Kirtland, Aug. 1831. Lyman Wight baptized nearly 100 people and formed first branch of LDS church in city, 1833. Second branch formed, 1840, by John E. Page and Orson Hyde. Hyde departed city for Jerusalem to dedicate Palestine, at JS's direction, for return of Jews. Third edition of Book of Mormon printed in city, 1840. Brigham Young, Heber C. Kimball, and Lyman Wight held conference in city, 27 May 1844.

Clay County, Missouri. MAP 4: C-1; MAP 5: D-3. Settled ca. 1800. Organized from Ray Co., 1822. Original size diminished when land was taken to create several surrounding counties. Liberty designated county seat, 1822. Population in 1830 about 5,000; in 1836 about 8,500; and in 1840 about 8,300. Refuge for Latter-day Saints expelled from Jackson Co., 1833. LDS population in 1834 about 900. Citizens demanded Saints leave, summer 1836. Most Saints immigrated to newly formed Caldwell Co., by 1838. During Mormon-Missouri conflict in Caldwell Co., militia from Clay Co. assembled to combat Mormons but did not fight. JS imprisoned in jail at Liberty, winter 1838–1839.

Commerce (now Nauvoo), Hancock County, Illinois. MAP 1: B-2; MAP 4: A-4; MAP 11: C-3; MAP 12. Located near middle of western boundary of state, bordering Mississippi River. European Americans settled area, 1820s. From bank of river, several feet above high-water mark, ground described as nearly level for six or seven blocks before gradually sloping upward sixty to seventy feet to level ground that later became temple block. Beyond this, ground remained level and continued into prairie. Laid out,

1834. Originally called Venus. Adjacent town, Commerce City, laid out, 1837. Both towns originally square with shore, as opposed to later east-west orientation of Nauvoo plat. Described in 1837 as having two stores, one grocery, and twelve or fifteen families. Panic of 1837 created buyers' market for land in Commerce and Commerce City. Latter-day Saints who resided at Quincy, Illinois (following expulsion from Missouri), planned settlement in area and purchased large tracts of land, including Commerce City and part of Commerce, 1839. JS moved with family to Commerce, 10 May 1839, into log house on bank of river. Stake organized at Commerce, 5 Oct. 1839, with William Marks as president. When post office name changed from Commerce to Nauvoo, Apr. 1840, entire area became known as Nauvoo.

Daviess County, Missouri. MAP 4: B-2; MAP 5: A-4; MAP 6: B-3. Area in northwest Missouri settled by European Americans, 1830. Sparsely inhabited until 1838. Created from Ray Co., Dec. 1836, in attempt to resolve conflicts related to Mormon settlement in that region. County is transected diagonally from northwest to southeast by Grand River, a principal tributary of Missouri River. Described as "equally divided between gently rolling prairie and fine timber lands." Small number of Mormons settled in Daviess Co., by 1837. JS led expedition into county to survey possible future settlements for Latter-day Saints, May 1838. Significant Mormon settlements in Daviess Co. were Adam-ondi-Ahman, Marrowbone, Honey Creek, and Lick Fork. As Mormon population grew, so did antagonism of neighboring Missourians who feared Saints would soon dominate county government. On election day, Whig candidate William Peniston denounced right of Saints to vote, and violence erupted on 6 Aug. 1838. JS and others soon arrived to help Saints. Vigilantes from neighboring counties joined Daviess Co. residents to harass and intimidate Saints. In absence of state protection, Saints made preemptive strike, plundering and burning property in Millport, Gallatin, and Grindstone Fork—settlements known to harbor vigilantes. Responding to reports of Mormon depredations, Missouri governor Lilburn W. Boggs ordered state militia to area and issued new order to exterminate Saints or drive them from state, Oct. 1838. Ultimatum was given, essentially compelling all Saints to leave county, early Nov. 1838. Many moved to Caldwell Co., where they stayed until moving to Illinois and Iowa Territory, winter–spring 1839. Population of Daviess Co. in 1840 about 2,800. JS last visited Daviess Co., early Apr. 1839, while a prisoner of state.

De Witt, Grand River Township (now in De Witt Township), Carroll County, Missouri. MAP 4: C-2; MAP 5: C-5. Located on bluffs north of Missouri River, about six miles above mouth of Grand River. Permanently settled, by 1826. Laid out, 1836. First called Elderport; name changed to De Witt, 1837, when town acquired by speculators David Thomas and Henry Root, who later interested church leaders in its strategic location. Although about seventy miles from Far West, it provided port at confluence of Grand and Missouri rivers for importing goods needed by Latter-day Saints in northern Missouri and for exporting their farm products. Zion high council commissioned George Hinkle and John Murdock to purchase almost half of town lots, 23 June 1838. Saints from Ohio and other areas began moving into area, summer 1838. Branch of LDS church organized in town shortly after. Latter-day Saint population by Oct. 1838 about 430. Saints faced sustained opposition upon arrival. Vigilantes besieged Saints in De Witt in attempt to expel them from area, beginning 1 Oct. 1838. JS and other Far West Saints came to De Witt to offer assistance, 5–6 Oct. 1838. After governor declined their appeal for aid, about 400 Saints abandoned homes and property, 11 Oct. 1838. Missouri River, which flowed near De Witt in 1830s, now lies more than a mile east of town.

Far West, Rockford Township (now in Mirabile Township), Caldwell County, Missouri. Map 1: C-1; Map 4: C-1; Map 5: B-3; Map 6: E-2; Map 7; Map 8. Originally called Shoal Creek. Located fifty-five miles northeast of Independence. Surveyed 1823; first settled by whites, 1831. Site purchased, 8 Aug. 1836, before Caldwell Co. was organized for Latter-day Saints in Missouri. William W. Phelps and John Whitmer held one square mile of land in trust for LDS church. Site described as "high rolling prairie" between Shoal and Goose creeks, and the homes as "very scattering, and small, being chiefly built of hewed logs." During Mormon period, population estimated at 3,000 to 5,000. JS moved to Far West, Mar. 1838. By 1838, town featured 150 houses, four dry-goods stores, three family groceries, six blacksmith shops, two hotels, a printing office (where *Elders' Journal* was printed), and at least two schoolhouses. Saints laid cornerstones for planned temple, 4 July 1838. Became church headquarters and center of Mormon activity in Missouri. JS dictated several revelations in area. JS arrested with other church leaders just outside of Far West, 31 Oct. 1838, following Missouri governor Lilburn W. Boggs's executive order to exterminate Saints or drive them from state. Served as center of evacuation effort for Saints fleeing from state into Iowa Territory and western Illinois, early 1839.

Fox Islands, Hancock County (now Knox County), Maine. Not mapped. Archipelago featuring two large islands about halfway along coast of Maine in center of Penobscot Bay. English ship captain Martin Pring named islands after indigenous silver-gray foxes, 1603. Established as part of Massachusetts Bay Colony, by 1658. First permanent English settlement established on islands, ca. 1765. Town of Vinalhaven, named for Boston attorney John Vinal, established on both islands; incorporated 25 June 1789; population in 1830 about 1,800 and in 1840 about 2,000. Maine, including Fox Islands, granted statehood, 1820. Quarrying of high-quality granite began on south island, 1826. North island officially set off as separate town, 1846; name changed to North Haven, 1847. Thereafter, Vinalhaven referred to south island only. First Latter-day Saint missionaries preached on islands, beginning 20 Aug. 1837. By winter 1837–1838, branches of LDS church established on both islands, with about 100 members.

Gallatin, Honey Creek Township (now in Union Township), Daviess County, Missouri. Map 1: C-2; Map 4: B-2; Map 5: B-4; Map 6: C-3. Founded and laid out, 1837. Identified as county seat, 13 Sept. 1837; officially recorded as seat, 3 Sept. 1839. After 1840 dispute in state legislature, reaffirmed as county seat, 1841. Several Latter-day Saints attempted to vote at Gallatin, 6 Aug. 1838, but were attacked by local residents. After Mormon-Missouri conflict erupted, Saints launched preemptive strike against vigilantes in Gallatin and other towns, Oct. 1838. See also "Daviess County."

Geauga County, Ohio. Map 3: B-4; Map 3: E-2. Located in northeastern Ohio, south of Lake Erie. Rivers in area include Grand, Chagrin, and Cuyahoga. Settled mostly by New Englanders, beginning 1798. Formed from Trumbull Co., 1 Mar. 1806. Chardon established as county seat, 1808. Population in 1830 about 16,000. Later formation of new counties, including Ashtabula, Cuyahoga, and Lake, considerably reduced original boundaries. Lake Co. formed from Geauga Co.'s seven northern townships, including Kirtland, 1840. JS moved to Geauga Co., Feb. 1831. See also "Kirtland Township."

Grand River. Map 4: B-1; Map 5: B-4; Map 6: B-2; Map 9: B-2; Map 10: B-2. Flows from current state of Iowa approximately 225 miles southeast through Daviess and Livingston counties in Missouri en route to its mouth at Missouri River near De Witt, Missouri. Adam-ondi-Ahman, Far West, Hawn's Mill, Whitney's Mill, Myers settlement, and De Witt were all located within thirty-five miles of this river. Grand River valley described in 1837 as "fertile, well-timbered country that is beginning to attract emigrants, and is now settling very fast." Lyman Wight purchased cabin along river near future site of Adam-ondi-Ahman, by Feb. 1838. JS and others surveyed land near river for future Mormon settlement, May 1838. River described in 1839 as "navigable for small vessels." However, farming along river caused heavy silting, making navigation increasingly difficult, and by 1870, navigation in Daviess Co. had entirely ceased.

Guymon's horse mill, Blythe Township, Caldwell County, Missouri. Map 6: E-2. Horse-powered mill owned by Latter-day Saint Thomas Guymon. Located near small Mormon branch. Built by Lyons brothers, fall 1833.

Hancock County, Illinois. Map 4: B-4; Map 11: E-4. Formed from Pike Co., 1825. Described in 1837 as predominantly prairie and "deficient in timber." Early settlers came mainly from mid-Atlantic and southern states. Population in 1835 about 3,200; in 1840 about 9,900; and in 1844 at least 15,000. Carthage designated county seat, 1833. Included town of Commerce (now Nauvoo) where Latter-day Saints settled, 1839, following expulsion from Missouri. Saints also settled in at least sixteen other communities throughout county. Mob shot and killed JS and brother Hyrum while they were imprisoned in Carthage, 27 June 1844.

Hawn's Mill, Grand River Township (now in Fairview Township), Caldwell County, Missouri. Map 5: B-4; Map 6: E-3. Located on north bank of Shoal Creek in eastern part of Caldwell Co., about sixteen miles east of Far West, Missouri. Jacob Hawn (Haun) settled in area, 1832; established mill, 1834. Location of branch of church, 1838. By Oct. 1838, about twenty Mormon families lived at mill and about seventy families lived in surrounding area. Site where seventeen Mormons were killed by non-Mormon vigilantes, 30 Oct. 1838. Settlement largely abandoned, by Feb. 1839. Mill torn down, 1845.

House of the Lord (planned site), Far West, Rockford Township (now in Mirabile Township), Caldwell County, Missouri. Map 8: E-1. Plans for Far West included temple on central block. Latter-day Saints in Caldwell Co. made preparations for construction and commenced excavating for foundation, 3 July 1837. However, while visiting Latter-day Saints in Far West, 6 Nov. 1837, JS gave instructions to postpone work on temple until "the Lord shall reveal it to be his will to be commenced." JS revelation, dated 26 Apr. 1838, directed that temple be built. According to John W. Rigdon, son of Sidney Rigdon, Far West temple was to have been similar to Kirtland temple in function, including lower floor auditorium and upper floor to be used for school. Excavation for foundation was reportedly 120 by 80 feet and 5 feet deep. Cornerstones of temple laid at northeast corner of public square, 4 July 1838. Foundation not completed when Saints expelled from state, Nov. 1838–Apr. 1839. Quorum of the Twelve Apostles commanded in July 1838 revelation to depart on overseas mission from temple site on 26 Apr. 1839. The Twelve returned to Far West on that date to officially commence mission to England.

House of the Lord, Kirtland Township, Geauga County (now in Lake County), Ohio. NOT MAPPED. JS revelation, dated Jan. 1831, directed Latter-day Saints to migrate to Ohio, where they would "be endowed with power from on high." In Dec. 1832, JS revelation directed Saints to "establish . . . an house of God." JS revelation, dated 1 June 1833, chastened Saints for not building house. Cornerstone laid, 23 July 1833, and temple completed, Mar. 1836. Had three stories with large rooms for assemblies on first two floors and five rooms or offices on attic floor. Included variety of pulpits in tiers at either end of assembly rooms for various priesthood offices. Used for variety of purposes, both before and after dedication, including confirmations, ordinations, quorum organizations, anointings, Elders School, and Hebrew School. Temple dedicated, 27 Mar. 1836 and again 31 Mar. 1836. Long-anticipated solemn assembly held, 30 Mar. 1836. In temple, 3 Apr. 1836, JS and Oliver Cowdery reported receiving priesthood "keys," or authority, from Old Testament prophets Moses, Elias, and Elijah and reported seeing Jesus Christ.

Illinois. MAP 1: B-3; MAP 2: B-4; MAP 4: A-5; MAP 11: E-4. Became part of Northwest Territory of U.S., 1787. Admitted as state, 1818. Population in 1840 about 480,000. Population in 1845 about 660,000. Plentiful, inexpensive land attracted settlers from northern and southern states. Following expulsion from Missouri, Mormons gathered in Quincy, Springfield, and other areas, winter 1838–1839. LDS church leaders and agents purchased land around Commerce (now Nauvoo), spring 1839, and JS and many Saints settled there. Mormons were politically united in area, leading to tension between Saints and local residents. JS and Hyrum Smith were shot by mob, 27 June 1844, while incarcerated at Carthage. Saints were expelled from Nauvoo, 1846, and began westward migration to present-day Utah.

Independence, Blue Township, Jackson County, Missouri. MAP 1: C-1; MAP 4: C-1; MAP 5: D-3. Located twelve miles from western Missouri border. Permanently settled, platted, and designated county seat, 1827. Hub for steamboat travel on Missouri River. Point of departure for Santa Fe Trail. Population in 1831 about 300. Mormon population by summer 1833 about 200. Oliver Cowdery and other missionaries arrived in area, by Jan. 1831, and proselytized among American Indians living nearby. JS revelation, dated 20 July 1831, designated area as "city of Zion," gathering place for Saints, and location of future temple. Revelation commanded Saints to purchase land for temple, storehouse, and printing press; storehouse and printing press established, by 1832. Growing Mormon presence opposed by earlier settlers. Mob violence erupted, July 1833. Gilbert and Whitney store vandalized, printing office destroyed, and Edward Partridge and Charles Allen tarred and feathered. Saints expelled from area by prior settlers, Nov. 1833.

Iowa Territory. MAP 1: B-2; MAP 2: B-4; MAP 4: A-3; MAP 11: B-2. Area originally part of Louisiana Purchase, 1803. First permanent white settlements established, ca. 1833. Organized as territory, 1838, containing all of present-day Iowa, much of present-day Minnesota, and parts of North and South Dakota. Population in 1840 about 43,000; in 1844 about 75,000; in 1846 about 96,000; and in 1850 about 192,000. Several Mormon settlements established in Iowa across Mississippi River from Commerce (now Nauvoo),

Illinois. Iowa stake created, 1839. Locations of key LDS church activities in territory include Montrose, Council Bluffs, and Zarahemla. During forced exodus from Nauvoo, 1846, approximately 15,000 Saints traversed territory westward from Montrose to Council Bluffs. While in area, about 500 Mormon men enlisted in U.S. Army of the West, July 1846, to provide support in Mexican War. Territory gained statehood, Dec. 1846.

Jackson County, Missouri. Map 4: C-1; Map 5: D-3. Settled at Fort Osage, 1808. County created, 16 Feb. 1825; organized 1826. Named after U.S. president Andrew Jackson. Featured fertile lands along Missouri River and was Santa Fe Trail departure point, which attracted immigrants to area. Area of county reduced considerably in 1833 by creation of Van Buren and Bates counties from southern portion. Population in 1830 about 2,800; in 1836 about 4,500; and in 1840 about 7,600. JS appointed missionaries to proselytize among American Indians west of Independence, fall 1830. Saints began settling in county, July 1831. JS revelation, dated 20 July 1831, designated area near Independence as "city of Zion" for gathering of Saints and building of temple. Saints were instructed to buy land from temple site to western border of county. Saints began settling in Independence and Kaw Township. Mormon population by 1832 about 850. Mormon population by summer 1833 about 1,000. As increasing numbers of Saints entered Missouri, mob violence by earlier settlers erupted, July 1833. Saints expelled from county into Clay and other counties, Nov. 1833. Efforts to seek justice through courts were unsuccessful. JS led Camp of Israel expedition to western Missouri in failed effort to recover Mormon lands in Jackson Co., summer 1834. JS and other Mormon prisoners taken temporarily to county, Nov. 1838.

Jail, Liberty, Clay County, Missouri. Not mapped. Two-story building containing dungeon on lower floor with access through trap door. Wood building constructed, ca. 1830. Outer stone wall added and building completed, 1833. JS and five others confined there for just over four months, beginning 1 Dec. 1838, while awaiting trial for charges in connection with Mormon-Missouri conflict. JS and others attempted to escape jail and failed, 7 Feb. and 4 Mar. 1839. JS and others transferred from jail to Daviess Co., Missouri, 6 Apr. 1839. While imprisoned in jail, JS wrote or coauthored at least twelve letters and two petitions.

Kirtland Township, Geauga County (now in Lake County), Ohio. Map 1: B-6; Map 3: B-4. Located ten miles south of Lake Erie. Settled by 1811. Organized by 1818. Population in 1830 about 55 Latter-day Saints and 1,000 others; in 1838 about 2,000 Saints and 1,200 others; in 1839 about 100 Saints and 1,500 others. Mormon missionaries visited township, early Nov. 1830; many residents joined LDS church. JS and New York Saints migrated to Kirtland, 1831. Organized as "stake of Zion," with presidency and high council, 17 Feb. 1834. House of the Lord built, 1833–1836. Rapid immigration of Saints posed difficulty for both Saints and other residents. JS and other Saints participated in School of the Prophets as well as other schools devoted to wide variety of subjects, including Hebrew. Latter-day Saint press in Kirtland published newspapers, hymnal, second edition of Book of Mormon, and Doctrine and Covenants. While in township, JS obtained several ancient Egyptian mummies and papyrus scrolls; JS's translation of some scrolls later published as Book of Abraham. JS also dictated at least forty-six revelations in township. JS appointed Heber C. Kimball to lead group of elders from Kirtland to serve first mission to England, 1837. With increased demand for land in Kirtland, prices rose. Need for capital led to establishment of Kirtland Safety Society, but failure to obtain state charter, negative publicity, and other problems led to failure of financial institution, 1837. Under threats from dissidents and outside antagonists, JS and other church leaders fled township, early 1838. Many loyal Saints followed. Kirtland stake reorganized with 300 to 400 members, 1841. Acting on directive from JS, organized effort to leave Kirtland was again made in 1843, but many Saints remained through 1845. After death of JS and departure of most Saints, schismatic activity became prevalent in Kirtland.

Liberty, Liberty Township, Clay County, Missouri. Map 1: C-1; Map 4: C-1; Map 5: D-3. Located in western Missouri, thirteen miles north of Independence. Settled 1820. Clay Co. seat, 1822. Incorporated as town, May 1829. Following expulsion from Jackson Co., 1833, many Latter-day Saints found refuge in Clay Co., with church leaders and other Saints taking up residence in and near Liberty. Camp of Israel disbanded six miles from Liberty, 22 June 1834. Under threat of violence, most Saints left area, 1836. Described in 1837 as having "fourteen stores and four groceries" and large brick courthouse. Residents in Liberty acquired printing press damaged during mob destruction of Saints' printing office (1833) in Independence, Missouri, and used press to print the *Upper Missouri Enquirer*. During eventual expulsion of all Mormons from Missouri, JS and other leaders were imprisoned in Liberty, Dec. 1838–Apr. 1839. While incarcerated, JS wrote or co-authored twelve letters, portions of two of which were later canonized, to family members, church leaders, and general church membership, providing council during the migration from Missouri.

Maine. Map 2: A-6. Initially established as district of Massachusetts, 1691. Admitted as state, 1820. Population in 1830 about 400,000. Population in 1840 about 500,000. Capital city and seat of government, Augusta. First visited by Mormon missionaries, Sept. 1832. Branches of LDS church located in Farmington and Saco, by 1832. Wilford Woodruff and others arrived at Fox Islands, by Aug. 1837, and established branch. Many converts emigrated with Woodruff to Illinois, 1838. By 1847, nearly 500 converts left Maine to gather with Saints in Missouri and Illinois.

Millport, Daviess County, Missouri. Map 5: B-4; Map 6: C-3. Village located three miles east of Gallatin, Missouri, between Grand River and Big Muddy Creek. First settled by Robert P. Peniston, ca. 1831. Named Millport after Peniston completed horse-powered corn mill, ca. 1834. Laid out as town, 1836. First town in Daviess Co.; served as unofficial county seat upon county's creation, Dec. 1836–summer 1837. Major local trade port, 1835–1837. Upon Gallatin's designation as county seat, much of Millport population moved to Gallatin, 1837. Among towns where Saints launched preemptive strike against vigilantes, 18 Oct. 1838, after Mormon-Missouri conflict erupted. Burned down during conflict; never rebuilt.

Mississippi River. Map 1: C-3; Map 4: C-5; Map 11: F-3; Map 12: B-1. Principal U.S. river running southward from Itasca Lake, Minnesota, to Gulf of Mexico. Covered 3,160-mile course, 1839 (now about 2,350 miles). Drains about 1,100,000 square miles. Steamboat travel on Mississippi very important in 1830s and 1840s for shipping, transportation, and recreation. At least four steamboat landings utilized in Nauvoo, Illinois: Upper Stone House Landing, Kimball Landing, Lower Stone House Landing, and Nauvoo House Landing. River also utilized by Saints for performing baptisms and as source of food. Church owned modest freighting steamer, *Maid of Iowa,* which traversed entire Mississippi. Thousands of British converts immigrated to Nauvoo on river steamers from New Orleans, 1840–1846.

Missouri. MAP 1: C-2; MAP 2: C-4; MAP 4: B-3; MAP 11: F-1. Area acquired by U.S. in Louisiana Purchase, 1803, and established as territory, 1812. Missouri Compromise, 1820, admitted Missouri as slave state, 1821. Population in 1830 about 140,000; in 1836 about 240,000; and in 1840 about 380,000. Mormon missionaries preached to American Indians just west of Missouri border, early 1831. JS revelation, dated 20 July 1831, designated Missouri as "land of Zion" and where "city of Zion" was to be built. Saints began immigrating to Jackson Co., summer 1831. Many Missouri immigrants came from southern states, while most Saints came from northeastern states. Regional and cultural differences, as well as religious and ideological differences, caused tension and eventual violence. Saints expelled from Jackson Co. into Clay and other counties, 1833. Clay Co. citizens demanded Saints leave county, 1836. Missouri state legislature consequently created Caldwell Co. specifically for Saints. JS moved to Far West in Caldwell Co., Mar. 1838. Saints' settlement expanded northward into Daviess Co. and eastward into Carroll Co., 1838. Conflict in these counties escalated quickly. Missouri governor Lilburn W. Boggs issued order to exterminate Saints or drive them from state, 27 Oct. 1838. JS and others taken prisoner by Missouri militia, 31 Oct. 1838, and incarcerated through winter in jail at Liberty while approximately 8,000 to 10,000 Saints evacuated eastward into Illinois. JS allowed to escape, Apr. 1839. Missouri officials continued attempts to extradite, arrest, or kidnap JS, 1841–1843.

Missouri River. MAP 1: C-2; MAP 4: D-4; MAP 5: D-4. One of longest rivers in North America, in excess of 3,000 miles. From headwaters in Montana to confluence with Mississippi River near St. Louis, Missouri River drains 580,000 square miles (about one-sixth of continental U.S.). Explored by Lewis and Clark, 1804–1806. Major pioneer trails (Santa Fe, California, Oregon, Mormon) began on river in western Missouri. After dedicating temple site in Jackson Co., JS traveled on river by canoe, Aug. 1831, as he returned to Ohio. During journey, JS dictated revelation cautioning Saints about dangers on water, after which some Saints finished journey by land rather than on river. Important river landing located about three miles from courthouse in Independence, Missouri, at which point group of Saints arrived by steamboat from Ohio, July 1832. After expulsion from Jackson Co., Nov. 1833, most Saints fled northward and crossed river to gain refuge in Clay Co.

Montrose Township, Lee County, Iowa Territory. MAP 4: A-4. Located in southern part of county on western shore of Mississippi River. Area settled by Captain James White, 1832, following Black Hawk War. Federal government purchased land from White to create Fort Des Moines, 1834. Fort abandoned; remaining settlement unofficially named Montrose, 1837. Township created by dividing Ambrosia Township, 1841. Important port on Mississippi River. Following expulsion from Missouri, some Saints (including Brigham Young family) settled in township at abandoned fort. Church membership in area grew rapidly from immigration. Iowa stake created, Oct. 1839, and centered at Montrose. Name changed to Zarahemla stake, 1841. Population of stake in 1841 about 700. As Saints gathered to Nauvoo, population dwindled and stake was reduced to a branch, Jan. 1842. On at least two occasions, JS took refuge in Montrose to avoid legal action from Missouri and

Illinois. He and brother Hyrum left town, 23 June 1844, to return to Nauvoo just prior to going to Carthage.

Nauvoo, Hancock County, Illinois. MAP 1: B-2; MAP 4: A-4; MAP 11: C-3. Principal gathering place for Saints after expulsion from Missouri. Beginning in 1839, LDS church purchased lands in earlier settlement of Commerce and planned settlement of Commerce City, as well as surrounding areas. Served as church headquarters, 1839–1846. With post office name change in Apr. 1840, area was officially named Nauvoo (Hebrew for "beautiful"). JS's home (Nauvoo House) and JS's red brick store located in lower portion of Nauvoo (the flats) on nearly level ground along bank of Mississippi River, several feet above high-water mark and extending eastward about one mile. Ground gradually sloped upward sixty or seventy feet to area known as the bluff, where Latter-day Saints designated temple block. After ascent, ground was level and continued into surrounding prairie. JS often preached and attended meetings at groves near temple. Numerous boat and ferry landings established in Nauvoo, including Upper Stone House Landing, Kimball Landing, Lower Stone House Landing, and Nauvoo House Landing. City incorporated and charter granted, Dec. 1840. Charter secured powers, including habeas corpus provision and authority to establish Nauvoo Legion and University of Nauvoo, and called for mayor, four aldermen, and nine councilmen to serve in municipal government. Number of aldermen could change as population grew. Construction on Nauvoo temple began, Mar. 1841, but was not completed until 1846, after JS's death. Nauvoo House construction commenced, spring 1841; cornerstone laid, Oct. 1841. Population by 1846 about 15,000. JS introduced many principles and institutions in Nauvoo, including plurality of gods, celestial marriage, temple endowments, proxy rituals for dead, Relief Society, Anointed Quorum, and Council of Fifty. Tension developed between Nauvoo Saints and neighbors in Hancock and surrounding counties. After JS and Hyrum Smith were murdered while in jail at Carthage, 27 June 1844, city charter repealed, 1845. Latter-day Saints in Nauvoo finished temple and received endowments, 1846. Majority of Saints, under leadership of Brigham Young, crossed Mississippi River, 1846, en route to Salt Lake Valley. Emma Smith and some Saints remained in Nauvoo. Population greatly decreased and Nauvoo became small town.

New York City, New York. NOT MAPPED. Dutch founded New Netherland colony, 1625. Incorporated under British control and renamed New York, 1664. Harbor contributed to economic and population growth of city; became largest city in American colonies. British troops defeated Continental Army under George Washington in city, 1776. Following eventual British withdrawal, city served as U.S. capital, 1785–1790. Population in 1830 about 200,000; in 1840 about 310,000; and in 1850 about 520,000. JS and Newel K. Whitney visited city, 1832; JS visited again, 1836. Missionary efforts by Parley P. Pratt and Elijah Fordham began, 1837, eventually resulting in several branches of LDS church with about 200 members. Members of Quorum of the Twelve preached in city en route to Great Britain, June 1837 and fall 1839–Mar. 1840. To assist European converts immigrating west, church stationed agents in city, 1844. About 240 Saints left city on *SS Brooklyn*, Feb. 1846, bound for Yerba Buena (now San Francisco, California).

Ohio. MAP 1: B-5; MAP 2: B-5; MAP 3: C-3. French explored area, 1669. British took possession following French and Indian War, 1763. Ceded to U.S., 1783. First permanent white settlement established, 1788. Northeastern portion maintained as part of Connecticut,

1786, and called Connecticut Western Reserve. Connecticut granted jurisdiction of Western Reserve to U.S. government, 1800. All of Ohio area partitioned from Northwest Territory and admitted to U.S. as state, 1803. State bordered by Lake Erie on north and Ohio River on south. Population in 1820 about 580,000; in 1830 about 940,000; and in 1840 about 1,500,000. Mormon missionaries preached in northeastern Ohio, Oct. 1830. Reformed Baptist preacher Sidney Rigdon and many of his congregants in state joined LDS church, late 1830. JS revelation, dated 30 Dec. 1830, directed church members in New York to migrate to Ohio. JS lived in Kirtland and Hiram, 1831–1838. JS dictated over sixty revelations in state. JS and most loyal Ohio Saints migrated to Missouri, 1838. However, some Saints remained, and Ohio became location of schismatic activity after death of JS.

Painesville Township, Geauga County (now in Lake County), Ohio. Map 1: B-6. Located on Grand River twelve miles northeast of Kirtland. Created and settled, 1800. Originally named Champion. Flourished economically from harbor on Lake Erie and as major route of overland travel for western immigration. Included Painesville village; laid out, ca. 1805; incorporated as town, 1832; designated county seat of newly formed Lake Co., 1840. Population in 1830 about 1,500. Latter-day Saints borrowed money from Bank of Geauga branch in township. JS visited Painesville often. Early center of anti-Mormon activities. *Painesville Telegraph* printed material critical of JS and LDS church. First major anti-Mormon book, *Mormonism Unvailed,* also published in township. JS was arrested and tried in township multiple times.

Pleasant Park, Grand River Township (now in De Witt Township), Carroll County, Missouri. Map 5: C-5. Village (no longer exists) located about three miles west of De Witt. Included post office, 1835–1882. Resident David Thomas wrote to JS, 31 Mar. 1838, offering part of his land in area for possible settlement.

Quincy, Adams County, Illinois. Map 1: C-2; Map 4: B-4. Located on high limestone bluffs east of Mississippi River, about forty-five miles south of Nauvoo. Settled 1821. Adams Co. seat, 1825. Incorporated as town, 1834. Received city charter, 1840. Population in 1835 about 800; in 1840 about 2,300; and in 1845 about 4,000. Important river port and shipping and manufacturing center. Point where JS, Brigham Young, and many other Saints crossed Mississippi River en route from Ohio to western Missouri, 1830s. Members of Camp of Israel also crossed Mississippi at Quincy en route to Independence, Missouri, June 1834. Mormon exiles from Missouri found refuge in town, winter 1838–1839. Democratic Association of Quincy organized relief committee to provide clothing, food, and shelter for at least 5,000 Saints. Conference of church held in town, Mar. 1839. Following Missouri imprisonment, JS joined Saints in Quincy, 22 Apr. 1839. General conference held in town to approve land purchases and missions of the Twelve to Europe, May 1839. On 10 May 1839, JS and family left Quincy to settle in Commerce (now Nauvoo), Illinois. Branch organized in Quincy, 21 June 1840; stake organized, 25 Oct. 1840. Stake reduced to branch, 1841; branch functioned through at least spring 1848. After death of JS, 27 June 1844, leading citizens of Adams Co. (later known as Quincy Committee) met to find way to end growing hostilities between Saints and other Illinois residents.

Ray County, Missouri. Map 4: C-2; Map 5: D-4. Located in northwestern Missouri. Area settled, 1815. Created from Howard Co., 1820. Initially included all state land north of Missouri River and west of Grand River. Population in 1830 about 2,700; in 1836 about 6,600;

and in 1840 about 6,600. Latter-day Saints who were driven from homes in Jackson Co., Missouri, 1833, moved northward across Missouri River and took refuge in Ray and other counties. Camp of Israel passed through Ray Co., June 1834. Missouri legislature created Caldwell and Daviess counties from Ray Co., 29 Dec. 1836. In attempt to rescue LDS prisoners, Caldwell Co. militia contended with Ray Co. militia at Crooked River in unorganized territory attached to Ray Co., 25 Oct. 1838. JS and about sixty other LDS men were incarcerated in Richmond, Ray Co., jail to await hearings on charges related to Mormon-Missouri conflict, Nov. 1838.

Richmond, Richmond Township, Ray County, Missouri. Map 1: C-1; Map 5: D-4. Area settled, ca. 1814. Officially platted as Ray Co. seat, 1827. Population in 1840 about 500. Seat of Fifth Judicial Circuit Court of Missouri; also location of courthouse. JS and about sixty other Mormon men were incarcerated here while awaiting hearing by Judge Austin A. King on charges connected with Mormon-Missouri conflict, Nov. 1838.

Schoolhouse, Far West, Caldwell County, Missouri. Not mapped. There were at least two schoolhouses in Far West. First was likely log building; located in southwest quarter of town. Second schoolhouse built, by Feb. 1838. Both functioned as LDS church or public meetinghouses, and first served as county's courthouse until second was built.

Shoal Creek. Map 5: B-4; Map 6: E-3. Stream that flows eastward for about forty-five miles from east-central Clinton Co. through Caldwell Co. to confluence with Grand River in central Livingston Co. Thousands of Saints moved from Clay Co. to sites along Shoal Creek in Caldwell Co., beginning summer 1836. Stream powered numerous mills within county, including those at Whitney's Mill, Far West, and Hawn's Mill settlements. JS and family arrived in area from Ohio, 14 Mar. 1838. JS reported attempt on his life while watering horse at Shoal Creek.

Springfield, Sangamon County, Illinois. Map 1: C-3; Map 4: B-6. Settled by 1819. Incorporated as town, 1832. Became state capital, 1837. Incorporated as city, 1840. Sangamon Co. seat. Population in 1840 about 2,600. Stake of LDS church organized in Springfield, Nov. 1840; discontinued May 1841; branch organized, Jan. 1842. After arrest on charge of being accessory in assassination attempt on former Missouri governor Lilburn W. Boggs, JS traveled to Springfield, late Dec. 1842, for habeas corpus hearing before federal judge Nathaniel Pope. After hearing, early Jan. 1843, JS was discharged.

St. Louis, St. Louis County, Missouri. Map 1: C-3; Map 4: D-5. Located on west side of Mississippi River about fifteen miles south of confluence with Missouri River. Founded as fur-trading post by French settlers, 1764. Incorporated as town, 1809. First Mississippi steamboat docked by town, 1817. Incorporated as city, 1822. Population in 1820 about 4,900; in 1830 about 5,900; in 1840 about 16,000; and in 1849 about 63,000. Because of location on Mississippi River, St. Louis quickly became a hub of trade for continental interior. JS traveled through St. Louis, June 1831 and 1832. Place of refuge for Saints expelled from western Missouri. During Mormon expulsion from western Missouri, St. Louis newspapers defended LDS church and condemned Governor Lilburn W. Boggs. Crossroads for hundreds of Latter-day Saint emigrants traveling from England to Nauvoo. Official branch of church formed in city, early 1844. Brigham Young and others campaigned in city for JS's candidacy for U.S. president, May 1844. St. Louis press strongly condemned JS's murder, June 1844. Designated by Brigham Young as gathering place for refugees from Nauvoo and for arriving European converts, 1847. *Latter Day Saint's Emigrant's Guide* printed in city, Feb. 1848. Mormon population by 1849 at least 3,000.

United States of America. MAP 2. North American constitutional republic. Constitution ratified, 17 Sept. 1787. Population in 1805 about 6,000,000; in 1830 about 13,000,000; and in 1844 about 20,000,000. Louisiana Purchase, 1803, doubled size of U.S. Consisted of seventeen states at time of JS's birth, 23 Dec. 1805, and twenty-six states at time of JS's death, 27 June 1844.

Washington, District of Columbia. MAP 2: B-5. Created as district for seat of U.S. federal government by act of Congress, 1790, and named Washington DC, 1791. Named in honor of George Washington. Headquarters of executive, legislative, and judicial branches of U.S. government relocated to Washington DC, 1800. Population in 1840 about 23,000. JS visited Washington DC, Nov. 1839–Feb. 1840, seeking redress for property losses and suffering by Saints during expulsion from Missouri. President Martin Van Buren and other government leaders refused assistance.

Zion (place). NOT MAPPED. JS revelation, dated 20 July 1831, designated Missouri as "land of Zion" for gathering of Saints and place where "City of Zion" was to be built, with Independence area as "center place" of Zion. Latter-day Saint settlements elsewhere, such as in Kirtland, Ohio, became known as "stakes" of Zion. About 1,200 Saints gathered in Jackson Co. but were expelled by other residents, 1833. After Saints settled in other counties, such as Clay and Caldwell, JS and church members continued to refer to main body of Saints in Missouri as Zion but still considered Independence to be center place and planned to return. JS dictated several revelations about "redeeming Zion" and recovering their lands in Jackson Co. In 1840, after Saints had left Missouri and settled in Nauvoo, Illinois, JS declared that Zion referred to all of North and South America and anywhere Saints gathered.

Maps

The following maps show nearly every town and city mentioned in this volume of *The Joseph Smith Papers,* along with other significant features and boundaries, as they existed during the period indicated on each map.

To locate a particular place on these maps, consult the Geographical Directory in this volume. The directory provides grid coordinates and other information for each place.

599

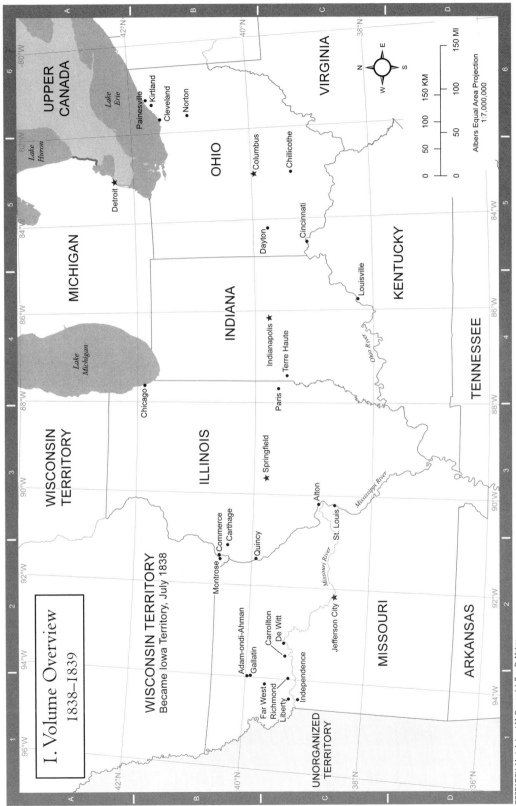

I. Volume Overview
1838–1839

RESEARCH: Mark Ashurst-McGee and Jeffrey D. Mahas
CARTOGRAPHY: Jonathan West

600

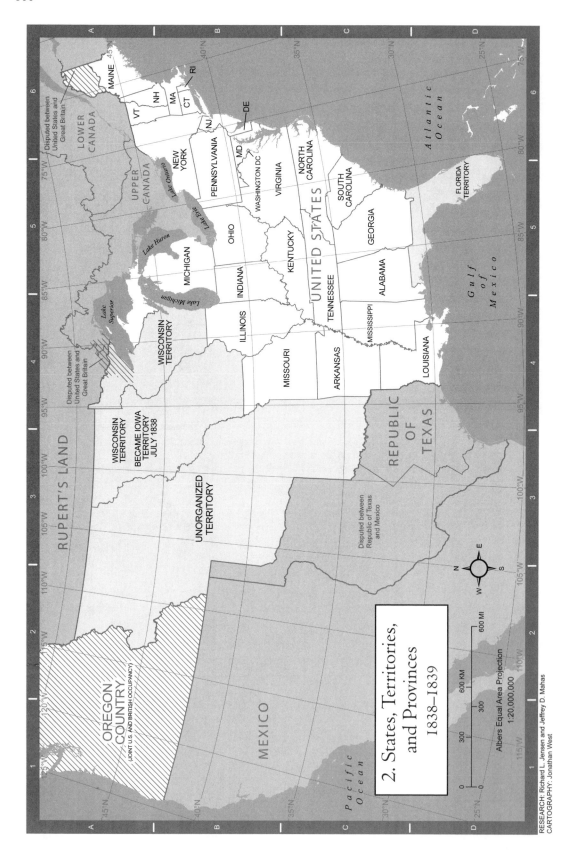

2. States, Territories, and Provinces 1838–1839

Albers Equal Area Projection
1:20,000,000

0   300   600 KM
0   300   600 MI

RESEARCH: Richard L. Jensen and Jeffrey D. Mahas
CARTOGRAPHY: Jonathan West

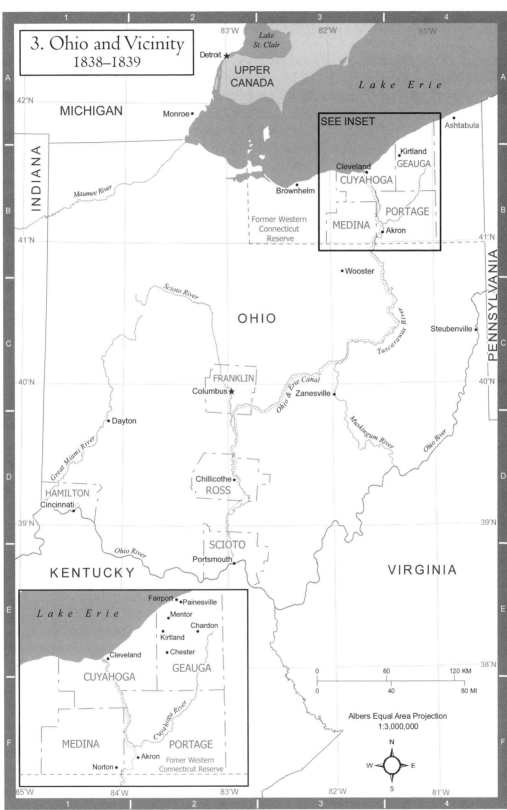

3. Ohio and Vicinity
1838–1839

83°W · *Lake St. Clair* · 82°W · 81°W

Detroit ★

UPPER CANADA

Lake Erie

42°N

MICHIGAN

Monroe •

SEE INSET

Ashtabula •

INDIANA

Maumee River

Cleveland •

Kirtland •
GEAUGA

CUYAHOGA

Brownhelm •

Former Western
Connecticut
Reserve

MEDINA

PORTAGE

41°N

Akron •

41°N

Wooster •

Scioto River

OHIO

Tuscarawas River

Steubenville •

PENNSYLVANIA

40°N

FRANKLIN

Columbus ★

Ohio & Erie Canal

Zanesville •

40°N

Dayton •

Great Miami River

Muskingum River

Ohio River

HAMILTON

Cincinnati •

Chillicothe •
ROSS

39°N

39°N

Ohio River

SCIOTO

Portsmouth •

KENTUCKY

VIRGINIA

Inset

Fairport •
Painesville •

Lake Erie

Mentor •

Chardon •

Kirtland •

Cleveland •

• Chester

CUYAHOGA

GEAUGA

38°N

Cuyahoga River

MEDINA

PORTAGE

Akron •

Fomer Western
Connecticut Reserve

Norton •

0   60   120 KM
0   40   80 MI

Albers Equal Area Projection
1:3,000,000

N
W ✦ E
S

85°W · 84°W · 83°W · 82°W · 81°W

RESEARCH: Jeffrey D. Mahas and Mark Ashurst-McGee
CARTOGRAPHY: Heidi Springsteed

602

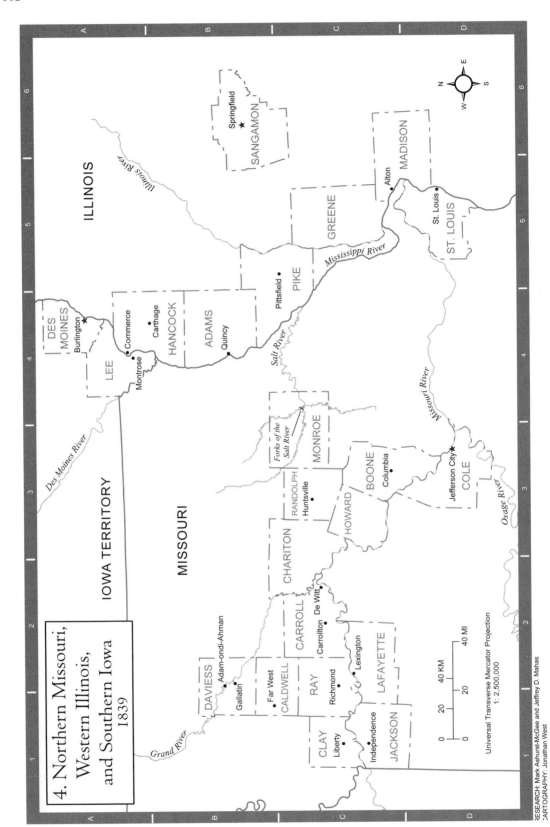

4. Northern Missouri, Western Illinois, and Southern Iowa 1839

RESEARCH: Mark Ashurst-McGee and Jeffrey D. Mahas
CARTOGRAPHY: Jonathan West

Universal Transverse Mercator Projection
1: 2,500,000

40 KM   20   40 MI

ILLINOIS

IOWA TERRITORY

MISSOURI

SANGAMON
Springfield

MADISON
Alton

GREENE

ST. LOUIS
St. Louis

PIKE
Pittsfield

DES MOINES
Burlington

LEE
Montrose

HANCOCK
Commerce
Carthage

ADAMS
Quincy

MONROE
Forks of the Salt River

RANDOLPH
Huntsville

BOONE
Columbia

COLE
Jefferson City

HOWARD

CHARITON

CARROLL
Carrollton   De Witt

DAVIESS
Adam-ondi-Ahman
Gallatin

CALDWELL
Far West

RAY
Richmond

LAFAYETTE
Lexington

CLAY
Liberty

JACKSON
Independence

Illinois River
Mississippi River
Salt River
Missouri River
Osage River
Des Moines River
Grand River

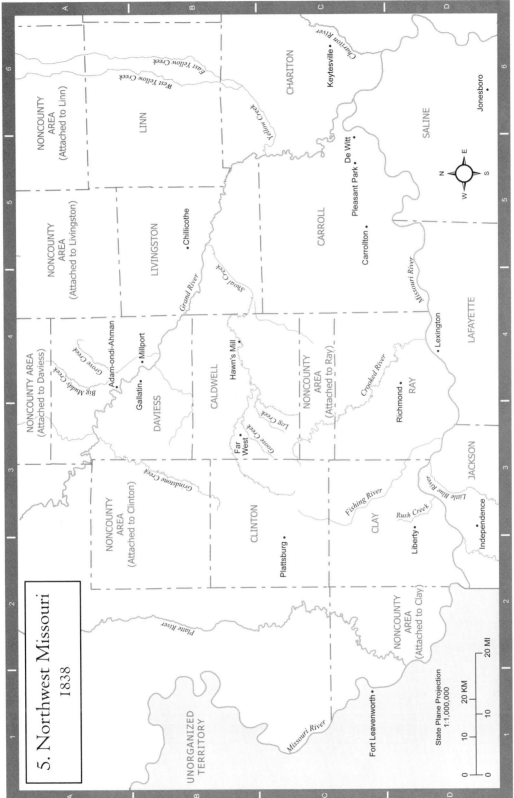

5. Northwest Missouri
1838

UNORGANIZED TERRITORY

NONCOUNTY AREA (Attached to Linn)

NONCOUNTY AREA (Attached to Livingston)

NONCOUNTY AREA (Attached to Daviess)

NONCOUNTY AREA (Attached to Clinton)

NONCOUNTY AREA (Attached to Ray)

NONCOUNTY AREA (Attached to Clay)

LINN

LIVINGSTON

CHARITON

SALINE

CARROLL

DAVIESS

CALDWELL

RAY

LAFAYETTE

CLINTON

CLAY

JACKSON

Keytesville •

Jonesboro •

De Witt •
Pleasant Park •

Chillicothe •

Carrollton •

Adam-ondi-Ahman •
Millport •

Gallatin •

Hawn's Mill •

Far West •

Richmond •

Lexington •

Plattsburg •

Liberty •

Independence •

Fort Leavenworth •

Chariton River

East Yellow Creek

West Yellow Creek

Yellow Creek

Grand River

Shoal Creek

Big Muddy Creek

Grove Creek

Log Creek

Goose Creek

Grindstone Creek

Missouri River

Crooked River

Fishing River

Rush Creek

Little Blue River

Platte River

Missouri River

State Plane Projection
1:1,000,000

20 KM 10 20 MI

RESEARCH: Mark Ashurst-McGee and Jeffrey D. Mahas
CARTOGRAPHY: Jonathan West

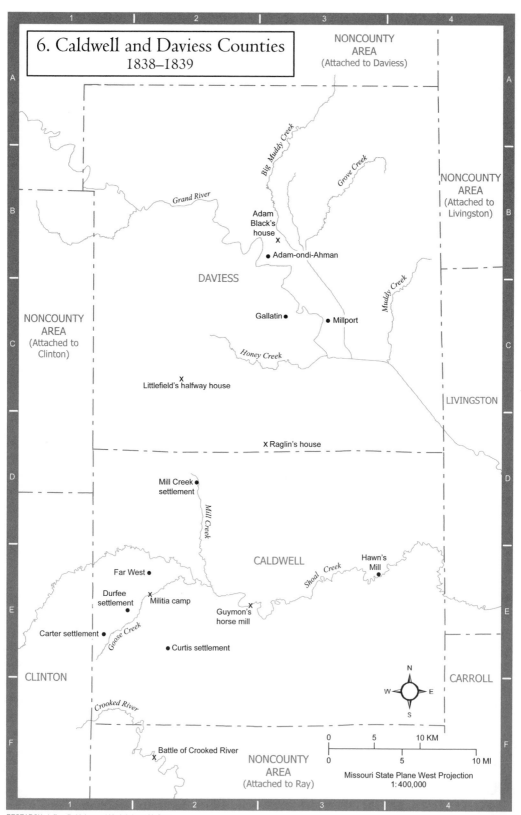

6. Caldwell and Daviess Counties
1838–1839

NONCOUNTY AREA
(Attached to Daviess)

NONCOUNTY AREA
(Attached to Livingston)

Big Muddy Creek

Grove Creek

Grand River

Adam Black's house
X

• Adam-ondi-Ahman

DAVIESS

Muddy Creek

NONCOUNTY AREA
(Attached to Clinton)

Gallatin •

• Millport

Honey Creek

X
Littlefield's halfway house

LIVINGSTON

X Raglin's house

Mill Creek • settlement

Mill Creek

CALDWELL

Hawn's Mill •

Shoal Creek

Far West •

Durfee settlement •

X Militia camp

X
Guymon's horse mill

Carter settlement •

Goose Creek

• Curtis settlement

CLINTON

CARROLL

N
W   E
S

Crooked River

Battle of Crooked River
X

NONCOUNTY AREA
(Attached to Ray)

0   5   10 KM
0   5   10 MI

Missouri State Plane West Projection
1:400,000

RESEARCH: Jeffrey D. Mahas and Mark Ashurst-McGee
CARTOGRAPHY: Jonathan West

7. Plat of Far West, Missouri, 1838

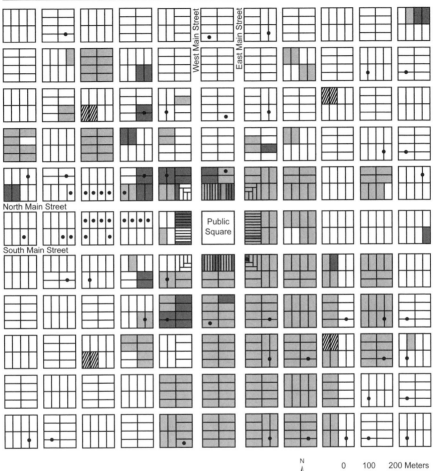

West Main Street

East Main Street

North Main Street

South Main Street

Public Square

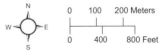

N
W — E
S

0   100   200 Meters

0   400   800 Feet

- **Possible structure.** An undated map labeled "Original Platte of Far West Caldwell Co Mo" contains penciled dots that seem to correspond with the location of known structures in Far West.

- **Public lots.** In the town plat William W. Phelps and John Whitmer registered in April 1837, these lots were reserved for public buildings. A schoolhouse was located on the public lot in the southwest quadrant of the town, and another schoolhouse was later built somewhere in the public square.

- **Lots apparently sold or reserved by 1838.** When William W. Phelps and John Whitmer sold the Far West plat to Edward Partridge on 17 May 1837, several lots were exempted, apparently because they had already been sold. Partridge likely sold some of the other lots after he took possession of the plat, as indicated by subsequent land sales by other individuals. Many of the lots near the town square were reserved for and possibly sold to Joseph Smith and other church leaders.

- **Lots not mentioned in extant land records.** Many of these lots were probably still held by Edward Partridge in 1838 and later sold by him or his estate.

- **Lots sold after 1838.** Edward Partridge retained title to most of the lots in Far West, possibly distributing them to Saints as stewardships. He estimated that he owned four-fifths of the lots in Far West at the time he left Missouri. In April 1839, Partridge sold several lots to church member Elias Smith. After Partridge died in 1840, most of the remaining lots in the city were sold by his estate. It is likely that more lots were sold after 1838 than those identified here, but records of these transactions are not extant.

RESEARCH: Jeffrey D. Mahas and Mark Ashurst-McGee
CARTOGRAPHY: Jeffrey D. Mahas and Suzy Bills

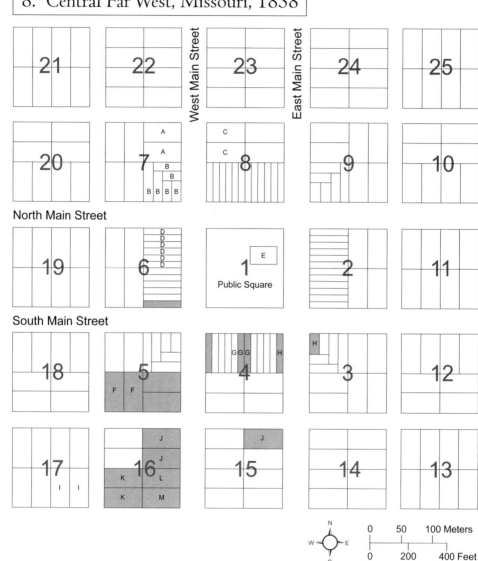

8. Central Far West, Missouri, 1838

Property and Sites

A. Joseph Smith Sr. property
B. JS property
C. Hyrum Smith property
D. Sidney Rigdon property (with home)
E. Site for temple
F. David Fullmer property
G. John Whitmer/John Burk property (with tavern)

H. Possible site of Samuel Musick/Smith family tavern
I. Probable location of George M. Hinkle/JS property (with home)
J. Elizabeth Gilbert property
K. Probable site of Jacob Whitmer property
L. Peter Laman property
M. Silas Maynard property

Property seized from John Whitmer on 21 July 1838

Note: numerals indicate block numbers.

RESEARCH: Jeffrey D. Mahas
CARTOGRAPHY: Jeffrey D. Mahas and Suzy Bills

607

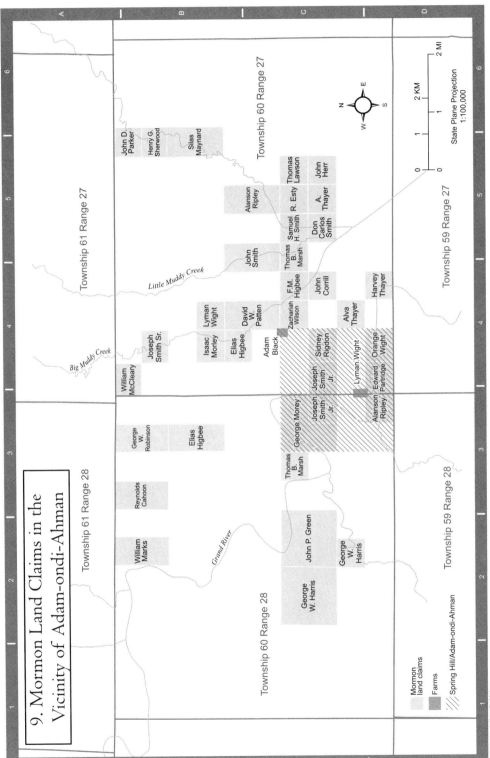

9. Mormon Land Claims in the Vicinity of Adam-ondi-Ahman

Township 61 Range 28

Township 61 Range 27

Township 60 Range 28

Township 60 Range 27

Township 59 Range 28

Township 59 Range 27

Big Muddy Creek

Little Muddy Creek

Grand River

William McCleary

Joseph Smith Sr.

Lyman Wight

Isaac Morley

Elias Higbee

David W. Patten

Adam Black

Zachariah Wilson

F.M. Higbee

John Smith

Thomas B. Marsh

Samuel H. Smith

Alanson Ripley

R. Esty

Don Carlos Smith

Thomas Lawson

John Herr

A. Thayer

John Corrill

Alva Thayer

Harvey Thayer

Sidney Rigdon

Joseph Smith Jr.

Lyman Wight

Orange Wight

Alanson Ripley

Edward Partridge

George Morey

Joseph Smith Jr.

Thomas B. Marsh

George W. Robinson

Elias Higbee

Reynolds Cahoon

William Marks

John P. Green

George W. Harris

George W. Harris

John D. Parker

Henry G. Sherwood

Silas Maynard

Mormon land claims

Farms

Spring Hill/Adam-ondi-Ahman

State Plane Projection 1:100,000

2 KM   2 MI

N

RESEARCH: Jeffrey D. Mahas
CARTOGRAPHY: Jonathan West

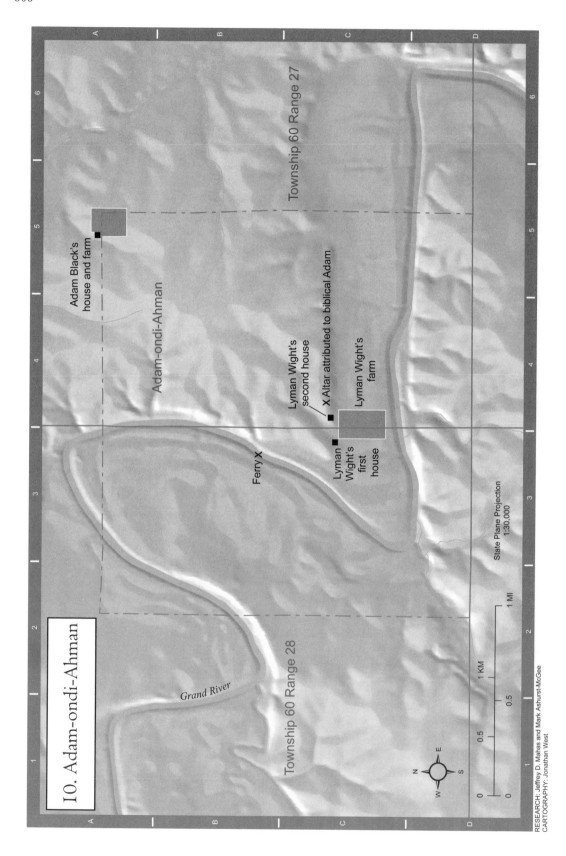

10. Adam-ondi-Ahman

Township 60 Range 28

Grand River

Township 60 Range 27

Adam-ondi-Ahman

Adam Black's house and farm

Lyman Wight's second house
X Altar attributed to biblical Adam

Lyman Wight's farm

Ferry X

Lyman Wight's first house

State Plane Projection
1:30,000

0   0.5   1 MI

0   0.5   1 KM

N
W E
S

RESEARCH: Jeffrey D. Mahas and Mark Ashurst-McGee
CARTOGRAPHY: Jonathan West

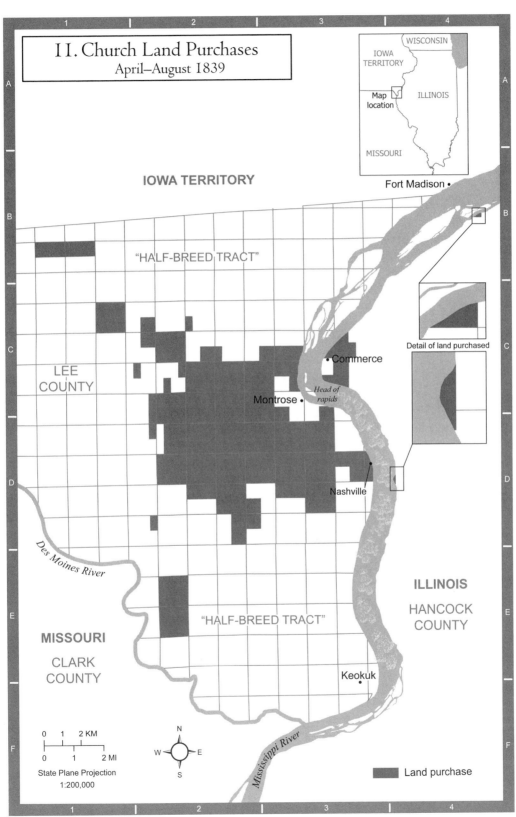

11. Church Land Purchases
April–August 1839

WISCONSIN

IOWA TERRITORY

Map location

ILLINOIS

MISSOURI

Fort Madison •

IOWA TERRITORY

"HALF-BREED TRACT"

Detail of land purchased

LEE COUNTY

• Commerce

Head of rapids

Montrose •

Nashville

Des Moines River

ILLINOIS

HANCOCK COUNTY

"HALF-BREED TRACT"

MISSOURI

CLARK COUNTY

Keokuk •

Mississippi River

0   1   2 KM

0   1   2 MI

State Plane Projection
1:200,000

N
W   E
S

■ Land purchase

RESEARCH: Robin Scott Jensen
CARTOGRAPHY: Jonathan West

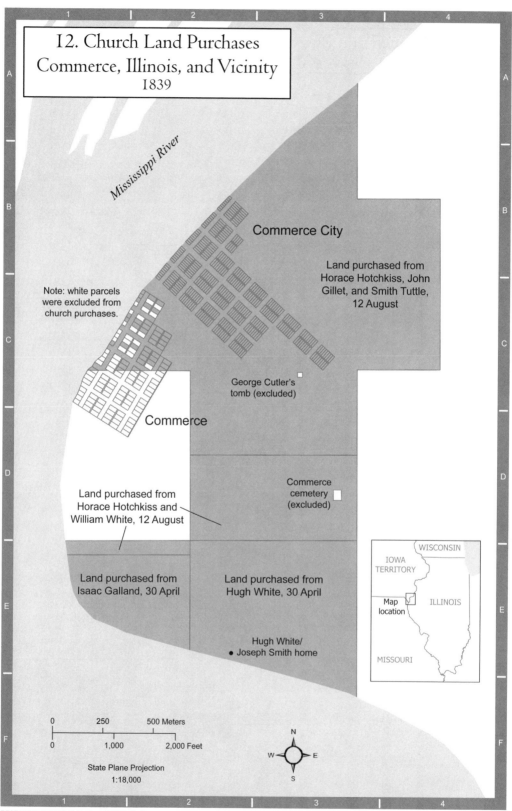

12. Church Land Purchases
Commerce, Illinois, and Vicinity
1839

Mississippi River

Commerce City

Land purchased from
Horace Hotchkiss, John
Gillet, and Smith Tuttle,
12 August

Note: white parcels
were excluded from
church purchases.

George Cutler's
tomb (excluded)

Commerce

Land purchased from
Horace Hotchkiss and
William White, 12 August

Commerce
cemetery
(excluded)

Land purchased from
Isaac Galland, 30 April

Land purchased from
Hugh White, 30 April

Hugh White/
● Joseph Smith home

WISCONSIN

IOWA
TERRITORY

Map
location

ILLINOIS

MISSOURI

0   250   500 Meters

0   1,000   2,000 Feet

State Plane Projection
1:18,000

N
W ◆ E
S

RESEARCH: Robin Scott Jensen and Richard L. Jensen
CARTOGRAPHY: Jonathan West

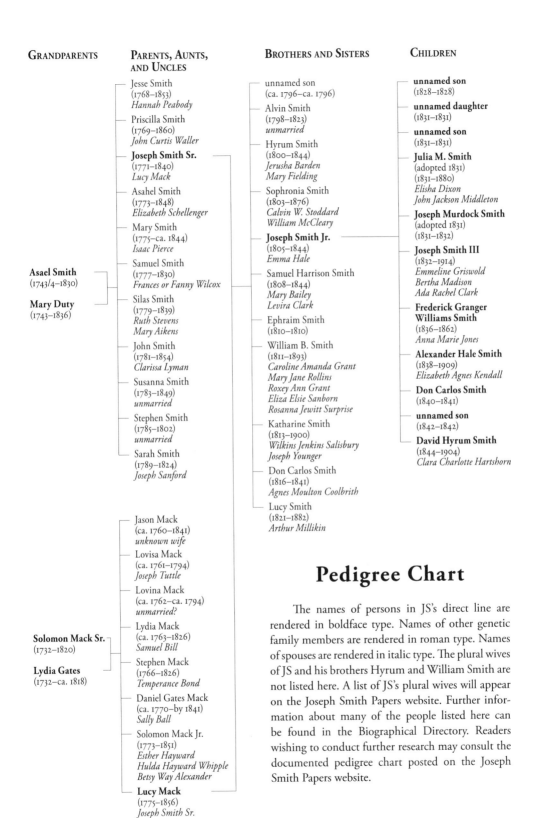

GRANDPARENTS	PARENTS, AUNTS, AND UNCLES	BROTHERS AND SISTERS	CHILDREN
	Jesse Smith (1768–1853) *Hannah Peabody*	unnamed son (ca. 1796–ca. 1796)	**unnamed son** (1828–1828)
	Priscilla Smith (1769–1860) *John Curtis Waller*	Alvin Smith (1798–1823) *unmarried*	**unnamed daughter** (1831–1831)
	Joseph Smith Sr. (1771–1840) *Lucy Mack*	Hyrum Smith (1800–1844) *Jerusha Barden* *Mary Fielding*	**unnamed son** (1831–1831)
	Asahel Smith (1773–1848) *Elizabeth Schellenger*	Sophronia Smith (1803–1876) *Calvin W. Stoddard* *William McCleary*	**Julia M. Smith** (adopted 1831) (1831–1880) *Elisha Dixon* *John Jackson Middleton*
	Mary Smith (1775–ca. 1844) *Isaac Pierce*	**Joseph Smith Jr.** (1805–1844) *Emma Hale*	**Joseph Murdock Smith** (adopted 1831) (1831–1832)
Asael Smith (1743/4–1830) **Mary Duty** (1743–1836)	Samuel Smith (1777–1830) *Frances or Fanny Wilcox*	Samuel Harrison Smith (1808–1844) *Mary Bailey* *Levira Clark*	**Joseph Smith III** (1832–1914) *Emmeline Griswold* *Bertha Madison* *Ada Rachel Clark*
	Silas Smith (1779–1839) *Ruth Stevens* *Mary Aikens*	Ephraim Smith (1810–1810)	**Frederick Granger Williams Smith** (1836–1862) *Anna Marie Jones*
	John Smith (1781–1854) *Clarissa Lyman*	William B. Smith (1811–1893) *Caroline Amanda Grant* *Mary Jane Rollins* *Roxey Ann Grant* *Eliza Elsie Sanborn* *Rosanna Jewitt Surprise*	**Alexander Hale Smith** (1838–1909) *Elizabeth Agnes Kendall*
	Susanna Smith (1783–1849) *unmarried*	Katharine Smith (1813–1900) *Wilkins Jenkins Salisbury* *Joseph Younger*	**Don Carlos Smith** (1840–1841)
	Stephen Smith (1785–1802) *unmarried*	Don Carlos Smith (1816–1841) *Agnes Moulton Coolbrith*	**unnamed son** (1842–1842)
	Sarah Smith (1789–1824) *Joseph Sanford*	Lucy Smith (1821–1882) *Arthur Millikin*	**David Hyrum Smith** (1844–1904) *Clara Charlotte Hartshorn*
	Jason Mack (ca. 1760–1841) *unknown wife*		
	Lovisa Mack (ca. 1761–1794) *Joseph Tuttle*		
	Lovina Mack (ca. 1762–ca. 1794) *unmarried?*		
	Lydia Mack (ca. 1763–1826) *Samuel Bill*		
Solomon Mack Sr. (1732–1820) **Lydia Gates** (1732–ca. 1818)	Stephen Mack (1766–1826) *Temperance Bond*		
	Daniel Gates Mack (ca. 1770–by 1841) *Sally Ball*		
	Solomon Mack Jr. (1773–1851) *Esther Hayward* *Hulda Hayward Whipple* *Betsy Way Alexander*		
	Lucy Mack (1775–1856) *Joseph Smith Sr.*		

Pedigree Chart

The names of persons in JS's direct line are rendered in boldface type. Names of other genetic family members are rendered in roman type. Names of spouses are rendered in italic type. The plural wives of JS and his brothers Hyrum and William Smith are not listed here. A list of JS's plural wives will appear on the Joseph Smith Papers website. Further information about many of the people listed here can be found in the Biographical Directory. Readers wishing to conduct further research may consult the documented pedigree chart posted on the Joseph Smith Papers website.

Biographical Directory

This register contains brief biographical sketches for most of the persons mentioned in this volume. These persons include church leaders, members of JS's family, people JS encountered on his travels, his acquaintances, and other figures from the earliest decades of the Latter-day Saint movement. Plural wives of JS and others are not listed here. A list of JS's plural wives will appear on the Joseph Smith Papers website.

The biographical entries identify persons by complete name (correctly spelled), birth and death dates, and additional information, such as parentage and birth place, migrations and places of residence, dates of marriage and names of spouses, occupation, denominational affiliation, religious and civic positions, and place of death. Occupations listed in an entry may not be comprehensive. Key figures with major significance to JS's activities receive the fullest biographical sketches. Others receive much briefer descriptions, often with less data than is available. Because unverified and sometimes incorrect data has been recirculated for decades, professional genealogists on the staff of the Joseph Smith Papers Project have utilized original sources whenever possible.

Entries for women are generally listed under their final married names, with appropriate cross-references under maiden names or earlier married names. Partial names in the text are not included in this directory when research could not determine the full name. In some cases, a footnote in the text provides possible identifications. The index found in this volume can often lead the reader to helpful information.

Locations that are noted include city or town, county, and state, when identified, for the first mention of a locale in each sketch. The counties and states of a handful of well-known cities have been omitted. "LDS church" refers to the church established by JS in 1830 and later known as the Church of Jesus Christ of Latter-day Saints. "RLDS church" refers to the church known originally as the New Organization and subsequently as the Reorganized Church of Jesus Christ of Latter Day Saints (1860–2001) and the Community of Christ (2001 to the present).

Even the fullest entries in this directory provide, of necessity, only a bare skeleton of a person's life. Readers wishing to conduct further research may consult the documented biographical directory posted on the Joseph Smith Papers website, josephsmithpapers.org.

Atchison, David Rice (11 Aug. 1807–26 Jan. 1886), lawyer, judge, agriculturist, politician, farmer. Born at Frogtown, near Lexington, Fayette Co., Kentucky. Son of William Atchison and Catherine Allen. About 1830, moved to Liberty, Clay Co., Missouri, where he became a prominent lawyer. Retained as lawyer to assist in preparing Mormon redress petitions during Jackson Co., Missouri, expulsion, 1833. Elected to lower house of Missouri legislature, 1834, 1838. Assisted Alexander W. Doniphan in working with state legislature to create Caldwell Co., Missouri, as haven for Mormons, 1836. Commanding officer of third division of state militia during Mormon conflict, 1838. Retained as lawyer to represent JS and other Mormons during conflict, 1838. Key prosecution witness at Nov. 1838 preliminary hearing for JS and others. Appointed judge of Twelfth Judicial Circuit of Missouri, which included Platte and Clinton counties, 1841. Served in U.S. Senate, 1843–1855; president pro tempore of Senate for several sessions. Died at Gower, Clinton Co., Missouri.

Avard, Sampson (23 Oct. 1800–15 Apr. 1869), physician. Born at St. Peter, Isle of Guernsey, Channel Islands, Great Britain. Migrated to U.S., by 1830. Married Eliza, a native of Virginia. Located at Washington DC, 1830. Moved to Virginia, by 1831. Moved to Freedom, Beaver Co., Pennsylvania, by 1835. A preacher for reformed Baptists (later Disciples of Christ or Campbellites). Baptized into LDS church and ordained an elder by Orson Pratt, 1835, at Freedom. Served mission near his home with Erastus Snow, 1836. Moved to Kirtland, Geauga Co., Ohio, 1836. Stockholder in Kirtland Safety Society. Ordained a high priest, before Oct. 1837. Migrated to Far West, Caldwell Co., Missouri, by 1838. Appointed general in Society of the Daughter of Zion (Danites) but was later demoted, summer 1838. Excommunicated, 17 Mar. 1839. Moved to Edwardsville, Madison Co., Illinois, by 1840. Died at Edwardsville.

Babbitt, Almon Whiting (Oct. 1812–Sept. 1856), postmaster, editor, attorney. Born at Cheshire, Berkshire Co., Massachusetts. Son of Ira Babbitt and Nancy Crosier. Baptized into LDS church, ca. 1830. Located in Amherst, Lorain Co., Ohio, July 1831. Served mission to New York, fall 1831. Served mission to Pomfret, Chautauque Co., New York, fall 1833. Married Julia Ann Johnson, 23 Nov. 1833, in Kirtland, Geauga Co., Ohio. Participated in Camp of Israel expedition to Missouri, 1834. Appointed member of First Quorum of the Seventy, Feb. 1835. Disfellowshipped, Dec. 1835. Restored to fellowship, Jan. 1836. Served mission to Upper Canada, 1837–1838. Led company of Canadian Latter-day Saints to Missouri, 1838. Appointed to gather reports and publications circulated against LDS church, 4 May 1839, at Quincy, Adams Co., Illinois. Appointed president of Kirtland stake, 3 Oct. 1840, at Nauvoo, Hancock Co., Illinois. Disfellowshipped, 1840, 1841. Moved to Ramus (later Webster), Hancock Co. Restored to fellowship and appointed presiding elder of Ramus, 1843. Appointed commander of Ramus militia. Admitted to Council of Fifty, 26 Mar. 1844. Appointed by Council of Fifty to serve mission to France, May 1844; mission never fulfilled. Elected to represent Hancock Co. in Illinois legislature, Dec. 1844. Appointed one of five trustees responsible for financial and temporal affairs in Nauvoo, 1846. Appointed postmaster of Nauvoo, 1846. Participated in battle at Nauvoo and signed surrender treaty, Sept. 1846. Migrated to Salt Lake Valley, 1849. Elected delegate to U.S. Congress for provisional state of Deseret, 5 July 1849. Disfellowshipped, 1849, 1851. Appointed secretary of Utah Territory, 1852. Excommunicated, May 1854. Was killed at Ash Hollow, Garden Co., Nebraska Territory.

Baldwin, Caleb (2 Sept. 1791–11 June 1849). Born in Nobletown (later Hillsdale), Orange Co., New York. Son of Philemon Baldwin and Esther. Served in War of 1812 in Ohio militia. Married Nancy Kingsbury, 7 Dec. 1814, in Cuyahoga Co., Ohio. Moved to Warrensville (later in University Heights), Cuyahoga Co., by June 1830. Baptized by Parley P. Pratt, 14 Nov. 1830, near Warrensville. Ordained an elder, by June 1831. Moved to Jackson Co., Missouri, by 1832. Moved to what became Caldwell Co., Missouri, ca. 1834. Served mission to Illinois, 1835; with Levi Jackman, established branch of church near Clear Creek, Union Co., Illinois. Participated in Mormon conflict, Oct. 1838. With JS in jail at Liberty, Clay Co., Missouri, Dec. 1838–Apr. 1839. Moved to Nauvoo, Hancock Co.,

Illinois, by 1840. Ordained a high priest. Moved to Salt Lake Valley, 1848. Died in Salt Lake City.

Ball, Joseph T. (21 Feb. 1804–20 Sept. 1861). Born at Boston. Son of Joseph Ball and Mary M. Drew. Moved to Kirtland, Geauga Co., Ohio, by 1836. Served missions to Orange Co., New York; to Fox Islands, Maine, 1838; and to Massachusetts, 1838. Moved to Nauvoo, Hancock Co., Illinois, by Mar. 1841. Served as presiding elder of Boston branch, 1844. Died at Boston.

Barlow, Israel (13 Sept. 1806–1 Nov. 1883), farmer, nurseryman, stockraiser. Born in Granville, Hampden Co., Massachusetts. Son of Jonathan Barlow and Anniss Gillett. Moved to New York. Baptized into LDS church by Brigham Young, 16 Mar. 1834, in Kirtland, Geauga Co., Ohio. Participated in Camp of Israel expedition to Missouri, 1834. Ordained a seventy, 1 Mar. 1835. Stockholder in Kirtland Safety Society. Moved to Missouri, by 1838. Served on church committee to locate land for potential settlement, Feb. 1839. Moved to Quincy, Adams Co., Illinois, by Mar. 1839. Married Elizabeth Haven, 23 Feb. 1840, in Quincy. Moved to Commerce (later Nauvoo), Hancock Co., Illinois, by 1840. Migrated to Salt Lake Valley, 1848; settled in what became Bountiful, Davis Co., Utah Territory, by 1849. Served mission to England, 1853–1855. Appointed commissioner to locate lands for university in Logan, Cache Co., Utah Territory, 1866. Ordained a patriarch, 1882, in Bountiful. Died at Bountiful.

Barnard, John Porter (28 Jan. 1804–28 July 1874), farmer, blacksmith. Born at New Hartford, Oneida Co., New York. Son of Ezra Barnard and Diadema Porter. Moved to Ulysses, Tompkins Co., New York, by Aug. 1826. Married Eliza Ann Wycoff, 31 Aug. 1826, at Ulysses. Moved to Barrington, Yates Co., New York, by June 1827. Moved to Greenwood, Steuben Co., New York, 1832. Baptized into LDS church, May 1835, in Greenwood. Migrated to Caldwell Co., Missouri, 1836. Expelled from Missouri; first located at Pike Co., Illinois, and then Nauvoo, Hancock Co., Illinois. Ordained a seventy, June 1839. Migrated to Salt Lake Valley, 1848. Moved to Centerville, Davis Co., Utah Territory; to Brigham City, Box Elder Co., Utah Territory; to Farmington, Davis Co., by 1860; to Box Elder, Box Elder Co., by 1870; and to Harper, Box Elder Co., after 1870. Died at Harper.

Barnes, Lorenzo Dow (22 Mar. 1812–20 Dec. 1842), teacher. Born in Tolland, Hampden Co., Massachusetts. Son of Phineas Barnes and Abigail Smith. Moved to eastern Ohio, 1815. Moved to Norton, Medina Co., Ohio, 1816. Baptized into LDS church, June 1833, in Norton. Ordained an elder by Sidney Rigdon, 18 July 1833. Served mission to western Ohio, 1833. Participated in Camp of Israel expedition to Missouri, 1834. Ordained a seventy, 2 May 1835, at Kirtland, Geauga Co., Ohio. Served mission to Virginia, 1835. Ordained a high priest, June 1838, at Adam-ondi-Ahman, Daviess Co., Missouri. Served as member of Adam-ondi-Ahman stake high council and as stake clerk. Appointed to serve mission to southern and eastern U.S., Sept. 1838. Served mission to England, beginning fall 1841. Presided over church conference in Bradford, Yorkshire, England. Died at Bradford.

Beebe, Calvin (1 July 1800–17 July 1861), farmer, merchant, postmaster. Born in Paris, Oneida Co., New York. Son of Isaac Beebe and Olive Soule. Moved to Chardon, Geauga Co., Ohio, by 1820. Married Submit Rockwell Starr, 19 Nov. 1823. Baptized into LDS church. Ordained an elder, by June 1831. Moved to Jackson Co., Missouri, Sept. 1831. Served mission to Illinois, Indiana, Michigan Territory, and Ohio, 1832. Ordained a high priest by Oliver Cowdery, 5 Oct. 1832, in Independence, Jackson Co. Clerk of church conference held at Jackson Co., 26 Sept. 1833. Moved near Fishing River, Clay Co., Missouri, 1833. Member of Zion high council in Clay Co., 1834. Appointed to serve mission to Kirtland, Geauga Co., Ohio, 1834. Moved to what became Caldwell Co., Missouri, ca. 1836. Served on Zion high council in Far West, Caldwell Co., 1837–1838. Moved to Daviess Co., Missouri; to Clinton Co., Missouri, 1838; and to Montrose, Lee Co., Iowa Territory, Mar. 1839. Excommunicated, 1841. Moved to Pottawattamie Co., Iowa, by 1850. Acting justice of the peace, 1857, at Mills Co., Iowa. Presided over branch of Alpheus Cutler's Church of Jesus Christ, 1859, at Farm Creek (later in Henderson), Mills Co. Appointed to high council of RLDS church, 6 Apr. 1860, in Amboy, Lee Co., Illinois. Moved to Mud Creek (later Anderson Township), Mills Co., by 1860. Moved to Farm Creek, by 1861.

Beman (Beaman), Sarah (Sally) Burt (27 Apr. 1775–29 Aug. 1840). Born at Lyme, New London Co., Connecticut. Daughter of Joseph Burt and Elizabeth Peck. Married Alvah Beman, 18 Aug. 1796. Moved from Massachusetts to Livonia, Ontario Co., New York, 1799. Moved to Avon, Livingston Co., New York, early 1830s. Baptized into LDS church, by 1835, in New York. Moved to Kirtland, Geauga Co., Ohio, after Oct. 1835. Died at Nauvoo, Hancock Co., Illinois.

Bigler, Mark (19 May 1785–23 Sept. 1839), farmer. Born in Enterprise, Harrison Co., Virginia (later in West Virginia). Son of Jacob Bigler and Hannah Booher. Married Susanna Ogden, 7 Nov. 1805, in Harrison Co. Baptized into LDS church, by 1837, in Harrison Co. Moved to Far West, Caldwell Co., Missouri, by July 1838. Died in Quincy, Adams Co., Illinois.

Billings, Titus (24 Mar. 1793–6 Feb. 1866), stonemason, carpenter, musician. Born in Greenfield, Hampshire Co., Massachusetts. Son of Ebenezer Billings and Esther Joyce. Moved to Mentor, Geauga Co., Ohio, by 1817. Married Diantha Morley, 16 Feb. 1817, in Geauga Co. Moved to Kirtland, Geauga Co., by 1820. Moved back to Mentor, 1827. Affiliated with Campbellite faith. Baptized into LDS church, 15 Nov. 1830, in Kirtland. Ordained a deacon, by Oct. 1831. Moved to Jackson Co., Missouri, 1832. Ordained an elder by Thomas B. Marsh, 10 Mar. 1832, in Jackson Co. Moved to Clay Co., Missouri, 1833. Moved back to Kirtland, ca. 1835. Labored on Kirtland temple. Moved to Caldwell Co., Missouri, by 1837. Ordained a high priest by Edward Partridge and Isaac Morley, 1 Aug. 1837, in Caldwell Co. Served as counselor to Bishop Edward Partridge, 1837–1840, in Missouri and Illinois. Fought in skirmish at Crooked River, 1838. Moved to Lima, Adams Co., Illinois, 1838. Moved to Yelrome (Morley's Settlement, later in Tioga), Hancock Co., Illinois, 1839. Member of Yelrome high council, 1839–1845. Appointed colonel in Nauvoo Legion, 1841. Appointed warden of Department of Music for University of Nauvoo, 1842. Served mission to New England, 1842. Moved to Nauvoo, Hancock Co., 1845. Migrated to what became Utah Territory, 1848; settled in Sessions Settlement (later Bountiful, Davis Co.). Member of Salt Lake stake high council, 1849. Moved to Manti (later in Sanpete Co., Utah Territory), 1849. Counselor in Sanpete stake presidency, 1851. Moved to Provo, Utah Co., Utah Territory, ca. 1864. Died in Provo.

Black, Adam (11 Sept. 1801–14 July 1890), farmer, sheriff, justice of the peace, judge. Born at Henderson Co., Kentucky. Son of William Black and Jane Wilson. Moved near

Booneville, Copper Co., Missouri Territory, and then to Ray Co., Missouri Territory, 1819. Elected sheriff of Ray Co., 1824. Married first Mary W. Morgan, 6 Sept. 1825, at Ray Co. Assessor of Ray Co., 1826. Served in Black Hawk War, 1832. Moved to what became Daviess Co., Missouri, 1833. Served as justice of the peace and county judge in Daviess Co. Prominent in anti-Mormon faction in Daviess Co., 1838. In 1844, moved to Gentry Co., Missouri, where he served as judge. Married second Margaret Grooms, ca. 1847. Married third Sarah (Sallie) Kelley, 15 Oct. 1857. In 1861, moved to Livingston Co., Missouri, where he served as county judge. Died in Jackson Township, Livingston Co.

Bogart, Samuel (2 Apr. 1797–11 Mar. 1861), preacher, military officer, farmer. Born in Carter Co., Tennessee. Son of Cornelius Bogart and Elizabeth Moffett. Served in War of 1812. Married Rachel Hammer, 19 May 1818, in Washington Co., Tennessee. Moved to Illinois and became Methodist minister. Served as commissioner in Schuyler Co., Illinois. Served as major in Black Hawk War, 1832. Located at Ray Co., Missouri, mid-1830s. Captain of company of mounted volunteers from Ray Co. during Mormon War, 1838; contended with Mormon militia at skirmish at Crooked River near Ray Co., 25 Oct. 1838. Appointed to arrest Mormons who participated in skirmish at Crooked River and to summon witnesses for court hearing at Richmond, Ray Co. Elected judge, Nov. 1839, at Caldwell Co., Missouri. Shot and killed opponent's nephew, Alexander Beatty, during election-day argument; fled to escape prosecution. Settled in Washington Co., Republic of Texas, 1839. Moved to what became Collin Co., Republic of Texas, 1845. Elected to Texas legislature, 1847, 1849, 1851, and 1859. Likely died near McKinney, Collin Co.

Boggs, Lilburn W. (14 Dec. 1796–14 Mar. 1860), bookkeeper, bank cashier, merchant, Indian agent and trader, lawyer, doctor, postmaster, politician. Born at Lexington, Fayette Co., Kentucky. Son of John M. Boggs and Martha Oliver. Served in War of 1812. Moved to St. Louis, ca. 1816, and engaged in business. Married first Julia Ann Bent, July 1817, at St. Louis. Moved to Franklin, Howard Co., Missouri, 1817; to Fort Osage, Howard Co., ca. 1818; to St. Louis, 1820; and back to Fort Osage, spring 1821. Married second Panthea Grant Boone, July 1823. Moved to Harmony Mission (Indian mission for Great Osage Nation; later near Papinville, Bates Co.), Missouri, by 1824. Located at Independence, Jackson Co., Missouri, 1826; elected to state senate on Democratic ticket, 1826, 1828. Elected lieutenant governor, 1832. Became governor upon resignation of predecessor, Daniel Dunklin, 1836, and served through 1840. Moved to Jefferson City, Cole Co., Missouri, 1836. Authorized 1838 expulsion of Mormons from Missouri under what was termed his "extermination order." Returned to Independence, before 1842. Severely wounded by would-be assassin, 6 May 1842; accused JS of complicity with Orrin Porter Rockwell in perpetrating the crime. Returned to Jefferson City, 1842. Served in state senate, 1842–1846. Moved to Cass Co., Missouri, by 1843; returned to Independence, by 1845. Migrated to Sonoma, Mexico (later in Sonoma Co., California), 1846. In 1852, moved to Napa Valley, Napa Co., California, where he died.

Bosley, Edmund (Edmond) (25 June 1776–15 Dec. 1846), miller. Born at Northumberland, Northumberland Co., Pennsylvania. Son of John P. Bosley and Hannah Bull. Married Ann Kelly of Northumberland Co. Lived at Livonia, Livingston Co., New York, 1792–1834. Moved to Kirtland, Geauga Co., Ohio, Mar. 1834. Stockholder in Kirtland Safety Society. Served as second counselor in Kirtland elders quorum, 1837. Moved to Missouri, by 1838. Located at Adams Co., Illinois, 1839. Ordained a high priest, 1844, at Nauvoo, Hancock Co., Illinois. Died at Winter Quarters, unorganized U.S. territory (now in Omaha, Douglas Co., Nebraska), during Mormon exodus to Salt Lake Valley.

Boynton, John Farnham (20 Sept. 1811–20 Oct. 1890), merchant, lecturer, scientist, inventor, dentist. Born at East Bradford (later Groveland), Essex Co., Massachusetts. Son of Eliphalet Boynton and Susanna Nichols. Baptized into LDS church by JS, Sept. 1832, at Kirtland, Geauga Co., Ohio. Ordained an elder by JS, 16 Nov. 1832. Served missions to Pennsylvania, 1832, with Zebedee Coltrin; to Maine, 1833–1834, with Evan Greene; and to Painesville, Geauga Co., Ohio, Nov. 1834, with William E. McLellin. Ordained member of Quorum of the Twelve, 15 Feb. 1835, in Kirtland. Served mission to eastern states and Canada with Quorum of the Twelve. Married first to Susannah (Susan) Lowell by JS, 20 Jan. 1836, at Kirtland. Disfellowshipped from Quorum of the Twelve, 3 Sept. 1837. Reinstated to church and membership in Quorum of the Twelve, 10 Sept. 1837. Excommunicated, 1837. Practiced dentistry in vicinity of Nauvoo, Hancock Co., Illinois, early 1840s. Graduated from St. Louis Medical College, 1845. Settled at Syracuse, Onondaga Co., New York, 1845. Wife died, 7 Aug. 1859. Married second Mary West Jenkins, Nov. 1865. Separated from wife, ca. 1869; divorced, 1880. Married third Caroline Foster Harriman, 20 Jan. 1883. Died at Syracuse.

Buell, Presendia Lathrop. See Kimball, Presendia Lathrop Huntington.

Brassfield, John (ca. 1812–after 29 June 1880), farmer. Born in Tennessee. Married Mahala Johnston, Jan. 1834, in Ray Co., Missouri. Appointed guard to assist Sheriff William Morgan transport Mormon prisoners from Daviess Co., Missouri, to Boone Co., Missouri; helped prisoners escape, Apr. 1839. Moved to North Fork, Izard Co., Arkansas, by 1850; to Mulberry, Johnson Co., Arkansas, by 1860; to Jackson Township, Newton Co., Arkansas, by 1870; and to Center Township, Sebastian Co., Arkansas, by 1880.

Breazeale, Hugh Lawson (ca. 1803–4 Nov. 1833), lawyer. Moved to Roane Co., Tennessee, by 1826. Married Amanda M. King, 15 Feb. 1827, in Roane Co. Traveled to Independence, Jackson Co., Missouri, to participate in expulsion of church members, possibly at urging of brother-in-law Austin A. King. Killed in skirmish near Blue River in Jackson Co.

Bullock, Thomas (23 Dec. 1816–10 Feb. 1885), farmer, excise officer, secretary, clerk. Born in Leek, Staffordshire, England. Son of Thomas Bullock and Mary Hall. Married Henrietta Rushton, 25 June 1838. Moved to Ardee, Co. Louth, Ireland, Nov. 1839; to Isle of Anglesey, Aug. 1840; and back to Leek, Nov. 1841. Baptized into LDS church by William Knight, 20 Nov. 1841, in Leek. Ordained a priest by Alfred Cordon, 28 Apr. 1842. Ordained an elder by James Riley and Robert Crooks, 3 July 1842. Emigrated from England, 8 Mar. 1843; arrived in Nauvoo, Hancock Co., Illinois, 31 May 1843. Participated in plural marriage during JS's lifetime. Served as scribe to JS, from 1843 until death of JS. Served as clerk of steamboat *Maid of Iowa,* beginning 1 May 1844. Made secretary of Nauvoo Masonic Lodge, 23 June 1844. Ordained a seventy by Joseph Young, 12 Jan. 1845; appointed president of Twenty-Seventh Quorum of the Seventy, 1 June 1845. Moved to Winter Quarters, unorganized U.S. territory (later in Omaha, Douglas Co., Nebraska), 1846. Served as clerk for Brigham Young pioneer company during migration to Salt Lake Valley, summer 1847. Returned to Winter Quarters, fall 1847; arrived back in Salt Lake Valley, Sept. 1848. Recorder for Salt Lake Co., Utah Territory, 1848–1856. Served as clerk to church historian and recorder. First proofreader for *Deseret News,* 1850. Appointed clerk of House of Representatives for provisional state of Deseret, 1850. Served mission to England, Aug. 1856–June 1858. Moved to Wanship, Summit Co., Utah Territory, 1868, where he served as clerk of probate court and recorder of Summit Co. Moved to Coalville, Summit Co., before June 1870, where he died.

Cahoon, Reynolds (30 Apr. 1790–29 Apr. 1861), farmer, tanner, builder. Born at Cambridge, Washington Co., New York. Son of William Cahoon Jr. and Mehitable Hodges. Married Thirza Stiles, 11 Dec. 1810. Moved to northeastern Ohio, 1811. Located at Harpersfield, Ashtabula Co., Ohio. Served in War of 1812. Moved near Kirtland, Geauga Co., Ohio, 1825. Baptized into LDS church by Parley P. Pratt, Nov. 1830. Ordained an elder by Sidney Rigdon and a high priest by JS, 4 June 1831. Appointed to serve mission to Missouri, 6 June 1831. Appointed counselor to Bishop Newel K. Whitney at Kirtland, 10 Feb. 1832. Appointed to serve mission with David W. Patten to Warsaw, Wyoming Co., New York, 23 Mar. 1833. Member of committee to oversee building of Kirtland temple. Stockholder in Kirtland Safety Society. Member of Kirtland stake presidency. Moved to Missouri, June 1838. Appointed counselor to stake president at Adam-ondi-Ahman, Daviess Co., Missouri, 28 June 1838. Located in Iowa Territory following exodus from Missouri. Appointed counselor in Iowa branch, Lee Co., Iowa Territory, 1839. Appointed guard in Nauvoo Legion, Mar. 1841. Served on building committee for Nauvoo temple. Member of Nauvoo Masonic Lodge. Admitted to Council of Fifty, 11 Mar. 1844. Resided at Winter Quarters, unorganized U.S. territory (later in Omaha, Douglas Co., Nebraska), 1846. Migrated to Salt Lake Valley, 1848. Died in Salt Lake City.

Carlin, Thomas (18 July 1789–14 Feb. 1852), ferry owner, farmer, sheriff, politician. Born in Fayette Co., Kentucky. Son of Thomas Carlin and Elizabeth Evans. Baptist. Moved to Missouri, by 1803. Moved to Illinois, by 1812. Served in War of 1812. Married Rebecca Hewitt, 13 Dec. 1814, in Madison Co., Illinois. Moved to Greene Co., Illinois, 1818. Appointed first sheriff of Greene Co., 1821. Served as state senator, 1824–1828. Donated land for construction of public buildings in Carrollton, Greene Co. Served in Black Hawk War as captain of spy battalion in Illinois Mounted Volunteers, 1832. Appointed receiver of public monies by U.S. president Andrew Jackson, 1834, in Quincy, Adams Co., Illinois. Affiliated with Church of Christ in Quincy. Served as governor of Illinois, 1838–1842. Issued warrant for arrest of JS for involvement in attempt to kill former Missouri governor Lilburn W. Boggs, 1842. Returned to Carrollton, 1842. Elected state representative, 1849. Died near Carrollton.

Carter, Jared (14 June 1801–6 July 1849). Born at Killingworth, Middlesex Co., Connecticut. Son of Gideon Carter and Johanna Sims. Moved to Benson, Rutland Co., Vermont, by 1810. Married Lydia Ames, 20 Sept. 1823, at Benson. Moved to Chenango, Broome Co., New York, by Jan. 1831. Baptized into LDS church by Hyrum Smith, 20 Feb. 1831, in Colesville, Broome Co. Moved with Colesville branch to Thompson, Geauga Co., Ohio, May 1831. Ordained a priest, June 1831. Ordained an elder, Sept. 1831. Appointed to serve missions to eastern U.S., 22 Sept. 1831 and 12 Mar. 1832. Left to serve mission to Michigan Territory, Dec. 1832. Appointed to serve mission to eastern U.S., Mar. 1833. Ordained a high priest, by May 1833. Appointed to obtain funds for Elders School, 4 May 1833. Member of Kirtland temple building committee, 1833. Appointed to first Kirtland high council, 17 Feb. 1834. Appointed to serve mission to Upper Canada, 20 Feb. 1834. Labored on

Kirtland temple. Stockholder in Kirtland Safety Society. Appointed president of Kirtland high council, 9 Sept. 1837. Removed family to Far West, Caldwell Co., Missouri, 1837. Appointed member of Far West high council, 3 Mar. 1838. Appointed captain general of Society of the Daughter of Zion (Danites) but was soon demoted, summer 1838. Moved from Far West to Commerce (later Nauvoo), Hancock Co., Illinois, 1839. Member of Nauvoo Masonic Lodge. Affiliated with James J. Strang's Church of Jesus Christ of Latter Day Saints, 1846. Excommunicated from Strangite movement, 8 Nov. 1846. Returned to LDS church. By June 1849, moved to DeKalb Co., Illinois, where he died.

Carter, Orlando Henry (27 Jan. 1820–before Oct. 1859). Born in Benson, Rutland Co., Vermont. Son of Simeon Carter and Lydia Kenyon. Moved to Amherst, Lorain Co., Ohio, by 1830. Baptized into LDS church, likely 1831. Moved to Far West, Caldwell Co., Missouri, before Mar. 1838. Married Sarah Vanblaracom, 3 Nov. 1842, in Scott Co., Illinois. Ordained a seventy, before 24 Dec. 1845. Migrated to Salt Lake Valley; arrived late Oct. 1849. Moved to Utah Co., Utah Territory, by 1850. Moved to San Bernardino, San Bernardino Co., California, by 1854. Left San Bernardino for Salt Lake City, 10 Sept. 1857.

Carter, Simeon (7 June 1794–3 Feb. 1869), farmer. Born at Killingworth, Middlesex Co., Connecticut. Son of Gideon Carter and Johanna Sims. Moved to Benson, Rutland Co., Vermont, by 1810. Married Lydia Kenyon, 2 Dec. 1818, at Benson. Moved to Amherst, Lorain Co., Ohio, by 1830. Baptized into LDS church, Feb. 1831. Ordained an elder. Ordained a high priest by Lyman Wight, 4 June 1831. Appointed to serve mission to Missouri with Solomon Hancock, June 1831. President of branch at Big Blue River, Kaw Township, Jackson Co., Missouri, 1833. Member of Zion high council in Clay Co., Missouri, 1834, and in Far West, Caldwell Co., Missouri, 1837. Expelled from Missouri, 1838. Located at Lee Co., Iowa Territory, by 1840. Served mission to England, 1846–1849. Arrived at Salt Lake Valley, 1849. Moved to Brigham City, Box Elder Co., Utah Territory, by 1860. Died at Brigham City.

Clark, John Bullock (17 Apr. 1802–29 Oct. 1885), lawyer, politician. Born at Madison Co., Kentucky. Moved to Howard Co., Missouri, 1818. Practiced law in Fayette, Howard Co., beginning 1824. Clerk of Howard Co. courts, 1824–1834. Appointed brigadier general in Missouri militia, 1830. Appointed major general in Missouri militia. Appointed to command Missouri militia operations against Mormon forces, 27 Oct. 1838; arrived in Far West, Caldwell Co., Missouri, 4 Nov. 1838, after Saints had surrendered. Insisted Saints leave Missouri; in conjunction with civil authorities, oversaw prosecution of Mormon prisoners at preliminary hearing, Nov. 1838. Member of Missouri House of Representatives, 1850–1851. Member of U.S. House of Representatives, 1857–1861. Died at Fayette.

Clark, Timothy Baldwin (15 Mar. 1778–29 May 1848). Born in Milford, New Haven Co., Connecticut. Son of John Clark and Elizabeth Rogers. Married Mary (Polly) Keeler, 3 May 1802, in Brookfield, Fairfield Co., Connecticut. Moved to Vienna Township, Trumbull Co., Ohio, by 1809. Served in War of 1812 and Black Hawk War. Moved to Edwards Co., Illinois, by 1820. Baptized into LDS church by Charles C. Rich, 7 May 1835. Lived near Far West, Caldwell Co., Missouri, late 1830s. Moved to Lee Co., Iowa Territory, by 1840. Buried at Bolingbrook, Will Co., Illinois.

Cleminson (Clemenson), John James (28 Dec. 1798–28 Nov. 1879), farmer, teacher, cabinet maker, carpenter, clerk. Born at Lancaster, Lancashire, England. Migrated to

St. John's, New Brunswick (later in Canada), 1812. Moved to Louisville, Jefferson Co., Kentucky. Moved to Lexington, Lillard Co., Missouri, by 1823. Married Lydia Lightner, 5 Jan. 1823, at Lillard Co. Baptized into LDS church and moved to Far West, Caldwell Co., Missouri, by 1837. Elected Caldwell Co. clerk and circuit clerk, 1837. Testified for prosecution at hearing in Richmond, Ray Co., Missouri, Nov. 1838. Moved to Rockport, Caldwell Co., by June 1840. Lived at Montrose, Lee Co., Iowa Territory, by Mar. 1842. Wrote to JS seeking reconciliation, May 1842. Ordained a high priest, by 31 Jan. 1846. Lived at San Diego Co., California, 1852. Moved to San Bernardino, Los Angeles Co., California, 1852. By June 1860, lived at El Monte, Los Angeles Co., where he died.

Cleveland, John (21 May 1790–24 Nov. 1860), farmer, wagon maker, carpenter, builder. Born in Duanesburg, Schenectady Co., New York. Son of Gardner Cleveland and Annis Durkee. Moved to Cincinnati, before 1826. Married Sarah Marietta Kingsley Howe, 1826, in Cincinnati. Moved to Millcreek Township, Hamilton Co., Ohio, by 1830. Moved to Quincy, Adams Co., Illinois, 1834. Gave lodging to JS's family when Saints were driven from Missouri, early 1839. Sold Quincy land to Emma Smith, 29 Sept. 1841, and moved to Plymouth, Hancock Co., Illinois. Purchased property from JS in Nauvoo, Hancock Co., 13 May 1843. Moved to Eden, Schuyler Co., Illinois, by 1850. Moved to Berlin Township, Delaware Co., Ohio, by 1860. Returned to Plymouth, where he died.

Cleveland, Sarah Marietta Kingsley (20 Oct. 1788–21 Apr. 1856). Born in Becket, Berkshire Co., Massachusetts. Daughter of Ebenezer Kingsley and Sarah Chaplin. Moved to New Haven, New Haven Co., Connecticut, by 1807. Married first John Howe, 7 Dec. 1807, in New Haven. Moved to Cincinnati, by 1826. Married second John Cleveland, 10 June 1826, in Cincinnati. Moved to Quincy, Adams Co., Illinois, 1834. Baptized into LDS church, likely in Quincy. Housed Emma Smith and Smith children after Saints were driven from Missouri, Feb.–May 1839. Sold Quincy land to Emma Smith, 29 Sept. 1841. Moved to Nauvoo, Hancock Co., Illinois, 1842. Appointed counselor to Emma Smith in Female Relief Society of Nauvoo, 17 Mar. 1842. Identified in some sources as a plural wife of JS. Moved from Nauvoo, ca. May 1843. Moved to Plymouth, Hancock Co., 1846, where she died.

Collins, William (25 Apr. 1797–18 Oct. 1894). Born in Fayette Co., Kentucky. Son of Robert Collins and Susanna Coons. Married Sally White, 10 Jan. 1820, in Fayette Co. Moved to Liberty, Clay Co., Missouri, 1828. Assisted Mormon prisoners at Independence, Jackson Co., Missouri, Nov. 1838. Died at Liberty.

Coltrin, John (July 1775–13 Aug. 1846). Born in Tolland, Tolland Co., Connecticut. Son of John Coltrin and Rebecca Maxon. Moved to Colrain, Hampshire Co., Massachusetts, by 1790. Married first Sarah Graham, ca. 1793–1794. Moved to New York, ca. late 1790s; to Ovid, Seneca Co., New York, by 1804; to Caledonia, Genesee Co., New York, by 1810; to Geauga Co., Ohio, 1814; and to Strongsville, Cuyahoga Co., Ohio, by 1820. Baptized into LDS church. Wife died, 20 Mar. 1841, at Strongsville. Moved to area near Nauvoo, Hancock Co., Illinois, ca. 1841. Married second Leah Van Duzen, ca. 1842. Received high priest license, 8 Apr. 1844. Died in Pottawattamie Co., Iowa Territory.

Corrill, John (17 Sept. 1794–26 Sept. 1842), surveyor, politician, author. Born at Worcester Co., Massachusetts. Married Margaret Lyndiff, ca. 1830. Lived at Harpersfield, Ashtabula Co., Ohio, 1830. Baptized into LDS church, 10 Jan. 1831, at Kirtland, Geauga Co., Ohio. Ordained an elder, Jan. 1831, at Kirtland. Served mission to New London,

Huron Co., Ohio, 1831. Ordained a high priest by Lyman Wight, 4 June 1831, at Kirtland. Appointed second counselor to Bishop Edward Partridge. Moved to Jackson Co., Missouri. Presided over group of church members in Independence, Jackson Co., 1831–1833. Appointed one of ten high priests to watch over the ten Missouri branches, 11 Sept. 1833. In Nov. 1833, expelled from Jackson Co. and located at Clay Co., Missouri, where he continued as counselor to Bishop Partridge. Returned to Kirtland and labored on temple, 1834–1836. Returned to Missouri and became a founder of Far West, Missouri, after Mar. 1836. Appointed "Keeper of the Lord's store House," at Far West, 22 May 1837. Released as counselor to Bishop Partridge, Aug. 1837. Elected state representative from Caldwell Co., Missouri, 1838. With Elias Higbee, appointed a church historian, 6 Apr. 1838. Testified for prosecution at JS's hearing in Richmond, Ray Co., Missouri, Nov. 1838. Moved to Illinois, 1839. Excommunicated, 17 Mar. 1839, at Quincy, Adams Co., Illinois. Published *A Brief History of the Church of Christ of Latter Day Saints, (Commonly Called Mormons),* 1839. Died in Adams Co.

Cowdery, Oliver (3 Oct. 1806–3 Mar. 1850), clerk, teacher, justice of the peace, lawyer, newspaper editor. Born at Wells, Rutland Co., Vermont. Son of William Cowdery and Rebecca Fuller. Raised Congregationalist. Moved to western New York and clerked at a store, ca. 1825–1828. Taught term as local schoolmaster at Manchester, Ontario Co., New York, 1828–1829. Assisted JS as principal scribe in translation of Book of Mormon, 1829. With JS, baptized and received priesthood authority, 1829. Moved to Fayette, Seneca Co., New York, and was one of the Three Witnesses of the Book of Mormon, June 1829. Helped oversee printing of Book of Mormon by E. B. Grandin, 1829–1830. Among six original members of LDS church, 6 Apr. 1830. Served as church recorder, 1830, 1835–1837. Led missionaries through Ohio and to Missouri, 1830–1831. Ordained a high priest by Sidney Rigdon, 28 Aug. 1831. With John Whitmer, left Ohio to take revelations to Missouri for publication, Nov. 1831. Assisted William W. Phelps in conducting church's printing operations at Jackson Co., Missouri, 1832–1833. Married Elizabeth Ann Whitmer, 18 Dec. 1832, in Kaw Township, Jackson Co. Edited *The Evening and the Morning Star,* 1833. Moved to Kirtland, Geauga Co., Ohio, by Sept. 1833. Member of United Firm, Literary Firm, and Kirtland high council. Appointed assistant president of church, 5 Dec. 1834. Edited Kirtland continuation of *The Evening and the Morning Star,* 1833, and edited reprint under modified title *Evening and Morning Star,* 1835–1836. Edited *LDS Messenger and Advocate,* 1834–1835, 1836–1837, and *Northern Times,* 1835. Stockholder in Kirtland Safety Society. Elected justice of the peace in Kirtland, 1837. Moved to Far West, Caldwell Co., Missouri, 1837. Excommunicated, 1838. Driven from Far West, late June 1838. Moved to Richmond, Ray Co., Missouri, summer 1838. Returned to Kirtland, 1838, and briefly practiced law. Moved to Tiffin, Seneca Co., Ohio, where he continued law practice and held political offices, 1840–1847. Attended Methodist Protestant Church at Tiffin. Moved to Elkhorn, Walworth Co., Wisconsin Territory, 1847. Ran unsuccessfully for Wisconsin State Assembly, 1848. Coeditor of *Walworth County Democrat,* 1848. Requested and received readmission to LDS church, 1848, at Kanesville (later Council Bluffs), Pottawattamie Co., Iowa. Died at Richmond.

Cowles, Ralph (16 May 1792–1 Aug. 1869), teacher, surveyor, auditor, jeweler. Born in New Hartford, Litchfield Co., Connecticut. Son of Asa Cowles and Sibyl Merrill. Moved to Chardon, Geauga Co., Ohio, July 1811. Elected clerk for Burlington Township (later

Claridon Township), Geauga Co., 7 Apr. 1817. Served as Geauga Co. auditor, 1818–1821, 1827–1835, 1839–1845. Married Delia Benton, 20 Aug. 1818, in Geauga Co. Served in various capacities for Geauga Co. Agricultural Society. Appointed counselor in Geauga Co. Anti-Slavery Society, 11 Sept. 1838. Served as recorder at trial proceedings of *Alpheus C. Russell v. JS et al.*, Mar. 1844, in Painesville, Geauga Co. Moved to Cleveland, by 1850. Elected trustee for Society of Savings, 1867–1868. Died in Cleveland.

Daniels, Cyrus (12 Sept. 1803–before May 1847), farmer, policeman. Born in Nelson, Chenango Co., New York. Son of Adam Daniels and Phoebe. Moved to Mentor, Geauga Co., Ohio, by 1826. Married Simira Colson, 21 Jan. 1828, in Cuyahoga Co., Ohio. Baptized into LDS church. Moved to Independence, Jackson Co., Missouri, fall 1831. Moved to Caldwell Co., Missouri, by Oct. 1838. Returned to Mentor, by 1840. Member of branch of church in Black River, Crawford Co., Wisconsin Territory, Feb. 1844. Admitted to Council of Fifty, 11 Mar. 1845. Member of police force in Nauvoo, Hancock Co., Illinois, by Apr. 1845. Ordained an elder, by 8 Jan. 1846. Moved to Winter Quarters, unorganized U.S. territory (later in Omaha, Douglas Co., Nebraska), by 1846. Probably died at or near Winter Quarters.

Decker, Isaac (29 Dec. 1799–14 June 1873), farmer, carpenter. Born in Columbia Co., New York. Son of Peter Decker and Hanna Snooks. Moved to Phelps, Ontario Co., New York, by Aug. 1820. Married first Harriet Page Wheeler, 1820, in Phelps. Moved to Freedom, Cattaraugus Co., New York. Moved to New Portage, Medina Co., Ohio, where baptized into LDS church. Received elder's license, 23 May 1836, in Kirtland, Geauga Co., Ohio. Moved to Kirtland, by fall 1837. Donated his wealth to church while in Ohio. Moved to Far West, Caldwell Co., Missouri, 1838; to Daviess Co., Missouri; back to Far West; to Quincy, Adams Co., Illinois; to Winchester, Scott Co., Illinois; and to Nauvoo, Hancock Co., Illinois, 1841. Member of Nauvoo Masonic Lodge. Divorced wife, before 1843, in Nauvoo. Ordained a high priest, before 24 Dec. 1845. Migrated to Salt Lake Valley, 1847. Moved to Midway, Wasatch Co., Utah Territory, by 1870. Moved to Salt Lake City, after 1870. Died in Salt Lake City.

Doniphan, Alexander William (9 July 1808–8 Aug. 1887), lawyer, military general, insurance/bank executive. Born near Maysville, Mason Co., Kentucky. Son of Joseph Doniphan and Ann Smith. Father died, 1813; sent to live with older brother George, 1815, in Augusta, Bracken Co., Kentucky. Attended Augusta College, 1822–1826. Studied law in office of jurist Martin Marshall in Augusta. Passed Kentucky and Ohio bar examinations, 1829. Located at St. Louis, Mar. 1830. Moved to Lexington, Lafayette Co., Missouri, and opened law office there, 1830. Moved to Liberty, Clay Co., Missouri, 1833. Employed as legal counsel by Latter-day Saints during their expulsion from Jackson Co., Missouri, 1833. Elected to Missouri General Assembly representing Clay Co., 1836, 1840, and 1854. Married Elizabeth Jane Thornton, 21 Dec. 1837. Appointed brigadier general in state militia. Prevented intended execution of JS and other church leaders at Far West, Caldwell Co., Missouri, Nov. 1838. Again defended JS and others in courts, 1838–1839. Served in Mexican War, 1846–1847. Returned to Liberty. Moved to St. Louis, 1863. Moved to Richmond, Ray Co., Missouri, ca. 1869. Died at Richmond.

Durfee, James (9 Sept. 1794–16/17 July 1844). Likely born in Tiverton, Newport Co., Rhode Island. Son of Perry Durfee and Annie Salisbury (Sulsbury). Moved with grandparents James and Ann Borden Durfee to Broadalbin, Montgomery Co., New York, 1801. Married Cynthia. Moved to Jackson Township, Wayne Co., Ohio, by Oct. 1818. Baptized into LDS church, by 1831. As a priest, attended a church conference in Geauga Co., Ohio, 3 June 1831. Appointed to serve mission to eastern U.S. with Edmund Marvin, 20 Feb. 1834. Ordained an elder, 26 Mar. 1836. Resided in Caldwell Co., Missouri, Sept. 1836–1 Nov. 1838. Fought in skirmish at Crooked River, 24 Oct. 1838, near Ray Co., Missouri. Member of branch of church, 23 Oct. 1840, in Lima, Adams Co., Illinois. Disfellowshipped, 23 Jan. 1842, in Lima; restored to fellowship, 4 Feb. 1842, at Nauvoo, Hancock Co., Illinois. Buried in Nauvoo.

French, Peter (ca. 1774–after 1850), farmer, tavern keeper, hotelier. Born in New York. Moved to Willoughby, Western Reserve (later Lake Co.), Ohio, 1799. Married Sally. Moved to Kirtland, Geauga Co., Ohio, 1811, as one of its earliest settlers. Named as one of town proprietors, 1818. Served as overseer of the poor, 1818, 1823, in Kirtland. Served as appraiser of property, 1818, in Kirtland. Among founders of Mentor Library Company, 1819, in Painesville, Geauga Co. Served as supervisor of highways, 1817, 1822, 1830; and as fence viewer, 1821, 1824, in Kirtland. Built hotel, 1827, in Kirtland. Sold hotel and other Kirtland property, including temple lot, to JS and church leaders, 1833, 1836. Moved to Mentor, Lake Co., by 1850.

Galland, Isaac (15 May 1791–27 Sept. 1858), merchant, postmaster, land speculator, doctor. Born at Somerset Co., Pennsylvania. Son of Matthew Galland and Hannah Fenno. Married first Nancy Harris, 22 Mar. 1811, in Madison Co., Ohio. Married second Margaret Knight, by 1816. Moved to Washington Co., Indiana, by 1816. Located at Owen Co., Indiana, by 1820, and at Edgar Co., Illinois, shortly after 1820. Moved to Horselick Grove (later in Hancock Co.), Illinois, 1824. Married third Hannah Kinney, 5 Oct. 1826. Moved to Oquawka, Henderson Co., Illinois, 1827. Established settlement later known as Nashville on west bank of Mississippi River, in unorganized U.S. territory, where he practiced medicine, established trading post, and founded first school in what later became Iowa Territory. Moved family to Fort Edwards (later Warsaw), Hancock Co., 1832. Served as colonel in Black Hawk War, 1832. Married fourth Elizabeth Wilcox, 25 Apr. 1833. Platted original town of Keokuk, Lee Co., Wisconsin Territory (later in Iowa), 1837. Moved to Commerce (later Nauvoo), Hancock Co., winter 1838–1839. Purchased land in "Half-Breed Tract" in Lee Co. and sold some 19,000 acres of it to Latter-day Saints, 1839. Also sold properties in Commerce to Latter-day Saints. Baptized into LDS church and ordained an elder by JS, 3 July 1839. Instructed in JS revelation to buy stock for building Nauvoo House, 19 Jan. 1841. Acted as authorized agent for church in settling certain land transactions involving property exchanges by eastern Latter-day Saints moving to Nauvoo. Withdrew from church activity, ca. 1842. Resident of Keokuk, Lee Co., Iowa Territory, 1842–1853. Moved to Sacramento, Sacramento Co., California, 1853; eventually settled in Petaluma, Sonoma Co., California. Moved to Fort Madison, Lee Co., 1856. Died at Fort Madison.

Gates, Thomas, Sr. (7 May 1776–22 June 1851), farmer. Born in Henniker, Hillsborough Co., New Hampshire. Son of Isaac Gates and Mary. Moved to Acworth, Cheshire Co., New Hampshire, by 1790. Married Patty Plumley, before 1805 and likely before 1800. Moved to St. Johnsbury, Caledonia Co., Vermont, by 1810; to Waterford, Caledonia Co., by 1820; and back to St. Johnsbury, by 1830. Baptized into LDS church,

1833. Ordained a seventy, by Apr. 1836. Member of Zion high council in Far West, Caldwell Co., Missouri, beginning 14 Mar. 1838. Appointed to high council of Crooked Creek branch, in Hancock Co., Illinois, 29 July 1840. Migrated to Salt Lake Valley, 1847. Moved to Weber Co., Utah Territory, by 1850. Died in Ogden, Weber Co.

Gillet (Gillett), John Dean (2 Aug. 1796–17 July 1848). Likely born in Connecticut. Son of Benoni Gillett and Phoebe Dean. Moved to Commerce, Hancock Co., Illinois, by May 1837. In Aug. 1839, with land-speculating partners Horace Hotchkiss and Smith Tuttle, sold land in Commerce (later Nauvoo), Hancock Co., Illinois, to JS. Moved to Logan Co., Illinois, by 1840, and settled at Bald Knob. Married Jemima Davis. Buried in Steenbergen Cemetery, Mount Pulaski Township, Logan Co.

Gordon, Thomas J. (8 Apr. 1805–10 Oct. 1889), farmer, shoemaker, justice of the peace, store clerk, carpenter. Born in New York. Married Mary Holmes. Resided at Norton, Medina Co., Ohio, by 1830. Listed as having appeared in one of several visions Joseph Bosworth recounted in a letter to JS dated 17 Feb. 1834. Baptized into LDS church. Attended church meetings held in New Portage, Medina Co., 8 Sept. 1834, 18 Nov. 1835, and 10 June 1836. Ordained a high priest, by 18 Nov. 1835. Moved to Ray Co., Missouri, summer 1836. As high councilor, attended meeting in Far West, Caldwell Co., Missouri, 28 May 1837. Appointed member of high council at organization of Adam-ondi-Ahman stake, 28 June 1838, in Daviess Co., Missouri. Moved to Quincy, Adams Co., Illinois, by late 1838. Returned to Norton, by 1840. Signed petition to U.S. Congress in Nauvoo, Hancock Co., Illinois, 28 Nov. 1843, to redress persecution and expulsion of Mormons from Missouri. Lived at Nauvoo, 1844. Moved to Washington Co., Iowa, by 24 Jan. 1849; to Marshall Co., Iowa, by 1850; and to Eldora, Hardin Co., Iowa, by 1856. Resided at Clay, Hardin Co., 1860. Moved to Cedar Falls, Black Hawk Co., Iowa, by 1870. Buried in Greenwood Cemetery, Cedar Falls.

Granger, Julius (16 Dec. 1805–26 Apr. 1871). Born in Phelps, Ontario Co., New York. Son of Pierce Granger and Clarissa Trumbull. Moved to Kent Co., Michigan Territory, by 1833. Moved to Geauga Co., Ohio, by 1838. Married Caroline H. Merrill, 20 Feb. 1840, in Geauga Co. Moved to Grand Rapids, Kent Co., by Apr. 1840. Helped organize Grand River Masonic Lodge in Grand Rapids, 19 Mar. 1849. Moved to Wyoming, Kent Co., by 1860. Returned to Grand Rapids, by 1870. Died at Grand Rapids.

Granger, Oliver (7 Feb. 1794–23/25 Aug. 1841), sheriff, church agent. Born at Phelps, Ontario Co., New York. Son of Pierce Granger and Clarissa Trumble. Married Lydia Dibble, 8 Sept. 1813, at Phelps. Member of Methodist church and licensed exhorter. Sheriff of Ontario Co. and colonel in militia. Nearly blind from 1827 onward. Lived at Phelps, 1830. Baptized into LDS church and ordained an elder by Brigham and Joseph Young, ca. 1832–1833, at Sodus, Wayne Co., New York. Moved to Kirtland, Geauga Co., Ohio, 1833. Served mission to eastern states with Samuel Newcomb. Ordained a high priest, 29 Apr. 1836, at Kirtland. Served mission to New York with John P. Greene, spring 1836. Appointed to Kirtland high council, 8 Oct. 1837. Appointed to settle JS's business affairs in Kirtland, 1838. Left Kirtland for Far West, Caldwell Co., Missouri, June 1838, possibly to confer regarding JS's Kirtland business affairs. Directed in July 1838 revelation to move to Far West. Returned to Kirtland to settle JS's affairs. Acted as agent in securing lands in Lee Co., Iowa Territory, May 1839. Appointed to preside over church in Kirtland, 4 May 1839. Died at Kirtland.

Greene, John Portineus (3 Sept. 1793–10 Sept. 1844), farmer, shoemaker, printer, publisher. Born at Herkimer, Herkimer Co., New York. Son of John Coddington Greene and Anna Chapman. Married first Rhoda Young, 11 Feb. 1813. Moved to Aurelius, Cayuga Co., New York, 1814; to Brownsville, Ontario Co., New York, 1819; to Watertown, Jefferson Co., New York, 1821; and to Mentz, Cayuga Co., 1826. Member of Methodist Episcopal Church; later, member of Methodist Reformed Church. A founder of Methodist Protestant Church, 1828. Moved to Conesus, Livingston Co., New York, 1829. Moved to Mendon, Monroe Co., New York, by 1832. Baptized into LDS church by Eleazer Miller, Apr. 1832, at Mendon; ordained an elder by Miller shortly after. Organized branch of church at Warsaw, Genesee Co., New York, 1832. Moved to Kirtland, Geauga Co., Ohio, Oct. 1832. Appointed to preside over branch in Parkman, Geauga Co., spring 1833. Returned to Kirtland, fall 1833. Ordained a high priest and left to serve mission to eastern U.S., 16 Sept. 1833. Left to serve mission to western New York and Canada, 25 Feb. 1834. Served mission to eastern U.S., 1835. Appointed member of Kirtland high council, 13 Jan. 1836. Served mission to Ohio to raise funds for Kirtland temple, Mar. 1836. Left to serve mission to New York, 13 July 1836. Stockholder in Kirtland Safety Society. Left to serve mission to Canada, 16 Nov. 1837. Moved to Far West, Caldwell Co., Missouri, 1838. Member of Caldwell Co. militia. Participated in skirmish at Crooked River, near Ray Co., Missouri, 25 Oct. 1838. Moved to Quincy, Adams Co., Illinois, Nov. 1838. Presided over church branches in New York and surrounding areas and collected donations for refugee Saints, 1839. Moved to Nauvoo, Hancock Co., Illinois, spring 1840. Member of Nauvoo City Council, 1841–1843. Married second Mary Eliza Nelson, 6 Dec. 1841, in Nauvoo. Member of Nauvoo Masonic Lodge. Member of Nauvoo Legion, 1842. Served mission to Ohio and New York, Aug. 1842. Elected Nauvoo city marshal, Dec. 1843. Assessor and collector of Nauvoo Fourth Ward. Admitted to Council of Fifty, 26 Mar. 1844. Carried out orders of JS and city council to suppress *Nauvoo Expositor* press, 10 June 1844. Died at Nauvoo.

Grover, Thomas (22 July 1807–20 Feb. 1886), farmer, boat operator. Born at Whitehall, Washington Co., New York. Son of Thomas Grover and Polly Spaulding. Married first Caroline Whiting of Whitehall, 1828. Became a Methodist preacher, by 1834. Moved to Freedom, Cattaraugus Co., New York, by 1834. Baptized into LDS church by Warren A. Cowdery, Sept. 1834, at Freedom. Moved to Kirtland, Geauga Co., Ohio, 1835. Ordained an elder, 2 Jan. 1836. Appointed to Kirtland high council, 1836. Removed his family to Far West, Caldwell Co., Missouri, where he served on high council, 1837. Member of committee at Far West to supervise removal of Latter-day Saints from Missouri, Jan. 1839. Moved to Adams Co., Illinois, by 7 May 1839. Located at Commerce (later Nauvoo), Hancock Co., Illinois, 1839. Appointed to Commerce high council, 1839. Member of Nauvoo Legion, 1841. Married second Caroline Nickerson Hubbard, 20 Feb. 1841, in Nauvoo. Served three short missions during early 1840s. Moved to Winter Quarters, unorganized U.S. territory (later in Omaha, Douglas Co., Nebraska), winter 1846–1847. Migrated to Salt Lake Valley, Oct. 1847; settled at Deuel Creek (later in Centerville), Davis Co., Utah Territory. Collected tithing in California, winter 1848–1849. Moved to Farmington, Davis Co., 1849. Moved to Kanesville (later Council Bluffs), Pottawattamie Co., Iowa, 1850; returned to Farmington, 1853. Member of Davis Co. high council. Served in Utah territorial legislature. Probate judge in Davis Co. Served mission to eastern U.S., 1874–1875. Died at Farmington.

Groves, Elisha Hurd (5 Nov. 1797–29 Dec. 1867), farmer. Born in Madison Co., Kentucky. Son of John Groves and Mary Hurd. Moved to Indiana, 1819. Married first Sarah Hogue, ca. 1825, in Indiana. Member of Presbyterian church. Baptized into LDS church by Calvin Beebe, 1 Mar. 1832, in Greene Co., Indiana; ordained an elder by Peter Dustin and Calvin Beebe shortly after in Greene Co. Divorced wife, by 1833. Moved to Jackson Co., Missouri, 1833. Served mission to Illinois, 1833–1834. Joined Camp of Israel expedition at Salt River, Monroe Co., Missouri, 1834. Ordained a high priest, 10 Sept. 1834, in Clay Co., Missouri. Served mission to Illinois, 1834. Moved to Kirtland, Geauga Co., Ohio, 1835. Labored on Kirtland temple. Served mission in Ohio, 1835. Appointed to Missouri high council, 1836, in Kirtland. Married second Lucy Simmons, 19 Jan. 1836, in Kirtland. Moved to Clay Co., 1836. Served mission to Kentucky to raise funds for church purchase of lands, 1836. Moved to what became Caldwell Co., Missouri, 1836. Served mission to Ohio to raise funds for construction of temple at Far West, Caldwell Co., 1836–1837. Moved to Daviess Co., Missouri, by spring 1838. Moved to Caldwell Co., Nov. 1838. Moved to Columbus, Adams Co., Illinois, 1839. Served mission to northern Illinois, 1839. Served mission to Wisconsin, 1841. Moved to Nauvoo, Hancock Co., Illinois, 1842. Served multiple missions in Illinois, 1842–1844. Appointed to settle Mount Pisgah, Clarke Co., Iowa Territory, 1846. Moved to Winter Quarters, unorganized U.S. territory (later in Omaha, Douglas Co., Nebraska), 1846. Migrated to Salt Lake City, 1848. Appointed to settle Iron Co., Utah Territory, 1850. Appointed to settle Harmony (later in New Harmony), Washington Co., Utah Territory, 1853. Died in Washington Co.

Hancock, Levi Ward (7 Apr. 1803–10 June 1882). Born at Springfield, Hampden Co., Massachusetts. Son of Thomas Hancock III and Amy Ward. Baptized into LDS church, 16 Nov. 1830, at Kirtland, Geauga Co., Ohio. Married Clarissa Reed, 20 Mar. 1831. Served mission to Missouri with Zebedee Coltrin, summer 1831. Appointed to serve mission to Missouri, Ohio, and Virginia, Jan. 1832. Attended organizational meeting of School of the Prophets, 22–23 Jan. 1833, in Kirtland. Participated in Camp of Israel expedition to Missouri, 1834. Ordained a seventy, 28 Feb. 1835; appointed a president of the Seventy shortly after. Moved to Missouri, 1838. Member of committee at Far West, Caldwell Co., Missouri, to supervise removal of Latter-day Saints from Missouri, Jan. 1839. Located at Commerce (later Nauvoo), Hancock Co., Illinois, 1839. Enlisted in Mormon Battalion at what became Council Bluffs, Pottawattamie Co., Iowa Territory; served 1846–1847. Only general authority of church on march; served as unofficial chaplain for battalion. Arrived in Salt Lake Valley, 1847. Member of Utah territorial legislature for three terms, beginning in 1851. Ordained a patriarch, 1872. Died at Washington, Washington Co., Utah Territory.

Hancock, Solomon (15 Aug. 1793/1794–2 Dec. 1847). Born at Springfield, Hampden Co., Massachusetts. Son of Thomas Hancock III and Amy Ward. Moved to Wolcott, Seneca Co., New York, by 1810. Joined Methodist church, 1814. Married first Alta Adams, 12 Mar. 1815. Moved to Columbia, Hamilton Co., Ohio, by 1823. Moved to Chagrin (later Willoughby), Cuyahoga Co., Ohio, by 1830. Baptized into LDS church, 16 Nov. 1830, in Ohio. Ordained an elder, by June 1831. Ordained a high priest by Lyman Wight, 4 June 1831, at Geauga Co., Ohio. Appointed to serve mission with Simeon Carter to Missouri, June 1831. Lived in Jackson Co., Missouri, by 1833. Appointed to Zion high council in Clay Co., Missouri, 1834. Served mission to eastern states, fall 1834. Wife died, 1836. Married second Phebe Adams, 28 June 1836. Moved to Caldwell Co., Missouri, by Dec. 1836. Served as member of Zion high council in Far West, Caldwell Co., 1837–1839. Expelled from Missouri, spring 1839; located at Adams Co., Illinois. Moved to Lima, Adams Co., 1841. Appointed member of Lima high council, 1843. Moved to Yelrome (Morley's Settlement, later in Tioga), Hancock Co., Illinois, ca. 1844, and presided over Yelrome branch of church. Died near what became Council Bluffs, Pottawattamie Co., Iowa.

Harris, George Washington (1 Apr. 1780–1857), jeweler. Born at Lanesboro, Berkshire Co., Massachusetts. Son of James Harris and Diana (Margaret) Burton. Married first Elizabeth, ca. 1800. Married second Margaret, who died in 1828. Moved to Batavia, Genesee Co., New York, by 1830. Married third Lucinda Pendleton, 30 Nov. 1830, at Batavia. Moved to Terre Haute, Vigo Co., Indiana, where baptized into LDS church by Orson Pratt, 1834. Moved to Far West, Missouri, by 1836. Appointed to Far West high council and ordained a high priest, 7 Apr. 1838. Owned land at Adam-ondi-Ahman, Daviess Co., Missouri, 1838. Expelled from Missouri; moved to Illinois, by 1839. Appointed to high council in Commerce (later Nauvoo), Hancock Co., Illinois, 5 Oct. 1839. Nauvoo city alderman, 1841–1845. President of Nauvoo Coach and Carriage Manufacturing Association. Started west with Mormon exodus from Nauvoo, 1846. Bishop and member of high council at Council Bluffs, Iowa Territory, 1846. Died at Council Bluffs.

Harris, Martin (18 May 1783–10 July 1875), farmer. Born at Easton, Albany Co., New York. Son of Nathan Harris and Rhoda Lapham. Moved with parents to area of Swift's Landing (later in Palmyra), Ontario Co., New York, 1793. Married first his first cousin Lucy Harris, 27 Mar. 1808, in Palmyra. Served in War of 1812 in New York militia. Became landowner of some 320 acres at Palmyra. Reportedly investigated Quakers, Universalists, Restorationists, Baptists, Methodists, and Presbyterians. Took transcript of Book of Mormon characters to Luther Bradish, Samuel Latham Mitchill, and Charles Anthon, Feb. 1828. Assisted JS as scribe during translation of first portion of Book of Mormon, ca. 12 Apr.–14 June 1828. One of the Three Witnesses of the Book of Mormon, June 1829. Separated from wife, after June 1830. Baptized into LDS church by Oliver Cowdery, 6 Apr. 1830. Ordained a priest, by 9 June 1830. Paid printing costs for publication of Book of Mormon through sale of 151 acres. Led members of Manchester, Ontario Co., branch from Palmyra to Kirtland, Geauga Co., Ohio, May 1831. Ordained a high priest by Lyman Wight, 4 June 1831, at Kirtland. Appointed to serve mission to Missouri, 6 June 1831. Appointed member of what became the Literary Firm, Nov. 1831. Appointed member of United Firm, Apr. 1832. Participated in Camp of Israel expedition to Missouri, 1834. Member of Kirtland high council, 1834. Married second Caroline Young, 1836/1837. Excommunicated, Dec. 1837. Rebaptized into LDS church, 1842, at Kirtland. Member of high council of James J. Strang's Church of Jesus Christ of Latter Day Saints at Kirtland, 7 Aug. 1846. Joined with William E. McLellin's religious movement, 1847. Initiated a new movement with William Smith and Chilton Daniels at Kirtland, likely 1855. Migrated to Salt Lake Valley, 1870. Rebaptized into LDS church, 1870. Died at Clarkston, Cache Co., Utah Territory.

Hawn (Haun), Jacob (13 Jan. 1804–27 Jan. 1860), miller, builder, carpenter. Born in Genesee Co., New York. Son of Henry Hawn. Consistently spelled surname as "Hawn" throughout life, but many contemporary records spelled name as "Haun." Married Harriet Elizabeth Pierson, 18 Nov. 1833, in either New Jersey or New York. Moved to Wisconsin. Moved to Shoal Creek area of what became Caldwell Co., Missouri, by Dec. 1835. Built mill and called settlement Hawn's Mill. Survived attack at Hawn's Mill, 1838. Moved to Oregon City, Clackamas District (later in Clackamas Co.), Oregon Country, 1843; to Moores Valley (likely near present-day Yamhill), Yamhill Co., Oregon Country, 1846; and to Lafayette, Yamhill Co., fall 1846. Died in Lafayette.

Higbee, Elias (23 Oct. 1795–8 June 1843), clerk, judge, surveyor. Born at Galloway, Gloucester Co., New Jersey. Son of Isaac Higbee and Sophia Somers. Moved to Clermont Co., Ohio, 1803. Married Sarah Elizabeth Ward, 10 Sept. 1818, in Tate Township, Clermont Co. Lived at Tate Township, 1820. Located at Fulton, Hamilton Co., Ohio, 1830. Baptized into LDS church, summer 1832, at Jackson Co., Missouri. Ordained an elder by Isaac Higbee, 20 Feb. 1833, at Cincinnati. Migrated to Jackson Co., Apr. 1833. Driven from Jackson Co. into Clay Co., Missouri, Nov. 1833. Ordained a high priest by Orson Pratt, 7 Aug. 1834, in Clay Co. Served mission to Missouri, Illinois, Indiana, and Ohio, 1835. Labored on Kirtland temple. Returned to Clay Co. Member of Zion high council in Clay Co., 1836. Moved to what became Caldwell Co., Missouri, spring 1836. Appointed county justice for Caldwell Co., 1837. Appointed presiding judge of court, Aug. 1838. Served on Zion high council in Far West, Caldwell Co., 1837–1838. With John Corrill, appointed a church historian, 6 Apr. 1838, at Far West. Appointed captain general of Society of the Daughter of Zion (Danites), summer 1838. Participated in skirmish at Crooked River, near Ray Co., Missouri, 25 Oct. 1838. Fled Missouri; located at Quincy, Adams Co., Illinois, 1839. Member of committee that investigated lands offered for sale by Isaac Galland, 1839. Settled at Commerce (later Nauvoo), Hancock Co., Illinois, 1839. Traveled to Washington DC with JS to seek redress for Missouri grievances, Oct. 1839–Mar. 1840. Appointed member of Nauvoo temple committee, 6 Oct. 1840. Appointed guard in Nauvoo Legion, Mar. 1841. Member of Nauvoo Masonic Lodge. Died at Nauvoo.

Higbee, Isaac (23 Dec. 1797–16 Feb. 1874), farmer, merchant, judge. Born in Galloway, Gloucester Co., New Jersey. Son of Isaac Higbee and Sophia Somers. Moved to Clermont Co., Ohio, ca. 1802. Married Keziah String, 11 Feb. 1819, in Clermont Co. Moved to Cincinnati, by 1830. Baptized into LDS church, May 1832. Ordained an elder by Lyman Wight and Calvin Wilson, 23 June 1832. Moved to Independence, Jackson Co., Missouri, spring 1833. Ordained a high priest, 22 Mar. 1835, in Clay Co., Missouri. Served mission in Illinois and Ohio, 1835–1838. Moved to Quincy, Adams Co., Illinois, Feb. 1839. Moved to Hancock Co., Illinois, by 1840. Appointed bishop by JS, 29 Feb. 1841, in Nauvoo, Hancock Co. Elected justice of the peace, Aug. 1843, in Nauvoo. Migrated to Salt Lake Valley; arrived 24 Sept. 1848. Appointed to preside over Saints in Utah Valley (later Provo, Utah Co., Utah), 28 May 1849. Served as first stake president in Provo, 1851–1852. Appointed probate judge in Utah Co., Dec. 1852. Appointed to serve mission to Europe, 1856. Died in Provo.

Hillman, Mayhew (Mahew) (4 Mar. 1793–2 Nov. 1839), farmer. Born at Chilmark, Dukes Co., Massachusetts. Son of Samson Hillman and Damaris Look. Married Sarah King, ca. 1818. Moved to Cambridge, Washington Co., New York, by Aug. 1820. Member of Freewill Baptist Church. Moved to Spafford, Onondaga Co., New York, 1823. Baptized into LDS church by Lyman E. Johnson, 10 Nov. 1832, at Spafford. Lived at Kirtland, Geauga Co., Ohio, 1833–1838. Ordained an elder, 29 Apr. 1836, in Kirtland. Stockholder in Kirtland Safety Society. Appointed to Kirtland high council, 3 Sept. 1837. Moved to western Missouri, 1838. Member of Adam-ondi-Ahman high council, 1838. Moved to Quincy, Adams Co., Illinois, spring 1839. Died at Commerce (later Nauvoo), Hancock Co., Illinois.

Hinkle, George M. (13 Nov. 1801–Nov. 1861), merchant, physician, publisher, minister, farmer. Born in Jefferson Co., Kentucky. Son of Michael Hinkle and Nancy Higgins. Married first Sarah Ann Starkey. Baptized into LDS church, 1832. Moved to Far West, Caldwell Co., Missouri. Served on high council at Clay Co., Missouri, and Caldwell Co., 1836–1838. Commissioned colonel in Missouri state militia, 1837. With John Murdock, purchased large number of lots for Mormon settlement in De Witt, Carroll Co., Missouri, 23 June 1838. During Missouri conflict in 1838, directed defense of De Witt and commanded Caldwell Co. militia and Mormon forces defending Far West. While assisting in negotiation of truce between state militia and Latter-day Saints at Far West, surrendered church leaders to General Samuel D. Lucas. Excommunicated, 17 Mar. 1839, at Quincy, Adams Co., Illinois. Moved to Duncan Prairie, Mercer Co., Illinois, 1839. Organized religious society named The Church of Jesus Christ, the Bride, the Lamb's Wife, 24 June 1840, at Moscow, Muscatine Co., Iowa Territory. Affiliated briefly with Sidney Rigdon and Church of Christ, 1845. Moved to Iowa Territory, by Dec. 1845. Wife died, 1 Dec. 1845. Returned to Mercer Co., by June 1850. Married second Mary Loman Hartman. Moved to Decatur Co., Iowa, by 1852. Moved to Adair Co., Iowa. Served in Civil War, 1861. Died at Decatur, Decatur Co.

Hitchcock, Reuben (2 Sept. 1806–9 Dec. 1883), attorney, judge, railroad executive. Born in Burton, Geauga Co., Ohio. Son of Peter Hitchcock and Nabby Cook. Moved to New Haven, New Haven Co., Connecticut. Graduated from Yale University, 1826. Taught at Burton Academy, ca. 1826–1829, in Burton. Admitted to Ohio bar, ca. 1831. Moved to Painesville, Geauga Co., ca. 1831. Married Sarah Marshall, 18 Sept. 1834, in Colebrook, Litchfield Co., Connecticut. Served as prosecuting attorney in Geauga Co., 1835–1839. Partner in law firm of Hitchcock & Wilder, 1837–1846. Involved in legal proceedings that included JS. President of First National Bank, 1838–1841, in Painesville. Served as presiding judge of court of common pleas for district that included Lake Co., Ohio, 1841. Moved to Cleveland and headed firm of Hitchcock, Wilson & Wade, 1846. Returned to Painesville, 1851. Served as judge of court of common pleas for district that included Geauga and Lake counties, 1852–1855. Served as vice president and legal advisor of Cleveland and Mahoning Railroad, 1855. Elected mayor of Painesville, 1874. Died in Clifton Springs, Ontario Co., New York.

Hotchkiss, Horace Rowe (15 Apr. 1799–21 Apr. 1849), merchant, land speculator. Born in East Haven, New Haven Co., Connecticut. Son of Heman Hotchkiss and Elizabeth Rowe. Moved to New Haven, New Haven Co., by 1815. Married Charlotte Austin Street, 22 Feb. 1824, in East Haven. Purchased land in and around Commerce (later Nauvoo), Hancock Co., Illinois, 1836; sold the land to JS and other church leaders, 1839, for development of Nauvoo. Died in New Haven.

Howden, John W. (ca. 1812–11 Sept. 1853), farmer, merchant, county clerk, American consul. Born in Vermont. Son of John Howden and Mary Smith. Moved to Geauga Co.,

Ohio, by Oct. 1836, and opened a dry goods store. Served as Geauga Co. clerk, 1840–1846. Married Elizabeth M. Adams, 30 Apr. 1844, in Lake Co., Ohio. Moved to Mentor, Lake Co., before 1850. Appointed American consul to Bermuda. Died at St. Georges, Bermuda.

Huntington, Dimick Baker (26 May 1808–1 Feb. 1879), farmer, blacksmith, shoemaker, constable, coroner, deputy sheriff, Indian interpreter. Born at Watertown, Jefferson Co., New York. Son of William Huntington and Zina Baker. Married Fannie Maria Allen, 28 Apr. 1830. Baptized into LDS church, 1 Aug. 1835. Ordained an elder at Kirtland, Geauga Co., Ohio. Constable at Caldwell Co., Missouri, and later deputy sheriff. Participated in skirmish at Crooked River, near Ray Co., Missouri, 25 Oct. 1838. Served as constable at Nauvoo, Hancock Co., Illinois. Drum major in Nauvoo Legion band, 1841. Appointed Nauvoo city marshal, 1841. Member of Nauvoo Masonic Lodge. Served as coroner, 1842–ca. 1846, in Nauvoo. Ordained a high priest by George Miller, 24/25 Sept. 1843, in Nauvoo. Arrested for destruction of *Nauvoo Expositor* press, 1844. Arrived in Salt Lake Valley, July 1847. Helped establish settlements at Utah and Sanpete counties. Served as interpreter in meetings between Indian tribes and settlers. Died at Salt Lake City.

Huntington, William, Sr. (28 Mar. 1784–19 Aug. 1846), farmer, brick maker, potash manufacturer. Born in New Grantham, Cheshire Co., New Hampshire. Son of William Huntington and Prescendia Lathrop. Married first Zina Baker, 28 Dec. 1806, in Plainfield, Sullivan Co., New Hampshire. Moved to Watertown Co., New York, by 1806. Joined Presbyterian church, 1816. Baptized into LDS church, Apr. 1835. Ordained an elder, 3 Sept. 1835. Moved to Kirtland, Geauga Co., Ohio, Oct. 1836. Appointed to Kirtland high council, fall 1837. Moved to Far West, Caldwell Co., Missouri, July 1838. Moved to Commerce (later Nauvoo), Hancock Co., Illinois, May 1839. Wife died, 8 July 1839, in Nauvoo. Married second Lydia Clisbee Partridge, 1840. Died in Pisgah, Harrison Co., Iowa.

Hyde, Orson (8 Jan. 1805–28 Nov. 1878), laborer, clerk, storekeeper, teacher, editor, businessman, lawyer, judge. Born at Oxford, New Haven Co., Connecticut. Son of Nathan Hyde and Sally Thorpe. Moved to Derby, New Haven Co., 1812. Moved to Kirtland, Geauga Co., Ohio, 1819. Joined Methodist church, ca. 1827. Later affiliated with reformed Baptists (later Disciples of Christ or Campbellites). Baptized into LDS church by Sidney Rigdon and ordained an elder by JS and Sidney Rigdon, Oct. 1831, at Kirtland. Ordained a high priest by Oliver Cowdery, 26 Oct. 1831. Appointed to serve mission to Ohio, Nov. 1831, in Orange, Cuyahoga Co., Ohio. Baptized many during proselytizing mission with Samuel H. Smith to eastern states, 1832. Attended organizational meeting of School of the Prophets, 22–23 Jan. 1833, in Kirtland. Appointed clerk to church presidency, 1833. Appointed to serve mission to Jackson Co., Missouri, summer 1833. Served mission to Pennsylvania and New York, winter and spring 1834. Member of Kirtland high council, 1834. Participated in Camp of Israel expedition to Missouri, 1834. Married to Marinda Nancy Johnson by Sidney Rigdon, 4 Sept. 1834, at Kirtland. Ordained member of Quorum of the Twelve by Oliver Cowdery, David Whitmer, and Martin Harris, 15 Feb. 1835, in Kirtland. Served mission to western New York and Upper Canada, 1836. Served mission to England with Heber C. Kimball, 1837–1838. Moved to Far West, Caldwell Co., Missouri, summer 1838. Sided with dissenters against JS, 1838. Lived in Missouri, winter 1838–1839. Removed from Quorum of the Twelve, 4 May 1839. Restored to Quorum of the Twelve, 27 June 1839, at Commerce (later Nauvoo), Hancock Co., Illinois. Served mission to Palestine to dedicate land for gathering of the

Jews, 1840–1842. Member of Nauvoo Masonic Lodge, 1842. Member of Nauvoo City Council, 1843–1845. Admitted to Council of Fifty, 13 Mar. 1844. Presented petition from JS to U.S. Congress, 1844. Participated in plural marriage during JS's lifetime. Departed Nauvoo during exodus to the West, mid-May 1846. Served mission to Great Britain, 1846–1847. Presided over Latter-day Saints in Iowa before migrating to Utah Territory. Appointed president of Quorum of the Twelve, 1847. Published *Frontier Guardian* at Kanesville (later Council Bluffs), Pottawattamie Co., Iowa, 1849–1852. Appointed to preside over church east of Rocky Mountains, 20 Apr. 1851, at Kanesville. Migrated to Utah Territory, 1852. Appointed associate judge of U.S. Supreme Court for Utah Territory, 1852. Elected to Utah territorial legislature, 27 Nov. 1852, 1858. Presided over church in Carson Co., Utah Territory (later in Nevada Territory), 1855–1856. Served colonizing mission to Sanpete Co., Utah Territory, by 1860; presided as ecclesiastical authority there, beginning 1860. Died at Spring City, Sanpete Co.

Jackman, Levi (28 July 1797–23 July 1876), carpenter, wainwright. Born at Vershire, Orange Co., Vermont. Son of Moses French Jackman and Elizabeth Carr. Moved to Batavia, Genesee Co., New York, 1810. Married first Angeline Myers Brady, 13 Nov. 1817, at Alexander, Genesee Co. Moved to Portage Co., Ohio, 1830. Baptized into LDS church by Harvey G. Whitlock, 7 May 1831, in Portage Co.; ordained an elder by Oliver Cowdery a few days later. Ordained a high priest by Oliver Cowdery, 25 Oct. 1831. Left for Jackson Co., Missouri, 2 May 1832. Moved to Clay Co., Missouri, Nov. 1833. Appointed member of Zion high council in Clay Co., summer 1834. Moved to Kirtland, Geauga Co., Ohio, July 1835. Labored on Kirtland temple, 1835–1836. Returned to Clay Co., 1836. Moved to Far West, Missouri, June 1836. Elected justice of the peace, 1836. Served on Zion high council in Far West, 1837–1839. Obtained land at Commerce (later Nauvoo), Hancock Co., Illinois, 1839. Labored on Nauvoo temple. Served mission, 1844. Married second Sally Plumb, 1846. Moved to Winter Quarters, unorganized U.S. territory (later in Omaha, Douglas Co., Nebraska), winter 1846–1847. Migrated with Brigham Young pioneer company to Salt Lake Valley, 1847. Appointed member of first high council in Salt Lake Valley. Ordained a patriarch. Moved to Salem, Utah Co., Utah Territory, Mar. 1864. Died at Salem.

Jackson, Sarah. See Lipstrap (Liptrap), Sarah.

Johnson, Luke (3 Nov. 1807–8 Dec. 1861), farmer, teacher, doctor. Born at Pomfret, Windsor Co., Vermont. Son of John Johnson and Alice (Elsa) Jacobs. Lived at Hiram, Portage Co., Ohio, when baptized into LDS church by JS, 10 May 1831. Ordained a priest by Christian Whitmer shortly after baptism. Ordained an elder, by Oct. 1831. Ordained a high priest by Oliver Cowdery, 25 Oct. 1831, at Orange, Cuyahoga Co., Ohio. Served missions to Ohio, Pennsylvania, Virginia, and Kentucky, 1831–1833. Married first Susan Harminda Poteet, 1 Nov. 1833, in Cabell Co., Virginia (later in West Virginia). Appointed to high council, 17 Feb. 1834, at Kirtland, Geauga Co., Ohio. Participated in Camp of Israel expedition to Missouri, 1834. Member of Quorum of the Twelve, 1835–1837. Served mission to eastern states, 1835, and to New York and Upper Canada, 1836. Constable in Kirtland. Stockholder in Kirtland Safety Society. Disfellowshipped, 3 Sept. 1837. Reinstated to church and membership in Quorum of the Twelve, 10 Sept. 1837. Excommunicated, 1838. Taught school in Virginia and also studied medicine, which he practiced at Kirtland. Rebaptized into LDS church by Orson Hyde, 8 Mar. 1846, at Nauvoo, Hancock Co.,

Illinois. Wife died, 1846. Married second America Morgan Clark, Mar. 1847. Member of Brigham Young pioneer company to Salt Lake Valley, 1847. Moved to St. John, Tooele Co., Utah Territory, 1858. Bishop at St. John. Died at Salt Lake City.

Johnson, Lyman Eugene (24 Oct. 1811–20 Dec. 1859), merchant, lawyer, hotelier. Born at Pomfret, Windsor Co., Vermont. Son of John Johnson and Alice (Elsa) Jacobs. Moved to Hiram, Portage Co., Ohio, Mar. 1818. Baptized into LDS church by Sidney Rigdon, Feb. 1831. Ordained an elder by Oliver Cowdery, 25 Oct. 1831, at Orange, Cuyahoga Co., Ohio. Ordained a high priest by Sidney Rigdon, 2 Nov. 1831. Served missions with Orson Pratt to eastern states and New England, 1832–1833, and to Upper Canada, 1834. Attended organizational meeting of School of the Prophets, 22–23 Jan. 1833, in Kirtland. Participated in Camp of Israel expedition to Missouri, 1834. Married Sarah Lang (Long), 4 Sept. 1834, in Geauga Co., Ohio. Member of Quorum of the Twelve, 1835–1838. Disfellowshipped, 3 Sept. 1837; restored to fellowship, 10 Sept. 1837. Migrated to Far West, Caldwell Co., Missouri. Excommunicated, 13 Apr. 1838. Member of Nauvoo Masonic Lodge, 1842. Lived in Iowa Territory, 1842. Practiced law at Davenport, Scott Co., Iowa Territory, and at Keokuk, Lee Co., Iowa Territory. Drowned near Prairie du Chien, Crawford Co., Wisconsin.

Kimball, Heber Chase (14 June 1801–22 June 1868), blacksmith, potter. Born at Sheldon, Franklin Co., Vermont. Son of Solomon Farnham Kimball and Anna Spaulding. Married Vilate Murray, 22 Nov. 1822, at Mendon, Monroe Co., New York. Member of Baptist church at Mendon, 1831. Baptized into LDS church by Alpheus Gifford, 15 Apr. 1832, at Mendon. Ordained an elder by Joseph Young, 1832. Moved to Kirtland, Geauga Co., Ohio, 1833. Participated in Camp of Israel expedition to Missouri, 1834. Ordained member of Quorum of the Twelve by Oliver Cowdery, David Whitmer, and Martin Harris, 14 Feb. 1835, at Kirtland. Served mission to the East with Quorum of the Twelve, 1835. Served mission to eastern states, 1836. Stockholder in Kirtland Safety Society. Presided over first Latter-day Saint missionaries to British Isles, 1837–1838. Moved to Far West, Caldwell Co., Missouri, 1838. Worked closely with Brigham Young and others in supervising removal of Latter-day Saints from Missouri, 1838–1839. Present at Far West temple site, 26 Apr. 1839, when members of Quorum of the Twelve formally began their missionary assignment to British Isles. In removing from Missouri, initially located at Quincy, Adams Co., Illinois, and then at Commerce (later Nauvoo), Hancock Co., Illinois, May 1839. Served mission with Quorum of the Twelve to British Isles, 1839–1841. Member of Nauvoo City Council, 1841–1845. Member of Nauvoo Masonic Lodge. Participated in plural marriage during JS's lifetime. Served mission to eastern states, 1843. Labored on Nauvoo temple. Admitted to Council of Fifty, 11 Mar. 1844. Joined exodus from Illinois into Iowa Territory, Feb. 1846. Member of Brigham Young pioneer company to Salt Lake Valley; arrived July 1847. Sustained as first counselor to Brigham Young in First Presidency at what became Council Bluffs, Pottawattamie Co., Iowa, 27 Dec. 1847. Elected lieutenant governor in provisional state of Deseret. Served in Utah territorial legislature. Died at Salt Lake City.

Kimball, Presendia Lathrop Huntington (7 Sept. 1810–1 Feb. 1892), schoolteacher, midwife. Born in Watertown, Jefferson Co., New York. Daughter of William Huntington and Zina Baker. Married first Norman Buell, 6 Jan. 1827, likely in Jefferson Co. Resided in Mannsville, Jefferson Co., for first few years of marriage. Moved to Lewis Co., New York, ca. 1829; to Ellisburg, Jefferson Co., by 1830; to Lorraine, Jefferson Co., ca. 1834; and to Kirtland, Geauga Co., Ohio, spring 1836. Baptized into LDS church, 1 June 1836, in Kirtland. Moved to Fishing River, Clay Co., Missouri, by 1838. Settled between Quincy, Adams Co., Illinois, and Nauvoo, Hancock Co., Illinois, fall 1840. Later identified herself as a plural wife of JS, married on 11 Dec. 1841. Joined Female Relief Society of Nauvoo, 19 Apr. 1842. Married third Heber C. Kimball, 1845, in Nauvoo. Left first husband, May 1846. Lived in Winter Quarters, unorganized U.S. territory (later in Omaha, Douglas Co., Nebraska), 1846–1847. Migrated to Salt Lake Valley, 1848. Joined board of health in Salt Lake City, ca. 1851. Moved to Springville, Utah Co., Utah Territory, 1858. Moved to Provo, Utah Co. Moved to Salt Lake City Seventeeth Ward, ca. spring 1859, and to Salt Lake City Sixteenth Ward, ca. fall 1859. Appointed secretary of Sixteenth Ward Relief Society at its organization, 15 June 1868. Died in Salt Lake City.

Kimball, Vilate Murray (1 June 1806–22 Oct. 1867). Born in Florida, Montgomery Co., New York. Daughter of Roswell Murray and Susannah Fitch. Moved to Bloomfield, Ontario Co., New York, by 1810. Moved to Victor, Ontario Co., by 1820. Married Heber Chase Kimball, 22 Nov. 1822, at Mendon, Monroe Co., New York. Baptized into LDS church by Joseph Young, Apr. 1832, in Mendon. Moved to Kirtland, Geauga Co., Ohio, fall 1833. Made clothes for workmen and veils of Kirtland House of the Lord, ca. 1834–1836. Moved to Far West, Caldwell Co., Missouri, July 1838; to Atlas and Quincy, Adams Co., Illinois, 1839; and to Commerce (later Nauvoo), Hancock Co., Illinois, ca. 1840. Joined Female Relief Society of Nauvoo, 24 Mar. 1842. Among first women to perform ordinances in Nauvoo temple. Moved to Winter Quarters, unorganized U.S. territory (later in Omaha, Douglas Co., Nebraska), 1846. Migrated to Salt Lake Valley; arrived Sept. 1848. Died in Salt Lake City.

King, Austin Augustus (21 Sept. 1802–22 Apr. 1870), attorney, judge, politician, farmer. Born at Sullivan Co., Tennessee. Son of Walter King and Nancy Sevier. Married first Nancy Harris Roberts, 13 May 1828, at Jackson, Madison Co., Tennessee. In 1830, moved to Missouri, where he practiced law at Columbia, Boone Co. Served as colonel in Black Hawk War, 1832. Elected to state legislature as Jacksonian Democrat from Boone Co., 1834, 1836. In 1837, removed to Richmond, Ray Co., Missouri, where he received appointment as circuit judge in northwestern Missouri by Governor Lilburn W. Boggs. Between 1837 and 1848, served as judge of Missouri's Fifth Judicial Circuit, consisting of counties of Clinton, Ray, Caldwell, Clay, Daviess, Carroll, and Livingston. In Nov. 1838, presided at preliminary hearing of JS and other Mormons at Richmond; committed them to jail pending trials to be held Mar. 1839. Governor of Missouri, 1848–1852. Married second Martha Anthony Woodson, 10 Aug. 1858, in Kingston, Caldwell Co. Represented Missouri in U.S. Congress, 1863–1865. Died at St. Louis.

Knight, Newel (13 Sept. 1800–11 Jan. 1847), miller, merchant. Born at Marlborough, Windham Co., Vermont. Son of Joseph Knight Sr. and Polly Peck. Moved to Jericho (later Bainbridge), Chenango Co., New York, ca. 1809. Moved to Windsor (later in Colesville), Broome Co., New York, 1811. Married first Sarah (Sally) Coburn, 7 June 1825. Became acquainted with JS when Knight's father hired JS, 1826. Baptized into LDS church by David Whitmer, last week of May 1830, in Seneca Co., New York. Ordained a priest, 26 Sept. 1830. President of Colesville branch of church; led Colesville branch from Broome Co. to

Thompson, Geauga Co., Ohio, Apr.–May 1831. Ordained an elder, before June 1831. Moved again with Colesville branch to Kaw Township, Jackson Co., Missouri, July 1831. Ordained a high priest, by July 1832. Expelled from Jackson Co. and moved to Clay Co., Missouri, Nov. 1833. Appointed member of Zion high council in Clay Co., July 1834. Wife died, Sept. 1834. Lived at Kirtland, Geauga Co., Ohio, spring 1835–spring 1836. Married second to Lydia Goldthwaite Bailey by JS, 24 Nov. 1835, at Kirtland. Lived at Clay Co., 1836. Served on Zion high council at Far West, Caldwell Co., Missouri, 1837–1838. Expelled from Missouri and moved to Commerce (later Nauvoo), Hancock Co., Illinois, 1839. Member of Commerce/ Nauvoo high council, 1839–1845. Left Nauvoo, 1846. Died at Fort Ponca (near present-day Niobrara in northern Nebraska).

Knight, Vinson (14 Mar. 1804–31 July 1842), farmer, druggist, school warden. Born at Norwich, Hampshire Co., Massachusetts. Son of Rudolphus Knight and Rispah (Rizpah) Lee. Married Martha McBride, July 1826. Moved to Perrysburg, Cattaraugus Co., New York, by 1830. Owned farm at Perrysburg when baptized into LDS church, spring 1834. Moved to Kirtland, Geauga Co., Ohio, by 24 June 1835. Ordained an elder, 2 Jan. 1836. Ordained high priest and appointed counselor to Bishop Newel K. Whitney, 13 Jan. 1836, at Kirtland. Stockholder in Kirtland Safety Society. Appointed township clerk, 1837. Traveled with JS and others to Far West, Caldwell Co., Missouri, 1837. Located at Adam-ondi-Ahman, Daviess Co., Missouri, summer 1838. Appointed acting bishop at Adam-ondi-Ahman, 28 June 1838. Expelled from Missouri; located at Quincy, Adams Co., Illinois, 1839. Church land agent; with others purchased approximately 19,000 acres of "Half-Breed Tract" in Lee Co., Iowa Territory, from Isaac Galland, and about 190 acres in Hancock Co., Illinois, from Galland and Hugh White, 1839. Appointed bishop in Commerce (later Nauvoo), Hancock Co., 4 May 1839. Appointed bishop of Lower Ward at Commerce, 5 Oct. 1839. Instructed in JS revelation to buy stock for building Nauvoo House, 19 Jan. 1841. Member of Nauvoo City Council, 1841–1842. Served as warden of Nauvoo common schools and member of Nauvoo University building committee, 1841–1842. Appointed guard in Nauvoo Legion, Mar. 1841. Member of Nauvoo Masonic Lodge. Died at Nauvoo.

Lipstrap (Liptrap), Sarah (ca. 1814–26 Sept. 1876). Born in Kentucky. Married first Mr. Jackson. Moved from Alton, Madison Co., Illinois, to area near Guymon's horse mill, Caldwell Co., Missouri, 1837. Submitted written testimony for appeal heard before Far West high council, 28 Apr. 1838. Lived at Kaw Township, Jackson Co., Missouri, 1850. Married second James Lipstrap (Liptrap), 28 May 1853, at Jackson Co. Lived at Kansas City, Jackson Co., 1860. Moved to Holton, Jackson Co., Kansas, by 1875. Died near Holton.

Lucas, Robert (1 Apr. 1781–7 Feb. 1853), surveyor, store owner, justice of the peace, military officer, politician. Born in Shepherdstown, Berkley Co., Virginia (later in Jefferson Co., West Virginia). Son of William Lucas and Susannah Barnes. Moved to Scioto Co., Northwest Territory (later Ohio), 1800. Appointed Scioto Co. surveyor, 1803. Served as Scioto Co. justice of the peace. Served in Ohio militia, 1804–1812. Served in Ohio House of Representatives, 1808–1809, 1831–1832. Married first Elizabeth Brown, 4 Apr. 1810. Wife died, 1812. Served in War of 1812. Served in Ohio Senate, 1814–1822, 1824–1830. Married second Friendly Ashley Sumner, 7 Mar. 1816. Moved to Piketon, Pike Co., Ohio, ca. 1816, and opened a general store. Joined Methodist church, 1819. Moved to Seal Township, Pike Co., by 1830. Served as chairman of Democratic National Convention, 1832. Served as governor of Ohio, 1832–1836. Appointed first governor of Iowa Territory, 1838. Moved near Iowa City, Johnson Co., Iowa Territory, by 1841. Died at Iowa City.

Lyman, Amasa Mason (30 Mar. 1813–4 Feb. 1877), boatman, gunsmith, farmer. Born at Lyman, Grafton Co., New Hampshire. Son of Boswell Lyman and Martha Mason. Baptized into LDS church by Lyman E. Johnson, 27 Apr. 1832. Moved to Hiram, Portage Co., Ohio, May–June 1832. Ordained an elder by JS and Frederick G. Williams, 23 Aug. 1832, at Hiram. Left to serve mission with Zerubbabel Snow to southern Ohio and Virginia, 24 Aug. 1832. Left to serve mission to New York and New Hampshire, 21 Mar. 1833. Ordained a high priest by Lyman E. Johnson and Orson Pratt, 11 Dec. 1833, in Elk Creek, Otsego Co., New York. Participated in Camp of Israel expedition to Missouri, 1834. Ordained a seventy by JS, Oliver Cowdery, and Sidney Rigdon, May/June 1835. Married Maria Louisa Tanner, 10 June 1835, at Kirtland, Geauga Co., Ohio. Served mission to New York, spring 1836. Stockholder in Kirtland Safety Society. Moved to Far West, Caldwell Co., Missouri, 1837; to McDonough Co., Illinois, winter 1839–1840; to Lee Co., Iowa Territory, spring 1840; and to Nauvoo, Hancock Co., Illinois, spring 1841. Served mission to northern Illinois and Wisconsin Territory, 1841. Appointed to serve mission to raise funds for construction of Nauvoo temple and Nauvoo House, Oct. 1841. Served mission to Tennessee, spring 1842. Member of Nauvoo Masonic Lodge. Member of Nauvoo City Council, 1842–1843. Ordained member of Quorum of the Twelve, 20 Aug. 1842, at Nauvoo. Elected a regent of University of Nauvoo, 20 Aug. 1842. Served mission to southern Illinois, 1842. Served colonizing mission to Shokokon, Henderson Co., Illinois, Feb.–June 1843; returned to Nauvoo, summer 1843. Counselor in First Presidency, 1843–1844. Admitted to Council of Fifty, 26 Mar. 1844. Served mission to reclaim Saints who followed James Emmett to vicinity of present-day Vermillion, Clay Co., South Dakota, Feb.–Mar. 1845. Trustee of Nauvoo House Association, Apr. 1845. Moved to Winter Quarters, unorganized U.S. territory (later in Omaha, Douglas Co., Nebraska), 1846. Captain of wagon companies to Salt Lake Valley, 1847, 1848. Appointed to establish settlement at San Bernardino, Los Angeles Co., California, 1851. Migrated to Salt Lake Valley, 1858. President of European mission, 1860–1862. Moved to Fillmore, Millard Co., Utah Territory, 1863. Deprived of apostleship, 6 May 1867, and excommunicated, 12 May 1870. President of Godbeite Church of Zion, 1870. Died at Fillmore.

Lyon, Aaron Child (ca. 1781–30 Sept. 1839). Born in Holland, Hampton Co., Massachusetts. Married Roxana (Rocksey) Palmer, 15 July 1804, at Orwell, Rutland Co., Vermont. Presumably baptized into LDS church. Acquired land at Caldwell Co., Missouri, including town lot at Far West. Helped found settlement near Guymon's mill in central Caldwell Co. Used claims of revelation to attempt to coerce Sarah Jackson to marry him. Jackson's husband brought charges. Appealed case to Zion high council in Far West, which stripped him of high priest office, 28 Apr. 1838. Expelled from Missouri, 1838. Died at Bear Creek, Hancock Co., Illinois.

Markham, Stephen (9 Feb. 1800–10 Mar. 1878), carpenter, farmer, stock raiser. Born at Rush (later Avon), Ontario Co., New York. Son of David Markham and Dinah Merry. Moved to Mentor, Geauga Co., Ohio, 1809. Moved to Unionville, Geauga Co., 1810. Married Hannah Hogaboom, before 1824. Moved to Chester, Geauga Co., by July 1824. Baptized into LDS church by Abel Lamb, July 1837, at Kirtland, Geauga Co. Led company of sixty Latter-day Saints to Far West, Caldwell Co., Missouri, 1838. Appointed member of committee at Far West to supervise removal of Latter-day Saints from Missouri, Jan. 1839. Escorted family of JS from Far West to Quincy, Adams Co., Illinois, Feb. 1839. Returned to Far West and assisted in disposal of Mormon properties. Moved to Nauvoo, Hancock Co., Illinois, before 1841. Commissioned a captain in Nauvoo Legion, Feb. 1841. Appointed counselor to Nauvoo priests quorum president Samuel Rolfe, 21 Mar. 1841. Elected lieutenant colonel in Nauvoo Legion, 1 May 1841. Member of Nauvoo Masonic Lodge. Elected Nauvoo city alderman, 8 Feb. 1843. Ordained an elder, Apr. 1843, in Nauvoo. Sent to serve mission to Berlin, Huron Co., Ohio, Apr. 1843. Appointed to serve mission to Illinois, 15 Apr. 1844. Ordained a high priest, 7 Oct. 1844, in Nauvoo. Captain in Brigham Young pioneer company migrating to Salt Lake Valley, 1847. Returned to Winter Quarters, unorganized U.S. territory (later in Omaha, Douglas Co., Nebraska), Aug. 1847. Settled in Davis Co., Utah Territory, 1850. Served colonizing mission to southern Utah Co., Utah Territory, 1851, and helped settle towns of Spanish Fork and Palmyra in Utah Co. Served colonizing mission to Fort Supply, near present-day Green River, Wyoming. Returned to Spanish Fork, Sept. 1857. Died at Spanish Fork.

Marks, William (15 Nov. 1792–22 May 1872), farmer, printer, publisher, postmaster. Born at Rutland, Rutland Co., Vermont. Son of Cornell (Cornwall) Marks and Sarah Goodrich. Married first Rosannah R. Robinson, 2 May 1813. Lived at Portage, Allegany Co., New York, where he was baptized into LDS church, by Apr. 1835. Ordained a priest, by 3 Apr. 1835. Ordained an elder, by 3 June 1836. Moved to Kirtland, Geauga Co., Ohio, by Sept. 1837. Appointed member of Kirtland high council, 3 Sept. 1837, and agent to Bishop Newel K. Whitney, 17 Sept. 1837. President of Kirtland stake, 1838. While at Kirtland, appointed stake president at Far West, Caldwell Co., Missouri, 8 July 1838. En route to Missouri when difficulties in that state were confirmed. Located with Latter-day Saints at Quincy, Adams Co., Illinois, 1839. Appointed president of stake in Commerce (later Nauvoo), Hancock Co., Illinois, 5 Oct. 1839. Instructed in JS revelation to buy stock for building Nauvoo House, 19 Jan. 1841. Nauvoo city alderman, 1841–1843. Appointed a regent of University of Nauvoo, 3 Feb. 1841. Appointed guard in Nauvoo Legion, Mar. 1841. Member of Nauvoo Masonic Lodge. Admitted to Council of Fifty, 19 Mar. 1844. Aligned himself with leadership claims of Sidney Rigdon following death of JS, 1844. Rejected from Council of Fifty, 4 Feb. 1845. Left Nauvoo, Mar. 1845. Appointed counselor to James J. Strang, 6 Mar. 1846. Located at Shabbona, De Kalb Co., Illinois, by June 1850. Affiliated with Charles B. Thompson, 1852–1853, and John E. Page, 1855, in leadership of new Mormon movements. Baptized into RLDS church, 10 June 1859, at Amboy, Lee Co., Illinois. Ordained a counselor in RLDS church presidency, 8 Apr. 1863. Married second Julia A. Muir, 5 Sept. 1866, in Shabbona. Moved to Little Rock, Kendall Co., Illinois, by June 1870. Died at Plano, Kendall Co.

Marsh, Thomas Baldwin (1 Nov. 1800–Jan. 1866), farmer, hotel worker, waiter, horse groom, grocer, type foundry worker, teacher. Born at Acton, Middlesex Co., Massachusetts. Son of James Marsh and Molly Law. Married first Elizabeth Godkin, 1 Nov. 1820, at New York City. Moved to Boston, 1822. Joined Methodist church at Boston. Migrated to Palmyra, Wayne Co., New York, by Sept. 1830. Baptized into LDS church by David Whitmer, 3 Sept. 1830, at Cayuga Lake, Seneca Co., New York. Ordained an elder by Oliver Cowdery, Sept. 1830. Moved to Kirtland, Geauga Co., Ohio, with Manchester, Ontario Co., New York, branch of church, May 1831. Ordained a high priest by Lyman Wight, 4 June 1831, at Kirtland. Served mission to Missouri, June 1831–Jan. 1832. Moved to Jackson Co., Missouri, 10 Nov. 1832. Appointed president of Big Blue River, Jackson Co., branch. Expelled from Jackson Co., 1833. Lived in Lafayette Co., Missouri, winter 1833–1834. Member of Zion high council in Clay Co., Missouri, 1834. Ordained member of Quorum of the Twelve, 26 Apr. 1835, at Kirtland. Sustained as president of Quorum of the Twelve, 2 May 1835. Served mission with the Twelve to eastern states, 1835. President pro tempore of church in Far West, Caldwell Co., Missouri, 10 Feb. 1838. Withdrew from church at Far West, 22 Oct. 1838. Excommunicated in absentia, 17 Mar. 1839, at Quincy, Adams Co., Illinois. Moved to Clay Co. and Ray Co., Missouri, before settling in Bonne Femme, Howard Co., Missouri, by June 1840. Moved to Grundy Co., Missouri, by 1854. Wife died, 1854. Sought readmittance into LDS church, Jan. 1857. Rebaptized at Florence, Douglas Co., Nebraska, 16 July 1857. Married second Hannah Adams, 4 Oct. 1857. Migrated to Utah Territory, 1857. Settled at Spanish Fork, Utah Co., Utah Territory, where he taught school. Moved to Ogden, Weber Co., Utah Territory, latter part of 1862. Died at Ogden.

McLellin, William Earl (18 Jan. 1806–14 Mar. 1883), schoolteacher, physician, publisher. Born at Smith Co., Tennessee. Son of Charles McLellin and Sarah (a Cherokee Indian). Married first Cynthia Ann, 30 July 1829. Wife died, by summer 1831. Baptized into LDS church by Hyrum Smith, 20 Aug. 1831, in Jackson Co., Missouri. Ordained an elder by Hyrum Smith and Edward Partridge, 24 Aug. 1831. Ordained a high priest by Oliver Cowdery, 25 Oct. 1831. Served two short-term missions. Married second Emeline Miller, 26 Apr. 1832, at Portage Co., Ohio. Left Ohio for Independence, Jackson Co., Missouri, 2 May 1832. Excommunicated, 3 Dec. 1832. Apparently reinstated; served mission to Missouri and Illinois with Parley P. Pratt, Jan.–June 1833. Fled with fellow Latter-day Saints from Jackson Co. into Clay Co., Missouri, Nov. 1833. Proselytized in Indiana on way to Kirtland, Geauga Co., Ohio, 1834. Appointed instructor in Kirtland School, 19 Nov. 1834. Ordained member of Quorum of the Twelve, 15 Feb. 1835. Disfellowshipped over difficulties arising during eastern mission with Quorum of the Twelve; reinstated 26 Sept. 1835. Wrote letter of withdrawal from church, Aug. 1836. Again sustained to Quorum of the Twelve, 3 Sept. 1837, at Kirtland. In Far West, Caldwell Co., Missouri, commissioned captain in First Company, Fifty-Ninth Regiment, Second Brigade, Third Division of Missouri state militia, 22 Nov. 1837. Excommunicated, 1838. Associated with factions organized under leadership of George M. Hinkle, William Law, Sidney Rigdon, James J. Strang, David Whitmer, and Granville Hedrick. Broke with all organized religion, 1869. Died at Independence.

McRae, Alexander (7 Sept. 1807–20 June 1891), tailor, sheriff, prison warden. Born in Anson Co., North Carolina. Son of John B. McRae and Mary. Moved to South Carolina; to Iredell Co., North Carolina; and back to South Carolina. Enlisted in U.S. Army, Mar. 1829, and served five years. Moved to Louisville, Jefferson Co., Kentucky, 1834. Married first Eunice Fitzgerald, 2 Oct. 1834, in New Castle, Henry Co., Kentucky. Moved to Ripley Co., Indiana, before June 1837. Baptized into LDS church, June 1837. Moved to Far West, Caldwell Co., Missouri, Sept. 1837. Participated in Mormon conflict, Oct. 1838. With JS in jail at Liberty, Clay Co., Missouri, 1 Dec. 1838–Apr. 1839. Moved to Quincy, Adams Co., Illinois, 1839. Ordained a seventy, 1839, at Quincy. Moved back to Ripley Co. Appointed aide-de-camp in Nauvoo Legion, 20 Feb. 1841. Moved to Nauvoo, Hancock Co., Illinois, before 1842. Served mission to North Carolina, 1844. Returned to Indiana after death of JS. Moved back to Nauvoo, spring 1845. Moved to Winter Quarters, unorganized U.S. territory (later in Omaha, Douglas Co., Nebraska), by May 1847. Moved to Kanesville (later Council Bluffs), Pottawattamie Co., Iowa, by Sept. 1850. Elected sheriff of Pottawattamie Co. Moved to Salt Lake City, 1852. Married second Caroline Amelia Webb, 1856, in Salt Lake City. Served mission to southern states, 1869–1870. Died in Salt Lake City.

Middleton, Julia Murdock Smith (30 Apr. 1831–12 Sept. 1880). Born in Warrensville, Cuyahoga Co., Ohio. Daughter of John Murdock and Julia Clapp. After death of mother, adopted by JS and Emma Smith at age of nine days. Lived in Hiram, Portage Co., Ohio, 1831. Moved to Kirtland, Geauga Co., Ohio, 1832; to Far West, Caldwell Co., Missouri, 1838; near Quincy, Adams Co., Illinois, 1839; and to Commerce (later Nauvoo), Hancock Co., Illinois, later that year. Member of Nauvoo Fourth Ward, 1842. Married first Elisha Dixon, by 1850. Moved to Galveston, Galveston Co., Texas, ca. 1851. Moved back to Nauvoo, 1853, following husband's death. Married second John Jackson Middleton, 19 Nov. 1856, in Hancock Co. Converted to Catholicism. Lived in Sonora Township, Hancock Co., by 1860. Likely died in Sonora Township.

Miles, Daniel Sanborn (23 July 1772–12 Oct. 1845). Born at Sanbornton, Belknap Co., New Hampshire. Son of Josiah Miles and Marah Sanborn. Married Electa Chamberlin, 30 Sept. 1813. Moved to Bath, Grafton Co., New Hampshire, by 1820. Baptized into LDS church by Orson Pratt and Lyman E. Johnson, Apr. 1832, at Bath. Moved to Kirtland, Geauga Co., Ohio, 1836. Ordained an elder by Reuben Hedlock, 28 Feb. 1836, in Kirtland. Ordained a seventy by Hazen Aldrich, 20 Dec. 1836. Stockholder in Kirtland Safety Society. Appointed a president of the Seventy, 6 Apr. 1837. Arrived at Far West, Caldwell Co., Missouri, Mar. 1838. Early settler at Commerce (later Nauvoo), Hancock Co., Illinois. Died in Hancock Co.

Morey, George (30 Nov. 1803–15 Dec. 1875), farmer. Born at Pittstown, Rensselaer Co., New York. Son of William Morey and Anda Martin. Moved to Collinsville, Butler Co., Ohio, 1814. Married Sylvia Butterfield, 29 Oct. 1825, at Butler Co. Moved to Vermillion Co., Illinois, 1831. Baptized into LDS church, 1833. Located in Clay Co., Missouri, 1834; in Kirtland, Geauga Co., Ohio, 1835–1836; and in Far West, Caldwell Co., Missouri, by Aug. 1837. Member of Zion high council in Far West, 1837–1838. Participated in skirmish at Crooked River, near Ray Co., Missouri, 25 Oct. 1838. Returned to Vermillion Co., by June 1840. Moved to Nauvoo, Hancock Co., Illinois, by 1841. Ordained a high priest, 1841. Constable in Nauvoo, 1841. Member of Nauvoo Legion. Supported Sidney Rigdon as successor to JS. Moved to Brown Co., Illinois, late 1844; to DeKalb Co., Illinois, 1849; and to Whiteside Co., Illinois, 1851. Settled at Hamilton Township, Decatur Co., Iowa, 1852. Presided over Little River branch of RLDS church, in Pleasanton, Decatur Co., 1859. Died near Pleasanton.

Morley, Isaac (11 Mar. 1786–24 June 1865), farmer, cooper, merchant, postmaster. Born at Montague, Hampshire Co., Massachusetts. Son of Thomas Morley and Editha (Edith) Marsh. Family affiliated with Presbyterian church. Moved to Kirtland, Geauga Co.,

Ohio, before 1812. Married Lucy Gunn, June 1812, at Montague; immediately returned to Kirtland. Served in War of 1812 as private and captain in Ohio militia. Elected trustee of Kirtland, 1818. Baptized into reformed Baptist (later Disciples of Christ or Campbellite) faith by Sidney Rigdon, 1828. Baptized into LDS church by Parley P. Pratt, 15 Nov. 1830. Saints migrating from New York settled on his farm at Kirtland, 1831. Ordained a high priest by Lyman Wight, 4 June 1831. Counselor to Bishop Edward Partridge at Kirtland, 1831, and in Missouri, 1831–1838. Lived at Independence, Jackson Co., Missouri, 1831. Appointed to set in order branches of church in Missouri, 3 Dec. 1832. Appointed bishop, 25 June 1833. Driven from Jackson Co. into Clay Co., Missouri, Nov. 1833. Member of Missouri high council, by 19 Dec. 1833. Served mission to eastern U.S. with Edward Partridge, June–Oct. 1835. Returned to Missouri and moved family to what became Far West, Caldwell Co., Missouri, Apr. 1836. Ordained a patriarch by JS, Sidney Rigdon, and Hyrum Smith, 7 Nov. 1837. Moved to Hancock Co., Illinois, 1839; founded Yelrome (Morley's Settlement, later in Tioga), where he served as bishop. Appointed president of stake at Lima, Adams Co., Illinois, 22 Oct. 1840. Member of Masonic lodge in Nauvoo, Hancock Co. Moved to Nauvoo, 1845. Admitted to Council of Fifty, 11 Apr. 1845. Moved to Winter Quarters, unorganized U.S. territory (later in Omaha, Douglas Co., Nebraska), 1846. Migrated to Salt Lake Valley, 1848. Elected senator of provisional state of Deseret, 12 Mar. 1849. Led initial settlement of Latter-day Saints at Sanpete Valley, unorganized U.S. territory (later in Sanpete Co., Utah Territory), 28 Oct. 1849, and presided at Manti, Sanpete Co., 1849–1853. Member of Utah territorial legislature, 1851–1857. Died at Fairview, Sanpete Co.

Mulholland, James (1804–3 Nov. 1839). Born in Ireland. Baptized into LDS church. Married Sarah Scott, 8 Feb. 1838/1839, at Far West, Caldwell Co., Missouri. Engaged in clerical work for JS, 1838, at Far West. Ordained a seventy, 28 Dec. 1838. After expulsion from Missouri, lived at Quincy, Adams Co., Illinois, spring 1839. Relocated at Commerce (later Nauvoo), Hancock Co., Illinois, May 1839. Scribe for two of JS's journals, fall 1838 and 1839. Scribe in dictation of JS's personal history, beginning 11 June 1839. Appointed clerk for land contracts and subtreasurer of church at Commerce, 20 Oct. 1839. Died at Commerce.

Murdock, John (15 July 1792–23 Dec. 1871), farmer. Born at Kortright, Delaware Co., New York. Son of John Murdock Sr. and Eleanor Riggs. Joined Lutheran Dutch Church, ca. 1817, then Presbyterian Seceder Church shortly after. Moved to Orange, Cuyahoga Co., Ohio, ca. 1819. Baptized into Baptist church, at Orange. Married first Julia Clapp of Mentor, Geauga Co., Ohio, 14 Dec. 1823. Joined reformed Baptist (later Disciples of Christ or Campbellite) faith, ca. 1827. Baptized into LDS church by Parley P. Pratt, 5 Nov. 1830, at Kirtland, Geauga Co. Ordained an elder by Oliver Cowdery, 7 Nov. 1830, at Mayfield, Cuyahoga Co. Organized branches of church at Orange and Warrensville, Cuyahoga Co., 1831. Wife died following birth of twins, 30 Apr. 1831, at Warrensville. JS and Emma Smith adopted the twins, Joseph and Julia. Ordained a high priest by JS, 4 June 1831, at Kirtland. Left to serve mission to Missouri with Hyrum Smith, June 1831. Appointed to serve mission to Missouri, Ohio, and Virginia, Jan. 1832. Attended organizational meeting of School of the Prophets, 22–23 Jan. 1833, in Kirtland. Left to serve mission to eastern states with Zebedee Coltrin, Apr. 1833. Participated in Camp of Israel expedition to Missouri, 1834. Member of Zion high council in Clay Co.,

Missouri, 1834. Served mission to Vermont and New York, 1835–1836. Appointed president of Zion high council, 1836. Married second Amoranda Turner, 4 Feb. 1836; she died, 1837. Married third Electra Allen, 3 May 1838. With George M. Hinkle, purchased large number of lots for Mormon settlement in De Witt, Carroll Co., Missouri, 23 June 1838. Forced out of De Witt by vigilantes, 11 Oct. 1838; returned to Far West, 14 Oct. 1838. Left Far West for Quincy, Adams Co., Illinois, 4 Feb. 1839. Lived near Lima, Adams Co., 1839–1841. Moved to Nauvoo, Hancock Co., Illinois, spring 1841. Bishop of Nauvoo Fifth Ward, 1842–1844. Served mission to Indiana, Nov. 1844–Mar. 1845. Wife died, 1845. Married fourth Sarah Zufelt, 13 Mar. 1846, in Fulton Co., Illinois. Arrived in Salt Lake Valley, 24 Sept. 1847. Member of Salt Lake high council, ca. 1847–1849, and appointed bishop of Salt Lake City Fourteenth Ward, 1849. Served in Utah territorial legislature, 1849–1851. Served mission to Australia, 1851–1853. Moved to Lehi, Utah Co., Utah Territory, ca. 1854. Served as patriarch, Apr. 1854–Mar. 1867. Moved to Beaver, Beaver Co., Utah Territory, fall 1867. Died at Beaver.

Musick, Samuel (23 Mar. 1804–after 1860), farmer, tavern keeper, store owner. Born in Virginia. Son of Abram Musick. Married first Elizabeth, ca. 1829. Baptized into LDS church, by 1834. Moved to Clay Co., Missouri, by Sept. 1834. Ordained a teacher, Sept. 1834. Moved to Far West, where he opened a tavern, by Nov. 1836. Rented or sold his tavern to JS, spring 1838. Ordained an elder, 5 Oct. 1839. Moved to Nauvoo, Hancock Co., Illinois, by 1842. Member of Nauvoo Legion. Ordained a seventy, by 31 Aug. 1845. Moved to St. Louis, by 1850. Married second Rachel, ca. 1852. Moved to Pike Township, Stoddard Co., Missouri, by 1860.

Newberry, James Washington (9 Dec. 1817–7 Mar. 1895). Born in Orange Co., New York. Son of James Newberry and Mary Smith. Moved with family to Brownhelm, Lorain Co., Ohio, by 1830; to Jackson Co., Missouri; to Clay Co., Missouri; to Caldwell Co., Missouri, by 1838; and to Lee Co., Iowa Territory, by 1840. Married Edith A. Benedict, 19 Sept. 1847. Joined RLDS church, 5 July 1861. Died at Argyle, Lee Co.

Newell, Grandison (2 May 1785–10 June 1874), farmer, clockmaker, furniture maker, manufacturer, merchant, banker. Born in Barkhamsted, Litchfield Co., Connecticut. Son of Solomon Newell and Damaris Johnson. Married Betsy Smith, 16 Apr. 1807. Moved to Winsted, Litchfield Co.; to Harpersfield, Delaware Co., New York, by Jan. 1808; back to Barkhamsted, by 1816; and to Mentor, Geauga Co., Ohio, June 1819. Accused JS of conspiring to assassinate him, Apr. 1837. Moved to Painesville, Lake Co., Ohio, ca. 1843. Died at Painesville.

Noble, Joseph Bates (14 Jan. 1810–17 Aug. 1900), farmer, miller, stock raiser. Born in Egremont, Berkshire Co., Massachusetts. Son of Ezekiel Noble and Theodotia Bates. Moved to Penfield, Monroe Co., New York, 1815. Moved to Bloomfield, Ontario Co., New York, ca. 1828. Baptized into LDS church, 1832. Participated in Camp of Israel expedition to Missouri, 1834. Moved to Kirtland, Geauga Co., Ohio, by 1834. Married Mary Adeline Beman, 11 Sept. 1834, in New York. Appointed member of First Quorum of the Seventy, 1835. Received elder's license, 7 Apr. 1836, at Kirtland. Served mission to southern Ohio, 1836–1838. Stockholder in Kirtland Safety Society. Moved to Far West, Caldwell Co., Missouri, 1838. Moved to Montrose, Lee Co., Iowa Territory, 1839. Served as counselor to Bishop Elias Smith in Montrose. Moved to Nauvoo, Hancock Co., Illinois, 1841. Served as bishop in Nauvoo Fifth Ward, beginning 1841. Member of Nauvoo Masonic Lodge. Commissioned second lieutenant in Iowa territorial militia, beginning 1841. Appointed quartermaster sergeant in Nauvoo Legion, 3 June 1842. Participated in plural marriage during JS's lifetime. Migrated to Salt Lake Valley, 1847. Resided in Bountiful, Davis Co., Utah Territory. Moved to Montpelier, Bear Lake Co., Idaho, by 1900. Died at Wardboro, Bear Lake Co.

Osborn, Salmon Spring (21 Oct. 1804–4 Mar. 1904), attorney, bank executive. Born in Walton, Delaware Co., New York. Son of Samuel Osborn and Polly Webster. Moved to Jefferson, Ashtabula Co., Ohio, 1813; to Erie, Erie Co., Pennsylvania, 1814; and to Sandusky, Huron Co., Ohio, 1816. Opened law office in Chardon, Geauga Co., Ohio, in partnership with R. Giddings, 1828. Married Maria Lucretia Loomis, 9 Apr. 1833, in Ypsilanti, Washtenaw Co., Michigan Territory. Moved to Painesville, Geauga Co., ca. 1833. Formed law firm of Perkins & Osborn with William L. Perkins, 18 Feb. 1834, in Painesville. Law firm represented JS in various lawsuits; also represented others in suits against JS. Elected cashier of First National Bank of Painesville, 18 June 1849. Moved to Illinois, ca. 1871. Moved to Chicago, by 1880. Died in Chicago.

Page, John Edward (25 Feb. 1799–14 Oct. 1867). Born at Trenton, Oneida Co., New York. Son of Ebenezer Page and Rachel Hill. Married first Betsey Thompson, 1831, in Huron Co., Ohio. Baptized into LDS church by Emer Harris, 18 Aug. 1833, at Brownhelm, Lorain Co., Ohio. Ordained an elder by Ebenezer Page, Sept. 1833, at Florence, Erie Co., Ohio. Married second Lavona Stevens, 26 Dec. 1833, in Huron Co. Moved to Kirtland, Geauga Co., Ohio, 1835. Proselytized in Upper Canada, 1836–1837, and led company of converts from Upper Canada to Missouri, 1838. Located at De Witt, Carroll Co., Missouri, and then Far West, Caldwell Co., Missouri, 1838. Ordained member of Quorum of the Twelve, 19 Dec. 1838, at Far West. Married third Mary Judd, ca. Jan. 1839. Moved to Warsaw, Hancock Co., Illinois, 1839. With others of the Twelve, returned to Far West to fulfill revelatory directive, 26 Apr. 1839. Preached in eastern U.S., 1841–1842. Member of Masonic lodge in Nauvoo, Hancock Co. Presided over church in Pittsburgh, 1843. Published *Gospel Light,* 1843–1844. Served mission to Washington DC, 1843–1844. Admitted to Council of Fifty, 1 Mar. 1845. Removed from Quorum of the Twelve, 9 Feb. 1846. Excommunicated, 26 June 1846. Supported James J. Strang's claim as successor to JS. Dropped from Council of Fifty, 12 Nov. 1846. Editor of Strangite newspaper *Zion's Reveille,* 1847. Affiliated with faction led by James C. Brewster, 1849. Moved to Walworth Co., Wisconsin, by 1850. Held own religious services with William Marks and other friends, by 1855. Joined Church of Christ (Hedrickites), Nov. 1862. Died near Sycamore, De Kalb Co., Illinois.

Parks, Hiram Gartrell (ca. 1807–after 1880), farmer, military officer, sheriff, real estate agent, hatter. Born in Tennessee. Married first Nancy McGhee, 22 Apr. 1828, in Knox Co., Tennessee. Resided in Knoxville, Knox Co., 1830. Moved to Richmond, Ray Co., Missouri, by 1835. Ray Co. treasurer, 1835–1836. Member of board of trustees, 1835, at Richmond. Brigadier general in Missouri militia. Served in Mormon War, 1838. Moved to California, 1849. Married second Louise, ca. 1854, in California. Married third Sarah Miller, 7 June 1858, at Analy (later in Sebastopol), Sonoma Co., California. Moved to Bodega, Sonoma Co., by 1860. Married fourth Louisa McDonald, 23 June 1865. Served intermittently as sheriff and deputy sheriff, 1865–1880, at Santa Rosa, Sonoma Co. Patient at Sonoma County Hospital, 1880.

Parrish, Warren Farr (10 Jan. 1803–3 Jan. 1877), clergyman, gardener. Born in New York. Son of John Parrish and Ruth Farr. Married first Elizabeth (Betsey) Patten of Westmoreland Co., New Hampshire, ca. 1822. Lived at Alexandria, Jefferson Co., New York, 1830. Purchased land at Chaumont, Lyme Township, Jefferson Co., 1831. Baptized by Brigham Young, 20 May 1833, at Theresa, Jefferson Co. Participated in Camp of Israel expedition to Missouri, 1834. Wife died of cholera at Rush Creek, Clay Co., Missouri, while accompanying him on expedition, 27 June 1834. Served mission to Missouri, Kentucky, and Tennessee with David W. Patten, 1834. Appointed member of First Quorum of the Seventy, 1835. Served mission to Kentucky and Tennessee with Wilford Woodruff, 1835. Worked as scribe for JS, 1835. Married second to Martha H. Raymond by JS, 3 Dec. 1835, at Kirtland, Geauga Co., Ohio. Appointed clerk of Kirtland Safety Society, 1836. Later appointed in place of JS as officer of society, July 1837. Accused of embezzlement and counterfeiting. Led movement of dissenters opposed to JS, 1837–1838. Excommunicated, Dec. 1837. Lived at Chardon, Geauga Co., 1840. Baptist clergyman in Fox River area of Wisconsin/Illinois, 1844. Clergyman at Mendon, Monroe Co., New York, 1850. Lived at Rockford, Winnebago Co., Illinois, 1860. Lived at Emporia, Lyon Co., Kansas, 1870. Wife died, 1875. Died at Emporia.

Partridge, Edward (27 Aug. 1793–27 May 1840), hatter. Born at Pittsfield, Berkshire Co., Massachusetts. Son of William Partridge and Jemima Bidwell. Moved to Painesville, Geauga Co., Ohio. Married Lydia Clisbee, 22 Aug. 1819, at Painesville. Initially a Universal Restorationist but adhered to reformed Baptist (later Disciples of Christ or Campbellite) faith when first contacted by Mormon missionaries in Nov. 1830. With Sidney Rigdon, visited JS at Fayette, Seneca Co., New York. Baptized into LDS church by JS, 11 Dec. 1830, in nearby Seneca River. Ordained an elder by Sidney Rigdon, by 15 Dec. 1830. Named first bishop in church, Feb. 1831, at Kirtland, Geauga Co. Ordained a high priest by Lyman Wight, 4 June 1831, at Kirtland. Accompanied JS to Independence, Jackson Co., Missouri, and appointed to oversee settlement of Saints in Missouri, summer 1831. Involved in administering stewardships of land under law of consecration. Appointed member of United Firm, Apr. 1832. Tarred and feathered during mob violence in Jackson Co., Missouri, July 1833. Fled with family to Clay Co., Missouri, Nov. 1833. Served as bishop in Clay Co. Served mission to Missouri, Illinois, Indiana, and Ohio, Jan.–Apr. 1835. Served mission to New York and New England, June–Oct. 1835. In fall 1836, forced to move from Clay Co. to what soon became Caldwell Co., Missouri, where he continued to serve as bishop. Jailed at Richmond, Ray Co., Missouri, fall 1838. Expelled from state, 1839. Appointed bishop of Upper Ward at Commerce (later Nauvoo), Hancock Co., Illinois, 1839. Died at Nauvoo.

Patten, David Wyman (14 Nov. 1799–25 Oct. 1838), farmer. Born in Vermont. Son of Benoni Patten and Edith Cole. Moved to Theresa, Oneida Co., New York, as a young child. Moved to Dundee, Monroe Co., Michigan Territory, as a youth. Married Phoebe Ann Babcock, 1828, in Dundee. Affiliated with the Methodists. Baptized into LDS church by his brother John Patten, 15 June 1832, at Fairplay, Greene Co., Indiana. Ordained an elder by Elisha H. Groves, 17 June 1832. Served mission to Michigan Territory, 1832.

Ordained a high priest by Hyrum Smith, 2 Sept. 1832. Served mission to eastern states, 1832–1833. Moved family from Michigan Territory to Florence, Erie Co., Ohio, 1833. With William Pratt, carried dispatches from JS to church leaders in Clay Co., Missouri, Dec. 1833. Served mission to southern U.S. with Warren F. Parrish, 1834–1835. Ordained member of Quorum of the Twelve, 15 Feb. 1835, at Kirtland, Geauga Co., Ohio. Served mission to Tennessee, spring 1835. With the Twelve, served mission to eastern states, summer 1835. Moved from Kirtland to Far West, 1836. Member of presidency pro tempore of church in Far West, 1838. Active in Mormon attempts to defend Caldwell Co., Missouri. Mortally wounded during skirmish at Crooked River, near Ray Co., Missouri, 25 Oct. 1838. Died near Far West.

Peck, Reed (1814–23 Aug. 1894), millwright, farmer. Born in Bainbridge Township, Chenango Co., New York. Son of Hezekiah Peck and Martha Long. Baptized into LDS church, ca. 1830. Moved from New York to Ohio and then to Kaw Township, Jackson Co., Missouri, Apr.–July 1831. Married Clarissa M. Member of Mormon delegation that attempted to negotiate equitable solution to Mormon War with General Samuel D. Lucas, 31 Oct. 1838. Disaffected from church. Prosecution witness at Nov. 1838 preliminary hearing of JS and others. Wrote extended account of his Missouri experience. Moved to Bainbridge, by 1840; to Cortlandville, Cortland Co., New York, by 1850; and to Afton, Chenango Co., by 1870. Died at Afton.

Perkins, William Lee (22 Jan. 1799–1 Dec. 1882), teacher, attorney, insurance agent, politician. Born in Ashford, Windham Co., Connecticut. Son of William Perkins and Mary Lee. Moved to Hartford, Hartford Co., Connecticut, to study law, ca. 1822. Admitted to Connecticut bar, May 1824. Moved to Windsor, Hartford Co., ca. 1824. Married first Julia Gillett, 8 Nov. 1826, in Windsor. Moved to Painesville, Geauga Co., Ohio, 1828. Formed law firm of Perkins & Osborn with Salmon S. Osborn, 18 Feb. 1834, in Painesville. Agent of Protection Insurance Company of Hartford, 1834. Married second Sarah Margaretta Oakley Waite, 12 Jan. 1837, in Geauga Co. Attorney for plaintiff in *Bank of Geauga v. JS et al.,* 5 June 1837. Attorney for plaintiff in *Hezekiah Kelley v. JS et al.,* 5 June 1837. Attorney for plaintiff in *Newbould v. JS et al.,* 24 Oct. 1837. Served as prosecuting attorney in Lake Co., Ohio, 1840, 1859–1863. Served in Ohio Senate, 1843–1847. Served as mayor of Painesville, 1853. Died in Painesville.

Phelps, William Wines (17 Feb. 1792–7 Mar. 1872), writer, teacher, printer, newspaper editor, publisher, postmaster, lawyer. Born at Hanover, Morris Co., New Jersey. Son of Enon Phelps and Mehitabel Goldsmith. Moved to Homer, Cortland Co., New York, 1800. Married Sally Waterman, 28 Apr. 1815, in Smyrna, Chenango Co., New York. Editor of *Western Courier.* Moved to Wooster, Wayne Co., Ohio, by 3 July 1819. Returned to Homer, by Nov. 1821. Moved to Trumansburg, Tompkins Co., New York, 1823. Edited Anti-Masonic newspaper *Lake Light.* Moved to Canandaigua, Ontario Co., New York, Apr. 1828, and there published Anti-Masonic newspaper *Ontario Phoenix.* Obtained copy of Book of Mormon, 1830. Met JS, 24 Dec. 1830. Migrated to Kirtland, Geauga Co., Ohio, 1831. Baptized into LDS church, 16 June 1831, at Kirtland. Ordained an elder by JS, June 1831, at Kirtland. Appointed church printer, 20 July 1831. Ordained a high priest by JS, 1 Oct. 1831. Appointed member of what became the Literary Firm, Nov. 1831. Moved to Jackson Co., Missouri, late 1831. Appointed member of United Firm, Apr. 1832. Became editor of *The Evening and the Morning Star* and *Upper Missouri Advertiser,* published 1832–1833 at Independence, Jackson Co. Published Book of Commandments, but most copies destroyed by mob when printing office was razed, 20 July 1833. Expelled from Jackson Co. to Clay Co., Missouri, Nov. 1833. Appointed counselor/assistant president to David Whitmer, president of church in Missouri, 3 July 1834. Returned to Kirtland and served as JS's scribe. Prolific writer of hymns. Helped compile Doctrine and Covenants and first Latter-day Saint hymnal, 1835, at Kirtland. Appointed to draft rules and regulations for Kirtland temple, 13 Jan. 1836. Returned from Kirtland to Clay Co., where he resumed duties with Missouri presidency, 1836. Appointed postmaster, 27 May 1837, at Far West, Caldwell Co., Missouri. Excommunicated, 10 Mar. 1838. Moved to Dayton, Montgomery Co., Ohio, before Mar. 1840. Reconciled with church; rebaptized into LDS church, late June 1840. Returned to Kirtland, by May 1841. Appointed to serve mission to eastern U.S., 23 May 1841. Appointed recorder of church licenses, 2 Oct. 1841, in Kirtland. Moved to Nauvoo, Hancock Co., Illinois, by Nov. 1842. Acted as clerk to JS and assisted John Taylor in editing *Times and Seasons* and *Nauvoo Neighbor.* Assisted Willard Richards in writing JS's history, by Jan. 1843. Elected fire warden, 11 Feb. 1843. Elected to Nauvoo City Council, early 1844. Admitted to Council of Fifty, 11 Mar. 1844. Migrated to Salt Lake Valley, 1848. Served as counselor to Parley P. Pratt on exploration mission to southern Utah Territory, Nov. 1849. Admitted to Utah territorial bar, 1851. Member of Utah territorial Legislative Assembly, 1851–1857. Died at Salt Lake City.

Pickett, Agnes Moulton Coolbrith (11 July 1811–26 Dec. 1876). Born at Scarborough, Cumberland Co., Maine. Daughter of Joseph Coolbrith and Mary Hasty Foss. Moved to Boston, by 1832. Baptized into LDS church, 1832, at Boston. Moved to Kirtland, Geauga Co., Ohio, summer 1833. Married Don Carlos Smith, 30 July 1835, at Kirtland. Moved to Norton, Summit Co., Ohio, by 1838. Moved to Missouri, summer 1838. Soon afterward located at Millport, Daviess Co., Missouri, near Adam-ondi-Ahman. Moved to Commerce (later Nauvoo), Hancock Co., Illinois, late summer 1839. Husband died, 7 Aug. 1841. Identified in some sources as a plural wife of JS, married on 6 Jan. 1842. Moved to St. Louis and married William Pickett, 1846. Migrated to Weber Co., Utah Territory, by 1850. Moved to California, 1852. Lived at Marysville, Yuba Co.; San Francisco; San Bernardino, San Bernardino Co.; Los Angeles; and Oakland, Alameda Co., California. Died at Oakland.

Post, Stephen (3 Jan. 1810–18 Dec. 1879), schoolteacher, blacksmith. Born in Greenwich, Washington Co., New York. Son of Samuel Post and Mary Sprague. Moved to Sparta Township, Crawford Co., Pennsylvania, after 1830. Married Jane Force, ca. 1835. Baptized into LDS church by Stephen Winchester, 14 July 1835. Moved to Kirtland, Geauga Co., Ohio, Nov. 1835, where he taught school. Ordained an elder by Alvah Beman, 27 Jan. 1836. Ordained a seventy by Sylvester Smith, 13 Feb. 1836, in Kirtland. Returned to Crawford Co., Apr. 1836. Served mission to Pennsylvania and New York, Sept. 1836–May 1837. Taught school at Venango Co., Pennsylvania, Dec. 1838–Mar. 1839. Served mission to Michigan, May–Sept. 1839. Taught school at La Harpe, Hancock Co., Illinois. Nov. 1843–Apr. 1844. Appointed to serve mission to Pennsylvania to campaign for JS as candidate for U.S. president, Apr. 1844. Returned to Crawford Co., Apr. 1844. Joined with James J. Strang's Church of Jesus Christ of Latter Day Saints, 1846. Affiliated with Sidney Rigdon's

Church of Christ, 1857. Moved to Attica, Marion Co., Iowa, Oct. 1864. Moved to West Lynne, Manitoba, Canada, where he died.

Pratt, Orson (19 Sept. 1811–3 Oct. 1881), farmer, writer, teacher, merchant, surveyor, editor, publisher. Born at Hartford, Washington Co., New York. Son of Jared Pratt and Charity Dickinson. Moved to New Lebanon, Columbia Co., New York, 1814; to Canaan, Columbia Co., fall 1823; to Hurl Gate, Queens Co., New York, spring 1825; and to New York City, spring 1826. Returned to Hurl Gate, fall 1826, and to Canaan, spring 1827. Moved to Lorain Co., Ohio, fall 1827; to Chagrin (later Willoughby), Cuyahoga Co., Ohio, spring 1828; and to Connecticut, fall 1828. Returned to Hurl Gate, winter 1828–1829, and to Canaan, spring 1829. Baptized into LDS church by Parley P. Pratt, 19 Sept. 1830, at Canaan. Ordained an elder by JS, 1 Dec. 1830, in Fayette, Seneca Co., New York, and appointed to serve mission to Colesville, Broome Co., New York. With Samuel H. Smith, traveled from New York to Kirtland, Geauga Co., Ohio; arrived, 27 Feb. 1831. Served mission to Missouri, summer 1831. Moved to Hiram, Portage Co., Ohio, Dec. 1831. Ordained a high priest by Sidney Rigdon, 2 Feb. 1832, in Hiram. Began mission with Lyman E. Johnson to the East from Kirtland, Feb. 1832. Participated in Camp of Israel expedition to Missouri, 1834. Ordained member of Quorum of the Twelve by David Whitmer and Oliver Cowdery, 26 Apr. 1835, at Kirtland. Married Sarah Marinda Bates, 4 July 1836, at Henderson, Jefferson Co., New York. Served mission to Upper Canada, 1836. Served mission to Great Britain with other members of Quorum of the Twelve, 1839–1841. Appointed assistant chaplain in Nauvoo Legion, 3 July 1841. Member of city council, 1841–1845, in Nauvoo, Hancock Co., Illinois. Member of Nauvoo Masonic Lodge. Excommunicated, 20 Aug. 1842, at Nauvoo. Rebaptized into LDS church, 20 Jan. 1843, and ordained to his former office in Quorum of the Twelve. Admitted to Council of Fifty, 11 Mar. 1844. Served mission to Washington DC and eastern U.S., 1844. Moved to what became Council Bluffs, Pottawattamie Co., Iowa Territory, 1846. Entered Salt Lake Valley with Mormon pioneers, 1847. Presided over church in Great Britain, 1848–1849, 1856–1857. Member of Utah territorial legislature. Appointed church historian, 1874. Died at Salt Lake City.

Pratt, Parley Parker (12 Apr. 1807–13 May 1857), farmer, editor, publisher, teacher, school administrator, legislator, explorer, author. Born at Burlington, Otsego Co., New York. Son of Jared Pratt and Charity Dickinson. Traveled west with brother William to acquire land, 1823. Affiliated with Baptist church at age eighteen. Lived in Ohio, 1826–1827. Married first Thankful Halsey, 9 Sept. 1827, at Canaan, Columbia Co., New York. Converted to reformed Baptist (later Disciples of Christ or Campbellite) faith by Sidney Rigdon, 1829. Baptized into LDS church and ordained an elder by Oliver Cowdery, 1 Sept. 1830, at Seneca Lake, Seneca Co., New York. Served mission to unorganized Indian Territory and Missouri with Oliver Cowdery and others, 1830–1831. En route, stopped at Kirtland, Geauga Co., Ohio, and vicinity; missionaries baptized some 130 individuals. Returned to Kirtland, 3 Apr. 1831. Ordained a high priest by Lyman Wight, 4 June 1831. Served mission to western U.S., 7 June 1831–May 1832. Moved to Jackson Co., Missouri, summer 1832. Appointed president of Elders School in Jackson Co. Left to serve mission to eastern U.S., Mar. 1834. Participated in Camp of Israel expedition to Missouri, 1834. Moved to Kirtland, Oct. 1834. Ordained member of Quorum of the Twelve by JS, David Whitmer, and Oliver Cowdery, 21 Feb. 1835. Served mission to eastern U.S., spring–28 Aug. 1835. Served mission to Canada, Apr.–June 1836. Stockholder in Kirtland Safety Society. Wife died, 25 Mar. 1837. Married second Mary Ann Frost Stearns, 14 May 1837, at Kirtland. Left to serve mission to New York City, July 1837. Moved to Far West, Caldwell Co., Missouri, Apr. 1838. Participated in skirmish at Crooked River, near Ray Co., Missouri, 25 Oct. 1838. Jailed at Richmond, Ray Co., and Columbia, Boone Co., Missouri, 1838–1839. Reunited with family, 11 July 1839, in Illinois. Served mission to England, 1839–1842. Edited first number of *LDS Millennial Star,* published in Manchester, England, 27 May 1840. President of British mission, 1841–1842. Arrived at Nauvoo, Hancock Co., Illinois, 7 Feb. 1843. Member of Nauvoo Masonic Lodge. Admitted to Council of Fifty, 11 Mar. 1844. Participated in plural marriage during JS's lifetime. Directed affairs of church in New York City, 1844–1845. Moved to what became Mount Pisgah, Clarke Co., Iowa Territory, 1846. Left to serve mission to England, 31 July 1846. Arrived at Winter Quarters, unorganized U.S. territory (later in Omaha, Douglas Co., Nebraska), 8 Apr. 1847. Arrived in Salt Lake Valley, 28 Sept. 1847. Led exploration party into southern Utah Territory, Nov. 1849–Feb. 1850. Served mission to Chile and California, 16 Mar. 1851–18 Oct. 1852. Served mission to eastern U.S., beginning Sept. 1856. Murdered at Van Buren, Crawford Co., Arkansas.

Price, Sterling (ca. Sept. 1809–29 Sept. 1867), farmer, merchant, military officer. Born near Farmville, Prince Edward Co., Virginia. Son of Pugh Williamson Price and Elizabeth Marshall Williamson. Moved to Missouri, 1831. Married Martha Head, 14 May 1833, in Randolph Co., Missouri. Member of Missouri House of Representatives, 1836–1838, 1840–1844. Served in Missouri militia, 1838–1839, and participated in Mormon War. Moved to Chariton Co., Missouri, by June 1840. Elected to U.S. Congress, 1844; resigned to serve in Mexican War, 12 Aug. 1846. Became military governor of Chihuahua, Mexico, 1847. Served as Missouri governor, 1852–1856. Commissioned major general in Confederate army in Civil War, 1862. Moved to Mexico. Moved to St. Louis, 11 Feb. 1867. Died in St. Louis.

Rich, Charles Coulson (21 Aug. 1809–17 Nov. 1883), schoolteacher, farmer, cooper. Born in Campbell Co., Kentucky. Son of Joseph Rich and Nancy O'Neal. Moved to Posey Township, Dearborn Co., Indiana, ca. 1810. Moved to Tazewell Co., Illinois, 1829. Baptized into LDS church by George M. Hinkle, 1 Apr. 1832, in Tazewell Co. Ordained an elder by Zebedee Coltrin, 16 May 1832, in Fountain Co., Indiana. Participated in Camp of Israel expedition to Missouri, 1834. Served mission to Illinois, 1835. Ordained a high priest by Hyrum Smith and John Smith, 12 Apr. 1836, in Kirtland, Geauga Co., Ohio. Moved to Far West, Missouri, 1836. President of high priests quorum, 1837, in Missouri. Married Sarah DeArmon Pea, 11 Feb. 1838. Moved to Quincy, Adams Co., Illinois, 1839. Moved to Commerce (later Nauvoo), Hancock Co., Illinois, fall 1839. Appointed member of Nauvoo stake high council, 5 Oct. 1839. Served in Nauvoo stake presidency, on Nauvoo city council, and on University of Nauvoo board of regents, 1841. Member of Nauvoo Legion. Member of Nauvoo Masonic Lodge. Served missions to Illinois and Michigan, 1842–1844. Admitted to Council of Fifty, 26 Mar. 1844. Appointed major general of Nauvoo Legion, 1844. Elected trustee of town of Nauvoo, Apr. 1845. Moved to Mt. Pisgah, Clarke Co., Iowa Territory, 1846, and served as presiding elder. Moved to Winter Quarters, unorganized U.S. territory (later in Omaha, Douglas Co., Nebraska), Mar. 1847. Migrated to Salt Lake Valley, 1847, and served as counselor in Salt Lake stake presidency. Moved to Deuel Creek (later Centerville), Davis Co., Utah Territory, by 1849. Ordained member of Quorum of the

Twelve by Brigham Young, 12 Feb. 1849, in Salt Lake City. Served mission to organize church in northern California, 1849. Moved to Utah Co., Utah Territory, by 1850. Left to serve colonizing mission to southern California, Mar. 1851; helped settle San Bernardino, Los Angeles Co., California. Returned to Utah during Utah War, 1857. Served mission to Europe, 1860–1862. Served colonizing mission to Bear Lake Valley, 1863; settled Paris, Owyhee Co., Idaho Territory, 1864. Delegate to Utah territorial legislature, 1864–1872. Served on construction committee for temple in Logan, Cache Co., Utah Territory. Died in Paris.

Richards, Willard (24 June 1804–11 Mar. 1854), teacher, lecturer, doctor, clerk, printer, editor, postmaster. Born at Hopkinton, Middlesex Co., Massachusetts. Son of Joseph Richards and Rhoda Howe. Moved to Richmond, Berkshire Co., Massachusetts, 1813. Moved to Chatham, Columbia Co., New York, by Nov. 1820; moved to Lanesborough, Berkshire Co., Massachusetts, by Nov. 1821. Moved to Nassau, Rensselaer Co., New York, by 6 Apr. 1823. Traveled through New England, giving lectures on scientific subjects for several years, beginning 1827. Practiced medicine at Thomsonian infirmary, beginning 1834, in Boston. Moved to Holliston, Middlesex Co., 1835. Moved to Kirtland, Geauga Co., Ohio, Oct. 1836. Baptized into LDS church by Brigham Young, 31 Dec. 1836, in Kirtland. Appointed to serve mission to eastern U.S., 13 Mar. 1837. Served mission to England, 1837–1841. Married Jennetta Richards, 24 Sept. 1838, in Walker Fold, Chaigley, Lancashire, England. Ordained member of Quorum of the Twelve, 14 Apr. 1840, at Preston, Lancashire. Traveled to Nauvoo, Hancock Co., Illinois, 16 Aug. 1841. Moved to Warsaw, Hancock Co., 7 Sept. 1841; moved to Nauvoo, 11 Dec. 1841. Member of Nauvoo City Council, 1841–1843. Appointed recorder for Nauvoo temple and JS's scribe, 13 Dec. 1841. Member of Nauvoo Masonic Lodge. Appointed JS's private secretary, Dec. 1842; church historian, ca. Dec. 1842; church recorder, 30 July 1843; Nauvoo city recorder, Aug. 1843; and clerk of municipal court. Admitted to Council of Fifty, 11 Mar. 1844, and served as recorder of council. Participated in plural marriage during JS's lifetime. Before death of JS, completed personal history of JS up to Aug. 1838. With JS in jail in Carthage, Hancock Co., when JS and Hyrum Smith were murdered. Moved to Winter Quarters, unorganized U.S. territory (later in Omaha, Douglas Co., Nebraska), 1846. Migrated to Salt Lake Valley and returned to Winter Quarters, 1847. Appointed second counselor to Brigham Young in church presidency, 27 Dec. 1847, at what became Council Bluffs, Pottawattamie Co., Iowa. Led company of Saints to Salt Lake Valley, 1848. Appointed secretary and president of legislative council for provisional state of Deseret. Secretary of Utah Territory, postmaster of Salt Lake City, and editor of *Deseret News.* Died at Salt Lake City.

Rigdon, Sidney (19 Feb. 1793–14 July 1876), tanner, farmer, minister. Born at St. Clair, Allegheny Co., Pennsylvania. Son of William Rigdon and Nancy Gallaher. Joined United Baptists, ca. 1818. Preached at Warren, Trumbull Co., Ohio, and vicinity, 1819–1821. Married Phebe Brooks, 12 June 1820, at Warren. Minister of First Baptist Church of Pittsburgh, 1821–1824. Later joined reformed Baptist (later Disciples of Christ or Campbellite) movement and became influential preacher. Moved to Bainbridge, Geauga Co., Ohio, 1826. Moved to Mentor, Geauga Co., 1827. Introduced to Mormonism by his former proselyte to reformed Baptist faith, Parley P. Pratt, who was en route with Oliver Cowdery and others on mission to unorganized Indian Territory. Baptized into LDS church by Oliver Cowdery, Nov. 1830. Scribe for JS, 1830. Ordained a high priest by Lyman Wight, 4 June 1831, in Kirtland, Geauga Co. Appointed to serve mission to Missouri, 6 June 1831. Moved to Hiram, Portage Co., Ohio, 1831. Appointed member of what became the Literary Firm, Nov. 1831. Counselor/assistant president in church presidency, 1832–1844. Appointed member of United Firm, Apr. 1832. Attended organizational meeting of School of the Prophets, 22–23 Jan. 1833, in Kirtland. Accompanied JS to Upper Canada on proselytizing mission and helped keep JS's diary during trip, 1833. Stockholder in Kirtland Safety Society. Arrived at Far West, Caldwell Co., Missouri, from Kirtland, 4 Apr. 1838. With JS in jail at Liberty, Clay Co., Missouri, Dec. 1838–Feb. 1839. After release, found refuge at Quincy, Adams Co., Illinois. Accompanied JS to Washington DC to seek redress for Missouri grievances, 1839–1840. Member of city council in Nauvoo, Hancock Co., Illinois, 1841. Appointed postmaster of Nauvoo, 24 Feb. 1841. Member of Nauvoo Masonic Lodge. Admitted to Council of Fifty, 19 Mar. 1844. Claimed right to lead church after death of JS; excommunicated, 1844. Moved to Pittsburgh to lead schismatic Church of Jesus Christ of Latter Day Saints, 1844; name of church changed to Church of Christ, 1845. Rejected from Council of Fifty, 4 Feb. 1845. Located near Greencastle, Antrim Township, Franklin Co., Pennsylvania, May 1846. Removed to Friendship, Allegany Co., New York, where he died.

Ripley, Alanson (8 Jan. 1798–before 1860), surveyor, lawyer. Born at New York. Son of Asa Ripley and Polly Deforest. Married Sarah Finkle. Resided in Massachusetts, 1827. Member of LDS church in Ohio. Participated in Camp of Israel expedition to Missouri, 1834. Landholder in Caldwell Co., Missouri, 1837. Ordained a seventy, 7 July 1838, at Far West, Caldwell Co. Surveyed Adam-ondi-Ahman, Daviess Co., Missouri. One of the committee for removing the poor from Missouri in 1839. Bishop in Lee Co., Iowa Territory, 1839–1841. Appointed city surveyor in Nauvoo, Hancock Co., Illinois, 1841. Appointed sergeant major in Nauvoo Legion, 3 June 1842. Moved to Pike Co., Illinois, by June 1850.

Robinson, Ebenezer (25 May 1816–11 Mar. 1891), printer, editor, publisher. Born at Floyd (near Rome), Oneida Co., New York. Son of Nathan Robinson and Mary Brown. Moved to Utica, Oneida Co., ca. 1831, and learned printing trade at *Utica Observer*. Moved to Ravenna, Portage Co., Ohio, Aug. 1833, and worked as compositor on the *Ohio Star*. Moved to Kirtland, Geauga Co., Ohio, May 1835, and worked in printing office. Baptized into LDS church by JS, 16 Oct. 1835. Married first Angelina (Angeline) Eliza Works, 13 Dec. 1835, at Kirtland. Ordained an elder, 29 Apr. 1836, and a seventy, 20 Dec. 1836. Served mission to Richland Co., Ohio, June–July 1836, and shortly after served mission to New York. Moved to Far West, Caldwell Co., Missouri, spring 1837. Assisted with publication of *Elders' Journal*, summer 1838. Appointed clerk and recorder for Zion and clerk of Zion high council at Far West, 6 Apr. 1838. Member of Zion high council at Far West, Dec. 1838. Justice of the peace, 1839. When driven from Missouri, moved to Quincy, Adams Co., Illinois, and worked on *Quincy Whig*, 1839. Became publisher, coeditor, and editor of *Times and Seasons*, 1839–1842, at Commerce (later Nauvoo), Hancock Co., Illinois. Member of Nauvoo Masonic Lodge. Justice of the peace in Hancock Co., by 1842. Served mission to New York, 1843. Moved to Pittsburgh, June 1844. Affiliated with Sidney Rigdon and served as his counselor. In May 1846, moved to Greencastle, Franklin Co., Pennsylvania, where he edited Rigdonite *Messenger and Advocate of the Church of Christ*.

Moved to Decatur Co., Iowa, Apr. 1855. Baptized into RLDS church by William W. Blair, 29 Apr. 1863, at Pleasanton, Decatur Co. Wife died, 1880. Married second Martha A. Cunningham, 5 Feb. 1885. Affiliated with David Whitmer's Church of Christ, 1888. Edited Whitmerite periodical *The Return,* 1889–1891. Died at Davis City, Decatur Co.

Robinson, George W. (14 May 1814–10 Feb. 1878), clerk, postmaster, merchant, clothier, banker. Born at Pawlet, Rutland Co., Vermont. Baptized into LDS church and moved to Kirtland, Geauga Co., Ohio, by 1836. Clerk and recorder for Kirtland high council, beginning Jan. 1836. Ordained a seventy, 20 Dec. 1836. Stockholder in Kirtland Safety Society. Married Athalia Rigdon, oldest daughter of Sidney Rigdon, 13 Apr. 1837, in Kirtland. In Sept. 1837, appointed general church recorder to replace Oliver Cowdery. Moved to Far West, Caldwell Co., Missouri, 28 Mar. 1838. Sustained as general church recorder and clerk to First Presidency at Far West, Apr. 1838. Imprisoned with JS and other church leaders in Missouri, Nov. 1838. Moved to Quincy, Adams Co., Illinois, winter 1839. Moved to Commerce (later Nauvoo), Hancock Co., Illinois, before 1840. Appointed first postmaster in Nauvoo, Apr. 1840. Member of Nauvoo Masonic Lodge. Left LDS church, by July 1842. Moved to Cuba, Allegany Co., New York, by 1846. Affiliated with Sidney Rigdon's Church of Christ as an apostle. Moved to Friendship, Allegany Co., 1847. Charter member of Masonic lodge in that community. Founder and president of First National Bank, 1 Feb. 1864. Died at Friendship.

Rogers, David White (4 Oct. 1787–21 Sept. 1881). Born in New Hampshire. Son of Samuel Rogers and Hannah Sinclair. Married Martha Collins, 5 Dec. 1811, in Montreal, Lower Canada. Moved to Pomfret, Chautauque Co., New York, by 1820. Moved to New York City, 1830. Baptized into LDS church by Parley P. Pratt, 25 Dec. 1837, in New York City. Ordained a teacher by Parley P. Pratt. Moved to Far West, Caldwell Co., Missouri, Sept. 1838. Moved to Quincy, Adams Co., Illinois, Nov. 1838. Ordained an elder by Lyman Wight, Apr. 1843, in Nauvoo, Hancock Co., Illinois. Ordained a seventy by George A. Smith, Oct. 1844, in Nauvoo. Appointed president of Thirty-Fourth Quorum of the Seventy, 5 Feb. 1846, in Nauvoo. Moved to Oskaloosa, Mahaska Co., Iowa, by 1850. Migrated to Salt Lake Valley, 1852. Moved to Provo, Utah Co., Utah Territory, by 1860. Served mission to eastern U.S. and Canada, 1854–1856. Died at Provo.

Root, Henry (14 June 1813–9 Apr. 1895), auctioneer, merchant, banker. Born at Clinton, Upper Canada. Son of Henry Ruth and Marie Overholt. Purchased interest in town of Eldersport (later De Witt), Carroll Co., Missouri, 1837. Sold lots in De Witt to Latter-day Saints. Moved to Quincy, Adams Co., Illinois, 1840. Married Sarah Ann Miller, 1844. Supplied provisions to U.S. Army during U.S. war with Mexico, 1847. Supplied horses to U.S. government during Civil War. Prominent banker at Quincy, beginning 1869. Died at Quincy.

Roundy, Shadrach (1 Jan. 1789–4 July 1872), merchant. Born at Rockingham, Windham Co., Vermont. Son of Uriah Roundy and Lucretia Needham. Married Betsy Quimby, 22 June 1814, at Rockingham. Lived at Spafford, Onondaga Co., New York. Member of Freewill Baptist Church in Spafford. Baptized into LDS church by William E. McLellin, 30 Jan. 1832. Ordained an elder by Orson Hyde and Samuel H. Smith, 16 May 1832. Lived at Elk Creek, Erie Co., Pennsylvania, 1833. Moved to Willoughby, Cuyahoga Co., Ohio, by 1834. Member of the Seventy, 1836. Migrated to Far West, Caldwell Co.,

Missouri. Located at Warsaw, Hancock Co., Illinois, 1839. Moved to Nauvoo, Hancock Co., 1840. Appointed member of a bishopric in Nauvoo, 19 Jan. 1841. Member of Nauvoo Legion. Member of Nauvoo Masonic Lodge. Joined Nauvoo police force, 1843. Admitted to Council of Fifty, 4 Mar. 1845. Ordained a high priest, by 25 Dec. 1845. Bishop of Winter Quarters Fifth Ward at Winter Quarters, unorganized U.S. territory (later in Omaha, Douglas Co., Nebraska). Member of Brigham Young pioneer company, arriving in Salt Lake Valley, July 1847. Bishop of Salt Lake City Sixteenth Ward, 1849–1856. Died at Salt Lake City.

Sagers, William Henry Harrison (3 May 1814/1815–19 June 1886), painter, farmer. Born in LeRoy, Genessee Co., New York. Son of John Sagers and Amy Sweet. Moved to Elk Creek Township, Erie Co., Pennsylvania, by 1830. Baptized into LDS church, 27 Jan. 1833. Served mission to eastern U.S., Apr.–June 1833. Appointed to serve mission to eastern U.S., Feb. 1834. Participated in Camp of Israel expedition, 1834. Ordained an elder, 10 Nov. 1837, at Far West, Caldwell Co., Missouri. Ordained a member of First Quorum of the Seventy, 6 Feb. 1838, at Kirtland, Geauga Co., Ohio. Ordained a high priest, by 28 June 1838. Appointed member of high council at Adam-ondi-Ahman, Daviess Co., Missouri, 28 June 1838. Appointed to serve mission to eastern states, Sept. 1838, to raise funds and recruit men to aid in purchasing property of church members who wanted to leave Daviess Co. Served mission to eastern states, 1839. Moved to Hancock Co., Illinois, by 1840. Served mission to New Orleans, 28 Mar.–May 1841. Appointed to serve mission to Jamaica, 1841. Member of Nauvoo Third Ward, 1842. Married Olive Amanda Wheaton, 22 Jan. 1846, in Nauvoo. Arrived in Salt Lake Valley, 13 Oct. 1850. Moved to what became Tooele, Tooele Co., Utah Territory, fall 1850. Died in Blackfoot, Bingham Co., Idaho Territory.

Salisbury, Wilkins Jenkins (6 Jan. 1809–28 Oct. 1853), lawyer, blacksmith. Born at Rushville, Yates Co., New York. Son of Gideon Salisbury and Elizabeth Shields. Baptized into LDS church in New York. Moved to Kirtland, Geauga Co., Ohio, by 1831. Married JS's sister Katharine Smith, 8 June 1831, at Kirtland. Settled at Chardon, Geauga Co. Participated in Camp of Israel expedition to Missouri, 1834. Appointed member of First Quorum of the Seventy, 28 Feb. 1835. Left Ohio for Far West, Caldwell Co., Missouri, May 1838. Expelled from Missouri; located near present-day Bardolph, McDonough Co., Illinois, Feb. 1839. Moved to Plymouth, Hancock Co., Illinois, by 1843; to Nauvoo, Hancock Co., by 1845; to Alexandria, Clark Co., Missouri, spring 1846; to Warsaw, Hancock Co., late 1846; and to Webster, Hancock Co., fall 1847. Died at Plymouth.

Sherman, Lyman Royal (22 May 1804–ca. 15 Feb. 1839). Born at Monkton, Addison Co., Vermont. Son of Elkanah Sherman and Asenath Hurlbut. Married Delcena Didamia Johnson, 16 Jan. 1829, at Pomfret, Chautauque Co., New York. Baptized into LDS church, Jan. 1832. Located at Kirtland, Geauga Co., Ohio, 1833. Participated in Camp of Israel expedition to Missouri, 1834. Appointed a president of First Quorum of the Seventy, 28 Feb. 1835. Issued elder's certificate, 30 Mar. 1836, at Kirtland. Ordained a high priest and appointed to Kirtland high council, 2 Oct. 1837. Moved to Far West, Caldwell Co., Missouri, by Oct. 1838. Appointed temporary member of Far West high council, 13 Dec. 1838. Appointed member of Quorum of the Twelve, 16 Jan. 1839, but died at Far West before notified and ordained.

Sherwood, Henry Garlick (20 Apr. 1785–24 Nov. 1867), surveyor. Born at Kingsbury, Washington Co., New York. Son of Newcomb Sherwood and a woman whose maiden name was Tolman (first name unidentified). Married first Jane J. McManagal (McMangle) of Glasgow, Lanark, Scotland, ca. 1824. Lived at Bolton, Warren Co., New York, 1830. Baptized into LDS church, by Aug. 1832. Ordained an elder by Jared and Simeon Carter, Aug. 1832. Moved to Kirtland, Geauga Co., Ohio, ca. 1834. Appointed to Kirtland high council, by 17 Aug. 1835. Married second Marcia Abbott of Windham Co., Vermont, ca. 1835. Served mission to Ohio, Kentucky, and Tennessee, 1836. Stockholder in Kirtland Safety Society. Migrated to Missouri; located at De Witt, Carroll Co., and then Daviess Co., 1838. Member of committee at Far West, Caldwell Co., Missouri, to supervise removal of Latter-day Saints from Missouri, Apr. 1839. Expelled from Missouri and located at Commerce (later Nauvoo), Hancock Co., Illinois, 1839. Member of Commerce high council, 6 Oct. 1839. Instructed in JS revelation to buy stock for building Nauvoo House, 19 Jan. 1841. Nauvoo city marshal, 1841–1843. Appointed guard in Nauvoo Legion, Mar. 1841. Member of Nauvoo Masonic Lodge. Member of Brigham Young pioneer company to Salt Lake Valley, 1847. Served colonizing mission to San Bernardino, Los Angeles Co., California, 1852. Returned to Utah Territory, 1855. Became disaffected with church and removed from high priests quorum, 27 Feb. 1856. Returned to San Bernardino, where he died.

Smalling, Cyrus (8 Feb. 1789–18 Feb. 1866), farmer. Born in Connecticut. Married Ruth. Moved to New York, by 1817. Baptized into LDS church, in Broome Co., New York. Moved to Kirtland, Geauga Co., Ohio, ca. 1833. Participated in Camp of Israel expedition to Missouri, 1834. Ordained a seventy, 30 June 1835. Received elder's certificate, 1 Apr. 1836, in Kirtland. Presided at conference held in Amity, Allegany Co., New York, 17 Sept. 1836. Directed to join high priests quorum, 6 Apr. 1837. Excommunicated, late 1837. Moved to Lapeer, Lapeer Co., Michigan, by 1850. Died in Attica Township, Lapeer Co.

Smith, Agnes Moulton Coolbrith. See Pickett, Agnes Moulton Coolbrith.

Smith, Alexander Hale (2 June 1838–12 Aug. 1909), photographer, carpenter, postmaster, minister. Born at Far West, Caldwell Co., Missouri. Son of JS and Emma Hale. Moved to Commerce (later Nauvoo), Hancock Co., Illinois, 1839. Married Elizabeth Agnes Kendall, 23 June 1861, at Nauvoo. Baptized into RLDS church by Joseph Smith III, 25 May 1862, at Nauvoo. Ordained an elder in RLDS church, 8 Apr. 1863. Served several missions for RLDS church. Ordained a high priest in RLDS church, 12 Apr. 1866. Moved to Colfax, Harrison Co., Missouri, 1870. Ordained an apostle in RLDS church, 10 Apr. 1873, at Plano, Kendall Co., Illinois. Moved to Stewartsville, De Kalb Co., Missouri, early 1882; to Independence, Jackson Co., Missouri, July 1882; and to Lamoni, Decatur Co., Iowa, 2 Apr. 1888. Ordained president of RLDS church Quorum of the Twelve, 15 Apr. 1890, at Lamoni. Appointed counselor to RLDS church president, 12 Apr. 1897; RLDS patriarch, 12 Apr. 1897. Moved to Fayette, Decatur Co., by June 1900. Died at Nauvoo. Buried at Lamoni.

Smith, Don Carlos (25 Mar. 1816–7 Aug. 1841), farmer, printer, editor. Born at Norwich, Windsor Co., Vermont. Son of Joseph Smith Sr. and Lucy Mack. Moved to Palmyra, Ontario Co., New York, 1816–Jan. 1817. Moved to Manchester, Ontario Co., 1825. Baptized into LDS church by David Whitmer, ca. 9 June 1830, at Seneca Lake, Seneca Co., New York. Accompanied his father on mission to Asael Smith family in St. Lawrence Co., New York, Aug. 1830. Lived at The Kingdom, unincorporated settlement near Waterloo, Seneca Co., Nov. 1830. Migrated to Kirtland, Geauga Co., Ohio, with

Lucy Mack Smith company of Fayette, Seneca Co., branch of Latter-day Saints, May 1831. Employed by Kirtland printing shop under Oliver Cowdery, fall 1833. Married Agnes Moulton Coolbrith, 30 July 1835, at Kirtland. Ordained a high priest and appointed president of Kirtland high priests quorum, 15 Jan. 1836. Served mission to Pennsylvania and New York, 1836. Continued working in Kirtland printing shop, including involvement with *Elders' Journal.* Moved to New Portage, Medina Co., Ohio, Dec. 1837. Served mission to Virginia, Pennsylvania, and Ohio, spring 1838. Left Ohio for Far West, Caldwell Co., Missouri, May 1838. Served mission to Kentucky and Tennessee, 1838. Expelled from Far West, Feb. 1839; moved to Quincy, Adams Co., Illinois. Lived at Macomb, McDonough Co., Illinois, and then moved to Commerce (later Nauvoo), Hancock Co., Illinois, 1839. President of high priests in Commerce, 1839. Editor and publisher of *Times and Seasons,* with Ebenezer Robinson, 1839–1841, at Nauvoo. Elected member of Nauvoo City Council, 1 Feb. 1841. Appointed a regent of University of Nauvoo, 3 Feb. 1841. Elected brigadier general in Nauvoo Legion, 5 Feb. 1841. Died at Nauvoo.

Smith, Elias (6 Sept. 1804–24 June 1888), teacher, printer, postmaster, bookkeeper, probate judge, newspaper editor. Born in Royalton, Windsor Co., Vermont. Son of Asahel Smith and Elizabeth Schellenger. Moved to Stockholm, St. Lawrence Co., New York, 1809. Baptized into LDS church by Hyrum Smith, 27 Aug. 1835, in Stockholm. Ordained an elder, 28 Aug. 1835, in Stockholm. Moved to Kirtland, Geauga Co., Ohio, May 1836. Appointed camp historian of Kirtland Camp, whose members moved to Far West, Caldwell Co., Missouri, Mar.–Oct. 1838. Moved to Commerce (later Nauvoo), Hancock Co., Illinois, ca. 1839. Moved to Nashville, Lee Co., Iowa Territory, June 1839. Ordained a bishop, July 1840, in Lee Co. Moved to Nauvoo to supervise printing office, 1843–1846. Admitted to Council of Fifty, 4 Apr. 1844. Postmaster of Nauvoo, 1844–1846. Married Lucy Brown, 7 Aug. 1845, in Nauvoo. Left Nauvoo for Iowa, May 1846. Migrated to Salt Lake Valley; arrived Sept. 1851. Served as probate judge of Salt Lake Co., Utah Territory, 1852–18 Mar. 1884; postmaster, July 1854–1858; and editor of *Deseret News,* 1856–Sept. 1863. Died in Salt Lake City.

Smith, Emma Hale (10 July 1804–30 Apr. 1879), scribe, editor, boardinghouse operator, clothier. Born at Willingborough Township (later in Harmony), Susquehanna Co., Pennsylvania. Daughter of Isaac Hale and Elizabeth Lewis. Member of Methodist church at Harmony (later in Oakland). Married first to JS by Zechariah Tarble, 18 Jan. 1827, at South Bainbridge (later Afton), Chenango Co., New York. Assisted JS as scribe during translation of Book of Mormon at Harmony, 1828, and joined him during completion of translation at Peter Whitmer Sr. farm, Fayette, Seneca Co., New York, summer 1829. Baptized into LDS church by Oliver Cowdery, 28 June 1830, at Colesville, Broome Co., New York. Migrated from New York to Kirtland, Geauga Co., Ohio, Jan.–Feb. 1831. Lived at John Johnson home at Hiram, Portage Co., Ohio, 1831–1832. Edited *A Collection of Sacred Hymns, for the Church of the Latter Day Saints,* published 1835, at Kirtland. Stockholder in Kirtland Safety Society. Fled Ohio for Far West, Caldwell Co., Missouri, Jan.–Mar. 1838. Exiled from Missouri, Feb. 1839; located near Quincy, Adams Co., Illinois. Moved to Commerce (later Nauvoo), Hancock Co., Illinois, 10 May 1839. Appointed president of Female Relief Society in Nauvoo, 17 Mar. 1842. Husband murdered, 27 June 1844. Fled to Fulton, Fulton Co., Illinois, Sept. 1846–Feb. 1847, then returned to

Nauvoo. Married second Lewis Crum Bidamon, 23 Dec. 1847, at Nauvoo. Affiliated with RLDS church, 1860. Died at Nauvoo.

Smith, Frederick Granger Williams (20 June 1836–13 Apr. 1862), farmer, merchant. Born at Kirtland, Geauga Co., Ohio. Son of JS and Emma Hale. Married Anna Marie Jones, 13 Sept. 1857, in Hancock Co., Illinois. Died in Nauvoo, Hancock Co.

Smith, George Albert (26 June 1817–1 Sept. 1875). Born at Potsdam, St. Lawrence Co., New York. Son of John Smith and Clarissa Lyman. Baptized into LDS church by Joseph H. Wakefield, 10 Sept. 1832, at Potsdam. Moved to Kirtland, Geauga Co., Ohio, 1833. Labored on Kirtland temple. Participated in Camp of Israel expedition to Missouri, 1834. Appointed member of First Quorum of the Seventy, 1 Mar. 1835, at Kirtland. Served mission to eastern states with Lyman Smith, 1835. Served mission to Ohio, 1836. Stockholder in Kirtland Safety Society. Arrived at Far West, Caldwell Co., Missouri, from Kirtland, 16 June 1838, and soon located at Adam-ondi-Ahman, Daviess Co., Missouri. Member of Adam-ondi-Ahman high council, 1838. In exodus from Missouri, located north of Quincy, Adams Co., Illinois. Ordained member of Quorum of the Twelve, 26 Apr. 1839, at Far West. Served mission to England, 1839–1841. Moved to Nauvoo, Hancock Co., Illinois, 1841. Married to Bathsheba W. Bigler by Don Carlos Smith, 25 July 1841, at Nauvoo. Moved to Zarahemla, Lee Co., Iowa Territory, 1841. Member of Nauvoo Masonic Lodge. Member of Nauvoo City Council, 1842–1843. Nauvoo city alderman, 1843–1844. Admitted to Council of Fifty, 11 Mar. 1844. Elected trustee of Nauvoo House Association, Apr. 1845. Member of Brigham Young pioneer company that journeyed to Salt Lake Valley, 1847. Appointed church historian and recorder, 1854. Member of Utah territorial supreme court, 1855. First counselor to Brigham Young in church presidency, 1868. Died at Salt Lake City.

Smith, Hyrum (9 Feb. 1800–27 June 1844), farmer, cooper. Born at Tunbridge, Orange Co., Vermont. Son of Joseph Smith Sr. and Lucy Mack. Moved to Randolph, Orange Co., 1802; to Tunbridge, before May 1803; to Royalton, Windsor Co., Vermont, 1804; to Sharon, Windsor Co., by Aug. 1804; to Tunbridge, by Mar. 1808; to Royalton, by Mar. 1810; to Lebanon, Grafton Co., New Hampshire, 1811; to Norwich, Windsor Co., 1813; and to Palmyra, Ontario Co., New York, 1816–Jan. 1817. Member of Western Presbyterian Church of Palmyra, early 1820s. Lived at Palmyra, 1817–1825. Lived at Manchester, Ontario Co., 1825–1826. Married first Jerusha Barden, 2 Nov. 1826, at Manchester. Returned to Palmyra, 1826. Baptized by JS, June 1829, at Seneca Lake, Seneca Co., New York. One of the Eight Witnesses of the Book of Mormon, June 1829. Assisted in arrangements for publication of Book of Mormon, 1829–1830, at Palmyra. Among six original members of LDS church, 6 Apr. 1830. Ordained a priest, 9 June 1830. Presided over branch of church at Colesville, Broome Co., New York, 1830–1831. Migrated to Kirtland, Geauga Co., Ohio, 1831. Ordained a high priest by JS, 4 June 1831. Left to serve mission to Missouri with John Murdock, June 1831. Appointed counselor to Bishop Newel K. Whitney, 10 Feb. 1832. Attended organizational meeting of School of the Prophets, 22–23 Jan. 1833, in Kirtland. Member of committee to supervise construction of Kirtland temple, 1833–1836. Participated in Camp of Israel expedition to Missouri, 1834. Appointed to Kirtland high council, 24 Sept. 1834. Ordained assistant president in presidency of the high priesthood, Dec. 1834. Stockholder in Kirtland Safety Society. Sustained as assistant counselor in presidency of church, 3 Sept. 1837. Wife died, 13 Oct. 1837. Appointed second counselor in First Presidency, 7 Nov. 1837. Married second Mary Fielding, 24 Dec. 1837, at Kirtland. Migrated to Far West, Caldwell Co., Missouri, Mar.–May 1838. Imprisoned at Liberty, Clay Co., Missouri, with his brother JS, 1838–1839. Allowed to escape during change of venue, 16 Apr. 1839, en route from trial in Gallatin, Daviess Co., Missouri, to Columbia, Boone Co., Missouri. Arrived at Quincy, Adams Co., Illinois, 22 Apr. 1839. Moved to Commerce (later Nauvoo), Hancock Co., Illinois, 1839. Succeeded Joseph Smith Sr. as church patriarch, 1840. In JS revelation dated 19 Jan. 1841, instructed to buy stock for building Nauvoo House, appointed patriarch of church, released as counselor in First Presidency, and appointed a prophet, seer, and revelator in First Presidency; instructed to "act in concert" with JS, who would "show unto him the keys whereby he may ask and receive, and be crowned with the same blessing, and glory, and honor, and priesthood, and gifts of the priesthood, that once were put upon . . . Oliver Cowdery." Elected to Nauvoo City Council, 1 Feb. 1841. Appointed chaplain in Nauvoo Legion, Mar. 1841. Member of Nauvoo Masonic Lodge; elected Worshipful Master, 10 Nov. 1842. Vice mayor of Nauvoo, 1842–ca. 1843. Appointed to replace Elias Higbee as member of Nauvoo temple committee, 10 Oct. 1843. Admitted to Council of Fifty, 11 Mar. 1844. Participated in plural marriage during JS's lifetime. Murdered at Carthage, Hancock Co.

Smith, John (16 July 1781–23 May 1854), farmer. Born at Derryfield (later Manchester), Rockingham Co., New Hampshire. Son of Asael Smith and Mary Duty. Member of Congregational church. Appointed overseer of highways at Potsdam, St. Lawrence Co., New York, 1810. Married Clarissa Lyman, 11 Sept. 1815. Baptized into LDS church by Solomon Humphrey, 9 Jan. 1832. Confirmed and ordained an elder by Joseph Wakefield and Solomon Humphrey, 9 Jan. 1832. Moved to Kirtland, Geauga Co., Ohio, 1833. Ordained a high priest, June 1833. Charter member of Kirtland high council, 17 Feb. 1834. Appointed president of Kirtland high council, 21 Jan. 1836. Served mission to eastern states with his brother Joseph Smith Sr., 1836. Stockholder in Kirtland Safety Society. Appointed assistant counselor in First Presidency, 3 Sept. 1837; member of Kirtland stake presidency, 1838. Left Kirtland for Far West, Caldwell Co., Missouri, 5 Apr. 1838. Appointed president of stake in Adam-ondi-Ahman, Daviess Co., Missouri, 28 June 1838. Expelled from Missouri; arrived in Illinois, 28 Feb. 1839. Moved to Commerce (later Nauvoo), Hancock Co., Illinois, June 1839. Appointed president of branch in Lee Co., Iowa Territory, 5 Oct. 1839. Moved to Nashville, Lee Co., Oct. 1839. Member of Nauvoo Masonic Lodge. Appointed to preside at Macedonia (later Webster), Hancock Co., Illinois, 1843–1844. Ordained a patriarch, 10 Jan. 1844. Admitted to Council of Fifty, 26 Mar. 1844. Appointed Nauvoo stake president, 7 Oct. 1844. Joined westward exodus of Latter-day Saints into Iowa Territory, 9 Feb. 1846. Arrived in Salt Lake Valley, 23 Sept. 1847. Presided over Salt Lake stake, 1847–1848. Ordained patriarch of church, 1 Jan. 1849. Died at Salt Lake City.

Smith, Joseph, III (6 Nov. 1832–10 Dec. 1914), clerk, hotelier, farmer, justice of the peace, editor, minister. Born at Kirtland, Geauga Co., Ohio. Son of JS and Emma Hale. Moved to Far West, Caldwell Co., Missouri, 1838; to Quincy, Adams Co., Illinois, 1839; and to Commerce (later Nauvoo), Hancock Co., Illinois, 1839. Baptized into LDS church by JS, Nov. 1843, at Nauvoo. Appointed clerk of city council in Canton, Fulton Co., Illinois,

Jan. 1855. Married first Emmeline Griswold, 22 Oct. 1856, at Nauvoo. Appointed president of RLDS church, 6 Apr. 1860, in Amboy, Lee Co., Illinois. Moved to Plano, Kendall Co., Illinois, 1865. Married second Bertha Madison, 12 Nov. 1869, at Sandwich, Kendall Co. Moved to Little Rock, Kendall Co., by June 1870. Returned to Plano, by June 1880. Moved to Lamoni, Decatur Co., Iowa, 1881. Founded Graceland College in Lamoni and served as chairman of board of trustees, 1893–1898. Married third Ada Rachel Clark, 12 Jan. 1898, at Amaranth, Dufferin Co., Ontario, Canada. Moved to Fayette, Decatur Co., by June 1900. Moved to Independence, Jackson Co., Missouri, 1906. Died at Independence.

Smith, Joseph, Sr. (12 July 1771–14 Sept. 1840), cooper, farmer, teacher, merchant. Born at Topsfield, Essex Co., Massachusetts. Son of Asael Smith and Mary Duty. Nominal member of Congregationalist church at Topsfield. Married to Lucy Mack by Seth Austin, 24 Jan. 1796, at Tunbridge, Orange Co., Vermont. Joined Universalist Society at Tunbridge, 1797. Entered mercantile business at Randolph, Orange Co., ca. 1802, and lost all in a ginseng root investment. Moved to Tunbridge, before May 1803; to Royalton, Windsor Co., Vermont, 1804; to Sharon, Windsor Co., by Aug. 1804; to Tunbridge, by Mar. 1808; to Royalton, by Mar. 1810; to Lebanon, Grafton Co., New Hampshire, 1811; to Norwich, Windsor Co., 1813; to Palmyra, Ontario Co., New York, 1816; and to Manchester, Ontario Co., 1825. One of the Eight Witnesses of the Book of Mormon, June 1829. Baptized into LDS church by Oliver Cowdery, 6 Apr. 1830, most likely at Seneca Lake, Seneca Co., New York. With his son Don Carlos, served mission to family of his father in St. Lawrence Co., New York, Aug. 1830. Lived at The Kingdom, unincorporated settlement near Waterloo, Seneca Co., Nov. 1830–1831. Moved to Kirtland, Geauga Co., Ohio, 1831. Ordained a high priest by Lyman Wight, 4 June 1831. Attended first meeting of School of the Prophets, 22–23 Jan. 1833, in Kirtland. Member of Kirtland high council, 1834. Ordained patriarch of church and assistant president, 6 Dec. 1834. Labored on Kirtland temple. Served mission to eastern states with his brother John Smith, 1836. Stockholder in Kirtland Safety Society. Sustained as assistant counselor in First Presidency, 3 Sept. 1837. Left Ohio for Far West, Caldwell Co., Missouri, May 1838. Expelled from Missouri; migrated to Quincy, Adams Co., Illinois, Feb. 1839. Located at Commerce (later Nauvoo), Hancock Co., Illinois, spring 1839. Died at Nauvoo.

Smith, Julia Murdock. See Middleton, Julia M. Smith.

Smith, Lucy Mack (8 July 1775–14 May 1856), oilcloth painter, nurse, fundraiser, author. Born at Gilsum, Cheshire Co., New Hampshire. Daughter of Solomon Mack Sr. and Lydia Gates. Moved to Montague, Franklin Co., Massachusetts, 1779; to Tunbridge, Orange Co., Vermont, 1788; to Gilsum, 1792; and to Tunbridge, 1794. Married to Joseph Smith Sr. by Seth Austin, 24 Jan. 1796, at Tunbridge. Moved to Randolph, Orange Co., 1802; to Tunbridge, before May 1803; to Royalton, Windsor Co., Vermont, 1804; to Sharon, Windsor Co., by Aug. 1804; to Tunbridge, by Mar. 1808; to Royalton, by Mar. 1810; to Lebanon, Grafton Co., New Hampshire, 1811; to Norwich, Windsor Co., 1813; and to Palmyra, Ontario Co., New York, 1816–Jan. 1817. Member of Western Presbyterian Church of Palmyra, early 1820s. Moved to Manchester, Ontario Co., 1825. Baptized into LDS church, 6 Apr. 1830, most likely at Seneca Lake, Seneca Co., New York. Lived at The Kingdom, unincorporated settlement near Waterloo, Seneca Co., Nov. 1830–May 1831. Led company of approximately eighty Fayette, Seneca Co., branch members from

Seneca Co. to Kirtland, Geauga Co., Ohio, May 1831. Stockholder in Kirtland Safety Society. Left Ohio for Far West, Caldwell Co., Missouri, May 1838. Fled to Quincy, Adams Co., Illinois, Feb. 1839. Located at Commerce (later Nauvoo), Hancock Co., Illinois, spring 1839. Husband died, 1840. Joined Female Relief Society, Mar. 1842, in Nauvoo. Lived with daughter Lucy Smith Millikin in Colchester, McDonough Co., Illinois, 1846–1852. Died in Nauvoo. Her narrative history of Smith family, published as *Biographical Sketches of Joseph Smith,* 1853, has been an invaluable resource for study of JS and early church.

Smith, Samuel Harrison (13 Mar. 1808–30 July 1844), farmer, logger, scribe, builder, tavern operator. Born at Tunbridge, Orange Co., Vermont. Son of Joseph Smith Sr. and Lucy Mack. Moved to Royalton, Windsor Co., Vermont, by Mar. 1810; to Lebanon, Grafton Co., New Hampshire, 1811; to Norwich, Windsor Co., 1813; and to Palmyra, Ontario Co., New York, 1816–Jan. 1817. Member of Western Presbyterian Church of Palmyra, early 1820s. Moved to Manchester, Ontario Co., 1825. Baptized by Oliver Cowdery, May 1829, at Harmony (later in Oakland), Susquehanna Co., Pennsylvania. One of the Eight Witnesses of the Book of Mormon, June 1829. Among six original members of LDS church, 6 Apr. 1830. Ordained an elder, 9 June 1830, at Fayette, Seneca Co., New York. Began mission to New York, 30 June 1830. Appointed to preach in Ohio, Dec. 1830. With Orson Pratt, journeyed from New York to Kirtland, Geauga Co., Ohio; arrived, 27 Feb. 1831. Ordained a high priest by Lyman Wight, 4 June 1831. Served mission to Missouri with Reynolds Cahoon, 1831. Served mission to eastern states with Orson Hyde, 1832. Attended organizational meeting of School of the Prophets, 22–23 Jan. 1833, in Kirtland. Appointed member of first Kirtland high council, 17 Feb. 1834. Married first Mary Bailey, 13 Aug. 1834, at Kirtland. Committee member and general agent for Literary Firm in Kirtland, 1835. Stockholder in Kirtland Safety Society. Appointed president of Kirtland high council, 2 Oct. 1837. Moved to Far West, Caldwell Co., Missouri, where he lived briefly before moving to Marrowbone, Daviess Co., Missouri, 1838. Participated in skirmish at Crooked River, near Ray Co., Missouri, 25 Oct. 1838. Among first Latter-day Saints to seek refuge at Quincy, Adams Co., Illinois, 1838. Hired to farm for George Miller near Macomb, McDonough Co., Illinois, Mar. 1839. Moved to Nauvoo, Hancock Co., Illinois, 1841. Wife died, Jan. 1841. Appointed a bishop at Nauvoo, 1841. Nauvoo city alderman, 1841–1842. Appointed guard in Nauvoo Legion, Mar. 1841. Married second Levira Clark, 30 May 1841, in Scott Co., Illinois. Appointed a regent of University of Nauvoo. Moved to Plymouth, Hancock Co., Jan. 1842. Member of Nauvoo Masonic Lodge. Member of Nauvoo City Council, 1842–1843. Died at Nauvoo.

Smith, William B. (13 Mar. 1811–13 Nov. 1893), farmer, newspaper editor. Born at Royalton, Windsor Co., Vermont. Son of Joseph Smith Sr. and Lucy Mack. Moved to Lebanon, Grafton Co., New Hampshire, 1811; to Norwich, Windsor Co., 1813; and to Palmyra, Ontario Co., New York, 1816–Jan. 1817. Moved to Manchester, Ontario Co., 1825. Baptized into LDS church by David Whitmer, ca. 9 June 1830, at Seneca Lake, Seneca Co., New York. Ordained a teacher, by 5 Oct. 1830. Lived at The Kingdom, unincorporated settlement near Waterloo, Seneca Co., Nov. 1830. Moved to Kirtland, Geauga Co., Ohio, May 1831. Ordained an elder by Lyman Johnson, 19 Dec. 1832, at Kirtland. Served mission to Erie Co., Pennsylvania, Dec. 1832. Attended organizational meeting of School of the Prophets, 22–23 Jan. 1833, in Kirtland. Married Caroline Amanda Grant, 14 Feb. 1833, likely in Erie Co. Ordained a high priest, 21 June 1833. Participated in Camp of Israel expedition to Missouri, 1834. Ordained member of Quorum of the Twelve, 15 Feb. 1835, at Kirtland. Left Ohio for Far West, Caldwell Co., Missouri, May 1838. Disfellowshipped, 4 May 1839. Restored to Quorum of the Twelve, 25 May 1839. Settled at Plymouth, Hancock Co., Illinois, ca. 1839, where he kept a tavern. Member of Masonic lodge in Nauvoo, Hancock Co. Member of Nauvoo City Council, 1842–1843. Editor of Nauvoo newspaper the *Wasp,* 1842. Represented Hancock Co. in Illinois House of Representatives, 1842–1843. Moved to Philadelphia to care for his sick wife, 1843. Admitted to Council of Fifty, 25 Apr. 1844. Participated in plural marriage during JS's lifetime. Moved to Nauvoo, 4 May 1845. Wife died, May 1845. Ordained patriarch of church, 24 May 1845. Married Mary Jane Rollins, 22 June 1845, at Nauvoo. Excommunicated, 12 Oct. 1845. Dropped from Council of Fifty, 11 Jan. 1846. Sustained James J. Strang as successor to JS, 1 Mar. 1846. Married Roxey Ann Grant, 19 May 1847, in Knox Co., Illinois. Ordained patriarch and apostle of Strang's Church of Jesus Christ of Latter Day Saints, 11 June 1846, at Voree, Walworth Co., Wisconsin Territory. Excommunicated from Strangite movement, 8 Oct. 1847. Affiliated briefly with Lyman Wight, 1849–1850. Initiated a new movement with Martin Harris and Chilton Daniels at Kirtland, likely 1855. Married Eliza Elsie Sanborn, 12 Nov. 1857, at Kirtland. Moved to Venango, Erie Co., Pennsylvania, by 1860, and to Elkader, Clayton Co., Iowa, shortly after. Enlisted in U.S. Army during Civil War and apparently adopted middle initial *B* at this time. Spent active duty time in Arkansas. Joined RLDS church, 1878. Wife died, Mar. 1889. Married Rosanna Jewitt Surprise, 21 Dec. 1889, at Clinton, Clinton Co., Iowa. Moved to Osterdock, Clayton Co., 1890. Died at Osterdock.

Snow, Erastus (9 Nov. 1818–27 May 1888), farmer, teacher, merchant, publisher, manufacturer. Born at St. Johnsbury, Caledonia Co., Vermont. Son of Levi Snow and Lucina Streeter. Baptized into LDS church by William Snow, 3 Feb. 1833, at Charleston, Orleans Co., Vermont. Ordained a teacher by John F. Boynton, 28 June 1834. Ordained a priest by William Snow, 13 Nov. 1834. Served mission to Vermont, New York, and New Hampshire, 1834–1835. Ordained an elder by Luke S. Johnson, 16 Aug. 1835. Arrived at Kirtland, Geauga Co., Ohio, Dec. 1835. Ordained a seventy by Lyman Sherman, early 1836. Served mission to Pennsylvania, Apr.–Dec. 1836. Stockholder in Kirtland Safety Society. Served mission to Pennsylvania, Ohio, and Maryland, May–Dec. 1837. Located with Latter-day Saints in Missouri, July 1838. Married Artimesia Beman, 13 Dec. 1838. Located at Montrose, Lee Co., Iowa Territory; appointed to high council of Iowa stake, Lee Co., 1839. Served mission to Pennsylvania, New Jersey, and Massachusetts, 1840–1843. Member of Nauvoo Masonic Lodge, 1844. Admitted to Council of Fifty, 11 Mar. 1844. Participated in plural marriage during JS's lifetime. Appointed to serve mission to eastern states, Apr. 1844. Member of Brigham Young pioneer company to Salt Lake Valley, 1847. Served mission to eastern states, 1847–1848. Appointed counselor in Salt Lake City stake presidency, Oct. 1848. Ordained member of Quorum of the Twelve, 12 Feb. 1849. Established Scandinavian mission, 1850. Appointed to serve colonizing mission to Iron Co., Utah Territory, Oct. 1852. Published and edited *St. Louis Luminary* in Missouri, 1854. Founded St. George, Washington Co., Utah Territory, 1861. Died at Salt Lake City.

Snow, Gardner (15 Feb. 1793–17 Nov. 1889), cooper. Born in Chesterfield, Cheshire Co., New Hampshire. Son of James Snow and Abigail Farr. Married Sarah Sawyer

Hastings, 30 Nov. 1814. Moved to St. Johnsbury, Caledonia Co., Vermont, 1818. Baptized into LDS church by Orson Pratt, 18 June 1833. Moved to Kirtland, Geauga Co., Ohio, 1836. Ordained an elder, 11 July 1836. Ordained a seventy, 20 Dec. 1836. Stockholder in Kirtland Safety Society. Moved to Adam-ondi-Ahman, Daviess Co., Missouri, 1838. Moved to Illinois, ca. winter 1839. Ordained a high priest, 23 Oct. 1840. Migrated to Salt Lake Valley, 1850. Moved to Sanpete Co., Utah Territory, 1850. Appointed probate judge for Sanpete Co., 24 Dec. 1860. Ordained a patriarch by Brigham Young. Died in Manti, Sanpete Co.

Stanton, Daniel (28 May 1795–26 Oct. 1872), farmer, carpenter. Born in Manlius, Onondaga Co., New York. Son of Amos Stanton and Elizabeth Wyman. Moved to Pompey, Onondaga Co., by 1800. Married Clarinda Graves, 16 Mar. 1816. Moved to Mayfield, Cuyahoga Co., Ohio, by 1820. Moved to Kirtland, Geauga Co., Ohio, by 1830. Baptized into LDS church by Parley P. Pratt, 3 Nov. 1830, in Kirtland. Ordained a priest by Lyman Wight, Jan. 1831, in Kirtland; an elder by JS, 6 June 1831, in Kirtland; and a high priest by Oliver Cowdery, 25 Oct. 1831, in Orange, Cuyahoga Co. Appointed to serve mission with Seymour Brunson, Jan. 1832. Moved to Jackson Co., Missouri, 1832. Recommended to be a counselor in a bishopric in Independence, Jackson Co., Missouri, by JS and other church leaders, 25 June 1833. Appointed to watch over branch "no. 2" in Independence, 11 Sept. 1833. Appointed to serve mission with Elias Eams, 6 Aug. 1834, at Clay Co., Missouri. Present at high council meeting, 10 Aug. 1835, in Kirtland. Served as acting counselor in Zion bishopric at general assembly of church, 17 Aug. 1835, in Kirtland. Moved to Daviess Co., Missouri, by 1838. Appointed member of high council at Adam-ondi-Ahman, Daviess Co., 28 June 1838. Expelled from Missouri; moved to Illinois, 1839. Appointed member of high council at Lima, Adams Co., Illinois, 11 June 1843. Appointed by Brigham Young to go abroad and preside over branches of church, 8 Oct. 1844. Moved to Kanesville (later Council Bluffs, Pottawattamie Co.), Iowa Territory, 1846; to Springville, Utah Co., Utah Territory, 1852; and to Fairfield, Cedar Co., Utah Territory, by 1860. Appointed by Brigham Young to help settle St. George, Washington Co., Utah Territory, 1861. Moved to Panaca, Washington Co. (later in Nevada), 1864. Buried in Panaca Cemetery.

Stollings, Jacob (22 Oct. 1804–14 May 1853), boardinghouse owner, farmer. Born in Pennsylvania. Son of Jacob Stollings and Sarah Ann Cooper. Married Jinsey Estes, 28 Mar. 1830, in Clay Co., Missouri. Moved to Daviess Co., Missouri, by 1837. Built first house in Gallatin, Daviess Co., 1838. Sold goods on credit to Mormons; store burned and receipt books confiscated by Mormon forces. Sought redress for his losses, Apr. 1839. Died in Henry Co., Missouri.

Swartzell, William (25 Dec. 1781–after 4 June 1841). Born in Green Co., Pennsylvania. Son of John Swartzell. Baptized into LDS church, by Mar. 1838. Ordained a deacon by Joseph Smith Sr., 1 Mar. 1838, in Rochester, Columbiana Co., Ohio. Moved to Pekin, Carroll Co., Ohio, before Apr. 1838. Moved to Missouri, Apr. 1838. Participated in Missouri Danite activities, 1838. Left church, Aug. 1838. Returned to Pekin, Oct. 1838. Married Catherine, before Dec. 1839. Wrote and published *Mormonism Exposed, Being a Journal of a Residence in Missouri from the 28th of May to the 20th of August, 1838,* 1840.

Tanner, John (15 Aug. 1778–13 Apr. 1850), farmer, timberland owner. Born at Hopkinton, Washington Co., Rhode Island. Son of Joshua Tanner and Thankful Tefft. Moved to Greenwich, Washington Co., New York, ca. 1791. Married first Tabitha Bentley,

1800. Wife died, Apr. 1801. Married second Lydia Stewart, fall 1801. Moved to Northwest Bay (near Bolton), Warren Co., New York, 1818. Moved to Bolton Landing, Warren Co., 1823. Wife died, 1825. Married third Elizabeth Beswick, 1825. Baptized into LDS church, 17 Sept. 1832, at Bolton Landing. Ordained a priest by Orson Pratt, 2 Feb. 1833, at Bolton. Moved to Kirtland, Geauga Co., Ohio, Dec. 1834. Loaned and donated substantial monies to JS and church. Stockholder in Kirtland Safety Society. Left Kirtland for Far West, Caldwell Co., Missouri, 1838. Severely beaten during conflict between Latter-day Saints and other Missourians, fall 1838. Moved to New Liberty, Pope Co., Illinois, Mar.–Apr. 1839. Located near Montrose, Lee Co., Iowa Territory, Mar. 1840. Materially assisted in building of temple in Nauvoo, Hancock Co., Illinois. Served mission to New York, 1844. Ordained a high priest, by Dec. 1845. Moved to what became Council Bluffs, Pottawattamie Co., Iowa Territory, spring 1846. Moved to Salt Lake Valley, 1848. Died at South Cottonwood, Salt Lake Valley.

Taylor, John (1 Nov. 1808–25 July 1887), preacher, editor, publisher, politician. Born at Milnthorpe, Westmoreland, England. Son of James Taylor and Agnes Taylor, members of Church of England. Around age sixteen, joined Methodists and was local preacher. Migrated from England to York, York Township, York Co., Home District, Upper Canada, ca. 1832. Married Leonora Cannon, 28 Jan. 1833, at York. Baptized into LDS church by Parley P. Pratt, 9 May 1836, and ordained an elder shortly after. Appointed to preside over churches in Upper Canada. Ordained a high priest by JS and others, 21 Aug. 1837. Moved to Kirtland, Geauga Co., Ohio. Moved to Far West, Caldwell Co., Missouri, 1838. Ordained member of Quorum of the Twelve by Brigham Young and Heber C. Kimball, 19 Dec. 1838, at Far West. Served mission to England, 1839–1841. In Nauvoo, Hancock Co., Illinois, served as member of city council, judge advocate of Nauvoo Legion, and editor of *Times and Seasons* and *Nauvoo Neighbor*. Member of Nauvoo Masonic Lodge. Admitted to Council of Fifty, 11 Mar. 1844. Participated in plural marriage during JS's lifetime. With JS when JS and Hyrum Smith were murdered in jail at Carthage, Hancock Co., 27 June 1844. Served mission to England, 1846–1847. Arrived in Salt Lake Valley, 1847. Elected associate judge of provisional state of Deseret, 12 Mar. 1849. Served mission to France and Germany, 1849–1852; arranged for translation of Book of Mormon into French and published *L'Etoile du Deseret* (The star of Deseret). In Germany, supervised translation of Book of Mormon into German and published *Zions Panier* (Zion's banner). Appointed to preside over branches in eastern states, 1854. Editor of the *Mormon,* New York City, 1855–1857. Member of Utah territorial legislature, 1857–1876. Following death of Brigham Young, presided over church from 1877 to 1887. Ordained president of church, 10 Oct. 1880. Died at Kaysville, Davis Co., Utah Territory. Buried in Salt Lake City.

Thayer, Ezra (14 Oct. 1791–6 Sept. 1862), farmer, gardener, builder. Born in New York. Married Elizabeth Frank. Lived at Bloomfield, Ontario Co., New York, 1820. Lived at Farmington, Ontario Co., 1830. Baptized into LDS church by Parley P. Pratt and confirmed by JS, fall 1830, at Ontario Co. or Palmyra, Wayne Co., New York. Ordained a high priest by Lyman Wight, 4 June 1831, at Kirtland, Geauga Co., Ohio. Appointed to serve mission to Missouri, 6 June 1831. Attended organizational meeting of School of the Prophets, 22–23 Jan. 1833, in Kirtland. Commissioned to superintend land purchases in Kirtland, 1833. Participated in Camp of Israel expedition to Missouri, 1834. Church membership suspended, 2 May 1835, at Kirtland. Apparently reinstated. Appointed member of high council at Adam-ondi-Ahman, Daviess Co., Missouri, 28 June 1838. Lived at Brighton, Monroe Co., New York, 1840. Admitted to Council of Fifty, 11 Apr. 1844. Served mission to Michigan, May–June 1844. Lived at Chili, Monroe Co., 1850. Affiliated briefly with James J. Strang at Voree, Walworth Co., Wisconsin, but soon returned to New York. Rebaptized into LDS church, Sept. 1854, in New York. Lived at Jefferson, Cass Co., Michigan, 1860. Baptized into RLDS church, 11 Sept. 1860, at Galien, Berrien Co., Michigan. Died in Cass Co.

Thomas, David (12 May 1797–25 Apr. 1845). Born at Flat Rock District, Bourbon Co., Kentucky. Son of Richard Thomas and Elizabeth Bowles. Married Martha Parker, 17 Mar. 1816. Migrated to Carrollton, Carroll Co., Missouri, 1833. With Henry Root, landowner at De Witt, Carroll Co., successfully solicited some seventy families of Latter-day Saints to purchase land and settle there in 1838. Died in Carroll Co.

Thompson, Mercy Rachel Fielding (15 June 1807–15 Sept. 1893). Born in Honeydon, Bedfordshire, England. Daughter of John Fielding and Rachel Ibbotson. Immigrated to Upper Canada, 1832. Baptized into LDS church by Parley P. Pratt, 21 May 1836, near Toronto. Moved to Kirtland, Geauga Co., Ohio, May 1837. Married Robert Blashel Thompson, 4 June 1837, in Kirtland. Returned to Canada with husband when he was appointed to serve a mission there. Moved to Far West, Caldwell Co., Missouri, May 1838; to Quincy, Adams Co., Illinois, Feb. 1839; and to Commerce (later Nauvoo), Hancock Co., Illinois, Apr. 1839. Husband died, 27 Aug. 1841. Joined Female Relief Society of Nauvoo, 24 Mar. 1842. "Married or sealed" to Hyrum Smith "for time," 11 Aug. 1843, in Nauvoo. Moved to Winter Quarters, unorganized U.S. territory (later in Omaha, Douglas Co., Nebraska), Sept. 1846. Migrated to Salt Lake City, 24 Sept. 1847. Died in Salt Lake City.

Thompson, Robert Blashel (1 Oct. 1811–27 Aug. 1841), clerk, editor. Born in Great Driffield, Yorkshire, England. Member of Methodist church. Immigrated to Upper Canada, 1834. Baptized into LDS church by Parley P. Pratt, May 1836, in Upper Canada. Ordained an elder by John Taylor, 22 July 1836, in Upper Canada. Resided at Churchville, Chinguacousy Township, York Co. (later in Ontario), Upper Canada, 24 Apr. 1837. Moved to Kirtland, Geauga Co., Ohio, May 1837. Married Mercy Rachel Fielding, 4 June 1837, in Kirtland. Began serving mission to Upper Canada, June 1837. Returned to Kirtland, Mar. 1838. Moved to Far West, Caldwell Co., Missouri, with Hyrum Smith's family, May 1838. Fought in skirmish at Crooked River, near Ray Co., Missouri, 25 Oct. 1838. After Missouri expulsion, moved to Quincy, Adams Co., Illinois, 1839. Appointed to gather reports and publications circulated against LDS church, 4 May 1839, at Quincy. Ordained a seventy, 6 May 1839. Moved to Commerce (later Nauvoo), Hancock Co., Illinois, 1839. Appointed to Nauvoo incorporation committee, 1840. Regent of University of Nauvoo, 1840. Appointed aide-de-camp to lieutenant general in Nauvoo Legion, Mar. 1841. Served as scribe to JS and church clerk, 1840–1841. Preached sermon at funeral for Joseph Smith Sr., 15 Sept. 1840. Elected Nauvoo city treasurer, 3 Feb. 1841. Associate editor of *Times and Seasons,* May–Aug. 1841. Died in Nauvoo, apparently from severe lung infection.

Tompkins, George O. (20 Mar. 1780–4 Apr. 1846), judge. Born in Fluvanna Co., Virginia. Son of Benjamin Tompkins and Elizabeth Goodloe. Moved to Jefferson Co.,

Kentucky, where he taught school, by 1806. Moved to Franklin, Howard Co., Missouri, and practiced law, 1816. Married Elizabeth Lientz, 9 Sept. 1824, in Boone Co., Missouri. Served as Missouri Supreme Court justice, 1824–1845. Petitioned by JS and others for release from jail, 15 Mar. 1839. Died near Jefferson City, Cole Co., Missouri.

Townsend, James (20 Feb. 1808–2 Apr. 1886), brick mason, hotel keeper. Born in Buxton, York Co., District of Maine. Son of Jacob Townsend and Abigail Elden. Married Susan Davis, 11 Apr. 1828, in Buxton. Baptized into LDS church, Aug. 1833. Preached with Wilford Woodruff at Bangor, Penobscot Co., Maine, 1838. Ordained a seventy, Feb. 1844. Migrated to Salt Lake Valley; arrived 13 Aug. 1852. Proprietor of Salt Lake House, 1854. Served mission to England, 1864. Proprietor of Townsend House hotel, in Salt Lake City. Died in Salt Lake City.

Turnham, Joel (23 Sept. 1783–24 Aug. 1862), judge, farmer. Born in Virginia. Married Elizabeth Rice, ca. Feb. 1806, in Jefferson Co., Kentucky. Moved to Jessamine Co., Kentucky, by 1810. Served in War of 1812 in Kentucky militia. Moved to Clay Co., Missouri, by 1822. Clay Co. court judge, 1827–1830, 1838–1844, 1854–1856. Built tobacco warehouse at Liberty Landing (later Liberty), Clay Co., winter 1830–1831. Lived in Fishing River, Clay Co., 1850. Moved to Milam Co., Texas, by 1860. Died in Milam Co.

Tuttle, Smith (12 Mar. 1795–7 Mar. 1865), shipping merchant, land speculator. Born in East Haven, New Haven Co., Connecticut. Son of Christopher Tuttle and Abigail Luddington. Moved to Wallingford, New Haven Co., by 1810. Married first Rachel Gillett. Married second Amarilla Sanford Gillett, 18 Jan. 1829, in New Haven, New Haven Co. Lived in New Haven, by 1830. In Aug. 1839, with land-speculating partners Horace Hotchkiss and John Gillet, sold land in Commerce (later Nauvoo), Hancock Co., Illinois, to JS. Died in New Haven.

Van Buren, Martin (5 Dec. 1782–24 July 1862), lawyer, politician, diplomat, farmer. Born in Kinderhook, Columbia Co., New York. Son of Abraham Van Buren and Maria Hoes Van Alen. Member of Reformed Protestant Dutch Church. Worked as law clerk, 1800, in New York City. Returned to Kinderhook, 1803. Married Hannah Hoes, 21 Feb. 1807, in Catskill, Greene Co., New York. Served as surrogate of Columbia Co., 1808–1813. Moved to Hudson, Columbia Co., 1809. Served as state senator, 1813–1820; as regent of University of New York, beginning 1815; and as attorney general of New York, 1816–1819. Moved to Albany, 1816. Served as U.S. senator, 1821–1828. Elected governor of New York, 1829. U.S. secretary of state, 1829–1831. Ambassador to Great Britain, 1831–1832. Served as vice president of U.S., 1833–1837, and as president of U.S., 1837–1841. Declined to assist JS and Saints in obtaining redress for losses in Missouri, 1839. Retired to Kinderhook to farm. Toured Europe, 1853–1855. Died in Kinderhook.

Wait, Truman (ca. 1810–1847), baptized into LDS church, before Jan. 1833. Ordained a priest by Hyrum Smith, 21 Jan. 1833, in Kirtland, Geauga Co., Ohio. Appointed to serve mission to eastern states, 12 Mar. 1833. Married Sarah Hodges, 12 Dec. 1833, in Cuyahoga Co., Ohio. Moved to Clay Co., Missouri, ca. 1834. Ordained an elder, before Aug. 1834. Served on Kirtland high council. Labored on Kirtland temple. Moved to Far West, Caldwell Co., Missouri, 1837; and to Illinois, 1839. Appointed to serve mission to Huron Co., Ohio, 10 Apr. 1843. Moved to Pittsburgh, after June 1844; and to St. Louis, 1846. Likely died in St. Louis.

West, Nathan Ayers (10 Apr. 1801–8 May 1888), joiner, farmer. Born in Hubbard, Trumbull Co., Ohio. Son of William West and Mary Ayers. Married first Mary Hulet, 25 Oct. 1828, in Portage Co., Ohio. Moved to Nelson, Portage Co., by 1830. Baptized into LDS church. Ordained an elder by Harvey Whitlock, 20 July 1833, in Jackson Co., Missouri. Married second Adaline Louisa Follett, 13 Mar. 1836, in Clay Co., Missouri. Moved to Caldwell Co., Missouri, by 1838. Appointed to serve mission to Illinois to campaign for JS as candidate for U.S. president, 15 Apr. 1844. Moved to Van Buren Co., Iowa, before 1847. Excommunicated, 20 Apr. 1851. Moved to Silver Creek, Mills Co., Iowa, before 1856. Married third Julia A. Flemming, 11 Nov. 1884, in Mills Co. Died in Malvern, Mills Co.

Whitmer, David (7 Jan. 1805–25 Jan. 1888), farmer, livery keeper. Born near Harrisburg, Dauphin Co., Pennsylvania. Son of Peter Whitmer Sr. and Mary Musselman. Raised Presbyterian. Moved to Ontario Co., New York, shortly after birth. Attended German Reformed Church. Arranged for completion of translation of Book of Mormon in his father's home, Fayette, Seneca Co., New York, June 1829. Baptized by JS, June 1829, in Seneca Lake, Seneca Co. One of the Three Witnesses of the Book of Mormon, 1829. Among six original members of church and ordained an elder, 6 Apr. 1830. Married Julia Ann Jolly, 9 Jan. 1831, at Seneca Co. Migrated from Fayette to Kirtland, Geauga Co., Ohio, 1831. Ordained a high priest by Oliver Cowdery, 25 Oct. 1831, at Orange, Cuyahoga Co., Ohio. Traveled to Jackson Co., Missouri, with Harvey G. Whitlock, 1831. Driven from Jackson Co. by vigilantes, Nov. 1833; located in Clay Co., Missouri. Appointed president of church in Missouri, 7 July 1834. Left for Kirtland, Sept. 1834. Stockholder in Kirtland Safety Society. Moved to Far West, Caldwell Co., Missouri, by 1837. Rejected as church president in Missouri at meetings in Far West, 5–9 Feb. 1838. Excommunicated, 13 Apr. 1838, at Far West. Expelled from Far West, late June 1838. In 1838, moved to Clay Co. and then to Richmond, Ray Co., Missouri, where he operated a livery stable. Ordained by William E. McLellin to preside over McLellinite Church of Christ, 1847, but later rejected that movement. Elected mayor of Richmond, 1867–1868. Founded Church of Christ (Whitmerite), 1875. Later set forth his religious claims in *An Address to All Believers in Christ, by a Witness to the Divine Authenticity of the Book of Mormon,* published 1887. Died at Richmond.

Whitmer, John (27 Aug. 1802–11 July 1878), farmer, stock raiser, newspaper editor. Born in Pennsylvania. Son of Peter Whitmer Sr. and Mary Musselman. Member of German Reformed Church, Fayette, Seneca Co., New York. Baptized by Oliver Cowdery, June 1829, most likely in Seneca Lake, Seneca Co. Acted as scribe during translation of Book of Mormon at Whitmer home. One of the Eight Witnesses of the Book of Mormon, June 1829. Ordained an elder, by 9 June 1830. Copied revelations as scribe to JS, July 1830. Sent by JS to Kirtland, Geauga Co., Ohio, ca. Dec. 1830. Appointed church historian, ca. 8 Mar. 1831. Worked on a church history, 1831–ca. 1847. Ordained a high priest by Lyman Wight, 4 June 1831, at Kirtland. With Oliver Cowdery, left Ohio to take revelations to Missouri for publication, Nov. 1831. Appointed member of United Firm, Apr. 1832. Married to Sarah Maria Jackson by William W. Phelps, 10 Feb. 1833, at Kaw Township, Jackson Co., Missouri. Expelled from Jackson Co. into Clay Co., Missouri, Nov. 1833. Appointed an assistant to his brother David Whitmer in Missouri church presidency, July 1834. Editor of *LDS Messenger and Advocate,* Kirtland, 1835–1836. Lived in

Clay Co., 1836. Helped establish Latter-day Saints at Far West, Missouri, 1836–1837. Excommunicated, 10 Mar. 1838, at Far West. Expelled from Far West; moved to Richmond, Ray Co., Missouri, June 1838. Returned to Far West after departure of Latter-day Saints. In Sept. 1847, met with his brother David Whitmer and William E. McLellin at Far West in an attempt to reconstitute Church of Christ under presidency of David Whitmer. Died at site of Far West.

Whitney, Newel Kimball (3/5 Feb. 1795–23 Sept. 1850), trader, merchant. Born at Marlborough, Windham Co., Vermont. Son of Samuel Whitney and Susanna Kimball. Moved to Fairfield, Herkimer Co., New York, 1803. Merchant at Plattsburg, Clinton Co., New York, 1814. Mercantile clerk for A. Sidney Gilbert at Painesville, Geauga Co., Ohio, ca. 1820. Opened store in Kirtland, Geauga Co., by 1822. Married Elizabeth Ann Smith, 20 Oct. 1822, in Geauga Co. Member of reformed Baptist (later Disciples of Christ or Campbellite) faith. Partner with A. Sidney Gilbert in N. K. Whitney & Co. store, by 1827. Baptized into LDS church by missionaries to unorganized Indian Territory, Nov. 1830. Appointed agent for church, 30 Aug. 1831. Ordained a high priest, by Dec. 1831. Appointed bishop at Kirtland, Dec. 1831. Traveled with JS to Missouri and then to New York City, Albany, and Boston, 1832. Appointed member of United Firm, Apr. 1832. Attended organizational meeting of School of the Prophets, 22–23 Jan. 1833, in Kirtland. En route to Missouri, fall 1838, when difficulties in that state were confirmed at St. Louis. Located his family temporarily at Carrollton, Greene Co., Illinois, and returned to Kirtland to conduct business. Moved family from Carrollton to Quincy, Adams Co., Illinois, and then to Commerce (later Nauvoo), Hancock Co., Illinois. Appointed bishop of Middle Ward at Commerce, Oct. 1839. Nauvoo city alderman, 1841–1843. Member of Nauvoo Masonic Lodge. Admitted to Council of Fifty, 11 Mar. 1844. Appointed trustee-in-trust for church following JS's death, Aug. 1844. Appointed "first bishop" of church, Oct. 1844. Joined exodus of Latter-day Saints into Iowa Territory and Winter Quarters, unorganized U.S. territory (later in Omaha, Douglas Co., Nebraska), 1846. Migrated to Salt Lake Valley, fall 1848. Bishop of Salt Lake City Eighteenth Ward, 1849. Elected treasurer and associate justice of provisional state of Deseret, 1849. Died at Salt Lake City.

Whitney, Samuel Franklin (17 Mar. 1804–22 Mar. 1886), farmer. Born in Fairfield, Herkimer Co., New York. Son of Samuel Whitney and Susanna Kimball. Moved to Kirtland, Geauga Co., Ohio, by Oct. 1828. Married first Eve Doane, 26 July 1829, in Geauga Co. Elected overseer of poor, 4 Apr. 1831, in Kirtland. Witness in case of *Ohio v. Hurlbut,* Mar. 1834. Married second Zama Jane Eddy, 8 Aug. 1861, in Cuyahoga Co., Ohio. Died at Kirtland.

Wight, Lyman (9 May 1796–31 Mar. 1858), farmer. Born at Fairfield, Herkimer Co., New York. Son of Levi Wight Jr. and Sarah Corbin. Served in War of 1812. Married Harriet Benton, 5 Jan. 1823, at Henrietta, Monroe Co., New York. Moved to Warrensville, Cuyahoga Co., Ohio, ca. 1826. Baptized into reformed Baptist (later Disciples of Christ or Campbellite) faith by Sidney Rigdon, May 1829. Moved to Isaac Morley homestead at Kirtland, Geauga Co., Ohio, Feb. 1830. Lived at Mayfield, Cuyahoga Co., when baptized into LDS church, 14 Nov. 1830. Ordained an elder by Oliver Cowdery, 20 Nov. 1830. Ordained JS and Sidney Rigdon high priests, 4 June 1831. Ordained a high priest by JS, 4 June 1831. Served mission to Jackson Co., Missouri, via Detroit and Pontiac,

Michigan Territory, June–Aug. 1831. Joined by family at Jackson Co., Sept. 1831; located at Prairie branch, Jackson Co. Appointed to serve mission to Missouri, Ohio, and Virginia, Jan. 1832. Moved to and presided over Big Blue settlement, Jackson Co. Driven from Jackson Co. into Clay Co., Missouri, Nov. 1833. Recruited volunteers for Camp of Israel expedition to Missouri, 1834. Member of Clay Co. high council, 1834. Moved to Caldwell Co., Missouri, 1837. Elected colonel at organization of Caldwell Co. militia, Aug. 1837. Moved to what became Adam-ondi-Ahman, Daviess Co., Missouri, 1838. Member of Adam-ondi-Ahman stake presidency, 1838. Prominent in Missouri Danite activities, 1838. Imprisoned with JS at Richmond, Ray Co., Missouri; Liberty, Clay Co.; and Gallatin, Daviess Co., 1838–1839. Allowed to escape Missouri imprisonment during change of venue to Columbia, Boone Co., Missouri. Moved to Quincy, Adams Co., Illinois, Apr. 1839. Counselor in Zarahemla stake presidency, Lee Co., Iowa Territory, Oct. 1839. Moved to Augusta, Des Moines Co., Iowa Territory, Nov. 1839. Trustee of Nauvoo House Association. Ordained member of Quorum of the Twelve, 8 Apr. 1841, at Nauvoo, Hancock Co., Illinois. Appointed aide-de-camp to major general in Nauvoo Legion, May 1841. Served fund-raising mission for Nauvoo House Association to Illinois, May–Sept. 1841. Served fund-raising mission for Nauvoo House Association to Illinois, Kentucky, Tennessee, Mississippi, and Louisiana, Jan.–Mar. 1842. Served mission to Tennessee, June–Aug. 1842. Member of Nauvoo City Council, 1841–1843. Member of Nauvoo Masonic Lodge. Served mission to New York and other eastern states, Sept. 1842–June 1843. Leader in procuring lumber for Nauvoo temple and Nauvoo House from pineries on Black River, Wisconsin Territory, 1843–1844. Added to Council of Fifty by JS, 18 Apr. 1844; formally admitted to council, 3 May 1844. Served mission to eastern states to campaign for JS as candidate for U.S. president, 1844. Returned to Wisconsin Territory, 1844–1845. Rejected from Council of Fifty, 4 Feb. 1845. Led company of some 150 Latter-day Saints from Wisconsin Territory to Republic of Texas, arriving in Nov. 1845. Moved to Zodiac, Gillespie Co., Texas, 1847. Excommunicated, 3 Dec. 1848. Died at Dexter, Medina Co., Texas, en route to Jackson Co., Missouri.

Wilder, Eli Trumbul (27 Nov. 1813–3 June 1904), lawyer, judge, realtor. Born in Hartland, Hartford Co., Connecticut. Son of Eli Wilder and Mary Johnson. Moved to Ashtabula Co., Ohio, 1837. Formed law partnership with Reuben Hitchcock, 11 July 1837, in Painesville, Geauga Co., Ohio. Married first Julia Wright Wakefield, 12 May 1839. Formed law partnership with Peter Hitchcock and Reuben Hitchcock as P & R Hitchcock & Wilder, 11 July 1842. Judge in Lake Co., Ohio, 1854. Judge in Court of Common Pleas in Ninth District (including Ashtabula, Lake, and Stark counties, Ohio), 1855. Opened real estate office in Dubuque, Dubuque Co., Iowa, 1855. Moved to Red Wing, Goodhue Co., Minnesota Territory, 1856. One of first members of Christ Church, in Red Wing. Partner with W. A. Williston in law firm of Wilder & Williston, in Red Wing. Married second Larissa Kendig, 1 Oct. 1868, in Waterloo, Seneca Co., New York. Died in Red Wing.

Williams, Frederick Granger (28 Oct. 1787–10 Oct. 1842), ship's pilot, teacher, physician, justice of the peace. Born at Suffield, Hartford Co., Connecticut. Son of William Wheeler Williams and Ruth Granger. Moved to Newburg, Cuyahoga Co., Ohio, 1799. Practiced Thomsonian botanical system of medicine as physician. Married Rebecca Swain, Dec. 1815. Lived at Warrensville, Cuyahoga Co., by 1816. Worshipped with Sidney Rigdon's reformed Baptist (later Disciples of Christ or Campbellite) congregation. Moved to Chardon, Geauga Co., Ohio, by 1828. Moved to Kirtland, Geauga Co., 1830. Baptized into LDS church and ordained an elder, Oct./Nov. 1830, by missionaries under leadership of Oliver Cowdery who were en route to Missouri and Indian reservations in unorganized U.S. territory. Accompanied Cowdery to Missouri frontier on mission. Ordained a high priest, 25 Oct. 1831, at Orange, Cuyahoga Co., Ohio. Appointed clerk and scribe to JS, 20 July 1832. Attended organizational meeting of School of the Prophets, 22–23 Jan. 1833, in Kirtland. Member of United Firm, 1833. Assistant president/counselor in presidency of church, 1833–1837. Consecrated by deed to JS roughly 142 prime acres in Kirtland, 1834. Participated in Camp of Israel expedition to Missouri, 1834. Editor of *Northern Times* and member of publications committee that printed Doctrine and Covenants and Emma Smith's *A Collection of Sacred Hymns, for the Church of the Latter Day Saints* under auspices of firm F. G. Williams & Co., 1835. Helped organize and was a trustee of School of the Prophets. Stockholder in Kirtland Safety Society. Elected justice of the peace, Kirtland, 1837. Elected officer of Kirtland Safety Society to replace Sidney Rigdon, July 1837. Removed from church presidency, 7 Nov. 1837. Moved to Far West, Caldwell Co., Missouri, 1837. An 8 July 1838 JS revelation directed that Williams be ordained an elder and preach abroad. Reconfirmed into LDS church, 5 Aug. 1838. Excommunicated, 17 Mar. 1839, at Quincy, Adams Co., Illinois. Restored to fellowship at Nauvoo, Hancock Co., Illinois, Apr. 1840. Died at Quincy.

Wilson, Moses Greer (1795–ca. 1868), farmer, merchant, land developer, postmaster. Born in Virginia. Moved to Greene Co., Tennessee, by Dec. 1818. Married first Margaret Guin, 23 Dec. 1829, in Greene Co. Moved to Pike Co., Illinois, by Apr. 1832. Served in Black Hawk War, 1832. Moved to Independence, Jackson Co., Missouri, by 1833. Operated store at Independence. Leader in movement to expel Saints from Jackson Co. Elected brigadier general in Missouri militia, Nov. 1833. Served as justice of Jackson Co. court, beginning 1834. Participated in Mormon War, 1838. A developer of Kansas City, Jackson Co., incorporated 14 Nov. 1838. Moved near McKinney, Collin Co., Texas, by 1846. Elected first district clerk, 13 July 1846, in Collin Co. Moved to Houston, after 17 Aug. 1847. Moved to Washington Co., Texas, by 1854. Married second Sophia Lewis, 1 Dec. 1857, in Washington Co. Served as postmaster in Vine Grove (near present-day Burton), Washington Co., ca. 1866.

Wilson, Robert (Nov. 1800–10 May 1870), politician, lawyer, farmer. Born near Staunton, Augusta Co., Virginia. Moved to Franklin, Howard Co., Missouri Territory, by 1820. Married Margaret (Peggie) Snoddy, 18 May 1826. Served as clerk of circuit and county courts in Randolph Co., Missouri, ca. 1828–1840. Admitted to the bar. Brigadier general in Missouri militia during Mormon War, ca. 1837. Elected U.S. senator, 1862. Died at Marshall, Saline Co., Missouri.

Winchester, Stephen (8 May 1795–1 Jan. 1873), farmer. Born in Vershire, Orange Co., Vermont. Son of Benjamin Winchester and Bethia Benjamins. Married Nancy Case, 31 July 1816, in Fort Edward, Washington Co., New York. Moved to Elk Creek, Erie Co., Pennsylvania, by 1820. Baptized into LDS church, 1833, in Erie Co. Moved to Kirtland, Geauga Co., Ohio, 1833. Participated in Camp of Israel expedition to Missouri, 1834. Ordained a seventy, after 2 May 1835. Moved near Far West, Caldwell Co., Missouri, 1837. Moved to Hancock Co., Illinois, by 1840. Appointed to serve mission to

Pennsylvania to campaign for JS as candidate for U.S. president, Apr. 1844. Moved to Winter Quarters, unorganized U.S. territory (later in Omaha, Douglas Co., Nebraska), 1846. Migrated to Salt Lake Valley, 1849. Died in Salt Lake City.

Woodruff, Wilford (1 Mar. 1807–2 Sept. 1898), farmer, miller. Born at Farmington, Hartford Co., Connecticut. Son of Aphek Woodruff and Beulah Thompson. Moved to Richland, Oswego Co., New York, 1832. Baptized into LDS church by Zera Pulsipher, 31 Dec. 1833, near Richland. Ordained a teacher, 2 Jan. 1834, at Richland. Moved to Kirtland, Geauga Co., Ohio, Apr. 1834. Participated in Camp of Israel expedition to Missouri, 1834. Ordained a priest, 5 Nov. 1834. Served mission to Arkansas, Tennessee, and Kentucky, 1834–1836. Ordained an elder, 1835. Appointed member of the Seventy, 31 May 1836. Stockholder in Kirtland Safety Society. Married to Phebe Carter by Frederick G. Williams, 13 Apr. 1837, at Kirtland. Served missions to New England and Fox Islands off coast of Maine, 1837–1838. Ordained member of Quorum of the Twelve by Brigham Young, 26 Apr. 1839, at Far West, Caldwell Co., Missouri. Served mission to Great Britain, 1839–1841. Appointed assistant chaplain in Nauvoo Legion, 3 July 1841. Member of city council, 1841–1843, in Nauvoo, Hancock Co., Illinois. Member of Nauvoo Masonic Lodge. Served mission to eastern states to raise funds for building Nauvoo temple, 1843. Admitted to Council of Fifty, 13 Mar. 1844. Served mission to eastern states to campaign for JS as candidate for U.S. president, 1844. Presided over British mission, Aug. 1844–Apr. 1846. Member of Brigham Young pioneer company that journeyed to Salt Lake Valley, 1847. Served mission to eastern states, 1848–1850. Member of Utah territorial legislature. Appointed assistant church historian, 7 Apr. 1856. President of temple in St. George, Washington Co., Utah Territory, 1877. President of Quorum of the Twelve, 1880. Sustained as church historian and general church recorder, 1883. President of church, 7 Apr. 1889–2 Sept. 1898. Died at San Francisco.

Young, Brigham (1 June 1801–29 Aug. 1877), carpenter, painter, glazier, colonizer. Born at Whitingham, Windham Co., Vermont. Son of John Young and Abigail (Nabby) Howe. Brought up in Methodist household; later joined Methodist church. Moved to Sherburne, Chenango Co., New York, 1804. Married first Miriam Angeline Works of Aurelius, Cayuga Co., New York, 8 Oct. 1824. Lived at Mendon, Monroe Co., New York, when baptized into LDS church by Eleazer Miller, 9/15 Apr. 1832. Wife died, 8 Sept. 1832. Served missions to New York and Upper Canada, 1832–1833. Migrated to Kirtland, Geauga Co., Ohio, 1833. Labored on Kirtland temple. Married second Mary Ann Angell, 31 Mar. 1834, in Geauga Co. Participated in Camp of Israel expedition to Missouri, 1834. Ordained member of Quorum of the Twelve by Oliver Cowdery, David Whitmer, and Martin Harris, 14 Feb. 1835, at Kirtland. Served mission to New York and New England, 1835–1837. Stockholder in Kirtland Safety Society. Fled Kirtland, 22 Dec. 1837. Joined JS en route to Far West, Caldwell Co., Missouri; arrived, 14 Mar. 1838. Member of presidency pro tempore of church in Far West, 1838. Helped direct Mormon evacuation from Missouri. Forced to leave Far West; reached Quincy, Adams Co., Illinois, Feb. 1839. Served mission to England, 1839–1841, departing from Montrose, Lee Co., Iowa Territory. Appointed president of Quorum of the Twelve, 14 Apr. 1840. Arrived in Nauvoo, Hancock Co., Illinois, 1 July 1841. Appointed assistant chaplain in Nauvoo Legion, 3 July 1841. Member of Nauvoo City Council, 1841–1845. Member of Nauvoo Masonic Lodge. Participated in plural marriage during JS's lifetime. Officiator in proxy baptisms for the dead in Nauvoo,

1843. Admitted to Council of Fifty, 11 Mar. 1844. Served mission to campaign for JS as candidate for U.S. president, 1844. With the Twelve, sustained to administer affairs of church after JS's death, 8 Aug. 1844, at Nauvoo. Reorganized Council of Fifty, 4 Feb. 1845. Recognized as "President of the whole Church of Latter Day Saints" at conference in Nauvoo, 7 Apr. 1845. Directed Mormon migration from Nauvoo to Salt Lake Valley, 1846–1848. Reorganized First Presidency of church, Dec. 1847. Governor of Utah Territory, 1850–1857. Superintendent of Indian affairs for Utah Territory, 1851–1857. Directed establishment of hundreds of settlements in western U.S. Died at Salt Lake City.

Young, Lorenzo Dow (19 Oct. 1807–21 Nov. 1895), farmer, plasterer, gardener, blacksmith, nurseryman. Born at Smyrna, Chenango Co., New York. Son of John Young and Abigail (Nabby) Howe. Married Persis Goodall, 6 June 1826, at Watertown, Jefferson Co., New York. Baptized into LDS church by John P. Greene, 1832. Moved to Kirtland, Geauga Co., Ohio, by 1834. Stockholder in Kirtland Safety Society. Moved to Missouri, Sept. 1837, and settled in Daviess Co., spring 1838. Moved to Far West, Caldwell Co., Missouri, Oct. 1838. Participated in skirmish at Crooked River, near Ray Co., Missouri, 25 Oct. 1838. Moved to Scott Co., Illinois, 1839; to Macedonia, Hancock Co., Illinois, 1841; and to Nauvoo, Hancock Co., 1842. Participated in plural marriage during JS's lifetime. Served mission to Ohio, 1844. Member of Brigham Young pioneer company that journeyed to Salt Lake Valley, 1847. Bishop of Salt Lake City Eighteenth Ward, 1851–1878. Ordained a patriarch, 1877. Died at Salt Lake City.

Organizational Charts

From 1837 to 1839, church leadership underwent substantial changes. In late 1837 and early 1838, JS oversaw or approved the removal and replacement of several officers because of their disaffection from or dissent against JS and other leaders. Also, beginning in early 1838, several officers in Kirtland, Ohio, followed JS in migrating to Missouri. The migration of leaders and the majority of other Latter-day Saints resulted in the need to fill positions in Kirtland and Missouri. The dynamics of leadership in the church's ecclesiastical organization were further disrupted by the imprisonment of JS and other leaders, the expulsion of the Latter-day Saints from Missouri, and the resettlement effort in Illinois and Iowa Territory.

The following charts provide information regarding the church and other relevant organizations between 1837 and 1839, particularly during the period covered in this volume: February 1838–August 1839. The charts depict the organizations and offices of the general leadership of the church and identify the men known to hold those offices. The charts also identify several local ecclesiastical leaders in Ohio, Missouri, and Illinois, as well as traveling authorities and other significant offices within the church's organization. Charts also identify offices in civic governments in Caldwell County, Missouri, which was widely recognized as a county set aside for Mormon settlement; the Caldwell County regiment of the state militia; the Society of the Daughter of Zion (also known as the Danite society); and the Mormon military.

This information has been compiled from minutes of meetings, other contemporaneous records, and later documents. In general, the charts present officers in the order they were listed in founding documents or as they were most commonly listed in documents from the period. Because not all organizational minutes and other administrative records are extant, in many cases the information in the charts has been pieced together from personal letters, journals, autobiographies, and other available documents. Readers wishing to conduct further research on specific groups or individuals may consult the annotated organizational charts and the glossary at the Joseph Smith Papers website, josephsmithpapers.org, as well as the Biographical Directory in this volume.

Church Structure, 1838–1839

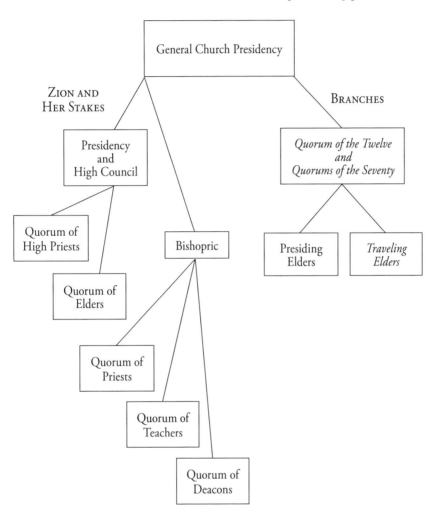

General Church Presidency

ZION AND HER STAKES

BRANCHES

Presidency and High Council

Quorum of the Twelve and Quorums of the Seventy

Quorum of High Priests

Bishopric

Presiding Elders

Traveling Elders

Quorum of Elders

Quorum of Priests

Quorum of Teachers

Quorum of Deacons

Key

MAJOR JURISDICTIONS
Standing organizations or officers
Traveling organizations or officers

General Church Officers

First Presidency

JS, as "President of the High Priesthood," and the men who served as counselors to him in that office formed a presidency of the high priesthood. This general church presidency, which was also called the First Presidency, oversaw all other administrative bodies in the church. Initially, the presidency was composed of JS as president and two other men as counselors. In 1834, the presidency was expanded to include additional members. On 3 September 1837, in a reorganization conference held in Kirtland, Ohio, JS was sustained as president of the church with two counselors and four assistant counselors. A revelation JS dictated on 26 April 1838 referred to Sidney Rigdon, Hyrum Smith, and other counselors, but extant minutes and other documents show no sign of men functioning as assistant counselors after JS moved from Ohio to Missouri in early 1838.

The following are notable events that occurred relative to the First Presidency from 3 September 1837 to 28 June 1838:

- 3 September 1837: JS sustained as president of the church with two counselors and four assistant counselors.
- 7 November 1837: Frederick G. Williams rejected from the First Presidency; replaced by Hyrum Smith.
- 12 April 1838: Oliver Cowdery excommunicated.
- 28 June 1838: John Smith was reassigned as president of Adam-ondi-Ahman stake.

3 September 1837	7 November 1837	6 April 1838
President Joseph Smith Jr.	*President* Joseph Smith Jr.	*President* Joseph Smith Jr.
First Counselor Sidney Rigdon	*First Counselor* Sidney Rigdon	*First Counselor* Sidney Rigdon
Second Counselor Frederick G. Williams	*Second Counselor* Hyrum Smith	*Second Counselor* Hyrum Smith
Assistant Counselors Oliver Cowdery Hyrum Smith Joseph Smith Sr. John Smith	*Assistant Counselors* Oliver Cowdery Joseph Smith Sr. John Smith	*Assistant Counselors* Oliver Cowdery Joseph Smith Sr. John Smith
		Scribe George W. Robinson

12 April 1838	28 June 1838
President Joseph Smith Jr.	*President* Joseph Smith Jr.
First Counselor Sidney Rigdon	*First Counselor* Sidney Rigdon
Second Counselor Hyrum Smith	*Second Counselor* Hyrum Smith
Assistant Counselors Joseph Smith Sr. John Smith	*Assistant Counselor* Joseph Smith Sr.
Scribe George W. Robinson	*Scribe* George W. Robinson

Other General Officers

Patriarch Joseph Smith Sr. (appointed 6 December 1834)	*Clerk and Recorder* George W. Robinson (appointed recorder 17 September 1837; appointed clerk and recorder 6 April 1838)	*Historians* John Whitmer (appointed 9 April 1831; excommunicated 10 March 1838) John Corrill (appointed 6 April 1838; disaffected November 1838; excommunicated 17 March 1839) Elias Higbee (appointed 6 April 1838)

Agents and Scribe for JS and the Church

As president of the church, JS appointed several men to act as scribes and agents. Scribes kept JS's journals, copied his correspondence, worked on his history, and produced and copied other papers. Agents acted on JS's behalf to purchase land and pay debts. After JS and Sidney Rigdon left Kirtland for Missouri in January 1838, church agents William Marks and Oliver Granger worked to resolve JS's and Rigdon's debts in Kirtland and to oversee church property there. As Latter-day Saints gathered in Illinois and Iowa Territory, agents purchased land for Mormon settlement, under the direction of church leaders.

By February 1838 William Marks Oliver Granger	*Circa April 1839* William Marks Oliver Granger Alanson Ripley George W. Robinson	*Circa June 1839* William Marks Oliver Granger Alanson Ripley George W. Robinson Vinson Knight

Scribe James Mulholland (circa 4 September–circa 5 October 1838; 22 April–3 November 1839)

Traveling Church Officers

Quorum of the Twelve Apostles

The Quorum of the Twelve Apostles originally had jurisdiction over all branches of the church outside of Zion and its stakes. In 1838, Zion was centered in Far West, Missouri. During early 1839, Zion and the Adam-ondi-Ahman stake were disbanded because church members were migrating out of the state under the terms of the expulsion order issued by Governor Lilburn W. Boggs. On 16 January, the members of the First Presidency, who were imprisoned in Clay County, Missouri, acknowledged in a letter to apostles Heber C. Kimball and Brigham Young that "the gathering of necessity stopt" and stated that the "management of the affairs of the [entire] church" temporarily fell to the quorum.

Dissent and disaffection, combined with the 1838 conflict between the Latter-day Saints and other Missourians, reduced the number of functioning apostles throughout 1838, but by the end of the year, quorum leaders began to ordain new apostles under the direction of the First Presidency. The quorum continued to stabilize in early and mid-1839, and its members embarked on a mission to Europe by the end of the year.

The original members of the quorum were ranked in seniority based on age. Newer members also were ordered by age, ranked below the original members. On 16 January 1839, the First Presidency instructed Kimball and Young to appoint the oldest of the original members to be the president of the quorum. Young, who was the oldest, acted as president of the quorum, although he was not sustained as president until April 1840.

The following are notable events that occurred relative to the Quorum of the Twelve Apostles from 7 November 1837 to 8 July 1839:

- Late December 1837: Luke Johnson and John F. Boynton excommunicated; John Taylor and John E. Page appointed (but not ordained).
- 13 April 1838: Lyman Johnson excommunicated.
- 11 May 1838: William E. McLellin removed.
- 8 July 1838: John Taylor and John E. Page reappointed (but not ordained); Wilford Woodruff and Willard Richards appointed (but not ordained).
- Circa 20 October 1838: Thomas B. Marsh and Orson Hyde disaffected.
- 25 October 1838: David W. Patten killed.
- 19 December 1838: John Taylor and John E. Page ordained.
- 16 January 1839: Brigham Young appointed as acting president.
- 26 April 1839: Wilford Woodruff ordained.
- 4 May 1839: Orson Hyde and William Smith suspended; George A. Smith ordained.
- 25 May 1839: William Smith restored.
- 27 June 1839: Orson Hyde restored.
- 8 July 1839: Willard Richards reappointed (but not ordained).

7 November 1837–19 December 1838

7 November 1837	Late December 1837	13 April 1838	11 May 1838
President	*President*	*President*	*President*
Thomas B. Marsh	Thomas B. Marsh	Thomas B. Marsh	Thomas B. Marsh
Members	*Members*	*Members*	*Members*
David W. Patten	David W. Patten	David W. Patten	David W. Patten
Brigham Young	Brigham Young	Brigham Young	Brigham Young
Heber C. Kimball	Heber C. Kimball	Heber C. Kimball	Heber C. Kimball
Orson Hyde	Orson Hyde	Orson Hyde	Orson Hyde
William E. McLellin	William E. McLellin	William E. McLellin	
Parley P. Pratt	Parley P. Pratt	Parley P. Pratt	Parley P. Pratt
William Smith	William Smith	William Smith	William Smith
Luke Johnson			
Orson Pratt	Orson Pratt	Orson Pratt	Orson Pratt
John F. Boynton			
Lyman Johnson	Lyman Johnson		

8 July 1838	Circa 20 October 1838	25 October 1838	19 December 1838
President	*President*	*President*	*President*
Thomas B. Marsh			
Members	*Members*	*Members*	*Members*
David W. Patten	David W. Patten		
Brigham Young	Brigham Young	Brigham Young	Brigham Young
Heber C. Kimball	Heber C. Kimball	Heber C. Kimball	Heber C. Kimball
Orson Hyde			
Parley P. Pratt	Parley P. Pratt	Parley P. Pratt	Parley P. Pratt
William Smith	William Smith	William Smith	William Smith
Orson Pratt	Orson Pratt	Orson Pratt	Orson Pratt
			John Taylor
			John E. Page

16 January 1839–8 July 1839

16 January 1839	26 April 1839	4 May 1839	25 May 1839
Acting President	*Acting President*	*Acting President*	*Acting President*
Brigham Young	Brigham Young	Brigham Young	Brigham Young
Members	*Members*	*Members*	*Members*
Heber C. Kimball	Heber C. Kimball	Heber C. Kimball	Heber C. Kimball
Parley P. Pratt	Parley P. Pratt	Parley P. Pratt	Parley P. Pratt
William Smith	William Smith		William Smith
Orson Pratt	Orson Pratt	Orson Pratt	Orson Pratt
John Taylor	John Taylor	John Taylor	John Taylor
John E. Page	John E. Page	John E. Page	John E. Page
	Wilford Woodruff	Wilford Woodruff	Wilford Woodruff
		George A. Smith	George A. Smith

27 June 1839	8 July 1839
Acting President	*Acting President*
Brigham Young	Brigham Young
Members	*Members*
Heber C. Kimball	Heber C. Kimball
Orson Hyde	Orson Hyde
Parley P. Pratt	Parley P. Pratt
William Smith	William Smith
Orson Pratt	Orson Pratt
John Taylor	John Taylor
John E. Page	John E. Page
Wilford Woodruff	Wilford Woodruff
George A. Smith	George A. Smith

Presidency of the Seventy

A quorum of seventy traveling elders was organized in 1835. The seventy were responsible for proselytizing and for administering to church members in branches outside of Zion and established stakes, under the direction of the Quorum of the Twelve Apostles. Unlike other quorums in the church, which were generally presided over by one president and two counselors, the First Quorum of the Seventy was presided over by seven presidents. It is unclear whether there was an order of seniority among the presidents. The Presidency of the Seventy had authority to organize further quorums of seventy "until seven times seventy" and was to preside over each quorum, functioning as a distinct group. Second and third quorums were organized in 1836. The members of the quorums occasionally met in general meetings for all seventies; there are no known records of members of an individual quorum meeting together in 1838 or 1839. The Presidency of the Seventy organized the "Kirtland Camp" of Ohio Saints migrating to Missouri in 1838 and renewed proselytizing efforts in 1839.

The following are notable events that occurred relative to the Presidency of the Seventy from circa 13 January to 13 March 1838

- Circa 13 January 1838: John Gaylord excommunicated.
- 6 February 1838: Henry Harriman appointed.
- 6 March 1838: Salmon Gee rejected; Zerah Pulsipher ordained.
- 13 March 1838: Elias Smith and Benjamin S. Wilber appointed pro tempore presidents to fill in for Daniel S. Miles and Levi Hancock, who apparently had relocated from Kirtland to Missouri.

By 3 September 1837	Circa 13 January 1838	6 February 1838
Presidents John Gaylord James Foster Salmon Gee Daniel S. Miles Joseph Young Josiah Butterfield Levi Hancock	*Presidents* James Foster Salmon Gee Daniel S. Miles Joseph Young Josiah Butterfield Levi Hancock	*Presidents* James Foster Salmon Gee Daniel S. Miles Joseph Young Josiah Butterfield Levi Hancock Henry Harriman

6 March 1838	13 March 1838	October 1838
Presidents James Foster Daniel S. Miles Joseph Young Josiah Butterfield Levi Hancock Henry Harriman Zerah Pulsipher	*Presidents* James Foster Daniel S. Miles Joseph Young Josiah Butterfield Levi Hancock Henry Harriman Zerah Pulsipher *Presidents pro tempore* Elias Smith Benjamin S. Wilber	*Presidents* James Foster Daniel S. Miles Joseph Young Josiah Butterfield Levi Hancock Henry Harriman Zerah Pulsipher *Presidents pro tempore* Elias Smith Benjamin S. Wilber

31 August 1839
Presidents James Foster Daniel S. Miles Joseph Young Josiah Butterfield Levi Hancock Henry Harriman Zerah Pulsipher

Local Church Officers

Within a few years after the church's organization, Missouri and Kirtland, Ohio, became the two approved places for church members to gather. In 1834 JS organized the presidencies and high councils in Zion (the church in Missouri) and the Kirtland stake of Zion. In Kirtland, where the members of the First Presidency resided, the First Presidency served as the presidency of the stake. By the end of 1837, the First Presidency was planning to move from Kirtland to Far West. Before they moved, they appointed a presidency for the Kirtland stake and emphasized their own role as the presidency over the entire church. Before the First Presidency arrived in Far West, the church there deposed the Zion presidency and appointed two of the resident apostles to serve as presidents pro tempore until the arrival of the First Presidency. After arriving, the First Presidency retained the new Zion presidency and reiterated the First Presidency's role of overseeing the entire church.

In the months after the First Presidency moved to Missouri, most of the Kirtland Saints also made the journey, as directed in a revelation JS dictated in January 1838. Several hundred of the migrating Saints were directed to settle at Adam-ondi-Ahman, where JS established a stake. In 1839, after the Saints were forcibly expelled from Missouri, they relocated to Commerce, Illinois, and across the Mississippi River in Lee County, Iowa Territory; these areas were organized into stakes by the end of the year.

Throughout the upheaval and displacement in 1838 and 1839, the church essentially maintained a pattern of two communities approved for Mormon settlement. Many of the same people served as the leaders in these gathering centers. For example, JS appointed William Marks and John Smith as members of the Kirtland presidency and later appointed Smith the president of Adam-ondi-Ahman and directed Marks to preside over the church in Far West. In May 1839, Marks was appointed president of the church in Commerce, and later that year John Smith was appointed president of the church in Lee County.

Kirtland Stake

The church organization at Kirtland, Ohio, began disintegrating in late 1837, when several leaders dissented from the course that JS and other leaders pursued. The Kirtland stake further dissolved in 1838 after most loyal Latter-day Saints followed the First Presidency to Missouri. Although a few leaders stayed behind to oversee stake matters and some of the other leaders were replaced, the last recorded action of the high council occurred in April 1838. It appears that the Kirtland presidency dissolved after William Marks left in October 1838. In May 1839, members at a general conference of the church voted that Kirtland be again considered "a stake of Zion," and Oliver Granger was appointed to preside. Because of widespread emigration and the lack of records, the changing leadership of the stake can be tracked only in part.

On 3 September 1837, ten men were sustained as members of the Kirtland high council. The council continued to function through at least April 1838, but by that time nearly half of the council members had left for Missouri or had become members of the Kirtland presidency. As there are no extant minutes of council meetings in 1838, there is no evidence that additional counselors were called to replace those who left for Missouri.

Presidency	
President William Marks (appointed January 1838; departed Kirtland October 1838) Oliver Granger (appointed 4 May 1839; certified 6 May 1839)	*Counselors* John Smith (appointed January 1838; departed Kirtland 5 April 1838) Reynolds Cahoon (appointed January 1838; departed Kirtland circa March 1838) [Hugh?] Cole (appointed by 22 July 1838) Hiram Kellogg (appointed by 22 July 1838)

High Council
Counselors John P. Greene (in Missouri by April 1838) Asahel Smith (in Iowa by October 1839) Mayhew Hillman (departed Kirtland circa late April 1838) Noah Packard (departed Kirtland after August 1838) Oliver Granger (appointed president over Kirtland, 4 May 1839) David Dort (in Missouri by December 1838) Lyman Sherman (departed Kirtland ca. late April 1838) Phineas Richards (departed Kirtland for Massachusetts 16 November 1837) Henry Sherwood (in Missouri by late summer 1838) Harlow Redfield (departed Kirtland circa late April 1838)

Bishop Newel K. Whitney (departed Kirtland fall 1838)

President of the High Priests Quorum Don Carlos Smith (appointed 15 January 1836; departed Kirtland between 12 January and 7 May 1838) Hiram Kellogg (appointed by 10 June 1838)

Presidency of the Elders Quorum
President Reuben Hedlock (appointed between 22 January and 26 February 1838; released 17 June 1838) John Morton (appointed 10 June 1838) *First Counselor* John Morton (appointed before 26 February 1838; appointed president 10 June 1838) Hezekiah Fisk (appointed 8 July 1838; departed Kirtland before summer 1839) *Counselor (unknown whether first or second)* Martin H. Peck (appointed 26 February 1838; departed Kirtland 5 July 1838) *Second Counselor* Lahasa Hollister (appointed 8 July 1838)

Zion

In 1834, David Whitmer was appointed president of the church in Zion (Missouri), with William W. Phelps and John Whitmer as assistant presidents. In early February 1838, the presidency members were removed from office by a "general assembly" of the church, and resident apostles Thomas B. Marsh and David W. Patten were appointed presidents pro tempore. When Phelps and John Whitmer were assistants to David Whitmer, they were also called presidents. Similarly, the minutes of a 10 February 1838 council meeting designate both Marsh and Patten as "Presidents, pro. tempor," but it was probably understood that Marsh, the president of the Quorum of the Twelve Apostles, was the preeminent president and Patten was his assistant. On 6 April, a few weeks after JS and apostle Brigham Young arrived in Far West (the center of Zion in 1838), the church in Zion appointed Marsh "President pro tempore of the Church in Zion," with Patten and Young as "his assistant presidents." Marsh, Patten, and Young were the three most senior apostles. On 8 July 1838, JS dictated a revelation that appointed William Marks, who was then in Kirtland, to preside over the Saints in Far West. Marks, however, did not arrive in Missouri prior to the armed conflict with other Missourians that erupted in fall 1838 and was therefore never ordained to the position. In late October 1838, during the height of the conflict, Marsh defected and Patten was killed, leaving only Young in the presidency. On 16 January 1839, Young met with the Zion high council for the last time on record, presumably because on the same day, the First Presidency wrote a letter directing the Quorum of the Twelve Apostles to take charge of the church since "the gathering of necessity [had] stopt." The Missouri Saints were emigrating from the state, and the organization of Zion was being dissolved. Shortly thereafter, the high council was effectively replaced by a committee directing the evacuation effort, further indicating that the usual church leadership structure in Zion was being disbanded.

The Zion high council consisted of twelve high counselors. John Murdock, as the oldest member of the council, was designated its president in 1836 and continued in this role until being released on 6 October 1838. On 12 April 1838, the council clarified that the president was "to receive charges and give notice to the defendant, also, to call the Council together and organize them." The president of the high council presided at council meetings except when a member of the Zion presidency or JS was present and presided. As counselors moved away from Far West, they were released and other men were called in their stead. Clerk Oliver Cowdery was also replaced because of dissension, which ultimately led to his excommunication. Substitutes also served frequently in the place of permanent counselors who were unavailable. When Murdock was released because he had moved to De Witt to help establish a new Mormon settlement there, Samuel Bent was appointed to the council and may have been designated president because he was the oldest high counselor. After the Saints were driven from De Witt, Murdock rejoined the high council. The last recorded meeting of the Zion high council occurred on 16 January 1839.

Don Carlos Smith, who had been president of the quorum of high priests in Kirtland, followed JS in migrating to Far West. In October 1839, he was sustained as president of the quorum in Zion at a general church conference in Commerce, Illinois, suggesting that he replaced Rich after arriving in Far West, possibly between 6 and 8 July 1838. Smith served a fund-raising mission from September to December 1838.

By 15 March 1838, Bishop Edward Partridge received authorization from the high council to organize the Aaronic, or lesser, priesthood quorums in Far West. As bishop, Partridge had authority to preside over the priests quorum. Additionally, as in 1836, a member of the quorum may have been appointed as a president of the quorum. Whereas extant records identify the president of the teachers quorum, extant sources do not name the president of the deacons quorum.

Presidency

7 July 1834–9 Feb. 1838	10 Feb.–6 Apr. 1838	6 Apr.–ca. 20 Oct. 1838	25 Oct.–16 Jan. 1839
President David Whitmer *Assistant Presidents* William W. Phelps John Whitmer	*Presidents pro Tempore* Thomas B. Marsh David W. Patten (possibly served as an assistant to Marsh)	*President pro Tempore* Thomas B. Marsh *Assistant Presidents* David W. Patten Brigham Young	*Acting President* Brigham Young

High Council

By 7 November 1837	6 April 1838	7 April 1838
President John Murdock	*President* John Murdock	*President* John Murdock
Counselors Solomon Hancock Elias Higbee Calvin Beebe George Morey Thomas Grover Simeon Carter Lyman Wight Newel Knight George M. Hinkle Levi Jackman Elisha H. Groves	*Counselors* Solomon Hancock Elias Higbee Calvin Beebe George Morey Thomas Grover Simeon Carter Lyman Wight Newel Knight George M. Hinkle Levi Jackman Elisha H. Groves	*Counselors* Solomon Hancock Elias Higbee George Morey Thomas Grover Simeon Carter Newel Knight George M. Hinkle Levi Jackman Jared Carter John P. Greene George W. Harris
Clerk Oliver Cowdery	*Clerk* Ebenezer Robinson	*Clerk* Ebenezer Robinson

6 October 1838	13 December 1838	16 January 1839
President Samuel Bent?	*President* Samuel Bent?	*President* Samuel Bent?
Counselors Solomon Hancock Elias Higbee George Morey Thomas Grover Simeon Carter Newel Knight George M. Hinkle Levi Jackman Jared Carter John P. Greene George W. Harris Isaac Higbee	*Counselors* Solomon Hancock Thomas Grover Simeon Carter Newel Knight Levi Jackman Jared Carter George W. Harris Isaac Higbee John Murdock David Dort John Badger Lyman Sherman	*Counselors* Solomon Hancock Thomas Grover Simeon Carter Newel Knight Levi Jackman Jared Carter George W. Harris Isaac Higbee John Murdock David Dort John Badger Lyman Sherman
Clerk Ebenezer Robinson	*Clerk* Ebenezer Robinson	*Clerk* Ebenezer Robinson

Bishopric

Bishop
Edward Partridge (appointed Feb. 1831; sustained 7 November 1837)

Counselors
Isaac Morley (appointed 3 June 1831; sustained 7 November 1837)
Titus Billings (appointed 1 August 1837; sustained 7 November 1837)

Keeper of the Lord's Storehouse
John Corrill (appointed 22 May 1837; disaffected October 1838)

Other Known Melchizedek Priesthood Leaders

Patriarch
Isaac Morley (appointed 7 November 1837)

Presidency of High Priests Quorum
Charles C. Rich, president (appointed by 20 August 1837)
Don Carlos Smith?, president (possibly appointed between 6 and 8 July 1838)
Samuel Bent, counselor (date of appointment unknown; until 6 October 1838)

President of Elders Quorum
Harvey Green (appointed between 20 August 1837–not after 6 October 1838)
Stephen Chase (appointed 6 October 1838)

Other Known Aaronic Priesthood Leaders

President of Priests Quorum
Edward Partridge

President of Teachers Quorum
Albert Petty (appointed 15 March 1838)

Licensing Officers

6 December 1837–10 February 1838	10 February 1838–8 April 1838
Chairman David Whitmer	*Chairman* Thomas B. Marsh (possibly)
Chairman pro Tempore Frederick G. Williams	
Clerk William W. Phelps	*Clerk* David W. Patten (possibly)
Clerk pro Tempore John Whitmer	
Recording Clerk Oliver Cowdery	

Other Officers

Clerk and Recorder Ebenezer Robinson (appointed 6 April 1838)
Recorder of Patriarchal Blessings Oliver Cowdery (appointed 6 December 1837; excommunicated 12 April 1838) Isaac Morley (appointed spring 1838; appointment rescinded 16 January 1839)

Adam-ondi-Ahman Stake

As Caldwell County, Missouri, filled with Latter-day Saints, immigration was steered northward to Adam-ondi-Ahman, Daviess County, Missouri, where a stake was organized on 28 June 1838. Because stake records are not extant, little is known regarding leadership changes before the stake was dissolved in mid-November 1838, when the Missouri state militia forcibly evacuated the Latter-day Saints from the county.

Presidency
President John Smith
First Counselor Reynolds Cahoon
Second Counselor Lyman Wight

High Council
John Lemon (excommunicated 10 August 1838) Daniel Stanton Mayhew Hillman Daniel Carter Isaac Perry Harrison Sagers Alanson Brown Thomas Gordon Lorenzo Barnes George A. Smith Harvey Olmstead Ezra Thayer

Bishop pro Tempore Vinson Knight

De Witt Stake

On 23 June 1838, George M. Hinkle and John Murdock, two members of the Zion high council, purchased half of the lots in the town plat of De Witt, Carroll County, Missouri, under the direction of the high council and JS. Shortly afterward, Hinkle and Murdock relocated there with their families. Church member Reed Peck later reported that the First Presidency intended to make De Witt "the fourth 'Stake of Zion,'" after Kirtland, Far West, and Adam-ondi-Ahman. On 17 September, JS and Sidney Rigdon wrote a letter stating that De Witt had been recently appointed a stake. Though designated as a stake, De Witt was apparently never formally organized with a presidency, high council, bishopric, or other stake officers. Charles H. Hales, a Latter-day Saint living in De Witt, later wrote that George M. Hinkle served as the "president of the Branch" at De Witt.

Removal and Settlement Committees

Of the several ad hoc committees established throughout the period covered in this volume, two were especially important: (1) the committee that supervised the evacuation of the Latter-day Saints from Missouri and (2) the committee that helped the Saints resettle in Illinois. These committees served as interim organizations for the church after the Saints were forced from their homes in Missouri and before they established new settlements in Illinois.

Removal Committee (29 January–14 April 1839)

29 January 1839	1 February 1839
William Huntington Charles Bird Alanson Ripley Theodore Turley Daniel Shearer Shadrach Roundy Jonathan Hale	William Huntington Charles Bird Alanson Ripley Theodore Turley Daniel Shearer Shadrach Roundy Jonathan Hale Elias Smith Erastus Bingham Stephen Markham James Newberry

Settlement Committee (circa January 1839–circa March 1839)

David Rogers Israel Barlow Samuel Bent (became sick and never served)

Commerce

Following the Saints' expulsion from Missouri in spring 1839, they regrouped in Illinois. After JS escaped from state custody and arrived in Illinois in April 1839, he began to reorganize the Saints at Commerce (later Nauvoo), Illinois, and across the river in Iowa Territory. On 6 May 1839, members at a church conference appointed a president and bishop—the two essential positions of stake organization—for the church members in Commerce, Illinois. Commerce was formally organized as a stake in October 1839.

President
William Marks

Bishop
Newel K. Whitney

Civic Officers in Caldwell County

The Missouri government organized Caldwell County in 1836 as a solution to the state's "Mormon problem." Missourians understood that the county was intended for Mormon settlement. Counties in Missouri were primarily governed by the county court, which consisted of three justices. These justices were initially appointed by the governor, but they were up for reelection or replacement every four years. One of the justices was appointed president of the court by his peers. The justices had the power to appoint a treasurer and a clerk/recorder for the court and county, while other county offices, such as assessor, sheriff, and coroner, were elected positions. Because of the lack of contemporaneous records, it is impossible to completely reconstruct the local governments of Caldwell County during the period this volume covers.

Before 6 August 1838	6 August 1838
Court Officers	*Court Officers*
William W. Phelps, president	Elias Higbee, president
Elias Higbee, justice	James Allred, justice
Unidentified justice	Arthur Morrison, justice
John Cleminson, clerk and recorder	John Cleminson, clerk and recorder
Unidentified treasurer	Unidentified treasurer
Assessors	*Assessors*
Unidentified	Alanson Ripley

Coroner
Unidentified
Sheriff
George W. Pitkin (appointed 1837; elected 6 August 1838)
John Skidmore (appointed before March 1839)
Deputies
Dimick B. Huntington (appointed June 1838)
William Allred (appointed 9 September 1838)

Rockford Township

Shortly after being organized, Caldwell County was subdivided into four municipal townships: Rockford, Blythe, Grand River, and Davis. Each township could elect up to four justices of the peace and a constable. Rockford Township included Far West, where many of the 1838 documents in this volume were produced.

Justices of the Peace
Levi Jackman (resigned by 9 April 1838)
David Frampton (served in 1838)
Harvey Green (served in 1838)
Isaac Higbee (served in 1838)
Albert Petty (serving as of 10 September 1838)
Amasa Lyman (elected 2 January 1839)
Ebenezer Robinson (elected 2 January 1839)

Constable
Dimick B. Huntington (elected spring 1838)

Far West

The town of Far West apparently was legally incorporated sometime between April and November 1837. Missouri law required that the town government begin with five trustees, initially appointed by the county court but elected thereafter. The trustees had the power to appoint an assessor, a collector, a constable, and other necessary officers. The initial appointments would have occurred in connection with the town's incorporation. The first election of trustees would have occurred on 2 April 1838. None of the trustees in 1837 or 1838 has been identified.

Trustees
Unidentified

Assessor
Philo Dibble

Collector
Dimick B. Huntington

Constable
Dimick B. Huntington

Military Authorities

Caldwell County Militia

Caldwell County supplied the soldiers for the Fifty-Ninth Regiment of the state militia. The militia's commander in chief was the governor, Lilburn W. Boggs. David R. Atchison served as the major general over the militia's Third Division, also called the "the northern division," which included several of the northwestern counties, such as Caldwell and Daviess counties. Within the Third Division, Hiram G. Parks served as the brigadier general over the Second Brigade, which included Ray, Caldwell, and possibly other counties. The Fifty-Ninth Regiment was organized in mid-1837 by Latter-day Saints William W. Phelps, George M. Hinkle, Lyman Wight, and Reed Peck.

Like other regiments, the Fifty-Ninth Regiment was commanded by a colonel and included several other officers and subdivisions. Hinkle and Wight were commissioned as colonels. There is conflicting evidence as to who was colonel and who was lieutenant colonel. A county history that appears to draw on militia records lists Hinkle as the colonel and Wight as lieutenant colonel. Regiments were divided into battalions, which were commanded by majors. Battalions were in turn divided into companies, which were commanded by captains. The battalion and company substructure of the Fifty-Ninth Regiment is not known. Missouri law allowed for a regiment to have as many as sixteen companies. The Fifty-Ninth Regiment consisted of at least seven companies. The officers in the companies are mostly unknown, except for those in the Second Company. Within the Second Company, it is possible that some of the men listed after Turner were corporals, not sergeants, matching the 3 October 1838 organization.

Fifty-Ninth Regiment

Colonel George M. Hinkle
Lieutenant Colonel Lyman Wight
Major Jefferson Hunt
Adjutant Reed Peck
Sergeant Major Philo Dibble

First Company

Captain William E. McLellin (apparently departed Caldwell County between late May and late June 1838)

Second Company

Circa early 1838	3 October 1838
Captain Seymour Brunson	*Captain* Seymour Brunson
Lieutenants Jerome Benson D. Chase	*Lieutenant* Jerome Benson
Ensign William Clark	*Ensign* Milo Andrus
Sergeants (or possibly Corporals) Chapman Duncan Lewis Turner Edward Larkey Perry Durfee Edmund Durfee Jr. William Hawk John Rudd Lyman Stevens	*Sergeants* Eli Chase, first sergeant William R. Cole, second sergeant James Daily, third sergeant Asa C. Earl, fourth sergeant
	Corporals William Jay, first corporal Uriah B. Powell, second corporal Nelson Mainard, third corporal Philo Allen, fourth corporal

Seventh Company

Captain Amasa Lyman
First Lieutenant Joseph Holbrook

Officers in One or More Unidentified Companies

Captain John Killian
Captain Arthur Morrison
Lieutenant George P. Dykes
Ensign Jacob Gates

Society of the Daughter of Zion (Danites)

The Society of the Daughter of Zion was an oath-bound military society organized among the Latter-day Saints in Missouri circa late June 1838 to defend the church from internal and external opposition. The members of this organization soon became known as Danites. The exact organizational structure of the society is difficult to reconstruct because of a scarcity of sources. A constitution for the society was presented in court in the Missouri government's case against JS. Although it is uncertain whether JS ever approved of this constitution, his journal and other contemporaneous sources confirm that the society implemented several organizational aspects that were articulated in the constitution. The society's constitution described an executive branch consisting of the First Presidency and a legislative branch consisting of the First Presidency as well as generals and colonels. The constitution also outlined the function of a secretary of war and specified that the military forces were to be led by a captain general. The general membership of the society was apparently organized in a military style, with generals, colonels, and other officers. Some participants described a command structure of captains of thousands, captains of hundreds, captains of fifties, and captains of tens. No captains of thousands or of hundreds have been identified. Given the size of these units and the general parallel between Danite offices and militia offices, captains of thousands and of hundreds may have gone by other military titles. The generals were apparently general officers over the Danites in both Caldwell and Daviess counties. Caldwell County probably had at least one captain of fifty, as did Daviess County, but none have been identified. The division in Daviess County may not have had a lieutenant colonel or a major because of the much smaller number of Saints in that county. The following charts show only the known officers.

Captain General
Jared Carter (removed early July 1838)
Elias Higbee (appointed early July 1838)

Major General
Sampson Avard (removed after 8 August 1838)

Brigadier General
Cornelius P. Lott

Adjutant
Reed Peck

Caldwell County	Daviess County
Colonel George W. Robinson	*Colonel* Lyman Wight
Lieutenant Colonel Philo Dibble	*Captains of Fifties* Reynolds Cahoon
Major Seymour Brunson	*Captains of Tens* James Sloan
Captains of Tens Unidentified	

War Department

It is unclear how long the original command structure of the Danites continued or whether or to what extent the small, secret, oath-bound society that started in summer 1838 had continuity with the much larger military force of mid-October, which included many if not most of the adult male members of the church. Multiple sources attest that the term *Danites* was being used—perhaps informally—to describe the large Mormon military force that was active in October. If this military force had continuity with the original Danite society, the original organization had significantly transformed. For example, in the October structure, Sampson Avard held the office of surgeon instead of his former position of major general. Further, the primary military leaders in October were Lyman Wight, David W. Patten, and Seymour Brunson instead of Generals Elias Higbee and Cornelius P. Lott, although Higbee may have continued in an executive capacity. It is also unclear how much overlap there was between positions in the church militia and the Caldwell County regiment of the Missouri state militia.

Albert Perry Rockwood, one of the men who used the term *Danites* to describe Mormon forces, more often used the term *armies of Israel,* perhaps as an informal title. In November, witnesses testifying in the court hearing about the October conflict also used the word *army* to describe the Mormon military. On 24 October, in a council meeting held in Sidney Rigdon's home, JS and other officers reorganized the command structure of the Mormon "war department," which included the officers in the following chart.

Caldwell County	Daviess County
Colonel Commander in Chief (Infantry) George M. Hinkle	*Colonel Commander in Chief (Infantry)* Lyman Wight
Captain (Cavalry) David W. Patten	*Captain (Cavalry)* Seymour Brunson

Officers in Unidentified Organizations

Historical accounts of the October 1838 conflict between the Latter-day Saints and other Missourians mention several officers without clarifying whether they held offices in the state militia, the Danite society, the Army of Israel, a posse comitatus, or some other well or loosely defined organization—or even some combination of these organizations.

Captains	*Lieutenants*
Charles C. Rich, captain of fifty	Parley P. Pratt, first lieutenant
John Murdock, captain of ten	Ebenezer Robinson, second lieutenant/ensign
William Allred	
Jonathan Dunham	
James Durfee	
David Evans	
Alexander McRae	
Ephraim Owen	
David W. Patten	

Essay on Sources

The featured texts found in this volume compose a significant collection of contemporary sources—including correspondence, minutes, discourses, JS revelations, and other documents—and often provide context for one another. More than one-third of the featured texts are letters. JS relied on letters to communicate with church leaders and missionaries in distant locations after he moved from Kirtland, Ohio, to Far West, Missouri, in early 1838. While incarcerated during winter 1838–1839, JS continued to compose epistles to counsel church members and govern the church during the forced migration of the Latter-day Saints from Missouri. He also exchanged several letters with his wife Emma Smith and other family members. Several original letters are extant and reproduced in this volume. Church clerks preserved other correspondence by copying the texts of the original letters into record books. For instance, general church clerk and First Presidency scribe George W. Robinson copied several letters into the "Scriptory Book," JS's March–September 1838 journal. Additionally, after JS's scribe James Mulholland relocated from Missouri to Illinois in spring 1839, he copied letters for JS into Letterbook 2 (1839–1843).[1]

This volume also features meeting minutes, discourses, and revelations. JS participated in meetings of the Zion high council in Far West, and clerk Ebenezer Robinson recorded minutes of the council's 1838 meetings on loose sheets. In 1842, Hosea Stout copied Robinson's minutes into Minute Book 2 (1838, 1842, 1844). In April and May 1839, James Mulholland kept minutes of church meetings over which JS presided in Quincy, Adams County, Illinois; the original minutes are featured here. JS also gave many discourses, and the scribes he employed to keep his journal, George W. Robinson and James Mulholland, sometimes recorded the discourses in JS's journal. Additionally, Wilford Woodruff wrote about several JS sermons in a summer 1839 journal as well as in a notebook titled "Book of Revelations," which Woodruff brought with him on his proselytizing mission in Europe. Willard Richards copied accounts of three additional JS discourses in his "Pocket Companion" notebook. Richards, who was in England when JS delivered these discourses in summer 1839, copied accounts from other missionaries after they arrived in England. JS also dictated several revelations during the period covered in this volume; the versions featured herein are early copies made by Edward Partridge and other early church leaders.

This volume also includes several financial and legal documents. When JS and Sidney Rigdon abruptly departed Kirtland in January 1838, they left their financial obligations to Ohio merchants and lawyers unsettled. Church agents William Marks and Oliver Granger worked to pay the debts the church leaders owed and to resolve litigation against them. Whereas Marks was instructed to move to Missouri in July 1838, Granger remained involved in Kirtland finances throughout 1838 and 1839. In Far West, receipts and promissory notes from fall 1838 suggest that Partridge paid several of JS's debts. The conflict with

---

1. For more information on source texts presented in this volume, see Source Notes for Multiple-Entry Documents, p. 563 herein.

anti-Mormons in Missouri during summer and fall 1838 led to legal charges against JS and other church leaders for treason and other crimes against the state of Missouri, resulting in court proceedings and a large corpus of legal papers. Several affidavits, petitions, and other legal documents that were either signed by JS or produced by scribes or attorneys on JS's behalf are featured herein. The case files for these legal proceedings will be available on josephsmithpapers.org. Once in Illinois, JS was involved in acquiring land for Mormon settlement. In late April 1839, he and the other members of the First Presidency acted as sureties for purchased land, and in August 1839, JS and other church leaders contracted with Horace Hotchkiss to acquire land in and around Commerce, Hancock County, Illinois.

Journals, letters, and newspapers were invaluable in annotating the documents in this volume. The content in the Scriptory Book manifests JS's optimism about Far West's potential, his struggles with dissenters, the establishment of Latter-day Saint settlements in Carroll and Daviess counties, and the outbreak of conflict with anti-Mormons in August and September 1838. Letters preserved in the George Albert Smith Papers at the Church History Library in Salt Lake City, Utah, and in Oliver Cowdery's letterbook at the Huntington Library in San Marino, California, contain valuable information on the activities of dissenters in Ohio and Missouri. Wilford Woodruff's missionary journal is an indispensable source for understanding his correspondence with JS. The church newspaper *Elders' Journal* (1837–1838) and regional and national periodicals provide additional information.

Most record keeping among church members ceased when the conflict between the Latter-day Saints and other Missourians climaxed in October 1838. The journals of Albert Perry Rockwood and John Smith are notable exceptions and provide contemporaneous Mormon perspectives on the conflict. In contrast to the dearth of Mormon records, Missouri militia officers produced substantial correspondence throughout the 1838 conflict, providing significant information. Copies of the militia leaders' letters and other documents were later compiled and preserved in the Mormon War Papers, housed in the Missouri State Archives in Jefferson City, Missouri.

In November 1838, following JS's arrest, Austin A. King of the fifth judicial circuit presided over a preliminary hearing in Richmond, Ray County, Missouri, where forty-two witnesses—several of whom were disaffected Latter-day Saints—testified for the prosecution. These testimonies provide important historical material, but given the adversarial proceedings in which they were produced, they have been used with caution when annotating documents herein. Two of the witnesses—John Corrill and Reed Peck, who were excommunicated along with other dissidents in March 1839—wrote detailed accounts of the conflict within a year of the cessation of violence. Although these accounts were shaped by disaffection and, at times, hostility toward JS and the Saints, they provide valuable information regarding the events in October 1838. For background on Corrill's history, see volume 2 in the Histories series of *The Joseph Smith Papers*. For images and transcripts of the November 1838 testimonies, see josephsmithpapers.org.

Primary sources also inform the annotation for the documents created during JS's winter 1838–1839 imprisonment in Clay County, his escape from state custody on 16 April 1839, and the Saints' migration to Illinois. Hyrum Smith kept a detailed journal and exchanged correspondence with his wife, Mary Fielding Smith, describing the prisoners' experiences. Fellow prisoner Lyman Wight also kept a useful journal in the jail. Although Wight's original journal is not extant, entries from the journal were preserved in volume 2 of *The History of the Reorganized Church of Jesus Christ of Latter Day Saints.* Another important source of information is the meeting minutes of a Far West committee formed in late January 1839 to oversee the migration of church members from Missouri to Illinois.

Contemporaneous sources have also been used to annotate documents that illuminate the Saints' resettlement in and around Quincy and then at Commerce, Illinois, and across the Mississippi River in Lee County, Iowa Territory. After Wilford Woodruff arrived in Quincy in April 1839, he kept a journal that has been referenced extensively in this volume. Another key source is JS's 1839 journal, which was kept by James Mulholland. Additionally, in July 1839 the Saints founded a new church newspaper, the *Times and Seasons,* which published letters from missionaries and articles chronicling events in Illinois. Regional newspapers also printed articles about the Latter-day Saints and their activities.

In 1839, the Saints launched a coordinated campaign to obtain redress for their losses in Missouri. As part of this effort, the Saints produced several historical narratives describing their experiences in the state during the time covered in this volume. Hundreds of church members wrote short affidavits and petitions documenting their losses in Missouri. In addition, Latter-day Saints John P. Greene, Parley P. Pratt, Sidney Rigdon, and Morris Phelps wrote detailed histories of the conflict from the Saints' perspective. In 1843, Hyrum Smith, Pratt, Rigdon, Wight, and others reported important details regarding the conflict when they testified before the Nauvoo, Illinois, municipal court in proceedings stemming from the efforts of Missouri officials to extradite JS.

For some events in this volume's time period, the only relevant sources are personal recollections and autobiographies written years later. In the mid-1840s, church historian Willard Richards and his clerks composed the portions of JS's manuscript history covering the 1838 conflict. The clerks' efforts included interviewing eyewitnesses of important events in Missouri. In 1844 and 1845, JS's mother, Lucy Mack Smith, dictated her autobiography, which includes details of the conflict that are found nowhere else. Apostle Heber C. Kimball, with the assistance of multiple scribes, composed his autobiography intermittently throughout the mid-nineteenth century. In general, reminiscences are helpful in filling gaps in the contemporaneous historical record. Such sources have been used when necessary and with caution to annotate some documents in this volume.

Works Cited

This list of sources serves as a comprehensive guide to all sources cited in this volume (documentation supporting the reference material in the back of this volume may be found on the Joseph Smith Papers website, josephsmithpapers.org). Annotation has been documented with original sources where possible and practical. In entries for manuscript sources, dates identify when the manuscript was created, which is not necessarily the time period the manuscript covers. Newspaper entries are listed under the newspaper titles used during the time period covered by this volume. Newspaper entries also provide beginning and ending years for the publication. Since newspapers often changed names or editors over time, such dates typically approximate the years the paper was active under a particular editor; when it is impractical to provide beginning and ending publication dates by an editor's tenure, dates may be determined by major events in the paper's history, such as a merger with another sizable newspaper.

Some sources cited in this volume are referred to on first and subsequent occurrences by a conventional shortened citation. For convenience, some documents are referred to by editorial titles rather than by their original titles or by the titles given in the catalogs of their current repositories, in which case the list of works cited provides the editorial title followed by full bibliographic information.

Transcripts and images of a growing number of Joseph Smith's papers are available on the Joseph Smith Papers website.

Scripture References

The annotation within volumes of *The Joseph Smith Papers* includes numerous references to works accepted as scripture by The Church of Jesus Christ of Latter-day Saints. The principal citations of Mormon scripture appearing in annotation are to JS-era published or manuscript versions. However, for reader convenience, these citations also include a bracketed reference to the current and widely available Latter-day Saint scriptural canon. Early extant copies of JS's revelations dictated during the period covered in this volume are transcribed in the main body of this volume. All versions of scripture cited in this volume, early or modern, are identified in the list of works cited.

The church's current scriptural canon consists of the King James (or Authorized) Version of the Bible (KJV), plus three other volumes: the Book of Mormon, the Doctrine and Covenants, and the Pearl of Great Price. The following paragraphs provide more detailed information about uniquely Mormon scriptures and how they are cited in this volume.

Book of Mormon. The first edition of the Book of Mormon was printed for JS in 1830. He oversaw the publication of subsequent editions in 1837 and 1840. The Book of Mormon, like the Bible, consists of a number of shorter books. However, the present volume cites early editions of the Book of Mormon by page numbers because these editions were not divided into numbered verses. The bracketed references to the modern (2013) Latter-day Saint edition of this work identify the book name with modern chapter and verse.

Doctrine and Covenants. JS authorized publication of early revelations beginning in 1832 in *The Evening and the Morning Star,* the church's first newspaper, and initiated the publication of a compilation of revelations, which first appeared in 1833 under the title Book of Commandments. Revised and expanded versions of this compilation were published in 1835 and 1844 under the title Doctrine and Covenants. Since JS's time, The Church of Jesus Christ of Latter-day Saints has continued to issue revised and expanded versions of the Doctrine and Covenants, as has the Community of Christ (formerly the Reorganized Church of Jesus Christ of Latter Day Saints). The bracketed references to the modern (2013) Latter-day Saint edition of the Doctrine and Covenants, which cite by section number and verse, use the abbreviation D&C in the place of Doctrine and Covenants. A table titled Corresponding Section Numbers in Editions of the Doctrine and Covenants, which appears after the list of works cited, aligns the corresponding section numbers of the three JS-era compilations and the current editions of the Doctrine and Covenants published by The Church of Jesus Christ of Latter-day Saints and by the Community of Christ. For more information about the format of Doctrine and Covenants citations, see the Editorial Method.

Joseph Smith Bible revision. Beginning in June 1830, JS systematically reviewed the text of the KJV and made revisions and additions to it. JS largely completed the work in 1833, but only a few excerpts were published in his lifetime. The Reorganized Church of Jesus Christ of Latter Day Saints published the entire work in 1867 under the title Holy Scriptures and included excerpts from the writings of Moses in two sections of its Doctrine and Covenants. The Church of Jesus Christ of Latter-day Saints, which today officially refers to JS's Bible revisions as the Joseph Smith Translation, has never published the entire work, but two excerpts are canonized in the Pearl of Great Price and many other excerpts are included in the footnotes and appendix of the modern (2013) Latter-day Saint edition of the KJV. In the *Papers,* references to JS's Bible revision are cited to the original manuscripts, with a bracketed reference given where possible to the relevant book, chapter, and verse of the Joseph Smith Translation.

Pearl of Great Price. The Pearl of Great Price, a collection of miscellaneous writings that primarily originated with JS, was first published in 1851 and was canonized by The Church of Jesus Christ of Latter-day Saints in 1880. The modern (2013) edition of this work consists of the following: selections from the Book of Moses, an extract from JS's Bible revision manuscripts; the Book of Abraham, writings translated from papyri JS and others acquired in 1835 and first published in the *Times and Seasons* in 1842; Joseph Smith—Matthew, another extract from JS's Bible revision manuscripts; Joseph Smith—History, a selection from the history that JS began working on in 1838; and the Articles of Faith, a statement of beliefs included in a JS letter to Chicago newspaper editor John Wentworth and published in the *Times and Seasons* in 1842. Except in the case of Joseph Smith—History, citations in this volume to early versions of each of these works also include a bracketed reference to the corresponding chapter and verse in the modern Latter-day Saint canon. The Pearl of Great Price is not part of the canon of the Community of

Christ. References to the history JS began work on in 1838 are cited to the original manuscript of that history (see entry on "JS History" in the list of works cited).

Legal References and Court Abbreviations

In this volume, citations to legal reporters documenting state or federal supreme court decisions are referred to by an abbreviated title and include the name of the deciding court and the year of the court's decision. For example, in the citation *In re* Clark, 9 Wendell 212 (N.Y. Sup. Ct. 1832), the case name is *In re* Clark, information about the case is located on page 212 in volume 9 of the legal reporter abbreviated as Wendell, and the case was decided by the New York Supreme Court in 1832. Full bibliographic information for each reporter is provided in the list of works cited, alphabetized under the abbreviated title.

Citations to legal cases in this volume usually reference the name of the case, the deciding court, and the year of the court's decision. Jurisdictions and court names used in legal citations are contemporary to the year of the cited case and do not necessarily correspond to modern courts or jurisdictions. The following abbreviations are used within this volume:

Chicago Mun. Ct.	Chicago Municipal Court
Clay Co. Cir. Ct.	Clay County, Missouri, Circuit Court
Daviess Co. Cir. Ct.	Daviess County, Missouri, Circuit Court
Geauga Co. C.P.	Geauga County, Ohio, Court of Common Pleas
Clay Co. J.P. Ct.	Clay County, Missouri, Justice of the Peace Court
Lee Co. Dist. Ct.	Lee County, Iowa Territory, District Court
Mo. 5th Jud. Cir.	Fifth Judicial Circuit of Missouri
Ray Co. Cir. Ct.	Ray County, Missouri, Circuit Court

Abbreviations for Frequently Cited Repositories

BYU	L. Tom Perry Special Collections, Harold B. Lee Library, Brigham Young University, Provo, Utah
CCLA	Community of Christ Library-Archives, Independence, Missouri
CHL	Church History Library, The Church of Jesus Christ of Latter-day Saints, Salt Lake City
FHL	Family History Library, The Church of Jesus Christ of Latter-day Saints, Salt Lake City
MSA	Missouri State Archives, Jefferson City

——— ❧ ———

Abraham (Book of). See *Pearl of Great Price.*

An Abridgment of the Book of Martyrs: To Which Are Prefixed, the Living Testimonies of the Church of God, and Faithful Martyrs, in Different Ages of the World; and the Corrupt Fruits of the False Church, in the Time of the Apostasy. New York: Samuel Wood, 1810.

Acts of a General Nature, Passed at the First Session of the Twentieth General Assembly of the State of Ohio, Begun and Held in the Town of Columbus, December 3, 1821; and in the Twentieth Year of Said State. Columbus: P. H. Olmsted, 1822.

Acts of a General Nature, Passed at the First Session of the Thirty-Third General Assembly of the State of Ohio, Begun and Held in the City of Columbus, December 1, 1834. In the Thirty-Third Year of Said State. Columbus: James B. Gardiner, 1835.

Acts of a General Nature, Passed at the First Session of the Thirty-Fifth General Assembly of the State of Ohio; Begun and Held in the City of Columbus, December 5th, 1836. And in the Thirty-Fifth Year of Said State. Columbus: S. R. Dolbee, 1837.

Acts of a General Nature, Passed by the Thirty-Seventh General Assembly of Ohio, at Its First Session, Held in the City of Columbus, and Commencing December 3, 1838, in the Thirty-Seventh Year of Said State. Columbus: Samuel Medary, 1839.

Adams, Dale W. "Grandison Newell's Obsession." *Journal of Mormon History* 30 (Spring 2004): 159–188.

Adams Sentinel. Gettysburg, PA. 1826–1867.

Ahlstrom, Sydney E. *A Religious History of the American People.* 2nd ed. New Haven, CT: Yale University Press, 2004.

Albany Journal. Albany, NY. 1830–1863.

Aldrich, Charles. Autograph Collection. State Historical Society of Iowa, Des Moines.

Allen, James B., Ronald K. Esplin, and David J. Whittaker. *Men with a Mission, 1837–1841: The Quorum of the Twelve Apostles in the British Isles.* Salt Lake City: Deseret Book, 1992.

Ambrosia Branch, Lee Co., Iowa Territory, Record Book, 1844–1846. CHL.

An American Dictionary of the English Language. . . . Edited by Noah Webster. New York: S. Converse, 1828.

American Slavery as It Is: Testimony of a Thousand Witnesses. New York: American Anti-Slavery Society, 1839.

Ames, Ira. Autobiography and Journal, 1858. CHL.

Anderson, Richard Lloyd. "Clarifications of Boggs's 'Order' and Joseph Smith's Constitutionalism." In *Regional Studies in Latter-day Saint Church History: Missouri,* edited by Arnold K. Garr and Clark V. Johnson, 27–83. Provo, UT: Department of Church History and Doctrine, Brigham Young University, 1994.

———. "What Changes Have Been Made in the Name of the Church?" *Ensign,* Jan. 1979, 13–14.

Andrus, Hyrum L., Chris Fuller, and Elizabeth E. McKenzie. "Register of the Newel Kimball Whitney Papers, 1825–1906," Sept. 1998. BYU.

Angell, Truman O. Autobiography, 1884. CHL. Also available in Archie Leon Brown and Charlene L. Hathaway, *141 Years of Mormon Heritage: Rawsons, Browns, Angells—Pioneers* (Oakland, CA: By the authors, 1973), 119–135.

Arrington, Leonard J., and Davis Bitton. *The Mormon Experience: A History of the Latter-day Saints.* 2nd ed. Urbana: University of Illinois Press, 1992.

Asbury, Henry. *Reminiscences of Quincy, Illinois, Containing Historical Events, Anecdotes, Matters concerning Old Settlers and Old Times, Etc.* Quincy, IL: D. Wilcox and Sons, 1882.

Ashurst-McGee, Mark. "Zion Rising: Joseph Smith's Early Social and Political Thought." PhD diss., Arizona State University, 2008.

Aurora. New Lisbon, OH. 1835–1837.

Axtell, James, and William C. Sturtevant. "The Unkindest Cut; or, Who Invented Scalping?" *William and Mary Quarterly* 37, no. 3 (July 1980): 451–472.

Bachman, Danel W. "New Light on an Old Hypothesis: The Ohio Origins of the Revelation on Eternal Marriage." *Journal of Mormon History* 5 (1978): 19–32.

Backman, Milton V., Jr. *The Heavens Resound: A History of the Latter-day Saints in Ohio, 1830–1838.* Salt Lake City: Deseret Book, 1983.

———, comp. *A Profile of Latter-day Saints of Kirtland, Ohio, and Members of Zion's Camp, 1830–1839: Vital Statistics and Sources.* 2nd ed. Provo, UT: Department of Church History and Doctrine and Religious Studies Center, Brigham Young University, 1983.

Baldwin, Caleb. Petition, Liberty, MO, 15 Mar. 1839. CHL.

Baldwin, Nathan Bennett. Account of Zion's Camp, 1882. Typescript. CHL.

Bank of Monroe. Account Statement, [Monroe, MI], for Kirtland Safety Society, ca. Apr. 1837. CHL.

Barlow Family Collection, 1816–1969. CHL.

Barnes, Lorenzo D. Reminiscences and Diaries, 1834–1839. CHL.

Baugh, Alexander L. "A Call to Arms: The 1838 Mormon Defense of Northern Missouri." PhD diss., Brigham Young University, 1996. Also available as *A Call to Arms: The 1838 Mormon Defense of Northern Missouri,* Dissertations in Latter-day Saint History (Provo, UT: Joseph Fielding Smith Institute for Latter-day Saint History; *BYU Studies*, 2000).

———. "The Final Episode of Mormonism in Missouri in the 1830s: The Incarceration of the Mormon Prisoners at Richmond and Columbia Jails, 1838–1839." *John Whitmer Historical Association Journal* 28 (2008): 1–34.

———. "Jacob Hawn and the Hawn's Mill Massacre: Missouri Millwright and Oregon Pioneer." *Mormon Historical Studies* 11, no. 1 (Spring 2010): 1–25.

———. "'We Took Our Change of Venue to the State of Illinois': The Gallatin Hearing and the Escape of Joseph Smith and the Mormon Prisoners from Missouri, April 1839." *Mormon Historical Studies* 2, no. 1 (Spring 2001): 59–82.

Bay, William Van Ness. *Reminiscences of the Bench and Bar of Missouri. . . .* St. Louis: F. H. Thomas, 1878.

Beneke, Chris. *Beyond Toleration: The Religious Origins of American Pluralism.* New York: Oxford University Press, 2006.

Benner, Martha L., Cullom Davis, Daniel W. Stowell, John A. Lupton, Susan Krause, Stacy Pratt McDermott, Christopher A. Schnell, and Dennis E. Suttles, eds. *The Law Practice of Abraham Lincoln: Complete Documentary Edition.* 2nd ed. Springfield, IL: Illinois Historic Preservation Agency, 2009. Accessed 3 Nov. 2016. http://www.lawpracticeofabrahamlincoln.org.

Bennett, Ella M. Collection, 1834–1910. CHL.

Bennett, Richard E. "'Quincy the Home of Our Adoption': A Study of the Mormons in Quincy, Illinois, 1838–1840." In *A City of Refuge: Quincy, Illinois,* edited by Susan Easton Black and Richard E. Bennett, 83–105. Salt Lake City: Millennial Press, 2000.

Bergera, Gary James. "The Personal Cost of the 1838 Mormon War in Missouri: One Mormon's Plea for Forgiveness." *Mormon Historical Studies* 4, no. 1 (Spring 2003): 139–144.

Berrett, LaMar C. "History of the Southern States Mission, 1831–1861." Master's thesis, Brigham Young University, 1960.

———, ed. *Sacred Places: A Comprehensive Guide to Early LDS Historical Sites.* 6 vols. Salt Lake City: Deseret Book, 1999–2007.

Best, Christy. "Register of the Revelations Collection in the Church Archives, The Church of Jesus Christ of Latter-day Saints," July 1983. CHL.

Bible. See *Holy Bible.*

Bigler, Jacob G. Autobiographical Sketch, 1907. Typescript. CHL.

Billings, Melvin, and Randy Shaw, comps. "Titus Billings," 1990. Typescript. Microfilm copy available at FHL.

Biographical Directory of the United States Congress, 1774–2005: The Continental Congress September 5, 1774, to October 21, 1788, and the Congress of the United States from the First through the One Hundred Eighth Congresses March 4, 1789, to January 3, 2005, Inclusive. Edited by Andrew R. Dodge and Betty K. Koed. Washington DC: U.S. Government Printing Office, 2005.

"Biographies of the Seventies of the Second Quorum," 1845–1855. In Seventies Quorum Records, 1844–1875. CHL.

Bitton, Davis. "Waning of Mormon Kirtland." *BYU Studies* 12, no. 4 (1972): 455–464.

Blackstone, William. *Commentaries on the Laws of England: In Four Books; with an Analysis of the Work. By Sir William Blackstone, Knt. One of the Justices of the Court of Common Pleas. In Two Volumes, from the Eighteenth London Edition. . . .* 2 vols. New York: W. E. Dean, 1838.

Block, Sharon. *Rape and Sexual Power in Early America.* Chapel Hill: University of North Carolina Press, 2006.

Blum, Ida. *Nauvoo—an American Heritage.* Carthage, IL: By the author, 1969.

Bodenhorn, Howard. *A History of Banking in Antebellum America: Financial Markets and Economic Development in an Era of Nation-Building.* New York: Cambridge University Press, 2000.

Bogart, Samuel. Letter, Elkhorn, MO, to the Postmaster, Quincy, IL, 22 Apr. 1839. CHL.

Bohn, Belle Cushman. "Early Wisconsin School Teachers." *Wisconsin Magazine of History* 23, no. 1 (Sept. 1939): 58–61.

The Book of Abraham. See *Pearl of Great Price.*

Book of Abraham Manuscript, Summer–Fall 1835. Book of Abraham Manuscripts, ca. Early July–ca. Nov. 1835, ca. 1841–1842. CHL.

Book of Doctrine and Covenants: Carefully Selected from the Revelations of God, and Given in the Order of Their Dates. Independence, MO: Herald Publishing House, 2004.

The Book of Mormon: An Account Written by the Hand of Mormon, upon Plates Taken from the Plates of Nephi. Palmyra, NY: E. B. Grandin, 1830.

The Book of Mormon: Another Testament of Jesus Christ. Salt Lake City: The Church of Jesus Christ of Latter-day Saints, 2013.

The Book of Moses (selections from). See *Pearl of Great Price.*

The Book of the Law of the Lord, Record Book, 1841–1845. CHL.

Boone County, Missouri, Circuit Court Records, 1839. State Historical Society of Missouri, Columbia.

Boston Recorder. Boston. 1830–1849.

Bouvier, John. *A Law Dictionary, Adapted to the Constitution and Laws of the United States of America, and of the Several States of the American Union; with References to the Civil and Other Systems of Foreign Law.* 2 vols. Philadelphia: T. and J. W. Johnson, 1839.

Bowman, Matthew. "Raising the Dead: Mormons, Evangelicals, and Miracles in America." *John Whitmer Historical Association Journal* 27 (2007): 75–97.

Bradford, Thomas G. Correspondence, 1822–1840. CHL.

Bradley, Don. "Mormon Polygamy before Nauvoo? The Relationship of Joseph Smith and Fanny Alger." In *Persistence of Polygamy: Joseph Smith and the Origins of Mormon Polygamy,* edited by Newell G. Bringhurst and Craig L. Foster, 14–58. Independence, MO: John Whitmer Books, 2010.

Bremer, Jeff. *A Store Almost in Sight: The Economic Transformation of Missouri from the Louisiana Purchase to the Civil War.* Iowa City: University of Iowa Press, 2014.

A Brief Account of the Life of the Hon. Emanuel Swedenborg, of the Senatorial Order of the Kingdom of Sweden; a Servant of the Lord; and the Messenger of the New Jerusalem Dispensation. Taunton, England: C. H. Drake, 1813.

A Brief Historical Sketch of the Town of Vinalhaven, from Its Earliest Known Settlement. Rockland, ME: Free Press Office, 1889.

Brigham Young Office Files, 1832–1878. CHL.

Brigham Young Office. Halsted, Haines & Co. File, 1867. Copy of case, Halsted, Haines & Co. v. Granger et al. (Geauga Co. C.P. 1841). CHL.

"British Channel Fisheries." *Tait's Edinburgh Magazine,* Mar. 1834, 125–127.

Brookes, Richard, comp. *A New Universal Gazetteer, Containing a Description of the Principal Nations, Empires, Kingdoms, States, Provinces, Cities, Towns, Forts, Seas, Harbours, Rivers, Lakes, Canals, Mountains, Volcanoes, Capes, Caverns, Cataracts and Grottoes. . . .* Philadelphia: W. Marshall, 1839.

Brown, Richard Maxwell. *Strain of Violence: Historical Studies of American Violence and Vigilantism.* Oxford: Oxford University Press, 1977.

Brown, Samuel M. *In Heaven as It Is on Earth: Joseph Smith and the Early Mormon Conquest of Death.* New York: Oxford University Press, 2012.

Bruce, Frederick F. *The Canon of Scripture.* Downers Grove, IL: Intervarsity Press, 1988.

Brunson, Lewis. Autobiography, 1861. CHL.

Buck, Charles. *A Theological Dictionary, Containing Definitions of All Religious Terms; a Comprehensive View of Every Article in the System of Divinity. . . .* New American ed., edited by George Bush. Philadelphia: James Kay Jr., 1830.

Burch, Thomas C. Letter, Keytesville, MO, to James L. Minor, Jefferson City, MO, 24 June 1839. Mormons Collection. Missouri History Museum Archives, St. Louis.

Burgess, Harrison. Autobiography, ca. 1883. Photocopy. CHL. Also available as "Sketch of a Well-Spent Life," in *Labors in the Vineyard,* Faith-Promoting Series 12 (Salt Lake City: Juvenile Instructor Office, 1884), 65–74.

Burnett, Peter H. *Recollections and Opinions of an Old Pioneer.* New York: D. Appleton, 1880.

Burritt, Elijah Hinsdale. *Burritt's Universal Multipliers for Computing Interest, Simple and Compound; Adapted to the Various Rates in the United States, on a New Plan; to Which Are Added, Tables of Annuities and Exchange.* Hartford, CT: D. F. Robinson, 1830.

Burton, W. E., ed. *Burton's Comic Songster: Being Entirely a New Collection of Original and Popular Songs, as Sung by Mr. Burton, Mr. Tyrone Power, Mr. John Reeve, Mr. Hadaway, &c. &c.* Philadelphia: James Kay Jr. and Brother, 1837.

Bushman, Katherine Gentry, comp. *Index of the First Plat Book of Clay County, Missouri, 1819–1875.* [Staunton, VA]: By the author, 1967.

Bushman, Richard Lyman. *Joseph Smith: Rough Stone Rolling.* With the assistance of Jed Woodworth. New York: Knopf, 2005.

Butler, John L. Autobiography, ca. 1859. CHL.

———. "A Short Account of an Affray That Took Place between the Latter Day Saints and a Portion of the People of Davis County Mo," 1859. CHL.

Butts, I. R. *The Business Man's Assistant, Part I. Containing Useful Forms of Legal Instruments: Enlarged by the Addition of Forms. . . .* Boston: By the author, 1847.

BYU Church History and Doctrine Department. Church History Project Collection, 1977–1981. Photocopy. CHL.

Cahoon, Reynolds. Letter, Far West, MO, to Newel K. Whitney, Kirtland, OH, 23 July 1838. CHL.

Cahoon, William F. Autobiography, 1878. Microfilm. CHL.

Call, Anson. Autobiography and Journal, ca. 1857–1883. CHL.

———. Statement, Bountiful, Utah Territory, 30 Dec. 1885. CHL.

Calvin, John. *Commentary on the Book of the Prophet Isaiah.* Translated by William Pringle. 4 vols. Grand Rapids, MI: William B. Eerdmans Publishing, 1948.

Cambridge Chronicle. Cambridge, MA. 1859–1873.

Cannon, Donald Q., and Lyndon W. Cook, eds. *Far West Record: Minutes of the Church of Jesus Christ of Latter-day Saints, 1830–1844.* Salt Lake City: Deseret Book, 1983.

Catalogue of the Utah Territorial Library, October, 1852. Great Salt Lake City, Utah Territory: Brigham H. Young, 1852.

Chace, J., D. Kelsey, D. H. Davidson, and W. H. Rease. *Map of Waldo County, Maine.* Portland, ME: J. Chace Jr., 1859. Copy at the Library of Congress.

Channing, W. H. "Outrages of Missouri Mobs on Mormons." *Western Messenger* 7, no. 3 (July 1839): 209–214.

Chapman, Raymond. "The Wheel of Fortune in Shakespeare's Historical Plays." *Review of English Studies* 1, no. 1 (Jan. 1950): 1–7.

"Charm of the Word Liberty." *Southern Lady's Companion* 2, no. 11 (Feb. 1849): 246–247.

Chase, Sherwin. "Events in the Life of Daniel Shearer," July 1983. Information concerning Daniel Shearer, ca. 1983. CHL.

Chenango Union. Norwich, NY. 1868–1890.

Chicago Daily Tribune. Chicago. 1872–1963.

Chitty, Joseph. *A Practical Treatise on Bills of Exchange, Checks on Bankers, Promissory Notes, Bankers' Cash Notes, and Bank Notes.* 6th American ed. Philadelphia: H. C. Carey and I. Lea, 1826.

Clark, A. Charles. "Timothy Baldwin Biography." Presented at the Dedication Ceremony of the Timothy Baldwin Clark Grave Site, Hillcrest Cemetery, Bolingbrook, IL, 7 May 2004. FamilySearch. Accessed 10 Oct. 2016. https://familysearch.org/photos/stories/10021886.

Clarke, Adam. *The New Testament of Our Lord and Saviour Jesus Christ. The Text Carefully Printed from the Most Correct Copies of the Present Authorised Version, Including the Marginal Readings and Parallel Texts. . . .* Vol. 1. New York: J. Emory and B. Waugh, 1831.

Clarke, H. *Fabulae Aesopi Selectae; or, Select Fables of Aesop; with an English Translation, More Literal Than Any Yet Extant, Designed for the Readier Instruction of Beginners in the Latin Tongue.* Boston: Samuel Hall, 1787.

Clay County, Missouri, Circuit Court Records, 1822–1878. Vol. 2, 1832–1841. Clay County Archives and Historical Library, Liberty, MO.

Clay County Archives and Historical Library. "About Us." Clay County Archives and Historical Library, Liberty, MO. Accessed 22 June 2016. http://www.claycountyarchives .org/index.php/about-us.

Clayton, William. Diary, 1840–1842. BYU.

———. History of the Nauvoo Temple, ca. 1845. CHL.

Cleveland, Edmund Janes, and Horace Gillette Cleveland, comps. *The Genealogy of the Cleveland and Cleaveland Families: An Attempt to Trace, in Both the Male and the Female Lines. . . .* 3 vols. Hartford, CT: By the authors, 1899.

Cole, Donald B. *Martin Van Buren and the American Political System.* Princeton, NJ: Princeton University Press, 1984.

Collected Works of Abraham Lincoln. 8 vols. Edited by Roy P. Basler, Marion Dolores Pratt, and Lloyd A. Dunlap. New Brunswick, NJ: Rutgers University Press, 1953.

Collection of Manuscripts about Mormons, 1832–1954. Chicago History Museum.

A Collection of Sacred Hymns, for the Church of the Latter Day Saints. Edited by Emma Smith. Kirtland, OH: F. G. Williams, 1835.

Compilation of Heber C. Kimball Correspondence, 1983. Typescript. CHL.

Complainant's Abstract of Pleading and Evidence. Lamoni, IA: Herald Publishing House, 1893.

Compton, Todd. *In Sacred Loneliness: The Plural Wives of Joseph Smith.* Salt Lake City: Signature Books, 2001.

Contributor. Salt Lake City. 1879–1896.

Cook, Lyndon W. "'I Have Sinned against Heaven, and Am Unworthy of Your Confidence, but I Cannot Live without a Reconciliation': Thomas B. Marsh Returns to the Church." *BYU Studies* 20, no. 4 (Summer 1980): 389–400.

———. "Isaac Galland—Mormon Benefactor." *BYU Studies* 19 (Spring 1979): 261–284.

———. *Joseph Smith and the Law of Consecration.* Provo, UT: Grandin Book, 1985.

Coray, Howard. Autobiographical Sketch, after 1883. Photocopy. CHL.

Corrill, John. *A Brief History of the Church of Christ of Latter Day Saints, (Commonly Called Mormons;) Including an Account of Their Doctrine and Discipline; with the Reasons of the Author for Leaving the Church.* St. Louis: By the author, 1839.

Cowdery, Lyman. Letter, Kirtland, OH, to Oliver Cowdery, Richmond, MO, 21 Aug. 1838. Western Americana Collection. Beinecke Rare Book and Manuscript Library, Yale University, New Haven, CT. Photocopy at CHL.

———. Papers, 1834–1858. CHL.

Cowdery, Oliver. Diary, Jan.–Mar. 1836. CHL. Also available as Leonard J. Arrington, "Oliver Cowdery's Kirtland, Ohio, 'Sketch Book,'" *BYU Studies* 12, no. 4 (Summer 1972): 410–426.

———. Docket Book, June–Sept. 1837. Henry E. Huntington Library, San Marino, CA.

———. Letter, Tiffin, OH, to Phineas Young, Nauvoo, IL, 23 Mar. 1846. CHL.

———. Letterbook, 1833–1838. Henry E. Huntington Library, San Marino, CA.

Cox, Cordelia Morley. "A Brief History of Patriarch Isaac Morley and Family Written by Mrs. Cordelia Morley Cox, Especially for Isaac Morley, Jr.," June 1907. CHL.

Crawley, Peter. *A Descriptive Bibliography of the Mormon Church*. 3 vols. Provo, UT: Religious Studies Center, Brigham Young University, 1997–2012.

Curtiss-Wedge, Franklyn, ed. *History of Goodhue County, Minnesota*. Chicago: H. C. Cooper, 1909.

Daily Cleveland Herald. Cleveland, OH. 1835–1837.

Daily Commercial Bulletin. St. Louis. 1838–1841.

Daily Herald and Gazette. Cleveland, OH. 1837–1839.

Daily Missouri Republican. St. Louis. 1839–1854.

Daily Pittsburgh Gazette. Pittsburgh. 1833–1841.

Daily Quincy Herald. Quincy, IL. 1865–1881.

D&C. See *Doctrine and Covenants of the Church of Jesus Christ of Latter-day Saints* (2013).

Darowski, Joseph F. "Seeking after the Ancient Order: Conferences and Councils in Early Church Governance, 1830–34." In *Brigham Young University Church History Symposium; A Firm Foundation: Church Organization and Administration,* edited by David J. Whittaker and Arnold K. Garr, 97–113. Provo, UT: Religious Studies Center, Brigham Young University; Salt Lake City: Deseret Book, 2011.

Daviess County, Missouri. Circuit Court Record, vol. A, July 1837–Oct. 1843. Daviess County Courthouse, Gallatin, MO.

Daviess County, Missouri. Circuit Court Records, 1839. State Historical Society of Missouri, Columbia.

Daviess County, Missouri. Legal Documents, 1838–1839. Photocopy. BYU.

Davis, Inez Smith. *The Story of the Church*. Independence, MO: Herald Publishing House, 1938.

Deatherage, Charles P. *Early History of Greater Kansas City, Missouri and Kansas: The Prophetic City at the Mouth of the Kaw. Vol. 1, Early History, from October 12, 1492, to 1870*. Kansas City, MO: By the author, 1927.

Derr, Jill Mulvay, Carol Cornwall Madsen, Kate Holbrook, and Matthew J. Grow, eds. *The First Fifty Years of Relief Society: Key Documents in Latter-day Saint Women's History*. Salt Lake City: Church Historian's Press, 2016.

Deseret News. Salt Lake City. 1850–.

Dibble, Philo. "Philo Dibble's Narrative." In *Early Scenes in Church History,* Faith-Promoting Series 8, pp. 74–96. Salt Lake City: Juvenile Instructor Office, 1882.

Dickinson, Donald C. *Dictionary of American Antiquarian Bookdealers*. Westport, CT: Greenwood Press, 1998.

A Digest of Patents, Issued by the United States, from 1790 to January 1, 1839: Published by Act of Congress, under the Superintendence of the Commissioner of Patents, Henry L. Ellsworth. To Which Is Added the Present Law relating to Patents. Washington DC: Peter Force, 1840.

A Directory for the City of Buffalo; Containing the Names and Residence of the Heads of Families and Householders, in Said City, on the First of May, 1836. Buffalo, NY: Charles Faxon, 1836.

A Directory for the City of Buffalo; Containing the Names and Residence of the Heads of Families, Householders, and Other Inhabitants, in Said City, on the 1st of May, 1837. Buffalo, NY: Sarah Crary, 1837.

Dixon, James D., comp. *History of Charles Dixon, One of the Early English Settlers of Sackville, N. B.* Sackville, New Brunswick: By the author, 1891.

Doctrine and Covenants, 2004 Community of Christ edition. See *Book of Doctrine and Covenants.*

Doctrine and Covenants of the Church of the Latter Day Saints: Carefully Selected from the Revelations of God. Compiled by Joseph Smith, Oliver Cowdery, Sidney Rigdon, and Frederick G. Williams. Kirtland, OH: F. G. Williams, 1835. Also available in Robin Scott Jensen, Richard E. Turley Jr., and Riley M. Lorimer, eds. *Revelations and Translations, Volume 2: Published Revelations.* Vol. 2 of the Revelations and Translations series of *The Joseph Smith Papers,* edited by Dean C. Jessee, Ronald K. Esplin, and Richard Lyman Bushman (Salt Lake City: Church Historian's Press, 2011).

The Doctrine and Covenants, of the Church of Jesus Christ of Latter-day Saints, Containing the Revelations Given to Joseph Smith, Jun., the Prophet, for the Building Up of the Kingdom of God in the Last Days. Salt Lake City: Deseret News Office, 1876.

The Doctrine and Covenants of the Church of Jesus Christ of Latter-day Saints: Containing Revelations Given to Joseph Smith, the Prophet, with Some Additions by His Successors in the Presidency of the Church. Salt Lake City: The Church of Jesus Christ of Latter-day Saints, 2013.

Document Containing the Correspondence, Orders, &c., in relation to the Disturbances with the Mormons; and the Evidence Given before the Hon. Austin A. King, Judge of the Fifth Judicial Circuit of the State of Missouri, at the Court-House in Richmond, in a Criminal Court of Inquiry, Begun November 12, 1838, on the Trial of Joseph Smith, Jr., and Others, for High Treason and Other Crimes against the State. Fayette, MO: Boon's Lick Democrat, 1841.

Documents Submitted by the Baltimore and Ohio Rail Road Company, in Behalf of Their Application to the Legislature of Virginia. Richmond, VA: Baltimore and Ohio Railroad Company, 1838.

Doty, William G. *Letters in Primitive Christianity.* Philadelphia: Fortress Press, 1973.

Doubleday, M. E. "The Wife of President Edwards." *Christian Parlor Magazine* 7 (1850): 134–138.

Doxey, Cynthia. "The Early Latter-day Saints in Livingston County, New York." In *Regional Studies in Latter-day Saint Church History: New York–Pennsylvania,* edited by Alexander L. Baugh and Andrew H. Hedges, 69–89. Provo, UT: Department of Church History and Doctrine, Brigham Young University, 2002.

The 1833 Ohio Gazetteer; or, Topographical Dictionary: Being a Continuation of the Work Originally Compiled by the Late John Kilbourn. Revised by a citizen of Columbus. 11th ed. Columbus, OH: Scott and Wright, 1833. Reprint, Knightstown, IN: Bookmark, 1978.

Eiserman, Rick. "Sterling Price: Solider—Politician—Missourian." In *Missouri Folk Heroes of the 19th Century,* edited by F. Mark McKiernan and Roger D. Launius, 115–134. Independence, MO: Independence Press, 1989.

Elders' Journal of the Church of Latter Day Saints. Kirtland, OH, Oct.–Nov. 1837; Far West, MO, July–Aug. 1838.

Ellsberry, Elizabeth Prather, comp. *Cemetery Records of Montgomery County, Missouri.* 2 vols. Chillicothe, MO: By the author, no date.

Encyclopaedia Americana. A Popular Dictionary of Arts, Sciences, Literature, History, Politics and Biography, Brought Down to the Present Time; Including a Copious Collection of Original Articles in American Biography; on the Basis of the Seventh Edition of the German Conversations-Lexicon. Edited by Francis Lieber, Edward Wigglesworth, and Thomas G. Bradford. New Edition. 13 vols. Philadelphia: Desilver, Thomas, 1836.

Encyclopedia of the History of Missouri, a Compendium of History and Biography for Ready Reference. Vol. 6. Edited by Howard L. Conard. New York: Southern History, 1901.

Ensign. Buffalo, Iowa Territory. 1844–1845.

Ensign of Liberty. Kirtland, OH. Mar. 1847–Aug. 1849.

Esplin, Ronald K. "The Emergence of Brigham Young and the Twelve to Mormon Leadership, 1830–1841." PhD diss., Brigham Young University, 1981. Also available as *The Emergence of Brigham Young and the Twelve to Mormon Leadership, 1830–1841,* Dissertations in Latter-day Saint History (Provo, UT: Joseph Fielding Smith Institute for Latter-day Saint History; *BYU Studies,* 2006).

———. "Hyrum Smith." In *United by Faith: The Joseph Sr. and Lucy Mack Smith Family,* edited by Kyle R. Walker, 122–163. American Fork, UT: Covenant Communications, 2006.

Evangelical Magazine and Gospel Advocate. Utica, NY. 1830–1850.

Evans, Max J. *Register of the Stephen Post Papers in the Church Archives, The Church of Jesus Christ of Latter-day Saints.* Salt Lake City: Historical Department of The Church of Jesus Christ of Latter-day Saints, 1975.

The Evening and the Morning Star. Independence, MO, June 1832–July 1833; Kirtland, OH, Dec. 1833–Sept. 1834.

Far West Committee. Minutes, Jan.–Apr. 1839. CHL.

Far West Stake High Council Minutes, Dec. 1837–Mar. 1838. CHL.

Faust, Drew Gilpin. *This Republic of Suffering: Death and the American Civil War.* New York: Knopf, 2008.

Feldberg, Michael. *The Turbulent Era: Riot and Disorder in Jacksonian America.* New York: Oxford University Press, 1980.

Fielding, Joseph. Journals, 1837–1859. CHL.

Firmage, Edwin Brown, and Richard Collin Mangrum. *Zion in the Courts: A Legal History of the Church of Jesus Christ of Latter-day Saints, 1830–1900.* Urbana: University of Illinois Press, 1988.

First Presidency (John Taylor). Correspondence, 1877–1887. CHL.

Fleming, Helen Vilate Bourne. Collection, 1836–1963. CHL.

Fluhman, J. Spencer. *"A Peculiar People": Anti-Mormonism and the Making of Religion in Nineteenth-Century America.* Chapel Hill: University of North Carolina Press, 2012.

Foote, David. Letter, Adams Co., IL, to Thomas Clement and Betsey Foote Clement, Dryden, NY, 14 May 1839. CHL.

Foote, Warren. Autobiography, not before 1903. 3 vols. Warren Foote, Papers, 1837–1941. CHL.

Foreman, Grant. *Advancing the Frontier, 1830–1860.* Norman: University of Oklahoma Press, 1933.

Frampton, David. Justice of the Peace Docket Entry, 12 July 1838. CHL.

Frederick S. Peck Collection of American Historical Autographs, and a Few Very Rare Books. Vol. 1. Philadelphia: Samuel T. Freeman, 1947.

Fuller, William Hyslop, comp. *Genealogy of Some Descendants of Edward Fuller of the Mayflower.* Palmer, MA: C. B. Fiske, 1908.

Galland, Isaac. Letter, Chillicothe, OH, to Samuel Swasey, North Haverhill, NH, 22 July 1839. CCLA.

Gates, Paul Wallace. "Southern Investments in Northern Lands before the Civil War." *Journal of Southern History* 5, no. 2 (May 1939): 155–185.

Gazette of the United States and Daily Advertiser. Philadelphia. 1800–1801.

Geauga County, Ohio, Court of Common Pleas, Journal N. Geauga County Archives and Records Center, Chardon, OH.

"General," Record Book, 1838. Verso of Patriarchal Blessings, vol. 5. CHL.

General Church Recorder. License Record Book, Dec. 1837–May 1862. CHL.

General Land Office Records. Bureau of Land Management, U.S. Department of the Interior. Accessed 1 July 2016. http://www.glorecords.blm.gov.

Gentry, Leland Homer, and Todd M. Compton. *Fire and Sword: A History of the Latter-day Saints in Northern Missouri, 1836–39.* Salt Lake City: Greg Kofford Books, 2011.

Gibbs, Josiah W. *Manual Hebrew and English Lexicon, Including the Biblical Chaldee. Designed Particularly for Beginners.* 2nd ed. New Haven, CT: Hezekiah Howe, 1832.

Gilje, Paul A. *Rioting in America.* Bloomington: Indiana University Press, 1999.

Gill, John. *A Complete Body of Doctrinal and Practical Divinity; or, A System of Evangelical Truths, Deduced from the Sacred Scriptures.* 3 vols. London: W. Winterbotham, 1796.

Givens, Terryl L. *Wrestling the Angel: The Foundations of Mormon Thought: Cosmos, God, Humanity.* New York: Oxford University Press, 2015.

Givens, Terryl L., and Matthew J. Grow. *Parley P. Pratt: The Apostle Paul of Mormonism.* New York: Oxford University Press, 2011.

Greene, Evan Melbourne. "A Biographical Sketch of the Life and Travels of John Portenus Greene," 1857. CHL.

Greene, John P. *Facts relative to the Expulsion of the Mormons, or Latter Day Saints, from the State of Missouri, under the "Exterminating Order." By John P. Greene, an Authorized Representative of the Mormons.* Cincinnati: R. P. Brooks, 1839.

Greensborough Patriot. Greensborough (now Greensboro), NC. 1839–1856.

Greenwood, Val D. *The Researcher's Guide to American Genealogy.* 3rd ed. Baltimore: Genealogical Publishing Company, 2000.

Gregg, Thomas. *History of Hancock County, Illinois, together with an Outline History of the State, and a Digest of State Laws.* Chicago: Charles C. Chapman, 1880.

Grimsted, David. *American Mobbing, 1828–1861: Toward Civil War.* New York: Oxford University Press, 1998.

———. "Rioting in Its Jacksonian Setting." *American Historical Review* 77, no. 2 (Apr. 1972): 361–397.

Grua, David W. "Memoirs of the Persecuted: Persecution, Memory, and the West as a Mormon Refuge." Master's thesis, Brigham Young University, 2008.

Gurley, Zenos H. "Questions Asked of David Whitmer at His Home in Richmond, Ray County, Mo.," 1885. CHL.

Guyatt, Nicholas. *Providence and the Invention of the United States, 1607–1876.* Cambridge: Cambridge University Press, 2007.

Hales, Brian C. "'Guilty of Such Folly?' Accusations of Adultery and Polygamy against Oliver Cowdery." *Mormon Historical Studies* 9, no. 2 (Fall 2008): 19–28.

———. *Joseph Smith's Polygamy.* 3 vols. Salt Lake City: Greg Kofford Books, 2013.

Hall, David D. *Ways of Writing: The Practice and Politics of Text-Making in Seventeenth-Century New England.* Philadelphia: University of Pennsylvania Press, 2008.

Hall, Florence Howe. *Social Customs.* Boston: Dana Estes, 1887.

Hamer, John. *Northeast of Eden: A Historical Atlas of Missouri's Mormon County.* [Mirabile, MO]: Far West Cultural Center, 2004.

Hamlin, L. B. "Selections from the William Greene Papers, I." *Quarterly Publication of the Historical and Philosophical Society of Ohio* 13, no. 1 (Jan.–Mar. 1918): 1–38.

Hammond, Charles. *Cases Decided in the Supreme Court of Ohio, in Bank, at December Terms, 1833, 1834.* Vol. 6. Cincinnati: Robert Clarke, 1872.

Hancock, Mosiah L. "Autobiography of Levi Ward Hancock," ca. 1896. CHL.

Hannibal Commercial Advertiser. Hannibal, MO. 1837–1839.

Harper, Steven C. "Oliver Cowdery as Second Witness of Priesthood Restoration." In *Days Never to Be Forgotten: Oliver Cowdery,* edited by Alexander Baugh, 73–89. Provo, UT: Religious Studies Center, Brigham Young University; Salt Lake City: Deseret Book, 2009.

Hartley, William G. "'Almost Too Intolerable a Burthen': The Winter Exodus from Missouri, 1838–39." *Journal of Mormon History* 18, no. 2 (Fall 1992): 6–40.

———. "Letters and Mail between Kirtland and Independence: A Mormon Postal History, 1831–1833." *Journal of Mormon History* 35, no. 3 (Summer 2009): 163–189.

———. "The Saints' Forced Exodus from Missouri, 1839." In *Joseph Smith: The Prophet and Seer,* edited by Richard Neitzel Holzapfel and Kent P. Jackson, 347–389. Provo, UT: Religious Studies Center, Brigham Young University; Salt Lake City: Deseret Book, 2010.

Hatch, Nathan O. *The Democratization of American Christianity.* New Haven, CT: Yale University Press, 1989.

Hawker, Robert. *Sermons on the Divinity and Operations of the Holy Ghost.* Holborn, England: S. Hazard, 1794.

Hening, William Waller, ed. *The Statutes at Large; Being a Collection of All the Laws of Virginia, from the First Session of the Legislature, in the Year 1619*. Vol. 12. Richmond, VA: George Cochran, 1823.

Henry, Matthew. *An Exposition of the Old and New Testament: Wherein Each Chapter Is Summed Up in Its Contents; the Sacred Text Inserted at Large, in Distinct Paragraphs; Each Paragraph Reduced to Its Proper Heads; the Sense Given, and Largely Illustrated; with Practical Remarks and Observations*. First American ed. 5 vols. Philadelphia: Ed. Barrington and Geo. D. Haswell, [1828].

Higbee, John S. Journal and Reminiscences, 1845–1849. John S. Higbee, Reminiscences and Diaries, 1845–1866. CHL.

Historian's Office. Brigham Young History Drafts, 1856–1858. CHL.

———. Catalogs and Inventories, 1846–1904. CHL.

———. Correspondence Files, 1856–1926. CHL.

———. General Church Minutes, 1839–1877. CHL.

———. Histories of the Twelve, 1856–1858, 1861. CHL.

———. Joseph Smith History, Draft Notes, ca. 1839–1856. CHL.

———. Joseph Smith History Documents, 1839–1860. CHL.

———. Journal, 1844–1997. CHL.

———. Obituary Notices of Distinguished Persons, 1854–1872. CHL.

Historical Department. Nineteenth-Century Legal Documents Collection, ca. 1825–1890. CHL.

Historical Department File, 1970s–1980s. CHL.

The Historical Record, a Monthly Periodical, Devoted Exclusively to Historical, Biographical, Chronological and Statistical Matters. Salt Lake City. 1882–1890.

History of Caldwell and Livingston Counties, Missouri, Written and Compiled from the Most Authentic Official and Private Sources. . . . St. Louis: National Historical, 1886.

History of Clay and Platte Counties, Missouri, Written and Compiled from the Most Authentic Official and Private Sources. . . . St. Louis: National Historical, 1885.

The History of Daviess County, Missouri: An Encyclopedia of Useful Information, and a Compendium of Actual Facts. . . . Kansas City, MO: Birdsall and Dean, 1882.

History of Geauga and Lake Counties, Ohio, with Illustrations and Biographical Sketches of Its Pioneers and Most Prominent Men. Philadelphia: Williams Brothers, 1878.

The History of Jackson County, Missouri, Containing a History of the County, Its Cities, Towns, Etc. . . . Kansas City, MO: Union Historical, 1881.

History of Ray County, Mo., Carefully Written and Compiled from the Most Authentic Official and Private Sources. . . . St. Louis: Missouri Historical, 1881.

History of the Church / Smith, Joseph, et al. *History of the Church of Jesus Christ of Latter-day Saints*. Edited by B. H. Roberts. Salt Lake City: *Deseret News*, 1902–1912 (vols. 1–6), 1932 (vol. 7).

The History of the Reorganized Church of Jesus Christ of Latter Day Saints. 4 vols. Lamoni, IA: 1896–1902. Reprint, Independence, MO: Herald Publishing House, [after 1976].

Hoffman, Anthony. Letter, Rushville, IL, to John Reid, Argyle, NY, 1 Nov. 1833. Abraham Lincoln Presidential Library, Springfield, IL.

Holifield, E. Brooks. *Theology in America: Christian Thought from the Age of the Puritans to the Civil War.* New Haven, CT: Yale University Press, 2003.

Holland, David F. *Sacred Borders: Continuing Revelation and Canonical Restraint in Early America.* New York: Oxford University Press, 2011.

Holt, Michael F. *The Rise and Fall of the American Whig Party: Jacksonian Politics and the Onset of the Civil War.* New York: Oxford University Press, 1999.

The Holy Bible, Containing the Old and New Testaments Translated Out of the Original Tongues: And with the Former Translations Diligently Compared and Revised, by His Majesty's Special Command. Authorized King James Version with Explanatory Notes and Cross References to the Standard Works of The Church of Jesus Christ of Latter-day Saints. Salt Lake City: The Church of Jesus Christ of Latter-day Saints, 2013.

Howe, Daniel Walker. *What Hath God Wrought: The Transformation of America, 1815–1848.* The Oxford History of the United States. New York: Oxford University Press, 2007.

Howe, Eber D. *Autobiography and Recollections of a Pioneer Printer: Together with Sketches of the War of 1812 on the Niagara Frontier.* Painesville, OH: Telegraph Steam Printing House, 1878.

———. *Mormonism Unvailed; or, A Faithful Account of That Singular Imposition and Delusion, from Its Rise to the Present Time. With Sketches of the Characters of Its Propagators, and a Full Detail of the Manner in Which the Famous Golden Bible Was Brought before the World. To Which Are Added, Inquiries into the Probability That the Historical Part of the Said Bible Was Written by One Solomon Spalding, More Than Twenty Years Ago, and by Him Intended to Have Been Published as a Romance.* Painesville, OH: By the author, 1834.

Huntington, Dimick B. Reminiscences and Journal, 1845–1847. Dimick B. Huntington, Journal, 1845–1849. CHL.

Huntington, Oliver B. "History of Oliver Boardman Huntington," 1845–1846. BYU.

Huntington, William D. Cemetery Records, 1839–1845. William D. Huntington, Records, 1839–1884. CHL.

Hyrum Smith Family Bible, 1834. In Hyrum Smith, Papers, ca. 1832–1844. BYU.

Illinois Office of Secretary of State. Enrolled Acts of the General Assembly, 1818–1993. Illinois State Archives, Springfield.

Illinois State Historical Society. Circuit Court Case Files, 1830–1900. Microfilm. CHL.

An Illustrated Historical Atlas of Caldwell County, Missouri. Compiled, Drawn and Published from Personal Examinations and Surveys. Philadelphia: Edwards Brothers, 1876.

Independent Press. Hartford, CT. 1833–1834.

"Inventory of President Joseph Fielding Smith's Safe," 23 May 1970. First Presidency, General Administration Files, 1921–1972. CHL.

Jefferson, Thomas. *A Manual of Parliamentary Practice. For the Use of the Senate of the United States.* Washington DC: Samuel Harrison Smith, 1801.

———. "Notes on the State of Virginia," 1783–1784. Massachusetts Historical Society, Boston.

Jeffersonian Republican. Jefferson City, MO. 1831–1844.

Jennings, Warren A. "Importuning for Redress." *Bulletin* 27, no. 1 (Oct. 1970): 15–29. Published by the Missouri Historical Society.

Jenson, Andrew. Collection, ca. 1841–1942. CHL.

———. Journals, 1864–1941. Andrew Jenson, Autobiography and Journals, 1864–1941. CHL.

———. *Latter-day Saint Biographical Encyclopedia: A Compilation of Biographical Sketches of Prominent Men and Women in the Church of Jesus Christ of Latter-day Saints.* 4 vols. Salt Lake City: Andrew Jenson History Co., 1901–1936.

Jessee, Dean C. "'Walls, Grates and Screeking Iron Doors': The Prison Experience of Mormon Leaders in Missouri, 1838–1839." In *New Views of Mormon History: A Collection of Essays in Honor of Leonard J. Arrington,* edited by Davis Bitton and Maureen Ursenbach Beecher, 19–42. Salt Lake City: University of Utah Press, 1987.

———. "The Writing of Joseph Smith's History." *BYU Studies* 11 (Summer 1971): 439–473.

Johnson, Benjamin Franklin. "A Life Review," after 1893. Benjamin Franklin Johnson, Papers, 1852–1911. CHL.

———. Papers, 1852–1911. CHL.

Johnson, Clark V., ed. *Mormon Redress Petitions: Documents of the 1833–1838 Missouri Conflict.* Religious Studies Center Monograph Series 16. Provo, UT: Religious Studies Center, Brigham Young University, 1992.

Johnson, Clark V., and Ronald E. Romig. *An Index to Early Caldwell County, Missouri, Land Records.* Rev. ed. Independence, MO: Missouri Mormon Frontier Foundation, 2002.

Johnson, Jeffery O. *Register of the Joseph Smith Collection in the Church Archives, The Church of Jesus Christ of Latter-day Saints.* Salt Lake City: Historical Department of The Church of Jesus Christ of Latter-day Saints, 1973.

John Whitmer Family Papers, 1837–1912. CHL.

Jones, Thomas. *The Principles and Practice of Book-Keeping, Embracing an Entirely New and Improved Method of Imparting the Science; with Exemplifications of the Most Concise and Approved Forms of Arranging Merchants' Accounts.* New York: Wiley and Putnam, 1841.

Jortner, Adam. "Cholera, Christ, and Jackson: The Epidemic of 1832 and the Origins of Christian Politics in Antebellum America." *Journal of the Early Republic* 27, no. 2 (Summer 2007): 233–264.

"Joseph Smith." *Collector* 17, no. 1 (Nov. 1903): 3–4.

Joseph Smith—Matthew. See *Pearl of Great Price.*

Joseph Smith Translation. See *Holy Bible.*

Journal, of the House of Representatives, of the State of Missouri, at the First Session of the Tenth General Assembly, Begun and Held at the City of Jefferson, on Monday, the Nineteenth Day of November, in the Year of Our Lord, One Thousand Eight Hundred and Thirty-Eight. Jefferson City, MO: Calvin Gunn, 1839.

Journal of Discourses. 26 vols. Liverpool: F. D. Richards, 1855–1886.

Journal of History. Lamoni, IA, 1908–1920; Independence, MO, 1921–1925.

Journal of the Senate of the United States of America, Being the First Session of the Twenty-Sixth Congress, Begun and Held at the City of Washington, December 2, 1839. And in the Sixty-Fourth Year of the Independence of the Said United States. Washington DC: Blair and Rives, 1839.

JS. In addition to the entries that immediately follow, see entries under "Smith, Joseph."

JS Collection / Joseph Smith Collection, 1827–1846. CHL.

JS Collection (Supplement) / Joseph Smith Collection (Supplement), 1833–1844. CHL.

JS History / Smith, Joseph, et al. History, 1838–1856. Vols. A-1–F-1 (originals), A-2–E-2 (fair copies). In Historian's Office, History of the Church, 1838–ca. 1882. CHL. The history for the period after 5 Aug. 1838 was composed after the death of Joseph Smith.

JS History, ca. Summer 1832 / Smith, Joseph. "A History of the Life of Joseph Smith Jr," ca. Summer 1832. In Joseph Smith, "Letterbook A," 1832–1835, 1–[6] (earliest numbering). Joseph Smith Collection. CHL.

JS History, 1834–1836 / Smith, Joseph, et al. History, 1834–1836. In Joseph Smith et al., History, 1838–1856, vol. A-1, back of book (earliest numbering), 9–20, 46–187. In Historian's Office, History of the Church, 1838–ca. 1882. CHL.

JS, Journal, Mar.–Sept. 1838 / Smith, Joseph, "The Scriptory Book—of Joseph Smith Jr.— President of the Church of Jesus Christ, of Latterday Saints in All the World," Mar.– Sept. 1838. In "General," Record Book, 1838, verso of Patriarchal Blessings, vol. 5. CHL.

JS Letterbook 1 / Smith, Joseph. "Letter Book A," 1832–1835. Joseph Smith Collection. CHL.

JS Letterbook 2 / Smith, Joseph. "Copies of Letters, &c. &c.," 1839–1843. Joseph Smith Collection. CHL.

JS Office Papers / Smith, Joseph. Office Papers, ca. 1835–1845. CHL.

JSP, D1 / MacKay, Michael Hubbard, Gerrit J. Dirkmaat, Grant Underwood, Robert J. Woodford, and William G. Hartley, eds. *Documents, Volume 1: July 1828–June 1831.* Vol. 1 of the Documents series of *The Joseph Smith Papers,* edited by Dean C. Jessee, Ronald K. Esplin, Richard Lyman Bushman, and Matthew J. Grow. Salt Lake City: Church Historian's Press, 2013.

JSP, D2 / Godfrey, Matthew C., Mark Ashurst-McGee, Grant Underwood, Robert J. Woodford, and William G. Hartley, eds. *Documents, Volume 2: July 1831–January 1833.* Vol. 2 of the Documents series of *The Joseph Smith Papers,* edited by Dean C. Jessee, Ronald K. Esplin, Richard Lyman Bushman, and Matthew J. Grow. Salt Lake City: Church Historian's Press, 2013.

JSP, D3 / Dirkmaat, Gerrit J., Brent M. Rogers, Grant Underwood, Robert J. Woodford, and William G. Hartley, eds. *Documents, Volume 3: February 1833–March 1834.* Vol. 3 of the Documents series of *The Joseph Smith Papers,* edited by Ronald K. Esplin and Matthew J. Grow. Salt Lake City: Church Historian's Press, 2014.

JSP, D4 / Godfrey, Matthew C., Brenden W. Rensink, Alex D. Smith, Max H Parkin, and Alexander L. Baugh, eds. *Documents, Volume 4: April 1834–September 1835.* Vol. 4 of the Documents series of *The Joseph Smith Papers,* edited by Ronald K. Esplin, Matthew J. Grow, and Matthew C. Godfrey. Salt Lake City: Church Historian's Press, 2016.

JSP, D5 / Rogers, Brent M., Elizabeth A. Kuehn, Christian K. Heimburger, Max H Parkin, Alexander L. Baugh, and Stephen C. Harper, eds. *Documents, Volume 5: October 1835– January 1838.* Vol. 5 of the Documents series of *The Joseph Smith Papers,* edited by Ronald K. Esplin, Matthew J. Grow, and Matthew C. Godfrey. Salt Lake City: Church Historian's Press, 2017.

JSP, H1 / Davidson, Karen Lynn, David J. Whittaker, Mark Ashurst-McGee, and Richard L. Jensen, eds. *Histories, Volume 1: Joseph Smith Histories, 1832–1844.* Vol. 1 of the Histories series of *The Joseph Smith Papers,* edited by Dean C. Jessee, Ronald K. Esplin, and Richard Lyman Bushman. Salt Lake City: Church Historian's Press, 2012.

JSP, H2 / Davidson, Karen Lynn, Richard L. Jensen, and David J. Whittaker, eds. *Histories, Volume 2: Assigned Histories, 1831–1847.* Vol. 2 of the Histories series of *The Joseph Smith Papers,* edited by Dean C. Jessee, Ronald K. Esplin, and Richard Lyman Bushman. Salt Lake City: Church Historian's Press, 2012.

JSP, J1 / Jessee, Dean C., Mark Ashurst-McGee, and Richard L. Jensen, eds. *Journals, Volume 1: 1832–1839.* Vol. 1 of the Journals series of *The Joseph Smith Papers,* edited by Dean C. Jessee, Ronald K. Esplin, and Richard Lyman Bushman. Salt Lake City: Church Historian's Press, 2008.

JSP, J2 / Hedges, Andrew H., Alex D. Smith, and Richard Lloyd Anderson, eds. *Journals, Volume 2: December 1841–April 1843.* Vol. 2 of the Journals series of *The Joseph Smith Papers,* edited by Dean C. Jessee, Ronald K. Esplin, and Richard Lyman Bushman. Salt Lake City: Church Historian's Press, 2011.

JSP, J3 / Hedges, Andrew H., Alex D. Smith, and Brent M. Rogers, eds. *Journals, Volume 3: May 1843–June 1844.* Vol. 3 of the Journals series of *The Joseph Smith Papers,* edited by Ronald K. Esplin and Matthew J. Grow. Salt Lake City: Church Historian's Press, 2015.

JSP, MRB / Jensen, Robin Scott, Robert J. Woodford, and Steven C. Harper, eds. *Manuscript Revelation Books.* Facsimile edition. First volume of the Revelations and Translations series of *The Joseph Smith Papers,* edited by Dean C. Jessee, Ronald K. Esplin, and Richard Lyman Bushman. Salt Lake City: Church Historian's Press, 2009.

JSP, R2 / Jensen, Robin Scott, Richard E. Turley Jr., and Riley M. Lorimer, eds. *Revelations and Translations, Volume 2: Published Revelations.* Vol. 2 of the Revelations and Translations series of *The Joseph Smith Papers,* edited by Dean C. Jessee, Ronald K. Esplin, and Richard Lyman Bushman. Salt Lake City: Church Historian's Press, 2011.

JSP, R3, Part 1 / Skousen, Royal, and Robin Scott Jensen, eds. *Revelations and Translations, Volume 3, Part 1: Printer's Manuscript of the Book of Mormon, 1 Nephi 1–Alma 35.* Facsimile edition. Part 1 of vol. 3 of the Revelations and Translations series of *The Joseph Smith Papers,* edited by Ronald K. Esplin and Matthew J. Grow. Salt Lake City: Church Historian's Press, 2015.

JS v. George M. Hinkle / Lee County, Iowa Territory, District Court. Joseph Smith v. George M. Hinkle, 1841–1842. CHL.

JS v. McLellin / Clay County, Missouri, Circuit Court. Joseph Smith v. William E. McLellin, 1839. Clay County Archives and Historical Library, Liberty, MO.

Judd, Zadoc Knapp. "Reminiscences of Zadoc Knapp Judd," 1902. Typescript. Mary F. Johnson Collection, 1878–1966. CHL.

Juvenile Instructor. Salt Lake City. 1866–1900.

Kilbourne, David W. *Strictures, on Dr. I. Galland's Pamphlet, Entitled, "Villainy Exposed," with Some Account of His Transactions in Lands of the Sac and Fox Reservation, etc., in Lee County, Iowa.* Fort Madison, IA: Statesman Office, 1850.

Kimball, Heber C. Autobiography, ca. 1856. Heber C. Kimball, Papers, 1837–1866. CHL.

———. Collection, 1837–1898. CHL.

———. Correspondence, 1837–1864. Private possession. Copy at CHL.

————. "History of Heber Chase Kimball by His Own Dictation," ca. 1842–1856. Heber C. Kimball, Papers, 1837–1866. CHL.

————. "The Journal and Record of Heber Chase Kimball an Apostle of Jesus Christ of Latter Day Saints," ca. 1842–1858. Heber C. Kimball, Papers, 1837–1866. CHL.

Kimball, Hiram. Collection, 1830–1910. CHL.

Kimball, Presendia Huntington. Reminiscences, 1881. CHL.

Kimball, Stanley B. *Heber C. Kimball: Mormon Patriarch and Pioneer.* Urbana: University of Illinois Press, 1986.

Kimball Family Correspondence, 1838–1871. CHL.

Kirtland Camp. Journal, Mar.–Oct. 1838. CHL.

Kirtland Egyptian Papers, ca. 1835–1836. CHL.

Kirtland Elders Quorum. "A Record of the First Quororum of Elders Belonging to the Church of Christ: In Kirtland Geauga Co. Ohio," 1836–1838, 1840–1841. CCLA.

Kirtland Safety Society. Stock Ledger, 1836–1837. Collection of Manuscripts about Mormons, 1832–1954, Chicago History Museum. Copy at CHL.

Kirtland Township Trustees' Minutes and Poll Book, 1817–1838. Lake County Historical Society, Painesville, OH.

Knight, Newel. History, ca. 1871. Private possession. Copy at CHL.

Knight, Vinson. Account Book, 1839–1842. Microfilm. CHL.

————. Letters, 1839 and 1842. Typescript. CHL.

Knodell, Jane. "Interregional Financial Integration and the Banknote Market: The Old Northwest, 1815–1845." *Journal of Economic History* 48, no. 2 (June 1988): 287–298.

Knox, Vicesimus. *Essays, Moral and Literary.* 15th ed. 3 vols. London: J. Mawman and Poultry, 1803.

Lake County, Ohio. Land Registry Records, 1840–1842. CHL.

Lass, William E. *Navigating the Missouri: Steamboating on Nature's Highway, 1819–1835.* Norman, OK: Arthur H. Clark, 2008.

Latter Day Saints' Messenger and Advocate. Kirtland, OH. Oct. 1834–Sept. 1837.

Latter-day Saints' Millennial Star. Manchester, England, 1840–1842; Liverpool, 1842–1932; London, 1932–1970.

Launius, Roger D. *Alexander William Doniphan: Portrait of a Missouri Moderate.* Columbia: University of Missouri Press, 1997.

Laws of the State of Missouri, Passed at the First Session of the Ninth General Assembly, Begun and Held at the City of Jefferson, on Monday, the Twenty-First Day of November, in the Year of Our Lord One Thousand Eight Hundred and Thirty-Six. 2nd ed. St. Louis: Chambers and Knapp, 1841.

Laws of the State of Missouri, Passed at the First Session of the Tenth General Assembly, Begun and Held at the City of Jefferson, on Monday, the Nineteenth Day of November, in the Year of Our Lord, One Thousand Eight Hundred and Thirty-Eight. Jefferson City, MO: Calvin Gunn, 1838.

Laws of the Territory of Utah, Passed at the Twenty-Ninth Session of the Legislative Assembly, Held at the City of Salt Lake, the Capital of Said Territory, Commencing January 13, A. D. 1890, and Ending March 13, A. D. 1890. Salt Lake City: Tribune Printing and Publishing, 1890.

Lazare, Edward, ed. *American Book-Prices Current, a Record of Literary Properties Sold at Auction in the United States during the Season of 1946–1947.* New York: R. R. Bowker, 1947.

——, ed. *American Book-Prices Current, a Record of Literary Properties Sold at Auction in the United States during the Seasons of 1950–1951.* New York: R. R. Bowker, 1951.

Lee, E. G. *The Mormons; or, Knavery Exposed, Giving an Account of the Discovery of the Golden Plates. . . .* Frankford, PA: By the author, 1841.

Lee, John D. *Mormonism Unveiled; or, The Life and Confessions of the Late Mormon Bishop, John D. Lee. . . .* St. Louis: Bryan, Brand, 1877.

Leonard, Glen M. *Nauvoo: A Place of Peace, a People of Promise.* Salt Lake City: Deseret Book; Provo, UT: Brigham Young University Press, 2002.

Lepler, Jessica M. *The Many Panics of 1837: People, Politics, and the Creation of a Transatlantic Financial Crisis.* Cambridge: Cambridge University Press, 2013.

LeSueur, Stephen C. *The 1838 Mormon War in Missouri.* Columbia: University of Missouri Press, 1987.

——. "Missouri's Failed Compromise: The Creation of Caldwell County for the Mormons." *Journal of Mormon History* 31, no. 3 (Fall 2005): 113–144.

——. "Mixing Politics with Religion: A Closer Look at Electioneering and Voting in Caldwell and Daviess Counties in 1838." *John Whitmer Historical Association Journal* 33, no. 1 (Spring/Summer 2013): 184–208.

Lewis, David. Autobiography, 1854. CHL.

Liberator. Boston. 1831–1865.

Liberty Hall and Cincinnati Gazette. Cincinnati. 1815–1857.

"Liberty Jail." *Liahona, the Elders' Journal* 12, no. 8 (18 Aug. 1914): 122–123.

Little, James Amasa. "Biography of Lorenzo Dow Young," 1890. Typescript. CHL.

Lloyd, James T. *Lloyd's Steamboat Directory, and Disasters on the Western Waters, Containing the History of the First Application of Steam, as a Motive Power. . . .* Cincinnati: James T. Lloyd, 1856.

Loehr, Rodney C. "Moving Back from the Atlantic Seaboard." *Agricultural History* 17, no. 2 (Apr. 1943): 90–96.

Longworth's American Almanac, New-York Register, and City Directory, of the Sixty-First Year of American Independence. . . . New York: Thomas Longworth, 1836.

Longworth's American Almanac, New-York Register, and City Directory, of the Sixty-Fourth Year of American Independence. . . . New York: Thomas Longworth, 1839.

Lord Sterling. Papers, 1835–1850. Lake County Historical Society, Painesville, OH.

Lynch, Bob D. *The Life and Times of Joshua W. Lynch Descendants.* Kansas City, MO: By the author, 2009.

Mace, Wandle. Autobiography, ca. 1890. CHL.

Madsen, Gordon A. "Joseph Smith and the Missouri Court of Inquiry: Austin A. King's Quest for Hostages." *BYU Studies* 43, no. 4 (2004): 93–136.

——. "Tabulating the Impact of Litigation on the Kirtland Economy." In *Sustaining the Law: Joseph Smith's Legal Encounters,* edited by Gordon A. Madsen, Jeffrey N. Walker, and John W. Welch, 227–246. Provo, UT: *BYU Studies,* 2014.

Madsen, Gordon A., Jeffrey N. Walker, and John W. Welch, eds. *Sustaining the Law: Joseph Smith's Legal Encounters*. Provo, UT: BYU Studies, 2014.

Marquardt, H. Michael. "Martin Harris: The Kirtland Years, 1831–1870." *Dialogue: A Journal of Mormon Thought* 35, no. 3 (Fall 2002): 1–41.

Maryland Gazette. Annapolis. 1827–1839.

Material relating to Mormon Expulsion from Missouri, 1839–1843. Photocopy. CHL.

Mauss, Armand. "In Search of Ephraim: Traditional Mormon Conceptions of Lineage and Race." *Journal of Mormon History* 25, no. 1 (Spring 1999): 131–173.

McBride, James. Autobiography, 1874–1876. Microfilm. CHL.

McBride, Reuben. Reminiscence, no date. CHL.

McCandless, Perry. *A History of Missouri*. 3 vols. Columbia: University of Missouri Press, 1971–1973.

McDannell, Colleen, and Bernhard Lang. *Heaven: A History*. New Haven, CT: Yale University Press, 1988.

McKay, David O. Diary Entries, 21–22 June 1961. Photocopy. CHL.

McLellin, William E. Letter, Independence, MO, to Joseph Smith III, [Plano, IL], July 1872. Letters and Documents Copied from Originals in the Office of the Church Historian, Reorganized Church, no date. Typescript. CHL. Original at CCLA.

McRae, Alexander. Petition, Liberty, MO, 15 Mar. 1839. CHL.

Mehling, Mary Bryant Alverson. *Cowdrey-Cowdery-Cowdray Genealogy: William Cowdery of Lynn, Massachusetts, 1630, and His Descendants*. [New York]: Frank Allaben Genealogical Company, 1911.

Meier, John P. "The Historical Jesus and the Historical Herodians." *Journal of Biblical Literature* 119, no. 4 (Winter 2000): 740–746.

Meigs, William M. *The Life of Thomas Hart Benton*. Philadelphia: J. B. Lippencott, 1904.

Memoirs of Matthias the Prophet, with a Full Exposure of His Atrocious Impositions and of the Degrading Delusions of His Followers. New York: The Sun, 1835.

Memorial of Ephraim Owen, Jr. H.R. Doc. no. 42, 25th Cong., 3rd Sess. (1838).

Merrill, J. L., ed. *History of Acworth, with the Proceedings of the Centennial Anniversary, Genealogical Records, and Register of Farms*. Acworth, NH: Town of Acworth, 1869.

Millennial Harbinger. Bethany, VA. Jan. 1830–Dec. 1870.

Miller, Lewis. Docket Book. Henry E. Huntington Library, San Marino, CA.

Miller, Richard Lawrence. *Lincoln and His World: Prairie Politician, 1834–1842*. Mechanicsburg, PA: Stackpole Books, 2008.

Minute Book 1 / "Conference A," 1832–1837. CHL.

Minute Book 2 / "The Conference Minutes and Record Book of Christ's Church of Latter Day Saints," 1838–ca. 1839, 1842, 1844. CHL.

Missouri, State of. "Evidence." Hearing Record, Richmond, MO, 12–29 Nov. 1838, State of Missouri v. Joseph Smith et al. for Treason and Other Crimes (Mo. 5th Jud. Cir. 1838). Eugene Morrow Violette Collection, 1806–1921. State Historical Society of Missouri, Columbia.

Missouri Argus. St. Louis. 1835–1841.

Missouri Republican. St. Louis. 1837–1839.

Moore, Andrew. Reminiscences, 1846. CHL.

Morgan, William. Papers, 1838–1839. CHL.

Morison, John. *Family Prayers for Every Morning and Evening throughout the Year. Additional Prayers for Special Occasions.* 2nd ed. New York: Fisher, Son, and Company, [1837].

Mormon Redress Petitions, 1839–1845. CHL.

Mormon War Papers, 1838–1841. MSA.

Moses (selections from the Book of). See *Pearl of Great Price.*

Mulholland, James. Journal, Apr.–Oct. 1839. In Joseph Smith, Journal, Sept.–Oct. 1838. Joseph Smith Collection. CHL.

———. Letter of Introduction, Commerce, IL, for Heber C. Kimball et al., 10 July 1839. CHL.

Mullen, E. Theodore. *The Divine Council in Canaanite and Early Hebrew Literature.* Harvard Semitic Monographs, no. 24. Chico, CA: Scholars Press, 1980.

Munson, Myron A. *The Munson Record: A Genealogical and Biographical Account of Captain Thomas Munson (a Pioneer of Hartford and New Haven) and His Descendants.* Vol. 2. New Haven, CT: Munson Association, 1895.

Murdock, John. Autobiography, ca. 1859–1867. John Murdock, Journal and Autobiography, ca. 1830–1867. CHL.

———. Journal, ca. 1830–1859. John Murdock, Journal and Autobiography, ca. 1830–1867. CHL.

———. Letter, Lima, IL, to Sister Crocker et al., 21 July 1839. CHL.

Myron H. Bond Folder. Biographical Folder Collection (P21, fd. 11). CCLA.

Naked Truths about Mormonism: Also a Journal for Important, Newly Apprehended Truths, and Miscellany. Oakland, CA. Jan. and Apr. 1888.

"Names of the Members of the Church in Missouri. Then Situated Most in Caldwell County," ca. early 1838. In Record Book, 1838. Verso of Patriarchal Blessings, vol. 5. CHL.

Nauvoo, IL. Records, 1841–1845. CHL.

Nauvoo City Council Draft Minutes, 1841–1844. Nauvoo, IL. Records, 1841–1845. CHL.

Nauvoo City Council Minute Book / Nauvoo City Council. "A Record of the Proceedings of the City Council of the City of Nauvoo Handcock County, State of Illinois, Commencing A.D. 1841," ca. 1841–1845. CHL.

Nauvoo High Council Minutes, 1839–1845. CHL.

Neibaur, Alexander. Journal, 1841–1862. CHL.

New Testament Revision 1 / "A Translation of the New Testament Translated by the Power of God," 1831. CCLA. Also available in Scott H. Faulring, Kent P. Jackson, and Robert J. Matthews, eds., *Joseph Smith's New Translation of the Bible: Original Manuscripts* (Provo, UT: Religious Studies Center, Brigham Young University, 2004), 153–228.

New Testament Revision 2, part 1 / New Testament Revision Manuscript 2, part 1, 1831. CCLA. Also available in Scott H. Faulring, Kent P. Jackson, and Robert J. Matthews, eds., *Joseph Smith's New Translation of the Bible: Original Manuscripts* (Provo, UT: Religious Studies Center, Brigham Young University, 2004), 235–298.

New Testament Revision 2, part 2 / New Testament Revision Manuscript 2, part 2, 1831–1832. CCLA. Also available in Scott H. Faulring, Kent P. Jackson, and Robert J. Matthews, eds., *Joseph Smith's New Translation of the Bible: Original Manuscripts* (Provo, UT: Religious Studies Center, Brigham Young University, 2004), 299–581.

New York City Branch History, no date. In High Priests Quorum Record, 1844–1845. CHL.

New-York Spectator. New York City. 1820–1867.

Niles' National Register. Washington DC. 1837–1849.

Nimer, Corwin L. "Sampson Avard: The First Danite." *Mormon Historical Studies* 5, no. 2 (Fall 2004): 37–60.

N. K. Whitney & Co. Daybook, Nov. 1836–Apr. 1837. Photocopy. CHL.

Noble, Joseph B., and Mary A. Noble. Reminiscences, ca. 1836. CHL.

The Northeastern Reporter, Volume 31, Containing All the Current Decisions of the Supreme Courts of Massachusetts, Ohio, Illinois, Indiana, Appellate Court of Indiana, and the Court of Appeals of New York. St. Paul, MN: West Publishing, 1892.

Northern Islander. St. James, MI. 1850–1856.

Northern Times. Kirtland, OH. 1835–[1836?].

"Notable Deaths." *Annals of Iowa* 6, no. 4 (Jan. 1904): 316–320.

Nuttall, L. John. "Extracts from Wᵐ Clayton's Private Book," 1880. L. John Nuttall, Papers, 1857–1904. BYU.

Obituary Notices and Biographies, 1854–1877. CHL.

O'Driscoll, Jeffrey S. *Hyrum Smith: A Life of Integrity.* Salt Lake City: Deseret Book, 2003.

Ohio Star. Ravenna. 1830–1854.

Old Testament Revision 1 / "A Revelation Given to Joseph the Revelator June 1830," 1830–1831. CCLA. Also available in Scott H. Faulring, Kent P. Jackson, and Robert J. Matthews, eds., *Joseph Smith's New Translation of the Bible: Original Manuscripts* (Provo, UT: Religious Studies Center, Brigham Young University, 2004), 75–152.

Oration Delivered by Mr. S. Rigdon, on the 4th of July, 1838. Far West, MO: Journal Office, 1838.

"The Original Prophet. By a Visitor to Salt Lake City." *Fraser's Magazine* 7, no. 28 (Feb. 1873): 225–235.

Osborn, David. Reminiscences and Journal, 1860–1893. CHL.

The Oxford English Dictionary. Edited by James A. H. Murray, Henry Bradley, W. A. Craigie, and C. T. Onions. 12 vols. 1933. Reprint. Oxford: Oxford University Press, 1970.

Page, John E. Journal Synopsis, ca. 1845. CHL.

Painesville Republican. Painesville, OH. 1836–1841.

Painesville Telegraph. Painesville, OH. 1831–1838.

Park, Benjamin E. "Developing a Historical Conscience: Wilford Woodruff and the Preservation of Church History." In *Preserving the History of the Latter-day Saints*, edited by Richard E. Turley Jr. and Steven C. Harper, 115–134. Provo, UT: Religious Studies Center, Brigham Young University; Salt Lake City: Deseret Book, 2010.

———. "'A Uniformity So Complete': Early Mormon Angelology." *Intermountain West Journal of Religious Studies* 2, no. 1 (2010): 1–37.

Parkin, Max H. "Conflict at Kirtland: A Study of the Nature and Causes of External and Internal Conflict of the Mormons in Ohio between 1830 and 1838." Master's thesis, Brigham Young University, 1966.

————. "Joseph Smith and the United Firm: The Growth and Decline of the Church's First Master Plan of Business and Finance, Ohio and Missouri, 1832–1834." *BYU Studies* 46, no. 3 (2007): 5–66.

Partridge, Edward. History, ca. 1839. In History of Joseph Smith (Coray copy), ca. 1841. CHL.

————. Papers, 1818–1839. CHL.

Patriarchal Blessings, 1833–. CHL.

The Pearl of Great Price: A Selection from the Revelations, Translations, and Narrations of Joseph Smith, First Prophet, Seer, and Revelator to The Church of Jesus Christ of Latter-day Saints. Salt Lake City: The Church of Jesus Christ of Latter-day Saints, 2013.

Peck, Reed. Letter, Quincy, IL, to "Dear Friends," 18 Sept. 1839. Henry E. Huntington Library, San Marino, CA.

Perkins, Keith W. "De Witt—Prelude to Expulsion." In *Regional Studies in Latter-day Saint Church History: Missouri,* edited by Arnold K. Garr and Clark V. Johnson, 261–280. Provo, UT: Department of Church History and Doctrine, Brigham Young University, 1994.

Pettegrew, David. "An History of David Pettegrew," not after 1858. Pettigrew Collection, 1837–1858, 1881–1892, 1908–1930. CHL.

Phelps, Morris. Reminiscences, no date. CHL.

Phelps, William W. Collection of Missouri Documents, 1833–1837. CHL.

————. Commissions, 1837–1838. CHL.

————. Letter, Far West, MO, to Sally Waterman Phelps, St. Louis, 1 May 1839. CHL.

————. Letter, Kirtland Mills, OH, to Sally Waterman Phelps, Liberty, MO, 16–18 Sept. 1835. Private possession. Copy at CHL.

————. Papers, 1835–1865. BYU.

Plewe, Brandon S., S. Kent Brown, Donald Q. Cannon, and Richard H. Jackson, eds. *Mapping Mormonism: An Atlas of Latter-day Saint History.* Provo, UT: Brigham Young University Press, 2012.

Pointer, Richard W. "Native Freedom? Indians and Religious Tolerance in Early America." In *The First Prejudice: Religious Tolerance and Intolerance in Early America,* edited by Chris Beneke and Christopher S. Grenda, 169–194. Philadelphia: University of Pennsylvania Press, 2011.

Porter, Larry C. "Beginnings of the Restoration: Canada, an 'Effectual Door' to the British Isles." In *Truth Will Prevail: The Rise of The Church of Jesus Christ of Latter-day Saints in the British Isles, 1837–1987,* edited by V. Ben Bloxham, James R. Moss, and Larry C. Porter, 3–43. Cambridge: The Church of Jesus Christ of Latter-day Saints, 1987.

————. "The Odyssey of William Earl McLellin: Man of Diversity, 1806–83." In *The Journals of William E. McLellin, 1831–1836,* edited by Jan Shipps and John W. Welch, 291–378. Provo, UT: BYU Studies; Urbana: University of Illinois Press, 1994.

Portrait and Biographical Record of Adams County, Illinois; Containing Biographical Sketches of Prominent and Representative Citizens, together with Biographies and Portraits of All the Presidents of the United States. Chicago: Chapman Brothers, 1892.

Post, Stephen. Journals, 1835–1879. Stephen Post, Papers, 1835–1921. CHL.

————. Papers, 1835–1921. CHL.

Pratt, Harry E. *The Personal Finances of Abraham Lincoln.* Springfield, IL: Abraham Lincoln Association, 1943.

Pratt, Orson. Journal, 1833–1837. Orson Pratt, Autobiography and Journals, 1833–1847. CHL.

Pratt, Parley P. *The Autobiography of Parley Parker Pratt, One of the Twelve Apostles of the Church of Jesus Christ of Latter-day Saints, Embracing His Life, Ministry and Travels, with Extracts, in Prose and Verse, from His Miscellaneous Writings.* Edited by Parley P. Pratt Jr. New York: Russell Brothers, 1874.

———. *History of the Late Persecution Inflicted by the State of Missouri upon the Mormons, in Which Ten Thousand American Citizens Were Robbed, Plundered, and Driven from the State, and Many Others Imprisoned, Martyred, &c. for Their Religion, and All This by Military Force, by Order of the Executive. By P. P. Pratt, Minister of the Gospel. Written during Eight Months Imprisonment in That State.* Detroit: Dawson and Bates, 1839.

———. *Late Persecution of the Church of Jesus Christ, of Latter Day Saints. Ten Thousand American Citizens Robbed, Plundered, and Banished; Others Imprisoned, and Others Martyred for Their Religion. With a Sketch of Their Rise, Progress and Doctrine. By P. P. Pratt, Minister of the Gospel, Written in Prison.* New York: J. W. Harrison, 1840.

———. Letters, 1838–1839. CHL.

———. *Mormonism Unveiled: Zion's Watchman Unmasked, and Its Editor, Mr. L. R. Sunderland, Exposed: Truth Vindicated: The Devil Mad, and Priestcraft in Danger!* New York: By the author, 1838.

———. *A Voice of Warning and Instruction to All People, Containing a Declaration of the Faith and Doctrine of the Church of the Latter Day Saints, Commonly Called Mormons.* New York: W. Sanford, 1837.

"A Provincial Vocabulary." *Monthly Magazine; or, British Register* 26, no. 5 (1 Dec. 1808): 421–423.

Public Land Survey Township Plats, Compiled 1789–1946, Documenting the Period 1785–1946. National Archives Microfilm Publications, microcopy T1234. 67 reels. Washington DC: National Archives, no date.

Public Statutes at Large of the United States of America, from the Organization of the Government in 1789, to March 3, 1845. . . . Edited by Richard Peters. 8 vols. Boston: Charles C. Little and James Brown, 1846–1867.

Pulsipher, Zerah. "Zerah Pu[l]siphers History." In Zerah Pulsipher, Record Book, ca. 1858–1878. CHL.

Quincy Argus. Quincy, IL. 1836–1841.

Quincy Whig. Quincy, IL. 1838–1857.

Quinn, D. Michael, ed. "The First Months of Mormonism: A Contemporary View by Rev. Diedrich Willers." *New York History* 54, no. 3 (July 1973): 317–333.

———. *The Mormon Hierarchy: Origins of Power.* Salt Lake City: Signature Books with Smith Research Associates, 1994.

Quorums of the Seventy. "Book of Records," 1837–1843. Bk. A. First Council of the Seventy, Records, 1837–1885. CHL.

Radke-Moss, Andrea G. "Beyond Petticoats and Poultices." Paper presented at annual Church History Symposium, Provo, UT, 3 Mar. 2016. Copy in editors' possession.

———. "'I Hid [the Prophet] in a Corn Patch': Mormon Women as Healers, Concealers, and Protectors in the 1838 Mormon-Missouri War." *Mormon Historical Studies* 15, no. 1 (Spring 2014): 25–40.

Recognizance, 7 Sept. 1838, State of Missouri v. JS et al. for Riot (Mo. 5th Jud. Cir. 1838). BYU.

Record Group 233, Records of the U.S. House of Representatives. National Archives, Washington DC.

Record of the Twelve / Quorum of the Twelve Apostles. "A Record of the Transactions of the Twelve Apostles of the Church of the Latter Day Saints from the Time of Their Call to the Apostleship Which Was on the 14th Day of Feby. AD 1835," Feb.–Aug. 1835. In Patriarchal Blessings, 1833–, vol. 2. CHL.

Records of the Bureau of Land Management, 1685–1993. National Archives, Washington DC.

Reeve, W. Paul. *Religion of a Different Color: Race and the Mormon Struggle for Whiteness.* Oxford: Oxford University Press, 2015.

"The Relation of Plumbing to Public Health." *Plumbers' Trade Journal* 24, no. 1 (1 July 1898): 24.

Relief Society Minute Book / "A Book of Records Containing the Proceedings of the Female Relief Society of Nauvoo," Mar. 1842–Mar. 1844. CHL.

Report and Collections of the State Historical Society of Wisconsin, for the Years 1873, 1874, 1875 and 1876. Vol. 7. Madison, WI: E. B. Bolens, 1876.

Republican Tribune. Union, MO. 1919–1937.

Return. Davis City, IA, 1889–1891; Richmond, MO, 1892–1893; Davis City, 1895–1896; Denver, 1898; Independence, MO, 1899–1900.

"Revelation Given 8 July 1838" [D&C 117]. BYU.

Revelations Collection, 1831–ca. 1844, 1847, 1861, ca. 1876. CHL.

The Revised Statutes of the State of Missouri, Revised and Digested by the Eighth General Assembly during the Years One Thousand Eight Hundred and Thirty-Four, and One Thousand Eight Hundred and Thirty-Five. . . . St. Louis: Argus Office, 1835.

Rich, Charles C. Journals, 1833–1862. Charles C. Rich Collection, 1832–1908. CHL.

Rich, Sarah Pea. Autobiography and Journal, 1885–1890. Sarah Pea Rich, Autobiography, 1884–1893. CHL.

Richards, Willard. Journals, 1836–1853. Willard Richards, Papers, 1821–1854. CHL.

———. Papers, 1821–1854. CHL.

———. "Willard Richards Pocket Companion Written in England," ca. 1840–1841. Willard Richards, Papers, 1821–1854. CHL.

Richards Family Collection, 1837–1961. CHL.

Rigdon, John Wickliff. "Life Story of Sidney Rigdon," no date. CHL.

[Rigdon, Sidney]. *An Appeal to the American People: Being an Account of the Persecutions of the Church of Latter Day Saints; and of the Barbarities Inflicted on Them by the Inhabitants of the State of Missouri.* Cincinnati: Glezen and Shepard, 1840.

———. Letter, Far West, MO, to Sterling Price, 8 Sept. 1838. CHL.

Rigdon, Sidney, JS, et al. Petition Draft ("To the Publick"), ca. Sept. 1838–ca. Oct. 1839. Joseph Smith Collection. CHL.

Rigdon, Smith & Co. Store Ledger, Chester, OH, 1836–1837. In Joseph Smith, "Copies of Letters, &c. &c.," 1839–1843. Joseph Smith Collection. CHL.

Riggs, Michael S. "The Economic Impact of Fort Leavenworth on Northwestern Missouri, 1827–1838. Yet Another Reason for the Mormon War?" In *Restoration Studies IV: A Collection of Essays about the History, Beliefs, and Practices of the Reorganized Church of Jesus Christ of Latter Day Saints,* edited by Marjorie B. Troeh and Eileen M. Terril, 124–133. Independence, MO: Herald Publishing House, 1988.

Riggs, Michael S., and John E. Thompson. "Joseph Smith, Jr., and 'the Notorious Case of Aaron Lyon': Evidence of Earlier Doctrinal Development of Salvation for the Dead and a Trigger for the Practice of Polyandry?" *John Whitmer Historical Association Journal* 26 (2006): 101–119.

Robbins, Lewis. Autobiographical Sketch, ca. 1845. Typescript. CHL.

Roberts, William Milnor. *Improvement of the Ohio River.* Pittsburgh: Pittsburgh Board of Trade, 1856.

Robinson, David M. "The Wheel of Fortune." *Classical Philology* 41, no. 4 (Oct. 1946): 207–216.

Robinson, George W. Papers, 1838. CHL.

Robison, Elwin C. *The First Mormon Temple: Design, Construction, and Historic Context of the Kirtland Temple.* Provo, UT: Brigham Young University Press, 1997.

Rockwood, Albert Perry. Journal Entries, Oct. 1838–Jan. 1839. CHL.

———. Mormon Letters and Sermons, 1838–1839. Western Americana Collection. Beinecke Rare Book and Manuscript Library, Yale University, New Haven, CT.

Rogers, David W. Statement, not before 1846. CHL.

Rohrbough, Malcom J. *The Land Office Business: The Settlement and Administration of American Public Lands, 1789–1837.* New York: Oxford University Press, 1968.

Ryan, Daniel J. *A History of Ohio, with Biographical Sketches of Her Governors and the Ordinance of 1787.* Columbus, OH: A. H. Smythe, 1888.

Saints' Herald. Independence, MO. 1860–.

Sandburg, Carl. *Lincoln Collector: The Story of Oliver R. Barrett's Great Private Collection.* New York City: Harcourt, Brace, 1950.

Sangamo Journal. Springfield, IL. 1831–1847.

Satz, Ronald N. *American Indian Policy in the Jacksonian Era.* Lincoln: University of Nebraska Press, 1975.

Scammon / Scammon, J. Young. *Reports of Cases Argued and Determined in the Supreme Court of the State of Illinois.* 4 vols. Chicago: Stephen F. Gale and Augustus H. Burley, 1841–1844.

"Schedule Setting Forth a List of Petitioner[']s Creditors, Their Residence, and the Amount Due to Each," ca. 15–16 Apr. 1842. CCLA.

Schmidt, Donald T. Correspondence, 1972–1982, 1984. CHL.

Scioto Gazette. Chillicothe, OH. 1835–1854.

Scioto Gazette and Independent Whig. Chillicothe, OH. 1834–1835.

Seixas, Joshua. *Manual Hebrew Grammar for the Use of Beginners.* 2nd ed., enl. and impr. Andover, MA: Gould and Newman, 1834.

Shepard, William, and H. Michael Marquardt. *Lost Apostles: Forgotten Members of Mormonism's Original Quorum of Twelve.* Salt Lake City: Signature Books, 2014.

Sherwood, Henry G. Record Book, ca. 1838–1844. CHL.

Shoemaker, Floyd Calvin. *Missouri and Missourians: Land of Contrasts and People of Achievements.* 5 vols. Chicago: Lewis Publishing, 1943.

Shurtleff, Stella Cahoon, and Brent Farrington Cahoon, comps. *Reynolds Cahoon and His Stalwart Sons: Utah Pioneers.* Salt Lake City: Paragon Press, 1960.

Shurtliff, Luman A. Autobiography, ca. 1852–1876. CHL.

"Sketch of an Elder's Life." In *Scraps of Biography,* Faith-Promoting Series 10, pp. 9–19. Salt Lake City: Juvenile Instructor Office, 1883.

Smart, Donna Toland, ed. *Mormon Midwife: The 1846–1888 Diaries of Patty Bartlett Sessions.* Logan: Utah State University Press, 1997.

Smith, Bathsheba Bigler. Autobiography, ca. 1875–1906. CHL.

Smith, Elias. Correspondence, 1834–1839. Elias Smith, Papers, 1834–1846. CHL.

———. Journals, 1836–1888. CHL.

Smith, George Albert. Autobiography, ca. 1860–1882. George Albert Smith, Papers, 1834–1882. CHL.

———. Papers, 1834–1877. CHL.

Smith, Hyrum. Collection, ca. 1839–1911. CHL.

———. Diary, Mar.–Apr. 1839, Oct. 1840. CHL.

———. Papers, ca. 1832–1844. BYU.

———. Petition, Liberty, MO, 9 Mar. 1839. CHL.

———. Petition, Liberty, MO, 15 Mar. 1839. CHL.

Smith, Hyrum, et al. Promissory Note, Kirtland, OH, to Halsted, Haines & Co., 1 Sept. 1837. Photocopy. CHL.

Smith, John. Journal, 1836–1840. John Smith, Papers, 1833–1854. CHL.

Smith, Joseph. In addition to the entries that immediately follow, see entries under "JS."

Smith, Joseph. Letter, Liberty, MO, to Emma Smith, Far West, MO, 1 Dec. 1838. CHL.

———. Letter, Liberty, MO, to the Church and Edward Partridge, Quincy, IL, 20–25 Mar. 1839. Copy. CHL.

———. Receipts and Accounts, 1838–1840. CHL.

Smith, Joseph, et al. Memorial to U.S. Senate and House of Representatives, 28 Nov. 1843. In Records of the U.S. Senate, Committee on the Judiciary, Records, 1816–1982. National Archives, Washington DC.

———. Promissory Note, Kirtland, OH, to Holbrook & Ferme, 1 Sept. 1837. Ohio Historical Society, Columbus. Copy at CHL.

———. Promissory Note, Kirtland, OH, to Holbrook & Ferme, 1 Sept. 1837. BYU.

Smith, Joseph, Sidney Rigdon, Hyrum Smith, and Elias Higbee. Authorization for Oliver Granger, Quincy, IL, 1 Nov. 1839. Photocopy. CHL. Original in private possession.

Smith, Joseph, III. Letter, Lamoni, IA, to "Dear Sirs," Keokuk, IA, 1 July 1901. Photocopy. CHL.

Smith, Lucy Mack. History, 1844–1845. 18 books. CHL.

———. History, 1845. CHL.

Smith, Mary Fielding. Collection, ca. 1832–1848. CHL.

Smith, Ophia D. "The Rise of the New Jerusalem Church in Ohio." *Ohio State Archaeological and Historical Quarterly* 61, no. 4 (Oct. 1952): 380–409.

Smith, Silas S. Autobiographical Sketch, ca. 1900. CHL.

Smith Family Genealogy Record, ca. 1840. CHL.

Snow, Eliza R. Letter, Caldwell Co., MO, to Isaac Streator, Streetsborough, OH, 22 Feb. 1839. Photocopy. CHL.

Snow, Erastus. Journals, 1835–1851, 1856–1857. CHL.

Snow, Lorenzo. Papers, ca. 1836–1896. CHL.

Spellberg, Denise A. *Thomas Jefferson's Qur'an: Islam and the Founders.* New York: Knopf, 2013.

Staker, Mark L. *Hearken, O Ye People: The Historical Setting of Joseph Smith's Ohio Revelations.* Salt Lake City: Greg Kofford Books, 2009.

———. "Raising Money in Righteousness." In *Days Never to Be Forgotten: Oliver Cowdery,* edited by Alexander Baugh, 143–253. Provo, UT: Religious Studies Center, Brigham Young University; Salt Lake City: Deseret Book, 2009.

Staker, Mark L., and Robin Scott Jensen. "David Hale's Store Ledger: New Details about Joseph and Emma Smith, the Hale Family, and the Book of Mormon." *BYU Studies* 53, no. 3 (2014): 77–112.

Stapley, Jonathan A., and Kristine Wright. "Female Ritual Healing in Mormonism." *Journal of Mormon History* 37, no. 1 (Winter 2011): 1–85.

Statements against William E. McLellin and Others, ca. 1838–1839. CHL.

State of Missouri v. Ripley et al. / State of Missouri v. Alanson Ripley, Jonathan Barlow, William D. Huntington, David Holman, and Erastus Snow (J.P. Ct. 1839). Clay County Archives and Historical Library, Liberty, MO.

The Statutes of Ohio and of the Northwestern Territory, Adopted or Enacted from 1788 to 1833 Inclusive: Together with the Ordinance of 1787; the Constitutions of Ohio and of the United States, and Various Public Instruments and Acts of Congress: Illustrated by a Preliminary Sketch of the History of Ohio; Numerous References and Notes, and Copious Indexes. 3 vols. Edited by Salmon P. Chase. Cincinnati: Corey and Fairbank, 1833–1835.

Stemberger, Günter. *Jewish Contemporaries of Jesus: Pharisees, Sadducees, Essenes.* Minneapolis, MN: Fortress Press, 1995.

Stevens, Walter B. *Centennial History of Missouri (the Center State): One Hundred Years in the Union, 1820–1921.* 5 vols. St. Louis: S. J. Clarke Publishing, 1921.

Stevenson, Edward. Autobiography, ca. 1891–1893. Edward Stevenson, Collection, 1849–1922. CHL.

Stevenson, Joseph Grant, ed. *Richards Family History.* 2 vols. Provo, UT: By the author, 1977–1981.

Stokes, Durward T., ed. "The Wilson Letters, 1835–1849." *Missouri Historical Review* 60, no. 4 (July 1966): 495–517.

Subpoena, Richmond, MO, for James Blakely, Nathaniel Blakely, James B. Turner, Laburn Morin, John Lockhart, and Timothy Lewis, 21 Nov. 1838. State of Missouri v. JS et al. for Treason and Other Crimes (Mo. 5th Jud. Cir. 1838). CHL.

"A Suit for Alleged Malpractice." *Cleveland Medical Gazette* 2, no. 4 (Feb. 1887): 117–132.

Sun. Baltimore. 1837–2008.

Susquehanna Register, and Northern Pennsylvanian. Montrose, PA. 1831–1836.

Swan, Joseph R. *The Practice in Civil Actions and Proceedings at Law, in Ohio, and Precedents in Pleading, with Practical Notes; together with the Forms of Process and Clerks' Entries.* 2 vols. Columbus: Isaac N. Whiting, 1845.

Swartzell, William. *Mormonism Exposed, Being a Journal of a Residence in Missouri from the 28th of May to the 20th of August, 1838, together with an Appendix, Containing the Revelation concerning the Golden Bible, with Numerous Extracts from the 'Book of Covenants,' &c., &c.* Pekin, OH: By the author, 1840.

Tafel, J. F. I. *Documents concerning the Life and Character of Emanuel Swedenborg, Late Member of the House of Nobles in the Royal Diet of Sweden, Assessor of the Royal Board of Mines, Fellow of the Royal Society of Upsala, and of the Royal Academy of Sciences of Stockholm, and Corresponding Member of the Academy of Sciences of St. Petersburg.* Manchester, England: Joseph Hayward, 1841.

Tanner, Elizabeth Beswick. Autobiography, not before 1885. Photocopy. CHL.

Tatum, Margaret Black. "'Please Send Stamps': The Civil War Letters of William Allen Clark, Part I." *Indiana Magazine of History* 91, no. 1 (Mar. 1995): 81–108.

Taylor, Alan. *The Civil War of 1812: American Citizens, British Subjects, Irish Rebels, and Indian Allies.* New York: Vintage Books, 2011.

Taylor, John. Collection, 1829–1894. CHL.

———. Letter, Quincy, IL, to "the Editor of the Argus," Quincy, IL, 1 May 1839. CHL.

———. *Short Account of the Murders, Rob[b]eries, Burnings, Thefts, and Other Outrages Committed by the Mob and Militia of the State of Missouri. . . .* [Springfield, IL]: By the author, [1839].

———. *Succession in the Priesthood: A Discourse by President John Taylor, Delivered at the Priesthood Meeting, Held in the Salt Lake Assembly Hall, Friday Evening, October 7th, 1881.* [Salt Lake City?], [1881?].

Taylor, Lori Elaine. "Telling Stories about Mormons and Indians." PhD diss., State University of New York at Buffalo, 2000.

Teachers Quorum Minutes, 1834–1845. CHL.

Thompson, Jason E. "'The Lord Told Me to Go and I Went': Wilford Woodruff's Missions to the Fox Islands, 1837–38," in *Banner of the Gospel: Wilford Woodruff,* edited by Alexander L. Baugh and Susan Easton Black, 97–148. Provo, UT: Religious Studies Center, Brigham Young University, 2010.

Thompson, John E. "A Chronology of Danite Meetings in Adam-ondi-Ahman, Missouri: July to September 1838." *Restoration* 4, no. 1 (Jan. 1985): 11–14.

Thompson, Leonard. *A History of South Africa.* 3rd ed. New Haven, CT: Yale University Press, 2001.

Thompson, Mercy Rachel Fielding. Autobiographical Sketch, 1880. CHL.

Thompson, Robert B. *Journal of Heber C. Kimball, an Elder of the Church of Jesus Christ of Latter Day Saints. Giving an Account of His Mission to Great Britain. . . .* Nauvoo, IL: Robinson and Smith, 1840.

Thornton, Tamara Plakins. *Handwriting in America: A Cultural History.* New Haven, CT: Yale University Press, 1996.

Tiffany's Monthly. New York City. 1856–1859.

Tillson, John. *History of the City of Quincy, Illinois.* Chicago: S. J. Clarke, 1900.

Times and Seasons. Commerce/Nauvoo, IL. Nov. 1839–Feb. 1846.

Troubat, Francis J., and William W. Haly. *The Practice in Civil Actions and Proceedings, in the Supreme Court of Pennsylvania, and in the District Court and Court of Common Pleas for the City and County of Philadelphia; and Also in the Courts of the United States.* 2 vols. Philadelphia: R. H. Small, 1837.

True Latter Day Saints' Herald. See *Saints' Herald.*

Trustees Land Books / Trustee-in-Trust, Church of Jesus Christ of Latter-day Saints. Land Books, 1839–1845. 2 vols. CHL.

Tullidge, Edward W. *The Women of Mormondom.* New York: Tullidge and Crandall, 1877.

Turley, Richard E., Jr. "Assistant Church Historians and the Publishing of Church History." In *Preserving the History of the Latter-Day Saints,* edited by Richard E. Turley Jr. and Steven C. Harper, 19–47. Provo, UT: Religious Studies Center, Brigham Young University; Salt Lake City: Deseret Book, 2010.

Tyler, Samuel D. Journal, July–Oct. 1838. CHL.

Underwood, Grant. *The Millenarian World of Early Mormonism.* Urbana: University of Illinois Press, 1993.

U.S. and Canada Record Collection. FHL.

U.S. Bureau of the Census. Population Schedules. Microfilm. FHL.

U.S. Department of the Interior. *Geological Survey Topographic Maps.* 7.5 Minute Series. 2012.

Utah Christian Advocate. Salt Lake City. 1884–1887.

Utah Genealogical and Historical Magazine. Salt Lake City. 1910–1940.

Van Wagoner, Richard S. *Sidney Rigdon: A Portrait of Religious Excess.* Salt Lake City: Signature Books, 1994.

Vogel, Dan. "The Locations of Joseph Smith's Early Treasure Quests." *Dialogue: A Journal of Mormon Thought* 27, no. 3 (Fall 1994): 197–231.

Waldo Patriot. Belfast, ME. 1837–1838.

Walker, Horatio N. *Walker's Buffalo City Directory, Containing a List of Civil and Military Officers, Religious, Benevolent and Philanthropic Societies, Local and Miscellaneous Statistics. With the Names, Residence and Occupation, of the Business Population, Heads of Families, &c. in the City of Buffalo.* Buffalo, NY: Lee and Thorp's Press, 1844.

Walker, Jeffrey N. "Habeas Corpus in Early Nineteenth-Century Mormonism: Joseph Smith's Legal Bulwark for Personal Freedom." *BYU Studies* 52, no. 1 (2013): 4–97.

———. "The Kirtland Safety Society and the Fraud of Grandison Newell: A Legal Examination." *BYU Studies* 54, no. 3 (2015): 32–148.

———. "Mormon Land Rights in Caldwell and Daviess Counties and the Mormon Conflict of 1838: New Findings and New Understandings." *BYU Studies* 47, no. 1 (2008): 4–55.

Walker, Ronald W. "Seeking the 'Remnant': The Native American during the Joseph Smith Period." *Journal of Mormon History* 19, no. 1 (Spring 1993): 1–33.

Warr, Helen C. History of the Carter Family, 1976–1978. CHL.

Washington, John E. *They Knew Lincoln.* New York: E. P. Dutton, 1942.

Welch, John W. "'All Their Creeds Were an Abomination': A Brief Look at Creeds as Part of the Apostasy." In *Prelude to the Restoration: From Apostasy to the Restored Church:*

The 33rd Annual Sidney B. Sperry Symposium, 228–249. Salt Lake City: Deseret Book; Provo, UT: Religious Studies Center, Brigham Young University, 2004.

Wells, Walter. *Provisional Report upon the Water-Power of Maine*. Augusta, ME: Stevens and Sayward, 1868.

Wesley, John. *Explanatory Notes upon the Old Testament*. 4 vols. Bristol, England: William Pine, 1765.

West, Elizabeth Howard. *Calendar of the Papers of Martin Van Buren*. Washington DC: U.S. Government Printing Office, 1910.

Western Intelligencer. Cleveland, OH, 1827; Hudson, OH, 1828–1830.

Whitmer, David. *An Address to All Believers in Christ*. Richmond, MO: By the author, 1887.

Whitmer, History / Whitmer, John. "The Book of John Whitmer Kept by Commandment," ca. 1835–1846. CCLA.

Whitmer, John. Daybook, 1832–1878. CHL.

———. Letter, Far West, MO, to Oliver Cowdery and David Whitmer, Kirtland Mills, OH, 29 Aug. 1837. Western Americana Collection, Beinecke Rare Book and Manuscript Library, Yale University, New Haven, CT.

Whitney, Newel K. Papers, 1825–1906. BYU.

Whitney, Newel K., Reynolds Cahoon, and Vinson Knight. *To the Saints Scattered Abroad, the Bishop and His Counselors of Kirtland Send Greeting*. [Kirtland, OH, ca. Sept. 1837]. Copy at CHL.

Whitney, Orson F. *Life of Heber C. Kimball, an Apostle; the Father and Founder of the British Mission*. Salt Lake City: Kimball Family, 1888.

Whitney Family Documents, 1843–1912. CHL.

Whittaker, David J. "The Book of Daniel in Early Mormon Thought." In *By Study and Also by Faith: Essays in Honor of Hugh W. Nibley on the Occasion of His Eightieth Birthday, 27 March 1990*, edited by John M. Lundquist and Stephen D. Ricks, 1:155–201. Salt Lake City: Deseret Book; Provo, UT: Foundation for Ancient Research and Mormon Studies, 1990.

Wight, Lyman. Petition, Liberty, MO, 15 Mar. 1839. CHL.

Wight, Orange L. Adam-ondi-Ahman Diagram, 1903. CHL.

———. Reminiscences, May–Dec. 1903. CHL.

Wilford C. Wood Collection of Church Historical Materials. Microfilm. CHL.

Williams, Edwin. *New-York Annual Register for the Year of Our Lord 1836. Containing an Almanac, Civil and Judicial List; with Political, Statistical and Other Information, respecting the State of New-York and the United States*. New York: Edwin Williams, 1836.

Williams, Frederick G. *The Life of Dr. Frederick G. Williams, Counselor to the Prophet Joseph Smith*. Provo, UT: *BYU Studies*, 2012.

Williams, Nancy Clement. *Meet Dr. Frederick Granger Williams, Second Counselor to the Prophet Joseph Smith in the Church of Jesus Christ of Latter-day Saints. . . .* Independence, MO: Zion's Printing and Publishing, 1951.

Withington, Mary C., comp. *A Catalogue of Manuscripts in the Collection of Western Americana Founded by William Robertson Coe, Yale University Library*. New Haven, CT: Yale University Press, 1952.

Woman's Exponent. Salt Lake City. 1872–1914.

Woodruff, Wilford. "Autobiography of Wilford Woodruff." *Tullidge's Quarterly Magazine* 3, no. 1 (Oct. 1883): 1–25.

———. "Book of Revelations," ca. 1837–1860. CHL.

———. Collection, 1830–1898. CHL.

———. Journals, 1833–1898. Wilford Woodruff, Journals and Papers, 1828–1898. CHL. Also available as *Wilford Woodruff's Journals, 1833–1898,* edited by Scott G. Kenney, 9 vols. (Midvale, UT: Signature Books, 1983–1985).

———. Journals and Papers, 1828–1898. CHL.

Woodson, William H. *History of Clay County, Missouri.* Topeka, KS: Historical Publishing, 1920.

The Works of the Rev. Isaac Watts. D. D. 9 vols. Leeds, England: William Baynes, 1812.

Yankee Farmer. Portland, ME. 1836–1837.

Young, Ann Eliza. *Wife No. 19; or, The Story of a Life in Bondage, Being a Complete Exposé of Mormonism, and Revealing the Sorrows, Sacrifices and Sufferings of Women in Polygamy.* Hartford, CT: Dustin, Gilman, 1876.

Young, Brigham. Journal, 1832–1877. Brigham Young Office Files, 1832–1878. CHL.

Young, Emily Dow Partridge. "Incidents in the Life of a Mormon Girl," ca. 1884. CHL.

Young, Lorenzo D. Statement, ca. 1894. CHL.

Young, Zina Huntington. Autobiographical Sketch, no date. Zina Card Brown Family Collection, 1806–1972. CHL.

Zion's Reveille. Voree, Wisconsin Territory. 1846–1847.

Zucker, Louis C. "Joseph Smith as a Student of Hebrew." *Dialogue: A Journal of Mormon Thought* 3, no. 2 (Summer 1968): 41–55.

Corresponding Section Numbers
in Editions of the Doctrine and Covenants

The Book of Commandments, of which a number of partial copies were printed in 1833, was superseded by the Doctrine and Covenants. Because the numbering of comparable material in the Book of Commandments and different editions of the Doctrine and Covenants varies extensively, the following table is provided to help readers refer from the version of a canonized item cited in this volume to other published versions of that same item. This table includes revelations announced by JS—plus letters, records of visions, articles, minutes, and other items, some of which were authored by other individuals—that were published in the Book of Commandments or Doctrine and Covenants in or before 1844, the year of JS's death. The table also includes material originating with JS that was first published in the Doctrine and Covenants after 1844. Such later-canonized material includes, for example, extracts of JS's 20 March 1839 letter written from the jail in Liberty, Missouri. These extracts, first canonized in 1876, are currently found in sections 121 through 123 of the Latter-day Saint edition of the Doctrine and Covenants.

The 1835 and 1844 editions of the Doctrine and Covenants included a series of lectures on the subject of faith, which constituted part 1 of the volume. Only part 2, the compilation of revelations and other items, is represented in the table. Further, the table does not include materials originating with JS that were not canonized in his lifetime and that have never been canonized by The Church of Jesus Christ of Latter-day Saints or by the Community of Christ. As only one of many examples, JS's journal entry for 3 November 1835 contains a JS revelation concerning the Twelve. This revelation has never been canonized and therefore does not appear in the table. More information about documents not listed on the table below will be provided in other volumes of *The Joseph Smith Papers* and on the Joseph Smith Papers website, josephsmithpapers.org.

Some material was significantly revised after its initial publication in the canon. For instance, the revelation in chapter 28 of the Book of Commandments included twice as much material when it was republished in the Doctrine and Covenants in 1835. As another example, chapter 65 of the Book of Commandments stops abruptly before the end of the revelation because publication of the volume was disrupted; the revelation was not published in its entirety until 1835. These and other substantial changes of greater or lesser significance are not accounted for in the table, but they will be identified in the appropriate volumes of the Documents series.

The far left column of the table gives the standard date of each item, based on careful study of original sources. The "standard date" is the date a revelation was originally dictated or recorded. If that date is ambiguous or unknown, the standard date is the best approximation of the date, based on existing evidence. The standard date provides a way to identify each item and situate it chronologically with other documents, but it cannot be assumed that every date corresponds to the day an item was first dictated or recorded. In some cases, an item was recorded without a date notation. It is also possible that a few items were first dictated on a date other than the date surviving manuscripts bear. The dates found in this table were assigned based on all available evidence, including later attempts by JS and his contemporaries to recover date, place, and circumstances.

Where surviving sources provide conflicting information about dating, editorial judgment has been exercised to select the most likely date (occasionally only an approximate month), based on the most reliable sources. In cases in which two or more items bear the same date, they have been listed in the order in which they most likely originated, and a letter of the alphabet has been appended, providing each item a unique editorial title (for example, May 1829–A or May 1829–B). Information on dating issues will accompany publication of these items in the Documents series.

The remaining five columns on the table provide the number of the chapter (in the case of the Book of Commandments) or section (in the case of editions of the Doctrine and Covenants) in which the item was published in one or more of five different canonical editions, the first three of which were initiated by JS. Full bibliographic information about these five editions is given in the list of works cited. See also the Scriptural References section in the introduction to Works Cited for more information about the origins of the Doctrine and Covenants and other Mormon scriptures.

Key to column titles

1833:   Book of Commandments
1835:   Doctrine and Covenants, 1835 edition, part 2
1844:   Doctrine and Covenants, 1844 edition, part 2[1]
2004:   Doctrine and Covenants, 2004 edition, Community of Christ[2]
2013:   Doctrine and Covenants, 2013 edition, The Church of Jesus Christ of
          Latter-day Saints[3]

| | JS-Era Canon | | | | |
Date	1833	1835	1844	2004	2013
21 Sept. 1823					2[4]
July 1828	2	30	30	2	3
Feb. 1829	3	31	31	4	4
Mar. 1829	4	32	32	5	5

1. The 1844 edition of the Doctrine and Covenants included one item written after the death of JS (section 111). That item is not included in this table.

2. The 2004 Community of Christ edition of the Doctrine and Covenants includes two extracts from JS's Bible revision (sections 22 and 36) and items written after the death of JS. Neither the extracts nor the later items are included in this table.

3. The 2013 Latter-day Saint edition of the Doctrine and Covenants includes some items written after the death of JS. Those items are not included in this table. Any item for which information appears only in the "2013" column and in the "Date" column is a later-canonized JS item, as discussed in the first paragraph of the preceding introduction.

4. This section, an extract from the history JS initiated in 1838, is here dated by the date of the event described in the section rather than the date of the document's creation.

	JS-Era Canon				
Date	**1833**	**1835**	**1844**	**2004**	**2013**
Apr. 1829–A	5	8	8	6	6
Spring 1829	9	36	36	3	10
Apr. 1829–B	7	34	34	8	8
Apr. 1829–C	6	33	33	7	7
Apr. 1829–D	8	35	35	9	9
15 May 1829					13[5]
May 1829–A	10	37	37	10	11
May 1829–B	11	38	38	11	12
June 1829–A	12	39	39	12	14
June 1829–B	15	43	43	16	18
June 1829–C	13	40	40	13	15
June 1829–D	14	41	41	14	16
June 1829–E		42	42	15	17
ca. Summer 1829	16	44	44	18	19
ca. Apr. 1830	24	2	2	17	20
6 Apr. 1830	22	46	46	19	21
Apr. 1830–A	17	45:1	45:1	21:1	23:1–2
Apr. 1830–B	18	45:2	45:2	21:2	23:3
Apr. 1830–C	19	45:3	45:3	21:3	23:4
Apr. 1830–D	20	45:4	45:4	21:4	23:5
Apr. 1830–E	21	45:5	45:5	21:5	23:6–7
16 Apr. 1830	23	47	47	20	22
July 1830–A	25	9	9	23	24
July 1830–B	27	49	49	25	26
July 1830–C	26	48	48	24	25
ca. Aug. 1830	28	50	50	26	27
Sept. 1830–A	29	10	10	28	29
Sept. 1830–B	30	51	51	27	28
Sept. 1830–C	31	52:1	52:1	29:1	30:1–4
Sept. 1830–D	32	52:2	52:2	29:2	30:5–8
Sept. 1830–E	33	52:3	52:3	29:3	30:9–11
Sept. 1830–F	34	53	53	30	31
Oct. 1830–A		54	54	31	32
Oct. 1830–B	35	55	55	32	33

5. This section, an extract from the history JS initiated in 1838, is here dated by the date of the event described in the section rather than the date of the document's creation.

| Date | JS-Era Canon | | | 2004 | 2013 |
	1833	1835	1844	2004	2013
4 Nov. 1830	36	56	56	33	34
7 Dec. 1830	37	11	11	34	35
9 Dec. 1830	38	57	57	35	36
30 Dec. 1830	39	58	58	37	37
1830		73	74	74	74
2 Jan. 1831	40	12	12	38	38
5 Jan. 1831	41	59	59	39	39
6 Jan. 1831	42	60	60	40	40
4 Feb. 1831	43	61	61	41	41
9 Feb. 1831[6]	44	13:1–19	13:1–19	42:1–19	42:1–72
Feb. 1831–A	45	14	14	43	43
Feb. 1831–B	46	62	62	44	44
23 Feb. 1831	47	13:21–23, 20	13:21–23, 20	42:21–23, 20	42:78–93, 74–77
ca. 7 Mar. 1831	48	15	15	45	45
ca. 8 Mar. 1831–A	49	16	16	46	46
ca. 8 Mar. 1831–B	50	63	63	47	47
10 Mar. 1831	51	64	64	48	48
7 May 1831	52	65	65	49	49
9 May 1831	53	17	17	50	50
20 May 1831		23	23	51	51
6 June 1831	54	66	66	52	52
8 June 1831	55	66[7]	67	53	53
10 June 1831	56	67	68	54	54
14 June 1831	57	68	69	55	55
15 June 1831	58	69	70	56	56
20 July 1831		27	27	57	57
1 Aug. 1831	59	18	18	58	58
7 Aug. 1831	60	19	19	59	59
8 Aug. 1831	61	70	71	60	60
12 Aug. 1831	62	71	72	61	61
13 Aug. 1831	63	72	73	62	62
30 Aug. 1831	64	20	20	63	63

6. See also the following entry for 23 Feb. 1831. In the 1835 edition of the Doctrine and Covenants, the last sentence of verse 19 (corresponding to verse 73 in the 2013 edition) was added to the revelation.

7. The second of two sections numbered 66. Numbering remains one off for subsequent sections within the 1835 edition.

| DATE | JS-Era Canon | | | 2004 | 2013 |
	1833	1835	1844		
11 Sept. 1831	65	21	21	64	64
29 Oct. 1831		74	75	66	66
30 Oct. 1831		24	24	65	65
1 Nov. 1831–A		22	22	68	68
1 Nov. 1831–B	1	1	1	1	1
ca. 2 Nov. 1831		25	25	67	67
3 Nov. 1831		100	108	108	133
11 Nov. 1831–A		28	28	69	69
11 Nov. 1831–B[8]		3 (partial[9])	3 (partial[10])	104 (partial[11])	107 (partial[12])
12 Nov. 1831		26	26	70	70
1 Dec. 1831		90	91	71	71
4 Dec. 1831–A		89:1–2	90:1–2	72:1–2	72:1–8
4 Dec. 1831–B		89:3–4	90:3–4	72:3–4	72:9–23
4 Dec. 1831–C		89:5	90:5	72:5	72:24–26
10 Jan. 1832		29	29	73	73
25 Jan. 1832–A		87:1–3	88:1–3	75:1–3	75:1–22
25 Jan. 1832–B		87:4–5	88:4–5	75:4–5	75:23–26
16 Feb. 1832		91	92	76	76
1 Mar. 1832		75	76	77	78
7 Mar. 1832		77	78	79	80
12 Mar. 1832		76	77	78	79
15 Mar. 1832		79	80	80	81
Between ca. 4 and ca. 20 Mar. 1832					77
26 Apr. 1832		86	87	81	82
30 Apr. 1832		88	89	82	83
29 Aug. 1832		78	79	96	99
22–23 Sept. 1832		4	4	83	84
27 Nov. 1832					85
6 Dec. 1832		6	6	84	86
25 Dec. 1832					87
27 and 28 Dec. 1832		7:1–38	7:1–38	85:1–38	88:1–126
3 Jan. 1833		7:39–46	7:39–46	85:39–46	88:127–137

8. See also the following entry for ca. Apr. 1835.

9. Verses 31–33, 35–42, 44.

10. Verses 31–33, 35–42, 44.

11. Verses 31–33, 35–42, 44.

12. Verses 59–69, 71–72, 74–75, 78–87, 91–92, 99–100.

| Date | JS-Era Canon | | | 2004 | 2013 |
	1833	1835	1844		
27 Feb. 1833		80	81	86	89
8 Mar. 1833		84	85	87	90
9 Mar. 1833		92	93	88	91
15 Mar. 1833		93	94	89	92
6 May 1833		82	83	90	93
1 June 1833		95	96	92	95
4 June 1833		96	97	93	96
2 Aug. 1833–A		81	82	94	97
2 Aug. 1833–B		83	84	91	94
6 Aug. 1833		85	86	95	98
12 Oct. 1833		94	95	97	100
16 and 17 Dec. 1833		97	98	98	101
18–19 Feb. 1834		5	5	99	102
24 Feb. 1834			101	100	103
23 Apr. 1834		98	99	101	104
22 June 1834			102	102	105
25 Nov. 1834		99	100	103	106
Between ca. 1 Mar. and ca. 4 May 1835[13]		3	3	104	107
ca. Aug. 1835 ("Marriage")		101	109	111	
ca. Aug. 1835 ("Of Governments and Laws in General")		102	110	112	134
26 Dec. 1835					108
21 Jan. 1836					137
27 Mar. 1836					109
3 Apr. 1836					110
6 Aug. 1836					111
23 July 1837			104	105	112
Mar. 1838					113
11 Apr. 1838					114
26 Apr. 1838					115
19 May 1838					116
8 July 1838–A					118

---

13. See also the preceding entry for 11 Nov. 1831–B.

| | JS-Era Canon | | | | |
Date	1833	1835	1844	2004	2013
8 July 1838–C[14]			107	106	119
8 July 1838–D					120
8 July 1838–E					117
20 Mar. 1839					121–123
19 Jan. 1841			[103]	107[15]	124
ca. Mar. 1841					125
9 July 1841					126
1 Sept. 1842			105	109[16]	127
7 Sept. 1842			106	110[17]	128
9 Feb. 1843					129
2 Apr. 1843					130
16–17 May 1843					131
12 July 1843					132

14. This table skips from 8 July 1838–A to 8 July 1838–C because the revelation not shown here, 8 July 1838–B, has never been canonized.

15. The 2004 Community of Christ edition provides the following note regarding this section: "Placed in the Appendix by action of the 1970 World Conference: the Appendix was subsequently removed by the 1990 World Conference."

16. The 2004 Community of Christ edition provides the following note regarding this section: "Placed in the Appendix by action of the 1970 World Conference: the Appendix was subsequently removed by the 1990 World Conference."

17. The 2004 Community of Christ edition provides the following note regarding this section: "Placed in the Appendix by action of the 1970 World Conference: the Appendix was subsequently removed by the 1990 World Conference."

Acknowledgments

This volume is made possible by the help and generosity of numerous people and institutions. We are particularly grateful for the administrators and officials of The Church of Jesus Christ of Latter-day Saints, Salt Lake City, which sponsors the project. We also express deep appreciation to the Larry H. Miller and Gail Miller Family Foundation for its continued support of the project. The foundation's generosity and encouragement have enabled us to meet an ambitious production schedule while adhering to the highest scholarly standards. In particular, we express the sincerest gratitude to Gail Miller Wilson. Her continued devotion to this work has made this and all other volumes of *The Joseph Smith Papers* possible.

The Joseph Smith Papers Project relies on the skills and dedication of employees and volunteers in the Church History Department of The Church of Jesus Christ of Latter-day Saints; on faculty, researchers, and editors at Brigham Young University; on our Editorial Board and National Advisory Board; and on independent scholars and editors. Employees from the Church History Department who have assisted us include Ronald Barney, Jeffrey G. Cannon, LaJean Purcell Carruth, Sherilyn Farnes, Nicole Fernley, Richard L. Jensen, Shannon Kelly, Scott D. Marianno, Spencer W. McBride, Adam McLain, Rachel Osborne, Alison Palmer, Sharon E. Nielsen, Jay Parry, Alex D. Smith, Mark L. Staker, Stephanie Steed, and Brent Westwood. We are especially grateful for Andrea Kay Nelson, whose research for this volume was invaluable, and for Joseph F. Darowski, who assisted with early drafts of annotation in this volume. We also thank Margaret A. Hogan and Nathan N. Waite for their help in proofreading the volume.

We are grateful to Jay R. Eastley and Naoma W. Eastley, volunteers at the Church History Library, who assisted with research and preliminary drafts for the geographical directory; Lee Ann Clanton and Eleanor Brainard, also volunteers, who helped with document transcription; and Noel R. Barton, Brian P. Barton, and Steven Motteshard, who provided professional genealogical research services in support of the biographical directory. Other research used in the biographical directory was provided by a volunteer team headed by Paddy Spilsbury and consisting of Barbara Ann Price, Beverly Jones, Judith Wight, Jeanine Ricketts, Cynthia Wood, and Kathleen Williams. We express thanks for their help. We are also very appreciative of Kate Mertes, who created the index for this volume and Carolyn Call of the Joseph Smith Papers, who skillfully typeset the volume.

Many independent scholars and academic interns provided valuable assistance. We are indebted to Andrea Radke-Moss for assistance with Latter-day Saint women's history in the Missouri era and to Samuel M. Brown, Stephen J. Flemming, Joseph Johnstun, Christopher J. Jones, Stephen C. LeSueur, H. Michael Marquardt, Benjamin E. Park, William V. Smith, Jonathan A. Stapley, and Bart Summerhays. We thank interns Robert M. Call, Carlin Cottam, Michael Duval, Ryan N. Freeman, Jason Grover, M. Jordan Kezele, Lane Lisonbee, Hannah E. Morse, Madison Nicole Porter, Arica Roberts, Stephen O. Smoot, Nathan Tresnak, and Noe Spencer Zapata.

We express our thanks to Glenn N. Rowe and Brandon Metcalf, Church History Department, The Church of Jesus Christ of Latter-day Saints, for their diligent assistance with the documents; to Gordon A. Madsen, Jeffrey N. Walker, Chad Foulger, and Peter J. Wosnik for their assistance with legal and financial documents; to Max H Parkin for his assistance with JS legal documents once housed in Daviess County, Missouri, several of which are now in private possession; and to Welden C. Andersen and Matthew Reier for their assistance with photographs published in this volume. We also thank Kiersten Olson for administrative assistance and Patrick Dunshee, Ben Ellis Godfrey, and Deb Xavier for their efforts in marketing the project and the volume.

In addition, we express special thanks to Kay Darowski, Joseph Smith Papers, who oversaw a talented team of student researchers at Brigham Young University from 2003 to 2012. They include Lisse L. Brox, Kendall Buchanan, Ethan J. Christensen, Matthew B. Christensen, Jared P. Collette, Justin Collings, Lia Suttner Collings, Renee Collins, Daniel J. Combs, Christopher K. Crockett, Eric Dowdle, Vanessa Ann Dominica Dowdle, James A. Goldberg, Angella M. Hamilton, Michael Jensen, Christopher C. Jones, Cort Kirksey, Mary-Celeste Lewis, Timothy Merrill, Crystal Moore-Walker, Kara Nelson, Amy Norton, Jason M. Olson, Benjamin E. Park, Daren E. Ray, Ryan W. Saltzgiver, David Harrison Smith, Kelli M. Smith, Todd M. Sparks, Timothy D. Speirs, Virginia E. Stratford, Kathryn Jensen Wall, and Stephen Whitaker.

Many libraries and repositories have provided essential assistance. We sincerely thank the management and staff of the Church History Library, The Church of Jesus Christ of Latter-day Saints, Salt Lake City, where the majority of Joseph Smith's papers are located; the Family History Library, The Church of Jesus Christ of Latter-day Saints, Salt Lake City; and Cindy Brightenburg and the staff of the L. Tom Perry Special Collections, Harold B. Lee Library, Brigham Young University, Provo, Utah. We express special thanks to the Community of Christ Library and Archives, Independence, Missouri, and to the historians and site directors of the Community of Christ; in particular, we thank Mark Scherer, Ronald E. Romig, Lachlan MacKay, Rachel Killebrew, and Richard Howard. We likewise extend gratitude to the Geauga County Archives and Records Center, Chardon, Ohio, and its staff; the Clay County Archives and Historical Library, Liberty, Missouri; the Missouri State Archives, Jefferson City, Missouri; Erika Van Vranken of the State Historical Society of Missouri; the Beinecke Rare Book and Manuscript Library, Yale University, New Haven, Connecticut; William R. Crawford, William R. Kreuger, and Karen L. Davies of the Iowa Masonic Library; the Western Reserve Historical Society, Cleveland, Ohio; the Henry E. Huntington Library, San Marino, California; Nan Lee, president of the North Haven Historical Society, North Haven, Maine; and George Shaner and the National Archives and Records Administration, Washington DC.

Many of the maps in this volume were developed by Geographic Information Services, The Church of Jesus Christ of Latter-day Saints, under the direction of David Peart, with cartography by Heidi Springsteed and Jonathan West. The maps are based on historical research; the names of those who performed the research are listed alongside the maps in this volume, and we thank these individuals for their contributions.

We also thank the management and staff at Deseret Book for the professional help and advice they provided regarding the design, printing, and distribution of this volume. We especially appreciate the contributions of Sheri L. Dew, Laurel Christensen Day, Lisa Roper, Amy Durham, Suzanne Brady, Richard Erickson, David Kimball, Derk Koldewyn, Rebecca B. Chambers, Ruth B. Howard, and Vicki Parry.

We would be remiss if we did not express the utmost gratitude to our families and friends for their love, support, and encouragement during the development and production of this volume. Thank you to all.

Index

In addition to the documents themselves, introductory essays, annotation, and most reference material have been indexed. Most maps are not indexed; map coordinates for specific locations are given in the Geographical Directory. Spelling, punctuation, and capitalization of quotations have been standardized. Personal names are listed by their correct spellings, not by variant spellings that may be found in the documents, unless the correct spelling is unknown. Entries for married women are generally listed under the names used during the period covered by the volume, with appropriate cross-references under maiden names or other married names. Unidentified individuals, such as "Sister Leonard," are included in this index. In subentry text, Joseph Smith (JS) and Emma Smith (ES) are referred to by their initials. Recurring locations in the volume are referenced in subentries without state identification; these include Adam-ondi-Ahman (Mo.), Caldwell Co. (Mo.), Clay Co. (Mo.), Commerce (Ill.), Daviess Co. (Mo.), Far West (Mo.), Jackson Co. (Mo.), and Kirtland (Ohio).

When found in an entry, "id." indicates an entry in the Biographical Directory or Geographical Directory or other text that summarizes the topic, "def." refers to a passage that defines the topic, "illus." indicates a photograph or other illustration, and "handwriting of" identifies documents that an individual inscribed.

Q

R

Additional Resources

The Joseph Smith Papers website, josephsmithpapers.org, offers many resources that enrich the documents presented in this volume and can aid further research. These include the following:

- High-resolution color images and searchable transcripts of documents
- A comprehensive calendar listing all known JS documents from the time period covered in this volume, including nonextant documents, forgeries, and a comprehensive collection of the licenses, deeds, mortgages, and promissory notes from this period
- A glossary of terms that have particular meaning in Mormon usage, defined as they were used in JS's time
- More maps, photographs, charts, and other media that contextualize the documents and events discussed herein
- A detailed chronology of JS's life
- Complete documentation for the reference material found in the back of this volume
- Finding aids that link to JS documents related to selected topics
- Updated errata for this and other volumes of *The Joseph Smith Papers*